MIRACLES

MIRACLES

The Credibility of
the New Testament Accounts

VOLUME 2

CRAIG S. KEENER

B
Baker Academic
a division of Baker Publishing Group
Grand Rapids, Michigan

Published by Baker Academic
a division of Baker Publishing Group
P.O. Box 6287, Grand Rapids, MI 49516-6287
www.bakeracademic.com

Printed in the United States of America

Library of Congress Cataloging-in-Publication Data

Keener, Craig S., 1960–
  Miracles : the credibility of the New Testament accounts / Craig S. Keener.
      p.   cm.
  Includes bibliographical references (p.   ) and index.
  ISBN 978-0-8010-3952-2 (cloth)
      1. Miracles. 2. Spiritual healing—Christianity. 3. Bible. N.T. Gospels—Evidences, authority, etc.
  4. Bible. N.T. Acts—Evidences, authority, etc. I. Title.
  BS2548.K44 2011
  226.7′06—dc23   2011020926

11 12 13 14 15 16 17   7 6 5 4 3 2 1

Contents

Abbreviations

Ancient Sources

Note: Most disputed works are listed under their putative or traditional authors.

General

ca.	circa
frg.	fragment
HB	Hebrew Bible
LXX	Septuagint
NT	New Testament
OT	Old Testament/Hebrew Bible
pref.	preface
Q	Quelle (hypothetical source behind much of Matthew and Luke)

Papyri and Inscriptions

CIJ	*Corpus Inscriptionum Iudaicarum*, ed. Frey
Epidauros inscr.	Epidauros inscriptions
I. Eph.	*Inscriften von Ephesos*
IG	*Inscriptiones Graecae*
PDM	*Papyri Demoticae Magicae*
PDM Sup.	*Papyri Demoticae Magicae Supplement*
PGM	*Papyri Graecae Magicae*
P. Grenf.	*Greek Papyri*, ed. B. P. Grenfell and A. S. Hunt
P. Oxy.	*Papyrus Oxyrhynchus*
P. Par.	*Les Papyrus grecs du Musée du Louvre*, ed. W. Brunet de Presle and E. Egger
SEG	*Supplementum Epigraphicum Graecum*
SIG	*Sylloge inscriptionum graecarum.* 3rd ed. Edited by W. Dittenberger. 4 vols. Leipzig, 1915–24

Hebrew Bible/Old Testament

Gen	Genesis	Josh	Joshua	2 Kgs	2 Kings
Exod	Exodus	Judg	Judges	2 Chr	2 Chronicles
Lev	Leviticus	1 Sam	1 Samuel	Neh	Nehemiah
Num	Numbers	2 Sam	2 Samuel	Job	Job
Deut	Deuteronomy	1 Kgs	1 Kings	Ps(s)	Psalm(s)

Prov	Proverbs	Ezek	Ezekiel	Mic	Micah
Eccl	Ecclesiastes	Dan	Daniel	Mal	Malachi
Isa	Isaiah	Jon	Jonah		

New Testament

Matt	Matthew	Gal	Galatians	Phlm	Philemon
Mark	Mark	Eph	Ephesians	Heb	Hebrews
Luke	Luke	Phil	Philippians	Jas	James
John	John	Col	Colossians	1 Pet	1 Peter
Acts	Acts	1 Thess	1 Thessalonians	2 Pet	2 Peter
Rom	Romans	2 Thess	2 Thessalonians	1 John	1 John
1 Cor	1 Corinthians	1 Tim	1 Timothy	Jude	Jude
2 Cor	2 Corinthians	2 Tim	2 Timothy	Rev	Revelation

Old Testament Apocrypha

Bar	Baruch	4 Macc	4 Maccabees	Wis	Wisdom of Solomon
Jdt	Judith	Sir	Sirach (Ecclesiasticus)		
2 Macc	2 Maccabees	Tob	Tobit		

Old Testament Pseudepigrapha

Apoc. Ab.	Apocalypse of Abraham	Liv. Pr.	Lives of the Prophets
Apoc. Adam	Apocalypse of Adam	Pr. Jos.	Prayer of Joseph
Apoc. Mos.	Apocalypse of Moses	Pss. Sol.	Psalms of Solomon
Apoc. Sedr.	Apocalypse of Sedrach	Ps.-Phoc.	Pseudo-Phocylides
Apoc. Zeph.	Apocalypse of Zephaniah	Sib. Or.	Sibylline Oracles
Ascen. Isa.	Ascension of Isaiah	Sim.	Similitudes (of 1 Enoch)
2 Bar.	2 Baruch	T. Ab.	Testament of Abraham
3 Bar.	3 Baruch	T. Adam	Testament of Adam
4 Bar.	4 Baruch	T. Jac.	Testament of Jacob
1 En.	1 Enoch	T. Job	Testament of Job
2 En.	2 Enoch	T. Sol.	Testament of Solomon
3 En.	3 Enoch	Tr. Shem	Treatise of Shem
Ezek. Trag.	Ezekiel the Tragedian Exagoge		
4 Ezra	4 Ezra		
Gr. Apoc. Ezra	Greek Apocalypse of Ezra		**Testaments of the Twelve Patriarchs**
Hist. Rech.	History of the Rechabites	T. Dan	Testament of Dan
Jan. Jam.	Jannes and Jambres	T. Iss.	Testament of Issachar
Jos. Asen.	Joseph and Aseneth	T. Jos.	Testament of Joseph
Jub.	Jubilees	T. Jud.	Testament of Judah
L.A.B.	Pseudo-Philo's Biblical Antiquities	T. Levi	Testament of Levi
L.A.E.	Life of Adam and Eve	T. Naph.	Testament of Naphtali
Let. Aris.	Letter of Pseudo-Aristeas	T. Reu.	Testament of Reuben
Odes Sol.	Odes of Solomon	T. Sim.	Testament of Simeon

Dead Sea Scrolls and Related Texts

CD	Damascus Document	1QS	Manual of Discipline / Community Rule
1Qap Gen^ar	Genesis Apocryphon		
1QM	Qumran War Scroll	4Q	Manuscripts from Qumran Cave Four
1QpHab	Qumran Pesher Commentary on Habakkuk	11QTemple	Qumran Temple Scroll

Targumic Texts

Tg. Jon.	*Targum Jonathan*	*Tg. Ps.-Jon.*	*Targum Pseudo-Jonathan*
Tg. Onq.	*Targum Onqelos*		

Mishnah, Talmud, and Related Literature

b.	Babylonian Talmud	*Maksh.*	*Makshirin*
bar.	baraita (i.e., a citation of earlier	*Meg.*	*Megillah*
	tradition)	*Meil.*	*Meila*
m.	Mishnah	*Men.*	*Menahoth*
p.	Palestinian (Jerusalem, Yerushalmi)	*Mid.*	*Middot*
	Talmud	*Mik.*	*Mikvaot*
tos.	Tosefta	*M.K.*	*Moed Katan*
		M.S.	*Maaser Sheni*
Ab.	*Aboth*	*Naz.*	*Nazir*
A.Z.	*Abodah Zarah*	*Ned.*	*Nedarim*
B.B.	*Baba Bathra*	*Neg.*	*Negaim*
Bek.	*Bekoroth*	*Nid.*	*Niddah*
Ber.	*Berakoth*	*Ohol.*	*Oholoth*
Bez.	*Bezah*	*Or.*	*Orlah*
Bik.	*Bikkurim*	*Pes.*	*Pesahim*
B.K.	*Baba Kamma*	*R.H.*	*Rosh Hoshana*
B.M.	*Baba Mezia*	*Sanh.*	*Sanhedrin*
Eduy.	*Eduyoth*	*Shab.*	*Shabbat*
Erub.	*Erubin*	*Sheb.*	*Shebuot*
Git.	*Gittin*	*Shebiith*	*Shebiith*
Hag.	*Hagigah*	*Sheq.*	*Sheqalim*
Hal.	*Hallah*	*Sot.*	*Sota*
Hor.	*Horayoth*	*Suk.*	*Sukkoth*
Hul.	*Hullin*	*Taan.*	*Taanit*
Kel.	*Kelim*	*Tam.*	*Tamid*
Ker.	*Keritot*	*Tem.*	*Temurah*
Ket.	*Ketuboth*	*Ter.*	*Terumoth*
Kid.	*Kiddushin*	*Toh.*	*Toharot*
Kip.	*Kippurim*	*Yad.*	*Yadaim*
Maas.	*Maaserot*	*Yeb.*	*Yebamot*
Mak.	*Makkot*	*Zeb.*	*Zebahim*

Other Rabbinic Works

Ab. R. Nat.	*Abot de Rabbi Nathan*	*Midr. Ps*	Midrash on Psalms (*Mid-*
A.M.	*Sipra Aharé Mot*		*rash Tehillim*)
Besh.	*Mekilta Beshallah*	*Num. Rab.*	*Numbers Rabbah*
Deut. Rab.	*Deuteronomy Rabbah*	*Pesiq. Rab.*	*Pesiqta Rabbati*
Eccl. Rab.	*Ecclesiastes (Koheleth)*	*Pesiq. Rab Kah.*	*Pesiqta de Rab Kahana*
	Rabbah	*Pesiq. Rab Kah. Sup.*	*Pesiqta de Rab Kahana*
Exod. Rab.	*Exodus Rabbah*		*Supplement*
Gen. Rab.	*Genesis Rabbah*	*Qed.*	*Sipra Qedoshim*
Lam. Rab.	*Lamentations Rabbah*	*Shir.*	*Mekilta Shirata*
Lev. Rab.	*Leviticus Rabbah*	*Sipre Deut.*	*Sipre Deuteronomy*
Mek.	*Mekilta*	*Song Rab.*	*Song Rabbah*

Patristic Sources

Ambrose

Ep.	*Epistles*

Apostolic Fathers

1 Clem.	*1 Clement*

Did.	*Didache*	
Herm.	*Shepherd of Hermas*	
Vis.	*Vision* (of Hermas)	

Athanasius

Inc.	*De incarnatione*
Vit. Ant.	*Life of St. Anthony*

Augustine

City of God	*De civitate Dei*
Conf.	*Confessions*
Ep.	*Epistles*
Retract.	*Retractions*
Util. cred.	*On the Advantage of Believing*

Chrysostom, John

Hom. Acts	*Homilies on Acts*
Hom. Cor.	*Homilies on 1–2 Corinthians*
Jul.	*In sanctum Julianum martyrem*

Clement of Alexandria

Quis div.	*Who Is the Rich Man That Shall Be Saved?*

Cyprian

Ep.	*Epistles*
Laps.	*On the Lapsed*

Eusebius

Praep. ev.	*Praeparatio evangelica*

Ignatius

Eph.	*To the Ephesians*

Irenaeus

Haer.	*Against Heresies*

Jerome

Vit. Hil.	*Vita S. Hilarionis eremitae*

Justin

Apol.	*Apology (1, 2)*
Dial.	*Dialogue with Trypho*

Lactantius

Epit.	*Epitome of the Divine Institutes*
Inst.	*Divine Institutes*

Origen

Cels.	*Against Celsus*
Hom. Jos.	*Homilies on Joseph*

Tertullian

An.	*On the Soul*
Apol.	*Apology*
Cor.	*De corona militis*
Idol.	*De idolatria*
Praescr.	*De praescriptione haereticorum*
Scap.	*Ad Scapulam*
Spect.	*De spectaculis*
Test.	*The Soul's Testimony*
Ux.	*Ad uxorem*

Theodoret of Cyr

Comm. 1 Cor.	*Commentary on 1 Corinthians*

New Testament Apocrypha and Pseudepigrapha

Acts Andrew	*Acts of Andrew*	*Acts Thom.*	*Acts of Thomas*
Acts John	*Acts of John*	*Apost. Const.*	*Apostolic Constitutions*
Acts Paul	*Acts of Paul*	*Gos. Nic.*	*Gospel of Nicodemus*
Acts Pet.	*Acts of Peter*		

Other Greek and Latin Works

Note: Texts that are an author's only known or surviving work are cited in this book by the author's name. Texts whose authorship is unknown are alphabetized by title in the list below, except when their traditional association with a particular corpus invites pseudepigraphic or some other works to be listed under a given author.

Achilles Tatius

Achilles Tatius	*Clitophon and Leucippe*

Aelius Aristides

Def. Or.	*Defense of Oratory*
Or.	*Oration to Rome*

Aeschines

Tim.	*Timarchus*

Aeschylus

Ag.	*Agamemnon*
Cho.	*Choephori (Libation-Bearers)*

Sept.	Septem contra Thebas (Seven against Thebes)

Alciphron

Farm.	Farmers

Aphthonius

Progymn.	Progymnasmata

Apollodorus

Bib.	Library
Epit.	Epitome

Apollonius Rhodius

Apollonius Rhodius	Argonautica

Appian

Bell. civ.	Civil War
Hist. rom.	Roman History

Apuleius

De deo Socr.	De deo Socratis
Metam.	Metamorphoses

Aristophanes

Ach.	Acharnians
Plut.	Rich Man/Plutus

Aristotle

De an.	De anima (Soul)
Div. somn.	De divinatio per somnum (Prophesying by Dreams)
Heavens	On the Heavens
Pol.	Politics
Rhet.	Rhetoric

Arius Didymus

Arius Didymus	Epitome of Stoic Ethics

Arrian

Alex.	Anabasis of Alexander

Artemidorus

Onir.	Onirocritica

Athenaeus

Deipn.	Deipnosophists

Athenagoras

Plea	A Plea for the Christians

Aulus Gellius

Aulus Gellius	Attic Nights

Bede

Comm. Acts	Commentary on Acts
H.E.G.A.	Historia Ecclesiastica Gentis Anglorum

Caesar

Bell. civ.	Civil War

Callimachus

Callimachus	Hymns

Callistratus

Descr.	Descriptions

Chariton

Chaer.	Chaereas and Callirhoe

Cicero

Att.	Letters to Atticus
Div.	De Divinatione
Fin.	De finibus
Inv.	De inventione rhetorica
Leg.	De legibus
Nat. d.	De Natura Deorum
Off.	De officiis
Pis.	In Pisonem
Rep.	De republica
Tusc.	Tusculan Disputations
Verr.	In Verrem

Cornutus

Nat. d.	Summary of Greek Theology

Digest

Dig.	Digest

Dio Cassius

Dio Cassius	Roman History

Dio Chrysostom

Or.	Orations

Diodorus Siculus

Diodorus Siculus	Library of History

Diogenes

Ep.	Epistle (in The Cynic Epistles, ed. A. Malherbe)

Diogenes Laertius

Diogenes Laertius	Lives of Eminent Philosophers

Dion. Hal. **Dionysius of**
                Halicarnassus
Ant. rom.   Roman Antiquities
Comp.   Literary Composition/De com-
                positione verborum
Epid.   Epideictic

Epictetus
Diatr.   Discourses

Eunapius
Lives   Lives of the Philosophers

Euripides
Alc.   Alcestis
Andr.   Andromache
Bacch.   Bacchanals
El.   Electra
Hec.   Hecuba
Herc. fur.   Madness of Heracles
Hipp.   Hippolytus
Orest.   Orestes

Fragments of Greek Historians
FrGrH   Fragments of Greek Historians

Fronto
Ad M. Caes.   Ad Marcus Caesarem
De Fer. Als.   De Feriis Alsiensibus
Eloq.   Eloquence

Gaius
Inst.   Institutes

Gregory of Tours
Hist.   History

Heliodorus
Aeth.   Aethiopica

Heraclitus
Hom. Prob.   Homeric Problems

Hermogenes
Inv.   On Invention
Issues   On Issues
Progymn.   Progymnasmata

Herodian
Herodian   History

Herodotus
Herodotus   Histories

Hesiod
Astron.   Astronomy
Op.   Works and Days
Theog.   Theogony

Homer
Il.   Iliad
Od.   Odyssey

Homeric Hymn
Hom. Hymn   Homeric Hymn

Hypostasis of the Archons
Hyp. Arch.   Hypostasis of the Archons

Iamblichus
Myst.   Mysteries
V.P.   Life of Pythagoras, or, Pythago-
                rean Life

Isaeus
Astyph.   Astyphilus
Menec.   Menecles

Isocrates
Paneg.   Panegyricus (Or. 4)

Josephus
Ant.   Antiquities of the Jews
Ag. Ap.   Against Apion
Life   Life
War   The Jewish War

Justinian
Inst.   Institutes

Juvenal
Sat.   Satires

Libanius
Narration   Sample Narrations
Speech in Character Sample Speeches in Character

Livy
Livy   Ab Urbe Condita

Longinus
Subl.   On the Sublime

Longus
Longus   Daphnis and Chloe

Lucan
Bell. civ.   Civil War

Lucian

Alex.	*Alexander the False Prophet*
Charid.	*Charidemus*
Critic	*The Mistaken Critic*
Dance	*The Dance*
Dem.	*Demonax*
Dial. D.	*Dialogues of the Dead*
Dial. G.	*Dialogues of the Gods*
Hermot.	*Hermotimus, or Sects*
Hist.	*How to Write History*
Icar.	*Icaromenippus, or Sky-Man*
Indictment	*Double Indictment/Bis accusatus*
Lover of Lies	*The Lover of Lies/Doubter/ Philopseudes*
Lucius	*Lucius or the Ass*
Men.	*Menippus, or Descent into Hades*
Peregr.	*Peregrinus*
Posts	*Salaried Posts in Great Houses*
Ship	*The Ship, or The Wishes/ Navigium*
Tim.	*Timon*
True Story	*A True Story*
Z. Rants	*Zeus Rants*

Lucretius

Nat.	*De Rerum Natura*

Macrobius

Sat.	*Saturnalia*

Marcus Aurelius

Marcus Aurelius	*Meditations*

Martial

Epig.	*Epigrams*

Maximus of Tyre

Maximus of Tyre	*Orations*

Menander Rhetor

Menander Rhetor	*Epideictic Speeches*

Minucius Felix

Oct.	*Octavius*

Orphic Hymns

Orph. H.	*Orphic Hymns*

Ovid

Am.	*Amores*
Fast.	*Fasti*
Metam.	*Metamorphoses*
Tristia	*Tristia*

Parthenius

L.R.	*Love Romance*

Pausanias

Pausanias	*Description of Greece*

Persius

Sat.	*Satires*

Petronius

Sat.	*Satyricon*

Philo

Ab.	*On Abraham*
Conf.	*On the Confusion of Languages*
Creation	*On the Creation of the World*
Giants	*On the Giants*
Migr.	*The Migration of Abraham*
Mos.	*Life of Moses (1–2)*
Names	*On the Change of Names*
Spec. Laws	*Special Laws (1–4)*

Philostratus

Ep. Apoll.	*Epistles of Apollonius*
Hrk.	*Heroikos*
Vit. Apoll.	*Life of Apollonius*
Vit. soph.	*Lives of the Sophists*

Pindar

Isthm.	*Isthmian Odes*
Pyth.	*Pythian Odes*

Plato

Epin.	*Epinomis*
Phaedr.	*Phaedrus*
Rep.	*Republic*
Symp.	*Symposium*

Pliny the Elder

Nat.	*Natural History*

Pliny the Younger

Ep.	*Epistles*

Plutarch

Alc.	*Alcibiades*
Alex.	*Alexander*
Bride	*Advice to Bride and Groom*
Br. Wom.	*Bravery of Women*
Cam.	*Camillus*
Cic.	*Cicero*
Cor.	*M. Coriolanus*
Dem.	*Demosthenes*
Dial. L.	*Dialogue on Love*
Face M.	*Face on the Moon*

Isis	*Isis and Osiris*
Luc.	*Lucullus*
Lys.	*Lysander*
M. Cato	*Marcus Cato*
Mor.	*Moralia*
Obsol.	*Obsolescence of Oracles*
Or. Delphi	*Oracles at Delphi no longer given in verse (De Pyth. Orac.)*
Pel.	*Pelopidas*
Pleas. L.	*Epicurus Actually Makes a Pleasant Life Impossible*
R.Q.	*Roman Questions*
Sign Soc.	*Sign of Socrates*
Sulla	*Sulla*
Them.	*Themistocles*
T.-T.	*Table-Talk*
Uned. R.	*Uneducated Ruler*

Polybius

Polybius	*History of the Roman Republic*

Porphyry

Marc.	*To Marcella*
Vit. Pyth.	*Life of Pythagoras*

Ps.-Callisthenes

Alex.	*Alexander Romance*

Pseudo-Clementine

Ps.-Clem. *Rec.*	*Recognitions*

Quadratus

Apol.	*Apology*

Quintilian

Decl.	*Lesser Declamations*
Inst.	*Institutes of Oratory*

Rhetorica ad Alexandrum

Rhet. Alex.	*Rhetorica ad Alexandrum*

Sallust

Bell. cat.	*War with Catiline*

Seneca the Elder

Controv.	*Controversiae*

Seneca the Younger

Ben.	*On Benefactions*
Dial.	*Dialogues*
Ep. Lucil.	*Epistles to Lucilius*
Nat.	*Natural Questions*

Sextus Empiricus

Math.	*Against the Professors (Adv. Math.)*
Pyr.	*Outlines of Pyrrhonism*

Silius Italicus

Silius Italicus	*Punica*

Socrates

Socrates *Ep.*	*Epistles (in Cynic Epistles)*

Sophocles

Antig.	*Antigone*
Phil.	*Philoctetes*

Soranus

Gynec.	*Gynecology*

Sozomen

H.E.	*Historia Ecclesiastica*

Statius

Silv.	*Silvae*
Theb.	*Thebaid*

Stobaeus

Ecl.	*Eclogae*

Strabo

Strabo	*Geography*

Suetonius

Aug.	*Augustus*
Claud.	*Claudius*
Jul.	*Julius*
Otho	*Otho*
Vesp.	*Vespasian*

Tacitus

Ann.	*Annals*
Germ.	*Germania*
Hist.	*History*

Theon

Progymn.	*Progymnasmata*

Theophilus

Autol.	*Ad Autolycum*

Thucydides

Thucydides	*History of the Peloponnesian War*

Valerius Flaccus

Valerius Flaccus   *Argonautica*

Valerius Maximus

Valerius Maximus   *Memorable Deeds and Sayings*

Varro

Lat. Lang.   *On the Latin Language*

Virgil

Aen.   *Aeneid*
Ecl.   *Eclogues*

Life of Aesop

Vit. Aes.   *Life of Aesop*

Vitruvius

Arch.   *Architecture*

Xenophon

Anab.   *Anabasis*
Cyr.   *Cyropedia*
Eq. mag.   *De equitum magistro (Cavalry Commander)*
Hell.   *Hellenica*
Mem.   *Memorabilia*

Xenophon of Ephesus

Eph.   *Ephesiaka*

Other Ancient and Medieval Works

AQHT	Aqhat Epic	*M. Takla Haym.*	*The Miracles of Takla Hâymânôt in the Version of Dabra Lîbânôs*
Incant. Texts	Aramaic incantation texts		
KRT	Keret Epic		
L. Takla Haym.	*The Life of Takla Hâymânôt in the Version of Dabra Lîbânôs*		

Modern Sources

AmJPsyc	American Journal of Psychiatry
AmJPsychT	American Journal of Psychotherapy
AmJTh	American Journal of Theology
AmPhilQ	American Philosophical Quarterly
AmPhilQMS	American Philosophical Quarterly Monograph Series
AmPsyc	American Psychologist
AmSocMissMonS	American Society of Missiology Monograph Series
AmSocMissS	American Society of Missiology Series
Analysis	Analysis
ANCTRTBS	Ashgate New Critical Thinking in Religion, Theology and Biblical Studies
ANES	Ancient Near Eastern Studies
ANET	Ancient Near Eastern Texts Relating to the Old Testament, ed. J. B. Pritchard, 1955 ed.
AnIntCare	Anaesthesia and Intensive Care
AnnBehMed	Annals of Behavioral Medicine
AnnEpid	Annals of Epidemiology
AnnIntMed	Annals of Internal Medicine
ANQ	Andover Newton Quarterly
ANRW	Aufstieg und Niedergang der Römischen Welt
ANTC	Abingdon New Testament Commentaries
AnthChr	Anthropology of Christianity
AnthConsc	Anthropology of Consciousness
AnthHum	Anthropology and Humanism
Anthropos	Anthropos
AnthrQ	Anthropological Quarterly
Anton	Antonianum
AnxSC	Anxiety, Stress and Coping
ANZJPsyc	Australian and New Zealand Journal of Psychiatry
APRC	Asia Pacific Research Center
ARAnth	Annual Review of Anthropology
Archaeology	Archaeology
ArchIntMed	Archives of Internal Medicine
ArchOd	Archaeology Odyssey
ArchRep	Archaeological Reports
ARG	Archiv für Reformationsgeschichte
ArIrMed	Archives of Iranian Medicine
AsEthn	Asian Ethnology
Asian Affairs	Asian Affairs
Asian Report	Asian Report
AsFolkSt	Asian Folklore Studies
AsTJ	Asbury Theological Journal
AT	Annales theologici
AThR	Anglican Theological Review
ATSSWCRMIS	Asbury Theological Seminary Series in World Christian Revitalization Movements in Intercultural Studies
ATSSWCRMPCS	Asbury Theological Seminary Series in World Christian Revitalization Movements in Pentecostal/Charismatic Studies
AUSS	Andrews University Seminary Studies
BA	Biblical Archaeologist
BAGB	Bulletin de l'Association Guillaume Budé
BangTF	Bangalore Theological Forum
BAR	Biblical Archaeology Review
BBR	Bulletin for Biblical Research
BehResTher	Behaviour Research and Therapy
BehSN	Behavior Science Notes
BeO	Bibbia e Oriente
BES	Biblical Encounters Series
BETL	Bibliotheca Ephemeridum Theologicarum Lovaniensium

Bib	*Biblica*
BibOr	*Biblia et Orientalia*
BibSham	Bibliotheca Shamanistica
BibT	The Bible Today
BibTh	*Biblical Theology*
BibW	*The Biblical World* (Journal)
Bijdr	*Bijdragen*
BIS	Biblical Interpretation Series
BJPhilSc	*British Journal for the Philosophy of Science*
BJPsy	*British Journal of Psychology*
BJRL	*Bulletin of the John Rylands University Library*
BJS	Brown Judaic Studies
BK	*Bibel und Kirche*
BL	*Bibel und Liturgie*
BMedJ	*British Medical Journal*
BMik	*Beth Mikra*
BN	*Biblische Notizen*
BollS	Bollingen Series
BR	*Biblical Research*
BrCanRes	*Breast Cancer Research*
Breast Journal	*Breast Journal*
BRev	*Bible Review*
BSac	*Bibliotheca Sacra*
BSClinPsyc	*British School of Clinical Psychology*
BTB	*Biblical Theology Bulletin*
BTCB	Belief: A Theological Commentary on the Bible
BTr	*Bible Translator*
BullHistMed	*Bulletin of the History of Medicine*
ByF	*Biblia y Fe*
BZ	*Biblische Zeitschrift*
BZNW	Beihefte zur Zeitschrift für die neutestamentliche Wissenschaft
CaÉ	Cahiers Évangile
CanJPhil	*Canadian Journal of Philosophy*
CanJPsy	*Canadian Journal of Psychiatry*
CanNur	*Cancer Nursing*
CBC	Cambridge Bible Commentary
CBQ	*Catholic Biblical Quarterly*
CBQMS	Catholic Biblical Quarterly Monograph Series
CBull	*Classical Bulletin*
C&C	*Cross and Crown*
CCRMS	Cross-Cultural Research and Methodology Series
CCTh	Cross Cultural Theologies
CCWJCW	Cambridge Commentaries on Writings of the Jewish and Christian World 200 BC to AD 200
CDSR	*Cochrane Database of Systematic Reviews*
CEC	The Context of Early Christianity
CGB	*Church Growth Bulletin*
CGl	*China Gleanings* (earlier issues simply *Gleanings*)
CGR	*Conrad Grebel Review*
Charisma	*Charisma*
CH	*Church History*
ChapT	*Chaplaincy Today*
ChGEv	*Church of God Evangel*
ChH	*Christian History* (continued as *Christian History and Biography*)
ChicSt	*Chicago Studies*
ChPsycHumDev	*Child Psychiatry and Human Development*
ChrCent	*Christian Century*

Churchman	*Churchman*
Circ	*Circulation*
CJ	*Classical Journal*
CJP	*Canadian Journal of Philosophy*
CJT	*Canadian Journal of Theology*
ClinGer	*Clinical Gerontologist*
ClinPsyRev	*Clinical Psychology Review*
CMAJ	*Canadian Medical Association Journal*
CMPsy	*Culture, Medicine, and Psychiatry*
CNS	*Cristianesimo nella Storia*
Coll	*Collationes*
CollAntr	*Collegium Antropologicum*
ColT	*Collectanea theologica*
ComMedRes	*Complementary Medical Research*
ComThClPrac	*Complementary Therapies in Clinical Practice*
Conf	*Confidence*
CounsSp	*Counseling and Spirituality*
CP	*Classical Philology*
CQ	*Classical Quarterly*
CrCareCl	*Critical Care Clinics*
CritInq	*Critical Inquiry*
CrQ	*Crozer Quarterly*
CSHSMC	Comparative Studies of Health Systems and Medical Care
CSIR	Cambridge Studies in Ideology and Religion
CSPhilRel	Cornell Studies in the Philosophy of Religion
CSR	*Christian Scholar's Review*
CT	*Christianity Today*
CulRel	*Culture and Religion*
CurAnth	*Current Anthropology*
CurTM	*Currents in Theology and Mission*
CV	*Communio Viatorum*
DACB	*Dictionary of African Christian Biography* (New Haven, Conn.: Overseas Ministries Study Center; a continuing online project)
Daphnis	*Daphnis*
DBM	*Deltion Biblikon Meleton*
DeathS	*Death Studies*
DécHell	*Décrets hellénistiques*
DepAnx	*Depression and Anxiety*
DiabC	*Diabetes Care*
Dial	*Dialogue*
Diál	*Diálogos*
DialAll	*Dialogue and Alliance*
Divinitas	*Divinitas*
DNTB	*Dictionary of New Testament Background.* Edited by Craig A. Evans and Stanley E. Porter. Downers Grove, Ill.: InterVarsity, 2000.
DoonTJ	*Doon Theological Journal*
DPL	*Dictionary of Paul and His Letters.* Edited by Gerald F. Hawthorne, Ralph P. Martin, and Daniel G. Reid. Downers Grove, Ill.: InterVarsity, 1993.
DRev	*The Downside Review*
DSD	*Dead Sea Discoveries*
DunRev	*Dunwoodie Review*
EAfSt	Eastern African Studies
ÉgT	*Église et Théologie*
EmmJ	*Emmaus Journal*
Enc	*Encounter*
Enr	*Enrichment*
ÉPROER	Études préliminaires aux religions orientales dans l'empire romain

EpwRev	Epworth Review
Eranos	Eranos
EstBib	Estudios Bíblicos
ÉtBib	Études Bibliques
EthDis	Ethnicity and Disease
EthHealth	Ethnicity and Health
Ethnology	Ethnology
Ethos	Ethos
EurJAg	European Journal of Ageing
EurJCC	European Journal of Cancer Care
EurZTh	Europäische Zeitschrift für Theologie
Evangel	Evangel
EvMissSS	Evangelical Missiological Society Series
EvQ	Evangelical Quarterly
EvT	Evangelische Theologie
ExAud	Ex auditu
Exchange	Exchange
Exp	The Expositor
ExpT	Expository Times
FamComHealth	Family and Community Health
FamMed	Family Medicine
FidHist	Fides et Historia
FoiVie	Foi et Vie
Forum	Forum
FourR	The Fourth R
FPhil	Faith and Philosophy
FSCS	Faith and Scholarship Colloquies Series
GeistLeb	Geist und Leben
Gerontologist	The Gerontologist
GNC	Good News Commentary
GosPersp	Gospel Perspectives. Edited by R. T. France and David Wenham. 6 vols. Sheffield: JSOT Press, 1980–86.
GOTR	Greek Orthodox Theological Review
Grail	Grail
GRBS	Greek, Roman and Byzantine Studies
Greg	Gregorianum
GrJ	Grace Journal
GTT	Gereformeerd theologisch tijdschrift
GynOnc	Gynecologic Oncology
HamIsl	Hamdard Islamicus
HastCRep	Hastings Center Report
HCPsy	Hospital and Community Psychiatry
HealthEdBeh	Health Education and Behavior
HealthPsy	Health Psychology
HealthSR	Health Services Research
Helios	Helios
Hen	Henoch
HeyJ	Heythrop Journal
HeyM	Heythrop Monographs
HistPhilQ	History of Philosophy Quarterly
HistTh	History and Theory
HJAsSt	Harvard Journal of Asiatic Studies
HMFT	Health/Medicine and the Faith Traditions
HR	History of Religions
HS	Hebrew Studies
HSW	Health and Social Work
HTIOPS	Hispanic Theological Initiative Occasional Paper Series

HTR	*Harvard Theological Review*
HTS	*Harvard Theological Studies*
HTS/TS	*HTS Teologiese Studies/Theological Studies*
HUCA	*Hebrew Union College Annual*
HumOrg	*Human Organization*
HumSt	*Hume Studies*
HvTS	*Hervormde Teologiese Studies*
Hypertension	*Hypertension*
IBMR	*International Bulletin of Missionary Research*
ICC	International Critical Commentaries
ICMR	*Islam and Christian-Muslim Relations*
IDS	*In die Skriflig*
IEJ	*Israel Exploration Journal*
IgViv	*Iglesia Viva*
IJAC	*International Journal for the Advancement of Counselling*
IJAHD	*International Journal of Aging in Human Development*
IJAHS	*International Journal of African Historical Studies*
IJGerPsyc	*International Journal of Geriatric Psychiatry*
IJGynC	*International Journal of Gynecological Cancer*
IJNeurSc	*International Journal of Neuroscience*
IJPhilRel	*International Journal for Philosophy of Religion*
IJSocPsyc	*International Journal of Social Psychiatry*
IJT	*Indian Journal of Theology*
IntArHistI	International Archives of the History of Ideas
Interp	*Interpretation*
IntJAd	*International Journal of the Addictions*
IntJAgHDev	*International Journal of Aging and Human Development*
IntJEpid	*International Journal of Epidemiology*
IntJGerPsyc	*International Journal of Geriatric Psychiatry*
IntJPsyMed	*International Journal of Psychiatry in Medicine*
IntJPsRel	*International Journal for the Psychology of Religion*
IntRevMiss	*International Review of Mission*
ITQ	*Irish Theological Quarterly*
JAACAP	*Journal of the American Academy of Child and Adolescent Psychiatry*
JAAR	*Journal of the American Academy of Religion*
JABFM	*Journal of the American Board of Family Medicine*
JAbSocPsy	*Journal of Abnormal and Social Psychology*
JAdDev	*Journal of Adult Development*
JAdHealth	*Journal of Adolescent Health*
JAfDis	*Journal of Affective Disorders*
JAgHealth	*Journal of Aging and Health*
JAlComMed	*Journal of Alternative and Complementary Medicine*
JAM	*Journal of Asian Mission*
JAMA	*Journal of the American Medical Association*
JAmGerAss	*Journal of the American Geriatrics Association*
JAmGerSoc	*Journal of the American Geriatric Society*
JANER	*Journal of Ancient Near Eastern Religions*
JANESCU	*Journal of the Ancient Near Eastern Society of Columbia University*
JAnthRes	*Journal of Anthropological Research*
JAppGer	*Journal of Applied Gerontology*
JASA	*Journal of the American Scientific Affiliation*
JATS	*Journal of the Adventist Theological Society*
JBehMed	*Journal of Behavioral Medicine*
JBiolRegHomA	*Journal of Biological Regulators and Homeostatic Agents*
JBL	*Journal of Biblical Literature*
JBSS	*Journal of Biosocial Science*
JCCAP	*Journal of Clinical Child and Adolescent Psychology*

JChrDis	Journal of Chronic Diseases
JCJQS	Joint Commission Journal on Quality and Safety
JClinEpid	Journal of Clinical Epidemiology
JClinOn	Journal of Clinical Oncology
JClinPsy	Journal of Clinical Psychiatry
JClPsychol	Journal of Clinical Psychology
JCommRel	Journal of Communication and Religion
JConClPsy	Journal of Consulting and Clinical Psychology
JContRel	Journal of Contemporary Religion
JCounsClPs	Journal of Counseling and Clinical Psychology
JECS	Journal of Early Christian Studies
JEH	Journal of Ecclesiastical History
JerPersp	Jerusalem Perspective
JEthS	Journal of Ethiopian Studies
JETS	Journal of the Evangelical Theological Society
JEurSt	Journal of European Studies
JewishHist	Jewish History
JFamPr	Journal of Family Practice
JFamPsych	Journal of Family Psychology
JFolkI	Journal of the Folklore Institute
JFSR	Journal of Feminist Studies in Religion
JGBSMS	Journals of Gerontology Series A: Biological Sciences and Medical Sciences
JGenIntMed	Journal of General Internal Medicine
JGenPsy	Journal of General Psychology
JGer	Journal of Gerontology
JGPSSS	Journal of Gerontology Series B: Psychological Sciences and Social Sciences
JGRCJ	Journal of Greco-Roman Christianity and Judaism
JHistSex	Journal of the History of Sexuality
JHPsych	Journal of Health Psychology
JHS	Journal of Hellenic Studies
JHSocBeh	Journal of Health and Social Behavior
Jian Dao	Jian Dao
JITC	Journal of the Interdenominational Theological Center
JJS	Journal of Jewish Studies
JMedPhil	Journal of Medicine and Philosophy
JMenSc	Journal of Mental Science
JNatCInst	Journal of the National Cancer Institute
JNeurSc	Journal of the Neurological Sciences
JNMedAss	Journal of the National Medical Association
JNMDis	Journal of Nervous and Mental Disease
JObGynNNurs	Journal of Obstetric, Gynecologic, and Neonatal Nursing
JOpPsyc	Journal of Operational Psychiatry
JPallMed	Journal of Palliative Medicine
JPastCare	Journal of Pastoral Care
JPers	Journal of Personality
JPerSocPsy	Journal of Personality and Social Psychology
JPFC	The Jewish People in the First Century: Historical Geography, Political History, Social, Cultural and Religious Life and Institutions. Edited by S. Safrai and M. Stern with D. Flusser and W. C. van Unnik. 2 vols. Section 1 of Compendia Rerum Iudaicarum ad Novum Testamentum. Vol. 1: Assen: Van Gorcum & Comp., B.V., 1974; Vol. 2: Philadelphia: Fortress Press, 1976.
JPHWMSM	J. Philip Hogan World Missions Series Monograph
JPsycHist	Journal of Psychohistory
JPsyChr	Journal of Psychology and Christianity
JPsycRes	Journal of Psychosomatic Research
JPsyTh	Journal of Psychology and Theology
JPT	Journal of Pentecostal Theology

JPTSup	Journal of Pentecostal Theology Supplement
JQR	Jewish Quarterly Review
JR	Journal of Religion
JRelAf	Journal of Religion in Africa
JRelGer	Journal of Religious Gerontology
JRelHealth	Journal of Religion and Health
JRepMed	The Journal of Reproductive Medicine
JResPer	Journal of Research in Personality
JRH	Journal of Religious History
JRitSt	Journal of Ritual Studies
JRS	Journal of Roman Studies
JRSHealth	Journal of the Royal Society of Health
JSHJ	Journal for the Study of the Historical Jesus
JSJ	Journal for the Study of Judaism in the Persian, Hellenistic, and Roman Periods
JSNTSup	Journal for the Study of the New Testament Supplement Series
JSocI	Journal of Social Issues
JSOT	Journal for the Study of the Old Testament
JSP	Journal for the Study of the Pseudepigrapha
JSQ	Jewish Studies Quarterly
JSRNC	Journal for the Study of Religion, Nature and Culture
JSS	Journal of Semitic Studies
JSSR	Journal for the Scientific Study of Religion
JStatPlInf	Journal of Statistical Planning and Inference
JStIJ	Jewish Studies: An Internet Journal
JStRel	Journal for the Study of Religion
JTIICC	Journal of Trauma-Injury Infection and Critical Care
Judaism	Judaism
Justice Quarterly	Justice Quarterly
JValInq	Journal of Value Inquiry
JWCDN	Journal of the World Christian Doctors Network
Kairos	Kairos
KD	Kerygma und Dogma
KEKNT	Kritisch-exegetischer Kommentar über das Neue Testament, begründet von H. A. W. Meyer
Lancet	Lancet
Laós	Laós
LCL	Loeb Classical Library
LD	Lectio Divina
LEC	Library of Early Christianity
Lig	Liguorian
Lit	Liturgy
LNTS	Library of New Testament Studies
Logia	Logia: A Journal of Lutheran Theology
Logos	Logos: A Journal of Catholic Thought and Culture
LouvS	Louvain Studies
LQ	Lutheran Quarterly
LRB	Library of Religious Biography
LRE	The Latter Rain Evangel
LumVie	Lumière et Vie
Man	Man
Maria	Maria: A Journal of Marian Studies
MBPS	Mellen Biblical Press Series
MedAnthQ	Medical Anthropology Quarterly
Medical Care	Medical Care
MedJAus	The Medical Journal of Australia
MedT	Medical Times
MHRC	Mental Health, Religion and Culture

MissFoc	Mission Focus
Missiology	Missiology: An International Review (continuing Practical Anthropology)
Missionalia	Missionalia: Southern African Journal of Missiology
MissSt	Mission Studies
MJT	Melanesian Journal of Theology
ModAnth	Module in Anthropology
ModCh	Modern Churchman
Month	The Month
MOrthS	Modern Orthodox Saints
MounM	Mountain Movers
MS	Mediaeval Studies
MScRel	Mélanges de Science Religieuse
MSJMed	Mount Sinai Journal of Medicine
MSMS	Modern Spiritual Masters Series
Muséon	Muséon
MusW	Muslim World
NatInt	The National Interest
Nature	Nature
NBf	New Blackfriars
NCamBC	New Cambridge Bible Commentary
NCBC	New Century Bible Commentary
NCCS	New Covenant Commentary Series
NCS	Noyes Classical Studies
NDST	Notre Dame Studies in Theology
NedTT	Nederlands Theologisch Tijdschrift
Neot	Neotestamentica
Neurology	Neurology
NewEngJMed	New England Journal of Medicine
NFTL	New Foundations Theological Library
NICNT	New International Commentary on the New Testament
NicTobRes	Nicotine and Tobacco Research
NIVAC	NIV Application Commentary
NKZ	Neue kirchliche Zeitschrift
Nous	Nous
NovT	Novum Testamentum
NovTSup	Supplements to Novum Testamentum
NRColPap	Nicholas Rescher Collected Papers
NRTh	Nouvelle Revue Théologique
NSPR	New Studies in the Philosophy of Religion
NTG	New Testament Guides
NTS	New Testament Studies
NTTS	New Testament Tools and Studies
Numen	Numen: International Review for the History of Religions
NYRB	New York Review of Books
OCD	The Oxford Classical Dictionary: The Ultimate Reference Work on the Classical World. 3rd rev. ed. Edited by Simon Hornblower and Antony Spawforth. Oxford: Oxford University Press, 2003.
OCPHS	Oxford Centre for Postgraduate Hebrew Studies
OEANE	The Oxford Encyclopedia of Archaeology in the Near East. Edited by E. M. Meyers. New York, 1997.
OHCC	Oxford History of the Christian Church
OIRSSA	Oxford in India Readings in Sociology and Social Anthropology
OrOnc	Oral Oncology
OTE	Old Testament Essays
OTP	The Old Testament Pseudepigrapha. Edited by James H. Charlesworth. 2 vols. Garden City, N.Y.: Doubleday, 1983–85.
OxBS	Oxford Bible Series

Pain	*Pain*
PallMed	*Palliative Medicine*
PallSCare	*Palliative and Supportive Care*
Parab	*Parabola*
Parac	*Paraclete*
PastPsy	*Pastoral Psychology*
PAST	Pauline Studies (Brill)
PatBibMon	Paternoster Biblical Monographs
PCPhil	Problems in Contemporary Philosophy
PedNurs	*Pediatric Nursing*
PentEv	*Pentecostal Evangel*
PentV	*The Pentecostal Voice* (Manila)
PEQ	*Palestine Exploration Quarterly*
PerIndDif	*Personality and Individual Differences*
PerMotSk	*Perceptual and Motor Skills*
Persp	*Perspective*
PHC	Penguin History of the Church
PhilChr	*Philosophia Christi*
PhilEW	*Philosophy East and West*
PhilFor	*Philosophical Forum*
Philo	*Philo*
Philosophy	*Philosophy: The Journal of the British Institute of Philosophical Studies*
PhilPhenRes	*Philosophy and Phenomenological Research*
PhilQ	*Philosophical Quarterly*
PhilRhet	*Philosophy and Rhetoric*
PhilSS	Philosophical Studies Series
PhilSt	*Philosophical Studies*
PhilTheol	*Philosophy and Theology*
PHNurs	*Public Health Nursing*
Phoenix	*Phoenix*
Phronesis	*Phronesis*
PhysOcTherGer	*Physical and Occupational Therapy in Geriatrics*
PIBA	*Proceedings of the Irish Biblical Association*
PNAS	*Proceedings of the National Academy of Sciences*
Pneuma	*Pneuma: Journal for the Society of Pentecostal Studies*
Pom	*Pomegranate*
PPAS	Publications of the Philadelphia Anthropological Society
PracAnth	*Practical Anthropology*
PrevMed	*Preventive Medicine*
PrMPhil	Princeton Monographs in Philosophy
PrPam	Princeton Pamphlets
PRSt	*Perspectives in Religious Studies*
PrTMS	Princeton Theological Monograph Series
PScChrF	*Perspectives on Science and Christian Faith*
PSocPsyBull	*Personality and Social Psychology Bulletin*
PsyAdBeh	*Psychology of Addictive Behaviors*
PsyAg	*Psychology and Aging*
PsycBull	*Psychological Bulletin*
PsychMed	*Psychosomatic Medicine*
Psycho-Oncology	*Psycho-Oncology*
Psychophysiology	*Psychophysiology*
Psychosomatics	*Psychosomatics*
PsychServ	*Psychiatric Services*
PsycRep	*Psychological Reports*
PsycRes	*Psychiatry Research*
PsycTRPT	*Psychotherapy: Theory, Research, Practice, Training*
PTMS	Pittsburgh Theological Monograph Series

PTR	Princeton Theological Review
PWS	Pietist and Wesleyan Studies
Qad	Qadmoniot
QR	Quarterly Review
RB	Revue Biblique
RBL	Review of Biblical Literature
RCB	Revista de Cultura Biblica
RefRenRev	Reformation and Renaissance Review
REJ	Revue des Études Juives
RelHHeal	Religion, Health, and Healing
Religion	Religion
RelL	Religion and Life
RelS	Religious Studies
RelT	Religious Traditions
RenJ	Renewal Journal
ResAg	Research on Aging
RevExp	Review and Expositor
RevMet	Review of Metaphysics
Re-Vision	Re-Vision
RevQ	Revue de Qumran
RGRW	Religions in the Graeco-Roman World
RHE	Revue d'histoire ecclésiastique
RHR	Revue de l'histoire des Religions
RHPR	Revue d'histoire et de philosophie religieuses
RivSAnt	Rivista storica dell'Antichita
RocT	Roczniki Teologiczne
RRelRes	Review of Religious Research
RSPT	Revue des Sciences Philosophiques et Théologiques
RSR	Recherches de Science Religieuse
RSSSR	Research in the Social Scientific Study of Religion
RStMiss	Regnum Studies in Mission
R&T	Religion and Theology
RThom	Revue Thomiste
RTL	Revue Théologique de Louvain
RTPC	Revue de théologie et de philosophie chrétienne
SAJPsyc	South African Journal of Psychology
SAOC	Studies in Ancient Oriental Civilization
SBEC	Studies in the Bible and Early Christianity
SBET	Scottish Bulletin of Evangelical Theology
SBFLA	Studii Biblici Franciscani Liber Annuus
SBLDS	Society of Biblical Literature Dissertation Series
SBLMS	Society of Biblical Literature Monograph Series
SBLSBL	Society of Biblical Literature Studies in Biblical Literature
SBLSemS	Society of Biblical Literature Semeia Studies
SBLSP	Society of Biblical Literature Seminar Papers
SBLSymS	Society of Biblical Literature Symposium Series
SBLWGRW	Society of Biblical Literature Writings from the Greco-Roman World
SBT	Studies in Biblical Theology
ScAm	Scientific American
ScChrB	Science and Christian Belief
ScDig	Science Digest
ScEs	Science et Esprit
SCEthn	Series in Contemporary Ethnography
SCHNT	Studia ad Corpus Hellenisticum Novi Testamenti
SCR	Studies in Comparative Religion
Scriptura	Scriptura
SEÅ	Svensk Exegetisk Årsbok

SEAJT	*South East Asia Journal of Theology*
SecCent	*Second Century*
SEHT	Studies in Evangelical History and Thought
Semeia	*Semeia*
XVIIᵉ siècle	*XVIIᵉ siècle*
Shamanism	*Shamanism*
SHCM	Studies in the History of Christian Mission
SHR	Studies in the History of Religions
SIFC	*Studi Italiani di Filologia Classica*
SICHC	Studies in the Intercultural History of Christianity
SixtCenJ	*Sixteenth Century Journal*
SJOT	*Scandinavian Journal of the Old Testament*
SJPhil	*Southern Journal of Philosophy*
SJRS	*Scottish Journal of Religious Studies*
SJT	*Scottish Journal of Theology*
SMedJ	*Southern Medical Journal*
SNTSMS	Society for New Testament Studies Monograph Series
SocAn	*Sociological Analysis*
SocCom	*Social Compass*
SocG	*Sociologische Gids*
SocQ	*Sociological Quarterly*
SocRel	*Sociology of Religion*
Soph	*Sophia*
SOTBT	Studies in Old Testament Biblical Theology
SP	Sacra Pagina
SpCh	*The Spirit and Church*
SPhilA	*Studia Philonica Annual (Studia Philonica)*
SPhilMon	Studia Philonica Monographs
SR/SR	*Studies in Religion/Sciences religieuses*
StChHist	Studies in Church History
StEv	Studies in Evangelicalism
StPB	Studia Post-Biblica
StrOnk	*Strahlentherapie und Onkologie*
SSAMD	Sage Series on African Modernization and Development
SSMed	*Social Science and Medicine*
ST	*Studia Theologica*
StChrMiss	Studies in Christian Mission
StHistEc	*Studia Historiae Ecclesiasticae*
StPatr	*Studia Patristica*
Stroke	*Stroke*
StThIn	Studies in Theological Interpretation
StWChr	*Studies in World Christianity*
SUNT	Studien zur Umwelt des Neuen Testaments
SvMT	*Svensk Missionstidskrift*
SwJT	*Southwestern Journal of Theology*
TANZ	Texte und Arbeiten zum neutestamentlichen Zeitalter
TDNT	*Theological Dictionary of the New Testament.* Translated by Geoffrey W. Bromiley. Edited by Gerhard Kittel and Gerhard Friedrich. 10 vols. Grand Rapids: Eerdmans, 1964–76.
TEFSG	Theological Education Fund Study Guide
TexJC	*Texas Journal of Corrections*
TheolEd	*Theological Education*
Theology	*Theology*
ThLife	*Theology and Life*
Thrakika	*Thrakika*
ThTo	*Theology Today*
Time	*Time*
TJ	*Trinity Journal*

TLZ	*Theologische Literaturzeitung*
TorStTh	Toronto Studies in Theology
TranscPsyc	*Transcultural Psychiatry*
TranscPsycR	*Transcultural Psychiatric Research*
TranscPsycRR	*Transcultural Psychiatric Research Review*
TS	*Theological Studies*
TwinResHumGen	Twin Research and Human Genetics
TynBul	*Tyndale Bulletin*
TZ	*Theologische Zeitschrift*
UF	*Ugarit Forschungen*
UJT	Understanding Jesus Today
UNDCSJCA	University of Notre Dame Center for the Study of Judaism and Christianity in Antiquity
UrbMiss	*Urban Mission*
VA Practitioner	*VA Practitioner*
VC	*Vigiliae Christianae*
VEE	*Verbum et Ecclesia*
Vid	*Vidyajyoti*
VidJTR	*Vidyajyoti Journal of Theological Reflection*
ViolWom	*Violence Against Women*
VitIndRel	Vitality of Indigenous Religions
VOH	*Voice of Healing*
VT	*Vetus Testamentum*
WBC	Word Biblical Commentary
WCDN	World Christian Doctors Network
WJBlSt	*Western Journal of Black Studies*
WMANT	Wissenschaftliche Monographien zum Alten und Neuen Testament
WMQ	*William and Mary Quarterly*
WPC	Westminster Pelican Commentaries
WPJ	*World Policy Journal*
WSCM	World Studies of Churches in Mission (World Council of Churches)
WTJ	*Westminster Theological Journal*
WUNT	Wissenschaftliche Untersuchungen zum Neuen Testament
WW	*Word and World*
WWit	*Word and Witness*
YSMT	York Studies in Medieval Theology
ZAW	*Zeitschrift für die Alttestamentliche Wissenschaft*
Zion	*Zion*
ZMR	*Zeitschrift für Missionswissenschaft und Religionswissenschaft*
ZNT	*Zeitschrift für Neues Testament*
ZNThG	*Zeitschrift für Neuere Theologiegeschichte*
ZNW	*Zeitschrift für die Neutestamentliche Wissenschaft*
ZTK	*Zeitschrift für Theologie und Kirche*
ZPE	*Zeitschrift für Papyrologie und Epigraphik*
ZR	*Zeitschrift für Religionswissenschaft*
ZRGG	*Zeitschrift für Religions- und Geistesgeschichte*
ZSNT	Zacchaeus Studies: New Testament
ZST	*Zeitschrift für systematische Theologie*
Zyg	*Zygon*

PART 4

Proposed Explanations

For a worldview that accepts both natural and supernatural factors (and attributes even nature's origin to supernatural causation), natural and supernatural explanations need not be incompatible. Nevertheless, uncommitted observers are generally more likely to acknowledge supernatural factors where natural factors prove insufficient to account for events. Often natural factors prove sufficient to account for recoveries, coincidences, and the like, even when some individual cases appear unusual. But is this always the case?

For most Western observers, the interpreter's assumptions determine *how* improbable natural explanations must be before supernatural explanations will be considered. Some rule out all evidence that they could explain by some other means, no matter how improbable the other explanations are, because they presuppose that supernatural explanations are always more improbable than even the weakest natural ones. In this case, they do not merely assign the burden of proof wholly to the supernaturalists, despite antisupernaturalism being the minority position historically and globally. They also demand a standard of evidence impossible for any position to meet, because evidence that contradicts one's position can virtually always be explained away. Those who reject this antisupernaturalistic bias, common though it may be, recognize that sometimes supernatural factors offer a more parsimonious explanation that skeptics dismiss too readily. In such cases, neutral observers should deem supernatural factors the best specific explanation available. That is the secondary, more controversial argument of the book, but I can address it more concisely than the arguments of previous sections because this argument builds on much of the information that I have already discussed in the previous chapters.

Nonsupernatural Causes

... magic, charms, spells and amulets. Cures, by these means, were recorded both in ecclesiastical and medical circles. The facts need not be questioned. It was the explanation of the facts which was wrong. They were mental and faith cures and not miracles. —George Gordon Dawson[1]

As we noted earlier, if even a handful of miracle claims prove far more probable than not, Hume's argument fails, removing the initial setting of wholesale skepticism against miracles. Without a special burden of proof against miracle claims, they can be evaluated on a case-by-case basis by normal laws of evidence like any other claims. Even on this basis, however, not all unusual claims require special divine action to be true; some may reflect the ordinary (or even unusual) process of nature.

Many cures stem from natural causes, even if, as most theists affirm, divine purpose stands somewhere behind nature. Many cures lack sufficient clear indications of divine activity to offer by themselves clear evidence for the latter for those who do not already believe it. Affirming the reality of miracles also does not give us the right to ignore the fact that miracles very often do not happen. Tragically and disappointingly, large numbers of people who seek supernatural (or natural) healing are not healed.[2] This observation seems to hold empirically true even in

---

1. Dawson, *Healing*, 188.
2. For examples and theological discussion, see further Crump, *Knocking*, 10–14, 42–45 and passim. For some further specific examples, see Benson, *Not Healed*; Eareckson with Musser, *Joni*; Bergunder, "Miracle Healing," 302 (noting that the same faith nevertheless enabled the woman to face death bravely). Joni Eareckson believed that she would be healed (Eareckson with Musser, *Joni*, 59, 62, 65, 69, 79, 113, 187–88); but while she recognizes that God sometimes does heal (187, 189–90), she was not physically healed herself. Instead she came to terms with her disability; indeed, few would doubt that her disability has allowed her to touch more lives than most other people touch (cf. e.g., 219–22, 228, and her subsequent advocacy for the disabled). Black, *Homiletic*, 52–53, 181, rightly emphasizes sensitivity toward the many persons not physically cured in healing services. Hiebert, *Reflections*, 200–201, notes his deep disappointment when

ministries that claim much supernatural healing, as most proponents of supernatural healing acknowledge.[3]

Likewise, some remissions prove disappointingly temporary, despite the short-
term benefit they do provide.[4] Testimonies from too soon after the cure[5] typically
do not leave room to test the permanence of the cure; even cases that a doctor
reasonably believed healed based on present evidence might prove temporary.[6] (It
should be noted, however, that even some early testimonies have been revisited
decades or even a half century later and proved enduring.[7]) Whether temporary
improvements can function as evidence of healing depends on the case and on

---

a child for whom he as a missionary prayed died, but that the funeral ended up glorifying God in the
community. By contrast, although Lindsay, *Not Healed*, allows for it to be someone's time to die (15–16),
he usually attributes a person's lack of healing to sin (8–12), unbelief (17–18), or the like, going beyond
biblical evidence; one might as well blame the healing ministers for inadequate faith (cf. Jas 5:14–15).

3. E.g., Gardner, *Healing Miracles*, 155–74, esp. 165–69; also 206; Neal, *Power*, x–xi, 1–8; Bennett,
Morning, 151; Stewart, *Only Believe*, 145, 147 (also 76 and 165, on the healing evangelists; also ibid., 152,
on a school for the deaf in Liberia founded by Stewart's ministry); Alexander, *Signs*, 10–13; Woldu, *Gifts*,
158–59; Tari, "Preface," 11 (noting that they pray for healing only when led to do so; cf. *Breeze*, 55–57);
Martin, *Healing*, 53; Ogilvie, *Healing*, 36–37; Lawrence, *Healing*, 43–44; Kirby, "Recovery," 119–20; Rogge,
"Relationship," 384–90; Benson, *Not Healed*, passim; Lucas, "Foundations," 31–37; Reyes, "Framework,"
114–43; Kraft, "Years," 120; Pytches, *Come*, 22, 162; cf. Winston, *Faith*, 47–49; Pytches, *Thundered*,
55, 82–83; Alamino, *Footsteps*, 51 (blind), 57–58 (deaf); Woodard, *Faith*, 48–58; Gee, *Trophimus* (in
McGee, *Miracles*, 196); helpful historical discussion in Hardesty, *Faith Cure*, 129–37; for Latin American
Pentecostalism, see Petersen, *Might*, 102–4 (noting trust in God's sovereignty, 102). This was clearly true
even of noted healing evangelists; for example, many close to Wigglesworth were not healed (Warner,
"Introduction," 19), and his own three-year agony with gallstones made his later ministry gentler than
before (Gee, "Foreword," 13; Warner, "Introduction," 22–23); Oral Roberts's informal estimate of 10
percent healed (Stewart, *Only Believe*, 58); in the modern faith movement, see Barron, *Gospel*, 125–36.
Van Brenk, "Wagner," 257, cites 29 percent completely healed for Wagner (which would be quite high).

4. E.g., Salmon, *Heals*, 113–16 (in ch. 16, "Disappointments"). Some also view even temporary
recoveries as often helpful, extending life at least partly (a view noted in Ogilbee and Riess, *Pilgrimage*,
49; cf. the incidents in Stibbe, *Prophetic Evangelism*, 2–3; Cunningham, *Holiness*, 154–55). Harry Hock
(*Miracles*) benefited greatly from his dramatic recovery in 1965, but he did pass away in late 1969 (when his
wife, at least, was in her sixties; see http://www.genealogybuff.com/pa/pa-mifflin-obits14.htm; accessed
Dec. 6, 2010); for another productive reprieve of three and a half years, see Hock, *Miracles*, 53–54, 69; in
Maddocks, *Call*, 36–37, a clearly dying man recovered after anointing, yet died of the same disease two
years later; in Ising, *Blumhardt*, 212, a man dying of lung disease returned to his work healthy but died two
years later. Baxter, *Healing*, 260–61, notes that some, especially older persons, not unexpectedly pass away
several years after healing; he emphasizes that present physical healings, in contrast to future resurrection,
are not intended to cure human mortality. Cf. also the report that Kimbangu warned one man named
Yankala not to sin again, and when Yankala did so his blindness returned (McClenon, "Miracles," 187).

5. Some testimonies come from soon after the cure (e.g., the cancer recovery testimony of J. W. Guthrie,
Akron, Ohio, "Healed," comes from only two years after the diagnosis; the testimony in Lederer, "Healing," of
Elyria, Ohio, comes only months after the remarkable tuberculosis recovery). Early Pentecostals recognized
that some recoveries were temporary and sought to explain these theologically (e.g., Clifford, "Permanent";
reprinted as Clifford, "Healings").

6. May, "Miracles," 151, points out that two of Gardner's twenty-two healing examples (about 9 percent)
died the year that Gardner's book (*Healing Miracles*) was published.

7. E.g., Warner, "Still Healed" (after fifty-two years); Warner, "Living by Faith" (after sixty-five to
seventy-five years). Clara Shannon, mentioned earlier, temporarily succumbed again to the affliction
from which she had been dying, but after more prayer, she remained healthy for at least forty more years
(Hurst, "Healings").

the bar the observer requires as evidence, but many would not establish the case by themselves.[8]

Finally, that everyone dies shows that no one, regardless of one's theology, will always be healed.[9] That is, whether remissions are permanent or not, death is inevitable for everyone. Not only are many not healed (as noted above), many have died without healing even in movements that emphasize healing, despite abundant prayer for them.[10] In some movements, a number of persons have even died precisely because, waiting for miraculous intervention, they neglected medical intervention already available to them.[11]

8. Bishop's dismissal of temporary cures as violating the definition of miracle (Bishop, *Healing*, 203) begs the question, since there is no agreed-on definition; moreover, even in medicine, when the original cause of an ailment is not removed, the ailment may return (e.g., one with a genetic predisposition to cancer may be genuinely cured and not merely in temporary remission but may succumb to cancer later). Even in some cases of relapses after a few years (such as rarely happen in connection with Lourdes), the original healing remains medically inexplicable (Cranston, *Miracle*, 185). But temporary cures, while beneficial, are often too ambiguous to function as evidence. Ancient conceptions of some kinds of miracles or magic allowed for reversal (see examples in Bertman, "Note"), but these were not normally eliminations of benefits conferred and therefore would not be relevant to this case.

9. So also Matthews and Clark, *Faith Factor*, 61; Choy, *Murray*, 158; Pink, *Healing*, 24; cf. Lim, "Evaluation," 189; Spraggett, *Kuhlman*, 109 (citing Dr. Don Gross); Robertson, *Miracles*, 109 (acknowledging that it is sometimes God's will to "take" someone); Christians being ready for death in Neal, *Power*, 12–17; some early Church of God Pentecostals in Alexander, *Healing*, 112–13. Some even cite cases where they believe sickness (German, "Mysterious Ways"; Numbere, *Vision*, 337 [sickness preventing taking a fatal flight]; Alamino, *Footsteps*, 48 [sickness protecting from false accusation]; Ten Boom, *Tramp*, 176; Bredesen, *Miracle*, 69) or other problems (Smith, "Breakdowns") proved providential, restraining them from a situation that could have led instead to death. In Anderson, *Miracles*, 156, the lack of supernatural healing saved the patient's marriage (the surgery brought the family together, preventing the divorce); earlier, J. Hudson Taylor experienced his greatest advances through physical affliction (Miller, *Miracle of Healing*, 66–67 [cf. also 87–89]; cf. Ps 119:67, 71), though he also experienced dramatic recoveries (ibid., 15–16, 87).

10. As a test case, during the 1918 flu epidemic, early Pentecostals claimed that many escaped death and were healed; their obituaries nevertheless show that many did die. At least some sources treated the deceased as having died in faith and overcome (Alexander, *Healing*, 222). For reports of both deaths and healings during that epidemic, see Olena, *Horton*, 43. The reality of death in spite of prayer clearly jarred a young and idealistic Aimee Semple MacPherson regarding her first husband (Blumhofer, *Sister*, 91–94); "faith" may have even encouraged the original deficiency in hygiene that helped precipitate the death (91). Charismatic leaders like David Watson have died from illness despite the prayers and faith of many (Storms, *Healing*, 34–35); note also, e.g., the godly Elberta Bennett (Bennett, *Morning*, 118–21). Though this present book emphasizes those who have been healed, many with whom I have talked during this period have shared about other loved ones who experienced tragic deaths despite fervent prayers; e.g., Genti Rexho (his mother; personal correspondence, May 25, 2009); Dick and Debbie Riffle (their son; personal correspondence, Dec. 13, 2007); cf. also Reed, *Surgery*, 16, 36. I am aware of a rare circle of teaching that has promised physical immortality (I have had particular concern regarding this version of "Manifested Sons" teaching), but such circles presumably die out over time with their most extreme advocates. Manifested Sons teachers like Bill Britton have died, though expecting elite Christians to be glorified on earth during the final tribulation (*Jesus the Pattern Son* [Springfield, Mo.: Bill Britton, 1967], 73–75; idem, *Sons of God—Awake!* [Springfield, Mo.: Bill Britton, 1966], 1–17, 64–83); the more radical Manifested Sons teacher Sam Fife died in 1979 ("Body Loses Head"; Taft, "Crash"; Scott, "Sect Leader"). Father Divine apparently taught that following him properly cured all sickness and could ideally prevent death (Fauset, *Gods*, 63).

11. E.g., Reed, *Surgery*, 41–42; Oursler, *Power*, 252; see esp. examples in May, "Miracles," 145; on Hobart Freeman, see, e.g., Barron, *Gospel*, 14–33; cf. Sweet, *Health*, 160; Wagner and Higdon, "Issues"; Alexander,

One cannot fairly count such observations against the testimony of the Gospels, however.[12] The Gospels nowhere imply continuous healing leading to immortality and have rarely been construed as implying this.[13] Nor do they appear to envisage a situation in this age where all the disabled are healed (cf. Luke 14:13–14); many of those who pray for the sick affirm that, no matter how many blessings of the kingdom are at work in the present, some still await the future era.[14] For early Christians, signs of the kingdom represented *samples* of the future age, not its fullness. Indeed, texts from the Pauline corpus indicate that even some persons in Paul's circle remained sick.[15] Paul apparently saw no contradiction between such illnesses and his claim that God performed signs through his ministry (2 Cor 12:12; Rom 15:19). Granted such observations, how should we respond to more dramatic healing claims such as many of those that we have noted?

Epistemological Premises

I believe that the book's primary and less controversial thesis, that eyewitnesses report healings (even rather dramatic ones), is already safely established. But how should these claims be understood? If one starts with the assumption that miracles happen, one will construe many of these reports as miracles. If one starts with the assumption that miracles do not happen, one will interpret all these stories differently. If we leave both options open and look for the most

---

Fire, 302. (Many of these writers critique an excess, not all charismatic healing; Reed's sister, for example, is charismatic leader Rita Bennett; Bennett, *Morning*, 141.) For some African churches' failure to address AIDS prevention adequately, see, e.g., Togarasei, "HIV/AIDS," 13–15; cf. Wanyama et al., "Belief." News stories about religiously based criminal neglect in cases of children's health abound: e.g., Rose French, "Courts Face New Challenges in Faith Healing Cases," Associated Press, June 30, 2009, http://news .yahoo.com/s/ap/20090630/ap_on_re/us_rel_faith_healing_law; accessed June 30, 2009; Robert Imrie, "Wis. Jury: Father Guilty in Prayer Death Case," Associated Press, Aug. 1, 2009, http://news.yahoo.com/s /ap/20090802/ap_on_re_us/us_prayer_death; accessed Aug. 1, 2009; Mensah M. Dean, "Faith-healing Parents Charged in Death of Infant Son," *Philadelphia Daily News*, http://www.philly.com/philly/hp /news_update/20091008_Faith-healing_parents_charged_in_death_of_infant_son.html; accessed Oct. 8, 2009; already a case in 1915 noted in Wacker, "Living," 434.

12. Some cite evil in the world as justification for rejecting theism (the position hypothetically noted in Basinger, "Evidence," 57–58; contrast Larmer, "Explanations," 11), but it is an idealized theism distinct from any form of theism offered in Jewish, Christian, or Islamic Scriptures.

13. Cho, "Foundation," 86, cites Oswald J. Smith (*Physician*, 57, 64), warning against building doctrine against healing on those who are not healed, since even Jesus did not heal all.

14. What many call the "already/not yet" of the kingdom, or "inaugurated" vs. consummated eschatology. See, e.g., Blue, *Authority*, 107–16; Lucas, "Foundations," 32; Dunkerley, *Healing Evangelism*, 51–55; Nolivos, "Paradigm," 233; Hudson, "British Pentecostals," 298 (though noting on 299–300 that this was not widely accepted in early British Pentecostalism); Cho, "Foundation," 94.

15. Many rightly cite Gal 4:13–14; Phil 2:27; 1 Tim 5:23; 2 Tim 4:20 (e.g., Blue, *Authority*, 107–8; Lucas, "Foundations," 31–32; Storms, *Healing*, 95–100). The thorn in the flesh of 2 Cor 12:7 that many cite, however, is more debatable (see Num 33:55; Josh 23:13; Judg 2:3; e.g., Keener, *Corinthians*, 240; Kwon, "Foundations," 164–65; Bartow, *Adventures*, 103), and while Gal 4:13 probably refers to sickness, it does not indicate an eye disease (*pace* many; see Keener, "Notes," 47–49). See also 1 Kgs 1:1; 14:4; 2 Kgs 13:14.

plausible explanation in any given case, different cases may require different explanations.

Regardless of one's assumptions about the possibility of supernatural causation, however, virtually everyone will agree that some claims are not miraculous and that many others do not offer evidence compelling enough by themselves to surmount a very high bar of evidence (for some starting with mostly Humean assumptions yet willing to accept strong evidence). Nevertheless, I will argue, especially in chapters 14–15, that there is some sufficiently strong evidence today to meet an open-minded nonsupernaturalist's bar of proof, if never that of a closed-minded antisupernaturalist. This is the secondary and more controversial argument of this book.

Epistemic Agnosticism

Thoroughgoing epistemological skepticism becomes impractically cumbersome when applied to daily life and often fails to allow for degrees of probability. For example, at an extreme, some aver that one cannot claim to have met with some-one else but only to have inferred that one met with someone else. Yet people in everyday life, as well as historians, do not and cannot function with such a narrow epistemological skepticism.[16] Demanding absolute certainty of the sort available in mathematics before making any sort of claims ignores the degrees of probability that we judge sufficient for various activities; it prejudices the case a priori against any assertions.[17] Many philosophers do not embrace such a limited epistemology, including regarding miracles.[18]

16. See Baxter, "Historical Judgment," 24–25. Baxter is critiquing those who so portray the disciples' resurrection experiences, noting that this epistemological skepticism so treats all encounters, transcendent or not. See also Maxwell, "Theories," 28–29, advocating a "structural realism" that accepts probable inferences, against an epistemological skepticism with which no one acts consistently. Descartes himself did not intend for skepticism to be applied with such rigor (Landesman, *Epistemology*, 78–81). Scientific theories involve both paradigms, which can be subjective, and data, on much of which observers usually agree (Barbour, *Religion and Science*, 127). Against extreme relativists, who treat scientific theories as more socially constructed than Kuhn, see Barbour, *Religion and Science*, 144–46; Baghramian, "Relativism"; against relativistic applications of Kuhn, cf. Musgrave, "Thoughts," 49; Stegmüller, "Theory Change," 86–87. Although social pragmatism is an inadequate epistemic foundation, it may also be worth noting that pure relativism would make it impossible to justify the Nuremberg trials (cf. Jaki, *Patterns*, 21) or to condemn the Nazi Holocaust and other atrocities except for social utility, itself ultimately difficult to justify without appeal to a higher principle. Between those who neglect social constructions and those who deny even the possibility of concrete data exist a range of "critical realist" positions (Templeton, "Introduction," 9; cf. Polkinghorne, *Physics*, 5–6, situating critical realism between modernism and postmodernism). On scientists' preference for critical realism, see Polkinghorne, *Reality*, 1–6, 15, 35; Devitt, "Realism."

17. Cf. Polanyi, *Knowledge*, 273–74, suggesting that Kant's demand for suspending judgment in pure mathematics in the absence of certain knowledge (though he accepted a prioris there) is itself a premise for which one cannot claim certain knowledge. Cf. also his argument about genuine patterns in nature, the degree of objectivity concerning which may be quantified by its order insofar as that differs from expectations of randomness (Polanyi, *Knowledge*, 33–40, esp. 36–37). On provisionality and probability in warrant, see also Templeton, "Introduction," 9–10.

18. Without embracing miracles, Levine, *Problem*, 186, concludes, "Contemporary epistemic theory, including reliabilism, is neutral with regard to the type of evaluative and normative question about the

According to one stringent modern approach to epistemology, we can describe human experiences, but we cannot know whether or what supernatural activity might stand behind them.[19] This supposedly neutral approach provides a common ground for academic discourse on history (namely, human experience open to investigators regardless of presuppositions), so it is useful. It does not, however, provide for dialogue regarding legitimate questions of theology or philosophy and is limited in the sphere in which it can make pronouncements. Such an approach, if its agnosticism functions as a definitive presupposition rather than as an adaptable heuristic tool, forecloses a priori the possibility of some potential interpretations. Though science labels potential grids for interpreting its data as hypotheses, it does not rule out the usefulness of such grids. Employing a common language for history need not require us to rule out a priori the possibility of some metahistorical hypotheses proving more satisfactory than others in explaining the data. In chapters 5–6, I argued that supernatural explanations like theism should not be a priori ruled out as potential explanatory hypotheses.

Since science depends on observation and experimentation, and since a "miracle is by definition an irreproducible" experience,[20] even documented miracle cures by definition cannot fit precisely the expectations of science as it has been most narrowly defined.[21] While affirming miracles, one scholar warns that "miracles cannot be investigated by the usual scientific methods since we cannot control the variables and perform experiments."[22] This does not mean that claims about such events are not falsifiable; it simply means that they must be investigated by means of the appropriate methodology, one suited for individual events.[23] Miracles are distinct acts in history (on theistic premises, actions of an intelligent agent) and thus no more subject to experimentation than other historical events like Napoleon's defeat at Waterloo.[24] As I noted earlier, science depends on predictions of the physical world; its method is not meant to provide mathematical predictions

possibility of justified belief in miracles that we have been examining." Hume could not accept miracles due to "his peculiarly narrow philosophical empiricism" (186; cf. 52).

19. Haacker, *Theology*, 9. In fact, there is no single consensus approach to epistemology today (Landesman, *Epistemology*, 191–92).

20. Hirschberg and Barasch, *Recovery*, 144; cf. Laato, "Miracles," 68. Hirschberg and Barasch note (*Recovery*, 277) that many scientists treat "miracles" as anomalies that need not be explained; they are statistically possible but not central for the practice of medicine. McClenon, *Events*, 7, notes that anomalous events "need not be experimentally validated" to have real sociological effects.

21. Definitions of science vary; see Okello, *Case*, 13. No one actually conducts his or her life along lines of the stricter definitions; virtually all knowledge on which we act in daily life involves probabilities of varying degrees. Between excessive caution and uncritical acceptance of all claims lie various critical approaches. Here I am simply specifying a methodological limitation of a particular approach to epistemology.

22. Wilson, "Miracle Events," 266.

23. If evaluated in a larger class of events, it would be the class of other miraculous events, once one has established the likelihood of a miracle in a given case. The closest one comes to a control group is nonmiraculous events; the closest one comes to predictions is that they occur more often in faith contexts, but firm specific predictions are not possible here (or in history more generally, which deals with individual events).

24. Clark, "Miracles and Law," 31.

of human (or divine) actions. Nevertheless, healing reports make claims about empirical reality that often can be tested,[25] and hypotheses may be formed about their most plausible explanations without necessarily unfairly prejudicing the case for or against faith. Their interpretation, however, is complicated by the evaluators' philosophic a prioris that often screen out possible explanations, as I suggested in chapters 5–6.

Genuine Anomalies

Although this chapter will explore natural explanations for many recoveries, some recoveries are anomalous. Whatever the reasons, extraordinary cures do occur and should not be minimized. Patrick McNamara, director of the Evolutionary Neurobehavior Laboratory at Boston University School of Medicine, and Reka Szent-Imrey, research associate at the Institute for the Biocultural Study of Religion, challenge the traditional intellectual goal of merely debunking miracle claims rather than learning from them. In this "scenario the hero-scientist" informs the recovering person that no real cure is occurring, "that instead he is gullible, stupid," and should appreciate the heroic scientist for informing the patient of this truth. By contrast, these authors contend, extraordinary healings do occur, especially in religious contexts. While agnostic about supernatural causation, they insist that scholars should study and learn from these cures.[26]

Statistically, extraordinary unexpected events sometimes happen; in ten million cases, one may expect to find about ten instances of any one-in-a-million unlikelihoods.[27] What makes such anomalies harder to accommodate as mere statistical deviations is when the quality or quantity of their occurrence in a given sort of setting is also statistically improbable to a high degree; this accumulation of irregularities becomes significant if there are patterns in their occurrence. Further, some events are too unexpected, contravening observed patterns of nature to such an extent that they exceed mere irregularities (e.g., perhaps the nonmedical raising of someone who has not breathed for hours). Critics might respond to such cases by citing apparently analogous cases of such anomalies. These proposed analogies, however, beg the question, since they might be further instances of the matter in

---

25. See Smedes, *Ministry*, 59: healing claims must be open "to objective, rigorous, and scientifically responsible testing . . . over an adequate period of time and . . . open to critical examination of skeptics." Like believers, skeptics can explain away evidence to fit contrary paradigms; but science can pass judgment on whether the person was sick and whether the person is now cured (cf. John 9:25). Ideally (if sufficient studies are available), with regard to the recovery's evidential value, science may also compare the probabilities of this happening in given cases where supernaturalist explanations are not invoked (esp. by chance). On NT epistemology treating miracles empirically, see Blessing, "Psychology," esp. 90–92, 97. Physical recoveries are not simply the subjective psychological experiences characterized as "mysticism" (cf. James, *Varieties*, 379–429; James himself allows supernatural reality but rejects miracles [520–21], concurring with dominant philosophic dispositions of his era).

26. McNamara and Szent-Imrey, "Learn," 208–9. The observation about religious contexts begins on 210.

27. One cannot calculate these with any mathematical precision, however; events that are too rare offer insufficient data for statistical predictions.

question (i.e., a possibly supernatural event), or at least much rarer outside the observed pattern of occurrence.

Likewise, the sort of event typically expected one in a million times may appear far more often (say, thirty cases in a million) under specified conditions (e.g., when prayer is offered), suggesting a pattern. When anomalies repeatedly surround particular persons, for example, multiple raising accounts in one circle (whether Mama Jeanne, Albert and Julienne Bissouessoue, or Jesus of Nazareth), the pattern of occurrence is itself statistically improbable unless one takes into account some relationship with the pattern (e.g., here, one explanatory hypothesis would be supernatural causation).

Explanations may vary depending on how anomalous events are. The disappearance of a headache or even an unexpected deathbed recovery are more easily explained as random statistical irregularities than, say, the full restoration of a person whose systems have already shut down or (still more unexpectedly) the raising of a person dead for forty minutes. A person recovering unexpectedly or living longer than the doctor predicted could be attributed to chance, since predictions are fallible estimates based on limited knowledge.[28] Anomalies are rarer than these, however, and the compounding of anomalies is itself anomalous. To simply dismiss such patterns as random irregularities is to evade the possibility of a supernatural explanation by fiat of definition ("anomalies" that do not require explanation rather than a possible miracle). The less common naturalistic alternative, to dismiss accounts as fabrications because they are too anomalous on naturalistic grounds, is simply to presuppose what one hopes to prove.

The Demand for Analogies

Before turning to natural causes, I must address a reason often given for accepting only natural causes and also address my reasons for questioning that approach. Some scholars will accept those extranormal claims in early Christian sources for which we have analogies today (such as healings and exorcisms), yet reject those that they regard as unparalleled and that cannot be explained naturalistically.[29] That is, only naturalistic explanations are acceptable from the start. One of the most obvious test cases for claims that cannot be explained without supernatural causation is walking on water. Marcus Borg accepts reports of Jesus's healings and exorcisms because we have such reports for others conducting these types of activities but rejects reports of raising someone long dead, walking on water, or multiplying food. "As a historian," he insists, "I cannot accept that Jesus's ability to 'do the spectacular' was unique and without parallel."[30] Likewise, Bart Ehrman

---

28. See, e.g., the case Joseph F. O'Donnell, an oncologist, cites in Lenzer, "Citizen" (the fifth page of my online version). The same page in Lenzer also correctly notes the "bias called the survivor effect": survivors offer testimonies, but even if they prayed beforehand, the dead tell no tales.

29. For a fuller discussion of Troeltsch and the principle of analogy in historiography, see ch. 6.

30. Borg, "Disagreement," 232; cf. similarly Price, Son of Man, 19–21, 131; Theissen and Merz, Guide, 310; particularly explicitly Montefiore, Miracles, 18: "it is difficult to believe that God intervened so often

points out that we know thousands of people, and they do not walk on water.[31] And it cannot be denied that water-walking claims remain quite rare (though not unheard of)[32] compared with healings and exorcisms.

Yet even here the inquiry starts from a premise that is not necessarily neutral. Evaluating Jesus by the standards of widespread practice may fail to account for the fact that what we *do* know about him even based on purely secular historiographic grounds[33] pushes him far beyond the category of "most people," even in terms of how he viewed himself.[34] As noted in chapters 2–3, we cannot even compare him in this respect with typical sign prophets of his era, who failed to perform the promised signs.[35] There are similarities and differences with other charismatic sages of his era (not least the historical attestation surrounding the latter),[36] but they were rare, none of them clearly offered the sort of self-claims that Jesus almost certainly offered for himself,[37] and for that matter, a supernaturalist might not a priori rule out the possibility that some of them experienced some supernatural agency as well. More important, most people with Jesus's self-claims do not offer healings, exorcisms, and the like, and if we compare Jesus with those who do, rather than people in general, this category includes few enough members that we cannot easily extrapolate from the others to Jesus. What if Jesus really was sent by God and attested by special supernatural signs? Is there more bias in raising the question or in dismissing it without examination?

---

in the ministry of Jesus if intervention only very rarely occurs elsewhere" (a position assuming both that Jesus was not extraordinary and that intervention everywhere else is rare). We do have some parallel claims for each of these categories, especially for resuscitating dead persons (as noted in the previous chapter), but all these categories of claims are admittedly rare. For feeding miracles, see Gardner, *Healing Miracles*, 38, and other sources discussed earlier. I also argued earlier that historians do not need to presuppose atheism or deism (i.e., to rule out an active God) to talk about history.

31. Ehrman, *Prophet*, 196.

32. See, e.g., Dermawan, "Study," 256; on a popular level, see Crawford, *Miracles*, 26; Tari, *Wind*, 43–47 (citing multiple eyewitnesses he knew), regarding West Timor.

33. For studies at this level particularly well informed about Jesus's Jewish environment, to name only a few, see, e.g., Vermes, *Jesus the Jew*; idem, *Jesus and Judaism*; idem, *Religion*; Sanders, *Jesus and Judaism*; idem, *Figure*; Meier, *Marginal Jew*; Charlesworth, *Jesus within Judaism*; Theissen and Merz, *Guide*; Flusser, *Sage*; I offered my own contribution in Keener, *Historical Jesus*, chs. 17–19, 22. Not all of these scholars would agree with the degree of uniqueness I would attribute to Jesus in this respect, but I think that all would agree (as would, I think, even Borg and Ehrman, noted above) at least that Jesus's activities differed considerably from average.

34. Cf. Eve, *Miracles*, 378, 384–86; from a different angle, Bartholomew, *Belief*, 112, as cited in Licona, *Resurrection*, 145n31. On the importance of the context of Jesus's life and claims for evaluating his miracle claims, cf. Swinburne, "Evidence," 205–6 (on the resurrection claim).

35. See further Eve, *Miracles*; Keener, *Historical Jesus*, 242–43, and the discussion in chs. 2–3 of the present book. The one ultimate promised sign in dispute is his resurrection (the most significant, and in my opinion the only viable, historical objection to considering which stems from antisupernaturalist assumptions); whether he expected the kingdom's consummation in tandem with judgment on Jerusalem chronologically or (as I think) only theologically is also a matter of dispute. But Jesus, unlike what we know of the sign prophets, performed many signs.

36. Again, see Eve, *Miracles*; our chs. 2–3.

37. See Keener, *Historical Jesus*, chs. 18–19, and sources cited there (notably Flusser, *Judaism*, 620).

If one does not start with the premise that Jesus *could* not be unique (or at least highly extraordinary),[38] the evidence does suggest that Jesus was sufficiently beyond the normal person for us to investigate unusual questions about him.[39] To start with the premise that Jesus could not be sufficiently extraordinary as to invite extraordinary explanations (such as those that his earliest followers affirmed) is merely to state an assumption, not to offer an argument. That assumption might be more readily entertained if it did not simply rule out by fiat the very position that it purports to refute.

Having noted this point, however, I will maintain my focus here on the less controversial and more clearly documented cases of healings and exorcisms, rather than arguing Borg's and Ehrman's point here. Neither walking on water nor multiplying food are common or typical in the Gospels. I have noted some modern claims to nature miracles (ch. 12), but the majority of miracle claims today, as in the Gospels and Acts, involve unusual recoveries. And as noted in the previous chapter, there are a number of claims of raising the dead today, though the majority of those, like most in the Bible, do not address those who have been dead for extended periods of time.[40]

Introducing Nonsupernatural Causes

Although experiences reported as miracle cures are significant to those who experience them, not all are genuinely anomalous medically. Moreover, whereas many observers will view some unusual recovery claims as quite plausible, virtually everyone will regard some miracle claims as fallacious, whether the error arises through deception or misunderstanding. Most of us have experienced either breaches of trust by some faulty witnesses (sometimes even deliberate con artists) or some witnesses' unsatisfactory interpretive assumptions about what must constitute supernatural activity. One cult leader,[41] Sam Fife, built much of his claim

38. Borg, "Disagreement," 232, is explicit about his premise: "if I became convinced that at least a few people have been able to walk on water, then I would be willing to take seriously that Jesus may have done so. But as a historian, I find myself unable to say that the life of Jesus involved spectacular happenings of a magnitude without parallel anywhere else."

39. Cf. Polkinghorne, *Reality*, 68. Certainly for Christians who affirm the Creator's special activity in Jesus of Nazareth, "it would not be surprising if some quite remarkable things happened around him" (Placher, *Mark*, 79, citing also Archbishop Rowan Williams, *Tokens*, 44–45). A priori accepting or rejecting this premise constitutes working from assumptions; to explore the *possibility* of the premise requires only an open mind.

40. Those resuscitated are not normally long dead (Price, *Son of Man*, 21: "the rotting dead"), but there is only one case of that even in biblical narrative (John 11:39, 43–44; cf. the urgency in 2 Kgs 4:29).

41. I define "cult" here in sociological rather than theological terms, though most theologians would consider both categories applicable in this case. Though resembling a radical charismatic group in some respects (and undoubtedly with much variation at the local level, and perhaps differing at different points in the movement's history), Sam Fife's "Body of Christ" went far beyond this, moving many people to wilderness farms (see, e.g., Taft, "Followers," 1; Watson, "Leader"; Buffington, "Leader"; "Body Loses Head"; Rudin and Rudin, *Prison*, 72–74, esp. 73; Scott, "Sect Leader," A5), allegedly breaking up families (e.g.,

for supernatural attestation of his ministry on an exorcism that he performed, supposedly delivering a woman from epilepsy, on account of which he was allegedly able to lecture the psychiatrists at Tulane University.[42] When I inquired at Tulane several years later, psychologist David Reed, then in private practice, responded that "no EEG readings satisfactorily established epilepsy" and noted significant exaggeration on the leader's part (for example, they dialogued with Fife; he did not teach them).[43]

Some accounts of miracles raise suspicions even for those who accept some other kinds of miracles. Thus, for example, in one report blood mysteriously spattered onto a woman's white dress during a church service, but the stains equally mysteriously disappeared soon afterward.[44] In another, people claimed to see "bloodstained crosses floating across the night sky."[45] Those prone to accept supernatural explanations can be tempted to explain more details than necessary in such terms. While one cannot a priori rule such unusual claims to be impossible, at the least they diverge from the pattern of the bulk of the analogies for more documented extranormal claims, and thus our first instinct, even on the premise that miracles do occur, will be to seek other explanatory categories.

Dunphy, "Marriage"; Taft, "Followers," 16) and on at least some farms beating, restraining, or otherwise abusing children (Dunphy, "Marriage," C1; Dettling, "Witness") and others (Watson, "Leader"; Buffington, "Leader"; idem, "Routine") who were supposedly possessed. Other materials are also in my file (mostly numerous newspaper clippings and copies of interviews with ex-members shared with me by some local anticult activists several years after the reported events).

42. Sam Fife, *Studies in Demonology* (North Miami, Fla.: North Bible Center, n.d.), 35, 40; see her own more nuanced testimony in a mainstream setting in Miller, "Story" (noting on 177 that she had remained delivered for nearly twenty-seven years). Fife also circulated a tape of the woman's deliverance ("The Jane Story: Deliverance from Demons").

43. Personal correspondence, May 27, 1980, noting that the staff there accurately predicted Fife's own breakdown, which followed soon after. Reed's clinical evaluation appears in Smucker and Hostetler, "Case," 182 and passim; he asked Fife to share at Tulane what happened (187), believed that psychotherapy helped prepare her (189), and argued that her belief system helped make her susceptible to this method of cure (190). Although with less direct information, what information Dr. Henry H. W. Miles at Tulane had available when I wrote them offered a quite different impression from Fife's exaggerated claims (personal correspondence, April 21, 1980). One might also note that most of Fife's specific prophecies (e.g., in his speech from Waynesboro, Pennsylvania, 1972, excerpts of which were provided me) did not come to pass. With regard to healing beliefs, "Tapes Prove," 1, quotes tapes in which sect leaders insist that one should believe the "truth" that one is already healed rather than the "facts" of one's sickness.

44. Wacker, *Heaven Below*, 93 (citing Robert A. Brown, in *Latter Rain Evangel* [July 1929]: 6). The "mysterious" character might reflect the incompleteness of the source and a misunderstanding at the source (e.g., she began menstruating unexpectedly, something ruptured, or communion wine was spilled; the garment was cleaned; and someone who did not check interpreted this outcome as miraculous); but of course I am supplying a rationalist explanation for the report.

45. Wacker, *Heaven Below*, 93; cf. the reportedly widely seen vision of a cross in the sky, interrupting nighttime firing of weapons on both sides, in Boddy, "Cross" (citing his eyewitness sources). These might evoke the tradition of the appearance of Constantine's celestial cross (Eusebius *Life of Constantine* 1.27–32; Smith, *Comparative Miracles*, 100–102). I have dealt elsewhere with the phenomenon of celestial apparitions, which seem most often susceptible to other explanations (above, 80–82; also Keener, *John*, 1187; cf. one modern discussion of classical examples in Strothers, "Objects").

The abundance of magical charms attested in both Christian and non-Christian medical literature from the late fourth century suggests to some interpreters that many of the healings of that era were "mental and faith cures." This does not mean that people in antiquity did not experience these cures as genuine events,[46] but a cure may be genuine without requiring direct supernatural causation. Many cure claims today can also reflect mental cures or fraud. I already noted (ch. 7) that a large proportion of on-the-spot healing testimonies in public meetings, at least in the West, involve matters that are not immediately visible to onlookers, and that some deceptive or self-deceived attention seekers may claim healings publicly that do not persist. In some cases, however, the healers themselves deceptively exploit their audiences.

Fraud

Josephus thought that the sign prophets in his day (who did not focus on healing) were fraudulent, arguing that they failed to deliver the signs and wonders they promised.[47] Such accusations continue to surface with regard to healers of various religious traditions.[48] While many examples are debatable, clearly many faith healers are neither sincere nor effective, and this has probably been true as long as faith healing has been practiced.[49] In extensive accounts of miracle stories,

---

46. Dawson, *Healing*, 188, citing evidence in Oribasius's *Medical Collection* in the late 300s; cf. Woolley, *Exorcism*, 25–26. Church leaders sometimes complained about superstition among many Christians on a popular level (Woolley, *Exorcism*, 66–67). As noted above, others have tried to explain NT miracles by analogy to "paranormal" telepathy, clairvoyance, and precognition (Montefiore, *Miracles*; Thouless, "Miracles," 255–56; cf. Perry, "Believing," 341, cautiously); while the differences are significant (NT accounts suggest divine dependence rather than innate abilities), the analogy at least represents another attempt to get beyond typical Western assumptions.

47. Josephus *Ant.* 20.167–68. In antiquity, cf. doctors in Toner, *Culture*, 40.

48. E.g., Hunter and Chan, *Protestantism*, 147, report the "gossip" about some *qigong* practitioners faking healings; for traditional healers faking phenomena, see Edwards, "Medicine," 21; Frank, *Persuasion*, 44; for both fraudulent shamans and authentic "supernormal" phenomena in other cases, see Oesterreich, *Possession*, 381; for charges of fraud in parapsychology, see, e.g., Charpak and Broch, *Debunked*, 127–28; in alternative medicine, Quackwatch (as cited in Lenzer, "Citizen"); in Theosophy, cf. Scott, "Publics." Allison and Malony, "Surgery," 56–57, note that James Randi and others have shown how Filipino psychic surgery could be faked and note (on 60) that businessmen hired fakes to exploit tourists, leaving it difficult to ascertain how authentic the original version would have been. McClenon, who has "observed over 1,000 psychic surgeries in the Philippines," also suspects fraud, though not citing concrete evidence ("Healing," 44). By contrast, Licauco, "Psychic Healing," 96, argues that despite some fraud the genuine phenomenon occurs (with too many patients simultaneously for Randi's techniques to work). For one study on psychic surgery (regarding Brazil), see Greenfield, *Spirits*.

49. Cf. Robertson, "Epidauros to Lourdes," 188; for King Edward the Confessor (ca. 1051), see Schwarz, *Healing*, 108–10. Also cf. the comparison of faith healing quacks and medical quacks in Frye, "Faith Healing," 16–17; but faith healing quacks are presumably more common, because, unlike their medical analogues, they are unregulated. For a particularly egregious example, Jim Jones faked miracles (Kerns, *People's Temple*, 47–50). For a fraudulent magnetism doctor, see Buskirk, *Healing*, 49–50. Some doubt that any faith healers cured (e.g., Boggs, *Faith Healing*, 35); others differentiate respectable versions such as Episcopalian Agnes Sanford from "extremes" like Father Divine and (on his view) Aimee Semple McPherson (Gross, *Spiritual Healing*, 23–33). Some distinguish those with genuine cures from those with more abuses (e.g., Dr. Hoyt in Spraggett, *Kuhlman*, 64; Spraggett himself in 16–34).

it is therefore not unlikely that some will prove fraudulent even if others are not.[50] One critical investigator, though his hostility openly betrays his own biases,[51] has rightly identified some fraudulent faith healers in the United States.[52] Others, who unlike Randi allow for genuinely supernatural and continuing gifts of healings, also acknowledge and challenge frauds and marketing gimmicks.[53] An honest investigator shared with me several accounts of healing testimonies and discovered two of these cases to be likely fraudulent during the editing process of my book.

Nevertheless, while frauds exist and are probably common, one cannot extrapolate from a number of fraudulent claims to the conclusion that all miracle claims are fraudulent,[54] since, as Philip Jenkins notes, "the great majority of churches work strenuously to suppress fraudulent claims."[55] That is, many people are ready to expose and discipline fraud when they discover it. Healing researcher Candy Gunther Brown offers psychological reasons that people tend to extrapolate from isolated cases of fraud to generalize about cure claims in general, but warns that the evidence does not support this generalization.[56] Extrapolating from some claims being false to all claims being false involves a common logical fallacy: generalizing based on specific cases, hence illegitimate transference, that is, guilt by association.[57] The fallacy is all the more suspect when those extrapolating have inflexibly rigid antisupernaturalist assumptions to defend. The logic is actually

50. E.g., Bredesen, *Miracle*, 128–30, cited a story from Michael Esses, presumably in good faith, but serious questions were later raised about Esses's veracity (esp. by DeBlase, *Survivor*).

51. While Randi accuses a physician of biases because he is charismatic (290; though the bias seems clear in this case), he ought to allow the charge of bias to cut the other way, since Randi himself is openly hostile. Pankratz, "Magician," and especially Schmidt, "Possession," place Randi's criticism in the historic context of magicians' conflict with charlatans. Schmidt, "Possession," 275, notes that modern magicians (P. T. Barnum, Houdini, and James Randi) as exposers of "supernatural" claims reflect a trend since the late eighteenth century for magicians to function as Enlightenment "celebrities" rather than purveyors of the supernatural (though on the other side Houdini's objectivity is questioned in a case in McClenon, *Events*, 196). For magicians' rationalist exposés, see Schmidt, "Possession," 297–300 (esp. 299, on Spiritualists); on Enlightenment use of ventriloquism as trickery, see 279–92 (for entertainment, 292–97).

52. Randi, *Faith Healers*; some he treats, like Leroy Jenkins (89–98; see also Bishop, *Healing*, 30–44, esp. 42–43) and most obviously W. V. Grant (Randi, *Faith Healers*, 78, 81–82, 99–137) and Peter Popoff (49, 76–78, 139–81; cf. Alnor, *Heaven*, 31; Carson, *Scandalous*, 150–51), are commonly regarded as fraudulent, although many would not go so far for some other evangelists that Randi lists, whatever their weaknesses. See also Pankratz, "Magician," 122, for some clear evidence for fraud. On mixed results for historical investigations of Spiritualists, see McClenon, *Events*, 189–96, and on a mixture of clear fraud and unexplained elements, see 226–27. Randi rejects miracles a priori (Prather, *Miracles*, 44).

53. E.g., Schwarz, *Healing*, 17–21, 46–47, 50–51, 53–66, 77, 84, 117, 185, 193–94; Oursler, *Power*, 253–56; cf. Witty, *Healing*, 18–19; Naswem, "Healing," 30–31; Frost, *Healing*, 183.

54. Probably implied in the argument of Hume, *Miracles*, 37; idem, "Miracles," 35.

55. Jenkins, *New Faces*, 122–23; cf. also Matthews and Clark, *Faith Factor*, 205, on "healing services"; Newman, *Essays*, 171; Ising, *Blumhardt*, 331. Mayhue, *Healing*, 90, gladly reports a charismatic magazine having to retract a healing story; but perhaps the proper lessons to be drawn might be that they were honest enough to retract what they found to be false and that they did not have to do so on a regular basis.

56. Candy Gunther Brown, personal correspondence, Jan. 1, 2011, based on forthcoming research.

57. This approach lumps all supernatural claims together as a single group, then evaluates the entire group based on some claims (essentially what Hume does in *Miracles*, 37); what members of the set share is simply supernatural claims (that is what defines the set), not necessarily fraud. Cf. the observation of

more apt to problematize the other position: if a single claim proved true, the *possibility* of some other genuine healings would have to be granted regardless of the occurrence of false claims.[58] Moreover, some of the fraudulent practices may have developed in imitation of authentic versions, reinforcing the danger of a generalization against genuine healing based on fraudulent or failed attempts. (From my reading of many historical accounts, I suspect that many authentic extranormal events take place at times of great spiritual intensity, what modern church historians often call revival—and that some later successors try to manufacture events that look similar without the same spiritual reality behind them.) It is likewise precarious to link together all extranormal claims in history without respect to the differing genres of the works that include them.[59]

In a different category from fraud, and more often relevant to self-descriptions of healings, are common reporting errors of anomalous experiences. Long-term memory usually preserves less detail than short-term memory;[60] memories may be "reconstructed" to conform them to ordinary or sometimes extraordinary experience;[61] the limitations of language for communicating experiences may inhibit full communication;[62] and the like. These problems are, however, much more relevant to reports of subjective internal states than to actual changes in physical condition on which most of this book focuses.

That observation is also relevant regarding hallucinations and other necessarily private experiences. Many reports of "alien abductions," for example, emerged as "repressed memories" during hypnosis.[63] Reports vary according to cultural expectations,[64] but most significantly, there are "almost no instances in which an individual has been observed during" the alleged abduction experience.[65] This situation is quite different from experiences of healing that are often public and often include changes in health before and after the cure.

---

one speaker in Euripides *Thyestes* frg. 396: not only are persuasive falsehoods common, but so are truths that are typically not believed.

58. E.g., Smart, *Philosophers*, 33–34; Licona, "Historicity of Resurrection," 100; Keener, *Gift*, 90; cf. Lawton, *Miracles*, 54; Frohock, *Healing Powers*, 135. Of course, those who inflexibly insist that such events cannot happen can claim that all evidence contrary to their position is false, just as such arguments can be offered to defend any strongly held assumptions against the possibility of contrary evidence.

59. An approach criticized in Licona, "Historicity of Resurrection," 100 (who contrasts the genre of the Gospels with that of Aesop's *Fables*; also in idem, *Resurrection*, 143).

60. Pekala and Cardeña, "Issues," 52. Studies of anomalous experiences often must depend on retrospective reporting (61). After noting such qualifications, however, Pekala and Cardeña are willing to use data with such qualifications in view.

61. Ibid., 52–53 (the character of "ordinary" sometimes being constructed according to culturally conditioned narratives, 52).

62. Ibid., 53.

63. See Appelle, Lynn, and Newman, "Experiences," 253–54 (for an example), 266 (for the observation that 70 percent of the stories involve hypnosis). The claims involve "subjectively real memories" (254). Cf. also Walsh, *Shamanism*, 169, noting the frequent unreliability of hypnotically shaped memories.

64. Appelle, Lynn, and Newman, "Experiences," 259–60 (noting also the biasing influence of investigators' cues, 259).

65. Ibid., 257.

Emotional Arousal

Here, however, we must look at some of the other natural explanations, which have varying degrees of explanatory power for various kinds of cases. Everyone is aware, for example, that some conditions heal on their own. Thus, for example, Dr. Peter May observes that one kind of birthmark that was supposedly healed miraculously was the sort of birthmark known to disappear naturally over time.[66] Likewise, while most theists affirm that God works through medical intervention,[67] we would not likely classify most such events as miraculous in a more specific sense.[68] May contends that a significant minority of those who develop epilepsy stop having seizures at some point in their lives.[69]

Inviting more discussion here, some apparent recoveries may stem from momentary excitement.[70] Thus one scholar points to a woman he met who claimed that she had been "'healed' at a meeting with a famous guru, when she stood up unaided and took a few paces for the only time since the accident." The scholar notes that "she reverted immediately to her paralyzed state," although she remained convinced that her temporary cure had benefited her.[71] Some examples suggest that such temporary cures may have a psychological benefit at times.[72]

Such incidents are reported among Christians as well. One scholar has warned against the phenomenon of designated wonder workers in some Indian Pentecostal circles, comparing analogous tactics of Hindu gurus.[73] He offers his eyewitness

---

66. May, "Miracles," 151. Assuming that he refers to this same case, he notes that the birthmark in question remained visible though the child was twelve, which is unusual (154).

67. Note, e.g., the phone survey of 1,052 households in eastern North Carolina, where 87 percent affirmed belief in miracles and 80 percent affirmed that God works through physicians (Mansfield, Mitchell, and King, "Doctor"; cited in Kub, "Miracles," 1275). Historically, see, e.g., Hickson in Mullin, *Miracles*, 241; Oral Roberts in Schwarz, *Healing*, 31–33; Kuhlman in *Miracles*, 15; others, e.g., Graham, *Spirit*, 160; Csordas, *Self*, 34–35 (Catholic charismatics); MacNutt, *Healing*, 14, 164–67; Martin, *Healing*, 34–35; Lawrence, *Healing*, 52–57; Baxter, *Healing*, 288; Witty, *Healing*, 17; Gorsuch, "Limits," 286, 297; Pugh, "Medicine"; Pytches, *Come*, 163; White, *Adventure*, 44–50; Dearing, *Healing*, 159–71; Wilkerson, *Beyond*, 126, 131; Neal, *Power*, 22–29; Althouse, *Healing*, 57; Sweet, *Health*, 160; Rasolondraibe, "Ministry," 348; Godwin, *Strategy*, 19, 32, 46; Numbere, *Vision*, 293, 345; Hanciles, *Beyond Christendom*, 360–61 (African Christianity generally); Ayegboyin, "Heal," 237, 246 (on the Aladura); see the summary in Harrell, "Divine Healing," 227.

68. May, "Miracles," 151, notes one advertised healing of this nature.

69. Ibid., 154. Others note that this is less likely for long-term, severe epilepsy.

70. Ibid., 148; May warns about the hype of healing meetings, involving music and "zealous rantings," though cultures and faith traditions that appreciate emotive preaching or worship may well take umbrage at the latter characterization.

71. Hunter and Chan, *Protestantism*, 147.

72. E.g., although Elena Modina's husband died a week after the public cure (transcript of Elena Modina, Jan. 7, 2005), he died now happy, converted, and no longer an invalid.

73. Bergunder, "Healing," 106–7, while acknowledging that the Pentecostal practice is not limited to India; he also notes on 103 that the formal parallels predominate in exorcism rather than healing proper; also idem, *Movement*, 126, 155, though some of his analogies, like Christians calling on Jesus's name or the afflicted falling to the ground, noted on 156, are already in the NT; idem, "Miracle Healing," 295. For rivalry between Hindu and Christian exorcists, see Bergunder, *Movement*, 157–58; Hinduism often expresses itself in different ways, however, e.g., a Hindu shaman having live coals poured over his head while in a state of possession trance (see Harper, "Pollution," 189). Cf. Hiebert, *Reflections*, 191; Sri Lankan Catholic

account of a disabled elderly man who, in the emotional intensity of the Christian meeting, took several steps and testified of healing, yet afterward was carried out the back, exhausted.[74] Nevertheless, the same researcher admits that such a case was exceptional[75] and contends that most reported recoveries appear to be authentic, with participants believing they have been cured through prayer.[76] (I have already noted people who were cured permanently at such meetings.) While Western scholars would attribute many of these to "psychosomatic diseases or spontaneous cures," he notes, some cannot be readily explained in such terms.[77] He notes that "healings do occur which are difficult to explain by the scientific means at present available to us."[78] Even the analogies sometimes most closely offered for the claim of emotional manipulation, then, should not be taken as representative.

Neither, however, is it purely anomalous or limited to any one culture. Thus researcher Allen Spraggett, who came to adore Kathryn Kuhlman, reported bluntly the sad story of one boy who walked boldly without crutches on stage at another evangelist's request, only to be back on crutches by the end of the service.[79] Some other apparent healings hailed by onlookers or hearers turned out to be something other than what they supposed.[80] Terence Nichols warns that "everyone" has heard of disabled persons walking at healing crusades and afterward collapsing, though he argues that many genuine miracles do occur.[81]

---

demonology at Kudagama drawing on Hinduism and especially Sinhalese Buddhism (Stirrat, "Possession," 137). One early Pentecostal Indian evangelist, unable to find other Western contacts, affiliated with William Branham (Bergunder, "Evangelist," 363) and afterward eventually developed Branham's questionable theological legacy beyond Christianity (365–74; cf. idem, "Miracle Healing," 295).

74. Bergunder, "Healing," 108; idem, "Miracle Healing," 296. He notes that the rallies promise healing to all "but many go home unhealed." The emphasis of my present interest, that some are dramatically healed, should not detract from recognizing this other element. A number of healing evangelists in India are said to promise healing to everyone, a promise not realized, though there seems to be a general understanding that everyone knows that despite the rhetoric only some persons are healed (Bergunder, *Movement*, 161–62; idem, "Miracle Healing," 296). For other criticisms of inauthentic activity, see Thomas, "Issues," 148–50.

75. Bergunder, *Movement*, 162.

76. Ibid., 161; cf. also idem, "Miracle Healing," 296.

77. Bergunder, *Movement*, 161; idem, "Miracle Healing," 296. With respect to Western Christians, cf. Stedman, *Life*, 65, noting that persons sometimes improve temporarily due to emotional stimulation, but noting that genuine, quick, and permanent divine healings are "too well attested and documented to challenge."

78. Bergunder, "Healing," 108; idem, *Miracles*, 161. He provides verbatim testimony of someone whose younger sister was cured at a rally (108–9).

79. Spraggett, *Kuhlman*, 18. For some other failed claims, see, e.g., Nolen, *Healing*, 99 (on Kuhlman herself); Randi, *Faith Healers*, 288; Jeffries, "Healing," 72.

80. Many of those in wheelchairs in the front of some mid-twentieth-century healing meetings were persons simply with back problems who could not be left standing in the healing line, but this sometimes left onlookers with the impression of a healing that did not take place (Stewart, *Only Believe*, 115, 130, arguing that this impression was normally not deliberate). A man who claimed to be cured at Lourdes in 1875 was able to walk with crutches even before his healing, and postmortem examination showed that some evidence of the original injury remained (West, *Miracles*, 9–10), though remaining evidence of an original injury, such as scars, need not impair the functions for which healing is normally sought (cf. even John 20:20, 25).

81. Nichols, "Miracles," 707.

Scientists could perhaps hire good actors to conduct a revival meeting in a setting where people were accustomed to this style of religion (perhaps university students in and from a heavily religious region). Emotional arousal and comfort, positive confidence, the placebo effect, and so forth might account for a number of cures. Such responses would not necessarily rule out supernatural activity in some cases—participants might encounter God where they expected to experience God regardless of the intention of the organizers. My point is merely that religious use of emotional stimulation can be employed with benevolent or exploitive intentions and does not by itself demonstrate supernatural activity.

The Power of Faith

In some cases of purported healing, another nonsupernatural factor is at work. Some convinced persons exercise what they believe is faith, but what some psychologists would consider denial. They act as though their symptoms do not exist, when in fact no medical change has taken place.[82] While hope and the power of suggestion can exert a positive curative influence in many sorts of cases, as doctors also observe, this influence does not prove supernatural intervention.[83] Suggestion can be effective even when the healing practitioner uses deception.[84]

More positively, science has clearly documented the power of faith, and most religious persons believe that God often works through faith, though God is not limited to it.[85] A secular observer, however, might reasonably protest that faith's effectiveness need not guarantee the reality of faith's object. Thus I survey here some of the studies involving health and religious practice, including the positive confidence that often comes from it, typically without clear indication of direct divine causation.[86] These helpful studies are not meant to address the question of supernatural miracles pro or con (their authors themselves hold a range of

82. Ludwig, *Order Restored*, 183. Some forms of teaching in the tradition of faith healing, going beyond more sober biblical examples of "acting on faith," contribute to this problem. Already this belief was causing problems in the late nineteenth century (Curtis, *Faith*, 113, 204). When sickness remained, early Pentecostal leader E. N. Bell advised one to continue claiming healing, yet not to "lie in their testimonies" (Reyes, "Framework," 85–86). Likewise, challenging the high cure rates some suppose for psychic healing, McClenon, "Healing," 44–45, warns that many healers practice denial. As we have noted, even some Christian healers believed to be effective on other occasions have on some other occasions practiced denial (Buckingham, *Daughter*, 129–32, 141, 149, 233–35).

83. Ludwig, *Order Restored*, 183. Ludwig himself emphasizes the value of psychological and emotional factors aiding the body's immune system and healing processes (141–59).

84. McClenon, "Healing," 46.

85. E.g., Benson, *Healing*, 204–6, attributes a remarkable cancer recovery to both faith *and* radiation therapy, though he notes (206) that neither place this in the category of miracle. For a psychological phenomenology of faith, see Brownell, "Faith," 219–26 (including developmental stages on 222; its relevance to belief in miracle on 231).

86. I should emphasize that the purpose of the medical studies is not to supplant faith in God with faith in faith (see, e.g., the caution of Benson, *Healing*, 190). I simply observe that demonstrating the healing effects of "faith" does not, by itself, prove supernatural or divine activity.

perspectives), but we may take them into account in cases where recoveries are simply somewhat faster or more complete than usual.

Because in Scripture God often works through natural means, a biblical theist would find nothing incompatible with her views in emphasizing the power of faith or other factors in nature understood as the created order.[87] Indeed, while God working through natural means would not fit Hume's definition of a miracle, it could certainly fit Augustine's. Yet insofar as miracles are defined as extraordinary, these natural factors by themselves do not demonstrate such extraordinary activity (unless they are carried out in an extraordinary way, say, e.g., a recovery that would naturally take ten months taking half an hour). They normally provide instead a more "ordinary" context for religious elements in some recoveries (e.g., social support or reduced anxiety).

Religious Practice and Health

When a religious person merely recovers faster than usual but not extraordinarily faster, sometimes this recovery may simply constitute a variation from the average. When this positive variation happens particularly frequently with religious people, it may reflect factors characteristic of the lifestyle or support systems of religious traditions. Thus studies suggest that some general health improvements may simply reflect the medically documented beneficial effects (on average) of religious conviction and practice;[88] this observation differs from arguing for specifically and demonstrably supernatural causation.[89] These general benefits do not of course explain cases of instantaneous or almost instantaneous bone regeneration or cataracts disappearing, but at least in the West these general benefits are probably more common than such striking miracles.

As Harold Koenig, Dale Matthews, David Larson, and many other medical scientists have publicized, a vast range of recent studies on religion and health

87. One would be hard-pressed to cite a biblical or modern miracle claim as dramatic as "DNA, a miraculous three-foot-long string curled up in its entirety in a cell no more than fifteen micrometers across" (Frankenberry, *Faith*, xiv, with reference to Stephen Jay Gould, undoubtedly rightly).

88. See, e.g., Matthews and Clark, *Faith Factor* (e.g., 15–23); for one brief popular account, Wallis, "Healing" (esp. 60); for a brief history, see Eames, "History." I have borrowed the vast majority of sources for this discussion from abstracts provided at http://www.dukespiritualityandhealth.org (accessed March 14, 2008), from the interdisciplinary Duke Center for Spirituality, Theology, and Health, brought to my attention by my student Barbara McCall, a nurse, and again later noted to me by Margie Shealy of the Christian Medical and Dental Associations. I have categorized them loosely here for readers who may wish the information without reading hundreds of abstracts. I cite only a fraction of the studies (about twelve hundred by the year 2000; see Koenig, McCullough, and Larson, *Handbook*, 514–89). In addition, see vast numbers of older resources not included here but abstracted at Duke Center's website; Matthews, Larson, and Barry, *Bibliography*; Benn, "Correlation," and sources cited there (including Levin and Schiller, "Factor," which uses more than "200 epidemiological studies"); and the bibliographies of the works cited. Many researchers pursuing integration of religion and health probably have a faith tradition (Plante, "Spirituality," 212–14), but this should not be assumed in all cases, especially given the vast number of them (so also Matthews and Clark, *Faith Factor*, 37).

89. Some scholars, however, do suggests links between the two; see Breggen, "Miracle Reports," 382, as well as sources cited there.

have frequently emphasized the positive benefits of religious activity. It has been increasingly recognized that religious issues cannot be avoided in medical treatment. Whereas less than 3 percent of North American medical schools had courses related to religion and spirituality in 1992, roughly 70 percent of them had such courses by 2006, and of these, 70 percent were mandatory courses.[90] Religious issues appear important to many patients in treatment,[91] and religion's social influence also often proves helpful for health education and intervention, especially in particular communities.[92]

In these studies, religion appears positively associated with psychological health[93] (particularly emphasized in studies of depression[94] and related sorts of

90. Koenig, *Medicine*, 24, 35–36. For some health curricula that now include a component on religion and health, see, e.g., Barnes, "Curriculum"; Glennon, "Religion."

91. Patients tended to value religious and spiritual concerns and dimensions of their illness or recovery (Steinhauser et al., "Factors"; Balboni et al., "Religiousness"; Miller et al., "Needs"; Hamilton and Levine, "Preferences" [regarding neopagans]; cf. Holmes, Rabow, and Dibble, "Screening") more than most of their physicians suspected or could easily accommodate (cf. Clark, Drain, and Malone, "Needs"; Curlin et al., "Association"; Huguelet et al., "Spirituality"; Monroe et al., "Preferences"; Silvestri et al., "Importance"; Matthews and Clark, *Faith Factor*, 271–72; though cf. McCauley et al., "Beliefs"). Frequently this disparity creates tension (Kub, "Miracles," 1273, on 1275–76 referring more specifically to Rushton and Russell, "Language"; Silvestri et al., "Importance"; Sulmasy, "Issues"). Matthews and Clark, *Faith Factor*, 4, cites studies that two-thirds of patients want to discuss spiritual matters with their physicians (nationally, in *USA Today Weekend* and *Time*), and 48 percent want doctors to pray with them (in North Carolina, in King and Bushwick, "Beliefs"). Doctors remain divided on such issues, though more are open than opposed (Koenig, *Medicine*, 26–27).

92. E.g., Daniels et al., "Effectiveness"; Young and Stewart, "Intervention"; cf. Catanzaro et al., "Health Ministries"; Falcone et al., "Development"; Koenig, *Medicine*, 34–35. Chaplain visitation was also associated with patients' lower anxiety and higher satisfaction (Iler, Obenshain, and Camac, "Impact") and reduced depression (Baker, "Investigation"); on the value of chaplains, see also Koenig, *Medicine*, 25.

93. E.g., Park, "Relations"; Matthews and Clark, *Faith Factor*, 83–104; Kendler and Liu et al., "Dimensions"; Saxena, "Study"; Krause, "Facets"; idem, "Meaning"; Dull and Skokan, "Model" (by providing meaning); Ciarrocchi and Deneke, "Hope"; Benjamins, "Religion"; Francis et al., "Correlation"; Francis and Kaldor, "Relationship"; Krupski et al., "Spirituality"; Rummans et al., "Quality"; Lechner et al., "Associations"; McIllmurray et al., "Needs"; Khouzam, Smith, and Bissett, "Therapy"; Willemsen et al., "Upbringing" (religious upbringing vs. neuroticism); Koenig, George, and Titus, "Ill Patients"; De Orio, "Phenomenology"; Jonas and Fischer, "Management" (decreased fear of death); Wink and Scott, "Religiousness" (decreased fear of death among the very religious, though increased among the more casually religious); Reyes-Ortiz et al., "Attendance" (decreased fear of falling); Bowen et al., "Religion" (reducing perceived stress and panic disorder); Ai et al., "Pathways" (optimism and prayer as a coping strategy); Galea et al., "Abuse" (the benefit of spirituality for those who had experienced child abuse); Hill et al., "Attendance" (cognitive functioning among older adults); Wollin et al., "Predictors" (a factor in children's preoperative anxiety); Schwartz et al., "Behaviors"; Geary, Ciarrocchi, and Scheers, "Spirituality" (though not large); Fisch et al., "Assessment"; Hamrick and Diefenbach, "Religion." Cf. weakened faith and increased need for mental health services (Fontana and Rosenheck, "Trauma"); religious involvement's inverse relationship with dementia (Koenig, *Medicine*, 120–22).

94. E.g., Koenig, *Medicine*, 68–73 (and sources cited there), 147 (noting it as one of the leading disabilities); Matthews and Clark, *Faith Factor*, 24–26 (and sources cited there), 86–95; Koenig, "Remission"; idem, "Inpatients"; Mofidi et al., "Spirituality"; Ai et al., "Depression"; Yi et al., "Religion"; Kristeller et al., "Study"; Tarakeshwar, Pearce, and Sikkema, "Development"; Pearce et al., "Symptoms"; Wink, Larsen, and Dillon, "Religion"; Smith et al., "Religiousness"; Gillum, Sullivan, and Bybee, "Importance"; Baetz et al., "Commitment"; Murray-Swank et al., "Religiosity"; Alderete et al., "Symptoms"; Olphen et al.,

issues),[95] and is often correlated with other healthy dispositions.[96] For example, in one 1990 study involving 451 African Americans, less religious men were nearly twice as prone to depression as their more religious peers.[97] Other studies show that religiously committed persons tended to adjust more healthily to the death of a child or spouse.[98] Religious commitment not only helps addiction prevention[99] but also strengthens addiction recovery.[100] For example, patients involved

"Involvement"; Miller and Gur, "Religiosity"; Patel et al., "Variables"; Drentea and Goldner, "Caregiving"; Watlington and Murphy, "Roles"; Lonczak et al., "Coping" (religious upbringing vs. depressive symptoms); Hebert, Dang, and Schulz, "Beliefs" (esp. consistently for religious attenders); McClain, Rosenfeld, and Breithart, "Effect" (on the terminally ill; cf. McNichols and Feldman, "Spirituality," 197–98); Murphy et al., "Relation" (mediated via hope); Carrico et al., "Model" (seeking to explain positive religious coping vs. depressive symptoms); Braam et al., "Climate" (trust in divine sovereignty among Calvinists vs. depressive symptoms). Cf. perhaps differently Borg et al., "System" (but the study curiously included only fifteen participants). Although I was not looking for such examples, I did receive a testimony of a spiritual experience that quickly liberated one woman from postpartum depression earlier than expected (Miyuki Yoshihara, interview, Jan. 30, 2009, regarding 2002; a testimony of instant deliverance from depression in 2007 appears on International House of Prayer's website); various psychological healings, including instant ones, have often been reported (e.g., Bosworth, Healer, 217–19); note also a progressive recovery from what was expected to be a lifelong, perhaps neurologically based, severe mental disorder in Lakshmi Devi, personal correspondence, Oct. 29, 2010 (referring to her young daughter).

95. For grief recovery, see Walsh et al., "Beliefs"; Murphy, Johnson, and Lohan, "Meaning"; for post-traumatic stress symptoms, Chen, "Expression"; Watlington and Murphy, "Roles"; Zehnder et al., "Study"; Schiff, "Shadow"; Key, Leppien, and Smith, "Model"; Matthews and Clark, Faith Factor, 153–56, 161–66.

96. Cf. the correlations of gratitude with emotional health and with religion or spirituality (McCullough et al., "Disposition"); religious commitment with optimism (Mattis et al., "Religiosity"; Koenig, Medicine, 79–80) and forgiveness (Mullet et al., "Involvement"); much earlier observations of regular attendance and health in Buskirk, Healing, 127–28.

97. Matthews and Clark, Faith Factor, 25 (citing Brown, Ndubuisi, and Gary, "Religiosity"). On average, African-Americans proved more apt than whites to affirm miracles and other theistic beliefs (see Johnson, Elbert-Avila, and Tulsky, "Influence," summarized in Kub, "Miracles," 1276).

98. Matthews and Clark, Faith Factor, 25–26 (citing Cook and Wimberley, "Commitment"; Rosik, "Impact"), 105–33.

99. Matthews and Clark, Faith Factor, 27, noting a study in which 89 percent of alcoholics had lost faith during adolescence in contrast to 20 percent of the control group (Larson and Wilson, "Religious Life"); and another study in which relatively nonreligious high schoolers were four to five times likelier than highly religious peers to abuse illegal drugs (Hadaway, Elifson, and Peterson, "Involvement"). See also the wide-ranging study of Wallace and Forman, "Role," cited in Koenig, Medicine, 59; also numerous studies in Koenig, Medicine, 60–62.

100. Among many other sources, see, e.g., Flynn et al., "Dependence"; Mohr et al., "Integration"; Benda, "Factors"; Walsh et al., "Transcendence" (gambling addiction); Winkelman, "Spirituality" (altered states of consciousness induced by shamanic drumming); for some anecdotal examples from various religious traditions, see Wakefield, Miracle, 94–117. For whatever reasons, religious disinterest correlates significantly with substance abuse (see Schoeneberger et al, "Abuse"), and both religiosity (Wills, Yaeger, and Sandy, "Effect") and particular religious values (Kendler and Liu et al., "Dimensions") correlate with lower substance abuse (cf. also lower alcohol consumption among religious Israeli youth, Schiff, "Shadow"). Syrdal, "Transcript," 18–19, observed the unusually high rate of addiction deliverance (compared with purely secular models in the West) through Christian faith in early twentieth-century China. For Christian testimonies of addiction deliverance, see, e.g., Wacker, Heaven, 65; Ramirez, "Faiths," 371; Khai, "Pentecostalism," 269; Green, Asian Tigers, 99–100 (instantaneous release from heroin addiction); Wilson, "Miracle Events," 274–75; Koch, Zulus, 128–32; Jones, Wonders, 73; Marszalek, Miracles, 118–19 (through the Salvation Army); Gutierrez, Mujer de Milagros, 12–13 (translated for me by Mayra Picos-Lee);

in religious programs proved nearly ten times likelier to continue abstaining from heroin a year after treatment.[101]

Somewhat fewer studies have examined the relationship between religious faith and physical health, but those that have done so fairly consistently correlate the two.[102] Examples of such studies reveal favorable health correlations in matters related to hypertension,[103] blood pressure,[104] and heart disease.[105] They also show correlations more generally to reduction in mortality,[106] now noted even in popular

---

Neal, *Power*, 56–57; Baxter, *Healing*, 103; Anderson, *Pelendo*, 34–36, 95; Bredesen, *Miracle*, 43–52, 100; DeGrandis, *Miracles*, 32; Robertson, *Miracles*, 67, 71–77, 92; for the therapeutic use of glossolalia in such deliverance, see Wilkerson, *Cross*, 154–68 (regarding Teen Challenge, the success rate of which has been supported by other studies; cf. Manuel, *Factor*; Wilson, "Miracle Events," 274); DeGrandis, *Miracles*, 46; and, regarding Jackie Pullinger's work in Hong Kong, Storms, *Guide*, 145–46; Pullinger, *Dragon*, 83, 149, 158–60, 166, 169, 173, and especially 174; external corroboration in sociologists Miller and Yamamori, *Pentecostalism*, 99–105 (esp. 104, 109; against any supposition of their starting with favorable bias, see 99, 147). On Alcoholics Anonymous, see, e.g., Oursler, *Power*, 302–10; B., "Challenge."

101. Matthews and Clark, *Faith Factor*, 26 (citing Desmond and Maddux, "Programs").

102. E.g., Maselko et al., "Attendance" (religious attendance predicting lower allostatic load in older women); Pargament et al., "Methods" (through positive coping); Tully et al., "Factors" (90 percent reduction in probability of meningococcal disease); Sephton et al., "Expression"; Kinney et al., "Involvement"; McCullough and Laurenceau, "Religiousness"; Dedert et al., "Practice"; Contrada et al., "Factors" (regarding postsurgical recovery); Krupski et al., "Spirituality"; Koenig, *Religion*, 77–99; cf. Harrison et al., "Pain" (religious attendance vs. pain); Rew and Wong, "Review" (regarding health behaviors); Koenig, George, and Titus, "Ill Patients" (though with less connection than with mental health); Benjamins, "Religion and Health" (though only positively connected to attendance); Olphen et al., "Involvement" (esp. with attendance); Messina et al., "Study." For slower disease progression, see Ironson et al., "Increase." Cf. also the earlier observations regarding loving care and hope facilitating recovery (or at least comfort), even in some terminally ill patients, in Reed, *Surgery*, 111–16. Reed also offers the example of a coma patient previously deemed terminal recovering through prayer and faith (84).

103. Gillum and Ingram, "Frequency" (lower hypertension).

104. Al-Kandari, "Religiosity." Matthews, Larson, and Barry, *Bibliography*, cite earlier studies, e.g., lowered blood pressure for regular church attenders in Graham et al., "Frequency"; Larson et al., "Impact" (with a small but significant decrease); Walsh, "Effect" (lower but not statistically significant).

105. King, Mainous, and Pearson, "Protein"; Benn, "Correlation," 141–43 (citing esp. Comstock and Partridge, "Attendance," with a 40 percent difference in mortality in a sample size of 91,000; Oxman, Freeman, and Manheimer, "Participation"); for the cardiovascular system generally, see Koenig, *Medicine*, 96–112, and the many sources cited there (including Koenig, George, Cohen et al., "Relationship"; Newlin et al., "Relationship"; Olphen et al., "Involvement"; Steffen and Hinderliter, "Coping"; Gillum and Ingram, "Frequency"). See the case study in Matthews and Clark, *Faith Factor*, 72–73, where prayer may have been a factor in the unexpectedly strong recovery.

106. Wong et al., "Factors"; Ellison et al., "Involvement"; Heuch, Jacobsen, and Fraser, "Study" (among Seventh-Day Adventists, not surprisingly); Matthews and Clark, *Faith Factor*, 158–61; Koenig, *Medicine*, 129–45; Lutgendorf et al., "Participation"; Musick, House, and Williams, "Attendance and Mortality"; Bagiella, Hong, and Sloan, "Attendance as Predictor"; Strawbridge et al., "Attendance"; Strawbridge et al., "Strength"; Cour, Avlund, and Schultz-Larsen, "Religion"; Hill et al., "Attendance and Mortality"; Helm et al., "Activity"; Krause, "Support"; Van Ness, Kasl, and Jones, "Religion"; Yeager et al., "Involvement"; Ironson et al., "Spirituality" (regarding AIDS); Eng et al., "Ties"; Oman et al., "Attendance"; Sears and Wallace, "Spirituality"; but cf. the more ambiguous results among Israelis in Kraut et al., "Association"; and negative results in Wrensch et al., "Factors" (though the sample size was fewer than 600 patients in one county). High attendance's association is indirect through lower levels of Interleukin-6 (Thoresen, "Health," 8). On will to live and "mature" religion, see Hedgespeth, "Power." It might appear ironic that the mortality test was initially proposed in the 1870s by a skeptic

media.[107] One may take, for example, the combination of faith and healthy lifestyle advocated among Seventh-day Adventists; in a 1983 study in the Netherlands,[108] male Adventists lived on average nine years longer than non-Adventist men (with a general average of four years in another study).[109] The longevity difference is even higher in some other reports.[110] One detailed statistical analysis concludes that the reduction in mortality associated with religious attendance in general is comparable to "regular physical exercise" and "statin-type therapy" (an average of two to five additional years of life).[111]

The following chart, adapted from Matthews, Larson, and Barry's *Annotated Bibliography of Clinical Research on Spiritual Subjects*, and Herbert Benson's *Timeless Healing*,[112] illustrates visually the effects of studies already known by the early 1990s:

Area of improvement, as defined by reduction in the following:	Number of studies	Number of studies in which religion correlated positively with improvements	Proportion of these studies in which religion correlated positively with improvements
Alcohol	18	16	89%
Anxiety	11	8	73%
Anxiety about death	15	10	67%
Blood pressure	5	4	80%
Depression	17	12	71%
Drugs	12	12	100%
Smoking	6	6	100%
Health (general)	5	4	80%
Life satisfaction	13	12	92%
Quality of life (cancer patients)	8	7	88%
Quality of life (heart patients)	6	4	67%
Survival rates	9	8	89%

eager to discredit any effects of faith (Opp, *Lord for Body*, 15), though his focus was prayer rather than religion more generally. On the logical coherency of prayer on theistic premises, see Stump, "Prayer" (esp. the summary on 186); Young, "Petitioning"; Brümmer, *Pray* (esp. 33–55); cf. Polkinghorne and Beale, *Questions*, 94–95.

107. Kluger, "Biology," 62.

108. Matthews and Clark, *Faith Factor*, 22 (citing for a Danish cancer study Jensen, "Risk"; and esp., for the life expectancy difference in the Netherlands, Berkel and Waard, "Mortality Pattern"). For an anecdotal observation, I was impressed with the proportion of healthy, active older Adventists in my visit to Andrews University, Berrien Springs, Michigan, Feb. 7–10, 2008.

109. Koenig, *Medicine*, 109 (Frazer et al., "Effects"). Adventists experience lower rates of stroke (Koenig, *Medicine*, 119) and cancer (124–25) than in the average population.

110. An article from *U.S. News and World Report* summarizes Seventh-day Adventists in the United States as averaging eighty-nine years in longevity, roughly a decade beyond the national average (http://health.yahoo.com/featured/7/10-health-habits-that-will-help-you-live-to-100; accessed April 20, 2009).

111. Hall, "Attendance," 106, 108.

112. Matthews, Larson, and Barry, *Bibliography*, ii–iii; also Benson, *Healing*, 174–75, who is adapting the identical material from Matthews, Larson, and Barry's *Bibliography* in chart form (arranged differently here). Benson seems to be using a later published version (1994) differing from the bound version now available to me (1993).

Factors in Healthy Religious Practice

The studies often note that the positive correlation usually remains even when other related factors are screened out.[113] Personality was often a larger factor when separated from religion,[114] but positive religious approaches presumably may affect that factor over time as well.[115]

Nevertheless, not all associations between religion (or aspects of religion) and better health need be causal.[116] Where they are,[117] some such effects may stem from social support[118] (which is positively correlated with religious involvement);[119] positive religious coping mechanisms[120] (versus negative

---

113. E.g., in the United States, religious practice tends to be inversely proportional to cigarette smoking and some other unhealthy habits (Timberlake et al., "Effects"; Hill et al., "Behaviors"; Elizabeth et al., "Factors"; Roff et al., "Religiosity" [but not obesity]; Benn, "Correlation," 145; studies in Koenig, *Medicine*, 111), but controlled studies usually account for such factors (though in one study nonsmoking explained the effects of religious attendance; King et al., "Relationship"). Frequency of religious practice also correlates with higher math and reading scores (Regnerus, "Success").

114. E.g., Ciarrocchi and Deneke, "Happiness," though affirming the importance of both elements; cf. also Golden et al., "Spirituality."

115. E.g., altruism (often positively correlated with religion, e.g., in 60 percent of studies noted in Matthews, Larson, and Barry, *Bibliography*, iii; with spiritual practices, among scientists, in Ecklund, *Science*, 64–65; 70 percent of older adult volunteers in Koenig, *Medicine*, 65) is associated with greater well-being (see, e.g., Benson, *Healing*, 181–82 [citing Luks, *Power*]; Koenig, *Medicine*, 49–52 [citing Hunter and Linn, "Differences"; Schwartz et al., "Behaviors"; Morrow-Howell et al., "Effects"; Liang, Krause, and Bennett, "Exchange"; Yuen, "Impact"; Moll et al., "Networks"; and many others]). Scholars debate the ultimate cause of altruism (cf. Haught, *Atheism*, 69–71).

116. Correlations are clear, but assertions of causality require a higher bar of proof (cf. Benn, "Correlation," 141, 146–47; Thoresen, "Health," 6).

117. E.g., Koenig, *Medicine*, 149 (citing Idler and Kasl, "Religion"), argues that attendance tends to prevent disability more than the reverse.

118. E.g., Litwin, "Association"; cf. Jaffe et al., "Neighborhood" (on living in religiously affiliated neighborhoods); Patel et al., "Variables"; Benn, "Correlation," 145; Epperly, *Touch*, 229 (support groups and churches); Matthews and Clark, *Faith Factor*, 248–50 (but with greater benefits in specifically *religious* social networks, 251–53). Social isolation significantly increases mortality (Eng et al., "Ties"); in Hughes et al., "Support," religiosity appears related to lower anxiety to the same degree that social support is. The massive study of Canadian adults in Baetz et al., "Association," associates religious attendance with fewer depressive symptoms, but spirituality, which may include an introspective component, with more depressive symptoms. "Spirituality" has proved difficult to define and measure, however (Matthews and Clark, *Faith Factor*, 185).

119. Koenig, *Medicine*, 56–57 (citing Koenig, McCullough, and Larson, *Handbook*, 525–26, noting this is the case in roughly 95 percent of studies). Nevertheless, only church-based social involvement displayed such outcomes, even when other factors were taken into account (Koenig, *Medicine*, 57, citing Cutler, "Membership"; Krause, "Exploring"; Salsman et al., "Link"; Watlington and Murphy, "Roles"; cf. Koenig, Moberg, and Kvale, "Activities").

120. Positive religious coping is associated with life satisfaction (Mendonca et al., "Spirituality"; after AIDS diagnosis, Szaflarski et al., "Modeling"; Kremer and Ironson, "Spirituality"; Cotton et al., "Spirituality"; with advanced cancer, Tarakeshwar et al., "Coping"; with ovarian cancer, Canada et al., "Coping"; during caregiving, Pearce, Singer, and Prigerson, "Coping"; Matthews and Clark, *Faith Factor*, 142–44; positive coping in Koenig, *Medicine*, 72, 153–54, and satisfaction in 78–79; anecdotal examples of coping with terminal illness in Lesslie, *Angels*, 45–46, 222–23; for help with schizophrenia, Rogers and Risher, "Religion," 290–93); feeling better during and after treatment (Becker et al., "Belief"; cf. Thoresen, "Health," 8; Masters, "Prayer," 20); and appears inversely related to depression (Bosworth et al., "Impact") and pre- and postoperative distress (Ai et al., "Mediation"). Adding a partner's positive religious coping

ones,[121] which appear to be much less common in the studies so far);[122] likelier family cohesion;[123] on-average better health behaviors;[124] and perhaps reduction in anxiety because of greater emotional security and dependence on the transcendent.[125] Outcomes usually varied according to the religious variables studied, with concrete factors such as religious attendance frequently being more prominent.[126] Emotional and social causes of stress weaken the immune system and increase susceptibility to most diseases;[127] positive religious practice can reduce such stress factors, with obviously positive health benefits.[128] One cause of some cases of better average health could be some answers to prayer, but given

apparently increases the effect (Yoshimoto et al., "Coping"). Matthews and Clark, *Faith Factor*, 31–32, notes that religion significantly facilitated coping with incarceration (Koenig, "Prison": 32 percent ranked it highest) and reduced recidivism (by more than three times; Johnson, Larson, and Pitts, "Programs"; cf. Johnson, "Impact"; though some other studies appear inconclusive).

121. Negative religious coping appears associated with greater depression (Schanowitz and Nicassio, "Predictors"), anxiety, and mortality (Pargament et al., "Religious Struggle"; more broadly, McConnell et al., "Links"). Some of the studies addressing positive effects of positive religious coping also underscore the harmful effects of negative religious coping (e.g., Tarakeshwar et al., "Coping"; Pargament et al., "Methods"; Mendonca et al., "Spirituality"; Lonczak et al., "Coping"; cf. Koenig, *Medicine*, 80; Schottenbauer, Rodriguez, Glass, and Arnkoff, "Coping Research"). Koenig, *Religion*, 104–11, notes that negative use of religion reflects a neurotic approach to religion rather than characteristics intrinsic to religion itself (the same features are used positively by others); see also Matthews and Clark, *Faith Factor*, 52–56. Definitions of both religion and mental health do affect studies' outcomes (Lotufo and Lotufo-Neto, "Religiosity," 287; Alcorta, "Adolescence," 61).

122. See, e.g., Mohr et al., "Integration." In Uganda, 1.2 percent of patients withdrew from AIDS treatment due to spiritual beliefs (Wanyama et al., "Belief"), and in the United States, religious beliefs can affect adherence to treatment positively or negatively (Parsons et al., "Beliefs"); but stronger religious or spiritual commitments are usually associated instead with willingness to seek examination and treatment (e.g., Friedman et al., "Predictors"; Hill et al., "Behaviors"; for mental health care, see Harris, Edlund, and Larson, "Involvement"). Faith generally affects AIDS favorably (Kluger, "Biology," 62).

123. See, e.g., Regnerus and Burdette, "Change."

124. E.g., Koenig, *Medicine*, 127.

125. On reduced anxiety, see the studies in Koenig, *Medicine*, 76–78. Beliefs in afterlife were inversely associated with the severity of symptoms in a range of psychiatric problems in Flannelly et al., "Belief"; beliefs in a positive afterlife also reduced bereavement stress in Japan in Krause et al., "Death." Cf. end-of-life "peace" (Steinhauser et al., "Peace"). For various factors, many framed in religious terms, see, e.g., Matthews and Clark, *Faith Factor*, 42–52.

126. See, e.g., Koenig et al., "Religion and Use"; Dezutter, Soenens, and Hutsebaut, "Religiosity"; Ardelt and Koenig, "Role"; Lesniak et al., "Distress"; Kaufman et al., "Decline" (private religiosity inversely associated with cognitive decline); Masters et al., "Orientation" (extrinsic vs. intrinsic religiosity). This variation sometimes appeared more prominently among Protestants, perhaps suggesting the influence of Protestant distinctions between intrinsic and extrinsic religiosity (Cohen et al., "Religiosity"). It also obtains "only if that attendance is not driven by anxiety" (Hill, Kopp, and Bollinger, "Measures," 35 [cf. 31–32]). Active compassion (minus the stress of continual caregiving) is also associated with health (Wachholtz and Pearce, "Compassion"), as is a sense of calling (i.e., purpose or motivation; Dreher and Plante, "Protocol").

127. Koenig, *Medicine*, 37–53; Alcorta, "Adolescence," 62–65. On psychosocial, apparently including religious, impact on healthy immune and endocrine function, see Koenig, *Medicine*, 82–95.

128. See Koenig, *Medicine*, 54–67. While not seeking cases of emotional healing (perhaps more common than dramatic physical healing) for this book, I encountered some, such as the significant testimony of Anglican deacon Anna Gulick (personal correspondence, May 4, 2009; interview, March 10, 2011).

other potential factors difficult to separate from positive religious faith, such as a spiritual sense of security, noted above, it seems difficult to demonstrate (or disprove) this claim by statistical means.

The general benefits of religious practice do not appear to be limited to Christian circles; those raised in or who find their home in many religious traditions find comfort and well-being there.[129] The beneficial effect of religion on health is attested in Jewish,[130] Islamic,[131] and other faiths,[132] as well as among Christians, although some studies so far are inconclusive[133] or indicate negative effects in some religious communities.[134] Meditation, emphasized more in some religious and cultural traditions than others (but usually valued, given an appropriate subject of meditation), generally offers significant health benefits.[135]

129. See Koenig, *Medicine*, 56. Some emphasize the role of religious experiences in restoring self-esteem (Valla and Prince, "Experiences," esp. 164).

130. E.g., Billig, Kohn, and Levav, "Stress"; Jaffe et al., "Neighborhood"; Litwin, "Association"; Schiff, "Shadow" (for post-traumatic stress disorder [PTSD] but not depression). One study associates religiosity with lower mortality for younger workers and higher mortality for older ones (Kraut et al., "Association," in a study of 3,638 Jewish Israeli men). Very religious Jewish Israeli physicians were more apt to prolong patients' life longer (Wenger and Carmel, "Religiosity").

131. Al-Sabwah and Abdel-Khalek, "Religiosity" (regarding lower death depression and anxiety); Abdel-Khalek, "Happiness" (regarding both psychological and physical health); Koenig, *Medicine*, 56 (citing Kesselring et al., "Attitudes," noting Egyptian Muslim patients finding comfort in their faith); on benefits to Muslims of hearing the Qur'an recited, see the claims in Makarfi, "Bedrock," 68–69 (apparently dependent on work by Ahmad Elkadi; cf. also Ademola, "Attitude," 111).

132. Among Latter-day Saints, religious factors significantly reduced mortality in Ostbye et al., "Investigators." Contrary to some expectations, in one study Jehovah's Witnesses appear to lack significantly increased risk of trauma fatality (Varela et al., "Risk").

133. Krisanaprakornkit et al., "Therapy," conclude that most Transcendental Meditation studies so far prove inconclusive; but for a different perspective contrast studies below. Acupuncture and sham acupuncture had the same effect on depression (Allen et al., "Acupuncture"). Religious attitudes apparently did not affect obsessive-compulsive disorder in Iran (Assarian, Biqam, Asqarnejad, "Study"). Some emotional health studies may work from a bias that evaluates religious content (see Sica et al., "Religiousness"). Blumenthal et al., "Spirituality," found no correlation with physical health but noted that the data sample was too narrow to offer conclusions. The correlation between exercise and religious attendance in women over sixty (Gillum, "Frequency") might link activity or social support more generally; see studies on religion and exercise in Koenig, *Medicine*, 110–11 (so far apparently limited in number). The Israeli sample in Schiff, "Shadow," shows reduced PTSD but not depression.

134. Cf. Yeager et al., "Involvement," for Taiwanese religious attendance (esp. among Taoists and Buddhists), though private religious practices and convictions were associated with worse health (on 2240, the researchers hypothetically attributed this to the specific nature of the beliefs). Naeem, "Culture," associates lack of control of diabetes partly with Islamic fatalism; less negatively, cf. Muslim submission to Allah's will in matters of health in Rozario, "Scientist." Results in Kraut et al., "Association," seem age-specific.

135. Buddhist meditation helped (Kabat-Zinn et al., "Influence"); use of mantras or prayers in any religion appear to have improved emotive states (Bormann et al., "Effects"; Bormann and Oman, "Repetition," 102–10; idem, "Mantram"); yoga and meditation also showed some possible positive effects in Harinath et al., "Effects"; Benson, *Healing*, 157, notes that Chinese *chi gong* helped relaxation in Huang, "Effects." For Transcendental Meditation, Paul-Labrador et al., "Effects," and earlier Castillo-Richmond et al., "Effects," cite positive effects; at Maharishi University, so also (in Koenig, *Medicine*, 105–6) Schneider et al, "Trial"; Wenneberg et al., "Study"; Schneider et al., "Year." For meditation more generally, cf. Shapiro and Walsh, "Meditation"; Flinders, Oman, and Flinders,

That the health benefit of religious practice is attested more in some ethnic communities[136] than others or more commonly with a particular gender (women)[137] may suggest cultural factors in how religion is appropriated.[138] Likewise, more people in highly religious countries will find comfort in religion than those in highly secularized societies.[139] For whatever reasons, religion in general could be a contributing factor in some gradual improvements in health, though it would not explain many of the sudden and dramatic changes I have noted, such as cases of instant healings of long-term blindness or deafness, the immediate repair of bones, or restoration to life after apparent death.

As I have noted, many religious observers would consider some positive benefits associated with religious involvement divinely designed; traditional Christian theology sees God as sovereign over and working through the course of nature as well as acting beyond it.[140] Most religious observers today would also believe that God provided humans the wisdom for medical science and that God works through it;[141] even in miracle stories in the Gospels, miracles seem to be reserved for when they are needed (cf. Mark 6:43–44; 8:11–12; John 6:12–13; elsewhere, cf. 1 Tim 5:23). Thus I have often received testimonies of those who attribute the

---

"Program"; idem, "Meditation"; Oman and Thoresen, "Spiritual," 47–48, 50. Benson, *Healing*, 163–64 (citing idem, "Temperature Changes"), reports direct observation and testing of Tibetan monks generating paranormal heat in cold settings and (*Healing*, 166) metabolism drops of as much as 64 percent, beyond previously documented human examples. For meditation and healing Portsmouth, *Prayer*, 56–61, draws on the contemplative Christian tradition. Particular forms of prayer, such as contemplation and thanksgiving, may correlate more with health benefits (Stanley, "Types," though the sample size is small).

136. Cf. Steffen and Hinderliter, "Coping"; Cooper et al., "Spirituality"; Balboni et al., "Religiousness"; Roff et al., "Limitations"; Drentea and Goldner, "Caregiving"; Koenig et al., "Care Use"; Kinney et al., "Involvement"; Kelly and Floyd, "Impact." Cf. the cultural variables in Franzini, Ribble, and Wingfield, "Religion."

137. Saxena, "Study"; Chen, "Expression"; Contrada et al., "Factors"; Strawbridge et al., "Strength"; McCullough and Laurenceau, "Religiousness"; cf. Wink and Dillon, "Development"; among Kuwaiti Muslims, Abdel-Khalek, "Happiness." This is not surprising, since women are on average more committed religiously than men (Matthews, Larson, and Barry, *Bibliography*, iii), though evangelical women scored lower in self-esteem than men (Aycock and Noaker, "Comparison," in Matthews, Larson, and Barry, *Bibliography*, 12–13).

138. For example, cultural differences affect the processing of pain (Sternbach and Tusky, "Differences"; Bates, Edwards, and Anderson, "Influences"; both cited in Benson, *Healing*, 56–57).

139. Koenig, *Medicine*, 56 (citing Kesselring et al., "Attitudes," in which 38 percent of Swiss patients found support in religion, compared with 92 percent of Egyptian Muslim patients); cf. Benn, "Correlation," 146.

140. Hiebert, *Reflections*, 234, notes that all healing is God's work, so to separate medical healing from prayer healing is to succumb to a dualistic worldview; see also Petersen, *Might*, 99–100 (on common Pentecostal perspectives in Latin America); and González, *Tribe*, 94 (also for a Latin American perspective; cf., e.g., Durand and Massey, *Miracles*, 164–65, 176–77). In biblical theology, God did miracles when necessary and to reveal God's greatness and compassion, not to satisfy spiritual sensationalism. Empirical studies in the United States suggest that the healthiest approach combines medical and spiritual methods (Koenig, "Afterword," 506).

141. Many argue persuasively for their compatibility, e.g., Matthews and Clark, *Faith Factor*, 53, 63, 67–68. Many conjoin prayer with medical procedures (e.g., Skinsnes, "Healed").

success of their uncertain treatments to God as well as to their doctors,[142] and complementary approaches to recovery are probably more common where medical means are available. The radical Enlightenment may have defined "natural" over against "supernatural" (or likelier the reverse), but a biblical perspective would approach "nature" as the sphere of God's activity in creation. My point here is not to question such theological claims (with which I personally agree) but to note here that some religiously connected recoveries involve natural elements to the extent that distinctly extranatural causation is difficult to demonstrate apart from such general theological considerations.

We cannot rule out that the overall average better recovery rate for religious practitioners may also involve many individual answers to prayer, but proving causal links from this general data would be difficult, since one could not easily screen other factors out and prayer does not always lead to this outcome. A rapid recovery or average lower mortality rate is not the same as cataracts instantly disappearing or a dead person being raised. In biblical terms, gifts of healings are for believers and need not be dramatic to be effective; their purpose is restoration, not evidence. Might not God answer prayers regarding health through medical means in medical cultures? By contrast, signs and wonders in the context of evangelism are often more dramatic, inviting attention toward the kingdom they represent; biblically we could allow for both kinds of healings without insisting that both have the same evidential value for extraordinary supernatural activity.

For that matter, how does one quantify effective prayer, and when prayers are backed by a life of faith and integrity, and whose prayers (out of multiple participants) proved particularly effective? I have known nonreligious persons, when faced with illness, to pray, and even agnostics to request prayer from deeply committed religious persons whose prayers *might* help. And theologically, who is to say that a deity would not reach out to a sincere agnostic who desperately prays or has a loved one pray for him or her? My point then is not that God is not at work, indirectly or even directly, in many cases in these surveys. My point is merely that interpreters will not all find here evidence for special divine action, especially if the data are taken in isolation from other evidence. These studies focus only on averages (as such studies by their nature must); many causal links are difficult to verify; scientific analysis is equipped to quantify natural rather than supernatural factors; and supernatural factors are impossible to fully quantify in any case,

---

142. E.g., my student Tamika Johnson, who twice received desperately needed liver transplants, one within sixteen hours after she had been given twenty-four to forty-eight hours to live (personal correspondence, Dec. 2, 3, 4, 2010); Joo Young Kim, interview, Jan. 24, 2009, after a prophecy about his recovery and treatment for serious chronic hepatitis B, which is sometimes, but not always, cured by treatment; in Uganda, Onesimus Asiimwe prayed for Henry Mugsha, who was blind (Onesimus Asiimwe, interview, Oct. 13, 2008), and the latter was able to have an operation that successfully complemented the prayer (Henry Mugsha, phone interview, Oct. 23, 2008). Mr. Mugsha no longer even needs glasses and now runs a nongovernmental organization (Onesimus Asiimwe, interview, Oct. 13, 2008; corroborated by Archbishop Henry Orombi, interview, Oct. 13, 2008).

because we cannot know all the factors that a greater intelligence might take into account in limiting human mortality.

Psychosomatic Elements of Faith Cures

Some recoveries clearly stem from emotional or mental cures, whether by strengthening the body's immune responses or by addressing psychological roots of the initial illness. This factor is widely recognized, including by commentators who also allow for organic supernatural cures.[143] Thus when one doctor falsely informed three patients that a faith healer would pray for them at a particular time, all three improved dramatically, though only one permanently.[144] But how far should such observations be pressed? After an extraordinary "faith cure" in 1889, some doctors pointed out that patients could be cured by faith in physicians no less than by faith in God—that "faith" brought healing regardless of its object.[145] Their argument stemmed from the psychological theories of "magnetism" dominant in their era, attributing healings to religious hysteria and explaining them naturalistically as "mental influence on the nervous system."[146]

Some writers have compared the effectiveness of shamans and other healers to hypnosis and altered states of consciousness.[147] Some early twentieth-century studies claimed that hypnotized patients could produce "blisters corresponding to imaginary burns" that could even bleed under suggestion, and that habitual bleeding could be cured by hypnosis.[148] More recent studies have suggested that

143. Pennington, "Relationship," 160–61; Frost, *Healing*, 183; Kelsey, *Healing*, 243–77; Hirschberg and Barasch, *Recovery*, 307; Rose, *Faith Healing*, 119–34, 176; Robertson, "Epidauros to Lourdes," 188 (though cf. also 189); McClenon, *Events*, 131 ("generally" psychosomatic); Bartow, *Adventures*, 43, 130–42; Robertson, *Miracles*, 144; Salmon, *Heals*, 33, 118; all those who pray for healing surveyed in Tilley, "Phenomenology," 565; on emotions' effects on the immune system and health, see Fountain, *Medicine*, 71–82; Siegel, *Medicine* (esp. 65–124, though he may overestimate cure rates); in a religious context, Koenig, *Medicine*, 82–95. Tournier, *Casebook*, 209–10, cites here principles in Prov 3:7–8; 4:20, 22; 17:22 (and on 213, Jas 5:16). The argument of Pattison, "Meaning," that many use belief in faith healing as a moral coping mechanism, interprets his data through the grid of his theory and works with a sample size representing only one social group, not necessarily representative.
144. Frank, *Persuasion*, 61, emphasizing that patients were helped by a false belief.
145. Opp, *Lord for Body*, 79. Cf. the relevance of physicians' confidence to the placebo effect, below. For the importance of the relationship between doctors and patients in healing, see Jonas and Crawford, "Presence."
146. Opp, *Lord for Body*, 80; cf. Duffin, *Miracles*, 132–34. The psychology of the era attributed many healings to mind over matter (Opp, *Lord for Body*, 165–66), many ministers so explained modern healings (Mullin, *Miracles*, 103), and many scholars so explained Jesus's healings (Tennant, *Miracle*, 31). Christian Science flourished in this context in the early twentieth century (Mullin, *Miracles*, 181–83), and a physician reading the founder's testimonials argued that the cures were largely psychosomatic (Buskirk, *Healing*, 60, though conceding some organic cures on 60–61, which he nevertheless attributes to psychological causes).
147. McClenon, *Healing*, 61, 67, though noting on 79 that it is not proved for all kinds of cases, but merely a reasonable hypothesis; Greenfield, *Spirits*, 88. The primary common factor seems to be that shamans and people who are easily hypnotized are predisposed to enter trance states (see here also clearly Pekala and Cardeña, "Issues," 71). In the example that McClenon, *Healing*, offers on 79–81, an easily hypnotizable person can be led even in a different culture's ritual trance state through suggestion.
148. West, *Miracles*, 19, citing (as authoritative) Schindler, *Nervensystem*; see also Heim, *Transformation*, 178. Note the hypnotically induced stigmata in Krippner and Kirkwood, "Bleeding," 168–69 (following

hypnosis can help treat burns, especially within the first two hours, by limiting inflammation and reducing pain.[149] They also may help skin conditions, warts, and psychosomatic problems; they do not, however, help every kind of ailment for which we have healing descriptions, and cannot explain most current reports of miraculous healings, which do not include dissociative states.[150] (By contrast, some recent studies have argued that most observed effects of hypnosis involve the subjects' desire to present themselves as "good subjects" in anticipated hypnotic situations.[151]) In any case, the controlled clinical conditions of hypnotism differ starkly from Jesus's public ministry, as do the repetitive rituals of typical shamans. Meanwhile, some documented cases of visual acuity improvement in spiritual contexts more like those in which Jesus ministered reveal effects on average far exceeding those in the most optimistic of hypnosis studies.[152]

More generally, however, some argue that culturally relevant images that communicate healing (by exorcism or the like) provide psychological codes that, converted biologically into neuropeptide signals, mobilize immune defenses and so forth.[153] Psychological factors may thus be helpful in cures. For example, a researcher notes that one woman in Puerto Rico who "had not walked for several years" found that she enjoyed the attention given to her state, yet in a prayer meeting she found strength to walk home.[154] While ability to walk with atrophied muscles is remarkable, a psychological factor might well also be at work in such a healing report. Similarly, a case of terminal, metastasized cancer remitted without surgery for eighteen years, the worst of it after a change in lifestyle;[155] another case of advanced terminal cancer gradually remitted (over the course of a year) after lifestyle changes and never returned.[156] Nevertheless, such remissions are quite

---

Lechler, *Ratsel*; Wilson, *Bleeding Mind*, esp. 97, 126); Heim, *Transformation*, 178 (who also cites abdominal swelling in imagined pregnancies).

149. McClenon, *Healing*, 75, citing Ewin, "Emergency Room Hypnosis"; idem, "Hypnosis in Surgery." Krippner and Achterberg, "Experiences," 378, note that shifting of blood flow can aid burn recovery and that it can be controlled to some extent through biofeedback (on 377 they note a 1931 study linking it to spontaneous disappearance of warts). Pekala and Cardeña, "Issues," 55, note pain reduction; a doctor in Mensah, "Basis," 176, cites the success of hypnotism in allowing a biopsy without anesthesia.

150. McNamara and Szent-Imrey, "Learn," 211 (citing for the areas of cure Bowers and LeBaron, "Hypnosis," and countering the relevance of McClenon's ritual healing theory to most modern reports).

151. Spanos, "Hypnosis," 97–102.

152. Brown, Mory, Williams, and McClymond, "Effects," 867: whereas improvements after hypnosis have averaged two to two and a half times' increase in the most optimistic studies (and none in others), "The average visual acuity improvement measured" for those receiving prayer through the earlier mentioned ministry in Mozambique "was over tenfold."

153. Greenfield, *Spirits*, 18, 180, 201; suggested to me also by John Pilch, personal correspondence, Nov. 13, 2009; cf. also Johnson, "Neurotheology," 223–24. On the belief that a factor may help communicating with the immune system, and altered states of consciousness (ASCs) functioning hypnotically, see Greenfield, *Spirits*, 189. Some allow for factors complementary to neurobiology (interpersonal psychology in Koss-Chioino, "Transformation," 64).

154. Laurentin, *Catholic Pentecostalism*, 119, emphasizing the psychological component of her cure.

155. Ellens, "Miracles and Process," 11, and idem, "God and Science," 13 (following Lenzer, "Citizen," 56).

156. Ellens, "Miracles and Process," 12 (following Lenzer, "Citizen," 58). Lenzer notes some conflicting studies, however, regarding cancer and mind-body connections (the fifth page of my online version).

rare (usually estimated at around one case in sixty thousand to one case in one hundred thousand,[157] though actual numbers may be higher),[158] so that one would not expect them to occur repeatedly in a particular ministry circle purely by chance.

Psychosomatic Elements in Jesus's Ministry?

Such explanations have been used as analogies for Gospel miracles; some have even employed them to defend the historical claims of the Gospels, albeit at the expense of a supernatural explanation.[159] Thus many have attributed Jesus's healing miracles to psychic abilities[160] or the ailments cured to psychosomatic causes.[161] As I have noted, this is a logical approach for those who explain all modern cures in these terms.[162] Others argue, however, that such approaches prove inadequate to accommodate all the data.[163] While we cannot rule out the curing of some psy-

157. Ellens, "Miracles and Process," 11 (following Lenzer, "Citizen," 56).

158. McNamara and Szent-Imrey, "Learn," 209, argue that real remission rates may be ten to twenty times greater than these estimates. Because anomalies do not fit reigning paradigms, they are inadequately reported and tracked. By contrast, some sources in Lenzer, "Citizen" (the second through fourth pages of my online version) appear to suggest that remission rates may be *lower* than usual estimates; she suggests (my sixth page) that early remissions are fairly common, whereas late remissions "are as rare as hens' teeth."

159. Through at least the mid-twentieth century, many continued to cite psychic parallels in support of miracles (e.g., views noted in Lawton, *Miracles*, 57, 90, 169; earlier, in Johnson, "Miracles and History," 544–45), though this could be viewed as grasping an available naturalistic explanation to continue denying a supernatural one.

160. Cf., e.g., M. C. van Mourik Broekman (1938; in Loos, *Miracles*, 30, 565–66); Jesus's expression of mana and the power of the unconscious mind in Tenzler, "Tiefenpsychologie." More recently Montefiore, *Miracles*, has sought to explain NT miracles by analogy to "paranormal" telepathy (23–40), clairvoyance (41–49), and precognition (51–65); this allows "natural" explanations (24), i.e., one acceptable within a Humean worldview. (He recognizes that his thesis will fail to persuade many [115–16], a point reiterated by a reviewer [Garrow, "Acts"].) Perry, "Miracles," 66–67, allows some but warns that such appeals can be "overdone." While the differences are significant (NT accounts suggest divine dependence rather than innate abilities), the analogy represents an attempt to get beyond typical Western assumptions. Heim, *Transformation*, 184–85, believes that a powerful mind can affect distant bodies and matter (though he distinguishes this effect from more specifically divine activity; cf., e.g., 187, 193, 195). For a collection of more than one hundred anomaly reports, see Long, *Ecology*.

161. Many have long attributed Jesus's cures to psychosomatic causes (Matthew Arnold [in Boobyer, "Miracles," 33–34]; Fenner, *Krankheit* [as cited in Sabourin, *Miracles*, 246; Loos, *Miracles*, 109]; Capps, *Village Psychiatrist*, 5; Ellens, "Miracles and Process," 5–6; views cited but not necessarily endorsed in Wilson, "Miracles," 13; Loos, *Miracles*, 105, 107, 111; Burkill, "Miracle"; Remus, *Healer*, 114; cf. the question in Jaeger, "Suggestionstherapeut" [cited in Metzger, *Index*, 18]). Some earlier writers noted the likelihood of some "nervous" diseases without attributing all of them to this cause (Wright, "Miracles," 189; Wilson, "Miracles," 28). Some argued that Jesus merely accommodated the opinions of his day, using mere psychosomatic healing; others objected that this explanation cannot account for some of the miracles (Dakin, "Belief," 38–39) or objected for theological reasons (Everts, "Exorcist," 357–59).

162. As I noted in the case of nineteenth-century discussions, the alternative is usually inconsistency. Thus May, "Miracles," 147, denies the plausibility of mere spontaneous remission in the healing of someone deaf and mute in the Gospels yet claims it in a more concretely documented case today (150–51).

163. E.g., Davey, "Healing," 62, noting the cluster of miracles surrounding Jesus and his theological interpretation; earlier, Johnson, "Miracles and History," 545–56. Carlston, "Question," 102, suggests that Jesus's miracles can be so construed, once "one strips away legendary accretions" (the criterion for what is legendary in this case presumably involving what is not plausible naturalistically). Carlston does not

chosomatic ailments in Jesus's ministry, the Gospel reports bear little resemblance to psychotherapy (or modern medicine); and if Jesus merely discerned which illnesses were psychosomatic, his widespread reputation as an *extraordinary* healer becomes more difficult to explain.[164]

Among the categories of disorders that multiple attestation suggests that Jesus cured are blindness, deafness, skin disorders ("leprosy"), and occasionally death.[165] Some summaries (e.g., in Q, Matt 11:5//Luke 7:22), not to mention specific cases, suggest that Jesus healed *multiple* cases of blindness, deafness, leprosy, inability to walk, and death. Would he have encountered so many psychosomatic cases, and primarily psychosomatic cases, of such dramatic ailments, in a one- to three-year ministry in Galilee? Some suggest that Jesus's cures of blindness, paralysis, and the like reflect his cure of a particular psychiatric disorder;[166] yet how many psychiatrists regularly cure cases of these afflictions (especially publicly and immediately)? If Jesus meanwhile would have regularly failed with irreversible organic cases of blindness and leprosy, yet could not distinguish which cases were organic beforehand, would we not find more defensive explanations (like the one in Nazareth, Mark 6:5–6)? Some detractors of the psychic powers line of interpretation also find it interesting that some observers are prepared to allow unproved psychic powers for humans that they reject as unacceptable violations of nature's uniformity if assigned to God.[167]

---

himself deny that God acted in Jesus but notes that "there are always alternative explanations." While not settling on this limitation, in 1905 Wilson, "Miracles," 28, allowed that social conditions in first-century Palestine probably made nervous conditions common. He argued that whether one believes that Jesus did more than psychosomatic healings depends on one's Christology (Wilson, "Miracles," 14); I would add that it can also depend on one's view of supernatural causation more generally. Dod, "Healer," 174–76, believes that God could work through psychosomatic healing both in Jesus's day and subsequently but that miracles involving nature ceased after the apostolic period. Others highlight the psychiatric value of Jesus's ministry to those with anxiety-related ailments (Capps, *Village Psychiatrist*, passim, esp. xii–xiv; Ellens, "Miracles and Process," 3–4).

164. Eve, *Healer*, 51–52.

165. E.g., blindness is cured in Q (Matt 11:5//Luke 7:22), Mark (8:22–25), Matthew (21:14), and John (9:6–7). All of these categories are also claimed today. For an argument in an ophthalmological journal that the descriptions of Jesus's eye healings in the Gospels appear plausible, see Mansour, Mehio-Sibai, Walsh et al., "Jesus and Eye" (summarized in Kub, "Miracles," 1273–74).

166. See Davies, *Healer*, 70–72; Capps, *Village Psychiatrist*, 8; for paralysis, see 37–55 (esp. 43–46); for blindness, 57–80; he suggests (xiv) that Jesus understood and worked through natural law (presumably on a much higher level than people today). Ralph Waldo Emerson's temporary blindness may have remitted due to prayer, but Capps believes it was psychological (64–65). Of course, while emotional miracles (cf., e.g., in Johnson, "Psychotherapy") would not meet Hume's standard, they could nevertheless function biblically as signs to people open to them. Because the Gospels rarely specify causes, one could allow psychiatric causes in some cases (with Capps) without ruling out organic cases, which remain pervasive in traditional societies. Yet we should avoid double standards: no one wants doctors to view all cases as psychological. Hoffman and Kurzenberger, "Miraculous," 81, note that this explanation for miracles of healing was a common modernist approach.

167. Cf. comments in Légasse, "L'Historien," 144. Parapsychology proponents tend to view the abilities as natural, yet have so far failed to offer natural mechanisms to account for claimed phenomena (Krippner and Achterberg, "Experiences," 380).

The Gospels often do connect faith with healings (Matt 8:10, 13; 9:2, 6–7, 22, 28–29; 15:28; Mark 2:5, 11–12; 5:34, 36; 9:23–24; 10:52; Luke 5:20, 24–25; 7:9; 8:48, 50; 17:19; 18:42; John 4:50; 11:40; cf. Mark 16:17–18; Acts 3:16; 14:9) or other answers to prayer (Mark 11:23–24; Matt 14:28–31; 21:21–22; Luke 17:6; cf. Mark 16:17–18), and sometimes shortage of healings due to a culture of disbelief (Mark 6:5–6; Matt 13:58; Luke 9:41) or Jesus's agents' disbelief (Matt 17:20; cf. Mark 9:29; Luke 9:41). (John more typically emphasizes basic faith *following* signs; John 1:50; 2:11, 23; 4:39, 48, 53; 7:31; 11:15, 42, 45, 48; 12:11; 14:29; 16:30; 20:30–31; cf. John 9:35–38; 10:25; Acts 13:12.)

Whether or not such receptivity plays a role in some cases, however, there is no thought that faith is efficacious only for events that could be explained psychosomatically (note secondary faith in Matt 8:13; 9:2; 15:28; Mark 2:5; Luke 7:9; John 4:50; death in Mark 5:36, 41–42; John 11:40–44; extrahuman effects in Mark 11:23–24; Matt 14:29; 21:21). Psychosomatic recovery is also not, as I have noted, the explanation most commonly applicable for some sorts of cures, such as the sudden stop of menorrhagia (Mark 5:34), long-term blindness (Mark 10:52), paralysis (Mark 2:11–12), and other conditions; had Jesus healed only psychosomatic ailments, he certainly would have failed publicly in many cases of organic blindness and the like, with no typical shamanic rituals to buffer the failure, and this could have reduced his crowds.

At least in the perspective of the Gospel writers, faith is not to be in one's amount of faith, as if it were a substance, but in God or Christ, who does the works (Mark 11:22; cf. Matt 18:6). Whereas Westerners after Kant tend to think of faith as a subjective feeling, the Gospels treat it more as a recognition of objective truth; the issue is less faith's finite possessor than its omnipotent object (Mark 11:22). The mention of faith is also missing in many accounts (e.g., Matt 8:14–15; 14:14; Mark 1:30–31; Luke 7:12–15; 13:11–13; John 5:6–9; 9:4–7); one dare not argue from silence, especially since Jesus himself supplied faith in many cases, but it is nevertheless clear that miracles can occur despite some participants' lack of faith (Matt 8:26; 14:17, 26; 16:8–10; Mark 4:40; 6:49; 8:4, 17–21; 9:24, 26; Luke 2:9; 5:4–9; 8:25; 11:14–15; especially Luke 1:20; cf. Luke 10:18). The disciples themselves are often the ones chided for their little faith (Mark 4:40; Luke 8:25; 12:28; cf. Luke 17:5), albeit especially in Matthew (6:30; 8:26; 14:31; 16:8; 17:20).[168]

While most historical Jesus scholars accept that Jesus performed acts that people believed to be cures, it is those drawing on medical anthropology (such as Pilch and Crossan) who most often emphasize that he did in fact cure illnesses. Their work offers extremely valuable insights from which I have learned. Yet some of these scholars contend that Jesus cured only culturally defined illnesses, not organic

---

168. Cotter's recent and excellent *Portrait*, thoroughly informed in ancient culture, helpfully highlights the petitioners and Jesus's response to them in some key Markan narratives and Q, often including the petitioners' boldness. For faith and its often bold expression in this work, see 6–7, 9, 12, 74–75, 100–102, 158, 254–55, 257.

disease.[169] More recently, drawing on psychoimmunology, scholars have begun to recognize that curing the former could also affect the latter.[170]

Nevertheless, while this recognition is welcome, challenges ethnocentric readings, and may discern processes that Jesus may have sometimes used, even it still leaves some questions unanswered.[171] Should we expect merely favorable immune responses to cure organic conditions like leprosy immediately? What of the raising of the dead? Such factors may be at work in many cures, but I believe that we still dance around an obvious question for some reports. It seems that scholarship is permitted to discuss any hypothesis—so long as we do not invoke God or other extrahuman intelligences.[172] Why are we obligated to observe that rule, which is itself an ethnocentric imposition from a particular subculture? Granted that we can work within a discipline's circumscribed boundaries by not asking the question, the question is not consequently epistemologically illegitimate. Granted that not all our colleagues accept this approach, is there any reason why the hypothesis should not be allowed on the table (like other hypotheses on which scholars disagree among ourselves)?

Appropriately for those who see the Gospels as biographies about a person who lived not long before, Stevan Davies accepts larger than usual portions of their portrayal of Jesus as historically accurate because these can fit his spirit possession thesis. For him, Jesus was a healer employing the placebo effect.[173] Yet the exclusion of anything genuinely supernatural is "a premise I accept absolutely," rendering impossible, for example, Jesus's resurrection.[174] Whenever we come across a principle that some take as axiomatic (e.g., the insistence of some popular writers on a "literal" interpretation of Revelation), I ask my students, "Who made up that rule?" That is, is it a rule that we are obligated to follow or merely an idea that we take for granted? If the answer to who made up the rule is in this case Hume, we have already surveyed evidence that raises serious questions about the logical value of his rule. Davies's careful approach allows him to accept more of the

169. Evaluating the dichotomy, see Capps, *Village Psychiatrist*, xv–xvi; Gaztambide, "Psychoimmunology," 95–97. Capps, *Village Psychiatrist*, xvii–xviii, counters that in psychosomatic illness, emotional roots can create physical problems.

170. Gaztambide, "Psychoimmunology," 97–99, following Felix Just, Marcus Borg, and Donald Capps; developing the evidence further on 99–108; cf. information in Lenzer, "Citizen." This approach is more culturally open to ancient conceptions than most academic readings have been. Capps, *Village Psychiatrist*, xii, does not deny the involvement of genuine physical conditions, but avers that these are generated psychologically.

171. No approach is obligated to answer questions outside its purview, so my questions here are intended as supplemental rather than denying insights in this approach.

172. I am not contending that all those who make the above arguments deny God or supernatural activity. I am complaining rather that the constraints that limit usual academic inquiry should be open to challenge in view of significant evidence (though I work within such constraints as needed).

173. Davies, *Healer*, 77 (addressing anxiety-suppressed immune systems and psychogenic illnesses, 76).

174. Ibid., 16. Thus he rejects nature miracles, unlike healings, as legendary (67), because they cannot fit his paradigm; in principle he allows raisings, but only insofar as the persons may have been comatose or perhaps just recently dead. Contrast those who argue (as I do below) that refusing nontheistic constraints may yield a fuller picture of reality (e.g., Polkinghorne, *Reality*, 83, 88).

early evidence than most scholars do; but admitting as possible also some cures that cannot be explained by the placebo effect would provide greater consistency in handling our sources. If it is natural to take most first- and second-generation reports as historically valuable, why screen out elements simply because they are contrary to a Humean worldview? Following the principle in logic known as Occam's razor, allowing supernatural activity provides the simplest interpretation for some of our other evidence that even Davies's interesting approach cannot accommodate.

The Placebo Effect

Having introduced the supernatural question, however, we must return to natural factors. One cannot deny that psychological factors play a role in many cures. While "magnetic" and many hypnotic explanations are now dated, the value of psychological factors in recovery is well documented. Some researchers have estimated that as many as half, or even more than half, of patients lack organic causes for their ailments,[175] although these estimates naturally include only those whose organic causes are diagnosed.[176] Most ailments do improve on their own with or without medical or other treatment.[177] The placebo effect often helps patients,[178] so that even some alternative medicines without proven chemical efficacy have benefited patients through this effect.[179] Some have even linked it to remission of

---

175. Frye, "Faith Healing," 18; Markle, "Body," 16–17; Baroody, "Healing," 87–88; Benson, *Healing*, 49; cf. Kelsey, *Healing*, 5; Buskirk, *Healing*, 25–44; Venter, *Healing*, 231; Robertson, *Miracles*, 144. Cf. even a reported case for deafness in Benson, *Healing*, 63. On psychosomatic cures, see also, e.g., Neal, *Power*, 77–78; Mayhue, *Healing*, 92–94; emotions in Frohock, *Healing Powers*, 133.

176. Remus, *Healer*, 109, notes that surveys suggest that clear diagnoses elude physicians in roughly half the occasions.

177. Frohock, *Healing Powers*, 133. Roberts, *Coburn*, 18, offers this observation based on his time in the Amazon rainforest, where most people lacked access to physicians.

178. See, e.g., Droege, *Faith Factor*, 15–33 (esp. 23–26; cf. also 9–12, on psychoneuroimmunology; on which see also Gaztambide, "Role," 303–6); Matthews and Clark, *Faith Factor*, 179–81; Gaztambide, "Role"; Frank, *Persuasion*, 65–74; Benson, *Healing*, 117; Bishop, *Healing*, 25–27; Buskirk, *Healing*, 45–49, 89–119; Hirschberg and Barasch, *Recovery*, 70; Eya, "Healing," 49 (citing, e.g., Beecher, "Placebo," though some of his work has subsequently generated controversy); Remus, *Healer*, 110–13; Beauregard and O'Leary, *Brain*, 144–50; Chesnut, *Born Again in Brazil*, 87; Schwarz, *Healing*, 169–70; Venter, *Healing*, 62; Wallis, "Healing," 51; Epperly, *Touch*, 35–36. Benson, *Healing*, 21, found that attitudes of wellness could prove two or three times as effective as an ordinary placebo. Benson, *Healing*, 184–87, found apparent but not adequately replicable effects of "healers" even on animals, hypothesizing (186) that positive human pheromones may have played a part. Randi, *Faith Healers*, 283–84, offers this complaint about "faith healing" claims, though he lays the same essential charge against psychotherapy (285–86); one might also wonder how spinal pressure could cure deafness (Bishop, *Healing*, 82–83, on early chiropractic). Cf. one comment (intended favorably) regarding African traditional healers: "The therapeutic effect comes basically from the client's belief that the healer is a powerful person" (Mkhwanazi, "Psychotherapist," 267).

179. Marilynn Marchione, "Experts: Placebo Power Behind Many Natural Cures," Associated Press, Nov. 10, 2009, http://news.yahoo.com/s/ap/20091110/ap_on_he_me/med_unproven_remedies_placebo; accessed Nov. 10, 2009. She cites sources claiming that the placebo effect accounts for a third of the benefits even in the case of accepted medicines.

some cases of cancer[180] or used it to explain faith cures of tuberculosis,[181] though it should be noted that confidence does not always produce such effects. In some cases, the placebo effect has made a genuine difference between life and death.[182] It is said that self-hypnosis has sometimes alleviated nonpsychosomatic, congenital ailments, though normally partially, gradually, and with need for the treatment to continue.[183]

Through history, many religio-medical folk practices offered no pharmaceutical benefit but apparently did provide significant placebo effects.[184] Thus on the medical side eighteenth-century patients often improved after bloodletting, which we now know to be harmful; patients *expected* to improve because the medical establishment of the day supported the practice.[185] Herbert Benson of Harvard Medical School notes that because of confidence in physicians' orders, participants in one five-year study who neglected most of their prescribed placebos were almost twice as likely to die as those who took them.[186] Other medically worthless treatments have displayed objectively documented higher improvement rates—until the treatments were shown to be ineffective.[187] Other personal factors can be important; for example, physicians' personal concern for patients aids the recovery process.[188] In the case of one ailment where placebos proved as effective as medicines, confident physicians proved some 30 percent more effective than skeptical ones.[189] Mental health helps mobilize immune responses and facilitate physical recovery, and various kinds of meditation or religiously sanctioned expressions of confidence can aid in this process.[190]

Whether the placebo effect stands behind a *particular* healing, of course, remains open to question. An Asian physician for whom a pastor prayed noted that before the prayer he could not bend down because his back had been sprained. After prayer, he was fine, with no need for pain medication, and went running

180. Hirschberg and Barasch, *Recovery*, 277–78; cf. Spraggett, *Kuhlman*, 40. Preliminary studies can suggest a generally positive correlation of spirituality with cancer coping and improvement, though more research is needed (cf. Sherman and Simonton, "Spirituality and Cancer" [for one ambiguity, see, e.g., 164]; Koenig, *Medicine*, 124–27).

181. Melinsky, *Miracles*, 98–100 (esp. the story of Pauline on 99–100), 163; Spraggett, *Kuhlman*, 39–40.

182. Althouse, *Healing*, 107–9.

183. Spraggett, *Kuhlman*, 47–48.

184. Benson, *Healing*, 107–10 (citing Shapiro, "History"; Hand, *Magical Medicine*; Vogel, *Medicine*).

185. Matthews and Clark, *Faith Factor*, 179. Bloodletting also appears in some Native American traditional medicine (Hultkrantz, *Healing*, 33–34, 66, 95).

186. Benson, *Healing*, 45 (citing Benson and McCallie, "Placebo Effect"; Horwitz et al., "Adherence"). For the negative version of the placebo effect, see, e.g., Benson, *Healing*, 39, 42, 53, 59, 62.

187. Benson, *Healing*, 34, 36–37. On other occasions, medicines or procedures work but not for the reasons theorists initially suppose (see, e.g., Clark, *Philosophy of Science*, 92–93, 112–13).

188. Cassell, *Miracles*, 215–18 (esp. 215, based on interviews with surgeons).

189. Moerman, *Meaning*, 38–39, as cited in Pilch, "Usefulness," 99–100.

190. See, e.g., Benson, *Healing*, 16–21 and passim; cf. Althouse, *Healing*, 117–21 (on Christian meditation); Krippner and Achterberg, "Experiences," 382 (on the biological benefits of "positive emotional changes" more generally); for Christian spirituality benefiting mental health, see, e.g., Joubert, "Spirituality"; Hoffman, Moriarty and Williamson, "Dynamics."

the next day. The doctor noted that he had originally thought that the placebo effect accounted for all healings but said that he could not explain his own case in those terms.[191] Some scientists recognize that extraordinary cures labeled miracles "go way beyond mere placebo effects," and even more powerful "expectation effects."[192] While in some cases psychosomatic explanations are probable, in some other cases they are futile: the healing of babies, the raising of the dead, or the stilling of storms.[193]

As for explanations that depend on psychic human abilities, these explanations grow weak in cases of cures where faith was lacking, as sometimes reported at Lourdes and elsewhere (note also various other examples throughout this book).[194] Appeal to latent human powers[195] (even to still storms), like appeal to God or other superhuman forces, is ultimately an appeal beyond materialistic naturalism as we know it. That some find it appealing as an alternative to divine or other superhuman explanations, even when cures immediately follow prayer, suggests again the presuppositions that I have noted stand behind much of the modern antipathy toward miracles: atheism and deism.

Religion and Psychological Elements in Healing

Religion may support psychological elements in healing. Suggestibility (or, on a less charitable reading, gullibility) may account for some psychic healing claims.[196] Many studies link spiritual healing to altered states of consciousness.[197] Confidence can produce relaxation, which provides an immune system advantage.[198] A Japanese hypnotherapist observing shamans and Christian healers compared the trance behavior involved with hypnosis, regarding these practices as potentially

191. Bruce Collins, phone interview, April 11, 2009. Bruce provided me the doctor's correspondence (dated Feb. 9, 2009) and the names involved, which I omit in print for the sake of privacy.

192. McNamara and Szent-Imrey, "Learn," 210, complaining that too little research has been done on the nature of religious faith in extraordinary cures. They use "costly signaling theory" to address forms of human illness and recovery in ibid., 213–18.

193. Cf. ibid., 213: "we have no [scientific] explanation for the miraculous healing of an infant."

194. E.g., the story of Elaine Panelo's raising in ch. 12.

195. Over half a century ago, Ikin, Concepts, 115–37, sought to bring together spiritual healing with the "new physics," suggesting a latent power within nature (perhaps as a religious attempt to bridge to secular language). With some others, she suggested that psychic processes were as normal as physical ones (151–58).

196. Allison and Malony, "Surgery," 54–55 (on Filipino psychic surgery; see also the sleight of hand argument in McClenon, Events, 107–15). McClenon and Nooney, "Experiences," 47, note the evolutionary approach in which more suggestible persons were more often cured in shamanic rituals, hence perpetuated their suggestibility genes.

197. See McClenon, Healing, 67, and sources in his notes. On 87–88 he notes the different brain activity during altered states of consciousness; on 89–91, brain activity and anomalous experiences; on 92, brain activity and hypnosis; on 92–93, hypnosis and anomalous experiences; and on 95–96, hypnosis and spiritual healing. Despite the empirical aspects of these studies, the specific configuration of connections may require more study. On altered states of consciousness, see brief discussions in appendixes B and E.

198. McClenon, Healing, 76, suggesting that rituals can facilitate this increased confidence.

therapeutic.[199] (One should note, however, that in a number of cultures it is the healer rather than the patient who typically enters a trance.)

In some cultures today, "indigenous folk-healers" offer a higher cure rate than Western medical practitioners there, especially in treating the many mental causes of illness.[200] Some studies found that most cases involving the studied shamans were cured, partly or fully, with significantly higher average patient satisfaction than in the West.[201] Certainly traditional healers are more affordable and accessible than Western medicine.[202] Noting the inadequate medical help available for most Africans, many modern Western scholars thus praise the health support offered by traditional African healers and African Independent Churches (AICs) as a significant benefit to society, whether or not it involves supernatural elements.[203] Some also complain that Western insensitivity toward nonorganic causes drives traditional Africans to faith healers and traditional healers, where such causes are taken seriously.[204] Health workers generally affirm that these healers help people and fulfill a genuine social role,[205] and many studies contend that they are even more effective in treating psychological disorders than psychotherapy is.[206] Zambia's

199. Cited in McClenon, Healing, 59.

200. Eve, Miracles, 354 (citing Kleinman, Healers, 71–82, 139–40, 366, especially regarding the Taiwanese shaman, or tâng-ki). This would not be relevant for many illnesses reported cured in the NT, however, such as leprosy or most cases of paralysis and blindness. Eve, Miracles, 355–56, also notes that the NT reports do not allow time for the sort of "folk psychotherapy" attested in these other accounts.

201. McClenon, Healing, 62–63, cites regarding patient satisfaction Kleinman and Sung, "Practitioners," though noting that their small study found no evidence for healing that could not be explained psychologically (and that half of doctors' caseloads in the West deal with similar issues). On most cases being cured in one study, again allowing psychological explanations, McClenon, Healing, 63, cites Curley, Elders.

202. See, e.g., Amutabi, "Pharmacology," 154, noting also that there are traditional practitioners for every two hundred to three hundred people, but only one trained medical person for thirty thousand people.

203. Many address the psychosomatic or positive psychotherapeutic value of traditional African healing forms: in AICs, see, e.g., Oosthuizen, "Healing," 87; idem, "Baptism," 187–88; idem, Healer-Prophet, 193; Mkhize, "Prayer-Healer"; Ayegboyin, "Heal," 244, 245 (while also noting serious problems, 244–45); Edwards, "Healing," 343–44; cf. Motala, "Influence"; in traditional religion, Mkhwanazi, "Psychotherapist" (on the therapeutic relationship, see 277); Ademilokun, "Contribution," 131; Adeyemi, "Healing Systems," 145–46; Cheetham and Griffiths, "Psychotherapist"; Benson, Healing, 110 (citing Gelfand, Witch Doctor). Given faith healing's benefit for mental care, Peltzer, "Faith Healing," 399, contends that it should be accepted as part of health care in South Africa (though noting on 404 that many of its remedies, even for STDs, are spiritual and essentially homeopathic). Cf., e.g., the South African Pentecostal cure of a woman's anorexia in Denis, "Religion," 187. Others also recommend sensitivity to local mental health taxonomies (e.g., for South African Muslims in Ally and Laher, "Perceptions"). Although some traditional diagnoses may simply defer problems or project them (hindering relationships), African traditional healing has an advantage from a systems perspective in that it treats the entire social context of a person's psychological distress, in contrast to traditional Western psychiatry (Crawford and Lipsedge, "Help," 143). Zionists and Pentecostals promote more faithful sexual behavior, helpful against HIV (Scorgie, "Weapons," 89); Zionists provide communal support and emotional catharsis (91–93), and some non-Zionists come for ministry also (96).

204. Daneel, Zionism, 22–23, 57. Cf. a similar Native American case in Hultkrantz, Healing, 151. Some doctors, however, have claimed that "fetish priests" have tried to attack them "spiritually since I was destroying their livelihood" (Mensah, "Basis," 177).

205. McClenon, Healing, 63.

206. See studies cited in McClenon, Healing, 62–67; for the placebo effect as a possible factor in shamanic healing, see Walsh, Shamanism, 212–14; West, Sorcery, 43–44, 92–93.

government legally certifies herbalist folk healers,[207] and the World Health Organization (WHO) has trained many "native healers, sometimes incorporating them into Western medical clinics and hospitals" to make health accessible to more people.[208] Nor are indigenous medicines limited to Africa; for example, one study of a tribe in the Philippines urges that folk medicine be continued there so long as scientific medicine remains unavailable.[209] (Some have suggested that charismatic Christian healing also should be accepted as an alternative therapy "in contexts where access to conventional treatment is limited."[210])

Even apart from the question of supernatural elements, however, not all effects of traditional African medicine are psychosomatic.[211] Some traditional herbal remedies, for example, are natural remedies that may be chemically effective.[212] Local experience may yield some substances that prove helpful in addressing local ailments;[213] some have even suggested that African medicine pioneered the use of immunizations even before Western medicine.[214] Herbal remedies are not, when employed only naturally, incompatible with the claims of different religions, including Christianity;[215] the questions are often more pharmaceuti-

207. Jules-Rosette, "Healers," 128–29 (cf. also acceptance of spirit healers there, in Luig, "Worlds," 132–33). Although illegal for a time in Mozambique, traditional healers are now legal there (Roque, "Mafumo," 186) and sometimes even celebrated (West, Sorcery, 39).

208. Krippner, "Medicine," 195. For differences, commonalities, and dialogue between Western medicine and African traditional practices in Africa, see Merwe, "Relevance," 61–62.

209. Angel, "Craft," 135 (again, based on herbal remedies, many of them not yet known or studied outside their context; cf. iv–v).

210. Brown, Mory, Williams, and McClymond, "Effects," 864, 868.

211. Religious healing usually coexists "with naturalistic treatment" (Frank, Persuasion, 37). Traditional herbalists often have belief systems about spirits (see, e.g., Jules-Rosette, "Healers," 128–29; Hultkrantz, Healing, 52, 94, 158) or practice divination (Jules-Rosette, "Healers," 132–33; mediums in Emmons, Ghosts, 224), but these may be distinguished from some of the herbs they use.

212. Cf. Amutabi, "Pharmacology," 155 (noting roots and herbs on 165–70); for "naturalistic" traditional medicine, including herbs and surgery, see Sofowora, Traditional Medicine. Sofowora distinguishes "occult" spirit activities from traditional medicine and treatments (43–44), though noting that they have often overlapped (e.g., 3–5, 44). For use of herbs, cf. also, e.g., Umeh, Dibia, 121–36 (esp. 126–30); Byaruhanga-Akiiki and Kealotswe, Healing, 164–74 (on some Asian remedies), 182–87 (in Africa); Crawford and Lipsedge, "Help," 138–39 (among the Zulu); Abioye, "Faith," 4; Akintan, "Priest," 137–38; Haar and Ellis, "Possession," 199–200; Roque, "Mafumo," 184–89; Katz, Energy, 39, 51 (among the !Kung); in Caribbean healing, Hurbon, "Pentecostalism," 134; in Haiti, Beauvoir, "Herbs," 115–25 (suggesting chemical effectiveness); Native American herbalists in Hultkrantz, Healing, 33, 36, 94, 111–12, 147, 158; cf. traditional Japanese herbal remedies in Nakasone, "Healing," 289; indigenous folk remedies in part of the Philippines in Castro, "Practices," 309–67, and Angel, "Craft," e.g., iv–v; some in indigenous Mexican culture in Heinrich, "Medicines." The majority of students at the University of Zululand believed that diviners and herbalists were helpful for the sick (Nene, "Analysis," 37–41, esp. 40), though some thought them more helpful for the "superstitious" (41).

213. Also other treatments, e.g., of snakebite by cutting open the wound and applying a tourniquet (Reynolds, Magic, 67).

214. McNaughton, Blacksmiths, 57–58, although the evidence cited is limited.

215. See, e.g., Gaiser, Healing, 57–58; the concession of William Wadé Harris in Walls, Movement, 98–99. Western Christians have sometimes collaborated with traditional healers (e.g., Seale, "Collaboration"; a missionary and an herbalist in Olson, Bruchko, 126–29), although generally more open to their more "naturalistic" methods such as herbs than competing supernatural approaches (Seale, "Collaboration,"

cal than religious.[216] (Some treatments involve water more than herbs.[217]) In an era when Western medicine was far less dependable than today, John Wesley, for example, advocated traditional herbs and other folk remedies.[218] When Wesley seemed on his deathbed at the age of fifty-one, at the hour that some were praying for him, he had a poultice of sulfur and egg white on brown paper applied to his side. "The pain ceased in five minutes," he declared, "the fever in half an hour,"

316–17). Kyomo, "Healing," 146–47, tells of Danieli Kamwela, a traditional medicine man who devoted his traditional medical practice to Christ's service after becoming a Christian (cf. the healing of a missionary's daughter through these means, and the missionary's subsequent support, 145–46). Members of some indigenous churches resort to both Christian faith healing and to herbalists, but to the latter as a later resort and with the emphatic caveat that the herbalists they consulted were not using non-Christian religion (Jules-Rosette, "Healers," 130). Some groups, like the church of John Maranke, reject both traditional and modern medicines (Jules-Rosette, "Healers," 134–35). Views of Muslims toward traditional medicine of various kinds varies also (see Kareem, "Attitude," 79–81; cf. Ademola, "Attitude," 110).

216. Emphasized to me by my brother-in-law Emmanuel Moussounga, who has a PhD in chemistry from Paris as well as a master's degree in pharmacology. He has explored these issues locally and hopes to pursue more research as the funding becomes available. Benson, *Healing*, 109 (citing Ackerknecht, *Medicine and Ethnology*), suggests that many local herbs contained agents useful for healing but that these agents were often delivered in an inadequately therapeutic way. That many committed Christians prescribe local herbal remedies, often with claims of supernatural discernment, was clear to me during my interviews in Congo (July 2008); other African Christians believe such traditional concoctions unnecessary (Onesimus Asiimwe, interview, Oct. 12, 2008, though he was not against genuinely medicinal substances). Some elements may be symbolic (Oosthuizen, *Healer-Prophet*, 76), and some who employ such substances regard them as merely props for faith, regarding faith as the important element (Mkhize, "Prayer-Healer," 289, on a woman who attributed her gift to both God and ancestors). Church history is replete with many such healing symbols (such as oil, e.g., Crisafulli and Nesbitt, *Miracles*, 22, 160–61; a revealed remedy of vinegar and salt, Crisafulli and Nesbitt, *Miracles*, 12; berries, in a dream, 222–25), often borrowed from surrounding cultures. With many herbs, however, a pharmacological element is also in view.

217. In some parts of Africa, indigenous church healers use holy water rather than herbs (Wessels, "Practices," 94, noting that they also avoid using bones, killing medicine, and snuff, probably more widespread prohibitions; for divergent views of traditional medicines among AIC prophets, see Oosthuizen, *Healer-Prophet*, 174). The Aladura view of water somewhat resembles its role in Yoruba traditional religion (Ayegboyin, "Heal," 238); for use of water and other substances in Zionist healing practices, see Dube, "Search," 122; Daneel, "Zionism," 29; Edwards, "Healing," 341; Oosthuizen, *Healer-Prophet*, 40, 59–60, 75, 76 (vinegar and brown sugar), 89; Okoye, "Healing," 23; sacred baptismal water in Oosthuizen, "Baptism," comparing Roman Catholic and Orthodox rituals; idem, *Healer-Prophet*, 149–64, 169 (for healing, esp. 44–46); among the Karanga, Shoko, *Religion*, 54 (sprinkling of holy water); among West African Seraphim, Parrinder, *Religion*, 121; for water and Vaseline among the amaNazaretha, see Moodley, *Shembe*, 173–75 (though Vimbeni Shembe attributes the healing to faith and prayer, 161); for oil, orange juice, eggs, and smoke in some "apostolic" churches, Shoko, *Religion*, 53. Traditional cults also emphasize water and washing (e.g., Beauvoir, "Herbs," 132, on Haiti), although Christians would look to other precedents (2 Kgs 5:10; John 9:7). The symbol is culturally intelligible in many cultures; baths (Pliny *Ep.* 7.21.3; Fronto *Eloq.* 1.4) and hot springs (Vitruvius *Arch.* 8.3.4; Pliny *Nat.* 31.31.59–61; Philostratus *Hrk.* 23.30) were considered therapeutic in the ancient Mediterranean world (see comment in ch. 2).

218. See Pickstone, "Systems," 171 (referring to his *Primitive Physick*). This approach in a sense empowered the poor with regard to their health, though we now know that many of these folk cures, like many of those of that era's medical establishment, were not dependable (see, e.g., Wigger, *Saint*, 67–68, 75, 229, 248–49, 275, 329–30). On the social context of the *Primitive Physick*, as an act of pastoral concern, see Rack, "Healing," 138–40, 143–46, though Asbury did not follow its prescriptions (Wigger, *Saint*, 264); for Wesley's mixed record on contemporary science, see Brooke, *Science*, 189–91. In North America, some traditional faith healers in Appalachia have also employed herbs alongside prayer (Wigginton, *Foxfire Book*, 356).

and he began to recover.[219] Today we would doubt that the poultice did much, at least physically, for his rapid recovery, but neither would we think that it harmed him or compromised his faith.[220]

Nevertheless, in many cases of recoveries associated with religion or traditional culture, Western observers believe that psychological elements play a role. One study in Switzerland showed that when a faith healer laid hands on 532 smokers to pray for their deliverance, fully 40 percent remained smoke-free after four months (compared with 2 percent success for "behavior-modification techniques" and "13% for those using nicotine-replacement therapy"), though this figure fell to 20 percent after five years, undoubtedly due to factors that made smoking attractive in the first place. While one could explain the outcomes in terms of extraordinary supernatural causation, one could also cite psychological factors. Those with stronger religious belief in the efficacy of laying on of hands had a higher long-term cure rate, perhaps suggesting the element many religious people call faith.[221] In keeping with such an approach, one paralysis cured by emotional change was assumed to be functional rather than organic.[222]

When some clearly organic conditions have been cured, however, it seems reductionist to reduce all reports of healings to psychosomatic cures of functional limitations. This allowance for mind cures of a functional nature, while denying organic ones, long persisted as a traditional compromise with antisupernaturalist assumptions.[223] Early twentieth-century modernist Christians could accept God acting by natural means through the human "mind and spirit" far more readily than God "intervening directly in physical nature."[224]

Reductionism aside, we readily acknowledge that many cures may involve these natural factors. Most theists, including those affirming miraculous healing, can

---

219. Wesley, *Journal* (1974), 198 (Nov. 28, 1753). He was healthy enough to begin riding the next day (198), but apparently recovered full strength only gradually (199).

220. By contrast, the decoction of bark he ingested on Dec. 20 of the same year apparently set him back a few days (Wesley, *Journal* [1974], 199). In Olson, *Bruchko*, 148, Motilone Indians successfully employed antibiotics and prayer against snake venom, unaware that the antibiotics were useless for snake poison. Like Wesley, they used the best medicine they knew while depending on God. Jones, *Wonders*, 110, notes a similar combination of a worthless remedy and helpful faith and (114–15, 126) acknowledges recoveries after remedies he considers unhelpful.

221. Matthews and Clark, *Faith Factor*, 28–29 (citing Gmur and Tschopp, "Factors"; for the 2 percent success rate, Law and Tang, "Analysis"); for an anecdotal report of instant supernatural healing from cigarette addiction, see Carothers, *Prison*, 49. Mainstream media also report the usefulness of religion in combating nicotine addiction; see Jeff Levine, "Study: Religion Helps Smokers Kick the Habit" (CNN, May 15, 1996), http://www.cnn.com/HEALTH/9605/15/nfm/holy.smokes/index.html; accessed June 22, 2009, via Dr. David Larson's website.

222. Hirschberg and Barasch, *Recovery*, 111–12. Note also the case in May, "Miracles," 148.

223. Mullin, *Miracles*, 183 (on 184 noting liberal Christians' earlier contrast made between healing and the more problematic nature miracles); cf. L. W. Grensted's critique of Hickson in Mews, "Revival," 330; also Wright, *Miracle*, 150–57, 167–69 (though he allows that Jesus's miracles may be of a different character, 145–46, 169–70). Thouless, "Miracles," 257, contends that "mental healing" can explain even organic cures but admits that the cases available so far had not yet proved amenable "to experimental study."

224. Mullin, *Miracles*, 184.

affirm that God frequently works through such psychological factors for recovery.[225] Indeed, some Christians focus especially on *spiritual* healing, with various degrees of efficacy.[226] Most persons with disabilities are not miraculously healed, but many find strength in their faith to cope with their disabilities (cf. 1 Kgs 14:4–6; 2 Kgs 13:14; Luke 14:13, 21); from a believer's or a friend's standpoint, this ability may reflect divine grace. Nevertheless, for the purposes under discussion here, in these cases unconvinced observers will not view such recoveries as indisputable empirical evidence for extranormal divine activity.[227]

In the middle of the twentieth century, British Methodist theologian Leslie Weatherhead acknowledged psychological means of healing, including Mesmerism,[228] hypnotism,[229] and suggestion.[230] Yet while psychological means were useful, he urged that the church must also "recover the lost art of healing through the direct activity of God."[231] While affirming the value of medicine and psychology, he lamented that the church "has lost the supernatural gift of healing." Though Christ used psychological principles, he insisted, psychology alone is not the fullness of Christ's supernatural power.[232]

Some narratives, such as raisings and nature miracles, are not as susceptible to this sort of explanation. These events are less frequent than faith cures but are often based on the same sort of eyewitness testimonies, often by individuals whose trustworthiness should not be in dispute. The frequent practice today of admitting the possibility of faith cures in the Gospels and Acts, while denying claims that would seem to require supernatural action (or at least highly improbable,

225. See, e.g., Mount, "Miracles?" 19; Brown, "Spiritual Healing," 115–17; cf. De Orio, "Phenomenology," 123–24. Some healings, MacNutt notes (*Power*, 68–70), work "through purely natural forces released in prayer," although he notes extraordinary activity (70–74), including healing of nerve damage and the straightening of teeth (76–77). The high proportion of ailments that have psychological roots will also require cures that address those roots (MacNutt, *Power*, 79). Even in Scripture, God typically worked through natural processes—which, after all, God created (problematizing the distinction between "natural" and "supernatural"); even in Exod 14:21, God swept back the sea through an east wind, though this was not a *random* event. Some contend that the historic combination of spiritual and medical approaches in healing has been enjoying a resurgence after several scientific studies (cited in Cherry, *Healing Prayer*, 3–17; cf. Neal, *Smoke*, 126–34).

226. Csordas, "Healing," recounts two case studies with a charismatic Catholic priest and psychologist; the second case (129–32) acknowledged minimal improvement, although the client's resistance would have made psychiatric progress equally difficult.

227. Some, of course, will not be convinced by any arguments. Moreover, even some unusual cures provide limited evidence. Spontaneous remission can happen with or without prayer (Mount, "Miracles?" 19). The exception would be a sufficient collocation of natural factors as to be too improbable naturally to attribute to coincidence (Corduan, "Miracle," 104). While this collocation may be miraculous, it is not as often disputed as the sort of event inexplicable without some sort of supernatural agency (see discussion in Dietl, "Miracles," 130). Moreover, even in the Gospels Jesus sometimes healed from compassion without a prior request when he was present (Luke 7:13–15).

228. Weatherhead, *Psychology*, 105–8.

229. Ibid., 109–21.

230. Ibid., 122–28.

231. Ibid., 485.

232. Ibid., 486.

extraordinary coincidences), is acceptable on nonsupernatural grounds. (Biblical supernaturalists can accept both miraculous and more natural faith cures, since, as I have repeatedly noted, God in Scripture often worked through nature, albeit usually doing so in extraordinary ways when the objective involved signs.) But if, as I argued in chapters 5–6, the case for antisupernaturalism is largely circular, then an open-minded approach should be willing to consider also those claims that do not fit this paradigm (including babies, raisings, and particularly extraordinary cures). One need not presuppose that miracles happen to be open to the possibility; by contrast, to foreclose the possibility a priori and without exploration rests on a closed-minded, hence uncritically held, presupposition. For an ideal, neutral observer not schooled in antisupernaturalism, which way would the totality of the evidence, including claims of raisings and nature miracles, point?

Conclusion

Based on the preceding discussion, even an atheist could affirm that many people believed themselves healed and experienced recovery through Jesus's and his first followers' ministry. That is, the primary, historical claim of this book would be sufficiently established even apart from a theistic perspective. Nevertheless, I believe that it is possible to strengthen the historical claim still further, as well as advance the book's secondary argument, by looking at the other side of some of the evidence.

14

Biased Standards?

The ground rules that the commissions established in order to validate a healing as miraculous—that is, that it could not merely be inexplicable, but also had to be unique and not found in the annals of either medicine or other religions—almost ensured that no healings would be deemed "miracles." —Robert Bruce Mullin[1]

... have concluded that she must have been misdiagnosed and mistreated for the past twenty years. These conscientious and competent doctors have risked a possible malpractice suit rather than admit the possibility of divine healing. —Ken Blue[2]

W e have looked at various plausible naturalistic factors in recoveries sometimes associated with faith. Since the God of Scripture most often appears
to work with natural factors, there is nothing in these observations that necessarily
challenges a position grounded in Scripture, even theologically. Neither, however,
would such activity convince an open-minded agnostic of a deity's extranormal
activity. Many Western Christian scholars in recent centuries have appropriately
discovered God's greatness in the regularity of nature, but those who take nature's
regularity for granted may find extraordinary works more persuasive than natural
ones. In general terms, how might such extraordinary works be identified?

Keep in mind this book's earlier discussion regarding Hume and Western skepticism toward miracles. Despite its shaky foundations, this Humean skepticism provides a starting bias in much of the traditional Western evaluation of the evidence
for miracles, a bias that often screens out all evidence not in its favor.

Reductionism?

Clearly natural factors are at work in much healing, but some observers contend that
attributing *all* medically unexplained recovery claims to exclusively psychological

1. Mullin, *Miracles*, 248.
2. Blue, *Authority*, 58.

causes, when other proposed factors may be at work, is reductionist.[3] This warning surely applies to a number of the sorts of extranormal recoveries recounted earlier in this book, including healings of babies and the restoration of dead persons, for which a theological explanation is normally more supportable than a psychosomatic one.

One should also consider the cumulative factor: a specific coincidence appears increasingly less coincidental as its incidence level increases; the explanatory power of coincidence is not unlimited (as even David Hume recognized).[4] One Western observer protests, "It strains the credulity of anyone who has seen literally countless instances of healing following prayer to be told that these instances are always" due to chance or psychological factors.[5] Thus in one report, when a girl immobilized in her lower limbs by polio was, after a prayer of faith, promptly able to walk "holding only her father's arm," one professor derided the experience as a coincidence. To this remark her father, also a professor, responded that if her healing was a coincidence, it was surely a miraculous one.[6] If some people find all of these reports incredible, they should remember that the basis for their skepticism is the premise that such events cannot happen. They should also remember, as I argued earlier, that premise is only an assumption, not the conclusion of an examination of all (or normally even of many) miracle claims.

Avoiding a reductionist approach, a recent academic work in the sociology of religion notes that some of the reports of miracles that the authors collected could involve spontaneous remission, psychosomatic illnesses, or exaggerated rumors, yet other reports defied such naturalistic explanations and would be regarded by believers as supernatural.[7] They allow that many cases may allow "*complementary* explanations"—both social and theological, both human and suprahuman elements.[8] One need not rule out the usual sociological variables, they note, by

3. Gardner, *Healing Miracles*, 29–31, acknowledging psychosomatic ailments, and that mental attitudes can improve cure rates but denying that these explanations cover many of the cases he notes; cf. Frohock, *Healing Powers*, 135–36. Hickson, *Heal*, 72, cites the published letter of Bishop Herbert J. Molony of Chekiang Province in China, dated June 14, 1921: "many of the cures are not to be accounted for on any theory of 'suggestion.' This plays its part, as in all hope-inspiring medical practice, but it cannot account for some of the things I have seen." Others have also claimed some healing of organic, congenital, or "incurable" ailments (e.g., Shaub, "Analysis," 85, regarding Price, "Healing," 13, in the early period of World War II). Against reductionism more generally, see, e.g., Davies, "Preface," xi–xii; Polkinghorne, *Reality*, 8–9, 29–30, 37 (observing that particle physics does not explain every level of reality).

4. Hume, *Miracles*, 31–32: healing is not always a miracle, but if it is conjoined causally with a specific command to be healed it is a miracle. It is not miraculous if the conjunction can be explained as coincidence, but miraculous if coincidence is disproved (presumably with respect to the frequency of collocation vis-à-vis the level of infrequency of comparable cures apart from such collocation).

5. Puxley, "Experience," 171. The context of prayer fits the sort of religious context often applied in evaluating miracles, noted in ch. 5.

6. Edmunds, "Sick."

7. Miller and Yamamori, *Pentecostalism*, 152–53, citing favorably also the similar opinion of a theologian in Hong Kong. They critique Durkheim's approach as too reductionist ("or at least a bit arrogant"; 219).

8. Miller and Yamamori, *Pentecostalism*, 158. Some others have also allowed this approach (e.g., Spraggett, *Kuhlman*, 40).

adding another that may be at work at times: what they call "the realm of the Spirit."[9] The stark division that some drive between such explanations, assuming them to be incompatible in all cases, reflects the milieu in which such a division originated.[10] That is, the division reflects historically conditioned assumptions that are not deemed self-evident to all cultures. It is that either-or, forced-choice logic that I seek to avoid in my evaluation of proposed explanations. Some cases are explicable purely naturally; some are not explicable purely naturally; many are cumulatively *more* explicable with supernatural elements, although the degree of their persuasiveness varies according to the observer's presuppositions more generally. From a theistic perspective, a divine act need not involve creation *ex nihilo* to be dramatic; signs could often expedite or employ natural processes or functions (whether psychological, physical, or both) to achieve results that chance in nature would not produce on its own.

A Historic Bias against Faith?

While natural factors such as those noted earlier caution us against taking all faith healing claims at face value, and even more so against using all of them as incontrovertible evidence of divine activity, unspoken factors are often at work in setting the bar of proof impossibly high. Hume's position demands "overwhelming evidence"[11] before accepting the validity of a miracle. Yet Hume deliberately sets the standard of "overwhelming" as virtually impossible, rejecting virtually any historical or present testimony. As one scholar points out, "In the nature of the case it is rarely possible to obtain such overwhelming evidence for any historical event." Hence, many presume "that the kinds of things that demonstrably do not happen most of the time, never have happened."[12] Following this paradigm, research sometimes works with an interpretive grid that dismisses potential evidence.[13]

---

9. Miller and Yamamori, *Pentecostalism*, 159; cf. also 219–20.

10. See Mullin, *Miracles*, passim, esp. 223–24. In addition to the intellectual milieu more generally, professional specialization and disciplinary boundaries augmented the dichotomy (103–4, 246–47). Research shows that most people who affirm divine healing accept medical explanations of disease and normal means of recovery but additionally affirm a higher metaphysical level; that is, they do not treat the spheres as incompatible or express hostility toward medicine (Poloma, *Assemblies*, 58–60).

11. The degree to which such evidence is deemed "overwhelming" varies according to the individual critic's standard; one presupposing supernatural activity may require less evidence in a particular case than someone more skeptical of this. Likewise, the more dogmatic one's antisupernaturalism the less any amount of documentation will appear convincing, regardless of its effect on a more neutral observer.

12. Hesse, "Miracles," 40. For a response to the presuppositions informing Hume's approach, see also Eddy and Boyd, *Legend*, 61–63; the summary of J. Houston's arguments, and my other treatments of Hume in chs. 5–6 earlier. Virtually no report persuades those unwilling to be persuaded; even the most public sort of claim, such as a reported event at Fatima in front of seventy thousand people (cited in Hoffman and McGuire, "Miracles," 225), is disputed (in this case, at least on the level of interpretation).

13. As warned by, e.g., Wink, "Write," 6.

The Biased Vancouver Study

Some scholars today still cite against miraculous healing claims a supposedly objective committee that dismissed as exaggerated or deceptive 350 Pentecostal healing claims—in a study conducted in 1925.[14] This study illustrates well the problem of bias against healing that effectively screens out any evidence potentially favoring it. The study conceded only five cures, all of which it claimed could have been effected medically, and thirty-eight cases of some improvement, while five persons, it reported emphatically, "had become insane."[15] Undoubtedly a large proportion of the claims did prove false or exaggerated,[16] but one also suspects that the study did not proceed without guiding premises and that it proved what its authors expected it to.

Historian James Opp has recently probed the presuppositions of this supposedly objective study, which concerned the results of Charles Price's 1923 meetings in Vancouver. Although the only public study of its era to collect much data on faith healers,[17] its approach to the data is deeply marred by a predetermined allegiance to the idea, explicitly stated in the study's introduction, that God works only through natural causes.[18] The reader will recall from my historical survey that this perspective reflected a dominant viewpoint in academic circles of that era.

Nearly "all of the ministers in Vancouver who had publicly opposed the faith healer" were members of this committee, the most prominent being A. E. Cooke.[19] Cooke had initially invited Price to the city but then turned against him as stoking false hopes. What Cooke did not say publicly, yet was understood by all who knew him, was that his daughter had failed to be cured in the meetings.[20] Cooke thus had understandable yet subjective personal incentive for his hostility—appropriately never directed, however, toward the medical establishment's inability

14. Anderson, *Vision*, 93; followed more recently by Hunter and Chan, *Protestantism*, 146. Academia and the cultural establishment more generally were largely hostile to Pentecostalism in 1925, in contrast to the generally more open posture today. Cf. the 1932 committee challenging healing claims of the heterodox A. H. Dallimore (Guy, "Miracles," 458–59). Journalist Margaret Macpherson claimed to have been instantly healed of twenty years of lumbago in his meetings (offering the claim three years later; 462), but doctors thought that Dallimore cured by suggestion (461).

15. Anderson, *Vision*, 93–94. Thus, for example, one patient with a previous history of mental illness had become "insane" after prayer and "died a week later from 'the exhaustion of acute mania'" (Opp, *Lord for Body*, 181). A very similar complaint was lodged against Bosworth, again reflecting older nineteenth-century psychological theories (Opp, *Lord for Body*, 165).

16. Anderson, *Vision*, 94, cites Stanley Frodsham and Donald Gee, early Pentecostal leaders who were in a position to know (but who also may have been stating their positions forcefully to make a point to uncritical members of their own faith community) as objecting to inadequate documentation and complaining that only a small proportion of miracle claims proved demonstrably true. One should note, however, that these authors nevertheless maintained that genuine miracles did occur (see, e.g., Frodsham, *Apostle*).

17. Opp, *Lord for Body*, 178.

18. Ibid., 179. The study did have the beneficial effect of making "Pentecostal editors . . . more careful in publishing reports without substantiation" (Reyes, "Framework," 88–89).

19. Opp, *Lord for Body*, 178.

20. Ibid., 162.

to cure the same daughter. The most significant physician on the committee had previously worked with Cooke in discrediting chiropractic.[21] The committee had an agenda to discredit both faith healing and Price[22] and urged that laws should be passed allowing only physicians, not ministers, to practice curative "hypnotism."[23]

Given the dominance of his critics on the committee, it is hardly surprising that Price and his supporters declined to cooperate with it; several ministers supportive of him withdrew from the committee once its predisposition was obvious. Likewise, the local Baptist Ministerial Association "passed a resolution refusing to cooperate and protested that too many critics of the campaign were now investigating it."[24] Because of the consequent shortage of cooperative subjects, the committee investigated not just claimed healings but anyone who had received prayer, depending on newspaper appeals for information.[25]

Two Methodist ministers who remained on the committee protested the majority perspective and issued a minority report. They noted that the committee investigated less than 6 percent of those anointed and that the study was not representative because those claiming cures viewed the committee as hostile and therefore refused to cooperate.[26] The minority report complained that the committee did not actually directly listen to the testimonies of those who claimed to be healed, and assumed that those claiming healing could not properly evaluate whether or not they had been cured.[27]

Even so, the committee found thirty-eight persons who experienced improvement after prayer (in addition to the five who recovered). Some of the "improvements" reported sound significant, but these were attributed to suggestion and mass hypnotism.[28] (Public hypnosis was a favorite explanation of the era for healing claims.[29]) The committee clearly implied that the celebrated case of Ruby Dimmick was purely psychological, enraging "her father, Rev. J. F. Dimmick," who noted that "no one on the committee had actually interviewed him or Ruby, nor did they even discuss the case with Dr Hall." Rev. Dimmick pointed out that the orthopedic hospital would hardly have admitted her to begin with had her condition been

21. Ibid., 178.
22. Ibid., 176.
23. Ibid., 181.
24. Ibid., 179.
25. Ibid.
26. Ibid., 182–83 (quotation from 183). They also challenged the committee's emphasis that 39 had died, showing this as nonrepresentative. Since those examined constituted only 6 percent of the total who received prayer, then 668 persons altogether should have died, yet "government statistics actually showed a decrease in the death rate over the seven months following the campaign when compared with the previous year" (183).
27. Ibid., 184. That this accusation accurately represents the perspective of the majority report is clear from Cooke's insistence that only "a trained expert" and not the patient could diagnose what if anything was wrong with the patient (184), and reflects the naturalistic medical premises then dominant (185).
28. Ibid., 180.
29. Ibid., 166–69. The claim also appears in Perry, "Reporting," 107.

considered "hysteria" rather than a spinal problem![30] Although her physician at first had been skeptical, by 1926 he conceded in writing that a miracle had in fact taken place.[31] The committee's ready dismissal of cases such as Dimmick's reveals the way that it sorted evidence.

One woman clearly had "improved motor function," but because X-rays showed that her bones were not healed, the "improved muscle function" that enabled her to walk better was dismissed as "functional" rather than "organic."[32] To this objection that the cures were of nonorganic causes, the minority report pointed out that most cures by physicians could be dismissed by the same standards.[33] Another observer who claimed to know members of the committee complained that they dismissed demonstrable healings "of previously diagnosed tuberculosis and cancer" by simply claiming "that the original diagnoses were mistaken"—so that they rejected even what empirical evidence they did have available.[34] Rev. W. J. Knott, well known in the city, "testified that he had been cured of [a] goiter from which he had been suffering for years," almost instantly; family members affectionately kissed "the place where the goiter had been."[35]

Understandably the committee emphasized the dashed hopes and disappointed faith of those not cured.[36] Price himself did not, however, claim that everyone for whom he prayed recovered;[37] people are not always cured medically, either. Some doctors supported Price,[38] but a central issue at conflict with many other doctors and ministers of the era was epistemological:[39] while faith healers (in contrast to Christian Science) did not deny the reality of natural causes, they also allowed (in contrast to antisupernaturalists) supernatural causes as well.

Similar Past Critiques of Other Public Healing Claims

Similarly, a committee produced a devastating critique of James Moore Hickson's healings in England. Contemporaries, however, recognized that the committee

30. Opp, *Lord for Body*, 186. In the nineteenth century, "hysteria" was a common female affliction and diagnosis, but this largely vanished when it became culturally unacceptable (Buskirk, *Healing*, 35–36).

31. Opp, *Lord for Body*, 186; for his former skepticism, see 157. He had initially pronounced her cured even soon after the meeting ("Healings at Victoria," 15); another observer declared "that her spine was perfectly straight and there was a complete healing of the foot" ("Healings at Victoria," 15).

32. Opp, *Lord for Body*, 186–87. If Price's detractors produced public X-rays, in this case, Price displayed photos of those healed, holding their previous bandages and so forth (191–95).

33. Ibid., 183.

34. Ibid., 187.

35. "Healings at Victoria," 15, citing (see 9) the *Victoria Daily Times*. According to the article, Knott was expected to die because the goiter was now constricting his breathing ("to strangle him").

36. Opp, *Lord for Body*, 181. Lourdes works to guard against this response, so that most of the uncured nevertheless go away encouraged (Cranston, *Miracle*, 156–60).

37. Opp, *Lord for Body*, 159, 182 (though he did associate swooning with faith, 159). Cf. accusations that Francisco Olazábal did not heal everyone who requested prayer, and his response that God does the healing and did not heal everyone he prayed for (Espinosa, "Healing in Borderlands," 141).

38. Opp, *Lord for Body*, 182. A small number of physicians even shifted from medical practice to emphasizing divine healing (177, 195–202).

39. Ibid., passim, e.g., 208–10.

began with the commitment to discredit Hickson and that most local doctors involved refused to verify cures, claiming that those healed must have been simply misdiagnosed to begin with.[40]

Less reported was a similar study of miracles in Bangor, Maine, reported by a biblical scholar undoubtedly interested in parallels with NT miracles. He identifies the possibility of fraud: the campaign advertisement listed fifteen testimonials, at least nine with "addresses unknown to the postal authorities, and only two had local addresses."[41] He rightly warned that an irrelevant cause could be attached to a person's recovery, and a person might not genuinely recover at all. Thus one girl with tuberculosis removed her cast to walk a week prematurely (Sept. 1925), and now she limps badly.[42] Another woman, able to walk but not well without a crutch, went a few days without it until she became disillusioned with the healing minister and started using her crutch again.[43] Clearly the reporter pinpoints those not healed who sometimes hope to be healed in such meetings.

The critic further viewed some recovery claims as too weak to count as favorable evidence: a man with a damaged knee had worn a bandage for three years; he removed the bandage, but he had been having no recurrence of symptoms.[44] A woman was cured from "periodic attacks of vertigo and severe nausea," which had not recurred since the meetings.[45] Although such cases do not provide strong evidence for supernatural healing, the examiner's verdict here is sarcastic: "Imaginary ailments, of course, disappear instantly."[46]

Even this critic is prepared to admit a few cures, yet he attributes these not to divine intervention but to encouragement. He complains about "self-deception": a young man with heart and lung problems, who had given up and was nearly bedridden, received so much courage from the meeting that he went back to work, though medically his condition was *presumably* unchanged.[47] Likewise he noted "an old woman almost completely crippled with rheumatism who is now doing her housework and knitting mittens."[48] Most strangely, he relegates to a footnote the observation that a woman "claimed to have been entirely blind in one eye. She described how her sight was instantly restored at the meeting. She was found to be now able-bodied and apparently had fair eyesight, though in need of glasses."[49] Later he places this testimony among psychological cures, despite her own claim:

40. Mews, "Revival," 330. Hickson accepted doctors (307), but while he praised doctors for what they accomplished, he also claimed that Jesus could cure what medicine could not (304).

41. Perry, "Reporting," 106n11. Maine had already seen some semi-cultic Pentecostal extremism; see, e.g., the account in Wacker, "Living," 432.

42. Perry, "Reporting," 105.

43. Ibid., 107. He attributes the healer's success to her "hypnotic personality."

44. Ibid., 106 and n. 5.

45. Ibid., 106 and n. 6.

46. Ibid., 106.

47. Ibid., 105–6 and n. 4, 108.

48. Ibid., 108.

49. Ibid., 105n3.

"One old woman who says she was nearly blind before, tells how the dazzling light broke upon her all at once with the restoration of the sight of her useless eye."[50] However one explains the other cures, restoration of sight to her eye seems like it should have given pause to someone not committed to an a priori skepticism.

Not everyone was cured, but assumptions about those who did claim healing do not seem to entertain all the possibilities. One further suspects some bias in reading the scholar's descriptions: such healing ideas "spread among the less intelligent all over the state, and even some of the educated clergy fell victims to it."[51] He concludes that most "who received or sought healing were not closely connected with organized religion, but rather were folk of little knowledge and superficial exposure to religion." Lest one suppose he does not mean the description to denigrate them, he also speaks of their "washed-out, second-hand faith which was little more than superstition."[52] That Jesus focused his ministry on outsiders, and that signs in Acts and subsequently appeared especially in the setting of outreach to nonbelievers, apparently escapes his notice. Nevertheless, his approach was common among members of the intellectual and often religious elite of his era.

In 1956, a British medical committee expressed skepticism about miraculous healing, although the report's own appendixes include statements from British physicians specifying some unusual recoveries. Thus, in one doctor's statement, two strokes had paralyzed and left speechless an aged woman; doctors diagnosed hemiplegia due to cerebral hemorrhage and counted her case hopeless. Within days after a healing service, she "was about again, and now thirteen years later, at the age of eighty-three, this patient is still walking to church twice every Sunday."[53] In another statement, a gynecologist had declared a case of cervical cancer inoperable because of its extent; after prayer, the pain left quickly and the cancer was completely gone within two months. The patient died from pneumonia eight years later, with no recurrence of cancer.[54] While cancers do remit, we should also remember that cancer treatments were far more limited in that era than today and that the cancer had already spread.

Nevertheless, the committee, while not denying a number of extraordinary cures,[55] concluded that such cures were probably the result of misdiagnosis, "remission, or possibly of spontaneous cure."[56] While the report plays down claims of healings by noting that most physicians responding to the query believed in divine healing and thus were "prejudiced in its favor,"[57] one physician is duly quoted as warning that in

---

50. Ibid., 108.
51. Ibid., 106.
52. Ibid., 108.
53. Oursler, *Power*, 230.
54. Ibid., 231.
55. Ibid., 243, pointing out that the report seems to suggest that divine healings are not significant because physicians can achieve comparable results—an argument that is beside the point.
56. Ibid., 232.
57. Ibid., 240. Oursler complains that if they genuinely considered these physicians so severely prejudiced, they ought to demand that their licenses be withdrawn, since such prejudice would affect

cases where something appeared to be a miracle, it might simply reflect a law of nature not yet discovered.[58] It was not the first time in history that those who presupposed the nonexistence of miracles questioned the competence of colleagues more directly acquainted with cases in question who had interpreted the evidence differently.[59]

While these nonsupernatural explanations are logically possible, one wonders what evidence, if any, even in cases much stronger than these, would be accepted for divine healing. Could not *any* unexplained recovery be simply called "spontaneous," without thereby explaining it?[60] The burden of proof seems stacked impossibly against divine healing: any recovery that could be explained otherwise excludes divine healing, yet nearly any restoration noted in Scripture or today could potentially be explained on such terms.[61] This criterion does not require the antisupernaturalist to offer a *plausible* explanation—just *any* explanation. Among viable explanations in the skeptic's arsenal is now that apparent miracles could reflect *unknown* laws of nature—a criterion that effectively excludes any appeal to evidence. Even if a person had been duly deemed dead by physicians and returned to life the next day (as in a case I noted earlier in the book), an antisupernaturalist might choose to insist that, despite lack of detectable cardiac or brain activity, the person was not really dead. The committee could dismiss the reports of most of the physicians responding to their query about healing as undoubtedly believing in healing and thus being biased, as in the case above. Could not a believer in divine healing ask the same question of the committee? Why was it stacked with those who would a priori rule out any claim to healing?

Are Nonsupernatural Interpretations Always Better?

More recently, one physician has studied a number of healing claims and dismissed all of them. His analysis is helpful on many points, since, as I have noted, fraud and false diagnoses occur, and I think it likely that he has identified some of these cases.[62] But just as advocates for miracles could force all proposed cases to fit their paradigm, it is possible to force all cases to fit a contrary paradigm, especially when driven by "moral outrage," as this physician describes his commitment.[63]

---

their practice (243). He also wonders why the doctors on the committee should be accepted as less prejudiced than the doctors whose testimonies they dismiss as prejudiced (243).

58. Ibid., 241. Further suggesting the committee's prejudice, they mention how rare are certified cures at Lourdes (while praising the thoroughness of the Medical Bureau there), yet mention nothing of the considerable documentation for the few cures proclaimed (241–42).

59. See Duffin, *Miracles*, 113, 133–34, where physicians not present during cures proved adamant against the judgment of attending physicians, on the grounds that miracles cannot happen.

60. Krippner and Achterberg, "Experiences," 358, cites Simonton, Matthews-Simonton, and Creighton, *Getting Well*, 21, to the effect that any normally inexplicable cure can be designated "spontaneous" "in much the same way as the term *spontaneous generation* covered medical ignorance during the late Middle Ages."

61. Cf. the same complaint regarding any paranormal claims more generally in McClenon, *Events*, 187; and the argument against other theistic claims addressed in Plantinga, "Science," 109, 112–13.

62. See esp. May, "Miracles," 145, 151.

63. Ibid., 146. May expresses this (often justifiable) "outrage" in comments about "bogus claims," healers doing "serious harm," and fund-raising techniques that "profoundly nauseate me" (and in many

While there seems reason to concur that his criticisms of some figures may be justified, I believe that he too readily dismisses the healing claims of his fellow physician Rex Gardner as having secured "spurious credibility."[64] He challenges Gardner's case of instant healing of sensorineural hearing loss (see discussion in ch. 12) on the grounds that it is not absolutely unique;[65] nevertheless, it is clearly extremely rare, not yet explained, and at least in this case (we do not hear details about others) instantaneous and associated with prayer.

This physician's study also works with the consistent approach of rejecting any supernatural claims for which a natural explanation is possible, even if the natural explanation is itself speculative.[66] For example, he dismisses a claim of healed long-term blindness as possibly reflecting merely the person feeling better about her sight[67] (though he would regard genuine restoration of sight as unusual).[68] He seems to hold a double standard in some cases: when Jesus healed someone blind or deaf, these are incurable disorders that do not "spontaneously remit,"[69] but as we have observed, he is less prepared to admit such claims today, even though they are sometimes better documented medically than the ancient cases could have been. While this author performs a useful service in challenging false or inadequate claims, therefore, I am inclined to suspect that his approach is too one-sided against contemporary healing claims.

Even his criticisms of healing evangelists' testimonies can appear one-sided. In one case he challenges the medical facts in an evangelist's video,[70] arguing that X-rays showed no change in a woman's spine after her healing; he also notes that some claims in the original video include exaggerations or material not strictly relevant to the claims (that is, not all the operations involved the woman's spine). Some of

---

cases the rest of us as well). Even some pure naturalists, however, recognize a valuable placebo effect in some healing beliefs (cf. even May himself, 155), so claims about "serious harm," while sometimes true, especially in the sorts of cases May emphasizes, should be balanced with benefits of some other ministries even aside from supernatural questions.

64. Ibid., 150.

65. Ibid., 150–51.

66. Ibid., 149–50, also challenges cases reported at Lourdes. While his argument regarding the lesion here is substantial, it is clearly one on which a number of doctors who certified the claim disagree, so the matter remains in dispute among experts. May has a newer article, too recent for me to obtain for this book, and it is possible that this approach is more balanced than in the earlier one.

67. Ibid., 154.

68. For genuine restoration being unusual, see, e.g., ibid., 147, 154.

69. Ibid., 147. The double standard also appears in Pullum, "Believe," 143, who notes that biblical miracles were empirically verifiable, whereas today "body parts are never regenerated like those cases in the Bible." I cannot think of cases of body parts regenerated in the Bible. This approach is virtually the opposite of that of Capps, Ellens, and others.

70. May, "Miracles," 152. Given May's one-sided approach, however (though to be fair, articulating one's thesis—in this case that the healing was not organic—does not require one to address every other issue), it is not surprising to me that the woman's physician, who on the video affirms the dramatic transformation and his own amazement, refused to cooperate with May. Also to be fair, my access to the woman's testimony is in sources more recent than May's, which may have clarified some matters in response to his or others' criticisms (I am working with the older article of May and the newer version of the cure account).

the ailments noted in the original video probably were not directly related to her spinal problems. While I am not qualified to comment on the specifically medical features of the case, however, the critic's argument seems one-sided. The woman clearly experienced a cure of some sort, whatever happened regarding her spine and some other details. Her family members, including a teenage daughter who had never known her to walk normally before and could not believe it when she bounded up the stairs, offer their testimony. Likewise, neighbors and others who witnessed the immediate change recount it; her own doctor also testifies to being astonished. Previously confined to walking sticks or a wheelchair for many years, she was immediately able to run, including when she returned home, and witnesses as well as video footage confirmed her regularly jogging, playing rugby, and swimming after the event. Any reader who might wish to criticize her transformation ought to give the footage a fair-minded viewing first.[71] Why would a critic's report (mostly read by people who would not see the video) focus exclusively on particular negative factors but not the obvious transformation, unless the critic simply had an agenda of disputing all miracle claims rather than a fair-minded approach that could grant credence to some elements of them? If he simply insists that a true miracle must be certifiably organic, if this case is not organic, one might want to dispute his definition of miracle. (Here the shadow of Hume's legacy—restricting miracles to violations of nature—is often difficult to evade.) But he also disputed the case of Gardner noted above, where the auditory nerve damage clearly *was* organic.

Such a prejudice sometimes continues to inform modern discussions of healing miracles. Ken Blue reports that one woman was healed through prayer from severe epilepsy and a brain disturbance that had plagued her from ages six to twenty-six. Afterward, her EEG reading was normal, and her doctors, unable to believe the change, repeated the test two more times over the next few weeks. Finally they accepted that she was well but denied the possibility that she was healed through prayer.[72] Now they "have concluded that she must have been misdiagnosed and mistreated for the past twenty years. These conscientious and competent doctors have risked a possible malpractice suit rather than admit the possibility of divine healing."[73] He reports a different case in which tests showed highly advanced uterine cancer; despite the sense of those praying that God healed the woman, the doctors removed the uterus—and then found it without cancer. "Though Brenda's doctors have no explanation themselves, they are not considering the possibility that God healed her."[74]

71. See *Miracle Investigation* (dated 2005), which includes the account; and *Miraculous Healing* (currently dated 2008, though including earlier elements). She had been scheduled for a fourth spinal surgery, with little hope of success, which was afterward canceled. She also cites a dream prior to the crusade, claiming that the evangelist (Reinhard Bonnke) and the location looked like what she saw in the dream; though the youth meeting was large, the evangelist independently felt that God had singled her out for a special healing.
72. Blue, *Authority*, 57.
73. Ibid., 58.
74. Ibid. In Dearing, *Healing*, 115–16, an urgent mastectomy was canceled due to healing; another case in Salmon, *Heals*, 38.

Seth Ablorh, a Christian doctor in Ghana mentioned in chapter 9, admits that he himself struggled with this antisupernatural bias from his training. He was working alongside a visiting oncological surgeon from the United States. The surgeon examined a woman already diagnosed with rectal cancer, exploring the lesion, doing a colostomy, and the like. The woman insisted that she believed that God would heal her, and they gave what would presumably normally be good advice: "God will heal you through surgery." When, however, they reached the theater to operate and the surgeon checked the lesion again, he could not discover it digitally or with a proctoscope. "We woke the patient up and discharged her saying we had missed the diagnosis though we were not the only ones who diagnosed her. She called it a miracle, but in our medical minds we were unwilling to accept that she had had divine healing."[75] Misdiagnosis and remissions occur, but when these attributions are overused to explain away any possible evidence, the evidence is not being treated fairly. In the short term any naturally unexplained recovery could be called a remission, without thereby explaining it.

When a doctor reports that a condition is not genuinely cured or that it often resolves on its own, she speaks within her expertise and we should give heed. When a doctor denies that a cure is miraculous based on a philosophic paradigm that excludes miracles, however, he speaks not as a doctor but as an amateur philosopher. In the latter case, the opinion merits no greater weight than that assigned to that of any other amateur philosopher.

The Demand for Medically Certified Testimony

I do cite some medically certified healings in this book, but limiting testimonies to those that are medically certified produces at best a critical minimum of a particular sort of evidence, not the sum total of evidence one would accept in normal circumstances. Clearly most patients do not experience extraordinary healings, so doctors do not have reason to expect them on a normal basis (they would otherwise be considered normal recoveries).

Nevertheless, it is possible to sort evidence in such a way as to screen out all alternative explanations. Some people accept *only* claims that are medically certified as valid, even if it means dismissing all eyewitness claims, of which there are numerous significant ones, as inauthentic. Granted, those who are healed should seek not only medical confirmation of their recovery but also (ideally) medical documentation. Nevertheless, various obstacles involved in securing such documentation around the world mean that refusal to accept any evidence without this kind of documentation will end up screening out a large proportion, probably the majority, of genuine cures. Moreover, as we noted above, even once claims are medically certified their relevance is often dismissed if any other explanation is

75. Mensah, "Basis," 178.

possible. Insofar as one may argue that "anything is possible," virtually any claim may thus be dismissed, conveniently allowing any evidence to be ignored.

Securing Medical Documentation

If one must have a doctor's certification that a recovery is a bona fide miracle, no recoveries will be classified as miracles provided one's doctor is reticent (whether out of skepticism or professional reserve) to deem it as such, or where no doctors were available to document the healing. Likewise, this approach refuses to grant even the slightest credence to any of the countless eyewitness testimonies from places where medical help was not available, yet on matters such as a person's previous blindness and subsequent ability to see, where one would expect intimate acquaintances to be reliable informants.[76]

Clearly medical documentation strengthens the case for a genuine healing, and some works I have cited by doctors have included such documentation.[77] But what of a case in a traditional village where someone was publicly raised from death through prayer after many hours without detectable respiration or pulse?[78] Even if we granted in each case the inability of people who live around death regularly to distinguish death from a coma with scarcely detectable pulse and respiration, we must grant their ability to recognize full recoveries from that state as unusual, and their observation of the rare event's significant association with prayer.[79] Does their eyewitness testimony of instant recovery count for nothing, simply because the witnesses in the village do not have medical degrees or instruments available?[80] Does not the probability of coincidence decrease with the rise in the number of such events during prayer, vis-à-vis how often they occur "spontaneously"? (Repeated statistical unlikelihood can make outcomes appear "fixed" by another source.[81] Others also complain about unmerited faith in "the unlimited possibili-

76. At least if all other factors are equal, an eyewitness's testimony should be preferred to a nonwitness interpreting the testimony (Levine, *Problem*, 111). If experience is reliable in knowing that water is normally not turned to wine, why would it not be reliable in recognizing when water is turned to wine? (Levine, *Problem*, 126, agreeing with Kellenberger, "Miracles," 148 n.)

77. I have noted among others the sources in Gardner, *Healing Miracles*; Casdorph, *Miracles*; among non-physicians, such investigation is claimed, e.g., in Spraggett, *Kuhlman*. I have also found medical documentation for some healings (see ch. 15), though many others were from parts of the world where this was not even possible.

78. On the difficulties of obtaining medical documentation in financially poorer nations, cf. also Duffin, *Miracles*, 136.

79. This is especially the case where consequent changes in religious affiliation demonstrate that observers experienced these events quite differently from the norm.

80. If one charges that eyewitnesses can lie, even colluding as a group, one could also contend that those in charge of medical documentation might forge it, or (more easily) colluding doctors could lie. (Doctors deliberately falsifying information could lose their licenses, but many other witnesses also have a stake in maintaining their own credibility.) That is, one could use this approach of skepticism toward the evidence to dismiss any evidence one wished. While one expects some claimants to be false, one should not expect that to be the case for all of the huge numbers of claimants available today, including for many substantive reports.

81. Beckwith, "History," 45.

ties of coincidence," such as in the familiar but statistically virtually impossible illustration of a million monkeys randomly typing the works of Shakespeare.[82]) The cumulative weight of the stronger cases seems compelling.[83]

Moreover, of the people I interviewed who had been examined both before and after their recovery, most had no idea how to obtain medical documentation or initially even what I meant by it. One of the notable exceptions, though a doctor, had to go to some trouble to obtain it, not having it already in his possession. That even the most sincere people rarely request and retain before-and-after medical records of their recovery does not surprise me; I failed to collect it myself in years before I anticipated writing a book on the subject.[84] Not only in cases of claims that I find weak but also in some that I find strong, some claimants (particularly in some cultures or subcultures) do not understand even my need as a researcher for such documentation.[85] Granted that a case is stronger with such documentation, it need not follow that all cases are completely worthless without it.

As an investigative reporter discovered, though he originally wanted indisputable medical documentation for every case, this standard ultimately proved unreasonable. Doctors often disagree with one another; reports in medical journals are often not "infallibly documented"; and a mother does not need to have medical competence to testify that doctors explained that her child had a clubfoot.[86] The

82. Bridge, *Signs*, 29–30. An event need not be impossible naturally to be improbable enough to elicit faith, depending on the degree of the burden of proof that one's assumptions require (Basinger and Basinger, "Concept," 167, allow it for believers). Ideally, a technical study could quantify how much more often extranormal cures occur in the context of prayers or specific kinds of or specific persons' prayers in contrast to such events in the general population (cf. the request for "quantitative [degree-yielding] criteria" for probabilities in Wykstra, "Problem," 156), but my sample size for the control group is too small, and I do not know of studies quantifying such events in the general population on these matters. A proper study would have to be massive, and the variables are probably too many for its success on these terms. Yet see comment on "coincidence" in ch. 15.

83. From a mathematical perspective, see De Poe, "Bayesian Approach." For the implausibility of cures at Lourdes being coincidental, see Cranston, *Miracle*, 259.

84. Though I was fairly aggressive in several cases where I hoped to get the documentation (and in some of these cases succeeded), I confess that my personality is not suited to pressing many busy informants beyond what they had already supplied. The very demand that people involved in cures adopt the researcher's critical posture can prove antithetical to the native faith that helped produce the cures (see Laurentin, *Miracles*, 95), and it is difficult for me to justify my "right to information" at that expense. Nevertheless, investigative reporters either confirming (e.g., Spraggett; Grazier; Neal) or debunking (Emery; again, Spraggett) healing claims have proved more successful in this area. Some people eagerly offered to supply me old documentation but subsequently failed to find it in their many boxes of old papers. Most people would not spend hours looking for it simply to help a professor writing a book; in one case, someone who knew me did spend more than a workday looking for it but had an entire garage full of boxes.

85. In their sphere of relationships, people take other people's word for what they have witnessed; to ask for documentation is to communicate hostile suspicion. I can eventually overcome much suspicion, but I cannot get them to re-create documentation they have long since discarded as irrelevant, even if they obtained it to begin with (which is usually not the case).

86. Spraggett, *Kuhlman*, 50. Spraggett himself doubted many healing evangelists but came to regard some evidence for supernatural healing as incontrovertible. Others also note that "instant medical confirmation" is rare but note that medical receptivity to allowing for divine healing is increasing (Lawrence, *Practice*, 32–33).

reporter provides an example where specialists disagreed about the sudden healing of a case of necrosis of the hip after prayer: an orthopedist insisted that "natural remissions" of this affliction "sometimes occur," whereas a radiologist insisted that, after "careful study of the case," that it was "medically extraordinary."[87] Sometimes the written records also fail to elaborate on some key details that, in retrospect, would have been helpful in terms of evidence.

The reporter also discovered that medical documentation could be difficult to procure for logistical reasons, such as one hospital destroying outpatient records after ten years, attending physicians having died, or particular physicians failing to respond to requests.[88] When trying to follow up medical documentation (even more so for people from particular cultures), I discovered that people often did not know that they had a right to access their medical records.[89] In some other cases, people requested documentation several times and were not able to obtain it within the months before my book was due to the publisher.[90] Obtaining records might be among patients' rights, but that does not mean that busy professionals will always hasten to their assistance (in some cases perhaps especially if they fear that they might be cited in support of a professionally unusual conclusion in which they have no stake, or if apparent irregularities could even be potentially cited legally against them). In some cultures, patients lacked access to medical records, as the hospitals refused to share them.[91] (In one unusual case, when the hospital finally acquiesced to give a copy, my friend who was to obtain it was obstructed because

87. Spraggett, *Kuhlman*, 51. He shows how a pathologist and a psychiatrist came to opposite conclusions as to which recoveries were genuinely remarkable (ibid.).

88. Ibid., 52. Spraggett notes all of these problems in the case on 82, but he found other nondocumentary corroborating evidence for the case in question (82–83, the type of braces earlier used counting as strong circumstantial evidence). My informants have also encountered some of these problems when seeking documentation for their situations.

89. Renae Yu-Ching Hsu noted that some international evangelical healing conferences and healed persons in Taiwan often seek medical confirmation (interview, Jan. 24, 2009), but also noted (based on her experience trying to secure information to help with my project) that many people do not know that they have a right to access their medical records (personal correspondence, May 10, 2009). Further, often "people cannot recognize that the [medical] documentation is part of their own testimonies," hence evidence provided often falls short of "the strict demand required for scientific proof" (personal correspondence, June 29, 2009). In view of the obstacles, she observed that accumulating such evidence would take time and might be accommodated through something like an ongoing "online library" (personal correspondence, June 13, 24, 2009), a valuable proposal that perhaps others will develop further.

90. As in some cases I know where, after several months and more than one attempt, an individual was still trying (phone follow-up, Dec. 15, 2009; another case, e.g., June 7; Sept. 1, 2010). Some institutions responded more quickly, as in the case of Carl Cocherell, though it took him time to get his information even from one of these institutions. Critics should not overestimate the ease of the process. One person had given his documentation away; at least two others who were sure that they had it discovered that they did not know which of their scores of boxes contained it; they naturally were not ready to expend days trying to help my research project.

91. This occurred in one case in Nigeria, where, however, through the intercession of another doctor we were able to secure at least a summary statement. This practice was also noted to me by Dr. Nonyem E. Numbere, who collected some sources but noted that unlike in the United States, Nigerian hospitals retain all the records (phone interview, Dec. 14, 2009). This was also the case for part of the documentation for Yazmin Hommer in Mexico (Dec. 1, 2009), though she was able to obtain and share a sufficient amount.

genuinely violent riots, widely documented in international media, broke out in that city for the duration of his visit there.)

With many of the same cultures I faced a language barrier; with some other cultures, medical help (and thus any form of medical documentation) was rarely available to begin with. Even sharing one's testimony was difficult for many individuals, more often in some cultures than in others, because it was so intensely personal. Other informants, often eager to help, have also gone to get records for me only to run into the problem of hospitals having already destroyed them.[92] One catch-22 is that we normally give more credence to cures that have persisted over many years; the farther in the past the cure happened, however, the less likely it is that one can secure medical records unless one has kept copies, which most people have not. All this to say that while it is reasonable to expect that some cases will be medically documented (and they are), it is not reasonable to dismiss all firsthand testimonies that lack such documentation, especially in places where people cannot be expected to have access to it (or perhaps even to treatment).

The difficulties can come from the other side, too, where some medical personnel have witnessed extraordinary recoveries but cannot provide documentation apart from their word. As noted earlier, Donald Moore is a speech language pathologist, a clinical director of voice and swallowing disorders, and has fifteen years of clinical experience working with patients who suffered cerebral vascular accidents (i.e., strokes). He is not lightly persuaded of miracles, regarding many stroke improvements as normal rehabilitation progress (on his advice I condensed and qualified some material in this book[93]). In February 2009, however, Donald had a fifty-two-year-old patient who had suffered a severe brain stem stroke in the region of the medulla. Research shows that damage in the ability to swallow caused by medulla brain stem strokes is irreversible, and this case was quite a serious one. A video fluoroscopic swallow study confirmed that his dysphagia (inability to swallow) was so severe that the patient could not protect his airway during swallowing and thus "required alternate means of nutritional intake."

Several months later the same man "returned to have his swallow function re-evaluated." Donald explained to him that he would not be able to resume eating, but the man replied that he had "been eating for the past few weeks." Donald protested "that this was impossible given the nature of his stroke." The man then explained that he and his family had been praying and that he had been eating ever since. Moved by the man's faith, but not anticipating significant improvement, Donald conducted the study. To the shock of both Donald and the radiologist, this person who had "suffered a large medulla brain stem stroke was able to swallow," now eating through the mouth without artificial means. Since the patient had already mentioned prayer, Donald began to comment, and the man finished his sentence

92. E.g., a hospital in Mexico after six years (Eduardo Lara Reyes, personal correspondence, Sept. 23, 2009).

93. Donald Moore (personal correspondence, Dec. 4, 2009; Jan. 3, 5, 2010).

with, "I know, it's a miracle." (This incident happened shortly before the story of Yesenia Robinson, whose story involving Donald I recount elsewhere in this book.)

Such cures are not common, at least in circles we know in the United States; Donald said that was the first case of it he had witnessed in fifteen years. Because of HIPAA laws protecting the release of a patient's information, however, Donald discovered that he could not request or obtain medical records. What he could offer me was his professional opinion about an anonymous case, and that is what he has done here. Had Donald not been taking my class and learned that I was interested in cases with medical documentation, I would not have had any access to this story, or it would have been dismissed by skeptics as merely the tale of another person claiming healing against the evidence.[94]

Beyond these matters, prejudiced approaches can deny the value of medical documentation even when it *is* available. Those who question supernatural healing claims often attribute the more convincing cases to an initial misdiagnosis.[95] Although genuine misdiagnosis does occur at times,[96] this approach sometimes has been used as a means to explain away extranormal healings retroactively,[97] and sometimes the initial evidence is too firm to aver a misdiagnosis.[98] (Recall the case above in which physicians preferred to claim that they must have misdiagnosed and mistreated the patient for twenty years rather than allow that the patient had been miraculously healed during prayer.[99]) To simply dismiss every cure as a case of prior misdiagnosis is to allow one's presupposition to determine the outcome, especially when it involves many cases and the prior diagnoses involve multiple physicians.[100] One healing evangelist reasonably complains that if critics really believe that so many hundreds of healing cases result from initial misdiagnosis, they should be raising an outcry against such widespread misdiagnosis instead of against divine healing.[101]

94. Donald Moore (personal correspondence, Oct. 28, 2009; follow-up correspondence, Oct. 31, 2009), officially following up our earlier conversations.

95. A possibility noted in Frohock, *Healing Powers*, 133. The same explanation is sometimes given for other spontaneous remissions; see Lenzer, "Citizen" (while conceding some cases noted by Quackwatch).

96. See the probable example in Bishop, *Healing*, 177; the uncertain possibility in Alexander, *Signs*, 18. Remus, *Healer*, 109, even cites surveys arguing "that about half the time a firm diagnosis of illnesses is not possible," noting that even advanced tests can give wrong results; Downing, *Death*, 61, cites figures for frequently even fatal medical error and side effects. Again, this problem would not cover all healing reports I have noted (e.g., most cases of blindness), but it could well account for some of them.

97. Gardner, *Healing Miracles*, 28–29; cf. Melinsky, *Miracles*, 157.

98. E.g., Gardner, *Healing Miracles*, 21. Among more recent cures at Lourdes, the standards of documentation for case histories are too stringent for possible misdiagnoses to pass (Cranston, *Miracle*, 259).

99. Blue, *Authority*, 58.

100. The complaint in Braden, "Study," 232 (noting on 227 multiple confirmations in one case and in another that the cancer had spread to many organs).

101. Stewart, *Only Believe*, 66. Matt Marsak, phone interview, Aug. 21, 2010, noted that his surgeon found no trace of cancer, even though all the lab tests showed cancer. When Matt suggested that God had answered prayer and healed him, the surgeon insisted that he must have been misdiagnosed, implying that all the previous experts were wrong. Matt suggested that if he really did accept such a position it could

Given the unpredictability of substantial healing claims and their dominance in places where they are most needed (i.e., where medical treatment is least available), it is not surprising that doctors are not usually personally present when a nonmedical healing occurs. (Many theists would argue that God in fact usually works through doctors when they are available.[102] Both Scripture and the pattern of nature suggest that God does not usually lavish explicit miracles when natural means God has provided are available.) In some cases doctors are present, but how they interpret the cure can depend not only on whether or not such a cure took place (sometimes it really did not) but also on the learned assumptions through which the evidence is framed. Doctors who believe in supernatural healing are perhaps more likely to be present in such settings and will be more open to this explanation in cases where it can account for a cure. Since scientific training has traditionally focused solely on natural causes, however, it is not surprising that many doctors would try to exhaust all remotely possible natural explanations first. While considering natural explanations helps guard against credulity, it also risks serious bias when it must overlook or explain away what could constitute larger patterns of anomalies in the circles in question.[103] I have already suggested in chapter 6, and argue more fully below, that creating an insurmountable burden of proof for only one position reflects bias, since it de facto rules out any opposing arguments a priori.

For example, could a baby who appeared dead start breathing again, without prayer?[104] Undoubtedly it could. But it does not happen very often, so if it happens a number of times during prayer, why not consider whether a supernatural factor could be involved? Someone could argue that if it happens to 0.001 percent of babies (though this is a number I have simply invented for the sake of the argument), out of billions of babies born it must sometimes happen during prayer, even during prayers of intense faith. It does not happen commonly enough to allow a statistical perspective on what proportion of these occasions happen during prayer,[105] but

---

invite a malpractice suit, whereupon, he reports, the doctor quickly backed down from the misdiagnosis proposal. My point here is not that misdiagnosis does not occur, but that the verdict can sometimes involve retroactive interpretation after eliminating supernatural activity or an anomaly as an option.

102. See, e.g., Crandall, *Raising*, 41.

103. Cf. Weintraub, "Credibility," 374: some rule out theistic explanations a priori by arguing that any event must be explained naturalistically even if it can be explained theistically. "But this behaviouristic bias is no more tenable in divine psychology than it is in its human counterparts." This analogy might, however, offer little help to those whose view of human personality is purely materialistic (arguable, but an analogy not applicable to a Creator external to the universe).

104. By this I mean not that the baby would go limp and stop breathing for a few seconds, raising concern, but that it would apparently stop breathing for a few minutes and give signs of being dead, such as discoloration, raising panic or (more dramatically) mourning.

105. Shermer, "Miracle," notes that "one-in-a-million miracles happen 295 times a day in America," arguing that rare coincidences are still bound to occur; see the helpful probability calculations in Charpak and Broch, *Debunked*, 48–49, 56–60, 133–35 (note the positive but qualified review in Dyson, "One"). My imaginary estimate is one in one hundred thousand altogether, rather than one in a million per day, but to my knowledge there is no precise estimation of such cases available. What is much more unusual is that such incidents happen to show up (connected with prayer) in my very limited sample size. I address

if it happens during prayer a number of times (cf., e.g., the cluster of examples of raising testimonies around Mama Jeanne in ch. 12, and another in the family of the person who happens to be writing this book for unrelated reasons), is it not closed-minded to just dismiss or peremptorily explain away a possible relationship in these cases? I have not gathered all possible cases but only those I have come across; and some of these I came across unexpectedly in interviews, out of fewer than two hundred people I interviewed (none of them famous healers).[106]

Working with the dominant nonsupernatural paradigm of Western academia, one can "explain" almost any cure as a spontaneous remission or, in the most difficult cases, an anomaly (which by definition is not yet explained). But observers not committed to a methodology that a priori privileges any remotely possible naturalistic explanation over any supernatural one (i.e., observers not committed to the approach challenged in chs. 5–6) will not foreclose the possibility of supernatural explanations. One philosopher cites as an analogy G. E. Moore's refutation of idealist skepticism concerning the material world: he "held up his hand and claimed, 'here is my hand.'" Moore understood that the argument was more complex, but he also recognized "that common sense places a significant burden on the Idealists." Denials of miracles can become strained under some circumstances.[107]

The Demand's Epistemological Premise

Again, some healing claims are medically documented. Here I merely address the question of why some critics will admit *only* this kind of evidence, and, as we have seen, often not even this. Naturally this observation is relevant to accounts in the Gospels and Acts. If we can accept cures as genuine only where modern Western medical documentation is available, then all cures in the Gospels and Acts, as well as any reported until perhaps a century ago, and the vast majority reported in most of the world's cultures today, can be dismissed by fiat. Such a methodology would not even allow one to offer educated guesses about what might have happened in the first century or in places where no medical documentation is available, but those employing a rigorously skeptical methodology sometimes employ it today.

In one case, for example, a woman testified to having "been miraculously healed after being blind for 16 years," yet a critic rejects this claim because no medical investigation was undertaken.[108] He agrees that registered blindness does not go

---

some sample probability calculations in ch. 15 and especially appendix E, but too many variables exist in the real world to quantify these with precision.

106. One might adjust this by noting that only a minority of people who knew that I was interested in information offered some; while some of these other people told me that they had miracle accounts (some of them dramatic, like raisings) and did not get back to me, I will ignore them for the sake of argument and multiply by as much as fifteen. Three thousand people still should not provide so many stories of this nature. Some were referrals from people I knew who knew them, but even if one multiplied by ten times more (a generous figure, since most cases were not referrals, and a number were merely confirmations of others' accounts), we are still talking about many extraordinary cases in a comparatively small sample size.

107. Kelly, "Miracle," 50.

108. May, "Miracle," 152–53.

away without medical intervention but suggests that perhaps her vision simply improved; perhaps "she was depressed and now isn't," hence "feels better about her vision."[109] I lack access to the source of the original report and therefore do not know the degree of blindness to which she refers; I grant that people sometimes make exaggerated claims, though, unless they are boldly lying, usually not *this* exaggerated. Nevertheless, I am more directly aware of some other claims of healed blindness (see ch. 12) where such charges would not hold up whether or not medical documents were available (in some cases they are).

In normal circumstances, we accept the claims of credible eyewitnesses who have much at stake; for most sorts of claims, no medical evidence or the like is available, but we do not for that reason disregard the claims.[110] For example, we would not require photographic evidence that a particular driver involved in an accident ran a red light if sufficiently credible witnesses attest this claim. As I have noted, many discussions in philosophy and law, including philosophic discussions of miracles, support the acceptance of a reliable witness, and still more the cumulative force of multiple independent witnesses. A number of healing claims are of the sorts of conditions that do not require an advanced degree in medicine to verify. If we will not grant the competence of a person who is blind or her family to attest that she was blind and received sight unless we possess a doctor's certification to that effect, are we actually saying that only a physician is competent to diagnose blindness? Physicians themselves would not make this claim,[111] which is essentially a now-disputed academic premise taken much too far.[112] Courts, unlike the rest of us, can subpoena records, but if records were unavailable (say in the case of a person in a part of the world who had never been able to afford medical treatment), would we not ordinarily accept testimony that the person was blind?[113]

In cases where medical expertise is not necessary to pronounce a genuine cure, is a critic implying that only a certain class of people, namely physicians, can constitute reliable witnesses? (Again, physicians would certainly not make this claim.) Even here, some accept the testimony of physicians normally, but when the physicians are verifying cures at Lourdes, some skeptics will then challenge these physicians' integrity, even though not all the physicians testifying are even persons of faith.[114]

109. Ibid., 154.

110. This observation is certainly true in historiography, where few claims can "be verified scientifically" (Licona, *Resurrection*, 171n119).

111. Dr. Tahira Adelekan, phone interview, April 24, 2009 (not in response to May's article, which I had not yet discovered). Indeed, when patients come to physicians for particular ailments, physicians normally ask their symptoms, although they can then run appropriately targeted medical tests to determine organic causes.

112. Tedlock, "Observation," 71, notes that traditional anthropology assumed "that a subject's way of knowing is incompatible with the scientist's way of knowing and that the domain of objectivity is the sole property of the outsider," an approach that has become increasingly controversial.

113. That we might be less inclined to do so if she or he were no longer blind, if she or he claimed divine rather than human medical intervention, works from the assumption that such divine interventions do not occur. Since that is the premise under dispute, it is not legitimate logically to assume it here.

114. See Cranston, *Miracle*, 186–87.

That is, one can never satisfy a closed mind, which can always find ways to exclude more and more evidence by narrowing the range of what is acceptable.

Yet if the reason for excluding nonphysicians' testimony about obvious cures is a matter not of competence but of testimonial reliability, one could apply this principle more broadly and admit as testimony in court only the verdicts of physicians. Such a practice would be absurd, hence should not be demanded in the sorts of healing accounts where the nature of the infirmity and its cure would be obvious, even without specialized training, to those involved (who sometimes, but not on average, happened to be physicians).

That some people will not accept a cure as genuine without medical documentation, and sometimes additionally reject medical documentation's validity if the doctor is known to accept the possibility of miracles, may say something about who has designed the rules of the game in their interests as well as about the nature of the evidence. Indeed, where some sort of medical documentation *has* been provided, some critics have rejected the appeal to "mere" medical documentation as unscientific without measurements of entire groups who seek healing.[115] This latter approach presumes that if supernatural healing is true, everyone who seeks it should be healed—a straw-man view held by few of supernatural healing's actual proponents. Neither Scripture nor Christian theology uses miracles as an excuse to neglect wisdom (for us including medical science) or avoid working for justice and peace in the world. Miracles are portrayed as merely sample signs of a future age, a reminder of what the world can be like; they are not intended as a large-scale panacea for the world's problems.

Yet critics sometimes will dismiss even medical testimony or documentation if occurrences are not common. Thus, in response to a medically documented case of a man dead for thirty or forty minutes being raised when a renowned cardiologist prayed for him, a critic dismisses the case as isolated, hence anecdotal, not able to be counted scientifically.[116] Technically, this objection may be correct for how the rules of science are written. Yet, as I have noted, no one in practice lives with such a constricted epistemology as if such rules are our only source of knowledge. The nature of some sorts of events remains significant even if they are documented only rarely. That is, simply because one epistemic method does not confirm something true does not mean that we cannot know it by other epistemic approaches that we

---

115. West, *Miracles*, 121; cf. Duffin, *Miracles*, 34. No large-scale study of such healings is possible, however, since the usual premises of scientific publication a priori exclude most cases from consideration (Llewellyn, "Events," 253).

116. Dr. Richard Sloan (on Fox News's coverage of the raising; http://video.google.com/videoplay ?docid=2684816148510273361&q=fox+news+miracle&to; http://www.youtube.com/watch?v=JUJiD _UFNCE; accessed May 9, 2009). Sloan reasonably protests that the man would not have revived without the additional electrical shock, and seems likely correct on this point. Nevertheless, the reverse is also true: had Dr. Crandall not felt compelled to raise the man who otherwise appeared beyond hope, no electrical shock would have been applied. (Certainly no one will make this case a new precedent for shocking bodies after forty minutes of death.) Moreover, a raising after so long a time is at best extraordinarily rare; the recovery and especially the lack of brain damage are medically inexplicable.

employ on a regular basis, since the first epistemic method may be limited in its scope or the data available to it may be limited. Regarding the matter in question, let us hypothesize a figure that one in a quarter million persons is supernaturally raised after certified death in the West today. Yet we would not expect controlled studies to shed much light on the matter, since even hundreds of studies would likely lack reported examples useful for comparison, and exceptions could again be deemed isolated, hence (again) essentially anecdotal.

Even solid medical documentation is not adequate by itself to surmount strongly held presuppositions, because one may insist in every case (even if there are thousands of them) that another explanation is possible. My colleague in Hebrew Bible, Emmanuel Itapson, was told that his third child had "the death chromosome" and would likely die before birth if not aborted. The family prayed, and the boy is now nine years old.[117] Because 1 percent of those with this chromosome are known to live beyond infancy,[118] one cannot prove beyond any doubt that prayer is the factor that helped him to live so long; yet I am prepared to grant that likelihood in view of the significant number of extraordinary answers to prayer in Emmanuel's circle, including one mentioned in chapter 9 and another in chapter 12.

Likewise, a child dying of fibrosing alveolitis was sent home to die but began to improve shortly after being taken to a British Pentecostal healing service. He eventually became a fully healthy boy. This diagnosis in a child's first year "is *almost* uniformly fatal," one physician notes, and the case is medically documented. The physicians involved believed that the cure "was the work of God, and it has been locally talked about as miraculous." Nevertheless, the writer, himself suspecting a miracle, warns that the expression "*almost* uniformly" is the catch. Demonstrating that a healing is miraculous is difficult because "medicine knows few absolutes," and a detractor can always claim an "inexplicable spontaneous remission."[119] If one's worldview does not allow for a connection between prayer and healing, one might ignore the connection, even when the connection would prove frequent. Still, this doctor notes that sufficient analogies can allow us to view "the direct intervention of God" as the most plausible explanation for those whose worldview allows this.[120] If medically impossible cases like bone restoration and cataract disappearance are granted, and if we allow or infer supernatural involvement in

117. Emmanuel Itapson, phone interview, Dec. 15, 2009.

118. Some of which might also be answers to prayer, but this becomes difficult to quantify, since certainly more than 1 percent of families have prayed for their children's healing.

119. Gardner, "Miracles," 1928. May, "Miracles," 150, attributes one of Gardner's clearest cases to "spontaneous remission," while admitting that "the phenomenon . . . is ill-understood" (presently inexplicable). Faith, prayer, and the like are often present in spontaneous remissions where these factors (or results) have been noted (see Roberts, "Contributions," 248–49, citing O'Regan and Hirschberg, *Remission*, 45). Speed, *Incurables*, 23, notes that when a woman was suddenly and permanently healed after fifteen years of inability to walk unaided, despite nerve and muscle degeneration, some other doctors (besides Speed) titled it a "remission."

120. Gardner, "Miracles," 1929, arguing that sources like Bede had sufficient reason to hold this perspective within their theological frame of reference.

such cases, we hardly dare assume that supernatural causes would be *limited* to cases where natural explanations are never possible.

Events in history are not repeatable in controlled studies; yet should we draw from that observation the inference that they are therefore not *true*? One is compelled to ask what kind of narrow epistemology would require us to rule out virtually any reliable information in history. When one employs a method of verifying miracles that insists that they be replicable in controlled settings, yet regards as natural and nonmiraculous any event that is so replicable,[121] one has framed the method so as to secure the expected antisupernatural outcome. Moreover, a miraculous raising report does not actually appear in complete isolation. If we have a significant number of raisings reported in the specific context of prayer, is it sounder research to explore the common factor in such cases or to ignore it because we have already presupposed that religious elements do not count?

As I have noted, some people also respond to medical certification of an incurable condition that is afterward cured by claiming that the condition must have been initially misdiagnosed.[122] The four consultants who examined a dying medical intern remain confident of their diagnosis, but because her subsequent healing is medically inexplicable, some critics still suggest that the doctors must have been mistaken.[123] Events that surprise doctors, as often narrated by informants in previous chapters, need not be supernatural; none of us is omniscient, and all of us are sometimes surprised in our various disciplines. But some unexpected recoveries challenge conventional paradigms more than others do: for example, pleasant surprise about a skin condition improving differs from astonishment about badly damaged organs being completely healthy. While misdiagnosis occurs and might even be frequent,[124] when it provides a ready answer to all healing claims one wonders if it is not simply used to sustain antisupernaturalistic presuppositions by dismissing all evidence.[125] Given all the claims of healings in the world, attributing most of them to misdiagnosis would also present a very incompetent medical industry meriting far more pervasive lawsuits—an evaluation I think as wrong as the antisupernaturalism it would be constructed to support.

---

121. Cf. how Laato, "Miracles," 68, describes the usual scientific approach; the complaint in Gorsuch, "Limits," 282; the suggestion in Pyysiäinen, "Fascination," 20, that naturally explicable events are not considered miracles. Llewellyn, "Events," 244, complains that skepticism is built into the usual scientific approach from the beginning.

122. E.g., Parker, "Suffering," 216; Blue, *Authority*, 58; Mews, "Revival," 330; Frohock, *Healing Powers*, 133.

123. Gardner, "Miracles," 1929.

124. Cf., e.g., Remus, *Healer*, 109. It is possible that I may have experienced at least one relevant case: after a doctor examined my swollen knee, which could not bend, he insisted I would never again be able to pray kneeling. At that time in my life, this verdict was unthinkable; the affliction departed after I prayed (ca. 1981) and never recurred, but his designation for the condition (cellulitis) does not seem to fit his verdict. Possibly I simply misunderstood him. In some parts of the Majority World, our family and friends know firsthand that misdiagnosis (sometimes deliberate, for pecuniary motives) and mistreatment are common, in spite of many other devoted physicians serving altruistically there.

125. Gardner, *Healing Miracles*, 28–29.

People who can explain away reliable eyewitness testimony of cataracts instantly disappearing (a recognition that should not require graduate training in ophthalmology) are people who have designed the rules so they can explain away whatever is necessary. In a culture shaped by Enlightenment assumptions about miracles, Western skeptics could conceivably deny tens of thousands of claims by attributing all of them to misdiagnosis, misinterpretation, and so forth. Such dismissal of any possible evidence, at the expense of viewing malpractice as pervasive and coincidence as extraordinarily rife during prayers, makes the collection of any eyewitness claims and medical documentation superfluous; such skepticism is impervious to correction. One wonders if many of the Majority World perspectives noted earlier in the book are not more epistemically open-minded on such matters.

At the same time, it cannot be denied that most nonprofessionals are not in a good position to verify how extraordinary most sorts of recoveries might be. Pursuing medical documentation also can helpfully explore whether some allegedly inexplicable healing claims are genuinely medically inexplicable; even many well-intentioned reports of better-than-expected recoveries can have plausible natural explanations, and some reports involve misunderstandings of the medical situation. Though I do think (and statistics suggest) that most of us would expect a pattern of multiple, instant cures of blindness, deafness, paralysis, and death to meet that standard, many different kinds of cures (e.g., headaches and insomnia, much as the cures are appreciated) may remain more debated ground. I shall return to these questions further below; I shall also call attention to some medical documentation with regard to Lourdes below and with regard to other cases in chapter 15. My point here is to note the dangers of bias.

Use of Videotapes?

I digress briefly to respond to the occasional complaint that more healings should be captured on videotape today if they are truly happening.[126] The problem here, as with medical documentation, is that since one usually cannot predict where a healing will occur, one usually cannot film it in process.[127] The exception could be mass healing meetings, which do produce some videos, but this is the sort of setting where critics also raise the most questions regarding motives and methods. Videotaping interviews with those claiming healing is much easier, because one has already narrowed down the range of where to look; such sources do exist.[128]

126. A science professor reasonably raised this question during a public lecture I gave on the subject of this book at Wheaton College, March 16, 2009.

127. Compare the semimythical chupacabra; people claimed sightings or capturings, but many have refused to believe the witnesses because they took no photographs. Finally, someone produced a video of a strange animal that fits some of the typical descriptions (Mike Krumboltz, "The Chupacabra Caught?" http://buzz.yahoo.com/buzzlog/92971?fp=1; accessed Sept. 2, 2009). My point is not whether the photographed animal is in fact the chupacabra but an observation about human nature: belief about the creature might change with the photograph, but its existence did not.

128. E.g., Dr. Candy Gunther Brown allowed me to view several tapes she had available, including one made immediately after the person's cure. Individual photos of testimonies, before-and-after healing

Most of the cures reported in this book also occur in places and at times when the average persons present lacked means to videotape, even had they known when to start videotaping. Moreover, medical documentation seems more reliable than what is normally observable on a video.

Nevertheless, for those interested in such sources, some cures in faith settings have been videotaped. Some may question the authenticity of all of these, but should not employ unfair standards: one should not ask for evidence that challenges one's worldview and then dismiss any evidence that does not easily fit it (however else they might explain it). Some of these appear, for example, on a popular DVD called *Finger of God*.[129] I have also noted some footage from a Baptist church in Ethiopia,[130] and local examples like the latter could undoubtedly be multiplied today. Yet, as my (then) eleven-year-old son perceptively pointed out to me, even if a skeptic demands videos, if his skepticism is inflexible he will reject their value once produced, claiming that the footage was faked.[131] In many kinds of cases, only those strongly committed to skepticism a priori would insist on such an approach. Fabrication can be fairly safely dismissed with *Finger of God*, whatever one's interpretation of some material in the film;[132] nor would one expect the Bakers, involved in highly sacrificial ministry, to have been involved in faked footage. (As we have noted, limited medical documentation also supports the existence of dramatic cures in their ministry.) Because the Ethiopian example came to me through a trusted friend who has witnessed such events at the church, I personally would not suspect fabrication in that video, either.

A video exists of a young man's instant healing from Guillain-Barré syndrome, in a midwestern U.S. church (though the camera is directed toward him only after commotion erupts). Previously, placing pressure on his feet caused intense pain, but he now left behind his wheelchair to run around the room. A friend of ours had known his condition for the previous few months and the genuineness of his recovery afterward, matching his own depiction of his condition before a minister prayed for him in faith.[133]

---

photos, and reproductions of X-rays are more common (e.g., Numbere, *Vision*, 152), and I have seen before-and-after photos even from close friends (Marie Brown, personal correspondence, May 31, 2006). Of course, this technology has been available longer.

129. *Finger of God*, most notably the healing of deafness in Mozambique.

130. Pastor Dawit Molalegn, Atsheber DVD 2.

131. Some have even compared traditional miracles functionally with special effects' impact on humans, as in Vries, "Miracles," 51–52. Some psychic healers also have videotapes (e.g., the one noted in McClenon, *Events*, 134; cf. psychic phenomena on 232).

132. For the most part it lacks dramatic special effects (cases involving "gold dust" as the only exceptions, and the part of the film most enigmatic to me) and involves people in informal, unplanned settings.

133. I viewed the video on May 3, 2010, at http://cmp.ihop.tv/gp.php?pid=zZzFzChe0FUVH7cy _PIH9uCDBehUxVx; and Jonathan's subsequent testimony on May 6, 2010, at http://cmp.ihop.tv/gp.ph p?pid=zYsSrFPhHn_612mVuiLx14weh7Dp0woc. Lauren Mason confirmed the events for us in personal correspondence, May 3, 5, 6, 8; interview, June 3, 2010; confirmed also by the young man himself, in Jonathan Pollard (personal correspondence, May 12, 13, 15, 16, 19, 20, 22, 2010), with some medical documentation (sent to me July 22, 2010).

Likewise, a video captures the healing of Randy McKenzie at a conference in Abbotsford, British Columbia, on September 22, 2006. Moments after experiencing healing, he bends over and sideways repeatedly, pain-free, noting that he has not been able to do this for four years. Then he actually picks up his wife. How can we guarantee that Randy McKenzie was actually unable to do something like this before? The video provides what usual journalistic standards would treat as compelling evidence for his previous condition, with X-rays, interviews with his family and friends, and so forth.[134] I was originally informed of this testimony and long-term healing through therapist and broadcaster Craig Miller, who knows the family, and Randy's wife, Susan, provided further information.[135]

Finally, a friend pointed me to an internet video of Delia Knox beginning to have feeling in her paralyzed legs and then walking with others supporting her, from August 30, 2010. Several days later, another video showed her walking several feet with no support. Such steps might not sound impressive, yet I discovered local news reports from two years earlier showing that she had indeed been organically paralyzed due to nerve damage from a car accident; in fact, she had not walked for more than two decades. Initially she was walking only haltingly while regaining strength. A new video on October 27, however, showed her walking normally as she prayed for others.[136]

Not knowing Hume, I do not know whether he would have balked at calling such an event a miracle (as his essay suggests) or would have altered his perspective had he been present and known the persons involved. Whatever nomenclature we use, Knox appears to have experienced an extraordinary change in her ability

---

134. The video ("McKenzie Story") also recounts earlier healing incidents; further information appears at http://www.teamfamilyonline.com/miracles/; www.RandyandSusan.org. The battery pack briefly mentioned in the video functioned only briefly (Susan McKenzie, personal correspondence, July 20, 2010).

135. Craig Miller (personal correspondence, July 12–13, 2010); Susan McKenzie (personal correspondence, July 14, 20, 2010).

136. These videos and other information appeared at http://www.youtube.com/watch?v=oYjM4xrw1ds, Aug. 30, 2010; accessed Sept. 2, 2010; Press-Register staff, "Miracle in Mobile? Singer Delia Knox Says She Can Walk Again after 22 Years Thanks to Revival," Sept. 2, 2010, http://blog.al.com/live/2010/09/miracle_in _mobile_singer_delia.html; accessed Sept. 2; http://blog.al.com/live/2010/09/delia_knox_revival .html, Sept. 4; accessed Sept. 4, 2010; http://www.youtube.com/watch?v=whk_14KIoKo&feature=player _embedded#!; accessed Oct. 28, 2010 (my thanks to Jeff Lundblad for tech help here). "Delia Knox Walks," *Thrive* Magazine (Buffalo, N.Y.), Sept. 8, 2010, http://www.thrivebuffalo.org/delia-knox-walks/2010/9/8 /delia-knox-walks.html; accessed Dec. 29, 2010; "Paralysed for 23 Yrs, Woman Walks Again," *The Times of India*, Dec. 23, 2010, http://timesofindia.indiatimes.com/articleshow/7148516.cms?prtpage=1; accessed Dec. 29, 2010. The paralyzing accident occurred on Dec. 25, 1987. I can imagine no way that her able locomotion in the Oct. 28 video could have been faked, and many suggestions of internet critics border on the absurd: the claim that she faked paralysis for twenty-two years for the sake of later claiming healing lacks any modicum of common sense; the suggestion that she was misdiagnosed for so many years and merely psychologically paralyzed would appear little better, attributing extraordinary incompetence to the medical profession (but I have not been able to obtain concrete information). The assertion of fraud by some unaware of her previous condition simply recycles presuppositions; aside from earlier public reports, I have reports from people who knew her when she was paralyzed (e.g., Alycia Wood, personal correspondence, Sept. 2 [via Michael Licona]; Nov. 1, 2010). Barring significant forthcoming evidence to the contrary, charges of fraud appear libelous special pleading.

to walk, and the earlier footage strongly suggests that this change began with a dramatic spiritual experience. The experience precedes the book's release too closely to allow further evaluation; unable to contact her (despite attempts) or view earlier medical records, I merely offer this example as a response to protests that cure experiences are never videotaped. Sometimes they are.

I defer to future researchers for their conclusions regarding videos circulated by some controversial circles with which I lack direct contact; for example, some have told me that, despite genuine healings occurring in Nigeria, evidence suggests faked documentation in at least some cases.[137] Because, as I have noted, some people are hostile to supernatural beliefs altogether, it is not surprising that controversy surrounds many figures who emphasize healing; but controversies can also arise for legitimate reasons. One case disputed at the time of this book's writing involves a large church in Lagos, Nigeria, that has videotaped a number of dramatic, visible disorders and corresponding healing claims.[138] Some critics have denied the church's credibility and argued that its videos are fabricated.[139] Conversely, a medical expert argued, with some significant evidence, that some videos of medically inexplicable visible healings there involve what appear to be genuine medical conditions (though sometimes mislabeled by the church) and noted that during his visits there he witnessed some healings similar to those on the videos.[140] Nor is his knowledge merely secondhand in this regard; he further noted that he himself was immediately healed of a chronic condition that had plagued him for seven years when he received prayer at the church.[141]

137. Dr. Gary Maxey, founder of West Africa Theological Seminary, affirms that many genuine miracles are occurring but that evidence is fairly compelling that at least one Nigerian preacher (different from the one in question in my context here) paid substantial money to have documentation faked (personal correspondence, May 25, 2009, and esp. May 26, 2009). See also the warning in Numbere, Vision, 433. Most churches, of course, could not afford such fake documentation, but neither is fraud surprising; fake documentation of sorts is not a new problem (e.g., Josh 9:4–6; Lucian Alex. 12, 14, 26; Acts Pet. 8/28; cf. Scherrer, "Signs").

138. From the Synagogue Church of All Nations, video footage that I have watched includes (from the internet; also reported in Jackson, "Back," including a neurosurgeon's observations; questioned by detractors) the apparent resuscitation of a dead man, Moses Marule; and (from video materials shared with me by Dr. David Zaritzky) the healing of a man unable to walk (who appears surprised himself but eventually runs), what are said to be visible cancers of the lip, buttocks, and anus (Dr. David Zaritzky, phone interview, May 24, 2009, notes that he and other doctors watching identified them instead as a sort of venereal disease affecting the lips, and that he saw the woman's healed condition in a later video; severe decuvibutus ulcers; and a severe, infected rectal prolapse), and others. Raising of the dead also occurs on a Reinhard Bonnke video mentioned earlier.

139. See discussion in the next paragraph. More positive assessments appear in, e.g., Ajaero, "Life"; Achi, "Joshua"; the report in Phillips, "Chiluba," is neutral. Many Brazilian Pentecostals believe that the IURD's televised exorcisms in Brazil are "stage managed" (Shaw, Awakening, 145).

140. Dr. David Zaritzky notes that he showed the videos to some other doctors, and that the graphic details were accurate and one would not expect these to be faked in Africa (David Zaritzky, phone interview, May 24, 2009). He had some even more graphic footage that he did not share with me.

141. David Zaritzky, personal correspondence, June 13, 2009, including his healing testimony that he plans as part of a forthcoming book. The condition involved both a serious back injury due to an

Most sources in Nigeria that I have consulted outside the church, while acknowledging that many miracles occur in Nigeria, have noted frequent criticisms of this particular church.[142] Some accusations that I have read could involve merely contextualization for an African setting; others, if true, are significant and could call into question the integrity of key leadership in the church.[143] At the same time, the church has responded in detail to some charges, including a videotaped confession of one who claimed to be the source for some false rumors.[144] I cannot offer firmer conclusions about this particular church without investigating personally on the scene, which I have not done.

In any case, herein lie limitations of videotapes. Even videotapes will not always persuade skeptics. Moreover, skepticism is not always unwarranted in particular cases. If less creditable evangelists of a former generation could fake healings,[145] we cannot rule out that some sources, especially those designed to promote a particular healing ministry, might do the same today. There is in fact reason to affirm that in some settings some documentation has been faked,[146] though the reasons

---

accident and consequent long-term sleeplessness; he also noted a fairly specific prophecy that addressed and healed a deep pain in his life.

142. Because of the controversy, I solicited confidential opinions from a range of Nigerian church sources, both Pentecostal and non-Pentecostal. Both Pentecostals and non-Pentecostals also affirmed that many genuine miracles do occur in Nigeria.

143. Of particular concern are the allegations of Bayo Ajede (including allegations concerning sexual immorality), whom T. B. Joshua in one interview denied knowing, yet who clearly was his close associate (Grady, "Followers," esp. 16). Further (and responded to in the next note) is a DVD circulated in Nigeria regarding *Deception of the Age: The Rise of a Nigerian Antichrist*, with accusations of sexual exploitation and fakery (from esp. two of his former associates, summarized in "Fear Grips T. B. Joshua," *Diamond Christian Magazine* (May 20, 2009): 6–7, though some articles in this issue resemble typical tabloid journalism). If true, these charges would effectively discredit this ministry; some elements do not appear to fit other footage I have seen, but I cannot speak to other charges. Lesser charges of authoritarian control appear likely (at least for the past) even from the church's responses.

144. See most extensively http://www.scoan.org/blasphemers.htm; accessed June 6, 2009; among other charges addressed here, charges of burying pregnant women for witchcraft at the church and (long ago) drug dealing seem trumped up. (Some have charged other churches with burying corpses and cult objects to gain power, as reported in Burgess, *Revolution*, 301n22. But while some do seek to gain power at the expense of others' welfare—see comments in appendix B—in a given case the charge seems more easily offered than proved.) Some responses appear to discredit the testimony of the accusers, focusing on those in the *Deception* video noted above, as effectively as any defense attorney would seek to do; some of this "discrediting" in these cases, however, depends on members' prior confessions, the circumstances of which are unclear (being largely limited to selections from what had been videotaped). David Zaritzky (personal correspondence, June 13, 2009) noted that some of these charges were unfamiliar to him, but he answered some others from personal knowledge of some who ministered there. False rumors and accusations against ministries are common (e.g., Numbere, *Vision*, 175–76, 456); in this case, I lack means to sort out much of what is true from what is untrue.

145. Pullum, "Selling," 154–55, suggests that earlier media captured some dramatic public expressions of healing, yet he does not appear persuaded by them.

146. Shared with me as a general observation by those who also affirm that many genuine miracles are occurring in Nigeria, including Dr. Gary Maxey (personal correspondence, May 26, 2009); Dr. Danny McCain (personal correspondence, June 1, 2009). At least in the past century and currently, I suspect that such faking has happened most often in settings of capitalist competition among healing ministers or individual claimants seeking to acquire attention. Yet, as I noted in ch. 13 and above, fraud has a long

for affirming this in some cases are irrelevant to the vast majority of documented cases I have cited. Having offered this concession, I would remind skeptics who will not accept *any* evidence to consider whether they may be privileging their presuppositions above evidence. At least some immediate healings have been recorded on videotape by creditable sources that should not be quickly dismissed.

How to Sort the Evidence

Many of the recoveries listed in chapters 7–12 are compatible with but do not require a supernatural explanation. That is, if one prays for a thousand generically sick patients, the odds are good that many will recover with or without prayer and even with or without medical treatment, though instant cures of something like blindness would belong to a different category. Even in the case of serious illnesses, many cures could be the sort of spontaneous remissions that occur with or without prayer.[147] While most believers would regard any recoveries as divine grace, directly or indirectly,[148] it is more difficult to utilize them as indisputable proof of specifically divine activity.

It should be noted, however, that at least some "natural" remissions without reported prayer surely do involve prayer. One person whose ability to see changed measurably after prayer noted her optometrist's remark that he had seen these "inexplicable" cures of eyesight only three times previously in his practice, all related to prayer.[149] But in many or most cures associated with prayer, this information is not shared with doctors. Research shows that those "who utilize non-medical forms of healing often do not tell their doctors for fear of irritating or losing them."[150] Some persons whom I had interviewed had instantaneous "spontaneous recoveries during prayer, including one case in which other cases of such spontaneous recoveries were not known, but their doctors classified the recoveries as anomalies and refused to admit that a miracle had occurred. One doctor also told me of a dramatic, medically inexplicable healing that occurred after prayer, in which

---

history; early Christian authors also felt uncomfortable with some miracle claims (Mark 13:22; Matt 7:22; 24:24; 2 Thess 2:9; Rev 13:13–15).

147. Cf. Frohock, *Healing Powers*, 134, countering one healing claimant's enthusiasm about his heart growing new veins by noting that this "is a common and natural phenomenon."

148. See, e.g., Rose, *Faith Healing*, 134–35; O'Connor, *Movement*, 163. Gardner, *Healing Miracles*, 14–15, notes that Christian theology could define as a miracle any answer to prayer; a definition acceptable to medical science, however, would be narrower.

149. Anna Gulick (personal correspondence, June 10, 2010, the day of the conversation). She reported that he said that "two were cataracts, and in one case the improvement was significant enough that surgery was canceled," though "in all three cases, the patient continued to receive some medical help" after the significant cure (hence explaining his continued knowledge of their situation).

150. Poloma, *Assemblies*, 57. Before reading Poloma's sociological study, I had already noted that some of those I interviewed had testified to their churches but admitted that they had not bothered to inform their physicians that they had prayed. Some patients on recovery have failed to even inform their doctors of their cure (see Duffin, *Miracles*, 131).

case he was an eyewitness, but the surgeon was content to label it a "spontaneous healing."[151] This approach to classifying data to fit existing naturalistic paradigms inevitably obscures all potential evidence in conflict with the paradigm. Because the specialist in one case was not willing to consider the recovery as miraculous, although it was unique and instantaneous during a prayer, the next time such a healing occurs, others could cite the first case as an anomaly and note that such remissions have "happened on other occasions." No mention of prayer is likely to appear in any of the medical records.[152]

Meanwhile, remissions and similar explanations cannot cover many other examples provided, such as most healings of blindness. Moreover, eliminating potential remissions can function as an unduly stringent criterion,[153] if it disallows the cumulative import of a disproportionate number of remissions after prayer in circles where such prayers appear to prove particularly effective. One Christian physician notes that most miraculous healings could be dismissed as remissions, but it is significant that they happen so often immediately after prayers of faith in Jesus's name.[154]

I have omitted many reports of healings of cancer due to critics who explain such healings in terms of natural remissions, especially when the same person later experiences cancer again, but long-term healings without treatment are not so common. Some have even estimated that "the spontaneous remission rate for cancer is about one in 100,000."[155] This figure could well overestimate the rareness of spontaneous remissions; yet because those diagnosed with cancer are normally taken into treatment immediately, hard figures for *spontaneous* remissions without

151. Tonye Briggs, phone interview, Dec. 16, 2009. In this case, a deep wound about 10–15 cm wide closed overnight, after prayer, a day before the medical student's arm was scheduled to be amputated, an instance for which there should be no medical explanation.

152. Similarly, talk about divine intervention is often screened out of public reports (as in the cases in, e.g., Malarkey, *Boy*, 201, 204–5; Gebru Woldu, interview, May 20, 2010). To correlate some anomalies with prayer is not to suggest a theology in which God acts only when people pray, or to suggest that all remissions involve prayer. But for the questions presently involved, prayer seems the most relevant potential factor to attempt to correlate.

153. The ways questions or assumptions are framed can affect outcomes. Thus, as I mention elsewhere in this book, one professor, when I asked him if he could believe in a genuine miracle if someone were raised from the dead in front of him, unhesitatingly responded, "No." Yet he considered me closed-minded for being a Christian, although I was a convert from atheism who had once myself discounted Christians' intelligence. Likewise, my brother, a physicist, tried to recount to a colleague his eyewitness knowledge of a healing personally known to him. His conversation partner refused to believe him and also refused to come meet the family or visit the circles where such phenomena appeared more frequent. Common as such an approach is, I believe that Gardner, *Healing Miracles*, 165, is right to contest its objectivity.

154. Ibid., 24–25. Most miracle reports involve prayer (Prather, *Miracles*, 214).

155. Flach, *Faith*, 92, though admitting that faith remissions are merely improbable naturally, not impossible. Flach is a physician here citing another doctor. The usual estimates range from one in sixty thousand to one in one hundred thousand (Ellens, "Miracles and Process," 11, following Lenzer, "Citizen," 56). Dr. Nicole Matthews (personal correspondence, April 14, 2009, extending discussion from April 1) emphasized to me that genuine malignancies (as opposed to benign tumors) require treatment (even homeopathic therapy uses "herbs that have some cell growth limiting factors"); disappearance without treatment is thus extraordinary.

medical treatment are difficult to come by.[156] The point is that they cannot be taken for granted; thus a case like the permanent healing of the three-year-old's untreated leukemia in Brazzaville, cited earlier,[157] and in a context with other numerous attested healings attributed to divine activity,[158] should still be deemed extraordinary. One must also account for the smaller proportion (yet strikingly large number) of dramatic recoveries suggested above that are not readily amenable to such explanations even on an individual level, such as suddenly regaining sight or life.

Critics of Lourdes

Because claims of cures associated with Lourdes cluster in one location rather than occur randomly throughout the world, Lourdes lends itself more readily to collecting medical documentation than most individual sources for healing claims do. This observation makes studies of Lourdes helpful for research even though the percentage of healing claims there is lower than the proportion in many other settings. Regardless of one's perspective on miracle claims at Lourdes, it thus offers a useful case study in methodology, as well as of both the importance and the difficulty of surmounting reductionism.[159] Theologians may debate whether healings took place because of Lourdes or whether the same healings could have taken place anywhere through faith, but this question (also relevant to other healing contexts) is not necessary for the point we are investigating here.

The Catholic Church has strict evaluation criteria in place at Lourdes and in most generations has left the burden of proof heavily on the miracle claim. As we shall see, some standards are *too* stringent.[160] Increasingly rigorous standards have reflected the Roman Catholic approach to all miracle claims since the Counter-Reformation. The approach does not imply that other claimed miracles may not have occurred, but seeks a secure minimum that withstands external scrutiny.[161]

156. Dr. Tahira Adelekan, phone interview, April 24, 2009; on spontaneous remission rates without treatment being unknown, see also Krippner and Achterberg, "Experiences," 358; for estimates of remissions being more common than the standard estimate, see McNamara and Szent-Imrey, "Learn," 209. Some clearly have recovered using alternate therapies of some sort, but natural recovery seems far from the norm.

157. From Jacques Vernaud, personal correspondence, Aug. 29, 2005.

158. Known to me far before I planned to write this book: Jacques Moussounga independently attested Jacques Vernaud's ministry in healing, sharing this with his daughter Médine; Médine spoke of it shortly after we met (in our first extended conversation, Oct. 1, 1989), long before we considered marriage but after I already knew of the healing of Jacques Vernaud's daughter (from that daughter, confirmed by her father).

159. Others have also raised the discussion of Lourdes in connection with studies of biblical miracles (cf., e.g., Légasse, "L'Historien," 141). Thus in his book regarding Jesus's miracles, Sabourin, *Miracles*, 162–63, suggests that miraculous cures there are likely but notes reasons for caution (esp. in the need to distinguish "normal" spontaneous cures from miraculous ones).

160. Cf. also Laurentin, *Catholic Pentecostalism*, 123–24; Williams, *Doctor*, 72, 75.

161. See Duffin, *Miracles*, passim. For the formative historical context of early Protestant skepticism and seminal medical thinkers in establishing the sorts of rigorous approach now in place (including the office of *promotor fidei*, i.e., "the devil's advocate"), see Duffin, *Miracles*, 19–35. On the minimalist evidential approach, without denying other miracles, see 35, 111. Critics today who, by contrast, reject any testimony without medical documentation, not merely for a minimally secure base of data but even to evaluate which claims might be deemed probable, rarely seek to defend their rejection of eyewitness testimony. This

One critic of supernatural healing at Lourdes, D. J. West, censures the bias of the Medical Bureau there, but his own evaluation seems open to the same charge. Since recoveries in real life are never instantaneous, West claims, doctors at Lourdes face "the necessity to distort facts to fit them in" and "fail utterly to preserve that detached frame of mind so essential to a fair consideration of the respective merits of all possible interpretations."[162] I defer conclusions on medical points to those with medical competence; yet it must be noted, against the critic's concern about bias, that members of the Medical Bureau have included not only Catholics but also Protestants and those who do not claim adherence to Christian faith or any faith.[163] The bureau's responsibility is not to certify miracles but to certify cures and to determine whether they can be explained naturalistically.[164] Three different panels of physicians examine each case, later panels screening out some cases accepted by the earlier panels.[165] Responding to criticisms, the bureau has become increasingly strict in its standards, excluding even many medically inexplicable cases.[166]

One also does not need any particular medical expertise to observe that West's own language reflects his starting assumptions in this case. Assuming that natural recoveries are never instantaneous, he simply disallows evidence from Lourdes for instantaneous *super*natural healing. That is, he will not accept as evidence what cannot be explained in purely natural terms, yet what can be explained in purely natural terms he can discount as not a true miracle. (Another example below will illustrate how his method effectively screens out evidence that does not match his presuppositions.) Further, he places the standard of proof so high that few ailments or recoveries can even be considered.[167] A psychiatrist and parapsychologist, West affirms that "psychological influence plays some part in almost all illnesses and a

---

behavior supports the suspicion that in most cases their epistemological approach is authority: accepting without argument a particular historically conditioned approach (while broadening its application).

162. West, *Miracles*, 123. Spraggett, *Kuhlman*, 33, calls West, a psychiatrist, a "friendly critic"; Sabourin, *Miracles*, 158, offers a cordial critique, noting West's predisposition for psychic explanations based on his previous work.

163. Cranston, *Miracle*, 73–74, 186; Garner, "Regressions," 1257, notes that they prefer "documentation by non-Catholics." More than fifteen hundred doctors from all religious or nonreligious backgrounds participated in the examinations in 1953, the year for which figures are reported in Cranston, *Miracle*, 74, 80. At that time the bureau was supported by the dues of some five thousand physicians from roughly thirty nations (82, emphasizing that no money came from the church); note the international composition of the twenty-seven members of the International Medical Committee as of 1986 in Cranston, *Miracle*, 335. Religious diversity is even more true of doctors involved outside Lourdes (see, e.g., the astonished report of one agnostic physician in Cranston, *Miracle*, 182–83; the opinion of the Dutch Jewish neurologist in Cranston, *Miracle*, 249).

164. Wakefield, *Miracle*, 41. Of course, some will explain any event naturalistically, even if it is by insisting that a naturalistic explanation will someday be found; but the bar of evidence at Lourdes seems quite high, probably thereby even excluding many cures for which a naturalistic explanation, while possible, is nowhere close to the simplest option for a theist.

165. Garner, "Regressions," 1255.

166. Ibid., 1259, accounting for some reduction of the numbers. It might also be possible that greater dependence on medicine and scientific worldview has decreased some of potential supplicants' dependence on miracles, just as established Pentecostal denominations tend to give less attention to signs than initially.

167. See, e.g., West, *Miracles*, 22.

large part in many," *including* "organic" diseases.[168] Since he attributes nearly anything to psychological factors, an approach that attributes to supernatural factors only what one cannot attempt to explain otherwise[169] will have few cases to work with. Despite his argument for psychosomatic cures, many who have been cured were not expecting it;[170] some were not Catholic; and some had no faith in any religion at the time of their cure.[171] Nor do the vast majority of doctors expect suggestibility to instantly cure organic lesions, as in some reported cases.[172]

Of the just eleven cases that West examines, some do indeed seem disputable, but the book includes considerable "explaining away." Thus he avers that "lay witnesses" to a woman rising from being bedridden do not count scientifically without medical documentation of an organic cure.[173] While strictly speaking this may mean that we cannot be sure of an organic cure (and I am not qualified to evaluate the case in question), few cases described as this one is in the records should be deemed purely psychological ailments. Because a person bedridden for six years cannot get up and immediately walk (even true of someone otherwise healthy who has been lying in bed for months), the author doubts this aspect of the claim.[174] That is, he denies the possibility of instant cures because these rarely occur naturally (i.e., if they occurred it would be miraculous), yet would deny as

168. E.g., ibid., 20. Langford, "Problem," 49, thinks that healings at Lourdes fit psychosomatic explanations; he allows (52) that God works in psychosomatic ways but is skeptical of other miracles. Suggesting psychological cures, Frank, *Persuasion*, 58, allows that Lourdes cures may be genuine without being miraculous; he emphasizes (59) that those cured were usually "simple" rather than critical people.

169. One feature implied in the dictionary definition cited by the person introducing Peter May in May, "Miracles," 144. As noted in ch. 5, definitions vary, but this one does not correspond well to any biblical conception.

170. Cranston, *Miracle*, 260 (and passim among examples in the book).

171. Ibid., 155. Note, e.g., Gabriel Gargam, a paralyzed atheist near death, was cured immediately, though still gaunt (gaining twenty pounds in days; 40–41, 269). Also Elie Auclair, an atheist before his cure, though in this case he later suffered physical relapse months after his conversion and maintained his postconversion faith (185–86). Louis Olivari, a half-paralyzed French Communist, was an atheist who went to Lourdes only at his Catholic wife's insistence; moved by the earnest faith of the ten-year-old blind boy next to him, praying for Olivari, he prayed that God, if he existed, would heal the boy; the boy was uncured, but the atheist was immediately and completely healed when he left the water. The Medical Bureau refused to certify the cure without a long process of verifying that the change was organic, but Olivari was convinced and became a Christian (Oursler, *Power*, 59–61; Rose, *Faith Healing*, 95). Catholic miracle stories in recent centuries typically include the element of patients' surprise at their cure (Duffin, *Miracles*, 177). Skeptics were also healed in Salmon's ministry (Salmon, *Heals*, 34). Similarly, a woman with eczema for thirty-five years decided two days after the healing meeting that she simply had lacked sufficient faith; the next morning she awoke healed (63–64).

172. See Cranston, *Miracle*, 260–61.

173. West, *Miracles*, 36.

174. Ibid., 41. Similarly, Hume dismissed a claimed miracle cure because a physician declared that such cures do not occur (*naturally*) as quickly as the eyewitnesses claimed; but this evaluation simply presupposes pure naturalism (deSilva, "Meaning," 14–15). For similar cases, see Duffin, *Miracles*, 133–34. Frank, *Persuasion*, 57–58, views Lourdes cures as gradual; although the paralyzed may walk immediately or the blind see immediately, subsequent "actual tissue healing takes hours, days, or weeks," and weight gain is gradual. Yet why should we require instant healing of what is curable naturally in order for the curing of the naturally incurable aspect to be considered genuinely extraordinary?

miraculous any cure that could happen naturally. In other words, he construes naturally explicable elements as pointing to a natural recovery but treats as false any elements that are not naturally explicable. This is a catch-22 in which the rules are so fixed as to rule out any evidence for miracles; the approach thus simply presupposes that no supernatural explanation is to be admitted.

Rigorous Standards at Lourdes

By any standards, most ailing pilgrims at Lourdes are not cured there,[175] but these numbers appear even smaller by Lourdes's own rigorous standards.[176] While most of the diseases healed at Lourdes are also those known to sometimes undergo spontaneous remission in "secular" settings,[177] the standards for evidence are very strict there.[178] On extremely rare occasions doctors there (and elsewhere) have been duped,[179] but in the vast majority of cases the Medical Bureau is able to screen out attempts at fraud immediately.[180]

Only a small minority of pilgrims reported healings, although not all pilgrims are ill to begin with. By some estimates, most groups of organized pilgrims in the first half century reported between 0.001 and 0.02 percent cures,[181] certainly

175. One doctor directed patients there for twelve years without seeing any recoveries, but he observed a positive change in their mental attitude (Buskirk, *Healing*, 51–52; cf. Frank, *Persuasion*, 56, who believes that most are psychologically benefited); another reported a tuberculosis recovery, which he attributed to mental attitudes (Buskirk, *Healing*, 52). Hay, "Concept," 193, notes that while the Medical Bureau at Lourdes does not exaggerate, many believers in Lourdes overestimate the actual number of cures. West, *Miracles*, 121, complains that merely giving medical documentation for cures is not scientific unless one studies entire groups; but this approach implicitly presupposes that Lourdes claims to cure everyone. Amiotte-Suchet, "Egaux," argues that Catholics accept the rareness of miracles, expecting them less often than Pentecostals do (though sometimes exaggerating the latter's expectations).

176. For their very difficult standards, designed to secure a minimum of assured results, see, e.g., Cranston, *Miracle*, 75–79. Doctors are advised to be as rigorous as possible, erring on the side of skepticism rather than credulity (81).

177. Hirschberg and Barasch, *Recovery*, 106–7; Melinsky, *Miracles*, 163 (on cancer and tuberculosis). West, *Miracles*, 42, complains that "spontaneous recoveries" happen and these may thus happen with respect to pilgrimage to Lourdes only coincidentally.

178. See, e.g., Rose, *Faith Healing*, 96; Dearmer, *Body and Soul*, 307, 308–15. Other Christian traditions also have used healing locations, including in the United States (see Ogilbee and Riess, *Pilgrimage*, 3–50).

179. Some healings, such as that of Gabrielle Durand in the early twentieth century, are well verified (Scherzer, *Healing*, 138–39), though on another occasion doctors there (as well as *other* doctors) were duped (139–40; Major, *Faiths*, 34–36).

180. See Cranston, *Miracle*, 186–90. In one case, a woman had been paid by an antireligious organization to claim a healing falsely that could then be publicized to discredit standards at Lourdes; instead, the examination physicians immediately recognized the falsehood (190). In his novel *Lourdes*, Zola deliberately fabricated external falsehoods about Lourdes (Cranston, *Miracle*, 190); nevertheless, he himself witnessed "the overnight disappearance of horrendous leg and facial ulcers" that he could not explain naturally (Garner, "Regressions," 1262).

181. See the statistics in Kselman, *Miracles*, 201–3. These figures do not specify how many pilgrims specifically *sought* cures and would not include all subsequent or any unreported cures; at the same time, they would include a number of cures that medical science would not find impressive. Warfield, *Miracles*, 107, who generously concedes as much as 10 percent cured (a much higher figure), focuses instead on the disappointment of those uncured, though this observation cannot discount genuine cures.

significantly lower than the expected reported cure rate through medical science. If the point of Lourdes is to function as a theological sign rather than as a medical institution, however, comparison with medicine's cure rate is beside the point (though comparison with rates of spontaneous remission need not be). Of millions of pilgrims over the years,[182] with probably more than half a million sick,[183] about five thousand miracle claims have been recorded (less than 1 percent). Of these, the medical committees evaluating cures there have judged a smaller number to be "medically inexplicable." Only these screened cures have been forwarded on to bishops for further discussion, and of these only sixty-five have survived the evaluation of all examiners and been pronounced certain "miracles."[184] If the only genuine cures are those that have been deemed both medically inexplicable[185] and religiously approved, the cure rate is abysmally low—perhaps no better than one would find in hospitals dealing with the same number of "incurable" patients. Even many who affirm that supernatural healings occur there do not contend that they should be expected very often.

When one examines the statistics, though, one should also examine the stringent criteria employed there—cures are more frequent than the critical minimum finally counted as miracles. The concern of many pilgrims is their travel and health, not obtaining documentation; to satisfy the Medical Bureau's investigation, however, they must have full medical documentation of their prior condition, including any available hospital records.[186] Investigators cannot always obtain sufficient

182. Critics may also have exaggerated the number of pilgrims (Melinsky, *Miracles*, 162, though unsympathetic to attempts to evaluate and document miracles) but the average number probably exceeds three million annually (Marnham, *Lourdes*, 183); room exists to hold only one hundred thousand at a time at the torchlight procession (Cranston, *Miracle*, 103). However, only some of these are ill, and of these only those with medical certification can be examined by the bureau if cured, which reduces the figures considerably (in 1954, this was 33,276; Cranston, *Miracle*, 75).

183. Cranston, *Miracle*, 113, estimated that half a million sick had visited in the first 128 years. This estimate may be too low; it would suggest an average of only four thousand a year, though smaller numbers in the early years would skew that average for later years. Oursler, *Power*, 65, estimates that only 1 percent of annual pilgrims are ill, of which two hundred to three hundred claim cures.

184. Varying slightly regarding the number of initial claims, Marnham, *Lourdes*, viii; Hirschberg and Barasch, *Recovery*, 107; MacNutt, *Power*, 66; Mullin, *Miracles*, 120. But apparently most do remain uncured (cf. similar pilgrimages in Oktavec, *Prayers*, 37–38; more positively, 52); for a severe critique, doubting any of the cures, see Randi, *Faith Healers*, 20–30; also skeptical, Schwarz, *Healing*, 61–62; Bishop, *Healing*, 143–54.

185. A common definition for "miracle" today is "a permanently inexplicable event" (Basinger and Basinger, "Concept," 165; idem, *Miracle*, 23), but on this definition one denying a miracle could simply deny the permanence of its (nonsupernatural) inexplicability (Basinger and Basinger, "Concept," 166; idem, *Miracle*, 71; Basinger, "Apologetics," 352–53); see discussion of "God of the gaps" arguments below. Apart from the question of actual supernatural causation, it is cognitively easier to explain apparently naturally inexplicable events in relation to known religious assumptions (Pyysiäinen, "Mind," in terms of mental processing of counterintuitive events; the article does not seek to resolve whether or not miracles in the strong sense might actually happen, which it avers [738–39] that science cannot address). On the neural and mental processing of such events, see also helpfully Paloutzian, Rogers, Swenson, and Lowe, "Attributions"; a theist can construe such psychological structures providentially (e.g., Lawal, "Psychology," 151–52). Recognizing events as miracles involves not a mere "feeling" of awe (Hume, *Miracles*, 35, notes that wonder tales feel pleasant) but a "cognitive process" (Rogers, "Miracles," 111).

186. Cranston, *Miracle*, 118; cf. Williams, *Doctor*, 72.

documentation to proceed, since many doctors do not respond to requests for it, lacking interest and/or time.[187] Tracking down the witnesses can be difficult if they have moved. If patients have taken medicine that could possibly have produced the cure, they are excluded from consideration.[188] Most patients today, however, will seek the best of medicine as well as prayer. If one's ailment is not demonstrably organic, one is excluded, even though this excludes from consideration many genuine afflictions.[189]

Many people thus find themselves cured, yet if their cures cannot pass all the stringent criteria to achieve certainty, they are not pronounced miraculous by the church.[190] For example, a Protestant doctor notes that he "saw with my own eyes" that a woman who had been suffering from "advanced ankylosing spondylitis of the spine" was now able to pick up objects from the floor "without the slightest pain or difficulty." Lourdes rejected this cure because X-rays showed that her spine remained diseased, but the doctor notes that her new ability defied scientific explanation.[191] More than twelve hundred cures accepted by the Medical Bureau after multiple examinations lacked some (though usually not all) of the requisite documentation and thus were never processed.[192] Anyone who has tried to collect medical documentation recognizes that factors beyond the researcher's control sometimes make this process difficult. Besides the fairly secure cures, the bureau knows of four thousand other probable cures.[193] Many others were cured and never submitted any information to the bureau.[194] Forty doctors confirmed the cure of a medically incurable, quadriplegic postencephalitic idiot—a child who went from complete insensibility and lack of control to intelligent normalcy—but because some documents were missing, the cure was never officially proclaimed.[195] By the minimalist standards employed at Lourdes, it is likely that many of Jesus's miracles reported in the Gospels would have been screened out had they occurred instead at Lourdes.[196]

Unfair skepticism at any point in the process, whether from doctors or church leaders, can skew the results just as credulity throughout the process would. The

187. Cranston, *Miracle*, 119.

188. Ibid.

189. Ibid., 125; cf. Williams, *Doctor*, 75.

190. Cranston, *Miracle*, 119.

191. Woodard, *Faith*, 53 (noting that she had remained healed three years at the time that he met her and reviewed her case records; pure willpower could not produce such results).

192. Cranston, *Miracle*, 153. Sometimes doctors' records are not sufficiently precise; some other doctors refuse to provide requested information, whether out of prejudice against Lourdes or for other reasons (154). More recently, Garner, "Regressions," 1257, notes "nearly 1500 well documented cures, with case-notes, X-ray films and photographs," with another three thousand to four thousand lacking adequate data but presumably including many cures.

193. Cranston, *Miracle*, 154.

194. Ibid.

195. Ibid., 242–46, noting on 245 that none of the doctors had ever seen such a case in their medical careers.

196. Cf. a similar observation in Miller, "Miracle Worker," 21.

makeup of the committee and their philosophic predispositions, as well as those of bishops and diocesan councils, apparently plays a noteworthy role; some eras and regions include a number of reported healings, whereas others report barely any.[197] For example, no healings were admitted "between 1913 and 1946."[198] Yet between 1925 and 1946, thousands of reported cures appear in the Medical Bureau's records, of which eighty-nine were viewed as inexplicable;[199] those responsible for evaluating them simply did not proclaim any of them as miracles during this period. After the long hiatus, twenty-four miracle proclamations cluster in thirty-four years, starting, as one writer observes, "at about the same time as the reorganization of the Medical Bureau and the decision to encourage the simultaneous development of the Marian shrine of Fatima."[200] The French church decided to acknowledge healings at Lourdes near the fiftieth anniversary; they proclaimed twenty-one cures, including some that had taken place earlier, over the span of a few months, a collection that even today remains roughly a third of those proclaimed there.[201] That is to say, discerning an individual miracle can involve subjectivity, whether in affirming or denying it.[202]

Some Dramatic Cures at Lourdes

Moreover, whatever one makes of some of the roughly six thousand claims offered, some (for which medical documentation remains available) seem rather impressive. Cures of tuberculosis peritonitis dominate many of the claims, and critics charge that these may reflect misdiagnosis or psychological recoveries.[203]

197. For those proclaimed miracles, by twenty-five-year periods: four appear in 1862–86; twenty-nine in 1887–1911 (twenty-eight proclamations, all between 1907–11); two in 1912–36; twenty in 1937–61; and two in 1962–79 (Marnham, *Lourdes*, 185). Meanwhile, Bishop, *Healing*, 148, highlights the "predominantly French Catholic" character of the medical committee, though one would expect Catholics to be those with the greatest interest in serving on the committee. Yet he also notes that the committee is suspicious even of healings where the person expected healing beforehand, since the healing *might* be explained psychologically (Bishop, *Healing*, 151–52). Bishop's complaint that the water itself is not chemically special nor efficacious elsewhere (152–53) focuses on water rather than divine activity hence risks missing the point of why they are considered miracles.

198. Melinsky, *Miracles*, 162. Some of this period's dearth reflects the limitations imposed by two world wars (Cranston, *Miracle*, 114–15), especially 1939–46 (Cranston, *Miracle*, 207).

199. Marnham, *Lourdes*, 186. West, *Miracles*, 8, warns that the documentation kept in the bureau before 1946 was inadequate, a problem that also limited the scientific evidence with which he could securely work in his 1957 book. The Medical Bureau passed seventy-one cures between 1947 and 1988.

200. Marnham, *Lourdes*, 186.

201. Ibid., suggesting "political" factors. He also notes the high proportion of nuns and priests. External political factors also influenced miracle collections for canonizing saints; see Duffin, *Miracles*, 33 (Napoleon's influence on suppression of religion), 39, 178.

202. Cf. the struggle of Alexis Carrel, an agnostic medical researcher, to interpret and come to terms with what he witnessed at Lourdes (Flach, *Faith*, 38–40).

203. West, *Miracles*, 122; Major, *Faiths*, 37–38. Even Warfield, *Miracles*, 110, concedes that genuine cures at Lourdes are undeniable yet (111) attributes them mostly to "hysterosis," while leaving other cures (117–18; such as the instant healing of a broken bone) as mere anomalies or falsehoods. One wonders why a theist must automatically prefer this kind of psychological explanations, which themselves lack experimental confirmation, to theological explanations.

Tuberculosis did not lend itself to medical cures in that era, however, and if genuine was not cured by such means.[204] Because scientists now know that tuberculosis sometimes is cured spontaneously (and medical treatments are now available), Catholic miracle records of the past half century no longer include new cases.[205] Nevertheless, some cases of cured cancer[206] or tuberculosis[207] seem too sudden, from near death to complete health in hours, to readily lend themselves to the suggestion of merely coincidental remissions. The clinical details of one cancer case were presented at a conference on bone sarcomata, with no one able to explain the case naturally; only afterward was it revealed that the cure occurred at Lourdes.[208]

Nevertheless, even if we explain these sorts of cures naturally, it is harder to naturally explain Francis Pascal, cured of "blindness" and "paralysis of the lower limbs," at the age of three years and ten months, on August 28, 1938.[209] While the keenness of his vision remained less than the average person's,[210] this child who had been completely blind before the cure was now an active reader and writer.[211] Other blind persons were also cured of documented, organic optic atrophy, able thereafter to see.[212] One might also consider Marie Bigot, cured of blindness, deafness, and hemiplegia, on October 10, 1954.[213]

A clear case of Hodgkin's disease was cured on May 31, 1950: the pilgrim felt warmth and was healed, with all traces of the disease gone from his body. The original diagnosis of the disease cannot be disputed, as "the original histological specimens have been repeatedly and thoroughly reviewed."[214] Vittorio Micheli vis-

204. Garner, "Regressions," 1259.

205. Duffin, Miracles, 75–76.

206. Keep in mind that healings from cancer include medically documented, naturally inexplicable cases like Mlle Delot, whose cancer had spread, who had been given up by her physicians to die and was nearly dead, and who was instantly cured of cancer, even her damaged organs reforming (Cranston, Miracle, 127–29).

207. Sometimes the tubercular patient had great abscesses and was dying, yet within hours was so fully healed that she could walk under her own power and the wounds had closed (Mlle Brosse, in Cranston, Miracle, 180–84, including the astonished report of an agnostic physician, 182–83); the case of Jeanne Fretel, cured Oct. 8, 1948 (209–16, 269), is also noteworthy. Nearly half the confirmed cures until 1948 involved tuberculosis, partly because this was a common and then not really curable disease that drew many pilgrims to Lourdes (281); cases of healed tuberculosis have also been verified at Lourdes in more recent times (284–85, 292–93, 300–302).

208. Ibid., 306. The full cure of a girl near death from Ewing's Sarcoma in 1976 is significant because it "had never been found to regress spontaneously" (311). May, "Miracles," 149–50, however, questions this diagnosis (citing a specialist's conclusion based on slides) and further objects that it was partial and gradual.

209. Recognized as a miracle in 1949 (Marnham, Lourdes, 189; see Cranston, Miracle, 233–39, including her interviews with Pascal and his family; cf. Woodard, Faith, 57). For the full list of the persons and ailments cured, and dates, see Marnham, Lourdes, 187–91.

210. West, Miracles, 6.

211. Cranston, Miracle, 236, 237.

212. Ibid., 42–44, 227–33 (the second case, of Gerard Baillie, healed Sept. 27, 1947, was of a seven-year-old).

213. Marnham, Lourdes, 190 (for more on her, see 192–94; Cranston, Miracle, 293–95). She happens to have been captured on film just before and after her cure (Cranston, Miracle, 295).

214. Marnham, Lourdes, 191; see also Cranston, Miracle, 289–90.

ited Lourdes on May 24, 1963; on June 1, he felt that he was healed, and subsequent X-rays showed "that the bony reconstruction of the parts destroyed was progressing steadily"—something that should not happen naturally.[215] Unable to work and deemed an invalid due to verified physical causes, the nearly blind Serge Perrin visited Lourdes and on May 1, 1970, was anointed. He unexpectedly "experienced some sensation, felt even in his feet"; within hours his vision returned fully, and he was able to walk unaided.[216] Doctors verified that no trace of his previous medical problems remained; six years later, in view of his continued health, the cure was recognized by the church as miraculous.[217] The medically documented instantaneous healing of a swollen and paralyzed arm drew public attention and television coverage in France in 1954 and 1960.[218] A paralyzed and nearly blind man was instantly, permanently, and unexpectedly cured on May 1, 1970.[219]

In 1902, Alexis Carrel, not believing in miracles himself but learning of his patients cured at Lourdes, decided to investigate. On the train he cared for a dying girl, Marie Bailly, who was also traveling there, noting that her abdomen was swollen and that she was in danger of dying at any moment. She had peritonitis and was deathly pale and skeletal.[220] At Lourdes, she was removed from the train by a stretcher, with almost no pulse. To the "stupefaction" of the physicians, she was cured, the "tumors" vanishing in front of them; one astonished medical observer added that such a serious affliction "has never been cured [naturally] in a few hours like the case on record here."[221] Because Carrel had become interested in miracles, the University of Lyons medical faculty rejected him in 1905; he joined the Rockefeller Institute instead and in 1912 received the Nobel Prize in physiology and medicine, his memoir of the healing being published only later.[222]

In an academic journal article, Terence Nichols also recounts an earlier cure from 1878. The "gangrenous ulcer" on Joachime Dehant's right leg was twelve inches by six inches and had "penetrated to the bone." Her companions on the

215. Marnham, *Lourdes*, 195 (see more fully 195–96; his full dossier appears on 198–216). X-rays and army records showed that sarcoma had nearly destroyed his left pelvis, disconnecting it from the femur; X-rays a few months later showed regression of the sarcoma and the pelvic bone regenerating. Many orthopedic surgeons were consulted who had dealt with bone cancer; none had "encountered a case of spontaneous cure of a malignant tumour of the bone" (Garner, "Regressions," 1259).

216. Marnham, *Lourdes*, 197. Mays, "Miracles," 150, thinks that this case was "psychosomatic," though on 155 he concedes that "it is very difficult to be sure whether a person is a hysteric or not."

217. Marnham, *Lourdes*, 197–98.

218. Cranston, *Miracle*, 295–96.

219. Ibid., 307–8.

220. Oursler, *Power*, 72; Nichols, "Miracles," 706.

221. Nichols, "Miracles," 706, citing the original sources (esp. in Carrel, *Voyage*; Boissarie, *Healing*). Boissarie was one of the early physicians examining cases at Lourdes. See also the account in Cranston, *Miracle*, 172–76; briefly, Woodard, *Faith*, 51.

222. Nichols, "Miracles," 707; Cranston, *Miracle*, 35. A Jewish neurologist became interested in Lourdes based on Carrel's testimony, noting that since he trusted his word on cardiological experiments he ought to trust his word on this matter as well (Cranston, *Miracle*, 249). Trusting his eyewitness testimony need not involve agreement with all his views; Carrel's advocacy of the then sometimes accepted idea of euthanasia for dangerous criminals would be at best extremely controversial today.

train, nauseated by the odor, vomited. Nevertheless, the second time she bathed in the pool at Lourdes, she was healed, leaving only a scar. Investigators gathered testimony not only from physicians at Lourdes and her own physicians who had treated her for more than a decade but also from her traveling companions, family, and others who knew her in her hometown.[223] Perhaps some skeptics would dismiss the evidence as being from a generation prior to our own, hence not directly observed by us; again, this approach would make historiography beyond the living memory of eyewitnesses impossible. Because the cure took two or three hours[224] or because it left a scar,[225] some critics might dismiss the supernatural element, but such criticisms seem petty in view of the recovery.

Only a small percentage of cures are officially pronounced, but many dramatic healings occur among the much larger body of healings that are not among the official cures. A Methodist visitor to Lourdes testifies of being instantly healed there of disabilities that are not known to be cured naturally in this way.[226] An investigative reporter spoke with a woman who had been diagnosed as having "an inoperable malignancy located between her pulmonary artery and her heart" and told that she had six months to live. She was cured during her second time bathing in the water at Lourdes.[227] She informed the reporter that about sixty cures had been reported in the half-year before his visit; one case involved the instant healing of a man whose cancer had eaten away "most of his hip bone," and she showed the reporter the X-rays confirming the full restoration of the bone.[228] In a half-year period, some sixteen hundred physicians from thirty-two different nations and a diverse range of religious or nonreligious perspectives visited the Medical Bureau, where they are welcomed to examine the evidence for themselves.[229] That infants and unbelievers have been healed works against purely psychosomatic explanations.[230]

223. Nichols, "Miracles," 707, following Boissarie, *Healing*, 2–9; see also Cranston, *Miracle*, 39.

224. Nichols, "Miracles," 708.

225. Many of the cures leave "some vestige to show that the original illness existed, e.g., scars or a bone in a slightly different position" (Cranston, *Miracle*, 119); cf. the dramatic case of Belgian Pierre De Rudder, where scarring indicated the injury but new, whiter bone tissue had connected what had been considered a medically incurable fracture (Oursler, *Power*, 71, noting on 72 that twenty-eight physicians were involved in certifying the cure). Vestiges of an original injury or illness do not seem objectionable from the standpoint of biblical theism (see Gen 32:25, 31–32; Lev 13:23, 28). In one account, however, a physician admits that he had refused to accept a cure as miraculous if he found a scar—and he found none (Duffin, *Miracles*, 137).

226. Heron, *Channels*, 142–43.

227. Spraggett, *Kuhlman*, 29. One dying woman had a massive tumor that was inoperable due to her heart condition; it disappeared immediately and without a period of convalescence, with visible changes (Cranston, *Miracle*, 177–78).

228. Spraggett, *Kuhlman*, 30.

229. Ibid., 31–32.

230. Ibid., 32 (cf. also in Kuhlman's meetings, unbelievers on 165 and infants on 171). Healings include those who denied the supernatural (until the cure) and also Muslims and Jews at an extension site (Garner, "Regressions," 1257). Frank, *Persuasion*, 59, counters that the skeptics healed at Lourdes probably had some "emotional conflict," thus explaining why they would become believers after they were cured. Since any but the most inflexible skeptic might find a cure persuasive (hence might well become a believer), one wonders if Frank's explanation does not force evidence (as in his complaints about psychoanalysis on 124).

Granted that most pilgrims are not healed, some extraordinary healings have been documented. What of those cures that have been excluded by the minimalist criteria in place? The exclusion of medically explicable cures is a time-honored approach, employed in the Middle Ages, when it did not limit as many claims.[231] But in this era, it is difficult for doctors to call any healing medically inexplicable, since any given cure might have a potential secular explanation, whether or not that is the most plausible explanation for a given case. One English Catholic defender of miracles in 1914 complained that critics reckoned miracles at Lourdes impossible, and when evidence that such cures had occurred proved overwhelming, "it is given a big long name and called natural."[232] Moreover, most people who might travel to Lourdes today could first seek medical treatment elsewhere, thereby usually removing them from the medical committee's potential list of "miracles."[233] Proclaimed cures have thus declined as medical standards have risen.[234] This trend might reflect not only more rigorous standards at Lourdes but also improved health in society; the extreme conditions often cured at Lourdes in the past, such as tuberculosis, are also much rarer than they once were.[235]

Whether one feels free to count the religious context at Lourdes affects one's interpretation of the results. One scholar skeptical of supernatural approaches readily grants that the healings occur. He affirms that "some utterly extraordinary cures" have occurred there,[236] noting that enemies of the Catholic Church and leading medical scientists like Alexis Carrel have been persuaded by the data.[237] He concedes that some cases cannot even be explained psychosomatically;[238] among examples, he lists "the instant healing of a terribly disfigured face, and the instantaneous healing of a club foot on a two and one half year old child," shown by non-Catholics to be permanent. Further, he cites a news article about a three-year-old with terminal cancer and the bones being eaten away; after the healing, even "the bones in her skull grew back. Her doctor, a Protestant, said that 'miracle' would not be too strong a word to use."[239]

Yet this same scholar notes that scientists can reject the supernatural interpretation at Lourdes by suggesting that some sort of naturalistic interpretation would

231. See Lugt, "*Incubus*," 175–76.

232. Hillaire Belloc, in Mullin, *Miracles*, 219 (citing Chesterton, *Miracles*, 4, 11). Cf. the complaint of Larmer, "Explanations," 9: simply "calling an event a nonrepeatable counterinstance does not really explain its occurrence," and by labeling an event such an antisupernaturalist is merely rejecting "the theist's explanation," not providing an alternative explanation. Larmer counts multiple healings through a healer against calling them "nonrepeatable" (9–10), though miracles, like human actions, are not repeatable (cf. discussion in, e.g., Kellenberger, "Miracles," 149) or predictable in the sense expected in physics. Others might call them "a unique series of non-repeatable events" (Levine, *Problem*, 37, noting that Hume's epistemology would not accommodate these).

233. Hirschberg and Barasch, *Recovery*, 108; Shorter, *Witch Doctor*, 218–19.

234. Cranston, *Miracle*, 115.

235. Ibid., 116.

236. Diamond, "Miracles," 311.

237. Ibid., 312; he notes on 313 that scientists "unanimously" concur that these healings take place there.

238. Ibid., 312.

239. Ibid., citing *Newsweek*, Aug. 9, 1971. For the cures of children at Lourdes, see Cranston, *Miracle*, 227–46.

arise if only we had sufficient evidence. The collocation of natural factors in this case might occur together only one in ten million times, he argues, but, because he assumes the miraculous impossible, must have occurred here.[240] Scientists need autonomy to do their work, he insists, not having to wait to see if theologians will pronounce some event miraculous.[241] Some theologians might wish to retort that they need some autonomy to evaluate miracles without the theological premise of their entire discipline being ruled out by thinkers committed to antisupernaturalist assumptions. The scholar's antisupernatural assumptions in this case have made a fair evaluation of the data impossible.

Rigorous Standards, Hostile Assumptions

Rigorous standards can reflect integrity, but to rule out any evidence that does not meet these standards risks giving too much ground to an antisupernaturalist worldview whose advocates generally assume rather than argue their case (see chs. 5–6). While allowing for a fairly certain critical minimum, such standards should not be used negatively, to argue that miracle claims not meeting these criteria are inauthentic. Exceptionally rigorous criteria may seek to meet an unreasonable standard required by skeptics who will accept very little evidence that could be construed as contrary to their case. Skeptics on the committee at Lourdes may reject even a particularly dramatic cure as "inexplicable" no matter how many tests are run, on the principle that one must always come up with a natural explanation, which can be produced sooner or later.[242]

One sociologist thus critiques the admitted methodology of a medical investigator who denies faith healing. If the person claiming healing has had any medical treatment (hence been deemed incurable before the healing), the investigator attributed the healing to this medical treatment no matter how unusual the recovery was. By contrast, if the person did not have medical treatment, the investigator dismissed the cure as not being properly diagnosed. In other words, the investigation demonstrated nothing except its own starting assumptions that had screened out the possibility of miraculous cures in advance.[243]

With reference to Lourdes, Francis MacNutt, a PhD in theology and a leader who has been influential in the healing ministry in the Roman Catholic Church,[244] notes,

---

240. Diamond, "Miracles," 314–15, 323.

241. Ibid., 321.

242. Laurentin, *Miracles*, 91. He critiques the excessive rigor in the process at Lourdes with reasonable examples (ibid., 35, 90–91).

243. Poloma, *Assemblies*, 57–58. It is because of such clearly hostile studies that some of those involved in divine healing today are unwilling to cooperate with researchers (since those who cooperate can be misrepresented) or even see value in collecting medical documentation. Some investigators now urge practitioners of healing not to cooperate with research, since the very mind-set that strips cures of divine involvement is antithetical to the faith necessary to produce them (cf. Laurentin, *Miracles*, 95).

244. Csordas, *Language*, 32, describes him as "the first and most widely known among American Catholic Charismatic healers"; see also MacNutt's influence in Csordas, *Self*, 25, 36, 42, 230–31. For his PhD in theology, see MacNutt, *Healing*, 24.

"The doctors themselves were frustrated. Although they could see consistent evidence of God's healing power, most of these cures could not be proven as absolutely beyond the natural curative power of nature."[245] Some sorts of healings I have noted also appear at times as medical anomalies.[246] MacNutt notes that, by the standards of proof some require, proof is hard to come by: "Once, when I described to a group of doctors how I prayed and a tumor disappeared within an hour, one doctor responded that I couldn't prove that the prayer was what *caused* the tumor to go down. All I could legitimately claim was that I prayed and *after* that the tumor disappeared."

MacNutt admits that this objection is technically true;[247] it fits the narrow epistemology used in some settings (though not in much of ordinary life). Nevertheless, MacNutt contends that this pattern occurs frequently enough when he prays to invite the belief that more is at work than mere coincidence.[248] As others have observed, the clustering of a significant number of occurrences around a particular factor logically reduces the likelihood of mere "coincidence."[249] To the degree that a particular person's[250] prayers (given a sufficient sample size) increases the likelihood of unusual recovery in a statistically significant way, the probability should to that degree favor a connection between that person's prayers (or something associated with them) and the outcome rather than favor mere coincidence—unless one's worldview excludes the former possibility. Naturally, some particularly dramatic miracles invite that consideration no matter how rare they may be.[251]

Yet even two external investigators who use the stringent criterion mentioned above (admitting as a demonstrable miracle only a claim that lacks a possible natural explanation) happened upon two extraordinary cases that they felt met it. A priest in a healing service told a man to walk; the man had been wheelchair-bound for

---

245. MacNutt, *Power*, 66.

246. Some of the recorded anomalies not specifically attributed to prayer may nevertheless occur in response to prayer; this connection is not normally noted in medical records.

247. MacNutt, *Power*, 66–67. For a defense of a miraculous interpretation of tumors disappearing when other explanations are less plausible, see Young, "Petitioning," 197.

248. MacNutt, *Power*, 79; at Lourdes, see Cranston, *Miracle*, 259. Similarly, Kraft, *Power*, 126–27, claims to have witnessed "hundreds of physical healings," though most were minor (he includes the healing of a neck injury, 78–79; a "serious 30-year back problem," 127; an ankle injury, 148).

249. See, e.g., Ashe, *Miracles*, 163–64, 185, though he attributes these patterns to "subconscious" knowledge and the realm of the mind (167, 190). While concurring with Ashe's principle regarding coincidence, I am less convinced by his particular example of Nostradamus, given ambiguities. In philosophy of science, cf. the frequent understanding that the whole is greater than the parts, with a higher level of complexity (Davies, "Preface," x).

250. I specify "a particular person" because it would be difficult to assume, including from biblical perspectives, that everyone shares equally a special sensitivity for this kind of prayer. That individuals are simply religious would not by itself constitute a certain basis for this sensitivity. Nevertheless, the most consistent settings for dramatic healing reports seem to be new evangelism contexts, which are not in statistically testable settings (bringing us back to the relevance of the case study approach for this kind of research). Many of those I interviewed concerning healings acknowledged God's sovereignty and recognized that healings were not disbursed according to merit.

251. Cf. Spraggett, *Kuhlman*, 61, arguing that paranormal healings were too common in Kuhlman's meetings to be attributed to mere chance. Avoiding theological explanations, Spraggett calls it simply, "anti-chance" (62).

twenty years, and his muscles and nerves could not sustain him walking. Yet he walked—though his astonished doctor found that his muscles and nerves still should be incapable of doing so—for three months until his muscles and nerves also were restored.[252] Likewise, one healing of a four-year-old attributed to Mother Seton was not written up in a medical journal because the hematologist said (in 1993) that he was afraid to do so.[253] The particular investigators to whom I refer here do not seem to offer these reports from the standpoint of traditional religious conviction: they allow that perhaps psychological factors were at work;[254] perhaps God acted, they opine, but perhaps "God" is simply some sort of "extrabiological energy."[255]

Prejudice in the Academy?

Assumptions help shape how we read evidence as well as what evidence we acknowledge. Hostility toward recognizing unusual healings and even toward respecting supernatural interpretations as a legitimate academic perspective is less intense than it once was but still exists in some quarters. Many have complained about such prejudices, but bias and academic politics have a long history in no wise limited to this issue. Philosophic assumptions have frequently shaped even scientific paradigms. It has therefore always been important (though not always popular) for some observers to call to the academy's attention the uneven criteria we sometimes employ in evaluating paradigms.

Prejudice against Religion and Meteorites

I have noted that a hematologist admitted that he feared to write about a religiously connected healing in a medical journal.[256] By now the reader should be aware that while faith is often assumed to be a controlling bias,[257] academic skepticism can also be a controlling and even coercive bias. This bias can include hostility toward faith perspectives, a demand for conformity with dominant academic beliefs,[258] and the risk of "losing prestigious appointments";[259] it has also been described as "the anti-tenure variable."[260]

252. Hirschberg and Barasch, *Recovery*, 113–15. At Lourdes the functionality of an organ the functionality of which is medically impossible, such as seeing through eyes the optic nerves of which remain atrophied, appears as a special miracle (Cranston, *Miracle*, 136).

253. Hirschberg and Barasch, *Recovery*, 137.

254. Ibid., 138 (but would this fit the four-year-old?).

255. Ibid., 144.

256. Ibid., 137.

257. Against treating faith as a bias that must be bracketed out (in contrast to biases such as anti-faith), see, e.g., Padgett, "Advice."

258. See nuanced discussion in Marsden, *Outrageous Idea*, 3–7, 13–24.

259. Matthews and Clark, *Faith Factor*, 58. For one example, see the physician (who later won a Nobel Prize elsewhere) in Nichols, "Miracles," 707; Cranston, *Miracle*, 35 (who also notes another medical student whose thesis was rejected because it studied cures at Lourdes).

260. David Larson, cited in Matthews, Larson, and Barry, *Bibliography*, ii; also see Sherrill and Larson, "Anti-Tenure Factor." A naturalistic philosopher points out that scientific journals, as opposed to philosophic ones, will not accept articles arguing from theistic premises (Smith, "Metaphilosophy," 197).

A recent sociological study concludes that most religious scientists remain silent about their faith, fearing disdain from peers and discrimination in their career.[261] Some whose convictions were known mentioned specific occasions of discrimination.[262] Those dissociating faith from science feel less pressure to "closet" their convictions,[263] even at times to the extent of warning that any students who might wish to express religious opinions should drop the class.[264] In one study, only a third of professors in the natural sciences professed belief in God (in contrast to perhaps 95 percent of the general population).[265] More than one-third of science professors at elite universities envisioned no "positive role for religious people, institutions, and ideas on their campuses."[266] Despite the religious roots of many Western universities and divinity schools at their own universities, some professors even maintain that the existence of divinity schools is dangerous, tantamount to endorsing religion and undermining science.[267] While such avidly antireligious voices in elite research universities account for only 5 percent of the interviewees in the research study, they are a very vocal minority.[268]

Some scholars warn that typical academic discourse, far from being neutral, represents its own subculture "of disbelief,"[269] and sociologist Andrew Greeley, who had also attended a pre-Vatican II seminary, complains that "the academy had its own dogmas at least as rigid" as in that seminary with respect to paranormal claims.[270] Some scholars complain that belief in miracles has been marginalized

261. Ecklund, Science, 43–45; cf. religious scientists' concerns about marginalization on 73; experience or perceptions of discrimination, 116–22; closeted faith, on 76, 79, 100–102; one hostile scientist's active suppression of religious voices on 78. Some criticize expressly religious schools for "considering religion in hiring decisions," yet feared allowing known religious individuals to obtain jobs in their own department (ibid., 95).

262. Ibid., 117. Although the numbers were only 8 percent in the natural sciences and 12 percent in the social sciences, these percentages account for a significant percentage of those whose religious convictions are known (only 9 percent of scientists profess no doubt about God's existence; see ibid., 16).

263. Cf. ibid., 79–80, 83–84.

264. Ibid., 84 (noting the professor's open disdain even for sociologists of religion who simply research people's beliefs); cf. ibid., 154.

265. Llewellyn, "Events," 241. For scientists in general, surveys published in Nature have suggested that roughly 40 percent affirm a personal, prayer-answering God, but the proportion is significantly lower among scientists in elite universities; see Brooke, "Secularized," 231, following especially Larson and Witham, "Keeping"; Larson and Witham, "Reject."

266. Ecklund, Science, 91; cf. also some examples in ibid., 94–95. Conversely, 42 percent allowed for a positive role (often "supporting the private expression of religion"; ibid., 110).

267. Ibid., 97. Some others felt that such schools could exist, but "not to be given the same legitimacy or resources as science departments" (104). That concern, at least, is unfounded; in view of funding sources, there seems little danger of resource equity.

268. Ibid., 105–6.

269. McClenon, Events, 20. Statistically, skepticism about the paranormal increases with status in the scientific community, making deviance problematic there (xii), but in the United States, scientific training does not decrease the incidence of anomaly reports, and skepticism among elite scientists and academics does not dominate science undergraduates (35).

270. Greeley, Sociology, 5; cf. the new discussion in Yancey, Scholarship (59, 64, 66, 98–101, 116–19, 142, 153–54, 173). A nonpracticing Jewish scientist urged more openness to religious voices in academia, complaining, "the only diversity they [academics] don't like is intellectual diversity" (Ecklund, Science, 124).

as virtually "heretical" in some academic circles.[271] A psychologist notes that peer review normally precludes the publication of events without natural explanations or that are not replicable, so that miracles almost by definition are anomalies excluded from appearing in scientific publications.[272] When their very possibility is in turn excluded in the name of science, because of self-restrictions in scientific epistemology, we are back to Hume's circular exclusion of miracles by definition. One doctor who recounts miracles that have occurred in his practice also notes that the prejudice against miracle reports is so strong that even doctors who have seen miracles are often reluctant to risk their reputation to verify them. To include mention of prayer in the notes, which go to referral doctors and can be used by malpractice lawyers, carries serious risks in some places.[273] More generally, beyond theistic premises, anthropologists have sometimes feared to publish "anomalous experiences" from their field work for fear of stigmatization.[274]

Less coercively, most of us in the academy (including myself) have been trained to work only with naturalistic methods. This training makes some sense in terms of dialogue on areas of common ground with our peers, yet it still predisposes us against attending to data that do not fit this paradigm or to viewing attempts to do so as of questionable academic value.[275] One doctor complains that historians fail to ask the obvious question that doctors would ask of miracle accounts: "Were these patients healed as described or not?" He attributes this reticence to ask the obvious question to fear of "academic suicide."[276]

Keep in mind that the bias that I describe here is not that found in religious ministries openly committed to the premise of supernatural healing but rather in academic circles that publicly pride themselves on objectivity and a supposed antithesis to religiously conditioned biases. Philosopher Robert Larmer recounted to me an occasion when he was dialoguing with another professor, who considered belief in miracles nothing more than a "two-thousand year-old superstition" incompatible with science. When Professor Larmer pointed out that there are

271. Gregory, "Secular Bias," 138. Basil Mitchell, a long-time professor at Oxford, notes the "prevailing orthodoxy" against faith and danger to one's academic reputation (Clark, *Philosophers*, 40–41); I recall during my doctoral work one of my favorite religion professors insisting that any professor who publicly acknowledged belief in God should be fired (a view happily not promulgated by the department more generally, which tolerated more diversity).

272. Llewellyn, "Events," 253; cf. also Gorsuch, "Limits," 282. Ellens, "Conclusion," 301–2, suggests that scientific journals should in fact publish, hence collect, reports of paranormal experience, so they can be documented and examined together; he notes a small number of journals studying these anomalies.

273. Chauncey Crandall, phone interview, May 30, 2010; cf. idem, personal correspondence, Oct. 8, 2010.

274. McClenon and Nooney, "Experiences," 50 (citing Salamone, "Bori," 15). Turner, "Advances," 37, notes that even as late as the 1970s, her husband, she, and other anthropologists felt the pressure to remain "mainstream" in print (i.e., avoiding paranormal claims) for the sake of job security. At the time, challenging the settled theories of Durkheim regarding religion was risky (Turner, "Advances," 39–40).

275. As one open-minded agnostic scientist honestly puts it, "As a result of my scientific studies, I have a deeply rooted belief in the philosophies of reductionism and materialism—the view that the whole is equal to the sum of the parts—even with respect to questions relating to life and mind" (Jastrow, "Forces," 48).

276. Gardner, "Miracles," 1928.

reports of miracles occurring today that can be subject to investigation, his detractor warned that it would waste scientists' time to check out such claims. Which of the two was really functioning on "blind faith"?[277]

Lest anyone (presumably outside the academy itself) suppose that scholarly consensus always follows data and proves impervious to bias, we can recall the history that I have already noted (ch. 6) concerning academic resistance to new scientific paradigms. Historically, many Enlightenment advances defined themselves over against popular superstition, which was often intertwined with popular religion. This background to the radical Enlightenment has unfortunately bequeathed a legacy of suspicion against claims more generally that could be associated with religion, regardless of other possible ways of reading the evidence.

What Michael Polanyi has observed about science is relevant to scholarship more generally. Science normally initially ignores claims that go against established consensus, he notes, thereby screening out of consideration a mass of claims or data likely to prove false or irrelevant. The problematic by-product of this necessary caution, however, is "the risk of occasionally disregarding thereby true evidence which conflicts (or seems to conflict) with the current teachings of science."[278] As noted earlier, paradigm shifts normally meet initial resistance.[279]

Thus, for example, whereas today scientists study the natural effects of hypnotism, early investigators were barred from medical and scientific circles because of the technique's public associations with Mesmer and his followers.[280] More dramatically, radical Enlightenment scientists reacted against popular supernaturalist interpretations of meteorites by denying the existence of meteorites altogether. Polanyi observes, "During the eighteenth century the French Academy of Science stubbornly denied the evidence for the fall of meteorites, which seemed massively obvious to everybody else. Their opposition to the superstitious beliefs which a popular tradition attached to such heavenly intervention blinded them to the facts in question."[281] Because Paris set the intellectual trends of the day, museums in at least five other European countries discarded their meteorites.[282] One need

---

277. Robert Larmer, personal correspondence, Aug. 5, 2009.

278. Polanyi, *Knowledge*, 138.

279. E.g., Kuhn, *Structure*, 64–65, 107, 133, 169.

280. McClenon, *Events*, 188–89; Walsh, *Shamanism*, 179–80. Mesmer witnessed the ministry of Father Gassner but attributed the cures to animal magnetism, by which he sought to produce his own cures (Major, *Faiths*, 180–88).

281. Polanyi, *Knowledge*, 138; noted again on 274; see also McClenon, *Events*, 2. On the wide variety of natural phenomena often construed as portents in sixteenth- and seventeenth-century popular sources, see Daston, "Facts," 102–3, 106; but theological agendas increasingly drove the rise of more natural interpretations for unexplained phenomena (Daston, "Facts," 107).

282. Polanyi, *Knowledge*, 138n2. This observation is not meant to deny that museums, like anyone else, are sometimes taken in by fraud; cf. Toby Sterling, "'Moon Rock' in Dutch Museum Is Just Petrified Wood," Associated Press, Aug. 27, 2009, accessed at http://news.yahoo.com/s/ap/20090827/ap_on _re_eu/eu_netherlands_not_moon_rock; accessed Aug. 27, 2009. Cf. Spraggett, *Kuhlman*, 54, regarding Lavoisier; on 53–55, he also notes how other published scientific statements of certainty—such as the impossibility of blood circulation, chloroform, air flight, and space travel—were ultimately and sometimes quickly overturned by facts conveniently ignored by existing theories. One may also compare the

not attach theological significance to meteorites to note that a bias against that interpretation functioned as a prejudice that disregarded facts. Would such a bias necessarily disappear in cases where facts might more readily support a supernatural interpretation than they did in the case of meteorites?

Philosophic Assumptions behind Scientific Paradigms

While surveys reveal that even most "elite" scientists are not antireligious (contrary to misinformed stereotypes), the proportion of those holding some particular religious views differs starkly from the general population.[283] Some members of the more hostile minority affirm a priori that no "supernatural" explanation should even be discussed at a university.[284] Scientists associated with top-ranked research universities are only about one-seventh as likely to strongly believe in God as the general U.S. population is.[285] Yet the *reasons* for those views usually have little to do with science itself, and sometimes lack an intellectual basis.[286] Sometimes they even reflect a stereotyping of religion based on its worst examples, expressing a form of "religious illiteracy."[287] Many scientifically inclined persons who rule out supernatural explanations a priori may do so not because the data in their specialties demand this approach but because their initial plausibility structures reflect philosophic assumptions borrowed from outside their discipline.[288] (Purely theological writers pontificating on matters of science naturally run the same risk.)

---

seventeenth-century religious belief in spirit possession with the alternative contemporary "scientific" belief in "black humors," which proved unverifiable (Azouvi, "Rationalité").

283. E.g., Catholics compose 27 percent of the U.S. population, but only 9 percent (one-third that figure) among elite scientists; evangelical Protestants, 28 percent and 2 percent, respectively; and, most strikingly, black Protestants, 8 percent and 0.2 percent, respectively; they are about three times more likely to be religiously unaffiliated (Ecklund, *Science*, 15, 33, 152). Still, about a fifth of elite scientists attend religious services (often mainline Protestant) regularly (ibid., 151), and 39 percent claim that their religion or spirituality influences their interpersonal behavior (ibid., 76).

284. Ecklund, *Science*, 96.

285. See ibid., 16. More generally, 36 percent of elite scientists believe in God (ibid., 35), compared to 94 percent of the general U.S. population (ibid., 36); that is, others are two or three times more likely to believe in God. Nevertheless, over 20 percent of these scientists who do not view themselves as religious view themselves as "spiritual" (ibid., 51), and the rising, younger generation of scientists tends to be more religious than their seniors (ibid., 48).

286. Ibid., 17, 151. One chemist, a religious believer, complained that some of his colleagues react against religion in an "anti-intellectual" manner (120). Examples of reasons for religious skepticism were the belief that religion let them down (20–21) and bad experiences with religion (21–22). For one extreme example: one scientist friend, one of the most brilliant people I have ever met, confided in me (Aug. 7, 1988) that he was an agnostic (at that time) because he could not believe in a god who would have let his girlfriend break up with him.

287. Ecklund, *Science*, 154 (for misconceptions, see 152–55).

288. See our discussion of the earlier influence of philosophy of religion in chs. 5 and 6. Ecklund, *Science*, 49, applies to the relationship between science and religion the sociological observation that groups with minimal contact tend to harbor greater prejudices. From a sociological standpoint, some scientists' critiques of religion serve a boundary function of exalting science at other disciplines' expense (Wuthnow, "Contradictions," 163–64).

Philosophic approaches drove many paradigm shifts in science, both positively and negatively.[289] Isaac Newton, for example, argued that matter was inert partly for theological reasons, to underline the distinction between creature and Creator.[290] One may illustrate the matter more extensively from Johannes Kepler, the heliocentric astronomer who discovered the elliptical paths of planets and founded the modern approach to optics. Early in his career, Kepler was a theological student who found a job teaching mathematics.[291] Like Galileo, he believed that science and the Bible could be harmonized without damage to either, partly by not taking every biblical passage literally.[292]

Kepler conceived some of his ideas by adopting alternative ancient philosophic premises that challenged current philosophic paradigms. Though not directly relevant to his famous discoveries, Kepler was obsessed "with the harmony of the [heavenly] spheres and the five Pythagorean solids."[293] His original reasons for preferring Copernicus's barely known heliocentric theory were "metaphysical," based on an analogy to the Trinity in the heavens, which served his understanding of how the "heavens declare the glory of God" (Ps 19:1).[294] Following ancient ideologies, Kepler sought to calculate the "music" of the "heavenly spheres"[295] and

289. On modern science's metaphysical foundations, see, e.g., Burtt, *Foundations*.

290. Murphy, "Apologetics," 116. He also managed to subsume cosmic history within Archbishop James Ussher's famous chronology, with creation in 4004 B.C.E. (Frankenberry, *Faith*, 103–4), a view we regard as astonishing today.

291. Koestler, "Kepler," 49. For Kepler, "perfect knowledge is always mathematical" (Burtt, *Foundations*, 67), though he insisted that the observable world would verify correct mathematical constructs (Burtt, *Foundations*, 71). His later conflict with the Lutheran Church involved the Lord's Supper, not science.

292. Frankenberry, *Faith*, 38; for some of his explanations, see Kepler, *Astronomy*, 59–66, 385–86 (reproduced in Frankenberry, *Faith*, 47–53). Francis Bacon assigned faith and science to distinct yet valid epistemic spheres, science dealing with empirical data and religion appealing "to revelation and final causes"; nature could not, however, reveal God's character (ibid., 61). Bacon spoke of "our Saviour Christ" and the Trinity (ibid., 64, 66, citing Bacon, *Advancement*, 112–13). Pascal was more emphatically Christocentric (Frankenberry, *Faith*, 80), valuing experience with God over science for human existence (material from *Pensées* in ibid., 100–101).

293. Koestler, "Kepler," 57; see also Frankenberry, *Faith*, 36–37. Copernicus's approach appealed to Pythagorean and Platonic principles as an alternative to Aristotelianism (Burtt, *Foundations*, 52–56). Copernicus was a Catholic Church canon (albeit not a priest) suspected of sympathy with Lutheranism (see Repcheck, *Secret*, 68–69, 106–7, 129–31, 163–68; Vanessa Gera, "Astronomer Copernicus reburied as hero," at http://news.yahoo.com/s/ap/20100522/ap_on_re_eu/eu_poland_copernicus_reburied; accessed May 22, 2010). He cited Scripture and, contrary to popular distortions, was supported by some Protestant church leaders and scholars (Gingerich, "Copernicus," adapted from the then-forthcoming Gingerich, *Book*). Copernicus also drew on prior heliocentric thought (Hart, *Delusions*, 60–62). Copernicus and those who embraced his views found no contradiction with their faith (Danielson, "Demoted"), including Kepler (Danielson, "Demoted," 55–56). Kepler was a Lutheran who preferred Calvin's approach to the Lord's Supper yet rejected predestination (Frankenberry, *Faith*, 38); he and Galileo both appealed to Plato as a source (Efron, "Christianity," 83), as did the later homology of Richard Owen, on which Darwin drew, and from which Owen inferred a form of theistic evolution (Rupke, "Theory," 140).

294. Koestler, "Kepler," 50; Gingerich, "Scientist," 28; Burtt, *Foundations*, 60–61; Frankenberry, *Faith*, 35–36.

295. Burtt, *Foundations*, 63; Frankenberry, *Faith*, 34–35 (cf. 56–57, citing Kepler, *Harmony*, 146–47). Pythagoras reportedly calculated planetary distances in terms of music (Pliny *Nat.* 2.20.84); he allegedly meditated on the harmony of the heavenly spheres (Iamblichus *V.P.* 15.65–66). For the rhythm or music

viewed as one of his crowning achievements his geometric calculations of planetary distances, which have proved faulty.[296] His view that mathematics could elucidate the harmony of nature, in accordance with divine design, rests on ancient Greek philosophy.[297] He also accepted the widespread notion of his day, astonishing to most readers today, that astrology offered some value.[298]

Yet despite the faulty premises of much of his sky physics, it led him to reject the widely accepted philosophic necessity of motion in circles, hence cosmic epicycles[299] (a view linked with incorrect traditional views of planets' movements). It also led him to articulate "the three correct laws of planetary motion."[300] By contrast, while he came up with the theory of universal gravitation, his ideology led him, like Galileo and Descartes, to reject this theory. It did not serve his system, and gravity as a mysterious force seemed to be a return to medieval mysticism.[301] That error could lead Kepler to reject truth is not surprising, but how did erroneous grounds lead him to some true conclusions? Rather than simply accepting consensus, Kepler followed intuitions, some accurate and some inaccurate, and allowed empirical facts to adjust his insights.[302]

Kepler's explorations illustrate Polanyi's insight about balancing competing tensions. "Unfettered intuitive speculation would lead to extravagant wishful conclusions; while rigorous fulfilment of any set of critical rules would completely paralyse discovery." Thus the scientist's conscience must arbitrate between the two.[303] Scholarship should be not reproached for appropriate caution, but it must also be open to a paradigm shift if sufficient neglected evidence is brought to scholars' attention. Contrary to what many people suppose, even the most empirically

---

of heavenly spheres, see, e.g., Cicero *Pub.* 6.18.18–19; Philo *Creation* 70; Lucian *Dance* 8; Maximus of Tyre 37.5 (citing Pythagoras); Menander Rhetor 2.17, 442.28–443.2; cf. Murray, *Stages*, 175. The praise of heavenly bodies in *1 En.* 41:7 might but need not allude to this concept. Aristotle knew the Pythagorean view (*Heavens* 2.9, 290b.12–29) and argued against it (2.9, 290b.30–291a.26).

296. Burtt, *Foundations*, 62.

297. Ibid., 69. Similarly, Galileo, ignoring Kepler on planets' elliptical orbits, maintained the mathematically unworkable circular orbits of Copernicus (Hart, *Delusions*, 66). Meanwhile, Copernicus had maintained them on the ancient grounds that whatever was perfect was circular (62)—what thinkers today might consider circular reasoning.

298. Burtt, *Foundations*, 69n45, citing here especially Kepler's *De Fundamentis Astrologiae Certioribus* (*Opera* 1.417ff.).

299. Koestler, "Kepler," 55.

300. Ibid., 54.

301. Ibid., 52–54, 57; cf. Frankenberry, *Faith*, 37.

302. Koestler, "Kepler," 56. For Kepler, error chanced on truth only rarely (McMullin, "Virtues," 499).

303. Polanyi, *Science*, 41. Licona, *Resurrection*, 104, cites MIT scientists who suggest that much exploration in science (like much in the humanities) follows the investigator's instincts. Polkinghorne, *Reality*, 95, notes that experience (e.g., the quantum world) sometimes exceeds expectations of coherence with conventional theories. Montgomery, "Science," 150–52, complains about a system that forces all data to fit a naturalistic paradigm. Subordinating all particulars to the general, he argues, precludes discovery, and explains why it took science an unnecessary extra half century to discover xenon tetrafluoride and other compounds with inert gases; generalizations based on the periodic table seemed to preclude it. By definition miracles involve particularities hence cannot be dismissed by appealing to general patterns (cf. Duffin, *Miracles*, 187).

minded disciplines must be open to revising hypotheses.[304] I believe that the data available today invite a challenge to Hume's antisupernaturalism; they certainly challenge a major assumption on which Hume builds his case, namely, the denial of credible eyewitnesses.

Academic politics has long played a role in the acceptability of views. Galileo suffered at the hands of fellow academics, in that case with much church backing;[305] others suffer from it today, often with much secular backing. Some seventeenth-century scientists gained cultural prestige for scientific epistemology by demonstrating its utility for religion (hence inadvertently "modernizing" religion), but the social power situation has now reversed, with scientific epistemology not surprisingly holding greater cultural prestige.[306] Cultural prestige helps shape the acceptability of views in circles that share those cultural predilections.

Not only philosophic shifts but also academic politics have created the common perception of hostility between science and faith. Yet it was the politics of knowledge, rather than an incompatibility between science and faith for many ordinary scientists and believers, that drove the dichotomy between science and faith.[307] The history of that dichotomy has been severely distorted in antireligious polemic.[308] Indeed, the myth of opposition between religion and science was cre-

304. Ecklund, *Science*, 108, cites physicist Sylvester James Gates Jr., director of String and Particle Theory at the University of Maryland, as noting that scientists can revise their beliefs in light of new evidence; "Science is about measuring things. It is not about truth, but it is about reducing the falsity of our beliefs"; Polkinghorne, *Reality*, 3. Similarly, Stephen Jay Gould recognized intuition and cultural shaping as factors in science and why its views change (*Mismeasure*, 21–23, as cited in Frankenberry, *Faith*, 259).

305. Galileo and his supporters were no less men of the church than their accusers were (cf. my 141n202; Brooke, *Science*, 78–79); academic politics drove much of the debate (see, e.g., Hart, *Delusions*, 62–66; Brooke, *Science*, 37; Hummel, *Connection*). Galileo insisted that it was Scripture's interpreters in the church hierarchy, and not Scripture itself, that erred (Frankenberry, *Faith*, 4, 10, quoting him). His real nemesis was the dominant Aristotelianism (ibid., 8), and he expressly borrowed Augustine's approach to accommodation to articulate and defend his astronomical views as compatible with Scripture (see Lee, "Galileo"; for Augustine's reading of Genesis in light of the science of his era, see Lindberg, "Rise," 18). For commonalities between Galileo and Jesuit thinkers, see, e.g., Brooke, "Science," 8. Frankenberry, *Faith*, 6, contends that the heliocentrism Galileo advocated "was gaining the day within the Catholic hierarchy," but Galileo's overzealous pronouncement on Scripture interpretation created a political reaction. Even the Inquisition torturing or jailing Galileo was a rationalist myth (see Finocchiaro, "Galileo"; sources in Ecklund, *Science*, 208n1), though he did endure house arrest (Frankenberry, *Faith*, 6). Meanwhile, painting all religion with the brush of the Inquisition is somewhat analogous (though not in degree) to painting science with the brush of Nazi doctors like Josef Mengele; others (like Wuthnow, "Contradictions," 166) cite the Tuskegee experiment on syphilis-infected African-American men. (Despite the negative legacy of the Inquisition, cf. comments qualifying popular misconceptions in Hart, *Delusions*, 80–86, following Kamen, *Inquisition*, 28–54, 73.) Similarly, many today underline the atheistic ideologies of Hitler and Stalin (e.g., Freeman Dyson's 2000 Templeton Speech [in Frankenberry, *Faith*, 379–80]; Polkinghorne, *Physics*, 14), but one can hardly fault all atheists for their atrocities.

306. Harrison, "Miracles," 510.

307. See Poewe, "Rethinking," 253–54.

308. Cf., e.g., observations in Brooke, "Science," 19; idem, *Reconstructing Nature*; Barbour, *Religion and Science*, 24–29, 64–65; Welch, "Myths," 32–33, 35, 37; Wildman, "Quest," 48–49; Lindberg and Numbers, *Essays*; Numbers, "Aggressors"; idem, *Galileo*; Livingstone, Hart, and Noll, *Perspective*; Livingstone, *Defenders*. Note especially biologist Asa Gray, Darwin's contemporary defender in the United States and

ated by some radical French Enlightenment thinkers in the eighteenth century to combat the conservative French Catholic Church, but it thoroughly misrepresents the history of science.[309] Two propagandistic books in the late nineteenth century, no longer accepted as accurate accounts, popularized the myth for Anglophone readers.[310] The arguments between many theologians and many scientists in some periods have been no greater than arguments among disciplines within the natural sciences themselves.[311] What conflicts existed long ago are minimal today;[312] indeed, whatever their personal faith, only about 15 percent of elite scientists today accept the conflict paradigm.[313] In view of such factors, one may lament that some

a committed evangelical; see Livingstone, *Defenders*, xi, 49, 60–64, 72–73, 76–77, 113, 171; Numbers, "Aggressors," 28–29. Many evangelicals of Darwin's era (including Gray, Charles Hodge, and B. B. Warfield) viewed evolution as the clearest evidence of design; it was only the attribution of such patterns to pure chance to which they objected (e.g., Livingstone, *Defenders*, 49, 63–64, 95, 104–5, 116, 135–38; cf. Polkinghorne, *Reality*, 39). Darwin himself originally marketed his theory as reflecting divine laws (Moore, "Darwin's Faith," 146); his *Origin of Species* (1859) employed "*creation*" and its cognates over one hundred times," opposing "miraculous creation" but affirming a theistic argument "for creation by law" (147). He lost his faith for personal theological reasons, not over evolution per se (146–48), but "never published a word directly against Christianity or belief in God" (151). The alleged witness of his deathbed conversion story is questionable, but she included personal details regarding Darwin's home life difficult for her to have known (148–49).

309. See Lindberg, *Beginnings*; concisely, idem, "Adversaries" (here esp. 44). On Rousseau and Voltaire and their different forms of deism, see concisely, e.g., Brown, *Philosophy*, 81–86 (on Voltaire, cf. also idem, *Thought*, 288–94; on Rousseau, 294–99; Burne, "Rousseau," 145–47; on Voltaire's racial hierarchies and anti-Semitism, see Herrick, *Mythologies*, 164); on the influence of English deists on such authors, see Loos, *Miracles*, 14. On the myth of opposition more recently, see also, e.g., Polkinghorne and Beale, *Questions*, 56, 141–42. Some see it as the dominant model (Wiebe, "Compatibility," 169, though going on to note various alternative models). Approaches to the relationship between "science" and "religion" often reify both categories into abstractions, severing them from actual scientists and persons of faith (Frankenberry, *Faith*, vii).

310. Hart, *Delusions*, 56, noting that Draper and White felt free to invent evidence as needed. See Numbers, "Introduction," 1–3, 6–7; idem, "Aggressors," 31–33; Shank, "Suppressed," 19; Cormack, "Flat," 28–29; Park, "Dissection," 43, 47–49; Shackelford, "Bruno," 60–61; Principe, "Catholics," 99–100; Schoepflin, "Anesthesia," 123, 129–30; Livingstone, "Huxley," 153–54; Brooke, *Science*, 34–36.

311. E.g., when in the nineteenth century physicists insisted (against geologists) that the earth was at most one hundred million years old, and physicists argued whether light consisted of particles or waves (Gerhart and Russell, "Mathematics," 127). See further Numbers, "Aggressors," 50.

312. So Woodward, *Miracles*, 22. One might except from this particular spheres of inquiry, particularly arguments raised by young-earth creationists, but most theistic academics (including myself) do not hold that view. Indeed, contrary to popular misperceptions based on a novelistic drama, even populist Democratic politician William Jennings Bryan, best known for his problematic response to evolution, did not hold that view (Larson, "Trial," 182–84).

313. Ecklund, *Science*, 19. Fewer than 5 percent are "extremely hostile" (78, 150). Stephen Jay Gould, a respectful agnostic, doubted that science and religion needed to experience conflict (although he denied any overlap in their spheres of inquiry; Gould, *Rocks*, 4, and *Dinosaur*, 48, as cited in Frankenberry, *Faith*, 254, 262; see also comment in Numbers, "Aggressors," 47–48). Although most scientists view fundamentalism (and evangelicalism, which they inaccurately identify with it) negatively, largely because of issues like young-earth creationism, most have a positive view of those seeking to reconcile science and religion (Ecklund, *Science*, 46–47, who also notes on 155 that evangelicalism itself is changing). Comparing the views of trained scientists with those of rank-and-file churchgoers might be like comparing biblical scholars with amateur scientists lacking graduate training in science. On average, religious leaders appear more approving of scientific endeavor than scientists of religion (Duffin, *Miracles*, 185).

earlier theologians bought into the Kantian dichotomy between objective reason and subjective faith[314] too easily.

Even apart from objections to defining away potential objective grounds for faith and treating God radically differently than less controversial objects of belief, many philosophers of science today recognize that even scientific inquiry is sometimes less than totally objective[315] and that theoretical models, necessary as they are in science, inevitably both structure data and ignore some data.[316] Although theories provide maps of data and correlations,[317] they structure them[318] and may be themselves semantically reframed in the light of new data.[319] These observations concerning the philosophy of science are also relevant to academic paradigms more generally. Even direct psychological experiments can be distorted by research bias, since researchers' framing of questions or nonverbal cues can inadvertently direct participants toward desired responses.[320] The widespread assumption of antisupernaturalism has been allowed to shape academic readings of the data, but scholars have rarely publicly revisited that data with alternative models in mind. For example, two anthropologists observe that scientists who confine their study to "normal" phenomena reinforce traditional paradigms, but taking into account extensive "anomalous" or extranormal data not readily explained by these paradigms invites "scientific innovations."[321]

Uneven Criteria

As I have attempted to illustrate (and will seek to illustrate concisely but more concretely in ch. 15), many scholars still explain away massive amounts of data based on Humean antisupernaturalism. This approach forces them to apply standards that are inconsistent (as well as hostile to the perspectives of most of the world's cultures). If one applied to the medical profession the criteria that most critics apply to supernatural claims—that is, discounting any cures or remissions that conceivably *could* occur without intervention—we might have few medical cures.[322] Such a test would of course be patently unfair; medical technology dramati-

---

314. Cf., e.g., Barbour, *Religion and Science*, 46–47, for summary; Brown, *Philosophy*, 94–97; McGowan, *Authenticity*, 53. The problem continues today; some speak of religion as "based on feeling" (e.g., d'Aubigne, "Force," 157, though going on to affirm some value in this; cf. Karle, "No Way," 181–82; perhaps Holley, "Existence").

315. Maxwell, "Theories," 31; Bird, "Turn," 76.

316. See Hesse, "Language," 72–73; Sankey, "Method," 249–50; cf. Worrall, "Change."

317. Hanson, "Theory," 273.

318. Ibid., 237. Empiricism observes facts, but arrangement and interpretation are necessary for significance (Lonergan, *Insight*, 411–12; cf. Meyer, *Realism*, 11–12).

319. Hanson, "Theory," 233–34. Barbour, *Religion and Science*, 108, warns that "*all data are theory-laden*" (emphasis his; cf. 125–27).

320. See Pekala and Cardeña, "Issues," 56 (on "demand characteristics").

321. McClenon and Nooney, "Experiences," 57.

322. In one study, treatment by prayer and laying on of hands (which was common, though not ubiquitous, in NT cases of healing) produced results regarding joint swelling comparable to that from some medical treatments and better than those of educational interventions, though this could be partly

cally improves cure rates for most physical disorders. Yet some critics dismiss all claims of supernatural healing by arguing that there are or may be natural analogies to such recoveries on some occasions, a dismissal that seems particularly forced when applied to multiple cases of blind eyes healed or the dead resuscitated after prayer. Likewise, in evaluating cure rates, it is inappropriate to lump genuine physicians with quacks. Yet all supernatural healing claims and claimants are generally lumped together, when in fact cure rates may differ among them.

Some critics of supernatural healing curiously exclude the significance of any healing claims if medical technology could produce the same result.[323] Yet this criterion makes little sense in cases where such medical technology was not applied. The criterion in effect claims that anything that humans could do (even though they did not) cannot be attributed to divine agency, in effect excluding most of the evidence. Most conditions can be cured at least sometimes by medical technology now, and such technology is happily always improving; does this improvement logically reduce the miraculous character of cures earlier or independently occurring *without* such technology? If so, one could exclude not only cures that can also be duplicated naturally and medically but also those that might conceivably be cured in the future—that is, any cure. But would not such a criterion for miracles, which could effectively eliminate appeal to any claims, ultimately screen out any genuine cases of supernatural causation if there were some?

If so, the criterion decides the debate's outcome by default on the basis of a logically unrelated question; there is no necessary logical relationship between the possibility of an illness being cured medically and the possibility of it being cured supernaturally. That is, one can argue that a person who received curative medical treatment may have been cured by such treatment, but one cannot argue that a person who did *not receive such treatment,* yet was cured, was cured by such treatment. The potentially medical curability of an illness is therefore not a legitimate criterion for determining the possibility of supernatural involvement in the ailment's cure, when the medical cure was not applied.

Yet a similar prejudicial line of argumentation has long been privileged. Thus, for example, one nineteenth-century skeptic designed his argument to a priori

---

psychosomatic (Matthews, Marlowe, and MacNutt, "Effects," 1185; for the susceptibility of rheumatoid arthritis to "psychosomatic improvements," see Lerman, "Arthritis," as cited in Brown, Mory, Williams, and McClymond, "Effects," 865). The analogy here is limited, since it is supernatural healing and not medical healing that is under dispute in much of our cultural setting. Moreover, it is precarious to cite the results of a single study as representative of what all studies would likely find. Nevertheless, it does illustrate how the criterion would unfairly screen out the vast majority of possible evidence. Further, metaphysical naturalism is disputed by more people in the world than supernatural cures are, so speaking of what is "under dispute" presupposes particular starting assumptions.

323. Cf. the complaint in Melinsky, *Miracles*, 157. Critics of supernatural healing might suggest moreover that medical technology reduces a population's overall mortality more than the sum total of individual healings do (cf. Henson, *Notes*, 18), and where such technology is widely available I presume that this observation normally would be correct. But one should not compare apples and oranges: in Christian tradition miracles are meant to draw attention to God's activity and portend the kingdom, not to cure every affliction in the present.

exclude consideration of miracle claims by noting that a naturalistic explanation might eventually emerge.[324] That the perpetual limitation of natural knowledge thereby unfairly screened out any possible evidence was not considered; he laid the burden of proof solely on supernatural claims and then placed the bar of proof for them impossibly high. Likewise, T. H. Huxley, following Hume's argument, doubted that any event could be extraordinary enough to justify the claim that its cause was supernatural.[325] Some church commissions in the 1920s reflected the same bias, as historian Robert Bruce Mullin observes: "The ground rules that the commissions established in order to validate a healing as miraculous—that is, that it could not merely be inexplicable, but also had to be unique and not found in the annals of either medicine or other religions—almost ensured that no healings would be deemed 'miracles.'"[326]

By this approach, a skeptic can reject a supernatural explanation even when lacking a specific, plausible natural one by simply averring that a natural explanation may be forthcoming.[327] The committed skeptic can then insist that this as-yet unfulfilled potentiality must be superior to any supernatural explanation. Yet with sufficient ingenuity and confidence that a naturalistic explanation is necessary, it is *inevitable* that naturalistic solutions (often competing, mutually contradictory ones) will emerge.[328] That inevitability does not, however, guarantee that they will be *good* explanations or that they will not force too much of the evidence. As one scholar suggests, appealing to "as yet unknown laws of nature" to explain "even raisings from the dead" yields "a tremendous implausibility."[329] Such deferred natural explanations are rendered the only possible interpretations merely by the a priori exclusion of the possibility of nonnatural interpretations.[330]

324. John Tyndall, in Mullin, *Miracles*, 42.
325. Ibid. Huxley's famous debate with Bishop Samuel Wilberforce reflected a generational conflict over how science should be conducted (Livingstone, "Huxley," 158); contrary to subsequent literary traditions, little is actually known of the content or outcome of the debate (Livingstone, "Huxley").
326. Mullin, *Miracles*, 248.
327. So Alexis Carrel regarding Lourdes, in Flach, *Faith*, 40; the position noted in Basinger and Basinger, "Concept," 166; Phillips, "Miracles," 35 (demurring); Larmer, "Criteria" (arguing against it). Cf. Frank, *Persuasion*, 58: the world is full of "inexplicable cures," so assumptions determine whether one views their cause as divine. Frank's objection (lodged against claims at Lourdes) is logically correct as far as it goes, but I believe that it neglects the *cumulative* weight of numerous such cures during prayer.
328. Because science by its historic nature is methodologically committed to finding natural explanations, it may view even the greatest of anomalies as having natural explanations (cf. Fern, "Critique," 347–48). Some go so far as to concede that instant healings occur (Diamond, "Miracles," 311) but refuse to interpret them supernaturally lest naturalistic science be stripped of its autonomy (321). Because we have compartmentalized epistemological approaches in different disciplines, science that seeks naturalistic explanations is doing what it is designed to do, but we must correspondingly recognize that it is not designed to answer or pronounce on other (nonnaturalistic) questions. As noted in chs. 5–6, the view that there *is* no reality outside of naturalistic explanations is simply a presupposition.
329. Purtill, "Proofs," 48 (regarding raisings in the Gospels). Revising laws of nature to explain anomalies is sometimes harder than simply accepting anomalies (Levine, *Problem*, 180); see discussion in ch. 5.
330. Larmer, "Evidence," 51; cf. Duffin, *Miracles*, 186–87, 189, highlighting the fideism involved in such an approach.

Thus, for example, one writer insists that cures at Lourdes so far never known to remit naturally might involve some exceedingly rare circumstance like the combination of a particular blood type with the chemical waters at Lourdes. Even if this combination went undetected because it occurred only "once in every ten million persons,"[331] the author contends, once eventually discovered it could be subsumed under a new scientific rule. The author considers such a yet-undiscovered scientific explanation, which allows prediction, preferable to accepting as divine mystery the question of why some are healed and others are not.[332] Despite possible theological solutions,[333] he considers the theological quandary more difficult than the extraordinarily low probability of his alternate explanation and uses the former to justify supporting the latter. That is, his approach simply rules out from the start the possibility of a supernatural explanation (the explanation normally offered by the event's immediate witnesses).

Nevertheless, perceptions of plausibility are shaped partly by presuppositions about what sorts of explanations are open to consideration. That is, the skeptic, as noted earlier, may in effect simply rule out the possibility of supernatural explanations a priori.[334] That seems to be the case in the hypothetical example just offered. Analyses show that there is nothing particularly unusual about the bathing water at Lourdes—except that it is heavily contaminated with bacteria that nevertheless seem to fail to infect the bathers.[335] I am not Catholic, but I think that attributing the cures to chemical properties in the shrine's water is an extraordinarily implausible explanation.

Presuppositions and Burden of Proof

Such a methodology typically dismisses appeals to supernatural explanations as a tenuous god-of-the-gaps approach, since a nonsupernatural explanation may eventually emerge.[336] But when a supernatural explanation seems the most plau-

---

331. Diamond, "Miracles," 314.

332. Ibid., 315.

333. While I defer that extensive discussion to theologians, one historical and philosophic factor already noted may be kept in mind. I argued earlier that the behavior of personal beings, which function at a high level of complexity, is not predictable in terms of scientific laws in the same way that less complex nature (e.g., particles) is. This unpredictability would be even more the case for a superintelligent personality not a part of nature. Miracles are meant to be special foretastes of the future kingdom rather than the new ordinary expectation of the present.

334. As noted in ch. 5, the skeptic who is inflexibly dogmatic against miracles in effect presupposes atheism or deism, hence cannot admit evidence contrary to his or her position.

335. Cranston, *Miracle*, 59, notes that "*chemically . . . the water of the Spring at Lourdes contains no curative or medicinal properties whatever*" (emphasis hers; cf. also 259); on 58–59, she gives reports showing that chemically it is merely normal mountain drinking water. One might expect the waters to breed infection rather than the reverse, with more than two thousand bathing per day, some afflicted by syphilis or tuberculosis (56–57); but she argues (56) that infections are not known to result. She notes (58–60) that the water is heavily polluted bacterially, yet testing showed that none of these microbes (some normally harmful) caused harm to test animals. On 60 she notes that test animals injected with water considered comparable did become infected. See also Woodard, *Faith*, 58–59.

336. E.g., Mott, "Science," 66, though he believes that theism is the only valid explanation for human consciousness, which he thinks will remain a permanent "gap." If "miracle" is defined only as what cannot be

sible explanation to the average observer genuinely not yet committed to either thoroughgoing naturalism or the possibility of supernatural action (in a case such as the raising of a dead person immediately after prayer), this objection may itself be susceptible to the label of a naturalism-of-the-gaps approach—except without any discernible gap.[337] It rejects a plausible theistic explanation on the grounds

---

explained based on current scientific knowledge, some argue, current "miracles of the gaps" could eventually be eliminated (Langford, "Problem," 47; cf. Basinger and Basinger, "Concept," 165–67). But again, even where natural explanations are possible for details, theism allows that God often (or even usually) works through nature; when this activity through nature cumulatively suggests purpose (as perhaps in the case of highly unusual miracles), the possibility of explaining mechanisms of particular details should not distract one from recognizing the larger structure of purpose (a recognition accepted, for example, with respect to cultivated fields or human inventions making intelligent use of natural substances).

337. See Moreland, "Miracles," 145–46; Licona, *Resurrection*, 586; cf. similar language on a different issue in Dembski and Wells, *Atheist*, 95. The objection is possible, but it is a defensive argument from silence and thus cannot be used to rule out the hypothesis of theism (esp. where an external intelligence best accounts for the composite activity of the first cells). A philosophically neutral approach cannot simply presuppose that there are no natural gaps (Collins, "Miracles," 26), any more than presupposing that there must be such gaps; cf. Geivett, "Value," 184: "Failure to eliminate the possibility of a naturalistic explanation does not entail that a naturalistic explanation currently exists or is close at hand." To rule out miraculous explanations a priori by appealing to as-yet undiscovered laws is to stack the deck of the debate unfairly. An article in 1924 noted that appeals to "latent laws of nature" constituted de facto tacit admissions of the lack of a satisfactory alternative (Everts, "Exorcist," 360). In 1925, Tennant, *Miracle*, 29–30, 65, 67, suggested that on an empirical approach one could not prove miracles, because nature is not exhaustively known (noting that science as such can neither affirm nor deny divine activity). Yet Tennant also allowed (cf. *Miracle*, 54–55, 58, 66) that miracles can more tentatively *suggest* faith. Without entering a debate about macroevolution more generally (many accept it as compatible with theism, though others have demurred), one may note that naturalistic critics of "god-of-the-gaps" approaches often fail to observe a similar tendency among some traditional evolutionary ethicists when they offer positive evolutionary "motives" for the emergence of each trait (cf. "teleonomy" in evolutionary biology, e.g., in Eccles, "Evolution," 117–18; complaint in Nickles, "Discovery," 447–48; against full "genetic determinism," see, e.g., Polkinghorne and Beale, *Questions*, 78–80, 149–50). That is, some evolutionary approaches almost suggest, despite their rejection of such language, positive evolutionary "design," in contrast to what one would expect from merely random mutations. In addition to some models today providing *too much* explanation, cf. the more explicitly goal-directed pre-Darwinian evolutionary models in Kuhn, *Structure*, 171; Barbour, *Religion and Science*, 54–55; or early theistic evolution in Livingstone, *Defenders*; Ramm, *View*, 186, 198–202. Many reject "laws" and speak only of evolutionary "trends" (e.g., Popper, *Historicism*, 107–8); nevertheless, even as a trend it seems significant that the complexity involved in human intelligence emerges (naturally much later in the process rather than earlier). Despite various levels of "conscious purpose" in higher mammals (cf. Eccles, "Evolution," 118–32), survival of the fittest alone seems an inadequate mechanism to explain high levels of abstract thinking, especially as achieved in a species less than a million years old. (Davies, "Effectiveness," 55, thus asks what value human mathematical ability had for survival in the jungle). (Although other explanations are possible, some also protest naturalistic evolutionary attempts to explain the persistence of religion; see Haught, *Atheism*, 58–59.) Some therefore find theistic teleology in evolution, against others who define it as purely nondirected; see, e.g., Gingerich, "Scientist" (a Harvard professor of astronomy and history of science; he objects to the necessity of assigning all development to randomness, 30); Polkinghorne and Beale, *Questions*, 51; see extended and nuanced discussion (emphasizing "directionality") in McGrath, *Universe*, 183–201. Evolution seems to work randomly at a smaller level, but there is increasing information and complexity in some forms (see Barbour, *Religion and Science*, 237–40, also addressing theological approaches to this data; on 246–47 he sees God as designer of the self-organizing system; cf. Templeton, "Introduction," 11–12, 17–19; Davies, "Effectiveness," 56), like homo sapiens (the intellectual capabilities of which do not surface randomly throughout evolutionary history; however explained, the increasing complexity of some forms is "directional"). Polkinghorne, "Universe,"

that a plausible nontheistic position may emerge. Nontheistic explanations frequently do emerge; while not all of these are indisputable (often they compete), often emerging natural solutions are correct (even if a theist would still see God ultimately behind them).

But to argue that because explanations based on special divine action have sometimes been rightly displaced that all supernatural explanations ought to be displaced reflects a logical fallacy (generalizing based on particular cases). Why then do we not have many cases of the reverse, nonsupernatural explanations being displaced in the academy by supernatural ones? One might suggest that some antisupernatural explanations for the instant healing of blind eyes or raising of dead persons might have been displaced by theistic explanations had the latter been an acceptable option within academia. When the academy explicitly excludes the possibility (or at least the academic respectability) of supernatural explanations, however, it is next to impossible to find an academic defense of such explanations, except in the few disciplines that allow them. This does not mean that such explanations are indefensible; it means that various specialties' exclusion of such an appeal from their purview at the start have made it impossible for them to address it. Recall again that those disciplines that often do allow evaluation of such explanations, such as theology, are often marginalized from the epistemological center of modern academia.

To rule out theistic explanations wherever a nontheist expects potential for a nontheistic explanation reflects a presupposed preference for any nontheistic explanation. Theists are within their epistemological rights to demur from such an approach. Were we to apply the principle of deferred certainty to knowledge in general, we could never offer claims about anything.[338] Indeed, our inadequate knowledge of nature's positive limits does not mean that there are no cases where we cannot appeal to its negative ones; we may be fairly confident, for example, that some things are not explicable in terms of mere human ability.[339] Thus, Christian

---

106, suggests that the place to discern design is "in the fundamental structure of the universe," the intelligence and benevolence implied in natural laws. Hearn, "Purpose," 69, employs the analogy between studying the chemical activity of pen, ink, and paper (for traditional scientific approaches) and the communication an author uses these mechanical processes to convey; cf. similarly Osmond, "Physiologist," 163–64 (following MacKay, *Science*), for analogies of large-scale purpose not always seen at the level of detail. On "organized" complexity, suggesting information input, see, e.g., Davies, "Effectiveness," 45–46; at length, Dembski, *Inference*. Many argue that mere genetic accumulation of information in the course of evolution does not readily explain the initial infusion of information into the most basic organisms, apart from (on a theistic view) a preexisting superintelligence. Gaps in our knowledge do limit the completeness of our explanations (cf. Osmond, "Physiologist," 164–65, citing Goudge, *Ascent*, 127–28). To posit explanations for phenomena after the event (whether in terms of survival of the fittest or intelligence) can make sense within a coherent philosophic system, but such explanations lack the scientific persuasiveness offered in accurate predictions. (Theists and randomness advocates could both prescind from requiring such predictions of themselves, although they would do so for different reasons.)

338. See Tonquédec, *Miracles*, 56–57. The appropriateness of tentativeness must vary according to the strength of the information we have available.

339. Sabourin, *Miracles*, 16, doubting that a human command stilling a storm will ever be explicable naturalistically (i.e., in terms of mere biology).

doctors often recognize cases where naturalistic explanations are inadequate and "cannot identify the parameters of knowledge within which these events *might* be explained in any future development of the scientific approach."[340]

Granted that a supernatural interpretation presupposes the existence of something supernatural, the ruling out of such an interpretation presupposes the nonexistence of anything supernatural, and in some cases a supernatural explanation (such as theism) provides a more plausible explanation than coincidence would.[341] The antisupernaturalist position assumes that a theist may claim an event to be miraculous in public discourse only if the skeptic is persuaded that there is no possible natural explanation, even though the ideal skeptic claims a priori that all events could have a possible natural explanation. That is, skeptics "have laid out the rules of the game in such a way that they cannot possibly lose."[342] To simply predicate naturalistic causes for all purported extranormal phenomena, even if a naturalistic explanation proves far less plausible than a supernatural one, is to make one's position unfalsifiable[343]—hence to withdraw from genuine participation in public discourse.[344]

Since science does not claim comprehensive knowledge of the universe, it cannot conclusively demonstrate that particular miracle claims are outside the realm of natural possibility.[345] Neither, however, can it exclude supernatural activity; in fact, affirming or denying divine activity requires a broader philosophic or theological framework than the questions that science as science is specifically competent to address. Such an observation suggests the limits of scientific epistemology rather than the impossibility or complete epistemic inaccessibility of miracles.[346] Nevertheless, we do have degrees of probability, and statistics suggest that most observers would conclude that some reports in this book, if authentic, make better sense on the premise of supernatural action than without it.

Although observers must periodically revise putative laws of nature to fit new data, this approach is sometimes more difficult than simply admitting anomalies.[347]

---

340. Lees and Fiddes, "Healed," 13.

341. On the assumption of theism in appeals to miracle, see Purtill, "Defining Miracles," 70. See my notes on coincidence as an explanation in chs. 14, 15 (esp. 736, 758) and appendix E.

342. Corduan, "Miracle," 101 (cf. also 106–7).

343. As noted by Geisler, "Miracles," 83. Likewise, Corduan, "Miracle," 110, complains that Flew's insistence on falsifiability for theism challenges the unfalsifiability of his own insistence on interpreting all miracle claims naturalistically.

344. Cf. also Corduan, "Miracle," 107.

345. See Carter, "Recognition." While some seek to dismiss miracle claims based on as-yet undiscovered laws, one could as easily appeal to unknown law to support them (e.g., Mozley, *Lectures*, 113) if the unknown law were a higher order representing divine activity (130).

346. Cf. comments in Ellens, "God and Science," 5.

347. Levine, *Problem*, 180. Such revision fits Hume's approach (Mumford, "Laws," 279) but is not always the most probable approach unless one must fit all evidence into an antisupernaturalist paradigm. Some seek coherence by finding theories to accommodate all the evidence within a naturalistic paradigm (a position noted in Weintraub, "Credibility," 372), but the limitation of the paradigm to metaphysical naturalism can (and in my view does) arbitrarily force the evidence.

In some cases, however, including, I believe, some miracle claims I have noted, allowing the hypothesis of a supernatural agent[348] might explain the circumstances better than either alternative. If allowance for supernatural agency is built into one's worldview, then miracles might be as much a part of the way things are as the ordinary course of nature is; they are simply not predictable based on lower-level physical laws because personal agents acting in history are not predictable based on those laws.

Other Complications

Even apart from such factors, it is difficult to procure statistics for supernatural healing claims here; although many pray for recoveries today and recoveries often follow, the heyday of large-scale and dramatic healing revivalism in the United States fell in the mid-twentieth century, and it is now far more popular in the Majority World.[349] The samples above also suggest that supernatural healing claims are and have always been more common in new evangelistic contexts,[350] thus in settings least accessible to modern controlled clinical studies.[351] Likewise, they are reported especially among the poor,[352] those with least access to medical in-

348. See discussion in chs. 5–6. As noted, scientific method tests hypotheses rather than ruling out their possibility without testing; what is illegitimate is refusal to allow one's hypothesis to be challenged (a refusal observed in instances above where no amount of evidence for supernatural activity is accepted). On "critical realism concerning theoretical models," see Barbour, *Myths*, 37–38.

349. On the shift, see Harrell, "Divine Healing," 227; also noted in Stewart, *Only Believe*, 106–7. In the Majority World, as in the U.S. revivals, the movement again is especially among the poor who are least likely to afford hospitals, where strict medical records are kept. (In Taiwan, tribal Christians reported many healings of cancer, whereas nontribal Christians reported them only rarely; see Chin, "Practices," 29.) Not every individual who prays necessarily exhibits the same charism of healing (cf. 1 Cor 12:9), nor are all settings equally conducive to it. I point this out with respect to some studies that I do not believe are looking in the most effective places.

350. So, e.g., Fant, *Miracles*, 108 ("on the mission fields"); McKenzie, "Miracles," 82–84; for applicability to church growth, e.g., Kwon, "Foundations," 187–90; for examples of the abundance in such settings, see, e.g., Grant, "Folk Religion" (cited in Filson, "Study," 137–38); Suico, "Pentecostalism," 356; Braun, *Here*, 160; Wilfred Mina, interview, Jan. 24, 2009 (on seeing miracles regularly in an evangelism context in rural northern Luzon, Philippines). Historically, see Latourette, *History of Christianity*, 344; Tucker, *Jerusalem*, 41; and comments in ch. 10. Many also expect them in such settings for theological reasons; see, e.g., Solomon, "Healing," 364; Dunkerley, *Healing Evangelism*, 17–33, 112; Lloyd-Jones, *Spirit*, 49; Go, "Ministry" (summary on ii); Gideon Achi, interview, May 25, 2009; cf. the connection with the kingdom in Cho, "Foundation," 90–94; with "outsiders" in Crump, *Knocking*, 43. Percy, "Miracles," 13–14, notes that Jesus focused on the excluded, and contrasts the frequent inward focus of modern healing movements. Many also argue that God performs miracles more typically where needs are greater (hence in Indonesia more than in the United States, in Tari, *Wind*, 104–5).

351. A Victorian skeptic posed the initial demand for controlled studies regarding prayer (Opp, *Lord for Body*, 15; Numbers, "Aggressors," 34–35; Mullin, *History*, 202, on John Tyndall). This approach perhaps characterized Victorian-era skepticism more generally; some "scientists publicly ridiculed church leaders who prayed for God's intervention against the cholera epidemic of 1866, denounced prayer as a form of superstition, and charged the church with" resisting progress (Wuthnow, "Contradictions," 163).

352. See, e.g., Währisch-Oblau, "Healthy," 97; Chevreau, *Turnings*, 16–17; MacNutt, *Healing*, 26–27; Bomann, *Faith in Barrios*; idem, "Salve."

tervention and thus the greatest need for supernatural intervention, but again among populations less apt to have doctors' reports than typical Westerners today would.[353] Thus one can accumulate thousands of testimonies and in some cases secure before-and-after medical documentation,[354] but these accounts do not easily yield to controlled experiments, just as some other sorts of evidence, such as any unrepeatable historical acts, do not.[355]

Another catch-22 in addressing antisupernaturalism is that the more dramatic and demonstrable the cure claim, the less likely it is to be accepted.[356] An antisupernaturalist would be more disposed to accept healing claims that can be explained psychosomatically, precisely because they need not entail belief in the supernatural.[357] An antisupernaturalist (albeit undoubtedly some others as well, given the claims' rareness) would thus be more disposed to reject claims such as these: a woman who had had her fingers partly amputated on one hand was healed of cancer. The fingers grew back after prayer, and "finger-nails are also forming."[358] At age twenty-seven, Agatha Okafor of Port Harcourt, Nigeria, still lacked adult breasts; during prayer one day her breasts fully formed, and she went on to mother

353. Laurentin, *Miracles*, 15, 38, 89–90, develops the difficulty of this problem.

354. Though in many of these healing settings, people are mostly poor and lack access to empirical medical treatment, probably another factor in their dependence on other forms of healing.

355. Probably even less to deliberately skeptical settings inimical to faith, which may be one reason why Randi, *Healers*, 309–10, has had few takers, despite his commendable exposés of some clearly fraudulent healers. On the difference between historical and scientific language, see, e.g., Ramsey, "Miracles," 10. Even sciences addressing the past, "such as cosmology and evolutionary biology," necessarily depend on observation rather than experimentation (Polkinghorne, *Physics*, 11; cf. 9).

356. Cf. Wei, "Young," 337: a "miracle" that resembles natural events is credible, but one cannot appeal to God as an explanation; if it is "incredible," like biblical miracles, it must normally be "suspect." That is, the verdict remains as rigged against the consideration of divine activity as it has remained since the Enlightenment. Hume claimed that if uniform experience counts against miracles, one should not believe them; if it does not, then one cannot know that it is a miracle (a position noted in Mumford, "Laws," 279; countered in Hambourger, "Belief," 600), a position that underestimates the potential role of greater frequency of such events in specifically theistic contexts. Warfield, *Miracles*, 191, contends that faith healing (as he knew it through Charles Cullis's views) could not and did not claim to cure broken bones or missing teeth—a limitation no longer applicable to all miracle healing claims.

357. Warfield, *Miracles*, 119, complains that the claim of a Jansenist who lacked legs, as attested by two surgeons, yet grew them miraculously, is simply unbelievable.

358. This amazed the neighbors, who knew she had had fingers missing—see "Amputated Fingers" (1926); I do not report this account with confidence that it is correct, given the inadequate verification offered. Poloma, *Assemblies*, 273n3, notes that claims of raisings and restored limbs in early Pentecostal literature do not appear in more recent U.S. Assemblies publications, whether due to a change in the movement or an increase in verification standards (one might factor into this discussion also a shift in plausibility structures; having sampled early Pentecostal literature, I am inclined to admit any of the three explanations, including the first, for various reports). Rumph, *Signs*, 131–36, cites a much more recent case of an adult's partly amputated finger gradually growing back after prayer and dreams about restoration, even though this is medically impossible by natural means. Cf. also the claim of restored appendages in Clark, *Impartation*, 166. Other astonishing claims include the survival of someone who had bled to death (though the recovery was not instantaneous; Marszalek, *Miracles*, 45–51), and full recovery of her completely brain-damaged infant within four days (Marszalek, *Miracles*, 50–51); the gradual re-formation of an adult's bones and leg after amputation beneath the knee (Marszalek, *Miracles*, 194–96).

five children.[359] A Western minister reports a case in Ghana of a leg severed beneath the knee miraculously growing back.[360] An eyewitness who prayed for a twelve-year-old boy in Bogota, Colombia, with a deformed hand reports seeing the half-inch fingers all grow out to three inches over the course of an hour and a half of prayer.[361] In another case, the morning after prayer for a different need, a nearly bald woman awoke with hair, now a few inches in length.[362] Another source reports that a partially severed thumb grew out instantly.[363] Witnesses, including quite reluctant but certain ones, report God filling the teeth of poor persons who could not afford fillings.[364] In one report, a misshapen skull was visibly healed.[365] Perhaps most dramatically, even a local newspaper reported a boy able to see through his artificial eye![366] Various eyewitnesses claim the instant and visible

359. An account attested both by the preacher and by Mrs. Okafor, now a grandmother, in Numbere, *Vision*, 78 (the photo on 150 attests her breasts and reveals that she was physically small). Alfred Cookey, himself soon converted at one of the crusades, was astonished by the public testimony of an obese woman who claimed she lost her obesity overnight; he knew that she had that weight the day before and no longer had it now (Numbere, *Vision*, 131); both continued as part of the new movement (132).

360. Robertson, *Miracles*, 176–77, providing further details from T. L. Osborn about a man in one of his meetings in Ghana; see also Harrell, *Robertson*, 317. Such reports are not common today and do not appear in the Gospels or Acts.

361. Videotaped interview from August 2007, provided courtesy of Dr. Candy Gunther Brown, who addresses healing claims from a sociological perspective. Salmon, *Heals*, 135–37, reports a basic hand and fingers beginning to form over a two-year period in a child that lacked a hand at age three; unlike the report in Brown's interview, Salmon's might be conceivable naturalistically, but developments even in the first month of growth (137) were remarkable. The healing of the deformed hand in 135 appears to be a different and also remarkable case.

362. Jackson, *Quest*, 85, recounting the experience of his wife's previous roommate after prayer in Calvary Chapel, San Diego. I am convinced of the integrity of both Bill Jackson and his wife, Betsy, whom I met and my brother knows well (hence I am personally inclined to take the informants for this report more seriously than the 1926 "Amputated Fingers" report noted above but for which I have no personal context).

363. Bill Johnson's church website, Oct. 9, 2007.

364. Gardner, *Healing Miracles*, 175–84 (for the reluctant witness, 176–77, 184); Bonnie Ortiz (interview, Jan. 10, 2009); Kumsook Cho, interview, Jan. 24, 2009; frequent claims in Argentina cited in Marostica, "Learning," 216; the old, unusual report in McGee, *Miracles*, 72. For what appears to be a fake case of such fillings, see Bishop, *Healing*, 199–203 (the healer's use of a dental mirror on 200); in the other accounts with which I am familiar, however, the minister did not touch the healed persons' teeth.

365. Lindsay, *Lake*, 57. Cf. also the gradual reshaping of a child's apparently Down syndrome features noted by Lee Don Coffee, phone interview, July 7, 2009.

366. "Ronnie Coyne," including information from a medical doctor and copies of the optometrist's report and the news article from *Chattanooga News-Free Press* [i.e., *Times Free Press*], which also quotes a doctor: "It's amazing. . . . There's absolutely nothing in the eye except fatty tissue. The organ has been entirely removed." Even *VOH* rarely has material this extraordinary with outside documentation. Among other exceptions, it does include a testimony of severed vocal cords being miraculously healed (Phillips, "Restored"); four years later the girl had even sung on the radio (idem, "Sings"). Mike Finley provided me access to these articles. As we have noted, at Lourdes the functionality of an organ the functionality of which is medically impossible, such as seeing through eyes the optic nerves of which remain atrophied, appears as a special miracle (Cranston, *Miracle*, 136). McGee, *Miracles*, 203, concisely lists Coyne among fraudulent claims, but unfortunately does not provide the reasons; one witness I trust noted what he suspected were spiritual deficiencies in Coyne's later meetings, but that he could not explain Coyne's visual ability (personal correspondence, Dec. 27, 2010).

disappearance of lumps.[367] We may deem such reports true or false (or some true and others false), but our usual intuitive response to such claims highlights our modern Western discomfort with them, providing some perspective regarding our presuppositions about how we approach ancient healing claims.[368] While some such reports may be false, to reject all eyewitness claims to such extraordinary miracles on the premise that they cannot occur returns to Hume's circular logic.

On the same sort of principle, scholars often a priori exclude the possibility of nature miracles, but this exclusion involves content criticism rather than any formal distinction in the Gospels; nature miracles are not *formally* different from others.[369] Indeed, the category is not only not formal but also is too arbitrary to function as a content category. As C. F. D. Moule observes, the category is unsatisfactory "because it implies . . . that there is an order of regularity and consistency in it different from that which obtains in the personal realm. It suggests an *a priori* assumption that you could not alter the weather but you might change a personality; and this is an arbitrary assumption."[370] Do healing a cancer within a person or restoring life after the brain has died *not* affect the course of nature simply because they involve the human body? (Our body is, after all, part of nature, as all of us who are aging can testify.) Like other miracle claims, those concerning nature miracles have appeared through history and today, as I have noted in chapter 12.[371] Decisions about their potential historicity depend on one's presuppositions about what is

367. Kim, "Prominent Woman," 205; Spraggett, *Kuhlman*, 141; Harris, *Acts Today*, 100–101; Moreland, *Triangle*, 169; Brown, "Awakenings," 363; Zagrans, *Miracles*, 100 (a visible facial tumor disappeared within five minutes of prayer); Bill Twyman, interview, Nov. 11, 2007; Eleanor Sebiano, interview, Jan. 29, 2009; Yusuf Herman, interview, July 10, 2011; Marie Brown (personal correspondence, May 31, 2006).

368. Cf. the convincing nature of such events, if proved, even to firm extreme cessationists, though in principle they would insist on rejecting them (see Ruthven, *Cessation*, 65). Whatever one makes of some of these examples, some even more radical claims reported in Wacker, *Heaven Below*, 93, would strike even the least skeptical readers as implausible.

369. See, e.g., Robinson, "Challenge," 329; for Bultmann's skeptical treatment of nature miracles, see, e.g., Bultmann, *Tradition* (1963 ed.), 227–28. Like many, Carlston, "Question," accepts the healing narratives (where he engages the question of divine activity) as more authentic than the nature miracles. Others have defended the nature miracles (e.g., Fonck, *Wunder*, 1:127–469, as cited in Sabourin, *Miracles*, 247), though some have relegated them only to the past, for theological reasons (Dod, "Healer," 176).

370. Moule, "Classification," 240; cf. similar criticisms in Neil, "Nature Miracles," 370; Best, "Miracles," 548. Collins, *Introduction*, 176, refers to Bultmann's distinction between nature and healing miracles as "a confusion in the categorization of the Gospel material on the basis of form and content." Wright, "Miracles," 190, treats "nature miracles" as a misnomer, since physical healings also involve nature. Eve, *Healer*, 113–16, argues for formal differences between nature miracles and other miracles in Mark but acknowledges that this argument is "cumulative," with no single criterion adequate to distinguish them (115). Eve uses OT echoes (Eve, *Healer*, 150–56) and other features to try to set these miracle stories apart from others historically, but such allusions (e.g., to Jonah in the lake-crossing account) seem inadequate to explain the composition of these full stories, within a generation after Jesus's execution.

371. E.g., Yung, "Integrity," 174; McGee, "Regions Beyond," 70; Hellestad, "Prayer," 16–17; Kinnear, *Tide*, 92–96; Khai, "Pentecostalism," 268; Peckham, *Sounds*, 106, 113; Koschorke, Ludwig, and Delgado, *History*, 223–24; Sanneh, *West African Christianity*, 181–83; Dayhoff, "Barros"; Bush and Pegues, *Move*, 54–55, 59, 64, 192; Koch, *Revival*, 143–46, 208–17; Wiyono, "Timor Revival," 285–86, 288; Crawford, *Miracles*, 28, 75; Harris, *Acts Today*, 66–67, 80; Chavda, *Miracle*, 9–10, 128–29; Numbere, *Vision*, 130, 206–7, 213, 266; Dunkerley, *Healing Evangelism*, 112; Castleberry, "Impact," 111–12; Paul Mokake,

possible and one's verdict on the general historical reliability of the traditions and narratives in which they occur.[372]

When healing or other miracle reports are ancient, new complications are added.[373] As one scholar observes, "The task is complicated as well by the simple fact that the historian must work with historical probabilities, while miracle stories are concerned by definition with the occurrence of historical improbabilities."[374] With ancient sources, medical documentation in the modern sense is never available, nor can one interrogate the eyewitnesses. One can work only on the basis of normal historiographic method and one's presuppositions about what is possible (formed partly from philosophic a prioris and partly from analogies with subsequent historical and current evidence).

It is important to take into account the observation that signs claims and skeptical studies usually focus on different kinds of examples. Although studies' conclusions vary, some studies suggest no effect when persons (at least those chosen for controlled studies) prayed for hospitalized people whom they did not know, without the hospitalized persons' knowledge, primarily for the purpose of scientific studies.[375] Several other studies have yielded more positive results, but all the studies are preliminary.[376] For example, one study of 990 coronary care patients showed an 11 percent difference in positive outcomes for those who received intercessory prayer,[377] but many have questioned the study. (Larger numbers might be needed to rule out coincidence and bias, but the larger the pool of data, the less obvious the effects of any genuinely supernatural individual cases, if these prove rare in such settings.) There are also significant individual cases of extraordinary, probably natural inexplicable, recoveries during distant intercessory prayer,[378] but these have not been identified in the fewer controlled studies.

---

interviews, June 3, 2006; May 13, 2009; Emmanuel Itapson, interview, April 29, 2008; Sandy Thomas, phone interview, Aug. 26, 2008; Donna Arukua, interview, Jan. 29, 2009; Kay Fountain, interview, Jan. 29, 2009.

372. Stanton, "Message and Miracles," 67; Blomberg, *Gospels*, 130–33.

373. With Jaki, *Miracles and Physics*, 95.

374. Williams, *Miracle Stories*, 143.

375. Bishop and Stenger, "Prayer," argue that prayer studies do not demonstrate the efficacy of prayer. Johnson and Butzen, "Prayer," 251–54, also find them inconclusive.

376. For one example, in a masked, random test of the effect of prayer on the success of in vitro fertilization in 219 patients, those who unknowingly received prayer had a 50 percent pregnancy rate as opposed to those who did not (26 percent; Cha, Wirth, and Lobo, "Prayer," esp. 786–87); on theistic premises, results might vary with different persons praying or other factors. When verifiable cures are rare, it "denies science the necessary frequency of occurrence of a phenomenon to warrant the use of statistical methods" (Eya, "Healing," 50; cf. Duffin, *Miracles*, 34–35). But Matthews and Clark, *Faith Factor*, 199–200, cite significant effects in Byrd, "Effects" (also noted in Matthews, Larson, and Barry, *Bibliography*, 44–45, as well executed but needing further studies); also in Collipp, "Efficacy" (45 percent higher among leukemia patients prayed for; but Collipp's sample size was too small for safe extrapolation; note Matthews, Larson, and Barry, *Bibliography*, 52); Beutler et al., "Healing."

377. Harris et al., "Trial" (also noted in "Prayer and Outcomes").

378. Note again the case of Matthew Dawson of New Zealand, cited earlier (based on Matthew Dawson, personal correspondence, March 29, 2009; April 3–4, 2009). Other cases of distant intercessory prayer having immediate effects have long been reported (e.g., cases in Glover, "Healings," 15; to his surprise,

Evaluating such studies can prove complicated. In one extensive study of 1,802 coronary patients, those who were notified that they would receive distant prayer fared worse in "post-operative complications" than those who were not (possibly due to performance anxiety),[379] and those who received prayer unknowingly fared worse than those who did not receive it.[380] No one, including skeptics about prayer's efficacy, would say that prayer itself made matters worse. But the study reveals the complications in seeking to measure such processes. In such studies, we cannot quantify the results of prayers from those personally committed to patients both inside and outside the control group, who were not among the study's intercessors.[381] Since 96 percent of participants in this study acknowledged that people they knew were praying for them (presumably praying more fervently than most strangers would have been), it is not clear that the distant intercessors added significantly to any effect of petitions already occurring.[382] Moreover, intercessors chosen for some studies came from various religions and traditions, and prayed in various ways.[383] A number of intercessors from the traditions emphasized in this book, accustomed to laying on hands and praying in particular ways, felt too constricted by the controls to pray in their usual way.[384] Nor do most Christians expect God's intervention to relate to prayer quantitatively, as if God were a mathematical function rather than a personal being.[385] Would God favor someone or not because they belonged to a control group?[386]

Clinical settings differ from the usual setting of both biblical[387] and subsequent healing claims, in terms of objectives, interest, and the infirm person's knowledge.[388]

Blumhardt found occasions he believed effective through his correspondence, in Ising, *Blumhardt*, 216, 218, 331–33), but even in the Gospels (Matt 8:13//Luke 7:10; John 4:50–53) and Acts (cf. Acts 12:5, not regarding healing) these were a small minority of cases, perhaps requiring special faith (Matt 8:8–10// Luke 7:6–9).

379. Fung and Fung, "Prayer Studies," 44, note that this is the hypothesis offered by the study's authors.

380. For this study, see Benson et al., "Study."

381. Cf. the concerns raised in one study cited in Masters, "Prayer," 17.

382. Fung and Fung, "Prayer Studies," 44.

383. E.g., of the distant intercessor groups in the study where patients fared worse, the only Protestant group represented belonged to the New Thought group Unity (Brown, Mory, Williams, and McClymond, "Effects," 865), although it is not possible to know whether the inclusion of different groups would have made a difference in this case.

384. Johnson and Butzen, "Prayer," 256–57.

385. For these and other concerns with criteria in prayer studies, including "dosage effects" (what kinds of prayer? what kinds of prayerful people are praying?), see Gorsuch, "Limits," 288–93. Gorsuch regards the view that God would simply add up the number of prayers as something like a prayer wheel or a magical approach (293–94).

386. Johnson and Butzen, "Prayer," 257 (citing also Masters, "Disconnect").

387. E.g., Byrne, "Miracles," 170: "biblical miracles are not set down as having taken place in scientifically controlled conditions."

388. While distant prayer has had at *best* mixed results (Matthews, Marlowe, and MacNutt, "Effects," 1177, 1180–82; no significant results in Krucoff et al., "Music"; Benson et al., "Study"; few in Koenig et al., "Care Use"; see the survey in Masters, "Prayer," 14–20), prayer with laying on of hands displays a higher improvement rate, including in a study on rheumatoid arthritis (Matthews, Marlowe, and MacNutt, "Effects"); religious commitment and expectancy did not affect the results (1183–84). Results concerning

For such reasons, many consider the accumulation of evidence from individual healings in their natural settings more compelling than the sorts of group studies so far conducted.[389] In such natural settings, in fact, a number of individual cures have been documented that far exceed normal expectations.[390] As I noted earlier, anomalies invite a case-study approach. The majority of the healing reports I cited in this book occurred in evangelistic contexts (that is, healings functioning as signs of the gospel) or, somewhat less frequently, pastoral contexts. Granted, the general lack of healing without the prayee's knowledge in controlled studies could suggest that some healings involve psychological factors. Nevertheless, these factors do not readily explain some dramatic healings accounts that I have noted, suggesting that the evangelistic and/or pastoral context also may play a significant role. As C. S. Lewis warned about controlled studies he expected to be conducted someday, "I do not see how any real prayer could go on under such conditions." Mere words need not constitute prayer whether offered by people or parrots; asking people to pray for an experiment, he argued, treats prayer "as if it were magic, or a machine—something that functions automatically."[391]

One wonders whether a deity acting like the God of the Gospels and Acts would be expected to offer "signs" by participating as an actor in a controlled experiment.[392] (Although not the agenda of most investigators today, the test of controlled hospital studies regarding prayer was originally designed to challenge faith.[393]) While evidence from controlled studies remains ambiguous, therefore, a

---

joint swelling were comparable to those from some medical treatments and exceeded those of educational approaches, though psychosomatic elements might play a role (1183). Seventy-eight percent "had at least a 20% reduction in the number of tender and swollen joints over the course of the study"; 55 percent "met full ACR20 criteria for clinical improvement" (1182). Some individuals experienced significant benefit (Matthews and Clark, *Faith Factor*, 77–79). Spraggett, *Kuhlman*, 26–29, recounts his personal knowledge of a woman completely crippled by rheumatoid arthritis whose swelling went down and she was completely cured after prayer; but he claims that rheumatoid arthritis is just a "psychosomatic disorder."

389. See Johnson and Butzen, "Prayer," 255–58.

390. See Brown, Mory, Williams, and McClymond, "Effects," reporting cures among several persons with auditory and visual impairments in rural Mozambique (cf. briefly Brown, "Awakenings," 363–64).

391. C. S. Lewis, as cited in Fung and Fung, "Prayer Studies," 44.

392. Cf. Polkinghorne and Beale, *Questions*, 29: "God is not an object on which one can do experiments." Cf. Mark 8:11–12 (despite Jesus's signs in other contexts); Luke 11:16, 29–30; Matt 12:38–39; 16:1, 4; 24:3, 30; perhaps John 6:30–36; Exod 17:2, 7. Jesus did not perform signs in front of the Sanhedrin or even for the Pharisees, but among the sick who needed them, a principle that coheres with his mission among the humble but in conflict with the elites (and not among those who resisted his claims, Mark 6:5). It is not then surprising that claims of miracles in his name would flourish more in the Majority World and among the poor than among the world's elites today. Still, God might respond to uninformed yet genuine inquirers (cf. 1 Sam 6:9–12 with 4:8–9, in contrast to Pharaoh in Exodus; John 4:48–53).

393. Mullin, *Miracles*, 45–46; Opp, *Lord for Body*, 15. Although one need not conduct such studies with this bias, the Gospels seem to often (not always) link healing with faith and rarely associate it positively with skepticism; see especially Mark 6:5–6. But while some suggest that faith healers often do not want skeptics present (Frohock, *Healing Powers*, 135), apparently only 30 percent of those surveyed in Tilley, "Phenomenology," 546, felt that the presence of nonbelievers was detrimental (recall also the story of onlookers in my accounts from Jeanne Mabiala and Albert and Julienne Bissouessoue). More detrimental was a rationalistic approach on the part of those needing to exercise faith (Tilley, "Phenomenology," 545–46).

significant number of extranormal, dramatic cures continue to invite our attention. The cumulative pattern of the spiritual context in a significant proportion of these "anomalies" invites more consideration than it has often received.

Conclusion

Although one cannot prove special divine action where natural factors can account for a healing, to assume by contrast that the presence of natural factors must exclude supernatural ones is reductionist. Some critics carry the reductionism so far that they attribute even healings without any currently explainable natural causes to natural causation that may someday be explained. Even when the most obvious common factor in some organic healings is prayer, these cases are often discounted by one means or another to achieve the desired conclusion, and those who postulate supernatural or even merely religious causes may face considerable bias in some academic circles. Many employ criteria specifically designed to screen out any evidence that might support the objectionable conclusion of supernatural causation.

Those who follow such a procedure rigidly will never acknowledge any evidence for supernatural activity, because they employ rules designed from the start to exclude such evidence. But what sort of evidence might open-minded observers count against their antisupernatural thesis? In addition to many examples offered sporadically in recent chapters, including this one, I will suggest some such evidence in the following chapter.

15

More Extranormal Cases

No one will ever know how much of the cure depends on the patient's desire and expectation that he be healed. But most physicians do recognize that motivation is a powerful force aiding recovery. In spite of this, there are surely few in the field of who have not, on some rare occasion at least, witnessed a recovery so contrary to the usual prognosis, and so apparently complete, that the word "miracle" seemed the only appropriate description of it. —David Robertson, MD[1]

In chapter 5 I noted the argument of many thinkers that if theism (a majority premise in our society) is accepted, the possibility of some miracles in particular theistic contexts becomes more probable than not; in that case, evidence from credible witnesses for genuine miracles should be accepted. If one starts from an agnostic position that does not a priori privilege theism, atheism, or deism, one may at least examine the evidence open to the possibility of such events. Only those for whom miracles are philosophically impossible are obligated to rule out this explanation in every case. If we are open to such events and to a supernatural explanation as a possible interpretation for them, is there any evidence that such events occur? Are there events that we would construe as miracles if a theistic premise is granted to a significant degree of probability?

If one allows for many natural causes in unusual recoveries yet avoids reductionism (the subjects of the previous two chapters), one remains free to examine a variety of claims that seem to significantly exceed what we can expect from solely natural causes. In recent chapters (particularly chs. 12 and 14), I have recounted some cases in which supernatural explanations appear to offer better explanatory power than naturalistic ones. Some healing accounts seem more ambiguous, such as partial and gradual healings. As we shall soon see, however, even some of these cases exhibit distinctly extranormal elements. In this chapter, I do not propose

1. Robertson, "Epidauros to Lourdes," 188–89. Admittedly, "few" may be an overstatement, and "miracle" is variously defined.

to rehearse all the plausible miracle reports already given but to survey some of them, to offer some new ones, and to conclude by evaluating a few of the stronger ones, especially among cases with which I have some connection.

Because many conditions improve on their own with or without prayer, anyone who prays for hundreds of people would see many of them recover even if the prayers lacked any efficacy. Yet we have also noted some other recoveries, such as instant cures of blindness, restoration from death, and so forth that do *not* normally simply improve on their own, and a number of cases fit a pattern of following immediately after prayer. After surveying some cases where more concrete medical documentation is available and some cases of partial and gradual healings, I will survey some other kinds of extranormal claims and turn to samples of eyewitness evidence for genuine miracles that I find credible.

Considering Medical Documentation

Anthropologists and sociologists studying beliefs about supernatural and paranormal phenomena only rarely provide medical documentation;[2] studies of beliefs do not require this sort of evidence, so it is not mandatory for the primary purpose of this book. When we move to the secondary academic question of what stands behind such beliefs, however, it is helpful to provide at least some additional analysis. Others have written and are researching works documenting some medically inexplicable healings. That is not the purpose of this book, and not being a medical doctor I again observe that I must defer discussion of such matters to those qualified to provide it. Roman Catholics have proved most careful about documenting healings, including medical testimony for many hundreds of cases in recent centuries.[3] Apart from these circles (and especially Lourdes, treated in ch. 14), few ministries are organized to provide medical documentation for healings; when one cannot predict where miracles will occur, it is difficult to know where to gather documentation of prior illness in advance. As a scholar, I have found myself frequently disappointed by this problem, wanting more *publicly* accessible documentation even when I know the circumstances firsthand or through the firsthand accounts of people I trust.[4] Meanwhile, in some cases my lack of expertise in medicine undoubtedly hindered access or understanding of records.

2. E.g., Greeley, *Sociology*; Miller and Yamamori, *Pentecostalism*; McClenon and Nooney, "Experiences"; Scherberger, "Shaman"; McClenon, *Events*, xiii, 57–74 (with testimonial evidence on 62–63, 64–66, 68–69, 70–72), 131; even in most cases where the writer advocates for the activity of genuine spirits, as in Turner, "Actuality"; idem, *Hands*. The most common exceptions are neurological studies of possession and mystic experiences (see appendix B); for fire walking, cf. also McClenon, *Events*, 121–26.

3. Duffin, *Miracles*, 8, 113–43.

4. Some have suggested that Protestants should establish an agency for certifying miracles analogous to the Medical Bureau at Lourdes ("Miraculous Truth"). That the locations of such cures is unpredictable, however, complicates matters, as does the lack of consensus among Protestants concerning the nature and frequency of miracles (hence the nature of evidence that would be deemed admissible). Surveying some

I noted in the previous chapter that it is unreasonable to reject eyewitness claims simply because we lack access to medical records in many cases, if other factors (such as multiple witnesses or the witness's known reliability) support their claims. I have also repeatedly noted that I will not focus on such material in this book because I am qualified neither to provide nor to evaluate it. Nevertheless, that medical documentation is not always available does not mean that it is never available. Below I mention some sample cases.

Some Medical Documentation

In some notes I have pointed out that some persons supplied medical documentation for their healings; I have also cited works by doctors[5] or other investigators[6] who found such documentation. Some researchers have shown how the subjects of some dramatic healing testimonies remained cured many decades later.[7] These sources are in addition to numerous works cited where the authors claimed to include only cases that they were relatively certain were reliable or where they noted the existence of medical evidence without citing or reproducing it. Nor do I include here many of the interviewees who spoke of medical recognition of their recoveries but, because of distance in time or other factors, could not provide me access to medical documents.

In addition to more publicly known cases of documentation at Lourdes, many others cite support. One of the doctors I have noted has cited cases of cancer that had already metastasized (spread) being healed abruptly after prayer.[8] Another of these doctors notes a clear case of instant healing of advanced tuberculosis of the spine, where there can be no question of either the diagnosis or the outcome.[9] Yet another doctor provided in his book more substantial medical documentation, including X-rays and the like, for the following cases of extraordinary healings after prayer, though some of these are more "medically inexplicable" than others:

- Lisa Larios, healed of reticulum cell sarcoma of the right pelvic bone[10]
- Elfrieda Stauffer, healed of chronic rheumatoid arthritis with severe disability[11]
- Marie Rosenberger, healed of malignant brain tumor of the left temporal lobe[12]

---

difficulties in verifying that inexplicable acts are caused by God, Basinger and Basinger, *Miracle*, 81–100, note lack of consensus among theists.

5. E.g., Gardner, *Healing Miracles*; Casdorph, *Miracles*; Reed, *Surgery*; Speed, *Incurables* (cases she witnessed directly); some material in Frazier, *Healing*; earlier, cf. Opp, *Lord for Body*, 196.

6. E.g., Spraggett, *Kuhlman*; Grazier, *Power Beyond*; Neal, *Reporter*; in an earlier era, see Hickson, *Heal*, 122–23, 129–30, 134–35; Mews, "Revival," 301–4.

7. See here Warner, "Still Healed"; Warner, "Living by Faith."

8. Reed, *Surgery*, 35, 52–53; cf. also 43–48. Prayer and faith also appear very likely to have contributed to recovery of the terminal coma patient in Reed, *Surgery*, 84.

9. White, "Lady," 72–73.

10. Casdorph, *Miracles*, 25–33.

11. Ibid., 37–45.

12. Ibid., 49–57.

- Marion Burgio, healed of multiple sclerosis[13]
- Marvin Bird, healed of arteriosclerotic heart disease[14]
- B. Ray Jackson, healed of carcinoma of the kidney (hypernephroma) with diffuse bony metastases[15]
- Pearl Bryant, healed of mixed rheumatoid arthritis and osteoarthritis[16]
- Anne Soults, healed of probable brain tumor vs. infarction of the brain[17]
- Paul Trousdale, instantly healed of massive GI hemorrhage with shock[18]
- Delores Winder, healed of osteoporosis of the entire spine with intractable pain requiring bilateral cordotomies[19]

The author of that work consulted also at least nine other named doctors and medical researchers to verify the diagnoses noted in his book.[20]

Such collections offer merely samples of extraordinary restorations that can be medically documented. I noted various examples, many treated more extensively earlier and thus merely summarized here. One was the case of Joy Wahnefried, who provided me clear documentation that her vision, previously so problematic that she suffered lengthy and disabling migraines for several years, suddenly became perfect (20/20) during prayer.[21] Anna Gulick, tested by both her eye doctor and optometrist, provided evidence for a sudden improvement in her vision after prayer, with physical changes in that eye, reversing years of macular degeneration.[22] Other cases with documentation include the Ethiopian couple healed of a condition that made it impossible for the husband to get his wife pregnant,[23] and Yazmin Hommer's recovery from her coma, although her organs had begun shutting down.[24] Jonathan Pollard, raised from a wheelchair and cured of what was thought to be Guillain-Barré syndrome, sent me medical evidence.[25] Others I knew also sent test results to support their testimony.[26]

13. Ibid., 61–72.
14. Ibid., 77–86.
15. Ibid., 91–100.
16. Ibid., 105–16.
17. Ibid., 121–32.
18. Ibid., 137–43.
19. Ibid., 147–57.
20. Named in ibid., 9–10.
21. The vision specialist's certification is dated Oct. 16, 2009, based on a test on May 27, 2009; the certification was provided to explain that she no longer requires corrective lenses for driving. She also provided documentation of her previous condition. Cf. another possible case in Prather, *Miracles*, 91.
22. Anna Gulick (personal correspondence, June 10, 12, 2010; Aug. 26, 2010; medical documentation from both doctors, received June 17 and July 6, 2010; more sent Sept. 11, 2010).
23. Tadesse Woldetsadik (closely known to me), with information and medical documentation from Tariku Kebede Woldeyes and Adanech Negash Tesema, personal correspondence, Sept. 28, 2009; follow-up correspondence, Oct. 1, 2009.
24. Yazmin Hommer (personal correspondence, with records, Dec. 1, 2009).
25. Personal correspondence, July 22, 2010.
26. E.g., Byron Klaus (documentation sent July 10, 2009).

I also noted Carl Cocherell's healing from a broken ankle bone. The radiology reports shared with me indicate a diagnosis on March 8, 2006, of "left cuboid avulsion fracture," which required overnight immobilization in the hospital. The radiology report from a different doctor on March 15 both notes that he was examined for a fracture and observed the splint that had been attached to his leg. Nevertheless, it declares that "fracture or dislocation is not suspected." Would a sixty-two-year-old man's bone heal so quickly naturally that in a single week not even a sign of the fracture would remain?[27]

Among better known testimonies, Ben Godwin's testimony of bone restoration without the planned bone graft surgery includes X-rays and medical reports.[28] Lee McDougald cites medical attestation for his total healing from advanced Parkinson's disease.[29] Although in much of the Majority World medical documentation is hard to come by, a research team in which I have confidence confirmed a number of cases of extraordinarily significant improvements in hearing and vision after prayer in the ministry surrounding Heidi and Rolland Baker and Global Awakening in Mozambique.[30] In another documented case, a middle-aged patient suffering for several years with Sjogren's syndrome, a currently incurable autoimmune disorder, neither produced saliva nor was expected to be able to ever produce it. After prayer, and without medication, her mouth began producing saliva.[31] Similarly, a doctor attests that due to cancer and surgery, Bob Bruce had no salivary glands. Nevertheless, after two and a half years without saliva, his mouth began spontaneously producing normal saliva, indicating new glands.[32] Among recoveries not noted earlier in this book, a woman in the United States was confined to bed most of the day with an incurable, progres-

27. Radiology reports from Skaggs Community Health Center (Branson, Mo.; CT results March 8, 2006); Oakwood Hospital Southshore (Michigan; March 15, 2006). One cannot charge pecuniary motives for an initial misdiagnosis (an unlikely proposal to begin with for a U.S. hospital); the original discharge summary noted that "the patient will followup [sic] with his primary care physician." The March 15 report indicates some unrelated, "minimal early spur formation," but "the osseous, articular, and soft tissue anatomy appears to be basically intact." I retain copies of these documents in my possession.

28. Godwin, *Strategy*, 62–64, 164–67. In personal correspondence dated May 28, 2009, Ben Godwin also provided me an updated report from the original orthopedic surgeon (dated Jan. 9, 2009). As noted earlier, the missing bone included three inches from his tibia.

29. In personal correspondence, May 24, 2009, Lee McDougald directed me to the statement of Dr. William Lightfoot, one of his physicians, at http://www.cbn.com/700club/features/amazing/Lee_McDougald122208.aspx?; accessed June 21, 2009: "Parkinson's is generally a progressive neurological disorder . . . I can only say that I have never seen a Parkinson's patient healed as completely as Lee was." The healing occurred in 2006, after many years of decline.

30. Brown, Mory, Williams, and McClymond, "Effects," in a medical journal; I was in correspondence with Dr. Brown both before and after their investigation, not related to my correspondence with the Bakers. Audiometric and visual acuity measurements of improved function closely matched self-reported improvements after prayer.

31. Documentation from June 2005 through Feb. 2009, in my possession, courtesy of Dr. David Zaritzky (sent in May 2009).

32. I received the doctor's report from him in Aug. 2010. See also Bob Bruce (personal correspondence, July 26, 2010); Bruce, *Care*, 25–29 (for the sickness), 67–68 (for the healing; other cures mentioned on 26). This case was referred to me very confidently by Gwladys Keating, whom I know and who belongs to the same Presbyterian church of which Bob Bruce is a member (personal correspondence, July 25; follow-up, Aug. 16, 2010). Nivedita Ghosh of Kolkata, India, offered another case of apparent regeneration of salivary glands destroyed by treatment (shared with me Oct. 13, 2010).

sive disease. In fall 2004, when friends in Nigeria called during the night and noted that they had prayed and she was healed, she ignored them and simply went back to sleep. The next day, however, she discovered to her astonishment that she was well, as new tests confirmed; tests also ruled out the possibility of initial misdiagnosis.[33]

In other kinds of cases, Christian doctors have sometimes expressed their confidence that various cures reflected divine intervention. For example, Dr. Chauncey Crandall reports the raising immediately after prayer of a person who had been dead for forty minutes, noting the presence of other witnesses;[34] similarly if less dramatically, Dr. Jenny Lai, a medical doctor who long worked with a healing ministry in Taiwan, sent me a number of cure reports known directly to her about which she felt confident.[35] Dr. Jeannie Lindquist notes a patient healed of kidney failure through prayer, and Dr. Raquel Burgos testified of her own medically documented healing as a child.[36] I reported earlier accounts regarding cures of severe epilepsy, tumors, and the like, that I received from Dr. Alex Abraham, a neurologist.[37] Dr. Mirtha Venero Boza provided her eyewitness report of a burn healing.[38] Dr. Tonye Briggs attested as an eyewitness a dramatic closing of a massive wound overnight after prayer in Nigeria.[39] Psychiatry professor William Wilson noted the healing after three hours of prayer of a Methodist pastor friend, who had previously had "75% occlusion of his major arteries."[40] He also reports a nurse healed of her depression and the asthma she had suffered for thirty years when he prayed;[41] a healing of severe ankylosing spondylitis mentioned earlier;[42] and other accounts.[43]

33. Michael McClymond, personal correspondence, unpublished manuscript and phone conversation, Jan. 3, 2011; extensive before-and-after medical documentation (including detailed Mayo Clinic test results) sent to me Jan. 5 (received Jan. 6), 2011 (also confirming trace antibodies confirming the initial diagnosis).

34. See television reports and my interview cited in ch. 12. Other doctors report healings (e.g., McAll, "Deliverance," 296), and others report the testimonies of still other doctors, such as Charles Woodhouse (ch. 11) and William Reed (see in Bredesen, *Miracle*, 36–38).

35. Sent to me in Aug. 2009, the reports mostly range from 1992 to 1997. At least nine records involve some sort of healing, though these are of varying evidential quality (e.g., a young man paralyzed from a spinal cord injury who began to walk at a healing meeting; chronic foot pain healed after prayer; a university lecturer in mechanical engineering whose heavy, chronic infection declined during prayer; and so forth). These reports are in the cured persons' own words and signed by them, though some were very soon after the event. Seminarian Renae Hsu initially provided my contact with Dr. Lai. My NT colleague at Palmer, Dr. Diane G. Chen, graciously translated the accounts from Chinese for me as we discussed them together (Aug. 17, 2009).

36. Llewellyn, "Events," 255, citing interviews with them. Both noted medical documentation, but I lack access to it. Llewellyn also notes a "miraculous" outcome reported by Dr. John T. Dearborn (ibid., 259), and his own healing (ibid., 260).

37. Interview, Oct. 29, 2009.

38. Mirtha Venero Boza (interview, Aug. 6, 2010).

39. Dr. Tonye Briggs, phone interviews, Dec. 14, 16, 2009.

40. Wilson, "Miracle Events," 269–70 (reporting that X-ray evidence confirmed the healing at this stage). His friend reported that the non-Christian doctor admitted that it was a miracle.

41. Ibid., 270.

42. Ibid., 272–73.

43. A friend he trusts supplied accounts of a man whose heart was found healthy and his bypass surgery canceled after prayer, and a seventy-year-old woman bound in a wheelchair and body braces healed so fully

In one videotaped interview, a neurologist reported observing cures associated with prayer, including a patient's return from brain death.[44] Even a popular television program hosted by Dr. Oz recently highlighted cases of unusual recovery after prayer and some attendant medical documentation evaluated by his colleagues.[45] A generation ago, respected doctor Christopher Woodard testified to a number of inexplicable healings after prayer, which he believed to be divine healing.[46] While most such cure reports are not medical records per se, they at least challenge some critics' skepticism about whether scientifically trained persons could affirm that they have witnessed supernaturally caused cures. As we noted earlier, the interpretation of such evidence involves not only science but the philosophic grids through which scientific evidence is read.

Benedict Heron and other authors cite medical confirmation for their healing reports,[47] some other healing ministries cite doctors' verification,[48] and some ministries have indicated medical documentation for some of those claiming healing.[49] Additionally, a minority of healing evangelists have had physicians working with them to verify the healings; the catch-22 for an external investigator is that a skeptic will view physicians working with an evangelist as biased, but most other physicians will not be present. Nevertheless, as we saw in the case of Kathryn Kuhlman, many of the claims withstood public scrutiny or required a dismissal that would not meet ordinary standards of evidence. The three testimonies noted from Ukraine included medical documentation.[50]

I have also noted medical documentation for a raising from the dead in the Democratic Republic of Congo;[51] a doctor's report of his own healing, in which

---

that by the fourth day she was dancing (Wilson, "Miracle Events," 271). (She rose from the wheelchair on the first day and was free of all braces by the third.)

44. The testimony of neurologist Karen Garnaas, http://www.globalawakening.com/Articles /1000039117/Global_Awakening/Media/Video_Podcast/Episode_28.aspx; accessed April 3, 2011.

45. Associated with Catholic doctor Issam Nemeh; brought to my attention after *The Dr. Oz Show*, Jan. 31, 2011 (http://www.doctoroz.com/videos/man-faith-healer; accessed Feb. 5, 2011). Although this information came to my attention too late in the process of this book for evaluation and follow-up, see the positive reports in Zagrans, *Miracles* (e.g., 5–9, 100, 175, 222–23); earlier and more critically, Harlan Spector at http://www.religionnewsblog.com/11928/not-everyone-is-believer-in-popular-faith-healer; Aug. 5, 2005; accessed Feb. 28, 2011.

46. Woodard, *Faith*, passim (esp. some cases in 63–99 passim; though the *majority* of his cases are not inexplicable, even there the cumulative weight in his immediate circle might be significant). Woodard was Anglo-Catholic, and a retired Anglican bishop wrote his foreword.

47. Heron, *Channels*, passim.

48. E.g., MacNutt, *Healing*, 36.

49. E.g., Hinn, *Miracle*, 12–13, 37, 42, 44, 50, 56, 70, 75, 79, 90, 101–2, 104, 111, 116, 118, 123, 131–32, 139, 142, 146, 157, 159, 161, 173, 175. Despite significant controversy about his ministry and about some claims, Hinn has at least sought to provide documentation where he could obtain it. Others have complained about lack of adequate documentation; some ministries provide none, sometimes because their goal is simply helping individuals and they lack concern to offer public evidence for healing.

50. "Healed from Trauma"; "New Spleen"; "Healed the Scar." My former student Yulia Kolodotchka Bagwell confirmed the relevance of the Russian documentation for me (July 1, 2010).

51. Chavda, *Miracle*, between 78–79.

he supplied me with medical documentation; several other individuals who did supply me documentation; and books that supplied further medical documentation, despite potential danger to the authors' reputation. The reader will again recall reports from (among others) Dr. Rex Gardner, including

- the medical trainee who was not only healed of severe meningitis and its complications but even of eye scarring;[52]
- the healing of a cardiac invalid;[53]
- the nine-year-old deaf girl, whose instant healing from severe nerve damage is medically confirmed.[54]

These are samples of the medical documentation that could be offered, although, as I have noted, many cases reported in this book occurred in locations where such documents would not even have been possible to obtain.

One reporter who investigated a range of healing claims observed that they derive independently from various kinds of circles. Moreover,

> some cures are of organic as well as functional illness. And some happen instantaneously, in mere minutes or hours. Records are available in many cases, with X-rays, statements of witnesses and hospital reports. Dismissing all of it as medical error, hypnotic suggestion or hysteria which will wear off, does not meet a scientific standard of objectivity. Psychosomatic medicine can explain some of the cures but not all.[55]

Not all doctors take into account any association between anomalous cures and prayer to identify them as miracles,[56] but some do. Dr. Crandall, a well-trained cardiologist with world-class credentials, explained to me that he initially did not believe in miracles but occasionally saw unexplained miracles in hospitals. At a critical point, he noted, he had to decide whether they were real. Once he decided that they were real, he had to act consistently with that belief, and began to pray for patients in addition to using conventional medicine.[57]

He acknowledges that most people are not immediately healed,[58] yet the cures he has often witnessed following prayer far exceed his most optimistic expectations based on past medical experience. He offered the example of a man whose lung

---

52. Gardner, *Healing Miracles*, 20–21 (cf. also 15).

53. Ibid., 104–6.

54. Ibid., 202–5.

55. Oursler, *Power*, 25.

56. A Humean might reject causal connections between prayer and anomalies, but consistent with skeptical Humean epistemology would also have to reject causal connections more generally. Such an approach would make medical and pharmaceutical research quite difficult. At the least, one can notice patterns between prayer and anomalies (such as raisings from the dead) in a large number of cases.

57. Phone interview (May 30, 2010).

58. He witnessed only three instantaneous, visible miracles out of perhaps a thousand people he prayed for in Nigeria, yet these were not explicable naturally (Crandall, *Raising*, 152–53, esp. 153).

cancer had metastasized to his brain; Crandall prayed with fairly little faith for him, knowing that little could be done for him medically. Months later he learned that after very minimal chemotherapy all the man's tumors had disappeared, and the man's doctors were calling it a miracle.[59]

He shared other recoveries. Thus, for example, he prayed for a man with a tumor on his forehead; the man came back the next day, and the tumor was gone.[60] I already mentioned his eyewitness accounts of a disabled woman, man, and child each instantly cured during prayer;[61] he also witnessed a child's deafness instantly cured during prayer.[62] A young woman was dying of an illness from which fewer than 10 percent of persons survive, and her organs had already begun shutting down; she recovered fully.[63] Crandall writes of another woman whose large, inoperable tumor disappeared spontaneously after prayer,[64] and of a man whose inoperable large lung tumor was quickly healed after prayer, as attested by CT scan results.[65]

He has seen the deaf healed (though especially overseas) and those unable to walk suddenly gain that ability.[66] One Thursday, a gentleman whom he had known for many years came to his office.[67] He had not seen the man in six months, but this patient had a grapefruit-sized flesh-eating ulcer, with the wound going down to the bone, eating through the calf muscles. Treatments had failed, and he was scheduled to have his leg amputated the next week. The family had come to Dr. Crandall for a second opinion, and he concurred with the other doctors: the wound was incurable. Nevertheless, he would pray. After unwrapping the leg, he placed his hand inside the wound and prayed for the wound to be healed. He then wrapped the leg up, and confessed, "I've done what I can do; the rest is up to God." Four days later the man's wife called, noting that the ulcer was melting away and new skin was forming. Should they amputate it anyway, she wondered? Because a miracle was clearly taking place, he advised against that. By the following week, the man's leg was completely whole.

"Can that happen on its own?" I probed.

"It can't happen on its own," Dr. Crandall replied, sounding astonished at my medical naiveté. "Impossible." As in the case of his own son Chad, who died from leukemia,[68] not everyone is healed; but he has seen so many miracles since he began

59. Phone interview (May 30, 2010); Crandall, *Raising*, 50–52.

60. Phone interview (May 30, 2010).

61. Crandall, *Raising*, 39, 152.

62. Ibid., 152–53.

63. He provided details in a phone interview (May 30, 2010); the media also interviewed her (available at http://www.youtube.com/watch?v=YYNNXs5rq9s; accessed May 9, 2009).

64. Crandall, *Raising*, 176–78.

65. Ibid., 181–82.

66. Phone interview (May 28, 2010).

67. Phone interview (May 28, 2010). The account also appears in Crandall, *Raising*, 171.

68. For Chad's valiant struggle over the years and finally death, see Crandall, *Raising*, 7–131, passim. The leukemia did regress at times (35, 45), but ultimately metastasized (81); nevertheless, Chad was healed instantly during prayer from another condition that could have been chronic (101–2). Nearing the end, Chad briefly died and revived as his mother prayed, astonishing the watching nurse and respiratory

praying for patients that he cannot doubt their reality.[69] For the past year before our interview, he had been keeping notes on the cases.[70] One could go on, but my point in all this survey is that modernity's simple dismissal of miracles on the basis of "modern knowledge" is in the eye of the beholder; some doctors qualified to evaluate extraordinary cures do contend that they have witnessed some. One should not attribute it to neglect of intellect when some favor what appears to be significant firsthand evidence over others' preferred interpretive grids.

Implications of and Prospects for Medical Documentation

Gardner insists that modern comparative examples can chasten our excessive tendency to skepticism of all ancient accounts. As an example of this approach, he analyzes one report of a missionary doctor in Pakistan where the patient is supposed to have recovered miraculously. Examining it as skeptically as possible based on the lacunae in the information, he concludes that the recovery could have occurred naturally (though not that it was invented). But because the source was a contemporary one, he was then able to obtain all the medical details and to show that the recovery was indeed extranormal (the woman may have "lost more than her total blood volume" in a forty-eight-hour period, with only two pints available to be added). He concludes that whereas "the normal techniques of historical scholarship" would have inclined us to dismiss the story, the availability of medical data in this case demonstrates that something quite unusual did (hence could) happen.[71]

That some doctors would testify to miracles is not as surprising as one might suppose if one assumed that all intellectuals accepted Hume's view on miracles. In one 2004 national study of 1,100 physicians, 74 percent responded that they believed "that miracles have occurred in the past," while almost the same number, 73 percent, affirm that they "can occur today." The majority of physicians (59 percent) pray for their patients, and roughly 46 percent encourage patients to pray at least partly for God to answer their prayers. What might be the largest surprise in the survey, however, is that 55 percent of physicians claimed to "have seen treatment results in their patients that they would consider miraculous."[72] Apparently most

---

therapist (127). Uncured from leukemia, however, he died again soon afterward; Crandall prayed for an hour and a half to raise him, but he remained dead (130). (This case differs from Markin's in that in the latter Crandall specifically felt God moving him to pray for the raising.) Crandall argues that perfect healing awaited Chad and others in heaven (133–34, 138, 192); others involved with healing also recognize death in Christ as healing (Hickson, *Bridegroom*, 326). (This approach of course involves a theological affirmation and not a belief regarding miracles per se.)

69. Phone interview (May 30, 2010). In our May 28 interview, he pointed out that obvious miracles do not happen every day, but they happen often enough.

70. Phone interview (May 30, 2010); whether due to time constraints or confidentiality concerns, he was not able to provide me access to the notes. For several local (Channel 7) media clips of interviews with Dr. Crandall's patients who experienced cures, including Jeff Markin, see http://www.youtube.com /watch?v=vGQmGGWzLQM&feature=related; accessed June 7, 2010.

71. Gardner, "Miracles," 1930.

72. See "Science or Miracle," summarizing results of a survey by HCD Research and the Louis Finkelstein Institute for Religious and Social Studies of The Jewish Theological Seminary. One could argue that

physicians are willing to acknowledge divine activity along with medical treatment, rather than viewing the two spheres as incompatible. Some may be reluctant to try to publicly surmount the Humean standards of proof demanded by colleagues, yet many are willing to acknowledge witnessing results that they personally consider supernaturally beneficial. While in many cases their "miraculous results" would not meet some conventional tests for miracles, I have already noted earlier that some claim to have witnessed cures that would.

One group that has recently sought to provide medical documentation for extranormal healings is the World Christian Doctors Network, with scores of cases from around the world posted at their website and newer ones in their journal.[73] Naturally the accounts for which they can provide documentation are limited by the currently narrow circles covered by their network; one could nevertheless fill a chapter with the material they provide. (A number of these cases admittedly involve gradual or partial healings, and the evidence is of varying quality.[74]) Some cases, however, are more substantial. A radiologist who looked through some of the documentation for me found some of it impressive. For example, in a case of calcified tendonitis of the elbow,[75] the calcification evident in an earlier X-ray had clearly disappeared, and it was not corrected by surgery, which would have left a scar. In another case, chronic tuberculosis had destroyed much of a singer's lung and led to the collapse of the upper lobe before the healing; this healing, too, exceeded natural recovery. In such cases, the radiologist confirmed from the bone structure that the X-rays involved the same person both before and after the healing.[76]

---

religious physicians could have been more ready to answer the survey than nonreligious physicians, but the figures are nevertheless revealing and at least give a basic estimate of belief and practice. Definitions of "miraculous" may have also varied among them; but again, most miraculous cures reported in this book are outside the normal range of treatment results, many in locations where medical help was unavailable. (I personally suspect that God typically works through medical means when these are available, though there are many reports of exceptions.) Many do not claim to have seen miracles (e.g., Lesslie, *Angels*, 105, who is not opposed to them); again, some define the term more rigorously than others.

73. Some significant claims seem to include documented healing of disk herniation (Case 1 in *JWCDN* 1 [1, 2009]: 15–18; Case 2 in *JWCDN* 1 [1, 2009]: 19–21); partial healing of deafness (http://www .wcdn.org/wcdn_eng/case/case_content.asp?id=23&page=4; accessed May 6, 2009; http://www.wcdn .org/wcdn_eng/case/case_content.asp?id=38&page=3; accessed May 6, 2009; *JWCDN* 1 [1, 2009]: 24–26); and other ailments. It also claims a thirty-year-old Taiwanese paraplegic finally able to walk without crutches after prayer in May 2004, twenty years after the injury. Those who recover from spinal cord injuries recover most rapidly in the first three months, and most recovery is completed in the first year. The source suggests that although her legs remained weak, she could now walk and live independently, and her gait pattern improved (*JWCDN* 1 [1, 2009]: 52–58, providing medical documentation). Yet I lack means to independently verify the information, to know what information might be missing in some cases; I had some initial concerns, but, lacking knowledge of the Korean language, was limited in pursuing them. I offer a very small number of specified and carefully selected examples elsewhere in the book (in most cases tentatively), but nowhere does my case rest on them.

74. My kind and helpful correspondent there also recognizes this and rightly pointed out that more recent accounts tended to be more rigorously documented.

75. The case involves Deaconess Ahn, a violinist in the Nissi Orchestra, from Jan. 31 to April 12, 2002.

76. David Zaritzky (phone interview, July 24, 2009), noting that the tuberculosis was specifically chronic. He was confident about the cures provided that the X-rays and dates on them (which originate

Not all of the material is this substantive, but some of it is, an observation that could swell the numbers of documented cures available. Unfortunately, the founding organization is quite controversial,[77] particularly in South Korea.[78] Without taking a position personally on more cases or questioning whether some genuine cures take place through faith in relation to that organization, I have felt it prudent not to exploit the material prematurely. I am thus not expending more extensive space here on the evidence cited there, pending further exploration by other scholars better acquainted with the evidence.[79]

At the same time, the cases and doctors attending the international conferences (now with more than 250 doctors attending) represent a wide range of denominations and nations. These doctors come not to support the founding organization but simply to bring and examine cases with other doctors. These doctors have the freedom to examine and debate cases, presenting those that the academic committee considers the best cases and coming to their own conclusions;[80] researchers can examine their evidence case by case. Moreover, whatever approach other doctors take to this particular organization, its model of doctors compiling a database of cases of extranormal healings seems quite useful and will, one hopes, be developed further also by others. (I have already surveyed the Medical Bureau at Lourdes, though documentation there is largely limited to a single site.) Although their work is not complete at the time of this book's writing, other writers I know are currently working to collect medical documentation for a number of healings at an optimum standard. It is good to have multiple and complementary studies on the subject, and all researchers on the subject should highly value such medical contributions.

Nevertheless, as I explained in chapter 14, it is unreasonable to expect medical documentation for most healings that eyewitnesses claim. A high proportion of those reported take place where medical cures are unavailable, perhaps often even occurring this way precisely because no other curative options are available. Are not these settings more analogous to what we find in the Gospels and Acts? Yet in most cases we lack reason to dismiss the reliability of these eyewitnesses any more than we would dismiss different claims by any other eyewitnesses. In a large

---

at the same time as the X-rays) are authentic, and he does not see how they could be otherwise. Hock, *Miracles*, 33, reports that the doctor believed that torn ribs had collapsed one of his lungs, but (38) after his healing a medical examination revealed his lungs perfectly healthy.

77. In contrast to the Medical Bureau at Lourdes, which is independent of Roman Catholic control, this network appears to include considerable oversight from the founding church.

78. Despite support from some sources and the generosity of WCDN in allowing me access to their material, which is fairly extensive, several trusted Korean friends and scholars discouraged me strongly from using this source, based on widespread views in South Korea. Because I cannot read Korean and have not traveled to South Korea to research these questions, I am not in an authoritative position to speak to the question myself and thus defer the matter to other researchers.

79. If doctors ultimately find the material persuasive, I will have at least erred on the side of caution, and others will have more material to work with. I pursue caution in the event that they might not find it persuasive; I do not rest my case on any one source I cite, but I emphasize in this section sources currently less controversial.

80. Chauncey Crandall (phone interviews, May 28, 30, 2010).

number of cases, in fact, large numbers of people radically changed their traditional beliefs after witnessing such cures, which suggests that these non-Christian witnesses did not view them as merely the sort of natural recoveries that they would know happen occasionally on their own.

Moreover, the majority of healings after prayer, even when medically documented, are of cures that have natural analogies, although this is not always the case (e.g., for the instant healing of eye scarring or broken bones). That is hardly surprising, since most ailments that need to be cured are often curable naturally. But medical documentation is sometimes available, and people's response to it (from eagerly accepting the weakest documentation to stubbornly rejecting the strongest) again tends to reflect the predispositions with which one approaches the data.

In my opinion, some testimonies of matters that the witnesses are qualified to attest firsthand is stronger than some medical documentation, either when the former is strong or the latter is weak. Trustworthy eyewitnesses recount clear miracles, such as the instant and visible disappearance of cataract-covered eyes, now able to see—an observation that requires no particular expertise. Individual cases of testimony cannot be dismissed on the basis of the assumption that miracles do not happen when we have so *many* cases of reliable and substantial testimony; even a few clear cases should remove bias against testimony and allow us to evaluate it on a case-by-case basis. I will return to many cases of eyewitness testimony below. Sometimes, however, as in some cases summarized above, we are fortunate enough to have both testimony and medical documents.

Partial and Gradual Healings

From a NT (especially Pauline) perspective, one might allow a theological distinction between gifts of healings, whose object was simply a person's wellness (cf. 1 Cor 12:9; Jas 5:14), and a more compelling "sign," which was meant to get the attention of outsiders for the message about Jesus, by means of its extraordinary character (Rom 15:19; 2 Cor 12:12; Acts 4:29–30; 14:3). That is, believers can find in some recoveries encouraging signs of God's grace without feeling compelled to appeal to them as extraordinary evidence that nonbelievers would necessarily find compelling. Discussions of miracles today usually focus on the extraordinary, but at times we may find extraordinary elements even in cures that have ordinary elements. I shall thus deliberately survey some evidence that can be construed as more ambiguous (such as partial and gradual healings) before turning to less disputable cases.

Although complete and instantaneous healings normally offer more compelling evidence for miracles, and I shall soon turn to more of these,[81] many healing claims involve partial and/or gradual recoveries. These differ in form from most

---

81. Roman physician Paolo Zacchia (1584–1659) proved influential in his emphasis on cures being instantaneous (Duffin, *Miracles*, 24); that is, this demand too has a historical context. Most recoveries of

healings reported in the Gospels and Acts. Nevertheless, even some partial or gradual cures differ from normal naturalistic expectations. Many people concede that they have failed to procure healing for those for whom they prayed more often than they succeeded, but appeal to the cumulative force of the many who were healed, some too dramatically to be explained as comparable to what might be achieved merely by positive thinking.[82] Although it may have less "sign" value for outsiders than an instant healing would, a partial or gradual recovery remains beneficial to the person who recovers.

Some cure claims are partial; for example, a healing removing the cause of the illness (cancer) but leaving the damage it had already done to be cured by medical intervention.[83] In another case, supposedly irreversible damage reversed, but other treatment remained necessary,[84] and one could add similar examples.[85] A Methodist woman was immediately healed at Lourdes from much of her naturally incurable blindness (due to macular degeneration), though she still cannot see perfectly.[86] (This incident was not among the proclaimed cures at Lourdes.) A four-year-old boy with a severe eye lesion was instantly healed during prayer, so that the astonished ophthalmologist canceled the operation.[87] Of the hundreds of lesions this ophthalmologist had seen, he had never seen one heal naturally and did not think that it was possible.[88] Yet the boy's vision in that eye, while better off than it would have been otherwise, remains only 10 percent due to the factors that were not healed.[89] After five years in a wheelchair, a woman who was paraplegic due to a spinal cord injury heard God tell her to rise and walk, and she

---

any sort, medical or otherwise, are not instantaneous, so some reasonably consider "instantaneous and complete" an unrealistic standard (West, *Miracles*, 123). Nevertheless, there are cases of just such healings.

82. White, "Lady," 84; MacNutt, *Healing*, 31; for an example, Bredesen, *Miracle*, 27, cites the recovery of Episcopal priest John Medaris. MacNutt, *Power*, 165–66, notes that, ironically, his own neck and shoulder problems have not been healed, though those of others for whom he has prayed have been.

83. Gardner, *Healing Miracles*, 45–46, on a bladder cancer.

84. Gary Best provided me with the written testimony of a person whose body had been severely rejecting a donated kidney, with doctors allowing absolutely no chance of the kidney surviving. Before the doctors could remove it, however, it began improving, the damage reversing itself. Despite this unexpected recovery, she still requires treatment once each week (personal correspondence, July 21, 2008, also listing some other partial recoveries).

85. Note Neal, *Power*, 65, on pain reduction in an illness that was not healed (cf. similarly Schlemon, *Prayer*, 29–30); gradual and partial restoration in DiOrio, *Signs*, 116–20 (esp. 119); partial healing in Salmon, *Heals*, 116. Matthews and Clark, *Faith Factor*, 71, note a prayerful patient living much longer than expected: a tumor remained yet became quiescent, in a kind of cancer that normally killed 99 percent of its patients. DeGrandis, *Miracles*, 32, notes that a dying man's atrophied leg was healed in the sight of witnesses (presumably as a sign) the night before his death.

86. Heron, *Channels*, 143. Charles McDonald was bedridden from certified tuberculosis but began to recover after his visit to Lourdes in 1936, with a medically demonstrable complete cure after a year (Oursler, *Power*, 74–75, noting that this was not, however, declared a miracle at Lourdes).

87. Spraggett, *Kuhlman*, 104–6.

88. Ibid., 106–7, noting not only the healing of the corneal laceration, but more significantly the healing of the severely prolapsed iris.

89. Ibid., 108. Another healing in a Kuhlman meeting allowed a boy to see colors and shapes through an eye previously unable to do so (Baxter, *Healing*, 243–44).

was immediately healed. A year later, however, she relapsed after another problem, until four months later, during prayer, she was healed again (and remained well as of four years later).[90]

Most of those who pray for healing acknowledge that it sometimes occurs progressively,[91] though they also aver that it can sometimes be instantaneous.[92] Even some progressive recoveries, however, may be significant. MacNutt, for example, concedes that healings are often partial and gradual,[93] yet contends that these healings may nevertheless appear much faster than natural recovery (e.g., eight hours of prayer for an ailment that might require months of medical treatment).[94] Some claims are dramatic even for gradual healings, for example, leprosy being healed over two days.[95] At Lourdes, a years-long wound of twelve inches by six inches healed, but over the course of half an hour; another person near death was cured but over the course of two or three hours.[96]

MacNutt offers an eyewitness example of a gradual but dramatic healing where he was present in Colombia.[97] In this case, the woman's right leg was six inches

90. Schiappacasse, *Heals*, 63. Some reported relapses are associated with returning to a preconversion lifestyle (McClenon, "Miracles," 187; Koch, *Zulus*, 79, 276–77, 279; Salmon, *Heals*, 113–16; probably not the primary sense of John 5:14), but this cannot always be the case.

91. All those surveyed in Tilley, "Phenomenology," 547–48; cf. Marshall, *Helper*, 178–84. John Alexander Dowie differed from most other contemporary leaders in the healing movement by insisting that healing must be instantaneous (Alexander, *Healing*, 60–61). I have one report of what appears to be a progressive healing of a Taiwanese internist's healing of a severe digestive disorder (her own report, with her name and photograph, from June 1997; shared with me by Dr. Jenny Lai).

92. Again, all those surveyed in Tilley, "Phenomenology," 548.

93. MacNutt, *Power*, 27–33, 57–62. For claims of gradual healings elsewhere, see, e.g., Lindsay, *Lake*, 11–12; Lambert, *Millions*, 113–16; Bush and Pegues, *Move*, 47–49; Yun, *Heavenly Man*, 174; Wilkerson, *Beyond*, 141–42; Neal, *Power*, 39–46; Chevreau, *Turnings*, 35–36, 166–67; cf. Teresa of Avila in Matthews and Clark, *Faith Factor*, 60–61. Some critics dismissed healings in Blumhardt's ministry that were merely gradual and through prayer (rather than commands of faith; Ising, *Blumhardt*, 268) or partial (279).

94. MacNutt, *Power*, 45; cf. Fant, *Miracles*, 149–50 (only a month of the expected two years of treatment); Neal, *Power*, 23–24; Schlemon, *Prayer*, 47–48; Nichols, "Miracles"; physicians' comments in Duffin, *Miracles*, 140, 142. Blumhardt saw answers to prayer in a dangerous throat swelling healed overnight; dropsy in eight days; and a swollen foot about to be amputated, instead healing in a few weeks (Ising, *Blumhardt*, 212). Augustine considered a miracle "chiefly as an unusual acceleration of natural processes" (Clark, "Miracles and Law," 25).

95. Sung, *Diaries*, 52. Some gradual or delayed healings have occurred within a few hours (e.g., Numbere, *Vision*, 130–31). Less dramatically, a case of severe ulcerative colitis requiring almost immediate removal of the colon was progressively healed over several months, allowing repeated postponement of the operation, until the healing was complete (Bennett, *Morning*, 96–97).

96. Nichols, "Miracles," 708, speaking of "a greatly accelerated natural process" that he regards as miraculous. A very serious illness, which included tuberculosis of the lungs and infected wounds of the shoulder, recovered fully within three weeks of bathing at Lourdes (Cranston, *Miracle*, 92). Normally Lourdes counts healings only that begin instantaneously, but full recovery may take weeks; e.g., a cancer may stop immediately, but the bones may recalcify over weeks (Cranston, *Miracle*, 119), something that is impossible by currently known natural processes. Nevertheless, to be counted, a cure must lack a period of convalescence; the organic functions are restored immediately (Cranston, *Miracle*, 131). May, "Miracles," 149, appears to demand a more instantaneous cure, to match the literary accounts in the Gospels. Needless to say, this criterion excludes from consideration many cures that might otherwise well be deemed miraculous.

97. MacNutt, *Power*, 51–54. Flach, *Faith*, 87–88, also alludes to this story.

shorter than the left, making it impossible to walk without crutches. But over the course of a few days of prayers, the leg grew to within half an inch of the other one, and finally—for the first time in fourteen years—she was able to walk again, unaided.[98] I do not think that anyone will argue that this cure could have occurred naturally. If we wanted to accuse MacNutt of hallucinating or lying,[99] we might need to accuse plenty of other witnesses of such events as well. Were MacNutt so inclined, however, he could have peppered his book with far more dramatic and instantaneous claims than he does. If we claim that this healing was necessarily psychosomatic, our claim betrays our naturalistic biases, since we lack evidence that mere belief can produce rapid bone growth. If we complain that we lack extensive medical documentation supporting the healing's cause being supernatural, we certainly also lack it for psychosomatic cures of this nature.[100]

Similarly, Emily Gardiner Neal noted that a blind woman was merely able to see light when they prayed; they prayed again, and she could see fully.[101] While such a recovery may have happened in (two) stages (cf. Mark 8:23–25), it remains extraordinary! Dr. Bennett Hill suffered a totally paralyzing stroke due to occlusion of the basilar artery, a normally terminal condition from which one is not supposed to recover. He began to recover within two days after one evangelist prayed for him, however, with rapid progress thereafter.[102] Although her recovery was gradual and scars remain, a woman in Mexico is said to have survived being shot roughly twenty times, after which she ran through the night, and thereafter recovered.[103] I have already recounted the story that Yesenia Robinson shared with me about her son; given the sort of brain damage involved, his ability to speak,

98. MacNutt, *Power*, 53. Also, on 52, "In a period of hours her toes on the right foot had nearly doubled in size!" Bill Jackson (interview, Nov. 13, 2007) told me of a woman wearing a lift of about one and a half inches in her shoe; when he prayed and lightly tapped her foot, it grew out, and she removed the lift and walked home without it. The leg of a man with a built-up shoe grew two inches in Neal, *Power*, 56; Bredesen, *Miracle*, 34, cites one report of nine inches; see also Osborn, *Healing*, first photograph between 258 and 259 (four inches); eighth photograph (five and a half inches, also noted in 309). Leg lengthening has often been visually fabricated, deliberately or not, but when doctors have placed lifts in the shoe and the leg visibly grows out, releasing one from years of pain (as also in Venter, *Healing*, 263–64; he offers other testimonies on 52, 188; also DeGrandis, *Miracles*, 100; Schiappacasse, *Heals*, 5; Prather, *Miracles*, 200–201; Seibert, *Church*, 99–100), the healing appears to be a genuine one (the sort that the failed attempts merely imitate). On the charismatic "genre" of "leg-lengthening," see Csordas, *Self*, 58–67 (with some treating it empirically as "spiritualized chiropractic," 61–65, words from 64).

99. While arguing that miracles in themselves do not convey meaning, Phillips, "Miracles," also notes that skeptics lack grounds to accuse witnesses of deception. As noted in ch. 5, Hume's approach, at least according to its ontological rather than epistemological interpretation, presumes that witnesses otherwise assumed to be reliable must be presumed to be lying or themselves deceived if testifying in support of events violating his stricture against miracles.

100. Indeed, I doubt that acupuncture, massage, or drug treatments would have produced this result.

101. Neal, *Power*, 40. Cf. the named person in Osborn, *Healing*, 285–86, cured of deafness one night and muteness the next morning (Jamaica, 1949); an elderly man's blindness cured in two stages on two different nights, 295 (Venezuela, 1952).

102. Spraggett, *Kuhlman*, 97–103 (on Kuhlman).

103. She was interviewed on videotape by my friend Obed Arango (personal correspondence, Aug. 27, 2008, and ensuing conversation).

swallow, and the like is extraordinary, something that should not happen naturally given our current knowledge of the human brain.

Dr. G. Wayne Brodland, a professor in the University of Waterloo's engineering faculty and a specialist in biomechanics, provided philosophy professor Robert Larmer his account of his medically documented, progressive hearing recovery. Suffering from a substantial hearing deficit in one ear as a child, he became functionally virtually deaf in his late forties, due to auditory nerve degeneration. After prolonged prayer from groups that believed in healing, he insisted that his hearing was beginning to improve, despite his doctor's assurance that "nerve damage does not heal." To the audiologist's astonishment, however, tests verified that his ability to hear had indeed improved substantially. Although it was not perfect, he was no longer functionally deaf, and test results revealed that he could hear as well as he had in much younger years.[104]

British Anglican James Moore Hickson reported that most healings in his ministry were gradual[105] and that many others were not healed.[106] But he cites also some extraordinary examples not amenable to purely naturalistic explanations. Thus one "man, whose deep, long-standing wound miraculously filled with flesh during the service, can now walk freely on his formerly lame foot."[107] Likewise in New Zealand, one "calf leg, shrunken, had filled out almost to normal within twelve hours of the service."[108] A few such extraordinary signs like these could prove quite compelling regardless of their comparative rareness (or taking twelve hours rather than twelve seconds). Moreover, such problems and healings cannot be readily attributed to what is purely psychosomatic.[109] Some believers suggest that sometimes progressive healings give time to develop faith and spiritual growth in ways that might not come through instant healings.[110] An automatic response, for many of us steeped in skeptical, Western Enlightenment thinking, is to question the witnesses' accuracy regarding these more dramatic sorts of cases. Granted, some reports are undoubtedly inaccurate. But what does our ready assumption about their inaccuracy, when applied automatically even to possibly special contexts, say about our own captivity to particular paradigms?

The Gospels and Acts do not specifically describe any signs as gradual,[111] although a few texts might allow for such cases.[112] (Normally they do not specify

104. Wayne Brodland wrote this account at the request of Robert Larmer, Oct. 13, 2007; I have greatly condensed the account (found in Larmer, "Manuscript") here (from eleven paragraphs to one).

105. Hickson, Heal, 50, 114; e.g., idem, Bridegroom, 268. Even some gradual healings were so numerous and of conditions considered so incurable that their effect proved dramatic (idem, Heal, 77, from a hospital matron in China, 1921).

106. Most who claim some healings note that many others were not healed (e.g., Deere, Power of Spirit, 128).

107. Hickson, Heal, 85, noting the witness from Japan in an area of many lepers in 1921.

108. Ibid., 218.

109. See again ibid., 72; Gardner, Healing Miracles, 29–31.

110. McKenna, Miracles, 51. She provides a nuanced perspective on gradual and medically aided healings (48–54).

111. Noted, e.g., by May, "Miracles," 147; Pullum, "Believe," 141.

112. Though the recovery in Mark 8:23–25 occurs in two stages, it also functions as an acted parable to teach the "half-blind" disciples (Mark 8:17). Perhaps "that hour" in Acts 16:18 allows for it; Acts 20:10–12

the dramatic restoration of missing flesh, as in some examples above, though they do specify restoration of sight, life, and so forth. But many of the mentions of healings we find in the Gospels are bare summaries.) Observers might pose theological, literary, or cultural explanations or a combination thereof to explain differences between those accounts and typical healing reports from our own era. For example, perhaps distinctively Jesus and those with fuller acquaintance with his healing ministry, such as the Twelve, were more prepared to experience dramatic, instant signs than most others are. Or perhaps (on theological grounds) their ministry invited fuller attestation than that of some others in our modern analogies.[113] Other factors in the comparative lack of gradual signs might include the narrative focus of the Gospels and Acts (undoubtedly reporting the most extraordinary cures);[114] or perhaps a culture more open to[115] extraordinary signs; or less cultural disposition to analyze and remember (or perhaps care about) the length of time for completion (perhaps because they were more prone to believe in miracles than to doubt them). The differences between *many* modern examples and those narrated in the Gospels and Acts are worth noting, but they need not detract from the central point that eyewitnesses can claim extranormal healings, on at least *some* occasions instantaneous and complete ones.

In any case, the cumulative effects of some particularly dramatic healings reported today seem to move beyond conventional naturalistic explanations. Certainly cases such as the healings of infants or claims of people restored from a state of death, when these events occur in the specific context of prayer, challenge purely psychosomatic explanations.[116] One could object that sudden recoveries happen

---

might suggest it; in the OT, 2 Kgs 20:5 probably suggests it. Paul in Phil 2:27 may allow for Epaphroditus's recovery gradually or even construe it as divine grace employing natural means; Jas 5:15–16 does not specify the time frame explicitly. The summaries are not specific; most of the individual stories chosen for inclusion in the Gospels and Acts are more dramatic. Regarding frequency, Van Brenk, "Wagner," 258, while affirming that healings "happen with enough regularity," rightly notes that they seem to happen less often today than in NT accounts (at least in circles we regularly encounter).

113. One could argue that modern healings are on a lesser level than those in the Gospels and Acts or that God would grant them on that level only for extraordinary, strategic moments in history. The former position is a moderate cessationism not easily established exegetically but perhaps plausible empirically outside new evangelistic contexts, but the latter noncessationist approach might better accommodate a common experience in new evangelistic contexts. Either might be helpful for those who conclude (as some do) that Jesus always healed all who came to him, in contrast to less uniform healing claims today. Robertson, *Miracles*, 114, suggests that we do not have the same level of faith that Jesus had.

114. Conciseness is a possible but less likely factor (cf., e.g., Matt 21:19 with Mark 11:14, 20—Matthew makes the miracle more instantaneous by abbreviating the account). One might cautiously compare later hagiography to this degree: a narrative praising its protagonist is less apt to report what might be construed as failures (cf. Goddu, "Failure," 7, on saints' exorcism failures, which [9–10] seem to have clustered in the sixth and seventh, eleventh through fourteenth, and sixteenth and seventeenth centuries). The sociology of paranormal claims favors successes (Charpak and Broch, *Debunked*, 50–51), though this explanation works better for sporadically correct predictions than for multiple cures of blindness and other major ailments through a single person.

115. And/or in need of them, physically and/or spiritually.

116. Many philosophers do accept the raising of the dead as significant evidence, if it occurs (Swinburne, *Miracles*, 32), and most thinkers have long recognized that infants cannot be healed psychosomatically

at times without prayer (certainly a correct observation), but again some of the examples (such as restoration from death hours after being pronounced dead, and at the moment of prayer) do not lend themselves as easily to such explanations. One could regard all such claims as fictitious, but that particular approach, applied indiscriminately, will not carry weight with those (including myself) who know some sincere claimants or have witnessed their changed condition. It is too convenient a tool for dismissing evidence inconvenient to rigidly held presuppositions.

Some Scholars' Testimonies, Explanations

Rather than include all testimonies earlier, I have reserved several new ones for this chapter (where I will also rehearse briefly some earlier examples). These are not all more substantive than all accounts offered earlier, but the sources fit Hume's profile of witnesses with much to lose. Although I cited testimonies of various scholars earlier, I have reserved some testimonies of some philosophers and my own accounts for here.

Philosophers' Interviews

Robert Larmer, professor and chair of the department of philosophy at the University of New Brunswick, generously shared with me some interviews that he conducted with persons who had experienced unusual recoveries.[117] One case involves Irene MacDonald of Fredericton, New Brunswick, who had been experiencing rapid deterioration from clearly diagnosed multiple sclerosis. A specialist warned her that her condition was terminal and that she would soon die. Soon bedridden, she needed spinal injections for pain every ten days. As the decline continued, however, one Friday afternoon a friend assured Irene that God was saying that he was going to heal her soon. Given all that she had been through, Irene was understandably skeptical of such an encouragement by this point. Nevertheless, a dream and increased strength encouraged her, and Sunday she asked to be carried into church. During prayer for her there, feeling suddenly returned to

---

(see the perspective noted in Mullin, *Miracles*, 209). Accounts of healed infants include Duffin, *Miracles*, 60 (noting multiple cases); Ising, *Blumhardt*, 207–8, 211; Koch, *Zulus*, 102–4; I offer many examples elsewhere in the book, including (though not by any means comprehensively) Duffin, *Miracles*, 145 (a raised infant); Llewellyn, "Events," 262; Gibbs, "Miracles," esp. 67–68, 70, 72; Ising, *Blumhardt*, 206–7; Hickson, *Heal*, 76; "Healed from Trauma"; Sabourin, *Miracles*, 165–67; Gardner, *Healing Miracles*, 25–27; Crandall, *Raising*, 155; Hock, *Miracles*, 47–49; Brown, "Healing Words," 278; Spraggett, *Kuhlman*, 76–83; O'Connor, *Movement*, 162–63; Tarango, "Physician," 112; Bush and Pegues, *Move*, 55–56; Montgomery, *Faith*, 109–12; DiOrio, *Signs*, 21–26; Pytches, *Come*, 121–22; DeGrandis, *Miracles*, 43; Harris, *Acts Today*, 100–101; Fant, *Miracles*, 141–44; Rumph, *Signs*, 49–52; Ikin, *Concepts*, 86–87; Jeanne Mabiala, July 29, 2008; Josiah Mataika, Jan. 29, 2009; Chester Allan Tesoro, Jan. 30, 2009; Sarah Speer, Jan. 7, Aug. 20, 2009; James Watson, Nov. 27, 2009; Mirtha Venero Boza, Aug. 6, 2010; Iris Lilia Fonseca Valdés, Aug. 11, 2010.

117. Robert Larmer (personal correspondence, Aug. 4, 2009), sharing the chapter in an unpublished manuscript that he hopes to publish. I have omitted the names of physicians where they occurred because I have not solicited permission to publish their names.

her arm and legs. Instantly she had full "control of her body and fully regained muscular strength." Although she had long been confined to bed, she walked from the church and returned to all her pre-illness activities. That was more than a quarter of a century ago, and none of the symptoms have ever returned. Dr. Larmer not only interviewed Irene but also knows well many of those who witnessed the original healing.[118]

Dr. Larmer also notes the healing of missionary Bill Drost, who was diagnosed with stomach cancer and informed by the specialist in New Brunswick that "even if the operation were successful Bill would need a tube in his side the rest of his life." Bill often fainted from the bleeding but had deferred the operation, against medical advice, to attend a conference. Because nothing had changed after previous occasions of prayer, he acquiesced when people at the conference wanted to pray for him, yet he expected nothing. The next morning, however, he realized that he had slept without pain and now felt hungry; "he had his first normal bowel movement in months." Although convinced that he was now healed, he kept his surgical appointment. The doctors found "no trace of cancer," and after nine days of extensive testing, they finally acknowledged his cure and sent him home. He passed away many years later, of unrelated causes.[119]

Larmer also notes Mary Ellen Fitch, who was hospitalized with hepatitis B. She was warned that she would need to remain in the hospital for a minimum of three months and likelier a year, with permanent liver damage. She turned yellow, and her swollen liver expanded her abdomen. Shortly beyond a week in the hospital, she had a deep experience with God and committed her condition to him to do as he chose. Blood tests the next morning showed that she was normal; the bewildered doctors kept testing her over time, but she continued to test normal. Many years have passed, and she has never had subsequent liver problems.[120]

Dr. Joseph Novak, a professor in the University of Waterloo's philosophy department, also provided a healing account to Larmer, concerning Novak's mother, Mary. Her serious leg ulcers over the years had required various treatments, but operation for a broken femur cut off the flow of blood in her right leg, and massive gangrene set in. Doctors wanted to amputate her leg below the knee, though they acknowledged that Mary, at eighty-one, might not survive the surgery. She refused the operation, so the doctors told the family that they could not help her further, and to arrange for her to die in a hospice. Mary's deterioration continued there, where she dropped to about eighty-six pounds. At this point, Dr. Novak contacted Joan Gieson, known for her ministry to the poor in St. Louis and also for a healing ministry. Joan flew in to pray for Mary personally and even missed

118. Larmer, "Manuscript," citing interviews with Irene and Norman MacDonald, Oct. 4, 2007, and the witness of "a number of people in the church which I attend."

119. Ibid., citing interviews with Drost's widow, Ruth Drost, and son Verner Drost, and the published account of Drost's healing.

120. Ibid., based on an interview with Mary Ellen Fitch, Oct. 29, 2007. Fitch is now middle-aged; she was nineteen when she fell sick with hepatitis.

her initial flight home due to delays at the nursing home. The day after her prayer, however, the leg was looking better, and soon the black spots turned red, then later disappeared. Gradually all the gangrene disappeared, to the astonishment of the doctors following the case. Mary lived on for nearly six more years before passing away from unrelated causes (a stroke) in 2005.[121]

Others report further interviews; for example, philosophy professor Hendrik van der Breggen, in his dissertation regarding the philosophic plausibility of miracle reports, mentions interviews with persons claiming eyewitness experience of miracles, including a university science professor and the former president of the Evangelical Missionary Church of Canada.[122]

One scholar I know, Dr. J. P. Moreland, who had long moved in cessationist circles, was astonished to find himself instantly healed in answer to prayer.[123] He and a colleague now also provide reports of instantly healed bones;[124] an instantly and completely healed knee;[125] healings of cancers in their own church, including some that were beyond medical help; and the healing of blindness and deafness there.[126]

Some Limited Eyewitness Experience

I have reserved this section for the final chapter not because my own experience is as dramatic as that of many others reported in the book but merely because Hume emphasizes direct experience and denies the likelihood of credible witnesses with much to lose by testifying. Anyone familiar with Western academia will recognize that my academic reputation would be far better served by not challenging conventional assumptions on this issue. It would be even better served by not claiming to have witnessed extranormal cures myself, since some consider more biased those claiming to be witnesses of what the critics do not believe than those who, not having experienced such cures, feel free to dismiss them based on their nonexperience. (One might compare their limitations to the ambit of Hume's circle against those of Pascal or Wesley.) Making claims about some particular subjects violates the current understanding of "neutrality," and violating it seems particularly imprudent for one advocating a minority philosophic position in the academy.[127]

---

121. Ibid., reproducing verbatim the account provided by Dr. Joseph Novak. Again, I have greatly condensed the account (from nineteen paragraphs to one).

122. Breggen, "Miracle Reports," 383.

123. Moreland, *Triangle*, 164–65. Experience has also reoriented some others previously inclined toward cessationism, such as the cessationist in India reported in Miller and Yamamori, *Pentecostalism*, 150–51 (cf. the effect on the theologian in Hong Kong on 153); or Presbyterian evangelist Don Dunkerley (*Healing Evangelism*, 28–30).

124. Moreland and Issler, *Faith*, 136.

125. Ibid., 138.

126. Ibid., 149. They also note the healing of a case of severe, long-term digestive sickness and insomnia (149–51).

127. Some of us challenge dominant Western academic perspectives not because we are ignorant of them but because we feel compelled to do so by evidence we believe that we have witnessed.

Nevertheless, an honest exploration of truth claims cannot simply dismiss claims merely to perpetuate scholarly consensus. I have noted, for example, an increasing chorus of voices among anthropologists challenging Western assumptions regarding traditional cultures' worldviews regarding extraordinary experience. Most obviously, although she has generally retained respect, Edith Turner potentially risked her reputation in the anthropological community to attest eyewitness experience of phenomena in a traditional African religious context, phenomena that, according to modern Western assumptions, should not have occurred.[128]

Moreover, from another perspective, firsthand stories are particularly credible, because they bring the reader closest to the eyewitness level and demand the greatest care on the part of the eyewitness.[129] I can also insist that my memories of miraculous events are not different in kind from my other memories: I do not recall, for example, a healing I witnessed three decades ago differently or with greater embellishment than I remember other events from that same time. The images of the setting and persons remain roughly equally clear. The only difference might be that I might remember the healing more clearly when it was such a dramatic event as to be seared into my memory, partly because it so challenged my cultural predispositions.

I began my own quite young philosophic explorations as an atheist, at which time I denied the possibility of miracles; as one who is currently a Christian and sometimes moves in circles where such phenomena are claimed, I would naturally personally affirm the possibility of miracles. At this point, however, I am not simply affirming that I believe that miracles are possible or that I believe that they occur; rather, I am affirming that I have witnessed some events myself that I believe may be most easily explained in such terms. By laying my integrity on the line, I join those who challenge Hume's denial of the existence of credible witnesses with something to lose.[130]

I risk stating this even though extranormal claims have been traditionally ruled out of bounds for discussion in academia, whereas the premise that such claims

128. See Turner, *Experiencing Ritual*, 149, 159; idem, "Reality." The academy traditionally followed Humean thought here as well; Hume's primary target was apparently Christian apologetic, but he a priori dismissed claims from traditional religions as "ignorant and barbarous."

129. Cf., e.g., Covell, "Foreword," x, noting that they have taken stories "from participants, from close observers," and, at times, even the personal involvement of one of the authors, adding "even further credibility to the stories." On the value placed on eyewitness experience and participation in ancient historiography, see, e.g., Byrskog, *History*, 153–57; Keener, *Historical Jesus*, ch. 7.

130. See Kee, *Miracle*, 11–12. Gardner, *Healing Miracles*, 11, a physician, notes several doctors who could refute Hume at this point and lays his own medical credibility on the line. Against Hume's a priori exclusion of the value of testimony (even of concrete examples that he himself admits as unimpeachable testimony; Twelftree, *Miracle Worker*, 42), sufficient testimony should challenge a prioris, since our lives regularly depend on others' experience claims (Twelftree, *Miracle Worker*, 41). Strelan, *Strange Acts*, 9, notes that few NT scholars have wanted to engage supranormal phenomena in the NT; after a century of a priori rejection of the supernatural, "few academics would put their credibility and academic acceptability on the line by publishing on this material. If they did publish on it, it was to debunk it as historically unreliable or as illustrative of precritical thought."

are inauthentic is deemed acceptable. Because of prejudices like those I have noted earlier, it is not surprising that some scholars with much to lose are reticent to challenge the status quo even when they do not agree with it. Their position is understandable, but I feel that my academic integrity would be more at risk if I entirely evade discussing my experience concerning the matters in question.

Hume's epistemology rejects testimony for events that more neutral observers would attribute to miracles (a rejection that I have argued is oversimplified and problematic); yet his epistemology grants much higher credence to one's direct experience. My direct experience is very limited; I have not directly experienced the most dramatic cases (like raisings from the dead) described in the book. Such experience would not be likely for me: given my normal primary professional focus on people who have been dead for two millennia, I do not spend much of my time in settings where I am frequently exposed to major health needs. Nevertheless, after completing my research, my own limited direct experiences seem in retrospect sufficient to incline me to regard many accounts that I have received from others as quite plausible. If this experience is a bias, it seems to me surely a better-grounded one than the nonexperience that some critics use as a basis for explaining away others' experiences.

I offer some more direct accounts in the next section but begin with some preliminary remarks. My wife is a non-Pentecostal, mainstream Congolese Protestant with her PhD from University of Paris 7;[131] she and her family come from a region where Christianity peacefully spread from a relatively small minority to become the dominant professed faith in less than a century.[132] In that context and elsewhere, we have personally witnessed some events no less extraordinary than those reported in the Gospels and Acts, even if not on a regular basis.[133] If we

---

131. Like her father, who was gifted in healing, she has never yet experienced tongues, though some other family members have. At the time of writing, I have been a minister for about two decades in the National Baptist Convention, USA, and teach in a mostly interdenominational seminary affiliated with the American Baptist Convention (NBC is largely African-American; NBC and ABC are both members of the National Council of Churches). While I appreciate these connections, they arose from specific circumstances. My personal spiritual commitments are unrelated to denominational boundaries; I mention these connections only because readers might wish to know why I have not highlighted these connections the way that I have highlighted my wife's (and to explain how I had access to testimonies in particular circles). This is not the context where I have witnessed most healings, though examples in earlier chapters will show that these occur among various kinds of Baptists as elsewhere; a few were in Pentecostal church contexts, but most were outside church settings altogether.

132. In my wife's nation, Christianity grew from 2.5 percent of the population in 1910 to 89.9 percent in 2010 (Johnson and Ross, *Atlas*, 120). In Africa as a whole, Christianity grew from 9.2 percent of the population (9.9 million people) in 1900 to 45 percent (360 million) by 2000 (Hanciles, *Beyond Christendom*, 45, 128, following Jaffarian, "Statistical State"; Barrett, Kurian, and Johnson, *Encyclopedia*, 5); for Christian growth in Africa from 1910 to 2010, see Johnson and Ross, *Atlas*, 110–33. "Islam and Christianity," i, estimates seventyfold growth from 7 million to 470 million between 1900 and 2010.

133. Some of our eyewitness accounts (mostly not of healings) may be in the published version of Médine's war testimony (in process), although our original version will be greatly abridged (probably esp. regarding my own accounts). If someone accuses my wife and me of cultural bias for heeding reports from Africa (an accusation many would view as ethnocentric), I would respond that we are not denigrating the

include only phenomena that one of us has witnessed[134] or those shared with us firsthand by those who claim to have experienced them, there is scarcely a report in the Gospels and Acts that I could not accept as at least potentially the claim of an eyewitness (water walking, turning water into wine, and permanent resurrection being admitted exceptions to our experience).

Thus, for example, I talked with an aged Nigerian evangelist, Baba Tambaya, who was widely known to have survived stoning and being left for dead in earlier years;[135] a pastor who was wounded in the same war where my wife was a refugee fled unseen past his assailants;[136] as I have noted, a member of my wife's immediate family (her sister Thérèse) was restored from roughly three hours of apparent death after prayer, among eyewitnesses my wife also knows;[137] consistent prophecies from people of prayer in different regions accurately foretold what appeared to be impossible details of the future;[138] both of us have witnessed some healings instantly following prayer and have close relationships with (or have been) the people so healed; and so forth. I also have close, trusted friends who have given eyewitness reports of healing miracles in which they were involved, and (as the reader by now knows) have interviewed a number of other eyewitnesses.[139] For

---

insights of eighteenth-century Western philosophy but that knowing multiple cultures provides a greater critical control than knowing only (or uncritically accepting the premises of only) Western culture. An anthropologist supporting a non-Christian worldview complains about the condescension of those who regard her convincing eyewitness experience (visibly witnessing a spirit during an African ritual) as merely "subjective" (Turner, *Experiencing Ritual*, 160).

134. Our shared type of experience, by the way, reflects the commonness of the experience, not any deliberate matching on our part. Our shared academic background and nonmiraculous elements of shared faith brought us together; apart from a generic comment about her father's healing gift, I began learning most of her miracle-type stories only after we were engaged.

135. I met with Tambaya Jibirin on July 2, 1998. Our interpreter was Emmanuel Itapson, now my colleague in Hebrew Bible at Palmer Theological Seminary; Emmanuel's father had worked closely with Baba Tambaya. Other cases of people being revived after being left for dead are reported (e.g., Numbere, *Vision*, 178; Lynch-Watson, *Robe*, 50, shocking the Tibetan witness's persecutors; Acts 14:19–20).

136. Pastor Massamba (told to Médine and others who visited him and recorded in Médine's journal, June 27, 1999).

137. Antoinette Malombé (July 12, 2008); Ngoma Moïse (May 14, 2009); see ch. 12.

138. In spite of some prophecies not being fulfilled, some, especially some from particular individuals, proved accurate in extraordinary details. These include several independent prophecies from different individuals that she would marry a white minister, in settings where barely anyone was white and no one knew even of our friendship (e.g., one on Feb. 27, 1999, when she was a refugee in the forest; and in 1990 and 1997, from a different person who did not know the other). At the time, she had no reason to believe that it was even possible that we would marry.

139. In the course of preparing this section, some people in my immediate circle as well as some who did not know of the project told me about cures, many of which (if they are less documented or distinctive) are not recorded elsewhere in the book. For example, my physicist-trained brother Chris reported to me (June 23, 2007, concerning an earlier event) the sudden, complete, and permanent healing of a friend's long-term pain from a shoulder injury during prayer for healing in which Chris was involved. Similarly during that time, J. P. Moreland, though trained in cessationist circles, also told me that he adopted an entirely different perspective after witnessing several dramatic healings in his church (see now his *Triangle*, 164–65). Such events necessarily appear anecdotal in isolation—but can appear more persuasive to those who know the persons and their integrity, and when they happen on multiple occasions.

what it is worth, because of our own settings, only a minority of these events near us took place in specifically identifiable Pentecostal or charismatic circles. I shall note some more concrete examples in the next section.

I reiterate again my awareness that extranormal healings do not occur every time petitioners seek them. Many are not healed; many others experience only temporary reprieves in remissions; and everyone eventually dies. Even in the Gospels and Acts, healings function as signs of the future kingdom, not as universal guarantees of perpetual health. Moreover, in most Christians' theology, depending on natural medicine no more contravenes faith than does working for one's daily bread in addition to praying for it; in the Gospels, Jesus multiplied food when necessary but expected his followers to use natural means for their next meal (Mark 6:43; John 6:12–13).

I also emphasize here that, like most people with access to medical resources, I resort to these medical resources regularly, and there have been a number of times, such as a series of miscarriages we have experienced, where no cure, medical or otherwise, occurred. The latter disappointments make me sympathetic toward those who, from their own experience, are skeptical of miracles; I have at times been quite tempted by such skepticism. But our own experience is too small a sample size from which to rule out what others may have experienced, and some of the incidents we have experienced, including those experienced by myself or people close to me, were dramatically extranormal, not simply normal recoveries.

Even if apparently extranormal recoveries might sometimes occur naturally, and I have not witnessed such recoveries on a uniformly regular basis, I believe that they occurred immediately after prayer far more frequently in our circles of acquaintance than one might easily attribute to coincidence.[140] Some philosophers note that one need not rule out supernatural claims in the case of "extraordinary coincidence," with an extraordinarily improbable collocation of factors.[141] Witnesses cite a large number of such cases.[142]

140. E.g., although Harnack accepted Luke's historical reliability highly (see Johnson, "Miracles and History," 535–37), Harnack reduces the miracles "by a rather free use of the theory of coincidence" (537), until it becomes cumulatively overwhelmingly improbable (538).

141. See Swinburne, Miracle, 10; Corduan, "Miracle," 104; as "signs," cf. 1 Sam 10:7; for divine explanations in ancient Greek thought, cf. "Coincidence," 1021–22. This principle might apply to highly unusual cases of prophecy (e.g., Newman, "Prophecy"). Clouds spelling out Scripture do not appear to require a violation of nature, technically, but the natural probability of such an event is so low as to virtually demand a supernatural explanation (cf. Langtry, "Probability," 71).

142. An example of such a "coincidence" would be David Wilkerson feeling led to seek a particular person in precisely the building in all of Spanish Harlem where it turned out that he lived, in Wilkerson, Cross, 31; for other leadings or cases of direction, see, e.g., 106, 109–11; Peckham, Sounds, 84, 227; Alexander, Signs, 1–2; Baxter, Healing, 102; Bennett, Morning, 106–7; Piper, Minutes, 160–62; Tournier, Casebook, 213; Numbere, Vision, 445–46; McKenna, Miracles, 129–30; Lesslie, Angels, 152–54; Ten Boom, Tramp, 84, 87–88; Koch, Zulus, 12–13, 108, 261–63, 279–81 (for coincidence; for guidance, 26, 28, 235–36, 239); Alamino, Footsteps, 67–68; Anderson, Miracles, 4–6, 15–16, 41–42, 44–46, 76–77, 92–93, 107–8, 232–34 (in this last case, the precise yet unknown phone number where the intended recipient was passing in another state); the unusually fortuitous circumstances in Duffin, Miracles, 147; Flint, "Accounts," 147; Sullivan, "Foreword," viii; Carothers, Prison, 87–88; Lesslie, Angels, 144,

Closer Eyewitness Examples and Alternative Explanations

That eyewitnesses claim to have witnessed extranormal recoveries should be safely beyond dispute; the existence of such claims and recoveries, however, cannot by itself conclusively resolve the question of their interpretation.[143] Even if we accept the use of modern analogies, scholars might differ concerning the particular analogies from which to draw: charlatans, theologically suspect or (alternatively) naturalistically explainable yet sincere claims, more credible claims, or some other approach to categorizing the reports.

Even when there can be no question that an event occurred, interpreters will differ as to the cause of the event. For example, I watched as a Christian group of college students preparing for a ministry outreach event prayed for the stilling of a heavy storm; the storm, which had continued for a couple hours and was expected to continue for much of the day, stopped within seconds.[144] In the West, the usual secular explanation for such an event would be coincidence[145]—though as one person skeptical about undue skepticism pointed out, "All I know is that when I stop praying, the coincidences stop happening!"[146]

On another occasion, also in the United States, I saw a sincere man whom I knew take the hand of an elderly woman who had never been able to walk since I had known her. To the horror of the rest of us in that nursing home room, including the woman, Don commanded Barbara to walk in the name of Jesus and lifted her by her hand from her wheelchair. (If skeptics charge that faith is a bias, I may be deemed innocent of that bias in this case: I was terrified that the poor woman would collapse on the floor.) She immediately began to walk, though

---

146–48 (cf. perhaps 203–4); Wright, *Acts*, 131–33; Yohannan, *Revolution*, 36–38; Robertson, *Miracles*, 18; Anderson, *Miracles*, 23–24, 32–33, 34–36, 40–41; Woodard, *Faith*, 57–58; Braun, *Way*, 80–82, 220, 243; Brian Stewart (interview, Aug. 14, 2010); David Gomero Borges and Yaíma Gutiérrez Valdés (interview, Aug. 13, 2010); Marszalek, *Miracles*, 113–14, 184–85; Aikman, *Jesus in Beijing*, 106; the providential circumstances deferring execution in ibid., 70–71. Still, unusual circumstances can accompany both positive and negative occurrences; see Crump, *Knocking*, 13–14. I have also on some occasions experienced precise leadings (a very few are recounted in *Gift*, 37, 44, 51, 57, 121; one from June 14, 1998, corroborated through correspondence with Jeff Power, July 24, 2010); one could fill volumes with claims of this nature.

143. I deliberately take the following two examples from the United States. In the West, such phenomena, which violate standard plausibility structures, seem far less frequent than in many parts of the world, but such claims are made in the West as well. Regarding interpretation, those with paranormal experiences usually interpret them within their own folk religious contexts (McClenon, *Events*, 5), as faith explanations provide contexts for reducing cognitive dissonance (10).

144. Mentioned also in Keener, *Gift*, 62; personal journal, Nov. 6, 1993. For much more dramatic examples of nature miracles, see ch. 12, although I did not witness most of those. The stopping of storms after prayer is not uncommon (for another example, see Bright, "Guest," 47), though it should be noted that storms eventually stop, and they do not always stop when people pray. I have thus given preference to more unusual cases.

145. One need not rule out supernatural claims in the case of "extraordinary coincidence" (see Swinburne, *Miracle*, 10), but my point here is that competing worldviews produce alternative explanations.

146. Elberta Bennett in Bennett, *Morning*, 101, in the context of prayers regarding the weather. The point is not that all prayers are answered, but that for those who move in this spiritual sphere the "coincidences" often seem extraordinary and large in number (with past or others' experience as a control).

at first hesitantly, scarcely believing it herself, and after that day began walking regularly and very happily, though initially using a walker for security.[147] At first too shocked to believe what was happening, after she found herself able to walk she regularly expressed appreciation that she had been cured that night. Because I saw her every week I knew that she did not relapse after the excitement of the moment; far from it, she walked from that time on.

Some would explain this recovery as a psychological cure of a psychosomatic illness; I am not qualified to speak to whether or not such factors were at work in this case and cannot deny the possibility. I can say that few in the room at that time, knowing her long-term complaints about her condition, would have doubted the reality of her changed condition, even though we were not prepared to do what Don did. More to the point, she appeared as horrified by his action initially as the rest of us; moreover, if her condition was psychosomatic, he had no natural way to know that. If only a psychosomatic illness could be cured and Don had no way to distinguish it from a physical one, it seems quite a happy coincidence that we witnessed Don's involvement in this public cure but never saw him attempt any cures that failed.

I have witnessed extraordinary events on a number of other occasions. I have not kept track, and am not listing here occasions beyond healings. Nevertheless, the following, all from before I began graduate work in religion and many from within my first two to four years as a Christian, are examples:

- the instant disappearance of a cyst in the ear of a woman I prayed for;[148]
- after two of us prayed, the immediate functioning again of a person's kidneys, which had failed;
- the immediate healing of lungs that had been bleeding, where the doctor previously suspected lung cancer;[149]
- the healing of my own limping, damaged ankle immediately thereafter able to run well;[150]

147. After being confined to a wheelchair so long, her muscles were undoubtedly atrophied in any case. On reading this account, my younger brother Chris reminded me that he was also present on that occasion and witnessed Barbara's rising and walking (personal correspondence, Jan. 30 and Feb. 8, 2009). I have not been able to locate Don, then a Fuller seminarian, who had been part of my church, to secure permission to print his full name.

148. By contrast, a more recent cyst of my own had to be addressed medically.

149. I recount this one, regarding Mabel Cooper, in somewhat more detail in *Gift*, 59.

150. I have always had weak ankles. Within two years of my conversion, I was healed of an injured ankle at the beginning of a cross-country race after a couple weeks of limping in pain; the pain vanished instantly and permanently, and that was (to my embarrassment) the only race in which I ever took first place. A few years later (ca. 1984), I twisted or broke an ankle in an accident, and, unable to afford medical help, for two years could only limp on it painfully if I overexerted it, after the swelling eventually went down. I can testify that for those years I had not been able to run on it more than at most a few meters without intense pain returning and stopping me. In late summer or early fall of 1986, after no change in the condition, my ankle was instantly healed after I sensed special faith for healing while I was praying,

- instant and complete healing of flu at its intense peak;[151]
- and so forth.[152]

Yet on other occasions of equally intense prayers, no suprahuman cures were forthcoming. No formula allowed one to predict the outcome in a given instance.

Interpreting the Evidence

Cumulatively, I believe that the evidence should be sufficient to challenge any rule based on Hume's denial of adequate eyewitness claims for miracles. The exception must be if one places the bar of adequacy so high that no evidence can meet it, but to do so is simply to restate a presupposition that miracles cannot occur. Is this the conclusion to which an observer neutral on the question would likely come?

Is a Nontheistic Interpretation Necessary?

Lack of a predicting formula does not mean that we lack an observable pattern. If, for example, eyewitnesses or even medical records attest that some persons have been raised from the dead (though this phenomenon is comparatively rare both today and in the Gospels and Acts), one could counter that people who appear to be dead do sometimes (very rarely) return to life, and coincidentally some might return to life when a person is expressing faith for that to happen. Yet this explanation does not easily account for the clustering of such events around those who expect it to occur at times. A person committed to antitheism or committed for some other reason to admitting only nontheistic explanations might counter that faith is itself some active power not yet understood, though this proposal would seem a high price for maintaining thoroughgoing naturalism (some might even view it as another form of supernaturalism).[153] That is, if one is inclined to doubt

---

and I tested it right away. The next day I had opportunity for a greater test with six flights of stairs, which I ran up; the pain from that injury never returned.

151. Twice in the first two years after my conversion, afflicted by the flu and ready to disgorge into a toilet basin, I prayed and was cured so instantly that there was suddenly not even anything to disgorge. I had not planned to mention these cures until reading that a doctor was persuaded of the efficacy of prayer when his own flu instantly dissipated after it (Spraggett, *Kuhlman*, 62–63), hence thought it could be appropriate to mention it. Accustomed to vomiting during flu in that period of my life, I prayed that God would remove that affliction from me; while I cannot predict the future, I have not vomited for over three decades since that time (though I have been sick plenty of other ways, including a brief period with reflux).

152. When as a young Christian I used to pray in a wooded area, my arms quickly filled up with mosquito bites; after I prayed for the bites (and for those of anyone praying with me, on occasions when anyone did), they vanished within a few minutes (at most half an hour), which had not been my usual experience before my conversion. This happened on numerous occasions and, at that time in my life, without exception.

153. In a Platonic worldview, the world of ideas exerts itself in the world of shadows (hence in later Platonism, matter). Cf. sixteenth-century alternatives to miraculous explanations that appealed instead to "causes almost as wondrous: occult virtues of animals, plants, and humans; astral influences; the power of the imagination on animate and inanimate bodies" (Daston, "Facts," 112). Bacon allowed that rigid

the possibility of divine activity, one can pose an alternative possibility without assurance that one's explanation is itself probable, so long as one deems a supernatural explanation impossible.

Yet is it really intellectually necessary to dismiss as possible the explanation that large numbers of actual observers believe far more consistent with the most relevant evidence—namely, the explanation of divine activity? The majority of those who assume as necessary Hume's argument or antitheism are not themselves professional philosophers. They seem to simply take for granted that philosophy has excluded the possibility of miracles, when in fact, contrary to the belief of some outside academic philosophy, theism remains an acceptable subject of discussion in that discipline.[154] Indeed, as one committed naturalistic philosopher unhappily but fairly points out, the vast *majority* of philosophers of religion addressing theism today write in *support* of it.[155] Appealing to a philosophic a priori against the possibility of God as a cause will not work as an a priori basis for rejecting supernatural explanations for miracle claims. Atheism is not currently the default philosophic position, so it must be argued for rather than assumed. And if one does not a priori rule out the possibility of a supernatural explanation, many will find a supernatural explanation the most compelling one available for some of the incidents that have been recounted.

Normally one places greater trust in hypotheses that make accurate predictions; some would thus attribute unpredictability in these matters to pure coincidence. But historical work and social sciences in general cannot make exact predictions,[156] precisely because intelligent agents are not always predictable.[157] Since too many of the examples above seem implausible to me as pure coincidence, particularly cumulatively, I prefer a different hypothesis: a personal God ready and able to heal,

---

corpses allegedly bleeding again when their murderers were present might be miraculous but deemed it likely due to mental causes (Daston, "Facts," 112).

154. See, e.g., among many others, Plantinga, *Minds*; Davies, *Physics*; Davis, *Proofs*; Dembski, *Inference*; Denton, *Destiny*; Gale and Pruss, "Argument"; Koons, *Realism*; Oderberg, "Argument"; Gale and Pruss, *Existence*; Manson, *Design* (for both sides); Swinburne, *Existence*; Nowacki, *Argument*; O'Connor, *Theism*; for helpful popular introductions to theistic philosophers, see Craig, "Not Dead"; Clark, *Philosophers*; for a summary of arguments, see also Beck, "Existence." Even the Platonic theistic perspective of some innate knowledge of God might find comfort in the modern suggestion that faith in the divine is a distinctly human, genetic survival instinct (Benson, *Healing*, 196–97, 208–11, though he leaves open the question whether it is divinely planted or projected by need).

155. Smith, "Metaphilosophy," 197 (brought to my attention by Licona, "Historicity of Resurrection," 110n82; accessed Nov. 28, 2008, and later in hard copy). Smith estimates that theists (mostly "orthodox Christians") compose a quarter to a third of philosophy professors (196), but that perhaps 98 percent of those publishing on philosophy of religion advance theism (197).

156. Popper, *Historicism*, 12–14. Indeed, one cannot predict the outcome of particular surgeries, though one can offer statistical probabilities (Cassell, *Miracles*, 214); the reasons for unpredictability, however, are different in the case of miracles.

157. Barbour, *Religion and Science*, 140; cf. Barrow and Tippler, *Principle*, 139. As Ward, "Miracles and Testimony," 137, notes, we do not speak of human actions as violating nature simply because the laws of physics do not predict them. He would apply this principle a fortiori to claims about divine action, since he denies that science can formulate laws about God as a nonphysical being (Ward, "Believing," 746–47).

but one who also often allows created nature to take its own course and who is not manipulated by formulas, as perhaps an impersonal or merely psychological force could be.[158] Although miracles are consistent with the character of the biblical God, we cannot always predict a personal deity's future actions, especially when our knowledge about the factors involved in those actions are limited.[159] If miracles happened with absolute regularity, we would view them as part of the course of nature; their occurrence beyond providence in nature allows them to function more specifically as signs revealing God's activity and character.[160]

158. Lourdes notes the unpredictability of cures, emphasizing that this places them outside the normal domain of scientific laws (Cranston, *Miracle*, 136, 264). C. S. Lewis, like many others, argued that one should expect the usual course of nature in general, with God intervening only selectively (e.g., Lewis, *Miracles*, 201). Although his book reflects its milieu (an older understanding of natural law and sometimes a Platonic perspective; note the concern in Sharp, "Miracles," 11), many of its considerations remain useful in (or even anticipate) the current discussion (Larmer, "Critique," 167, thinks them "worthy of more attention and respect by professional philosophers"). I think the evidence today suggests more miracles than Lewis expected, but it is true that they seem not to occur evenly or pervasively throughout human experience. In terms of what is *conceivable*, miracles would not even need to be "rare" (Landrum, "Miracle," 56–57; Fitzgerald, "Miracles," 61–62); if they function as signs, they simply need to communicate something from personal suprahuman intelligence.

159. See the discussion in Smart, *Philosophers*, 39–42.

160. Detractors of Christianity sometimes protest that a genuinely good God would provide far more miracles than are claimed (also deists, cf., e.g., Mott, "Science," 66); some consider this a complex problem that challenges the theistic hypothesis (cf., e.g., Weintraub, "Credibility," 372; counting biblical miracles as arbitrary and biased, see Overall, "Miracles," 351–52, but McGrew, "Miracles," 4.1, shows why most philosophers do not follow Overall's argument; cf. Overall, "Larmer"; Larmer, "Apology"). Taliaferro, "Argument," 225–26 (responding to Sobel, *Logic*, 309), posits eschatological justice and asks how far Sobel would push the fairness argument, since skills and so on are also inequitably distributed. Some argue that miracles for a few are unfair (Keller, "Argument," 69–70; he allows that only God might know why, but only *if* one has other reasons for believing this, 73; cf. his process approach in "Power"). (As an analogy regarding complaints about God's limited benefits, one might note a writer's claim about a government leader who expressed concern about foreigners giving out candy if there was not enough for all the children. Resources being limited, however, it is said that the leader sometimes had had to do similar things [Corbett, *Cuba*, 186, 188]. Most theists would appeal not to God's lack of resources but to miracles needing to be distinguishable from usual providence in nature; my point is simply that we ought not to complain about benefits even when they are not universal.) McKenzie responds ("Miracles," 77) that miracles are unmerited, like all grace or election; that (77–78) different benefits may be conferred on others; that (76) their limited occurrence fits the Christian understanding of grace and mystery; and most important, that (82) there is a nonarbitrary pattern as to where miracles are reported, often associated with faith (82) or mission (82–84). Some argue that God could be good and allow suffering to prevent greater harm to the recipient (cf. Stump and Kretzmann, "Being," 312). Some argue for God allowing a measure of chance, so that misfortune generally (more than average incidents of it) serves a purpose (Inwagen, "Chance," 234–35; but while Inwagen allows for miracles [217], the viability of this approach remains contingent on his theological perspective not shared by all). Parker, "Suffering," 215–16, contends that if God *always* did miracles, human self-interest would overwhelm human moral freedom (cf. John 6:26, 30–31). Wei, "Meaning," 254, contends that if miracles always happened in given circumstances, we would see them as divine regularity; but since they are rare, they could be simply anomalies, like a spontaneous recovery. If, however, they were standard, one might subsume them under the ordinary course of nature (specific associations with prayer or the like perhaps constituting the distinguishing factor); Hume (as quoted in Mawson, "Miracles," 33) noted, "Nothing is esteemed a miracle, if it ever happen in the common course of nature." From a theistic approach, divine providence in nature is widely distributed, but miracles function more specifically as *signs* of God's activity and character (cf. very similarly O'Grady,

Hume ruled out miracles and thus circularly ruled out the reliability of any witnesses who reported them.[161] Hume's line of argument has cast its influence far beyond his discipline and even beyond those who are aware of its intellectual pedigree. Thus, as I noted in an earlier chapter, one professor, when I asked him if he could believe in a genuine miracle if someone were raised from the dead in front of him, unhesitatingly responded, "No." Yet he considered me closed-minded for being a Christian, although I was a convert from atheism who had once myself discounted all Christians' intelligence on grounds no better than his. Why do many academicians consider a theistic explanation biased,[162] yet one that presupposes atheism or deism neutral? I have repeatedly suggested that atheistic or deistic premises are no more neutral than theistic ones and merely pose as such because of their hegemony in academic modernity.

Suprahuman Explanations?

On the subject of miracles, William P. Wilson, professor emeritus of psychiatry at Duke University Medical Center, concludes, "In spite of protestations by some scientists, documented events occur regularly both in this country and in the rest of the world," and many are similar in kind to those reported about Jesus and his early followers.[163] My primary critique in this book has been directed toward those who deny that credible eyewitnesses can report such events, not against those who simply reduce the question to one of interpretation of the observations (as often in many anthropological accounts that nonjudgmentally report such phenomena). Among Western scholars aware of the many healing claims in the world today, the second approach is far more common than the first.

Yet I also offer a secondary argument in this book regarding the interpretation of such events. I suggested earlier that scholars ought not to close off suprahuman explanations a priori, even if we did lack an overwhelming sample size of relatively dramatic, well-attested, and extraordinarily improbable (from the standpoint of naturalistic assumptions) events to completely establish the degree of burden of proof properly assigned to a particular position.[164] I believe that we have sufficient credible testimonies and other evidence (and that much more could be added) that cumulatively favor the probability that cases of suprahuman causation exist. As in civil law, most historians accept "more probable than not" as the standard for the burden of proof, and I have argued that unless one presupposes from the start that they cannot be valid this is the appropriate standard to apply when evaluating

---

"Miracles," 373). For a psychological critique of those who reject miracles unless everyone receives them, see Montgomery, *Trusting*, 117–18.

161. See Licona, "Historicity of Resurrection," 95, 97.

162. Hume denied the credibility of miracle stories recounted in religious contexts, which he deemed irrational (Larmer, *Water*, 105).

163. Wilson, "Miracle Events," 278.

164. Cf. Licona, "Historicity of Resurrection," 135, who notes that he would believe his wife's testimony even about a highly unusual event, such as meeting the president of the United States, because he trusts the integrity of her testimony.

miracle claims.[165] As I noted earlier, *hundreds of millions* of people claim to have witnessed miracles, and as I have also illustrated, a number of these claims (though not by any means all of them) are significant and multiply attested.

The radical Enlightenment (as opposed to the early Enlightenment thinkers) excluded even the hypothesis of divine intervention from consideration in explaining the data of even the best-attested miracle claims. Yet could it not be culturally elitist to simply dismiss from consideration the credibility of traditions stemming from most cultures and eras in history, based on a presupposition for which those who hold it rarely seek to even offer evidence? Granted, as I have noted, many individual claims, especially those far removed from the eyewitnesses, are inauthentic or misinterpreted. But does critical thinking always support an all-or-nothing mentality on other matters of debate?[166] Science and history address whether some people genuinely recovered; they do not need to rule out the question of why they recovered or the option of divine causation, although this question has usually been assigned only to theologians.

Those who start from theistic assumptions may view all recoveries as divine grace, whether demonstrably supernatural (i.e., not readily admitting naturalistic explanations) or not. By contrast, as I have noted, those who start from antisupernaturalist assumptions sometimes rule out all supernaturalist explanations even if no purely natural explanation is readily available, by merely postulating that a naturalistic explanation may be possible when more is known about nature or about the particulars of the recovery. Antisupernaturalists and antitheists should be clear, however, that they are filtering information through an interpretive grid no less than the theist is.[167] Those who do not a priori rule out supernatural factors, awaiting some evidence, will neither dismiss nor endorse all cases. They will find some cases more compelling than others and thus need to critically evaluate claims on a case-by-case basis.

Dramatic Recoveries

Although most people do not experience recoveries inexplicable in view of what is known of natural processes, the numbers of such reports may give skeptics pause, and some of these reports have strong claim to authenticity. I believe that some dramatic recoveries in the context of prayer do suggest evidence of divine activity. Some include medical documentation; a much larger number are, like claims in the Gospels and Acts, just eyewitness claims.

---

165. Ibid., 134, and idem, *Resurrection*, 193–94, noting that the different standard in criminal cases, "beyond reasonable doubt," would make witnesses for Jesus's resurrection even more difficult to challenge, rather than less.

166. With regard to claims of angelic experiences, Moolenburgh, *Meetings*, 203, notes that even if one explains away some stories as natural phenomena, hallucinations, hypnosis, or fabrication, too many remain to explain away all of them. Moolenburgh refers to his own collection of roughly one hundred accounts; the principle obtains far more when one addresses millions of claims.

167. What I earlier called a naturalism-of-the-gaps approach, in these cases without the gaps.

Although not all of the following claims share equal attestation, I wish to recall here some claims of dramatic recoveries that cannot be easily explained (if accurate) without supernatural explanations. Examples include reports of complete healings of severely broken bones and bone chips.[168] Other reports include someone who was said to have been brain-dead for months yet was restored through prayer;[169] healings from AIDS or HIV infection;[170] and a huge number of immediate healings of long-paralyzed limbs or inability to walk, even though genuine, long-term paralysis (the case in some of these instances) is not normally reversible.[171] I noted independent researchers who marveled at someone wheelchair-bound for twenty years who rose and walked even before his muscles should have been able to permit this activity.[172] A midwife reportedly gave birth to two sets of twins in years following a hysterectomy;[173] that this claim is impossible on natural terms goes without saying, but that is the point. In a similar report, a young woman was healed in Canada in 1922 and, though the doctor insisted that he had removed her reproductive organs, she bore two sons.[174] Others claim teeth instantly and miraculously filled.[175] Pastor Raju Mathew prayed for a woman expected to die the next day, who was completely healed;[176] a person dying of kidney failure was healed and then lived another quarter century, to the age of eighty-nine.[177]

Although cancers sometimes do go into remission, for which reason I have not offered as many of those accounts here, even some of these accounts are dramatic, such as the lady healed of throat cancer, without an operation, who now sings daily.[178] In another case an esophagus eaten by cancer is said to have been restored when the cancer was healed.[179] In another account (by the healed person's daughter, an eyewitness), a woman who had died from throat cancer that had destroyed her

168. Carl Cocherell (phone interview, May 2, 2009; medical documentation received, June 17, 2009); claiming X-ray support, Schiappacasse, *Heals*, 12–13 (bones), 31 (virtually new hip joints, after twenty years' deterioration); cf. ibid., 30–31.

169. Baker, *Enough*, 65.

170. Ibid., 160; Jeanne Mabiala, interview, July 29, 2008; Schiappacasse, *Heals*, 27–28.

171. E.g., Augustine *City of God* 22.8; De Wet, "Signs," 103–4; Ma, "Encounter," 137; idem, "Vanderbout," 129, 132; Castleberry, "Impact," 112; Daniel, "Labour," 160; Filson, "Study," 154; Bush and Pegues, *Move*, 56; Khai, "Pentecostalism," 270; Green, *Thirty Years*, 104; Dunkerley, *Healing Evangelism*, 18–20; Harris, *Acts Today*, 104–5; Marie Brown, correspondence, May 31, 2006; Bernard Luvutse, personal correspondence, Aug. 17, 2006; Shelley Hollis, phone interview, Jan. 10, 2009; Mina KC, interview by John Lathrop, March 2, 2010.

172. Hirschberg and Barasch, *Recovery*, 113–15.

173. Jeanne Mabiala, interview, July 29, 2008. For other testimonies of childbearing after a hysterectomy, see Lindsay, *Lake*, 56; Antoinette Malombé, interview, July 13, 2008.

174. Cadwalder, "Healings," testifying of his personal knowledge of the event, more than four decades earlier.

175. E.g., Castleberry, "Impact," 112 (from his interview with Benjamin LaFon), 143 (an interview with the mother, a physician); Gardner, *Healing Miracles*, 175–84; Bonnie Ortiz, interview, Jan. 10, 2009.

176. Raju Mathew, interview, Aug. 29, 2008.

177. Harris, *Acts Today*, 70–71.

178. Lambert, *Millions*, 114. Cf. also the woman raised from the dead and healed after cancer had eaten away her voice box, in Barachias Irons, personal correspondence, Sept. 13, 2009.

179. Johnson, *Heaven*, 53–54; idem, *Mind*, 36.

voice box was both raised and healed, thereafter able to speak.[180] I will not rehearse here the claims where the cancer had spread and was inoperable.[181]

Some have claimed instant healings of afflictions that were clearly visible, such as a misshapen skull becoming normal.[182] Hickson cites a case of organic troubles caused by an accident, including a crooked face, the removal of part of the tongue, and inability to speak articulately; instantly healed, the woman's "face was straightened and her speech restored."[183] One evangelist claims that he saw with his "own eyes" advanced cancer disappear instantly after prayer: the wound ran from the chest to the intestines, but he saw the color and texture suddenly change and the wound begin to close.[184] At Lourdes, the abdominal swelling of a woman with tuberculosis "immediately disappeared before the eyes of the examining doctors."[185]

More often, witnesses, including some I know, have described lumps instantly disappearing on various occasions.[186] A number of others cite the instant, public disappearance of goiters during prayer.[187] For example, Julie Ma recounts how she

180. Barachias Irons (personal correspondence, Sept. 13, 2009), passing on the information for me directly from her mother, from whom she had it and whom she consulted, Mother Katherine Taylor. Robertson, *Miracles*, 145–48, 156–58, reports nonmedical healings of cancer that had already spread throughout the body.

181. E.g., Reed, *Surgery*, 35, 52–53; Oursler, *Power*, 135, 231; Baxter, *Healing*, 184, 194–206; DiOrio, *Miracle*, 37–43, 97–105. Healings of cancers and tumors are common in Roman Catholic canonization records (Duffin, *Miracles*, 87).

182. Lindsay, *Lake*, 57.

183. Hickson, *Bridegroom*, 301.

184. Stewart, *Only Believe*, 75, portraying a cure of this character as highly unusual. He recounts also how two members of their team felt the place where a hole had been in someone's side before prayer and now found it gone (175), X-rays afterward confirming that removed ribs had been restored (176; it is not clear from the account whether Stewart himself saw the X-rays, though it sounds like it).

185. Woodard, *Faith*, 57, noting that she had been suffering for eight years "from tuberculosis peritonitis and also tuberculosis of the bones"; now she was spontaneously recovering.

186. Kim, "Prominent Woman," 205; Brown, "Awakenings," 363; Spraggett, *Kuhlman*, 141 (a probably cancerous growth on the ear, disappearing instantly); Harris, *Acts Today*, 100–101; Huyssen, *Saw*, 146–48; Llewellyn, "Events," 257 (cf. the visible, immediate disappearance of scars in ibid., 256); Osborn, *Healing*, 281, 293, 301 (a hunchbacked person instantly healed); Iris Lilia Fonseca Valdés (interview, Aug. 11, 2010); Zagrans, *Miracles*, 100; Moreland, *Triangle*, 169; Bill Twyman, interview, Nov. 11, 2007; Eleanor Sebiano, interview, Jan. 29, 2009; Yusuf Herman, July 10, 2011; Marie Brown, personal correspondence, May 31, 2006 (on Tanzania); earlier, Duffin, *Miracles*, 37 (a cancerous breast lump the size of an egg disappearing overnight, 1844); cf. Schiappacasse, *Heals*, 43–44, 47; Tari, *Wind*, 113–15 (a boil breaking); Koch, *Zulus*, 115 (a visible tumor healing—perhaps he means a boil—but the speed of full healing is not as clear). Anna Gulick (correspondence, Jan. 14, 2010; June 6, 2011; interview, March 11, 2011) recounts that after being bitten, one parishioner's wrist swelled to "the size of a small football"; Anna felt led to simply touch the wrist, saying something like, "In the name of Jesus," "and immediately the edema collapsed."

187. Sung, *Diaries*, 58; Yeomans, *Healing*, 123; Jamieson, "Healings"; Frodsham, "Victories" (a particularly severe goiter substantially reduced, though in this case apparently over a few days); "Healings at Victoria," 15; Tari, *Breeze*, 160 (a cantaloupe-sized goiter vanishing during prayer in his presence); Gebru Woldu (interview, May 20, 2010: "plenty of goiters" disappearing before his eyes); Blackman, "Miracles," 9; Spraggett, *Kuhlman*, 139; Osborn, *Healing*, 281; in the Philippines, Stewart, *Only Believe*, 143–44, 153; Gervacio Tovera, interviewed by Rose Engcoy, July 6, 2001; Bruce Kinabrew, personal correspondence, June 24, 2008; Dwight Palmquist, personal correspondence, Feb. 2, 2009; Osborn, *Healing*, 307; cf. Ma, "Encounter," 136; elsewhere in Asia, Jones, *Wonders*, 107. In Ma, "Vanderbout," 130, and idem, *Mission*,

and her husband, Wonsuk, who are both scholars, prayed for a woman who had been dying from a toxic goiter. Neither doctors nor local cultic practices had been able to cure it; it had simply grown worse over the past year. "While we were praying," Ma attests, "she felt something in her neck and was able to swallow her saliva, which she could not do before. The goiter disappeared in the sight of many witnesses."[188]

Similarly, Gail Randolph, one of my coworkers at Palmer Seminary, found a raised welt on her calf about four inches long and two or three inches wide, and as hard as wood. She and her husband, concerned about the obvious abnormality, prayed immediately for healing, and when she checked in less than an hour, she found that it had vanished.[189] From the basic description, Dr. Nicole Matthews explained to me that this was probably cellulitis, but that it would not naturally vanish so quickly. In fact, it usually spreads quickly and requires antibiotics; its sudden disappearance is therefore not normal based on purely natural causes.[190]

Some have claimed instant spinal or neck healings so that a mandatory brace was suddenly rendered superfluous.[191] A teenager was instantly healed of a deadly condition, and testing revealed that even her bones had been healed—clearly an organic rather than merely "functional" healing.[192] Other reports of instant or un-naturally rapid bone healings also appear.[193] In other reports, a young man's severely broken leg, with no expectation of ever walking normally, was instantly healed, after which he went to college on a basketball scholarship.[194] A man long disabled with Parkinson's disease reports instant healing when prayed for, with complete and continuing mobility thereafter.[195] A child's broken neck, with the prognosis of permanent paralysis, was fully healed during prayer.[196] Severe burns were healed.[197] Some skeptics about healing argue (beyond the evidence) that almost anything can be psychosomatic, whereas clearly organic restorations of limbs are never reported.

64, a large goiter started shrinking when they prayed and disappeared overnight. Spraggett, *Kuhlman*, 36, lists goiters among psychosomatic ailments, but it seems unimaginable that purely psychological factors account for these visible features disappearing instantly.

188. Ma, *Mission*, 65–66 (quotation from 66). During several following weeks of continued prayer, the woman, Edna, recovered her strength fully; Edna and many others became Christians.

189. Gail Randolph, personal correspondence, Oct. 9, 2009, following up personal conversation, narrating events of the evening of Oct. 4, 2009; my "less than an hour" allows for a margin of error, but her description is more precisely "some minutes." The incident is not spiritually isolated in this period of Gail's life. Although very competent doctors were essential to the process, her son's survival and complete recovery after a life-threatening injury exceeded optimum prior medical expectations.

190. Nicole Matthews, personal discussion, Oct. 10, 2009.

191. Opp, *Lord for Body*, 193–94, including a photograph of the woman holding her brace; O'Connor, *Movement*, 162; Johnson, *Heaven*, 27.

192. Casdorph, *Miracles*, 30–32.

193. Williams, *Signs*, 140–41; Godwin, *Strategy*, 16–66; idem, personal correspondence, May 23, 2009; Grazier, *Power Beyond*, 95–97, 125–27; Moreland and Issler, *Faith*, 136; Jackson, *Quest*, 256; Bill Johnson's church website, Nov. 7, 2006.

194. Wilkerson, *Beyond*, 149–51.

195. Lee McDougald, at http://www.thehealedguy.com, and personal correspondence, Aug. 28, 2008.

196. Rumph, *Signs*, 119–24.

197. Harris, *Acts Today*, 71–74; less immediately, Joshua Obeng, interview, Jan. 28, 2009; Chevreau, *Turnings*, 143–44.

Certainly there are not many such reports (including in the Bible), but they do appear occasionally; in one extraordinary report, for example, a leg severed beneath the knee grew back.[198] Elsewhere, useless or shriveled limbs have become functional and filled out miraculously quickly.[199] Those committed to disbelief that such miracles can happen will, of course, dismiss such claims;[200] but while the rareness of such claims (hence limited possible analogies) does invite caution, one might also get the impression that some skeptics' demands for particular kinds of evidence become stricter whenever evidence of the demanded sort appears.

I have noted a huge number of eyewitness claims of immediate healings from deafness (often long-term deafness) during prayer, in Africa,[201] Asia,[202] Latin America,[203] and the West.[204] I will not rehearse all the cases of the healings of deafness I have noted, but healing of this affliction is a common *pattern* in one ministry that we surveyed in Mozambique.[205] People who visited there specifically

198. Robertson, *Miracles*, 176–77, providing further details from T. L. Osborn about a man in one of his meetings in Ghana. (He does not specify details such as whether the entire restoration occurred immediately, but it appears to have at least begun immediately and visibly.) Such reports are not common today and do not appear in the Gospels or Acts. Clark, *Impartation*, 166, speaks of other "missing parts" being restored.

199. Osborn, *Healing*, 300, on a meeting in Ibadan, Nigeria (Jan. 1957): "a man, who had dragged his body on the ground with his hands for over thirty years.... His legs looked like poles; but as he walked, they developed." Because all Ibadan knew him, "It took over an hour to calm the multitude" (301); he reports other useless legs becoming functional (e.g., 298). Tari, *Breeze*, 44–45, notes shriveled and useless legs healed enough to walk within a few minutes, and filling out within a few days (with himself as eyewitness). Cf. Rumph, *Signs*, 110–11; other accounts above.

200. Hume, *Miracles*, 42–43, notes the abundant local witnesses for such a cure in Aragon and praises Cardinal de Retz for dismissing them. Hume's point, which we have earlier challenged, is that miracle claims should not be accepted no matter how many witnesses claim to attest them.

201. Hickson, *Heal*, 121, 122–24, 129–30, 134–35; Salmon, *Heals*, 75–76; Koch, *Zulus*, 80–84; Numbere, *Vision*, 210; Baker, *Enough*, 157, 169, 173; idem, *Miracles*, 7–8, 39, 43, 78, 108, 114, 163, 172, 180, 183, 192–93; Chevreau, *Turnings*, 142, 145, 174, 182; Marie Brown, personal correspondence, May 31, 2006; Kathy Evans, personal correspondence, Nov. 10, 2008; Shelley Hollis, phone interview, Jan. 10, 2009; *Finger of God*.

202. Sung, *Diaries*, 40, 91, 109, 111, 116, 155, 161; Khai, "Pentecostalism," 268; Daniel, "Signs and Wonders," 105; Ma, "Encounter," 137; idem, "Vanderbout," 132; idem, *Mission*, 63–64; Marie Brown, personal correspondence, May 31, 2006 (on Papua New Guinea); cf. the summary statement in Pospisil, "Deliverances."

203. Castleberry, "Impact," 108, 112; Steve and Sheila Heneise, correspondence, Aug. 20–21, 2008; Doleshal, "Healings"; among U.S. Latinos, Espinosa, "Healing in Borderlands," 136. In the Caribbean, note the Jamaican example in Miller, *Miracle of Healing*, 94.

204. Gardner, *Healing Miracles*, 202–4 (noting significant medical documentation); Ising, *Blumhardt*, 210 (partial deafness; from eyewitnesses); "Miracle Woman," 62; Buckingham, *Daughter*, 128, 132; Best, *Supernatural*, 88; Wagner, "World," 81; Reiff, "Los Angeles Campmeeting," 13; idem, "Later Healings"; "Revival in England"; "Healings in Australia"; Miller, *Miracle of Healing*, 48 (who knows the healed person), 49–50; DeGrandis, *Miracles*, 99 (involving a permanently damaged ear bone); cf. Tallman, *Shakarian*, 76 (apparently partial); Schiappacasse, *Heals*, 15–16, 21; Zagrans, *Miracles*, 5, 57. More generally, Bush and Pegues, *Move*, 51–52; for the Osborns' ministry around the world, see, e.g., Osborn, *Evangelism*, 1:938; 21:368–69; 22:536, 782; 23:440–41, 593, 720–21; Osborn, *Healing*, 280, 281 ("hundreds," with "as many as 125" in one campaign), 285–86, 290, 293, 294, 296, 298, 300 (seven), 304, 308, 309, 310, 312, 319, 327 (multiple cases).

205. E.g., Shelley Hollis, phone interview, Jan. 10, 2009; *Finger of God*; Kathy Evans, personal correspondence, Nov. 10, 2008; Baker, *Enough*, passim.

yet independently told me about witnessing this phenomenon, and one team of researchers has now gathered some medical documentation that supports the eyewitness accounts.[206] Lest we be tempted to dismiss the healings as psychological recoveries of psychosomatic ailments, most of those healed were being personally exposed to Christianity for the first time. Some were healed without even being specifically prayed for or promised healing; they simply were present as the new message was being preached. Their fellow villagers knew their deafness, recognized that they could now hear, and were sufficiently persuaded that many permanently changed their lifelong beliefs and practice immediately. Is it possible that this pattern of healing tells us something?

Recall also the number of cures of blindness during prayer that I have noted, most of them immediate, many reported in the early twentieth century[207] as well as today. A vast number of recent reports of healed blindness involve the Majority World,[208] including Africa,[209] Asia,[210] and Latin America,[211] and in the West.[212] In the modern period, I have come across claims of perhaps four hundred healings of blindness through prayer, the majority of them from sources that I trust (some of them from eyewitnesses I personally interviewed or know personally),[213] and

206. Brown, Mory, Williams, and McClymond, "Effects," noted earlier.

207. Cf., e.g., Sung, *Diaries*, 28, 36, 56, 111 (multiple cases), 116 (multiple cases), 153, 158 (multiple cases), 161; Hickson, *Heal*, 29, 31–32, 37–38, 53, 54, 62, 65–66, 74, 76, 78, 85, 87, 118, 124, 126, 128–29, 135, 141 (noting thirty-six cases), 151, 162, 180–82, 191, 196, 205–6, 213; Rabey, "Prophet"; Lindsay, *Lake*, 32, 40.

208. E.g., Chavda, *Miracle*, 122–23; Osborn, *Evangelism*, 1:930, 938, 941–42; 21:370, 400; 22:65; 22:67 (two cases); 22:783; 23:592; 23:713–15 (twenty-five cases, with photos of five testifying of restored sight); 23:722; Osborn, *Healing*, 281 (as many as ninety in one crusade), 287–88, 291, 293, 295, 296 (the sister of a worker), 298 (two), 300 (multiple cases), 301, 302 (two), 304, 306 (two), 308, 310, 313, 316, 317, 326; crossed eyes on 296, 297, 300.

209. Protus, "Latunde"; idem, "Chukwu"; Menburu, "Mekonnen Negera"; Negash, "Demelash"; Numbere, *Vision*, 121, 186, 210; Baker, *Enough*, 76, 145, 169, 171–74, 182 (with further accounts of eyes white with blindness changing color as they were being healed, 76, 171–72, 173; idem, *Miracles*, 189); idem, *Miracles*, 8, 39–40, 68, 78 (often), 108, 113, 159, 160, 192; De Wet, "Signs," 93–96; Jackson, *Quest*, 254; Bruce Collins, phone interview, April 11, 2009; Shelley Hollis, phone interview, Jan. 10, 2009; Daniel Kolenda in a Nigeria crusade, Oct. 9, 2008; Yolanda McCain, personal correspondence, Oct. 3, 2008; Paul Mokake, interview, May 13, 2009; and others.

210. E.g., Ma, "Encounter," 137; idem, "Vanderbout," 130, 132; idem, *Mission*, 64; Khai, "Pentecostalism," 268; Daniel, "Labour," 160; *C&C* 37 (5, May 2008): 9; Bush and Pegues, *Move*, 61; Wiyono, "Timor Revival," 286; Aikman, *Jesus in Beijing*, 274; De Wet, "Signs," 121–23; Stewart, *Only Believe*, 139–41, 151; Angela Salazar Aragona, interview by Rosanny D. Engcoy, April 14, 2002; Chester Allan Tesoro, interview, Jan. 30, 2009; Flint McGlaughlin, personal correspondence, Feb. 6–7, 2009; Robin Shields, personal correspondence, Feb. 7, 2009; Jacob Beera, personal correspondence, Nov. 2, 2009.

211. De Wet, "Signs," 103–4; Castleberry, "Impact," 108, 112; Ramirez, "Faiths," 94–95; Doleshal, "Healings," 7; Harris, *Acts Today*, 22–23.

212. E.g., Parker, "Suffering," 216; Gardner, *Healing Miracles*, 31–35; Spraggett, *Kuhlman*, 26; Harris, *Acts Today*, 8, 18; Neal, *Power*, 40, 57; Best, *Supernatural*, 125; Laurentin, *Catholic Pentecostalism*, 103–4; Jackson, *Quest*, 255; Stewart, *Only Believe*, 1–2, 43.

213. E.g., Yolanda McCain, personal correspondence, Oct. 3, 2008; Shelley Hollis, phone interview, Jan. 10, 2009; Bungishabaku Katho, interview, March 12, 2009; Flint McGlaughlin, personal correspondence, Feb. 6–7, 2009; Paul Mokake, interview, May 13, 2009.

these can be regarded as merely a representative sample. Certainly a vastly larger number of blind persons are not healed, but the healings of blindness nevertheless remain significant. Some of these healings have included medical documentation of organic problems, including, as noted earlier, scarring of the eye tissue, which disappeared during the healing.[214] In some cases of healings from blindness, the eyewitness reporters have observed eyes white from cataracts immediately change as the cataracts have disappeared.[215] As noted earlier, cataracts can normally be removed medically only by surgery.[216]

Again, recall the accounts of raisings from death surveyed earlier, which I will recall but not elaborate again here. A number of claims date from the early twentieth century,[217] but again I focus on the far more numerous more recent ones.[218] These accounts also involve Africa,[219] Asia,[220] Latin America,[221] and the

214. E.g., Gardner, *Healing Miracles*, 15, 20–21; Warner, *Kuhlman*, 132–34. Although not supplying medical documentation, Peterman, *Healing*, 2–3, cites a case where a specialist could do nothing for a scratched cornea. The woman knelt at the altar at Philadelphia's St. Stephen's Episcopal Church for prayer for healing, and "arose with a healed eye"; the specialist acknowledged it as a miracle.

215. Baker, *Enough*, 76, 171–72, 173; Brown, "Awakenings," 363 (on one eye, citing the testimony of a retired radiologist); Chester Allan Tesoro, interview, Jan. 30, 2009; Gebru Woldu (interview, May 20, 2010); cf. the "flat and clouded" eyes restored in Robin Shields, personal correspondence, Feb. 7, 2009; cf. the claim in Ogilbee and Riess, *Pilgrimage*, 43.

216. Dr. Nicole Matthews, personal correspondence, April 1, 2009.

217. Maddocks, *Ministry*, 101–2; Tarango, "Physician," 112; "Saw God"; Fant, *Miracles*, 143; Woodworth-Etter, *Diary*, 156–57; Lindsay, *Lake*, 12–13, 32–33; Pytches, "Anglican," 194; cf. Yeomans, *Healing*, 120–21; and numerous other cases noted in ch. 12.

218. E.g., Lewis, *Healing*, 64–65; Osborn, *Evangelism*, 1:940–41; Wagner, *Acts*, 476–77 (and less dramatically, 321–22); Wilkerson, *Beyond*, 14–21, 25–32 (esp. 32), 47–54 (esp. 53), 56–58, 89–97 (esp. 94–95), 97–104 (esp. 101–3; his father-in-law's story), 105–6, 107–9 (esp. 108), 109–14 (esp. 113–14); Clark, *Impartation*, 203; Rutz, *Megashift*, 3–14, 21–22, 29–34, 79, 104–5; Rumph, *Signs*, 155–73 (including a small number of North American examples); Smith, "Baby"; Conn, "Visit to Heaven"; Carpenter, "Death"; Harris, *Acts Today*, 98–99, 101–3.

219. E.g., Bush and Pegues, *Move*, 52 (about raisings being common in Ethiopia); Chevreau, *Turnings*, 53–56; Baker, *Enough*, 74–76; idem, *Miracles*, 89 (at least fifty-three by 2007), 169; Chavda, *Miracle*, 9, 13–15, 131–41; Numbere, *Vision*, 136–37, 140–42; Tarr, *Foolishness*, 329–30; Pytches, *Come*, 241; Wilkerson, *Beyond*, 114–15; Venter, *Healing*, 294–95; Antoinette Malombé, interview, July 12, 2008; Jeanne Mabiala, interview, July 29, 2008; Albert Bissouessoue, interview, July 29, 2008; Sarah Speer, phone interview, Jan. 7, 2009; Leo Bawa, personal correspondence, Aug. 10, 2009, p. 5; Gebru Woldu, interview, May 20, 2010; personal correspondence, May 21, 2010; June 3, 2010. Earlier, Anderson, *Pelendo*, 69–70; Deere, *Power of Spirit*, 123–24; Daneel, *Zionism*, 15–16.

220. Gardner, *Healing Miracles*, 138; Miller and Yamamori, *Pentecostalism*, 152; Jenkins, *New Faces*, 114; Ma, "Encounter," 137; Khai, "Pentecostalism," 270; Zhaoming, "Chinese Denominations," 451; Kim, "Pentecostalism," 32; Bush and Pegues, *Move*, 57–58, 59, 60; De Wet, "Signs," 110–11; Koch, *Zulus*, 167; Crawford, *Miracles*, 26–28; Lambert, *Millions*, 109, 118–19; Venter, *Healing*, 294–95; Pytches, *Come*, 242–44; Cagle, "Power"; Thollander, *Mathews*, 88; Tari, *Wind*, 76–78; Wilkerson, *Beyond*, 77, 81–83; Pullinger, *Dragon*, 224–25; Elaine Panelo, interview, Jan. 30, 2009; Mervin Ascabano, correspondence, Jan. 9, 2009; Feb. 6, 2009; Chester Allan Tesoro, interview, Jan. 30, 2009; Willie Soans, personal correspondence, Nov. 3, 2010.

221. Sánchez Walsh, *Identity*, 44; Chesnut, *Born Again in Brazil*, 86; Bomann, "Salve," 195–96; Gardner, *Healing Miracles*, 139–40; Pytches, *Come*, 245; Alamino, *Footsteps*, 63–65; Wilkerson, *Beyond*, 84–88; Iris Lilia Fonseca Valdés, interview, Aug. 11, 2010. Earlier, Sánchez Walsh, *Identity*, 43–44.

West.[222] A number of these accounts involve persons who have been dead for many hours[223] or sometimes even more than a day.[224] Some are from people I not only interviewed but also knew personally, or met through my wife's family knowing them personally;[225] where possible I cross-checked interviewees' testimony with other witnesses. Witnesses range from those participating in the prayers to a person raised herself. While writing this book I have come across claims of nearly three hundred raisings, from well over 150 different sources. Again, these are merely a representative sample; some others have discovered far more reports that I have not included in this count,[226] and I found some of my own sources by randomly interviewing persons with healing accounts in a few sample locations in the Majority World. Because their stories have never before been printed, I presume that I would have found numerous other accounts had I traveled and interviewed more widely.

These sources may vary in their reliability, but a high proportion reflect reports from eyewitnesses that one would normally deem reliable. I am particularly impressed with reports from individuals whose character I know and trust. I do not include in the count cases of which I was informed (in some instances with accompanying names, dates, and locations) yet not permitted by my sources to use because of the security situation in their countries. I am also not including at this point claims of nature miracles apart from human bodies (which are, I have noted, also part of nature), but in chapter 12 I have noted such claims as well.[227] This chapter would of course be much longer had I included much of chapter 12 and some other earlier material in it. I have offered merely a summary of some

222. E.g., Dunkerley, *Healing Evangelism*, 45; Stegeman, "Faith"; Koch, *Zulus*, 169–70; Piper, *Minutes*, 44–45; Pytches, *Come*, 239, 244–45; Johnson, *Mind*, 122; Chauncey Crandall's account (in ch. 12); Barachias Irons, personal correspondence, Sept. 13, 2009; Dick and Debbie Riffle, personal correspondence, Dec. 13, 2007.

223. E.g., Wilkerson, *Beyond*, 105–6; Antoinette Malombé, interview, July 12, 2008.

224. E.g., Bush and Pegues, *Move*, 118–19; Chevreau, *Turnings*, 54–56; Wilkerson, *Beyond*, 81; cf. Tari, *Wind*, 76–78; Miller and Yamamori, *Pentecostalism*, 151–52; about twenty-four hours in Shelley Hollis, phone interview, Jan. 10, 2009.

225. Especially (in order of my knowing them) Leo Bawa; Antoinette Malombé; Jeanne Mabiala; Albert Bissouessoue.

226. Mike Finley, whose book is forthcoming, has spent years collecting reports; he knows of some five hundred to a thousand reports from the twentieth century alone. While he is not able to verify all of them, he is confident of many of them (phone interview, Oct. 2, 2010); in more than forty cases, "medically trained personnel (doctors, nurses, EMTs) were present when the individual was determined dead, and then came back to life" (personal correspondence, Sept. 23, 2010). Hebert, *Raised*, cites four hundred accounts (few overlapping with my count), though only a minority are both from modern times and have strong attestation (those with weakest attestation he assigns to an appendix, 319–29).

227. E.g., Koschorke, Ludwig, and Delgado, *History*, 223–24; Sanneh, *West African Christianity*, 181–83; Castleberry, "Impact," 111–12; Daniel, "Labour," 157; Sung, *Diaries*, 143, 158, 161; Bush and Pegues, *Move*, 54–55, 59, 64, 192; Kinnear, *Tide*, 92–96; Dunkerley, *Healing Evangelism*, 112; Dayhoff, "Barros"; Khai, "Pentecostalism," 268–69; Wiyono, "Timor Revival," 288; Harris, *Acts Today*, 66–67, 80; Lindsay, *Lake*, 48–49; Emmanuel Itapson, interview, April 29, 2008; Sandy Thomas, phone interview, Aug. 26, 2008; Donna Arukua, interview, Jan. 29, 2009; Kay Fountain, interview, Jan. 29, 2009.

material here to challenge the notion that all healing claims must involve only psychosomatic ailments.

Examples Nearer the Author

I list below some further examples used earlier in the book. Although I could have recalled many more, these should be sufficient to illustrate that many claims warrant serious attention. I limit the number employed here, because the reader can readily pick out some other examples from the earlier material, and repetition is not a virtue in a book of this length. I have selected these particular cases from among interviews with people whom I know on some level and have good reason to trust (e.g., they are intelligent observers without financial or other incentive to deceive),[228] to reduce the need for the additional criterion of evaluating the claimant's integrity. I personally have no doubts about the integrity of many of my other informants—to name just a few, the Bonillas, Marie Brown, Bruce Collins, Matthew Dawson, Bonnie Ortiz, the several Vineyard interviewees I noted, and Ed and Brad Wilkinson. In fact, there are far more of those whom I interviewed whom I have good reason to trust than any reason to question. Some that I have not cited below yet trust are some long-term friends; most lacked anything possible to gain by telling their stories; some, especially those who ministered in cessationist circles, like Bungishabaku Katho, risked possible things to lose; and most whom I did not know initially were referred to me by trustworthy persons or were part of a larger community of witnesses to whom they had to be accountable.

Again I could have chosen more such examples, but I have selected for the samples below mainly a limited number of examples from persons I know on some level in person. I exclude here most strong cases that I interviewed, for example, only by phone or had contact with exclusively for discussion of healing claims (i.e., did not know or get to know outside that context); I also exclude those with well-known ministries who might be discussed by others; and I include only a sample of those who remain. While I thus apply the following grid only to some sample claims, a reader could use the same sort of grid to evaluate healing claims cited by others in the book. Not all of those claims carry equal evidential weight, but a number of them appear strong. Theists need not apply these tests with equal rigor, since some of the caveats I applied earlier will exclude many recoveries that those customarily allowing for divine activity would admit as divine activity. Those who need to be persuaded, however, and remain open to persuasion, may find at least some of the following cases persuasive. Some may quibble with some of my decisions below, and those with varying presuppositions will approach them with

---

228. In many cases, like Jeanne Mabiala, the person does not live in an Anglophone nation, thus would not likely gain even publicity from the places of this book's circulation (even if it is translated, which they have no reason to expect).

various degrees of openness, but I personally believe that most of the following cases are best explained by supernatural activity.

Healing claim	How do I know the witness?[*]	Psychosomatic element possible?	How frequent are such events normally (given an accurate description by the witness)?	Supernatural explanation seems more plausible than not, if not a priori ruled out?[†]
I witnessed: A woman whom I knew previously unable to walk began walking after commanded to rise in Jesus's name	I am the witness, and there were other witnesses present in the room (including my younger brother, who also recalls the occasion); I continued to see the woman walking (initially with a walker) in following weeks	Possible but not probable (she lacked any expectation of healing and the man who prayed lacked any reason to believe that her condition was not organic)	Rare	Plausible to (in my view) very probable (depending on one's starting assumptions)
I was present: a woman's cyst was instantly healed when I prayed; failed kidneys healed when I prayed	The healed person was a friend and member of my church; she claimed medical verification[‡]	No	At best, quite rare	Very probably yes
Flint McGlaughlin and Robin Shields witnessed a blind man whose eyes were clouded with cataracts instantly healed, his eyes visibly changing	Extensive personal conversation with Flint McGlaughlin on other issues; Robin Shields also independently provided post-healing photographs	No	Medically impossible	Yes
Bungishabaku Katho witnessed the immediate and permanent healing of a blind woman's eyes	Long-term correspondence, friendship, and meetings around other issues; supernatural claims also are not in his interest	Not at all likely	Unless the entire village conspired to deceive Katho and his associates over a period of years about her initial blindness, this is probably medically inexplicable	Very probably
Professor J. Ayodeji Adewuya witnessed his baby son being restored to life through prayer after twenty minutes with no vital signs; the son has now completed a master's degree	A friend and colleague with whom I converse regularly at biblical studies meetings	No	Should be impossible (the midwife certified that the baby was dead the entire time)	Yes

Healing claim	How do I know the witness?*	Psychosomatic element possible?	How frequent are such events normally (given an accurate description by the witness)?	Supernatural explanation seems more plausible than not, if not a priori ruled out?†
Elaine Panelo, pronounced dead from liver cancer, was raised nearly two hours later, simultaneously healed, immediately and permanently, of liver cancer	Working together regularly during my time in the Philippines; recommendation from a long-term friend with whom she works regularly; she was personally reticent to share so much of her private life, but agreed to do so (and to allow use of her name) only out of gratitude to God	No (she was initially not even convinced that she was healed)	If she was truly dead (as in her report the hospital staff certainly believed), the raising is impossible by natural means; conjoined with the immediate disappearance of symptoms, and eventual confirmation that the cancer was gone, virtually impossible	Yes
Eleanor Sebiano, witnessed a sizable lump disappear instantly during prayer	Interviews, conversation on other issues, correspondence, recommendation from a trusted source	No	Impossible	Yes
Danny McCain witnessed a baby's severe burns from the previous day suddenly disappear during prayer, leaving no scar	Correspondence from a trusted friend with whom I lived for some eighteen weeks; in a divided country, he is widely respected by all peoples and religions	No	Impossible (given the severity of burns described and the instant, rather than merely quick, healing)	Yes
Gail Randolph, my coworker, witnessed a sizable, hard mass disappear from her leg in less than an hour ("some minutes")	Conversation, follow-up correspondence, with a trusted coworker	No	Not normal	Probable (in a theistic context)
Melesse Woldetsadik prayed for the disappearance of an as-yet untreated pulmonary mass; tests confirmed its disappearance	A long-term, close friend; medical documentation provided by the doctor who was healed	No	Proportionately rare	More probable than not (though one's verdict will depend on one's openness to supernatural phenomena)
Leo Bawa prayed for a dead child for a few hours, and the boy returned to life	A long-term friend; he offered this account, along with some others, only when I specifically asked about healings	No	Extremely rare (with close contact for hours, it is unlikely the child had merely *apparently* stopped breathing)	Yes
Yolanda McCain and Paul Mokake independently attested a blind man receiving sight when Paul prayed, and his sight remaining thereafter	Both have been my students with whom we have had close contact (Yolanda is also a close friend of our family)	Not likely	Barely conceivable	Almost certainly yes

Healing claim	How do I know the witness?*	Psychosomatic element possible?	How frequent are such events normally (given an accurate description by the witness)?	Supernatural explanation seems more plausible than not, if not a priori ruled out?†
Mama Jeanne Mabiala: Marie was dead when brought, was raised after prayer (though she remained weak) and recovered fully	Interviews; close and continuing friend of family; my brother-in-law attests that such accounts about her are known to others; a confirming eyewitness	Very unlikely	Very rare (impossible, if she had been genuinely dead for some time, as appears likely)	Very probably yes
Mama Jeanne Mabiala: another woman believed to be dead raised in a prayer meeting	Interviews; close friend of family; my brother-in-law knows the woman said to be raised	No	Very rare (impossible, if she had been genuinely dead for some time, as appears likely)	Very probably yes
Mama Jeanne Mabiala: baby born dead and already white, fully restored during prayer and remains healthy	Interviews; close friend of family; noted continuing contact with the family involved	No	Medically impossible; the baby had already turned white, and, Mama Jeanne, with midwife experience and training, recognized that she had been dead for some time	Very probably yes
Mama Jeanne Mabiala: a midwife who had had a hysterectomy bore children	Interviews; close friend of family	No	Medically impossible (if she is correct that a hysterectomy had occurred; she seemed quite sure, and had had extensive contact with the woman and her situation)	Yes
Mama Jeanne Mabiala: a young woman convulsing and apparently dying was completely healed during prayer	Interviews; close friend of family; my brother-in-law was an eyewitness to the event	Not likely	Not probable	Probably yes
Mama Jeanne Mabiala: a couple was healed of a positive HIV status	Interviews; close friend of family; my brother-in-law knows the family in question and had heard the story	No	No (unless we might speculate that the first test results were inaccurate)	Very probably yes
Albert Bissouessoue reported the raising of a child clearly dead for about eight hours	Interviews; close friend of family; a humble couple with no reason to deceive	No	No	Yes
Julienne Bissouessoue reported the raising of another person	Interviews; close friend of family; a humble couple with no reason to deceive	No	No (at least everyone present, including the hospital's dispensary manager, believed her dead)	Yes

Healing claim	How do I know the witness?[*]	Psychosomatic element possible?	How frequent are such events normally (given an accurate description by the witness)?	Supernatural explanation seems more plausible than not, if not a priori ruled out?[†]
Douglas Norwood's paralyzed wife able to walk despite a severed spinal cord	Interviews, conversation on other issues, correspondence, recommendation from a trustworthy source, readiness to supply all requested information	No	Medically impossible	Yes
Douglas Norwood: aged skeptic from completely non-Christian background, with almost lifelong arm paralysis, suddenly healed when confronting Christians	Interviews, correspondence, recommendation from a trustworthy source, readiness to supply all requested information	Extremely unlikely (given lifelong condition and hostility)	At best *extremely* rare	Yes
Bruce Kinabrew: healing of the lame, the blind, and the instant disappearance of a goiter	One of my closest friends from college, with whom I have maintained contact	Not at all likely (especially in conjunction with one another); the goiter seems impossible	Not at all likely (especially in conjunction with one another); the goiter seems impossible	Yes
Antoinette Malombé, on the raising and full recovery of her daughter after perhaps three hours without breathing	Interview with my mother-in-law, others who had already known the story; confirmed the story with another eyewitness; the raised daughter (Thérèse) is my sister-in-law	No	Impossible if (as we have every reason to believe) no respiration occurred for some three hours (after six minutes without air, the brain begins to die)	Yes
Jacques Moussounga: after twenty-one years with mouth abscesses, was healed after Suzanne Makounou (without prior knowledge of the condition) dreamed of and prayed for his problem	Personal correspondence from my father-in-law; the story is known to others close to him, and Suzanne Makounou remains a close friend of the family	Not likely	Improbable (not so much because the abscesses went away, but because they did so in connection with Suzanne Makounou's dream)	Probably yes
Jacques Moussounga and Antoinette Malombé: after a night of prayer, an infant daughter survived cerebral meningitis when strongly expected to die; she recovered fully (albeit gradually)	Personal correspondence with my father-in-law, interview with mother-in-law, conversation with grown daughter (Gracia)	No	Not usual for an infant in this setting (though enough unexpected recoveries occur)	Debatable, but in the context of a number of such unexpected recoveries, plausible (in a theistic context, more probable than not)

Healing claim	How do I know the witness?[*]	Psychosomatic element possible?	How frequent are such events normally (given an accurate description by the witness)?	Supernatural explanation seems more plausible than not, if not a priori ruled out?[†]
Stephen and Sheila Heneise: permanent healing during prayers of congenital deafness and limp	Personal acquaintance; we know their children (continuing relationship with their son); supernatural claims also are not in their interest[§]	No (birth defects)	No (a leg genuinely lengthened over the course of several minutes)	Yes
Several of my students healed of serious conditions in childhood (especially, Melaina Marshall, of a bone disease; Danielle Moffatt; Jonathan Turner)	My students (also confirmed in two cases with their relatives, who were witnesses; too long ago for medical records, but long enough to confirm the cures' durability)	Very unlikely in some cases	Quite unusual to extraordinary	Very probably yes
Joy Wahnefried: healed of lifelong debilitating migraines and light sensitivity, and accompanying eyesight problem with a documented organic cause, instantly during prayer	Referred by a long-term friend, Dr. Bill Heth, who also (with another source) attested the change, having been present during the healing and known her condition both before and after it; continued correspondence	No (medically documented improvement of vision)	No natural analogies known to us	Yes

[*]Admittedly my report of the claim adds another layer of distance for the reader, who in the vast majority of cases will not know the person in question. I also know some of the witnesses better than others, and even when the witness is my own wife (or myself), another person may consider my attribution of reliability to be subjective. Nevertheless, such decisions are necessary when dealing with any historical or contemporary sources, and (as we noted in ch. 5) only inflexibly antisupernatural presuppositions will rule out all testimony, since historical inquiry would become nearly impossible without the use of testimony.

[†]Note that these cases are not simply claims that the extranormal happened, but each is linked with a specific occasion of prayer or "power encounter" (which could constitute another criterion had I space for further columns). That such extranormal events happen so much more often in connection with prayer, even when psychosomatic elements are ruled out, raises the plausibility of a supernatural explanation.

[‡]This was when I had been a Christian for less than three years; not expecting to write a book on miracles until recently, I never asked Jeannie to let me see the medical verification. Without grounds to infer that she was lying, however (in which case she would have been lying about her pre-prayer condition), I accept her claim. She had no motive to deceive me on the matter, and in principle I could have asked to see the documentation for myself.

[§]Most of their supporting circles in the United States are not accustomed to such reports.

I could have also added eyewitness reports of significant nature miracles from people I know from other settings, such as Sandy Thomas, Emmanuel Itapson, Ayo Adewuya, Benjamin Ahanonu, or Donna Arukua (whom I met more briefly; see ch. 12). In some cases, like the one reported by Emmanuel Itapson, the events so convinced non-Christian observers that large numbers of them abandoned centuries of religious tradition and became followers of the new faith they believed confirmed by these events. Perhaps I could have added the healing of blindness attested by Gary Dickinson, reports of blindness and death healed from Gebru Woldu, and so forth.

Had I chosen to include more interviewees or other testimonies here, and had I traveled to collect more international eyewitness claims, I could have continued with such information virtually indefinitely. In the case of many of the circles where such recoveries occurred, a larger pattern lends weight to individual testimonies, though for many of these witnesses I have offered only a single account. One may note also that the accumulation of some events, normally rare in themselves, around particular persons reduces the likelihood of coincidence as an explanation.[229]

For example, someone might object that a person deemed dead (somehow wrongly) more than ten minutes occasionally returns to life without prayer or medical intervention, say (to simply make up a number) in one out of five hundred thousand cases. Yet I asked the one Pentecostal minister with whom I happened to remain in contact from my earlier visits to Nigeria if he had any healing stories, and he happened to have a case of a resuscitation "after a few hours."[230] This would appear an extraordinary coincidence by itself; as a control, think how few people are eyewitnesses of the hypothetical situation above (someone returning to life without medical intervention or prayer). Of the fifteen or so people in the Philippines that I got to know best during my time there, one had a firsthand account of a raising (her own; after being dead more than one hundred minutes). One must then compound the improbability of the first "coincidence" by this next one. Of those who volunteered stories in Cuba, one, a nurse and eyewitness, recounted the raising of her own baby after more than an hour. One of my handful of friends from Ethiopia shared an eyewitness account of a raising.

Even more improbably as coincidence, my wife's family had a firsthand account of a raising (her sister, after about three hours), and their immediate circle of acquaintances offered six others (with perhaps still others from other acquaintances that we did not interview). Even in the United States, I asked my brother if he had any healing accounts; he put me in touch with a family from his former church who had experienced what they understood as a raising. Moreover, even one of my seminary students shared a raising account, although we were not able to get together officially afterward so I could obtain explicit permission to use her story. Admittedly, none of the several Chinese pastors who shared healing stories with me volunteered a raising (despite some other extraordinary cures),[231] but the numbers remain extraordinary.

229. One could object that such particular persons are simply good storytellers. But while some of my sources are good at recounting their stories, in many of these cases, including persons I interviewed in Congo, other eyewitnesses were available to confirm their accounts and that a pattern of healings surrounded their prayers.

230. Leo Bawa, personal correspondence, Aug. 10, 2009. This was one of only two dead persons that Leo prayed for, the other being a friend (personal correspondence, Oct. 13, 2010); it should go without saying that 50 percent is higher than we would expect by coincidence. I knew Ayo Adewuya from biblical scholars meetings in the United States, but as probably the one Nigerian present at my paper addressing miracles at an SBL seminar, he also ended up recounting as an eyewitness the raising of his son twenty minutes after he had been pronounced dead, and with no subsequent impairment (Nov. 22, 2009; follow-up phone interview, Dec. 14, 2009).

231. I am not counting for this argument the Chinese accounts in published sources. In my earlier travels, no one (including Leo at that time) had reasons to share accounts with me; I was not researching or talking about the question, and other issues of discussion were more relevant at that time.

A philosopher might seek to quantify the likelihood of such coincidences mathematically.[232] By estimating how rarely such events happen or could be expected to happen in the course of nature, one might estimate their natural improbability. Whatever the improbability of the events occurring in a given circle, that improbability is compounded exponentially when such events occur multiple times in the same circle. That is, if coincidence appears a plausible explanation for a single case, the plausibility declines with the next level of coincidence, the accumulation of statistically improbable coincidences in a single sample. Multiple extraordinary events like raisings in the same circle seem massively improbable as pure coincidences.[233] Given such considerations, it seems hardly irrational for me or others in my circle to believe that more than coincidence is at work.[234]

Is coincidence the most compelling explanation for my circle of experience? Or is the cumulative evidence that raisings occur sufficient that I should accept that as a likelier explanation than Hume's belief from "uniform human experience" against miracles? Again, one could argue that my immediate circle of friends and family include a disproportionate number of liars, but I would regard this charge as too high a price to defend Hume's generalization from his own circle, which essentially argues from silence about the far more vast circles he did not know.[235] After all, I know these people and believe I have good reason for confidence in their testimony; the critic excludes their testimony circularly, on the grounds that he or she does not agree with the content of their testimony (perhaps because he or she does not similarly know such witnesses).

It is my point here only to address unusual healings, not what appears to be in most settings the more common lack thereof. Some critics raise understandable theological objections such as, "If God/a supernatural force were involved, why allow the death/sickness in the first place?" or similar objections. These are,

232. Such estimates would need to include upper and lower ranges for most of the figures; most of the figures involved cannot be precisely known, which is why I do not attempt to calculate them here. Nevertheless, even the lower figures would prove cumulatively significant. On the limiting side, one would need to take into account the likelihood that the witnesses report true information insofar as they know it; one cannot however fairly rule them out on the presupposition that such events can never happen, since that is the premise under dispute. The cumulative impact of reliable claims, however, would prove significant.

233. If one's starting estimate were as high as one chance in ten that one would come across a particular event in one's circle, one might think of one chance in ten billion for ten such claims. This approach over-simplifies, but then again, an estimate of one chance in ten seems impossibly high for claims like raisings (Hume presumably had none in his circle). One might claim that one has merely happened across a circle that by itself is an improbable sample; yet there are multiple such circles where such extraordinary reports cluster, and they share some common spiritual characteristics.

234. Hume allowed that his fictional prince was right to believe his own (limited) experience; if no one else believes the experiences of our circle, at least we may do so. Hume mistrusted causal explanations for events, but most thinkers today allow that some hypotheses provide better explanations than others.

235. One might also add other such coincidences: when visited for other reasons by a university president from Congo-Kinshasa, I asked if he had eyewitness accounts of healings, and he offered an account of instantly healed blindness. Other accounts of healed blindness in my circle seem too many for coincidence. Though I personally know more blind persons not healed, it is healing rather than nonhealing that is extraordinary and the point under consideration.

however, at root theological objections that would need to be addressed theologically. Such questions may well have persuasive answers from within a specific theistic framework (e.g., a Christian biblical perspective), but those are questions for a different book, by a different kind of author.

By contrast, I am asking especially historical questions in this book—whether healings happen and what can be their plausible causes, not why they sometimes do or do not happen. My point here is that there are a significant number of instant, nonpsychosomatic healings after prayer, with prayer being a common factor. In these cases, supernatural explanations should be respected as one viable interpretive option among genuinely open-minded academics.

Conclusion

I am not claiming that all recoveries demonstrate extraordinary supernatural activity. Some claims of supernatural healing are clearly false; many others are not clearly false, but normal natural factors cannot be ruled out. Biblically informed Christians, as well as members of some other faiths, affirm that God often works through natural factors, but the greater the likelihood of natural factors, the less one can cite such recoveries as distinctive evidence for special divine activity, especially to those not predisposed to accept such claims.

Some other miracle claims, however, are dramatically extranormal (such as the instant disappearance of cataracts on blind eyes or the raising of someone dead without medical intervention) and are more simply explained by their frequent connection with prayer or faith than by the usual course of natural events. Rather than pursuing a reductionist, one-size-fits-all explanation, we should explore which explanations are most useful in particular sorts of cases. Given differing presuppositions, including those formed by prior experiences with religiously associated recoveries or failures to recover, different observers will understand some cases differently. What I do hope that most readers find persuasive is that there are many cases where a purely naturalistic explanation is not the only or even the most easily intellectually defensible one if supernatural explanations are not ruled out. Many may be persuaded, as I am, that a supernatural explanation in some cases makes better sense than any explanation that omits the likelihood of supernatural causation.

Conclusion

M iracle claims, especially regarding healings, are by Western standards surprisingly common (though by no means universal) in regions of the world where such events are expected. These claims include, as in the Gospels and Acts, the healing of the blind, those unable to walk, and the raising of the dead, among many others. To acknowledge the frequency of such claims is not to pass judgment on their accuracy or to prejudge their theological meaning. Their frequency does, however, at least bring into question some traditional critics' suppositions that any such claims must reflect a lengthy period of legendary accretion. That eyewitnesses can cite dramatic cures does not mean that all other claims of dramatic cures stem from eyewitnesses; but it should remove the persistent prejudice that such claims cannot stem from eyewitnesses. Most of the claims I have cited are from sources claiming to represent eyewitnesses or voices at most one remove from eyewitnesses. There therefore seems no reason, based on the principle of historical analogy, to deny that first-century eyewitnesses could have believed that they saw Jesus heal blind eyes, make paralytics walk, or raise the dead, all of which cures eyewitnesses also claim today.

The frequency of such cures also challenges some scholars' working hermeneutical assumption that no one in the modern world believes in miracles. That assumption has always rested on an elitist exclusion from the "modern world" of the voices of the Majority World, as well as a sizable proportion of Western voices outside of a traditional academic and cultural elite. This observation does not by itself prove that miracles exist; it does show that the assumption that modern people cannot believe in miracles is plainly false. In today's postmodern climate, those who would deny the possibility of miracles need to provide supporting arguments more effective than an appeal to a nonexistent consensus or an appeal to the "uniformity" of human experience (the traditional basis for rejecting miracles).

The Western intellectual tendency is to regard most cultures in history and in today's world as precritical, without so much as undertaking a critical analysis of any of their claims.[1] Yet it seems to me that such disdain for vast numbers of claims (apparently hundreds of millions of them) from other cultures, purely on the basis of unproved presuppositions inherited from the radical wing of the Enlightenment, risks the charge of ethnocentric elitism. Even on the level of interpretation, the radical Enlightenment is not a certain guide. Scientific endeavor by virtue of its nature must work with the concept of an orderly and predictable universe, but it is both reductionist and reflects a logical fallacy to leap from a normally effective method applied to purely natural phenomena to the epistemological and ontological conclusion that no intelligence exists, whether human or nonhuman, that cannot be addressed solely on the basis of known physical laws.

When we have not an isolated instance but a pattern of a number of highly extraordinary events accompanying prayer that do not normally occur without it, it may seem logical to explore prayer as a factor in the anomalous events. I think of circumstances like a number of persons apparently dead for hours abruptly recovering; cataracts immediately disappearing; long-term impaired hearing becoming normal; or the more unusual of the nature miracles I have mentioned. Some of these cases are strongly attested to by reliable eyewitnesses. Because some witnesses inevitably prove unreliable, some readers may be prepared to dismiss all eyewitness claimants as liars. I know many of the eyewitnesses personally, however, and am ready to depend on their integrity—far more than I would be willing to dismiss them as liars because some people's philosophic assumptions require them to dismiss witnesses who arouse for them cognitive dissonance. At the very least, must not arguments based on the "uniformity of human experience" be reconsidered?

Of course, many recoveries claimed as miracles have ready natural explanations. Others, however, are far more difficult on these terms. Even if cases as surely extranormal as those just mentioned are a small proportion of the total claims, I believe that they are cumulatively too numerous to be simply dismissed. (One should keep in mind that I have not necessarily collected the strongest cases—simply the ones that were available without me taking time off for extensive world travels.) I believe that the evidence is sometimes compelling enough to warrant the suggestion of supernatural causation as the simpler explanation, and I hope that most readers will share my opinion that a number of miracle claims press far enough beyond currently plausible naturalistic explanations to invite at least consideration of the possibility of supernatural causation.

Even if some readers committed to the Humean paradigm are not persuaded by my secondary argument supporting divine or at least supernatural activity, is the evidence not compelling enough to allow at least the verdict that, in view of the inadequacy of current naturalistic explanations for a number of miracle claims, we should leave other possibilities open? Is a scholar who is unwilling to grant even that possibility at least willing to grant that fellow scholars who do allow

1. As noted in ch. 10, Davies and Allison, *Matthew*, 2:62–65, cite various eyewitness claims through history and today and contend that such claims cannot be dismissed as merely "antique naïveté."

for supernatural explanations may indeed be genuine scholars with a respectable case for their position? The primary philosophic arguments against supernatural causation, often accepted a priori and uncritically, were formulated mostly in the absence of our current abundant testimony regarding such claims.

Admittedly, those who are committed to an antisupernatural worldview may propose alternate explanations for virtually any purportedly suprahuman phenomenon (certainly the limited sort that appear in the Gospels and Acts). And as I have already conceded, in a number of instances natural explanations are preferable, though in others I believe that such attempts become strained. If one's worldview disallows a miraculous interpretation of all claims, one must, and therefore will, come up with purely natural explanations. Yet I have argued, following many others, that the philosophic foundation for this less charitable reading of miracle claims rests on an argument that is circular; certainly it is too disputed in philosophy today to provide a simple basis for all evaluations. A Humean approach is not neutral, and no examination of miracle claims undertaken with these presuppositions can arrive at its conclusions genuinely open-mindedly. Since almost anything can have a *possible* natural explanation (for example, for whatever reason, someone apparently dead has on *occasion* revived), one need not accept any proposed evidence for miracles; but a possible explanation is not always the most plausible or probable explanation. For example, multiple raisings following prayer in the same circles would seem to defy any reasonable probability of mere accident.

What if, instead of a priori ruling them in or out as a class of claims, one examines individual supernatural claims, using the same criteria we use for other claimed events? I believe that a reader without Humean premises, who allows for the possibility of supernatural explanations among others, would find sufficient cases to render the hypothesis of a supernatural explanation probable in those cases, hence challenging prejudice against such a possibility.

Again, I recognize that some genuine scholars will demur from my secondary argument that some cases of supernatural causation are likely, as I myself once did. What I do not believe is intellectually legitimate is to simply dismiss on the basis of preexisting assumptions the sincerity of all the millions of persons who claim to have witnessed such phenomena, or to insist that such claims could arise only gradually in legend or through a writer's imagination. Such insistence flies in the face of an extraordinary amount of evidence, denying voluminous and cross-cultural testimony merely on the basis of a dogmatic theory forged in a very different era and context (one dependent, in fact, on a much narrower range of evidence). In view of even the very limited number of cases I have offered above, I would consider such sweeping claims (or the claim that no one in the modern world believes in miracles) to be impossibly naive and misinformed. At the very least, then, we need not attribute the key aspects of miracle accounts in the Gospels and Acts to legend.

Any finite number of firsthand observations may be technically anecdotal, but the witnesses are surely no more biased for believing that they have *seen* some unusual dramatic recoveries immediately following prayer than are those who, not having seen them, deny that anyone else could have seen them either. Their a priori skepticism appears plausible when forged in contexts where such phenomena are not observed; but it seems less than charitable when they presuppose universal nonexperience on the basis of their own. Most important, it is no longer plausible to tout "uniform human experience" as a basis for denying miracles, as in the traditional modern argument. Hundreds of millions of claims would have to be satisfactorily explained in nonsupernatural terms for this appeal to succeed; while many may be so explained, one cannot adopt the conclusion of uniformity as a premise without investigating all of them.[2]

In the climate of current scholarship, one might do well to write merely like Josephus, urging caution with particular miracle claims while leaving open the possibility that some could occur. Several statements, however, are possible and, I hope, widely agreeable:

1. Most people in Mediterranean antiquity believed that miracles occurred, and the Gospels and Acts include a relatively high proportion of such claims.
2. Modern scholars may question the interpretations of such ancient reports, yet regard some of them as genuine experiences for those who claim them. (That many other reports were fraudulent, of course, no scholar in antiquity or today would deny.)
3. The a priori modernist assumption that genuine miracles are impossible is a historically and culturally conditioned premise. This premise is not shared by all intelligent or critical thinkers, and notably not by many people in non-Western cultures. The assumption is an interpretive grid, not a demonstrated fact; contrary to what appeared to be the case to many Western intellectuals one or two centuries ago, history does not support a linear evolution of all cultures toward this position.
4. Even the vast majority of those who always reject suprahuman interpretations of ancient miracle reports do not uncritically otherwise reject the value of ancient historians who include them.
5. Without prejudice based on one's views regarding the possibility of divine causation, we must recognize that enormous numbers of eyewitnesses claim to have witnessed such phenomena. We should therefore acknowledge that many such claims (certainly regarding cures during prayer) can belong even to the eyewitness level of our sources and need not be attributed to a long process of oral development.

In view of such conclusions, one should not a priori reject the possibility of eyewitness testimony behind reports of cures in the Gospels and Acts; whatever one's

2. One might argue for a probable premise based on what one deemed a representative sample, but that sample should include an impartial investigation of the strongest and not simply the weakest cases (e.g., should include medical evidence from Lourdes and elsewhere).

explanation for eyewitness testimony of cures, this phenomenon is too common to merely dismiss. Whatever one's other tools for evaluating these reports, skepticism that eyewitnesses could offer them should not be among them. Further, I would also argue that scholars need not rule out the possibility of divine activity in all such claims, although this argument technically involves a philosophic and theological question rather than a historical one in the narrow sense. Finally, given the presence of such claims in ancient historical sources, even if one were to remain skeptical about miracle claims one would not need to reject the rest of the testimony of the Gospels and Acts regarding other events.

Whether in the end one shares the early Christian worldview concerning signs, it is ethnocentric simply to despise it. And whether in the end one despises it, one cannot objectively expunge from the record the clear evidence that early Christians (and many people since then) believed that they witnessed these phenomena.

Oxford scholar G. B. Caird long ago remarked regarding Luke, the first Christian historian:

> Luke has often been accused of credulity because he has packed his narrative with signs and wonders, but it would be more in keeping with the evidence to commend him for his faithful reproduction of one of the major constituents of early Christianity. For the Epistles bear their concurrent witness that the preaching of the Gospel was everywhere accompanied by exorcisms and healing and by other forms of miracle.[3]

---

3. Caird, *Apostolic Age*, 64, citing Rom 15:19; 1 Cor 12:9–10, 28–30; 2 Cor 12:12; Gal 3:5; and (I believe less clearly) Heb 2:4.

Concluding Unscientific Postscript

In Brazzaville and Kinshasa, in July 2008, I saw a number of men using their arms to pedal themselves in the roads on something like tricycles, an improvement over the means of locomotion available to them in the past. In one particular case, as I noticed the man's legs hanging down like shriveled sticks, I longed to be able to follow the example of Jesus in the Gospels, or some of the miracle claims collected for this book.

When I started writing the book, I felt some competition between my theistic theological sympathies (favoring and even articulating the possibility of miracles in principle) and the intellectual skepticism and reservations characteristic of my academic training (reluctant to credit most particular examples, especially those not susceptible to naturalistic explanations). My earlier background as an atheist who valued only naturalistic empiricism probably reinforced some of the latter predilections. Despite having witnessed some healings in conjunction with prayer, especially in earlier years, more recent disappointments and (in my academic work, especially recently) imbibing an Enlightenment hermeneutic of suspicion had me primed for a significant degree of skepticism. (Sometimes we academicians use the hermeneutic of suspicion as a surrogate for faith: doubt all that you can, and if anything is left at the end, you may tentatively accept it.)

As a Christian I believed in miracles in principle but wondered about the veracity of many claims today. In a number of cases, further research reinforced my suspicion about particular claims (though not, of course, about the fact that people make them). Enough other cases, however, have rendered untenable for me personally my initial, knee-jerk predisposition to doubt any given claim to supernatural activity at the outset. My training makes it easier to evaluate critically than to trust, but at some point the intellectual honesty valued in my training also compelled me to go back and critically evaluate the reasons why I found it so much easier to exercise skepticism than to exercise faith, even in the face of enormous evidence in favor of faith. While I may question or reject particular claims, I ought to be free to acknowledge other occasions that I find quite persuasive, even if they are not my own regular experience and even if they do not appeal to the conclusions that the academy expects one to find.

My personal questions today are not whether God heals people, sometimes in demonstrable ways. My struggles now are for the vast numbers of people in the world—probably the majority—who need healing of some sort or another and do not have it, most of whom have little access to medical help. In the week before I saw this man in Brazzaville, I prayed for my sick father-in-law and arthritic mother-in-law in Dolisie, Congo, and for the deaf ears of a happy little girl there. I did not see any immediate changes, and my heart broke for their need. (Happily, by God's mercy, my father-in-law did not die as we expected, and gradually he regained much of his health, though he died a year later from an unrelated infection.) Nevertheless, as a Christian, I believe that the Jesus of the Gospels is alive and still has compassion for the suffering. I yearn to watch God touch the broken today.

Witnessing suffering in parts of the Majority World has increased my gratitude for doctors and medical science, which are helping to meet these heartbreaking needs on an impressive scale. In many parts of the Majority World, however, scarcity or expense of resources means that many or most people do not have access to doctors. Even when doctors sacrificially seek to help (I have heard grateful accounts about Doctors without Borders, the International Red Cross, and medical missionaries), they may face unusual obstacles. While I was in Congo, corrupt local officials in one region shut down a mission hospital under the threat of violence, leading to a large number of needless deaths (but the corrupt officials' profit—unless they happen to fall sick). We learned that in another town, a corrupt American had absconded with Congolese government funds designated for rebuilding a hospital. That sizable town to this day has only inadequate medical resources.

The universality of human mortality demonstrates that even the most optimistic construal of miracles will not eradicate human suffering; miracles do not always occur. The physical benefits that they confer when they do occur are necessarily temporary; but in the context of the Gospels' theology, they are also signs of a better, eschatological kingdom for all who hope in Jesus. In the full context of Jesus's ministry, such signs reveal a kingdom that also involves suffering and is currently overshadowed by the cross, the necessary gateway to the resurrection. They function as promises of a better future, of ideal wholeness, because they reveal the God of the cross, who understands and embraces suffering and can be trusted to be found even there. As signs of kingdom power, however, the miracles foreshadow the hope that lies beyond the cross. While Jesus's unjust execution unveils the world's injustice, his ministry to the broken summons his followers to address the same concerns on which Jesus acted.

People are hurting and are in tremendous need. Like Elisha, I want to cry out, "Where is the God of Elijah?" The point of this book has been to demonstrate the plausibility of miracle claims in the Gospels and Acts, with a secondary purpose of suggesting that these claims need not all be explained solely by recourse to natural causation. My starting concerns involved a matter of biblical interpretation rather than practical theology. But for me personally as a convert to the Christian faith, work on this book has also brought afresh to my attention the dramatic, moving character of human need, as well as the desire of a compassionate and living God to meet those needs. It has reminded me how the Gospel accounts' emphasis on healings is consistent with a God of compassion who cares about real issues of human life and death, issues that theology, philosophy, and exegesis in their most academic forms sometimes forget. I know that miracles often do not happen and that not every prayer is answered affirmatively. But whether through using medicine, prayer, or both, I now long more than ever to see those desperate human needs met.

Appendix A

Demons and Exorcism in Antiquity

One category of healing story that I have largely excluded from the main body of the book is exorcism, since it involves a distinct set of problems for modern interpreters. Nevertheless, exorcism narratives in the Gospels fit the form of other miracle narratives.[1] This appendix summarizes ancient demonology and exorcisms, minus the early Christian sources, many of which I have treated at relevant points in my commentaries on Matthew and Acts. It is intended mostly as a concise prolegomenon to the following appendix, which introduces modern anthropological literature for a point of comparison.

Ancient Views of Demons

The Greek term δαιμόνιον had a wide range of meaning, but the negative aspects of that range made it one of the most suitable terms for hostile spirits in early Judaism. A wide range of opinions about demons existed in early Judaism, a repertoire that expanded as centuries passed. Demonology became increasingly prominent in late antiquity.

---

1. Guillemette, "Forme" (persuasively, *pace* Bultmann). One cannot distinguish between historical information and legend based on form (see Rüsch, "Dämonenaus-Treibung"). Mark is the dominant extant source for our knowledge of Jesus's exorcisms, with Matthew and Luke usually following Mark (Robinson, "Challenge," 326; Best, "Exorcism," 2; cf. Finger and Swartley, "Bondage," 18–20). Nevertheless, a summary of Jesus's exorcism ministry also appears in Q, indicating that Jesus was known for casting out demons, obviously on multiple occasions (Matt 12:27–28//Luke 11:19–20).

Demons' most direct attack on an individual was through possession.[2] Various prophylactic methods were meant to ward off demonic attacks of diverse kinds, but in the case of possession a cure took the form of exorcism. Although those practicing exorcism sometimes employed commands, as Jesus did, even their commands usually belonged to a larger context of incantations and often accompanied various rituals (such as fumigation).

Daimones

Greeks could picture gods[3] or other spirits[4] entering a person. The Greek term translated "demon" is not in itself necessarily negative,[5] and the meaning of the term evolved over time.[6] It could refer to the spirits of the deceased,[7] including prominent heroes of the past;[8] it could involve good or ill fortune;[9] it could denote a particular

---

2. Our English terminology of "possession" is potentially misleading, because of the term's semantic range (Johnson and Keller, "Possession"), because it fails to allow degrees of effects, and because it subsumes so many diverse human actions or experiences. I employ the term "possession" because of its common usage, but its nuances are very imprecise (cf. Theron, "Beste"; Carter, "Demon Possession"; idem, "Possession"; Gildea, "Possession"); it assumes "ownership," hence implies no variation among degrees and types of control, in contrast to the more general Greek term δαιμονίζομαι in the NT. Arguing for degrees of demonization, see, e.g., Warner, "Position," 84–86; Davies, "Exorcism," 25–28.

3. Homer *Il.* 17.210–11.

4. Epictetus *Diatr.* 1.14.14.

5. For a survey of Greek views on demonology and *daimones*, see especially Ferguson, *Demonology*, 33–67 (beginning on 33–35 with the three views in Plutarch *Obsol.* 10–15, *Mor.* 415A–418D); Barrett-Lennard, *Healing*, 337–44; cf. more briefly Ferguson, *Backgrounds*, 184–86; Alexander, *Possession*, 259–65; Finger and Swartley, "Bondage," 10; for the ancient Near East, see, e.g., sources cited in Carpenter, "Deuteronomy," 518, 542. On the Greek term, see further Sánchez, "Daimones"; Burkert, *Religion*, 179–81; Liddell and Scott, *Lexicon*, 365.

6. See Rives, *Religion*, 18 (citing Apuleius *De deo Socr.* 13–16). In Heraclitus, the *daimon* shapes the person's character (Darcus, "Daimon") or generates one's ordered speech (Darcus, "Logos"); for Empedocles, the divine mind parallels the human *daimon* (Darcus, "*Phren*"). Following Plato more closely than Neoplatonists did, Plutarch viewed *daimon* as a higher component of the soul (Brenk, "Doctrine"); Von Franz, "Daimons," shows how Stoic and Middle Platonic views of spirits developed and how spirits related to "self." For a collection of relevant texts, see Cotter, *Miracles*, 75–105.

7. E.g., Dio Chrysostom *Or.* 3.54; Maximus of Tyre 9.6; Menander Rhetor 2.9, 414.25–27 (when consoling the bereaved); *PGM* 4.1965–69; Philostratus *Vit. Apoll.* 3.38; perhaps Dio Chrysostom *Or.* 25 (but this appears more novel and may be a rhetorical exercise); see further discussion in Bolt, "Daimons," 76–96. Even many intellectuals believed stories of ghosts (Pliny *Ep.* 7.27.1–14), though others lampooned them (Lucian *Lover of Lies* 29–32). Lucian doubts spirit stories generally (*Lover of Lies* 16–20, 29–31), including those explicitly involving *daimones* (*Lover of Lies* 13, 16, 29). Although the Furies often appear (e.g., Ovid *Tristia* 4.4.70), Cicero attributes them to one's feelings of guilt (Cicero *Pis.* 20.46–47) or employs them figuratively (*Att.* 10.18).

8. Pythagoras was thus a *daimon* (Philostratus *Ep. Apoll.* 50), as were Achilles (Maximus of Tyre 9.7) and Protesilaos (Philostratus *Hrk.* 43.3). The deceased golden race had become benevolent *daimones* (Hesiod *Op.* 121–23).

9. Dio Chrysostom *Or.* 23.6; Chariton *Chaer.* 6.2.9; Philostratus *Hrk.* 12.1 (cf. Burkert, *Religion*, 180). The application to ill fortune (e.g., Menander Rhetor 2.11; 419.18, 32) lent itself to the increasingly pejorative sense of the term (Ferguson, *Backgrounds*, 134).

deity,[10] or even deity more generally.[11] One could even pun on multiple senses of the term.[12] On a popular level, Greeks close to the early Christian period applied the term increasingly often to the many forces intermediate in character between deities and nature.[13] These spirits were thus highly useful for magic,[14] and even some Jewish texts mention protagonists exploiting the usefulness of "demons."[15]

Greeks often applied the term to deities like the Olympians,[16] but more commonly to lower, superhuman spirits and demigods or deified mortals.[17] Sometimes they even used it as the equivalent of the Roman *genius*.[18] Not everyone concurred with the appropriateness of this intermediary category between deities and mortals, but it was widely held.[19] Probably reflecting Diaspora Judaism's common adap-

10. E.g., *I. Eph.* 1255 (ἀγαθοῦ δαίμονος, the "good *daimon*," linked here with Artemis); Menander Rhetor 1.1.342.6–9 (personified jealousy).

11. E.g., Dio Chrysostom *Or.* 76.5; Epictetus *Diatr.* 3.22.53; for "supernatural," see, e.g., Philostratus *Hrk.* 25.4; 48.19; 55.4. Socrates was accused of having introduced new "divinities" to Athens (e.g., Philostratus *Vit. Apoll.* 7.11, δαιμόνια καινά; see comment on Acts 17:18 in my commentary on Acts); his own spirit-guide is also called a *daimon* (Plutarch *Alc.* 17.4; *Sign Soc.* 10, *Mor.* 580C; Socrates *Ep.* 1; for modern views on this, see, e.g., Kleve, "Daimon"; cf. Brickhouse and Smith, "Sign"), which was a deity (Xenophon *Mem.* 1.1.2; 1.4.2, 10, 13; 4.8.1, 5–6).

12. Lucian *Lover of Lies*, 32 (meaning "supernatural," but in the context of a ghost story).

13. See Nilsson, *Piety*, 170–72; Sánchez, "Daimones."

14. E.g., *PGM* 4.1965–69; Ps.-Callisth. *Alex.* 1.5; Aune, *Prophecy*, 45; Nilsson, *Piety*, 171; Smith, *Magician*, 97–99; Yamauchi, "Magic," 140–41; perhaps Philostratus *Hrk.* 25.13. From a (hostile) Jewish perspective, see *1 En.* 9:6–7; *L.A.B.* 34:2–3; *T. Jud.* 23:1; *b. Sanh.* 67b; cf. Gaster, *Scriptures*, 85 (on CD XII, 2–3, if we take the Hebrew term as "ghost"; cf. Jastrow, *Dictionary*, 21). Those who used demons magically sometimes had trouble getting rid of them afterward (Klauck, *Context*, 229).

15. See Solomon in *T. Sol.* 22; *b. Git.* 68ab; *Eccl. Rab.* 2:8, §1. It was said that a demon helped God's people (*b. Meil.* 17b, if, as is very likely, this is a demon; *Gen. Rab.* 63:8) and that one spirit sought local people's help driving away an evil spirit (*Lev. Rab.* 24:3); later rabbis sometimes learned from and cited demons (e.g., *b. Pes.* 110a), and some considered particular categories of spirits, whether in the house or field, to be benevolent (*Gen. Rab.* 24:6). Cf. the Watchers coming, like the Greek Prometheus (cf. Achilles Tatius 3.8), to teach (*Jub.* 4:15). Jewish magical texts (or syncretistic texts employing Jewish motifs?) appealed to angels and deities (Goodenough, *Symbols*, 2:153–295).

16. E.g., Homer *Il.* 1.561 (Hera); *Orph. H.* 17.8 (Poseidon); 50.2 (Dionysus); 73.1–2 (Zeus). Nilsson, *Piety*, 172, notes that the definition shifted between Homer and Plato.

17. E.g., Ps.-Plato *Epin.* 984DE; Isaeus *Menec.* 47; Dionysius of Halicarnassus *Ant. rom.* 1.31.1; Plutarch *Isis* 26, *Mor.* 361A; *Obsol.* 10–22, *Mor.* 415B–422C (e.g., 13, *Mor.* 416E); *Sign Soc.* 24, *Mor.* 593D; Arius Didymus 2.7.11s, pp. 98–99.18–19; Artemidorus *Onir.* 2.40; Pausanias 9.22.7; Maximus of Tyre 8.6; 9.2; Menander Rhetor 1.1.333.21–24; 1.1.341.1–4; Achilles Tatius 3.10.1; Diogenes Laertius 8.1.32; Philostratus *Hrk.* 48.15; Iamblichus *Myst.* 1.5, 20; Libanius *Narration* 7.1 (sea deities). Sometimes one could translate the term in more than one manner, e.g., in Chariton *Chaer.* 3.1.4; 6.2.9; cf. Circe in Philostratus *Hrk.* 25.13; a sea *daimon* who loved a mortal in *Hrk.* 45.2 (on uses in Philostratus, see Puiggali, "Démonologie").

18. Epictetus *Diatr.* 1.14.12, 14; Plut *Mor.* 564F (in Betz, Dirkse, and Smith, "Numinis," 225); the LCL translation of Diogenes Laertius 8.1.32; cf. the popular view of everyone having either a good or a bad *daimon* (Dio Chrysostom *Or.* 23.6; in 23.9, he notes that this is not his own view; cf. again *Or.* 4.79–80, 83). A *daimon* could be a beneficial guardian spirit (as in Iamblichus *V.P.* 2.10). On the *genius* (often as an individual's tutelary deity), see Maharam, "Genius"; the view was widespread (as noted in Seneca *Ep. Lucil.* 110.1).

19. Dionysius of Halicarnassus *Ant. rom.* 1.77.3. Such intermediate powers contributed to the "demonizing of religion" (Ferguson, *Backgrounds*, 134).

tation of broader religious vocabulary, Josephus freely employs this Hellenistic language for the divine.[20]

In Middle Platonism, humans could become heroes, *daimones*, and finally divine; or the *daimones* could also regress back into mortal bodies and eventually face death.[21] They were intermediaries connecting and communicating between the divine and human realms.[22] As in other sources, *daimones* were associated with oracles, filling, for example, the Delphic priestess before she would speak.[23] Because these intermediary spirits could be either good or bad, however, the semantic range includes a negative usage. Thus at times,[24] and increasingly in a later period,[25] the term could refer to an evil spirit.[26]

In the early empire, such views seem to have flourished already around Palestine and among Arabs.[27] These views may well have come from farther east. Persian demonology, involving massive numbers of evil demons, bears some resemblance to the common Jewish and Christian perspective,[28] though none of the relevant extant sources come from the Parthian period (250 B.C.E.–250 C.E.).[29] Many Jewish people believed that the gods of the pagans were demons in any case;[30] some Middle Eastern religions demonized the deities of those they supplanted.[31] Such demons could prove hostile to mortals.[32]

20. Isaacs, *Spirit*, 33–34 (though noting that he also applies it to demons more strictly in *War* 7.185).

21. Klauck, *Context*, 424; see categories of *daimones* in Dillon, *Middle Platonists*, 317–19. Some Stoics also allowed that the soul rose to the heavens (Seneca *Dial*. 11.9.3) before its ultimate resolution back into the primeval fire (Marcus Aurelius 4.21).

22. Maximus of Tyre 8.8; 9.2 (see further Trapp, *Maximus*, 67, on 9.1–7); Aelius Aristides *Def. Or.* 424, §144D (citing Plato). Maximus believed there were many of them (8.8, citing Hesiod *W.D.* 252–53 for thirty thousand). Iamblichus believed that all apparitions were *daimones* (*Myst*. 2.10).

23. Maximus of Tyre 8.1 (Trapp, *Maximus*, 69n1, cites also Plato *Symp*. 202e; Apuleius *De Deo Socr.* 6.133; Plutarch *Face* 944cd and esp. *Obsol*. 415a ff.).

24. E.g., Valerius Maximus 1.7.7 (switching here from Latin to the Greek "κακὸν δαίμονα"; it tormented one at night as a portent of impending death).

25. E.g., *P. Grenf.* 2.76.3–4 (from 305–6 C.E.); Philostratus *Vit. Apoll*. 3.38; 4.20; Porphyry *Marc.* 11.201–2; 19.322; 21.331–33, 336–39; Xenophon *Eph*. 1.5.

26. Much later, Iamblichus *Myst*. 2.3, classifies angels as benevolent, demons as unpleasant, and heroes as kinder than demons.

27. Lucian *Lover of Lies* 16–17 (not using the term but depicting possession and exorcism); for Egypt and exorcism, 31 (cf. 33).

28. Olmstead, *Persian Empire*, 18, 96, 195, 232. Many have assumed that Judaism simply adopted the Persian perspective (e.g., Foakes Jackson and Lake, "Teaching," 287); as I note here and in appendix B, however, the experiences are fairly transcultural.

29. Yamauchi, "Magic," 118. Among the Persians, a "demon" could involve one touched by madness (cf. Olmstead, *Persian Empire*, 53). Our demonstrably datable, extant Jewish sources appear earlier, but we cannot be sure whether or not this is simply because more Jewish sources from the period survive.

30. Ps 106:37 (esp. LXX); Bar 4:7; *1 En*. 19:1; *Jub*. 1:11; 22:17; 4Q243–245, line 18; *Sib. Or*. 8.43–47; *T. Job* 3:3; *T. Sol*. 5:5; 6:4; *Sipre Deut*. 318.2.1–2; cf. perhaps 4Q560 1 I, 5; 4Q491 A, 15 8–10; *2 Bar.* 10:8. In the early Christian movement, e.g., 1 Cor 10:20 (cf. Deut 32:17); 2 Pet 2:4 (if it associates fallen angels with Titans); Rev 9:20; Justin *1 Apol*. 5; Athenagoras 26; Tertullian *Apol*. 23.5–6. The attribution of the pagan to the demonic also served a useful social demarcation to maintain the small Christian sect's boundaries against paganism (Leeper, "Exorcism," 59–60).

31. Gordon, *Civilizations*, 246–47; Alexander, *Possession*, 19; for fallen angels, cf. the fallen gods of Enuma Elish, the Greek Titanomachy (see, e.g., West, "Introduction," 27), and the Hittite account in Gurney, *Aspects*, 15.

32. Cf. Chariton *Chaer*. 3.1.4; 6.2.9, though these may be divine.

Jewish Demonology[33]

Demonology is rare in the OT,[34] and a renewed focus on demons, which appeared in surrounding cultures, may have been occasioned by the experience of the exile.[35] A variety of Jewish conceptions of demonology developed, probably most of them overlapping at the level of popular religion, although it is difficult to know at what period various strands originated. In Josephus, some deadly demons are spirits of wicked persons that enter and kill the living.[36] In *1 Enoch*, many evil spirits are spirits of the deceased giants;[37] later rabbis thought that such spirits became more powerful after the flood generation.[38] For some later rabbis, demons impassioned by Adam and Eve used them to reproduce more demons.[39]

Some Jewish traditions may have adapted Greek concepts, such as reference to avenging spirits resembling the Greek Furies (Sir 39:28);[40] in some other early texts, however, angels of destruction appear to be spirits serving the evil prince

33. For a fuller survey of early Jewish demonology, see Ferguson, *Demonology*, 69–104, who treats especially intertestamental texts on 74–81; Philo and Josephus (who employ the full range of the Greek *daimon*) on 81–86; and rabbinic sources on 86–93; also Barrett-Lennard, *Healing*, 331–36. Briefly, e.g., Ford, "Response"; Finger and Swartley, "Bondage," 10–12; Kotansky, "Demonology," 270–71. Naturally the conceptions are more diverse than this summary allows me to detail; even the Qumran scrolls and *Jubilees*, which reflect a similar worldview, may have some differences (Noack, "Qumran and Jubilees," 200; for similarities, see Fröhlich, "Invoke"; Ibba, "Spirits"), though *Jubilees* was probably authoritative at Qumran (see Hopkins, "Status"). Given the summary nature of this appendix, I have not distinguished the different periods involved, but those familiar with the sources will recognize the sources in the endnotes and the respective periods to which they belong.

34. Akkadian and Arabic cognates do confirm the LXX interpretation of Lev 17:7 (cf. Deut 32:17; Ps 106:37) as referring to demons (as my colleague Emmanuel Itapson persuaded me, in addition to his Nigerian perspective on the evidence). Possession by a hostile spirit may appear in 1 Sam 16:14 (e.g., Oesterreich, *Possession*, 168–69; the meaning is debated—see, e.g., discussion in Ma, "Presence," 21–22; Arnold, *Samuel*, 239–42). But such references are rare. Note the survey of themes in Finger and Swartley, "Bondage," 12–17.

35. Cf. Propp, "Demons" (attributing it to disillusionment with the covenant's control over ill fortune; it could also be attributed, however, to a wider acquaintance with alternative paradigms). Hittites and other peoples employed some purity rituals resembling ancient Israel's, applying them prophylactically against demons.

36. Josephus *War* 7.185. In Josephus they are usually souls of the dead (Ferguson, *Demonology*, 85). Traditional paganism expected netherworld spirits to plague or possess tomb robbers (Trombley, "Paganism," 204). For associations of tombs with spirits, see *PGM* 101.1–3; Nineham, *Mark*, 153; Alexander, *Possession*, 29; cf. *Jub.* 22:17; *'Ab. R. Nat.* 3A; *T. Sol.* 8:9; Lewis, *Life*, 96; for use of corpses in witchcraft, e.g., Apuleius *Metam.* 2.20.

37. *1 En.* 15:9; 16:1; cf. the spirits that impregnated their mothers in Philo *Giants* 6, 16; the Greek Titanomachy (e.g., Hesiod *Theog.* 717–19; Menander Rhetor 2.17, 438.31–32), of which various Jewish sources show awareness (e.g., *Sib. Or.* 3.121, 155; cf. Jdt 16:7). For demons in Jewish apocalyptic sources, see the collection of material in Cotter, *Miracles*, 106–19 (also noting the absence of exorcisms in these texts, probably due to their genre, 119).

38. *Lev. Rab.* 5:1; their idolatry rendered them susceptible to demons (*Gen. Rab.* 23:6).

39. So *Pesiq. Rab Kah.* 5:3; *b. Erub.* 18b; *Gen. Rab.* 24:6.

40. God also sends demons as agents of destruction in later texts, e.g., *Tg. Onq.* to Deut 32:24; *Tg. Ps.-Jon.* to Deut 28:24.

of darkness.[41] A few texts may also reflect the later Platonic notion[42] of demons as disembodied souls.[43] Magical texts reflecting some folk religion specify among other types of demons groups such as "liliths."[44] Some texts also call demons "unclean spirits."[45]

People associated demons with various afflictions, from which deliverance could be sought.[46] People also occasionally associated them with particular or specialized sins,[47] like demons of deceit associated with witchcraft and divination,[48] jealousy,[49] promiscuity,[50] arrogance,[51] lying,[52] and anger.[53] "The spirit of error" seems a more pervasive title, found in Qumran dualism and elsewhere in early Judaism.[54] Named demons

41. 1QM XIII, 11–12; perhaps *p. Shebu.* 6:6, §3. On the angelology of 1QM, see Yadin, *Scroll of War*, 229–42.

42. Cf. Dillon, *Middle Platonists*, 317–19.

43. Philo *Giants* 6, 16; *Gen. Rab.* 7:5 (in this case, nonembodied, because the Sabbath prevented God from completing creation). But angels, too, could be viewed as bodiless (*T. Ab.* 3:6; 4:9; 9:2; 15:4, 6; 16:2 A).

44. E.g., 4Q510 1 5 (singular, but listing various kinds of demons); Aramaic incantation texts 1.6, 8; 3.14; 6.11; 10.2; 11.1–3, 9; 12.2, 8; cf. Isa 34:14; *2 Bar.* 10:8 (among the desert spirits); a modern Yemenite amulet in Hes, "Role," 376; in older Canaanite religion, see Kaiser, "Pantheon," 131. For headless demons, cf., e.g., *PGM* 2.11; 5.98, 125, 145–46; 7.233, 243, 442; 8.91; 102.5; *T. Sol.* 9:1; Dickie, "Headless Demons." For satyrs (cf. Lev 17:7; 2 Chr 11:15), see *Sipra A.M.* pq. 9.188.3.6 (demythologized). Modern cults also sometimes delineate types of spirits, e.g., in Umbanda (Pressel, "Possession," 335) or others (Colson, "Possession," 70–72).

45. *T. Sol.* 3:7 (later); cf. *Jub.* 10:1 ("polluted demons"); 4Q230 1 1 (but this is reconstructed); and, differently, "unclean spirit" in 1QS IV, 22 (vs. the "spirit of truth in IV, 21); 4Q444 1 4i + 5.8 (possibly the human spirit); clearly 11QS XIX, 15 (and the reconstructed text in 11Q6 4 V, 16; here an unclean spirit acts like Satan); Mark 1:23; Luke 8:29; cf. Klutz, *Exorcism Stories*, 134–38 (citing esp. *Pesiq. Rab Kah.* 4:7). "Unclean" could sometimes represent "sinful" (1QpHab VIII, 13); Klawans ("Impurity"; idem, "Idolatry") emphasizes the links between sin and impurity in the Scrolls; Himmelfarb, "Impurity and Sin," warns against overgeneralizing this link (while conceding that 1QS and 4Q512 exceed OT perspectives). Those dominated by Belial's spirits also are more apt to defile the temple (CD XII, 1–2; 4Q271 5 I, 17–18).

46. See Eve, *Miracles*, 174–216. In other cultures, see discussion below.

47. Most prominently in the Testaments of the Twelve Patriarchs, e.g., *T. Reu.* 2:1–2; 3:3ff.; *T. Jud.* 16:1–4; earlier, in the Qumran scrolls, see Tigchelaar, "Names of Spirits." Cf. specializing spirits in the Middle Platonic tradition in Maximus of Tyre 8.8; 9.7; πνεῦμα can, however, include psychological dispositions (Chevallier, *Souffle*, 39). Angels, too, could specialize (e.g., the angel over repentance in *1 En.* 40:9). In one modern discussion, see Instone-Brewer, "Psychiatrists," 142. They appear in the Zoroastrian Denkard (Yamauchi, *Persia*, 439–40), but this was probably not compiled before the ninth century C.E. (ibid., 410). The association appears in both Hinduism and contemporary Indian charismatic Christianity (Bergunder, "Miracle Healing," 290). This is probably *not* the point of 1 Cor 2:12; 2 Tim 1:7.

48. *T. Jud.* 23:1. The association of demons with witchcraft might stand behind accusations against Jesus (see Keener, *Spirit*, 104; idem, *Matthew*, 361–62; idem, *John*, 714–15, and many sources cited there); for "possession" in deviance labeling there, see the discussion in Guijarro, "Politics," 118, 122–23.

49. *T. Sim.* 2:7; *T. Dan* 1:6.

50. *T. Dan* 5:6.

51. *T. Dan* 5:6.

52. *T. Dan* 2:1; 5:5.

53. *T. Dan* 2:1; cf. *Pesiq. Rab Kah.* 5:3. Cf. also destroying demons against Israel, "Wrath," "Anger," etc. (*Tg. Ps.-Jon.* on Deut 9:19).

54. 1QS III, 18–19; IV, 21–23 (see Charlesworth, "Comparison," 418; Keener, *John*, 970); *T. Jud.* 14:8; 20:1 (cf. *T. Sim.* 3:1; contrast the seven spirits of deception in *T. Reu.* 2:1; cf. *T. Iss.* 4:4; *T. Sol.* 8:3, 9).

appear early;[55] one persistent name in Jewish texts is Lilith.[56] Demons also could cause physical afflictions, as at times in the Gospels,[57] or even kill people.[58] Demons could specialize in oil, in causing headaches, or in imbibing excessive alcohol.[59] Some sources suggest a special unleashing of demons in the eschatological time before the end.[60]

One kind of evil spirit dwelled in reed stalks,[61] and others might be found in palm and other trees;[62] various trees and bushes harbored various sorts of demons,[63] as did most vegetables.[64] Demons might be found in ruins,[65] in bathhouses,[66] in graveyards,[67] and elsewhere. Apparently they could not attack anyone in the holy city of Jerusalem, however.[68] Rabbis reportedly learned some of these traditions from reports offered by demons themselves,[69] a source, one might think, of dubitable veracity, however firsthand its information.[70]

---

55. 4Q560 1 I, 4; Penney and Wise, "Beelzebub"; Penney, "Devils," 41–51; cf. Mark 5:9. See the possible incantation against Resheph (pestilence?) in 11Q11 V, 5, but the Hebrew may read "heavens." On the origin of many demon names, see, e.g., Barton, "Origin" (though he omits Mastema). Other traditional religions also may have named demons, spirits, or malevolent forces (e.g., Umeh, *Dibia*, 197–200; in *bori*, see Echard, "Possession Cult," 71–80), though in some cultures most are not known by name (Shorter, "Spirit Possession," 117).

56. See 4Q510 1 5, and some identify with her the evil figure in 4Q184 (Baumgarten, "Seductress"; White Crawford, "Folly"). In late talmudic and especially medieval texts, "Lilith" becomes a frequently mentioned demon, eventually queen of the female demons (see Morel-Vergniol, "Ève et Lilith"; Gaines, "Lilith"; *lilin* were night spirits). Cf. the demoness Agrath in *b. Pes.* 112b (Eve, *Miracles*, 290–91).

57. *T. Sol.* 1:1–4; 18; *Midr.* Ps 17:8; Luke 13:11; Kotansky, "Demonology," 271–72. Schwab, "Psychosomatic medicine," suggests that the demonological explanation for sickness in medieval times reduced psychosomatic treatments; still, one would expect exorcism, at least, to have worked in many of these cases. Curses invite sicknesses in various societies, later cured by exorcism (see MacNutt, *Power*, 74–75, in this case a Christian exorcism in Colombia). Many traditional South American societies affirm possession illness (without possession trance), which is thought to be cured only by exorcism (Bourguignon, "Spirit Possession Belief," 20–21); see also discussion at Acts 10:38 in my Acts commentary.

58. Tob 3:8 (Sara's first seven husbands); Josephus *War* 7.185; *Num. Rab.* 12:3; for regular demonic attacks against humans, not necessarily lethal, see *1 En.* 69:12; cf. *Tr. Shem* 2:9. Satan is an "angel of destruction" in *p. Shebuot* 6:6, §3.

59. Alexander, *Possession*, 32.

60. *2 Bar.* 27:9; perhaps relevant to their prevalence in the Gospels as the kingdom is at hand (cf. Alexander, *Possession*, 249; Hultgren, "Stories," 133). For the possible linking of exorcism with eschatology, cf. perhaps *T. Sim.* 6:6; with the kingdom, 4Q510 1 4 (Vermes, *Religion*, 130).

61. *Gen. Rab.* 56:6.

62. *B. Pes.* 111a, bar.; 111ab.

63. *B. Pes.* 111b.

64. *B. Sanh.* 101a, bar.

65. *B. Ber.* 3ab. For views concerning spirits haunting abandoned places, cf. also Lewis, "Possession," 191.

66. *Tos. Ber.* 6:25 (by implication); *b. Ber.* 62a; *Kid.* 39b–40a; *Shab.* 67a; *Eccl. Rab.* 2:8, §1 (Solomon heating his baths with demons); *Song Rab.* 3:7, §5.

67. See, e.g., sources in Alexander, *Possession*, 29; cf. Mark 5:2–3; this may refer merely to madness in *b. Hag.* 3b. One could hear spirits of the dead talking there at night (*b. Ber.* 18b). Because of their association with the dead, spirits remain associated with burial grounds even in some cultures today (Schmidt, "Psychiatry," 147; Edwards, "Possession," 211).

68. *Ab. R. Nat.* 35 A, if the translator has correctly construed the original. The tradition probably idealizes Jerusalem after its destruction.

69. *B. Pes.* 110ab.

70. Perhaps obtained by interrogation, as in some modern examples; cf. Fuchs, "Techniques," 135–36.

Later rabbis thought that some kinds of demons could look like people.[71] Some opined that demons could see people but not the reverse, and angels could see demons but not the reverse.[72] Some felt that particular demons might prove helpful.[73] But of course such spirits were subject to and recognized God's sovereignty; God was sovereign over all spirits in the vast majority of early Jewish literary sources.[74] Demons could also be arranged in ranks or legions.[75] (I am leaving aside here Jewish teaching about angels of nations.[76])

Possession

Greeks and Romans believed that mantic ecstasy often involved possession by a deity.[77] The presence of the numinous could generate dread and trembling.[78] Such madness might be sent by a deity and result in killing of loved ones;[79] after a bout of madness, one might have no recollection of the mad behavior.[80] Madness was

---

71. *B. Git.* 66a; Satan in *T. Job* 23:2. Others resembled Greeks' monsters (e.g., the late *Apoc. Zeph.* 4:2–4; for pagan monsters, see, e.g., one of the Furies in Statius *Theb.* 1.103–9).

72. *Pesiq. Rab.* 6:5; cf. *Ab. R. Nat.* 40A.

73. *B. Meil.* 17b; *Gen. Rab.* 24:6; 63:8.

74. *Jub.* 49:2; CD VIII, 2–3; 1Qap Gen[ar] XX, 16–17; 1QM XIV, 9–10; *T. Adam* 1:1; *Num. Rab.* 14:3; cf. VanderKam, "Traditions," 245; *Pr. Jos.* 7. Cf. Islamic Somali tradition in Lewis, "Possession," 192.

75. *T. Sol.* 11:3 (if not modeled after Mark 5:9 or Eph 6:12, this may be modeled after angelic ranks; *1 En.* 69:3; 75:1; *2 En.* 21:1; 22:2, 6, J; 33:10; *3 En.* 5:2; *3 Bar.* 11:4, 6, 8; *Gr. Apoc. Ezra* 1:4, 7; perhaps 2 Kgs 6:15; 4Q529 II–III). One could host multiple spirits (Mark 5:9; Luke 8:2; four in Lewis, "Possession," 212; seventeen in Abdalla, "Friend," 38; multiple spirits in Rahim, "*Zar*," 144; Last, "*Bori*," 51; a medium could host multiple spirits in succession in Firth, *Ritual*, 306). For hierarchies of spirits in some Islamic cults, see Abdalla, "Friend," 41–42.

76. Briefly, cf. Deut 32:8 LXX; Dan 10:13–12:1; *Jub.* 15:30–32; *1 En.* 89:59–90:19; later *1 En.* 40:9 (Knibb; contrast Isaacs); 61:10; *2 En.* 20:1 (longer version); *T. Levi* 3:8; *T. Job* 49:2; *3 Bar.* 12:3; *Ascen. Isa.* 1:3; 2:2 (but probably Christian material; cf. 1:4); *Tg. Ps.-Jon.* on Gen 11:8; in early gnostic texts, e.g., *Apoc. Adam* 1:4; *Hyp. Arch.* The Daniel and early Enoch material shows that the language precedes Christianity (Stuckenbruck, "Angels of Nations"; cf. Caragounis, *Mysterion*, 157–61; Cullmann, *State*, 68; *pace* the concerns of Carr, *Angels*, 40); Paul's source may be apocalyptic tradition (Lee, "Powers"; cf. Benoit, "Angelology"). For the LXX of Deuteronomy, see Russell, *Apocalyptic*, 244–49; Peake, "Colossians," 479; Dodd, *Bible and Greeks*, 18–19. Jewish sources usually treat them as angelic authorities appointed by God (*Jub.* 15:31–32; 35:17; *Mek. Shir.* 2:112ff.; *b. Ber.* 16b–17a; *Yoma* 77a; *Exod. Rab.* 32:3; *Pesiq. Rab.* 17:4; *3 En.* 29:1; 30:1–2), but in some sources, God appointed them to lead the nations astray (*Jub.* 15:31), or they had become malevolent powers and would be judged at the end of the age (e.g., 1QM XIV, 15–16; XV, 13–14; XVII, 5–8; Kobelski, "Melchizedek," 123; cf. *3 En.* 26:12; *Sipre Deut.* 315.2.1; *Gen. Rab.* 77:3; 78:3).

77. Graf, "Ecstasy," 800 (citing, e.g., Virgil *Aen.* 6.77–80); Dionysius of Halicarnassus *Ant. rom.* 1.31.1; the state is negative but probably faked, in Menander *Theophoroumene* (cf. discussion in 20–25). Thus one might think Dio mad, but he warns that it may be (prophetically) inspired by a *daimon* (Dio Chrysostom *Or.* 34.4).

78. Suetonius *Aug.* 6.

79. Strelan, *Strange Acts*, 103, citing Diodorus Siculus 4.11.1; see Euripides *Herc. Fur.* passim.

80. Achilles Tatius 4.17.4; but contrast Dan 4:36. Lack of recollection also characterizes many of those described as "possessed" today (e.g., Gelfand, *Religion*, 166, 169; Field, "Possession," 3, 6).

routinely associated with *daimones*.[81] A ghost might be thought to impart epilepsy, which was often viewed as a form of divine possession.[82]

Possession trance often appeared to outsiders as madness when witnessed outside the cultic context.[83] A cultic context, however, could make such possession appear more positive. Plato envisioned four kinds of ecstasy, one of the most important being prophetic, associated with Apollo;[84] although also linked with the unattached Sibyl and Bacis, prophetic ecstasy was primarily linked to oracle locations, especially Delphi, Didyma, and Claros.[85] Virgil associates this prophetic ecstasy with divine possession.[86]

Some thinkers claimed that the sort of "madness" that came from the gods was superior to sanity.[87] Being prophetically seized by the divine was periodic rather than continuous.[88] The δαίμονες spoke "through human bodies, just as the pipe player Ismenias used his skill to produce notes from his pipe."[89] (Some Christian writers argued that Christian prophecy, unlike "possession," was controllable.[90]) Josephus might presuppose the idea of such δαίμονες possessing persons with fury or passionate zeal.[91]

One may compare, for example, ancient accounts of the Pythia's possession.[92] In most sources, the Pythian priestess would prophesy from a tripod seat.[93] Plutarch claims that she went into mad ecstasy but returned to calm sobriety after leaving "her tripod and its exhalations."[94] Plutarch described the Pythian spirits by a term that came to mean "ventriloquist," making one's voice seem to come from elsewhere, but probably

81. Nilsson, *Piety*, 172. Chrysostom *Hom. Acts* 17, also cited similarities between the possessed and the intoxicated (referring to their eyes, but perhaps also alluding to a lack of personal motor control).

82. Xenophon *Eph.* 5.7. Many ancients believed that epilepsy involved (divine) possession (though Hippocratics ascribed it to physical causes; see Capps, *Village Psychiatrist*, 92). Epilepsy is now understood to be neurologically based (and distinguished from demonization in Matt 4:24); for one African query about the relation between the two, cf. Ikeobi, "Healing," 67–70.

83. E.g., Alexander, *Possession*, 98–99 (citing Euripides *Bacch.* 241; Plato *Phaedr.* 47), 115 (specifically on the Pythia); cf. Mbiti, *Religions*, 227. A few people opined that deities were not localized in their temples and thus need not be approached there (Lucian *Dem.* 27).

84. Plato *Phaedr.* 265B.

85. Graf, "Ecstasy," 800. Alexander the false prophet seems to imply that his own prophecies are more accurate than these more famous cult centers (Lucian *Alex.* 43); Lucian himself, our main source for this figure, was unimpressed with any of them (*Dial. G.* 244 [18/16, *Hera and Leto* 1]).

86. Virgil *Aen.* 6.77–80. Graf, "Ecstasy," 800.

87. Aelius Aristides *Def. Or.* 53, §17D, perhaps employing the rhetorical technique of shocking speech.

88. E.g., Arrian *Alex.* 4.13.5–6.

89. Maximus of Tyre 9.1 (trans. Trapp, 77).

90. 1 Cor 14:32; Chrysostom *Hom. Cor.* 29.2 (ACCS-Cor, 118); Severian of Gabala *Pauline Commentary from the Greek Church* (NTA 15:262; ACCS-Cor, 118; again, NTA 15:270; ACCS-Cor, 144).

91. Twelftree, *Triumphant*, 34, cites Josephus *War* 3.485; 7.389.

92. See also Keener, "Possession," 233–35.

93. E.g., Callimachus *Hymn* 4 (to Delos), 89–90; Lucian *Z. Rants* 30 (jesting that Apollo cannot prophesy without his tripod); some people in Iamblichus *Myst.* 3.11 (others claimed a four-footed stool); for a figurative allusion, Lucian *Critic* 10. Aune, *Prophecy*, 28, thinks that the tripod probably represented Apollo's throne.

94. *Dial. L.* 16, *Mor.* 759B (LCL 9:367).

it originally meant "pregnant" with the deity, perhaps at least implying speech with a strange voice.[95] Plutarch, however, elsewhere reports the view that the inspiration came only to her mind, so that the voice and all physical features stemmed from the woman.[96] Valerius Maximus claims that Appius forced the Pythia to descend to the

> innermost part of the sacred cave, from which, while definite answers are sought for those who consult, the breath of the divine spirit is deadly to those who give the replies. So, driven by the impulse of the power she had seized, the girl prophesied the fate of Appius in a terrifying sounding voice and obscure riddles.[97]

Others also described this inspiration. Apollo's power "impregnated" and then inspired the Pythia.[98] The priestess would prophesy when ἐκστῶσιν, "ecstatic," and afterward remembered nothing.[99] Seated on the tripod, she was filled with the divine breath.[100] She was possessed by a divine spirit and the divine fire from the cavern.[101] Some claimed that there were different kinds of prophetic inspiration, with the Pythian priestess at Delphi being inspired (*incitabat*) by the power of the earth as the Sibyl was by nature's power.[102] A δαίμων filled her before she prophesied; these spirits were associated with other important oracles, including Dodona, Ammon, and Claros as well.[103] A Jewish source also speaks of the Pythia's frenzy.[104]

Lucan paints this frenzy most graphically, although he certainly exaggerates;[105] he depicts full possession, controlling the virgin priestess's soul and lips.[106] Without signs

95. *De defect. Orac.* 9, *Mor.* 414E. Lake and Cadbury, *Commentary*, 192; Aune, *Prophecy*, 40–41; cf. Conzelmann, *Acts*, 131; Fitzmyer, *Acts*, 586; Witherington, *Acts*, 494. Apollo's voice comes from the cavern in Valerius Maximus 7.1.2. For strange voices in possession accounts today, see appendix B; for a spirit speaking from the belly, see, e.g., Ising, *Blumhardt*, 104.

96. Plutarch *Or. Delphi* 7, *Mor.* 397C; for Apollo using the priestess's body to reveal his thoughts, see *Or. Delphi* 21, *Mor.* 404E. Plutarch has some specialized knowledge of Delphi because of his priesthood there (see Jaillard, "Plutarque et divination," esp. on *Mor.* 438AB).

97. Valerius Maximus 1.8.10 (trans. Wardle, 60). Other sites also provided subterranean encounters with a *daimonion* (e.g., Maximus of Tyre 8.2); cf. the oracular chasm for Orpheus in Philostratus *Hrk.* 28.9.

98. Longinus *Subl.* 13.2.

99. Aelius Aristides *Def. Or.* 34–35, §11D.

100. Dio Chrysostom *Or.* 79.12 (LCL 5:187).

101. Iamblichus *Myst.* 3.11.

102. Cicero *Div.* 1.36.79 (cf. Iamblichus *Myst.* 3.11: at Colophon, the prophetess drinks water from a sacred fountain). Some believed that the subterranean exhalations that once inspired the Pythia no longer worked (Cicero *Div.* 2.57.117), though in the first century c.e. Pliny the Elder compares them with other unusual vapors supposed to arise from the earth (Pliny *Nat.* 2.95.207–8). Most today doubt the claims of "mephitic vapours" (Cary and Haarhoff, *Life*, 317); cf. Pytho's association with the "earth" (Menander Rhetor 2.17, 441.16–17).

103. Maximus of Tyre 8.1. For δαιμονες and other oracles, see, e.g., Plato *Symp.* 202E; Apuleius *De deo Socr.* 6.133 (Trapp, *Maximus*, 69n1). On Claros, see Robert, *Claros*; Potter, "Claros"; Klauck, *Context*, 193; archaeological reports summarized in Mitchell, "Archaeology," 148–49; note also the Apollo oracle at Korope in Thessaly (Klauck, *Context*, 193–95).

104. *Sib. Or.* 11.315, 318.

105. This is Lucan's dramatization, and Lucan himself claims that this was an unusual event (*Bell. civ.* 5.166–67; see Klauck, *Context*, 187–88).

106. Lucan *Bell. civ.* 5.97–101.

of stirring and divine frenzy, she could be faking her inspiration; when genuinely possessed, however, her voice would fill the whole cavern; her hair would bristle, and the wreath would rise from her head.[107] Apollo "forced his way into her body," banishing her thoughts as he seizes possession of her; her head tosses, her hair bristles, things are overturned, and the fire of Apollo's wrath burns inside her. This possession tortures her from within, yielding frenzy and foaming lips, inarticulate panting and groans, wailing, and finally articulate speech.[108]

We should not read too much into Lucan's epic poetry. Archaeology shows that despite literary references, no "mephitic vapors" beneath the Delphic tripod inspired the Pythian priestess.[109] Nevertheless, neither should we attribute the depiction of her possession behavior altogether to Lucan.[110] Although lacking Lucan's elaborate description, both earlier and later sources indicate that she was possessed by a spirit[111] and went into mad ecstasy.[112] Jewish people believed that demons would enter people, forcing them to do what the demons desired.[113] Nevertheless, against the assumptions of some scholars, the speech of Apollo's priestess at Delphi was intelligible, not gibberish.[114] That her utterances were obscure allowed for professional interpretation. This practice was useful for the temple's cultic staff, who could benefit from the fee involved.[115] Interpreters have long compared such ancient depictions of possession with those in more recent eyewitness sources.[116]

Prophylaxis against Demons

In popular culture, people sought various means of protection from hostile spirits; though much of our documentation comes from one or more centuries after the first century (the heyday of emphasis on demonology is the third century and later), enough evidence attests that demons were a matter of practical concern to popular folk religion already by the first century. A foul-smelling fish product

---

107. Lucan *Bell. civ.* 5.148–57. Firth, "Foreword," xii, notes cases of faked trances but that genuine trances (those that the "possessed" person genuinely believes) are common (cf. also Verger, "Trance," 64–65; Beattie, "Mediumship," 166–67).

108. Lucan *Bell. civ.* 5.165–93.

109. Cary and Haarhoff, *Life*, 317; Klauck, *Context*, 187.

110. As some appear to do: Klauck, *Context*, 187–88, noting that it depends solely on Lucan *Bell. civ.* 5.116–20, 161–74, 190–97, and that Lucan himself claims that this possession was more powerful than ever before (*Bell. civ.* 5.166–67). Also others (e.g., Witherington, *Corinthians*, 278–79).

111. Valerius Maximus 1.8.10; Maximus of Tyre 8.1.

112. Plutarch *Dial. L.* 16, *Mor.* 759B (regaining tranquility afterward); Aelius Aristides *Def. Or.* 34–35, §11D.

113. *Sipre Deut.* 318.2.1–2.

114. See Aune, "Magic," 1551; Witherington, *Corinthians*, 54–55 (following Fontenrose, *Oracle*); cf. Maurizio, "Pythia's role."

115. Klauck, *Context*, 189–90.

116. E.g., Oesterreich, *Possession*, 153–60, 383–89 (allowing some genuine parapsychic abilities for the Pythoness).

could drive off a demon in Tobit (6:17; 8:3);[117] in Josephus, a particular root was useful for driving off deadly demons from an afflicted person.[118]

Amulets were widespread.[119] Common enough in the republic,[120] they became even more widespread under the empire.[121] Magical practices designed to protect against the influence of demons in Sassanian Babylonia (third to seventh centuries C.E.) crossed religious boundaries, as popular syncretism naturally does.[122] Superstition readily crossed folk boundaries and from there would eventually permeate more sophisticated systems as well; for example, Mesopotamian rabbis' fears about even numbers rendering one susceptible to demons[123] reflect a broader ancient superstition.[124]

A Jewish charm might mention hostile demons from which a person needed exorcism.[125] Later magical amulets in Israel[126] and incantation texts guaranteeing protection from specific demons[127] indicate how widespread such views became: beginning no later than the third century, many rabbis thought that the very air around them was crowded with demons,[128] a view more widely shared in the culture.[129] Demons were thought to attack people,[130] but later rabbis often viewed them as mortal.[131] Before the first century, some Jews believed that particular medicines could protect people from evil spirits,[132] and later rabbis used various folk remedies to ward off such spirits;[133] some might even hope that warriors could protect them.[134]

---

117. For Tobit, see the discussion in Eve, *Miracles*, 218–32; Twelftree, *Triumphant*, 28–30. Foul odors against demons (Tob 6:17; 8:3) also appear in some traditional cures of more recent times (e.g., Mbiti, *Religions*, 196, though this is not exorcism). Cf. also fumigation in Ferdinando, "Demonology," 118; Colson, "Possession," 71; Lewis, "Possession," 199; striking the possessed in an old Russian Jewish account in Oesterreich, *Possession*, 209.

118. Josephus *War* 7.180, 185. For medicines to protect against demons, see also *Jub.* 10:1–14.

119. MacMullen, *Enemies*, 103–4; in pre-Hellenistic Egypt, Frankfurter, *Religion in Egypt*, 275; for numerous examples of Jewish spiritual prophylaxis, see, e.g., Alexander, *Possession*, 34.

120. Varro *Lat. Lang.* 7.6.107.

121. Nilsson, *Piety*, 167; cf. Greek magic against demons in Betz, "Fragments."

122. Gordon, "Incantations," 231.

123. *B. B.M.* 86a; *Kid.* 29b; *Pes.* 110a, bar.

124. Virgil *Ecl.* 8.75; Plutarch *R.Q.* 102, *Mor.* 288D.

125. *PGM* 4.3007–86 (e.g., 4.3039–40).

126. E.g., Rahmani, "Amulet."

127. *Incant. Texts* 17.1–2; 19.2; 34.1, 6; 47.1; earlier, see 4Q510 1 4–7; 11Q11.

128. *B. Ber.* 6a; *Num. Rab.* 11:5; 12:3; *Deut. Rab.* 4:4; *Pesiq. Rab.* 5:10; *Midr.* Ps 17:8. Demons could sometimes fly (*b. Git.* 68b; *Num. Rab.* 12:3; *Deut. Rab.* 6:6).

129. Earlier, Pythagoras (Diogenes Laertius 8.1.32) and Heraclitus (Diogenes Laertius 9.1.7) both reportedly believed that the air was filled with *daimones* and souls of the deceased (not necessarily hostile); so also Philo *Giants* 9; the powers in *Conf.* 174; angels in Wolfson, *Philo*, 1:366–85. In Middle Platonism generally, see Dillon, *Middle Platonists*, 288. Cf. spirits in the air in *PGM* 1.179–81; 4.3043–44; 12.67.

130. *1 En.* 69:12; *Tr. Shem* 2:9.

131. *Ab. R. Nat.* 37A; *b. Pes.* 110a; 111b; *Lev. Rab.* 24:3; perhaps *Jub.* 10:5; cf. Alexander, *Possession*, 33. Cf. the Titans in *Sib. Or.* 3.156–58, but here they were just humans anyway (cf. *Sib. Or.* 1.307–23; 2.231).

132. *Jub.* 10:10–13.

133. *B. Ber.* 6a.

134. *Song Rab.* 3:7, §5; *Pesiq. Rab.* 15:3.

Various sages came to urge proper precautions against demonic assaults. Drinking water at night rendered one susceptible to demons;[135] going out on particular nights of the week was dangerous;[136] different demons exercised their dangers during different times of the year.[137]

Rabbinic piety suggested that prayer could render many demons impotent or destroy them, though dealing with them was never pleasant.[138] Other pious acts, like the erection of the tabernacle, could destroy demons;[139] fear of God could protect one from them.[140] As early as Qumran, Jewish people prayed for protection against demonic activity;[141] in later sources, the protection sought in the Aaronic benediction included protection from demons.[142] Paul's sample extant letters do not articulate a full demonology, but what they do include probably presupposes one, although the extent of its overlap with contemporary understandings is not specified (see, e.g., 1 Cor 10:20; Rom 8:38).[143]

Exorcism

Although there are many significant exceptions,[144] most texts about exorcism come from after the first, and often even after the second, century c.e. Although to some extent this reflects the proliferation of the demonic worldview in a later period,[145] it also likely reflects the slowness of the elite (sources of most of our literature) to address phenomena that were already concerning the masses more widely.[146] Examples in Tobit and 1QapGen XX, 16–17, 28–29 are clearly pre-Christian, and Josephus's example probably presupposes that these practices had been circulating

135. *B. A.Z.* 12b, bar. For special dangers at night, see, e.g., Lewis, "Possession," 191.

136. *B. Pes.* 112b, bar.; other peoples also recognized unlucky days, e.g., Aulus Gellius 5.17; Ovid *Fast.* 1.8, 45–48; Plutarch *Alc.* 34.1; *Cam.* 19.1; Dionysius *Epideictic* 3.266–67; Iamblichus *V.P.* 28.152 (see further Keener, *John*, 496).

137. *Num. Rab.* 12:3.

138. *B. Kid.* 29b.

139. *Num. Rab.* 12:3; *Pesiq. Rab.* 5:10.

140. *Gen. Rab.* 36:1.

141. 11Q5 XIX, 13–16; cf. songs for warding off demons in 11Q11 II–V; cf. *Jub.* 19:28. God was protecting his people, who kept his covenant, against such demons (1QM XIV, 9–10).

142. E.g., *Sipre Num.* 40.1.5; *Num. Rab.* 11:5; *Tg. Ps.-Jon.* on Num 6:24. This is an intertextual reading employing Ps 91:11.

143. Cf. Eph 1:20–2:3; 6:12; Col 2:15; discussion in, e.g., Adeyemi, "Θέσεις"; Paige, "Demons," esp. 211.

144. See much earlier Egyptian models in Twelftree, *Triumphant*, 21–22 (who, however, notes on 22 that the temporal and geographic distance from Jesus's day is too great to assume dependence); Hull, *Magic*, 63 (following Franz Cumont).

145. The majority of magical papyri do stem from the later period.

146. Cf., e.g., Klutz, *Exorcism Stories*, 6. Thus Abrahams, *Studies 1*, 110, doubts that possession and exorcism were common in first-century Palestine, based on Tannaitic literature, despite acknowledging the demonology of *1 Enoch* (which is much earlier).

well before his own time.[147] In addition to the importance of expelling demons from people, spirits also had to be removed from haunted houses, often by appeasing a ghost or burying its bones there.[148]

One of the earliest pagan reports of wonder workers casting out demons is placed in second-century Palestine. In this satirical account, the victims "fall down and roll their eyes and fill their mouths with foam," but then the wonder worker heals them and takes a good bit of their money.[149] The exorcist asks the demon through which body part it entered, and it answers either in Greek or another language; he then adjures the spirit (cf. the Legion's attempt in Mark 5:7) and threatens it, thus compelling it to leave; the unreliable narrator claims to have seen one smoke-colored *daimon* emerge.[150] Origen's Celsus (in the late second century) attacks Jesus as nothing more than a cheap magician of the Egyptian sort in the market, who for a few obols would drive away people's demons, cure diseases, and teach esoteric doctrines.[151]

Beyond this, few extant stories of pagan wonder workers offer much in the way of exorcisms apart from Philostratus's *Life of Apollonius*, which probably draws on Christian as well as other widespread miracle stories of the day.[152] Apollonius confronts a youth scoffing at his teaching by identifying the demon in him and ordering it out.[153] Quite different from the early Christian accounts, he identifies a blind beggar as a demon and orders it stoned, despite the beggar's pleas; but once it is dead, it turns into a giant dog.[154] A homosexual demon, the ghost of a man betrayed by his wife, was pursuing and possessing an attractive boy, threatening to kill him if exorcism was attempted. Apollonius, however, sent a threatening letter, after which the demon desisted.[155] (Other texts also speak of sexually interested

---

147. On 1QapGen, see, e.g., Twelftree, *Triumphant*, 32–33; he addresses Tobit on 29 (though allowing that this may not be a full-scale exorcism). On pre-Christian examples, see also Hull, *Magic*, 63–64.

148. E.g., Pliny *Nat.* 7.27.7–11; Lucian *Lover of Lies* 31; cf. a haunted schoolhouse in *b. Kid.* 29b. One African scholar reports a (disembodied) spirit that attacked anyone who tried to live on the property a deceased man had left to his widow (Mbiti, *Religions*, 113). Cf. also the Chinese exorcism from a haunted house in Währisch-Oblau, "Healthy," 89–90; another Asian account in Yung, "Case Studies," 142; exorcising a curse from a house in India in Bergunder, "Miracle Healing," 293.

149. Lucian *Lover of Lies* 16 (LCL 3:345); cf. Mark 9:20 for foam.

150. Lucian *Lover of Lies* 16. Lucian knew of Christians, though what he knew of them was probably mixed with other sources (cf. *Peregr.* 11–13). Someone claims to see hundreds of spirits, and to see them all the time, by means of a ring secured from an Arab (Lucian *Lover of Lies* 17).

151. Origen *Cels.* 1.68 (noted in Eve, *Miracles*, 347).

152. Blackburn, "ΑΝΔΡΕΣ," 192. The commonalities are often observed (e.g., Klutz, *Exorcism Stories*, 121–25; Strelan, *Strange Acts*, 103, citing Philostratus *Vit. Apoll.* 2.14; 3.38; 4.10, 25, 40).

153. Philostratus *Vit. Apoll.* 4.20 (probably dependent on earlier models from the Gospels, despite differences).

154. Ibid., 4.10.

155. Ibid., 3.38. Cf. Asmodaeus, who killed Sara's first seven husbands, in Tob 3:8; 6:14; homosexually inclined spirits in *PGM* 2.55–56; *PDM* 14.68, 287 (cf. also *PGM* 1.86; 5.376–7.544). In traditional religions, the supposed correlation between possession and male homosexual behavior may appear but is not common (see Beattie and Middleton, "Introduction," xxv), sometimes appearing in societies that associate possession with women (e.g., Lee, "Possession," 143–44).

spirits.[156]) Another source claims that Porphyry cast a demon from a bath.[157] But pagan exorcism is clearly earlier than these literary sources.[158]

Exorcism is attested more strongly and from an earlier period in Jewish sources,[159] which came from the East.[160] Exorcism, in contrast to the mention of demons, admittedly appears much less often in the early period than its emphasis in the Gospels could suggest.[161] This may be simply a matter of what literature has survived, however;[162] it already appears in Qumran and Josephus,[163] and in our earliest traditions Jesus recognized the existence of other Jewish exorcists (Matt 12:27// Luke 11:19).[164] It might involve smoking out a demon with a special substance,[165]

156. Elsewhere Apollonius combats a phantom vampire, who had seduced a young philosopher so she could kill him (Philostratus Vit. Apoll. 4.25). On the sexual interests of spirits in early Judaism, cf., e.g., 1 En. 6:2; 16:2; 69:5; 106:5–6, 13–14; Jub. 4:22; 5:1; 7:21; CD II, 16–18; 4Q180 1 7–9; 1Qap Gen^ar II, 15–16; T. Reu. 5:6; 2 Bar. 56:12; T. Sol. 4; 5:3; 6:3; Apoc. Ab. 14:6; 2 En. 18:5; Gen. Rab. 24:6; Incant. Text 1.12–13; Wolfson, Philo, 1:384–85; Alexander, "Sons of God"; Delcor, "Mythe." Cf. also Greek deities raping or seducing mortals, e.g., in Sophocles Searchers 212–15; Euripides Antiope 69–71; Pirithous 22–24; Alope frg. 107; Antiope frg. 223.72–77; Archelaus frg. 228a.15–16; Danae frg. 1132.26–34; Andromeda frg. 136 (Stobaeus Ecl. 4.20.42); Menander Heros frg. 2 (Stobaeus Ecl. 5.20a.21); Apollodorus Bib. 1.5.1; 1.7.8–9; 1.9.3; 3.1.1; 3.2.1; 3.4.3; 3.5.5; 3.7.6; 3.8.2; 3.10.1, 3; 3.12.2, 5–6; 3.15.2, 4; Epit. 1.9, 22; Thebaid frg. 11 (from scholiast D on Iliad, 23.346); Cypria frg. 10 (from Athenaeus Deipn. 8.334b); frg. 11 (from Philodemus Piety B 7369); Varro Lat. Lang. 5.5.31; Ovid Metam. 2.714–47; 3.1–2, 260–61; 4.234–44; 5.391–408; 14.765–71; Silius Italicus 13.615; Lucian Dial. G. 250 (23/19, Aphrodite and Eros 1); Pausanias 8.25.7–8; Parthenius L.R. 15.3; Achilles Tatius 1.5.5–7; Apuleius Metam. 6.22; Libanius Speech in Character 27.3; Narration 1; 4.1–2; 17; 31; 32; 39; 41. Cf. one type of medieval incubus, in Lugt, "Incubus," 177; for spirit spouses and intercourse today, cf. Mbiti, Religions, 111; Firth, Ritual, 319–21; Horton, "Possession," 35, 38–40; Crapanzaro, "Mohammed," 162–64; Rosny, Healers, 185; spirits "riding" their "horses," their "spouses," in Montilus, "Vodun," 3 (cf. spirits mounting persons as "horses" also in Michel, Bellegarde-Smith, and Racine-Toussaint, "Mouths," 82); or attractive spirits in Ritchie, Spirit, 25. Cf. also sexually excessive spirits in Stoller, "Change," 277–80 (which Stoller views as a protest against the republic's neoconservative Islam); spirits that entice shamans sexually, sometimes even jealous of a wife (Sandner, "Psychology," 281).

157. Eunapius Lives 457; the event probably occurs in Syria. Like Philostratus, Eunapius (late fourth century) and Porphyry (234–ca. 305 C.E.) are both much later than the first century.

158. Ferguson, Backgrounds, 185, cites, e.g., Plutarch T.-T. 5, Mor. 706E; Lucian Lover of Lies 16. In subsequent rabbinic sources, see, e.g., Hruby, "Perspectives Rabbiniques," 82–83.

159. E.g., Josephus Ant. 8.46–48 (on Josephus, see further Eve, Miracles, 339–43); in Qumran sources, see, e.g., 4QNab (4Q242) I, 4; perhaps 4Q243–45; 4Q552–53; 4Q560 (see Wise, "Introduction" to 4Q242, p. 266); cf. Leicht, "Mashbia'"; on the limited Qumran evidence, cf. Kirchschläger, "Exorzismus"; Eve, Miracles, 343–45. Some apparently used "healing" as appropriate language for exorcism (11Q11 II, 7; 1Qap Gen^ar XX, 21–29; cf. 4Q242 4 1; Josephus Ant. 8.45).

160. On the Middle Eastern origin of exorcism stories, see further Williams, Miracle Stories, 23–25 (noting on 24 that exorcism stories appear in Greco-Roman settings only later, for which he cites Plutarch T.-T. 7.5.4; Lucian Lover of Lies 16; Philostratus Vit. Apoll. 4.20).

161. Eve, Miracles, 244; idem, Healer, 26–27.

162. Eve argues (255–59) that early Judaism exhibited little interest in forming narratives about exorcists, but this verdict could also reflect the limitations of our evidence. See the broader early Jewish context of Gospel exorcisms in Eshel, "Exorcist."

163. 1Qap Gen^ar XX, 21–29; Josephus Ant. 8.47. See further sources and discussion in Koskenniemi, Miracle-Workers, 290 (who includes also 11Q11; L.A.B. 60:1–3; and what he views as related ideas in Jub. 11:15–22; Apoc. Ab. 13:4–14; Liv. Pr. 4:10).

164. On early Christian attestation of other exorcists, cf. also Grelot, "Démonologie," 63 (citing also Acts 19:13–16); Dakin, "Belief," 38; Best, "Exorcism," 1; Rollins, "Miracles," 45 (adding Matt 7:22).

165. Tob 6:7–8, 16–17; 8:2–3; cf. T. Sol. 5:13; Parshall, Bridges, 85.

invoking other spirits to expel it,[166] or even laying on one's hands in prayer.[167] As in paganism,[168] the visible proof of departure by some outward act often remained important.[169] Solomon,[170] and to a lesser extent David,[171] was associated with exorcism or authority over demons in sources spanning a long range of time. A pre-Christian writer reports how Abraham cast out a demon that Pharaoh's magicians could not.[172]

Because exorcism in this period was more common in the East, the Greek milieu of most extant Gospels does not account for the Gospel narratives of exorcisms;[173] moreover, redaction-critical analysis shows that neither Matthew nor Luke, writing in different parts of the empire, made major changes in their sources about exorcism.[174] All of this suggests that the substance of the Gospels' exorcism portrayal remains authentic. Whereas many question Jesus walking on water, few doubt that he exorcised, even if they do not believe that actual spirits were involved.[175] Most scholars believe that Jesus historically gained a reputation as an exorcist,[176] although the Gospels omit most magical exorcism techniques dominant among

166. *Incant. Text* 3.8–9; 50.7–8; *T. Sol.* 2:4; 5:5; 8:5–11; 18. Eve, *Miracles*, 347, notes that the names used for invocation in Origen *Cels.* 1.24 are Persian or Egyptian (suggesting Gentile usage); but in *Cels.* 5.45, they submit to the name of God of Abraham, Isaac, and Jacob (presumably a Jewish formula).

167. 1Qap Gen[ar] XX.

168. Later, Philostratus *Vit. Apoll.* 4.20. See more fully Theissen, *Miracle Stories*, 66–67 (who also cites Lucian *Lover of Lies* 16; still relevant but less so, Philostratus *Vit. Apoll.* 4.10). In traditional Navajo exorcism, the moth flying inside the mentally ill person may be expelled in part by vomiting (Kaplan and Johnson, "Navajo Psychopathology," 211).

169. Josephus *Ant.* 8.48; in modern times, Hes, "Role," 376; Bergunder, "Miracle Healing," 293 (Hindu and Christian exorcism in India); an old Russian Jewish account in Oesterreich, *Possession*, 209–10 (where the departing spirit knocked a small hole in the window).

170. 11Q11 II, 2–12; Josephus *Ant.* 8.45–49; *CIJ* 1:394, §534; 2:374, §1448; *PGM* 4.850–929, 3039–41; *T. Sol.* Greek title; 2:1–7; 5:10; 6:11; *incant. text* 47.1–3; 48.4–5; *Pesiq. Rab Kah.* 5:3 (before he sinned); *b. Git.* 68ab; *Eccl. Rab.* 2:8, §1; *Song Rab.* 3:7, §5 (before his sin); *Pesiq. Rab.* 15:3 (before his sin); cf. *p. Ket.* 12:3, §11; Betz, "Miracles in Josephus," 220–21; Mills, *Agents*, 49–61; Duling, "Introduction," 948; in Islamic tradition, Qur'an 27.17, 39–40; in some folk Islam, Butler, "Materialization," 267. That *2 Bar.* 77:25 relates to this tradition is not impossible.

171. *L.A.B.* 60; cf. 1 Sam 16:23, the closest precedent for exorcism in the Hebrew Bible (cf. Kotansky, "Demonology," 269–70, comparing a Greek conception).

172. 1Qap Gen[ar] XX, 19–29. As in analogous examples in ancient literature, the physicians' and magicians' failure highlights Abraham's superiority all the more (XX, 19–20).

173. McCasland, *Finger*, 65–82 (see esp. 76, 82); also, as noted above, Williams, *Miracle Stories*, 23–25.

174. McCasland, *Finger*, 51, 53. More generally on miracle stories in Luke-Acts, see Williams, *Miracle Stories*.

175. Best, "Exorcism," 2. Hedrick, "Miracles," 312, allows that Jesus may have been a faith healer but denies real demons, hence real exorcism (cf. also Best, "Exorcism," 4–8).

176. Sanders, *Figure*, 149, 154; Meier, *Marginal Jew*, 2:646–77; Dunn, *Jesus and Spirit*, 44; Miller, *Seminar*, 56–57 (though doubting individual accounts); Michaels, *Servant*, 174; Twelftree, "ΕΚΒΑΛΛΩ"; idem, *Miracle Worker*, 281–92 (esp. 282–83); Achtemeier, *Miracle Tradition*, 140; Sears, "View," 101–2. One Christian writer suggests that possession phenomena peaked in Jesus's day as part of a demonic counterattack (Alexander, *Possession*, 249; further and less plausibly, Keyser, "Rationale," 362–63, compares their increase in activity through humans with Jesus's incarnation); we may note, however, that claims of spirit possession are widespread in numerous cultures (see discussion below).

other reported exorcists, such as rings, roots, incantations, and so forth.[177] Unlike other forms of healing at times in the Gospels, exorcism is not associated with the ailing person's faith.[178] Exorcism is connected closely with the gospel of the kingdom, as a concrete manifestation of the deliverance it brings.[179] Christian exorcism shares some other aspects in common with some Jewish exorcisms,[180] but especially transformed them by using Jesus's name.[181] Justin complains that Jewish exorcists, like Gentiles, depend on "fumigations and incantations," but Christians successfully employ the name of Jesus. No other name, he declared, could accomplish the same effects.[182]

Second-century patristic sources unabashedly report Christianity spreading especially through exorcisms, claiming Christians' success in exorcisms as a matter of common knowledge.[183] Tertullian even challenges the authorities to bring in a demon-possessed person to court; any Christian will make short work of the demon, forcing it to confess its deceit.[184] If the demons do not immediately confess their identity, he insists, then execute that impudent Christian immediately![185] Tertullian elsewhere reports a demon being exorcised from a Christian who had gone to the theater. The exorcist demanded how the demon dare enter a Christian; the spirit replied that he "found her on my own ground."[186] By the time of Hippolytus (ca. 215 C.E.), exorcism was often practiced in connection with baptism,[187] and it

---

177. Kee, "Terminology," 239; Vermes, *Jesus the Jew*, 23, 65; Twelftree, "ΕΚΒΑΛΛΩ," 383–84; Witherington, *Christology*, 159; Eve, *Miracles*, 349. A few later rabbis were also said to have exercised authority over demons with commands (*b. Pes.* 112b; Vermes, *Jesus the Jew*, 66; cf. Kee, "Terminology," 246; but Eve, *Miracles*, 290–91, notes that Hanina ben Dosa confronts but does not exorcise a demon in *b. Pes.* 112b). The form of many exorcism accounts in the Synoptics resembles many miracle stories (cf. Guillemette, "Forme"). Like many others, Grelot, "Démonologie," 71–72, suggests that Jesus employed the exorcistic language of his era to communicate; as we shall see in appendix B, however, such practice is by no means limited to antiquity.

178. Robinson, "Challenge," 326, noting that even in other cases Jesus required faith not because he depended on it but because he wanted at least some present who would understand his point.

179. Ladd, *Kingdom*, 47; see further Hiers, "Satan"; Kallas, *View*; Evans, "Kingdom"; idem, *Fabricating Jesus*, 141.

180. E.g., Vermes, *Jesus the Jew*, 66; Sanders, *Jesus and Judaism*, 135; cf. perhaps Kee, "Terminology," 246.

181. Edwards, "Exorcisms," noting also that pagans usually viewed Christian exorcism as trickery.

182. Justin *Dial.* 85 (*Ante-Nicene Fathers*, 241); cf. *Dial.* 76. Eve, *Miracles*, 347, notes Justin's complaint but also presents Iren. *Her.* 2.6.2 (who mentions Jewish prayers before Christ's coming).

183. MacMullen, *Christianizing*, 27–28, 40–41, 60–61; Lampe, "Miracles," 215–17; Young, "Miracles in History," 107–8; cf. McCasland, *Finger*, 55; patristic sources in Martin, "Resisting," 49–50, 58–59; Sears, "View," 103–4. Various sources (Ferguson, *Backgrounds*, 185; Talbert, *Acts*, 143; Haines in Marcus Aurelius LCL, pp. 5–6n6) cite, e.g., Justin *Dial.* 30, 85; *2 Apol.* 5–6; *Acts Pet.* 2; Tertullian *Test.* 3; Origen *Cels.* 1.46; Best, "Exorcism," 3, cites *Acts Pet.* 4.11. Ferguson, *Backgrounds*, 185, also thinks that the condemnation of superstitious exorcists in Marcus Aurelius 1.5 refers to Christians. On ante-Nicene demonology, see further Frost, *Healing*, 141–61.

184. Tertullian *Apol.* 23.4–5; MacMullen, *Christianizing*, 27. Cf. similarly the power encounter in the 350s reported in Athanasius *Vit. Ant.* 80 (MacMullen, *Christianizing*, 112).

185. Tertullian *Apol.* 23.6.

186. Tertullian *Spect.* 26 (LCL p. 291).

187. See "Ceremony." This may reflect the perceived rise in demons in the wider culture.

continued to be common in the early church.[188] Augustine reports cases of effective exorcisms, sometimes attested with affidavits.[189]

Those who worked with spirits questioned them and for some reason expected honest answers.[190] Incantations were a common means for removing unwanted spirits,[191] including in early Jewish circles.[192] A potentially more problematic approach was appealing to higher spirits to manipulate lower ones.[193] Sometimes demons express willingness to leave in return for a sacrifice.[194] Josephus reports that he personally witnessed, in the presence of Vespasian and others, a Jewish exorcist drawing out a demon through a man's nose by the odor of a special root under his ring's seal, using Solomon's incantations.[195] (Rings that control spirits appear in some Eastern sources, although not pervasively.[196]) In a Qumran text, Abraham is said to have just laid hands on Pharaoh and prayed, thereby curing him from his evil spirit.[197] In some, often later, sources, Solomon[198] or others[199] command demons, perhaps sometimes

188. See, e.g., Hillgarth, *Paganism*, 11–12, 183; Daniélou and Marrou, *Six Hundred Years*, 313; Casiday, "Sin," 503, 514; Frank, "Devotion," 539; Frankforter, *History*, 60; Spinks, "Growth," 603, 610; Brenk, "Art," 706; MacMullen, *Second Church*, 4–5. Scholars (esp. here Talbert, *Acts*, 143) provide an extensive list of examples (including Lact. 2.16; 5.2; *Apost. Const.* 8.1; Eusebius *H.E.* 5.7.4; 6.43.11; 8.6.9; Cyril of Jerusalem *Catechesis* 16.15–16; Athanasius *Inc.* 48; *Vit. Ant.* 63; Gregory of Nyssa *Life of St. Gregory the Wonderworker* [PLG 46, col. 916A]; Jerome *Vit. Hil.* 22). Talbert, *Acts*, 143, also cites early Christian novels (*Acts Pet.* 11; *Acts John* 56; *Acts Thom.* 5; 7; 8; *Acts Andrew* [beginning of martyrdom]; Ps.-Clem. *Rec.* 4.7; 9.38). For the office of exorcists, see also Ambrose 1.216 (in Greer, "Care," 573). From a different perspective, see the survey in Oesterreich, *Possession*, 161–68; in medieval sources, Oesterreich, *Possession*, 177–86.

189. *City of God* 22.8; *Conf.* 9.7.16; Herum, "Theology," 63–65.

190. E.g., *PGM* 4.3043–44. Acquiring accurate knowledge was necessary for manipulating spirits usefully (Arnold, *Power*, 18).

191. E.g., in the haunted house in Lucian *Lover of Lies* 30–31 (claiming satirically that Egyptian curses are the best, 31).

192. E.g., 4Q560; cf. 4Q510 1 4–7.

193. E.g., *PGM* 101.38–39. The higher ones are angels in *T. Sol.* 2:4; 5:5, 9; 8:5–11; 11:5; *incant. text* 3:8–9; 50:7–8.

194. Theissen, *Miracle Stories*, 57; cf. the slaughter of a sheep in modern Yemenite exorcism in Israel (Hes, "Role," 376).

195. Josephus *Ant.* 8.47; the exorcist also bound the demon by oath (ὥρκου); cf. Mark 5:7; *PGM* 1.80–82, 167; 36.307; 39.19–20; Aune, *Prophecy*, 273; *T. Sol.* 11:6; cf. also use of ἐξορκίζω (Kotansky, "Remnants"). On this Josephus passage, see, e.g., Twelftree, *Triumphant*, 34–36. Smoking the demon out also appears in Tob 6:17–18; 8:3; also an account attributed, probably fictitiously, to Johanan ben Zakkai, and noting the use of the roots, as in paganism and Josephus (*Num. Rab.* 19:8; *Pesiq. Rab.* 14:14); and apparently later in some Islamic folk practice (Parshall, *Bridges*, 85, following Jones and Jones, *Women*, 349–50, for a case of smoking the *jinn* out, then beating the boy unconscious, in this case with tragic consequences). Perhaps the roots idea was originally related to the prophylactic herbs of *Jub.* 10:12–13. Fumigation for exorcism appears in some traditional African societies (Ferdinando, "Demonology," 118; Colson, "Possession," 71; Lewis, "Possession," 199; incense fumigation in Granjo, "Rituals," 282); in Somali tradition, fragrant incense can protect from or exorcise malevolent sprites (Lewis, "Possession," 192–93, 199).

196. E.g., Lucian *Lover of Lies* 17 (the source being an Arab); Josephus *Ant.* 8.47; *b. Git.* 68a.

197. 1Qap Gen^ar XX, 21–29. Theissen, *Miracle Stories*, 62n18, thinks that this laying on of hands works for an illness caused by a demon but is not attested for possession; perhaps this is because the possessed would not allow it.

198. *T. Sol.* 3; 6:11. Some early Jewish sources also portray Solomon as a prophet (see Embry, "Solomon").

199. Cf. threats in Theissen, *Miracle Stories*, 63–64; exorcistic texts commanding "wandering wombs" (Faraone, "New Light"), and behavior resembling that involved in exorcisms in Soranus *Gynec.* 3.4.29.

reminiscent of the Jesus tradition. In the later (probably third-century) *Testament of Solomon*, the demons bargain for reduced sentences.[200] Particular angels could thwart particular demons and those under them, and demons might be compelled to name which angels thwarted them.[201] Solomon even was said to keep Asmodeus's strength down by maintaining a fire beneath him.[202]

In appendix B, I turn to especially anthropological observations concerning beliefs and practices of spirit possession and exorcism today.

Barrett, *Documents*, 34, thinks (from an occurrence in *PGM*) that "come out" (cf. Luke 4:35) was probably a frequent command of exorcists; yet its occasional occurrence in the vast corpus of *PGM* (4.1243, 1245, 3013; 5.158) does not suggest its frequency (cf. Aune, "Magic," 1531), and its context there differs (with incantations; Yamauchi, "Magic," 133).

200. *T. Sol.* 2:6. A minority of scholars, however, attribute *T. Sol.* to a Christian author (Albrile, "*Sigilla*"); at the very least it contains Christian interpolations.

201. *T. Sol.* 2:4; 5:5, 9; 8:5–11; 11:5. Learning demons' names was also crucial, e.g., *T. Sol.* 5:2, 6–7.

202. *T. Sol.* 5:13. The name Asmodeus, who first appears in Tobit, probably originates with the Persian demon *Aeshma daeva* (Yamauchi, *Persia*, 460).

Appendix B

Spirit Possession and Exorcism
in Societies Today

In chapter 1 we noted that most scholars associate Jesus with healings and exorcisms; there is little doubt that people experienced Jesus as an exorcist, although details are debated and few have explored what exorcism looks like in eyewitness reports. My approach in these first two appendixes on spirits and exorcism differs from the main body of the work. Because anthropologists have provided a large body of material on spirit possession, even though usually not from a perspective that affirms the existence of spirits, the comparative documentary sources are so rich that I have cast the net more widely here, drawing especially from their literature rather than popular Christian sources.[1] What I hope to show is that the accounts of possession and exorcism in the Gospels and Acts are plausible from a cross-cultural standpoint.[2]

Anthropological studies permit us to place possession behavior in ancient texts in a wider context, since such behavior appears in a wide range of societies. Although some expressions of possession vary from one culture to another, some features appear more widely, apparently often even on the neurophysiological level. I treat these matters more fully below.

1. Although we explored briefly accounts of healing in traditional religions (ch. 7), the anthropological approach to spirits appears more distinctive. I treat some of the material here in Keener, "Possession," albeit less fully and with a more direct application to NT historiography; more briefly, idem, "Comparisons," 3–4. A likely helpful work still forthcoming and unavailable to me at the time of this manuscript's completion is Kay and Parry, Exorcism.

2. Even some early modern research recognized the continuity among the phenomena reported in the Gospels, those reported in later history, and those characteristic of current reports (see Oesterreich, Possession, 3–11).

Cross-Cultural Evidence for Possession Experiences

However one explains them, experiences analogous to ancient depictions of possession by an alien spirit are impossible to deny. Although many modern Western students of early Judaism and early Christianity doubt the reality of spirit possession, they admit that ancients believed in such phenomena.[3] Explanations (explored later in this appendix) diverge: for example, most academicians discount the involvement of actual spirits in such experiences;[4] some, however, question modern Western presuppositions about such phenomena.[5] Globally, views diverge even further, with many cultures affirming the moral neutrality or diversity of spirits.

Whether one accepts the historically and culturally widespread explanation of invasive spirits or prefers the modern Western materialist rejection of such explanations' tenability, the transcultural character of the *experience* of possession behavior is impossible to evade. At least a few NT scholars cognizant of anthropological research have recognized this fact and applied some conclusions from social-science studies to the Gospels.[6] Studies have shown "an altered neurophysiology" during many possession states.[7] While neurophysiological studies cannot determine whether possession phenomena derive from an "an invading alien being" or from other psychological factors,[8] clearly neurophysiological changes, including hyperarousal, do frequently occur.[9] Incidents of possession on a notable

3. See Wrede, *Secret*, 26–27.

4. E.g., Best, "Exorcism," 4–8 (on 5 considering Jesus's misunderstanding on the matter as a limitation imposed by the nature of the incarnation; on 6 linking the belief with superstition).

5. E.g., Robinson, "Challenge," 323–25; Yamauchi, "Magic," 142–47; Wenham, *Bible*, 64; Montgomery, "Exorcism"; cf. Borg, *Vision*, 62, 72n16. See a much more complete survey of Western theological skepticism and the suggested problems with it in Twelftree, *Triumphant*, 135–70.

6. E.g., Borg, *Vision*, 62 (citing Lewis, *Ecstatic Religion*); Borg, *Jesus*, 149–50; Crossan, *Historical Jesus*, 315–17; Loubser, "Possession"; more extensively Davies, *Healer* (introducing spirit possession, 22–42); see further Keener, "Possession."

7. Prince, "EEG," 127–29. For example, persons in altered states of consciousness (ASC) fall in the theta range during an EEG, found in children but not normally in awake adults (Davies, *Healer*, 141–42, following Goodman, *Ecstasy*, 39). Tibetan heat yoga provides an extreme and paranormal example (see Benson, "Temperature Changes"; idem, *Healing*, 163–64). For various studies on the brain and consciousness relevant to "anomalous experiences" (visions, etc.), see McClenon and Nooney, "Experiences," 48, with fuller details in appendix E.

8. Goodman, *Demons*, 126; cf. Ladd, *Theology*, 51. For comparison with multiple personality disorder, cf., e.g., Firth, "Foreword," ix–x (also noting suggestibility on xiii); Bourguignon, "Multiple Personality"; Field, "Possession," 3; for earlier "possession" diagnosis and the sometimes consequent development of "secondary personality," see Oesterreich, "Possession," 111, 140; idem, *Possession*, 127. Psychiatric expectations may often contribute to this disorder (Spanos, "Hypnosis," 109–18, emphasizes the role-playing function). For earlier discussions of neurosis versus demonology, see, e.g., Freud, "Neurosis" (though Freud's diagnosis is problematic; see Midelfort, "Reactions," 139, 143–44); Anne Chevreau in 1598 viewed Marthe's "possession" in terms resembling neurosis (Walker and Dickerman, "Woman," 554). For possession as a religiously meaningful shared cultural idiom for sorts of mental illness, sometimes helpful to the possessed person, see Obeyesekere, "Idiom."

9. Goodman, *Demons*, 1–24, 126.

scale have also been documented, although Westerners may tend to attribute these to mass hysteria,[10] including in earlier Western history.[11]

Anthropological Reports of Possession Experiences

We thus do not need to assume that ancients invented all experiences of possession and deliverance, although writers probably schematized many and invented some of them. Whatever one makes of such experiences, they are inescapably widely attested;[12] seeking to deny phenomena like possession, trances, and so forth has been regarded as the anthropological equivalent of "being a 'flat-earther.'"[13] Although anthropologists do not all share a common cross-cultural conceptual metanarrative with which to frame them, possession states "are among the most commonly discussed behavior disorders in the anthropological literature."[14] Indeed, although I here address primarily those cases defined by their cultures as possession (control by alien spirits), the "behavior patterns" of many possession cases occur widely even in societies that do not construe them as possession.[15] Cross-cultural comparison is admittedly complicated by whether we are comparing merely altered states of consciousness, however defined, or experiences indigenously defined as possession, regardless of neurological state.[16]

10. E.g., when 120 people in a factory in Malaysia were "possessed" in 1978 and the factory had to be shut down while a local "spirit healer" sought to placate the spirits, to the U.S. director's embarrassment (Keller, *Hammer*, 107, citing Ong, *Spirits*, 204, 209, though interpreting the incident differently from Ong); about four hundred students during a possession epidemic in Transkei (1981–83; Edwards, "Possession," 220; cf. similar mass possession hysteria in factories in 1787 and in the nineteenth and twentieth centuries in Rosen, "Psychopathology," 245); possession of Kenyan schoolgirls in the 1990s (Smith, "Possession," 442 [earlier, cf. 442–45]); possession epidemics in public and private Madagascar schools in the late 1970s (Sharp, "Power of Possession," 3; cf. the "laughing" epidemic in Tanzania in 1962 (Capps, *Village Psychiatrist*, 10).

11. Mass possessions in Europe appear commonly only after 1500 (Midelfort, "Reactions," 136), though a major outbreak (the dance frenzy) occurred in 1374 (Rosen, "Psychopathology," 221–22; these dance epidemics continued in the fifteenth and sixteenth centuries, 226–27). From 1491 to 1881, see Oesterreich, *Possession*, 187–90. On the convent at Loudun in 1633, see Baskin, "Devils"; Oesterreich, "Possession," 112–13; Keller, "Glimpses," 277–80 (for one psychoanalytic approach, Lietaer and Corveleyn, "Interpretation," 266–73, noting the case of 259, 262–63; for this as pseudo-possession as opposed to genuine possession, see Gildea, "Possession," 298); at Carpi in the late 1630s, Watt, "Demons" (noting that the cardinals faulted the exorcists for the problem). Sociologists also compare mass hysteria in frontier revivals; cf. the multiplication of visions at Lourdes in 1858 (Taylor, "Letters from Lourdes," 472).

12. See, e.g., the bibliography in Boddy, "Spirit Possession," 428–34; earlier, Zaretsky, *Bibliography*.

13. Burridge, *New Earth*, 4n2 (as cited in Lewis, *Healing*, 321–22n15). As early as 1921, Oesterreich, *Possession*, 389, complained that the simple rationalist denial of ancient accounts of spirit possession, as in the case of the Pythoness, "is frankly no longer possible to-day" (though his appeal to the possibility of parapsychological powers need not be granted to uphold this conclusion). Some anthropologists emphasizing participant observation have also entered into shamanic trances (Turner, "Advances," 48, cites, e.g., Friedson, *Prophets*, 20–22).

14. Guthrie, *Disorder*, 8, as cited in Bourguignon, *Possession*, 9. Not all anthropologists today would view all "possession" as a disorder (see, e.g., Hoffman and Kurzenberger, "Miraculous," 84–85; similarly, Bourguignon, "Self," 56, argues that it is not "deviant" in a Haitian context).

15. Bourguignon, *Possession*, 9–10.

16. Cf. problems of various approaches surveyed in Ward, "Cross-Cultural Study," 27–31.

The anthropological literature demonstrates conclusively that many peoples do experience possession trance, even while the perception, interpretation, and sometimes expression of such experiences vary culturally.[17] Anthropologists today generally try to study the phenomenon from the perspective of societies that claim it, rather than imposing a Western interpretive grid on it.[18] In contrast to theologians and parapsychologists, most anthropologists seek to study not spiritual phenomena but indigenous *beliefs* about spirits.[19] Thus one study offers as a working definition of spirit possession "*any altered state of consciousness indigenously interpreted in terms of the influence of an alien spirit.*"[20] More recent studies work harder than most of their predecessors to take into account the indigenous frame of reference;[21] while traditional Western categories, often from a medical perspective, make cross-cultural comparison easier, more contextualized and phenomenological approaches prove more epistemologically open.[22]

As Erika Bourguignon points out, belief in spirit possession is widespread in varied cultures around the world, "as any reader of ethnographies knows."[23] She sampled 488 diverse, ethnographically representative societies and discovered spirit possession beliefs in 360 societies, that is, in 74 percent (nearly three-quarters) of those

17. Illnesses are often "oriented to and shaped by" cultural conceptions (Kaplan and Johnson, "Navajo Psychopathology," 203); cf., e.g., a form of possession associated with initial encounters with overhead airplanes (Colson, "Possession," 79, 85). Groups can experience revelatory trance states that they distinguish from possession (cf. Surgy, *L'Église*, 216–17).

18. Tippett, "Possession," 143–44. For a brief historical overview of anthropological approaches to spirit possession, see Prince, "Foreword," xi; Crapanzaro, "Introduction," 5–7; more thoroughly for recent studies, Boddy, "Spirit Possession," 410–14.

19. Bourguignon, *Possession*, 14. Some scholars warn of the impropriety of applying some Western diagnostic categories cross-culturally, since some behaviors considered disordered by therapists in one society may be norms in others (Hoffman and Kurzenberger, "Miraculous," 84–85).

20. Crapanzaro, "Introduction," 7 (emphasis his; cited also by others, e.g., Davies, *Healer*, 23); for those including any state indigenously interpreted as possession, cf. Bourguignon, *Possession*, 7; Lewis, "Spirits and Sex War," 627. With respect to shamans, Harner, *Way of Shaman*, xiii, 46–50, speaks of this altered state as a "shamanic state of consciousness" (noting on xiii that shamans can move back and forth between ordinary and shamanic consciousness). Typical shamans depend on guardian spirits (43 and passim).

21. Thus, Keller, *Hammer*, 39–40, notes that earlier anthropologists tended to explain possession in psychosocial terms, not commenting on possessing agents, but more recent research "does take seriously the agency of possessing ancestors, deities, and spirits."

22. See Boddy, "Spirit Possession," 408, 410–14, 427.

23. Bourguignon, "Spirit Possession Belief," 18; cf. also Bourguignon, "Introduction," 17–19; idem, "Self"; Boddy, "Spirit Possession," 409; Firth, "Foreword," ix; Morsy, "Possession," 189; Chandra shekar, "Possession Syndrome," 80; an earlier intuition in Robbins, "Exorcism," 201; Oesterreich, *Possession*, 376; on belief in spirits being found in most cultures, Turner, "Reality," 30 (distinguishing this from mere "energy," *ki* or *chi*). For the geographic distribution of cultures practicing trance, possession trance, and spirit possession, with maps, see Bourguignon, "Distribution," 18–32. Most occur in every geographic region, though some more in some regions than others. Lewis, *Ecstatic Religion*, 100–126, shows that negatively perceived spirit possession occurs in a wide range of societies, as do efforts to contain or exorcise it. In addition to anthropologists, missionaries widely report the phenomena, although construing them differently (Mooneyham, "Demonism," 210–14). I have heard many examples orally from African scholar friends, who sometimes have firsthand or secondhand experiences with these phenomena.

studied. The beliefs are most attested in the Pacific islands (88 percent); 77 percent around the Mediterranean; and less in the Americas (64 percent in the aboriginal population of North America and 64 percent in South America).[24] Sixteen percent of the 360 societies have possession trance only; 22 percent have other forms of possession; and 35 percent have both.[25] One could thus provide examples from a wide variety of societies in most regions of the world,[26] among them Africa[27] (including the northeast,[28] central east,[29] south,[30] northwest,[31] and west[32]), the Middle East,[33] Asia,[34]

24. Bourguignon, "Spirit Possession Belief," 19–21; idem, "Appendix"; followed also in Kaplan and Sadock, Psychiatry, 259, 1237; Ward, "Possession," 126 (noting that possession or trance states occur in 90 percent; Pilch, Dictionary, 81–82, also cites 90 percent for trances or altered states of consciousness); see, e.g., Wetering, "Effectiveness" (in Suriname). It occurs in the West, though often interpreted less benignly (Macklin, "Yankee," esp. 42).

25. Bourguignon, "Spirit Possession Belief," 21, noting that possession trance is rarer in the Americas (5 percent in North America, 12 percent in South America); more have possession without trance (27 percent of North American societies; 34 percent of South American societies). Possession trance is common in African tradition (Ferdinando, "Demonology," 120; Turner, Experiencing Ritual, 183).

26. For samples of those studied, see, e.g., Crapanzaro and Garrison, Case Studies; Goodman, Demons, 1–24, 126; Lewis, Ecstatic Religion; Oesterreich, Possession; Alexander, Possession, 105–6. In addition to those I have surveyed directly, some of the following samples come from the bibliography in Boddy, "Spirit Possession," 428–34 (with 221 sources, it provides a useful starting point for further research); for zar, tumbura, and bori cults, see Makris and Natvig, "Bibliography"; Lewis, Al-Safi, and Hurreiz, Medicine, 283–91.

27. E.g., Mbiti, Religions, 106, 111 (noting an "epidemic" of possession among the Akamba in the early twentieth century), 113, 249–50; Beattie and Middleton, Mediumship, passim. In Africa's early Western diaspora through slavery, see Raboteau, Slave Religion, 10–11, 17, 19, 27–28, 35–37, 63–73.

28. In Egypt, Saunders, "Zar Experience"; Natvig, "Zar Cult" (including early history, 178–80); idem, "Rites"; in Ethiopia, Somalia, and the Sudan (including the zar cult there), see Leiris, Possession; Lewis, "Possession"; Morton, "Dawit"; Messing, "Zar Cult"; Natvig, "Zar Spirits"; Tubiana, "Zar"; Makris and Al-Safi, "Spirit Possession Cult"; Boddy, "Spirits and Selves"; idem, Wombs; Kahana, "Zar Spirits"; Kennedy, "Zar Ceremonies"; Constantinides, "Zar" (for history); Kenyon, "Zar"; Luling, "Possession Cults." For earlier Western reports on zar cults, see Oesterreich, Possession, 230–35.

29. E.g., Smith, "Possession"; Harris, "Possession Hysteria"; Noble, "Possession"; Giles, "Possession Cults"; idem, "Spirits"; idem, "Possession"; Gomm, "Spirit Possession"; Beattie, "Mediumship."

30. Among Shona peoples, see, e.g., Gelfand, "Disorders"; Fry, Spirits; Garbett, "Mediums"; in Transkei, O'Connell, "Possession"; among the !Kung of the Kalahari, Katz, "Healing"; among the Valley Tonga of Zambia, Colson, "Possession"; Luig, "Worlds"; in Zambia generally, including in urban areas, Haar and Ellis, "Possession" (e.g., 204); Binsbergen, Change, 75–99; in Madagascar, Sharp, "Possessed"; idem, Possessed; idem, "Power of Possession"; Mayotte in the Indian Ocean, Lambek, Knowledge; idem, "Disease," 40–45.

31. E.g., in Morocco, Crapanzaro, "Mohammed"; in Mali, Colleyn, "Horse"; in Tunisia, Ferchiou, "Possession Cults."

32. E.g., among the Wolof of Senegal, Zempleni, "Symptom"; in Ghana, Field, "Possession"; Platvoet, "Communication" (analyzing aspects of Akan rites recorded in 1922); in Niger, Echard, "Possession Cult"; Stoller, "Change"; Masquelier, "Invention"; in Hausaland, Abdalla, "Friend"; among traditional Yorubas, Prince, "Possession Cults."

33. E.g., the zar cult in Iran, Modarressi, "Zar Cult"; in Kuwait, Ashkanani, "Zar"; see also northeast Africa.

34. E.g., in Nepal, Gray, "Exorcism"; Peters, Healing in Nepal; Hitchcock and Jones, Spirit Possession; in India, Chandra shekar, "Possession Syndrome"; Basso, "Music" (in Orissa); McDaniel, "States" (on goddess possession in West Bengal); Indo-Tibetan Buddhism, in Wayman, "Meaning"; in Sri Lanka and Sinhalese Buddhism, Kapferer, Exorcism; Obeyesekere, "Possession"; Yalman, "Healing Rituals," 128; Halverson, "Dynamics" (esp. 334–42); Oesterreich, Possession, 216–17; Pieris, "Humour"; in Hong Kong,

the Pacific,[35] and the Americas.[36] I will draw further on anthropological research below.

Cultural Elements of Possession Behavior

The actual experiences involved in possession behavior vary, sometimes even within cultures that have multiple forms of possession. One scholar suggests several categories. These include an intense, temporary state usually induced externally (e.g., by drums), which can either involve "psycho-physiological changes" (e.g., ecstasy or trance states) or not. The scholar also elaborates three suggested categories of permanent possession and allows for other types as well. Thus "the empirical facts underlying possession can be anything between a permanent backache and the most expert, breathtaking performance of less than one hour's duration."[37]

Possession behavior does not result from all purported interaction with spirits, though I also survey some claims of the latter experience in this appendix. Shamans in many parts of the world, for example, claim to communicate with spirits but are not taken over by them; some other shamans, however, become completely possessed, whether temporarily or long-term.[38] Thus in many traditional African societies mediums are normally in their own minds except when possessed by a spirit; only during the trance state do they function as mediums.[39] Spirit possession can be induced or solicited for such purposes by drumming

---

Yap, "Syndrome"; in the Philippines, Guthrie and Szanton, "Diagnosis"; in Malaysia, Kessler, "Conflict"; Ackerman and Lee, "Communication"; Lee, "Self-Presentation" (esp. 253–57); Keller, *Hammer*, 106–7; in Myanmar (then Burma), see Oesterreich, *Possession*, 218; Spiro, *Supernaturalism*; in Indonesia, Stange, "Configurations"; in Japan, Lebra, *Patterns*; McVeigh, "Possession." In early Buddhist tradition, see, e.g., Oesterreich, *Possession*, 174.

35. E.g., in the pre-Christian Solomon Islands, see Tippett, *Solomon Islands Christianity*, 14, 250–51; in Fiji, Hoare, "Approach," 124–46; among traditional aboriginal Australians, see Berndt, "Role," 269; in New Guinea, Salisbury, "Possession."

36. In New England, Macklin, "Yankee"; in Puerto Rico, Koss, "Spirits"; Garrison, "Syndrome"; Harwood, *Spiritist*; in Montserrat, Dobbin, *Dance*; some groups in St. Vincent, Henney, "Belief"; in a group in Yucatan, Goodman, "Disturbances"; in Haiti, Douyon, "L'Examen"; Kiev, "Value"; in the Brazilian cult of Umbanda, Pressel, "Umbanda"; idem, "Trance"; idem, "Possession"; in this and other Brazilian cults, cf. Krippner, "Call"; Hayes, "Limits"; in a Canadian Native American group, cf. Jilek, "Brainwashing"; idem, "Therapeutic Use"; in a U.S. Native American group, cf. Kaplan and Johnson, "Navajo Psychopathology," 211; cf. Fogelson, "Theories," 78, 84.

37. Binsbergen, *Change*, 90–91, also noting mediumship with some but not other kinds.

38. Eliade, *Shamanism*, 6 (cf. possession in 346); Tippett, "Possession," 165 (following Eliade); Peters, *Healing in Nepal*, 10–11. Guardian spirits are essential for shamanism (Harner, *Way of Shaman*, 43). Shamanism is not itself associated with mental illness (Hoffman and Kurzenberger, "Miraculous," 85). Shorter, *Witch Doctor*, 177, notes that those most susceptible to dissociation after initiation may become shamans themselves. Krippner, "Perspectives," surveys a variety of proposed models and data, including the traditional Christian model of shamans' "demon possession" (963–64; noting on 964 that shamans sometimes make these claims about rival shamans), which he rejects, and the various attentional states of different kinds of shamans (967).

39. Mbiti, *Religions*, 225–26 (in most other situations, spirit possession can be harmful, 106); cf. Firth, *Ritual*, 298. In some societies, only the medium will enter a trance (e.g., Colson, "Possession," 76).

and dancing.[40] (Dancing or drumming can also be associated with healing and exorcism.[41]) Some societies believe in possession but lack trance states; others link the two or have only the latter,[42] though those lacking only the latter could employ possession in connection with spirits.[43]

Some practices are common in particular regions. For example, in Brazilian spiritism,[44] in more than half the cults some see spirits of the dead; in all but one some see supernatural beings; most cults include possession of mediums, and most include possession of initiates; most include ecstatic trance; more often the possessed are unconscious than conscious; and in most cults possession can be either spontaneous or induced.[45] In rural Ghana, possession often includes

40. For drumming, see Mbiti, *Religions*, 106; Harner, *Way of Shaman*, 50–53, 142–43 (its repetition useful for the shamanic state); Peters, *Healing in Nepal*, 46, 49; Pressel, "Possession," 344; Shorter, "Spirit Possession," 114; Bourguignon, *Possession*, 19–20 (with dancing); Firth, "Foreword," xiii; Beattie and Middleton, "Introduction," xxvi; Horton, "Possession," 19; Binsbergen, *Change*, 90; Verger, "Trance," 55–59; Southall, "Possession," 233, 236, 240–42, 248, 269; Constantinides, "*Zar*," 89, 91 (for *bori*, but not *tumbura* possession); Luling, "Possession Cults," 173 (Somalia); Field, "Possession," 4, 7 (Ghana); Gelfand, "Disorders," 156, 162; idem, *Religion*, 166–67 (traditional Shona culture); Musi, "Shaman," 55 (Asian vs. European); Jilek, "Therapeutic Use," 182 (acoustic rhythm, "kinetic stimulation," "sleep deprivation," etc.); Hultkrantz, *Healing*, 36, 66, 163 (drumming to induce the proper state in northern North America and among Native Americans on the Plains); Fleurant, "Music," 49–50 (Haitian Vodun); in the Dionysus cult in antiquity, Plutarch *T.-T.* 1.5.2, *Mor.* 623B. Music aids possession in Basso, "Music"; for music and trance, see Alcorta, "Music," 243–47; for drumming and dancing to induce altered states of consciousness in a Zionist church, see Edwards, "Healing," 340–42; for sacred dance and healing in a contextualized South African church, see Mthethwa, "Music," 253–55; dancing and spiritual power in South African African Independent Churches (AICs), Oosthuizen, *Healer-Prophet*, 55–56; shamanic dancing in Hultkrantz, *Healing*, 63–65; possession dance in Stoller and Olkes, *Shadow*, 85. Others have appropriated the shamanic use of drumming to induce altered states of consciousness for therapeutic purposes (Winkelman, "Spirituality," 459–60; suggesting the psychobiological bases, see 461–62; but Walsh, *Shamanism*, 148, complains that Winkelman fails to cite empirical data for his neurophysiological claims). For fasting altering conscious perceptions, see, e.g., Kluger, "Biology," 64; for the use of psychoactive plants to achieve altered states of consciousness (ASC), see, e.g., Dobkin de Rios, "Power."

41. For healing in Siberia, Turner, *Hands*, 59, 71; in one African context, Turner, *Hands*, 71; drumming in an exorcism ceremony in Gray, "Cult," 177–79; Lewis, "Possession," 206; Edwards, "Possession," 215; Schuetze, "Role," 41–43 (rhythm, with clapping, in addressing spirits); Mthethwa, "Music," 254 (driving away demons at church); music to set the tone for exorcism in a São Paulo (Brazil) Pentecostal service in Miller and Yamamori, *Pentecostalism*, 154; in African Pentecostalism, cf. Cox, "Miracles," 91. Cf. sacred dance and healing in a contextualized South African church, see Mthethwa, "Music," 253–55. Music aids in exorcism in *L.A.B.* 60:2–3.

42. See Bourguignon, *Possession*, 42–49.

43. Ibid., 48, notes that 48 percent of Native American societies (among the highest percentages anywhere) lacked belief in possession, yet "all but one had a pattern of ritual trance, mostly of a hallucinatory or visionary type, in which communication with spirits could be established." Native Americans had the highest percentages of trance states or altered states of consciousness (Pilch, *Dictionary*, 81).

44. See Johnson, "Authority," 15–65, including a careful chart of the belief structures of the different groups (64, table 2) and beliefs about possession in these groups (65, table 3); I use especially 65 here. Claims to "see" spirits also appear elsewhere (McNaughton, *Blacksmiths*, 11). Spiritists are highly influential in Brazil and undergo formal training; see Lotufo-Neto, "Influences," 201.

45. Using sacrifices, drums, singing, dancing, tobacco, prayer, and often drinking. (Such means are not universal; see, e.g., Field, "Possession," 7; but cf. use of tobacco and rum in Scherberger, "Shaman," 62,

an initial stupor followed by excited, ecstatic activity;[46] an established diviner may become possessed to divine what deity is possessing another person.[47] In traditional Mozambique, a healer drew spirits from the patient's body and then became a mouthpiece for the spirits, which would speak through him.[48] Among traditional Valley Korekore, spirit possession is common and "danced out" in cult groups, but mediums, who speak by spirit possession, are rarer.[49]

Possession behavior varies in some respects among different cultures.[50] Possession often follows conventions particular to the culture where it occurs,[51] and some possessed persons seem to exhibit stereotyped responses.[52] Thus, for example, Somali possession cults lack the emphasis on different spirits with distinct behaviors, in contrast to related Sudanese cults; the possessed dance but do not speak much, in contrast to, say, Comoro Islands possession.[53] By contrast, forms of possession trance vary considerably among individual mediums in Palau.[54]

64–65.) For trance-inducing practices in the Afro-Brazilian cults, see Lotufo-Neto, "Influences," 198–200. In Candomblé, an African-oriented cult in Brazil, the Orixás that are invoked "are assumed to dwell in Africa and are summoned from there" (Johnson, "Authority," 32). Shamans also "see" physically invisible "spirit" in Scherberger, "Shaman," 59. Greenfield, *Spirits*, 75, notes possession of mediums and (88–90) hypothesizes a hypnotic state for the patients as well.

46. Field, "Possession," 3–4.

47. Ibid., 8. On possession facilitating ability to diagnose (among the Karanga), see Shoko, *Religion*, 71–72; on comparable dependence on the Holy Spirit in an AIC, see Shoko, *Religion*, 122–23. In the Philippines, some divine by means of the saints as spirits (Licauco, "Realities," 266–67); Vodun also identifies some traditional spirits with the saints (Fleurant, "Music," 47). Roman Catholic missiologist and anthropologist Louis Luzbetak articulated problems with such syncretic forms that he has called Christopaganism (*Church and Cultures*, 239–48, esp. here 239–40, with sources cited).

48. Roque, "Mafumo," 181.

49. Garbett, "Mediums," 105, noting that mediums, unlike members of possession cults, had to remain in the vicinity belonging to their possessing spirit.

50. See, e.g., Platvoet, "Rule"; Keener, "Possession," 221–24; note also common cultural characteristics in some features of traditional African spirit possession and patterned responses to religious activity in the African diaspora, including many African-American churches (e.g., Jules-Rosette, "Spirituality"). For traditional Japanese spirit possession and other patterns in their cultural context, see, e.g., Lebra, *Patterns*. Some societies lack even dissociation in some cases, so that the common element in possession in these societies tends to be the belief that a spirit is overpowering one's personality (Shorter, *Witch Doctor*, 180). Possession accounts focus on children in Europe primarily after 1600, and group possession appears mostly after 1500 (Midelfort, "Reactions," 136). Trance and possession seem more common where members play more responsible roles in collective experience (Swanson, "Trance," 272–73).

51. See, e.g., Verger, "Trance," 64; Southall, "Possession," 243; Firth, *Ritual*, 313–14 (noting the possessing spirits' use of "conventional Tikopia concepts and . . . ordinary Tikopia norms of etiquette and morality"); Binsbergen, *Change*, 92, on temporary possession, as opposed to long-term afflictions classified as possession.

52. E.g., among the southeastern Bantu in Gussler, "Change," 123–24, to at least some degree apparently reflecting traditional beliefs; loss of eye control in Navajo mental illness (Kaplan and Johnson, "Navajo Psychopathology," 206).

53. Luling, "Possession Cults," 175.

54. Leonard, "Spirit Mediums," 176, also noting that most remaining possession trance is found among the elderly.

Even within a single culture (as just noted for Palau), possession behavior sometimes varies widely.[55] For example, in Mayotte, there is wide variation in susceptibility to and expression of trance or possession.[56] As Bourguignon summarizes, "Because of its psychobiological substrate, it reveals constants wherever we find it. Yet it is subject to learning and by this means, it is amenable to cultural patterning. As such, it takes on a striking variety of forms."[57] Moreover, travelers can take particular forms of spirit possession and mediumship with them to societies previously unfamiliar with them.[58] The nature of cults can change over time;[59] in some societies a traditionally serious, therapeutic possession cult has been harnessed increasingly in the direction of entertainment.[60]

Some Special Forms of Possession Behaviors

I focus here on some forms of possession behavior, found in some locations, that may be of special interest to students of the Gospels and Acts. In a wide range of societies, possession results in a major change of personality and sudden and dramatic shifts in "behavior, timbre and pitch of voice."[61] Those

---

55. Nevius, *Possession*, 46, noting wild activity, apparently normal activity except in a different voice, or speaking for a deceased relative or a fox (although all these reactions may have been accepted as stereotyped responses within the culture. On fox spirits, see, e.g., Matsuoka, "Fox Possession"; cf., e.g., one economic interpretation in Miyamoto, "Possessed." On possession supposedly by an animal, see also, e.g., Oesterreich, *Possession*, 28, 144–45, 191, 364, 220, 224–28 (noting the prevalence of fox spirits in Japan and claiming, on 226, oxen in southeast Asia; cf. the snake spirit in Emmons, *Ghosts*, 185, and snakelike action in Koch, *Zulus*, 294; lion spirits in 33; monkey spirits of some sort in Tari, *Breeze*, 63). In Tari, *Breeze*, 131–32, when children cast spirits from a local traditional priest, the spirits appeared like a long black snake coming from his mouth; other animal figures emerge from the mouth in Ising, *Blumhardt*, 170.

56. Lambek, "Disease," 41–43.

57. Bourguignon, "Assessment," 337; cf. similarly McClenon, *Healing*, 60.

58. See, e.g., Shorter, "Possession and Healing," 47 (on coastal beliefs reaching the interior of Tanzania through one Kipakulo in the mid-twentieth century); idem, "Spirit Possession," 122; Binsbergen, *Change*, 96–98. The same system collapsed in 1970 (49). Scholars have tried to reconstruct the spread of the *zar* cult (e.g., Morsy, "Possession," 192–93). *Amafufunyana* possession came to Zululand in the late 1920s or 1930s and spread elsewhere in South Africa (Edwards, "Possession," 209; cf. Oosthuizen, *Healer-Prophet*, 88). Spirits are now globalized, with spirits from Brazil or Ghana or Nigeria possessing persons elsewhere, and spirits that helped an antigovernment cult once based in northern Uganda now called Hitler or Mussolini (Behrend and Luig, "Introduction," xiii, citing for the latter Behrend, *Geister*). Some *bori* spirits in West Africa are "European" (Krings, "History," 53).

59. E.g., Natvig, "Zar Cult," 181; and often in the literature. Syncretism is common (e.g., Constantinides, "Zar," 91) and other factors, such as Islam, have forced a measure of change (e.g., Last, "Bori," 57; Giles, "Spirits," 76), though elements of continuity also appear to exist (Echard, "Possession Cult," 67). Cf. haziri possession at Islamic shrines (Bellamy, "Person"); Islamic possession and spiritual power in Ally and Laher, "Perceptions." Like Christianity, Islam faces syncretism on many local levels; see, e.g., between African tradition and Sufism, Ferchiou, "Possession Cults," 213; Islamic and pre-Islamic beliefs in Mindanao, Williams, "Bwaya," 122–25; in East Africa, Giles, "Spirits," 61–62, 71; Nicolini, "Notes," 121; West Africa, in Butler, "Materialization"; Islam elsewhere, e.g., Accoroni, "Healing Practices," 7–11. Coastal Swahili culture distinguishes between Muslim spirits and the "uncivilized" pagan spirits (Giles, "Possession," 148).

60. Cf., e.g., Last, "Bori," 49–50; Hurreiz, "Zar" (esp. 154); Sellers, "Zar" (esp. 156–57, 163). Some exorcistic language and ritual can become "domesticated" (cf. Versteeg and Droogers, "Typology").

61. Tippett, "Possession," 162 (following Herskovits; elaborated further on 162–64, with thorough documentation from anthropological literature). See, e.g., Oesterreich, *Possession*, 19–22 (offering many

leaving the possession state often have no recollection of how they acted while possessed.[62] Thus Raymond Firth notes that social anthropologists, approaching spirit possession from a very different standpoint from missionaries, spiritualists, or psychics,

> have been faced in the field by dramatic changes of personality in men or women they were studying—startling yet evidently accustomed alterations of behaviour, with trembling, sweating, groaning, speaking with strange voices, assumption of a different identity, purporting to be a spirit not a human being, giving commands or foretelling the future in a new authoritative way. Sometimes it has been hard for the anthropologist to persuade himself that it is really the same person as before whom he is watching or confronting, so marked is the personality change.[63]

Some of these descriptions appear relevant to examples of violent or self-destructive expressions of possession in the Gospels and Acts (Mark 5:4–5; 9:18, 22; Acts 19:16).[64] In a number of diverse cultures where it has been observed in the modern world, spirit possession sometimes yields superhuman strength that makes restraint

---

examples), 97, 208; Ising, *Blumhardt*, 104–5, 168, 169, 171–72, 174–75, 178, 183; Mbiti, *Religions*, 225–26, including (on 225) a case he witnessed; Dayhoff, "Guiva" (a girl speaking in a deep, unnatural voice before exorcism); Gelfand, *Religion*, 169 (regarding Shona examples); Shorter, *Witch Doctor*, 177; Greenfield, *Spirits*, 40 (new persona); Emmons, *Ghosts*, 193 (a medium imitating the voice and gestures of the deceased); Stacey, "Practice," 294 (change in voice and the elongation of facial features); Grof, "Potential," 144 (change in voice and superhuman knowledge); Wilson, "Miracle Events," 275 (two male voices from a woman); Instone-Brewer, "Psychiatrists," 140 (a case he witnessed while studying psychiatry); Ma, *Mission*, 67 (a woman's voice becoming male); Emmanuel Itapson, interview, April 1, 2011; Pastor Ricky Sayco of Metro Manila, interview, Jan. 27, 2009; Scherberger, "Shaman," 62 (change of voice and personality through spirit helpers); Turner, "Advances," 50 (citing also Earle, "Borders," 3); McClenon, *Events*, 134–35 (a right-handed Chinese non-artist painting with his left hand when entranced), 226 (trance and altered personality in a spiritualist context); cf. the trance behavior of a shaman in Evans-Pritchard, *Witchcraft*, 165; Veronica Steiner's possession in 1574 (Midelfort, "Possession," 127).

62. E.g., Field, "Possession," 3, 6; Horton, "Possession," 23; Gelfand, *Religion*, 166, 169; Bourguignon, "Self," 53, 56; Grof, "Potential," 145; Rosny, *Healers*, 185–86; Chandra shekar, "Possession Syndrome," 87; Bellamy, "Person," 40; Betty, "Evidence," 14; cf. Singleton, "Spirits," 477; Oesterreich, *Possession*, 13 ("posterior amnesia"); but contrast Shorter, "Spirit Possession," 113. Some claim to know little about the spirits that possess them, claiming to be "powerless in their hands" (Shorter, "Possession and Healing," 48). In some studies, hypnotic amnesia involves role playing rather than genuine neurological amnesia (see Spanos, "Hypnosis," 101–2, persuasively; cf. 116–17).

63. Firth, "Foreword," x (adding his own shock when first encountering spirit mediumship among the Tikopia four decades earlier). Possession typically displaces the normal personality (Mbiti, *Religions*, 106; Montilus, "Vodun," 3–4); for the possessed acting like the spirits believed to possess them, see, e.g., Verger, "Trance," 50–51, 53.

64. See also Keener, "Possession," 231–33. Exorcising a "legion" of demons in Mark 5:9–13 appears an unusual case on a dramatic scale (though cf. Luke 8:2; Mark 16:9), though Blumhardt believed that many demons left his parishioner, with a spiritual effect on the region (Ising, *Blumhardt*, 170–71), and Tari, *Wind*, 38–40, reports a sort of mass exorcism in a village in Indonesia.

difficult or impossible[65] and often yields "violent thrashing"[66] or destructiveness[67] (sometimes requiring isolation[68]), including at times self-laceration.[69]

For example, among traditional !Kung bushmen, younger and less experienced trancers have to be restrained from injuring themselves or others; they are known for grabbing live coals and smearing them on their bodies, contact with fire from one to five seconds producing burns.[70] One African scholar describes a case of possession trance he witnessed near Kampala, where the medium banged his head on the floor without injury, and after possession returned to normalcy.[71] In many African societies, spirit possession drives the person to live in the forest, to jump into fire, or to use sharp objects to hurt oneself.[72] According to one report, a possessed child being exorcised of an ancestor spirit hurled "a huge burning log from the fire place" at the prophets, who dodged it and expelled the spirit.[73]

65. E.g., Kaplan and Johnson, "Navajo Psychopathology," 208; Murphy, "Aspects of Shamanism," 58; Field, "Possession," 5; Oesterreich, *Possession*, 22–23; Filson, "Study," 154; Betty, "Evidence," 16, 20; Koch, *Zulus*, 45, 191 (seven men could not restrain her); cf. Edwards, "Possession," 210; Borg, *Vision*, 62; Ising, *Blumhardt*, 174; Mark 5:4 (but more positively, 1 Sam 11:6–7; 14:6, 19; 15:14; *T. Jud.* 2:1–7); perhaps breaking chains after alleged madness in Quintilian *Decl.* 295 intro; on other occasions, though, a possessed person could be tied up (Gray, "Cult," 182; Osborn, *Healing*, 315). Pastor Ricky Sayco of Manila recounted an incident where four strong men were unable to hold down an eighteen-year-old woman in Davoa City, Mindanao. She had become possessed in response to a curse from her father but was permanently delivered after they had spent five hours in prayer (interview, Jan. 27, 2009). Betty, "Evidence," 16, 20, following a report from a Western Taoist observer in 1920s China, recounts that the person visibly swelled in front of the eyewitnesses like a balloon and then deflated during the exorcism (something not known to happen naturally). Curiously, an account of an exorcism in India from May 2009, obviously independent from the report just mentioned, notes one bloating and becoming heavy during possession; the person's exorcism converted the village (a report involving a Filadelphia Bible College graduate, sent by Finny Philip, June 19, 2009).

66. Beauvoir, "Herbs," 129, also noting "'wild' behavior," but further a quieter form of possession; Wilson, "Miracle Events," 275.

67. Eliade, *Rites*, 71; Gelfand, "Disorders," 165, 170; Schmidt, "Psychiatry," 145; Kaplan and Johnson, "Navajo Psychopathology," 227; Matt 8:28; for possession yielding threats and aggression, see Obeyesekere, "Possession," 251. For spirits cursing and berating the possessed, see, e.g., Morton, "*Dawit*," 221.

68. When possessed persons become unmanageable, they might be confined to a cave, where they would die of dehydration, or (more often) be driven into the woods (Gelfand, "Disorders," 170).

69. Fox, "Witchcraft," 185; Ising, *Blumhardt*, 174, 326–27; cf. Evans-Pritchard, *Witchcraft*, 162; Mark 5:5; 1 Kgs 18:28. For various maladaptive responses, see Ludwig, "Altered States," 86 (including voodoo death, on which see also Benson, *Healing*, 40).

70. Lee, "Sociology," 41–42, 47 (though they believed that fire would not burn them, 43); Katz, *Energy*, 121–22. One may also run headlong into a tree; on occasion one has been known to violently attack a dog or to engage in despised sexual behavior (Lee, "Sociology," 42). In some cultures, shamans can walk on "red hot coals" (Filson, "Analysis," 76).

71. Mbiti, *Religions*, 225–26.

72. Ibid., 106, noting that sometimes the victim also hurts others; cf. "wandering through the bush" with danger of injury in Gray, "Cult," 178. In antiquity, cf. Mark 5:5; 9:18; Acts 19:16; cf. also the Galli, who were said to emasculate themselves in frenzy (on them see my *Acts*, at Acts 8:27). For throwing themselves into the fire, see also, e.g., Kaplan and Johnson, "Navajo Psychopathology," 211 (noting multiple cases); cf. Mark 9:22; Southall, "Possession," 234.

73. Shoko, *Religion*, 125, recounting the report from within a Karanga AIC in Zimbabwe. Some Kenyan members of AICs experiencing ASCs are able "to run along the road for hours beating drums" or perform exorcisms and the like (Harries, "Nature," 403).

Such feats appear more widely than in Africa. At a traditional Taiwanese festival, "spirit mediums" become possessed and flail themselves with instruments of "self-mutilation," allowing them to show immunity to the pain of their wounds.[74] Some Indian mediums display apparently superhuman character in fire walking or enduring beatings with swords, and some "carry heavy rocks that cannot be lifted by three or four people."[75] Some fire walkers in Indonesia have displayed immunity to pain in rapid contact with burning substances and slashing of their tongues.[76] Haitian possession is said to sometimes involve "glass- or fire-eating" or other feats.[77] One study suggests that those in trance states can become less susceptible to burns and the like.[78] It is reported, however, that some persons "have died of post-possession exhaustion" or in the height of ecstasy.[79]

The Christian collectors and their informants in one wide-ranging study on possession phenomena in traditional China, from the final decade of the nineteenth

74. Jochim, *Religions*, 154. Although Ghanaian possession examples lack cases of self-injury noted in many cultures, they appear to lack hunger and many other normal sensations (Field, "Possession," 6). For cases of immunity to pain or heat, see McClenon, *Events*, 97–100 (esp. photographs of Sufi dervishes vs. pain [98], heat [99], and snake venom [100]); heat immunity in McClenon, *Healing*, 71–74. The Sioux doing Ghost Dancing in the snow (Brown, *Wounded Knee*, 409–10) may have experienced immunity to cold. Less commonly, some have prescribed substances supposed to provide invulnerability even against bullets (Brown, *Wounded Knee*, 408; Stoller and Olkes, *Shadow*, 176; Owusu, "Strings," 146; Oritsejafor, "Dealing," 89; protective charms during battle in Burgess, *Revolution*, 84; cf. a mark for protection from sorcery in West, *Sorcery*, 33–34); my wife tells me that it is reported that some young men from one of her nation's southern regions smeared with such an ointment cried desperately as they found themselves gunned down during a war in her country. When bullets succeed, it is believed that their users employ a more expensive magic that outweighs the protective charms (Owusu, "Strings," 133).

75. Chandra shekar, "Possession Syndrome," 89, though noting that these mediums appeared to remain conscious; cf. Betty, "Evidence," 15–16. For techniques for feigning some kinds of immunity, see Charpak and Broch, *Debunked*, 29–36.

76. Bourguignon, *Possession*, 12, citing Pfeiffer, *Psychiatrie*, 121–22, noting that the cases discussed were not indigenously interpreted as possession, though all participants from one culture entered an altered state of consciousness. Cf. the claim of lack of burns in Koch, *Revival*, 31 (who speaks of various forms of possession trance, also in Bali, in 34–36); study of genuine fire walking in McClenon, *Events*, 115–26 (with fewer blisters for those relying on an outside force, 121; for scientific considerations possibly mitigating the heat distribution with respect to ordinary coals, 121–26; McClenon, *Healing*, 72–73, 75); for scientific reasons why fire walking, properly done, would not produce severe burns, see Charpak and Broch, *Debunked*, 37–41; for denial of mass hypnosis in some Asian fire walking, see Licauco, "Realities," 266. Bourguignon, *Possession*, 12, notes that Greek fire walking assumes possession (by St. Constantine; following Michael-Dede, "Anastenari"), whereas Bulgarian fire walking "appears to be linked to a hallucinatory state" (following Schipkowensky, *Feuertanz*). For fire walking in antiquity, see Trombley, "Paganism," 192 (citing Strabo 12.2.7).

77. Beauvoir, "Herbs," 130.

78. After noting scientific explanations for lesser cases of heat immunity (McClenon, *Healing*, 72–73, 75), and that many fire walkers blister afterward, regardless of religious commitment (74), McClenon (72–73) notes anomalous cases during trance. Whereas McClenon after his first experiment found that his own blisters took three weeks to heal (74), after hypnosis he was able to walk the coals safely multiple times and to take others so hypnotized across the coals (76). McClenon (94) contends that shamans control bleeding, show heat immunity, and the like through processes similar to hypnosis.

79. Field, "Possession," 5. In other cases as well, exhaustion commonly follows ecstasy (e.g., Lewis, "Possession," 202). A Tikopia medium might not feel tired after his spirit control entered, yet feel exhausted through the coming of other spirits (Firth, *Ritual*, 311).

century,[80] naturally read their data through the grid of their own traditional Christian worldview. Nevertheless, much of the study's data remains informative to a range of scholars[81] because major shifts in Chinese culture since that time have made comparable data less accessible.[82] Some spirits reportedly spoke with the voice of a fox or a bird; others with the voice of a deceased spouse; some persons normally weak in singing or poetry could sing or compose rhyme under possession.[83] The Chinese Christian observers, the study's informants, also claimed "northerners speaking the languages of the South, which they did not know";[84] often they knew information that they could not have known normally, including other languages unknown to the speaker in his or her normal state; they also knew of Jesus as divine and feared him.[85] Inexplicable knowledge also appears in some current eyewitness descriptions of reported spirit activity,[86] including one

80. Nevius, *Possession*. Other scholars have also compared Nevius and biblical portraits to various accounts of possession behavior today (e.g., Heth, "Demonization"; for Nevius, Oesterreich, *Possession*, 219–20; for biblical portraits, also Oesterreich, *Possession*, 3–11; cf. summary of Nevius in Collins, *Exorcism*). Oesterreich, *Possession*, 13–16, cites sources from the 1500s forward, especially favoring some observations by two nineteenth-century doctors (in his book, passim, he provides countless case studies, though the reporters behind his sources held a range of interpretations). More than a century ago Alexander, *Possession*, argued for the reality of possession, using medical as well as historical sources (cited also with appreciation in Wilson, "Miracles," 29; I believe that Alexander's rabbinic evidence comes largely from A. Edersheim or other secondary sources).

81. As Oesterreich, *Possession*, 13, observes, the data collected are useful whether the sources attribute the possession behaviors to psychological or demonic sources (thus he includes, among others, missionary reports, e.g., 143–46, 213–15, 219–23, 229, 362–64). Others also find missionary reports useful, though limited, windows into earlier cultures (Kasten, "Shamanism," 65).

82. Even mostly nonreligious university students who grew up during the Cultural Revolution, however, "reported levels of anomalous experience equivalent to U.S. national samples" (McClenon, *Events*, xiii–xiv).

83. Nevius, *Possession*, 46–47, 58; some also noted in Tippett, "Possession," 153. Nevius, *Possession*, 140–43, defends the reliability of his Chinese informants, especially noting on 143 that the reports cohere with reports received from other cultures and eras. Nevius reports that he himself was persuaded of the reality of spirit possession only gradually, through his field experience (ix, 9–13), as others have also pointed out (e.g., Ramsay, *Teaching*, 105–6).

84. Nevius, *Possession*, 58, noted in Tippett, "Possession," 153, also noting that some spirits bargained over the price of their departure. (The entire section in Nevius, "circular letter and responses," is 41–59.)

85. Tippett, "Possession," 154. Cf. also MacPhail, "Path," 190, claiming Indian experience that Hindus, Muslims, and Christians, when possessed, speak of Jesus Christ as the true God. Isaacs, "Disorder," 269, addressing possession disorder in the West, notes frequent revulsion against "religion or religious objects." Allison, "Doubt," 117–18, notes that demons (whether imaginary or real) he encountered in his practice with patients "cowed in fear when I spoke the words 'Jesus Christ,'" and the demons left. Wilson, "Miracle Events," 275, notes that an attempt to say, "Jesus is Lord," was cut short by a demonic manifestation, but after deliverance the woman accepted and confessed Jesus freely.

86. Earle, "Borders," 3 (as cited in Turner, "Advances," 50); McClenon, *Events*, 137 (in a trance, without knowledge of the man, painting a requested picture of a long-deceased man that relatives regarded as "an exact representation"), 138 (accurately answering McClenon's thoughts; but McClenon himself was not persuaded, ibid.); Krippner and Achterberg, "Experiences," 353–54; unusually accurate (but not infallible) knowledge of spirit mediums in Emmons, *Ghosts*, 193–96, 198–207; Koch, *Zulus*, 143, 146 (cf. the shaman in 294); a possession state described in Grof, "Potential," 144–45; an occult practitioner's continual knowledge of his wife's whereabouts (Alamino, *Footsteps*, 36); cf. Keener, "Possession," 226; alleged occasional parapsychologic phenomena in Oesterreich, *Possession*, 381–82; supernatural knowledge in

by then-psychiatric student (now rabbinics scholar) David Instone-Brewer,[87] and others have reported the possessed speaking languages unknown to them, or the beliefs that something like this occurs.[88]

In the early twentieth century, some reports elsewhere in China continued to envision some sort of spirit phenomena; thus one Lutheran observer reports an evil spirit that kept trying to strangle a woman, leaving physical signs of the attacks. After shamans failed to cure the woman of the spirit, Christians tried to help her, but with limited success; everyone noticed that objects started being removed from the house, and she claimed to witness the spirit carrying them away.[89] (Local Chinese culture believed in haunted houses and in ghosts,[90] although these appear

---

Numbere, *Vision*, 344. But this does not appear to be always the case (cf., e.g., Firth, *Ritual*, 310; Emmons, *Ghosts*, 208; test cases in McClenon, *Events*, 138).

87. Instone-Brewer, "Psychiatrists," 140–41, where the apparently possessed person knew the psychiatric student's (Instone-Brewer's) thoughts.

88. Cf. the "alien tongue" frequent in Kalabari possession (in Horton, "Possession," 29); alleged strange tongues in some nuns' possession ca. 1611 (Rosen, "Psychopathology," 231); the illiterate George Lukyns speaking Latin during possession (exorcised by Methodists in 1788; Rack, "Healing," 148); the possessed speaking what hearers took to be Italian or French in Ising, *Blumhardt*, 181; the girl speaking Zulu—not her language—before exorcism (in Dayhoff, "Guiva"); a non-English speaker speaking English (in Hickson, *Heal*, 65, Calcutta, March 1921; idem, *Bridegroom*, 163; though knowledge of English would have been accessible there); again English (in Koch, *Zulus*, 55, though again access is not impossible); an alleged non-Latin speaker using some Latin (Kreiser, "Devils," 63–64—though she undoubtedly had heard Latin); a woman speaking her parents' home language (Malagasy) rather than her usual language (Wilson, "Miracle Events," 275); some elements of High German (possibly mixed with gibberish, Oesterreich, *Possession*, 208); various languages (Koch, *Zulus*, 143, 146); "unrecognizable words" in Stacey, "Practice," 294; nonsense syllables mixed with African fragments in one Haitian case of a "possessed" person's mind (Bourguignon, "Self," 50); occasional supposed African languages in Freston, "Transnationalisation," 211; Hausa-speaking spirits that include (known) elements of Pidgin English and French in Krings, "History," 55–58; other supposed languages in prophetic frenzy in Naipaul, *Masque*, 121. Shorter, *Witch Doctor*, 183, recounts a case from Tanzania of an elderly, illiterate vagrant woman, who could have had no exposure to Flemish, accusing a startled Belgian in fluent Flemish (following Robert, *Croyances*, 152–53). Stewart, *Only Believe*, 96, notes a young woman who knew no English speaking perfect English when possessed (though we might note that in her country English was widely known). An eyewitness account notes a demon speaking with a foreign accent (from the Levant in 1936, in McCasland, *Finger*, 57), and speaking with a strange voice may occur in possession accounts (Eliade, *Shamanism*, 365); the possessed may also address exorcists with unexpected theological sophistication (though Midelfort, "Possession," 118–19, attributes this to the reporters). Cf. perhaps the secret spirit languages of some Asian shamans (Eliade, *Shamanism*, 347, 440).

89. Lee, "Rulers," esp. 5–6. Given the account's brevity, I cannot venture an explanation, but analogous, independent accounts of spirits trying to strangle their hosts appear (e.g., Alamino, *Footsteps*, 40, in Cuba; Koch, *Zulus*, 278; cf. also the invisible burning hand leaving burn marks in Ising, *Blumhardt*, 170; biting in Sumrall, *Story*, 7–36, passim, in the Philippines).

90. On local beliefs in houses haunted by evil spirits, see Ronning, "Mission"; in Hong Kong, Emmons, *Ghosts*, 117–43; on Chinese haunting incidents in medieval sources, see McClenon, *Events*, 154–55. Claimed experiences of haunted locations and associated paranormal phenomena, whatever their causes, are documented in various cultures; see Favret-Saada, *Witchcraft*, 139; Koch, *Zulus*, 161–63 (with a narrative of deliverance); Ising, *Blumhardt*, 164–67, 175; more broadly, McClenon, *Events*, xiii, 57–74, esp. specific claims on 62–63, 64–66, 68–69, 70–72, 210–19, with apparitions on, e.g., 70, 72; the story in Davies, "Exorcism," 47. On a more popular level, early twentieth-century Chinese Christians also report some encounters with demons in Baker, *Visions* (2006), 101–4 (also noting their relationship with indigenous

in a more nuanced form among traditional intellectuals.[91]) An earlier theological-journal-article writer noted that every Western missionary in China whom he knew affirmed the reality of possession and that the phenomenon was well authenticated by doctors working there. He noted that these claims reflected the indigenous understanding of diseases caused by evil spirits, which were distinguished from mental illnesses.[92] One of his sources, who consulted many missionaries, noted that the local Chinese Christians would command these spirits to depart in Jesus's name and were regularly successful.[93] I am not satisfied that observers have always interpreted these phenomena or reports reliably (some reports appear particularly dissatisfying), but we should listen to them carefully before trying to fit them all into our predetermined interpretive grids.

Spirits, Sickness, and Seers

Some other associations with spirits, not all of them associated with possession, will be of interest to students of the Gospels and Acts (cf. Luke 13:11; Acts 10:38; 16:16).[94] Shamans are sometimes viewed as healers, addressing the spiritual problem by spiritual means.[95] Sickness is sometimes associated with pos-

folk beliefs, 106). Buddhist monks in Hong Kong exorcised a building "under government auspices on May 19, 1963" (Emmons, *Ghosts*, 177). Beliefs do not automatically generate reports; whereas belief in ghosts has been much higher in Hong Kong (ca. 50 percent) than in the United States, reported incidents are lower (ca. 4 percent; Emmons, *Ghosts*, 39–40).

91. The Neo-Confucian Chu Hsi (1130–1200) sought to explain ghosts and spirits as part of a larger worldview that did not divide nature from spirit (Gardner, "Ghosts"); spirits could express cosmic *ch'i* and appear as dangerous ghosts or as honorable ancestor spirits (Gardner, "Ghosts," 599; on ancestral spirits, 606–10). While he dismisses many popular rumors about spirits (602), he affirms their existence, along with nature demons, spirit possession, exorcism, and the like (601). Some later claimed to see ghosts (Chan, "Narrative," 37–38); others debated or defended these people (38–39). Many scholars doubt that Ji Yun (1724–1805) believed in ghosts (Chan, "Narrative," 60), but more likely he demonstrated sincerity by acknowledging naturalistic explanations where possible, while arguing especially for the necessity of the reality of spirits based on many bizarre events (e.g., 60–62).

92. Wilson, "Miracles," 30. Among his missionary sources was Dr. Howard Taylor (30), and he cites at greater length Ms. Gordon Cumming, who collected and published information from missionaries working in close relationships with the Chinese people (30–31). He follows her also in the observation that Taoist and Buddhist priests perform exorcisms, though not always successfully (31).

93. Ibid., 31 (still following Cumming). He notes one poor Chinese "Bible woman" asked to pray for a woman who was violently thrashing, foaming at the mouth, and struggling against "the holy one"; after the Bible woman (who refused payment, for the gospel's sake) prayed, the other woman was delivered and asked for baptism. Keyser, "Rationale," 363, cites accounts from China and elsewhere by Presbyterian missionary "Dr. Hugh W. White." More recent popular sources also recount successful exorcisms (Danyun, *Lilies*, 132).

94. Luke associates sickness generally with the devil's activity (Acts 10:38; cf. Thomas, *Deliverance*, 227; Twelftree, *Name*, 154; Pilch, *Healing*, 105; Boyd, *War*, 182–83), but he normally distinguishes sickness from possession (Thomas, *Deliverance*, 191–228, esp. 227–28), perhaps especially in Acts (cf. Weissenrieder, *Images*, 338–39). Although evil spirits can bring some disease in the NT accounts, they are not usually mentioned (Borgen, "Miracles," 101); they constitute only one of the possible causes of illness in the NT (Thomas, "Health," 92–98, for demons or the devil, 95–97).

95. E.g., Lyon, "Prophecies," 71. The presence of their own spirit can make them resistant to diseases (Harner, *Way of Shaman*, 69).

session or demonic attacks, and this has long been the case.[96] Medical anthropology distinguishes cultures where sickness is caused only naturally from cultures where it can be caused by personal agents such as deities, spirits, or the use of witchcraft.[97] Although some cultures do not associate spirits with sickness,[98] a vast number of cultures do.[99] (Still, in some cultures where many still attribute sickness to spirits, people nevertheless depend more on medicine than on spiritual remedies.[100]) In Hmong culture, a kind of evil spirit constricts breathing at night during nightmares. A number of Hmong refugees in the United States have died in their sleep from heart failure with "no structural heart abnormalities,"

96. See the sources in Ward, "Possession," 126; Shoko, *Religion*, 57–63; earlier, Rivers, *Medicine*, 7–8 (as cited in Loos, *Miracles*, 94, and other sources on 94–99); cf. Keener, "Possession," 225–26. Pre-Christian Gikuyu attributed sickness to ancestor spirits and witches; the biblically influenced indigenous Arathi movement redefined the cause as Satan (Githieya, "Church," 241). Whereas in some societies in West and East Africa exorcism may resolve possession-induced sickness (Bourguignon, "Self," 43, 56), in some others (such as Haiti) spirits may cause sickness without possession (56). For sickness and "spirit substance," which must be removed, see Turner, *Hands*, 227–28 (based on Iñupiat and some other cultures); for the removal of intrusive substances in much shamanic healing, see Harner, *Way of Shaman*, 115–30 (emphasizing sucking); some Indian charismatics in Bergunder, "Miracle Healing," 293 (though regarded by other Indian charismatics as fraud); objects emerging by vomiting (Ising, *Blumhardt*, 172) or from other orifices or the skin (173, 185, 327).

97. Borgen, "Miracles," 94; Foster, "Etiologies" (noting exceptions on 775–76). From 186 cultures, Murdock, *Theories*, surveys theories of natural (8–16) and supernatural (17–27) causation. Favret-Saada, *Witchcraft*, 195, describes magic from an indigenous perspective (understanding its function within a culture), rather than denigrating it as illogical; in 250–66, she argues against the older psychiatric view that treats it as mere delirium. Some now attribute the virus attacks to witchcraft (in Brooke, *Science*, 36).

98. Keller, *Miracles*, 243, argues that whereas ancients believed that forces like demons caused sickness, today we understand that bacteria and viruses do. This is somewhat forced-choice logic, since many today who posit demons and witchcraft as causes of sickness would not rule out bacteria and viruses as agents through which those forces at least sometimes work.

99. Bourguignon, "Spirit Possession Belief," 20–21; idem, "Distribution," 17; Murdock, *Theories*, 72–76 (on 72 noting 135 of 139, more than 97 percent of the societies he surveyed); Neyrey, "Miracles," 30–31; for examples, see Bourguignon, *Possession*, 7, 24; Hien, "Yin Illness"; Cho, "Healing," 123–24; Eliade, *Shamanism*, 215, 363; Ejizu, "Exorcism," 13, 15, 21; Gray, "Cult," 171, 178; Lewis, "Possession," 193; Southall, "Possession," 259, 262; Welbourn, "Spirit Initiation," 292; Haar and Ellis, "Possession," 197–98; Firth, *Ritual*, 319; Ikeobi, "Healing," 57; Saunders, "Zar Experience," 179; Morton, "*Dawit*," 193, 220; Pressel, "Possession," 339; Umeh, *Dibia*, 200; Hammond-Tooke, "Aetiology," 54–58; Berends, "African Healing Practices," 278–79; Mashau, "Occultism"; Evans-Pritchard, *Religion*, 98; Turner, *Drums*, 34, 119, 296; Colson, "Possession," 71–72; Beattie, "Mediumship," 164; Peters, *Healing in Nepal*, 65–68; Shorter, *Witch Doctor*, 174–76 (regarding what are considered morally neutral water spirits); idem, "Spirit Possession," 124; Rosny, *Healers*, 116–19; Luling, "Possession Cults," 175; Ferchiou, "Possession Cults," 214–15; Bate, "Mission," 77 (some traditional Zulu association with ancestors); Forsberg, "Medicine" (on supernatural powers, 35–64; on medicine effective against them, 76–147, 158–63); Kham, "Story," 207 (traditional Chin beliefs); Koch, *Zulus*, 56 (some Zulu shamans), 146–47; Espinosa, "Healing in Borderlands," 133–34 (late nineteenth-century Mexican folk Catholicism); Bergunder, "Miracle Healing," 288; Wright, *Miracle*, 143; McGavran, "Healing," 76; Lake, *Healer*, 118–19 (some but not all sickness).

100. See, e.g., Wyllie, "Effutu." Many Zulu people appreciate Western treatment but depend on traditional or faith healers to discern illness's causes (such as sorcery or problems with the ancestors; Crawford and Lipsedge, "Help"). Many members of the Apostolic Church of John Maranke apparently employ herbalists and Western medicine, though both are prohibited (Jules-Rosette, "Healers," 135). Many Indian Pentecostals recognize natural causes for many illnesses as well as spiritual ones (Bergunder, "Miracle Healing," 290). In Shoko, "Healing," 52–53, African Pentecostals demonize ancestor spirits.

and those "who have been revived" from these heart attacks have described the above-mentioned nightmare.[101] More generally, a variety of cultures attribute occasions of "sleep paralysis" to evil presences, sometimes accompanied with apparitions.[102]

In a different but sometimes related conception (given the frequent use of spirits in witchcraft), many cultures associate sickness with witchcraft or sorcery,[103] which are pervasive beliefs in Africa.[104] (Although some writers distinguish witchcraft from sorcery, many use them interchangeably, and I do not make any technical distinction here.[105] They can be used as explanations for misfortune more generally.[106]) Witchcraft accusations are thus common

101. Benson, *Healing*, 85–86, citing Adler, "Pathogenesis," and attributing the real cause to a sense of powerlessness. One seeking a broader context might consider night terrors and especially the cross-cultural approach of Hufford, *Terror*.

102. McClenon and Nooney, "Experiences," 53 (noting that some respond by reciting incantations, some by calling on Jesus), also citing esp. Hufford, *Terror*. See also McClenon, *Healing*, 129–30.

103. See, e.g., Murdock, *Theories*, 64–71; Ajibade, "Hearthstones," 198; Eliade, *Shamanism*, 363; Foster, "Etiologies," 773, 775, 777; Daneel, "Zionism," 30, 40–41; Jules-Rosette, "Healers," 128, 131–33, 141, 145; Sofowora, *Traditional Medicine*, 26–27; Uzukwu, "Address," 8; Ejizu, "Exorcism," 13–15, 21; Ikeobi, "Healing," 57; Lee, "Possession," 144; Beattie, "Mediumship," 164; Middleton, "Possession," 225; Rosny, *Healers*, 74, 80, 83, 85; Turner, *Drums*, 14–15, 34, 119, 128–29, 296, 298; McClenon, *Events*, 133; Shorter, *Witch Doctor*, 94 (a lion attack); Ayegboyin, "Heal," 236; Dube, "Search," 114–15; Ritchie, *Spirit*, 26, 230; Crawford and Lipsedge, "Help," 133–35 (mental illness); Gaiser, *Healing*, 136n9 (mental illness); Hultkrantz, *Healing*, 29–31, 53–54, 82, 89, 111, 151, 162 (among Native Americans); Maclean, "Misconceptions" (as a source of death in Papua New Guinea); Turnbull, *Forest People*, 48–49 (as an explanation for some untimely deaths); Shoko, *Religion*, 63–67, 97–98; Espinosa, "Healing in Borderlands," 133–34; Bergunder, "Miracle Healing," 288–89; cf. Fogelson, "Theories," 82–85 (affliction with a sort of psychosis, among some Native American peoples). On the harm caused by African witchcraft belief and practice, see, e.g., Manala, "Witchcraft." Sorcery is often blamed for spirit possession in traditional Sri Lankan Catholicism at Kudagama (Stirrat, "Possession," 137–38). Debates exist; Foster, "Etiologies," 775, rightly notes naturalistic ancient Mediterranean systems (as well as those in India and China), whereas Murdock, *Theories*, 57–63, emphasizes witchcraft in the circum-Mediterranean area (too narrowly and with some irrelevant "correlates"); spiritual and herbalist practices coexist in most of Africa (as Foster, "Etiologies," 776, notes, *the two etiologies are rarely if ever mutually exclusive*," emphasis his).

104. Binsbergen, "Witchcraft," 254. He concedes that this affirmation is not politically correct in some circles (230); surveys also suggest that a number of Christians or Muslims reject its reality ("Islam and Christianity," 178–79; though we should also note that out of courtesy African informants sometimes answer the way they think Western inquirers would expect, Debrunner, *Witchcraft*, 3). But while witchcraft is neither exclusive to Africa nor the majority practice, my West and Central African informants offer vivid examples of its occurrence and belief in it.

105. Murdock, *Theories*, 64–71, like Evans-Pritchard, distinguishes witchcraft from sorcery, the latter associated with the New World; but against this being a widely usable distinction, see sources in Welton, "Themes," 13–15, esp. V. Turner; Bond and Ciekawy, "Introduction," 26n1; for other distinctions, Krippner, "Medicine," 191–92; on the lack of a standard definition, see, e.g., Eze, "Issues," 265–66.

106. E.g., Bond, "Ancestors," 132; thus deaths are rarely assigned solely to natural causes (138), AIDS is often blamed on witchcraft (154–55), and an epidemic could lead to many witchcraft accusations (152, though on 153 Christian beliefs led to a consensus of divine or satanic activity in addition to witches). Binsbergen, "Witchcraft," 232–33, argues against witchcraft being an "explanation" (as opposed to a cause). Some traditional Western settings less influenced by modernity have also used witchcraft to explain misfortunes (e.g., Favret-Saada, *Witchcraft*, 137), some of them admittedly quite unusual (see the progression of unusual events in Favret-Saada, *Witchcraft*, 137–39).

in many societies today,[107] as in some earlier periods in Western history.[108] In some places, accused witches are forced to undo their curses.[109] In South Africa, such accusations, often targeting single elderly women, have led to tragic public burnings.[110] They have also occurred elsewhere[111] and were frequent in

107. E.g., West, *Sorcery*, 15–17, 55, 60, 88; Evans-Pritchard, *Witchcraft*, 31–32, 122–26; Shorter, *Witch Doctor*, 94; Singleton, "Spirits," 471; Gray, "Cult," 183–84; Bongmba, "Witchcraft," 53; Koch, *Zulus*, 152–53, 157 (emphasizing their falsity); cf. Welbourn, "Healing," 353–55; earlier, Berger, "Women," 25; for some witch beliefs, see also Hammond-Tooke, "Aetiology," 51–54. Brand, "Beliefs," 43–44, reports an indigenous perspective that witchcraft accusations can serve a useful social function of controlling envy and reducing genuine witchcraft practice. In most societies, however, they breed distrust (Harries, "Worldview," 493; Kgatla, "Moloi"). In antiquity, too, people could attribute untimely death to witchcraft and invoke divine vengeance (Graf, "Death"). Cf. campaigns to eradicate witchcraft in Kenya, by both colonial and independent governments (noted in, e.g., Benjamin, "Squatters," 260); postcolonial hostility toward and sometimes killing of witches in Zimbabwe (Ranger, "Religion," 369–71). The modern introduction of newer witchcraft models like Wicca (on its historic discontinuity with older traditions, see, e.g., Hutton, "Status"; Magliocco, "Spells"; Hayes, "Responses," 340–42) make societal approaches to traditional witchcraft more complex (cf. Wallace, "Debating").

108. Cotton Mather claimed to have personally known cases of witchcraft (e.g., Scherzer, *Healing*, 98; more fully, Mather, *Providences*), but his later involvement in the hanging of Rev. George Burroughs (Scherzer, *Healing*, 99) seriously risks discrediting his testimony on this subject. In 1598, a woman claiming to be possessed blamed another woman for bewitching her, but her possession was ultimately deemed inauthentic (see discussion in Walker and Dickerman, "Woman," 551–52; reprinted in idem, "Influence"). "Possessed" Ursuline novices succeeded in getting their confessor condemned and executed and reestablished their virtuous status (Marshman, "Exorcism"). For discussion of eighteenth-century French perspectives regarding witchcraft and possession, see Wilkins, "Attitudes." Some have explained some physiological afflictions of the possessed at Salem in 1692 on the basis of grain contaminated with toxic ergot (Caporael, "Ergotism"); others demur (Spanos and Gottlieb, "Ergotism"). One deranged preacher accused Francis Asbury and his early Methodist colleagues of witchcraft against him (Wigger, *Saint*, 136).

109. Shoko, *Religion*, 123 (on one AIC), noting that patients often recover after this action; but sometimes putative witches reluctant to reverse their spells are beaten to secure their compliance.

110. E.g., Msaba Zungu and Thabitha Thusi, in KwaZulu-Natal province, South Africa (http://news .bbc.co.uk/go/pr/fr/-/2/hi/africa/6980439.stm; published and accessed Sept. 5, 2007). Kgatla, "Moloi," 84, estimates more than six hundred lynchings (often with kangaroo courts, 89) in one province in South Africa (where others also emphasize witch burning, e.g., Hayes, "Responses," 347; witch attacks in South Africa in Wyk, "Witchcraft," 1202–3). For how witchcraft and sorcery are practiced in South Africa, see Wyk, "Witchcraft," 1210–17, though it appears to me that the popular version with which we are acquainted in Congo-Brazzaville differs in some significant respects from South African witchcraft customs. In contrast to some positive portrayals in earlier South African media (e.g., Rüther, "Representations," 390–93), some inaccurately lumped together all traditional healers as murderous witches (401, 405–6). Elderly women are sometimes marginalized as witches in Congo-Brazzaville (where some virtuous people we know have suffered this treatment) and elsewhere (for Mozambique, cf. Lubkemann, "Ancestor," 344); among the Karanga of Zimbabwe, light-skinned ("red") and night-dark women are most suspected of witchcraft (Shoko, *Religion*, 43).

111. A young woman burned alive in Papua New Guinea (despite opposition to such burnings from government and churches; http://news.bbc.co.uk/go/pr/fr/-/2/hi/asia-pacific/7825511.stm; published and accessed Jan. 1, 2009). Cf. the abuse of "witch-children" in southeast Nigeria (http://news.bbc .co.uk/go/pr/fr/-/2/hi/africa/7764575.stm; published and accessed Dec. 4, 2008) and Congo-Kinshasa (Phiri, "Witches"; Thomson, "Sorcery"); executions of accused witches among Dagomba Muslims in northern Ghana (Hill, "Witchcraft," 332); legal issues in Saudi Arabia (Abdullah Al-Shihri, "Saudi Court Rejects Death Sentence for TV Psychic," http://news.yahoo.com/s/ap/20101113/ap_on_re_mi_ea /ml_saudi_witchcraft; accessed Nov. 13, 2010); earlier execution of witches among Native Americans (Hultkrantz, *Healing*, 53); in Zanzibar (Arnold, "Conflicts," 223, 225). The rise of accusations against

an earlier period of Western history;[112] locally, some form of witch persecution and sometimes execution appeared as a traditional part of local South African cultures in their fear of witches.[113] Some cultures employ divination to identify sorcery or witchcraft,[114] and many traditional African healing practices are directed against them.[115]

Nevertheless, despite frequent abuses and exaggerations, some people in many African societies do seek to practice malevolent sorcery, as is inevitable in cultures that believe in sorcery.[116] On occasion, Western academicians have even come to entertain the potential efficacy of such practices. Certainly it is difficult to deny

---

children seems a largely new phenomenon associated especially with urbanization and war (http://www
.bbc.co.uk/news/world-africa-10671790).

112. Priests accused of bewitching nuns were burned alive in 1611, 1634, and 1647 (Rosen, "Psychopathology," 231; cf. Baskin, "Devils," 18–19; idem, "Nuns," 199), whereas a politically connected priest in 1730 evaded the charge (Kreiser, "Devils"); for some other tragic burnings, see the older account in Reville, "History," 245–47. Hart, *Delusions*, 76, notes that the dominant period of witch burning was not medieval but early modern, and that the Catholic Church more often than not worked to suppress witch hunts. Some Reformers like Knox assumed but did not emphasize inherited views about witchcraft and demonology (Goodare, "Knox"), but the 1563 Scottish Witchcraft Act, to which he contributed with perhaps different issues in mind, eventually led to as many as two thousand executions (Goodare, "Act"). Warning against executing witches in South Africa, Hayes, "Responses," 343, contends that Christian involvement in the execution of witches was limited to a six-century (and mostly two-century) period in one part of the world and that it was more commonly a pre-Christian practice suppressed with the rise of Christianity (on its geographic limitations to particular regions of Europe, see Wyk, "Witchcraft," 1206). In 1437, a Dominican linked witchcraft to myths about people forming pacts with the devil, and in 1487, two members of the Inquisition wrote on it, propagating this notion and consequent action (Wyk, "Witchcraft," 1207). On false Western witchcraft accusations more recently, see, e.g., in Favret-Saada, *Witchcraft*, 192, 263.

113. See Kirkaldy, "*Vhuloi*," on late nineteenth-century Vendaland, and the abundant evidence cited there. Missionaries, though not always understanding the local culture sympathetically, sometimes intervened to save the lives of the accused (see in Kirkaldy, "*Vhuloi*," 106–7). In many societies, African traditional religion opposes witchcraft as harming rather than helping (Ranger, "Religion," 353–58).

114. E.g., Eliade, *Shamanism*, 363–64; Beattie and Middleton, "Introduction," xxiii; Field, "Possession," 11; Beattie, "Mediumship," 164; Gray, "Cult," 183; Middleton, "Possession," 225; Craig, "Divination"; Jules-Rosette, "Healers," 142; Wyk, "Witchcraft," 1217–19; cf. Garbett, "Mediums," 123; Adeyemi, "Healing Systems," 140, 142; Numbere, *Vision*, 39. In indigenous churches, prophecy can be used to identify witchcraft (Ayegboyin, "Heal," 238), not always accurately (e.g., Jules-Rosette, "Healers," 137, 139). Alice Auma felt possessed by the "Italian" spirit Lakwena to discern witches and heal (and eventually lead bloody guerilla warfare; Kassimir, "Politics," 250). Behrend, "Power," 21–29, shows that she combined Christian discourse (communication with the Virgin Mary and deceased good people, 23–26, perhaps analogous to saints or martyrs) with indigenous spirit possession; meanwhile, Arabic spirits were drafted to help with killing (26). Her rival and enemy Joseph Kony adapted her discourse to suit his genocidal activities (29–31).

115. Wyk, "Witchcraft," 1201.

116. Shorter, *Witchcraft*, 99; Wyk, "Witchcraft," 1202; note confessions in Shoko, *Religion*, 46; Mayrargue, "Expansion," 286. Our family also has unpleasant, direct acquaintance with this reality, albeit not as practitioners. Witchcraft is flourishing in Africa (Harries, "Worldview," 492; Hill, "Witchcraft," 323–25; in South Africa, Bähre, "Witchcraft," 300, 329; Wyk, "Witchcraft," 1203–4). African Christians can adapt their approach to practitioners somewhat flexibly (cf. Wild, "Witchcraft," 462, observing Congolese Christians for a time allowed some good through the Mai-Mai, "despite their occult practices"). Witchcraft in the West may often be a very different phenomenon, but some who work with youth have argued that it is more common and harmful than is widely known (Campolo, *Pentecostal*, 141).

that there are practitioners who believe in their practices and endanger others by natural means, some of which have been widely reported.[117] Thus one Western lecturer, after having denied the reality of witches, was corrected by an African student who noted that he was a witch and believed that he had an effective record of killing people through witchcraft.[118] An anthropologist studying witchcraft observed uncomfortably that soon after some spiritually powerful people uttered curses ("death wishes") against particular individuals, those individuals died in car accidents.[119] Western missionaries from desupernaturalized Europe, which had declared belief in witchcraft heretical because of its own earlier excesses, often taught ideas unworkable for an African context.[120] Some missiologists even argue that many missionaries' claims that believers are immune from the effects of witchcraft simply reinforce the sort of immunity-to-suffering thinking found in prosperity theology.[121] Missiologists are also concerned for syncretism: witchcraft

117. Note, e.g., obvious physical dangers such as the killing of albinos resulting from a premium on their body parts for charms (see the claim, from the International Federation for the Red Cross and Crescent societies, in Tom Odula, "10,000 E. African Albinos in Hiding after Killings," http://news.yahoo.com/s/ap /af_africa_albino_killings; accessed Nov. 28, 2009; the account in "Burundi Albino Boy 'Dismembered,'" http://www.bbc.co.uk/news/world-africa-11614957; accessed Oct. 24, 2010). Some claim that they or others have killed victims (in one example one's granddaughter) to consume them or to obtain parts of their flesh, especially genitals, for rituals (Reynolds, *Magic*, 44–47). In late 2010, a friend of ours from southern Africa reported to us that her cousin was recently murdered to procure some of his body parts (quickly removed) for witchcraft.

118. Hair, "Witches," 140 (an interaction that repays reading). For poisoning as well as occult means (sometimes reported by self-acknowledged sorcerers) with intent to kill, see Reynolds, *Magic*, 41–44; Kapolyo, *Condition*, 77. Most Africans are familiar with the use of charms and the like to seek to kill (in southern Nigeria, see, e.g., Numbere, *Vision*, 81, 96, 132–33), in some cases believed efficaciously (Numbere, *Vision*, 136; Oritsejafor, "Dealing," 97–98); some deaths are believed homicides through witchcraft (e.g., Grindal, "Heart," 66; among a northern Alaskan people, see Turner, "Actuality," 5; via lion attacks, West, *Sorcery*, 3–5, 9–10; a fatality within hours after confronting the sorcerer, West, *Sorcery*, 88; cf. Osborn, *Healing*, 313, citing a converted witch doctor but attributing the fatal effects to fear). For the belief that negative shamanism is used to harm or kill among an indigenous people in Guyana, see Scherberger, "Shaman," 57–59; in Africa, Azenabor, "Witchcraft," 30–31; McNaughton, *Blacksmiths*, 69; Koch, *Zulus*, 151–52, 292–93 (witchcraft practitioners' confessions); in India, Bergunder, "Miracle Healing," 293–94; Yohannan, *Revolution*, 21–22, 204; in Indonesia, Tari, *Breeze*, 23 (even through lightning), 135 (Tari saw their instruments), 137 (one claimed to have killed more than one hundred people); for the sacrifice by witchcraft of relatives to achieve success, see Binsbergen, "Witchcraft," 243; for some traditional European witches seeking to harm enemies magically, see, e.g., Alison Mutler, "Curses! Romania's witches forced to pay income tax," http://news.yahoo.com/s/ap/20110105/ap_on_re_eu/eu_romania_witchcraft; accessed Jan. 5, 2011. Mensah, "Basis," 171, warns that while people in Africa blame deaths on witchcraft too often, sometimes genuinely spiritual as well as medical factors are involved.

119. Favret-Saada, *Witchcraft*, 124–27. She finally concludes that actually bewitching rituals were probably normally rare in that culture, noting that the only ones she was able to uncover related to the more open "unwitchers" (135n18). Favret-Saada's temporary concern that unwitchers might practice witchcraft (123, 126) should perhaps not be too readily dismissed, if witchcraft can be a defensive act (123) and is socially unacceptable enough to remain secretive.

120. Lagerwerf, *Witchcraft*, 14–15. He notes the failure of conventional Western medicine to be able to treat witchcraft affliction because it isolates it from its traditional social framework (16–17), and how local people often mistrusted the missions for ignoring sorcery (18).

121. Harries, "Worldview," 497–98. He argues that (499) "to relegate magic to backward people and bygone years is to misunderstand its nature and to underestimate its power." Most missionaries

beliefs fulfill roles within societies that if unaddressed by newer religious cultures can persist and grow.[122]

While traditional cultures often seek a beneficial use of power, they frequently retain also malevolent spiritual expressions of conflict.[123] In Sri Lanka, for example, people seek sorcerers at shrines of various religions to bring harm to their enemies.[124] After a chief in Fiji was accused of killing four villagers through witchcraft, he remarkably admitted to this claim, despite cultural stigmas now in place.[125] Voodoo deaths, associated with spirits, are a real phenomenon,[126] though Western observers, usually seeking psychological rather than spiritual explanations, typically associate them with terror.[127]

---

tend to underestimate witchcraft's prevalence (Hill, "Witchcraft," 323–25); early missionaries brought an Enlightenment denial of witchcraft implausible in an African context (Hayes, "Responses," 344–45; Lagerwerf, *Witchcraft*, 1). Koch, *Zulus*, 154–56, contends that believers whose ancestors practiced witchcraft are more susceptible, and (151–52, 158, citing two incidents) that thwarted witchcraft attacks may bring the intended suffering against the witch.

122. Cf. the return to traditional practices among some former Christians in Nigeria (Danfulani, "Conflict"). Some argue that understanding witchcraft customs is important for contextualizing; how to contextualize without religious syncretism (and where the boundaries lie; some, like Brand, "Beliefs," and Hill, "Witchcraft," 337, may go too far; cf. syncretism in Shoko, "Healing," 52) remains a significant problem in missiology. Some African Pentecostal churches have appeared culturally relevant by addressing witchcraft (Maxwell, "Witches," 334); Hayes, "Responses," 346–47, 352, views positively the approach of Zionists like Bishop Nyasha, who simply baptizes, exorcises, and reintegrates those who confess to witchcraft. Most African Catholics, Anglicans, and Presbyterian pastors condemn witchcraft, though their parishioners do not always hear them this way (Ross, "Preaching," 12–13).

123. The conflict sometimes entails competition for life ("kill or be killed"); see, e.g., Favret-Saada, *Witchcraft*, 123.

124. Obeyesekere, "Sorcery" (sampling Muslim, Hindu, and Buddhist shrines on 9). Though the intention is deliberately homicidal (3), harm to the desired objects was reported in only one in every thirty-seven cases (and these included retrospective cases and those who suffered only much later; 21). Obeyesekere thinks that in societies practicing sorcery, premeditated (as opposed to spontaneous) lethal aggression may get channeled into sorcery rather than more conspicuous means (22); it is normally (80 percent) practiced anonymously, aggressors seeking distant rather than nearby shrines (5). By its usual definition, sorcery is employed especially to harm others (see, e.g., Krippner, "Medicine," 193).

125. Hoare, "Approach," 127–28. Some do confess to witchcraft to honor their power, however (Azenabor, "Witchcraft," 27).

126. For suffering and death caused by curses, see, e.g., Prince, "Yoruba Psychiatry," 91; Dawson, "Urbanization," 328–29; Mbiti, *Religions*, 258; cf. Remus, *Healer*, 110; Welbourn, "Healing," 364; voodoo and taboo deaths in Benson, *Healing*, 40–41; esp. Knapstad, "Power," 84, 89; for a healing through breaking a voodoo curse, see Blue, *Authority*, 146. Most people in the ancient Mediterranean world also accepted the efficacy of curses (e.g., Aeschylus *Cho.* 912; *Sept.* 70, 656, 695–97, 709 [it was irresistible— see 692–711, 725–26, 833–34]). Widespread beliefs in curses' efficacy appear in rural Africa (e.g., Azevedo, Prater, and Lantum, "Biomedicine"; Lienhardt, "Death"; Chinwokwu, "Localizing," 12–13) but also in sixteenth- and seventeenth-century Netherlands (see Waardt, "Witchcraft") and in some parts of the West more recently (e.g., Sebald, "Witchcraft").

127. Note voodoo and taboo deaths in Cannon, "Voodoo Death" (cited in Benson, *Healing*, 40–41; Remus, *Healer*, 109); taboo and especially curse deaths in Frank, *Persuasion*, 39–42. Cf. the "nocebo effect," the negative opposite of the placebo effect (in Beauregard and O'Leary, *Brain*, 145–47; Benson, *Healing*, 39, 53, 59, 63, 267–69; Epperly, *Touch*, 36); sudden deaths from emotive trauma in Engel, "Death" (as cited in Benson, *Healing*, 42; cf. Weisman and Hackett, "Predilection," in Benson, *Healing*, 53; Phillips, Van Vorhees, and Ruth, "Birthday," in Benson, *Healing*, 62; Adler, "Pathogenesis," in Benson, *Healing*,

In some traditional societies today, spirits are also believed to be involved in prophetic activity.[128] Even where spirits are considered generally destructive, they may be reckoned as necessary intermediaries with deities.[129] In traditional African societies, those possessed virtually always claim to speak for lower spirits, never (in contrast to Christian and Islamic circles) for the supreme Creator God.[130] In contrast to early Christians but analogous to many Greeks, the traditional African worldview typically views some spirits as good, some others bad, but most neutral, like most people.[131] Defending this worldview, some scholars complain that most Christians "insensitively" classify all possessing spirits, except for God's Spirit, as evil and demonic.[132] But this complaint is a case of one religious worldview critiquing another's critique; competing frameworks determine their respective classifications.[133] African culture often applies this approach of allowing moral ambiguity also to magical power more generally.[134]

---

85). Negative astrological predictions appear to hasten the death of believers in Chinese astrology, but not nonbelievers (Walsh, *Shamanism*, 213 [elsewhere showing the impossibility of astrology, 233]). Ancient sorcerers also sought to terrify victims by leaving physical evidence of their intent (Trombley, "Paganism," 198).

128. E.g., Mbiti, *Religions*, 233; Evans-Pritchard, *Religion*, 96, 303; Field, "Possession," 6; Middleton, "Possession," 224; Southall, "Possession," 242–43; Fitzgerald, "Speech"; cf. shamans and predictions, Lyon, "Prophecies," 73. In old Shona tradition, various kinds of spirits can possess mediums (Gelfand, *Religion*, 166), and possession gives the medium powers (177–78).

129. Ohnuki-Tierney, "Shamanism," 194–96; cf. Mbiti, *Religions*, 233.

130. Mbiti, *Religions*, 249–50; Field, "Possession," 9.

131. Mbiti, *Religions*, 111; Beattie and Middleton, "Introduction," xxi–xxii, xxvii; Brand, "Beliefs," 47; Lema, "Chaga Religion," 47; cf. Shorter, *Witch Doctor*, 188–89; idem, "Possession and Healing," 48–49, 52; on the amorality of fetishes in Nuer religion, see Evans-Pritchard, *Religion*, 100; on the neutrality of Ga possession, see Field, "Possession," 13; on the diverse morality of spirits in traditional Yanomamö shamanism (in South America), see Ritchie, *Spirit*, 59; on neutral Mayan mountain spirits, see Garrard-Burnett, "Demons," 218. On spirits in African tradition, see Ferdinando, "Demonology," 110–20 (on their ambiguity between good and bad, esp. 114). For a supreme God above these spirits in traditional African and other cosmologies, see Boyd, *War*, 124–27. For one chart comparing Western worldviews (both secular and Christian) with NT and traditional African ones, see Loewen, "Possession," 128–33).

132. E.g., Shorter, *Witch Doctor*, 188–89; cf. Achebe, "Ogbanje Phenomenon," 35–36. Grundman, "Inviting," 66, also rejects the biblical opposition to other spirits; Stabell, "Modernity," 462–63, 470, opposes the usual Christian connection between witchcraft and demons. Cf. the nominally Islamic Segeju identification of *shetani* with Qur'anic demons in Gray, "Cult," 173–75. Most of the newer churches do view all spirits as harmful (Ranger, "Religion," 352, complaining about "Apostolic and Pentecostal churches in Southern Africa"); Korean Christians also treated all the older spirits as demons (Kim, "Healing," 268–69).

133. For example, my Baptist student Paul Mokake, from Cameroon, has experienced power encounters regarding what local people regard as water spirits and ancestral spirits that some others considered neutral (interview, May 13, 2009). In one exorcism of such spirits that he recounted, the person acted like a serpent and different animals as the spirits departed (ibid.). For other exorcisms of water spirits ("mermaids," or "mammy" spirits), see Numbere, *Vision*, 163–64, 186, 231; cf. discussion in Oritsejafor, "Dealing," 80–85, 94–95; for (often excessive) beliefs about water spirits (Mami Wata) in eastern Nigerian Pentecostalism, see Burgess, *Revolution*, 80, 226 (some Pentecostals warning against the excesses, 228); Csordas, "Global Perspective," 339; for Pentecostals addressing concerns about these spirits that traditional churches had ignored, see Marshall-Fratani, "Mediating," 99; for indigenous beliefs about mermaid spirits in Zimbabwe, see Shoko, *Religion*, 41.

134. Bond and Ciekawy, "Introduction," 13; cf. Devisch, "Forces," 108 (for defensive use of power, 115–18; for retaliation, 113–15). In some places spirits and spiritual power are considered neutral (e.g.,

Exorcism in Recent Times

Continuing my approach in much of the book, I initially suspend academic judgment on the meaning of these phenomena in order to recount some common views of them today. Just as belief in malevolent spirit possession is common, so are various attempts to cure, control, or exorcise it.[135] Those who view all possession behavior as the result of the belief that one is possessed see exorcism as succeeding through the belief that one is possessed no longer;[136] most who practice exorcism, however, believe that real spirits are being expelled (see many examples below). Some recognize the possibility of either explanation for a given case (see discussion below).

Non-Christian Exorcism Practices

Noted anthropologist Edith Turner argues for the success of an exorcism that she witnessed; I shall address her account more fully below.[137] Her account is, however, by no means unique, though the forms used to try to rid persons of harmful spirits vary from one culture to another. Thus, for example, the pre-Christian Solomon Islands used various elaborate rituals to try to exorcise spirits.[138] In traditional African society, cultic personnel might exorcise harmful spirits, and ceremonies could be employed to drive off spirits endangering a village.[139] For example, traditional Segeju in Tanzania cajole or force a spirit to leave its victim, most frequently by a ritual dance.[140] Conceptualizing the problem differently, vomiting may help expel the moth that causes mental illness among traditional Navajo.[141] In nineteenth-century China, the following means of exorcism are reported: "enticing them to leave by burning charms, and paper money; or by begging and exhorting them; or by frightening them with magic spells and incantations; or driving them away by pricking with needles, or pinching with the fingers, in which case they cry out and promise to go."[142] A Muslim Somali holy man exorcises demons using Qur'anic

---

Ciekawy, "Utsai," 176; McNaughton, *Blacksmiths*, 12), but they are potentially dangerous and can be harnessed for harm (McNaughton, *Blacksmiths*, 12, 15; cf. 3; Ciekawy, "Utsai," 180). Anthropologists typically reserve the label "witchcraft" for the negative use of the power (Bond and Ciekawy, "Introduction," 26n1).

135. E.g., Lewis, *Ecstatic Religion*, 100–126; Turner, *Experiencing Ritual*, 183–87 (including various kinds of spirit healers in 185–87); in popular level Christian sources, cf., e.g., Schlink, *World*, 28–53; Williams, *Signs*, 140; for a study of some popular approaches, see, e.g., Wright, "Interpretations." See, e.g., shamanistic exorcism among the Aymara in Bolivia (Bourguignon, "Spirit Possession Belief," 20); other cultures in Kaplan and Johnson, "Navajo Psychopathology," 211; Fuchs, "Techniques," 135–37; Mbiti, *Religions*, 106; a successful Buddhist Sinhalese exorcism in Obeyesekere, "Possession," 259–89.

136. Oesterreich, *Possession*, 100.

137. Turner, *Experiencing Ritual*, 149.

138. Tippett, *Solomon Islands Christianity*, 14.

139. Mbiti, *Religions*, 106; for an example, see Turner, *Drums*, 204.

140. Gray, "Cult," 171. For dances used in expelling spirits, see also, e.g., Garbett, "Mediums," 105; Lewis, "Possession," 201.

141. Kaplan and Johnson, "Navajo Psychopathology," 211.

142. A Chinese report in Nevius, *Possession*, 54. Sometimes demons would leave if given what they demanded; also through "written charms, or chanted verses," or puncturing "the body with needles" (53).

passages.[143] On May 23, 1936, a missionary in the Levant reported that locals had tried unsuccessfully to remove long-standing demons by beating the possessed woman and applying hot irons to her.[144]

In many societies, spirit possession is employed to drive out a lower, afflicting spirit or to appease an offended spirit.[145] Shamans or mediums in a number of societies enter trance and/or possession states themselves to expel or control spirits.[146] Thus a Balahi Hindu traditional healer, empowered by a spirit's magic power, questions and rhetorically duels with a hostile possessing spirit until successfully expelling it.[147] Filipino psychic healers enter trances that they associate with spirits.[148] Shamans or mediums often have to negotiate with possessing spirits, who speak through the victim's mouth.[149] Thus a Muslim traditional healer, having struck a bargain with local spirits but unable to expel some visiting Fulani ones, had to leave the room and let his wife convince these spirits that it was culturally

---

In China, Taoist priests until recent times battled spirits to expel them (Betty, "Evidence," 14; for reports of observations of a Taoist exorcism near Shanghai in the 1920s, see 16). Resembling the pain compliance techniques here, some extreme Christian sects have also been reputed to forcibly detain or beat those suspected of possession (for one sect, see Dunphy, "Marriage," C1; Dettling, "Witness"; Watson, "Leader"; Buffington, "Leader"; idem, "Routine"), although the vast majority of Christians and others condemn such behavior. Among the Karanga of Zimbabwe, disease spirits are weakened or expelled by techniques "such as blood-letting, emetics or purgatives, and sniffing" (Shoko, *Religion*, 97).

143. Lewis, "Possession," 199 (noting the special utility of sûra 66), 213; cf. the use of verses of the Qur'an drunk in water (Abdalla, "Friend," 38). In the Kuwaiti version of the *zar* cult, the healer also recites sûras (Ashkanani, "*Zar*," 224–25).

144. The narrative is reproduced in McCasland, *Finger*, 57–58 (here 57). Afterward the missionaries gradually cast the demons out and she recovered her health. For flogging to remove a demon, see also the example of the Indian Muslim exorcist in Williams, "*Bwaya*," 127.

145. Beattie and Middleton, "Introduction," xxv. Cf. appendix A for ancient Mediterranean cases of invoking higher spirits to drive away lower ones (e.g., *PGM* 101.38–39).

146. Klutz, *Exorcism Stories*, 196–97, citing especially (197) examples from eastern Siberia; Peters, *Healing in Nepal*, 14–15; possession for healing in Southall, "Possession," 237–38; Hien, "Yin Illness," 307 (in "the Mother Goddess religion of the Viêt"); Licauco, "Psychic Healing," 95; cf. Obeyesekere, "Idiom," 108. By young adulthood, more than half of !Kung males become spirit healers, and roughly 10 percent of the women do (Katz, "Healing," 213). On shamans sending spirits to work harm, see, e.g., Peters, *Healing in Nepal*, 61 (noting on 63 that some reject limiting one's powers to only benevolent acts); on mediums able to work harm (sending dangerous spirits) as well as good, see also Beattie, "Mediumship," 169; Somali holy men in Lewis, "Possession," 189; shamans among a people in Guyana, Scherberger, "Shaman," 57–59. For claims of traditional healers offering relief from spirit forces, see, e.g., Achebe, "Ogbanje Phenomenon," 34–35; cf. Shorter, "Possession and Healing," 48. In some cases healers "are mentally disordered" or display psychotic traits (McClenon, "Healing," 40, 45–46), but other psychological approaches exist (e.g., Koss-Chioino, "Transformation," 56–63).

147. Fuchs, "Techniques," 135–37. The ritual typically concludes with the patient swooning, after which she is cured (137). Hindu shamans could also be possessed for acts of power or involuntarily possessed via impurity from an "Untouchable" (Harper, "Pollution," 189). For possessed persons in Hindu sources, see, e.g., Oesterreich, *Possession*, 175; McDaniel, "States."

148. Licauco, "Psychic Healing," 95; idem, "Realities," 263 (on 265 noting local attribution to the Holy Spirit).

149. E.g., Singleton, "Spirits," 473; Schuetze, "Role," 47 (for an agreement with the spirits, 39–49); for spirits departing if they get what they wanted, Gray, "Cult," 181. Likewise, traditional Tanzanian *migawo* specialists have to "persuade" spirits to depart (Shorter, "Spirit Possession," 119). By contrast, Pentecostals and charismatics usually just cast out spirits without negotiation (Schuetze, "Role," 50–53).

rude for them to possess a guest visiting in their home.[150] Various forms of exorcism have continued among some traditional Jewish groups into the modern period.[151] Some cultures fear that possessing spirits can be transferred to exorcists or bystanders during exorcism.[152]

Christian Movements and Exorcisms

Some argue that a major reason for the proliferation of Pentecostal, charismatic, and evangelical Christianity in tropical Africa today involves "their perceived ability to provide the believer ultimate protection against the ever-present evils of magic, witchcraft and sorcery."[153] Christians in the Majority World often practice exorcism,[154] able to draw on the church's heritage of exorcism often neglected today in the West.[155] I noted the frequency of exorcisms in patristic sources in chapter 10; one may also compare accounts in Augustine's *City of God* 22.8. Early Pentecostals were also quick to reclaim this emphasis throughout the world,[156] an emphasis that often persists today. When those from Afro-Spiritist groups enter their typical trances while visiting Brazilian Pentecostal churches, for example, the leaders command the spirits out.[157]

150. Abdalla, "Friend," 38–39. The Sudanese culture of hospitality applies to treatment of *zar* spirits, as to people (Kenyon, "*Zar*," 108). Similarly, in sixteenth-century Europe many believed that some types of spirits (nymphs, sprites, fairies, and so forth) were limited to particular locales (Midelfort, "Possession," 115).

151. Cf., e.g., Hes, "Role," 376, 380; Oesterreich, *Possession*, 207–10. Burning the skin with a heated nail, or extracting blood, provides an aperture for the spirits' departure (Hes, "Role," 380).

152. Cf., e.g., Obeyesekere, "Possession," 253.

153. Owusu, "Strings," 129; earlier, healing churches in Debrunner, *Witchcraft*, 2, 149, 160–61. Even where Western missionaries have denied the existence of witchcraft, local peoples often refuse to believe them (e.g., Smythe, "Creation," 139).

154. As often noted, e.g., Alexander, *Signs*, 103; in Nigeria, see Folarin, "State," 85–87 (including examples of excesses); among Costa Rican Pentecostals, e.g., in Bastian, "Pentecostalism," 171; a case in Mongolia noted to me by Korean Presbyterian pastor Mun Kil Kim (July 24, 2010); cases in Cuba noted by Dr. Mirtha Venero Boza (Aug. 6, 2010); India, Devadason, "Band," 64; the West, e.g., Robertson, *Miracles*, 93–94, 98, 101–2. Pentecostals usually prefer terms like "deliverance" or "liberation" to "exorcism," emphasizing freeing individuals rather than emphasizing the hostile spirits (Brown, "Introduction," 5), but I retain the older term typical in anthropological literature for various cultures.

155. For contemporary Anglican approaches to exorcism, see, e.g., Malia, "Look"; Milner, "Exorcism"; Hexham, "Exorcism" (esp. 115–16); for a contemporary Catholic perspective, Li, "Theology of Exorcism"; concisely, Davies, "Exorcism"; discussion of the Catholic Rituale Romanum in Landmann, "Agape." Addressing the Anglican report, Welbourn, "Exorcism," 596, contends that the magical worldview involved in exorcism is impossible for technological people but makes sense for other peoples. In the sixteenth and seventeenth centuries, Calvinists, in contrast to Lutherans, deleted the traditional baptismal exorcism rite (Nischan, "Baptism"; reprinted as idem, "Controversy"; cf. Martin, "Resisting," 57); for a Lutheran case in 1546, see Wengert and Krey, "Exorcism." Christians might need to adapt some of the traditional ritual (some of which might even reflect the influence of Valentinus; see Leeper, "Connection") in view of NT exegesis (see Schloz-Durr, "Exorzismus").

156. Early twentieth-century Pentecostals practiced exorcism in various places, e.g., a case in Syria in Malick, "Sowing" (though the "symptoms" explicitly reported are not particularly compelling); Kucera, "South India"; Ruesga, "Healings" (noting prayer and fasting); Otero, "Convention"; indirectly in Reiff, "Los Angeles Campmeeting," 14; among non-Pentecostals, see, e.g., Anderson, *Pelendo*, 97–98, 133.

157. Greenfield, *Spirits*, 141–42; cf. Shaw, *Awakening*, 145.

Such practices are frequent in Africa; in many African countries a third of Christians claim to have witnessed exorcisms, and in some that figure rises to roughly half (Uganda, Mozambique), 65 percent (Ghana), or 74 percent (Ethiopia).[158] Exorcism is common, for example, in Ethiopia[159] and in Ambanja in Madagascar[160] and appears in various settings, including contemporary healing evangelism modeled after Acts.[161] A range of Christian movements in Africa employ exorcism, including among Catholics[162] and African Independent Churches.[163] One African scholar writing for an African theological journal associated with a mainline denomination recommends the use of exorcism for some situations, citing the case of a woman tormented for years by spirits. The article claims that at her exorcism in 1982 other voices were heard calling through her mouth, and then she was permanently free.[164] A German scholar reported many exorcisms among the Zulu people of southern Africa, often resulting in permanent deliverance and healing.[165] Paul Mokake, a Baptist from Cameroon who obtained both master's and doctor's degrees at my institution, shared with me various firsthand exorcism accounts; in one example, when in the village of Nguti they cast the spirits from a woman who had worshiped spirits of the sea, she acted like a serpent and different animals in succession as the spirits were departing.[166]

Jorum Mugari from Zimbabwe, now studying at Gordon-Conwell's Charlotte campus, was a traditional exorcist before his conversion to Christianity. He noted that whereas particular rituals (typically including singing, instruments, lotions,

158. "Islam and Christianity," 214. My colleague in Hebrew Bible, Emmanuel Itapson, attests witnessing such events firsthand in Nigeria (interview, April 1, 2011).

159. For exorcism in Ethiopia, see Geleta, "Demonization."

160. Klutz, *Exorcism Stories*, 142, citing Sharp, *Possessed*. For a much older account of possession in Madagascar, see Oesterreich, *Possession*, 138; for Christian approaches to healing in Madagascar, see Rasolondraibe, "Ministry" (mentioning exorcism on 349).

161. E.g., Sung, *Diaries*, 23, 30, 34 (though Sung reports very few exorcisms compared with other forms of healing; for the principle, Sung, *Diaries*, 90); also see Hickson, *Heal*, 65, 70–71 (on events in India and China in 1921; cf. idem, *Bridegroom*, 212–13, in Japan); Lindsay, *Lake*, 22, 28, 39–40 (early twentieth century); Menberu, "Regassa Feysa" (on events in 1965); cf. Pullinger, *Dragon*, 210; Storms, *Convergence*, 69–71; Best, *Supernatural*, 158–59 (Wimber). Long histories of different forms of exorcistic practice appear in Catholicism (e.g., Toner, "Exorcism") and Eastern Orthodoxy (e.g., Papademetriou, "Exorcism"); for some patristic prayers of exorcism, see Stephanou, "Exorcisms," 57–66; for Eastern Orthodox accounts of possession over the past nearly three centuries, see Stephanou, "Exorcisms," 66–72.

162. On exorcism in an African Catholic context, see Ikeobi, "Healing," 73–75, 78–82; Eneja, "Message," 164–66; cf. Manus, "Healing," 101.

163. See, e.g., in AICs, in Oosthuizen, "Healing," 79–80, 89; idem, *Healer-Prophet*, 117–48. On the linkage of most sorts of events with spirits in AICs, see, e.g., Molobi, "Knowledge," 85.

164. Mchami, "Possession" (esp. 31), who notes the case of "Esther" in the Evangelical Lutheran Church in Tanzania (her entire account is 31–34; the article is also cited in Jenkins, *New Faces*, 105–7). Elsewhere, an alleged ghost followed a woman wherever she fled, tormenting her, and others witnessed the phenomena until she was delivered (Koch, *Zulus*, 160–61; cf. an analogous nineteenth-century experience reported in Ising, *Blumhardt*, 166–67).

165. Koch, *Zulus*, 55 (permanent deliverance of a witchcraft practitioner), 56–58 (healings during conversion/deliverance), 132–35, 163–65 (uniquely effective).

166. Paul Mokake, interview, May 13, 2009. Others have independently described similar behavior elsewhere (e.g., Koch, *Zulus*, 54–55).

and the like) led to possession manifestations in traditional settings, even a simple prayer could trigger such manifestations in Christian settings. Christians exorcised all spirits; traditional practitioners sought to get harmful spirits to leave but solicited information from those they considered beneficial. Traditional exorcists sought to torment the spirits, sometimes handling the patients roughly; Christians normally would command the spirit to leave until it complied.

Possession behavior, which was the same in both settings, sometimes included having immunity to pain and fire, rolling on the ground, acting like snakes or animals, or even moving up through a roof. In one case he noted in a Christian setting, a person who had descended several steps into a baptismal pool suddenly became violent and then slithered like a snake out of the pool (not using the steps). The church members then exorcised the spirit.[167]

Whatever explanations one prefers (see discussion below), some exorcisms have a therapeutic effect.[168] Some systems that attribute everything to spirits appear to generate their own supply of possession and demand for deliverance;[169] nevertheless, serious cases of disturbance not manufactured by exorcists also appear. A boy in Indonesia, possessed after he was given an amulet by a witch doctor, terrorized the area, killing chickens. Even five men together could not restrain him, but evangelists cast the spirit from him, leading to his freedom.[170] Likewise, Marino Shed wandered around terrorizing people in Madolenihmw, Pohnpei Island, in the Pacific for two decades. Finally, Steve Malakai, a pastor on this island, and another believer cast the spirits from him. Now Marino, transformed, is loved by his community,[171] and he is involved in a respectable profession.[172] An Anglican minister in Southeast Asia, from a Buddhist background, notes that his sister was delivered from demon possession.[173]

Ajith Fernando, a well-known Methodist Bible expositor, recounted to me that a woman who had found no deliverance from some local non-Christian exorcists in Sri Lanka was delivered in their church and has remained well since that time fifteen years ago.[174] In Nepal, non-Christian religious teachers sometimes refer cases of spirit

167. Jorum Mugari, discussion, March 27, 2010; personal correspondence, April 1, 2, 5, 2010. For a possessed person acting like a snake in a different African culture, see Koch, *Zulus*, 294 (in the context of snakes associated with sorcery, 294–95).

168. See, e.g., Ma, *Mission*, 67–68, offering two examples in the Philippines; earlier, cf. Ising, *Blumhardt*, 185.

169. See, e.g., the decline in possession when exorcism services became insufficient to meet the demand, in Csordas, *Language*, 38 (citing Ackerman, "Language").

170. Filson, "Study," 154; Indonesian exorcisms also appear in Crawford, *Miracles*, 62–65, 70–72. My friend John Lathrop shared with me a local account of exorcism, producing the person's dramatic healing and conversion, that he heard while in Indonesia (personal correspondence, Dec. 11, 2008).

171. Bozarth, "Demons." Steve Malakai had a similar impact on a young man named Andy Titirik (Cagle, "Happened"; Wayne Cagle, personal correspondence, Feb. 10, 2009).

172. Wayne Cagle, Jan. 25, 2009 (based on conversation with Marino several years earlier).

173. Green, *Asian Tigers*, 99. Anglicans in Southeast Asia value deliverance from the demonic as an important ministry (110–11).

174. Phone interview, Oct. 1, 2008; personal correspondence, March 13, 2009.

possession to Pentecostal churches for deliverance.[175] In another case, Nepali pastor Mina KC heard of three girls (Pramila, Rita, and Sunita) who, bound by a hostile spirit, were mute for three years.[176] They were released when she prayed for them, and the cure was so dramatic that "their whole village came to know Christ"; the three girls also began bringing others to Christ through their testimony.[177] A South African psychology professor, head of the Department of Industrial Psychology at Nelson Mandela Metropolitan University in Port Elizabeth, explains his own former case of possession, with another personality controlling him and institutionalization proving ineffective, until his spontaneous exorcism by a Christian.[178]

As noted in chapter 8, I had an opportunity, while briefly visiting a country in Asia before lecturing in another location in 2007, to talk with some Chinese pastors. Although these pastors were not charismatics or Pentecostals, when I spontaneously asked if any of them had firsthand accounts of healings, several offered exorcism accounts. For example, one eyewitness recounted that in 1994 a woman could not remember her identity and began having hallucinations. When the believers prayed, two spirits began speaking to them through the woman; the spirits threw her down before them, crying, "Please leave us! We can't bear more about Jesus!" The spirits tried to negotiate conditions, finally settling on eating a meal through the woman. The possessed woman ate an inordinate amount of food, and then the spirits left, never returning.[179]

Similarly, an elderly woman pastor mentioned a thirty-year-old woman with a psychological problem, to whom everything seemed unreal. Sometimes she felt pressed down on the floor; now she was pale, not having eaten for several days. Half an hour after the pastor's prayer, casting out a demon in Jesus's name, the woman felt ready to eat and was completely cured of her sickness. This was no merely temporary cure without the possibility of long-term verification; she is now the worship leader in the pastor's church.[180]

A sociologist reports the account of one Christian minister in Japan. A spirit had given a woman strikingly accurate precognition, but both her own spirit and a

175. Sharma, "History," 304.

176. Mina KC, interview by John Lathrop, provided to me March 3, 2010.

177. Ibid.

178. Venter, *Healing*, 249–52, providing the written testimony of Robin Snelgar, his brother-in-law.

179. I was curious about the Christians allowing the negotiation and about the eating, but I simply recount the story that the man gave me. Jesus made one concession (Mark 5:12–13), but it seems not to have been to the spirits' benefit (Mark 5:13). Claims of spirits requesting meals to eat through their hosts appear elsewhere (e.g., Turner, *Healers*, 115, following J. Boddy).

180. The pastor also offered another exorcism account involving a person whose parents practiced necromancy. This account included a sudden and extreme drop in temperature in the room to below freezing during the exorcism. Neither I nor my informant could understand the reason for this phenomenon. (Contrast the generation of heat in a form of Tibetan yoga, in Benson, *Healing*, 164, citing idem, "Temperature Changes.") Some accounts do include a stench, as of a corpse, accompanying spirits (Eshleman, *Jesus*, 120). For another exorcism account from contemporary China, see Lambert, *Millions*, 116, and the mention of Christian nurses there who could readily distinguish demonization from mental illness, 117. For other accounts, see Yamamori and Chan, *Witnesses*, 47; Aikman, *Jesus in Beijing*, 85.

shaman warned her that she would soon die unless she became a shaman herself. Wishing to avoid this destiny, she allowed the minister to pray for her. According to the minister's account, she collapsed with a shriek and unconsciously defied the minister in a man's voice, refusing to leave. He appealed to Jesus's name and for hours kept commanding the spirit to depart; during this time she even "levitated above her bed." Finally, however, she returned to normalcy, the spirit and her psychic abilities gone. She accepted the Christian faith and attended the church regularly after that.[181]

Some report even physical recoveries in connection with exorcism (see comments on spirits and sickness above).[182] For example, witnesses attest the recovery after exorcism over the course of several days of a boy who had been near death.[183] In another account, a Zulu boy cursed by a witch doctor at the age of seven had not grown in the seven years since that time and acted like an animal. Shortly after exorcism, however, he recovered fully.[184] In Cuba, Eusbarina Acosta Estévez told me that years ago she was invoking other spirits and was too sick to walk. When two pastors prayed for her in 1988, she recounts, she fell to the ground and all the chairs around her were also thrown back by the force of the spirits coming out.[185] She was converted, and her severe heart and kidney malfunctions ended instantly. Likewise, Leonel Camejo Tazé experienced paranormal phenomena just before falling very sick for months; his deliverance from these spiritual forces shortly preceded his healing.[186]

When visiting a Cameroonian student from our seminary, Paul Mokake, in summer 2006, Yolanda McCain, one of our American students, was shocked to witness a blind man's sight restored during exorcism of what purported to be a spirit partly controlling his nervous system.[187] Paul Mokake, who performed that exorcism, offered other sample accounts. Among them was the exorcism of a woman who was said to have spiritual power in her nails; when they were cut (as a way of renouncing the connections with the spirits), she became largely blind for two months, able to see only with special lenses. At the end of those two months, her sight returned, and she never again needed the lenses.[188]

181. McClenon, Events, 144–45; idem, Healing, 59.

182. Daniel Mekonnen notes this in his ministry (phone interview, Dec. 10, 2009).

183. Bush and Pegues, Move, 47–49; they also note (59) the exorcism of a girl in north India.

184. Jackson, Quest, 256–57 (with further details; following Wimber, Power Evangelism, 175–76). For another exorcism involving Wimber, see Venter, Healing, 126–27.

185. Eusbarina Acosta Estévez (interview, Aug. 7, 2010).

186. Interview (Aug. 11, 2010). He was nonreligious himself before his conversion; but his grandfather practiced Santeria; phenomena that he reported included something invisible sitting by him, visibly indenting the mattress, and (later) a force grabbing his feet and chest.

187. It is difficult for me to conceive of a witness more trustworthy than Yolanda, who also conveyed the report with genuine astonishment. She reported this account orally in 2006 and confirmed it for me in writing Oct. 3, 2008; Paul confirmed this for me again on May 13, 2009. Both Yolanda and the person who performed the exorcism, Paul Mokake, are Baptist (I mention this to counter the possible prejudice that those who report such phenomena are only, say, Pentecostals, Catholics, or AICs).

188. Paul Mokake, interview, May 13, 2009. Ancient Israelites might have understood such conceptions better than modern Western readers; for an implied symbolic connection between a physical state (there apparently reflecting a Nazirite vow) and spiritual power, cf. possibly Judg 16:19–20.

Perspectives on Exorcisms

Current perspectives on exorcisms vary, including among those who doubt the reality of spirits.[189] Some argue that minority religious movements in regions, such as contextually relevant, indigenous Pentecostal Christianity in parts of India, may adapt elements of non-Christian indigenous exorcism forms in their competition with local traditional beliefs.[190] Whatever the particulars, Indian Pentecostalism,[191] like African Pentecostalism,[192] clearly appeals to people in a context of belief in the pervasive experience of oppression by spirits. Some affirm any neutral, "client-centered" therapy that "works within the belief structure of the patient";[193] others question the ethics of an approach that encourages a belief such as exorcism that the therapist rejects.[194] In one case, when a psychiatrist referred what he believed a possessed person to a minister, the minister refused to help, denying the reality of demons; the client "then became profoundly depressed and attempted suicide."[195] While false diagnosis of possession would surely exacerbate problems, failure to treat possession beliefs seriously also carries potential problems.

Some have argued that exorcism might constitute the most culturally sensitive therapy for those for whom possession is the most culturally intelligible explanation for their condition.[196] One psychiatrist has found exorcisms effec-

189. For its usefulness, Bull, "Model"; Bull et al., "Exorcism," 194 (on 191 noting eight with exclusively positive, and seven with partly positive, and none with fully negative experiences). Page, "Role," 129; idem, "Exorcism," 143, affirms exorcism but insists qualified medical help should identify whether the person is possessed; for arguments that the warnings contain overreactions, see, e.g., Wilson, "Possession"; cf. Beck and Lewis, "Counseling." Wilson, "Exorcism," addresses the use of shared language (whether "possession" or "psychological disorders"), noting that society shapes how it is viewed but that wide use of possession language would increase cases of "possession" (295; Wilson himself views it in sociological, not demonic, terms, 292–93).

190. The view of Bergunder, "Healing," 103–5; idem, Movement, 125–26, 155–58; cf. idem, "Miracle Healing," 292–94 (on demonology, but noting fundamental theological differences on 294–95); Csordas, "Global Perspective," 335, on Catholic exorcism in India; MacPhail, "Path," 187–99 (suggesting syncretism in Catholic Jebakulam, from an explicitly outsider perspective). In Brazil, cf. Lehmann, Struggle, 145, though highlighting important differences (esp. Pentecostals' demonization of possession cults' spirits, and the former having followers in contrast to the latter having clients). Cf. also comparisons of the function of prophets in AIC churches with traditional diviners (Oosthuizen, Healer-Prophet, 165–93, while recognizing differences, 166–70). In antiquity, too, exorcism could symbolize triumph over competing religious claims (see, e.g., Frankfurter, "Christianity and Paganism," 184; Trombley, "Paganism," 192).

191. See Frykenberg, "Globalization," 127. Bergunder, "Miracle Healing," 288, contends that Tamil Pentecostalism's demons are largely derived from popular Hinduism.

192. Maxwell, "Witches," 325. Pentecostal exorcism has displaced some traditional religions in some regions (326), just as many adherents of spirit-possession cults have now turned instead to Pentecostalism (Berger, "Women," 44, on women).

193. Bull et al., "Exorcism," 195, noting the large proportion of Christian clients who affirm the reality of spirits.

194. Shorter, Witch Doctor, 184–85; cf. Ikeobi, "Healing," 66; zar therapy in Rahim, "Zar," 145–46.

195. McAll, "Deliverance," 298.

196. E.g., Martínez-Taboas, "Seizures" (after inability to change the patient's beliefs about possession, Martínez-Taboas, "World," 18; responding to Castro-Blanco, "Sensitivity," who prefers challenging "the utility of the belief in spiritual possession" [15]); Singleton, "Spirits," 478; Hexham, "Exorcism"; Heinze,

tive for multiple personality disorder (MPD; what he considers "internalized imaginary companions" conceptualized by patients as demons) but ineffective for altered personalities created by dissociation.[197] Others, by contrast, note differences from multiple personality disorder (now usually called dissociative identity disorder [DID]), contending that the spirit-possessed generally do not have alternate personalities,[198] and warn that misdiagnosing it as possession is harmful.[199] Not every therapist would necessarily explain or treat every case so labeled by others in the same way; I lack clinical expertise, but it appears that even most clinicians who allow for genuine cases of possession would recognize the disorder as existing apart from possession. Most would recognize that culture may shape the expression and labeling of conditions; some psychiatrists in India note that possession syndrome is common there (largely among women) whereas MPD/DID is rarely diagnosed there. They suggest that these are "parallel dissociative disorders with similar etiologies despite some major differences in clinical profiles."[200]

Some sociologists studying routine "deliverance" services have suggested that some cases involve more metaphoric issues[201] but note that even full exorcism sometimes helps those "suffering from psychologically induced traumas."[202] Indeed, one anthropologist specializing in the study of spirit possession points out

---

"Introduction," 14 (as a helpful fiction allowing the experience of multiple personality disorder to be objectified); cf. Ashkanani, "Zar," 225 (some Kuwaitis more receptive to zar therapy than modern therapies). Krippner, "Perspectives," 972, emphasizes that understandings will vary from one culture to another and Western therapists need to be culturally sensitive. For one case of treatment blending psychiatric help with traditional practices, see Hammerschlag, "Offering."

197. Allison, "Doubt," 116, 119. Initially he denied genuine spirits (110) but gradually discovered that exorcism worked, though he did not fully believe in it (110–13); he offers examples of successful exorcisms on 116–19. Many psychiatrists believe that the other personality is purely human (cf. discussion in Betty, "Evidence," 23); others (below) suggest that cases might differ, since causes might differ. Cf. the discussion in Lesher, "Response," 168–72.

198. Eve, Healer, 64 (following Davies, Healer, 86–89); Bourguignon, Possession, 38–39.

199. Friesen, Mystery (who does believe that genuine possession also occurs), as summarized in Hoffman and Kurzenberger, "Miraculous," 78. Cf. Young, "Miracles in History," 118, affirming that cases of genuine possession exist but warning that often exorcists are misdiagnosing psychological disorders.

200. Adityanjee, Raju, and Khandelwal, "Status," 1609–10 (quote from 1610), as quoted in Davies, Healer, 87. Whereas DID is more often linked with child sexual abuse, in anthropological literature possession more often appears in contexts of current family problems (Davies, Healer, 88, noting that these circumstances naturally often overlap). Davies (89) associates Mary Magdalene's condition more with DID than with anthropological possession reports, since the latter usually lack the appearance of multiple personalities (Luke 8:2; later, Mark 16:9).

201. Miller and Yamamori, Pentecostalism, 155, for cases in Thailand and especially Brazil (contrasting "curses" with actual "spirit possession" and giving an example of an experience of child abuse dominating one's life). For older exorcism accounts from local physicians in Siam (Thailand), see Oesterreich, Possession, 217–18.

202. Miller and Yamamori, Pentecostalism, 156, suggesting that it is "at least as effective as some forms of Western psychotherapy, which, when spontaneous remission is excluded, have relatively low cure rates." Whatever one's view about this, they suggest that deliverance either is a "form of psychotherapy" significantly effective beyond Western models or that it is at least sometimes genuinely effects a spiritual deliverance (156–57). They believe that it also has positive long-range economic effects (170).

that only exorcism works as a strategy for removing possession.[203] Some Western observers, writing for *African Affairs*, lament the failure of more traditional churches to provide the exorcisms needed to confront the epidemics of spirit possession in some African societies.[204] Some others appreciate healthy, cathartic aspects of exorcism in some African indigenous churches[205] while warning that their exorcistic practice can at times reinforce unhealthy aspects of traditional worldviews.[206] Some observers attribute this effectiveness to the placebo effect.[207] This verdict presumably would be accurate for psychological disorders socially defined as possession but would equally presumably prove insufficient in cases of genuine spirits.

Several examples help make these generalizations more concrete. One girl in Nigeria, tormented day and night by spirits and unable to improve through a psychiatrist, was freed through the help of an indigenous healing movement.[208] Immediate cures of severe psychiatric disorders attributed to spirits are reported in India.[209] (Of course, exorcisms do not always resolve all problems, either.[210]) One may also recall many of the accounts offered above.

203. Goodman, *Demons*, 125; for the effectiveness of exorcism in particular kinds of cases, see also Shorter, "Possession and Healing," 51; Allison, "Doubt"; Lagerwerf, *Witchcraft*, 55–56. For one story of an effective deliverance of an early twentieth-century man detained in an asylum, see John Lake's diary, cited in Wacker, *Heaven Below*, 64–65; for a mid-twentieth-century doctor's claims of exorcisms successfully resolving what appeared to be neurological problems, see Woodard, *Faith*, 24–29. Some witch doctors have complained that other witch doctors cheat by merely bargaining with witches to remove curses (Evans-Pritchard, *Witchcraft*, 195, skeptically).

204. Haar and Ellis, "Possession," 205–6 (favoring Emmanuel Milingo's approach, while archbishop, over that of other elements of the Zambian church hierarchy).

205. Daneel, "Exorcism," 239–41 (positive features more generally on 237–45).

206. See Daneel, "Exorcism," 243–44 (the fowl's blood and other symbols evoking older traditions). Newell, "Witchcraft," contends that much of the structure of African witchcraft ideology has been imported in local Pentecostal witchcraft polemic.

207. Ward, "Exorcism," 134–37. For the influence of a culture's beliefs on traditional exorcism's effectiveness, see also Wetering, "Effectiveness."

208. Ejizu, "Exorcism," 14 (on the girl's experience with the Christ Healing Sabbath Church), noting that "her case is one out of so many hundreds" (this article also appears in Ejizu, "Perspective"). Among African immigrants in Germany, see Währisch-Oblau, "Healthy," 92.

209. See Bergunder, *Movement*, 162, 164, though he warns on 151 that diagnoses probably attribute too much to demons; see one early Pentecostal example in Kucera, "South India"; exorcism in Marszalek, *Miracles*, 34–35. Some have portrayed the spirits as those of repressed deceased humans (Selvanayagam, "Demons"; Bergunder, "Miracle Healing," 288; on possession as a form of Dalit protest, cf. Tajkumar, "Reading"; spirits of the deceased in Korean Pentecostalism, Kim, "Healing," 281; earlier, a case in Ising, *Blumhardt*, 109, 178), but I am relatively sure that the majority Pentecostal perspective globally would involve demons who were not deceased humans.

210. Some late medieval exorcists blamed their failures on the victim's pact with the devil (Goddu, "Failure," 2; for earlier accounts of difficulties, though rarely explicit failures, in exorcism, see 7). For a survey of some medieval German accounts of exorcism and Satan, see Nauman, "Exorcism," 73–85; other medieval accounts, Caesar of Heisterbach, "Encounters"; Keller, "Glimpses," 266–75; Catholic accounts of the sixteenth and seventeenth centuries, Robbins, "Exorcism," 204–15; for Jewish accounts from the 1500s forward, see, e.g., Lieberman, "Dybbuk," 101–4; on the golem, Lieberman, "Golem." Contrary to some earlier portrayals, however, modern scholars usually doubt that medieval Europe viewed all mental disorders as demonization (Kemp, "Ravished," 67, 76–77).

Interpreting Spirit Possession

The matter of interpreting possession experiences is a question distinct from reporting them,[211] but even here we should note that a traditional modern Western reading, which is naturally materialistic, is not the only possible interpretation, nor do even modern Western interpreters all share precisely the same interpretive framework.[212] As one anthropologist notes, worldviews, including those of anthropologists, offer grids to "introduce order" to our data; "as our frameworks shift, our creation and use of data shifts."[213] The approaches of anthropologists, psychiatrists, psychologists, and indigenous interpreters often vary considerably from one another.[214]

Natural Elements and Western Academic Explanations

In 1871, E. B. Tylor recognized that most cultures still held possession to be the main cause of inspiration and sickness. Nevertheless, he held that this interpretation was simply a necessary stage in the development of religion, eventually supplanted by medical knowledge.[215] In 1971, M. J. Herskovits took possession seriously but regarded it as unexplained; mere psychopathological explanations, however, he viewed as inadequate.[216] Some interpreters who lack a commitment to purely materialistic worldviews are more apt to allow that, once spurious and psychopathological cases are removed, some cases of genuine possession by invasive entities do occur, as suggested by cross-cultural, consistent motor behavior.[217]

211. Thus, e.g., Smith, *Magician*, 9, reports his own eyewitness encounter with possession behavior but does not genuinely regard it as involving a spirit. Cf. similarly Peters, *Healing in Nepal*, 47, of his own "possession" state. For the range of interpretations, see also Keener, "Possession," 227–31.

212. "Modern Western" might need to be defined. Joseph Glanvill, for example, a leader in early moderate empiricism, warned that open-minded science ought to recognize rather than disparage evidence for witchcraft and spirits (Burns, *Debate*, 49–50), and Robert Boyle (father of chemistry) agreed with him (51). Deists like Toland expressly demurred (75).

213. Silverman, "Ambiguation," 228 (see also 204). On presuppositions in social sciences, see also Murphy, "Social Science," 33–37.

214. E.g., Wendl, "Slavery," 120, criticizes psychoanalytic (Crapanzaro), sociological (Lewis), and feminist approaches for imposing grids instead of analyzing indigenous functions for possession experience.

215. Tippett, "Possession," 144. His interpretation seems to fit the evolution of religion paradigm dominant in that era. Even half a century later, Henson, *Notes*, 140, viewed exorcism as sometimes useful, but only as "a suggestive fiction adapted to" the "ignorant superstition" of "primitive societies" (on 140–42 noting that Hickson's successful use of it occurred esp. among peoples whom Henson deemed primitive).

216. Herskovits, *Life*, 147–48 (as summarized in Tippett, "Possession," 146). Social context often determines whether possession is perceived as pathological (Peters, *Healing in Nepal*, 14–16). Johnson, "Model," 19–30, contends that the dissociation involved in shamanism is useful rather than pathological, the pathological model imposing a Western cultural construal of shamanistic cultures as pathological; researchers in shamanism today normally reject the pathological model (Walsh, *Shamanism*, 8, 93–99; Hoffman and Kurzenberger, "Miraculous," 85). Note Hood and Byrom, "Mysticism," 174 on the diverse psychological and religious evaluations of mysticism.

217. Tippett, "Possession," 147–48. I use "materialistic" for "matter" in the ordinary sense (e.g., distinct from energy); one could allow for superhuman beings that were "material" as part of the natural order.

Aspects of some concretely documented forms of possession experience are not limited to states indigenously interpreted as possession. Various "secular" stimuli not normally connected with possession can induce trance states in normal people.[218] Dissociation and altered states of consciousness (ASC) are universal phenomena, but interpretations vary:[219] the primary mystical interpretations (though not all are mystical) are soul loss and spirit possession.[220] Further, a range of altered states of consciousness exists, from rapid eye movement to a trance state to "possession trance linked to impersonation behavior."[221] Others have pointed to neurological parallels in psychomotor epilepsy,[222] sleepwalking,[223] and hysterical fugue states.[224] Studies have shown that people (as well as dogs) experiencing an overload of stresses (among humans, e.g., battle fatigue) may experience a collapse of their nervous systems; an induced collapse may in fact relieve stresses and aid mental health.[225] Some have

218. Lewis, *Ecstatic Religion*, 39. This may be described as "mental dissociation" (44); but not all "possession" involves trance, so the two should not be identified (45). Possession is not inherently "mentally dissociated" but is a particular cultural construction of the person's state in terms of an invasive spirit (46; cf. Bourguignon, *Possession*, 7). Thirty-five percent of people in the United States claim to have felt a force lift them outside themselves, 12 percent reporting "several times" and 5 percent often (Swanson, "Trance," 273).

219. Worldview affects dissociation's description in various societies, though the degree of acculturation is often a common factor (Maquet, "Shaman," 3; Peters, *Healing in Nepal*, 11–16, 46–47, 50; Frey and Roysircar, "Acculturation and Worldview," citing other studies, most relevantly Castillo, "Possession"; Hollan, "Culture"; Krippner, "Disorders"; Leavitt, "Trance"; Prince, "Variations"; Schumaker, "Suggestibility"; Sodowsky and Lai, "Variables"; for variations in posttraumatic stress responses, Marsella et al., "Aspects"; Oquendo, Horwath, and Martinez, "Ataques"). Lack of suggestibility may render "possession" difficult (cases in Last, "*Bori*," 52–53). For common features through history and in diverse societies, see McClenon, *Events*, 36–56; idem, *Healing*, 60; McClenon and Nooney, "Experiences," 47–48 (citing further McClenon, "Shamanic Healing"; allegedly in Paleolithic art in Lewis-Williams and Dawson, "Signs"); even animals can be susceptible to hypnotic experiences (McClenon and Nooney, "Experiences," 48, citing McClenon, *Healing*; on common characteristics of "mammalian consciousness," Hobson, *Chemistry*).

220. Lewis, *Ecstatic Religion*, 64.

221. Bourguignon, "Introduction," 14; cf. also examples in Finkler, "Religion," 52; Johnson, "Neuro-theology," 223.

222. Prince, "EEG," 122–24. For studies linking temporal lobe epilepsy with religious experiences (due to the temporal lobe's association with such experiences), see McClenon, *Healing*, 90. Some traditional African culture attributes epilepsy to spirits of ancestors (Gaiser, *Healing*, 139). It should be noted that some medieval Christian writers distinguished possession from epilepsy (Kemp, "Ravished," 74). Some could attribute epilepsy, as illness more generally, to demonic sources (e.g., Aramaic Incantation Text 53:12; cf. Yamauchi, "Magic," 100–113); by contrast, however, Matthew distinguishes the two in Matt 4:24 (cf. Alexander, *Possession*, 32, 63; Gaiser, *Healing*, 138), though demonization apparently causes this condition in the specific case of 17:15, 18. The term he uses did have a broader usage than epilepsy alone (cf. Ross, "Epileptic"; Yamauchi, "Magic," 129). Dr. John Wilkinson, noting that physiological factors are sometimes, but not always, identifiable, allows that a spirit could be a cause in some cases but not in others (*Healing*, 73).

223. Prince, "EEG," 124–25; cf. Field, "Possession," 4–5. Cf. the Haitian association of sleep talking with possession (Bourguignon, "Self," 50, 56). Obeyesekere, "Idiom," 108, compares "hypnotic sleep" to aspects of possession; but while lucid dreams appear especially during REM sleep (LaBerge and Gackenbach, "Dreaming," 158–60; brain patterns in REM sleep resemble waking—Greenfield, *Spirits*, 186), McClenon distinguishes brain activity during hypnosis from REM sleep (McClenon, *Healing*, 88).

224. Prince, "EEG," 125–27. Herbert Benson likewise offers a range of experiences comparable to meditation/relaxation, including athletic euphoria (*Healing*, 137–38, 167).

225. Prince, "EEG," 129–30. (Against Sargent, he thinks [130, 132] the convulsions during Wesley's preaching on June 15, 1739, represent suggestion rather than emotional collapse. White, *Spirit*, 181, notes

pointed to experiential parallels with hypnosis (at the least, both shamanism and hypnosis involve trance states, or altered states of consciousness).[226] Hallucinogenic drugs can also induce altered states of consciousness.[227]

Neurophysiological studies do not ultimately address the possibility of invasive spirits but do help explain the human neurological side of possession behavior. Societies that believe in spirit possession could naturally expect the activity of such spirits on the human nervous system to often produce results no less traumatic than other stimuli; likewise, they could believe that neurophysiological stimuli that produce susceptibility to suggestion or harsher stresses might well also render a person more susceptible to the activity of invasive spirits.[228] Such studies need not rule out the possibility of other factors in various cases but may help us understand how many forms of possession experience function neurologically.[229]

Some have linked possession experience to social frameworks (an explanatory paradigm that need not be incongruent with some others);[230] this approach has also been applied to Jesus's setting.[231] Increase in occurrences of possession often

that Wesley expected such emotional expressions as works of the Spirit, and some occurred, in a more restrained fashion, in Whitefield's meetings.) Drumbeats at the right intervals, like photic driving, can produce emotional and neurological shifts (Prince, "EEG," 133–34).

226. Cardeña, "Hypnosis," 290 (observing "similarities between shamanism and deep hypnotic phenomena" in 292–99; on possible genetic factors in the predisposition to hypnotizability, see 293). In general, the most hypnotizable 10 percent of people (those most prone to dissociative states) are six times more prone to anomalous experiences than the least hypnotizable 10 percent (Pekala and Cardeña, "Issues," 71). Some studies also associate past life memories with hypnotizability (Spanos, "Enactments"; idem, "Identities," as cited in Mills and Lynn, "Experiences," 287); such memories also appear culturally shaped (e.g., the likelihood of gender change from a past life varies widely based on cultural attitudes; Mills and Lynn, "Experiences," 292; Mills, "Investigation," 244 [though Mills herself believes that reincarnation best explains some data, 263]; cf. the cultural variations in reincarnation as males or females [243] or the gap between death and reincarnation [245]).

227. Cf. Pinkson, "Pilgrimage," 165, for an ASC through LSD; for hallucinogens and shamans, see Metzner, "Hallucinogens," 170–75; for experiences of "evil entities" through drugs, see Grof, "Potential," 141–42; for religious experiences and drugs, see Roberts, "Contributions," 244–46, 258; idem, "Study"; Hood, "Mysticism," 33; in some Amazonian indigenous practices, Tupper, "Healing." Some have argued for drug use at ancient Eleusis (Ruck, "Solving," 48–50), but this approach has faced serious challenges (Burkert, *Mystery Cults*, 108–9; Klauck, *Context*, 96).

228. While familiarity with local traditions of possession offer the primary factor for it in one study in Trinidad, stress or emotional conflict provide the immediate trigger (Ward and Beaubrun, "Psychodynamics," 206); stress being a precipitating factor appears in numerous studies (cited by Ward and Beaubrun, "Psychodynamics," 206), e.g., Douyon, "L'examen"; Freed and Freed, "Possession"; Leiris, *Possession*; Pressel, "Trance"; Warner, "Witchcraft." Case #2 in Ward and Beaubrun, "Psychodynamics," 203, lends itself especially readily to psychological explanations (at the least in terms of susceptibility). Some exorcisms probably prove effective by correcting hysterical disorders (Instone-Brewer, "Psychiatrists," 134–35), although this explanation proves inadequate for some of the phenomena recorded in the NT and other sources (see the analysis by Instone-Brewer, "Psychiatrists," 135–40).

229. The presence of physiological elements in anomalous experience, as well as its frequency in a range of unrelated cultures, clearly shows that purely cultural explanations are often inadequate (McClenon and Nooney, "Experiences," 47).

230. E.g., Prince, "Possession Cults."

231. Cf., e.g., Hollenbach, "Demoniacs"; Crossan, *Historical Jesus*, 318. While affirming anthropological observations regarding intrafamily conflicts and possession (Davies, *Healer*, 81–84), Davies

accompany dramatic changes in society.[232] Even in the nineteenth century, observers noted that "cases of possession are less frequent in peaceful times, and more frequent in times of civil commotion; also less frequent in prosperous families" and "among educated people."[233] Possession without a trance is more common in hunter-gatherer societies; increasing societal stratification and complexity increases the likelihood of added trance states.[234] Some others have also concurred that it appears more commonly in stratified slave societies.[235] Some societies use trances under controlled, ritualized situations; when society becomes uncontrolled, the instability creates crisis for the individual and his or her surroundings.[236] (Shamanic rituals involve the group, in contrast to usual Western medical practice focused on the individual in isolation.[237]) In at least some cases, people are socialized into the role of possession; certainly their behavior was often structured according to expectations.[238] (Thus, for example, some Haitian parents have encouraged

---

views Hollenbach's approach (emphasizing a sociological response to pervasive Roman oppression) as "preposterous" in view of the Galilean context (79–80). In any case, sociological factors seem to influence susceptibility but do not by themselves appear adequate to explain the phenomena surrounding the more anomalous cases (i.e., it appears reductionist to appeal solely to such factors).

232. See Wetering, "Effectiveness." Cf. also the increase in witchcraft and anti-witchcraft movements, e.g., in Li, "Abirewa."

233. Nevius, *Possession*, 58. For their greater frequency among the uneducated, see Field, "Possession," 4; Oesterreich, *Possession*, 99, 121, 165, 203, 205.

234. Bourguignon, "Spirit Possession Belief," 22. In "Introduction," 22, she notes that it is more common in stratified slave societies but on 23 thinks that rigidity also affects its occurrence (on 31, 33, relating possession behavior to release from societal strictures without changing the strictures). The data do not seem to fit readily a single consistent model, and correlation might reflect common factors rather than causation; but they might also reveal some conditions most conducive to possession states. In some settings, some trance states might perform a cathartic function (though Prince, "Foreword," xiii, warns that this approach fails to account for societies where the healer rather than the patient "becomes dissociated"). When working among highly marginalized people living on the street years ago, I also observed a much higher than usual incidence of dissociative states (sometimes with explicit possession claims), though whether social marginalization helped produce the state or whether the state led to marginalization (as it inevitably would; more generally, federal cuts in assistance for the mentally ill did increase homelessness, hence our contacts) I am not qualified to guess.

235. Greenbaum, "Societal Correlates," 54; idem, "Possession Trance," 84; for emphasis on demonology in periods of "social oppression and loss of social integration" (Pattison, "Interpretations," 217).

236. Bourguignon, "Assessment," 339; for the stress of social change and possession in one African society, see, e.g., Stoller, "Change"; in another, Smith, "Possession," 452–53 (the informants claimed that unemployment led to the spirits not being fed, hence protesting through schoolgirls). Cf. the relation to ferment in sixteenth-century cases suggested in Sluhovsky, "Apparition," 1053. But mediums initially uncontrollably possessed may learn to control the impulses (Horton, "Possession," 36, 41; Verger, "Trance," 51), though this varies (cf. Berenbaum, Kerns, and Raghavan, "Experiences," 30).

237. Kasten, "Shamanism," 68.

238. See, e.g., some of the examples in Spanos, "Hypnosis," 103–8 (e.g., on 108, demonized Catholics denouncing the pope and praising Calvin, whereas demonized Puritans avoided Calvin but read Catholic and other non-Puritan texts; on anti-Huguenot exploitation of Catholic possession, see also Walker, "Propaganda," 285–94; Walker and Dickerman, "Woman," 550–51). That public, ritual expressions of possession differ from private cases also suggests frequent performance according to expectations in such cases (Lee, "Self-Presentation," 251–52); similarly, conformity to anticipated behavioral patterns can enhance a medium's credibility (Lee, "Self-Presentation," 257). For the possibility of adopting "roles" informed by beliefs about the devil, see discussion in Wikstrom, "Possession," 32–33 (noting that possession includes a religious interpretation system).

children adopting new roles and playing at spirit possession as a sort of game.[239])
Social contexts also provide the shared vocabulary for articulating the experiences.[240]
Including ecstatic Christian experiences in her analysis, Bourguignon suggests
that possession trance is most common among the more marginalized members
of a society; groups that once experienced it, such as early Methodists,[241] that
have now become respectable are far less likely to display it.[242] It often appears
among those marginalized from other means of power in their society,[243] especially
women,[244] although this pattern varies from one society to another.[245]

239. Bourguignon, "Self," 48.

240. Lee, "Self-Presentation," 251.

241. On revelatory claims among early Methodists, see, e.g., Noll, Shape, 46; for popular "enthusiasm" among them, see, e.g., Wigger, Saint, 58–59, 78, 81–83, 166–67, 170, 307, 311–12, 320, 322. Marginalized Christian groups experiencing such phenomena (cf., e.g., Ghanaian "Holy Spirit" movements in Field, "Possession," 9–10) could view it as God's favor toward the marginalized (cf. healings in Chevreau, Turnings, 16–17; Jesus's healings in Percy, "Miracles," 13–14). Lewis, Healing, 293, notes that most of the charismatic participants in his study on healings were middle-class professionals and that many did experience some ecstatic phenomena like "shaking or falling over." But he also observes (268) that healings seem to have occurred more often among those of "lower social classes" present, suggesting perhaps divine bias for the weak. In Zambia those self-reporting possession included many educated, urban professionals (Haar and Ellis, "Possession," 189, 191, 195, though mentioning the influence of national poverty on 202); cultural factors may be involved in the varied acceptability of such diagnoses.

242. Bourguignon, "Epilogue," 342–43. Bourguignon, Possession, 55–58, compares other ecstatic phenomena in the history of U.S. revivals and contemporary Christian movements in North America and (56–57) attributes the more subdued ecstasy of middle-class charismatics vis-à-vis many other groups to their respective social status. Csordas, Self, 32, compares "resting in the Spirit" among charismatic Catholics; Haar and Platvoet, "Bezetenheid," compare Milingo's exorcism ministry. Barnett, "Answer," 280, compares a traditional spirit trance with "similar seizures at evangelistic revival meetings."

243. Lewis, "Possession," 189–90; Sharp, "Power of Possession," 4; cf. Rahim, "Zar," 138–45; Morsy, "Possession," 204–5. Some explain some Pentecostal activity in these terms (cf. discussion in Alexander, "Ritual").

244. Kessler, "Conflict," 301–2; Berger, "Women," 41, 55; Shorter, "Spirit Possession," 115 (cf. 119); Obeyesekere, "Idiom," 103; Horton, "Possession," 41–42; Colson, "Possession," 90–92, 99–100; Lee, "Possession," 143–44, 150–51, 154; Southall, "Possession," 244; Abdalla, "Friend," 41, 44; Last, "Bori," 58–59; Hammond-Tooke, "Aetiology," 57; Oosthuizen, Healer-Prophet, 88; Midelfort, "Possession," 124 (in the period 1490–1579, though not the following period); Sluhovsky, "Apparition" (1054–55, on Nicole Obry as well as others, 1565–66); Walker and Dickerman, "Woman," 539, 554; Stirrat, "Possession," 138, 151 (80 percent; of these, 70 percent are adolescents or in "early maturity"), 154; Oesterreich, Possession, 121; Giles, "Spirits," 77; Sousa, "Women"; Kenyon, "Case"; cf. Chandra shekar, "Possession Syndrome," 85 (surveying several approaches); Gray, "Cult," 171; Lewis, "Possession," 216–17; idem, "Introduction," 5; idem, "Deprivation Cults," 313–25; Constantinides, "Zar," 89; Ashkanani, "Zar," 228–29; probably even among Greeks, in Kraemer, "Ecstasy"; varied evidence in Haar and Ellis, "Possession," 193–95. Wilson, "Ambiguity," 366, suggests that the tension in these cases more often involves other women rather than other men (e.g., 370, when the husband is acquiring an additional wife); but Lewis, "Spirits and Sex War," 627, thinks this less clear. On spirit possession and gender, note the survey in Behrend and Luig, "Introduction," xvii–xviii. Among Christians, women outnumber men among participants in Catholic charismatic prayer groups, although their experiences were comparable (Csordas, Self, 31–32); also among Zulu faith healers (Crawford and Lipsedge, "Help," 138). Likewise, they account for the majority of cures at Lourdes (three to one), but this is in proportion to their participation in pilgrimage there (Cranston, Miracle, 154; for examples, see 247–58; for notable men, see, e.g., names on 137).

245. E.g., in one study of the Azande, women rarely became witch doctors (Evans-Pritchard, Witchcraft, 155–56); a masculine cult in Mali conceptualized as defending against feminine witchcraft in Colleyn,

Perhaps often because of this marginalization, possession behavior sometimes can gain desires otherwise inappropriate to express.[246] Possession trance may provide a socially sanctioned outlet for aggression where other such outlets are lacking[247] and has historically been exploited to target enemies.[248] Claims of possession can reduce guilt by projecting it on the invasive spirit;[249] in some societies, possession can generate more sympathy than acknowledgment of mental illness would, inviting some mentally ill persons to "seek shelter" under this diagnosis.[250] Because spirit possession and exorcisms fulfill a sociological function, some factors supposed to abolish such practices (such as urbanization or Western education) do not always do so.[251] Others, however, warn about the ideological underpinnings of the deprivation hypothesis about possession.[252] Moreover, many studies have overplayed the social benefits of possession to the possessed at the expense of noting the problems it causes them.[253]

"Horse," 72; mixed data on witches' gender in Crawford and Lipsedge, "Help," 134; more traditional Sukuma spirit mediums are male (Tanner, "Theory," 274) but the possessed patients female (Tanner, "Theory," 281). Pre-Islamic Hausa women played a stronger role in healing rituals than they do today (Abdalla, "Friend," 40–41). Morsy, "Possession," 208, argues that societies that allow women to express resistance through possession continue to subordinate them.

246. Successful, e.g., in Chandra shekar, "Possession Syndrome," 88, 91; Bourguignon, "Self," 50, 53; cf. Ward, "Possession," 130–32; Sharp, "Power of Possession," 4; Eve, Healer, 67. In the zar cult, the genie usually asks for something the adolescent has been wanting anyway, so it provides a safe outlet for expressing feelings (Modarressi, "Zar Cult," 154–55; cf. Lewis, "Possession," 201–4, 210–12, 216–17; Southall, "Possession," 243); elsewhere, possession may yield less pleasant eruptions "of forbidden impulses" (Ludwig, "Altered States," 86) or can express "frustrated love and passion" (Lewis, "Deprivation Cult," 315–16) or supposed neglect (Lewis, "Deprivation Cult," 317–18; cf. perfumes, etc., to compensate for a husband taking another wife, Wilson, "Ambiguity," 370); a culturally accepted outlet for relieving frustration (Beauvoir, "Herbs," 129). The spirits in Abdalla, "Friend," 39, demand special treatment for their mount. A "trance attack" or possession in India is described as "essentially a culturally sanctioned mechanism" (Raguraman et al., "Presentation").

247. This has been proposed, e.g., for women in Samoan society (Lazar, "Aggression") and in Sri Lanka (Obeyesekere, "Idiom," 104–5).

248. Kreiser, "Devils," 71–73 (though the civil courts disregarded the charges as unproved, 83–84); cf. also anti-Jewish (Walker, "Propaganda," 284–85) and anti-Huguenot and other anti-Protestant use of exorcisms (Walker, "Propaganda," 285–94; Walker and Dickerman, "Woman," 550–51).

249. Ward and Beaubrun, "Possession," 201. From the descriptions in the article (esp. case #2 on p. 203), the psychological explanations appear more persuasive than others in these cases.

250. Chandra shekar, "Possession Syndrome," 92.

251. Jacobs, "Possession," 186–87 (focusing on two East African cultures); Shorter, Witch Doctor, 179; Makris and Al-Safi, "Spirit Possession Cult," 118; Emmons, Ghosts, 191; Behrend and Luig, "Introduction," xiii–xiv; healing practices, Jules-Rosette, "Healers," 127–29; for shamanism in Korean cities, see Hard, "Animism"; for the pervasiveness of spirits in pre-Christian Korean life, see Kim, "Healing," 269–70. Likewise, witchcraft remains a significant problem in South Africa, not resolved by political freedom (Bähre, "Witchcraft," 300, 329). Still, a comparison of the few (three) epidemiological studies cited in Chandra shekar, "Possession Syndrome," 80–81, could suggest that it is more prevalent in rural than semi-urban areas. Cf. the unanticipated failure of modernity to eradicate religion in Cladis, "Modernity"; Butler, "Theory"; Haught, Atheism, 58–59.

252. Binsbergen, Change, 86–87 (cf. 24–25, 77–86). Wilson, "Ambiguity," 377, suggests that the jeopardization or ambiguity of status is more precise than general "deprivation" or marginality.

253. See Hayes, "Limits."

Diverse Approaches

Diverse cultures offer an array of different interpretive matrixes for these experiences,[254] although their experiences do produce some similar beliefs even in a number of very different societies.[255] Some societies employ naturalistic explanations for possession trance; others, supernaturalist ones.[256] Naturalist expectations are more common in the West[257] but occasionally appear elsewhere;[258] supernaturalist explanations include soul absence[259] or the presence of a spirit.[260] Some observers warn that "natural" interpretations are unlikely to be credible in much of Africa, where "nature" is never autonomous.[261]

Likewise, both voluntary and involuntary possession states could exist;[262] sometimes they coexist in the same culture (e.g., voluntary for the shaman and "hysterical" for the patient),[263] and various anomalous experiences may shift from voluntary to involuntary or the reverse.[264] Cultures that believe in possession by a spirit are more likely to generate more cases of the phenomenon so interpreted.[265] Evaluations of trance behavior can be positive or negative,[266] and the explanatory

---

254. See, e.g., Lewis, *Ecstatic Religion*, 44; cf. also Maquet, "Shaman," 3; Peters, *Healing in Nepal*, 11–16, 46–47, 50. Deprivation theories often are reductionist (cf. Hunt, "Sociology," 183–84).

255. McClenon and Nooney, "Experiences," 47.

256. Bourguignon, "Distribution," 4–11; Pattison, "Interpretations," 205–6. Technically, one might better speak of material and nonhuman-but-personal explanations (in the biblical worldview, for example, such spirits are not supernatural, though they are not material in any traditional sense).

257. E.g., many offer psychological explanations, such as the emergence of repressed subconscious thoughts (e.g., Singleton, "Spirits," 475); certainly this appears to be the case in some instances (see, e.g., Lewis, "Possession," 201–3, regarding suppressed erotic desire; cf. guilt in Ferchiou, "Possession Cults," 215–17). Cf. the naturalistic discussion of one semi-naturalistic practitioner of altered states of consciousness in Zusne, "States."

258. Bourguignon, "Distribution," 6. Ivey, "Discourses," finds evil and possession to be useful metaphors; he explains the basis as an internal "splitting," a defense mechanism (56), which causes the destructive "spirit" to function "as an autonomous suborganisation of the psyche," projected onto the mythical demon (57; some view religion more generally as a defense mechanism; see Spiro, "Systems"). But Ivey, "Discourses," follows Freud in regarding psychoanalytic language as itself no less "mythical" than the older demonic terminology; it is simply a different construction of reality (58–59); Pattison, "Interpretations," 217, treats "psychoanalytic psychotherapy" as a secular form of "exorcism" (for an analogous understanding of eighteenth- and nineteenth-century Mesmerism, see Spanos and Gottlieb, "Possession"); Kauffman, "Representations," 157, questions the idea that psychotherapy is a simple "successor" of exorcism. For one attempt to borrow Jungian language for the demonic, see Cook, "Manticores," 165–74.

259. Bourguignon, "Distribution," 7–9.

260. Ibid., 9–12.

261. Harries, "Nature," 404, noting that the experience in Africa is typically associated with the divine (or, one might add, the realm of spirits). For one African view, see Kapolyo, *Condition*, 56, 103–4.

262. Lewis, *Ecstatic Religion*, 64.

263. Peters, *Healing in Nepal*, 147–48; see also Basso, "Music."

264. Berenbaum, Kerns, and Raghavan, "Experiences," 30.

265. Kemp, "Ravished," 75; cf. also the prognosis for Western churches accepting the diagnosis in Wilson, "Exorcism," 295.

266. Bourguignon, "Distribution," 6–7, 13–15. Thus some societies seek possession whereas others seek deliverance from it (Bourguignon, "Self," 42–43). Some societies have trance without possession; others possession without trance; and still others, possession trance (Bourguignon, "Distribution," 18; idem, "Spirit Possession Belief," 21–22).

systems attached to trance behavior inevitably affect the behavior.[267] Some peoples, for example, regard spirit affliction as a danger caused by an ancestor spirit;[268] possession by deceased relatives is one of the most common conceptualizations of spirit possession.[269] Not all peoples, however, view ancestor spirits as malevolent or dangerous.[270]

267. Bourguignon, "Distribution," 12. Popular literature also suggests culturally defined conduits for possession behavior, such as the "werewolf" in Argentina (see Bottari, *Free*, 30–31; such zooanthropy reflects an older belief documented in the Middle Ages, Oesterreich, *Possession*, 191; it appears in various settings today, Berenbaum, Kerns, and Raghavan, "Experiences," 31). Ancients also believed that witches could turn themselves or sometimes others (as in Homer's Circe) into animals (Ovid *Am.* 1.8.13–14; Apuleius *Metam.* 1.9; 2.1, 5, 30; 3.21–25; 6.22; Ps.-Callisth. *Alex.* 1.10; Libanius *Encomium* 2.18; cf. Blackburn, "ΑΝΔΡΕΣ," 190, 193); for the belief today, especially for turning themselves into animals, see also West, *Sorcery*, 20; Oesterreich, *Possession*, 144; Lowie, *Religion*, 33; Mbiti, *Religions*, 256–58; Nicolini, "Notes," 119; Nanan, "Sorcerer"; Umeh, *Dibia*, 132; Zempleni, "Symptom," 99; Dobkin de Rios, "Power," 293–94; Wyk, "Witchcraft," 1210–11. For familiars used for witchcraft, see Turner, *Drums*, 206; Bond, "Ancestors," 138, 141; Shoko, *Religion*, 44–45 (animals in Zimbabwe); Debrunner, *Witchcraft*, 50; witch familiars or assistants as particular kinds of animals or half-animals in South African witchcraft in Bähre, "Witchcraft," 301; Crawford and Lipsedge, "Help," 134–35; beating by something with a tail in Koch, *Zulus*, 275; animal familiars in northern Zimbabwe (and elsewhere, 36), see Reynolds, *Magic*, 34–39; for shamanic spirits in many societies envisioned as power animals, Harner, *Way of Shaman*, 81, 87–88, 98; cf. the belief that ghosts can possess animals (Emmons, *Ghosts*, 176; cf. Mark 5:12–13); the demonic animals in southern Nigeria in Numbere, *Vision*, 118–19, 171–72, 233.

268. Turner, *Experiencing Ritual*, 182; Obeyesekere, "Possession," 239; Garbett, "Mediums," 123; Reynolds, *Magic*, 62; cf. Bate, "Mission," 77; ancestor possession in Beattie and Middleton, "Introduction," xxvii; Field, "Possession," 9; Lee, "Possession," 131–32; Keller, *Hammer*, 131–32, 155; Zempleni, "Symptom," 92; Barrington-Ward, "Spirit Possession," 456; Jules-Rosette, "Healers," 133, 142; Loewen, "Possession," 121 (causing sickness); on non-trance, Haitian possession by spirits of the dead (causing sickness by sorcery), see Bourguignon, *Possession*, 24–27; possession by dead relatives in Melanesia in Eliade, *Shamanism*, 365–66; possession by souls (in the West, esp. after decline in belief in the devil) in Oesterreich, *Possession*, 26–27, 186, 209; ghost possession in Hien, "Yin Illness," 312, 316; Emmons, *Ghosts*, 171–72, 175–76; on spirits of the dead more generally, see, e.g., Beattie and Middleton, "Introduction," xix–xxii; Beattie, "Mediumship," 162 (dangerous ghosts, including ancestors); Ma, "Types," 207 (on the need to appease ancestral spirits); Tenibemas, "Folk Islam," 23 (they disturb people); Horton, "Possession," 15; Southall, "Possession," 233 (spirits of deceased soldiers), 246–49, 255 (spirits of earlier chiefs); Welbourn, "Spirit Initiation," 291–92 (on dangerous ghosts); Byaruhanga-Akiiki and Kealotswe, *Healing*, 111–12 (for consulting spirits of the dead for healing, see 113); Barnett, "Answer," 277 (white people appearing like pale spirits of the dead to some traditional peoples in New Guinea); Shoko, *Religion*, 45 (witches exploit spirits of the dead to steal for them). Among the Valley Tonga, possession by ghosts can be fatal (Colson, "Possession," 71). In Prussian folklore, a ghost might attack the living until the ghost's offensive corpse was burned (Straight, *Miracles*, 142).

269. See Chandra shekar, "Possession Syndrome," 81 (following Salisbury, "Highlands," in noting that it usually follows a relative's death within two weeks). Ancestor possession appears even in Zimbabwean novels (see Vambe, "Possession") and something apparently analogous to it in some sixteenth-century Jewish mysticism (Schwartz, "Possession"). Many charismatic Christians who would not speak of ancestor possession nevertheless speak of "generational [ancestral] curses"; in India, see Bergunder, "Miracle Healing," 290.

270. They provide good things in Turner, *Drums*, 14; they provide helpful information in Garbett, "Mediums," 105; also (but normally only for the recently dead) Last, "*Bori*," 51; protection even in some AICs (Oosthuizen, "Baptism," 185); they must be propitiated to be kept neutral rather than harmful in Tanner, "Theory," 274; Ma, "Veneration," 168; in contrast to many kinds of spirits, in most but not all cultures they do not possess in Hammond-Tooke, "Aetiology," 55–56. On ancestor spirits, see also, e.g., Koss, "Spirits," 372; and numerous other sources. Traditional Shonas' "ancestor" spirits effectively

Religious interpretations may flourish where possession behavior occurs in cultic contexts, as it often does.[271] Many cases of spirit possession are reported in connection with Vodun in Haiti[272] and various forms of spiritism in Brazil.[273] Possession trance is also said to occur in the *zar* cult (which occurs in Iran, Sudan, Egypt, and some parts of Arabia);[274] among traditional Yorubas;[275] in some fundamentalist cults in St. Vincent;[276] and in Indo-Tibetan Buddhism,[277] for example. In nineteenth-century Fuchow, a Taoist priest would take the pose of a worshiped image, then tremble, and then begin to speak for the spirit, receiving incense and veneration.[278] Not all trances, however, have particular religious connection.[279]

Even in the West, there is no unanimity on the meaning of possession experiences. Thus, for example, anthropologists have criticized psychologists and psychiatrists for ethnocentric understanding of altered states of consciousness, whereas others have criticized anthropologists' limited competence in psychological and psychiatric matters.[280] Confronted with some anthropologists' macrosocial interpretations of possession as resistance against dominant social power structures, one Japanese hypnotherapist objected, "Don't anthropologists understand what

---

include only grandparents and parents (Gelfand, *Religion*, 173). Even many South African independent churches venerate ancestors (Molobi, "Veneration"), and some theologians support elements of this practice (Kahakwa, "Theology"). Many other Christians argue that attempted contact with (as opposed to respect for) ancestors is syncretistic (see Gehman, "Communion").

271. Tippett, "Possession," 148–51; often in the literature, e.g., Gray, "Cult," 171; the religious context of the 1374 European outbreak of the "dance frenzy" in Rosen, "Psychopathology," 224; cf. Keener, "Possession," 224–25. In antiquity cf. perhaps Persius *Sat.* 5.185–89 on demons related to the Cybele cult.

272. See Bourguignon, *Possession*, 15–27 (esp. the ritual described in 18–21); Tippett, "Possession," 155–56; Douyon, "L'Examen"; Kiev, "Value"; Perkinson, "Iron," 574–75.

273. Tippett, "Possession," 157–58; Pressel, "Umbanda"; idem, "Possession," 333–35. Cf. also the Spiritist Church, in Puerto Rico (Garrison, "Syndrome," 393–94; for mediums, see 398–403); New England (Macklin, "Yankee"); and elsewhere.

274. Modarressi, "Zar Cult."

275. Prince, "Possession Cults."

276. Henney, "Belief"; Raboteau, *Slave Religion*, 63–64.

277. Wayman, "Meaning." Cf. a Buddhist monk's exorcism and the pervasiveness of spirit propitiation in traditional Sinhalese Buddhism in Ames, "Magical-animism," 40–41; exorcism in Sinhalese Buddhism in Ames, "Magical-animism," 33; exorcism of troubling spirits from the home in Korean shamanism that overlaps with local Buddhism in Ma, "Worldviews," 9.

278. A Chinese report in Nevius, *Possession*, 47 (the reporter seems skeptical about the supernatural element). Cultic contexts often produce social pressure on particular persons to enter possession trance (Firth, "Foreword," xiii; Horton, "Possession," 24, 25, 35; Verger, "Trance," 52).

279. Shorter, "Possession and Healing," 48 (Maji-ya-Soda viewing the water spirits as neutral and adapting the ritual to fit his various clientele's religious sensibilities). Water spirits are frequent in discussions of African spirits (e.g., Horton, "Possession," 15, 17, 45); they are hostile and require exorcism in Numbere, *Vision*, 163–64; Paul Mokake (interview, May 13, 2009).

280. Ward, "Introduction," 9. Ward, "Cross-Cultural Study," 17, notes that psychologists' focus on "objective, quantifiable data" must be complemented by anthropologists' "incorporation of subjective experiential data." While she favors most often social approaches emphasizing adaptive responses, she recognizes that a variety of psychiatric conditions also appear under the cultural umbrella of possession (Ward, "Possession," 132–33). For a wide range of modern scientific (esp. psychiatric) classifications, see Chandra shekar, "Possession Syndrome," 82–83. Many psychologists view "demons" as just repressed parts of the psyche (Hoffman and Kurzenberger, "Miraculous," 84).

people actually feel?" and noted that this explanation omits a significant proportion of cases.[281] Interdisciplinary exploration is important.

Possession experiences are widely attested in anthropological literature. But whereas the leading collectors of data on the subject have been anthropologists, whether actual spirits could be involved in some extreme cases is a matter of the *interpretation* of the data and can vary according to the philosophic assumptions of the interpreter. That is, anthropologists are not the only community qualified to interpret their data; social, psychiatric, and spiritual factors may each be accorded a role in many cases without necessarily excluding the others. Genuine (sometimes organic) psychiatric problems in some cases can be channeled behaviorally in culturally conditioned patterns that can be used for other purposes by other members of society; there is no inherent reason why cases involving the activity of genuine spirits could not be expected to fit into a larger social matrix as well.

While Western scholars lack unanimity on particular approaches, however, in most disciplines there remains a prejudice against considering and especially articulating the possibility of nonmaterial personal agents, that is, a common indigenous understanding of the experience. Contexts make a difference in the interpretations that can be articulated: some interpretations in some circles would be academic suicide, whereas criticism of such interpretations is politically advantageous. Nevertheless, some anthropologists like Edith Turner (treated below) have attempted a critique of the materialist interpretation of such experiences common in Western thought, which she regards as ethnocentric and reductionist on this point.

Possession and Spirits

Various anthropologists sometimes offer contrasting readings of possession experiences based on the same data and sometimes concede that the data can be read in different ways.[282] While anthropological literature normally seeks to adopt a neutral stance,[283] simply describing phenomena and the views of the subjects, some anthropologists today press beyond traditional paradigms.[284]

---

281. Noted in McClenon, *Healing*, 59–60. Postcolonial approaches tend to emphasize such factors, but while they might help explain the dominance of possession trance in some societies, they do not explain its much more widespread incidence. Although West, *Sorcery*, 66–67, notes some local relationships between social settings and sorcery accusations, he recognizes (1–5, 14, 24–25, 35–38, 83) how such Western social and economic models often distort data and neglect genuinely indigenous perceptions.

282. See, e.g., Wilson, "Spirits" (against I. M. Lewis), conceding at the end (on 629) that both interpretations discuss "'good ideas' in a subjective manner in which speculation plays as large a part as investigation." While most postmodernists remain inclined toward skepticism, they are more open to spirits being actual than modernists were (Hoffman and Kurzenberger, "Miraculous," 84).

283. Despite efforts at value neutrality, however, social sciences as typically practiced presuppose some values that tend to dictate their conclusions (Murphy, "Social Science," 33–37; using esp. Murphy and Ellis, *Nature*; Milbank, *Social Theory*).

284. Probably most would concur at least with Werbner, "Truth," 190–91: anthropologists as outsiders may be skeptical of witchcraft, but they must suspend their skepticism to enter sympathetically into the culture. Out of innate courtesy, most African informants would not challenge their Western interrogators' skepticism; the vocal Western critic would thus not learn indigenous beliefs (Debrunner, *Witchcraft*, 3).

Thus, for example, one anthropologist with psychological training notes that the category "hallucination" fails to cover some clear experiences, such as his own experience of two apparitions in the context of Native American religion.[285] Even further from traditional approaches, a minority[286] of anthropologists specializing in such observations have dared contravene the usual assumptions of academia, publicly contending that the spirits are real.[287] (They do not, however, all view these spirits in the same manner.) Some anthropologists have noted the transformation of a number of other anthropologists' beliefs through their anomalous experiences.[288]

One obvious example of this pattern is the noted anthropologist Edith Turner,[289] who describes her gradual transformation from skeptical observer to convinced observer and finally participant, now rejecting her former stance as cultural imperialism.[290] In 1980, she and her husband, Victor Turner, were leading some students at New York University in some rituals addressed to Yoruba deities, with drumming and songs; right there a street theater director went into a trance and made accurate predictions afterward. The Turners had not expected the ritual to function this way outside its original context.[291] Her "experience of seeing a spirit" began her experiential research,[292] following what her husband called "coexperience"

285. Young, "Visitors," 174.

286. Most anthropologists deny the existence of spirits (Goulet and Young, "Issues," 323); some advocate simply accepting local beliefs about them (324); Goulet and Young "reject both of these extremes" (324), noting that both approaches require taking a particular worldview literally to the exclusion of others (325). Fictional elements in Carlos Castaneda's work (Marton, "Legacy," 281–82, though cf. some possibly truthful elements on 284) also stirred a reaction in some circles against better-documented claims by some other anthropologists (275; cf. 273–74); researchers of shamanism today question his material (see Walsh, *Shamanism*, 6).

287. See examples cited below; of course a larger number will contend that they are *psychologically* real from the standpoint of the patient (e.g., Singleton, "Spirits," 477).

288. McClenon and Nooney, "Experiences." In their view, these findings support evolution of religion (e.g., 46).

289. A lecturer in anthropology at the University of Virginia and editor of *Anthropology and Humanism: Journal of the Society for Humanistic Anthropology*, known for her earlier fieldwork in Africa beside Victor Turner, her late husband.

290. See Turner, "Reality of Spirits" (from a pro-shamanist perspective); cf. idem, "Reality." Cf. also the earlier gradual shift of German philosophy professor Traugott Konstantin Oesterreich from positivism to neo-Platonism under the influence of studying paranormal phenomena (Gregory, "Introduction," vi). Valuing participation, see, e.g., Scherberger, "Shaman," 66; Turner, "Advances," 43; Earle, "Borders," 2 (as cited in Turner, "Advances," 50). Even several decades ago, many anthropologists recognized that while much objectivity is necessary for writing, for better or for worse it is difficult to avoid becoming involved emotionally in relationships in the host culture (see, e.g., Nunez, "Objectivity," 167–71, a negative example; cf. also Firth, "Anthropologist," 31; Barnett, "Answer," 280; Forge, "Anthropologist," 297), and some early examples of participation were being reclaimed (e.g., Gronewold, "Cushing"; cf. Tedlock, "Observation," 70–71). For most of the twentieth century, the Anglophone anthropological ideal of "participant observer" (with some Jesuit antecedents; Poewe, "Nature," 8) created considerable dissonance between the ideals of empathy and detachment (Tedlock, "Observation," 69).

291. Turner, "Field," 9.

292. Turner, *Hands*, xxii.

with the people whose culture an anthropologist is researching.[293] Turner notes that anthropologists normally regard their subjects' beliefs as significant culturally and do not care whether they are true, but in the past have at times assumed that needs for psychological compensation simply drove "underprivileged people" to "hallucinations."[294] She complains that some academics "believe that trained anthropologists . . . understand aspects of a culture better than field subjects."[295] She further complains that anthropologists repeatedly "witness spirit rituals" and hear explanations from indigenous experts concerning the activity of spirits and the centrality of such rituals to their culture, yet the anthropologist continues to interpret the data according to a Western framework.[296] Often Western observers genuinely disrespect indigenous views, for all their pretense of sympathetic understanding.[297]

Moreover, she charges, anthropologists have often responded to paranormal events by simply remaining silent about them.[298] By contrast, she insists that she is unwilling to be silent. She notes that when she sought to be more sympathetic to local interpretations than in the past,[299] during a Zambian spirit ritual in 1985 to eject an *ihamba*, she was stunned by an unexpected experience: "I *saw* with my own eyes a giant thing emerging out of the flesh of her back. This thing was a large gray blob about six inches across, a deep gray opaque thing emerging as a sphere."[300]

293. Ibid., xxiii. She warns that "the usual policy of using 'the scientific method'" (i.e., distancing from the subject) is inadequate for this kind of research (xxiii).

294. Turner, *Experiencing Ritual*, 3 (for such "compensation," cf., e.g., Firth, "Foreword," xii).

295. Turner, *Experiencing Ritual*, 4, noting that today many recognize this approach as ethnocentric, ignoring other logics. Yet (15) she denies using postmodern or neocolonial postures, which often provide a Western grid through which fieldwork subjects' "traditional religion" is viewed as oppressive to them. Cf. Swarz, "Changed," 209: while claiming neutrality, Western interpreters select and rearrange data to fit their grids rather than hearing the fuller story of local informants.

296. Turner, "Reality," 30. She compares Western psychoanalytic approaches concerning dream figures from the imagination but thinks traditional cultures' explanations of external spirits even more plausible and certainly no less deserving of respect. Anthropological approaches have become much more open to indigenous categories, however (see Keller, *Hammer*, 39–40; Wilson, "Seeing," 198–206).

297. After her experience, she concluded (Turner, "Reality," 28) that many members of her guild had "perpetuated an endless series of put-downs about the many spirit events in which they participated—'participated' in a kindly pretense. They might have obtained valuable material, but they have been operating with the wrong paradigm, that of the positivist's denial." Anthropologists have sometimes devalued Native American medicine (Hultkrantz, *Healing*, 163–64; cf. 3 for frequent Native American distrust of anthropologists).

298. Turner, *Experiencing Ritual*, 3.

299. Turner, "Reality," 28.

300. Turner, *Experiencing Ritual*, 149; similarly, idem, "Field," 9; idem, "Advances," 43; idem, "Actuality," 2; idem, *Healers*, 1–23; idem, "Spirit Form." Although she allows some sleight-of-hand regarding other parts of the ritual (Turner, *Experiencing Ritual*, 165; on such tricks, see Frank, *Persuasion*, 44–45), she insists that she knows what she saw and that she was "not in trance" (Turner, *Experiencing Ritual*, 159). Wanting to keep the tradition intact, the person leading the ritual did not want any Christians (advocates of a hostile belief system) around (Turner, *Experiencing Ritual*, 155). Cf. Turner, "Religious Healing," 403: "There *are* spirit figures and forms: some of us have seen them." For one Christian claim of unexpectedly seeing a demonic form, see, e.g., Storms, *Convergence*, 67; for a claim of a cure through expelling (in spittle) a visible "witchcraft" substance, see Bergunder, *Movement*, 157. On the *ihamba* more generally, cf. Turner,

She says that she realized that there is genuine "spirit affliction: it isn't a matter of metaphor and symbol, or even psychology."[301] She afterward entered sympatheti-cally into the spirit experiences of her traditional Eskimo hosts in 1987.[302] She questions the ethics, in a multicultural world, of imposing a traditional positivist paradigm on local cultures (even to the extent of reforming indigenous elite per-spectives) "at all costs," despite the evidence favoring indigenous interpretations.[303] After surveying some of her research findings, she concludes one book regarding the Iñupiat people and their spirit experiences: "We may have to come to terms with the fact that we are not the only souls occupying this earth, that there are indeed other entities."[304] Elsewhere she offers claims of healings involving spirits,[305] affirming that she experienced one herself.[306]

Some other anthropologists and NT scholars have also noted with apprecia-tion Turner's challenge to traditional Western reductionist approaches to such claims.[307] (Some anthropologists teaching about spirit possession today even introduce students directly to such experiences.[308]) Two sociologists observed what appeared to be socially patterned, apparently culturally learned expressions of possession behavior. Their interviews with many educated observers who had

---

Drums, 156–97 (on the *ihamba* tooth, cf., e.g., 175–83, 298–99); on extractions of harmful objects and spirits from persons, see Shoko, *Religion*, 48, 97, 127–28 (regarding the Karanga of Zimbabwe).

301. Turner, "Reality," 28.

302. Ibid., 29. Wilkie, "Imagination," 163–64, invokes spirits because it is effective but leaves open for further exploration their nature and categories.

303. Turner, "Reality," 30, comparing this anthropological approach with that of missionaries, whose role she also dislikes; questioning the ethics, cf. also idem, "Field," 10–11. She concedes ("Reality," 30) that some anthropologists are more respectful than others, trying to "bend over backward to accord their people a much fuller sympathy" but announces that "in this paper I really go over the edge" of traditional boundaries for the discipline (also "Field," 11). One should note that many of our disciplines were formed in an era in which positivist (and more to the point in this case, in my opinion, antisupernaturalist) influence was inevitable. Some missiologists also warn against reductionist dismissal of cultural idiom (Hoare, "Approach") or reality (Hill, "Witchcraft," 325); others affirm the transcultural truth claims of possession (see discussion below).

304. Turner, *Hands*, 232.

305. Turner, *Healers*, 103–40.

306. Ibid., 103.

307. See Strelan, *Strange Acts*, 51, citing Hume, *Ancestral Power*; cf. Walsh, *Shamanism*, 144 (a psychiatrist); respectful discussion of this pedagogic strategy in Barnes, "Introduction," 19–20. Among scholars in theological disciplines, see, e.g., Eddy, "Reality of Spirits," not yet published. His paper, which pointed me to many sources on this subject, provides additional sources that I have not followed up for this appendix; see a sampling of this research in Eddy and Boyd, *Legend*, 67–69.

308. Turner ("Anthropology," 203) and others (Winkelman and Carr, "Approach," 177–78; Goodman, "Workshop"; Wilkie, "Imagination," 137–40, corporately invoking Greek deities; cf. Millay, "Time Travel"; Harner, *Way of Shaman*, 65–68, 76–85) actually introduce students to shamanic experiences in classes, an approach that many (including myself) find deeply problematic (note voices summarized in Barnes, "Introduction," 20). Less problematic would be observing rituals of their choice outside class (as in Payne-Jackson, "Magic," 232–35) or participating in class field trips (Mosher and Jacobs, "Seminar," 270–71). Some anthropologists now advocate sympathetically entering "witchcraft" experiences as learners, while keeping in mind scholarly obligations (Salomonsen, "Methods"). Although not accepting the indigenous epistemological framework in many respects, Peters, *Healing in Nepal*, 37–54, also supports an experiential anthropological approach (Peters underwent shaman training).

a wider range of experience, however, brought to their attention "manifestations that simply did not fit secular categories of explanation."[309] Some other Westerners initially skeptical of the reality of spirit powers in traditional religions, viewing them as mere superstition, have gradually become convinced otherwise through experience.[310] Turner notes that the discipline has moved so far that even some more "old-school" anthropologists "concede place to the new ethos with a kind of shrug—'We're not supposed to call spirits "metaphors" anymore.'"[311]

A growing minority of scholars are challenging the recent Western academic consensus against spirits.[312] The modern Western assumption of pure materialism has counted against exploring other interpretations, but it has not disproved them.[313] Paul Stoller, an anthropologist working among Songhay Muslims, was warned that he would face an attack of sorcery; that night he felt a suffocating weight on him and heard threatening creatures on his roof. The affliction stopped only when he recalled the prescribed cure in that culture (some Qur'anic verses). This changed his perspective; indigenous understandings rather than his anthro-

309. Miller and Yamamori, *Pentecostalism*, 156, citing one example of an especially "difficult deliverance of a woman who was well known as a medium," "who skidded across the floor of the church in a prone position, apparently being propelled by some supernatural force." Cf. the apparently difficult position of the body in Ising, *Blumhardt*, 175. Moreland and Issler, *Faith*, 157–59, also note occult phenomena in which, for example, objects were moved across the room.

310. E.g., Steyne, *Gods of Power*, 14–19; Nevius, *Possession*, ix, 9–13. Cf. Peters, *Healing in Nepal*, above; on 50, when he lost motor control and in a vision or dream saw a green figure, the shaman interpreted this as a spirit possessing him, though (47) Peters himself does not believe in spirit possession. McClenon, *Events*, 236–37, notes that he experienced the paranormal but allows that this experience could be purely subjective.

311. Turner, "Advances," 45. She notes (ibid.) that shamanism is now "the fastest growing field" in anthropology. I should note, however, that many recent works do continue to treat spirits and witchcraft discourse as political metaphors. Some areas of anthropology seem susceptible to "political reductionism" (a phrase borrowed by Burgess, *Revolution*, 261, from Jean Copans and Ruth Marshall); Wuthnow, "Contradictions," 157, suggests this tendency in sociology of religion.

312. See, e.g., Betty, "Evidence," and sources cited there; Isaacs, "Disorder"; Johnson, "Possession"; Sall, "Possession"; and sources cited below. Baker, "Believes," 211–13, notes that in U.S. society generally, belief in demons or personalized, spiritual evil, which a majority of people in the United States hold, on average tends to decrease with rise in income and education, possibly because of greater comfort. But he also notes (216–17) that religious attendance is a stronger prediction of such beliefs (with a positive correlation). He further notes (212, 218) that it tends to run higher among women, probably because they are more often religious, and African-Americans, both because of religious tradition and the experience of social marginalization. His statistics appear to suggest those with graduate education are only 75 percent as likely to believe this as those with only a high school education, but this figure may also suggest that *most* who believe in these entities do not lose that belief despite the materialistic training characteristic of most education. My focus here, however, is not on these sources of belief more generally but the narrower category of those who claim to have encountered embodied examples of such belief.

313. With Tonquédec, *Miracles*, 64–65; cf. similarly Wilson, "Miracles," 32–33, noting on 33 that there is no specifically logical reason to discount the possibility; Goulet and Young, "Issues," 325, questioning whether "any scientific experiment" can settle the question of spirits. As to whether such entities could be subsumed under materialism, this might depend on how we define materialism (e.g., the material universe includes energy and can be defined as including human intellect).

pological training enabled him to cope with the local reality.[314] Publication of his experience initially stirred controversy and disdain from some peers, though it eventually led to accolades.[315]

Likewise, Solon Kimball, a noted anthropologist,[316] notes his own completely unexpected experience of encountering an apparition during his fieldwork in Ireland.[317] He was just outside his hotel when an apparition began moving toward him; when he tried to strike it, thinking it a human aggressor, his foot passed through empty air, and the apparition quickly vanished.[318] Shaken, he reported his experience to the hotel porter, and in the morning others in the hotel, especially long-term residents, began to share their own "ghost" experiences.[319] One land commissioner had found "a figure standing at the foot of his bed"; another resident had been rid of a "persistent visitor" only through the intervention of "the Franciscan fathers." When a man from the town heard the story, he recounted seeing the same "apparition on a number of occasions" in the same vicinity.[320]

Recounting his experience later, Kimball notes that in subsequent years he had "puzzled" over the experience. Transcendentalists might suggest a ghost, whereas materialists would suggest a hallucination, but there was no way to resolve which was correct.[321] From a neutral anthropological perspective, he concludes, it does not matter whether the encounter involved a ghost or a hallucination; the important point is that the experience reveals the influence of local culture on the observer.[322] Some other anthropologists have reported unusual apparitions of deceased persons while awake.[323] But we should remember that Kimball had no knowledge of the

---

314. Stoller, "Eye," 110 (as cited in Turner, "Advances," 41). That the experience occurs at night is consistent with the belief that witches are thought to go out at night (Bond, "Ancestors," 141; in classical antiquity, see, e.g., Ovid *Am.* 1.8.3–8).

315. Turner, "Advances," 42.

316. Coeditor of the volume in which the essay was offered, he was at the time of its publication graduate research professor in anthropology at the University of Florida, and had been visiting professor in such institutions as the University of Chicago and University of California at Berkeley; he had also been president of the American Ethnological Society and of the Society for Applied Anthropology. Dr. Paul Eddy, personal correspondence, Oct. 26, 2009, directed me to this source.

317. He notes that Irish culture when he was there embraced the supernatural, so that no one doubted the experience (Kimball, "Learning," 188, 190–92). Turner, "Advances," 37, confesses that "anthropology marveled briefly at Solon Kimball's ghost story" but then neglected its implications until other such stories began to be published. She also notes (Turner, "Advances," 40) "a strange public apparition" in Trinidad during the time that Joseph Long, a medical anthropologist, was there; for other claims of apparitions, see McClenon, *Events*, xiii, 70, 72 (noting also some apparitions to groups of people, 75).

318. Kimball, "Learning," 189.

319. Ibid., 189–90.

320. Ibid., 190.

321. Ibid.

322. Ibid., 191, noting that "the capacity for supernatural experience as well as its form and content is culturally learned." While the shape of interpretations may be culturally learned, however, anomalous experiences appear in a wide range of cultures (McClenon and Nooney, "Experiences," 46–47).

323. McClenon and Nooney, "Experiences," 51, cite Goulet, "Ways of Knowing," 129–30 (also cited in Turner, "Advances," 47). McClenon and Nooney, "Experiences," 51, also cite Young, "Visitors," 168–69, for one twice awakened by visiting apparitions (note in Young, "Visitors," 172, that a local Cree healer

familiar "ghost" sightings nearby. If one does not need to explain his experience in materialistic terms, is that the *most* plausible explanation for it?[324]

Certainly many intelligent observers from many other cultures do not share the dominant Western interpretations. This is no less true among Christians than among other indigenous interpreters. Thus, one Chinese church leader of a previous generation reproved Western critics with the observation that their theological hairsplitting would benefit them little in his country "if when the need arose you could not cast out a demon."[325] As one Lutheran writer in Tanzania notes, "The phenomenon of demon possession is a hard reality with which a good number of East African Christians struggle daily." Whereas Westerners tend to denigrate such views as "primitive," he notes, East Africans take them for granted, and "the biblical accounts are read not as myths, but as objective accounts of actual experiences."[326]

A generation ago noted missiologist Stephen Neill warned that it was next to impossible to convince most Majority World Christians "that evil spirits do not exist"; he noted that they cited examples of local possession cults. He further observed that most missionaries who lived in traditional areas similarly refused to reduce all cases of possession to hysteria.[327] Many early Presbyterian missionaries to Korea had learned in seminary that spirits were not real, but most came to believe otherwise in the context of ministry alongside indigenous believers.[328] Thus for example Charles Clark was astonished in the face of a violent demonstration of spirit possession; quickly changing his doctrine, he invoked Jesus's name and the man quickly became rational, completely unaware of his prior state.[329] Other missionaries also reported exorcisms (usually led by Korean believers), and noted that in the early, groundbreaking years exorcisms similar to those in the NT accompanied the start of many or most churches.[330]

More recently, Peruvian missiologist Samuel Escobar reports a conversation with an indigenous teacher from the Peruvian jungle. When local people noticed

---

recognized his description of the first apparition as a spirit regularly encountered there). McClenon, *Events*, 39–45, shows that "apparitions" are attested in a wide variety of cultures.

324. Paul Eddy, who supplied the source, suggested that a materialistic or even cultural explanation seems to fall "very flat in light of his own report of the event" (personal correspondence, Oct. 26, 2009), and I am inclined to agree, especially if such experiences could be multiplied (and they can be, though that is not the subject of this book). I do not personally believe in ghosts but also doubt that the conventional denial of extrahuman forces can explain all our evidence.

325. Watchman Nee in Kinnear, *Tide*, 152; on 318n10, he notes "an account of an exorcism." One Chinese minister, Pastor Hsi, became known as "Shengmo," the "demon overcomer" (McGee, "Regions Beyond," 70).

326. Mchami, "Possession," 17 (while conceding that East African interpretation could use more exegesis).

327. Neill, "Demons," 161.

328. Kim, "Healing," 270.

329. Ibid., 270–71. In 1908 the same missionary reported an exorcism, after extended prayer, of a spirit so powerful that three nonbelievers outside were hurled to the ground when it came out (271, citing Clark's report).

330. Ibid., 272–73. The best known Korean exorcist was also the most popular Korean Protestant preacher of the day, Presbyterian Kim Ik-tu (Kim, "Healing," 273–74).

demons in the Western linguist's translation of Mark, the Western linguist explained that such spirits were only for the first century. While the local teacher respected the linguist, however, he insisted that their local environment matched better what they found in Mark: "We know that there really are demons and spirits; they're around here."[331]

Other indigenous interpreters have rejected conventional Western explanations, contending that some spiritual power is at work. As John S. Mbiti points out, "Every African who has grown up in the traditional environment will, no doubt, know something about this mystical power which often is experienced, or manifests itself, in [the] form of magic, divination, witchcraft, and mysterious phenomena that seem to defy even immediate scientific explanations."[332] He notes even documented cases of Westerners who experienced these powers at close hand and were therefore forced to acknowledge and deal with them.[333] Ohene Kweku Opare-Sem, a U.S.-trained hematologist and oncologist working in Ghana, notes that when he went to touch one patient who had been to "fetish priests," something "like a bolt of electricity" jolted his arm, paralyzing it "for several hours." When he tried to visit her again in the morning, as soon as their eyes met, it happened again, and subsided only as he retired "to the doctor's room to pray."[334]

One of my Nigerian students in the United States, Benjamin Ahanonu, told me of confronting spiritual powers in his home village. Others who had been cursed by those known to harness such powers often died suddenly soon afterward; after his own confrontation, he found himself in the hospital in the capital the next day. A village elder finally traveled to the capital because, he informed Benjamin, they had been surprised not to get word that he had died; the elder was now even more shocked to find him alive. Benjamin recovered and has since returned to the village many years to preach.[335]

Various personal experiences and reports from some close and trusted African friends also predispose me to be among those who accept the reality of nonhuman spirits behind some (but by no means all) contemporary possession claims.[336] Generally when I have asked educated persons from Africa and many other parts of the

331. Escobar, *Tides*, 86.

332. Mbiti, *Religions*, 253–54. I am more skeptical of some of Mbiti's individual anecdotes (e.g., 256–57), but not all of them.

333. Ibid., 254–56. I am tempted to recount also my own few, involuntary experiences with these practices in Africa, experiences that I think would surprise most Western readers, but will offer only a bare minimum, preferring to reserve my credibility for points where it matters more.

334. Mensah, "Basis," 176.

335. Interview, Dec. 1, 2009. We and our immediate relatives in Africa have some similar stories, some of which I myself experienced in that context.

336. Without knowing where to draw the line, I am aware of circles that attribute all mental illness or personal problems to the direct effects of indwelling demons, a perspective that is neither biblical nor sensible. One cannot by any means identify with demonization all kinds or cases of mental illness, which in the Gospels overlaps with demonization in at most some cases (see Songer, "Possession," esp. 121; on 119 counting "naïve" the simple equation of ancient demons and modern neuroses; cf. Gaiser, *Healing*, 136n10). Against excess deliverance ideology, see, e.g., Onyinah, "Deliverance," 133.

Majority World whether they believed in the reality of spirits, occult activity, and the like, their response has been, "Of course," sometimes with a caveat that they are careful with whom they discuss such matters, especially among skeptical Westerners.[337]

I recognize that some who follow the secondary argument of the main book (that God sometimes does miracles) will not share my openness to some other cultures' affirmation existence of other spirits in addition to one God. Still, one clearly monotheistic NT scholar has suggested that accepting the possibility of malevolent spirits is no more a priori implausible than accepting the possibility of "a good spirit—God."[338] Another, who has researched the issues extensively, remains "convinced by the testimony of credible witnesses and reasonable arguments, as well as personal experience, that it is judicious to entertain the idea of the existence of some form of destructive spiritual entities not unreasonably designated 'evil spirits.'"[339] While not all cultures treat these subordinate spirits as hostile, some post-Holocaust Western theology has affirmed a dimension of personal superhuman evil that allows for such hostility.[340]

Regardless of interpretation, however, possession behavior is well documented cross-culturally, and there is no reason to automatically doubt reports of it in our ancient sources. There is no inherent reason to suppose such reports are necessarily fictitious or legendary rather than potentially based on eyewitness claims.

Western Psychiatrists and Belief in Genuine Spirits

Reports of spirit possession have been less frequent in most of mainstream Western society,[341] yet not so infrequent as to occasion no comment. From popular reports to the public claims of a small number of psychiatrists[342] willing to defy

---

337. Cf. the similar observation about educated Africans' affirmation of these realities in Hart, *Delusions*, 102. I say "generally" not because there have yet been any exceptions but because I recognize that my sample size is anecdotal. Many Africans today apparently do not believe in "evil spirits" ("Islam and Christianity," 177) or "witchcraft" (ibid., 178; cf. 179; elsewhere, cf. Friedrich, "Fighter," 141), though some may have construed "believe in" differently from how the questioners intended the questions ("demand effects" and the desire in some hospitable African settings to please questioners, who often may not have believed in such spirits, may also have affected the results; cf. the observation in Debrunner, *Witchcraft*, 3). Thus in Ethiopia, where 31 percent of Christians "believe in evil spirits" ("Islam and Christianity," 177), 74 percent claim to have experienced or witnessed evil spirits being cast out of someone (214); figures for other countries likewise reveal this sort of disparity.

338. Ladd, *Theology*, 51.

339. Twelftree, *Name*, 293.

340. See discussion in Boyd, *War*, 70–71. Cf. also the reasoning in Hultgren, "Stories," 133; calling for countering the neglect of this theme, see earlier Stewart, "Emphasis." Africans are sometimes especially cognizant of the reality of evil (Oduyoye, "Value," 113).

341. Berends, "Criteria," 347–48, suggests that possession could be rare as in the OT era; restricted especially to areas with little influence from the good news of the kingdom; or increasing because of the "last days." On 348–52, he suggests that it would be expected most in pagan environments (and [351] where people are particularly interested in spirits; he compares missionary reports). He concludes (364) that they will predominate in pagan societies.

342. E.g., Wilson (then a psychiatry professor at Duke University), "Hysteria," 225–30, providing three case studies; Isaacs, "Disorder," 265–66 (noting both psychologists and psychiatrists); Johnson,

the conventions of modern Western intellectual thought,[343] some even in the Western world report not only cases of possession but also cases of successful expulsion of spirits.

Many cases of apparent possession have more direct psychological explanations.[344] I noted earlier in the book my concern with a particular documented exorcism detailed as an example in one generally useful academic work.[345] Charismatic psychiatrist John White, noted earlier in the book, treats psychosis as the result of chemical imbalance rather than demons.[346] Even when one allows for the possibility of spiritual explanations, they do not supplant psychological ones. Behavior may be the same whether a person has psychiatric problems from material or emotional causes or because these are caused by an invasive spirit, leaving the burden of proof on the latter claim; when preternatural phenomena accompany the apparent possession, however, the presence of another spirit becomes more plausible.[347]

Scott Peck, a noted psychiatrist, dismisses most claims of possession and exorcism but claims that he has encountered rare cases for which he found this the only explanation.[348] (Peck does believe that most cases of malevolence, however, are of purely human character.[349]) He became certain enough of one case of possession that he risked endorsing the need for exorcism despite the disdain for this practice in his profession;[350] it was this encounter that convinced him that personal nonhu-

---

"Possession"; cf. McAll, "Taste"; idem, "Deliverance"; see further Peck, *Glimpses*, below; cf. Friesen, *Mystery* (as summarized in Hoffman and Kurzenberger, "Miraculous," 78); for Christian doctors, Lees and Fiddes, "Healed," 22; for some popular claims, see Harris, *Acts Today*, 140–45. White, "Lady," 75, notes that he struggled not to come to this conclusion, but some phenomena in his patients compelled him to arrive at this conviction (for one exorcism account, see White, *Spirit*, 203–7). Walsh, *Shamanism*, 147–48, notes that different paradigms explain the evidence differently and allows (148–49) that different cases may have different explanations (cf. similarly Moreau, "Possession Phenomena," 772).

343. I assume that a head count would show more psychiatrists denying than affirming the reality of genuine spirits. Nevertheless, those supporting a currently dominant paradigm are normally the majority until detractors challenge the adequacy of the paradigm to cover all the data.

344. Cf. "pseudo-possession" in Gildea, "Possession," 296–98.

345. Miller, "Story"; more critically evaluated in Smucker and Hostetler, "Case." My concern about the exorcist Sam Fife (or at least about what he became subsequently) is not intended to deny the genuineness of Miller's experience.

346. Loewen, "Possession," 137–38. John Wilkinson, also a medical doctor, warns that psychiatric knowledge cannot exclude "possession as a possible cause" of psychosis, but also that it is not always a cause (*Healing*, 73).

347. Cf. Gildea, "Possession," 299, though he questions the accuracy of reports of such phenomena (310) and allows that those who regard psychic powers as inherent in the human personality may regard even these as not identifying a foreign spirit (301). I have received oral reports of preternatural phenomena from a number of eyewitnesses, but more often in connection with claims of witchcraft than with possession.

348. In *Glimpses*, providing fuller detail (as he notes on xvii) for two accounts of exorcism merely summarized (and with some more potentially controversial details omitted) in his widely read *People of the Lie*. Others also cite Peck (e.g., Betty, "Evidence," 17; Loewen, "Possession," 138–39; less favorably, Collins, *Exorcism*, 166–70). Cf. Grof, "Potential," 144–45, for one rare case that exceeded normal psychiatric (or human) bounds (Roberts, "Study," 51–52, tries to interpret this report in light of mysticism).

349. Peck, *Glimpses*, 239–41.

350. Ibid., 237–38.

man malevolent beings do exist.[351] He suggests that enough empirical information is already available "to make demonology a respectable field of research and study." But he doubts that science will undertake such an objective study, "at least not until . . . a 350-year-old separation of the world of supposed natural phenomena from the assumed world of supernatural phenomena is revisited, and recognized by all concerned as having been a gigantic mistake."[352] Some other NT scholars cite his approach respectfully.[353]

William P. Wilson, professor emeritus of psychiatry at Duke University Medical Center, regards as purely psychological many problems popularly attributed to demons today, but insists that there are real cases, including some that he has encountered, of actual spirits.[354] He offers as an example a Malagasy woman whose parents practiced the occult. On various occasions, she "would be violently thrown to the floor, whereupon two male voices" would speak through her in what was not her normal language. Confronted with this behavior, Wilson commanded the spirits to leave her, invoking Jesus. She regained normalcy immediately, and remained healthy during the year of follow up.[355]

Another psychiatrist warns against viewing most sorts of emotional problems as demonic[356] but notes that he has seen a few clear cases of possession by a genuine spirit "even in my own psychiatric practice."[357] Still another psychiatrist notes that 70 percent of his work deals with psychosomatic cases, but in 4 percent of the cases he has treated, he has needed to undertake exorcism. He notes roughly 280 cases that required exorcism, especially resulting from the occult practices of the person or their family (such as Ouija boards, witchcraft, horoscopes, etc.).[358] In one case, the timing of a mother's deliverance correlated with the instant curing of her son (who, unknown to them, was suffering schizophrenia in a hospital four hundred miles away), as well as the son's wife's tuberculosis.[359] He describes an instant release from schizophrenia through exorcism removing the curse of an occult group; the complete healing through exorcism of a violent woman in

---

351. Ibid., 238.
352. Ibid., 249.
353. See esp. Borg, *Jesus*, 322n9, allowing for this paradigm.
354. Wilson, "Miracle Events," 268.
355. Ibid., 275.
356. Johnson, "Possession," 150–51.
357. Ibid., 152. On 152–53, he offers three examples; all these patients were involved with the occult. Similarly, a Mennonite pastor in Pennsylvania notes that he runs into "two to three demonized persons a year"; the first occasion was a "high priestess of a satanic coven" (Winslow, "Care," 192). Before deliverance ministries became excessive, early Igbo Pentecostal deliverance especially occurred in evangelistic contexts among those previously involved in spiritual power in traditional religions (Burgess, *Revolution*, 153).
358. McAll, "Deliverance," 296. A counselor in Ball, "View," 127–28, also reports the deliverance of someone demonized who apparently had a background in the occult; so also a report from Portugal, among reports sent to me by Douglas LeRoy, Nov. 9, 2009. Occult background also figures in two confrontations with spirits noted by Samson Uytanlet in personal correspondence (Dec. 15, 2009); cf. also concerns with the occult mentioned in Davies, "Exorcism," 17–19, 23, 29, 46, 50.
359. McAll, "Deliverance," 296–97.

a padded cell who had not spoken for two years; and the instant deliverance of another woman in a padded cell, when several prayed at a distance from her and without her knowledge.[360]

Occult connections appear in many of his accounts. Although possession could "mimic epilepsy," he noted, it differed from it. Three adults tried to restrain one six-year-old, but in contrast to epilepsy, the boy remained conscious; the boy was cured when his father renounced Spiritualism. A heroin addict whose mother was a Spiritualist medium was through exorcism completely freed from addiction despite his initial "lack of cooperation." Another boy was healed through exorcism when his mother renounced her role as a fortune-teller. The daughter of a witchcraft practitioner who had cursed her was freed immediately from alcoholism when (unknown to her) some people prayed for her release.[361] Likewise, an emergency room physician notes a case that appeared to be possession by some extraordinary evil, in a person allegedly promoting voodoo.[362]

One counseling professor, while insisting that most claims of possession are inauthentic,[363] observes in a professional journal that he encountered what he believed to be a genuine one. When a sixteen-year-old boy involved with the occult started "snarling like an animal," a crucifix fell from the wall, its nails hot and melted.[364] The father, a physician, decided that the son was possessed; nominal, mainline Protestants, the family asked a team of ministers and psychological professionals to help. A minister on the team asked the boy to repeat "Jesus Christ, son of God," but before the young man could finish, his visage and voice altered.[365] "You fools," he uttered, "he can't say that."[366] The exorcism was, however, ultimately successful.[367] Several

---

360. Ibid., 297, noting in the last case that unknown to them at the time, her aunt had been "a patient in a mental hospital" in another country and was delivered simultaneously. Healing during deliverance, whether from physical or mental affliction, appears in many accounts. For an example of the former, see, e.g., a report by D. F. Rodrigo of Sri Lanka, in which the Hindu family became Christians and joined the church (sent to me by Douglas LeRoy, Nov. 9, 2009). In an account from Benin illustrating the latter, people brought to a Pentecostal church for prayer a woman considered insane; once there, she fell into a coma for six hours, but after much prayer she revived, "healed from her insanity" (a report from Pastor Achille Todego, sent to me by Douglas LeRoy, Nov. 9, 2009; on Pentecostalism's anti-witchcraft posture in Benin, see Mayrargue, "Expansion," 283; for its growth through healings, 287). A clinical psychologist, Russ Llewellyn, "Events," 252–53, reports a healing of schizophrenia and two resolutions of Dissociative Identity Disorder through prayer (citing no involvement from other spirits).

361. McAll, "Deliverance," 297.

362. Lesslie, *Angels*, 155–66 (voodoo is mentioned esp. on 160). The woman had torn out her tongue, with shockingly minimal bleeding, and apparently swallowed it.

363. Van Gelder, "Possession," 160. Van Gelder was at the time associate professor of pastoral counseling at Erskine Theological Seminary.

364. Ibid., 151–52 (depending on both parents for this information). The son had been involved with the occult since age ten (152). For the claim of a dangerously hot cross in a "haunting" context, see McClenon, *Events*, 68.

365. Van Gelder, "Possession," 153.

366. Ibid., 154. Similarly, in Crandall, *Raising*, 164, whenever a demonized person attempted to utter Jesus's name she appeared to become temporarily catatonic; this changed immediately after exorcism. In Tari, *Breeze*, 61–62, demons were upset to hear about Jesus.

367. Van Gelder, "Possession," 154.

of those present were professionals, the professor notes, and he also notes his own ample acquaintance with psychiatric disorders; it was clear that they were not dealing with epilepsy, psychosis, or other conditions that they knew how to recognize.[368]

Another professional claims that whereas standard treatments can help hallucinations and psychosis, demonization can be cured only by prayer or exorcism.[369] One study, noting that typical cases of possession do not fit other diagnoses, identified seven common characteristics in possession cases.[370] A number of the individuals saw "dark figures" and would "hear audible and coherent voices" outside themselves but as part of otherwise normal reality.[371] They often exhibited revulsion toward religious objects;[372] in contrast to psychological disorders, "there is an impact on others in the vicinity of the patient," who may also "experience odd phenomena."[373] The study's sample size, however, is small (fourteen individuals),[374] and some different characteristics may have been screened out circularly by the "possession" definition employed. If an alien spirit did affect the psyche or the central nervous system, would it not sometimes produce some effects comparable to problems those areas of a person could also experience apart from it?[375] The examples identified as possession here, however, offer at least some perspectives on criteria used by some professionals to identify a minimum number of cases of possession by a genuine spirit.

Francis MacNutt, a figure in Catholic and Episcopal renewal circles mentioned earlier in the book, notes that he has witnessed "what purport to be demons speaking through the person (e.g., 'You will never drive us out; we are too many and too

368. Ibid., 158.

369. Sall, "Possession," 289, also noting other clinical contrasts, though conceding that most deviance in the West reflects natural causes. Gebru Woldu named a hospital psychiatrist in Ethiopia, as well as some Western doctors he has taken to Ethiopia with him, who treat genuine medical and/or psychiatric cases but expect Gebru and his team to pray for the genuinely demonized (interview, May 20, 2010).

370. Isaacs, "Disorder," 266. On it not fitting other diagnoses, see 265–66.

371. Ibid., 268.

372. Ibid., 269. Woodard, *Faith,* 25, cites blasphemy among the behaviors of one he describes as possessed; cf. earlier Ising, *Blumhardt,* 171, 183, 326, 337.

373. Isaacs, "Disorder," 270, noting "poltergeist-type phenomena and the feeling of suffocation while praying."

374. The study took subjects referred by four Episcopal exorcists (two of them priests) who distinguished these cases from psychological ones; then the cases were referred to one psychiatrist and four psychologists for diagnosis (ibid., 264).

375. Some proposed criteria for distinguishing possession are thus subjective (see, e.g., Bach, "Possession," 25, noting that they may overlap and mistrusting the distinctions in Sall, "Possession"; Sall offers an able reply in "Response"), though suprahuman knowledge, strength, and so forth are not (see Gildea, "Possession"). Monden, *Signs,* 163, thinks that the line between the natural and demonic exploitation of psychopathology is not easily discerned psychologically. Some warn that some Christians now carry deliverance too far, so that "preoccupation with demons and witches" becomes "an affirmation of the old order" (Onyinah, "Deliverance," 133). In contrast to Third Wave theology, Western Pentecostals normally doubt that Christians can have demons (Wright, "Profiles," 287; Carter, "Demon Possession"; idem, "Possession"; Collins, "Perspective 1"; idem, "Perspective 2"; Macchia, "Deliverance"; historically, see Collins, *Exorcism,* 22, 46–47n169), as do some other circles (e.g., Berends, "Criteria," 364; cf. varying views among Mennonites in Burkholder, "Foundations," 42).

strong for you')—often much to the speaking person's surprise." Entirely rational people sometimes find themselves hurled to the ground while being exorcised, as astonished as anyone else. Other explanations remain possible, he suggests, but the simplest is the best: in cases like these, a spirit is actually speaking through them.[376] A Western medical doctor, shocked to find a new voice from his patient insisting, "Let her alone, she's ours!" reports that he decided that something spiritual was happening for which even his psychiatric colleagues had little training. After some hesitation, he succeeded in expelling the spirits by invoking Jesus's name.[377]

Obviously exorcism has a severely tarnished history of extremism, an excessive tendency that continues frequently in many settings today.[378] When exorcism captures Western public attention, it is usually in this malignant form.[379] Others, however, convinced that some spirits are real, have reported confrontations with what they believe are genuine spirits (among Christians, probably more frequent in missiological power encounters than in ritualistic "exorcistic" settings).[380] Although

376. MacNutt, *Healing*, 214 (though even MacNutt has been accused of seeing demons too widely; cf. Collins, *Exorcism*, 56–63). For a charismatic Protestant report, see Wimber, *Healing*, 98; in India, see Yohannan, *Revolution*, 30.

377. Mullen, *Feel*, 151–52.

378. Faddish approaches have developed in some charismatic circles (see criticism in Stackhouse, "Foreword," xv; Robertson, *Miracles*, 94–95), with roots in practices by figures like W. Branham (Collins, *Exorcism*, 28–30); A. A. Allen (37); Derek Prince (43–53, with idiosyncratic views such as demons being pre-Adamite humans, 48); and further extremes in F. and I. Hammond (authors of *Pigs in the Parlor*; 64–69) and Bill Subritzky (87–89); in addition to pure fabrications (99–100, 142–47). Extreme demonology also appears in some noncharismatic circles (e.g., 154–66), where it sometimes has been wielded against Pentecostals and charismatics (117–26, 131, 149–50). Collins's critique is generally helpful, despite his reliance on the category of "enthusiasm" (and excessive epistemic reticence toward experience, *pace* Hume!). Cf. the harmful practice of psychologically induced vomiting in a church in Bowler, "Bodies," 90 (perhaps reflecting the pastor's initial experience with exorcism; cf. 87); disputed claims in Bergunder, "Miracle Healing," 293. Some African charismatics express concerns that others' deliverance ministries have become extreme (Gifford, "Provenance," 70, 73; Burgess, *Revolution*, 228); charismatics from different cultures and movements often hold strongly divergent views (Brown, "Awakenings," 360). One may demur from beliefs and practices of many deliverance ministries without viewing all practices as equally extreme; some focus on correcting demonic influence on thinking much more than on what most would mean by exorcism or possession (cf., e.g., Lozano, *Unbound*, 12). Yet in more extreme cases, when prosperity teachings failed, for example, many resorted to challenging "spirits of poverty" (Burgess, *Revolution*, 229–30).

379. E.g., the extremism reported in Collins, *Exorcism*, 70; according to some media reports, also in a recent case in Guyana (http://news.yahoo.com/s/ap/20100402/ap_on_re_la_am_ca/cb_guyana_exorcism_death; accessed April 2, 2010). In general, few reports of more positive outcomes would likely survive the journalistic publication process (in contrast to anthropologists' notes), since some Western editor or publisher along the way would probably object to it, whereas negative reports can be viewed as enlightening the public (in favor of a conventional modern Western worldview). The exceptions might be an occasional more thoroughly documented investigative report or (unhelpfully and counterproductively) sensational entertainment media catering to popular fascination with the lurid and the occult. Yet there are certainly enough genuine instances of extremism to fill volumes with negative examples.

380. If some Western critics would accuse me of ideological bias for admitting Christian reports about spiritual confrontations, I would note that most of my critics have an ideological bias against local informants' claims concerning spirits and spiritual power. Sometimes Western observers have simply transmuted these spiritual claims into sociological critiques of political power; while such critiques may be necessary, they are hardly the traditional point of most village witchcraft discourse—at least not insofar

many Westerners look askance at the practice, missiologists collecting field data today have sometimes reported a strong success rate for exorcisms conducted in Jesus's name in various cultures.[381] Power encounters of various kinds have been influential in church growth in cultures where spiritual power is emphasized.[382] (Although from a different perspective and not my focus here, some sorts of spiritual power conflicts undoubtedly occur in competition among adherents of traditional religious worldviews as well, and supernatural claims have generated growth among such groups.[383] Some of these also appeal to supernatural means to display hostility toward Christian conversion.[384])

Missiologists on Power Encounters

Karl Barth appealed to Christ's victory in an exorcism performed by J. C. Blumhardt as encapsulating the gospel message of Christ's triumph.[385] Nevertheless, modern Western Christians often consider only one spirit, God, and dismiss the reality of other spirits; Christians in many parts of the world, however, have experience with what they believe are multiple spirits and look to biblical models for showing why their God should be preferred to other spirits. Missionary anthropologist Paul Hiebert notes that Christians in India addressed a cultural blind spot

---

as I may trust my informants who grew up in such settings rather than Western visitors who read all such accounts through a purely materialist grid.

381. Johnson, "Authority," 105–6 (on Brazil); cf. the observations in Instone-Brewer, "Psychiatrists," 140–41. I cannot ascertain from Johnson's report the extent to which experiences of spirit possession (as defined above, as opposed to mere confrontation of spiritual ideologies and practices) are involved (without which the NT, at least, lacks examples of exorcism). Others have also reported the efficacy of Jesus's name in exorcising spirits (e.g., earlier Chinese reports in Nevius, *Possession*, 13, 33–35, 55–57); cf. demons' fear of the rosary in traditional Sri Lankan Catholicism at Kudagama (Stirrat, "Possession," 138, though the goal is simply to make "life so unpleasant for the demon that it eventually leaves," 140). A former Yanomamö shaman came to view the Creator God of whom Christians spoke as more powerful than all the spirits (Ritchie, *Spirit*, 113–232, esp. 159, 214–15, 226–28, 237–38) and claims that spirits could desert or kill old shamans who were no longer useful (ibid., 226–27; cf. the fear in Koch, *Zulus*, 143).

382. E.g., Johnson, "Growing Church," 54–58; cf. De Wet, "Signs," passim; cf. accounts in Alexander, *Signs*, 95–114 (esp. 110–14). Anderson, "Exorcism," argues that "deliverance ministry" meets a felt need in Africa, helping fuel Pentecostal growth in Africa (see also Newell, "Witchcraft").

383. Cf. "contest stories," e.g., the Buddha competing with the Brahmin tradition, Hindu stories about Hindu sages overpowering Buddhist ones, and the like (Woodward, *Miracles*, 25). Fulani and Turawa spirits dislike each other (Krings, "History," 63). For the revival of Taiwanese folk religion since World War II, see Chin, "Practices," 1 (noting that 85 percent of people in Taiwan follow folk religion). Cf. various religions' practice of exorcism (e.g., Hien, "Yin Illness," 313–18; other sources in this appendix).

384. For possessing spirits complaining about Christian conversions, see, e.g., Field, "Possession," 8; spirits hostile to missionaries, e.g., Sandgren, "Kamba Christianity," 176 (in the late nineteenth century); Lema, "Chaga Religion," 55–56; conversion as a danger, Maddox, "Cigogo," 156; for Nkai (divinity) punishing a woman with blisters for attending church until she desisted, see Straight, *Miracles*, 171. Spirits are said to dislike Protestantism conversion, which some in Haiti undertake to escape "indebtedness" to uncooperative spirits, but some disillusioned with Protestantism convert back to Vodou (Michel, "Worlds," 35).

385. Barth, *Dogmatics*, 4.3:165ff., noted in Kauffman, "Introduction," 7–8.

that he carried: his scientific training stressed a naturalistic, empirical approach; his theological training emphasized theistic explanations. But he had lacked a functional category for superhuman activity other than that of the supreme God, despite its prevalence in parts of Scripture as well as belief in it in many cultures. In recent centuries, Western thought had left no intermediate category between God and the natural world, but in his dialogue with Indian Christians he came to believe that such a sphere existed.[386]

Presumably a significant proportion of this book's readers will have particularly Christian or biblical studies interests and will be interested in the sorts of conflictual encounters with spirits or those involved with them depicted in the Gospels and Acts (cf., e.g., Mark 1:21–28; 5:1–20; Acts 8:5–13; 13:8–11; 19:13–20). Missiologists frequently approach spirit phenomena very differently than nonmissionary anthropologists, often from the standpoint of what they call "power encounters."[387] Historically, Irenaeus attests that many nonbelievers in his day became Christians after experiencing successful exorcisms.[388]

More specifically missiological encounters are reported of ancient and medieval missionaries such as Patrick in Ireland, Columba in Scotland, and Boniface in Germany.[389] Boniface, for example, felled Thor's sacred oak and suffered no harm (a setting resembling "trial by ordeal").[390] Although the Enlightenment was increasingly viewing the speaking of other voices through individuals as mere deception,[391] John Wesley encountered persons he believed genuinely possessed,[392] and was reported to have cast out demons from those involuntarily possessed,

386. Hiebert, "Excluded Middle," 43. This omission of the preternatural that he notes is traced more fully in Daston, "Facts," 100–113.

387. Because missiologists' accounts are normally told from the Christian perspective and with Christian interests, they normally describe the advance of Christian faith rather than the advance of other, often competing movements.

388. Barrett-Lennard, *Healing*, 229. Barrett-Lennard concludes an examination of exorcism in Irenaeus and Athanasius by noting that in both sources full-scale exorcism seems to have been limited to nonbelievers (228, Athanasius allowing that Christians could be attacked but not possessed). But some ancient sources suggest that a spirit might remain until "the time of the final exorcism on the day before baptism" (266); the bishop functioned as the chief exorcist (274). Cf. also the probably fourth-century *Sacramentary of Sarapion* (277–323), in which Christians could "suffer from less serious forms of demonic attack," though probably not possession (323). The grandfather of fifth-century historian Sozomen was converted through the family witnessing a Christian instantly exorcise a spirit in Jesus's name, whereas pagans and others had failed to accomplish this by any means (Frend, "Place of Miracles," 11, citing Sozomen *H.E.* 5.15.14–17).

389. De Wet, "Signs," 87.

390. See Neill, *History of Missions*, 75; Latourette, *History of Christianity*, 348; Tucker, *Jerusalem*, 47. In the East, in Central Asia, the missionary Elijah likewise felled a sacred tree in a power encounter during the patriarchate of Timothy I (780–823; Young, "Miracles in History," 112, also noting his effectiveness in exorcisms).

391. Schmidt, "Possession," 279–92.

392. Ibid., 281; see, e.g., Wesley, *Journal* (1974), 81–83. Earlier, martyrologist John Foxe was known for successful exorcisms (Freeman, "Famous Miracle," 309). Wesley's father, Samuel, like many of his contemporaries, believed in ghosts (Handley, "Ghosts," esp. 345, 355); preachers employed these stories moralistically (Handley, "Ghosts," 348–49). Generally cf. idem, *Visions*.

yielding deliverance.[393] Early Methodist preachers in Wesley's day expelled demons from some who were possessed.[394] Lutheran pastor Johann Christian Blumhardt undertook a lengthy struggle in prayer until a person believed severely possessed and with an occult background was freed; this deliverance impacted the entire area and, he believed, broke a spiritual barrier.[395] Historians document reports of possession and exorcism throughout the history of the church but most commonly "on the border of the church with paganism," that is, when confronting power-related traditional religions.[396] Missiologists often cite the relevance of power encounters for reaching cultures today that affirm superhuman powers.[397]

Modern Examples of Power Encounters

Power encounters appear commonly in modern accounts of evangelization,[398] and both popular and academic literature offer numerous fairly recent examples of such power encounter claims, usually yielding conversions. For example, a recent convert to Catholicism, John Chukwu (1902–86), was cursed by witch doctors[399] and awoke blind; although physicians could not help him, he was healed when Father John (the priest) prayed and sprinkled on him consecrated water.[400] In the first quarter of the twentieth century, some villagers in southern Africa during a drought mocked the allegedly foreign Christian god who could not bring rain; Letwaba, the evangelist, promised rain the next day, after which the next day's

393. Tomkins, *Wesley*, 72.

394. Rack, "Healing," 147–49. For Wesley's views about the demonic world in their eighteenth-century context, see Webster, "Terrors." Cf. Baer, "Bodies," 47, for an early Free Methodist exorcism.

395. Ising, *Blumhardt*, 162–89, with clearly therapeutic results (175–76); cf. the gradual deliverance in 327 (and perhaps 327–28). He did not accept all alleged exorcisms, but eyewitness experience opened him to the reality of some (104). See further Macchia, *Spirituality*, 65–68.

396. Skarsaune and Engelsviken, "Possession" (quote from 85).

397. E.g., Hiebert, "Power Encounter," 56; Musk, "Popular Islam," 214–15; Parshall, "Lessons," 255–56.

398. E.g., De Wet, "Signs," 91, notes the following for more examples of power encounters: Johnson, "Authority," 102–11; Klassen, "Fire," 176–82; in Guatemala, Thomas, "Report," 252–55; in India, several studies (Devadason, "Missionary Societies," 179–91; Middleton, "Growth," 109–11; Sargunam, "Churches," 194–95; Shinde, "Animism," 261–62; Zechariah, "Factors," 122–23, 162–65); in Indonesia, Bruckner, "History," 137–87; in Mexico, Aulie, "Movement," 128–85; in Sri Lanka, both Chandy, "Discipling," 117–36, and Daniel, "Labour," 147–72; in the Solomon Islands, Tippett, *Solomon Islands Christianity*, 3–19, 42–44, 57–62, 100–111, 190–200; idem, *Verdict Theology*, passim; cf. recent claims of more ambiguous value in Bentley, *Miraculous*, 264, 284, 291, 300. For some recent power encounters in Asia, see Pothen, "Missions," 305–8; Yung, "Case Studies"; Ma, "Planting," 331–35; Khai, *Cross*, 143–44; Gulick, June 8, 13, 2011; cf. the summary about the effectiveness of power encounters in Guthrie, "Breakthrough," 26.

399. For the pervasiveness of witchcraft in Africa (so viewed by fellow Africans), sometimes even among Christians (to the dismay of other Christians), see, e.g., Jenkins, *New Faces*, 110–13 (including stories of conversions from occult backgrounds, some more plausible than others, 112–13). Divination is sometimes used to identify sorcery or witchcraft (e.g., Beattie and Middleton, "Introduction," xxiii; Field, "Possession," 11; Beattie, "Mediumship," 164; Gray, "Cult," 183; Middleton, "Possession," 225; cf. Garbett, "Mediums," 123); on witchcraft accusations, see discussion above. Nevertheless, despite exaggerations and many false accusations, some people do seek to practice malevolent sorcery (Shorter, *Witchcraft*, 99).

400. Protus, "Chukwu."

rainfall generated many converts.[401] Likewise, in early twentieth-century West Africa, Prophet Braide went against traditional religions and competed with the older powers; on one occasion when the dibia challenged him to see if his God could bring rain, he knelt and began praying, and within five minutes the rains fell.[402] He and the William Wadé Harris both succeeded in winning tens of thousands of their fellow Africans to Christianity especially through power encounters.[403]

My friend and coworker Dr. Rodney Ragwan recounted a story from his grandfather, Kisten Ragwan, an Indian Baptist tailor in Durban, northern KwaZulu-Natal, South Africa.[404] One morning a man entered Kisten's tailor shop and said, "Uncle, I will give you some 'medicine.'" (The "medicine" in this case was not merely herbal but related to traditional religion.) Kisten refused, noting that he was a Christian and accepted only the power of God. The man responded that his own power was superior to the power of the God of the Bible, and in the ensuing discussion Kisten agreed to the man's claim that that evening they would see which god was greater. "Around 12:00 tonight I will send a spirit," the man promised, "and you will see which god is more powerful." Being a man of prayer, Kisten fasted that day and then gathered his family around 11:30 to pray. Around 11:45, they heard giant footsteps around the house, which continued for about twenty minutes; Rodney's father remembers these vividly. The steps gradually subsided, and the family went to bed. The next morning at the tailor shop, the man shook Kisten's hand. "Uncle," he said, "my spirits could not get into your house—when they got there, there was fire around your house. Indeed, your God is powerful." Similar, independent reports appear elsewhere.[405]

These accounts fit larger patterns in confrontations claiming to represent competing forms of spiritual power.[406] Confrontations between different religious groups or individuals with an active view of spiritual power fit into a more general missiological use of the expression "power encounters."[407] In many traditional societies, such power encounters in more recent times have, as sometimes earlier, taken the

401. Lindsay, Lake, 48–49.
402. Koschorke, Ludwig, and Delgado, History, 223–24.
403. Hanciles, "Conversion," 170.
404. Rodney Ragwan, interview, Dec. 15, 2009. Rodney confirmed these details with his father (Kisten Ragwan's son) on Dec.16, in turn confirming this with me Dec. 17.
405. Koch, Zulus, 272–76, reports that another Indian in South Africa, suffering spiritual attacks from a Zulu sorcerer, was being physically "beaten by invisible powers" each night; temporarily delivered but unwilling to submit fully to Christ, he finally died from the spiritual abuse. Ayo Oritsejafor, a Nigerian preacher, reports that a man sent by spirits to disrupt his meeting found himself surrounded by a ring of fire; he gave up his charms and is now an usher in Oritsejafor's church (Oritsejafor, "Dealing," 97). When evangelizing an area known for pervasive witchcraft, Tari and his colleagues regularly heard "strange noises" outside their door, but nothing could penetrate it (Tari, Breeze, 136).
406. See, e.g., Olaiya, "Praying," 105–8. Asbury PhD student Samson Uytanlet (personal correspondence, Dec. 15, 2009) recounted two incidents in the Philippines where persons resisted Christians and their ability to free them from the spirits because the people would lose their "power"; in one case the person had angered the spirits by letting the Christians begin to drive the spirits back.
407. Of the three definitions in De Wet, "Signs," 82–83, I include the second (such as burning fetishes) but refer especially to the third, the "challenge-oriented power encounter in public." In traditional thought,

form of burning fetishes or felling a sacred tree or totem, without suffering the promised harmful effects.[408] Often when those who doubt a religious system defy its taboos and escape unscathed, many insiders are convinced and abandon the taboos.[409]

In one example from Indonesia, it was said that everyone who touched the bark of a particular sacred tree died within twenty-four hours. One Indonesian evangelist cut down and burned the tree; after he suffered no harm, a church was started there.[410] Power encounters are also reported with the spread of the Christian message in other parts of Asia, such as India.[411] People have burned fetishes and abandoned witch doctors due to power encounters in African nations[412] and elsewhere.[413]

The number of Protestants grew enormously in Haiti through confronting Vodun[414] and through power encounters there.[415] In one account, fifteen of the children of a polygynous voodoo priest[416] fell sick, and he found his rituals ineffective for curing them. Finally he solicited the prayers of Church of God pastor Edouard Joseph; the children were healed and became followers of Christ.[417] In one relatively recent report from Africa, when shamans gathered around a sacred

tales of power "help connect life narratives to the larger narrative, more holistic than the dominant scientific approach" (Kremer, "Tales of Power," esp. 45–46).

408. De Wet, "Signs," 82–83; Hiebert, "Power Encounter," 52–53; for some African examples, see Numbere, *Vision*, 96, 119, 124–25, 133–37, 142–43, 169–71, 191, 203, 209–11; cf. Burton, "Evangelism" (the final paragraph); William Wadé Harris in Shaw, *Awakening*, 56; Bartels, *Roots*, 174–78 (burning fetishes). For the spiritual power dimension in current missiology more generally (noting negative but esp. positive features), see Pocock, Van Rheenen, and McConnell, *Face*, 183–208. For Christian spiritual conflict with Umbanda, particularly involving Christian conversions, see Itioka, "Umbanda"; for conflict when dealing with folk religion, see Burnett, "Conflict."

409. See, e.g., Tippett, *People Movements*, 80–84, 164–67; De Wet, "Signs," 81; an example in Anderson, *Pelendo*, 49–55, 71–76, 139–43, 146–55, 158–59. In some cultures, to burn ancestral witchcraft paraphernalia is to invite an effective familial curse (Favret-Saada, *Witchcraft*, 130, 133); surviving such an action thus undermines the entire system of witchcraft belief. Traditional societies often attribute illness to ritual violations (e.g., Lake, *Healer*, 118).

410. Crawford, *Miracles*, 144–45.

411. Pothen, "Missions," 305–8.

412. In Uganda, see, e.g., Dunkerley, *Healing Evangelism*, 86; in an East African AIC, see Githieya, "Church," 241; in West Africa, see, e.g., Burgess, *Revolution*, 151 (among Igbo revivalists of the 1970s); Merz, "Witch," 203; Mayrargue, "Expansion," 286; in southern Africa, Koch, *Zulus*, 148, 152, 153, 199, 279; Braun, *Here*, 160–61. Burning fetishes has a long history (e.g., among nineteenth- and early twentieth-century Ghanaian Methodist converts, in Southon, *Methodism*, 99, 150; Joseph Babalola's preaching in 1930 Nigeria, in Davies and Conway, *Christianity*, 118; more recently, cf. the conversion of juju priests in early 1970s Nigeria in Numbere, *Vision*, 96, 134).

413. In some Asian contexts, see, e.g., Danyun, *Lilies*, 331; Park, "Spirituality," 52–53; Jones, *Wonders*, 104; Samuel, "Gatherings," in India; Koch, *Zulus*, 111, digressing on Indonesia; Tari, *Wind*, 27, 43; idem, *Breeze*, 21, 137. For a Western equivalent, cf. Crandall, *Raising*, 78, 86–88.

414. Johnson, "Growing Church," 54–58.

415. E.g., destroying an "indestructible" sacred rock, in Johnson, "Growing Church," 55–56.

416. Although often treated as unique in Western Christian reports, Vodun preserves large measures of traditional African religion from what is now Benin and from the Congo-Angola region (Fleurant, "Music," 47; Clérismé, "Vodoun," 60; Michel, Bellegarde-Smith, and Racine-Toussaint, "Mouths," 75).

417. A report from Lloyd Frazier, among reports sent to me by Douglas LeRoy, Nov. 9, 2009.

tree were cursing the Christians' God (during a meeting of Christians seven miles away), lightning destroyed the tree, apparently producing a widespread response.[418]

Such confrontations have occurred in the Philippines. Some mountain families in the Philippines would spend several years' wages to buy sacrificial pigs prescribed by traditional exorcists to seek deliverance for a possessed family member. A local Christian leader began successfully exorcising the possessed without fees, and often accomplishing what traditional exorcists could not.[419] Traditional Kankana-eys (a tribal group in the northern Philippines) practice animism and ancestor worship, but when people are healed through Christian prayer rather than through contact with ancestors, families and even communities sometimes turn to Christian faith.[420]

In Manila in 1953, the possession of seventeen-year-old Clarita Villanueva, who had been repeatedly bitten by spirits in the Bilibid prison, attracted national media attention. The observed and well-documented exorcism that followed was likewise publicized, resulting in what some estimate were many thousands of conversions.[421] In a church known for healings and exorcisms in Mindanao, Philippines, one informant who saw some other miracles firsthand related an incident he heard about from shortly before his arrival there. A possessed person announced, "We will come at 7:00 p.m." At 7:00 p.m., the power went out, and the person declared, "See, I told you, there are more of us now." But despite their show of power, the spirits were all cast out.[422]

---

418. Chavda, *Miracle*, 9–10, 128–29, including photographs (between 78 and 79) and the claim of eyewitnesses. In Nigerian evangelism, extraordinary lightning attacks have also been construed as power encounters (Numbere, *Vision*, 165), as also storms and other phenomena for which wizards claimed credit (Numbere, *Vision*, 209). Koch, *Zulus*, 157, portrays some witch doctors as able to cause storms (cf. Rev 13:13), though here countered by Christ (with lightning). One of my students, Paul Mokake, has shared several eyewitness accounts of power encounters in his homeland of northern Cameroon (noting demonstrations of supernatural power from both sides, including those involving weather conditions). Claims of weather conditions changing during some traditional religions' rituals also appear (Turner, "Advances," 43, although the connection between the ritual and the weather is only implicit, and only one case is cited; cf. Kinnear, *Tide*, 92–96).

419. Cole, "Model," 264, regarding his friend, Rev. Antonio Caput Sr., who also demands the destruction of fetishes (265).

420. Ma, "Encounter," 136; see more fully idem, *Spirit*. The forms of Christianity most relevant in such traditional religious contexts emphasizing spiritual power are those that also emphasize spiritual power (Ma, "Worldviews," 20).

421. The ministry of Lester Sumrall in May 1953, in Johnson, *History*, 77–78 (brought to my attention in idem, personal correspondence, Feb. 20, 2009); Stewart, *Only Believe*, 94–97. The reports claim that a physician, police, and reporters were in attendance at the time of the exorcism and name some of them. Sumrall, *Story*, 7–36, extensively quotes Manila newspapers by name and date, including concerning the biting phenomenon, which many took to be genuine spirit activity. Dr. Mariano B. Lara, then chief medical examiner of the Manila Police Department and a university professor of pathology and legal medicine, was convinced of the genuineness of the possession and exorcism and provided his own description, recounted at length in Sumrall, *Story*, 37–83; more concisely, see Lara, "Report." For spirit-afflicted persons being assaulted by the spirits elsewhere, see also the brief accounts by Dr. H. C. Moolenburgh (*Meetings*, 154). More recently in Manila, see "Priest in war."

422. Chester Allan Tesoro, interview, Jan. 30, 2009.

A missionary doctor reports that someone who wished to stab him was unable to withdraw the knife from its scabbard, and that such incidents convinced many locals that Christ was more powerful than the spirits.[423] Cameroonian Christians exorcised a person known to be insane; his immediate and full recovery led to many conversions in the community.[424] Many Indian evangelists pray and fast, then minister to those who are held to be possessed; word of deliverances from spirits spreads, opening the community to the gospel.[425] After Micronesian pastor Steve Malakai began to rebuke the spiritual powers dominant in the ruins of an ancient sacrificial site, widespread healings, deliverances, and conversions followed.[426] A Sri Lankan evangelist notes that he cast out demons, and converts turned over talismans and charms; people expected him to suffer harm, but he did not.[427] *Jesus Film* workers around the world have also frequently reported power encounters.[428]

Power Encounters That Persuade Religious Competitors

Some accounts involve conflict between religious practitioners or narrate the superiority of one over another. I noted above the report of Garrick Braide's success against the dibia.[429] In 1971, when a juju priestess was influencing his family, young Nigerian Christian Geoffrey Numbere confronted her in Jesus's name. She began staggering, lost her powers, and permanently lost her mind; Geoffrey's family was converted.[430] In an account not involving direct confrontation, a South African witch doctor told a mute, new Christian that he could not help her, but when her Christian friends prayed for her, she was healed.[431]

Displays of spiritual power have sometimes led practitioners of one religion to switch allegiances. Thus, for example, in the late 1940s, a Congolese evangelist named Peter faced opposition from a witch doctor named Kasumba. When Kasumba fell sick and his fellow witch doctors could not help him, someone robed in white instructed him in a dream to have Peter pray for him; although Kasumba was healed, he immediately reverted to his opposition. The pattern was repeated three

---

423. Lees and Fiddes, "Healed," 25.

424. Paul Mokake (interview, May 13, 2009), as one of the people who prayed and witnessed the healing. Other societies can also associate possession with "madness"; see, e.g., Kasule, "Possession," 299, 303 (for Uganda); Mbiti, *Religions*, 227; for ancient Mediterranean associations, see appendix A.

425. Dunkerley, *Healing Evangelism*, 169–70; in many of these communities, this is the only available inroad for teaching a message differing from the traditional one. Yohannan, *Revolution*, 21, 30, also notes frequent deliverance from demonization in India.

426. Wayne and Judy Cagle supplied me with their written reports from fall 1992, which they confirmed for me orally (Jan. 25, 2009).

427. Daniel, "Labour," 158–59.

428. E.g., Eshleman, *Jesus*, 108 (Indonesia), 110–11 (India), 111–12 (Thailand).

429. Koschorke, Ludwig, and Delgado, *History*, 223–24.

430. Numbere, *Vision*, 40–41. For other encounters, see 125–26, 170.

431. Johns, "Name." I include the story here and not in the part of the book recounting healing narratives because no organic cause for her six months of muteness was found.

times, but the third time Kasumba became a committed Christian and eventually an elder in the young village church.[432]

Albert Bissouessoue told us various accounts of spiritual conflict, including one already recounted (where Jesus raised a dead girl in Etoumbi that traditional spirit practitioners could not).[433] Here I focus on his account from Etoumbi, March 1987, when an anguished man confessed that he belonged to a traditional cult and had made a pact with the spirits to have a good life provided they could take his life on a particular date and time. Now the date was three days away, at midnight, and he wanted to confess to someone because he lamented leaving behind his family. Papa Bissouessoue explained that Jesus Christ could free him from this evil bondage; the man returned in twenty minutes with all the objects related to the pact, and Papa Bissouessoue burned them. When the appointed time came, Papa Bissouessoue and his wife experienced a deep spiritual battle, and Papa Bissouessoue says that he witnessed the devil himself. But they were crying out to Jesus, and the time passed with no harm to the man, who quickly entrusted himself to Christ. Today he is an influential lay leader in the Catholic parish of Brazzaville.

Likewise, Korean shaman Bok-hee Lim viewed the prayers of Christians in her neighborhood as a confrontation between their God and her "demigods." Ultimately persuaded that the one God of the Christians is greater, she finally gathered five carloads of "the clothes and equipment that she used for her practice and burned them all," and then she "destroyed the little temple for her god of shamanism in her backyard."[434]

Similarly, when a woman in northern Thailand became the first Christian in her village in 1963, the traditional priest mocked her as she fell sick and apparently died. When the Christians who had joined her prayed, however, she recovered and began telling villagers "their previously unknown secrets"; the priest's son became a Christian and eventually an elder in that church.[435] In Tibet, a former priest (once attached to a lamasery) was dying after seven years of sickness, unable to eat; when a Christian invited to pray did so, and the family responded to his admonitions to destroy ties with other spirits, the man recovered and all his friends attributed this recovery to Jesus.[436] In Myanmar, it is reported that a village priest close to death was healed and converted.[437]

---

432. Hodgson, "Sorcerer" (referring to Belgian Congo, now the Democratic Republic of Congo). On the second occasion, the recovery appears natural, but the protection from death appears supernatural.

433. Another account involved his recognition, in late 1986, that something was wrong with the pastor in training; eventually the man began to lose his mind and was delivered only when he confessed and allowed Papa Bissouessoue to burn the fetishes he had kept for protection. He now has a thriving ministry (Papa Bissouessoue named the man, his location, and many details that I am not using here). All of these accounts are from the interview by Emmanuel Moussounga, Dec. 17, 2009.

434. Park, "Spirituality," 52–53.

435. Remaining an elder at the time of writing in Gardner, *Healing Miracles*, 138.

436. William Christie (the person who prayed) in Fant, *Miracles*, 110–12. The restored man joined the missionaries in evangelizing and lived healthily twelve years until his sudden death, which some attributed to poisoning (Fant, *Miracles*, 112–13).

437. Khai, "Pentecostalism," 269.

Early in the Timor revival in Indonesia, many destroyed their charms and fetishes.[438] Indonesian Christians tell of a traditional priest who saw the spirits with
which he had worked depart after visiting Christians prayed; the priest and village
were converted.[439] One powerful witch doctor in central Java, who claims that her
magic had killed at least a thousand people and describes the normal manner of
their death,[440] was informed of Jesus through a vision, never having known Christians or about Christianity. When she became a Christian and faced hostility from
her relatives, she sold everything that she had.[441] When a witch doctor stood against
a Maasai believer's witness, the witch doctor fell to the ground and was converted.[442]

During the healing campaign of black South African evangelist Isak Thlape in
Viljoenskroon in 1978, an influential shaman knotted many charms into his hair,
then got in the healing line so he could see what was happening. When Thlape
prayed, everyone in line fell to ground at the same time—including the shaman.
He was semiconscious for more than five minutes, and when he recovered full
consciousness, he found "that all his hair into which the amulets and charms were
knotted, had literally fallen out of his head." He quickly became a public follower
of Christ.[443]

Converted to Christianity, a witch in West Africa destroyed his witchcraft paraphernalia[444] and eventually experienced greater spiritual power, which he claims to
have used to deliver others from witchcraft.[445] Ineba Ojuka, a priestess of the sea

438. Wiyono, "Timor Revival," 278–79, 282; York, "Indigenous Missionaries," 250–51. Indonesian
shamans converted to Christianity burned their fetishes (Tari, Breeze, 21, 24).

439. Tari, Wind, 37–40.

440. In Knapstad, "Power," 84, she mixed "black magic" with verses from the Qur'an and a mantra "and
use[d] the spirit of the dead to cause the persons to die. After I said the mantra, the people would vomit
blood and then die." Two other informants also confirmed her description of killing by witchcraft (84).
The daughter of a witch doctor, being trained to be his successor but converted to Christianity, attested
that her father had killed many through witchcraft (89).

441. Knapstad, "Power," 83–85 (based on his interview with her).

442. Eshleman, Jesus, 14–15.

443. De Wet, "Signs," 84–85, noting (91n2) that the evangelist narrated the event to him and eyewitnesses later confirmed it. For southern African conversions of those confessing that they had practiced
witchcraft, see also stories in Koch, Zulus, 136–37, 143–44, 144–45, 147–48, 150, 153. Venter, Healing,
253, notes the exorcism of some African spiritists, effective only once their fetishes were burned. Pothen,
"Missions," 189, reports that in Gujarat and Maharashtra in the 1980s, many sorcerers turned instead to
Christ; in Africa, Baker, Miracles, 53, notes occasions (including six former shamans in one church); also
the conversion of shamans mentioned in Alexander, Signs, 89, 110; those converted in Anderson, Pelendo,
119, 155–58; a case in Miracle Investigation; another apparent case in Marszalek, Miracles, 160; hundreds
of Alauts (local practitioners of witchcraft) converted in Tari, Breeze, 136. A report sent to me by Asian
evangelist Vasanth Edward (March 10, 2007, about events of the preceding weeks) notes that one day he
warned against witchcraft; one woman, long paralyzed by witchcraft, was healed as she heard that message, and that night someone known for witchcraft died, leading to many conversions. Eshleman, Jesus,
108, describes the inversion of a witch doctor's curse (harming opponents rather than supporters of the
Jesus Film workers). Some market witch conversion testimonies (Ukah and Echtler, "Witches," 77–79).

444. Merz, "Witch," 203.

445. Ibid., 213. In his cultural worldview (but not in Scripture; cf., e.g., Acts 8:19–23), he had a sort of
spiritual charisma naturally, which could be used for evil witchcraft or God's service (213–14, Merz warning
also on 214 that some Nigerian Pentecostals have acted in ways very much like the witches they condemn).

goddess Akaso, was instantly healed of long-standing ailments (arthritis, a decade of chronic coughing, and near blindness) and converted in an evangelism meeting in southern Nigeria.[446] Converted through a dream, a witch doctor in Borneo burned his charms, and, against his culture's traditional expectations, he remains well.[447] Finding himself and his colleagues unable to attack a Cuban evangelist, the leader of an occult group publicly converted.[448]

When Indian village priests who had previously used witchcraft to kill found themselves unable to harm an Indian Christian, they became believers.[449] One local priestess in India, though known for power to inflict sickness and death, became completely paralyzed below the neck for three years. Sacrifices and petitions failed to alleviate her condition, but when an Indian Christian prayed for her, she was instantly healed, and soon was running, praising the Christian God. She was the first of many in her village to become a believer in Jesus.[450]

Readers in contexts of confrontation with traditional power religions thus find valuable relevance in ancient power encounters like those described in Acts 8:9–13; 13:8–12; 19:11–20; or other narratives like Exod 7:10–12.[451] Ancient Christians accepted the reality of spirits besides God but believed that in any confrontation, their God would readily overcome all other spirits not submitted to him.[452]

Some Personal and Family Experiences

While I personally believe that God often works with people in terms that they understand, I also find much current discussion about spiritual warfare inconsistent with biblical teaching and am uncomfortable with the explanations of many who practice "deliverance" routinely in popular settings. (I do not deny that some experience these occasions positively for psychological or spiritual reasons.) Nevertheless, to simply reject the possibility of genuine spirit experiences because of plentiful abuses, as many do, risks an uncritical overreaction.

I long resisted including any of my or my family's accounts here, because for some reason some consider experiences from one or one's immediate circle (like those of Pascal) more of a bias than extrapolation from nonexperience (like that of Hume's circle). Nevertheless, I have ultimately decided to follow the example

---

446. Numbere, *Vision*, 189–90. She maintained her new faith despite the hostility of other members of her former religion.

447. Green, *Asian Tigers*, 108.

448. Alamino, *Footsteps*, 34–35; another dramatic power encounter and deliverance of an occult priest appears on 40.

449. Yohannan, *Revolution*, 21. The priests reported fire and angels protecting the believer.

450. Ibid., 204–5.

451. That the Egyptians would have understood Moses's signs so differently from the Israelites (as more like a circus performance) suggests the importance of perspective (or "faith") in power encounters (cf. LaCocque, "Competition," 95). For ancient Egyptian snake charming, see Currid, *Egypt*, 94–95.

452. On early biblical miracles in competition with claims of other deities, starting with the paradigmatic plagues in Exodus, see, e.g., Tucker, "Miracles," 378. For the plagues from Egypt's religious perspective (cf. Exod 12:12), see, e.g., Hoffmeier, *Israel*, 149–53; cf. *Pesiq. Rab.* 17:5.

of the experientially oriented anthropologists and offer some experiences, the interpretations of which may be debated by others. I do not care to report all my or my family's experiences that could be relevant, but I narrate some samples here to illustrate why I take seriously some African and other reports about spirits, although these particular examples do not involve possession behavior.

Nearly four years after my conversion from atheism and several years before I had reimbibed much academic skepticism, I was visiting a recently converted widow when I felt that God's Spirit led me to a door, which I found then led me into a dark basement. As I descended the stairs, I felt that the widow's husband's "ghost" was behind another door in the basement, but according to the basic theology I had imbibed, this spirit could only really be a demon. Once I commanded it to leave in Jesus's name, it departed; the widow then informed me that her husband's belongings were stored in that room and that he had been involved with the occult. She also informed me that a year earlier she had dated a man who claimed to have psychic powers, who claimed that the ghost of her husband was in that room and tried to exorcise it; it chased him away instead.[453]

While that experience fit my theological and cultural understanding at the time, the following experiences of myself or my relatives did not.[454] In September 2006, one of my Congolese brothers-in-law, Dr. Jacques Emmanuel Moussounga, was the object of hostility from some people openly known to employ witchcraft. During this period, in a dream a snake bit his heels, and he awoke to find two physical holes in his heels. His legs gradually became immobilized as the poison spread up his legs, until he prayed with a person known for her prayerfulness; then he recovered. A PhD in chemistry from a French university, he noted that he never would have believed it had he not experienced it himself.

One of these hostile people insisted that Emmanuel visit him; because he was a relative[455] and it was therefore a family obligation, Emmanuel went. No sooner

453. See further Keener, *Gift*, 64–65.

454. Lagerwerf, *Witchcraft*, 62, speaks of experience with possession altering a minister's prior theological approach.

455. Although I do not know the full motivation in this case, witchcraft is usually believed to be directed against relatives and neighbors (Bond, "Ancestors," 142; Reynolds, *Magic*, 44; in nineteenth-century Germany, cf. perhaps Ising, *Blumhardt*, 177, though Ising seems skeptical). Binsbergen, "Witchcraft," 243, notes that one very widespread belief in Africa is the assumption that among those who achieve significant power in any domain, political or otherwise, "a close kinsman needs to be sacrificed or to be nominated as victim of occult, antisocial forces," and he further notes that he has "extensive reasons" for viewing this as reflecting real practices. Africans I know cite numerous examples, and it is difficult to believe otherwise: if such a belief is pervasive, then given human nature it is likely that some would indulge in it, especially concerning relatives they do not like. Even without occult connections and a recognized tradition of kin jealousy, many Westerners are ready to sacrifice family for success. The only grandparent my wife knew growing up was her mother's father, after he was reconciled with his daughter. The man had seemed very nice, but the family usually avoided his brother, who openly boasted about practicing witchcraft. One day the brother demanded all the possessions of Médine's grandfather, who was not a Christian. The grandfather refused, to which the brother replied, "We'll see." Her grandfather fell sick with a fever that night and died the next day. This was widely understood as being due to witchcraft. We know more recent, closer and multiply attested examples of witchcraft attempts on family members. Witchcraft

had he left their domicile than he felt so sick that he thought that he would die, recovering only after much prayer. Later, discounting the matter as coincidence, he visited the man again at the latter's insistence and suffered the same overwhelming, nearly paralyzing sickness. Seeking prayer, he stumbled into the home of another member of his church, known for the gift of prophecy. No sooner had he entered than she demanded, "Where have you been that you should not have gone?" Although she had no natural means of knowing about the person who had sought his harm, she declared that the Lord had shown her the person's name; it was the right name.[456]

Emmanuel recounted an incident in which a boy in his Sunday school was dying of the same mysterious sickness that had claimed the lives of the boy's two close friends. Fearful about his prognosis, the boy confessed what the three had done. An older man they met on the street had promised that they would become powerful government ministers, provided they kept this pact secret from anyone else. Then he had taken blood from each of them (not entirely voluntarily, especially for the youngest).[457] Soon after this event, the oldest of the three boys dreamed that this older man and three others stabbed him; he awoke ill that morning and died in December. The day that the first boy died, the second boy had the same dream, then fell sick; he died in February. That day the third boy had the same dream and fell sick, and he was so afraid that in about May he confessed this information. The Sunday school teachers who knew him, including Emmanuel, fasted during the day for nine days, then came together to pray for the boy. Emmanuel felt the Spirit strongly as they prayed, and the boy was healed that night.[458]

In July 2008, my wife and I spent time in Congo, so our marriage and support for the family became a matter of common knowledge even to those who wished to harm the family. A few months later, on December 6, I was experiencing what felt like such an unusual and unnaturally dramatic spiritual assault I was literally not

---

claims are not, of course, limited to families. In 2000, my then-future wife told me the story of a church in Congo where the new pastor killed a "sacred" animal being kept for rituals in the sanctuary, and the next day eight or nine deacons, who had syncretistically bound their lives with its life, died. The story, though secondhand, illustrates local beliefs.

456. Oct. 29, 2008 (I believe the visit may have been on Oct. 28). She also said she saw him being "electrocuted." That was not literal, but it was relevant. We had previously warned him not to go, in connection with a nightmare in which I had seen him being detained and being electrocuted. On another occasion (reported to us on Oct. 16, 2008; the events very probably happened that day or possibly the day before), both this woman and a child independently heard the same spiritual warning about the child's safety at the same time; unknown to the woman, the child had fallen very sick, but was able to recover once extricated from the situation.

457. As I discovered later, some other African peoples also appear to report this practice for some witchcraft rituals; see Koch, *Zulus*, 118.

458. Interview (Brazzaville, July 25, 2008), concerning events from that year. On April 16, 2010, we confirmed (phone interview) that the boy remains well. Western Christians who deny the possibility of any non-Christian spiritual power ought not attribute their skepticism to the biblical authors. At the same time, although many texts do link such power with individuals (e.g., Exod 7:12; Mark 13:22; 2 Thess 2:9; Rev 13:13–15), the larger picture considers the powers behind such activity (Eph 6:12). Moreover, Christians can cite biblical limits in Num 23:8; 2 Sam 16:12; Prov 26:2.

sure that I would survive the day. The next day, as I was recovering, I was walking with my wife and son, and we stopped under a particular strong tree, about three stories tall. No sooner had we followed my son's advice to walk a few steps away than the tree fell without warning, precisely where we had been standing, blocking the small road. Had it fallen a few seconds earlier, all three of us would have been crushed to death. I believe that this is the only tree I have ever witnessed falling (though I have of course seen fallen trees), yet out of hundreds of trees in view that day, and all the different ways that it could have fallen, it fell precisely where we had been standing seconds before. We came back and happily photographed the tree before the property owners called in a crew for it to be sawed and removed. The roots had not come up, but it looked as if the trunk had been cut through, and the wood appeared completely healthy.[459]

When Médine's brother went for prayer, the person prophesied that those employing witchcraft had tried to target us, to eliminate our support for the family; when the attack on my psyche proved ineffective, the hostile spirit settled in a tree that was twisting about, an image that made little sense to this woman until Médine's brother explained what had happened. She said that God had protected us, in part because of what God had called me to do. On December 15, 2008, an Ethiopian Pentecostal prophet prophesied about spirits having tried to kill me but being thwarted by God. He also gave various other relevant details about my life, including about this and another book, which something did not want written, without knowing anything about me, that I am an author, or the recent events.

To my recollection, no one had ever prophesied to me previously about spirits trying to kill me, or even about spirits per se; certainly no one had prophesied to me about a demon-afflicted tree. While I was fairly unfamiliar with African discourse about witchcraft, however, I was quite familiar with particular individuals who sometimes prophesied quite accurately (as opposed to random persons whose prophecies were more hit-and-miss). These were among the more accurate prophets. I felt deeply shaken by these events and their interpretation, which challenged elements of my worldview. For me as a Western Christian academician, these African-related experiences represented an entirely different world.

Of course there are the terribly frequent abuses, exaggerations, and psychological projections involved in many spirit beliefs and practices; after a few frightening experiences, it is easy for one to begin wrongly reading every mishap as a sign of witchcraft, especially within a cultural sphere that would reinforce that belief. Is it possible, however, that at least some actual spirit experiences lay originally and occasionally behind these wider beliefs? Like any of us when we fit evidence within an interpretive grid, those who invariably prefer purely materialistic explanations regularly prove resourceful and creative and would undoubtedly explain some of the above events as the result of suggestion and the others as mere coincidence. Because it is not impossible to construe them differently if necessary, my examples

459. I recorded the incidents in some notes at the time, in addition to the photographs.

do not offer incontrovertible proof to the contrary. Nevertheless, given our cumulative experiences (including but not limited to those narrated above), I hope that I can be forgiven for personally suspecting that, whatever the excesses, Africa may yet know some things that the West has forgotten.

Conclusion

Possession experiences are documented so widely that their appearance in ancient sources such as the Gospels and Acts should not surprise us. Although some ancient descriptions appear in fictitious sources, even these sources likely depend ultimately on information derived from traditions of genuine possession behavior, and we cannot rule out the possibility of eyewitness traditions in other ancient descriptions. We may interpret these claims in various ways, but they do call into question the curiously modern Western idea, held by some, that exorcism reports (replete with speaking spirits) can represent only legend and never eyewitness claims. Regardless of who stands behind Acts' "we" source, for example, Paul's stay in Philippi was part of it, and the first-person narrator persists at least long enough to know of the pythoness's proclamation (Acts 16:16–17).[460]

The meaning of possession experiences is debated, and possibly multiple, complementary models are helpful for explaining different aspects of such experiences or different kinds of cases. Exorcism is reported in many societies, often with therapeutic effects (at least sometimes due to local expectations, but in some reports possibly involving paranormal factors). Missiologists show, however, that power encounters often occur when worldviews that depend on spiritual power come into conflict. Along with other information, this perspective makes sense of the widespread tradition of Jesus's and his early followers' frequent use of exorcism.

460. The "we" is not explicit on the day of the event (Acts 16:18) but also does not figure into any of the action reported there, so it would not have reason to be mentioned. Even assuming that the narrator had taken that day off (which is not clear but is possible), it is difficult to suppose that he would not have heard the firsthand report afterward (Acts 16:40).

Appendix C

Comparisons with Later Christian Hagiography

The usual historiographic procedure is to examine proposed parallels from the milieu of the works in question, not from a milieu that existed only centuries later. Although I have addressed healing claims in this book from a much later period than those in the Gospels and Acts (most frequently from our own era), these comparisons are for the purpose of addressing philosophic questions specifically regarding miracles and the possibility of eyewitness claims, not for adducing literary parallels. Medieval hagiography is not a genuine literary parallel, nor does it often provide the sociological sort of parallel to eyewitnesses and secondhand sources claiming miracles that the modern reports I have included do. It can illustrate that late accounts can include substantial elaboration or fiction, but that premise is not in dispute, though given the dates of our documents, it is also less relevant than some suppose. I must, however, survey some examples of later Christian hagiography because these have been cited by others as a determinative grid for interpreting first-century miracle accounts.

Methodological Questions

On occasion, some scholars have compared the Gospels and Acts not only with pagan and Jewish accounts from their own time or the centuries immediately following but also with medieval hagiography and later German folktales.[1] The

1. Cf. medieval saints' lives in Dibelius, *Tradition*, 177 (following K. L. Schmidt); anchorite traditions in Dibelius, *Tradition*, 172–76; German and other folktales in, e.g., Bultmann, *Tradition* (1963), 229 (or

nature of these stories' preservation and growth differs substantially from that of first-century biographies (like the Gospels) and historical monographs (like Acts). Scholars have long recognized a significant difference between legends often accumulated over centuries, on the one hand, and first- and second-generation sources, on the other.[2] As one writer a century ago noted, "As a rule, the miraculous element is exhibited in these medieval biographies of saints very much in proportion to the interval of time between the events and the date of writing."[3] He contrasts the more modest claims offered for Martin of Tours nearer his decease with more fantastic claims offered by Ailred centuries after his protagonist Ninian,[4] though he finds significant oral elaboration even in the life of Columba, written a century after his passing.[5] Yet stories of Jesus's healings appear in Mark within a generation, and healings appear in "we" material even in the final chapter of Acts, closer in time to that work's composition. As such, closer functional analogies for the rapid rise of claims in the Gospels and Acts should be with the sorts of modern signs claims I cite later in this book, which appeal to eyewitnesses.

One can hardly call such first-generation claims "legendary accretions" such as we have in the hagiographic literature. Even a cursory reading of the healing accounts that I have noted in the book will reveal that some of them, including my own, are recalled years or even decades after the event. While this means that some details will be vague or forgotten, however, it hardly means that the events were invented; neither I nor any of my informants was suffering from dementia. In fact, the more dramatic the experience, and the more often it has been rehearsed, the more that it will be remembered, albeit in the fixed form surrounding the details most often rehearsed.[6] Records of firsthand memories from the witness's lifetime, particularly recent years, differ from second- or thirdhand accounts often generations later and without identifiable witnesses. The first two generations are far less likely to generate legendary accretions on average than are later sources.

"fairy" stories, e.g., 6, 229, 236); elaboration in Renaissance artwork in Bultmann, *Tradition*, 317; also comparison with a Buddhist tale of water walking in Dibelius, *Tradition*, 116; idem, *Jesus*, 84; Bultmann, *Tradition*, 237. Early form critics readily identified many Gospel materials as legends, often through content criticism (e.g., Dibelius, *Tradition*, 104–32l; in Acts, Dibelius, *Studies in Acts*, 24–25). Karris, *Saying*, 41, calls Luke "the first hagiographer," though not necessarily implying that Luke follows the later elaborative techniques. More recently, Borg, *Vision*, 74n37, has compared a third-century bishop who, after his decapitation, carried his head to his church and "sang the mass"; he does not provide a date for the tradition. None of these analogies is as extreme as Schamoni, *Parallelen*, who (according to Sabourin, *Miracles*, 265) uses later practices for canonizing saints as parallels to early Christian miracles.

2. E.g., Bernard, "Miracle," 392, who dates most Gospel reports within a half century of the events narrated (390); cf. Young, "Miracles in History," 115. In the early Roman Empire, biographies of persons from the previous generation or two tend to be substantially historical (see data in Keener, "Otho"; cf. "Assumptions"), as opposed to works involving characters from centuries past.

3. Wilson, "Miracles," 22.

4. Ibid., 22–23.

5. Ibid., 23–26 (esp. 23).

6. See Bauckham, *Eyewitnesses*, 331–34. I can often recall faces, feelings, and other details of such events three decades ago that I never deliberately memorized, though of course I cannot recall all the events and conversations that I would recall had the events taken place only last night.

Of course, we do see hagiographic embellishment in various ancient sources, whether second-century apocryphal gospels and acts[7] or in pseudepigraphic stories valorizing the patriarchs or *1 Enoch* reporting Noah's miraculous birth. But second-century gospels and acts (using the model of more accurate first-century sources) are generally more than a century later than the characters they depict,[8] and haggadah about earlier Jewish heroes many centuries after the sources first reporting those characters. Embellishment becomes more common in third- and fourth-century descriptions of earlier works,[9] and the tendency grew in time. Especially following ca. 1000 C.E., when hagiographic miracle collections became part of the growing canonization process, miracle accounts were used propagandistically by those campaigning for a location's or order's saint.[10] These included not only claims of miracles worked during the saint's life (the greater analogy to be made with the Gospels and Acts) but also claims of posthumous miracles.[11] Some of these traditions will be earlier and more reliable than others,[12] but historians must approach them very critically, especially in cases where sources date from many generations after the miracle in question.

Because some scholars have employed medieval hagiography for comparisons (at least pleasantly, since it offers graphic ones), I want to offer the reader here a taste of later hagiography, including at greatest length a case from one of my favorite later stories.[13] It is admittedly more fanciful than most of the second- and third-century apocryphal works, though even these are far enough removed from our first-century sources about Jesus and his first followers (see the fuller discussion of these sources in the introduction to my commentary on Acts).[14] Clearly hagiographic

7. Cf., e.g., Bultmann, *Tradition*, 241 (citing *Gos. Nic.* 7); Dibelius, *Tradition*, 106 (citing, e.g., *Acts John* 38ff.; *Acts Paul* 33); cf. Dibelius, *Tradition*, 273 (citing *Odes Sol.* 24; Ignatius *Eph.* 18.2; Justin *Dial.* 28.3).

8. Cf. also discussion in Blomberg, *Gospels*, 113–15, and the sources he cites. Their heyday, like that of Greek novels, is the late second and early third centuries (Aune, *Dictionary of Rhetoric*, 322).

9. Frost, *Healing*, 162.

10. See Andric, *Miracles*, 2. Analogous techniques in inquisition procedures show how testimony was often selected and shaped to fit objectives (Goodich, "History," 135–37), though much valuable information nevertheless survived (see, e.g., Goodich, "History," 152–56). For medieval understanding of miracles ca. 1000–1215, see Ward, *Miracles*. For the development of the conception of miracles ca. 1150–1350, see Goodich, *Miracles*; for their apologetic use against theological competitors such as Waldensians, Cathars, and Jews, see Goodich, *Miracles*, 69.

11. Andric, *Miracles*, 3.

12. Cf. also other cautions, e.g., in Goodich, *Miracles*, 87: "in canonization cases the canon lawyers, notaries, and theologians who were charged with determining the authenticity of miracles received a list of questions to which witnesses testifying under oath were asked to respond." The requirement of sworn depositions arose under Innocent III (1198–1216; Bolton, "Signs," 165); note also "vivid local details" in some accounts (Bolton, "Signs," 168).

13. Elsewhere, while hagiographies can echo the Gospels and Acts, they also can include fanciful tales not originally meant to be taken seriously. Such "pure fairy-tale incidents" include "when a missionary crosses the sea on a floating altar, or a monk hangs his clothes on a sunbeam" (Ashe, *Miracles*, 66, noting that such folklore is "often adapted from pre-Christian legend").

14. Keener, *Acts*, introduction ch. 2. Most scholars recognize the similarities of these later works to novels; see, e.g., Aune, *Environment*, 151–52; Lalleman, "Apocryphal Acts," 67; Rebenich, "Historical Prose," 307–8; Bauckham, "Acts of Paul"; Keylock, "Distinctness," 210; Krasser, "Reading," 554; Hofmann,

practices grew over time. Some critics occasionally cite later hagiography against our first-century sources' reliability,[15] but I would cite such material, if at all, to the opposite effect, believing that contrasts should be obvious. That is, while modern Western antisupernaturalists may lump all miracle accounts together, a more critical approach should be able to distinguish among different kinds of miracle reports, including the usual contrast between first- or second-generation sources and later ones that reflect considerable development. I have already argued that the NT accounts preserve the basic core of the events.[16] The tendency of some hagiography to emphasize the saints more than the God who answered their prayers drew some reactions even in antiquity[17] and may reflect the milieu of hero cults in late antiquity.[18]

Various Tales

Stories of saints written closer to their time in general carry more historical reminiscences; those written centuries later can sometimes be almost pure fiction.[19] Later accounts were also often contextualized for local interests; Andean culture, which had flying religious figures, envisioned St. Francis as flying.[20] Probably an early case of hagiography surrounds St. Helena's discovery of Jesus's true cross at Golgotha. There is very strong evidence that the site of the Holy Sepulchre is near the place of Jesus's original tomb, in the early second century already venerated as a holy site that Hadrian sought to desecrate.[21] Notwithstanding such evidence, there is no clear connection to Helena having a revelation about this site, or discovery of three crosses, the nails, and the crown of thorns, until at least seven decades later.[22] This deficiency is particularly striking in view of the silence of a contemporary source on this matter that describes her pilgrimage to the holy

---

"Novels: Christian," 846–48; Perkins, "World." Bultmann notes novelistic development of Jesus's miracles in these later sources and retrojects it into first-century sources (*Tradition*, 241). I have offered one more sustained contrast with novels in Keener, "Official."

15. I.e., to argue that if one accepts reports of phenomena attributed to supernatural sources in the canonical Gospels or Acts, one may as well believe such hagiography.

16. See again Keener, *Historical Jesus*; idem, *Acts*.

17. Haldon, "Essay," 46.

18. See, e.g., Philostratus *Hrk.* passim, and comments in Maclean and Aitken, *Heroikos*. Even some specific traditions like halos had ancient pagan counterparts (though one could postulate divine contextualization); see, e.g., Valerius Maximus 1.6.1, 2; Pliny *Nat.* 36.70.204. The veneration of Christian saints apparently developed from the veneration of Christian martyrs, ca. 160 C.E. (Fröhlich, "Saints," 871).

19. See examples in Bentley, *Relics*, 67–68 (esp. comments on St. Ithamar, used to restore English pride in the twelfth century). The story of holy anointing oil brought to St. Remi by a heavenly dove is first attested three centuries after Remi's time (83). Some miracle stories about Brigit (written perhaps two centuries after her) are tamer (see in Davies, *Spirituality*, 127).

20. Much to the disdain of contemporary Protestant critics; see Lara, "Joachim," 268–69.

21. For a number of details supporting the genuine antiquity of the site, see, e.g., Brown, *Death*, 1279–83; Charlesworth, *Jesus within Judaism*, 124; Wahlde, "Archaeology," 578–79; Keener, *John*, 1134–35, 1165–66; McRay, *Archaeology and New Testament*, 206–17.

22. Bentley, *Relics*, 48–49.

land.[23] In this case, rumor and pious speculation apparently hardened into tradition in less than a century. These conditions differ, however, from the earlier situation of the apostolic church, which remained small enough, with sufficiently identifiable guarantors of the Jesus tradition (as I argue elsewhere). Likewise, the early miracle tradition is on some of the most dramatic points attested early enough (especially in Paul) to render later hagiographic comparisons with the Gospel tradition of Mark and Q tenuous.[24] Mark stems to within four decades, and Q probably less, of the events narrated, within not only living memory but probably also the lifetime of, as well as continued leadership of, some eyewitnesses.

Somewhere around 635, Princess Osyth of Essex is said to have resisted pirates' sexual advances and been beheaded. As the story goes, she picked up her severed head, walked three leagues to a holy church, and there offered her head to God.[25] Many people were subsequently healed through her relics.[26] While some of the subsequent claims to healings may be authentic, most people today would doubt the story of her headless perambulation. Unlike healings, the purported event seems to lack any purpose beyond itself.

Many miracles attributed to St. George are associated ultimately with the holy mother of God.[27] Written by St. George's disciple Antony ca. 634, *The Life of Saint George of Choziba* is what its modern editors call "subdued hagiography."[28] When an old monk was cruel to George as a boy, the man's arm stiffened; George took him to the tomb of the saints, where they prayed and the man's arm was restored.[29] As a young monk, he prayed, and a man's dead only son was restored to life.[30] More unusually (though not in tales of monks), George was disturbed by a lion who would not get out of his way and felt around in the lion's mouth before sending it on its way.[31] An arrogant brother was assailed by ants while resting, as Abba George had warned, and repented.[32] A demon who would not cooperate properly was forced to do a chore for a monk and learned not to disobey them.[33] A monk

23. Ibid., 49.
24. See fuller discussion in Keener, *Historical Jesus*, and sources cited there.
25. Bentley, *Relics*, 68.
26. Ibid., 68–69. Cf. an early Muslim saint whose decapitated head was said to perform miracles (Sindawi, "Head"). Relic veneration and miracle claims remained common throughout the medieval period; see, e.g., Denomy and Bruckmann, "Version," on St. Magloire.
27. Vivian and Athanassakis, "Introduction," 28–30; see esp. *Miracles of the Holy Mother of God at Choziba*, e.g., a healing in 1; deliverance from a snake in 4. Antony's work speaks also of more direct faith in God (e.g., Antony *Life of St. George* 5.20). For one artistic survey with many Marian miracle claims, albeit without critical analysis of their dates, see Durham, *Miracles of Mary*. Some are implausible legends (e.g., the sick man healed by milk from her breast in Durham, *Miracles of Mary*, 160–61), but others refer to recent, dated events such as the healing of Sister Agnes's "incurable" deafness (178) on May 30, 1982.
28. Vivian and Athanassakis, "Introduction," 27. For archaeological treatment of the early monastery and known historical context, see 3–27.
29. Antony *Life of St. George* 1.4–5.
30. Ibid., 2.8.
31. Ibid., 2.10.
32. Ibid., 3.14
33. Ibid., 5.20

witnessed the mother of God miraculously put out a dangerously spreading fire by touching it.[34] Such accounts are more sober than some of those composed centuries after their protagonists' deaths. The section to which the narrator, Antony, was an eyewitness, however, consists mostly of St. George's teachings.[35]

Artemios died some time after 360 C.E., a death first recorded or transformed into a martyrdom less than a century later.[36] The author of the *Miracles of St. Artemios* probably completed his work between 658 and 668, probably roughly three centuries after Artemios's death.[37] The miracles recorded are posthumous ones and thus could be closer to the time of writing; many are similar to, and probably replace, earlier incubation miracles at Asclepius sanctuaries.[38] One supplicant with terrible foot pain dreamed that St. Artemios was squeezing his testicles; when he awoke, he found himself cured.[39] Another was gradually cured of a painful boil on his testicles through Artemios's gift of a poultice.[40] Another, unable to be helped by physicians, had seven sores on his male organ; Artemios appeared to him in a dream and prescribed white vinegar with salt on the sore, which cured it in two days.[41] (For some reason, many tales of this saint specialize in restoring the health of this valuable organ.) In yet another case, Artemios appears in a dream as a butcher, slices the patient open, removes and cleans his innards, and restores them, and the man awakes to find himself cured.[42]

Although the earliest extant source indicates that James son of Zebedee was martyred in Judea no later than 44 C.E. (Acts 12:2), in other words, probably within fourteen years of Jesus's execution, this fate did not spare him from being pressed into hagiographic service in local medieval traditions, in his case associated with Spain.[43] According to a popular legend, early ninth-century shepherds dug at a site in Galicia over which a bright star shone and discovered a tomb, which the local bishop attributed to James.[44] Because this site was the only apostolic tomb

34. Ibid., 5.24.

35. Ibid., 8–10.

36. Crisafulli and Nesbitt, *Miracles*, 1–3.

37. Ibid., 6–7 (on 7 allowing for one sign of a post-680 date being an interpolation). Some material may have been added later (33).

38. For incubation here, see ibid., 23–25.

39. *Miracles of Artemios* 2 (Crisafulli and Nesbitt, *Miracles*, 78.23–80.20).

40. *Miracles of Artemios* 3 (Crisafulli and Nesbitt, *Miracles*, 80.21–82.18). A vast number of the cures involve the touching or curing of testicles (e.g., *Miracles of Artemios* 12, 13, 14, 21, 25, 28, 29, 30, 32, 35, 41, 42, 43, 44, 45; Crisafulli and Nesbitt, *Miracles*, 100–103, 124–27, 144–47, 154–63, 166–67, 184–89, 210–11, 216–17, 218–19, 222–23); hernias also appear particularly commonly (e.g., *Miracles of Artemios* 37; Crisafulli and Nesbitt, *Miracles*, 192–93; see the index, 313). St. Artemios seems to have specialized in particular kinds of cures.

41. *Miracles of Artemios* 20 (Crisafulli and Nesbitt, *Miracles*, 122–25).

42. *Miracles of Artemios* 25 (Crisafulli and Nesbitt, *Miracles*, 144–47).

43. See Coffey, Davidson, and Dunn, *Miracles*, xxiii–xxiv. For later development of some medieval miracle-working Spanish traditions, see Lappin, "Miracles."

44. Coffey, Davidson, and Dunn, *Miracles*, xxiv. Excavations in 1878–79 uncovered a sarcophagus with bones from three distinct persons; in 1884, Pope Leo XIII officially proclaimed these the bones of St. James and two of his disciples (xxxiii).

farther west than Rome, it became a key pilgrimage site by the middle of the eleventh century.[45] Miracle tales associated with the saint spread widely throughout the late Middle Ages and subsequent centuries.[46] Comparing geographically and chronologically divergent versions of the miracle stories attests how they grew over time.[47] James interceded with the Virgin Mary, and miracles were attributed to the relic of his hand.[48] Posthumous miracles include a pilgrim hanged on the gallows for thirty-six days, whom St. James kept alive;[49] a dead boy that James (though himself dead) raised, after the boy's mother threatened suicide if he were not;[50] a pilgrim who killed himself at the instigation of a demon purporting to be St. James was restored to life by the apostle, with the mother of God's aid;[51] another man, captured by Saracens, was sold as a slave thirteen times yet freed thirteen times by James.[52]

Another Example: Takla Hâymânôt

But posthumous miracles, especially those accomplished through incubation at a healing site (like those attributed to St. Artemios), bear closer resemblance to the Asclepian tradition than to the charismatic healer tradition, so I return to hagiography about a saint's life. My favorite (and significantly later) example is the story of the Ethiopian saint Takla Hâymânôt (ca. 1215–ca. 1313).[53] Takla Hâymânôt very probably was reputed as a miracle worker during his lifetime, but the form in which we have the stories, from at least two centuries after his death,[54] includes considerable folklore.[55]

45. Ibid., xxix.
46. Ibid., xxxi–xxxii.
47. See ibid., xlv–xlvi, xlix–l.
48. Ibid., lviii.
49. *Miracles of St. James* ch. 5 (in Coffey, Davidson, and Dunn, *Miracles,* 69–70). Cf. other hanging survival miracle claims in Walsham, "Miracles," 298–99.
50. *Miracles of St. James* ch. 3 (in Coffey, Davidson, and Dunn, *Miracles,* 64–65).
51. *Miracles of St. James* ch. 17 (in Coffey, Davidson, and Dunn, *Miracles,* 84–89).
52. *Miracles of St. James* ch. 22 (in Coffey, Davidson, and Dunn, *Miracles,* 95–96). Many of the stories claim to reflect eyewitness information, the dominant source being Callixtus, whose reports would not be much earlier than the likely date of this collection (Coffey, Davidson, and Dunn, *Miracles,* xlvi–xlix). Multiple elements, however, show conclusively that the introductory letter attributed to Pope Callixtus is fabricated (xxxix–xl), which raises questions about the integrity of the collection's editing as a whole. Despite its dependence at many points on earlier tradition, the late authorial claims of knowledge may be as fabricated as the introduction.
53. These are the dates often given; Huntingford, "Takla," 37, gives "the twelfth and thirteenth centuries" and notes manuscript variation in his age of death. Both major versions of the story agree on their central features, despite diverging on details (35).
54. For this time lapse, cf. ibid., 35 (dating the earlier *Life* to the early fifteenth century) with 37.
55. Huntingford finds some reliable information in the accounts. This was a time of literary revival; thus, for example, Ethiopian texts in Ge'ez were reaching a peak in the thirteenth and fourteenth centuries C.E. (Ricci, "Ethiopian Literature," 977).

According to a lavishly illustrated story of this Ethiopian saint, his miracles began in his infancy. Three days after his birth he offered praise to the Father, Son, and Holy Spirit.[56] At about the age of one year and three months, he signaled to his mother to bring him the basket with wheat flour, and when he inserted his hand, it suddenly overflowed;[57] he also turned water to wine as a child.[58] When judgment came on a person who did evil to his father and himself, Takla Hâymânôt healed him.[59] St. Michael the archangel appeared to Takla Hâymânôt, who fell before him like a dead man; Michael then promised to be his guardian angel.[60] Jesus appointed him to be a new prophet,[61] and he drove out demons,[62] including by dealing with demonized trees[63] and serpents.[64] He also healed the sick,[65] raised the dead,[66] and in the course of his conflict with magicians died and returned to life forty times.[67]

Climaxing his conflict with magicians, the earth swallowed them.[68] Demons stoned him, but St. Michael healed him.[69] Although his opponents threw him over a cliff more than once, St. Michael rescued him on each occasion.[70] After King Matalômê had killed thousands of Christians,[71] he was converted through seeing wonders,[72] and Takla Hâymânôt baptized more than one hundred thousand people.[73] Takla Hâymânôt convinced the king to believe in resurrection by raising from death one thousand men—who had died by lightning on an occasion twenty-five years earlier.[74] Using a chariot of light, Takla Hâymânôt traveled, healing the sick on the way.[75] He made a nonbelieving woman's "house to be as bright as the

56. M. Takla Haym. introduction (in Budge, Takla Hâymânôt, 270).

57. L. Takla Haym. ch. 22 (in Budge, Takla Hâymânôt, 45); more briefly, M. Takla Haym. introduction (p. 270).

58. L. Takla Haym. ch. 23 (pp. 49–51). For water turned to olive oil, see M. Takla Haym. 8, 37.

59. L. Takla Haym. 26.

60. L. Takla Haym. 29 (after this Jesus appeared to him, on Michael's wings). In Jewish tradition, Michael was Israel's guardian angel (3 En. 44:10; 1QM XVII, 6–7 [see further Delcor, "Guerre," 374]; cf. 1 En. 20:5 [trans. M. Knibb, 107; but contrast E. Isaac, 24); certainly he was among the chief angels (1 En. 9:1; 54:6; 3 En. 17:1–3; 3 Bar. 11:2; 1QM VIII, 15–16; Sib. Or. 2:214–20; Gen. Rab. 78:1; Lam. Rab. 3:23, §8; Pesiq. Rab. 46:3; cf. 1 En. 40:9; b. B.M. 86b; Deut. Rab. 5:12; Song Rab. 2:4, §1; 6:10, §1; Pesiq. Rab. 21:9; Coptic charm in Goodenough, Symbols, 2:174–88), sometimes the chief angel (2 En. 22:6; 33:10; probably T. Ab. 1:13A; 2:1, 13–14 and passim A; 4:6; 14:7B).

61. L. Takla Haym. 33.

62. E.g., L. Takla Haym. 31, 43.

63. Ibid., 37, 40.

64. Ibid., 89, 100 (a sixty-cubit-long serpent).

65. E.g., L. Takla Haym. 43; M. Takla Haym. 2, 3, 28, 29, 42, 46. Cf. the woman who conceived after drinking rainwater (M. Takla Haym. 18).

66. E.g., L. Takla Haym. 38, 61, 82. With St. Michael's help, he also walked on a lake (L. Takla Haym. 77).

67. Ibid., 44.

68. Ibid., 44–45 (the earth swallows them in 45).

69. Ibid., 45.

70. Ibid., 51–52.

71. Ibid., 53.

72. Ibid., 54–58.

73. Ibid., 59.

74. Ibid., 61. European hagiography also includes raising accounts (Loos, Miracles, 563–64).

75. L. Takla Haym. 65. He and a monk travel in the chariot of light in 67.

day," and when she was terrified, he gave her a cross that led her, as if by a pillar of fire, to the land of the Christians, where she was converted.[76] We also learn of children who emerged unharmed from a fiery furnace[77] and cattle that spoke.[78] Takla Hâymânôt became bishop of half of Ethiopia;[79] miraculously, his monks and nuns could sleep in the same beds without succumbing to any temptation.[80]

It should be obvious that the level of elaboration contrasts with what we find in our earliest Christian accounts; medieval Christians had a much more thoroughly developed tradition of a hagiographic genre than did first-century biographers and especially historians, particularly those about recent characters. Indeed, it tended to be more elaborate even than other narrative genres of that earlier period.[81] The legends develop some miracle motifs from both canonical and later stories about Jesus and others, but their magnitude knows few bounds. (In fact, the combination of elements omits few of the individual sorts of feats of Takla's predecessors.) Medieval European Christian hagiography also grew through assimilating motifs from various European traditional religions and tales.[82] Even with medieval accounts, one cannot always arrange versions chronologically based on wondrous elements; some hagiography *reduced* miraculous elements, favoring theological explication.[83] Hagiography nevertheless tends to include more elaborate wonders, as we have seen, generally increased over time.

Conclusion

If we read the Gospels and Acts in light of tales developed over centuries and in a milieu with few historical controls, we will read them skeptically (as we should read the majority of these later tales, historically speaking), but this approach is

76. *M. Takla Haym.* 1 (quote from 276).

77. Ibid., 10.

78. Ibid., 30. Cf. the stopped flood in *M. Takla Haym.* 45. For talking animals, see earlier, e.g., Livy 24.10.10; 27.11.4; Arrian *Alex.* 3.3.5; Statius *Silv.* 2.4.1–2; Pliny *Nat.* 10.117; as omens, Homer *Il.* 19.404–7; Livy 24.10.10; 27.11.4; 35.21.4; 41.13.2; 41.21.13; Valerius Maximus 1.6.5; Appian *Bell. civ.* 4.1.4; Lucan *Bell. civ.* 1.561; the talking tree of *T. Ab.* 3:1–4 A; 3:1–4 B might evoke Greek examples like Dodona's oak (Allison, "Tree"; cf. Apollodorus *Bib.* 1.9.16; Apollonius Rhodius 1.526–28; Ps.-Dionysius *Epideictic* 1.258–59). Yet even statues were held to speak at times (see Aune, *Revelation*, 762–64).

79. *L. Takla Haym.* 96.

80. Ibid., 103. He himself became a hermit (*L. Takla Haym.* 105), undoubtedly following the paradigm of the Egyptian St. Anthony, as also when he gave up his possessions (*L. Takla Haym.* 30).

81. Again, this is not to deny some hagiography in Philostratus's Apollonius or rabbinic stories of holy sages, but to invite us to keep comparisons analogous. In general, the more generations (and esp. centuries) that pass, the more hagiographic accretions one finds. Our extant first-century Christian biographic or historic documents were composed within living memory of the witnesses of most of their subjects. Also, medieval reports were more fanciful because they employed a genre that had developed conventions accommodating such portrayals, far more than ancient historiography about the recent past would. The genres are quite different, apart from being narratives with theological interest.

82. See Porterfield, *Healing*, 73.

83. See Crostini, "Miracles" (esp. 86–87).

less useful historically than reading the Gospels and Acts in light of sources composed at comparable remove from the events that they depict and of comparable genre. I have suggested in this book that even modern accounts, if they are from relatively soon after the events they depict, offer stronger analogies from a *sociological* standpoint. While medieval hagiography and the Gospels may both involve claims of what is extranormal, an eyewitness account of an extranormal event is historically worth much more than an account from a significantly later generation.

Given the much greater span of time involved in the development of the legends (which tend to proliferate more quickly once the eyewitnesses are deceased or fail to function as successors), I treated early in the book the more pressing issue of ancient Mediterranean parallels, both Jewish and Gentile, and later analogies to first- and secondhand sources. Western children of the Enlightenment are not entitled to blend all miracle accounts together simply because they claim miracles (a procedure that assumes what a critic of miracles claims to prove); it is the denial of the supernatural that is more idiosyncratic historically, and we need to distinguish more critically among various miracle accounts. The premedieval parallels tend to prove closer in chronology, form, and content, though some are closer than others. Thus it is on these earlier parallels that I focused in the book's first section. Historical analogies for first- and second-generation sources, the focus of much of this book, provide the sort of parallels in function most relevant to the accounts in the Gospels and Acts.

Appendix D

Ancient Approaches to Natural Law

I have critiqued Hume's idea of natural law, but Enlightenment ideas of natural law borrowed, via the humanist and Renaissance emphasis on classical sources, a more ancient vocabulary.[1] While the Enlightenment used the language, however, Hume employed it differently from its normal classical application. Whether or not ancient theorists of natural law believed in the activities of deities, they did not see them as incompatible with the law of nature; if deities existed, their activities belonged to nature.[2]

The idea of a universal law was widely appealing. The early Stoic Zeno reportedly urged people to live according to nature, following "the common law," that is, the law common to all, which he identifies as the pervasive Logos and Zeus.[3] For early Stoics, this law involved motivations that yielded perfect behavior, rather than focusing on particular actions.[4] In the first century c.e., the Stoic philosopher Seneca uses "natural law" in various ways;[5] in one of these, nature's law makes virtue evident and attractive even to those who disobey it.[6] Musonius Rufus claims that

---

1. Although I have drawn the material in this appendix from material already composed for my commentary on Acts, see in greater detail Grant, *Miracle*, 19–28.

2. Cf. also poets in Saler, "Supernatural," 41–42.

3. Diogenes Laertius 7.1.88. On divine law meaning living according to nature, see also Epictetus *Diatr.* 2.16.28; on one law and Logos in the universe, see Marcus Aurelius 7.9. For a full discussion of natural law in Stoicism, see Watson, "Natural Law." For the connotative difference between *logos* and *physis* (Nature), see Long, *Philosophy*, 120, 148–49.

4. Vander Waerdt, "Theory." For Chrysippus (and later for Epictetus as well) humans had some innate ethical knowledge (Jackson-McCabe, "Implanted Preconceptions"). Thus intentions were important (cf. Seneca *Controv.* 10.1.9; Hermogenes *Issues* 61.16–18; 66.12–13; 72.14–73.3; Porphyry *Marc.* 25.401–2; p. *Ber.* 2:1).

5. Especially related to human physicality; Inwood, "Natural Law." For the wide variety of understandings of "natural law" in antiquity, see, e.g., Stowers, *Rereading of Romans*, 109–10.

6. Seneca *Ben.* 4.17.4.

the law of Zeus orders a person to be "good."[7] For Epictetus, "the divine law" summarizes human responsibility before God.[8] One epitome of Stoic ethics portrays the law as "right reason," which only the wise person obeys.[9]

Yet this "natural law" existed in other philosophical circles outside Stoicism,[10] as well as among nonphilosophers.[11] Socrates recognized universal, unwritten laws observed by people everywhere.[12] For Aristippus, if all human laws were repealed, philosophers would keep living as they did.[13] For Aristotle, whereas written laws varied, a law based on nature was constant.[14]

A Hellenistic rhetorician defined as "just" customs on which most of humanity agrees.[15] For Cicero, the law of nature implants in people innate religion, including duty to gods, parents, country, and others;[16] what is universally agreed throughout humanity is the law of nature.[17] Justice must be based not on human opinion but on the law of nature;[18] humans share a common sense of justice.[19] This law that teaches what is right based on nature is as old as the divine mind, existing long before being written down.[20] For Seneca the Elder, unwritten laws are less changeable than writ-

7. Musonius Rufus 16, p. 104.35–36. Reason is from the gods and enables one to distinguish good from bad (Musonius Rufus 3, p. 38.26–30). A perfect king would embody law in himself (Musonius Rufus 8, p. 64.11–12). Others also opined that kings must have the law of reason within them (Plutarch *Uned. R.* 3, *Mor.* 780C) or that some could embody a living law (e.g., Aristotle *Pol.* 3.8.2, 1284a [in Bruce, "All Things," 98n7]; the patriarchs in Philo *Abr.* 5).

8. Epictetus *Diatr.* 2.16.27–28.

9. Arius Didymus 2.7.11d, pp. 68–69.1–8; 2.7.11i, pp. 76–77.30–37.

10. In Plato, e.g., Diogenes Laertius 3.8, 86. Porphyry distinguished the law of nature from the law of God (*Marc.* 25.384–86); the former related to bodily need (*Marc.* 25.387–88), and the latter was known by the mind (*Marc.* 25.392–93). Knowing the law of nature helps one ascend to the divine law, which established nature's law (*Marc.* 27.420–22); they superseded a written law (*Marc.* 27.422–25). The mind knows the divine law (*Marc.* 26.409–11; cf. 26.413–14, 417–20; 32.485–88), though it is inaccessible to the impure (*Marc.* 26.402–3), and the wicked reject it (*Marc.* 16.272–73). The law of nature teaches deliverance from passion (*Marc.* 31.484), and one freed from passion has access to divine law (*Marc.* 26.403–4). Cf. "divine writings" placed in a person (*Marc.* 9.164–65).

11. Cf. Cicero in Frank, *Aspects*, 109; Ovid *Metam.* 15.6; Maximus of Tyre 6.5–6; 11.12 (comparing mind and law; in 27.8 he regards God as pure Mind); even Lucan *Bell. civ.* 7.1. Cf. in Palestinian Judaism, *1 En.* 72:2; 73:1; 74:1; 76:14; 78:10; 79:1–2; 1QM X, 12–13.

12. Xenophon *Mem.* 4.4.19. Skeptics like Sextus Empiricus would have appealed to exceptions to disprove this thesis.

13. Diogenes Laertius 2.68. The best morality was one not dictated by laws (Virgil *Aen.* 7.204–25, citing instead self-control and divine custom; Gal 5:23; 1 Tim 1:9). In the golden age, a mythographer could claim, people did right without needing a law (Ovid *Metam.* 1.89–90).

14. Aristotle *Rhet.* 1.15.6, 1375ab. Aristotle assigned the universe's rationality to necessity but not design (Saler, "Supernatural," 37).

15. *Rhet. Alex.* 1, 1421b.36–1422a.2. Cf. the sense of justice common to humanity in Apuleius *Metam.* 3.8.

16. Cicero *Inv.* 2.22.65; 2.53.161.

17. Cicero *Tusc.* 1.13.30.

18. Cicero *Leg.* 1.10.28. For Cicero, nature was the source of right (*Off.* passim, e.g., 3.17.72; 3.28.101) and itself equivalent to true law (*Leg.* 3.1.3); those who obeyed nature's laws would always do right (*Off.* 1.28.100).

19. Cicero *Leg.* 1.12.33. Society's common bonds came from nature (*Off.* 1.16.50).

20. Cicero *Leg.* 2.4.10.

ten ones.[21] For Dio Chrysostom, it is not the laws inscribed on stone but the law of nature, the laws of Zeus, that matter.[22] The idea of natural, universal law became so widespread that some Roman legal codes began by distinguishing laws particular to given states from the law of nature (*ius naturale*),[23] that is, the law due to natural reason (*naturalis ratio*).[24] More generally, divine law came to be applied even to days of ill omen[25] or heavenly decrees;[26] "eternal law" could apply to such natural matters as the sun rising on time.[27] It had long been a commonplace that laws of the gods (like burial of the dead) took precedence over laws of the state when the two conflicted.[28]

Diaspora Jews apparently used the concept of universal law to help shape how they presented their moral convictions.[29] Some Diaspora Jews believed that God would establish a common law for all humanity.[30] Like Cicero, Philo adopts the Stoic image of universal law of nature, which is essentially identical with reason;[31] his Logos governs creation as a law would rule a city.[32] Although the law of nature was by normal definition unwritten and universal rather than particular, Philo regarded Moses's law as a written copy of the law of nature.[33] Natural law is widespread in most ancient intellectual sources except the rabbis;[34] and as I have observed, expectation of a universal ethic appeared even there (though few Gentiles would have included abstaining from food with blood in it). The Stoic idea of natural law also persisted in late antiquity and is evident even in Aquinas.[35] Enlightenment thinkers who applied this language to mechanistic rules ruling the system of nature were developing the language in a distinctive direction.

21. Seneca *Controv.* 1.1.14.

22. Dio Chrysostom *Or.* 80.5–6. For Dio, humans have an innate knowledge of deity reinforced by nature (*Or.* 12.27–29, 32). Customs were "unwritten laws" of particular societies (*Or.* 76.1), but they could differ from universal unwritten laws.

23. Justinian *Inst.* 1.2.1–2 (tr., 36–37), a later compilation of earlier laws.

24. Gaius *Inst.* 1.1 (tr., 19–20). In the Hellenistic period, *Rhet. Alex.* pref. 1420a.26–28 defined law as reason (λόγος) specified by common agreement, a sort of social contract. Stoicism influenced Roman law in looking for a universal, rational basis for law (Jervis, "Law," 635); Remus, "Authority," suggests that in the period of the empire "nature" helped sustain or supplant laws, which had been losing their moral authority.

25. Tacitus *Hist.* 2.91.

26. Silius Italicus 6.120 (poetic).

27. Lucan *Bell. civ.* 7.1. Lucan believes that even the Creator is bound by eternal law (*Bell. civ.* 2.10).

28. Sophocles *Antig.* 450–57, 913–14.

29. See Sterling, "Universalizing the Particular." Cf. LXX translators in Roetzel, *Paul*, 52.

30. *Sib. Or.* 3.757–59.

31. See Horsley, "Law of Nature"; cf. Wolfson, *Philo*, 1:332–47; Tobin, *Rhetoric in Contexts*, 114–15. Koester, *Paul and World*, 126–42, treats Philo's contribution to natural law as particularly significant.

32. Myre, "Loi." Stoics also emphasized God's rule of the universe as a state (Cicero *Fin.* 3.19.64).

33. Najman, "Written Copy"; idem, "Authority." Whereas Greek epitaphs often spoke of natural law, 4 Maccabees identifies the "law" with the Pentateuch (Redditt, "*Nomos*").

34. Bockmuehl, "Law." Unwritten law in Philo resembles Greek concepts more than later rabbis' oral law (Martens, "Unwritten Law," on Philo *Spec. Laws* 4.149–50). Rabbis could envision a central unifying principle to the law (as in *b. Shab.* 31a; cf. Zipor, "Talebearers"; Keener, *Matthew*, 249), which some relate to Greek unwritten law (Jeremias, *Sermon*, 3).

35. Mitsis, "Stoics and Aquinas." Seagrave, "Cicero," finds in Aquinas's understanding of natural law a continuation of Cicero's Aristotelian approach.

Appendix E

Visions and Dreams

Visions and dreams do not strictly count as miracles[1] and therefore do not belong to the primary subject of this book. Nevertheless, I will cover them briefly here to illustrate further how many cultures, including elements within Western culture, demur from the dominant Western academic skepticism about suprahuman, extranormal phenomena. (One could have also addressed claims regarding glossolalia, but I have reserved that treatment exclusively, and a discussion of prophecy almost exclusively, for relevant points in my commentary on Acts.)

Although few critics deny that people experience visions and no one denies that people have dreams, Western academics usually treat them as subjective experiences not to be taken seriously.[2] A majority of people in the United States do, however, believe that dreams can sometimes foretell the future, and well over one hundred million of them claim to have had a dream that accurately predicted the future.[3] (I use these figures as statements of belief, not evidence of paranormal activity; it would be quite surprising if, out of the thousands of dreams the average person has, some of them did not somehow "come true."[4]) Here I primarily want to reinforce

1. Though most who prayed for the sick surveyed in Tilley, "Phenomenology," 555, had "visions" or "images" relevant to the healings.
2. See Young and Goulet, "Introduction," 9, arguing that this approach reflects anthropology's earlier complicity with Western imperialism. Increasingly a number of anthropologists are taking them more seriously (Young, "Visitors," 168–69, noting also Jung's insights on 169–70; in psychology, see, e.g., Blessing, "Psychology," 97–98); although they appear among all cultures, they tend to be dismissed in Western academia by classifying them with hallucinations (Young, "Visitors," 190).
3. Alexander, *Signs*, 117 (citing Baylor Institute, *Piety*, 45–46).
4. Indeed, that a higher proportion did not claim at least accidental correspondences suggests that many respondents must have ruled out cases they deemed coincidence, or that they do not remember their dreams. "Paranormal" dreams tend to involve the future, in contrast to paranormal knowledge while awake (McClenon and Nooney, "Experiences," 49, 54, and sources cited there). Some claims, however, appear

the point that claims in ancient historical sources should not be dismissed simply because they are foreign to Enlightenment expectations.

Cross-cultural studies show that altered states of consciousness are a frequent phenomenon; indeed, brain research suggests that the human brain is open to such experiences.[5] In fact, from dreams during REM sleep, to sleepwalking, to occurrences of psychomotor epilepsy, and to possession trance, a continuum of altered states of consciousness overlaps at some points with "normal" life.[6] While such phenomena do not all involve identical external causes, they do suggest that the common wiring of human nervous systems allows for similar symptoms due to a variety of causes, often experienced by the nervous system as something analogous to emotional stresses.[7] In religious contexts, various cultures often construe such altered states positively.[8] Heavenly visions in ancient Jewish apocalyptic and mystic sources show some parallels with shamanic sky journeys in various cultures.[9] Clini-

---

too precise to be explained as coincidence (e.g., Tari, *Wind*, 146–47). Shorter, *Witch Doctor*, 152–53, notes that some have argued for genuine precognition in some dreams (citing Dunne, *Experiment*, 37ff., 50, 59; and esp. Rycroft, *Innocence*, 36); see also Targ, Schlitz, and Irwin, "Experiences," 219–20 (a Latina's dream correctly predicted a husband's death by being hit by a bus two weeks before it happened, though [220] the psychiatric resident attributed this connection to coincidence); McClenon, *Events*, 45–47, 113–14; idem, *Healing*, 121–22; discussion of dreams involving accurate but previously unknown information allegedly from the deceased in Greeley, *Sociology*, 34–35.

5. So Pilch, *Visions*, passim, esp. 158–59; idem, "Trance Experience"; Malina and Pilch, *Acts*, 185–87; idem, *Letters*, 331–33. Wulff, "Experience," 410–14, notes that mysticism is not in itself psychopathological and surveys some neuropsychological models for it (416–18), as well as other approaches (418–27). Although alternative explanations merit more consideration, Beauregard and O'Leary, *Brain*, argue that such mystic experiences reflect genuine connections with the primordial ground of being (e.g., 293–94). Such hypotheses aside, the brain is susceptible to such experiences; McClenon, *Healing*, 90–91, notes that such experiences can be stimulated artificially. McClenon and Nooney, "Experiences," 48, cite Persinger and Makarec, "Signs"; Persinger and Valliant, "Signs"; Ramachandran and Blakeslee, *Phantoms*; Newberg, d'Aquili, and Rause, *Brain Science*. Strelan, *Strange Acts*, 131, suggests that ancients were less concerned than moderns to distinguish visual from visionary sight; while that was probably true in some cases, many ancient writers would have recognized the distinction.

6. Bourguignon, "Introduction," 14; for psychomotor epilepsy, Prince, "EEG," 122–24; for sleepwalking, 124–25; for hysterical fugue states, 125–27. Lucid dreaming appears especially during REM sleep (LaBerge and Gackenbach, "Dreaming," 158–60) and bears no connection with psychopathology (167).

7. Whether humans suffering battle fatigue or experimental dogs overwhelmed by stresses, the nervous system may collapse (Prince, "EEG," 129). Cathartic release of emotion, or at a more extreme level, emotional collapse, seems to reset human emotional circuits; whether ecstasies during Wesley's preaching (June 15, 1739) or brainwashing techniques, emotional collapse yields a suggestible state to which some also compare possession trance (130). Prince himself (132) thinks that ecstasies in Wesley's meetings were caused by suggestion, lacking neurophysiological causes as in some other cases. But other studies have shown that intense religious emotion can produce altered neurophysiological states (see, e.g., Goodman, *Speaking in Tongues*; on mystical "call" trances, cf. Lewis, *Ecstatic Religion*, 37–44). Prince, "EEG," 133–34, notes neurophysiological changes due to rhythmic drumming, as in West Africa and Haiti, and in "photic driving," "light flashing at or near the alpha rhythm of the brain."

8. Ludwig, "Altered States," 88. Cf. Goodman, *Trance Journeys*; idem, *Ecstasy*.

9. See Pilch, "Sky Journeys," including Paul (104) but especially the author of *1 Enoch* (106–10). Extracorporeal and mystical corporeal translocation experiences are reported in various cultures (see, e.g., Berenbaum, Kerns, and Raghavan, "Experiences," 31). "Hypnotic susceptibility" helps predict these (Alvarado, "Experiences," 208); while some evidence links these with parapsychological experiences, these

cal studies have shown that anomalous experiences do not by themselves indicate any psychopathology; where experiences formally resemble pathologies, they often involve different causes.[10] For theists who recognize God working in nature, neurological approaches need not prove incompatible with belief in revelation. Thus psychological or physiological factors in understanding need not rule out genuine communication from persons distinct from the recipient, divine as well as human.[11]

Ancient Dream Reports

I focus more on dreams here because they appear more frequently in the sources. (They presumably appear more frequently because most people dream far more regularly than they see visions.) Throughout history, many people have believed that dreams provided them with divine direction.[12] Whether in Greece and Macedonia,[13] Rome,[14] Egypt,[15] Carthage,[16] the East,[17] and Palestine;[18] among Diaspora Jews[19] or later rabbis;[20]

---

could occur without actual separation from the body (Alvarado, "Experiences," 209). Despite similarities, magic in some cultures does not employ sky-journeys (Musi, "Shaman," 55).

10. Cardeña, Lynn, and Krippner, "Experiences," 17; Berenbaum, Kerns, and Raghavan, "Experiences," 32. Noting connections, see Berenbaum, Kerns, and Raghavan, "Experiences," 32–40, but they also note (32) that "there is not good empirical support" for associating some kinds of anomalous experiences with psychopathology. In cases of hallucinatory audition, "inner speech" is projected externally (Bentall, "Experiences," 99–100), with activity in parts of the brain associated with speech production (100–101; note also subvocalization, 100).

11. For Martin Buber, signs could come not only from the unconscious mind, but also from God as revelation, while utilizing the same mental forms (Merkur, "Revelation," 294). Neurological features of the experience of communication could be identical whether or not extrahuman persons are involved; for some theists, revelatory inspiration could imply God working in nature, perhaps at a special level of providence.

12. See generally Croy, "Religion, Personal," 927; Theissen, *Erleben*, 138. On Greek and Roman dreams, see also Miller, *Convinced*, 23–39 (noting both acceptance and criticism); Bovon, *Studies*, 145–49; on Jewish dreams, Miller, *Convinced*, 40–61; Bovon, *Studies*, 149–52; on post-NT Christian dreams up through Augustine, see Bovon, *Studies*, 155–61 (e.g., *Acts Thom.* 154; *Acts John* 48); in the ancient Near East, see, e.g., sources noted in Long, "Samuel," 283.

13. Homer *Il.* 1.63; 5.150; Xenophon *Anab.* 3.1.11; 4.3.8; 6.1.22; *Eq. mag.* 9.9; Pausanias 4.19.5–6; 9.26.4; Longus 1.7; 2.23, 26–27; 3.27; 4.35; Appian *Hist. rom.* 11.9.56; 12.12.83; Quintus Curtius 4.2.17; Arrian *Alex.* 2.18.1; Babrius 136.3–4; Achilles Tatius 1.3.2; 4.1.4; 7.12.4; Chariton *Chaer.* 1.12.5; 2.9.6; 3.7.4; 4.1.2; 5.5.5–7; 6.2.2; 6.8.3; cf. *Orph. H.* 85–87; Epidauros inscriptions; Hadas, *Aristeas*, 184–85; Reinhold, *Diaspora*, 35; Oberhelman, "Dreams"; Mackay, "Plutarch," 104–6; Hanson, "Dreams and Visions"; Martin, *Religions*, 48–50; idem, "Artemidorus."

14. Tacitus *Ann.* 2.14; Marcus Aurelius 1.17.8; van der Horst, "Macrobius," 221–22; cf. Virgil *Aen.* 4.556–57; 7.415–20; Ovid *Metam.* 9.685–701; 15.653–54.

15. Ezek. Trag. 68–89; *Sib. Or.* 3.293; Philo *Migr.* 190; Deissmann, *Light*, 154; Lewis, *Life*, 99; Wright, *Archaeology*, 53.

16. Dio Cassius bk. 13, frg. in Zonaras 8.22.

17. Herodotus 1.34, 107, 127; Quintus Curtius 3.3.2–3 (but probably a non-Persian literary invention).

18. Josephus *War* 1.328; 2.116; *Life* 208–10.

19. *Sib. Or.* 3.293.

20. *Ab. R. Nat.* 40 A; 46, §§128–29 B; *Pesiq. Rab Kah.* 5:2; *b. B.B.* 10a; *Ber.* 55a–58a; *Hag.* 14b; *Gen. Rab.* 17:5; 44:17; 89:5–6, 8; *Lev. Rab.* 3:5; 34:12; *Eccl. Rab.* 1:1, §1; 3:2, §2; 5:2, §1; 5:6, §1; *Lam. Rab.* 1.1.16–18; Zeitlin, "Dreams"; Alexander, "Dreambook."

or in magical papyri,[21] people often believed that dreams conveyed divine messages. So compelling was trust in dreams' warnings that they could be employed to bolster an army's courage;[22] a fabricated dream reportedly precipitated an innocent man's execution;[23] and some found it important to warn of false dream tellers and interpreters.[24]

God revealed information to biblical heroes in Jewish tradition,[25] and later stories amplified the frequency of such revelations.[26] Later rabbis believed that revelatory dreams could be secured through fasting[27] or their ill pronouncements revoked through fasting.[28] Ancients also emphasized dreams experienced in a sacred place. The ancient Near Eastern practice of incubation—receiving a dream by sleeping in a temple[29]—continued in the Mediterranean world of the Hellenistic and Roman periods.[30] On occasion visions or dreams were believed confirmed by two persons having the same vision;[31] such confirmations are sometimes reported today as well.[32]

Still, even in antiquity people realized that not all dreams were divine revelations, and those who were more skeptical dismissed most dreams from being revelations.[33] Thus, what one had been thinking about during the day could cause

21. *PGM* 4.2076–80, 2444–45, 2625, 3172; *PDM Sup.* 117–30.

22. E.g., Quintus Curtius 4.2.17.

23. Dio Cassius 60.14.4–15.1; cf. Appian *Hist. rom.* 12.2.9.

24. Juvenal *Sat.* 6.542–47; *Lam. Rab.* 1:1, §14–15; cf. Virgil *Aen.* 5.636.

25. E.g., Gen 28:12; 37:5–9; Dan 2:19; cf. Josephus *Ant.* 2.13–16, 63–73.

26. E.g., 1Qap Gen^ar XIX, 14–23; *Jub.* 27:1–3; 32:1; 41:24; Ezek. Trag. 68–89; Josephus *Ant.* 2.216–19; 6.38; 7.147; *L.A.B.* 9:10; 42:3; *4 Ezra* 10:59; *T. Ab.* 4:8 A; 4:16; 6:1–2 B; *L.A.E.* 23:2/*Apoc. Mos.* 2:2; Endres, *Interpretation*, 207.

27. *P. Ket.* 12:3, §7.

28. *Pesiq. Rab Kah.* 28:2. Fasting for revelations appears in a variety of texts (e.g., Dan 10:3; *2 Bar.* 20:5; 43:30; Hermas 1.3.10; 9.2 [*Vis.* 3.1.2]; 18.6–7 [*Vis.* 3.10.6–7]; see sources in Lincoln, *Paradise*, 111; Keener, *Acts*, at Acts 13:2).

29. Cf. Gen 15:12–13; 1 Sam 3:3–4 (though this was certainly not deliberate); 1 Kgs 3:4–5; Keret in KRT A I (*ANET* 143); Aqhat in AQHT A I (*ANET* 150).

30. E.g., Diodorus Siculus 1.25.3–4; 1.53.8; Pausanias 1.34.5; 2.27.2; Herodian 4.8.3; Grant, *Religions*, 16, 38; Oepke, "Ὄναρ," 223–24; Grant, *Gods*, 66–67; cf. Rousselle, "Cults"; in Josephus, Gnuse, "Temple Experience."

31. Plutarch *Alex.* 24.3; Valerius Maximus 1.7.3; Apuleius *Metam.* 11.13; Boring et al., *Commentary*, 319–20, cites Epidauros inscr. 21; Parsons, *Acts*, 129, cites Dionysius of Halicarnassus *Ant. rom.* 1.57.4; Josephus *Ant.* 11.327; *Jos. Asen.* 14–15; Hermas *Vis.* 3.1.2; Apuleius *Metam.* 11.1–3, 6, 21–22, 26–27; Heliodorus *Aeth.* 3.11–12, 18; Chariton *Chaer.* 1.12; for other examples, see Wikenhauser, "Doppelträume" (cited in Brawley, *Luke-Acts and Jews*, 59, noting esp. Livy 8.6.8–16; Dionysius of Halicarnassus *Ant. rom.* 1.55–59); in Scripture, see Exod 4:27–28; Judg 7:9–15; Luke 1:8–38; Acts 9:1–16; 10:3–16. Less dramatically, visions or dreams could also be doubled to individuals; see Gen 37:7, 9; 41:1–7; Polybius 10.4.5; Valerius Maximus 1.7.7; the inscription in Horsley, *Documents* 1, §6, pp. 29–32.

32. Talbot, "Vision," 275 (Evan Roberts and a friend involved with the Welsh Revival); Yun, *Heavenly Man*, 28–30, 123, 263–64; Tari, *Breeze*, 25 (three people having the same vision simultaneously), 42–43 (the entire group having the same vision simultaneously), 91 (several, but not all, saw Jesus); Koch, *Zulus*, 221; Fever, "Delegation," 34 (a public vision); cf. Crandall, *Raising*, 17–18; a parapsychological explanation for one non-Christian example, Emmons, *Ghosts*, 46.

33. Sir 34[31]:1–8; *Let. Aris.* 213–16; Josephus *Ag. Ap.* 1.207–8; Homer *Od.* 19.559–67; Herodotus 7.12–19; Aristotle *De an.*; *Div. somn.*; Artemidorus *Onir.* 1.1; Herodian 2.9.3; cf. *b. Hor.* 13b; Cicero *Div.* 2.58.119–72.150; Diogenes Laertius 6.2.43; probably Polybius 33.21.1–2 (see LCL 6:290–91). See further discussion especially in Miller, *Convinced*, 29–36.

dreams.[34] Orators could invent "dreams" for effect,[35] even noting that they could be caused by eating particular kinds of food.[36] Some considered dreams less likely to be true during autumn[37] but more common in spring and autumn, and especially when lying on one's back.[38] Some dreams were even intended or regarded as divine deceptions.[39]

Biblical dreams typically differed from many of their counterparts in terms of who delivered the message. Pagan[40] and Jewish[41] dreams often included apparitions of deceased persons; like the biblical tradition, however, the NT writers usually limited apparitions to God and Christ or angels (though cf. Acts 16:9).[42] Matthew and Luke (exclusively in Acts) stress revelation through dreams more frequently than other extant first-century Christian writers do (Matt 2:12, 13, 19, 22; 27:19; Acts 16:9–10; 18:9–10; 23:11; 27:23–24; cf. 2:18).[43] Vision and dream reports feature also in subsequent Christian history,[44] for example, Augustine's reports of his mother's experiences[45] or experiences in early Methodism.[46] They occur

34. Artemidorus *Onir.* 1.1. White, *Artemidorus,* 67–68n6, provides many parallels to this conception. Cf. perhaps Eccl 2:23.

35. Menander Rhetor 2.4, 390.4–10 allows orators to invent dream-revelations for effect (cf. the value of *visiones* in Quintilian *Inst.* 6.2.29, though he applies this to emotive, descriptive language, e.g., 2.32).

36. Plutarch *M. Cato* 23.4. Thus a king's prophets might claim to interpret a dream that he had merely made up (Chariton *Chaer.* 6.8.3; cf. Dan 2:9; of course, political expediency could dictate the outcome of many prophecies, as in 1 Kgs 22:13).

37. Alciphron *Farm.* 2 (Iophon to Eraston), 3.10, ¶3; Plutarch *T.-T.* 8.10, *Mor.* 734D.

38. Pliny *Nat.* 28.14.54.

39. Homer *Il.* 2.20–21; Virgil *Aen.* 5.893–96; *Vit. Aes.* 33; *P. Par.* 47; cf. the prophecy in 1 Kgs 22:22–23. 4Q560 1 I, 5 is an incantation to protect against dreams, presumably recognizing that not all are from God.

40. E.g., Homer *Il.* 23.65, 83–85; Euripides *Hec.* 30–34, 703–6; Virgil *Aen.* 1.353–54; 2.268–97, 772–94; 4.351–52; 5.721–23; Ovid *Metam.* 11.586–88, 635, 650–73; Plutarch *Sulla* 37.2; *Br. Wom.,* *Mor.* 252F; Apuleius *Metam.* 8.8; 9.31; cf. Homer *Od.* 4.795–839; 19.546–49; Appian *Hist. rom.* 8.1.1; Arrian *Alex.* 7.30.2.

41. *Ab. R. Nat.* 40A; *Pesiq. Rab. Kah.* 11:23; *p. Hag.* 2:2, §5; *Ket.* 12:3, §7; *Sanh.* 6:6, §2; *Eccl. Rab.* 9:10, §1; to my knowledge, the earliest Christian example is *Acts Paul* 11:6.

42. Greek tradition also allowed for apparitions of deities, not restricted to incubation (see, e.g., Plutarch *Luc.* 10.2–3; 12.1; *Sulla* 9.4; 28.6). Christian reports of visions or dreams of loved ones being in heaven (e.g., Bennett, *Morning,* 121) or saying good-bye before departing for heaven (sometimes before arrival of news of their deaths, as my wife experienced at Pastor Ndoundou's passing) are not uncommon; sometimes they also convey information, as in the early Methodist experience in Webster, "Salvation," 379. For sociological analyses of apparitions and their contexts, see McClenon, *Healing,* 116–21.

43. On Luke's dream and vision reports, see esp. now Miller, *Convinced;* for a survey of Lukan scholarship on dreams and visions, see 81–90.

44. See, e.g., Bovon, *Studies,* 155–61; later, Constantine's claimed vision or dream (for discussion, see, e.g., Price, "*Signo*"), and later allegedly revelatory dreams (e.g., in 1097 in Hamilton, "Signs," 98); vision accounts appear even among women who knew that men were skeptical of women's reports (see Van Dijk, "Miracles," 248). Sixteenth-century physician Girolamo Cardano found portents in dreams (Duffin, *Miracles,* 22–23); Waldensians accepted visions and prophecies (Toon, "Waldenses," 1026).

45. Herum, "Theology," 35–36, cites Monica's dream of Augustine in *Conf.* 3.11.19; her vision of safety despite the storm in 6.1.1. Augustine's own ecstasies (Herum cites *Conf.* 7.10.16; 7.17.23; 9.10.24–25) resemble Neoplatonist contemplation of the divine.

46. See Webster, "Salvation"; Asbury's prophetic dream in Wigger, *Saint,* 188; John Wesley's reports of visionary experiences of some people he knew (Huyssen, *Saw,* 106–7).

among some noted figures even in recent Western Christian history,[47] including in foundational periods of even some fairly conservative Christian movements.[48]

Visions and Dreams in Global Christianity

Although in the West consideration of dreams is often relegated to the realm of Jungian psychotherapists[49] and (more empirically) neurologists, the divinatory or prophetic use of dreams and visions continues to play a role in many societies and religions.[50] This remains true in Asian and African Christianity;[51] as historian

47. Besides examples in medieval mystics; some mid-eighteenth-century Baptists (revelatory dreams, Kidd, *Awakening*, 246); the Welsh Revival of 1904 (Pytches, *Come*, 133; esp. Harvey, "Agony"; for Evan Roberts, e.g., White, "Revival," 1); and the like. Note, e.g., Salvation Army founder William Booth (Huyssen, *Saw*, 80–82). In some cases, the vision experience is explicitly subjective or appears ambiguous, yet real to the person experiencing it: Charles Finney (91, an extended experience; Prather, *Miracles*, 126–28); F. B. Meyer (Huyssen, *Saw*, 111–12, less subjective); in some cases the language might be partly figurative, but may point to visionary experiences: John Bunyan (109, at conversion); Catherine Marshall (125–26); Reinhard Bonnke (140). Cf. also Alcoholics Anonymous founder Bill Wilson's transforming experience of heaven (Kent and Waite, *Beyond*, ch. 28, citing Robert Thomsen's biography of Wilson).

48. E.g., they were common in early evangelicalism (Noll, *Rise*, 267), a movement that has been in the twentieth century traditionally more shy concerning extrabiblical "revelation." One may note particularly early Methodists' use of "dreams, portents and special revelations" (idem, *Shape*, 46), but early radical Puritans also claimed direct revelations, including in dreams and visions (Kidd, "Healing," 160).

49. Shorter, *Witch Doctor*, 152–53, notes Jung's "big dream" (Jung, "Symbolic Life," 556); that Freud conceded his inability to explain accurate premonitory dreams (Freud, *Interpretation*, 61); and that some have argued for genuine precognition in some dreams (citing Dunne, *Experiment*, 37ff., 50, 59; and esp. Rycroft, *Innocence*, 36). On Jung's emphasis on the divine and spirituality, see Rollins, "Wholeness."

50. Dreams have played a part in the Mayan cultural revival in the face of massive displacement and suffering (Tedlock, "Dreams," esp. 453–54, 471); for diagnosis through dreams among the Karanga of Zimbabwe, see Shoko, *Religion*, 75–76, 78; in much shamanism, see Harner, *Way of Shaman*, 99–101. In African tradition, see Evans-Pritchard, *Witchcraft*, 137, 378–86; Shorter, *Witch Doctor*, 149–61 (esp. 152–54); apparitions of Nkai among the Samburu (resembling biblical accounts but with precolonial origins, Straight, *Miracles*, 47); altered states of consciousness visions in Haitian Vodun in Crosley, "Universes," 9–10. Cf. also attacks from witches in dreams (against a former witch, but noting that they eventually gave up after failing to harm him; Merz, "Witch," 203); a witch could expect to kill by this means (Hair, "Witches," 140). Many Mande "claim to have seen" spirits (McNaughton, *Blacksmiths*, 11).

51. In the late nineteenth century, see, e.g., McGee, *Miracles*, 32, 34, 36; early twentieth century, e.g., Hickson, *Heal*, 149 (cf. Hickson's own visions in idem, *Bridegroom*, 35, 102–5); Sung, *Diaries*, 9–10, 15–16, 28, 55, 99, 102, 109, 110, 189–90; for summaries regarding the Majority World, see, e.g., Mullin, *History*, 279; Pierson, "Context," 21. In African Christian movements, see, e.g., Adeyemo, "Dreams"; Clark, "Challenge," 83; Dayhoff, "Machava"; idem, "Mthethwa"; idem, "Mucavele"; idem, "Vilakoti"; Fuller, "Harman"; idem, "Taiwo"; Gaiya, "Gindiri"; Koschorke, Ludwig, and Delgado, *History*, 221 (on Isaiah Shembe), 222; Mkhize, "Prayer-Healer," 288 (also related to Shembe's movement); Magaji and Danmallam, "Magaji"; Manana, "Magaji"; Menberu, "Abraham"; Odili, "Okeriaka"; Quinn, "Kivebulaya" (on an Anglican, 1864–1933); Daneel, *Zionism*, 13–14; Oosthuizen, *Healer-Prophet*, 27–28 (on southern African AICs); Zvanaka, "Churches," 70 (on the Zion Apostolic Church); Bongmba, "Visions" (an AIC in Texas); Sundkler, "Worship," 552–53; Wodi, "Wodi"; Kalu, *African Pentecostalism*, 288; Baker, *Enough*, 21, 58–59, 62–65, 72, 76, 142, 157, 182; idem, *Miracles*, 173; Clark, *Impartation*, 208; Numbere, *Vision*, 65–69, 74–75, 493. Dreams and visions characterized part of the East African revival (1935–45; see Shaw, *Awakenings*, 104). In Asia, cf. Prather, *Miracles*, 66; Ma, "Santuala," 66, notes a syncretistic group in which all members seek visions (comparing the visionary emphasis also among mountain Pentecostals); Tari,

Mark Noll points out, African Christians "are not surprised when Jesus speaks to them in dreams and visions," a pattern consistent with narratives in Acts.[52] Asian examples appear in a range of countries that include Myanmar,[53] China,[54] India,[55] Indonesia,[56] Singapore,[57] and the Philippines.[58] For example, dreams and visions figured heavily in the Nias revival in Indonesia in 1916.[59] They also appear in orphanages and among other groups of children in Asia.[60] They flourished in China some time ago particularly conspicuously during a particularly intense period of

---

Wind, 13, 146, and *Breeze*, 87–88, notes guidance through visions in Indonesia. Shorter, *Witch Doctor*, 160–61, cites an example of what he took to be accurate African precognition through a dream.

52. Noll, *Shape*, 23–24. In much of Africa, between one-fifth and one-third of Christians claim to have prophesied ("Islam and Christianity," 212), and even more to have received direct revelation from God (ibid., 213). Koch, *Zulus*, 138–39, 200–201, reports cases where God provided visionary revelation to illiterate new believers who lacked full access to Scripture. These experiences flourish in spite of many early missionaries' condemnation of attending to dreams (Lagerwerf, *Witchcraft*, 17–18).

53. See Khai, "Pentecostalism," 269, 270.

54. Yamamori and Chan, *Witnesses*, 9, 39, 59; Aikman, *Jesus in Beijing*, 101; Wagner, "World," 85; popular-level claims about dreams in China, Yun, *Heavenly Man*, 32, 35, 135, 137, 178, 180, 181, 189, 197, 305–6, 315, 341; Danyun, *Lilies*, 84; Jones, *Wonders*, 75, 103 (recognizing the foreigner, a missionary, seen in a dream); about visions, Yun, *Heavenly Man*, 58, 60, 68–69, 73, 103, 108–9, 122–23, 124, 254; Baker, *Visions* (2006); Danyun, *Lilies*, 43, 49–50, 195, 210, 351–52. For visions in the Manchurian revival of 1908, see Shaw, *Awakening*, 185.

55. E.g., nineteenth-century and early twentieth-century examples in McGee, *Miracles*, 34, 36, 82. See also Sadhu Sundar Singh in Lynch-Watson, *Robe*, 82–83, 136, 138 (though it is difficult for a biblical scholar to avoid voicing reservations about the content of some of the later ones, esp. related to Swedenborg; see in more detail here Appasamy, *Sundar Singh*, 214–19); in some cases information conveyed in his visions seems to have proved genuine when tested objectively (Appasamy, *Sundar Singh*, 220–21). For contemporary reports of and comments on his visions, based on his own words, see Streeter and Appasamy, *Message*, 86–123, though these writers considered suppressing this information for their Western audience, 87; Appasamy, *Sundar Singh*, 162–64, 211–21 (for a nuanced evaluation, see Appasamy, *Sundar Singh*, 165, 221). He distinguished these experiences from his one, converting vision of Christ (Prakash, *Preaching*, 23; Appasamy, *Sundar Singh*, 212; narrated in, e.g., Adeney, *Kingdom*, 121–22); the visions, sometimes more than ten times a month, included conversations with spiritual beings and started after his fast (Prakash, *Preaching*, 70). These came especially in his later years, in 1926–29 (Appasamy, *Sundar Singh*, 211).

56. In Timor, see, e.g., Wiyono, "Timor Revival," 284 (following, e.g., Brougham, "Work," 167); Wilkerson, *Beyond*, 76, 78, 81 (on a popular level).

57. Green, *Asian Tigers*, 56, 96.

58. Ma, "Manifestations"; idem, "Vanderbout," 135.

59. Dermawan, "Study," 260.

60. In an orphanage in early twentieth-century China, see also Baker, *Visions* (2006, passim; the vision on 131 is actually more biblically accurate without the footnote, which did not belong to the original edition; cf. also comment in McGee, *Miracles*, 147); among other children in Szechuan, China, see Holder, "Revival" (along with much prophesying); among children in the Philippines, Ma, "Vanderbout," 135; among young women at Ramabai's mission for "orphan brides," see, e.g., Anderson, "Signs," 201; in Myanmar, see Khai, "Pentecostalism," 270, noting that the pastor's theological training has predisposed him against it, but that he was compelled by the unexpected phenomena to accept it; Indonesia, see Koch, *Zulus*, 207 (prophecies); Tari, *Wind*, 51–54 (various experiences, including visions). In Africa, see Koch, *Zulus*, 208–16 (a girl's accurate visions), 217–18 (prophecy through a child). In the United States, see, e.g., Marszalek, *Miracles*, 43–44; the child's vision in connection with the Azusa Street Revival, in Olena, *Horton*, 34–36. Children have also proved susceptible to revival phenomena more generally (cf. their presence at Cane Ridge; Wolffe, *Expansion*, 59; Wacker, "Living," 426–27); traditional cultures also report preteen children being possessed (Southall, "Possession," 242).

persecution over about three years.[61] Despite skepticism in parts of the society, such claims also do appear in the West.[62] Visions and dreams seem to proliferate particularly in times of spiritual intensity, for example, the Presbyterian revivals in the Hebrides in 1939.[63]

Dreams sometimes figure in the rise of new religious movements[64] and appear in call experiences in various religious cultures.[65] Not surprisingly, many clergy in Africa, both Catholic and Protestant, are called to ministry through dreams.[66] For example, Margaret Wanjiru had a vision calling her to ministry; her humble ministry in healing, prophecy, and deliverance gained much attention in Nairobi, and her Sunday morning

61. Aikman, *Jesus in Beijing*, 83.

62. See, e.g., Ten Boom, *Tramp*, 189 (Ten Boom's vision of angels); Malarkey, *Boy*, 94; vision examples (fairly ecumenically distributed) in Huyssen, *Saw*, 24, 79, 118–19 (including for a founder's business), 122, 127, 132–33, 150, 183, 186, 195–201; dreams in ibid., 102–3, 119–20, 137; cf. Llewellyn, "Events," 251–52, 258–59. In early modern Pentecostalism, see, e.g., Woodworth-Etter, *Diary*, 111; idem, *Miracles*, 109–10; Menzies, *Anointed*, 30 (a girl in a cataleptic state during Swedish revival meetings in 1896 Minnesota); McGee, *People of Spirit*, 269; cf. Jones, *Wonders*, 17; more recently in the West, e.g., White, *Spirit*, 98 (a call to urban ministry through a vision); Alexander, *Signs*, 124–25 (urging ethnic reconciliation); Rumph, *Signs*, 83–90; Deere, *Voice*, passim; Williams, *Signs*, 141–42; Storms, *Convergence*, 60–61, 64, 78–80; Stibbe, *Prophetic Evangelism*, 95; Baker, *Enough*, 49–50, 55, 181; idem, *Miracles*, 31, 199; Moreland and Issler, *Faith*, 198–99; Clark, *Impartation*, 120, 145–48, 200; Anderson, *Miracles*, 94–95; Bentley, *Miraculous*, 185; Alexander, *Signs*, 115–30 (esp. 115–17); dreams in Pullinger, *Dragon*, 28, 106, 123, 135; visions in ibid., 29, 200, 232; dreams in Jackson, *Quest*, 176, 335; visions in ibid., 70–71, 298. Though perhaps rightly suspecting that many vision claims were the product of human imagination, Baxter, *Healing*, 256–57, recounts a genuine and thrice-repeated vision he experienced.

63. Peckham, *Sounds*, 107, 234. Although such phenomena are often associated particularly with Pentecostals today, this revival occurred among strict Calvinistic Presbyterians. Cf. visionary trances during Scottish awakenings in 1859–60 (Bebbington, "Clash," 79).

64. Lanternari, "Dreams"; Shorter, *Witch Doctor*, 153; among African Zionist movements and independent churches, see Green, *History*, 318; for the visionary call of Steven Tafa Shava, founder of one AIC, see Shoko, *Religion*, 115; cf. the dream that, according to one tradition, stood behind Sardar Birsa's movement, in Singh, "Prophet," 107.

65. Among Mayans today, see Tedlock, "Dreams," 455–59. Dreams sometimes recruit priests in traditional religions (e.g., Verger, "Trance," 51, though noting that this was not the most common method; one method in Krippner, "Call," 191; after a quest, in Hultkrantz, *Healing*, 62–63) or portend possession (Colson, "Possession," 73); a healer's calling in a dream in Binsbergen, "Witchcraft," 225–26. Lewis, *Ecstatic Religion*, 37, notes that mystical call experiences appear in some form of many major religions, as well as in tribal religions (including Eskimo shamans, the focus there); in Majority World Christian movements, see, e.g., Akinwumi, "Idahosa"; Dayhoff, "Vilakati"; Hayes, "Mthembu"; Khai, "Pentecostalism," 269 (the vision of Kam Cin Hau, in Myanmar).

66. Sundkler, *Bara Bukoba*, 98 (cited in Shorter, *Witch Doctor*, 153); in Zionism, Daneel, *Zionism*, 13–14; examples of callings in dreams in Burgess, *Revolution*, 160; Adelaja, "Land," 43–44; Walls, *Movement*, 88; Emmanuel Itapson, interview, April 8, 2011; visions in Numbere, *Vision*, 33–34; Adeboye with Mfon, "Preparing," 206; Sammy Wanyonyi's childhood vision in Marszalek, *Miracles*, 237; a Maasai prophet figure in Fischer, "Orishi," 24–25 (esp. 25); an AIC founder in Githieya, "Church," 232; in Latin America, see, e.g., Alamino, *Footsteps*, 23; Marostica, "Learning," 210 (Annacondia); in India, e.g., Yohannan, *Revolution*, 127–28; Huyssen, *Saw*, 93–94; in Korea, Kim, "Healing," 275 (Yonggi Cho's vision); in the West, e.g., the vision reported in Poloma, *Assemblies*, 73–74; Ten Boom, *Hiding Place*, 234–36; Osborn, *Healing*, 276; Shaw, *Awakening*, 138; Huyssen, *Saw*, 54–55, 80–82 (William Booth), 176; Tallman, *Shakarian*, 147; McGee, *Miracles*, 70; Zagrans, *Miracles*, 4; Seymour's dream in Alexander, *Fire*, 114. Note also a visionary call behind the Indonesian Timor revival in Wiyono, "Timor Revival," 278; the call of Indonesian evangelist Petrus Octavianus by a vision (Crawford, *Miracles*, 73); another in Indonesia in Tari, *Wind*, 159.

services draw about five thousand.[67] One doctoral student from Burkina Faso whom I interviewed, Elisée Ouoba, was called to ministry through a repeated, audible voice.[68] Some report that in some regions, large numbers or even most of those converted to Christianity today testify that they were converted through dreams or visions;[69] individual examples could be multiplied around the world[70] (with cases from many

67. Kalu, *African Pentecostalism*, 151; Alexander, *Signs*, 123.

68. Elisée Ouoba, interview, March 16, 2009. He is a PhD student at Wheaton College; he is from the Evangelical Church of SIM in Burkina Faso (Église Évangélique SIM au Burkina Faso), which was heavily influenced by earlier cessationist Western teachers. For other callings through an audible voice in Africa, see, e.g., Burgess, *Revolution*, 79; Hanciles, *Beyond Christendom*, 329; in Asia, Tari, *Wind*, 142–43 (noting on 143 that most of the ministry teams in Timor had heard God's audible voice at times); in the United States, e.g., John Stewart, who ministered among the Wyandot people in 1816 (McGee, *Miracles*, 10); Anna Gulick, on her experience (interview, March 10, 2011). Sister Briege McKenna also felt called to a healing ministry through a voice that she at first thought was from a human, though no one else was present (McKenna, *Miracles*, 5–6); so also Amanda Berry Smith (Pope-Levison, *Pulpit*, 89) and perhaps (the narrative is not quite clear if this occasion was audible) Jarena Lee (Riggs, *Witness*, 6; Pope-Levison, *Pulpit*, 27; Andrews, *Sisters*, 35).

69. E.g., Moreland, *Triangle*, 169; Moreland and Issler, *Faith*, 151–53; Kraft, *Worldview*, 493; Otis, *Giants*, 157–60; cf. Becken, "Healing Communities," 233; Guthrie, "Breakthrough," 26; Morgan, "Impasse," 61; Kure, "Light," 184 (revelations); Hausfeld, "Understanding," 75; cf. Anonymous, "History in Indonesia," 147 (through dreams and other supernatural means, in Indonesia); Crawford, *Miracles*, 92, 94 (in Indonesia, through a dream); for some examples claiming conversions through visions or auditions, see, e.g., Knapstad, "Power," 82 (a vision), 83 (a vision), 87–88 (a recurring dream).

70. E.g., Kwan, "Argument," 499 (conversion through a vision in nineteenth-century China); Goforth, *Goforth*, 216 (a conversion through a dream, after a request for one, in early twentieth-century China); Anderson, *Pelendo*, 33–36 (a voice, in Central Africa, with an attendant sign); Mohammad, "Saw"; Burgess, *Revolution*, 250; Chesnut, "Exorcising," 181–82 (apparently; Brazil); Kim, "Healing," 273 (Korea); Olson, *Bruchko*, 151 (a vision, leading to most of a Yuko village's conversion in South America); Bush and Pegues, *Move*, 53, 62; Yun, *Heavenly Man*, 50; Stearns, *Vision*, 17, 151, 185 (many among unevangelized peoples); Filson, "Study," 150 (a postmortem vision; after the woman returned to life she was converted and [151] engaged in evangelism), 154 (a dream preparing one for a particular witness); Tari, *Wind*, 143–45; idem, *Breeze*, 19; Koch, *Zulus*, 34, 143, 150, 202, 224 (through dreams; converted through visions in 141–42, 159, 225; cf. dreams for repentance in 227–31); Osborn, *Healing*, 298–99; Stibbe, *Prophetic Evangelism*, 5–6, 17–20 (in the West, 101–2), 98 (a vision; in the West, 104–5); McCallie, *Trophy*, 5–6 (a vision, if literal); Pope-Levison, *Pulpit*, 51 (Sojourner Truth); Marszalek, *Miracles*, 57–58 (a Native American's NDE vision, ultimately leading to conversion), 133; dreams in the *Jesus Film* newsletter, Jan. 15, 2010; regarding dreams, Bush and Pegues, *Move*, 54, 62; a dream in Bredesen, *Miracle*, 154–58 (also in Llewellyn, "Events," 249); visions associated with (before, during, or immediately after) conversions in Huyssen, *Saw*, 35–36 (Graham Kerr's wife), 42 (ca. 1900), 48–49, 54–55 (for thirty minutes), 89, 104–5, 170–72, 175; Levitt, *Beef*, 1–3, 48; cf. the revelatory light in Guldseth, "Power," 4; a voice in the heart in Steil, "Ears," 8; Eduardo Lara Reyes and Nimsi A. Arcila Leal (interview, Feb. 10, 2010), regarding a contact's new commitment through two persons' independent but same dreams over a period of two days. Jan Nylund, a PhD student, shared with me how a figure spoke words to his Iranian wife, Maria, that she later learned (before becoming a Christian) belonged to Jesus in the Gospels (Nov. 23, 2009). My former student Henry Baldwin, one of the Tuskegee Airmen, also told me of a light that filled the room at the time of his commitment to Christ, but at the time I hoped he would write his entire account and I neglected to record the exact date of our conversation. Cf. an example in early Methodism (Wigger, *Saint*, 93); Ekechi, "Medical Factor," 294, notes the influence of a vision on corporate conversion in 1873 Onitsha. Some argue that some religious experiences can be self-authenticating (as epistemic miracles; Oakes, "Experience").

years, for example, in India).[71] On one occasion, it is reported that many persons who venerated the sun were converted through the Indonesian preaching team when a vision of Jesus appeared just above the sun, seen by everyone present.[72] On another, a Hausa man recounted that an angel appeared to him three times and read to him from a book, then sent him on a long journey for an explanation to Christians, where he heard the same passage as they discipled him.[73]

Healings are also reported in conjunction with visions[74] and dreams.[75] For example, when Anna Gulick was a Lutheran missionary in Japan in the mid-1950s, she was receiving penicillin in various forms for her allergies. One night after spraying it in her nose, however, her "heart went into fibrillation due to anaphylactic shock from penicillin." She knew she had only five minutes to live in this state, and it was too late for her friends to get help, but suddenly she could see only Jesus at the foot of her bed. Without speaking, she communicated from her heart that "if He still had work for me to do, I was willing to stay." Then the room returned to normal, and her heart was beating fine. The next day the doctor warned her not to take penicillin again in any form. From that time forward she lost her fear of death, knowing that Jesus would be with her again.[76] That was more than fifty years

71. E.g., McBane, "Bhils," 139 (two people both having visions the same night urging them to accept Christ, leading to twenty-two baptisms in Nov. 1901); Lynch-Watson, *Robe*, 18 (Sadhu Sundar Singh, Dec. 17, 1904; also in Davey, *Robe*, 23–24); Flint, "Brahman's Son"; "Healings in India" (probably the same person as "Healeth: in India"); Boehr, *Medicine*, 55–56; Huyssen, *Saw*, 56–58, citing J. T. Seamands (a Hindu priest).

72. Koch, *Revival*, 143. An account is also told of Jesus's sorrowful face appearing on the wall in sight of an entire congregation shortly before the Great War began, with many witnesses and many conversions (Boddy, "Face," noting on 114 that nothing was unusual about the lighting).

73. Talbot, "Vision," 276–77, from her interview with Sue Davis, who had interpreted for the man (who became a pastor). Talbot compares as analogous an independent account in Bede.

74. E.g., Duffin, *Miracles*, 172–74; Zhaoming, "Chinese Denominations," 450–51; Yamamori and Chan, *Witnesses*, 59–60; Young, "Miracles in History," 117; McGee, *Miracles*, 219; Bush and Pegues, *Move*, 51, 61; Polkinghorne, *Science and Providence*, 55; Beadle, "Healings," 6; Chesnut, *Born Again in Brazil*, 87–88; Glew, "Experience," 81; Tari, *Breeze*, 58–59 (raising); Anderson, *Pelendo*, 111–12; Hiatt, "Vision"; Eusbarina Acosta Estévez, interview, Aug. 7, 2010; Wilson, "Miracle Events," 271; Karnofsky, "Vision," 15–16 (a medieval example); Bredesen, *Miracle*, 24; DeGrandis, *Miracles*, 89–90; Anderson, *Miracles*, 179–81; Huyssen, *Saw*, 27–28, 144–48, 157–62; Moolenburgh, *Meetings*, 72–84 (though none here are naturally inexplicable); Schiappacasse, *Heals*, 20 (cf. also 60); a non-Western testimony sent to me by Douglas LeRoy, Nov. 9, 2009; cf. Chesnut, *Born Again in Brazil*, 87–88; Jones, *Wonders*, 73; Marszalek, *Miracles*, 19–21; in other circles, Beard, *Mission*, 10. It is reported that Julian of Norwich, thought to be lying on her deathbed, saw visions of Jesus and recovered in 1373 (Llewellyn, "Events," 244).

75. For dreams and healings (or prescriptions or instructions where to seek healing), see, e.g., Shorter, *Witch Doctor*, 153–54; Zempleni, "Symptom," 119; Duffin, *Miracles*, 170–72 (incubation, 168–69); Bush and Pegues, *Move*, 51, 61; Szabo, "Healings"; Tomkins, *Wesley*, 60 (Charles Wesley's healing); Burgess, *Revolution*, 224; Alexander, *Fire*, 114; Salmon, *Heals*, 131–32; Ikin, *Concepts*, 106–7; Woodard, *Faith*, 94; Koch, *Zulus*, 76, 121 (marital reconciliation); Hodgson, "Sorcerer," 5. Cf. Jacques Moussounga, Sept. 8, 2005; Joshua Obeng, interview, Jan. 28, 2009; Antoinette Malombé, interview, July 13, 2008; Jeanne Mabiala, interview, July 29, 2008; Lakshmi Devi, personal correspondence, Oct. 29, 2010; Anonymous, "History in Indonesia," 137. Cf. also the Muslim physician alerted to the lymphoma in his body at stage 1, when it was treatable, through a dream he attributes to Allah, in Matthews and Clark, *Faith Factor*, 74–75.

76. Anna Gulick, personal correspondence, Aug. 10, 2009; further details, Aug. 13, 2009; interview, March 10, 2011. I was introduced to Anna through our mutual friend Onesimus Asiimwe. Dr. Nicole

ago; Anna is still going strong, now an Anglican deacon with a lively and articulate sense of humor, at age ninety-two.[77]

Similarly, Australian Markan scholar Rikk E. Watts recounts an incident that followed an extended time of prayer when he was about eighteen years old. A man visiting his family's church noted that he was not a Christian but that he had seen the church's name in a dream, in which he also heard that he would be healed there. Although the man had not identified his specific health problem and Rikk had not observed his entrance, he felt led to pray for the man's lower legs. Suddenly the man began shouting that he was healed, and afterward inquired how Rikk knew that the problem was with his feet.[78]

My wife, a second-generation Christian from Central Africa, collected in her journal various examples of Christians' dreams and visions that were taken very seriously and often proved (albeit in retrospect) strikingly accurate. Such dreams included those portending imminent war, before it was commonly known that war was coming, and only shortly before war came. (One may observe that some such dreams continued after the war as well, though this time they might have reflected posttraumatic stress syndrome.) When my wife was a girl, another person had a vision of her leaving the country, not a common practice in Congo for people of her family's means at the time. She was seen returning while the airport was being bombed, also an uncommon thought at the time, since the nation had long been at peace, so the family prayed that God would avert this crisis. Some twenty years later, when she finished her PhD and was returning to Congo, her flight plans were diverted while shooting and bombing occurred in the airport where she would have landed.[79] Others had visions when she was in her country, including when she was a refugee in the forest, that she would eventually marry a white minister from the West. They did not know about our friendship, and we became engaged only after the war ended; nor did she reveal the prophecies to me until we were engaged.[80] Not all dreams are taken as predictive, however, and even many who regularly look for meanings often find their sense obscure.

Matthews notes that the arrhythmia can often be reversed medically through electric shock or high-dose steroids, but it would not normally reverse itself spontaneously, as here (personal correspondence, Aug. 16–17, 2009).

77. At the time she shared the testimony with me, she was only about one month shy of ninety-one (personal correspondence, Aug. 14, 2009).

78. Rikk E. Watts, interview, Nov. 17, 2010.

79. Coco Moïse still remembered her especially by this prophecy when they talked around Nov. 30, 2008. Among other long-range prophecies, one might compare the prophecy given to Moses Tay's mother when she was pregnant with him about his significant future ministry; he became a doctor but eventually became the Anglican archbishop of the province of South East Asia (Green, *Asian Tigers*, 101–2). Many Christians could offer many reports of even such long-range prophecies, although again many prophecies are uttered that do not come to pass. One could dismiss many examples as coincidence, but some are precise and come from those who regularly prophesy accurately. Nevertheless, I lack means to quantify the relative probabilities.

80. As of the time she supplied this information to me, she has never been charismatic or Pentecostal; she belonged to her country's major Protestant church. I could cite additional examples of this sort of

Such reports are frequent. Thus Dr. Horace Russell, mentioned in chapter 9, shared the recent experience of a Baptist deacon he knows near Philadelphia, originally from Trinidad. She dreamed that her approximately twelve-year-old grandson was abducted by a white man and taken away, yet remained safe. Not knowing what the dream meant, she simply prayed. Four weeks later (and less than two months before he shared the account with me), a white man claiming to be a police officer told the boy to get in his car. The boy complied, yet was released unharmed; the police afterward insisted that none of their officers would have done that and promised to investigate. The dream, it is suggested, may have invited prayer to protect the boy in a coming dangerous situation.[81]

Besides visions and dreams, accurate prophecies are widely attested (with a higher degree of accuracy apparently in some circles than in others),[82] although

---

experience that I have witnessed firsthand (even from my own journal over the years), but the above examples should suffice to illustrate that many people do take such experiences very seriously.

81. Horace Russell (interview, Oct. 26, 2009).

82. For popular modern claims of charismatic Christian prophecy, sometimes accurate to the detail, see, e.g., Anderson, *Pentecostalism*, 71–72; White, *Spirit*, 185–86 (noting both accuracy and inaccuracy), 213; McKenna, *Miracles*, 6–7, 9–13, 23; Libersat, "Epilogue," 140; Gutierrez, *Mujer de Milagros*, 76–77 (including a severe hurricane); Jones, *Wonders*, 67; Crandall, *Raising*, 137–38 (a vision); Tari, *Wind*, 31–32, 54, 147; *Breeze*, 15; Martell-Otero (interview, April 22, 2010, regarding her father); Koch, *Zulus*, 219–20, 232 (vision), 234–35, 240–41; Marszalek, *Miracles*, 43–44, 166, 244–45; Bennett, *Morning*, 105; Deere, *Power of Spirit*, 36–37, 133, 210–12; Alexander, *Signs*, 121; Jackson, *Quest*, 179, 197–98, 211 (but also inaccurate ones, 208, 236–37); Pytches, *Come*, 97–100; idem, *Thundered*, 10–11, 18, 20–21, 82–84, 136 (some more controversial than others; inaccurate ones on 4–10, 109, 113–14, 150–51; and in Buckingham, "Afterword," 150–51); Storms, *Convergence*, 52, 60, 64, 66, 76–77, 78–80, 86–87; idem, *Guide*, 37–38, 44, 45–47, 81–84, 85, 94, 100; Yun, *Heavenly Man*, 79, 81; Stibbe, *Prophetic Evangelism*, 1–3, 4–5, 14–17, 49–50, 59–60, 62–64, 66–67, 70, 107, 129–30, 134–35, 159, 163, 166, 167, 195; Baker, *Enough*, 27; Moreland and Issler, *Faith*, 198–99; Best, *Supernatural*, 54–57, 92–93, 101–2, 107, 109–11, 125, 127–28, 199; Clark, *Impartation*, 134, 200; Johnson, *Heaven*, 102; Venter, *Healing*, 127; Numbere, *Vision*, 453; Robertson, *Miracles*, 57; Anderson, *Miracles*, 232–34; Osborn, *Christ*, 83 (firsthand experience with John Sung's prophetic gift); cf. Brownell, "Experience," 218; Pullinger, *Dragon*, 129; Malarkey, *Boy*, 175; Brian Stewart (interview, Aug. 7, 2010); Kayon Murray Johnson, interview, Oct. 14. 2010; Simon Hauger, phone interview, Dec. 4, 2009, about another person; note also false prophecies (for two among many possible examples) in Alnor, *Heaven*, 102; Numbere, *Vision*, 436. Storms also points to occasions in history (here Spurgeon's ministry) where the phenomenon of prophecy occurred by other names (*Guide*, 89–90, citing Spurgeon, *Autobiography*, 2:226–27; also in Storms, "View," 201–3); see Lloyd-Jones, *Spirit*, 45, 88, for prophecy among the Scottish Covenanters. For claims of accurate non-Christian prophecy, see, e.g., Ashe, *Miracles*, 165–66 (attributing the accuracy not to the tarot cards but to "unconscious" knowledge; but McClenon, *Events*, 139, argues that statistically tarot readings seem to prove correct only coincidentally); Harner, *Way of Shaman*, 97–98 (accurate shamanic precognition); Kibicho, "Continuity," 381 (Akikuyu prophecy); Salamone, "Bori," 18 (knowledge of the anthropologist's thoughts); Grindal, "Heart," 72 (mysterious knowledge, in northwestern Ghana); Scherberger, "Shaman," 60 (mysterious knowledge, among a people in Guyana); Turner, "Advances," 36 (a Native American divining where an archaeologist would find material); Turner, "Actuality," 7 (her experience of what she afterward viewed as precognition, through shamanic meditation, also in Turner, *Healers*, 161); McClenon, *Events*, 135 (a Protestant Chinese psychic claiming the help of Buddhist spirits, with extraordinary knowledge, sometimes including diagnosing problems before medical tests had done so); see Montefiore, *Miracles*, 23–24, on arguments for telepathy; 41–42, for clairvoyance; 51–52, for precognition; and 107–9, on veridical hallucinations. Although the laboratory basis for psychic ability seems questionable to me, even some scientists as respected as Freeman Dyson accept human psychic abilities (Herrick, *Mythologies*, 152).

these must be balanced with prophecies that did not prove accurate.[83] In such settings, people may use the predictive element as a warning rather than assuming an unalterable future;[84] the retrospective component may also be used at times to interpret dreams and presumably to distinguish what are believed to be accurate dreams (more apt to be revelatory) and revelations from inaccurate ones.[85]

Some predictions, however, are specific and narrow enough to seem more unusual.[86] For example, in some cases prophecies have been said to expose government agents secretly infiltrating services.[87] I have no way to provide a statistical comparison,[88] but I can at least say that the probability of coincidence seems very low when (as in one example above) various persons independently prophesied to my future wife that she would marry a white minister.[89] Very few white people lived in her country, and at least one of the several, independent prophecies was given to her while she was a refugee in the forest, with little natural prospect of the prophecy being fulfilled. (Those who offered the prophecy independently did not even know one another.)

I offer just one of a number of dreams that could be considered significant that occurred during the course of working on this book, which I happened to write down in my calendar: on November 10, 2008, I dreamed of a truck from the oncoming lane forcing Médine off the road; I warned her and then prayed. As she was driving to the university, a car from the oncoming lane pulled out from behind a truck and nearly hit her. Out of thousands of dreams, of course, some will coincide with events; moreover, it was not precisely a truck that almost struck her, and I must concede that we do have quite a lot of reckless drivers in this area.

Divination is typically a matter of probabilities, requiring repetition of the procedures to achieve greater confidence (among the Mande, see McNaughton, *Blacksmiths*, 56).

83. Examples in McGee, *Miracles*, 106–7, 125; and often. On the problems of coincidence within large samples and confirmation bias, see, e.g., Shermer, "Miracle," although some events are too improbable or difficult naturally to be explained in such terms, and such an approach can discount larger patterns among particular people and groups of people.

84. E.g., Burgess, *Revolution*, 161. Cultures that regard some dreams as revelatory usually do not regard the revelations as irreversible (in the ancient Near East, see, e.g., Walton, "Genesis," 121); similarly, omens in Pliny *Nat.* 28.4.17.

85. Cf. the experiment in Charpak and Broch, *Debunked*, 2–3, where 69 percent of students thought their "individualized" personality profiles based on their dreams were fairly accurate—though all the assigned profiles were identical.

86. Koch, *Zulus*, 232, notes that he had preached for years against visions, dreams, and the like until he encountered genuine revelatory ones in places of revival.

87. In postwar Nigeria, during a military government, in Numbere, *Vision*, 81.

88. Chandra shekar, "Possession Syndrome," 89, observes that many prophecies of Indian spirit mediums are vague; the medium elicited praise if the prediction came true, and if it did not the recipients blamed their own fate rather than the medium. In such cases, accuracy is not readily falsifiable; one might draw analogies for some prophecies in Christian circles.

89. E.g., her journal on Feb. 27, 1999. On other occasions, two different people without direct contact independently prophesied the same thing about one of our family members on the same day (e.g., two prophecies recounted to us around Nov. 13, 2008).

Statistically, even specific and unlikely coincidences are likely to happen some-times. Thus some critics offer the example of thinking about someone one has not seen for a long time just a few minutes before learning of the person's death, and they point out that we would expect, out of a U.S. population of (at the time) some 295 million, for this coincidence to happen to about seventy-seven people each day.[90] Such observations are especially important with vague dreams, low-level coincidences, and so forth; it does not, however, easily explain the coincidence of such events within our particular sample size. (For example, out of roughly 300 million people in the United States, the odds of a given person being one of those seventy-seven in a given day over the course of one's life, even just once, are less than one-tenth of 1 percent. For it to happen multiple times to the same person, or the same event to multiple persons at once, as in the example below, makes the odds *significantly* lower.[91]) One could appeal to a variation of the gambler's fal-lacy: If one comes across a roulette wheel that always yields a particular number, is it more probable that one has chanced upon the one roulette wheel of putative millions that yield this number, or that the wheel is fixed?

Regarding the particular sort of example offered by critics, examples might be provided. In one case in our family, when Pastor Ndoundou, known in Congo for miracles, passed, my wife, then a student in France, and many others dreamed of his passing.[92] Not knowing of others' dreams, my wife dreamed of his passing the night that it occurred, hearing about his passing only the next morning; in the dream, Pastor Ndoundou gestured farewell to her and those with her. On the other side of the discussion, everyone knew that Pastor Ndoundou had been ill, so for some this factor could mitigate the unusual character of the possible revela-tions. Such coincidences are difficult to quantify. Similarly, on January 23, 2011, I dreamed that I visited my first pastor and his wife and found them very happy. I cannot recall dreaming of them in the roughly thirty-five years since I had met them; I had not been in contact or received information about them for a long time, except hearing perhaps a year earlier that the wife had passed away. That evening his granddaughter wrote to inform me that he had passed away two days before.[93] Again, how would one quantify this probability?

When, however, inexplicably accurate knowledge happens repeatedly in the same circle or to the same person (as is the case with some persons I know), we

---

90. Shermer, "Miracle." He adjusts the "premonition" probability calculations in Charpak and Broch, *Debunked*, 61–62, who argue that a premonition of this sort is statistically likely to happen sixty-five times a day in the United States. I suspect that the odds may be higher but work with their odds, since the cumulative, exponential weight of multiple cases with a particular person would render the improbability significantly greater than what I note.

91. I work generously from an eighty-year lifetime with about 29,200 days.

92. Médine learned about one of the many cases only years later, when a family friend, Papa Nzouhou, reported that dream (roughly five days before Pastor Ndoundou's passing) on the occasion of the only other time he had such a dream, about Médine's father perhaps two months before his passing. She learned of many others' dreams, however, soon after Pastor Ndoundou had passed.

93. Lisa Prysock, personal correspondence, Jan. 23, 2011.

are talking about an extremely improbable occurrence, difficult to account for purely naturalistically. In such cases, it might seem more probable that the "roulette wheel" is "fixed." Those who prophesy accurately most regularly inspire the most trust, though even the intensely pneumatic early Christian movement apparently recognized that prophets remained fallible (1 Cor 14:29).

Bibliography of Secondary Sources

N ote: Bibliographic entries are keyed to the short titles from the notes. For the sake of space this bibliography omits the ancient works from which most primary references are taken, but full citation information for these may be found in the primary sources bibliographies of Keener's John and Acts commentaries, listed below.

Aarde, "Rabbits." Aarde, Andries van. "'Anthropological Rabbits' and 'Positivistic Ducks': An Experiential Reflection on Peter Craffert's 'Shamanistic Jesus.'" *HvTS* 64 (2, 2008): 767–98.

Abdalla, "Friend." Abdalla, Ismail H. "Neither Friend Nor Foe: The *Malam* Practitioner—*Yan Bori* Relationship in Hausaland." Pages 37–48 in *Women's Medicine: The* Zar-Bori *Cult in Africa and Beyond.* Edited by I. M. Lewis, Ahmed Al-Safi, and Sayyid Hurreiz. Edinburgh: International African Institute, Edinburgh University Press, 1991.

Abdel-Khalek, "Happiness." Abdel-Khalek, Ahmed M. "Happiness, Health, and Religiosity: Significant Relations." *MHRC* 9 (1, 2006): 85–97.

Abioye, "Faith." Abioye, S. A. "Christian Faith and Traditional Medicine in Conflict: The Nigerian Experience." Pages 1–5 in *Religion, Medicine, and Healing.* Edited by Gbola Aderibigbe and Deji Ayegboyin. Lagos: Nigerian Association for the Study of Religions and Education, 1995.

Abogunrin, *Corinthians.* Abogunrin, Samuel O. *The First Letter of Paul to the Corinthians.* Nairobi: Uzima, 1988.

Abogunrin, "Search." Abogunrin, Samuel O. "The Modern Search of the Historical Jesus in Relation to Christianity in Africa." *AfThJ* 9 (3, 1980): 18–29.

Abraham, "Spirit." Abraham, Shaibu. "Holy Spirit, Holiness, and Liberation: A Theology of Liberation in Pentecostal Perspective." *DoonTJ* 5 (1, 2008): 86–106.

Abrahams, *Studies 1.* Abrahams, I. *Studies in Pharisaism and the Gospels.* 1st series. Prolegomenon by Morton S. Enslin. Library of Biblical Studies. New York: KTAV, 1967.

Abrahamsen, "Reliefs." Abrahamsen, Valerie Ann. "The Rock Reliefs and the Cult of Diana at Philippi." ThD diss., Harvard University, May 1986. Ann Arbor, Mich.: University Microfilms International, 1986.

Accoroni, "Healing Practices." Accoroni, Dafne. "Healing Practices among the Senegalese Community in Paris." Pages 3–17 in *Studies in Witchcraft, Magic, War, and Peace in Africa.* Edited by Beatrice Nicolini. Lewiston, N.Y.: Edwin Mellen, 2006.

Achebe, "Ogbanje Phenomenon." Achebe, Chinwe C. "The Ogbanje Phenomenon—An Interpretation." Pages 24–43 in *Healing and Exorcism: The Nigerian Experience.* Proceedings, Lectures, Discussions, and Conclusions of the First Missiology Symposium on Healing and Exorcism, organized by the Spiritan International School of Theology, Attakwu, Enugu, May 18–20, 1989. Edited by Chris U. Manus, Luke N. Mbefo, and E. E. Uzukwu. Attakwu, Enugu: Spiritan International School of Theology, 1992.

Achi, "Joshua." Achi, Louis. "Joshua: What Manner of Healer?" *ThisDay* online (Nov. 16, 2004). http://www.thisdayonline.com/archive/2004/06/26/20040626tri01.html. Accessed June 13, 2009.

Achtemeier, "Divine Man." Achtemeier, Paul J. "Gospel Miracle Tradition and the Divine Man." *Interp* 26 (2, 1972): 174–97.

Achtemeier, *Miracle Tradition.* Achtemeier, Paul J. *Jesus and the Miracle Tradition.* Eugene, Ore.: Cascade, 2008.

Ackerknecht, *Medicine and Ethnology.* Ackerknecht, Erwin H. *Medicine and Ethnology.* Baltimore: Johns Hopkins University Press, 1971.

Ackerman, "Language." Ackerman, Susan E. "Language of Religious Innovation: Spirit Possession and Exorcism in a Malaysian Catholic Pentecostal Movement." *JFolkI* 8 (1972): 75–94.

Ackerman and Lee, "Communication." Ackerman, Susan E., and Raymond L. M. Lee. "Communication and Cognitive Pluralism in a Spirit Possession Event in Malaysia." *AmEthn* 8 (4, 1981): 789–99.

Adeboye, "Running." Adeboye, Olufunke. "Running with the Prophecy: The Redeemed Christian Church of God in North America, 1992–2005." *Missionalia* 36 (2/3, Aug./Nov. 2008): 259–79.

Adeboye with Mfon, "Preparing." Adeboye, Enoch A., with Eskor Mfon. "Preparing a People for Great Works." Pages 203–17 in *Out of Africa: How the Spiritual Explosion Among Nigerians Is Impacting the World.* Edited by C. Peter Wagner and Joseph Thompson. Ventura, Calif.: Regal, 2004.

Adelaja, "Land." Adelaja, Sunday. "Go to a Land That I Will Show You!" Pages 37–55 in *Out of Africa: How the Spiritual Explosion Among Nigerians Is Impacting the World.* Edited by C. Peter Wagner and Joseph Thompson. Ventura, Calif.: Regal, 2004.

Ademilokun, "Contribution." Ademilokun, M. K. "The Contribution of Traditional Healers to the Health-Care Delivery System among the Yoruba." Pages 127–32 in *Religion, Medicine, and Healing.* Edited by Gbola Aderibigbe and Deji Ayegboyin. Lagos: Nigerian Association for the Study of Religions and Education, 1995.

Ademola, "Attitude." Ademola, O. M. "Attitude of Muslims toward Traditional Medicine." Pages 109–12 in *Religion, Medicine, and Healing.* Edited by Gbola Aderibigbe and Deji Ayegboyin. Lagos: Nigerian Association for the Study of Religions and Education, 1995.

Adeney, *Kingdom.* Adeney, Miriam. *Kingdom Without Borders: The Untold Story of Global Christianity.* Downers Grove, Ill.: InterVarsity, 2009.

Adeniyi, "Interaction." Adeniyi, M. O. "Interaction Through Medicine, Charms, and Amulets: Islam and the Yoruba Traditional Religion." Pages 58–62 in *Religion, Medicine, and Healing.* Edited by Gbola Aderibigbe and Deji Ayegboyin. Lagos: Nigerian Association for the Study of Religions and Education, 1995.

Adewuya, *1–2 Corinthians.* Adewuya, J. Ayodeji. *A Commentary on 1 and 2 Corinthians.* SPCK International Study Guide 42. London: SPCK, 2009.

Adewuya, *Holiness.* Adewuya, J. Ayodeji. *Holiness and Community in 2 Cor 6:14–7:1: Paul's View of Communal Holiness in the Corinthian Correspondence.* New York: Peter Lang, 2001.

Adewuya, *Transformed.* Adewuya, J. Ayodeji. *Transformed by Grace: Paul's View of Holiness in Romans 6–8.* Eugene, Ore.: Cascade, 2004.

Adeyemi, "Healing Systems." Adeyemi, B. "Traditional Healing Systems in African Societies: A Socio-Cultural Analysis." Pages 144–46 in *Religion, Medicine, and Healing.* Edited by Gbola Aderibigbe and Deji Ayegboyin. Lagos: Nigerian Association for the Study of Religions and Education, 1995.

Adeyemi, "Θέσεις." Adeyemi, M. E. "Οι θέσεις του Απ. Παύλου για τη σωτηρία από τις δυνάμεις του κακού." *DBM* 20 (1, 2001): 82–96.

Adeyemo, "Dreams." Adeyemo, Tokunboh. "Dreams." Page 993 in *Africa Bible Commentary.* Edited by Tokunboh Adeyemo. Grand Rapids: Zondervan; Nairobi: WordAlive, 2006.

Adinolfi, "Lago." Adinolfi, Marco. "Il lago di Tiberiade e le sue città nella letteratura greco-romana." *SBFLA* 44 (1994): 375–80.

Adityanjee, Raju, and Khandelwal, "Status." Adityanjee, G. S., P. Raju, and S. K. Khandelwal. "Current Status of Multiple Personality Disorder in India." *AmJPsyc* 146 (12, 1989): 1607–10.

Adler, "Pathogenesis." Adler, Shelley R. "Ethnomedical Pathogenesis and Hmong Immigrants' Sudden Nocturnal Deaths." *CMPsy* 18 (1994): 23–59.

Adogame, "Walk." Adogame, Afe. "'A Walk for Africa': Combating the Demons of HIV/AIDS in an African Pentecostal Church—The Case of the Redeemed Christian Church of God." *Scriptura* 89 (2, 2005): 396–405.

Agosto, "Publics." Agosto, Efrain. "Who Is It For? The Publics of Theological Research." *TheolEd* 43 (2, 2008): 11–20.

Ahern, "Evidential Impossibility." Ahern, Dennis M. "Hume on the Evidential Impossibility of Miracles." Pages 1–31 in *Studies in Epistemology.* Edited by Nicholas Rescher. AmPhilQMS 9. Oxford: Blackwell, 1975.

Ahern, "Physical Impossibility." Ahern, Dennis M. "Miracles and Physical Impossibility." *CanJPhil* 7 (1, March 1977): 71–79.

Ai et al., "Depression." Ai, Amy L., C. Peterson, S. F. Bolling, and W. Rodgers. "Depression, Faith-Based Coping, and Short-Term Postoperative Global Functioning in Adult and Older Patients Undergoing Cardiac Surgery." *JPsycRes* 60 (1, 2006): 21–28.

Ai et al., "Mediation." Ai, Amy L., Crystal L. Park, Bu Huang, Willard Rodgers, and Terrence N. Tice. "Psychosocial Mediation of Religious Coping Styles: A Study of Short-Term Psychological Distress Following Cardiac Surgery." *PSocPsyBull* 33 (6, 2007): 867–82.

Ai et al., "Pathways." Ai, A. L., C. Peterson, T. N. Tice, S. F. Bolling, and H. G. Koenig. "Faith-Based and Secular Pathways to Hope and Optimism Sub-Constructs in Middle-Aged and Older Cardiac Patients." *JHPsych* 9 (3, 2004): 435–50.

Aichele, "Fantasy." Aichele, George. "Biblical Miracle Narratives as Fantasy." *ATR* 73 (1, Winter 1991): 51–58.

Aikman, *Jesus in Beijing.* Aikman, David. *Jesus in Beijing: How Christianity Is Transforming China and Changing the Global Balance of Power.* Washington, D.C.: Regnery, 2003.

Ajaero, "Life." Ajaero, Chris. "Life in the Occult World." *Newswatch* (Apr. 6, 2009). http://www .newswatchngr.com/index2.php?option=com_con tent&task=view&id=803&pop=1&page=0&Ite mid=1. Accessed June 13, 2009.

Ajayi, "Sacrament." Ajayi, M. O. "The Sacrament of Extreme Unction and Its Relevance to the Contemporary Situation in Nigerian Churches." Pages 52–57 in *Religion, Medicine, and Healing.* Edited by Gbola Aderibigbe and Deji Ayegboyin. Lagos: Nigerian Association for the Study of Religions and Education, 1995.

Ajibade, "Hearthstones." Ajibade, George Olusola. "Hearthstones: Religion, Ethics, and Medicine in the Healing Process in the Traditional Yorùbá Society." Pages 193–213 in *Studies in Witchcraft, Magic, War, and Peace in Africa.* Edited by Beatrice Nicolini. Lewiston, N.Y.: Edwin Mellen, 2006.

Akhtar, "Miracles." Akhtar, Shabbir. "Miracles as Evidence for the Existence of God." *SJRS* 11 (1, 1990): 18–23.

Akintan, "Priest." Akintan, O. A. "The Traditional Priest and Healing in Ijebu-Igbo." Pages 137–43 in *Religion, Medicine, and Healing.* Edited by Gbola Aderibigbe and Deji Ayegboyin. Lagos: Nigerian Association for the Study of Religions and Education, 1995.

Akinwumi, "Babalola." Akinwumi, Elijah Olu. "Babalola, Joseph Ayodele." *DACB.* http://www.dacb.org /stories/nigeria/babalola2_joseph.html.

Akinwumi, "Idahosa." Akinwumi, Elijah Olu. "Idahosa, Benson Andrew." *DACB.* http://www.dacb .org/stories/nigeria/idahosa_bensona.html.

Akinwumi, "Orimolade." Akinwumi, Elijah Olu. "Orimolade Tunolase, Moses." *DACB.* http://www .dacb.org/stories/nigeria/orimolade_moses.html.

Akinwumi, "Oschoffa." Akinwumi, Elijah Olu. "Oschoffa, Samuel Bilewu." *DACB.* http://www.dacb .org/stories/nigeria/oschoffa_samuelb.html.

Akogyeram, "Ministry." Akogyeram, Humphrey. "Ministry of Good News Theological College and Seminary." *MissFoc* 17 (2009): 147–57.

Alamino, *Footsteps.* Alamino, Carlos. *In the Footsteps of God's Call: A Cuban Pastor's Journey.* Translated by Osmany Espinosa Hernández. Edited by David Peck and Brian Stewart. Mountlake Terrace, Wash.: Original Media Publishers, 2008.

Alamino, "Perseverance." Alamino, Carlos. "The Perseverance of the Saints." Sermon, First Baptist Church, Everett, Wash., Feb. 1, 2009.

Albright and Mann, *Matthew.* Albright, William Foxwell, and C. S. Mann. *Matthew.* AB 26. Garden City, N.Y.: Doubleday, 1971.

Albrile, "Sigilla." Albrile, Ezio. "*Sigilla Anuli Salomonis.* Mito e leggenda nella tradizione magica su Salomone." *Anton* 82 (2, 2007): 351–72.

Alcorta, "Adolescence." Alcorta, Candace S. "Adolescence, Religion, and Health: A Developmental Model." Pages 56–79 in *Psychodynamics.* Vol. 3 of *The Healing Power of Spirituality: How Faith Helps Humans Thrive.* Edited by J. Harold Ellens. Santa Barbara, Calif.: Praeger, 2010.

Alcorta, "Music." Alcorta, Candace S. "Music and the Miraculous: The Neurophysiology of Music's Emotive Meaning." Pages 230–52 in *Parapsychological Perspectives.* Vol. 3 of *Miracles: God, Science, and Psychology in the Paranormal.* Edited by J. Harold Ellens. Westport, Conn.; London: Praeger, 2008.

Alderete et al., "Symptoms." Alderete, E., et al. "Depressive Symptoms among Women with an Abnormal Mammogram." *Psycho-Oncology* 15 (1, 2006): 66–78.

Alexander, *Context.* Alexander, Loveday C. A. *Acts in Its Ancient Literary Context: A Classicist Looks at the Acts of the Apostles.* Early Christianity in Context, LNTS 298. London: T&T Clark, 2005.

Alexander, "Dreambook." Alexander, Philip S. "Bavli Berakhot 55a–57b: The Talmudic Dreambook in Context." *JJS* 46 (1995): 230–48.

Alexander, *Fire.* Alexander, Estrelda Y. *Black Fire: One Hundred Years of African American Pentecostalism.* Downers Grove, Ill.: InterVarsity, 2011.

Alexander, *Healing.* Alexander, Kimberly Ervin. *Pentecostal Healing: Models in Theology and Practice.*

JPTSup. Blandford Forum, Dorset: Deo Publishing, 2006.

Alexander, "Marvelous Healings." Alexander, Orville. "Marvelous Healings at Indian Mission." *PentEv* (June 22, 1969): 13.

Alexander, *Possession*. Alexander, William Menzies. *Demonic Possession in the New Testament: Its Historical, Medical, and Theological Aspects*. Grand Rapids: Baker, 1980.

Alexander, "Ritual." Alexander, Bobby C. "Pentecostal Ritual Reconsidered: Anti-Structural Dimensions of Possession." *JRitSt* 3 (1, 1989): 109–28.

Alexander, *Signs*. Alexander, Paul. *Signs and Wonders: Why Pentecostalism Is the World's Fastest Growing Faith*. Foreword by Martin E. Marty. San Francisco: Jossey-Bass, 2009.

Alexander, "Sons of God." Alexander, Philip S. "The Targumim and Early Exegesis of 'Sons of God' in Genesis 6." *JJS* 23 (1, 1972): 60–71.

Al-Kandari, "Religiosity." Al-Kandari, Yagoub-Yousif. "Religiosity and Its Relation to Blood Pressure among Selected Kuwaitis." *JBSS* 35 (2003): 463–72.

Allen, "Miracle." Allen, Diogenes. "Miracle Old and New." *Interp* 28 (3, 1974): 298–306.

Allen, *Price*. Allen, A. A. *The Price of God's Miracle Working Power*. Lamar, Colo.: A. A. Allen, 1950.

Allen, "Whole Person Healing." Allen, E. Anthony. "Whole Person Healing, Spiritual Realism, and Social Disintegration: A Caribbean Case Study in Faith, Health, and Healing." *IntRevMiss* 90 (356/357, Jan./Apr. 2001): 118–33.

Allen et al., "Acupuncture." Allen, J. B., et al. "Acupuncture for Depression: A Randomized Controlled Trial." *JClinPsy* 67 (2006): 1665–73.

Alleyne, *Gold Coast*. Alleyne, Cameron Chesterfield. *Gold Coast at a Glance*. Rev. ed. Introduction by Bishop Paris Arthur Wallace. Norfolk, Va.: Woman's Home and Foreign Missionary Society, A. M. E. Zion Church, 1936.

Allison, "Doubt." Allison, Ralph B. "If in Doubt, Cast It Out? The Evolution of a Belief System Regarding Possession and Exorcism." *JPsyChr* 19 (2, 2000): 109–21.

Allison, *Jesus of Nazareth*. Allison, Dale C., Jr. *Jesus of Nazareth: Millenarian Prophet*. Minneapolis: Fortress, 1998.

Allison, "Tree." Allison, Dale C., Jr. "Abraham's Oracular Tree (T. Abr. 3:1–4)." *JJS* 54 (1, 2003): 51–61.

Allison and Malony, "Surgery." Allison, S. H., and H. N. Malony. "Filipino Psychic Surgery: Myth, Magic, or Miracle." *JRelHealth* 20 (1, 1981): 48–62.

Ally and Laher, "Perceptions." Ally, Yaseen, and Sumaya Laher. "South African Muslim Faith Healers' Perceptions of Mental Illness: Understanding,

Aetiology, and Treatment." *JRelHealth* 47 (1, 2008): 45–56.

Alnor, *Heaven*. Alnor, William M. *Heaven Can't Wait: A Survey of Alleged Trips to the Other Side*. Foreword by Tal Brooke. Grand Rapids: Baker, 1996.

Al-Sabwah and Abdel-Khalek, "Religiosity." Al-Sabwah, Mohammed N., and Ahmed M. Abdel-Khalek. "Religiosity and Death Distress in Arabic College Students." *DeathS* 30 (4, 2006): 365–75.

Alsop, "Analysis." Alsop, A. A. "An Analysis of the IELU of Argentina." MA project, Fuller Theological Seminary, 1974.

Alston, "Action." Alston, William P. "How to Think about Divine Action." Pages 51–70 in *Divine Action: Studies Inspired by the Philosophical Theology of Austin Farrer*. Edited by Brian Hebblethwaite and Edward Henderson. Edinburgh: T&T Clark, 1990.

Alston, "Divine Action." Alston, William P. "Divine and Human Action." Pages 257–80 in *Divine and Human Action: Essays in the Metaphysics of Theism*. Edited by Thomas V. Morris. Ithaca, N.Y.: Cornell University Press, 1988.

Althouse, *Healing*. Althouse, Lawrence W. *Rediscovering the Gift of Healing*. Nashville: Abingdon, 1977.

Alvarado, "Experiences." Alvarado, Carlos S. "Out-of-Body Experiences." Pages 183–218 in *Varieties of Anomalous Experience: Examining the Scientific Evidence*. Edited by Etzel Cardeña, Steven Jay Lynn, and Stanley Krippner. Washington, D.C.: American Psychological Association, 2000.

Alvarez, "South." Alvarez, Miguel. "The South and the Latin America Paradigm of the Pentecostal Movement." *AJPS* 5 (1, 2002): 135–53.

Amadi, "Healing." Amadi, G. I. S. "Healing in 'The Brotherhood of the Cross and Star.'" Pages 367–83 in *The Church and Healing: Papers Read at the Twentieth Summer Meeting and the Twenty-first Winter Meeting of the Ecclesiastical History Society*. StChHist 19. Edited by W. J. Sheils. Oxford: Basil Blackwell, 1982.

Ames, "Magical-animism." Ames, Michael M. "Magical-animism and Buddhism: A Structural Analysis of the Sinhalese Religious System." Pages 21–52 in *Religion in South Asia*. Edited by Edward B. Harper. Seattle: University of Washington Press, 1964.

Amiotte-Suchet, "Egaux." Amiotte-Suchet, Laurent. "Tous égaux devant Dieu? Reflexions sur les logiques d'éligibilité des miraculés." *SocCom* 52 (2, June 2005): 241–54.

Ammerman, "Sociology." Ammerman, Nancy T. "Sociology and the Study of Religion." Pages 76–88 in *Religion, Scholarship, Higher Education: Perspectives, Models, and Future Prospects*. Edited by Andrea Sterk. Notre Dame, Ind.: University of Notre Dame Press, 2001.

"Amputated Fingers." "God Restores Amputated Fingers." *LRE* (Jan. 1926): 11.

Amutabi, "Pharmacology." Amutabi, Maurice N. "Recuperating Traditional Pharmacology and Healing among the Abaluyia of Western Kenya." Pages 149–70 in *Health Knowledge and Belief Systems in Africa*. Edited by Toyin Falola and Matthew M. Heaton. Durham, N.C.: Carolina Academic Press, 2008.

Anderson, *Angels*. Anderson, Joan Wester. *Where Angels Walk: True Stories of Heavenly Visitors*. New York: Ballantine, 1993; London: Hodder & Stoughton, 1995.

Anderson, "Exorcism." Anderson, Allan. "Exorcism and Conversion to African Pentecostalism." *Exchange* 35 (1, 2006): 116–33.

Anderson, "Face." Anderson, Allan. "The Charismatic Face of Christianity in Asia." Pages 1–12 in *Asian and Pentecostal: The Charismatic Face of Christianity in Asia*. Edited by Allan Anderson and Edmond Tang. Foreword by Cecil M. Robeck. Regnum Studies in Mission, AJPSS 3. Oxford: Regnum; Baguio City, Philippines: APTS Press, 2005.

Anderson, *Mark*. Anderson, Hugh. *The Gospel of Mark*. NCBC. London: Oliphants (Marshall, Morgan & Scott), 1976.

Anderson, *Miracles*. Anderson, Joan Wester. *Where Miracles Happen: True Stories of Heavenly Encounters*. Brooklyn, N.Y.: Brett Books, 1994.

Anderson, *Pelendo*. Anderson, Alpha E. *Pelendo: God's Prophet in the Congo*. Chicago: Moody Press, 1964.

Anderson, *Pentecostalism*. Anderson, Allan. *An Introduction to Pentecostalism: Global Charismatic Christianity*. Cambridge: Cambridge University Press, 2004.

Anderson, *Philostratus*. Anderson, Graham. *Philostratus: Biography and Belles Lettres in the Third Century* A.D. London: Croom Helm, 1986.

Anderson, *Quest*. Anderson, Paul N. *The Fourth Gospel and the Quest for Jesus: Modern Foundations Reconsidered*. LNTS 321. New York: T&T Clark, 2006.

Anderson, *Raised*. Anderson, Kevin L. *'But God Raised Him from the Dead': The Theology of Jesus' Resurrection in Luke-Acts*. PatBibMon. Milton Keynes, UK: Paternoster, 2006.

Anderson, "Review." Anderson, E. N. Review of Linda H. Connor and Geoffrey Samuel, eds., *Healing Powers and Modernity*. *PhilEW* 56 (4, Oct. 2006): 702–3.

Anderson, "Signs." Anderson, Allan. "Signs and Blunders: Pentecostal Mission Issues at 'Home and Abroad' in the Twentieth Century." *JAM* 2 (2, Sept. 2000): 193–210.

Anderson, "Sojourners." Anderson, Palmer. "The Sojourners." *CGl* 9 (1932): 18–20.

Anderson, "Structure." Anderson, Allan. "Structures and Patterns in Pentecostal Mission." *Missionalia* 32 (2, Aug. 2004): 233–49.

Anderson, "Varieties." Anderson, Allan. "Varieties, Taxonomies, and Definitions." Pages 13–29 in *Studying Global Pentecostalism: Theories and Methods*. Edited by Allan Anderson, Michael Bergunder, André Droogers, and Cornelis van der Laan. Berkeley: University of California Press, 2010.

Anderson, *Vision*. Anderson, Robert M. *The Vision of the Disinherited: The Making of American Pentecostalism*. New York: Oxford University Press, 1979.

Anderson, Bergunder, Droogers, and Laan, *Studying*. Anderson, Allan, Michael Bergunder, André Droogers, and Cornelis van der Laan, eds. *Studying Global Pentecostalism: Theories and Methods*. Berkeley: University of California Press, 2010.

Anderson, Ellens, and Fowler, "Way Forward." Anderson, Paul N., J. Harold Ellens, and James W. Fowler. "A Way Forward in the Scientific Investigation of Gospel Traditions: Cognitive-Critical Analysis." Pages 247–76 in *From Christ to Jesus*. Vol. 4 of *Psychology and the Bible: A New Way to Read the Scriptures*. Edited by J. Harold Ellens and Wayne G. Rollins. Westport, Conn.: Praeger, 2004.

Andrews, "Healings." Andrews, Winifred. "Healings in Australia." *Conf* 129 (Apr. 1922): 27.

Andrews, *Singh*. Andrews, C. F. *Sadhu Sundar Singh: A Personal Memoir*. New York: Harper & Brothers, 1934.

Andrews, *Sisters*. Andrews, William L., ed. *Sisters of the Spirit: Three Black Women's Autobiographies of the Nineteenth Century*. Bloomington: Indiana University Press, 1986.

Andric, *Miracles*. Andric, Stanko. *The Miracles of St. John Capistran*. Budapest: Central European University Press, 2000.

Anfinsen, "Power." Anfinsen, Christian B. "There Exists an Incomprehensible Power with Limitless Foresight and Knowledge." Pages 138–40 in *Cosmos, Bios, and Theos: Scientists Reflect on Science, God, and the Origins of the Universe, Life, and Homo Sapiens*. Edited by Henry Margenau and Roy Abraham Varghese. La Salle, Ill.: Open Court, 1992.

Angel, "Craft." Angel, Angelita O. "Folk Medicine Craft of the Kankana-eys." EdD diss., Baguio Central University, 1989.

Anonymous, "History in Indonesia." Anonymous. "A History of the Pentecostal Movement in Indonesia." *AJPS* 4 (1, 2001): 131–48.

Antony, *Life of St. George*. Antony of Choziba. *Life of Saint George of Choziba; and, the Miracles of the Most Holy Mother of God at Choziba*. Translated by Tim Vivian and Apostolos N. Athanassakis. San Francisco: International Scholars Publications, 1994.

Appasamy, *Sundar Singh*. Appasamy, A. J. *Sundar Singh: A Biography*. London: Lutterworth, 1958.

Appelle, Lynn, and Newman, "Experiences." Appelle, Stuart, Steven Jay Lynn, and Leonard Newman. "Alien Abduction Experiences." Pages 253–82 in *Varieties of Anomalous Experience: Examining the Scientific Evidence*. Edited by Etzel Cardeña, Steven Jay Lynn, and Stanley Krippner. Washington, D.C.: American Psychological Association, 2000.

Arai, "Spirituality." Arai, Paula K. R. "Medicine, Healing, and Spirituality: A Cross-Cultural Exploration." Pages 207–18 in *Teaching Religion and Healing*. Edited by Linda L. Barnes and Inés Talamantez. AARTRSS. Oxford: Oxford University Press, 2006.

Arakelova, "Practices." Arakelova, Victoria. "Healing Practices among the Yezidi Sheikhs of Armenia." *AsFolkSt* 60 (2, 2001): 319–29.

Arav and Rousseau, "Bethsaïde." Arav, Rami, and J. Rousseau. "Bethsaïde, ville perdue et retrouvée." *RB* 100 (1993): 415–28.

Ardelt and Koenig, "Role." Ardelt, Monika, and Cynthia S. Koenig. "The Role of Religion for Hospice Patients and Relatively Healthy Older Adults." *ResAg* 28 (2, 2006): 184–215.

"Argentina Campaign." "400,000 in Single Service: Hicks' Argentina Campaign Sees Largest Evangelical Service in World History." *VOH* (Aug. 1954): 19, 30.

Argyle, *Matthew*. Argyle, A. W. *The Gospel According to Matthew*. Cambridge: Cambridge University Press, 1963.

Arles, "Appraisal." Arles, Nalini. "Pandita Ramabai— An Appraisal from Feminist Perspective." *BangTF* 31 (1, July 1999): 64–86.

Arles, "Study." Arles, Nalini. "Pandita Ramabai and Amy Carmichael: A Study of Their Contributions toward Transforming the Position of Indian Women." MTh thesis, University of Aberdeen, 1985.

Armstrong, "Wimber." Armstrong, John. "Wimber, John (1934–1997)." Pages 466–67 in vol. 1 of *Encyclopedia of Religious Revivals in America*. Edited by Michael McClymond. Westport, Conn.: Greenwood, 2007.

Arnold, "Conflicts." Arnold, Nathalie. "With 'Ripe' Eyes You Will See: Occult Conflicts in Pemba's Days of Caning, Zanzibar 1964–1968." Pages 215–26 in *Studies in Witchcraft, Magic, War, and Peace in Africa*. Edited by Beatrice Nicolini. Lewiston, N.Y.: Edwin Mellen, 2006.

Arnold, *Power*. Arnold, Clinton E. *Ephesians: Power and Magic. The Concept of Power in Ephesians in Light of Its Historical Setting*. SNTSMS 63. Cambridge: Cambridge University Press, 1989.

Arnold, *Samuel*. Arnold, Bill T. *1 and 2 Samuel*. NIVAC. Grand Rapids: Zondervan, 2003.

Arowele, "Signs." Arowele, P. J. "This Generation Seeks Signs. The Miracles of Jesus with Reference to the African Situation." *AfThJ* 10 (3, 1981): 17–28.

Arrington, *Acts*. Arrington, French L. *The Acts of the Apostles: An Introduction and Commentary*. Peabody, Mass.: Hendrickson, 1988.

Asamoah-Gyadu, "Hearing." Asamoah-Gyadu, Kwabena. "'Hearing in Our Own Tongues the Wonderful Works of God': Pentecost, Ecumenism, and Renewal in African Christianity." *Missionalia* 35 (3, Nov. 2007): 128–45.

Asamoah-Gyadu, "Leadership." "'Touch Not the Lord's Anointed': Leadership in Ghana's New Charismatic Communities." Pages 142–57 in *A New Day: Essays on World Christianity in Honor of Lamin Sanneh*. Edited by Akintunde E. Akinade. Foreword by Andrew F. Walls. New York: Peter Lang, 2010.

Ashe, *Miracles*. Ashe, Geoffrey. *Miracles*. London: Routledge & Kegan Paul, 1978.

Ashkanani, "Zar." Ashkanani, Zubaydah. "Zar in a Changing World: Kuwait." Pages 219–30 in *Women's Medicine: The Zar-Bori Cult in Africa and Beyond*. Edited by I. M. Lewis, Ahmed Al-Safi, and Sayyid Hurreiz. Edinburgh: International African Institute/ Edinburgh University Press, 1991.

Ashton, *Religion*. Ashton, John. *The Religion of Paul the Apostle*. New Haven: Yale University Press, 2000.

Aspinal, "Church." Aspinal, H. R. "The Brethren Church in Argentina." MA thesis, Fuller Theological Seminary, 1973.

Assarian, Biqam, Asqarnejad, "Study." Assarian, F., H. Biqam, and A. Asqarnejad. "An Epidemiological Study of Obsessive-Compulsive Disorder among High School Students and Its Relationship with Religious Attitudes." *ArIrMed* 9 (2, 2006): 104–7.

Atieno, *Movement*. Atieno, Abamfo Ofori. *The Rise of the Charismatic Movement in the Mainline Churches in Ghana*. Accra: Asempa Publishers, Christian Council of Ghana, 1993.

Atmore, Stacey, and Forman, *Kingdoms*. Atmore, Anthony, Gillian Stacey, and Werner Forman. *Black Kingdoms, Black Peoples: The West African Heritage*. London: Orbis, 1979.

Augustine *City of God*. Augustine. *Concerning the City of God against the Pagans*. Translated by Henry Bettenson. Edited by David Knowles. Harmondsworth: Pelican, 1972.

Aulie, "Movement." Aulie, H. Wilbur. "The Christian Movement among the Chols of Mexico, with Special Reference to Problems of Second-Generation Christianity." DMiss diss., Fuller Theological Seminary, 1979.

Aune, *Cultic Setting*. Aune, David Edward. *The Cultic Setting of Realized Eschatology in Early Christianity*. NovTSup 28. Leiden: Brill, 1972.

Aune, *Dictionary of Rhetoric*. Aune, David E. *The Westminster Dictionary of New Testament and Early Christian Literature and Rhetoric*. Louisville: Westminster John Knox, 2003.

Aune, *Environment*. Aune, David Edward. *The New Testament in Its Literary Environment*. LEC 8. Philadelphia: Westminster, 1987.

Aune, "Magic." Aune, David Edward. "Magic in Early Christianity." *ANRW* II (Principat).23 (1980): 1.1507–57.

Aune, "Problem of Genre." Aune, David E. "The Problem of the Genre of the Gospels: A Critique of C. H. Talbert's *What Is a Gospel?*" Pages 9–60 in *Studies of History and Tradition in the Four Gospels*. Vol. 2 of *GosPersp*. Edited by R. T. France and David Wenham. Sheffield: JSOT Press, 1981.

Aune, *Prophecy*. Aune, David Edward. *Prophecy in Early Christianity and the Ancient Mediterranean World*. Grand Rapids: Eerdmans, 1983.

Aune, *Revelation*. Aune, David E. *Revelation*. 3 vols. WBC 52, 52b, 52c. Dallas: Word, 1997.

Aurenhammer, "Sculptures." Aurenhammer, Maria. "Sculptures of Gods and Heroes from Ephesos." Pages 251–80 in *Ephesos: Metropolis of Asia. An Interdisciplinary Approach to Its Archaeology, Religion, and Culture*. Edited by Helmut Koester. HTS. Valley Forge, Pa.: Trinity Press International, 1995.

Austin-Broos, "Pentecostalism." Austin-Broos, Diane J. "Jamaican Pentecostalism: Transnational Relations and the Nation-State." Pages 142–62 in *Between Babel and Pentecost: Transnational Pentecostalism in Africa and Latin America*. Edited by André Corten and Ruth Marshall-Fratani. Bloomington: Indiana University Press, 2001.

Avalos, *Health Care*. Avalos, Hector. *Health Care and the Rise of Christianity*. Peabody, Mass.: Hendrickson, 1999.

Avalos, "Health Care." Avalos, Hector. "Health Care." Pages 760–64 in vol. 2 of *The New Interpreter's Dictionary of the Bible*. Edited by Katharine Doob Sakenfeld et al. 5 vols. Nashville: Abingdon, 2007.

Avalos, "Medicine." Avalos, Hector Ignacio. "Medicine." *OEANE* 3:450–59.

Avery-Peck, "Charismatic." Avery-Peck, Alan J. "The Galilean Charismatic and Rabbinic Piety: The Holy Man in the Talmudic Literature." Pages 149–65 in *The Historical Jesus in Context*. Edited by Amy-Jill Levine, Dale C. Allison Jr., and John Dominic Crossan. Princeton Readings in Religions. Princeton, N.J.: Princeton University Press, 2006.

Avi-Yonah, *Hellenism*. Avi-Yonah, Michael. *Hellenism and the East: Contacts and Interrelations from Alexander to the Roman Conquest*. Jerusalem: Institute of Languages, Literature and the Arts, The Hebrew University; University Microfilms International, 1978.

Aycock and Noaker, "Comparison." Aycock, D. W., and S. Noaker. "A Comparison of the Self-Esteem Levels in Evangelical Christian and General Populations." *JPsyTh* 13 (3, 1985): 199–208.

Ayegboyin, "Heal." Ayegboyin, Deji. "'Heal the Sick and Cast Out Demons': The Response of the Aladura." *StWChr* 10 (2, 2004): 233–49.

Ayers, "Eczema." Ayers, A. E. "Eczema Healed." *WWit* 9 (6, June 20, 1913): 7.

Ayuk, "Transformation." Ayuk, Ayuk Ausaji. "The Pentecostal Transformation of Nigerian Church Life." *AJPS* 5 (2, 2002): 189–204.

Azenabor, "Witchcraft." Azenabor, Godwin Ehi. "The Idea of Witchcraft and the Challenge of Modern Science." Pages 21–35 in *Studies in Witchcraft, Magic, War, and Peace in Africa*. Edited by Beatrice Nicolini. Lewiston, N.Y.: Edwin Mellen, 2006.

Azevedo, Prater, and Lantum, "Biomedicine." Azevedo, Mario J., Gwendolyn S. Prater, and Daniel N. Lantum. "Culture, Biomedicine, and Child Mortality in Cameroon." *SSMed* 32 (12, 1991): 1341–49.

Azouvi, "Rationalité." Azouvi, François. "Possession, Révélation et Rationalité Medicale au Debut du XVIIᵉ siècle." *RSPT* 64 (3, 1980): 355–62.

B., "Challenge." B., Dick. "The Healing Challenge in Recovery Groups Today." Pages 267–86 in *Religion*. Vol. 2 of *The Healing Power of Spirituality: How Faith Helps Humans Thrive*. Edited by J. Harold Ellens. Santa Barbara, Calif.: Praeger, 2010.

Babalola, "Impact." Babalola, E. O. "The Impact of African Traditional Religion and Culture upon the Aladura Churches." *AJT* 6 (1, 1992): 130–40.

Babbage, "Argument." Babbage, Charles. "Ninth Bridgewater Treatise (2nd ed. 1838), Chapter 10, 'On Hume's Argument against Miracles.'" Pages 203–12 in John Earman, *Hume's Abject Failure: The Argument against Miracles*. Oxford: Oxford University Press, 2000.

Babbage, *Treatise*. Babbage, Charles. *The Ninth Bridgewater Treatise: A Fragment*. 2nd ed. London: John Murray, 1938.

Bach, "Possession." Bach, Paul J. "Demon Possession and Psychopathology: A Theological Relationship." *JPsyTh* 7 (1, Spring 1979): 22–26.

Backhaus, "Falsehood." Backhaus, Wilfried K. "Advantageous Falsehood: The Person Moved by Faith Strikes Back." *PhilTheol* 7 (1993): 289–310.

Bacon, *Advancement*. Bacon, Francis. *The Advancement of Learning*. Edited by David Price. London: Cassell and Co., 1893.

Badía Cabrera, "Nota." Badía Cabrera, Miguel A. "Nota introductoria a la transcripción en inglés y a la traducción al español." *Diál* 83 (2004): 209–23.

Baer, "Bodies." Baer, Jonathan R. "Perfectly Empowered Bodies: Divine Healing in Modernizing America." PhD diss., Yale University, 2002.

Baetz et al., "Association." Baetz, Marilyn, Ronald Griffin, Rudy Bowen, Harold G. Koenig, and Eugene Marcoux. "The Association between Spiritual/Religious Involvement and Depressive Symptoms in the Canadian Population." *JNMDis* 192 (2004): 818–22.

Baetz et al., "Commitment." Baetz, Marilyn, David B. Larson, et al. "Canadian Psychiatric Inpatient Religious Commitment: An Association with Mental Health." *CanJPsy* 47 (2, 2002): 159–66.

Bagatti, *Church*. Bagatti, Bellarmino. *The Church from the Circumcision*. Jerusalem: Franciscan Printing Press, 1971.

Baghramian, "Relativism." Baghramian, Maria. "Relativism about Science." Pages 236–47 in *The Routledge Companion to Philosophy of Science*. Edited by Stathis Psillos and Martin Curd. New York: Routledge, 2008.

Bagiella, Hong, and Sloan, "Attendance as Predictor." Bagiella, Emilia, Victor Hong, and Richard P. Sloan. "Religious Attendance as a Predictor of Survival in the EPESE Cohorts." *IntJEpid* 34 (2005): 443–51.

Bähre, "Witchcraft." Bähre, Erik. "Witchcraft and the Exchange of Sex, Blood, and Money among Africans in Cape Town, South Africa." *JRelAf* 32 (3, 2002): 300–334.

Bainton, *Stand*. Bainton, Roland. *Here I Stand: A Life of Martin Luther*. New York: Abingdon, 1950.

Baird, "Analytical History." Baird, H. R. "An Analytical History of the Church of Christ Missions in Brazil." DMiss diss., Fuller Theological Seminary, 1979.

Baker, "Believes." Baker, Joseph. "Who Believes in Religious Evil? An Investigation of Sociological Patterns of Belief in Satan, Hell, and Demons." *RRelRes* 50 (2, Winter 2008): 206–20.

Baker, *Enough*. Baker, Rolland, and Heidi Baker. *There Is Always Enough: The Story of Rolland and Heidi Baker's Miraculous Ministry among the Poor*. Kent, England: Sovereign World, 2001. Published in the United States as *Always Enough: God's Miraculous Provision among the Poorest Children on Earth*. Grand Rapids: Chosen, 2003.

Baker, "Investigation." Baker, D. C. "The Investigation of Pastoral Care Interventions as a Treatment for Depression among Continuing Care Retirement Community Residents." *JRelGer* 12 (2000): 63–85.

Baker, *Miracles*. Baker, Heidi, and Rolland Baker. *Expecting Miracles: True Stories of God's Supernatural Power and How You Can Experience It*. Grand Rapids: Chosen, 2007. Also published as *The Hungry Always Get Fed: A Year of Miracles*. West Sussex: New Wine Ministries.

Baker, *Visions*. Baker, H. A. *Visions Beyond the Veil*. New Kensington, Pa.: Whitaker House, 2006. Earlier 12th ed.: Minneapolis: Osterhus Publishing House, n.d.

Balboni et al., "Religiousness." Balboni, Tracy A., L. C. Vanderwerker, S. D. Block, M. E. Paulk, C. S. Lathan, J. R. Peteet, and H. G. Prigerson. "Religiousness and Spiritual Support among Advanced Cancer Patients and Associations with End-of-Life Treatment Preferences and Quality of Life." *JClinOn* 25 (2007): 555–60.

Balch, "Genre." Balch, David L. "The Genre of Luke-Acts: Individual Biography, Adventure Novel, or Political History." *SwJT* 33 (1990): 5–19.

Balch, "Gospels (forms)." Balch, David L. "Gospels (literary forms)." Pages 947–49 in vol. 5 of *Brill's New Pauly: Encyclopaedia of the Ancient World*. Edited by Hubert Cancik and Helmuth Schneider. 20 vols. English ed. Christine F. Salazar. Leiden: Brill, 2010.

Balch, "ΜΕΤΑΒΟΛΗ ΠΟΛΙΤΕΙΩΝ." Balch, David L. "ΜΕΤΑΒΟΛΗ ΠΟΛΙΤΕΙΩΝ—Jesus as Founder of the Church in Luke-Acts: Form and Function." Pages 139–88 in *Contextualizing Acts: Lukan Narrative and Greco-Roman Discourse*. Edited by Todd Penner and Caroline Vander Stichele. SBLSymS 20. Atlanta: Society of Biblical Literature, 2003.

Ball, "Professors." Ball, Karen, comp. "What Professors Think." Pages 107–14 in *Signs and Wonders Today: The Story of Fuller Theological Seminary's Remarkable Course on Spiritual Power*. Rev. ed. Edited by C. Peter Wagner. Altamonte Springs, Fla.: Creation House, Strang Communications, 1987.

Ball, "View." Ball, Karen, comp. "The Students' View." Pages 125–35 in *Signs and Wonders Today: The Story of Fuller Theological Seminary's Remarkable Course on Spiritual Power*. Rev. ed. Edited by C. Peter Wagner. Altamonte Springs, Fla.: Creation House, Strang Communications, 1987.

Balling, *Story*. Balling, Jakob. *The Story of Christianity from Birth to Global Presence*. Grand Rapids: Eerdmans, 2003.

Baltzly, "Stoic Pantheism." Baltzly, Dirk. "Stoic Pantheism." *Soph* 42 (2, 2003): 3–33.

Barbour, *Myths*. Barbour, Ian G. *Myths, Models, and Paradigms: A Comparative Study in Science and Religion*. New York: Harper & Row, 1974.

Barbour, *Religion and Science*. Barbour, Ian G. *Religion and Science: Historical and Contemporary Issues*. San Franscisco: HarperSanFrancisco, 1997.

Barclay, *Acts*. Barclay, William. *The Acts of the Apostles*. Rev. ed. Philadelphia: Westminster, 1976.

Barclay, "Church in Nepal." Barclay, John. "The Church in Nepal: Analysis of Its Gestation and Growth." *IBMR* 33 (4, Oct. 2009): 189–94.

Barnes, "Chinese Healing." Barnes, Linda L. "Multiple Meanings of Chinese Healing in the United States." Pages 307–31 in *Religion and Healing in America*. Edited by Linda L. Barnes and Susan S. Sered. New York: Oxford University Press, 2005.

Barnes, "Curriculum." Barnes, Linda L. "A Medical School Curriculum on Religion and Healing." Pages 307–25 in *Teaching Religion and Healing*. Edited by Linda L. Barnes and Inés Talamantez. AARTRSS. Oxford: Oxford University Press, 2006.

Barnes, "History." Barnes, Linda L. "Teaching the History of Chinese Healing Traditions." Pages 95–109 in *Teaching Religion and Healing*. Edited by Linda L. Barnes and Inés Talamantez. AARTRSS. Oxford: Oxford University Press, 2006.

Barnes, "Introduction." Barnes, Linda L. "Introduction." Pages 3–26 in *Teaching Religion and Healing*. Edited by Linda L. Barnes and Inés Talamantez. AARTRSS. Oxford: Oxford University Press, 2006.

Barnes, "Miracles." Barnes, L. Philip. "Miracles, Charismata and Benjamin B. Warfield." *EvQ* 67 (3, 1995): 219–43.

Barnes, "World Religions." Barnes, Linda L. "World Religions and Healing." Pages 341–52 in *Teaching Religion and Healing*. Edited by Linda L. Barnes and Inés Talamantez. AARTRSS. Oxford: Oxford University Press, 2006.

Barnes and Talamantez, *Religion and Healing*. Barnes, Linda L., and Inés Talamantez, eds. *Teaching Religion and Healing*. AARTRSS. Oxford: Oxford University Press, 2006.

Barnett, "Answer." Barnett, Homer G. "The Answer to a Prayer." Pages 274–80 in *Crossing Cultural Boundaries: The Anthropological Experience*. Edited by Solon T. Kimball and James B. Watson. San Francisco: Chandler, 1972.

Barnett, *Birth*. Barnett, Paul. *The Birth of Christianity: The First Twenty Years*. Grand Rapids: Eerdmans, 2005.

Barnett, "Eschatological Prophets." Barnett, Paul. "The Jewish Eschatological Prophets." PhD diss., University of London, 1977.

Barnett, "Feeding." Barnett, Paul W. "The Feeding of the Multitude in Mark 6/John 6." Pages 273–93 in *The Miracles of Jesus*. Edited by David Wenham

and Craig Blomberg. Vol. 6 of *GosPersp*. Sheffield: JSOT Press, 1986.

Barnett, "Prophets." Barnett, Paul W. "The Jewish Sign Prophets—A.D. 40–70—Their Intentions and Origin." *NTS* 27 (5, Oct. 1981): 679–97.

Barnett, "Sign Prophets." Barnett, P. W. "The Jewish Sign Prophets." Pages 444–62 in *The Historical Jesus in Recent Research*. Edited by James D. G. Dunn and Scot McKnight. Winona Lake, Ind.: Eisenbrauns, 2005.

Barnum, *Silent*. Barnum, Thaddeus. *Never Silent: How Third World Missionaries Are Now Bringing the Gospel to the U.S.* Colorado Springs: Eleison Publishing, 2008.

Baroody, "Healing." Baroody, Naseeb B. "Spiritual Healing in Psychosomatic Disease." Pages 87–92 in *Faith Healing: Finger of God? Or, Scientific Curiosity?* Compiled by Claude A. Frazier. New York: Thomas Nelson, 1973.

Barr, *Physics and Faith*. Barr, Stephen M. *Modern Physics and Ancient Faith*. Notre Dame, Ind.: University of Notre Dame Press, 2003.

Barr, Leonard, Parsons, and Weaver, *Acts*. Barr, Beth Allison, Bill J. Leonard, Mikeal C. Parsons, and C. Douglas Weaver, eds. *The Acts of the Apostles: Four Centuries of Baptist Interpretation. The Baptists' Bible*. Waco: Baylor University Press, 2009.

Barrett, *Acts*. Barrett, C. K. *A Critical and Exegetical Commentary on the Acts of the Apostles*. 2 vols. Edinburgh: T&T Clark, 1994–98.

Barrett, *Documents*. Barrett, C. K. *The New Testament Background: Selected Documents*. New York: Harper & Row, 1961.

Barrett, *Encyclopedia*. Barrett, David B. *World Christian Encyclopedia*. 2nd ed. New York: Oxford University Press, 2001.

Barrett, "Renewal." Barrett, David B. "The Worldwide Holy Spirit Renewal." Pages 381–414 in *The Century of the Holy Spirit: One Hundred Years of Pentecostal and Charismatic Renewal, 1901–2001*. Edited by Vinson Synan. Nashville: Thomas Nelson, 2001.

Barrett, "Statistics." Barrett, David B. "Statistics, Global." Pages 810–29 in *Dictionary of Pentecostal and Charismatic Movements*. Edited by Stanley M. Burgess, Gary B. McGee, and Patrick H. Alexander. Grand Rapids: Zondervan, 1988.

Barrett, Johnson, and Crossing, "Missiometrics 2005." Barrett, David B., Todd M. Johnson, and Peter F. Crossing. "Missiometrics 2005: A Global Survey of World Mission." *IBMR* 29 (1, Jan. 2005): 27–30.

Barrett, Johnson, and Crossing, "Missiometrics 2006." Barrett, David B., Todd M. Johnson, and Peter F. Crossing. "Missiometrics 2006: Goals,

Resources, Doctrines of the 350 Christian World Communions." *IBMR* 30 (1, Jan. 2006): 27–30.

Barrett, Johnson, and Crossing, "Missiometrics 2007." Barrett, David B., Todd M. Johnson, and Peter F. Crossing. "Missiometrics 2007: Creating Your Own Analysis of Global Data." *IBMR* 31 (1, Jan. 2007): 25–32.

Barrett, Johnson, and Crossing, "Missiometrics 2008." Barrett, David B., Todd M. Johnson, and Peter F. Crossing. "Missiometrics 2008: Reality Checks for Christian World Communions." *IBMR* 32 (1, Jan. 2008): 27–30.

Barrett, Kurian, and Johnson, *Encyclopedia.* Barrett, David B., Thomas Kurian, and Todd M. Johnson. *World Christian Encyclopedia: A Comparative Survey of Churches and Religions in the Modern World.* 2nd ed. New York: Oxford University Press, 2001.

Barrett-Lennard, *Healing.* Barrett-Lennard, R. J. S. *Christian Healing after the New Testament: Some Approaches to Illness in the Second, Third, and Fourth Centuries.* Lanham, Md.: University Press of America, 1994.

Barrington-Ward, "Spirit Possession." Barrington-Ward, Simon. "'The Centre Cannot Hold . . .': Spirit Possession as Redefinition." Pages 455–70 in *Christianity in Independent Africa.* Edited by Edward Fasholé-Luke, Richard Gray, Adrian Hastings, and Godwin Tasie. Bloomington: Indiana University Press, 1978.

Barron, *Gospel.* Barron, Bruce. *The Health and Wealth Gospel: What's Going on Today in a Movement That Has Shaped the Faith of Millions?* Downers Grove, Ill.: InterVarsity, 1987.

Barrow, "Spiritualism." Barrow, Logie. "Anti-Establishment Healing: Spiritualism in Britain." Pages 225–47 in *The Church and Healing: Papers Read at the Twentieth Summer Meeting and the Twenty-first Winter Meeting of the Ecclesiastical History Society.* StChHist 19. Edited by W. J. Sheils. Oxford: Basil Blackwell, 1982.

Barrow and Tipler, *Principle.* Barrow, John D., and Frank J. Tipler. *The Anthropic Cosmological Principle.* Foreword by John A. Wheeler. Oxford: Clarendon; New York: Oxford University Press, 1986.

Bartels, *Roots.* Bartels, F. L. *The Roots of Ghana Methodism.* Cambridge: Cambridge University Press, 1965.

Barth, *Dogmatics.* Barth, Karl. *Church Dogmatics: The Doctrine of Reconciliation.* 4.3. Edinburgh: T&T Clark, 1961.

Barth, *Letters.* Barth, Karl. *Letters 1961–1968.* Translated and edited by Geoffrey W. Bromiley. Grand Rapids: Eerdmans, 1981.

Barth, *Theology.* Barth, Karl. *Protestant Theology in the Nineteenth Century.* London: SCM, 1972; Valley Forge, Pa.: Judson, 1973.

Bartholomew, *Belief.* Bartholomew, D. J. *Uncertain Belief: Is It Rational to Be a Christian?* New York: Oxford University Press, 2000.

Bartholomew, *Chance.* Bartholomew, David J. *The God of Chance.* London: SCM, 1984.

Bartleman, *Azusa Street.* Bartleman, Frank. *Azusa Street.* Foreword by Vinson Synan. Plainfield, N.J.: Logos, 1980.

Bartlett, *Hanged Man.* Bartlett, Robert. *The Hanged Man: A Story of Miracle, Memory, and Colonialism in the Middle Ages.* Princeton, N.J.: Princeton University Press, 2004.

Barton, "Feedings." Barton, Stephen C. "The Miraculous Feedings in Mark." *ExpT* 97 (4, Jan. 1986): 112–13.

Barton, "Origin." Barton, George A. "The Origin of the Names of Angels and Demons in the Extra-Canonical Apocalyptic Literature to 100 A.D." *JBL* 31 (1912): 156–67.

Bartow, *Adventures.* Bartow, Donald W. *The Adventures of Healing.* Canton, Ohio: Life Enrichment Publishers, 1981.

Basinger, "Apologetics." Basinger, David. "Miracles and Apologetics: A Response." *CSR* 9 (4, 1980): 348–53.

Basinger, "Evidence." Basinger, David. "Miracles as Evidence for Theism." *Soph* 29 (1, April 1990): 56–59.

Basinger and Basinger, "Concept." Basinger, David, and Randall Basinger. "Science and the Concept of Miracle." *JASA* 30 (4, 1978): 164–68.

Basinger and Basinger, *Miracle.* Basinger, David, and Randall Basinger. *Philosophy and Miracle: The Contemporary Debate.* PCPhil 2. Lewiston, N.Y.: Edwin Mellen, 1986.

Baskin, "Devils." Baskin, Wade. "The Devils of Loudun." Pages 15–20 in *Exorcism Through the Ages.* Edited by St. Elmo Nauman. New York: Philosophical Library, 1974.

Baskin, "Nuns." Baskin, Wade. "The Nuns of Aix-en-Provence." Pages 195–200 in *Exorcism Through the Ages.* Edited by St. Elmo Nauman. New York: Philosophical Library, 1974.

Basser, "Interpretations." Basser, Herbert W. "Superstitious Interpretations of Jewish Laws." *JSJ* 8 (2, Oct. 1977): 127–38.

Basso, "Music." Basso, Rebecca. "Music, Possession, and Shamanism among Khond Tribes." *CulRel* 7 (2, 2006): 177–97.

Bastian, "Pentecostalism." Bastian, Jean-Pierre. "Pentecostalism, Market Logic and Religious Transnationalisation in Costa Rica." Pages 163–80 in *Between Babel and Pentecost: Transnational Pentecostalism in Africa and Latin America.* Edited by André

Corten and Ruth Marshall-Fratani. Bloomington: Indiana University Press, 2001.

Bate, "Mission." Bate, Stuart C. "The Mission to Heal in a Global Context." *IntRevMiss* 90 (356/357, Jan./Apr. 2001): 70–80.

Batens, "Role." Batens, Diderik. "The Role of Logic in Philosophy of Science." Pages 47–57 in *The Routledge Companion to Philosophy of Science*. Edited by Stathis Psillos and Martin Curd. New York: Routledge, 2008.

Bates, Edwards, and Anderson, "Influences." Bates, M. S., W. T. Edwards, and K. O. Anderson. "Ethnocultural Influences on Variation in Chronic Pain Perception." *Pain* 52 (1993): 101–12.

Bauckham, "Acts of Paul." Bauckham, Richard J. "The Acts of Paul as a Sequel to Acts." Pages 105–52 in *The Book of Acts in Its Ancient Literary Setting*. Edited by Bruce W. Winter and Andrew D. Clark. Vol. 1 of *The Book of Acts in Its First Century Setting*. Grand Rapids: Eerdmans, 1993.

Bauckham, *Eyewitnesses*. Bauckham, Richard. *Jesus and the Eyewitnesses: The Gospels as Eyewitness Testimony*. Grand Rapids: Eerdmans, 2006.

Bauckham, "John." Bauckham, Richard. "John for Readers of Mark." Pages 147–72 in *The Gospels for All Christians: Rethinking the Gospel Audiences*. Edited by Richard Bauckham. Grand Rapids: Eerdmans, 1998.

Bauckham, "Visions." Bauckham, Richard. "Early Jewish Visions of Hell." *JTS* 41 (2, 1990): 355–85.

Bauckham, "Visiting." Bauckham, Richard. "Visiting the Places of the Dead in the Extra-Canonical Apocalypses." *PIBA* 18 (1995): 78–93.

Baum, "Heilungswunder." Baum, Armin D. "Die Heilungswunder Jesu als Symbolhandlungen Ein Versuch." *EurZTh* 13 (1, 2004): 5–14.

Bauman, "Response." Bauman, Harold E. "Response to Robert T. Sears." Pages 115–17 in *Essays on Spiritual Bondage and Deliverance*. Edited by Willard M. Swartley. Occasional Papers 11. Elkhart, Ind.: Institute of Mennonite Studies, 1988.

Baumgarten, "Fragments." Baumgarten, Joseph M. "The 4Q Zadokite Fragments on Skin Disease." *JJS* 41 (1990): 153–65.

Baumgarten, "Miracles." Baumgarten, Albert I. "Miracles and Halakah in Rabbinic Judaism." *JQR* 73 (3, Jan. 1983): 238–53.

Baumgarten, "Seductress." Baumgarten, Joseph M. "The Seductress of Qumran." *BRev* 17 (5, 2001): 21–23, 42.

Baxter, *Healing*. Baxter, J. Sidlow. *Divine Healing of the Body*. Grand Rapids: Zondervan, 1979.

Baxter, "Historical Judgment." Baxter, Anthony. "Historical Judgment, Transcendent Perspective, and

'Resurrection Appearances.'" *HeyJ* 40 (1, 1999): 19–40.

Baylor Institute, *Piety*. Baylor Institute for Studies of Religion. *American Piety in the Twenty-first Century: New Insights into the Depths and Complexity of Religion in the U.S.* Waco: Baylor Institute for Studies of Religion, 2006.

Bays, "Revival." Bays, Daniel H. "Christian Revival in China, 1900–1937." Pages 161–79 in *Modern Christian Revivals*. Edited by Edith Blumhofer and Randall H. Balmer. Urbana: University of Illinois Press, 1993.

Beadle, "Healings." Beadle, Wilbur. "Healings Lead Baptist Minister to Baptism in the Holy Spirit." *PentEv* (International Edition, Aug. 1968): 6–7.

Beals, *Culture*. Beals, Alan R. *Culture in Process*. New York: Holt, Rinehart & Winston, 1979.

Beard, *Mission*. Beard, Rebecca. *Everyman's Mission: The Development of the Christ-Self*. Philadelphia: Merrybrook, 1952.

Beasley-Murray, *John*. Beasley-Murray, George R. *John*. WBC 36. Waco: Word, 1987.

Beattie, "Mediumship." Beattie, John. "Spirit Mediumship in Bunyoro." Pages 159–70 in *Spirit Mediumship and Society in Africa*. Edited by John Beattie and John Middleton. Foreword by Raymond Firth. New York: Africana Publishing Corporation, 1969.

Beattie and Middleton, "Introduction." Beattie, John, and John Middleton. "Introduction." Pages xvii–xxx in *Spirit Mediumship and Society in Africa*. Edited by John Beattie and John Middleton. Foreword by Raymond Firth. New York: Africana Publishing Corporation, 1969.

Beattie and Middleton, *Mediumship*. Beattie, John, and John Middleton, eds. *Spirit Mediumship and Society in Africa*. Foreword by Raymond Firth. New York: Africana Publishing Corporation, 1969.

Beauregard and O'Leary, *Brain*. Beauregard, Mario, and Denyse O'Leary. *The Spiritual Brain: A Neuroscientist's Case for the Existence of the Soul*. New York: HarperCollins, 2007.

Beauvoir, "Herbs." Beauvoir, Max-G. "Herbs and Energy: The Holistic Medical System of the Haitian People." Pages 112–33 in *Haitian Vodou: Spirit, Myth, and Reality*. Edited by Patrick Bellegarde-Smith and Claudine Michel. Bloomington: Indiana University Press, 2006.

Bebbington, "Clash." Bebbington, D. W. "Revival and the Clash of Cultures: Ferryden, Forfarshire, in 1859." Pages 65–94 in *Revival, Renewal, and the Holy Spirit*. Edited by Dyfed Wyn Roberts. SEHT. Eugene, Ore.: Wipf & Stock, 2009.

Bebbington, *Dominance*. Bebbington, David W. *The Dominance of Evangelicalism: The Age of Spurgeon and*

Moody. A History of Evangelicalism: People, Movements, and Ideas in the English-Speaking World. Downers Grove, Ill.: InterVarsity, 2005.

Bebbington, *Evangelicalism*. Bebbington, David. *Evangelicalism in Modern Britain: A History from the 1730s to the 1980s*. Grand Rapids: Baker, 1989.

Beck, "Existence." Beck, W. David. "God's Existence." Pages 149–62 in *In Defense of Miracles: A Comprehensive Case for God's Action in History*. Edited by R. Douglas Geivett and Gary R. Habermas. Downers Grove, Ill.: InterVarsity, 1997.

Beck and Lewis, "Counseling." Beck, James R., and Gordon R. Lewis. "Counseling and the Demonic: A Reaction to Page." *JPsyTh* 17 (2, 1984): 132–34.

Becken, "Healing Communities." Becken, Hans-Jürgen. "African Independent Churches as Healing Communities." Pages 227–39 in *Afro-Christian Religion and Healing in Southern Africa*. Edited by G. C. Oosthuizen, S. D. Edwards, W. H. Wessels, and I. Hexham. AfSt 8. Lewiston, N.Y.: Edwin Mellen, 1989.

Becker, "Laws." Becker, Ulrich J. "Who Arranged for These Laws to Cooperate So Well?" Pages 28–30 in *Cosmos, Bios, and Theos: Scientists Reflect on Science, God, and the Origins of the Universe, Life, and Homo Sapiens*. Edited by Henry Margenau and Roy Abraham Varghese. La Salle, Ill.: Open Court, 1992.

Becker et al., "Belief." Becker, Gerhild, et al. "Religious Belief as a Coping Strategy: An Explorative Trial in Patients Irradiated for Head-and-Neck Cancer." *StrOnk* 182 (5, 2006): 270–76.

Beckwith, *Argument*. Beckwith, Francis J. *David Hume's Argument against Miracles: A Critical Analysis*. Lanham, Md.: University Press of America, 1989.

Beckwith, "Epistemology." Beckwith, Francis J. "Hume's Evidential/Testimonial Epistemology, Probability, and Miracles." *Logos* 12 (1991): 87–104.

Beckwith, "History." Beckwith, Francis J. "On History and Miracles." *PhilChr* 3 (1, 2001): 42–45.

Beckwith, "History and Miracles." Beckwith, Francis J. "History and Miracles." Pages 86–98 in *In Defense of Miracles: A Comprehensive Case for God's Action in History*. Edited by R. Douglas Geivett and Gary R. Habermas. Downers Grove, Ill.: InterVarsity, 1997.

Bediako, "African Culture." Bediako, Kwame. "Jesus in African Culture: A Ghanaian Perspective." Pages 93–121 in *Emerging Voices in Global Christian Theology*. Edited by William A. Dyrness. Grand Rapids: Zondervan, 1994.

Bediako, *Christianity in Africa*. Bediako, Kwame. *Christianity in Africa: The Renewal of a Non-Western Religion*. Edinburgh: Edinburgh University Press; Maryknoll, N.Y.: Orbis, 1995.

Beecher, "Placebo." Beecher, Henry K. "Surgery as Placebo: A Quantitative Study of Bias." *JAMA* 176 (1961): 1102–7.

Behe, *Box*. Behe, Michael J. *Darwin's Black Box: The Biochemical Challenge to Evolution*. New York: Free Press, 1997.

Behrend, *Geister*. Behrend, Heike. *Alice und die Geister. Krieg im Norden Ugandas*. Munich: Trickster Verlag, 1993.

Behrend, "Power." Behrend, Heike. "Power to Heal, Power to Kill: Spirit Possession & War in Northern Uganda (1986–1994)." Pages 20–33 in *Spirit Possession, Modernity and Power in Africa*. Edited by Heike Behrend and Ute Luig. Madison: University of Wisconsin Press, 1999.

Behrend and Luig, "Introduction." Behrend, Heike, and Ute Luig. "Introduction." Pages xiii–xxii in *Spirit Possession, Modernity and Power in Africa*. Edited by Heike Behrend and Ute Luig. Madison: University of Wisconsin Press, 1999.

Beit-Hallahmi, "Signs." Beit-Hallahmi, Benjamin. "Through Signs and Wonders: Religious Discourse and Miracle Narratives." Pages 159–85 in *Religious and Spiritual Events*. Vol. 1 of *Miracles: God, Science, and Psychology in the Paranormal*. Edited by J. Harold Ellens. Westport, Conn.; London: Praeger, 2008.

Bellamy, "Person." Bellamy, Carla. "Person in Place: Possession and Power at an Islamic Saint Shrine." *JFSR* 24 (1, 2008): 31–44.

Ben-Amos and Mintz, "Introduction." Ben-Amos, Dan, and Jerome R. Mintz, eds. and trans. *In Praise of the Baal Shem Tov (Shivhei ha-Besht): The Earliest Collection of Legends about the Founder of Hasidism*. Bloomington: Indiana University Press, 1970; New York: Schocken, 1984.

Benavidez, "Church of God." Benavidez, Doreen Alcoran. "The Early Years of the Church of God in Northern Luzon (1947–1953): A Historical and Theological Overview." *AJPS* 8 (2, July 2005): 255–69.

Benda, "Factors." Benda, B. B. "Factors Associated with Rehospitalization among Veterans in a Substance Abuse Treatment Program." *PsychServ* 53 (2002): 1176–78.

Benjamin, "Squatters." Benjamin, Jesse. "Squatters, Resistance to 'Development,' and Magic as a Tool of Subaltern Power: A Case from Coastal Kenya." Pages 239–62 in *Studies in Witchcraft, Magic, War, and Peace in Africa*. Edited by Beatrice Nicolini. Lewiston, N.Y.: Edwin Mellen, 2006.

Benjamins, "Religion." Benjamins, Maureen Reindl. "Does Religion Influence Patient Satisfaction?" *AmJHBeh* 30 (1, 2006): 85–91.

Benjamins, "Religion and Health." Benjamins, Maureen R. "Religion and Functional Health among the

Elderly: Is There a Relationship and Is It Constant?" *JAgHealth* 16 (3, 2004): 355–74.

Benn, "Correlation." Benn, Christoph. "Does Faith Contribute to Healing? Scientific Evidence for a Correlation between Spirituality and Health." *IntRevMiss* 90 (356/357, Jan./Apr. 2001): 140–48.

Bennett, *Miracle.* Bennett, George. *Miracle at Crowhurst.* Evesham: Arthur James, 1970.

Bennett, *Morning.* Bennett, Dennis J. *Nine O'Clock in the Morning.* Plainfield, N.J.: Logos, 1970.

Bennett, "Multiplication." Bennett, Charles T. "Notable Church Multiplication in Columbia." *CGB* 7 (1, 1970): 85–87.

Bennett, "Tinder." Bennett, Charles T. "Tinder in Tabasco." MA thesis, Fuller Theological Seminary, 1972.

Benoit, "Angelology." Benoit, Pierre. "Pauline Angelology and Demonology: Reflexions on the Designations of the Heavenly Powers and on the Origin of Angelic Evil According to Paul." *RSB* 3 (1, 1983): 1–18.

Benoit, *Jesus.* Benoit, Pierre. *Jesus and the Gospel.* 2 vols. Translated by Benet Weatherhead. Vol. 1: New York: Herder & Herder; London: Darton, Longman and Todd, 1973. Vol. 2: New York: Seabury (Crossroad); London: Darton, Longman and Todd, 1974.

Benor, "Survey." Benor, Daniel J. "Survey of Spiritual Healing Research." *ComMedRes* 4 (1990): 9–33.

Benson, *Healing.* Benson, Herbert, with Marg Stark. *Timeless Healing: The Power and Biology of Belief.* New York: Scribner, 1996.

Benson, *Not Healed.* Benson, Carmen. *What about Us Who Are Not Healed?* Plainfield, N.J.: Logos, 1975.

Benson, "Temperature Changes." Benson, Herbert. "Body Temperature Changes During the Practice of g Tum-mo Yoga." *Nature* 298 (1982): 402.

Benson and McCallie, "Placebo Effect." Benson, Herbert, and D. P. McCallie Jr. "Angina Pectoris and the Placebo Effect." *NewEngJMed* 300 (1979): 1424–29.

Benson et al., "Study." Benson, Herbert, Jeffrey A. Dusek, Jane B. Sherwood, et al. "Study of the Therapeutic Effects of Intercessory Prayer (STEP) in Cardiac Bypass Patients: A Multi-Center Randomized Trial of Uncertainty and Certainty of Receiving Intercessory Prayer." *AmHeartJ* 151 (2006): 934–42.

Bentall, "Experiences." Bentall, Richard P. "Hallucinatory Experiences." Pages 85–120 in *Varieties of Anomalous Experience: Examining the Scientific Evidence.* Edited by Etzel Cardeña, Steven Jay Lynn, and Stanley Krippner. Washington, D.C.: American Psychological Association, 2000.

Bentley, *Miraculous.* Bentley, Todd, with Jackie Macgirvin. *Journey into the Miraculous.* Victoria, B.C.: Hemlock Printers, 2003.

Bentley, *Relics.* Bentley, James. *Restless Bones: The Story of Relics.* London: Constable & Company, 1985.

Berceville, "L'étonnante." Berceville, Gilles. "L'étonnante Alliance: évangile et miracles selon Saint Thomas d'Aquin." *RThom* 103 (1, 2003): 5–74.

Berenbaum, Kerns, and Raghavan, "Experiences." Berenbaum, Howard, John Kerns, and Chitra Raghavan. "Anomalous Experiences, Peculiarity, and Psychopathology." Pages 25–46 in *Varieties of Anomalous Experience: Examining the Scientific Evidence.* Edited by Etzel Cardeña, Steven Jay Lynn, and Stanley Krippner. Washington, D.C.: American Psychological Association, 2000.

Berends, "African Healing Practices." Berends, Willem. "African Traditional Healing Practices and the Christian Community." *Missiology* 21 (3, 1993): 275–88.

Berends, "Criteria." Berends, Willem. "The Biblical Criteria for Demon Possession." *WTJ* 37 (3, 1975): 342–65.

Berger, "Faces." Berger, Peter L. "Four Faces of Global Culture." Pages 419–27 in *Globalization and the Challenges of a New Century: A Reader.* Edited by Patrick O'Meara, Howard D. Mehlinger, and Matthew Krain. Bloomington: Indiana University Press, 2000.

Berger, *Rumor.* Berger, Peter L. *A Rumor of Angels: Modern Society and the Rediscovery of the Supernatural.* Garden City, N.Y.: Doubleday, 1969.

Berger, "Women." Berger, Iris. "Women in East and Southern Africa." Pages 5–62 in *Women in Sub-Saharan Africa* by Iris Berger and E. Frances White. Restoring Women to History. Bloomington: Indiana University Press, 1999.

Bergunder, "Evangelist." Bergunder, Michael. "From Pentecostal Healing Evangelist to Kalki Avatar: The Remarkable Life of Paulaseer Lawrie, alias Shree Lahari Krishna (1921–1989)—A Contribution to the Understanding of New Religious Movements." Pages 357–75 in *Christians and Missionaries in India: Cross-Cultural Communication Since 1500, with Special Reference to Caste, Conversion, and Colonialism.* Edited by Robert Eric Frykenberg with Alaine Low. SHCM. Grand Rapids: Eerdmans; London: RoutledgeCurzon, 2003.

Bergunder, "Healing." Bergunder, Michael. "Miracle Healing and Exorcism: The South Indian Pentecostal Movement in the Context of Popular Hinduism." *IntRevMiss* 90 (356/357, Jan./Apr. 2001): 103–12.

Bergunder, "Miracle Healing." Bergunder, Michael. "Miracle Healing and Exorcism in South Indian Pentecostalism." Pages 287–305 in *Global Pentecostal and Charismatic Healing.* Edited by Candy Gunther Brown. Foreword by Harvey Cox. Oxford: Oxford University Press, 2011.

Bergunder, *Movement*. Bergunder, Michael. *The South Indian Pentecostal Movement in the Twentieth Century.* SHCM. Grand Rapids: Eerdmans, 2008.

Bergunder, "Turn." Bergunder, Michael. "The Cultural Turn." Pages 51–73 in *Studying Global Pentecostalism: Theories and Methods.* Edited by Allan Anderson, Michael Bergunder, André Droogers, and Cornelis van der Laan. Berkeley: University of California Press, 2010.

Berkel and Waard, "Mortality Pattern." Berkel, J., and F. de Waard. "Mortality Pattern and Life Expectancy of Seventh-Day Adventists in the Netherlands." *IntJEpid* 12 (4, 1983): 455–59.

Bernard, "Miracle." Bernard, J. H. "Miracle." Pages 379–96 in vol. 3 of *A Dictionary of the Bible Dealing with Its Language, Literature, and Contents Including the Biblical Theology.* Edited by James Hastings. 5 vols. New York: Charles Scribner's Sons, 1898–1909. Vol. 3 is 1900.

Bernasek, "Mechanism." Bernasek, Steven L. "The Mechanism of the World and the Why of It." Pages 149–51 in *Cosmos, Bios, and Theos: Scientists Reflect on Science, God, and the Origins of the Universe, Life, and Homo Sapiens.* Edited by Henry Margenau and Roy Abraham Varghese. La Salle, Ill.: Open Court, 1992.

Berndt, "Role." Berndt, Catherine H. "The Role of Native Doctors in Aboriginal Australia." Pages 264–84 in *Magic, Faith, and Healing: Studies in Primitive Psychiatry Today.* Edited by Ari Kiev. Foreword by Jerome D. Frank. New York: Free Press, 1964.

Bertman, "Note." Bertman, Stephen. "A Note on the Reversible Miracle." *HR* 3 (1964): 323–27.

Best, "Exorcism." Best, Ernest. "Exorcism in the New Testament and Today." *BibTh* 27 (1977): 1–9.

Best, "Miracles." Best, Ernest. "The Miracles in Mark." *RevExp* 75 (4, Fall 1978): 539–54.

Best, *Supernatural*. Best, Gary. *Naturally Supernatural: Joining God in His Work.* Cape Town: Vineyard International, 2005.

Bettenson and Knowles, *City of God*. Augustine. *Concerning the City of God against the Pagans.* Translated by Henry Bettenson. Edited by David Knowles. New York: Penguin, 1972.

Betty, "Evidence." Betty, Stafford. "The Growing Evidence for 'Demonic Possession': What Should Psychiatry's Response Be?" *JRelHealth* 44 (1, Spring 2005): 13–30.

Betz, "Fragments." Betz, Hans Dieter. "Fragments from a Catabasis Ritual in a Greek Magical Papyrus." *HR* 19 (1980): 287–95.

Betz, *Jesus*. Betz, Otto. *What Do We Know about Jesus?* Philadelphia: Westminster; London: SCM, 1968.

Betz, "Miracles in Josephus." Betz, Otto. "Miracles in the Writings of Flavius Josephus." Pages 212–35 in

Josephus, Judaism, and Christianity. Edited by Louis H. Feldman and Gohei Hata. Detroit: Wayne State University Press, 1987.

Betz, Dirkse, and Smith, "Numinis." Betz, H. D., Peter A. Dirkse, and E. W. Smith Jr. "De sera numinis vindicta (Moralia 548–568A)." Pages 181–235 in *Plutarch's Theological Writings and Early Christian Literature.* Edited by Hans Dieter Betz. SCHNT 3. Leiden: Brill, 1975.

Beutler et al., "Healing." Beutler, Jaap J., et al. "Paranormal Healing and Hypertension." *BMedJ* 296 (1988): 1491–94.

Bhatti, "Review." Bhatti, Faqir M. Review of Angela Hobart, *Healing Performance of Bali: Between Darkness and Light. Asian Affairs* 35 (3, Nov. 2004): 429.

Bhengu, "South Africa." Bhengu, Nicholas. "Taking South Africa for God." *PentEv* (March 6, 1955): 3.

Bieler, *Theios anēr*. Bieler, Ludwig. *Theios anēr. Das Bild des "göttlichen Menschen" in Spätantike und Frühchristentum.* Vienna: Höfels, 1935–36.

Biers, *Bath*. Biers, Jane C. *The Great Bath on the Lechaion Road.* Vol. 17 of *Corinth: Results of Excavations Conducted by the American School of Classical Studies at Athens.* Princeton, N.J.: The American School of Classical Studies at Athens, 1985.

Biller, "*Curate infirmos*." Biller, Peter. "*Curate infirmos*: The Medieval Waldensian Practice of Medicine." Pages 55–77 in *The Church and Healing: Papers Read at the Twentieth Summer Meeting and the Twenty-first Winter Meeting of the Ecclesiastical History Society.* StChHist 19. Edited by W. J. Sheils. Oxford: Basil Blackwell, 1982.

Biller and Ziegler, *Medicine*. Biller, Peter, and Joseph Ziegler, eds. *Religion and Medicine in the Middle Ages.* YSMT 3. Woodbridge, Suffolk: York Medieval Press, The University of York (with Boydell Press), 2001.

Billig, Kohn, and Levav, "Stress." Billig, Miriam, Robert Kohn, and Itzhak Levav. "Anticipatory Stress in the Population Facing Forced Removal from the Gaza Strip." *JNMDis* 194 (3, 2006): 195–200.

Binsbergen, *Change*. Binsbergen, Wim M. J. van. *Religious Change in Zambia: Exploratory Studies.* London: Kegan Paul, 1981.

Binsbergen, "Witchcraft." Binsbergen, Wim van. "Witchcraft in Modern Africa as Virtualized Boundary Conditions of the Kinship Order." Pages 212–63 in *Witchcraft Dialogues: Anthropological and Philosophical Exchanges.* Edited by George Clement Bond and Diane M. Ciekawy. Athens: Center for International Studies, Ohio University, 2001.

Bird, "Medicine." Bird, Jessalynn. "Medicine for Body and Soul: Jacques de Vitry's Sermons to Hospitallers and Their Charges." Pages 91–108 in *Religion and Medicine in the Middle Ages.* Edited by Peter Biller and Joseph Ziegler. YSMT 3. Woodbridge, Suffolk:

York Medieval Press, The University of York (with Boydell Press), 2001.

Bird, "Texts." Bird, Jessalynn. "Texts on Hospitals: Translation of Jacques de Vitry, *Historia Occidentalis* 29, and Edition of Jacques de Vitry's Sermons to Hospitallers." Pages 91–108 in *Religion and Medicine in the Middle Ages*. Edited by Peter Biller and Joseph Ziegler. YSMT 3. Woodbridge, Suffolk: York Medieval Press, The University of York (with Boydell Press), 2001.

Bird, "Turn." Bird, Alexander. "The Historical Turn in the Philosophy of Science." Pages 67–77 in *The Routledge Companion to Philosophy of Science*. Edited by Stathis Psillos and Martin Curd. New York: Routledge, 2008.

Birnbaum, "Polemic." Birnbaum, Ruth. "The Polemic on Miracles." *Judaism* 33 (4, 1984): 439–47.

Bishop, *Healing*. Bishop, George. *Faith Healing: God or Fraud?* Los Angeles: Sherbourne Press, 1967.

Bishop and Stenger, "Prayer." Bishop, Jeffrey P., and Victor J. Stenger. "Retroactive Prayer: Lots of History, Not Much Mystery, and No Science." *BMedJ* 329 (2004): 1444–46.

Bitzer, "Prince." Bitzer, Lloyd F. "The 'Indian Prince' in Miracle Arguments of Hume and His Predecessors and Early Critics." *PhilRhet* 31 (3, 1998): 175–230.

Blaauw, "Verdediging." Blaauw, Martijn. "Een verdediging van de mogelijkheid van wonderern." *Bijd* 64 (2, 2003): 165–78.

Black, *Homiletic*. Black, Kathy. *A Healing Homiletic: Preaching and Disability*. Nashville: Abingdon, 1996.

Black, "Preaching." Black, Kathleen. "Preaching the Miracle Healing Narratives." *QR* 16 (3, 1996): 253–64.

Blackburn, "ΑΝΔΡΕΣ." Blackburn, Barry L. "'Miracle Working ΘΕΙΟΙ ΑΝΔΡΕΣ' in Hellenism (and Hellenistic Judaism)." Pages 185–218 in *The Miracles of Jesus*. Vol. 6 of *GosPersp*. Edited by David Wenham and Craig Blomberg. Sheffield: JSOT Press, 1986.

Blackburn, "Miracles." Blackburn, Barry L. "The Miracles of Jesus." Pages 353–94 in *Studying the Historical Jesus: Evaluations of the State of Current Research*. NTTS 19. Edited by Bruce Chilton and Craig A. Evans. Leiden: Brill, 1994.

Blackman, "Impossibility." Blackman, Larry Lee. "The Logical Impossibility of Miracles in Hume." *IJPhilRel* 10 (1979): 179–87.

Blackman, "Miracles." Blackman, E. "Miracles of Healing in England." *PentEv* 338–39 (May 1, 1920): 9.

Blaising and Bock, *Progressive Dispensationalism*. Blaising, Craig A., and Darrell L. Bock. *Progressive Dispensationalism*. Grand Rapids: Baker, 1993.

Blenkinsopp, "Miracles." Blenkinsopp, Joseph. "Miracles: Elisha, and Hanina ben Dosa." Pages 57–81 in *Miracles in Jewish and Christian Antiquity: Imagining Truth*. Edited by John C. Cavadini. NDST 3. Notre Dame, Ind.: University of Notre Dame Press, 1999.

Blessing, "Healing." Blessing, Kamila. "Healing in the Gospels: The Essential Credentials." Pages 186–207 in *Religious and Spiritual Events*. Vol. 1 of *Miracles: God, Science, and Psychology in the Paranormal*. Edited by J. Harold Ellens. Westport, Conn.; London: Praeger, 2008.

Blessing, "Psychology." Blessing, Kamila. "Thaumaturgical Psychology: The Healing Constitution of Human Being." Pages 80–101 in *Psychodynamics*. Vol. 3 of *The Healing Power of Spirituality: How Faith Helps Humans Thrive*. Edited by J. Harold Ellens. Santa Barbara, Calif.: Praeger, 2010.

Blomberg, *Gospels*. Blomberg, Craig L. *The Historical Reliability of the Gospels*. 2nd ed. Downers Grove, Ill.: InterVarsity, 2008.

Blomberg, "Miracles." Blomberg, Craig L. "New Testament Miracles and Higher Criticism: Climbing up the Slippery Slope." *JETS* 27 (4, 1984): 425–38.

Blomberg, "Miracles as Parables." Blomberg, Craig L. "The Miracles as Parables." Pages 327–59 in *The Miracles of Jesus*. Vol. 6 of *GosPersp*. Edited by David Wenham and Craig Blomberg. Sheffield: JSOT Press, 1986.

Blomberg, "Reflections." Blomberg, Craig L. "Concluding Reflections on Miracles and Gospel Perspectives." Pages 443–57 in *The Miracles of Jesus*. Vol. 6 of *GosPersp*. Edited by David Wenham and Craig Blomberg. Sheffield: JSOT Press, 1986.

Blomberg, *Reliability*. Blomberg, Craig L. *The Historical Reliability of John's Gospel: Issues and Commentary*. Downers Grove, Ill.: InterVarsity, 2001.

Blowers, "Interpreting." Blowers, Paul M. "Interpreting Scripture." Pages 618–36 in *Constantine to c. 600*. Edited by Augustine Casiday and Frederick W. Norris. Vol. 2 of *The Cambridge History of Christianity*. 9 vols. Cambridge: Cambridge University Press, 2007.

Blue, *Authority*. Blue, Ken. *Authority to Heal*. Foreword by John White. Downers Grove, Ill.: InterVarsity, 1987.

Blumenthal et al., "Spirituality." Blumenthal, James A., et al. "Spirituality, Religion, and Clinical Outcomes in Patients Recovering from an Acute Myocardial Infarction." *PsychMed* 69 (2007): 501–8.

Blumhofer, "Apostolic Church." Blumhofer, Edith L. "The Christian Catholic Apostolic Church and the Apostolic Faith: A Study in the 1906 Pentecostal Revival." Pages 126–46 in *Charismatic Experiences in History*. Edited by Cecil M. Robeck Jr. Peabody, Mass.: Hendrickson, 1985.

Blumhofer, "Invasion." Blumhofer, Edith L. "A Pentecostal Branch Grows in Dowie's Zion: Charles F. Parham's 1906 Invasion." *AGHer* 6 (3, Fall 1986): 3–5.

Blumhofer, "McPherson." Blumhofer, Edith L. "McPherson, Aimee Semple (1890–1944)." Pages 263–67 in vol. 1 of *Encyclopedia of Religious Revivals in America*. Edited by Michael McClymond. 2 vols. Westport, Conn: Greenwood, 2007.

Blumhofer, "Portrait." Blumhofer, Edith. "Portrait of a Generation: Azusa Street Comes to Chicago." *Enr* 11 (2, Spring 2006): 95–102.

Blumhofer, "Restoration." Blumhofer, Edith L. "Restoration as Revival: Early American Pentecostalism." Pages 145–60 in *Modern Christian Revivals*. Edited by Edith Blumhofer and Randall H. Balmer. Urbana: University of Illinois Press, 1993.

Blumhofer, *Sister*. Blumhofer, Edith L. *Aimee Semple McPherson: Everybody's Sister*. Grand Rapids: Eerdmans, 1993.

Bockmuehl, "Law." Bockmuehl, Markus. "Natural Law in Second Temple Judaism." *VT* 45 (1, 1995): 17–44.

Bockmuehl, *Theology*. Bockmuehl, Klaus. *The Unreal God of Modern Theology. Bultmann, Barth, and the Theology of Atheism: A Call to Recovering the Truth of God's Reality*. Translated by Geoffrey W. Bromiley. Colorado Springs: Helmers & Howard, 1988.

Boddy, "Cross." Boddy, Alexander A. "A Cross in the Sky in War Time." *Conf* 9 (7, July 1916): 115.

Boddy, "Experiences." Boddy, Alexander A. "Transatlantic Experiences: A Visit to Zion City (Ill.)." *Conf* 6 (2, Feb. 1913): 33, 36–39.

Boddy, "Face." Boddy, Alexander A. "The Face of Christ: A Miraculous Appearance. Had It Any Reference to the War?" *Conf* 9 (7, July 1916): 113–14.

Boddy, "Spirit Possession." Boddy, Janice. "Spirit Possession Revisited: Beyond Instrumentality." *ARAnth* 23 (1994): 407–34.

Boddy, "Spirits and Selves." Boddy, Janice. "Spirits and Selves in Northern Sudan: The Cultural Therapeutics of Possession and Trance." *AmEthn* 15 (1, 1988): 4–27.

Boddy, *Wombs*. Boddy, Janice. *Wombs and Alien Spirits: Women, Men, and the Zar Cult in Northern Sudan*. Madison: University of Wisconsin Press, 1989.

"Body Loses Head." "'The Body' Loses Its Earthly Head." *CT* (June 29, 1979): 43.

Boer, "Introduction." Boer, Roland. "Introduction: Secularism and the Bible." Pages 1–12 in *Secularism and Biblical Studies*. Edited by Roland Boer. London: Equinox, 2010.

Boehr, *Medicine*. Boehr, Marian. *Medicine and Miracles amid the Multitudes: The Adventures of a Missionary Doctor in India*. Valley Forge, Pa.: American Baptist International Ministries, 2002.

Boggs, "Cults." Boggs, Wade H., Jr. "Faith Healing Cults." *Interp* 11 (1957): 55–70.

Boggs, *Faith Healing*. Boggs, Wade H., Jr. *Faith Healing and the Christian Faith*. Richmond, Va.: John Knox, 1956.

Boismard and Lamouille, *Actes*. Boismard, M.-É., and A. Lamouille. *Les Actes des Deux Apôtres*. ÉtBib, n.s. 12. 3 vols. Paris: Librairie Lecoffre, 1990. Vol. 1: Introduction and Texts. Vol. 2: The sense of the récits. Vol. 3: Literary Analyses.

Boissarie, *Healing*. Boissarie, P. G. *Healing at Lourdes*. Baltimore: John Murphy, 1933.

Bokser, "Wonder-Working." Bokser, Baruch M. "Wonder-Working and the Rabbinic Tradition: The Case of Hanina ben Dosa." *JSJ* 16 (1, June 1985): 42–92.

Bolt, "Daimons." Bolt, Peter G. "Jesus, the Daimons, and the Dead." Pages 75–102 in *The Unseen World: Christian Reflections on Angels, Demons, and the Heavenly Realm*. Edited by Anthony N. S. Lane. Grand Rapids: Baker, 1996.

Bolton, "Signs." Bolton, Brenda. "Signs, Wonders, Miracles: Supporting the Faith in Medieval Rome." Pages 157–78 in *Signs, Wonders, Miracles: Representations of Divine Power in the Life of the Church. Papers Read at the 2003 Summer Meeting and the 2004 Winter Meeting of the Ecclesiastical History Society*. Edited by Kate Cooper and Jeremy Gregory. Rochester: Boydell & Brewer, for the Ecclesiastical History Society, 2005.

Bolton, "Wife." Bolton, Robert. "A Smiling Wife and a Living Son." *MounM* (Jan. 1995): 28–29.

Bomann, *Faith in Barrios*. Bomann, Rebecca Pierce. *Faith in the Barrios: The Pentecostal Poor in Bogotá*. Boulder, Colo.: Lynn Rienner, 1999.

Bomann, "Salve." Bomann, Rebecca Pierce. "The Salve of Divine Healing: Essential Rituals for Survival among Working-Class Pentecostals in Bogotá, Colombia." Pages 187–205 in *Global Pentecostal and Charismatic Healing*. Edited by Candy Gunther Brown. Foreword by Harvey Cox. Oxford: Oxford University Press, 2011.

Bond, "Ancestors." Bond, George Clement. "Ancestors and Witches: Explanations and the Ideology of Individual Power in Northern Zambia." Pages 131–57 in *Witchcraft Dialogues: Anthropological and Philosophical Exchanges*. Edited by George Clement Bond and Diane M. Ciekawy. Athens: Center for International Studies, Ohio University, 2001.

Bond and Ciekawy, "Introduction." Bond, George Clement, and Diane M. Ciekawy. "Introduction: Contested Domains in the Dialogues of 'Witchcraft.'" Pages 1–38 in *Witchcraft Dialogues: Anthropological and Philosophical Exchanges*. Edited by George Clement Bond and Diane M. Ciekawy. Athens: Center for International Studies, Ohio University, 2001.

Bongmba, "Visions." Bongmba, Elias. "Visions and Dreams in an African Initiated Church." Pages 158–76 in *A New Day: Essays on World Christianity in Honor of Lamin Sanneh*. Edited by Akintunde E. Akinade. Foreword by Andrew F. Walls. New York: Peter Lang, 2010.

Bongmba, "Witchcraft." Bongmba, Elias. "African Witchcraft: From Ethnography to Critique." Pages 39–79 in *Witchcraft Dialogues: Anthropological and Philosophical Exchanges*. Edited by George Clement Bond and Diane M. Ciekawy. Athens: Center for International Studies, Ohio University, 2001.

Bonk, "Engaging." Bonk, Jonathan. "Engaging Escobar . . . and Beyond." Pages 47–55 in *Global Missiology for the 21st Century: The Iguassu Dialogue*. Edited by William D. Taylor. Grand Rapids: Baker Academic, 2000.

Bonnell, "Valid." Bonnell, John Sutherland. "Is Faith Healing Valid Today?" *PastPsy* 1 (10, 1950): 7–10.

Bonsirven, *Judaism*. Bonsirven, Joseph. *Palestinian Judaism in the Time of Jesus Christ*. New York: Holt, Rinehart & Winston, 1964.

Boobyer, "Miracles." Boobyer, G. H. "The Gospel Miracles: Views Past and Present." Pages 31–49 in *The Miracles and the Resurrection: Some Recent Studies by I. T. Ramsey, G. H. Boobyer, F. N. Davey, M. C. Perry, and Henry J. Cadbury*. Theological Collections 3. London: SPCK, 1964.

Booth-Clibborn, "John the Baptist." Booth-Clibborn, William E. "Is Another John the Baptist Due? Significance of the Pentecostal Outpouring." *LRE* 20 (9, June 1928): 6–9.

Borchert, *John*. Borchert, Gerald L. *John 1–11*. NAC 25A. Nashville: Broadman & Holman, 1996.

Borg, *Conflict*. Borg, Marcus J. *Conflict, Holiness, and Politics in the Teachings of Jesus*. SBEC 5. New York: Edwin Mellen, 1984.

Borg, "Disagreement." Borg, Marcus J. "An Appreciative Disagreement." Pages 227–43 in *Jesus and the Restoration of Israel: A Critical Assessment of N. T. Wright's Jesus and the Victory of God*. Edited by Carey C. Newman. Downers Grove, Ill.: InterVarsity, 1999.

Borg, "Experience." Borg, Marcus J. "The Spirit-Filled Experience of Jesus." Pages 302–14 in *The Historical Jesus in Recent Research*. Edited by James D. G. Dunn and Scot McKnight. Winona Lake, Ind.: Eisenbrauns, 2005.

Borg, *Jesus*. Borg, Marcus J. *Jesus: Uncovering the Life, Teachings, and Relevance of a Religious Revolutionary*. New York: HarperOne, 2006.

Borg, *Vision*. Borg, Marcus J. *Jesus: A New Vision (Spirit, Culture, and the Life of Discipleship)*. San Francisco: Harper & Row, 1987.

Borg et al., "System." Borg, Jacqueline, Bengt Andrée, Henrik Soderstrom, and Lars Farde. "The Serotonin System and Spiritual Experiences." *AmJPsyc* 160 (2003): 1965–69.

Borg-Breen, "Clutch." Borg-Breen, E. "In the Clutch of the Robbers." *CGl* 4 (2, Jan. 1923): 1–7.

Borgen, "Miracles." Borgen, Peder. "Miracles of Healing in the New Testament." *ST* 35 (2, 1981): 91–106.

Borgen, "Paul to Luke." Borgen, Peder. "From Paul to Luke: Observations toward Clarification of the Theology of Luke-Acts." *CBQ* 31 (1969): 168–82.

Boring, *Sayings*. Boring, M. Eugene. *Sayings of the Risen Jesus: Christian Prophecy in the Synoptic Tradition*. SNTSMS 46. Cambridge: Cambridge University Press, 1982.

Boring et al., *Commentary*. Boring, M. Eugene, Klaus Berger, and Carsten Colpe, eds. *Hellenistic Commentary to the New Testament*. Nashville: Abingdon, 1995.

Bormann and Oman, "Mantram." Bormann, Jill E., and Doug Oman. "Mantram, or Holy Name Repetition: Healing Power of a Portable Spiritual Practice." Pages 83–104 in *Personal Spirituality*. Vol. 1 of *The Healing Power of Spirituality: How Faith Helps Humans Thrive*. Edited by J. Harold Ellens. Santa Barbara, Calif.: Praeger, 2010.

Bormann and Oman, "Repetition." Bormann, Jill E., and Doug Oman. "Mantram or Holy Name Repetition: Health Benefits from a Portable Spiritual Practice." Pages 94–112 in *Spirit, Science, and Health: How the Spiritual Mind Fuels Physical Wellness*. Edited by Thomas G. Plante and Carl E. Thoresen. Foreword by Albert Bandura. Westport, Conn.: Praeger, 2007.

Bormann et al., "Effects." Bormann, J. E., A. L. Giffor, M. Shively, T. L. Smith, L. Rdwien, A. Kelly, et al. "Effects of Spiritual Mantram Repetition on HIV Outcomes: A Randomized Clinical Trial." *JBehMed* 29 (2006): 359–76.

Born, "Churches." Born, Bryan. "Christian Churches in Southern Africa—Challenge of Rebuilding Civil Society." *MissFoc* 17 (2009): 113–30.

Borzì, "L'accostamento." Borzì, S. "L'accostamento fra Apollonio di Tiana e Cristo." *Laós* 8 (1, 2001): 19–24.

Bosworth, *Healer*. Bosworth, F. F. *Christ the Healer*. Grand Rapids: Revell, 1973.

Bosworth et al., "Impact." Bosworth, H. B., K. S. Park, et al. "The Impact of Religious Practice and Religious Coping on Geriatric Depression." *IntJGerPsyc* 18 (10, 2003): 905–14.

Bottari, *Free*. Bottari, Pablo. *Free in Christ: Your Complete Handbook on the Ministry of Deliverance*. Foreword by Carlos Annacondia. Lake Mary, Fla.: Creation House, Strang Communications, 2000.

Boublik, "Finalita." Boublik, Vladimir. "La Finalita Dei Miracoli second S. Tommaso D'Aquini (Contra Gentes, III, 98)." *Divinitas* 11 (2, 1967): 651–60.

Bourgeois, "Spittle." Bourgeois, Sarah L. "Mark 8:22–26: Jesus and the Use of Spittle in a Two-Stage Healing." ThM thesis, Dallas Theological Seminary, 1999.

Bourguignon, "Appendix." Bourguignon, Erika. "Appendix." Pages 359–76 in *Religion, Altered States of Consciousness, and Social Change*. Edited by Erika Bourguignon. Columbus: Ohio State University Press, 1973.

Bourguignon, "Assessment." Bourguignon, Erika. "An Assessment of Some Comparisons and Implications." Pages 321–39 in *Religion, Altered States of Consciousness, and Social Change*. Edited by Erika Bourguignon. Columbus: Ohio State University Press, 1973.

Bourguignon, "Distribution." Bourguignon, Erika. "World Distribution and Patterns of Possession States." Pages 3–34 in *Trance and Possession States*. Proceedings of the Second Annual Conference, R. M. Bucke Memorial Society, March 4–6, 1966. Edited by Raymond Prince. Montreal: R. M. Bucke Memorial Society, 1968.

Bourguignon, "Epilogue." Bourguignon, Erika. "Epilogue: Some Notes on Contemporary Americans and the Irrational." Pages 340–56 in *Religion, Altered States of Consciousness, and Social Change*. Edited by Erika Bourguignon. Columbus: Ohio State University Press, 1973.

Bourguignon, "Introduction." Bourguignon, Erika. "Introduction: A Framework for the Comparative Study of Altered States of Consciousness." Pages 3–35 in *Religion, Altered States of Consciousness, and Social Change*. Edited by Erika Bourguignon. Columbus: Ohio State University Press, 1973.

Bourguignon, "Multiple Personality." Bourguignon, Erika. "Multiple Personality, Possession Trance, and the Psychic Unity of Mankind." *Ethos* 17 (1989): 371–84.

Bourguignon, *Possession*. Bourguignon, Erika. *Possession*. Chandler & Sharp Series in Cross-Cultural Themes. San Francisco: Chandler & Sharp, 1976.

Bourguignon, "Self." Bourguignon, Erika. "The Self, the Behavioral Environment, and the Theory of Spirit Possession." Pages 39–60 in *Culture and Meaning in Cultural Anthropology: In Honor of A. Irving Hallowell*. Edited by Melford E. Spiro. New York: Free Press; London: Collier-Macmillan, 1965.

Bourguignon, "Spirit Possession Belief." Bourguignon, Erika. "Spirit Possession Belief and Social Structure." Pages 17–26 in *The Realm of the Extra-Human: Ideas and Actions*. Edited by Agehananda Bharati. The Hague: Mouton, 1976.

Bourke, "Miracle Stories." Bourke, Myles M. "The Miracles Stories of the Gospels." *DunRev* 12 (1972): 21–34.

Bousset, *Kyrios Christos*. Bousset, William. *Kyrios Christos: A History of the Belief in Christ from the Beginnings of Christianity to Irenaeus*. Translated by John E. Steely. Nashville: Abingdon, 1970.

Bovon, "Miracles." Bovon, François. "Miracles, magie et guérison dans les Actes apocryphes des apôtres." *JECS* 3 (3, 1995): 245–59.

Bovon, *Studies*. Bovon, François. *Studies in Early Christianity*. Tübingen: Mohr Siebeck; Grand Rapids: Baker Academic, 2003.

Bovon, *Theologian*. Bovon, François. *Luke the Theologian: Thirty-three Years of Research (1950–1983)*. Translated by Ken McKinney. Allison Park, Pa.: Pickwick, 1987.

Bowald, *Rendering*. Bowald, Mark Alan. *Rendering the Word in Theological Hermeneutics: Mapping Divine and Human Agency*. Burlington, Vt.: Aldershot, 2007.

Bowen, *Return*. Bowen, Eleanor [pseudonym for Laura Bohannan]. *Return to Laughter*. New York: Harper, 1954.

Bowen et al., "Religion." Bowen, R., M. Baetz, and C. D'Arcy. "Self-Rated Importance of Religion Predicts One-Year Outcome of Patients with Panic Disorder." *DepAnx* 23 (5, 2006): 266–73.

Bowers and LeBaron, "Hypnosis." Bowers, Kenneth S., and S. LeBaron. "Hypnosis and Hypnotizability: Implications for Clinical Intervention." *HCPsy* 37 (5, May 1986): 457–67.

Bowersock, *Fiction as History*. Bowersock, G. W. *Fiction as History: Nero to Julian*. Berkeley: University of California Press, 1994.

Bowie, "Apollonius." Bowie, Ewen L. "Apollonius of Tyana: Tradition and Reality." *ANRW* 2.16.2 (1978): 1652–99.

Bowie, "Philostratus." Bowie, Ewen L. "Philostratus: Writer of Fiction." Pages 181–96 in *Greek Fiction: The Greek Novel in Context*. Edited by J. R. Morgan and R. Stoneman. London: Routledge, 1994.

Bowker, *Sense*. Bowker, John. *The Sense of God*. Oxford: Clarendon, 1973.

Bowler, "Bodies." Bowler, Catherine. "Blessed Bodies: Healing Within the African American Faith Movement." Pages 81–105 in *Global Pentecostal and Charismatic Healing*. Edited by Candy Gunther Brown. Foreword by Harvey Cox. Oxford: Oxford University Press, 2011.

Boyd, *Sage*. Boyd, Gregory A. *Cynic Sage or Son of God?* Wheaton: BridgePoint, 1995.

Boyd, *War*. Boyd, Gregory A. *God at War: The Bible and Spiritual Conflict*. Downers Grove, Ill.: InterVarsity, 1997.

Bozarth, "Demons." Bozarth, Tom. "Demons Out, God In." *MounM* (Feb. 1993): 16–17.

Braam et al., "Climate." Braam, A. W., A. T. Beekman, D. J. Van den Eeden, K. P. Knipscheer, and W. van Tilburg. "Religious Climate and Geographical Distribution of Depressive Symptoms in Older Dutch Citizens." *JAfDis* 54 (1–2, 1999): 149–59.

Braden, "Study." Braden, Charles S. "Study of Spiritual Healing in the Churches." Pages 224–35 in *New Concepts of Healing: Medical, Psychological, and Religious* by Alice Graham Ikin. Introduction by Wayne E. Oates. New York: Association Press, 1956. Reprinted from *PastPsy* (May 1954): 19–23.

Bradley, "*Apologia.*" Bradley, Keith. "Law, Magic, and Culture in the *Apologia* of Apuleius." *Phoenix* 51 (2, 1997): 203–33.

Brand, "Beliefs." Brand, Gerrit. "Witchcraft and Spirit Beliefs in African Christian Theology." *Exchange* 31 (1, 2002): 36–50.

Braun, *Here.* Braun, Willys K. *Here Am I: An Autobiography.* Wilmore, Ky.: Evangelism Resources, 2003.

Braun, *Way.* Braun, Thelma M. *On the Way: Joyful Jottings from a Missionary's Pen; A Devotional Autobiography.* Nappanee, Ind.: Evangel Publishing House, 2009.

Brawley, *Luke-Acts and Jews.* Brawley, Robert L. *Luke-Acts and the Jews: Conflict, Apology, and Conciliation.* SBLMS 33. Atlanta: Scholars Press, 1987.

Bray, "Angel." Bray, Jasmine. "An Angel in the Ravine." *MounM* (July 1993): 16–17.

Bray, *Corinthians.* Bray, Gerald, ed. *1–2 Corinthians.* ACCS, NT 7. Downers Grove, Ill.: InterVarsity, 1999.

Brayer, "Psychosomatics." Brayer, Menahem M. "Psychosomatics, Hermetic Medicine, and Dream Interpretation in the Qumran Literature (Psychological and Exegetical Consideration)." *JQR* 60 (2, 1969): 112–27; 60 (3, 1970): 213–30.

Bredero, *Christendom.* Bredero, Adriaan H. *Christendom and Christianity in the Middle Ages.* Translated by Reinder Bruinsma. Grand Rapids: Eerdmans, 1994.

Bredesen, *Miracle.* Bredesen, Harald, with James F. Scheer. *Need a Miracle?* Old Tappan, N.J.: Fleming H. Revell, 1979.

Breggen, "Miracle Reports." Breggen, Hendrik van der. "Miracle Reports, Moral Philosophy, and Contemporary Science." PhD diss., University of Waterloo, 2004.

Breggen, "Scale." Breggen, Hendrik van der. "Hume's Scale: How Hume Counts a Miracle's Improbability Twice." *PhilChr* 4 (2, 2002): 443–53.

Breggen, "Seeds." Breggen, Hendrik van der. "The Seeds of Their Own Destruction: David Hume's Fatally Flawed Arguments against Miracle Reports."

Christian Research Journal 30 (1, 2007): 5 pages, available online at http://www.equipresources .org/atf/cf/%7B9C4EE03A-F988-4091-84BD -F8E70A3B0215%7D/JAH225.pdf.

Bremback and Howell, *Persuasion.* Bremback, Winston L., and William S. Howell. *Persuasion: A Means of Social Influence.* 2nd ed. Englewood Cliffs, N.J.: Prentice-Hall, 1976.

Brenk, "Art." Brenk, Beat. "Art and *Propaganda fide*: Christian Art and Architecture, 300–600." Pages 691–725 in *Constantine to c. 600.* Edited by Augustine Casiday and Frederick W. Norris. Vol. 2 of *The Cambridge History of Christianity.* 9 vols. Cambridge: Cambridge University Press, 2007.

Brenk, "Doctrine." Brenk, Frederick E. "A Most Strange Doctrine: *Daimon* in Plutarch." *CJ* 69 (1973–74): 1–11.

Brickhouse and Smith, "Sign." Brickhouse, Thomas C., and Nicholas D. Smith. "'The Divine Sign Did Not Oppose Me.' A Problem in Plato's *Apology.*" *CJP* 16 (1985): 511–26.

Bridge, *Signs.* Bridge, Donald. *Signs and Wonders Today.* Leicester: Inter-Varsity, 1985.

Bright, "Guest." Bright, Bill. "The Uninvited Guest." *Worldwide Challenge* (Sept. 1997): 47–48.

Brinkman, *Non-Western Jesus.* Brinkman, Martien E. *The Non-Western Jesus: Jesus as Bodhisattva, Avatara, Guru, Prophet, Ancestor or Healer?* Translated by Henry Jansen and Lucy Jansen. London; Oakville, Conn.: Equinox, 2009.

Brockingham, "Miracles." Brockingham, A. Allen. "Miracles as Signs." *ExpT* 17 (1905–6): 493–95.

Brockman, "Braide." Brockman, Norbert. "Braide, Garrick Sokari Marian." *DACB.* http://www.dacb .org/stories/nigeria/braide1_garrick.html.

Brockman, "Kimbangu." Brockman, Norbert. "Simon Kimbangu." *DACB.* http://www.dacb.org/stories /demrepcongo/kimbangu1_simon.html.

Brockman, "Kivuli." Brockman, Norbert. "Kivuli, David Zakayo." *DACB.* http://www.dacb.org/stories /kenya/kivulidavidz1.html.

Brodie, "Unravelling." Brodie, Thomas L. "Towards Unraveling Luke's Use of the OT: Luke 7.11–17 as an *Imitatio* of 1 Kings 17.17–24." *NTS* 32 (2, April 1986): 247–67.

Brooke, *Reconstructing Nature.* Brooke, John Hedley, with Geoffrey Cantor. *Reconstructing Nature: The Engagement of Science and Religion.* Edinburgh: T&T Clark, 1998.

Brooke, *Science.* Brooke, John Hedley. *Science and Religion: Some Historical Perspectives.* Cambridge History of Science Series. New York: Cambridge University Press, 1991.

Brooke, "Science." Brooke, John Hedley. "Science and Theology in the Enlightenment." Pages 7–27 in *Religion and Science: History, Method, Dialogue.* Edited by W. Mark Richardson and Wesley J. Wildman. Foreword by Ian G. Barbour. New York: Routledge, 1996.

Brooke, "Secularized." Brooke, John Hedley. "That Modern Science Has Secularized Western Culture." Pages 224–32 in *Galileo Goes to Jail and Other Myths about Science and Religion.* Edited by Ronald L. Numbers. Cambridge, Mass.: Harvard University Press, 2009.

Brooks, *Moments.* Brooks, John W. *Might Moments: God's Leading Through a Life of Faith.* Franklin Springs, Ga.: Advocate Press, 1987.

Brougham, "Training." Brougham, David Royal. "The Training of the Chinese in Indonesia for the Ministry." MA thesis, Fuller Theological Seminary, 1970.

Brougham, "Work." Brougham, David R. "The Work of the Holy Spirit in Church Growth as Seen in Selected Indonesian Case Studies." DMiss diss., Fuller School of World Mission, 1988.

Brown, "Afterword." Brown, Candy Gunther. "Afterword." Pages 371–78 in *Global Pentecostal and Charismatic Healing.* Edited by Candy Gunther Brown. Foreword by Harvey Cox. Oxford: Oxford University Press, 2011.

Brown, "Asclepius." Brown, Michael L. "Was There a West Semitic Asklepios?" *UF* 29 (1998): 133–54.

Brown, "Awakenings." Brown, Candy Gunther. "Global Awakenings: Divine Healing Networks, and Global Community in North America, Brazil, Mozambique, and Beyond." Pages 351–69 in *Global Pentecostal and Charismatic Healing.* Edited by Candy Gunther Brown. Foreword by Harvey Cox. Oxford: Oxford University Press, 2011.

Brown, *Death.* Brown, Raymond E. *The Death of the Messiah: From Gethsemane to Grave. A Commentary on the Passion Narratives in the Four Gospels.* 2 vols. New York: Doubleday, 1994.

Brown, "Dowie." Brown, Candy Gunther. "Dowie, John Alexander (1847–1907)." Pages 144–45 in vol. 1 of *Encyclopedia of Religious Revivals in America.* Edited by Michael McClymond. 2 vols. Westport, Conn: Greenwood, 2007.

Brown, "Elisha." Brown, Raymond E. "Jesus and Elisha." *Persp* 12 (1971): 85–104.

Brown, *Essays.* Brown, Raymond E. *New Testament Essays.* Garden City, N.Y.: Doubleday, 1968.

Brown, *Healer.* Brown, Michael L. *Israel's Divine Healer.* SOTBT. Grand Rapids: Zondervan, 1995.

Brown, "Healing Words." Brown, Candy Gunther. "Healing Words: Narratives of Spiritual Healing and Kathryn Kuhlman's Uses of Print Culture, 1947–1976." Pages 271–97 in *Religion and the Culture of Print in Modern America.* Edited by Charles

L. Cohen and Paul S. Boyer. Madison: University of Wisconsin Press, 2008.

Brown, *Historians.* Brown, Truesdell S. *The Greek Historians.* Lexington, Mass.: D. C. Heath and Company, 1973.

Brown, "Introduction." Brown, Candy Gunther. "Introduction: Pentecostalism and the Globalization of Illness and Healing." Pages 3–26 in *Global Pentecostal and Charismatic Healing.* Edited by Candy Gunther Brown. Foreword by Harvey Cox. Oxford: Oxford University Press, 2011.

Brown, *Israel and Greece.* Brown, John Pairman. *Ancient Israel and Ancient Greece: Religion, Politics, and Culture.* Minneapolis: Fortress, 2003.

Brown, *John.* Brown, Raymond E. *The Gospel According to John.* 2 vols. AB 29 and 29A. Garden City, N.Y.: Doubleday, 1966–70.

Brown, "Kuhlman." Brown, Candy Gunther. "Kuhlman, Kathryn." Pages 235–36 in vol. 1 of *Encyclopedia of Religious Revivals in America.* Edited by Michael McClymond. 2 vols. Westport, Conn: Greenwood, 2007.

Brown, *Late Antiquity.* Brown, Peter. *The World of Late Antiquity.* London: Thames and Hudson, 1971.

Brown, *Miracles.* Brown, Colin. *Miracles and the Critical Mind.* Grand Rapids: Eerdmans, 1984.

Brown, *Philosophy.* Brown, Colin. *Philosophy and the Christian Faith: A Historical Sketch from the Middle Ages to the Present Day.* Downers Grove, Ill.: InterVarsity, 1968.

Brown, "Spiritual Healing." Brown, Allen W. "Spiritual Healing." Pages 113–17 in *Healing and Religious Faith.* Edited by Claude A. Frazier. Philadelphia: Pilgrim Press, United Church Press, 1974.

Brown, "Tent Meetings." Brown, Candy Gunther. "From Tent Meetings and Store-front Healing Rooms to Walmarts and the Internet: Healing Spaces in the United States, the Americas, and the World, 1906–2006." *CH* 75 (3, Sept. 2006): 631–47.

Brown, *Thought.* Brown, Colin. *From the Ancient World to the Age of the Enlightenment.* Vol. 1 of *Christianity and Western Thought: A History of Philosophers, Ideas and Movements.* Downers Grove, Ill.: IVP Academic, 1990.

Brown, *Walking on Water.* Brown, William Norman. *The Indian and Christian Miracles of Walking on the Water.* Chicago: Open Court, 1928.

Brown, "Woodworth-Etter." Brown, Candy Gunther. "Woodworth-Etter, Maria Beulah (1844–1924)." Pages 471–72 in vol. 1 of *Encyclopedia of Religious Revivals in America.* Edited by Michael McClymond. 2 vols. Westport, Conn: Greenwood, 2007.

Brown, "Worshipping." Brown, Kenneth I. "Worshipping with the African Church of the Lord (Aladura)." *PracAnth* 13 (2, 1966): 59–84.

Brown, *Wounded Knee*. Brown, Dee. *Bury My Heart at Wounded Knee: An Indian History of the American West*. New York: Bantam, 1970.

Brown, Mory, Williams, and McClymond, "Effects." Brown, Candy Gunther, Stephen C. Mory, Rebecca Williams, and Michael J. McClymond. "Study of the Therapeutic Effects of Proximal Intercessory Prayer (STEPP) on Auditory and Visual Impairments in Rural Mozambique." *SMedJ* 103 (9, Sept. 2010): 864–69.

Brown, Ndubuisi, and Gary, "Religiosity." Brown, D. R., S. C. Ndubuisi, and L. E. Gary. "Religiosity and Psychological Distress among Blacks." *JRel Health* 29 (1, 1990): 55–68.

Brownell, "Experience." Brownell, Philip. "Personal Experience, Self-Reporting, and Hyperbole." Pages 210–29 in *Parapsychological Perspectives*. Vol. 3 of *Miracles: God, Science, and Psychology in the Paranormal*. Edited by J. Harold Ellens. Westport, Conn.; London: Praeger, 2008.

Brownell, "Faith." Brownell, Philip. "Faith: An Existential, Phenomenological, and Biblical Integration." Pages 213–34 in *Medical and Therapeutic Events*. Vol. 2 of *Miracles: God, Science, and Psychology in the Paranormal*. Edited by J. Harold Ellens. Westport, Conn.; London: Praeger, 2008.

Bruce, *Acts*. Bruce, F. F. *The Acts of the Apostles: The Greek Text with Introduction and Commentary*. 3rd rev. and enlarged ed. Grand Rapids: Eerdmans, 1990.

Bruce, *Acts: Greek*. Bruce, F. F. *The Acts of the Apostles: The Greek Text with Introduction and Commentary*. Grand Rapids: Eerdmans, 1951.

Bruce, "All Things." Bruce, F. F. "'All Things to All Men': Diversity in Unity and Other Pauline Tensions." Pages 82–99 in *Unity and Diversity in New Testament Theology: Essays in Honor of George E. Ladd*. Edited by Robert A. Guelich. Grand Rapids: Eerdmans, 1978.

Bruce, *Care*. Bruce, Bob, and Gloria Bruce. *Does God Really Care?* N.p.: Xulon, 2008.

Bruce, "Date." Bruce, F. F. "The Date and Character of Mark." Pages 69–89 in *Jesus and the Politics of His Day*. Edited by Ernst Bammel and C. F. D. Moule. Cambridge: Cambridge University Press, 1984.

Brucker, "Wunder." Brucker, Ralph. "Die Wunder der Apostel." *ZNT* 4 (7, 2001): 32–45.

Bruckner, "History." Bruckner, L. I. "The History and Character of the Niasan People Movement in Indonesia." DMiss diss., Fuller Theological Seminary, 1979.

Brueggemann, *Astonishment*. Brueggemann, Walter. *Abiding Astonishment: Psalms, Modernity, and the Making of History*. Louisville: Westminster John Knox, 1991.

Brümmer, *Pray*. Brümmer, Vincent. *What Are We Doing When We Pray? On Prayer and the Nature of Faith*. Burlington, Vt.: Ashgate, 2008.

Bruns, "Ananda." Bruns, J. Edgar. "Ananda: The Fourth Evangelist's Model for 'the Disciple Whom Jesus Loved'?" *SR/SR* 3 (3, 1973): 236–43.

Bruns, *Art*. Bruns, J. Edgar. *The Art and Thought of John*. New York: Herder & Herder, 1969.

Bruns, *Buddhism*. Bruns, J. Edgar. *The Christian Buddhism of St. John*. Foreword by Gregory Baum. New York: Paulist, 1971.

Brusco, *Reformation*. Brusco, Elizabeth E. *The Reformation of Machismo: Evangelical Conversion and Gender in Colombia*. Austin: University of Texas Press, 1995.

Bryson, "Angels." Bryson, Sue. "Angels among Us." *Guideposts* (July 1994): 46.

Buchan and Waldeck, *Faith*. Buchan, Angus, and Val Waldeck. *Faith Like Potatoes*. Greytown: Shalom Ministries, 1998.

Buchwalter, "Asking." Buchwalter, Ada R. "Asking for Teachers." *PentEv* 647 (May 15, 1926): 10.

Buckingham, "Afterword." Buckingham, Jamie. "Afterword." Pages 145–54 in *Some Said It Thundered: A Personal Encounter with the Kansas City Prophets* by David Pytches. Foreword by John White. Nashville: Thomas Nelson, 1991.

Buckingham, *Daughter*. Buckingham, Jamie. *Daughter of Destiny: Kathryn Kuhlman . . . Her Story*. Plainfield, N.J.: Logos, 1976.

Buckingham, *Summer*. Buckingham, Jamie. *Summer of Miracles*. Lake Mary, Fla.: Creation House, 1991.

Budge, *Takla Hâymânôt*. Budge, E. A. Wallis. *The Life of Takla Hâymânôt in the Version of Dabra Lîbânôs, and The Miracles of Takla Hâymânôt in the Version of Dabra Lîbânôs, and The Book of the Riches of Kings*. The Ethiopic Texts, from the British Museum Ms. Oriental 723, edited with English translations, to which is added an English translation of the Waldebbân Version, with one hundred and sixty-five colored plates. London: privately printed for Lady Meux, 1906.

Buel, *Lincoln Myth*. Buel, Oliver Price. *The Abraham Lincoln Myth*. New York: The Mascot Publishing Co., 1894.

Buffington, "Leader." Buffington, Rex. "Cult Leader Convicted in Woman's Kidnapping." *Memphis Commercial Appeal* (June 2, 1977): 1, 3.

Buffington, "Routine." Buffington, Rex. "Daily Routine Appears Undisturbed at Commune of Convicted Leader." *Memphis Commercial Appeal* (June 5, 1977): A-1.

Bührmann, "Religion and Healing." Bührmann, M. V. "Religion and Healing: The African Experience."

Pages 25–34 in *Afro-Christian Religion and Healing in Southern Africa.* Edited by G. C. Oosthuizen, S. D. Edwards, W. H. Wessels, and I. Hexham. AfSt 8. Lewiston, N.Y.: Edwin Mellen, 1989.

Bull et al., "Exorcism." Bull, Dennis L., et al. "Exorcism Revisited: Positive Outcomes with Dissociative Identity Disorder." *JPsyTh* 26 (2, 1998): 188–96.

Bull, "Model." Bull, Dennis L. "A Phenomenological Model of Therapeutic Exorcism for Dissociative Identity Disorder." *JPsyTh* 29 (2, 2001): 131–39.

Bultmann, "Demythologizing." Bultmann, Rudolf. "On the Problem of Demythologizing (1952)." Pages 95–130 in *New Testament Mythology and Other Basic Writings.* Edited by Schubert Ogden. Philadelphia: Fortress, 1984.

Bultmann, "Exegesis." Bultmann, Rudolf. "Is Exegesis Without Presuppositions Possible?" Pages 145–53 in *New Testament Mythology and Other Basic Writings.* Edited by Schubert Ogden. Philadelphia: Fortress, 1984.

Bultmann, *Kerygma and Myth.* Bultmann, Rudolf. *Kerygma and Myth: A Theological Debate.* Edited by H. W. Bartsch. Edited, revised, and translated by R. H. Fuller. New York: Harper & Row, 1961.

Bultmann, "Mythology." Bultmann, Rudolf. "New Testament and Mythology." Pages 1–43 in *New Testament Mythology and Other Basic Writings.* Edited by Schubert Ogden. Philadelphia: Fortress, 1984.

Bultmann, "Problem of Miracle." Bultmann, Rudolf. "The Problem of Miracle." *RelL* 27 (1958): 63–75.

Bultmann, "Study." Bultmann, Rudolf. "The Study of the Synoptic Gospels." Pages 7–76 in *Form Criticism: Two Essays on New Testament Research* by Rudolf Bultmann and Karl Kundsin. Translated by Frederick C. Grant. New York: Harper & Brothers, 1962.

Bultmann, *Theology.* Bultmann, Rudolf. *Theology of the New Testament.* 2 vols. Translated by Kendrick Grobel. New York: Charles Scribner's Sons, 1951.

Bultmann, *Tradition.* Bultmann, Rudolf. *The History of the Synoptic Tradition.* 2nd ed. Translated by John Marsh. Oxford: Basil Blackwell, 1968.

Bultmann, *Word.* Bultmann, Rudolf. *Jesus and the Word.* Translated by Louise Smith and Erminie Lantero. New York: Charles Scribner's Sons, 1958.

Bundy, "Blumhardt." Bundy, David. "Blumhardt, Johann Christian." Pages 110–11 in *Dictionary of Evangelical Biography, 1730–1860.* Edited by Donald M. Lewis. 2 vols. Peabody, Mass.: Hendrickson, 2004; Oxford: Blackwell, 1995.

Bundy, "Trudel." Bundy, David. "Trudel, Dorothea." Pages 1121–22 in *Dictionary of Evangelical Biography, 1730–1860.* Edited by Donald M. Lewis. 2 vols. Peabody, Mass.: Hendrickson, 2004; Oxford: Blackwell, 1995.

Buntain, *Miracle.* Buntain, Mark, Ron Hembree, and Doug Brendel. *Miracle in the Mirror.* Minneapolis: Bethany House, 1982.

Burgess, "Evidence." Burgess, Stanley M. "Evidence of the Spirit: The Medieval and Modern Western Churches." Pages 20–40 in *Initial Evidence: Historical and Biblical Perspectives on the Pentecostal Doctrine of Spirit Baptism.* Edited by Gary B. McGee. Peabody, Mass.: Hendrickson, 1991.

Burgess, "Pandita Ramabai." Burgess, Ruth Vassar. "Pandita Ramabai: A Woman for All Seasons: Pandita Ramabai Saraswati Mary Dongre Medhavi (1858–1922)." *AJPS* 9 (2, July 2006): 183–98.

Burgess, "Pentecostalism in India." Burgess, Stanley M. "Pentecostalism in India: An Overview." *AJPS* 4 (1, Jan. 2001): 85–98.

Burgess, "Proclaiming." Burgess, Stanley M. "Proclaiming the Gospel with Miraculous Gifts in the Postbiblical Early Church." Pages 277–88 in *The Kingdom and the Power: Are Healing and the Spiritual Gifts Used by Jesus and the Early Church Meant for the Church Today?* Edited by Gary S. Greig and Kevin N. Springer. Ventura, Calif.: Regal, 1993.

Burgess, *Revolution.* Burgess, Richard. *Nigeria's Christian Revolution: The Civil War Revival and Its Pentecostal Progeny (1967–2006).* RStMiss. Eugene, Ore.: Wipf & Stock, 2008.

Burhenn, "Miracles." Burhenn, Herbert. "Attributing Miracles to Agents—Reply to George D. Chryssides." *RelS* 13 (4, 1977): 485–89.

Burkert, *Mystery Cults.* Burkert, Walter. *Ancient Mystery Cults.* Carl Newell Jackson Lectures. Cambridge, Mass.: Harvard University Press, 1987.

Burkert, *Religion.* Burkert, Walter. *Greek Religion.* Translated by John Raffan. Cambridge, Mass.: Harvard University Press, 1985.

Burkholder, "Foundations." Burkholder, Lawrence. "The Theological Foundations of Deliverance Healing." *CGR* 19 (1, 2001): 38–68.

Burkill, "Miracle." Burkill, T. A. "The Notion of Miracle with Special Reference to St. Mark's Gospel." *ZNW* 50 (1959): 33–48.

Burkitt, *Sources.* Burkitt, F. Crawford. *The Earliest Sources for the Life of Jesus.* Boston: Houghton Mifflin, 1910.

Burne, "Rousseau." Burne, John R. "Jean-Jacques Rousseau and the Bible." *EvQ* 28 (1956): 141–47.

Burnett, *Clash.* Burnett, David. *Clash of Worlds.* Rev. ed. Foreword by Peter Cotterell. Grand Rapid: Monarch, 2002.

Burnett, "Conflict." Burnett, David G. "Spiritual Conflict and Folk Religion." Pages 243–58 in *Deliver Us from Evil: An Uneasy Frontier in Christian Mission.* Edited by A. Scott Moreau, Tokunboh Adeyemo,

David G. Burnett, Bryant L. Myers, and Hwa Yung. Monrovia, Calif.: Lausanne Committee for World Evangelization, 2002.

Burns, *Debate.* Burns, Robert M. *The Great Debate on Miracles: From Joseph Glanvill to David Hume.* London: Associated University Presses; Lewisburg, Pa.: Bucknell University Press, 1981.

Burns, "Hume." Burns, Robert M. "David Hume and Miracles in Historical Perspective." PhD diss., Princeton University, 1971.

Burridge, "Biography, Ancient." Burridge, Richard A. "Biography, Ancient." Pages 167–70 in *DNTB.*

Burridge, *Gospels.* Burridge, Richard A. *What Are the Gospels? A Comparison with Graco-Roman Biography.* SNTSMS 70. Cambridge: Cambridge University Press, 1992.

Burridge, *New Earth.* Burridge, Kenelm. *New Heaven, New Earth.* Oxford: Basil Blackwell, 1969.

Burridge, "People." Burridge, Richard A. "About People, by People, for People: Gospel Genre and Audiences." Pages 113–46 in *The Gospels for All Christians: Rethinking the Gospel Audiences.* Edited by Richard Bauckham. Grand Rapids: Eerdmans, 1998.

Burton, "Evangelism." Burton, William F. P. "Native Evangelism in Congo." *PentEv* 851 (June 7, 1930): 11.

Burton, "Villages." Burton, William F. P. "How God Planted Pentecost in the Congo: Closed Villages Opened Thru Divine Healing." *LRE* 15 (8, May 1922): 5–9.

Burtt, *Foundations.* Burtt, Edwin Arthur. *The Metaphysical Foundations of Modern Science.* Reprint, Garden City, N.Y.: Doubleday, 1954.

Bush, *Readings.* Bush, L. Russ. *Classical Readings in Christian Apologetics: A.D. 100–1800.* Grand Rapids: Zondervan, 1983.

Bush and Pegues, *Move.* Bush, Luis, and Beverly Pegues. *The Move of the Holy Spirit in the 10/40 Window.* Edited by Jane Rumph. Seattle: YWAM Publishing, 1999.

Buskirk, *Healing.* Buskirk, James Dale van. *Religion, Healing, and Health.* New York: Macmillan, 1953.

Butler, "Materialization." Butler, Noah. "The Materialization of Magic: Islamic Talisman in West Africa." Pages 263–76 in *Studies in Witchcraft, Magic, War, and Peace in Africa.* Edited by Beatrice Nicolini. Lewiston, N.Y.: Edwin Mellen, 2006.

Butler, "Theory." Butler, Jon. "Theory and God in Gotham." *HistTh,* theme issue 45 (4, Dec. 2006): 47–61.

Buys and Nambala, "Hambuindja." Buys, Gerhard, and Shekutaamba Nambala. "Thusnelda Hambuindja." *DACB.* http://www.dacb.org/stories /namibia/hambuindja_thusnelda.html.

Buys and Nambala, "Kanambunga." Buys, Gerhard, and Shekutaamba Nambala. "Alfeus Kanambunga." *DACB.* http://www.dacb.org/stories/namibia /kanambunga_alfeus.html.

Byaruhanga-Akiiki and Kealotswe, *Healing.* Byaruhanga-Akiiki, A. B. T., and Obed N. O. Kealotswe. *African Theology of Healing: The Infinite Oneness.* Gaboroni: University of Botswana Press, 1995.

Byrd, "Effects." Byrd, Randolph B. "Positive Therapeutic Effects of Intercessory Prayer in a Coronary Care Unit Population." *SMedJ* 81 (1988): 826–29.

Byrne, "Miracles." Byrne, Peter. "Miracles and the Philosophy of Science." *HeyJ* 19 (1978): 162–70.

Byrskog, *History.* Byrskog, Samuel. *Story as History— History as Story: The Gospel Tradition in the Context of Ancient Oral History.* Boston: Brill, 2002.

Cadbury, *Acts in History.* Cadbury, Henry J. *The Book of Acts in History.* London: Adam & Charles Black, 1955.

Cadbury, "Intimations." Cadbury, Henry J. "Intimations of Immortality in the Thought of Jesus." Pages 79–104 in *The Miracles and the Resurrection: Some Recent Studies by I. T. Ramsey, G. H. Boobyer, F. N. Davey, M. C. Perry, and Henry J. Cadbury.* Theological Collections 3. London: SPCK, 1964.

Cadbury, "We in Luke-Acts." Cadbury, Henry J. "'We' and 'I' Passages in Luke-Acts." *NTS* 3 (1956–57): 128–32.

Cadwalder, "Healings." Cadwalder, Hugh M. "I Was There: Miraculous Healings in a Canadian Family." *PentEv* (Oct. 9, 1966): 9.

Caesar of Heisterbach, "Encounters." Caesar of Heisterbach. "Demonic Encouters." Pages 143–73 in *Exorcism Through the Ages.* Edited by St. Elmo Nauman. New York: Philosophical Library, 1974.

Cagle, "Church." Cagle, Judy. "The Church of Mighty Mana." *PentEv* (Oct. 25, 1992): 17.

Cagle, "Happened." Cagle, Judy. "What Happened to Andy?" *PentEv* (March 7, 1993): 11.

Cagle, "Power." Cagle, Wayne. "Resurrection Power in Urintogum." *PentEv* (April 15, 1990): 11.

Cagle, "Pray." Cagle, Wayne. "Pastor, We Have to Pray!" *MounM* (March 1991): 16–17.

Cain, "Miracles." Cain, Andrew. "Miracles, Martyrs, and Arians: Gregory of Tours' Sources for His Account of the Vandal Kingdom." *VC* 59 (4, 2005): 412–37.

Caird, *Apostolic Age.* Caird, George B. *The Apostolic Age.* London: Gerald Duckworth & Company, 1955.

Caldwell, "Prayers." Caldwell, Debbie. "We Depend on Your Prayers." *MounM* (Nov. 1995): 5–6.

Calley, "Healed." Calley, Viola Vice. "Healed of Tuberculosis." *Pent Ev* 738 (March 10, 1928): 5.

Campbell, *We Passages*. Campbell, William Sanger. *The "We" Passages in the Acts of the Apostles: The Narrator as Narrative Character*. SBLSBL 14. Atlanta: Society of Biblical Literature, 2007.

Campolo, *Pentecostal*. Campolo, Tony. *How to Be Pentecostal Without Speaking in Tongues*. Dallas: Word, 1991.

Campos M., "Power." Campos M., Bernardo L. "In the Power of the Spirit: Pentecostalism, Theology, and Social Ethics." Pages 41–50 in *In the Power of the Spirit: The Pentecostal Challenge to Historical Churches in Latin America*. Edited by Benjamin F. Gutiérrez and Dennis A. Smith. Mexico City: Asociación de Iglesias Presbiterianias y Reformadas en América Latina; Guatemala City: Centro Evangélico Latinoamericano de Estudios Pastorales; Louisville: Presbyterian Church (U.S.A.), 1996.

Canada et al., "Coping." Canada, Andrea L., et al. "Active Coping Mediates the Association between Religion/Spirituality and Quality of Life in Ovarian Cancer." *GynOnc* 101 (1, 2006): 102–7.

Cannon, "Voodoo Death." Cannon, Walter B. "'Voodoo' Death." *AmAnth* 44 (1942): 169–81.

Caporael, "Ergotism." Caporael, Linnda R. "Ergotism: The Satan Loosed in Salem?" Pages 251–56 in *Possession and Exorcism*. Vol. 9 of *Articles on Witchcraft, Magic, and Demonology: A Twelve-Volume Anthology of Scholarly Articles*. Edited by Brian P. Levack. New York: Garland, 1992. Reprinted from *Science* 192 (1976): 21–26.

Capps, *Village Psychiatrist*. Capps, Donald. *Jesus the Village Psychiatrist*. Louisville: Westminster John Knox, 2008.

Caragounis, *Mysterion*. Caragounis, Chrys C. *The Ephesian Mysterion: Meaning and Content*. CBNTS 8. Lund: C. W. K. Gleerup, 1977.

Carastro, "Divination et magie." Carastro, Marcello. "Quand Tirésias devint un *mágos*. Divination et magie en Grèce ancienne (Vᵉ-Ivᵉ siècle av. n. è.)." *RHR* 224 (2, 2007): 211–30.

Cardeña, "Hypnosis." Cardeña, Etzel. "Deep Hypnosis and Shamanism: Convergences and Divergences." Pages 289–303 in *Proceedings of the Fourth International Conference on the Study of Shamanism and Alternate Modes of Healing, Held at the St. Sabina Center, San Rafael, California, September 5–7, 1987*. Edited by Ruth-Inge Heinze. N.p.: Independent Scholars of Asia; Madison, Wis.: A-R Editions, 1988.

Cardeña, Lynn, and Krippner, "Experiences." Cardeña, Etzel, Steven Jay Lynn, and Stanley Krippner. "Introduction: Anomalous Experiences in Perspective." Pages 3–21 in *Varieties of Anomalous Experience: Examining the Scientific Evidence*. Edited by Etzel Cardeña, Steven Jay Lynn, and Stanley Krippner.

Washington, D.C.: American Psychological Association, 2000.

Carlson, *Hoax*. Carlson, Stephen C. *The Gospel Hoax: Morton Smith's Invention of Secret Mark*. Waco: Baylor University Press, 2005.

Carlston, "Question." Carlston, Charles E. "The Question of Miracles." *ANQ* 12 (2, Nov. 1971): 99–107.

Carnegie, Andrew. *The "Gospel of Wealth" and Other Writings*. London: Penguin, 2006.

Carothers, *Prison*. Carothers, Merlin. *Prison to Praise*. Escondido, Calif.: Merlin R. Carothers, 1970.

Carpenter, "Death." Carpenter, Harold. "Holding Death in My Arms." *MounM* (Dec. 1990): 16–17.

Carpenter, "Deuteronomy." Carpenter, Eugene E. "Deuteronomy." Pages 418–547 in vol. 1 of *Zondervan Illustrated Bible Backgrounds Commentary: Old Testament*. Edited by John H. Walton. 5 vols. Grand Rapids: Zondervan, 2009.

Carr, *Angels*. Carr, Wesley. *Angels and Principalities*. Cambridge: Cambridge University Press, 1981.

Carr, *Profession*. Carr, Jess. *The Second Oldest Profession: An Informal History of Moonshining in America*. Englewood Cliffs, N.J.: Prentice-Hall, 1972.

Carr, *Saint*. Carr, Jess. *The Saint of the Wilderness: A Biographical Novel Depicting the Life and Works of Robert Sayers Sheffey*. Radford, Va.: Commonwealth Press, 1974.

Carrel, *Voyage*. Carrel, Alexis. *The Voyage to Lourdes*. New York: Harper & Brothers, 1950.

Carrico et al., "Model." Carrico, A. W., G. Ironson, M. H. Antoni, S. C. Lechner, R. E. Duran, M. Kumar, and N. Schneiderman. "A Path Model of the Effects of Spirituality on Depressive Symptoms and 24-h Urinary-Free Cortisol in HIV-Positive Persons." *JPsycRes* 61 (1, 2006): 51–58.

"Carried but Walked." "He Was Carried in but Walked Out!" *MounM* (Nov. 1994): 14–15.

Carson, *Scandalous*. Carson, D. A. *Scandalous: The Cross and Resurrection of Jesus*. Wheaton: Crossway, 2010.

Carson, *Spirit*. Carson, D. A. *Showing the Spirit: A Theological Exposition of 1 Corinthians 12–14*. Grand Rapids: Baker, 1987.

Carter, "Demon Possession." Carter, Steven S. "Demon Possession and the Christian." *AJPS* 3 (1, Jan. 2000): 19–31.

Carter, "Possession." Carter, Steven S. "Demon Possession and the Christian." *Evangel* 19 (2, Summer 2001): 45–50.

Carter, "Recognition." Carter, James C. "The Recognition of Miracles." *TS* 20 (1959): 175–97.

Cary and Haarhoff, *Life*. Cary, M., and T. J. Haarhoff. *Life and Thought in the Greek and Roman World*. 4th ed. London: Methuen, 1946.

Casdorph, *Miracles*. Casdorph, H. Richard. *The Miracles: A Medical Doctor Says Yes to Miracles!* Plainfield, N.J.: Logos, 1976.

Casiday, "Sin." Casiday, Augustine. "Sin and Salvation: Experiences and Reflections." Pages 501–30 in *Constantine to c. 600*. Edited by Augustine Casiday and Frederick W. Norris. Vol. 2 of *The Cambridge History of Christianity*. 9 vols. Cambridge: Cambridge University Press, 2007.

Cassell, *Miracles*. Cassell, Joan. *Expected Miracles: Surgeons at Work*. Philadelphia: Temple University Press, 1991.

Casson, *Travel*. Casson, Lionel. *Travel in the Ancient World*. London: George Allen & Unwin, 1974.

Castillo, "Possession." Castillo, R. J. "Spirit Possession in South Asia, Dissociation or Hysteria? Part I: Theoretical Background." *CMPsy* 18 (1994): 1–21.

Castillo-Richmond et al., "Effects." Castillo-Richmond, Amparo, et al. "Effects of Stress Reduction on Carotid Atherosclerosis in Hypertensive African-Americans." *Stroke* 31 (3, 2000): 568–73.

Castleberry, "Impact." Castleberry, Joseph Lee. "It's Not Just for Ignorant People Anymore: The Future Impact of University Graduates on the Development of the Ecuadorian Assemblies of God." EdD diss., Teachers College, Columbia University, 1999.

Castro, "Practices." Castro, Marcelina T. "Folk Medical Practices of the Ibalois of Benguet." EdD diss., Baguio Central University, 1988.

Castro-Blanco, "Sensitivity." Castro-Blanco, David R. "Cultural Sensitivity in Conventional Psychotherapy: A Comment on Martínez-Taboas (2005)." *PsycTRPT* 42 (1, Spring 2005): 14–16.

Catanzaro et al., "Health Ministries." Catanzaro, Ana Maria, K. G. Meador, H. G. Koenig, M. Kuchibhatla, and Elizabeth Clipp. "Congregational Health Ministries: A National Study of Pastors' Views." *PHNurs* 24 (1, 2007): 6–17.

Cavadini, "Note." Cavadini, John C. "A Note on Gregory's Use of Miracles in The Life and Miracles of St. Benedict." *AmBenRev* 49 (1, 1998): 104–20.

Cavarnos, *St. Arsenios*. Cavarnos, Constantine. *St. Arsenios of Paros: Remarkable Confessor, Spiritual Guide, Educator, Ascetic, Miracle Worker, and Healer. An Account of His Life, Character, Message, and Miracles*. MOrthS 6. Belmont, Mass.: Institute for Byzantine and Modern Greek Studies, 1978.

Cavarnos, *St. Methodia*. Cavarnos, Constantine. *St. Methodia of Kimolos: Remarkable Ascetic, Teacher of Virtue, Counselor, Comforter, and Healer (1865–1908). An Account of Her Life, Character, Miracles,* and Influence, Together with Selected Hymns from the Akolouthia in Honor of Her, and a Letter to Her Sister Anna. MOrthS 9. Belmont, Mass.: Institute for Byzantine and Modern Greek Studies, 1978.

Cavarnos and Zeldin, *St. Seraphim*. Cavarnos, Constantine, and Mary-Barbara Zeldin. *St. Seraphim of Sarov: Widely Beloved Mystic, Healer, Comforter, and Spiritual Guide. An Account of His Life, Character, and Message, Together with a Very Edifying Conversation with His Disciple Motovilov on the Acquisition of the Grace of the Holy Spirit, and the Saint's Spiritual Counsels*. MOrthS 5. Belmont, Mass.: Institute for Byzantine and Modern Greek Studies, 1980.

"Ceremony." "An Awe-Inspiring Ceremony." *ChH* 37 (1993): 41.

"Certainty of Healing." "The Certainty of Healing for Our Bodies." *WWit* 8 (8, Oct. 20, 1912): 1.

César, "Babel." César, Waldo. "From Babel to Pentecost: A Social-Historical-Theological Study of the Growth of Pentecostalism." Pages 22–40 in *Between Babel and Pentecost: Transnational Pentecostalism in Africa and Latin America*. Edited by André Corten and Ruth Marshall-Fratani. Bloomington: Indiana University Press, 2001.

César, "Life." César, Waldo. "Daily Life and Transcendence in Pentecostalism." Pages 3–111 in *Pentecostalism and the Future of the Christian Churches: Promises, Limitations, Challenges* by Richard Shaull and Waldo César. Grand Rapids: Eerdmans, 2000.

Cha, Wirth, and Lobo, "Prayer." Cha, Kwang Y., Daniel P. Wirth, and Rogerio A. Lobo. "Does Prayer Influence the Success of in Vitro Fertilization-Embryo Transfer? Report of a Masked, Randomized Trial." *JRepMed* 46 (9, Sept. 2001): 781–87.

Chadwick, "Miracles." Chadwick, G. A. "The Miracles of Christ." *Exp*, 4th ser., 5 (1892): 39–50, 126–39, 270–80.

Chalmers, "Emergence." Chalmers, David J. "Strong and Weak Emergence." Pages 244–54 in *The Re-Emergence of Emergence: The Emergentist Hypothesis from Science to Religion*. Edited by Philip Clayton and Paul Davies. Oxford: Oxford University Press, 2006.

Champ, "Holywell." Champ, Judith F. "Bishop Milner, Holywell, and the Cure Tradition." Pages 153–64 in *The Church and Healing: Papers Read at the Twentieth Summer Meeting and the Twenty-first Winter Meeting of the Ecclesiastical History Society*. StChHist 19. Edited by W. J. Sheils. Oxford: Basil Blackwell, 1982.

Chan, "Narrative." Chan, Leo Tak-Hung. "Narrative as Argument: The *Yuewei coatang biji* and the Late Eighteenth-Century Elite Discourse on the Supernatural." *HJAsSt* 53 (1, June 1993): 25–62.

Chandra shekar, "Possession Syndrome." Chandra shekar, C. R. "Possession Syndrome in India." Pages 79–95 in *Altered States of Consciousness and Mental*

Health: A Cross-Cultural Perspective. Edited by Colleen A. Ward. CCRMS 12. Newbury Park, Calif.: Sage, 1989.

Chandy, "Discipling." Chandy, V. "The Discipling of Muslims in Sri Lanka." MA thesis, Fuller Theological Seminary, 1981.

Chappell, "Healing Movement." Chappell, Paul Gale. "The Divine Healing Movement in America." PhD diss., Drew University Graduate School, 1983.

Charlesworth, "Comparison." Charlesworth, James H. "A Critical Comparison of the Dualism in 1QS III,13–IV,26 and the 'Dualism' Contained in the Fourth Gospel." NTS 15 (4, July 1969): 389–418.

Charlesworth, Jesus within Judaism. Charlesworth, James H. Jesus within Judaism: New Light from Exciting Archaeological Discoveries. ABRL. New York: Doubleday, 1988.

Charlesworth, "Origin." Charlesworth, James H. "Conclusion: The Origin and Development of Resurrection Beliefs." Pages 218–31 in Resurrection: The Origin and Future of a Biblical Doctrine by James H. Charlesworth, C. D. Elledge, J. L. Crenshaw, H. Boers, and W. W. Willis Jr. New York: T&T Clark, 2006.

Charlesworth, "Resurrection." Charlesworth, James H. "Resurrection: The Dead Sea Scrolls and the New Testament." Pages 138–86 in Resurrection: The Origin and Future of a Biblical Doctrine by James H. Charlesworth, C. D. Elledge, J. L. Crenshaw, H. Boers, and W. W. Willis Jr. New York: T&T Clark, 2006.

Charlesworth, "Sketch." Charlesworth, James H. "The Historical Jesus: Sources and a Sketch." Pages 84–128 in Jesus Two Thousand Years Later. Edited by James H. Charlesworth and Walter P. Weaver. Faith and Scholarship Colloquies Series. Harrisburg, Pa.: Trinity Press International, 2000.

Charlier, "Notion." Charlier, J.-P. "La notion de signe (semeion) dans le IVe Évangile." RSPT 43 (3, 1959): 434–48.

Charpak and Broch, Debunked. Charpak, Georges, and Henri Broch. Debunked! ESP, Telekinesis, and Other Pseudoscience. Translated by Bart K. Holland. Baltimore: Johns Hopkins University Press, 2004.

Chaván de Matviuk, "Growth." Chaván de Matviuk, Marcela A. "Latin American Pentecostal Growth: Culture, Orality, and the Power of Testimonies." AJPS 5 (2, July 2002): 205–22.

Chavda, Miracle. Chavda, Mahesh, with John Blattner. Only Love Can Make a Miracle: The Mahesh Chavda Story. Ann Arbor, Mich.: Servant, 1990.

Cheetham and Griffiths, "Psychotherapist." Cheetham, R. W. S., and J. A. Griffiths. "The Traditional Healer/Diviner as Psychotherapist." Pages 305–17 in Afro-Christian Religion and Healing in Southern Africa. Edited by G. C. Oosthuizen, S. D.

Edwards, W. H. Wessels, and I. Hexham. AfSt 8. Lewiston, N.Y.: Edwin Mellen, 1989.

Chen, "Expression." Chen, Yung Y. "Written Emotional Expression and Religion: Effects on PTSD Symptoms." IntJPsyMed 35 (3, 2005): 273–86.

Chen, "Facts." Chen, Marcus. "Some First-Hand Facts about Marshal Feng Yu-Hsiang [Yuxiang]." CGl 6 (4, June 1925): 26–29.

Cherry, Healing Prayer. Cherry, Reginald, MD. Healing Prayer: God's Divine Intervention in Medicine, Faith, and Prayer. Nashville: Thomas Nelson, 1999.

Chesnut, Born Again in Brazil. Chesnut, R. Andrew. Born Again in Brazil: The Pentecostal Boom and the Pathogens of Poverty. New Brunswick, N.J.: Rutgers University Press, 1997.

Chesnut, "Exorcising." Chesnut, Andrew. "Exorcising the Demons of Deprivation: Divine Healing and Conversion in Brazilian Pentecostalism." Pages 169–85 in Global Pentecostal and Charismatic Healing. Edited by Candy Gunther Brown. Foreword by Harvey Cox. Oxford: Oxford University Press, 2011.

Chesterton, Miracles. Chesterton, G. K., et al. Do Miracles Happen? London: Christian Commonwealth, 1914.

Chevallier, Souffle. Chevallier, Max-Alain. Souffle de Dieu: le Saint-Esprit dans le Nouveau Testament. Vol. 1: Ancien Testament, Hellénisme et Judaïsme, La tradition synoptique, L'oeuvre de Luc. Le Point Théologique 26. Paris: Éditions Beauchesne, 1978.

Chevreau, Turnings. Chevreau, Guy. Turnings: The Kingdom of God and the Western World. Foreword by Rolland Baker and Heidi Baker. Kent: Sovereign World, 2004.

Chien-Kuei, "Life." Chien-Kuei, Feng. "My Life—In Sin and Under Grace." CGl 12 (4, Oct. 1935): 12–13.

Chin, "Practices." Chin, Shirley Shih-Hsin. "Healing Practices of Folk Religion and Christianity in Taiwan." ThM thesis, Fuller School of World Mission, 1985.

Chinwokwu, "Localizing." Chinwokwu, Emmanuel Nlenanya. "Localizing the Global: Revisiting New Testament Christology in African Context." Paper presented at the Society of New Testament Studies, Bard College, Aug. 5, 2011.

Chiquete, "Healing." Chiquete, Daniel. "Healing, Salvation, and Mission: The Ministry of Healing in Latin American Pentecostalism." IntRevMiss 93 (370–71, July/Oct. 2004): 474–85.

Chireau, Magic. Chireau, Yvonne. Black Magic: Religion and the African American Conjuring Tradition. Berkeley: University of California Press, 2003.

Chireau, "Natural." Chireau, Yvonne P. "Natural and Supernatural: African-American Hoodoo Narratives of Sickness and Healing." Pages 3–15 in Faith,

Health, and Healing in African-American Life. Edited by Stephanie Y. Mitchem and Emilie M. Townes. RelHHeal. Westport, Conn.: Praeger, 2008.

Chitando, "Prophetesses." Chitando, Anna. "Prophetesses and Healing in Zimbabwe." *AfThJ* 32 (1, 2009): 1–17.

Cho, "Foundation." Cho, Sung Hyun. "A Theoretical Foundation for a Healing Ministry in the Context of the Korean Evangelical Holiness Church." ThM thesis, Fuller School of World Mission, 1995.

Cho, "Healing." Cho, Il-Koo. "Healing in the Context of Korean Pentecostalism, 1950s to the Present: Historical and Ethnographic Approaches." PhD diss., Claremont Graduate University, 2002.

Choi, *Korean Miracles.* Choi, Jashil. *Korean Miracles.* Foreword by Paul Yonggi Cho. Seoul: Young San Publications; La Canada, Calif.: Mountain Press, n.d.

Choi, *Rise.* Choi, Meesaeng Lee. *The Rise of the Korean Holiness Church in Relation to the American Holiness Movement: Wesley's "Scriptural Holiness" and the "Fourfold Gospel."* PWS 28. Lanham, Md.: Scarecrow, 2008.

Chomsky, *Syntactic Structures.* Chomsky, Noam. *Syntactic Structures.* The Hague: Mouton, 1966.

Choy, *Murray.* Choy, Leona. *Andrew Murray: Apostle of Abiding Love.* Fort Washington, Pa.: Christian Literature Crusade, 1978.

Chrétien, "Exchange." Chrétien, Jean-Pierre. "Confronting the Unequal Exchange of the Oral and the Written." Pages 75–90 in *African Historiographies: What History for Which Africa?* Edited by Bogumil Jewsiewicki and David Newbury. SSAMDI 12. Beverly Hills, Calif.: Sage, 1986.

Chryssides, "Miracles." Chryssides, George D. "Miracles and Agents." *RelS* 11 (3, 1975): 319–27.

"Church of Scotland Report." Church of Scotland. *Report of Panel of Doctrine to the General Assembly. V: The Charismatic Movement Within the Church of Scotland.* Edinburgh: Church of Scotland, 1974.

Ciarrocchi and Deneke, "Happiness." Ciarrocchi, Joseph W., and Erin Deneke. "Happiness and the Varieties of Religious Experience: Religious Support, Practices, and Spirituality as Predictors of Well-Being." *RSSSR* 15 (2004): 209–33.

Ciarrocchi and Deneke, "Hope." Ciarrocchi, Joseph W., and Erin Deneke. "Hope, Optimism, Pessimism, and Spirituality as Predictors of Well-Being Controlling for Personality." *RSSSR* 16 (2006): 161–83.

Ciekawy, "Utsai." Ciekawy, Diane M. "Utsai as Ethical Discourse: A Critique of Power from Mijikenda in Coastal Kenya." Pages 158–89 in *Witchcraft Dialogues: Anthropological and Philosophical Exchanges.* Edited by George Clement Bond and Diane M. Ciekawy. Athens: Center for International Studies, Ohio University, 2001.

Cirillo, "Valore." Cirillo, Antonio. "Il valore rivelative dei miracoli di Cristo in San Tommaso." *AT* 4 (1, 1990): 151–73.

Cladis, "Modernity." Cladis, Mark S. "Modernity in Religion: A Response to Constantin Fasolt's 'History and Religion in the Modern Age.'" *HistTh,* theme issue 45 (4, Dec. 2006): 93–103.

Clapano, "Perspective." Clapano, Esperanza Y. "The Indigenous Perspective." *IntRevMiss* 90 (356/357, Jan./Apr. 2001): 113–17.

Clark, "Apostolic Faith Mission." Clark, Mathew. "Contemporary Pentecostal Leadership: The Apostolic Faith Mission of South Africa as Case Study." *AJPS* 10 (1, 2007): 42–61.

Clark, "Challenge." Clark, Mathew. "The Challenge of Contextualization and Syncretism to Pentecostal Theology and Missions in Africa." *JAM* 3 (1, March 2001): 79–99.

Clark, *Impartation.* Clark, Randy. *There Is More: Reclaiming the Power of Impartation.* Foreword by Bill Johnson. Mechanicsburg, Pa.: Global Awakening, 2006.

Clark, "Miracles." Clark, David K. "Miracles in the World Religions." Pages 199–213 in *In Defense of Miracles: A Comprehensive Case for God's Action in History.* Edited by R. Douglas Geivett and Gary R. Habermas. Downers Grove, Ill.: InterVarsity, 1997.

Clark, "Miracles and Law." Clark, Gordon H. "Miracles, History, and Natural Law." *EvQ* 12 (1940): 23–34.

Clark, *Parallel Lives.* Clark, Andrew C. *Parallel Lives: The Relation of Paul to the Apostles in the Lucan Perspective.* Carlisle: Paternoster, 2001.

Clark, *Philosophers.* Clark, Kelly James. *Philosophers Who Believe: The Spiritual Journeys of Eleven Leading Thinkers.* Downers Grove, Ill.: InterVarsity, 1993.

Clark, *Philosophy of Science.* Clark, Gordon H. *The Philosophy of Science and Belief in God.* Jefferson, Md.: Trinity Foundation, 1964.

Clark, "Religions." Clark, David K. "Miracles in the World Religions." *PhilChr* 3 (1, 2001): 61–63.

Clark, Drain, and Malone, "Needs." Clark, Paul Alexander, Maxwell Drain, and Mary P. Malone. "Addressing Patients' Emotional and Spiritual Needs." *JCJQS* 29 (12, 2003): 659–70.

Clarke, "Definition." Clarke, Steve. "Hume's Definition of Miracles Revised." *AmPhilQ* 36 (1, Jan. 1999): 49–57.

Clarke, "Luck." Clarke, Steve. "Luck and Miracles." *RelS* 39 (4, 2003): 471–74.

Clarke, "Response." Clarke, Steve. "Response to Mumford and Another Definition of Miracles." *RelS* 39 (4, 2003): 459–63.

Clarke, "Wine." Clarke, Clifton R. "Old Wine and New Wine Skins: West Indian and New West African Pentecostal Churches in Britain and the Challenge of Renewal." *JPT* 19 (1, 2010): 143–54.

Clayton, "Appraisal." Clayton, Philip. "Emergence from Quantum Physics to Religion: A Critical Appraisal." Pages 303–22 in *The Re-Emergence of Emergence: The Emergentist Hypothesis from Science to Religion.* Edited by Philip Clayton and Paul Davies. Oxford: Oxford University Press, 2006.

Clayton, "Foundations." Clayton, Philip. "Conceptual Foundations of Emergence Theory." Pages 1–31 in *The Re-Emergence of Emergence: The Emergentist Hypothesis from Science to Religion.* Edited by Philip Clayton and Paul Davies. Oxford: Oxford University Press, 2006.

Cleary and Stewart-Gambino, *Pentecostals.* Cleary, Edward L., and Hannah W. Stewart-Gambino. N.p.: Westview Press, HarperCollins, 1997.

Clérismé, "Vodoun." Clérismé, Rénald. "Vodoun, Peasant Songs, and Political Organizing." Pages 58–69 in *Haitian Vodou: Spirit, Myth, and Reality.* Edited by Patrick Bellegarde-Smith and Claudine Michel. Bloomington: Indiana University Press, 2006.

Clifford, "Healings." Clifford, Walter H. "Are Healings Permanent?" *PentEv* 770 (Oct. 27, 1928): 9.

Clifford, "Permanent." Clifford, Walter H. "Are Healings Permanent?" *PentEv* 660 (Aug. 14, 1926): 4.

Cody, "Miracle." Cody, Sadie. "A Miracle of Healing: Fractured Spine and Separated Vertebrae Healed; Short Leg Lengthened." *LRE* 3 (6, May 1911): 19–22.

Coe, *Coe.* Coe, Juanita. *The Jack Coe I Know.* N.p.: Herald of Healing, 1956.

Coffey, Davidson, and Dunn, *Miracles.* Coffey, Thomas F., Linda Kay Davidson, and Maryjane Dunn. *The Miracles of Saint James: Translations from the Liber Sancti Jacobi. First English Translation, with Introduction.* New York: Italica Press, 1996.

Cohen, *Maccabees.* Cohen, Shaye J. D. *From the Maccabees to the Mishnah.* LEC 7. Philadelphia: Westminster, 1987.

Cohen et al., "Religiosity." Cohen, Adam B., John D. Pierce, Rachel Meade, Jacqueline Chambers, Benjamin J. Gorvine, and Harold G. Koenig. "Intrinsic and Extrinsic Religiosity, Belief in the Afterlife, Death Anxiety, and Life Satisfaction in Young Catholic and Protestant Adults." *JResPer* 39 (2005): 307–24.

"Coincidence." "Coincidence." Pages 1020–22 in vol. 15 of *Brill's New Pauly: Encyclopaedia of the Ancient World.* Edited by Hubert Cancik and Helmuth Schneider. 20 vols. English ed. Christine F. Salazar. Leiden: Brill, 2010.

Cole, "Model." Cole, Harold R. "A Model of Contextualized Deliverance Ministry: A Case Study: The Cordillera Rehabilitation Center." *JAM* 5 (2, Sept. 2003): 259–73.

Coleman, *Globalisation.* Coleman, Simon. *The Globalization of Charismatic Christianity: Spreading the Gospel of Prosperity.* CSIR 12. Cambridge: Cambridge University Press, 2000.

Coleman, "Probability." Coleman, Dorothy. "Baconian Probability and Hume's Theory of Testimony." *HumSt* 27 (2, Nov. 2001): 195–226.

Coleman, "Wealth." Coleman, Simon. "Why Health *and* Wealth? Dimensions of Prosperity among Swedish Charismatics." Pages 47–60 in *Global Pentecostal and Charismatic Healing.* Edited by Candy Gunther Brown. Foreword by Harvey Cox. Oxford: Oxford University Press, 2011.

Colleyn, "Horse." Colleyn, Jean-Paul. "Horse, Hunter and Messenger: The Possessed Men of the *Nya Cult* in Mali." Pages 68–78 in *Spirit Possession, Modernity and Power in Africa.* Edited by Heike Behrend and Ute Luig. Madison: University of Wisconsin Press, 1999.

Collins, "Argument." Collins, Robin. "The Teleological Argument: An Exploration of the Fine-Tuning of the Universe." Pages 202–81 in *The Blackwell Companion to Natural Theology.* Edited by William Lane Craig and J. P. Moreland. Malden, Mass.: Blackwell, 2009.

Collins, "Artapanus." Collins, John J. "Introduction to Artapanus." Pages 889–96 in vol. 2 of *OTP.*

Collins, *God of Miracles.* Collins, C. John. *The God of Miracles: An Exegetical Examination of God's Action in the World.* Wheaton: Crossway, 2000.

Collins, *Exorcism.* Collins, James M. *Exorcism and Deliverance Ministry in the Twentieth Century: An Analysis of the Practice and Theology of Exorcism in Modern Western Christianity.* Foreword by Ian Stackhouse. Studies in Evangelical History and Thought. Colorado Springs: Paternoster, 2009.

Collins, "Hypothesis." Collins, Robin. "The Multiverse Hypothesis: A Theistic Perspective." Ch. 26 in *Universe or Multiverse?* Edited by Bernard Carr. Cambridge: Cambridge University Press, 2007.

Collins, *Introduction.* Collins, Raymond F. *Introduction to the New Testament.* Garden City, N.Y.: Doubleday, 1983.

Collins, *Language of God.* Collins, Francis S. *The Language of God: A Scientist Presents Evidence for Belief.* New York: Free Press, 2006.

Collins, "Miracles." Collins, Jack. "Miracles, Intelligent Design, and God-of-the-Gaps." *PScChrF* 55 (1, March 2003): 22–29.

Collins, "Perspective 1." Collins, W. Duane. "An Assemblies of God Perspective on Demonology, part 1." *Parac* 27 (4, 1993): 23–30.

Collins, "Perspective 2." Collins, W. Duane. "An Assemblies of God Perspective on Demonology, part 2." *Parac* 28 (1, 1994): 18–22.

Collip, "Efficacy." Collip, P. H. "The Efficacy of Prayer: A Triple-Blind Study." *MedT* 97 (1969): 201–4.

Colodny, "Introduction." Colodny, Robert G. "Introduction." Pages xi–xv in *The Nature and Function of Scientific Theories: Essays in Contemporary Science and Philosophy*. Edited by Robert G. Colodny. Pittsburgh: University of Pittsburgh Press, 1970.

Colson, "Possession." Colson, Elizabeth. "Central and South Africa: Spirit Possession among the Tonga of Zambia." Pages 69–103 in *Spirit Mediumship and Society in Africa*. Edited by John Beattie and John Middleton. Foreword by Raymond Firth. New York: Africana Publishing Corporation, 1969.

Colwell, "Defining Away." Colwell, Gary. "On Defining Away the Miraculous." *Philosophy* 57 (1982): 327–37.

Colwell, "Miracles and History." Colwell, Gary G. "Miracles and History." *Soph* 22 (1983): 9–14.

Comoro and Sivalon, "Ministry." Comoro, Christopher, and John Sivalon. "The Marian Faith Healing Ministry: An African Expression of Popular Catholicism in Tanzania." Pages 275–95 in *East African Expressions of Christianity*. Edited by Thomas Spear and Isaria N. Kimambo. EAfSt. Athens: Ohio University Press; Oxford: James Currey; Dar es Salaam: Mkuki na Nyota; Nairobi: East African Educational Publishers, 1999.

Comstock and Partridge, "Attendance." Comstock, G. W., and K. B. Partridge. "Church Attendance and Health." *JChrDis* 25 (1972): 665–72.

"Congressman Walks." "Crippled Congressman Walks." *VOH* (April 1951): 2–3.

Conn, "Visit to Heaven." Conn, Sallee J. "A Visit to Heaven." *MounM* (Feb. 1991): 16–17.

Connor and Samuel, *Healing Powers*. Connor, Linda H., and Geoffrey Samuel, eds. *Healing Powers and Modernity: Traditional Medicine, Shamanism, and Science in Asian Societies*. Westport, Conn.: Bergin & Garvey, 2001.

Constantelos, "Physician-Priests." Constantelos, Demetrios J. "Physician-Priests in the Medieval Greek Church." *GOTR* 12 (1, Summer 1966): 141–53.

Constantinides, "Zar." Constantinides, Pamela. "The History of Zar in the Sudan: Theories of Origin, Recorded Observation, and Oral Tradition." Pages 83–99 in *Women's Medicine: The Zar-Bori Cult in Africa and Beyond*. Edited by I. M. Lewis, Ahmed

Al-Safi, and Sayyid Hurreiz. Edinburgh: International African Institute, Edinburgh University Press, 1991.

Contrada et al., "Factors." Contrada, Richard J., et al. "Psychosocial Factors in Outcomes of Heart Surgery: The Impact of Religious Involvement and Depressive Symptoms." *HealthPsy* 23 (2004): 227–38.

Conybeare, "Introduction." Conybeare, F. C. "Introduction." Pages v–xv in vol. 1 of *The Life of Apollonius of Tyana* by Philostratus. Translated by F. C. Conybeare. 2 vols. LCL. Cambridge, Mass.: Harvard University Press, 1912.

Conzelmann, *Acts*. Conzelmann, Hans. *A Commentary on the Acts of the Apostles*. Edited by Eldon Jay Epp with Christopher R. Matthews. Translated by James Limburg, A. Thomas Kraabel, and Donald H. Juel. Philadelphia: Fortress, 1987.

Conzelmann, *Theology*. Conzelmann, Hans. *An Outline of the Theology of the New Testament*. New York: Harper & Row, 1969.

Cook, *Interpretation*. Cook, John Granger. *The Interpretation of the New Testament in Greco-Roman Paganism*. Peabody, Mass.: Hendrickson, 2002.

Cook, "Manticores." Cook, Robert. "Devils and Manticores: Plundering Jung for a Plausible Demonology." Pages 165–84 in *The Unseen World: Christian Reflections on Angels, Demons, and the Heavenly Realm*. Edited by Anthony N. S. Lane. Grand Rapids: Baker, 1996.

Cook, "Simpson." Cook, Jeffrey. "Simpson, Albert Benjamin (1843–1919)." Pages 401–2 in vol. 1 of *Encyclopedia of Religious Revivals in America*. Edited by Michael McClymond. 2 vols. Westport, Conn: Greenwood, 2007.

Cook and Wimberley, "Commitment." Cook, J. A., and D. W. Wimberley. "If I Should Die Before I Wake: Religious Commitment and Adjustment to the Death of a Child." *JSSR* 22 (3, 1983): 222–38.

Cooper, "Ventriloquism." Cooper, Kate. "Ventriloquism and the Miraculous: Conversion, Preaching, and the Martyr Exemplum in Late Antiquity." Pages 22–45 in *Signs, Wonders, Miracles: Representations of Divine Power in the Life of the Church. Papers Read at the 2003 Summer Meeting and the 2004 Winter Meeting of the Ecclesiastical History Society*. Edited by Kate Cooper and Jeremy Gregory. Rochester: Boydell & Brewer, for the Ecclesiastical History Society, 2005.

Cooper et al., "Spirituality." Cooper, L. A., C. Brown, et al. "How Important Is Intrinsic Spirituality in Depression Care? A Comparison of White and African-American Primary Care Patients." *JGenIntMed* 16 (9, 2001): 634–38.

Copleston, *Philosophy*. Copleston, Frederick. *Contemporary Philosophy: Studies of Logical Positivism and Existentialism.* Rev. ed. London: Search Press; Paramus, N.J.: Newman Press, 1972.

Coquery-Vidrovitch, "French Africa." Coquery-Vidrovitch, Catherine. "French Black Africa." Pages 329–92 in *From 1905–1940.* Translated by Elizabeth Edwards and Andrew Roberts. Edited by A. D. Roberts. Vol. 7 of *The Cambridge History of Africa.* Edited by J. D. Fage and Roland Oliver. 8 vols. Cambridge: Cambridge University Press, 1986.

Corbett, *Cuba.* Corbett, Ben. *This Is Cuba: An Outlaw Culture Survives.* Cambridge, Mass.: Westview, Perseus, 2004.

Cormack, "Flat." Cormack, Lesley B. "That Medieval Christians Taught That the Earth Was Flat." Pages 29–34 in *Galileo Goes to Jail and Other Myths about Science and Religion.* Edited by Ronald L. Numbers. Cambridge, Mass.: Harvard University Press, 2009.

Corduan, "Miracle." Corduan, Winfried. "Recognizing a Miracle." Pages 99–111 in *In Defense of Miracles: A Comprehensive Case for God's Action in History.* Edited by R. Douglas Geivett and Gary R. Habermas. Downers Grove, Ill.: InterVarsity, 1997.

Cornelius, "Growth." Cornelius, G. "Urban Church Growth." MA thesis, Fuller Theological Seminary, 1971.

Corten, "Obéissance." Corten, André. "Miracles et obéissance: Le discours de la guérison divine à l'Eglise Universelle." *SocCom* 44 (2, 1997): 283–303.

Corten and Marshall-Fratani, "Introduction." Corten, André, and Ruth Marshall-Fratani. "Introduction." Pages 1–21 in *Between Babel and Pentecost: Transnational Pentecostalism in Africa and Latin America.* Edited by André Corten and Ruth Marshall-Fratani. Bloomington: Indiana University Press, 2001.

Corten and Marshall-Fratani, *Pentecostalism.* Corten, André, and Ruth Marshall-Fratani, eds. *Between Babel and Pentecost: Transnational Pentecostalism in Africa and Latin America.* Bloomington: Indiana University Press, 2001.

Costa, "Review." Costa, Tony. Review of Robert M. Price, *Jesus Is Dead. RBL* 10 (2009); online at http://www.bookreviews.org/pdf/7049_7653.pdf.

Cotter, "Miracle." Cotter, Wendy. "Miracle." Pages 99–106 in vol. 4 of *The New Interpreter's Dictionary of the Bible.* Edited by Katharine Doob Sakenfeld et al. 5 vols. Nashville: Abingdon, 2009.

Cotter, *Miracles.* Cotter, Wendy. *Miracles in Greco-Roman Antiquity: A Sourcebook for the Study of New Testament Miracle Stories.* CEC. London: Routledge, 1999.

Cotter, "Miracle Stories." Cotter, Wendy. "Miracle Stories: The God Asclepius, the Pythagorean Philosophers, and the Roman Rulers." Pages 166–78 in *The Historical Jesus in Context.* Edited by Amy-Jill Levine, Dale C. Allison Jr., and John Dominic Crossan. Princeton Readings in Religions. Princeton, N.J.: Princeton University Press, 2006.

Cotter, *Portrait.* Cotter, Wendy J. *The Christ of the Miracle Stories: Portrait through Encounter.* Grand Rapids: Baker Academic, 2010.

Cotton et al., "Spirituality." Cotton, Sian, et al. "Spirituality and Religion in Patients with HIV/AIDS." *JGenIntMed* 21 (Suppl. 5, 2006): S5–13.

Cour, Avlund, and Schultz-Larsen, "Religion." Cour, P. la, K. Avlund, and K. Schultz-Larsen. "Religion and Survival in a Secular Region. A Twenty-Year Follow-up of 734 Danish Adults Born in 1914." *SSMed* 62 (2006): 157–64.

Covell, "Foreword." Covell, Ralph. "Foreword." Pages ix–xi in *Witnesses to Power: Stories of God's Quiet Work in a Changing China* by Tetsunao Yamamori and Kim-kwong Chan. Waynesboro, Ga.: Paternoster, 2000.

Cox, *Fire.* Cox, Harvey. *Fire from Heaven: The Rise of Pentecostal Spirituality and the Reshaping of Religion in the Twenty-first Century.* Reading, Mass.: Addison-Wesley, 1995.

Cox, "Foreword." Cox, Harvey. "Foreword." Pages xvii–xxi in *Global Pentecostal and Charismatic Healing.* Edited by Candy Gunther Brown. Oxford: Oxford University Press, 2011.

Cox, "Miracles." Cox, Harvey. "Into the Age of Miracles: Culture, Religion, and the Market Revolution." *WPJ* 14 (1, Spring 1997): 87–95.

Cracknell and White, *Introduction.* Cracknell, Kenneth, and Susan J. White. *An Introduction to World Methodism.* New York: Cambridge University Press, 2005.

Craffert, "Healer." Craffert, Pieter F. "Crossan's Historical Jesus as Healer, Exorcist, and Miracle Worker." *R&T* 10 (3–4, 2003): 243–66.

Craffert, "Origins." Craffert, Pieter F. "The Origins of Resurrection Faith: The Challenge of a Social Scientific Approach." *Neot* 23 (1989): 331–48.

Craffert and Botha, "Walk." Craffert, Pieter F., and Pieter J. J. Botha. "Why Jesus Could Walk on the Sea but He Could Not Read and Write: Reflections on Historicity and Interpretation in Historical Jesus Research." *Neot* 39 (1, 2005): 5–35.

Cragg, *Reason.* Cragg, Gerald R. *The Church and the Age of Reason, 1648–1789.* PHC 4. Rev. ed. Baltimore: Penguin, 1970.

Craig, *Assessing.* Craig, William Lane. *Assessing the New Testament Evidence for the Historicity of the Resurrection of Jesus.* SBEC 16. Lewiston, N.Y.: Edwin Mellen, 1989.

Craig, "Divination." Craig, Barry. "Sorcery Divination among the Abau of the Idam Valley, Upper Sepik, Papua New Guinea." *JRitSt* 22 (2, 2008): 37–51.

Craig, "Empty Tomb." Craig, William Lane. "The Empty Tomb of Jesus." Pages 173–200 in *Studies of History and Tradition in the Four Gospels*. Vol. 2 of *GosPersp*. Edited by R. T. France and David Wenham. 6 vols. Sheffield: JSOT Press, University of Sheffield, 1981.

Craig, *Faith*. Craig, William Lane. *Reasonable Faith: Christian Truth and Apologetics*. Rev. ed. Wheaton: Crossway, 1994.

Craig, "Historicity." Craig, William Lane. "The Historicity of the Empty Tomb of Jesus." *NTS* 31 (1985): 39–67.

Craig, "Miracles." Craig, William Lane. "The Problem of Miracles: A Historical and Philosophical Perspective." Pages 9–48 in *The Miracles of Jesus*. Vol. 6 of *GosPersp*. Edited by David Wenham and Craig Blomberg. Sheffield: JSOT Press, 1986.

Craig, "Not Dead." Craig, William Lane. "God Is Not Dead Yet: How Current Philosophers Argue for His Existence." *CT* (July 2008): 22–27.

Craig, "Resurrection." Craig, William Lane. "The Bodily Resurrection of Jesus." Pages 47–74 in *Studies of History and Tradition in the Four Gospels*. Vol. 1 of *GosPersp*. Edited by R. T. France and David Wenham. Sheffield: JSOT Press, 1980.

Craig, "Review." Craig, William Lane. Review of Colin Brown, *Miracles and the Critical Mind*. *JETS* 27 (4, 1984): 473–85.

Craig, "Rise?" Craig, William Lane. "Did Jesus Rise from the Dead?" Pages 141–76 in *Jesus Under Fire*. Edited by Michael J. Wilkins and J. P. Moreland. Grand Rapids: Zondervan, 1995.

Craig, "Tomb." Craig, William Lane. "On the Empty Tomb of Jesus." *PhilChr* 3 (1, 2001): 67–76.

Cramer, "Miracles." Cramer, John A. "Miracles and David Hume." *PScChrF* 40 (3, Sept. 1988): 129–37.

Crandall, *Raising*. Crandall, Chauncey W., IV. *Raising the Dead: A Doctor Encounters the Miraculous*. New York: FaithWords, 2010.

Cranston, *Miracle*. Cranston, Ruth. *The Miracle of Lourdes: Updated and Expanded Edition by the Medical Bureau of Lourdes*. New York: Image Books, Doubleday, 1988.

Crapanzaro, "Introduction." Crapanzaro, Vincent. "Introduction." Pages 1–40 in *Case Studies in Spirit Possession*. Edited by Vincent Crapanzaro and Vivian Garrison. New York: John Wiley & Sons, 1977.

Crapanzaro, "Mohammed." Crapanzaro, Vincent. "Mohammed and Dawia: Possession in Morocco." Pages 141–76 in *Case Studies in Spirit Possession*. Edited by Vincent Crapanzaro and Vivian Garrison. New York: John Wiley & Sons, 1977.

Crapanzaro and Garrison, *Case Studies*. Crapanzaro, Vincent, and Vivian Garrison, eds. *Case Studies in Spirit Possession*. New York: John Wiley & Sons, 1977.

Crawford, "Healing." Crawford, Suzanne J. "Religion, Healing, and the Body." Pages 29–45 in *Teaching Religion and Healing*. Edited by Linda L. Barnes and Inés Talamantez. AARTRSS. Oxford: Oxford University Press, 2006.

Crawford, *Miracles*. Crawford, Don. *Miracles in Indonesia: God's Power Builds His Church!* Wheaton: Tyndale, 1972.

Crawford, *Shantung Revival*. Crawford, Mary K. *The Shantung Revival*. Shanghai: China Baptist Publication Society, 1933.

Crawford and Lipsedge, "Help." Crawford, Tanya A., and Maurice Lipsedge. "Seeking Help for Psychological Distress: The Interface of Zulu Traditional Healing and Western Biomedicine." *MHRC* 7 (2, June 2004): 131–48.

"Cripples Walk." "Notable Cripples Walk." *VOH* (April 1950): 8–9.

Crisafulli and Nesbitt, *Miracles*. Crisafulli, Virgil S., and John W. Nesbitt. *The Miracles of St. Artemios: A Collection of Miracle Stories by an Anonymous Author of Seventh-Century Byzantium*. Translated by Virgil S. Crisafulli. Introduction by John W. Nesbitt. Commentary by Virgil S. Crisafulli and John W. Nesbitt. Leiden: Brill, 1997.

Cronan et al., "Prevalence." Cronan, T. A., et al. "The Prevalence of Religious Coping among Persons with Persistent Mental Illness." *PsychServ* 52 (5, 2001): 660–65.

Crosby, *History*. Crosby, Thomas. *The History of the English Baptists, from the Reformation to the Beginning of the Reign of King George I*. 4 vols. London: John Robinson, J. Hodges, and A. Ward, 1740.

Crosley, "Universes." Crosley, Reginald O. "Shadow-Matter Universes in Haitian and Dagara Ontologies: A Comparative Study." Pages 7–18 in *Haïtian Vodou: Spirit, Myth, and Reality*. Edited by Patrick Bellegarde-Smith and Claudine Michel. Bloomington: Indiana University Press, 2006.

Cross, "Genres." Cross, Anthony R. "Genres of the New Testament." Pages 402–11 in *DNTB*.

Cross and Crown 36 (2, July 2007): 6, 21; 37 (1, Sept. 2007): 4, 19; 37 (5, May 2008): 9.

Crossan, *Historical Jesus*. Crossan, John Dominic. *The Historical Jesus: The Life of a Mediterranean Jewish Peasant*. San Francisco: HarperSanFrancisco, 1991.

Crossan, "Necessary." Crossan, John Dominic. "Why Is Historical Jesus Research Necessary?" Pages 7–37 in *Jesus Two Thousand Years Later*. Edited by James H. Charlesworth and Walter P. Weaver. FSCS. Harrisburg, Pa.: Trinity Press International, 2000.

Crostini, "Miracles." Crostini, Barbara. "Mapping Miracles in Byzantine Hagiography: The Development of the Legend of St Alexios." Pages 77–88 in *Signs, Wonders, Miracles: Representations of Divine Power in the Life of the Church. Papers Read at the 2003 Summer Meeting and the 2004 Winter Meeting of the Ecclesiastical History Society.* Edited by Kate Cooper and Jeremy Gregory. Rochester: Boydell & Brewer, for the Ecclesiastical History Society, 2005.

Croy, "Religion, Personal." Croy, N. Clayton. "Religion, Personal." Pages 926–31 in *DNTB.*

Crump, *Knocking.* Crump, David. *Knocking on Heaven's Door: A New Testament Theology of Petitionary Prayer.* Grand Rapids: Baker Academic, 2006.

Crumplin, "Cuthbert." Crumplin, Sally. "Modernizing St Cuthbert: Reginald of Durham's Miracle Collection." Pages 179–91 in *Signs, Wonders, Miracles: Representations of Divine Power in the Life of the Church. Papers Read at the 2003 Summer Meeting and the 2004 Winter Meeting of the Ecclesiastical History Society.* Edited by Kate Cooper and Jeremy Gregory. Rochester: Boydell & Brewer, for the Ecclesiastical History Society, 2005.

Csordas, "Gender." Csordas, Thomas J. "Gender and Healing in Navajo Society." Pages 291–304 in *Religion and Healing in America.* Edited by Linda L. Barnes and Susan S. Sered. New York: Oxford University Press, 2005.

Csordas, "Global Perspective." Csordas, Thomas. "Catholic Charismatic Healing in Global Perspective: The Cases of India, Brazil, and Nigeria." Pages 331–50 in *Global Pentecostal and Charismatic Healing.* Edited by Candy Gunther Brown. Foreword by Harvey Cox. Oxford: Oxford University Press, 2011.

Csordas, "Healing." Csordas, Thomas. "Elements of Charismatic Persuasion and Healing." *MedAnthQ* 2 (1988): 121–42.

Csordas, *Language.* Csordas, Thomas J. *Language, Charisma, and Creativity: Ritual Life in the Catholic Charismatic Renewal.* Berkeley: University of California Press, 1997; New York: Palgrave, 2001.

Csordas, *Self.* Csordas, Thomas J. *The Sacred Self: A Cultural Phenomenology of Charismatic Healing.* Berkeley: University of California Press, 1994.

Cullis, *Trüdel.* Cullis, Charles. *Dorothea Trüdel or The Prayer of Faith.* Boston: Willard Tract Repository; London: Morgan & Chase, 1872.

Cullmann, *State.* Cullmann, Oscar. *The State in the New Testament.* New York: Charles Scribner's Sons, 1956.

Culpepper, "Problem of Miracles." Culpepper, Robert H. "The Problem of Miracles." *RevExp* 53 (2, April 1956): 211–24.

Cunningham, *Holiness.* Cunningham, Floyd T. *Holiness Abroad: Nazarene Missions in Asia.* PWS 16. Lanham, Md.: Oxford: Scarecrow, 2003.

Cunningham, "Holiness." Cunningham, Raymond J. "From Holiness to Healing: The Faith Cure in America, 1872–1892." *CH* 43 (Dec. 1974): 499–513.

Cunningham, *World.* Cunningham, Loren, Janet Benge, and Geoff Benge. *Into All the World.* Seattle, Wash.: YWAM Publishing, 2005.

Cunville, "Evangelization." Cunville, R. R. "The Evangelization of Northeast India." DMiss diss., Fuller Theological Seminary, 1975.

Curley, *Elders.* Curley, Richard T. *Elders, Shades, and Women: Ceremonial Change in Lango, Uganda.* Berkeley: University of California Press, 1973.

Curlin et al., "Association." Curlin, F. A., M. H. Chin, S. A. Sellergren, C. J. Roach, and J. D. Lentos. "The Association of Physicians' Religious Characteristics with Their Attitudes and Self-Reported Behaviors Regarding Religion and Spirituality in the Clinical Encounter." *Medical Care* 44 (2006): 446–53.

Currid, *Egypt.* Currid, John D. *Ancient Egypt and the Old Testament.* Foreword by Kenneth A. Kitchen. Grand Rapids: Baker, 1997.

Curtis, "Character." Curtis, Heather D. "The Global Character of Nineteenth-Century Divine Healing." Pages 29–45 in *Global Pentecostal and Charismatic Healing.* Edited by Candy Gunther Brown. Foreword by Harvey Cox. Oxford: Oxford University Press, 2011.

Curtis, *Faith.* Curtis, Heather D. *Faith in the Great Physician: Suffering and Divine Healing in American Culture, 1860–1900.* Baltimore: Johns Hopkins University Press, 2007.

Curtis, "Houses of Healing." Curtis, Heather D. "Houses of Healing: Sacred Space, Spiritual Practice, and the Transformation of Female Suffering in the Faith Cure Movement, 1870–90." *CH* 75 (3, Sept. 2006): 598–611.

Curtis, "Lord for Body." Curtis, Heather D. "The Lord for the Body: Pain, Suffering, and the Practice of Divine Healing in Late-Nineteenth-Century American Protestantism." ThD diss., Harvard University, 2005.

Cutler, "Membership." Cutler, Stephen J. "Membership in Different Types of Voluntary Associations and Psychological Well-Being." *Gerontologist* 16 (1976): 335–39.

Cutrer, "Miracle." Cutrer, Corrie. "Come and Receive Your Miracle." *CT* 45 (2, 2001): 41–49.

Daggett, "Miracles." Daggett, Mabel Potter. "Are There Modern Miracles?" *Ladies' Home Journal* (June 1923): 166.

Dairo, "Healing." Dairo, A. O. "Christianity and Healing: The Yoruba Experience." Pages 6–11 in *Religion, Medicine and Healing.* Edited by Gbola Aderibigbe and Deji Ayegboyin. Lagos: Nigerian Association for the Study of Religions and Education, 1995.

Dakin, "Belief." Dakin, Arthur. "The Belief in the Miraculous in New Testament Times." *ExpT* 23 (1911–12): 37–39.

Dal Santo, "Gregory." Dal Santo, Matthew. "Gregory the Great and Eustratius of Constantinople: The Dialogues on the Miracles of the Italian Fathers as an Apology for the Cult of Saints." *JECS* 17 (3, 2009): 421–57.

Daneel, "Churches." Daneel, Marthinus L. "African Initiated Churches in Southern Africa: Protest Movements or Mission Churches?" Pages 181–218 in *Christianity Reborn: The Global Expansion of Evangelicalism in the Twentieth Century.* Edited by Donald M. Lewis. SHCM. Grand Rapids: Eerdmans, 2004.

Daneel, "Exorcism." Daneel, M. L. "Exorcism As a Means of Combating Wizardry: Liberation or Enslavement?" *Missionalia* 18 (1, 1990): 220–46.

Daneel, *Zionism.* Daneel, M. L. *Zionism and Faith Healing in Rhodesia: Aspects of African Independent Churches.* Translated by V. A. February. Communications 2. Leiden: Afrika-Studiecentrum; The Hague: Mouton, 1970.

Danfulani, "Conflict." Danfulani, Umar Habila Dadem. "Religious Conflict on the Jos Plateau: The Interplay between Christianity and Traditional Religion During the Early Missionary Period." *SvMT* 89 (1, 2001): 7–40.

Daniel, "Dynamics and Strategy." Daniel, Christopher G. "Church Growth: Its Dynamics and Strategy. A Challenge to the Church in Sri Lanka Today." MA thesis, Fuller School of World Mission, 1977.

Daniel, "Labour." Daniel, Christopher G. "Indentured Labour and the Christian Movement in Sri Lanka." DMiss diss., Fuller School of World Mission, 1978.

Daniel, "Signs and Wonders." Daniel, Christopher G. "Signs and Wonders in Sri Lanka." *CGB* (Jan. 1977): 103–8.

Daniélou and Marrou, *Six Hundred Years.* Daniélou, Jean, and Henri Marrou. *The First Six Hundred Years.* Vol. 1 of *The Christian Centuries: A New History of the Catholic Church.* Translated by Vincent Cronin. New York: McGraw-Hill, 1964.

Daniels, "Differences." Daniels, David D., III. "God Makes No Differences in Nationality: The Fashioning of a New Racial/Nonracial Identity at the Azusa Street Revival." *Enr* 11 (2, Spring 2006): 72–76.

Daniels et al., "Effectiveness." Daniels, Nicholas A., Teresa Juarbe, Gina Moreno-John, and Eliseo J. Perez-Stable. "Effectiveness of Adult Vaccination Programs in Faith-Based Oorganizations." *EthDis* 17 (1, Suppl. 1, 2007): S15–22.

Danielson, "Demoted." Danielson, Dennis R. "That Copernicanism Demoted Humans from the Center of the Cosmos." Pages 50–58 in *Galileo Goes to Jail and Other Myths about Science and Religion.* Edited

by Ronald L. Numbers. Cambridge, Mass.: Harvard University Press, 2009.

Danyun, *Lilies.* Danyun. *Lilies Amongst Thorns.* Translated by Brother Dennis. Tonbridge: Sovereign World, 1991.

Dapila, "Role." Dapila, Fabian N. "The Socio-Religious Role of Witchcraft in the Old Testament Culture: An African Insight." *OTE* 11 (2, 1998): 215–39.

Dar and Applebaum, "Road." Dar, Shimon, and Shimon Applebaum. "The Roman Road from Antipatris to Caesarea." *PEQ* 105 (1973): 91–99.

Darcus, "Daimon." Darcus, S. M. "Daimon as a Force Shaping Ethos in Heraclitus." *Phoenix* 28 (1974): 390–407.

Darcus, "Logos." Darcus, S. M. "Logos of Psyche in Heraclitus." *RivSAnt* 9 (1979): 89–93.

Darcus, "*Phren.*" Darcus, S. M. "*Daimon* Parallels the Holy *Phren* in Empedocles." *Phronesis* 22 (1977): 175–90.

Darling, *Healing.* Darling, Frank C. *Christian Healing in the Middle Ages and Beyond.* Boulder, Colo.: Vista Publications, 1990.

Darling, *Restoration.* Darling, Frank C. *The Restoration of Christian Healing: New Freedom in the Church Since the Reformation.* Boulder, Colo.: Vista Publications, 1992.

Darnall, *Heaven.* Darnall, Jean. *Heaven—Here I Come! A Down-to-earth, Death-to-life Story.* Mukilteo, Wash.: Wine Press, 1998. Rev. from *Heaven, Here I Come: A Brief Biography.* London: Lakeland, 1974.

Daston, "Facts." Daston, Lorraine. "Marvelous Facts and Miraculous Evidence in Early Modern Europe." *CritInq* 18 (Autumn 1991): 93–124.

Dasuekwo, "Charms." Dasuekwo, L. S. "Charms and Amulets in Christian and Muslim Homes." Pages 13–18 in *Religion, Medicine, and Healing.* Edited by Gbola Aderibigbe and Deji Ayegboyin. Lagos: Nigerian Association for the Study of Religions and Education, 1995.

Daube, "Enfant." Daube, David. "Enfant Terrible." *HTR* 68 (3–4, July–October 1975): 371–76.

Daube, "Witnesses." Daube, David. "The Law of Witnesses in Transferred Operation." *JANESCU* 5 (1973): 91–93.

d'Aubigne, "Force." d'Aubigne, R. Merle. "How Is It Possible to Escape the Idea of Some Intelligent and Organizing Force?" Pages 157–59 in *Cosmos, Bios, and Theos: Scientists Reflect on Science, God, and the Origins of the Universe, Life, and Homo Sapiens.* Edited by Henry Margenau and Roy Abraham Varghese. La Salle, Ill.: Open Court, 1992.

Dauphin, "Apollo and Asclepius." Dauphin, Claudine. "From Apollo and Asclepius to Christ: Pilgrimage and Healing at the Temple and Episcopal Basilica of Dor." *SBFLA* 49 (1999): 397–430, plates 1–4.

Davey, "Healing." Davey, F. N. "Healing in the New Testament." Pages 50–63 in *The Miracles and the Resurrection: Some Recent Studies by I. T. Ramsey, G. H. Boobyer, F. N. Davey, M. C. Perry, and Henry J. Cadbury*. Theological Collections 3. London: SPCK, 1964.

Davey, *Robe*. Davey, Cyril J. *The Yellow Robe: The Story of Sahdu Sundar Singh*. London: SCM, 1950.

Davidson, "Pacific." Davidson, Allan K. "'The Pacific Is No Longer a Mission Field?' Conversion in the South Pacific in the Twentieth Century." Pages 133–53 in *Christianity Reborn: The Global Expansion of Evangelicalism in the Twentieth Century*. Edited by Donald M. Lewis. SHCM. Grand Rapids: Eerdmans, 2004.

Davies, "Downward Causation." Davies, Paul C. W. "The Physics of Downward Causation." Pages 35–52 in *The Re-Emergence of Emergence: The Emergentist Hypothesis from Science to Religion*. Edited by Philip Clayton and Paul Davies. Oxford: Oxford University Press, 2006.

Davies, "Effectiveness." Davies, Paul. "The Unreasonable Effectiveness of Science." Pages 44–56 in *Evidence of Purpose: Scientists Discover the Creator*. Edited by John Marks Templeton. New York: Continuum, 1994.

Davies, "Exorcism." Davies, Jeremy. "Exorcism: Understanding Exorcism in Scripture and Practice." London: Catholic Truth Society, 2008.

Davies, *Healer*. Davies, Stevan L. *Jesus the Healer: Possession, Trance, and the Origins of Christianity*. New York: Continuum, 1995.

Davies, *Invitation*. Davies, W. D. *Invitation to the New Testament: A Guide to Its Main Witnesses*. Garden City, N.Y.: Doubleday & Company, 1966.

Davies, *Mind*. Davies, Paul. *The Mind of God: The Scientific Basis for a Rational World*. New York: Simon & Schuster, 1992.

Davies, *Physics*. Davies, Paul. *God and the New Physics*. New York: Simon & Schuster, 1983.

Davies, "Preface." Davies, Paul. "Preface." Pages ix–xiv in *The Re-Emergence of Emergence: The Emergentist Hypothesis from Science to Religion*. Edited by Philip Clayton and Paul Davies. Oxford: Oxford University Press, 2006.

Davies, "Prophet/Healer." Davies, Stevan L. "The Historical Jesus as a Prophet/Healer: A Different Paradigm." *Neot* 30 (1, 1996): 21–38.

Davies, *Rhetoric*. Davies, Margaret. *Rhetoric and Reference in the Fourth Gospel*. JSNTSup 69. Sheffield: JSOT Press, 1992.

Davies, "Roberts." Davies, Gaius. "Evan Roberts: Blessings and Burnout." Pages 107–28 in *Revival,*

Renewal, and the Holy Spirit. Edited by Dyfed Wyn Roberts. SEHT. Eugene, Ore.: Wipf & Stock, 2009.

Davies, *Sermon*. Davies, W. D. *The Sermon on the Mount*. Cambridge: Cambridge University Press, 1966.

Davies, *Spirituality*. Davies, Oliver, with Thomas O'Loughlin. *Celtic Spirituality*. New York: Paulist, 1999.

Davies and Allison, *Matthew*. Davies, W. D., and Dale C. Allison. *A Critical and Exegetical Commentary on the Gospel According to Saint Matthew*. ICC. 3 vols. Vol. 1: *Introduction and Commentary on Matthew I–VII*. Edinburgh: T&T Clark, 1988. Vol. 2: *Commentary on Matthew VIII–XVIII*. Edinburgh: T&T Clark, 1991. Vol. 3: *The Gospel According to Saint Matthew*. Edinburgh: T&T Clark, 1997.

Davies and Conway, *Christianity*. Davies, Noel, and Martin Conway, *World Christianity in the Twentieth Century*. SCM Core Text. London: SCM, 2008.

Davis, "Actions." Davis, Stephen T. "God's Actions." Pages 163–77 in *In Defense of Miracles: A Comprehensive Case for God's Action in History*. Edited by R. Douglas Geivett and Gary R. Habermas. Downers Grove, Ill.: InterVarsity, 1997.

Davis, "Cosmology." Davis, Edward B. "That Isaac Newton's Mechanistic Cosmology Eliminated the Need for God." Pages 115–22 in *Galileo Goes to Jail and Other Myths about Science and Religion*. Edited by Ronald L. Numbers. Cambridge, Mass.: Harvard University Press, 2009.

Davis, *Proofs*. Davis, Stephen T. *God, Reason, and Theistic Proofs*. Grand Rapids: Eerdmans, 1997.

Dawid and Gillies, "Analysis." Dawid, Philip, and Donald Gillies. "A Bayesian Analysis of Hume's Argument Concerning Miracles." *PhilQ* 39 (1989): 57–65.

Dawson, *Healing*. Dawson, George Gordon. *Healing: Pagan and Christian*. London: SPCK; New York: Macmillan, 1935.

Dawson, "Urbanization." Dawson, John. "Urbanization and Mental Health in a West African Community." Pages 305–42 in *Magic, Faith, and Healing: Studies in Primitive Psychotherapy Today*. Edited by Ari Kiev. Introduction by Jerome D. Frank. New York: Free Press, 1964.

Dawtry, "*Modus Medendi*." Dawtry, Anne F. "The *Modus Medendi* and the Benedictine Order in Anglo-Norman England." Pages 25–38 in *The Church and Healing: Papers Read at the Twentieth Summer Meeting and the Twenty-first Winter Meeting of the Ecclesiastical History Society*. StChHist 19. Edited by W. J. Sheils. Oxford: Basil Blackwell, 1982.

Dayhoff, "Barros." Dayhoff, Paul S. "de Barros, Luciano Gomes." *DACB*. http://www.dacb.org/stories/capeverde/barros_luciano.html.

Dayhoff, "Guiva." Dayhoff, Paul S. "Guiva, Esther Danisane." *DACB.* http://www.dacb.org/stories /mozambique/guiva_esther.html.

Dayhoff, "Machava." Dayhoff, Paul S. "Machava, Sumão." *DACB.* http://www.dacb.org/stories /mozambique/machava_simao.html.

Dayhoff, "Marais." Dayhoff, Paul S. "Marais, Christopher." *DACB.* http://www.dacb.org/stories/south africa/marais_christopher.html.

Dayhoff, "Mthethwa." Dayhoff, Paul S. "Mthethwa, Johanne Patisa." *DACB.* http://www.dacb.org/stories /southafrica/mthethwa_johanne.html.

Dayhoff, "Mucavele." Dayhoff, Paul S. "Mucavele, Timoteo Umelwane Njanje." *DACB.* http://www .dacb.org/stories/mozambique/mucavele_timoteo .html.

Dayhoff, "Vilakoti." Dayhoff, Paul S. "Vilakati, Norman Magodzi." *DACB.* http://www.dacb.org/stories /swaziland/vilikati_norman.html.

Dayton, *Roots.* Dayton, Donald W. *Theological Roots of Pentecostalism.* Peabody, Mass.: Hendrickson, 1987.

Deacon, "Emergence." Deacon, Terrence W. "Emergence: The Hole at the Wheel's Hub." Pages 111–50 in *The Re-Emergence of Emergence: The Emergentist Hypothesis from Science to Religion.* Edited by Philip Clayton and Paul Davies. Oxford: Oxford University Press, 2006.

"Dead Raised to Life." *Weekly Evangel* 112 (Oct. 23, 1915): 1.

"Deaf Rear." "Deaf Rear" [*sic*]. *PentEv* (Dec. 10, 1921): 26.

Dearing, *Healing.* Dearing, Trevor. *Supernatural Healing Today.* Plainfield, N.J.: Logos, 1979.

Dearmer, *Body and Soul.* Dearmer, Percy. *Body and Soul: An Enquiry into the Effects of Religion upon Health, with a Description of Christian Works of Healing from the New Testament to the Present Day.* London: Sir Isaac Pitman & Sons, 1910.

DeBlase, *Survivor.* DeBlase, Betty Esses. *Survivor of a Tarnished Ministry: The True Story of Mike and Betty Esses.* Santa Ana, Calif.: Truth, 1983.

Debrunner, *Witchcraft.* Debrunner, Hans W. *Witchcraft in Ghana: A Study on the Belief in Destructive Witches and Its Effect on the Akan Tribes.* 2nd ed. Accra: Presbyterian Book Depot, 1961.

Deconinck-Brossard, "Acts of God." Deconinck-Brossard, Françoise. "Acts of God, Acts of Men: Providence in Seventeenth- and Eighteenth-Century England and France." Pages 356–75 in *Signs, Wonders, Miracles: Representations of Divine Power in the Life of the Church. Papers Read at the 2003 Summer Meeting and the 2004 Winter Meeting of the Ecclesiastical History Society.* Edited by Kate Cooper

and Jeremy Gregory. Rochester: Boydell & Brewer, for the Ecclesiastical History Society, 2005.

Dedert et al., "Practice." Dedert, Eric A., Jamie L. Studts, et al. "Private Religious Practice: Protection of Cortisol Rhythms among Women with Fibromyalgia." *IntJPsyMed* 34 (2004): 61–77.

Deere, "Being Right." Deere, Jack. "Being Right Isn't Enough." Pages 101–15 in *Power Encounters Among Christians in the Western World.* Edited by Kevin Springer. Introduction and afterword by John Wimber. San Francisco: Harper & Row, 1988.

Deere, *Power of Spirit.* Deere, Jack. *Surprised by the Power of the Spirit.* Grand Rapids: Zondervan, 1993.

Deere, *Voice.* Deere, Jack. *Surprised by the Voice of God.* Grand Rapids: Zondervan, 1996.

DeFelice, "Legend." DeFelice, John F. "The Rain Miracle Legend: Investigating the Dichotomy of the Pagan and Christian Traditions." *FidHist* 26 (2, 1994): 36–49.

DeGrandis, *Healing.* DeGrandis, Robert, with Linda Schubert. *Healing Through the Mass.* Rev. ed. Mineola, N.Y.: Resurrection Press, 1992.

DeGrandis, *Miracles.* DeGrandis, Robert, with Linda Schubert. *The Gift of Miracles: Experiencing God's Extraordinary Power in Your Life.* Ann Arbor, Mich.: Servant, 1991.

Deiros and Wilson, "Pentecostalism." Deiros, Pablo A., and Everett A. Wilson. "Hispanic Pentecostalism in the Americas." Pages 293–323 in *The Century of the Holy Spirit: One Hundred Years of Pentecostal and Charismatic Renewal, 1901–2001.* Edited by Vinson Synan. Nashville: Thomas Nelson, 2001.

Deissmann, *Light.* Deissmann, G. Adolf. *Light from the Ancient East.* Grand Rapids: Baker, 1978.

De Jong, *Rasputin.* De Jong, Alex. *The Life and Times of Grigorii Rasputin.* London: Collins, 1982.

Delaygue, "Grecs." Delaygue, M.-P. "Les Grecs connaissaient-ils les religions de l'Inde à l'époque hellénistique?" *BAGB* 54 (2, 1995): 152–72.

Delcor, "Guerre." Delcor, Mathias. "La guerre des dils de lumière contre les fils de ténèbres." *NRTh* 77 (4, April 1955): 372–99.

Delcor, "Mythe." Delcor, Mathias. "Le mythe de la chute des anges et de l'origine des géants comme explication du mal dans le monde, dans l'apocalyptique juive. Histoire des traditions." *RHR* 190 (1, 1976): 3–53.

De Leon, *Pentecostals.* De Leon, Victor. *The Silent Pentecostals: A Biographical History of the Pentecostal Movement among the Hispanics in the Twentieth Century.* Taylors, S.C.: Faith Printing Company, 1979.

D'Elia, *Place.* D'Elia, John A. *A Place at the Table: George Eldon Ladd and the Rehabilitation of Evan-*

gelical Scholarship in America. New York: Oxford University Press, 2008.

Delling, "Verständnis." Delling, Gerhard. "Das Verständnis des Wunders im Neuen Testament." ZST 24 (1955): 265–80.

Dembski, "Critique." Dembski, William A. "Schleiermacher's Metaphysical Critique of Miracles." SJT 49 (4, 1996): 443–65.

Dembski, Design. Dembski, William A. Intelligent Design: The Bridge between Science and Theology. Foreword by Michael Behe. Downers Grove, Ill.: InterVarsity, 1999.

Dembski, "Faith." Dembski, William A. "Faith and Healing—Where's the Evidence?" Posted July 11, 2008. http://www.bpnews.net/Bpnews.asp?ID=28460. Accessed May 12, 2009.

Dembski, Inference. Dembski, William A. The Design Inference. Cambridge: Cambridge University Press, 1998.

Dembski and Wells, Atheist. Dembski, William A., and Jonathan Wells. How to Be an Intellectually Fulfilled Atheist (Or Not). Wilmington, Del.: ISI Books, 2008.

Dempsey, "Lessons." Dempsey, Corinne G. "Lessons in Miracles from Kerala, South India: Stories of Three Christian Saints." HR 39 (2, 1999): 150–76.

Dempster, Klaus, and Petersen, Globalization of Pentecostalism. Dempster, Murray W., Byron D. Klaus, and Douglas Petersen, eds. The Globalization of Pentecostalism: A Religion Made to Travel. Foreword by Russell P. Spittler. Carlisle: Paternoster; Oxford: Regnum, 1999.

Denis, "Religion." Denis, Philippe. "African Traditional Religion and Christian Identity in a Group of Manyano Leaders." Missionalia 32 (2, Aug. 2004): 177–89.

Dennison, "Signs." Dennison, William David. "Miracles as 'Signs': Their Significance for Apologetics." BTB 6 (2, 1976): 190–202.

Denomy and Bruckmann, "Version." Denomy, Alex J., and J. Bruckmann. "An Old French Poetic Version of the Life and Miracles of Saint Magloire, Part 2." MS 21 (1959): 52–128.

Denton, Destiny. Denton, Michael. Nature's Destiny: How the Laws of Biology Reveal Purpose in the Universe. New York: Free Press, 1998.

De Orio, "Phenomenology." De Orio, Anthony R. "The Phenomenology of Transformation and Healing: The Disciples as Miracle Workers and Other Biblical Examples." Pages 114–33 in Medical and Therapeutic Events. Vol. 2 of Miracles: God, Science, and Psychology in the Paranormal. Edited by J. Harold Ellens. Westport, Conn.; London: Praeger, 2008.

D'Epinay, "Conquest." D'Epinay, Christian LaLive. "The Pentecostal 'Conquest' of Chile: Rudiments

of a Better Understanding." Pages 176–83 in Latin American Religions: Histories and Documents in Context. Edited by Anna L. Peterson and Manuel A. Vasquez. New York: New York University Press, 2008.

DePoe, "Bayesian Approach." DePoe, John. "Vindicating a Bayesian Approach to Confirming Miracles: A Response to Jordan Howard Sobel's Reading of Hume." PhilChr 10 (1, 2008): 229–38.

Derickson, "Cessation." Derickson, Gary W. "The Cessation of Healing Miracles in Paul's Ministry." BSac 155 (255, 1998): 299–315.

Dermawan, "Study." Dermawan, Julia Theis. "A Study of the Nias Revival in Indonesia." AJPS 6 (2, 2003): 247–63.

Derrett, Law. Derrett, J. Duncan M. Law in the New Testament. London: Darton, Longman and Todd, 1970.

Derrett, "Walked." Derrett, J. Duncan M. "Why and How Jesus Walked on the Sea." NovT 23 (4, 1981): 330–48.

Derrett, "Woman." Derrett, J. Duncan M. "The Samaritan Woman in India c. A.D. 200." ZRGG 39 (4, 1987): 328–36.

Desai, "Health." Desai, Prakash N. "Health, Faith Traditions, and South Asian Indians in North America." Pages 423–37 in Religion and Healing in America. Edited by Linda L. Barnes and Susan S. Sered. New York: Oxford University Press, 2005.

deSilva, Introduction. deSilva, David A. An Introduction to the New Testament: Contexts, Methods, and Ministry Formation. Downers Grove, Ill.: InterVarsity, 2004.

deSilva, "Meaning." deSilva, David A. "The Meaning of the New Testament and the Skandalon of World Constructions." EvQ 64 (1, Jan. 1992): 3–21.

Desjardlais, Body. Desjardlais, Robert. Body and Emotion: The Aesthetics of Illness and Healing in the Nepal Himalayas. Philadelphia: University of Pennsylvania Press, 1992.

Desmond and Maddux, "Programs." Desmond, D. P., and J. F. Maddux. "Religious Programs and Careers of Chronic Heroin Users." AJDAA 8 (1, 1981): 71–83.

Dettling, "Witness." Dettling, Jim. "Witness Testifies about Fear at Cult's Farm." Akron Beacon Journal (July 9, 1977): A-7.

Devadason, "Band." Devadason, Samuel. "Friends Missionary Prayer Band India: A Study of Its Origin, Growth, Achievements, and Future Strategy." ThM thesis, School of World Mission, Fuller Theological Seminary, 1977.

Devadason, "Missionary Societies." Devadason, Samuel. "Indian Missionary Societies." DMiss diss., Fuller Theological Seminary, 1978.

"Devin." "Ralph Devin Succumbs to Malaria." *PentEv* 1944 (Aug. 12, 1951): 13.

Devisch, "Forces." Devisch, René. "Sorcery Forces of Life and Death among the Yaka of Congo." Pages 101–30 in *Witchcraft Dialogues: Anthropological and Philosophical Exchanges*. Edited by George Clement Bond and Diane M. Ciekawy. Athens: Center for International Studies, Ohio University, 2001.

De Wet, "Basis." De Wet, Christiaan. "Biblical Basis of Signs and Wonders." Pages 51–58 in *Signs and Wonders Today: The Story of Fuller Theological Seminary's Remarkable Course on Spiritual Power*. Rev. ed. Edited by C. Peter Wagner. Altamonte Springs, Fla.: Creation House, Strang Communications, 1987.

De Wet, "Signs." De Wet, Christiaan Rudolph. "Signs and Wonders in Church Growth." MA thesis, Fuller School of World Mission, Dec. 1981.

Dezutter, Soenens, and Hutsebaut, "Religiosity." Dezutter, Jessie, Bart Soenens, and Dirk Hutsebaut. "Religiosity and Mental Health: A Further Exploration of the Relative Importance of Religious Behaviors vs. Religious Attitudes." *PerIndDif* 40 (4, 2006): 807–18.

Dhanis, "Miracle." Dhanis, Edouard. "Qu'est ce qu'un Miracle?" *Greg* 50 (1959): 201–41.

Diamond, "Miracles." Diamond, Malcolm L. "Miracles." *RelS* 9 (3, 1973): 307–24.

Dibb, "Revival." Dibb, Ashton. "The Revival in North Tinnevelly." *CMR* 5, n.s. (Aug. 1860): 178.

Dibelius, *Jesus*. Dibelius, Martin. *Jesus*. Translated by Charles B. Hedrick and Frederick C. Grant. Philadelphia: Westminster, 1949.

Dibelius, *Studies in Acts*. Dibelius, Martin. *Studies in the Acts of the Apostles*. Edited by H. Greeven. Translated by M. Ling. New York: Charles Scribner's Sons, 1956.

Dibelius, *Tradition*. Dibelius, Martin. *From Tradition to Gospel*. Translated from the 2nd (1933) German ed. by Bertram Lee Woolf. Cambridge: James Clarke; Greenwood, S.C.: Attic Press, 1971.

Dickie, "Evil Eye." Dickie, Matthew W. "Heliodorus and Plutarch on the Evil Eye." *CP* 86 (1, 1991): 17–29.

Dickie, "Headless Demons." Dickie, Matthew W. "Bonds and Headless Demons in Greco-Roman Magic." *GRBS* 40 (1, 1999): 99–104.

Dickie, "Who Practised Love Magic." Dickie, Matthew W. "Who Practised Love Magic in Classical Antiquity and in the Late Roman World?" *CQ* 50 (2, 2000): 563–83.

Dickson, *Theology*. Dickson, Kwesi A. *Theology in Africa*. London: Darton, Longman and Todd; Maryknoll, N.Y.: Orbis, 1984.

Dietl, "Miracles." Dietl, Paul. "On Miracles." *AmPhilQ* 5 (2, April 1968): 130–34.

Dijk, "Technologies." Dijk, Rijk van. "Time and Transcultural Technologies of the Self in the Ghanaian Pentecostal Diaspora." Pages 216–34 in *Between Babel and Pentecost: Transnational Pentecostalism in Africa and Latin America*. Edited by André Corten and Ruth Marshall-Fratani. Bloomington: Indiana University Press, 2001.

Dilley, "Act." Dilley, Frank B. "Does the 'God Who Acts' Really Act?" *AThR* 47 (1965): 66–80.

Dillon, *Middle Platonists*. Dillon, John. *The Middle Platonists: 80 B.C. to A.D. 220*. Ithaca, N.Y.: Cornell University Press, 1977.

DiOrio, *Miracle*. DiOrio, Ralph A. *A Miracle to Proclaim: Firsthand Experiences of Healing*. Garden City, N.Y.: Image Books, Doubleday, 1984.

DiOrio, *Signs*. DiOrio, Ralph A. *Signs and Wonders: Firsthand Experiences of Healing*. New York: Doubleday, 1987.

Dobbin, *Dance*. Dobbin, Jay D. *The Jombee Dance of Montserrat: A Study of Trance Ritual in the West Indies*. Columbus: Ohio State University Press, 1986.

Dobkin de Rios, "Power." Dobkin de Rios, Marlene. "Power and Hallucinogenic States of Consciousness among the Moche: An Ancient Peruvian Society." Pages 285–99 in *Altered States of Consciousness and Mental Health: A Cross-Cultural Perspective*. Edited by Colleen A. Ward. CCRMS 12. Newbury Park, Calif.: Sage, 1989.

"Doctor Healed." "Doctor Healed of Leukemia." *Cry of Calcutta* (Sept. 1989): 4–5.

Dod, "Healer." Dod, Marcus. "Jesus as Healer." *BibW* 15 (1900): 169–77.

Dodd, *Bible and Greeks*. Dodd, C. H. *The Bible and the Greeks*. London: Hodder & Stoughton, 1935.

Dodd, "Herrnworte." Dodd, C. H. "Some Johannine 'Herrnworte' with Parallels in the Synoptic Gospels." *NTS* 2 (2, Nov. 1955): 75–86.

Dolan, *Catholic Revivalism*. Dolan, Jay P. *Catholic Revivalism: The American Experience, 1830–1900*. Notre Dame, Ind.: University of Notre Dame Press, 1978.

Doleshal, "Healings." Doleshal, Frank. "Miraculous Healings in Chile." *PentEv* 2093 (June 20, 1954): 6–7.

Dollar, "Theology of Healing." Dollar, Harold Ellis. "A Cross-Cultural Theology of Healing." DMiss diss., Fuller Theological Seminary School of World Mission, 1981.

Dorier-Apprill, "Networks." Dorier-Apprill, Elisabeth. "The New Pentecostal Networks of Brazzaville." Pages 293–308 in *Between Babel and Pentecost: Transnational Pentecostalism in Africa and*

Latin America. Edited by André Corten and Ruth Marshall-Fratani. Bloomington: Indiana University Press, 2001.

Dormeyer, "Historii." Dormeyer, Detlev. "Pragmatyczne i patetyczne pisanie historii w historiografii greckiej, we wczesnym judaizmie i w Nowym Testamencie." *ColT* 78 (2, 2008): 81–94.

Douyon, "L'Examen." Douyon, Emerson. "L'Examen au Rorschach des Vaudouisants Haitiens." Pages 97–119 in *Trance and Possession States*. Proceedings of the Second Annual Conference, R. M. Bucke Memorial Society, March 4–6, 1966. Edited by Raymond Prince. Montreal: R. M. Bucke Memorial Society, 1968.

Downing, *Cynics*. Downing, F. Gerald. *Cynics, Paul, and the Pauline Churches: Cynics and Christian Origins II*. London: Routledge, 1998.

Downing, *Death*. Downing, Raymond. *Death and Life in America: Biblical Healing and Biomedicine*. Foreword by Jason Byassee. Scottsdale, Pa.: Herald, 2008.

Downs, *History*. Downs, F. S. *The Mighty Works of God: A Brief History of the Council of Baptist Churches in North East India: The Mission Period 1836–1950*. Panbazar, Assam: Christian Literature Center, 1971.

Drane, "Background." Drane, John W. "The Religious Background." Pages 117–25 in *New Testament Interpretation: Essays on Principles and Methods*. Edited by I. Howard Marshall. Grand Rapids: Eerdmans, 1977.

Draper, "Land." Draper, Jonathan A. "A Broken Land and a Healing Community: Zulu Zionism and Healing in the Case of George Khambule (1884–1949)." *StHistEc* 36 (1, 2010): 95–122.

Draper, "Orality." Draper, Jonathan A. "Orality, Literacy, and Colonialism in Antiquity." Pages 1–6 in *Orality, Literacy, and Colonialism in Antiquity*. Edited by Jonathan A. Draper. SBLSemS 47. Atlanta: Society of Biblical Literature, 2004.

Dreher and Plante, "Protocol." Dreher, Diane E., and Thomas G. Plante. "The Calling Protocol: Promoting Greater Health, Joy, and Purpose in Life." Pages 129–40 in *Spirit, Science, and Health: How the Spiritual Mind Fuels Physical Wellness*. Edited by Thomas G. Plante and Carl E. Thoresen. Foreword by Albert Bandura. Westport, Conn.: Praeger, 2007.

Drentea and Goldner, "Caregiving." Drentea, Patricia, and Melinda A. Goldner. "Caregiving Outside of the Home: The Effects of Race on Depression." *EthHealth* 11 (2006): 41–57.

Driver, *Scrolls*. Driver, G. R. *The Judaean Scrolls: The Problem and a Solution*. Oxford: Basil Blackwell, 1965.

Droege, *Faith Factor*. Droege, Thomas A. *The Faith Factor in Healing*. Philadelphia: Trinity Press International, 1991.

Droogers, "Globalisation." Droogers, André. "Globalisation and Pentecostal Success." Pages 41–61 in *Between Babel and Pentecost: Transnational Pentecostalism in Africa and Latin America*. Edited by André Corten and Ruth Marshall-Fratani. Bloomington: Indiana University Press, 2001.

Droogers, "Normalization." Droogers, André. "The Normalization of Religious Experience: Healing, Prophecy, Dreams, and Visions." Pages 33–49 in *Charismatic Christianity as a Global Culture*. Edited by Karla Poewe. SCR. Columbia: University of South Carolina Press, 1994.

Drury, *Design*. Drury, John. *Tradition and Design in Luke's Gospel: A Study in Early Christian Historiography*. London: Darton, Longman and Todd, 1976.

D'Souza, *Christianity*. D'Souza, Dinesh. *What's So Great about Christianity*. Washington, D.C.: Regnery, 2007.

Du Bois, *World*. Du Bois, W. E. B. *The World and Africa: An Inquiry into the Part Which Africa Has Played in History*. Rev. ed., including new writings of W. E. B. Du Bois, 1955–61. New York: International Publishers, 1965.

Dube, "Formations." Dube, Saurabh. "Formations." Pages 75–78 in *Historical Anthropology*. Edited by Saurabh Dube. OIRSSA. New Delhi: Oxford University Press, 2007.

Dube, "Past." Dube, Saurabh. "A Contested Past." Pages 173–89 in *Historical Anthropology*. Edited by Saurabh Dube. OIRSSA. New Delhi: Oxford University Press, 2007.

Dube, "Search." Dube, D. "A Search for Abundant Life: Health, Healing, and Wholeness in Zionist Churches." Pages 109–36 in *Afro-Christian Religion and Healing in Southern Africa*. Edited by G. C. Oosthuizen, S. D. Edwards, W. H. Wessels, and I. Hexham. AfSt 8. Lewiston, N.Y.: Edwin Mellen, 1989.

Duffin, *Miracles*. Duffin, Jacalyn. *Medical Miracles: Doctors, Saints, and Healing in the Modern World*. Oxford: Oxford University Press, 2009.

Duling, "Introduction." Duling, Dennis C. Introduction to "Testament of Solomon." Pages 935–59 in vol. 1 of *OTP*.

Dull and Skokan, "Model." Dull, V. T., and L. A. Skokan. "A Cognitive Model of Religion's Influence on Health." *JSocI* 51 (2, 1995): 49–64.

Dumsday, "Locke." Dumsday, Travis. "Locke on Competing Miracles." *FPhil* 25 (4, 2008): 416–24.

Dunand, *Religion en Égypte*. Dunand, Françoise. *Religion Populaire en Égypte Romaine*. ÉPROER 77. Leiden: Brill, 1979.

Duncan Hoyte, "Plagues." Duncan Hoyte, H. M. "The Plagues of Egypt: What Killed the Animals and the Firstborn?" *MedJAus* 158 (1993): 706–8.

Dunkerley, *Healing Evangelism*. Dunkerley, Don. *Healing Evangelism: Strengthen Your Witnessing with Effective Prayer for the Sick*. Foreword by J. I. Packer. Grand Rapids: Chosen, 1995.

Dunn, "Demythologizing." Dunn, James D. G. "Demythologizing—The Problem of Myth in the New Testament." Pages 285–307 in *New Testament Interpretation: Essays on Principles and Methods*. Edited by I. Howard Marshall. Grand Rapids: Eerdmans, 1977.

Dunn, *Jesus and Spirit*. Dunn, James D. G. *Jesus and the Spirit: A Study of the Religious and Charismatic Experience of Jesus and the First Christians as Reflected in the New Testament*. London: SCM, 1975.

Dunn, *New Perspective*. Dunn, James D. G. *A New Perspective on Jesus: What the Quest for the Historical Jesus Missed*. Grand Rapids: Baker Academic, 2005.

Dunn, *Remembered*. Dunn, James D. G. *Jesus Remembered*. Vol. 1 of *Christianity in the Making*. Grand Rapids: Eerdmans, 2003.

Dunne, *Experiment*. Dunne, J. W. *An Experiment with Time*. New York: Macmillan: 1927.

Dunphy, "Marriage." Dunphy, John. "'Marriage Torn Apart by Religious Cult.'" *Akron Beacon Journal* (May 18, 1975): C1, 3.

Dupont, *Sources*. Dupont, Jacques. *The Sources of the Acts: The Present Position*. Translated by Kathleen Pond. New York: Herder & Herder, 1964.

Durand and Massey, *Miracles*. Durand, Jorge, and Douglas S. Massey. *Miracles on the Border: Retablos of Mexican Migrants to the United States*. Tucson: University of Arizona Press, 1995.

Durham, *Miracles of Mary*. Durham, Michael S. *Miracles of Mary: Apparitions, Legends, and Miraculous Works of the Blessed Virgin Mary*. San Francisco: HarperSanFrancisco, 1995.

Dvorak, "Relationship." Dvorak, James D. "The Relationship between John and the Synoptic Gospels." *JETS* 41 (2, 1998): 201–13.

Dvorjetski, "Healing Waters." Dvorjetski, Esti. "Healing Waters: The Social World of Hot Springs in Roman Palestine." *BAR* 30 (4, 2004): 16–27, 60.

Dyrness, *Theology*. Dyrness, William A. *Learning about Theology from the Third World*. Grand Rapids: Academie, Zondervan, 1990.

Dyson, "One." Dyson, Freeman. "One in a Million." *NYRB* 51 (5, March 25, 2004): 4–5.

Eames, "History." Eames, Kevin J. "History of Research on Faith, Prayer, and Medical Healings." Pages 82–93 in *Medical and Therapeutic Events*. Vol. 2 of *Miracles: God, Science, and Psychology in the Paranormal*. Edited by J. Harold Ellens. Westport, Conn.; London: Praeger, 2008.

Eareckson with Musser, *Joni*. Eareckson, Joni, with Joe Musser. *Joni*. Grand Rapids: Zondervan, 1976.

Earle, "Borders." Earle, Duncan. "The Borders of Distinctions: Dog Days." Paper read at the Society for Humanistic Anthropology Invited Session on Practice, Performance, and Participation, American Anthropological Association Annual Meeting, Chicago, Nov. 2003.

Earman, "Bayes." Earman, John. "Bayes, Hume, and Miracles." *FPhil* 10 (3, 1993): 293–310.

Earman, *Failure*. Earman, John. *Hume's Abject Failure: The Argument against Miracles*. Oxford: Oxford University Press, 2000.

Earman, "Hume." Earman, John. "Bayes, Hume, Price, and Miracles." Pages 91–109 in *Bayes's Theorem*. Edited by Richard Swinburne. Oxford: Oxford University Press, 2005.

Eastwell, "Voodoo Death." Eastwell, Harry D. "Voodoo Death and the Mechanism for Dispatch of the Dying in East Arnhem, Australia." *AmAnth* 84 (1, March 1982): 5–18.

Eaton, "AIDS." Eaton, David. "Understanding AIDS in Public Lives: Luambo Makiadi and Sony Labou Tansi." Pages 315–32 in *Health Knowledge and Belief Systems in Africa*. Edited by Toyin Falola and Matthew M. Heaton. Durham, N.C.: Carolina Academic Press, 2008.

Eberhardt, "Fruit." Eberhardt, Anne. "Fruit of the Gospel in the Leper Work." *PentEv* 938 (March 5, 1932): 9.

Eby, *Paradise*. Eby, Richard E. *Caught Up Into Paradise*. Old Tappan, N.J.: Revell, 1978.

Eccles, "Design." Eccles, John. "A Divine Design: Some Questions on Origins." Pages 160–64 in *Cosmos, Bios, and Theos: Scientists Reflect on Science, God, and the Origins of the Universe, Life, and Homo Sapiens*. Edited by Henry Margenau and Roy Abraham Varghese. La Salle, Ill.: Open Court, 1992.

Eccles, "Evolution." Eccles, John C. "The Evolution of Purpose." Pages 116–32 in *Evidence of Purpose: Scientists Discover the Creator*. Edited by John Marks Templeton. New York: Continuum, 1994.

Echard, "Possession Cult." Echard, Nicole. "The Hausa *Bori* Possession Cult in the Ader Region of Niger." Pages 64–80 in *Women's Medicine: The Zar-Bori Cult in Africa and Beyond*. Edited by I. M. Lewis, Ahmed Al-Safi, and Sayyid Hurreiz. Edinburgh: International African Institute, Edinburgh University Press, 1991.

Eckey, *Apostelgeschichte*. Eckey, Wilfried. *Die Apostelgeschichte: Der Weg des Evangeliums von Jerusalem nach Rom*. 2 vols. Neukirchen-Vluyn: Neukirchener Verlag, 2000. Teilband I: 1,1–15,35; Teilband II: 15,36–28,31.

Ecklund, "Religion." Ecklund, Elaine Howard. "Religion and Spirituality among Scientists." *Contexts* 7 (1, 2008): 12–15.

Ecklund, *Science*. Ecklund, Elaine Howard. *Science vs. Religion: What Scientists Really Think.* Oxford: Oxford University Press, 2010.

Eddy, "Reality of Spirits." Eddy, Paul R. "The Reality of Spirits." Unpublished paper in the author's possession.

Eddy and Beilby, "Introduction." Eddy, Paul Rhodes, and James K. Beilby. "The Quest for the Historical Jesus: An Introduction." Pages 9–54 in *The Historical Jesus: Five Views.* Edited by Paul Rhodes Eddy and James K. Beilby. Downers Grove, Ill.: IVP Academic, 2009.

Eddy and Boyd, *Legend*. Eddy, Paul Rhodes, and Gregory A. Boyd. *The Jesus Legend: A Case for the Historical Reliability of the Synoptic Jesus Tradition.* Grand Rapids: Baker Academic, 2007.

Edelstein and Edelstein, *Asclepius*. Edelstein, Emma J., and Ludwig Edelstein. *Asclepius: A Collection and Interpretation of the Testimonies.* 2 vols. Baltimore: Johns Hopkins University Press, 1945.

Eder, *Wundertäter*. Eder, Gottfried. *Der göttliche Wundertäter: Ein exegetischer und religionswissenschaftlicher Versuch.* Passau: Selbstverl, 1957.

Edmunds, "Sick." Edmunds, P. K. "Is Any Sick Among You." Pages 69–74 in *Faith Healing: Finger of God? Or, Scientific Curiosity?* Compiled by Claude A. Frazier. New York: Thomas Nelson, 1973.

Edwards, *Christianity*. Edwards, David L. *Christianity: The First Two Thousand Years.* Maryknoll, N.Y.: Orbis, 1997.

Edwards, "Exorcisms." Edwards, M. J. "Three Exorcisms and the New Testament World." *Eranos* 87 (2, 1989): 117–26.

Edwards, "Healing." Edwards, F. S. "Healing: Xhosa Perspective." Pages 329–45 in *Afro-Christian Religion and Healing in Southern Africa.* Edited by G. C. Oosthuizen, S. D. Edwards, W. H. Wessels, and I. Hexham. AfSt 8. Lewiston, N.Y.: Edwin Mellen, 1989.

Edwards, "Medicine." Edwards, S. D. "Traditional and Modern Medicine in Southern Africa: Some Reflective and Research Considerations." Pages 13–24 in *Afro-Christian Religion and Healing in Southern Africa.* Edited by G. C. Oosthuizen, S. D. Edwards, W. H. Wessels, and I. Hexham. AfSt 8. Lewiston, N.Y.: Edwin Mellen, 1989.

Edwards, "Possession." Edwards, Felicity S. "Amafufunyana Spirit Possession: Treatment and Interpretation." Pages 207–25 in *Afro-Christian Religion and Healing in Southern Africa.* Edited by G. C. Oosthuizen, S. D. Edwards, W. H. Wessels, and I. Hexham. AfSt 8. Lewiston, N.Y.: Edwin Mellen, 1989.

Efron, "Christianity." Efron, Noah J. "That Christianity Gave Birth to Modern Science." Pages 78–89 in *Galileo Goes to Jail and Other Myths about Science and Religion.* Edited by Ronald L. Numbers. Cambridge, Mass.: Harvard University Press, 2009.

Église Évangélique, *Ngouédi*. Église Évangélique du Congo. *Ngouédi a 60 ans; historique des 90 ans d'évangélisation par la Mission Evangélique Suédoise et l'Église Évangélique du Congo.* Pointe Noire, Congo: Imprimerie IAD, Congo, 1991.

Ehrhardt, *Acts*. Ehrhardt, Arnold. *The Acts of the Apostles.* Manchester: Manchester University Press, 1969.

Ehrman, *Brief Introduction*. Ehrman, Bart D. *A Brief Introduction to the New Testament.* New York: Oxford University Press, 2004.

Ehrman, *Historical Introduction*. Ehrman, Bart D. *The New Testament: A Historical Introduction to the Early Christian Writings.* 4th ed. New York: Oxford University Press, 2008.

Ehrman, *Prophet*. Ehrman, Bart D. *Jesus: Apocalyptic Prophet of the New Millennium.* Oxford: Oxford University Press, 1999.

Ehrman, "Response." Ehrman, Bart D. "Response to Charles Hedrick's Stalemate." *JECS* 11 (2, Summer 2003): 155–63.

Ejizu, "Exorcism." Ejizu, Christopher I. "Cosmological Perspective on Exorcism and Prayer Healing in Contemporary Nigeria." Pages 11–23 in *Healing and Exorcism: The Nigerian Experience.* Proceedings, Lectures, Discussions, and Conclusions of the First Missiology Symposium on Healing and Exorcism, organized by the Spiritan International School of Theology, Attakwu, Enugu, May 18–20, 1989. Edited by Chris U. Manus, Luke N. Mbefo, and E. E. Uzukwu. Attakwu, Enugu: Spiritan International School of Theology, 1992.

Ejizu, "Perspective." Ejizu, Christopher I. "Cosmological Perspective on Exorcism and Prayer Healing in Contemporary Nigeria." *MissSt* 8 (2, 1991): 165–76.

Ekechi, "Medical Factor." Ekechi, Felix K. "The Medical Factor in Christian Conversion in Africa: Observations from Southeastern Nigeria." *Missiology* 21 (3, 1993): 289–309.

Elbert, "Themes." Elbert, Paul. "Pentecostal/Charismatic Themes in Luke-Acts at the Evangelical Theological Society: The Battle of Interpretive Method." *JPT* 12 (2, 2004): 181–215.

Eliade, *Rites*. Eliade, Mircea. *Rites and Symbols of Initiation: The Mysteries of Birth and Rebirth.* Translated by Willard R. Trask. New York: Harper & Row, 1958.

Eliade, *Shamanism*. Eliade, Mircea. *Shamanism: Archaic Techniques of Ecstasy.* Translated by Willard R. Trask. BollS 76. New York: Bollingen Foundation, Pantheon Books (Random House), 1964.

Elizabeth et al., "Factors." Elizabeth, Jesse D., Marilyn Graham, and Mel Swanson. "Psychosocial and

Spiritual Factors Associated with Smoking and Substance Use During Pregnancy in African American and White Lower-Income Women." *JObGynNNurs* 35 (1, 2006): 68–77.

Elizondo, "Response." Elizondo, Virgil. "The Response of Liberation Theology." Pages 51–56 in *Pentecostal Movements as an Ecumenical Challenge.* Edited by Jürgen Moltmann and Karl-Josef Kuschel. Concilium 3. Maryknoll, N.Y.: Orbis, 1996.

Ellenburg, "Review." Ellenburg, B. Dale. "A Review of Selected Narrative-Critical Conventions in Mark's Use of Miracle Material." *JETS* 38 (2, June 1995): 171–80.

Ellens, "Conclusion." Ellens, J. Harold. "Conclusion." Pages 301–3 in *Religious and Spiritual Events.* Vol. 1 of *Miracles: God, Science, and Psychology in the Paranormal.* Edited by J. Harold Ellens. Westport, Conn.; London: Praeger, 2008.

Ellens, "God and Science." Ellens, J. Harold. "God and Science." Pages 1–16 in *Medical and Therapeutic Events.* Vol. 2 of *Miracles: God, Science, and Psychology in the Paranormal.* Edited by J. Harold Ellens. Westport, Conn.; London: Praeger, 2008.

Ellens, "Miracles and Process." Ellens, J. Harold. "Biblical Miracles and Psychological Process: Jesus as Psychotherapist." Pages 1–14 in *Religious and Spiritual Events.* Vol. 1 of *Miracles: God, Science, and Psychology in the Paranormal.* Edited by J. Harold Ellens. Westport, Conn.; London: Praeger, 2008.

Ellin, "Again." Ellin, Joseph. "Again: Hume on Miracles." *HumSt* 19 (1, April 1993): 203–12.

Ellingsen, *Roots.* Ellingsen, Mark. *Reclaiming Our Roots: An Inclusive Introduction to Church History.* 2 vols. Vol. 1: *The Late First Century to the Eve of the Reformation.* Vol. 2: *From Martin Luther to Martin Luther King Jr.* Harrisburg, Pa.: Trinity Press International, 1999.

Elliot, "Fear." Elliot, John H. "The Fear of the Leer: The Evil Eye from the Bible to Li'l Abner." *Forum* 4 (4, 1988): 42–71.

Ellis, "Action." Ellis, Robert. "God and 'Action.'" *RelS* 24 (4, 1988): 463–82.

Ellis, "Nature." Ellis, George F. R. "On the Nature of Emergent Reality." Pages 79–107 in *The Re-Emergence of Emergence: The Emergentist Hypothesis from Science to Religion.* Edited by Philip Clayton and Paul Davies. Oxford: Oxford University Press, 2006.

Ellison et al., "Involvement." Ellison, Christopher G., R. A. Hummer, et al. "Religious Involvement and Mortality Risk among African American Adults." *ResAg* 22 (6, 2000): 630–67.

Emery, "Cured." Emery, C. Eugene, Jr. "Are They Really Cured? Putting the Claims of Faith Healer Ralph DiOrio to the Test." Providence *Sunday Journal Magazine* (Jan. 15, 1989): 6–17.

Emmel, "Process." Emmel, Thomas C. "The Creative Process May Well Be What We Observe, Deduce, and Call Evolution." Pages 166–71 in *Cosmos, Bios, and Theos: Scientists Reflect on Science, God, and the Origins of the Universe, Life, and* Homo Sapiens. Edited by Henry Margenau and Roy Abraham Varghese. La Salle, Ill.: Open Court, 1992.

Emmons, *Ghosts.* Emmons, Charles F. *Chinese Ghosts and ESP: A Study of Paranormal Beliefs and Experiences.* Metuchen, N.J.: Scarecrow, 1982.

Endres, *Interpretation.* Endres, John C. *Biblical Interpretation in the Book of Jubilees.* CBQMS 18. Washington, D.C.: Catholic Biblical Association of America, 1987.

Eneja, "Message." Eneja, M. U. "Goodwill Message from His Lordship Rt. Rev. Dr. M. U. Eneja, Bishop of Enugu." Pages 163–68 in *Healing and Exorcism: The Nigerian Experience.* Proceedings, Lectures, Discussions, and Conclusions of the First Missiology Symposium on Healing and Exorcism, organized by the Spiritan International School of Theology, Attakwu, Enugu, May 18–20, 1989. Edited by Chris U. Manus, Luke N. Mbefo, and E. E. Uzukwu. Attakwu, Enugu: Spiritan International School of Theology, 1992.

Eng et al., "Ties." Eng, P. M., E. B. Rimm, G. Fitzmaurice, and I. Kawachi. "Social Ties and Change in Social Ties in Relation to Subsequent Total and Cause-Specific Mortality and Coronary Heart Disease Incidence in Men." *AmJEpid* 155 (2002): 700–709.

Engel, "Death." Engel, George. "Sudden and Rapid Death During Psychological Stress: Folklore or Folk Wisdom?" *AnnIntMed* 74 (1971): 771–82.

Engels, "Grammaire." Engels, Jens Ivo. "Une grammaire de la vérité. Les miracles jansénistes en province d'après les Nouvelles Ecclésiastiques, 1728–1750." *RHE* 91 (2, 1996): 436–64.

Engels, *Roman Corinth.* Engels, Donald W. *Roman Corinth: An Alternative Model for the Classical City.* Chicago: University of Chicago Press, 1990.

Englund, "Quest." Englund, Harri. "The Quest for Missionaries: Transnationalism and Township. Pentecostalism in Malawi." Pages 235–55 in *Between Babel and Pentecost: Transnational Pentecostalism in Africa and Latin America.* Edited by André Corten and Ruth Marshall-Fratani. Bloomington: Indiana University Press, 2001.

Enns, "Profiles." Enns, A. "Profiles of Argentine Church Growth." MA thesis, Fuller Theological Seminary, 1967.

Entz, "Encounter." Entz, Donna Kampen. "Mennonite Encounter with the Changing Dynamics of Christian Churches in the Burkina Faso Context." *MissFoc* 17 (2009): 131–46.

"Episcopal Ministers." "Episcopal Ministers Baptized in the Spirit." *PentEv* 696 (May 7, 1927): 6.

Epperly, "Miracles." Epperly, Bruce. "Miracles Without Supernaturalism: A Process-Relational Perspective." *Enc* 67 (1, 2006): 47–61.

Epperly, *Touch.* Epperly, Bruce G. *God's Touch: Faith, Wholeness, and the Healing Miracles of Jesus.* Foreword by John B. Cobb Jr. Louisville: Westminster John Knox, 2001.

Epstein, *Aimee.* Epstein, Daniel Mark. *Sister Aimee: The Life of Aimee Semple McPherson.* New York: Harcourt Brace, 1993.

Erlandson, "Miracles." Erlandson, Douglas K. "A New Look at Miracles." *RelS* 13 (4, 1977): 417–28.

Escobar, "Scenario." Escobar, Samuel. "The Global Scenario at the Turn of the Century." Pages 25–46 in *Global Missiology for the 21st Century: The Iguassu Dialogue.* Edited by William D. Taylor. Grand Rapids: Baker Academic, 2000.

Escobar, *Tides.* Escobar, Samuel. *Changing Tides: Latin America and World Mission Today.* AmSoc MissMonS 31. Maryknoll, N.Y.: Orbis, 2002.

Eshel, "Exorcist." Eshel, Esther. "Jesus the Exorcist in Light of Epigraphic Sources." Pages 178–85 in *Jesus and Archaeology.* Edited by James H. Charlesworth. Grand Rapids: Eerdmans, 2006.

Eshleman, *Jesus.* Eshleman, Paul, with Carolyn E. Phillips. *I Just Saw Jesus.* Foreword by Billy Graham. Laguna Niguel, Calif.: The Jesus Project, 1985. Special edition: San Bernardino, Calif.: Campus Crusade for Christ, 1991.

Espinosa, "Borderland Religion." Espinosa, Gastón. "Borderland Religion: Los Angeles and the Origins of the Latino Pentecostal Movement in the U.S., Mexico, and Puerto Rico, 1900–1945." PhD diss., University of California at Santa Barbara, 1999.

Espinosa, "Contributions." Espinosa, Gastón. "'The Holy Ghost Is Here on Earth?': The Latino Contributions to the Azusa Street Revival." *Enr* 11 (2, Spring 2006): 118–25.

Espinosa, "Healing in Borderlands." Espinosa, Gastón. "Latino Pentecostal Healing in the North American Borderlands." Pages 129–49 in *Global Pentecostal and Charismatic Healing.* Edited by Candy Gunther Brown. Foreword by Harvey Cox. Oxford: Oxford University Press, 2011.

Espinosa, "Olazábal." Espinosa, Gastón. "El Azteca: Francisco Olazábal and Latino Pentecostal Charisma, Power, and Faith Healing in the Borderlands." *JAAR* 67 (3, Sept. 1999): 597–616.

Espinosa, "Revivals." Espinosa, Gastón. "Latino(a) Protestant and Pentecostal Revivals." Pages 237–40 in vol. 1 of *Encyclopedia of Religious Revivals in America.* Edited by Michael McClymond. 2 vols. Westport, Conn: Greenwood, 2007.

Espiritu, "Ethnohermeneutics." Espiritu, Daniel L. "Ethnohermeneutics or Oikohermeneutics? Questioning the Necessity of Caldwell's Hermeneutics." *JAM* 3 (2, Sept. 2001): 267–81.

Etienne, "Diangienda." Etienne, Byaruhanga Kabarole. "Diangienda, Ku-ntima Joseph." *DACB.* http://www.dacb.org/stories/demrepcongo/f-diangienda_joseph.html.

Evans, "Apollonius." Evans, Craig A. "Apollonius of Tyana." Pages 80–81 in *DNTB.*

Evans, *Fabricating Jesus.* Evans, Craig A. *Fabricating Jesus: How Modern Scholars Distort the Gospels.* Downers Grove, Ill.: InterVarsity, 2006.

Evans, "Judgment." Evans, C. Stephen. "Critical Historical Judgment and Biblical Faith." *FPhil* 11 (2, April 1994): 184–206.

Evans, "Kingdom." Evans, Craig A. "Inaugurating the Kingdom of God and Defeating the Kingdom of Satan." *BBR* 15 (1, 2005): 49–75.

Evans, "Mythology." Evans, Craig A. "Life-of-Jesus Research and the Eclipse of Mythology." *TS* 54 (1993): 3–36.

Evans, *Narrative.* Evans, C. Stephen. *The Historical Christ and the Jesus of Faith: The Incarnational Narrative as History.* Oxford: Clarendon, 1996.

Evans, "Naturalism." Evans, C. Stephen. "Methodological Naturalism in Historical Biblical Scholarship." Pages 180–205 in *Jesus and the Restoration of Israel: A Critical Assessment of N. T. Wright's Jesus and the Victory of God.* Edited by Carey C. Newman. Downers Grove, Ill.: InterVarsity, 1999.

Evans, "Prophet." Evans, Craig A. "Prophet, Sage, Healer, Messiah, and Martyr: Types and Identities of Jesus." Pages 1217–43 in *Handbook for the Study of the Historical Jesus.* Edited by Tom Holmén and Stanley E. Porter. 4 vols. Boston: Brill, 2010.

Evans, "4Q521." Evans, Craig A. "Messianic Apocalypse (4Q521)." Pages 695–98 in *DNTB.*

Evans and Manis, *Philosophy of Religion.* Evans, C. Stephen, and R. Zachary Manis. *Philosophy of Religion: Thinking about Faith.* 2nd ed. Downers Grove, Ill.: IVP Academic, 2009.

Evans-Pritchard, *Religion.* Evans-Pritchard, E. E. *Nuer Religion.* Oxford: Clarendon, 1956.

Evans-Pritchard, "Séance." Evans-Pritchard, E. E. "A Séance among the Azande." *Tomorrow* [Quarterly Review of Psychical Research] 5 (4, 1957): 11–26.

Evans-Pritchard, *Witchcraft.* Evans-Pritchard, E. E. *Witchcraft, Oracles, and Magic among the Azande.* Foreword by C. G. Seligman. Oxford: Clarendon, 1937.

Eve, "Meier." Eve, Eric. "Meier, Miracle, and Multiple Attestation." *JSHJ* 3 (1, 2005): 23–45.

Eve, *Healer*. Eve, Eric. *The Healer from Nazareth: Jesus' Miracles in Historical Context*. London: SPCK, 2009.

Eve, *Miracles*. Eve, Eric. *The Jewish Context of Jesus' Miracles*. JSNTSup 231. London: Sheffield Academic Press, 2002.

Eve, "Spit." Eve, Eric. "Spit in Your Eye: The Blind Man of Bethsaida and the Blind Man of Alexandria." *NTS* 54 (1, 2008): 1–17.

Everitt, "Impossibility." Everitt, Nicholas. "The Impossibility of Miracles." *RelS* 23 (3, 1987): 347–49.

Everts, "Exorcist." Everts, William W. "Jesus Christ, No Exorcist." *BSac* 81 (323, July 1924): 355–62.

Ewald, "Healings." Ewald, Ferdinand. "Healings in Poland." *PentEv* 641 (April 3, 1926): 11.

Ewin, "Emergency Room Hypnosis." Ewin, D. M. "Emergency Room Hypnosis for the Burned Patient." *AmJClinHyp* 29 (1986): 7–12.

Ewin, "Hypnosis in Surgery." Ewin, D. M. "Hypnosis in Surgery and Anesthesia." Pages 210–35 in *Clinical Hypnosis: A Multidisciplinary Approach*. Edited by W. C. Wester and A. H. Smith. Philadelphia: Lippincott, 1984.

Eya, "Healing." Eya, Regina. "Healing and Exorcism: The Psychological Aspects." Pages 44–54 in *Healing and Exorcism: The Nigerian Experience*. Proceedings, Lectures, Discussions, and Conclusions of the First Missiology Symposium on Healing and Exorcism, organized by the Spiritan International School of Theology, Attakwu, Enugu, May 18–20, 1989. Edited by Chris U. Manus, Luke N. Mbefo, and E. E. Uzukwu. Attakwu, Enugu: Spiritan International School of Theology, 1992.

Eze, "Issues." Eze, E. C. "Epistemological and Ideological Issues about Witchcraft in African Studies: A Response to René Devisch, Elias Bongmba, and Richard Werbner." Pages 264–82 in *Witchcraft Dialogues: Anthropological and Philosophical Exchanges*. Edited by George Clement Bond and Diane M. Ciekawy. Athens: Center for International Studies, Ohio University, 2001.

Fadda, "Miraculous." Fadda, Anna Maria Luiselli. "*Constat Ergo Inter Nos Verba Signa Esse*: The Understanding of the Miraculous in Anglo-Saxon Society." Pages 56–66 in *Signs, Wonders, Miracles: Representations of Divine Power in the Life of the Church. Papers Read at the 2003 Summer Meeting and the 2004 Winter Meeting of the Ecclesiastical History Society*. Edited by Kate Cooper and Jeremy Gregory. Rochester: Boydell & Brewer, for the Ecclesiastical History Society, 2005.

Falcone et al., "Development." Falcone, R. A., Jr., A. L. Brentley, C. D. Ricketts, S. E. Allen, and V. F. Garcia. "Development, Implementation, and Evaluation of a Unique African-American Faith-Based Approach to Increased Automobile Restraint Use." *JNMedAss* 98 (8, 2006): 1335–41.

Family Medical Guide. *The American Medical Association Family Medical Guide*. 3rd rev. ed. Edited by Charles B. Clayman. New York: Random House, 1994.

Fant, *Miracles*. Fant, David J., ed. *Modern Miracles of Healing: Personal Testimonies of Well-Known Christian Men and Women to the Power of God to Heal Their Bodies*. Harrisburg, Pa.: Christian Publications, 1943.

Fape, *Powers*. Fape, Michael Olusina. *Powers in Encounter with Power: Paul's Concept of Spiritual Warfare in Ephesians 6:10–12: An African Christian Perspective*. Ross-shire, Scotland: Christian Focus Publications, 2003.

Farah, *Pinnacle*. Farah, Charles, Jr. *From the Pinnacle of the Temple*. Plainfield, N.J.: Logos International, 1978.

Faraone, "New Light." Faraone, Christopher A. "New Light on Ancient Greek Exorcisms of the Wandering Womb." *ZPE* 144 (2003): 189–97.

Faraone, "Spells." Faraone, Christopher A. "When Spells Worked Magic." *Archaeology* 56 (2, 2003): 48–53.

Faris, "Healed." Faris, Charles. "Healed of Bone Cancer." *PentEv* (April 9, 2000): 27.

Farley, "Mission." Farley, A. Fay. "A Spiritual Healing Mission Remembered: James Moore Hickson's Christian Healing Mission at Palmerston North, New Zealand, 1923." *JRH* 34 (1, 2010): 1–19.

Farmer, *Verses*. Farmer, William R. *The Last Twelve Verses of Mark*. SNTSMS 25. Cambridge: Cambridge University Press, 1974.

Fasolt, "History and Religion." Fasolt, Constantin. "History and Religion in the Modern Age." *HistTh*, theme issue 45 (2006): 10–26.

Faupel, *Gospel*. Faupel, William D. *The Everlasting Gospel: The Significance of Eschatology in the Development of Pentecostal Thought*. Sheffield: Sheffield Academic Press, 1996.

Fauset, *Gods*. Fauset, Arthur Huff. *Black Gods of the Metropolis: Negro Religious Cults of the Urban North*. PPAS 3. Philadelphia: University of Pennsylvania Press; London: Oxford University Press, 1944.

Favre, "Action." Favre, Alexandre. "How Is It Possible to Exclude Action Coming from a Transcendent Order of Being?" Pages 37–39 in *Cosmos, Bios, and Theos: Scientists Reflect on Science, God, and the Origins of the Universe, Life, and Homo Sapiens*. Edited by Henry Margenau and Roy Abraham Varghese. La Salle, Ill.: Open Court, 1992.

Favret-Saada, *Witchcraft*. Favret-Saada, Jeanne. *Deadly Words: Witchcraft in the Bocage*. Translated by Catherine Cullen. Cambridge: Cambridge University Press, 1980.

Feaver, "Delegation." Feaver, Karen M. "What Chinese Christians Taught a U.S. Congressional Delegation." *CT* (May 16, 1994): 33–34.

Fee, "Disease." Fee, Gordon D. "The Disease of the Health and Wealth Gospel." Costa Mesa, Calif.: The Word for Today, 1979.

Fee, *Gospel*. Fee, Gordon D. *Gospel and Spirit: Issues in New Testament Hermeneutics*. Peabody, Mass.: Hendrickson, 1991.

Fee, *Paul, Spirit, and People*. Fee, Gordon D. *Paul, the Spirit, and the People of God*. Peabody, Mass.: Hendrickson, 1996.

Fee, *Presence*. Fee, Gordon D. *God's Empowering Presence: The Holy Spirit in the Letters of Paul*. Peabody, Mass.: Hendrickson, 1994.

Feldman, "Elijah." Feldman, Louis H. "Josephus' Portrait of Elijah." *SJOT* 8 (1, 1994): 61–86.

Feldman, "Hellenizations." Feldman, Louis H. "Hellenizations in Josephus' *Jewish Antiquities*: The Portrait of Abraham." Pages 133–53 in *Josephus, Judaism, and Christianity*. Edited by Louis H. Feldman and Gohei Hata. Detroit: Wayne State University Press, 1987.

"Fell Sixteen Feet." "Fell Sixteen Feet." *PentEv* (March 19, 1921): 10.

Fenner, *Krankheit*. Fenner, Friedrich. *Die Krankheit im Neuen Testament. Eine Religiös- und Medizingeschichtliche Untersuchung*. Edited by H. Windisch. Untersuchungen zum Neuen Testament 18. Leipzig: J. C. Hinrichs, 1930.

Ferchiou, "Possession Cults." Ferchiou, Sophie. "The Possession Cults of Tunisia: A Religious System Functioning as a System of Reference and a Social Field for Performing Actions." Pages 209–18 in *Women's Medicine: The Zar-Bori Cult in Africa and Beyond*. Edited by I. M. Lewis, Ahmed Al-Safi, and Sayyid Hurreiz. Edinburgh: International African Institute, Edinburgh University Press, 1991.

Ferdinando, "Demonology." Ferdinando, Keith. "Screwtape Revisited: Demonology Western, African, and Biblical." Pages 103–32 in *The Unseen World: Christian Reflections on Angels, Demons, and the Heavenly Realm*. Edited by Anthony N. S. Lane. Grand Rapids: Baker, 1996.

Ferguson, *Backgrounds*. Ferguson, Everett. *Backgrounds of Early Christianity*. Grand Rapids: Eerdmans, 1987.

Ferguson, *Demonology*. Ferguson, Everett. *Demonology of the Early Christian World*. Symposium Series 12. New York: Edwin Mellen, 1984.

Ferm, "Miracles." Ferm, Vergilius. "Miracles—Possible or Probable?" *CrQ* 26 (3, July 1949): 215–18.

Fern, "Critique." Fern, Richard L. "Hume's Critique of Miracles: An Irrelevant Triumph." *RelS* 18 (3, 1982): 337–54.

Fernando, *Attitude*. Fernando, Ajith. *The Christian's Attitude toward World Religions*. Wheaton: Tyndale, 1987.

Fernando, "God." Fernando, Ajith. "God: The Source, the Originator, and the End of Mission." Pages 191–205 in *Global Missiology for the 21st Century: The Iguassu Dialogue*. Edited by William D. Taylor. Grand Rapids: Baker Academic, 2000.

Feyerabend, "Problems 1." Feyerabend, Paul K. "Problems of Empiricism." Pages 145–260 in *Beyond the Edge of Certainty: Essays in Contemporary Science and Philosophy*. Edited by Robert Colodny. Englewood Cliffs, N.J.: Prentice-Hall, 1965.

Feyerabend, "Problems 2." Feyerabend, Paul K. "Problems of Empiricism." Pages 275–353 in *The Nature and Function of Scientific Theories: Essays in Contemporary Science and Philosophy*. Edited by Robert G. Colodny. Pittsburgh: University of Pittsburgh Press, 1970.

Fiebig, "Wunder." Fiebig, P. "Die Wunder Jesu und die Wunder der Rabbinen." *ZWissTh* NF 19 (54, 1912): 158–79.

Field, "Possession." Field, Margaret J. "Spirit Possession in Ghana." Pages 3–13 in *Spirit Mediumship and Society in Africa*. Edited by John Beattie and John Middleton. Foreword by Raymond Firth. New York: Africana Publishing Corporation, 1969.

"Fifteen Years." "Fifteen Years." *PentEv* 566 (Oct. 4, 1924): 9.

Filson, "Analysis." Filson, William Robert. "An Analysis of the Relationship of Pre-Christian Beliefs of the Ibaloi Pentecostal Christians to Their Beliefs and Practices Concerning the Verbal Gifts of 1 Corinthians 12:8–12." MDiv thesis, Asia Pacific Theological Seminary, 1993.

Filson, *History*. Filson, Floyd V. *A New Testament History*. Philadelphia: Westminster, 1964.

Filson, "Study." Filson, William R. "A Comparative Study of Contextualized and Pentecostal Approaches to Nominal Muslims in Indonesia." DMin diss., Asia Pacific Theological Seminary, 2006.

Finegan, *Records*. Finegan, Jack. *Hidden Records of the Life of Jesus*. Philadelphia: Pilgrim Press, 1969.

Finger of God. DVD. Produced by Darren Wilson. Wanderlust Productions, 2007.

Finger and Swartley, "Bondage." Finger, Thomas, and Willard Swartley. "Bondage and Deliverance: Biblical and Theological Perspectives." Pages 10–38 in *Essays on Spiritual Bondage and Deliverance*. Edited by Willard M. Swartley. Occasional Papers 11. Elkhart, Ind.: Institute of Mennonite Studies, 1988.

Finkler, "Religion." Finkler, Kaja. "Teaching Religion and Healing at a Southern University." Pages 47–57 in *Teaching Religion and Healing*. Edited by Linda L. Barnes and Inés Talamantez. AARTRSS. Oxford: Oxford University Press, 2006.

Finlay, *Columba*. Finlay, J. *Columba*. London: Victor Gollancz, 1979.

Finlay, "Miracles." Finlay, Katherine. "Angels in the Trenches: British Soldiers and Miracles in the First World War." Pages 443–52 in *Signs, Wonders, Miracles: Representations of Divine Power in the Life of the Church. Papers Read at the 2003 Summer Meeting and the 2004 Winter Meeting of the Ecclesiastical History Society*. Edited by Kate Cooper and Jeremy Gregory. Rochester: Boydell & Brewer, for the Ecclesiastical History Society, 2005.

Finney, *Memoirs*. Finney, Charles G. *Memoirs of Rev. Charles G. Finney*. New York: A. S. Barnes & Company, 1876.

Finocchiaro, "Galileo." Finocchiaro, Maurice A. "That Galileo Was Imprisoned and Tortured for Advocating Copernicanism." Pages 68–78 in *Galileo Goes to Jail and Other Myths about Science and Religion*. Edited by Ronald L. Numbers. Cambridge, Mass.: Harvard University Press, 2009.

Finucane, *Rescue*. Finucane, Ronald. *The Rescue of the Innocents: Endangered Children in Medieval Miracles*. New York: St. Martins, 1997.

Firth, "Anthropologist." Firth, Rosemary. "From Wife to Anthropologist." Pages 10–32 in *Crossing Cultural Boundaries: The Anthropological Experience*. Edited by Solon T. Kimball and James B. Watson. San Francisco: Chandler, 1972.

Firth, "Foreword." Firth, Raymond. "Foreword." Pages ix–xiv in *Spirit Mediumship and Society in Africa*. Edited by John Beattie and John Middleton. Foreword by Raymond Firth. New York: Africana Publishing Corporation, 1969.

Firth, *Ritual*. Firth, Raymond. *Tikopia Ritual and Belief*. Boston: Beacon Press, 1967.

Fisch et al., "Assessment." Fisch, Michael J., et al. "Assessment of Quality of Life in Outpatients with Advanced Cancer: The Accuracy of Clinician Estimations and the Relevance of Spiritual Well-Being—A Hoosier Oncology Group Study." *JClinOn* 21 (2003): 2754–59.

Fischer, "Orishi." Fischer, Moritz. "'Orishi'—Maasai-Diviner and Paradigmatic Contextualisation of Christianity." *AfThJ* 31 (2, 2008): 24–45.

Fitzgerald, "Miracles." Fitzgerald, Paul. "Miracles." *PhilFor* 17 (1, Fall 1985): 48–64.

Fitzgerald, "Speech." Fitzgerald, Dale K. "Prophetic Speech in Ga Spirit Mediumship." Paper presented at the sixty-eighth Annual Meeting of the American Anthropological Association, New Orleans, La., Nov. 1969.

Fitzmyer, *Acts*. Fitzmyer, Joseph A. *The Acts of the Apostles: A New Translation with Introduction and Commentary*. AB 31. New York: Doubleday, 1998.

Fitzmyer, *Apocryphon*. Fitzmyer, Joseph A. *The Genesis Apocryphon of Qumran Cave 1: A Commentary*. 2nd rev. ed. BibOr 18A. Rome: Biblical Institute Press, 1971.

Flach, *Faith*. Flach, Frederic. *Faith, Healing, and Miracles*. New York: Hatherleigh Press, 2000.

Flanders, "Deliverances at Sea." Flanders, Danny J. "'It Shall Not Come Nigh Thee': Some Remarkable Stories of Deliverances at Sea." *PentEv* 1571 (June 17, 1944): 1, 8.

Flannelly et al., "Belief." Flannelly, Kevin J., Harold G. Koenig, Christopher G. Ellison, Kathleen Galek, and Neal Krause. "Belief in Life-after-Death and Mental Health: Findings from a National Survey." *JNMDis* 194 (2006): 524–29.

Fleurant, "Music." Fleurant, Gerdès. "Vodun, Music, and Society in Haiti: Affirmation and Identity." Pages 46–57 in *Haïtian Vodou: Spirit, Myth, and Reality*. Edited by Patrick Bellegarde-Smith and Claudine Michel. Bloomington: Indiana University Press, 2006.

Flew, "Arguments." Flew, Antony. "Neo-Humean Arguments about the Miraculous." Pages 45–57 in *In Defense of Miracles: A Comprehensive Case for God's Action in History*. Edited by R. Douglas Geivett and Gary R. Habermas. Downers Grove, Ill.: InterVarsity, 1997.

Flew, "Evidence." Flew, Antony. "Scientific Versus Historical Evidence." Pages 97–102 in *Miracles*. Edited by Richard Swinburne. New York: Macmillan; London: Collier Macmillan, 1989.

Flew, *God*. Flew, Antony, with Roy Abraham Varghese. *There Is a God: How the World's Most Notorious Atheist Changed His Mind*. New York: HarperOne, HarperCollins, 2007.

Flew, "Introduction." Flew, Antony. "Introduction." Pages 1–23 in *Of Miracles* by David Hume. La Salle, Ill.: Open Court, 1985.

Flew, "Response." Flew, Antony. "Response to Lewis." Pages 241–42 in *Cosmos, Bios, and Theos: Scientists Reflect on Science, God, and the Origins of the Universe, Life, and Homo Sapiens*. Edited by Henry Margenau and Roy Abraham Varghese. La Salle, Ill.: Open Court, 1992.

Flichy, "État des recherches." Flichy, Odile. "État des recherches actuelles sur les Actes des Apôtres." Pages 13–42 in *Les Actes des Apôtres: Histoire, récit, théologie*. Edited by Michel Berder. XXe congrès de l'Association catholique française pour l'étude de la Bible (Angers, 2003). Lecto divina 199. Paris: Cerf, 2005.

Flichy, *L'oeuvre de Luc*. Flichy, Odile. *L'oeuvre de Luc: L'Évangile et les Actes des Apôtres*. CaÉ 114. Paris: Cerf, 2000.

Flinders, Oman, and Flinders, "Meditation." Flinders, Tim, Doug Oman, and Carol L. Flinders. "Meditation as Empowerment for Healing." Pages 213–40 in *Personal Spirituality*. Vol. 1 of *The Healing Power of Spirituality: How Faith Helps Humans Thrive*. Edited by J. Harold Ellens. Santa Barbara, Calif.: Praeger, 2010.

Flinders, Oman, and Flinders, "Program." Flinders, Tim, Doug Oman, and Carol Lee Flinders. "The Eight-Point Program of Passage Meditation: Health Effects of a Comprehensive Program." Pages 72–93 in *Spirit, Science, and Health: How the Spiritual Mind Fuels Physical Wellness*. Edited by Thomas G. Plante and Carl E. Thoresen. Foreword by Albert Bandura. Westport, Conn.: Praeger, 2007.

Flint, "Accounts." Flint, Thomas P. "Two Accounts of Providence." Pages 147–81 in *Divine and Human Action: Essays in the Metaphysics of Theism*. Edited by Thomas V. Morris. Ithaca, N.Y.: Cornell University Press, 1988.

Flint, "Brahman's Son." Flint, Marguerite. "Wealthy Brahman's Son Turns to Christ." *PentEv* 696 (May 7, 1927): 4–5.

Flusser, *Judaism*. Flusser, David. *Judaism and the Origins of Christianity*. Jerusalem: Magnes Press, The Hebrew University, 1988.

Flusser, "Laying on of Hands." Flusser, David. "Healing Through the Laying on of Hands in a Dead Sea Scroll." *IEJ* 7 (1957): 107–8.

Flusser, "Love." Flusser, David. "Jesus, His Ancestry, and the Commandment of Love." Pages 153–76 in *Jesus' Jewishness: Exploring the Place of Jesus Within Early Judaism*. Edited by James H. Charlesworth. New York: The American Interfaith Institute, Crossroad, 1991.

Flusser, *Sage*. Flusser, David, with R. Steven Notley. *The Sage from Galilee: Rediscovering Jesus' Genius*. Introduction by James H. Charlesworth. Grand Rapids: Eerdmans, 2007.

Flynn et al., "Dependence." Flynn, Patrick M., George W. Joe, Kirk M. Broome, D. Dwayne Simpson, and Barry S. Brown. "Looking Back on Cocaine Dependence: Reasons for Recovery." *American Journal on Addictions* 12 (5, 2003): 398–411.

Foakes Jackson and Lake, "Teaching." Foakes Jackson, F. J., and Kirsopp Lake. "The Public Teaching of Jesus and His Choice of the Twelve." Pages 267–99 in vol. 1 of *The Beginnings of Christianity*. Edited by F. J. Foakes Jackson and Kirsopp Lake. 5 vols. Grand Rapids: Baker, 1979.

Fogelin, *Defense*. Fogelin, Robert J. *A Defense of Hume on Miracles*. PrMPhil. Princeton, N.J.: Princeton University Press, 2003.

Fogelin, "Hume." Fogelin, Robert J. "What Hume Actually Said about Miracles." *HumSt* 16 (1, April 1990): 81–87.

Fogelson, "Theories." Fogelson, Raymond D. "Psychological Theories of Windigo 'Psychosis' and a Preliminary Application of a Models Approach." Pages 74–99 in *Culture and Meaning in Cultural Anthropology: In Honor of A. Irving Hallowell*. Edited by Melford E. Spiro. New York: Free Press; London: Collier-Macmillan, 1965.

Folarin, "State." Folarin, George O. "Contemporary State of the Prosperity Gospel in Nigeria." *AJT* 21 (1, April 2007): 69–95.

Folger, "Alternative." Folger, Tim. "Science's Alternative to an Intelligent Creator: The Multiverse Theory." *Discover Magazine* (Dec. 2008). Online: http://discovermagazine.com/2008/dec/10-sciences-alternative-to-an-intelligent-creator/article_view?b_start:int=2.

Föller, "Luther on Miracles." Föller, O. "Martin Luther on Miracles, Healing, Prophecy, and Tongues." *StHistEc* 31 (2, Oct. 2005): 333–51.

Foltz, "Healer." Foltz, Tanice G. "The Life History of a Kahuna Healer." Pages 147–65 in *Proceedings of the Fourth International Conference on the Study of Shamanism and Alternate Modes of Healing, Held at the St. Sabina Center, San Rafael, California, September 5–7, 1987*. Edited by Ruth-Inge Heinze. N.p.: Independent Scholars of Asia; Madison, Wis.: A-R Editions, 1988.

Folwarski, "Point of Contact." Folwarski, Shirley. "Point of Contact." *Guideposts* (July 1994): 28–29.

Fonck, *Wunder*. Fonck, Leopold. *Die Wunder des Herrn im Evangelium*. Vol. 1. Innsbruck: F. Rauch, 1907.

Fontana and Rosenheck, "Trauma." Fontana, Alan, and Robert Rosenheck. "Trauma, Change in Strength of Religious Faith, and Mental Health Service Use among Veterans Treated for PTSD." *JNMDis* 192 (2004): 579–84.

Fontenrose, *Oracle*. Fontenrose, Joseph E. *The Delphic Oracle: Its Response and Operations*. Berkeley: University of California Press, 1978.

Force, "Breakdown." Force, James E. "The Breakdown of the Newtonian Synthesis of Science and Religion: Hume, Newton, and the Royal Society." Pages 143–63 in *Essays on the Context, Nature, and Influence of Isaac Newton's Theology*, by James E. Force and Richard H. Popkin. IntArHistI 129. Dordrecht: Kluwer Academic, 1990.

Force, "Deism." Force, James E. "The Newtonians and Deism." Pages 43–73 in *Essays on the Context,*

Nature, and Influence of Isaac Newton's Theology, by James E. Force and Richard H. Popkin. IntArHistI 129. Dordrecht: Kluwer Academic, 1990.

Force, "Dominion." Force, James E. "Newton's God of Dominion: The Unity of Newton's Theological, Scientific, and Political Thought." Pages 75–102 in *Essays on the Context, Nature, and Influence of Isaac Newton's Theology*, by James E. Force and Richard H. Popkin. IntArHistI 129. Dordrecht: Kluwer Academic, 1990.

Force, "Gentleman." Force, James E. "Sir Isaac Newton, 'Gentleman of Wide Swallow'? Newton and the Latitudinarians." Pages 119–41 in *Essays on the Context, Nature, and Influence of Isaac Newton's Theology*, by James E. Force and Richard H. Popkin. IntArHistI 129. Dordrecht: Kluwer Academic, 1990.

Force, "Interest." Force, James E. "Hume's Interest in Newton and Science." Pages 181–206 in *Essays on the Context, Nature, and Influence of Isaac Newton's Theology*, by James E. Force and Richard H. Popkin. IntArHistI 129. Dordrecht: Kluwer Academic, 1990.

Ford, "Response." Ford, Josephine Massynbaerde. "Response to Thomas Finger and Willard Swartley." Pages 39–45 in *Essays on Spiritual Bondage and Deliverance*. Edited by Willard M. Swartley. Occasional Papers 11. Elkhart, Ind.: Institute of Mennonite Studies, 1988.

Forge, "Anthropologist." Forge, Anthony. "The Lonely Anthropologist." Pages 292–97 in *Crossing Cultural Boundaries: The Anthropological Experience*. Edited by Solon T. Kimball and James B. Watson. San Francisco: Chandler, 1972.

Forsberg, "Campaign." Forsberg, Simon E. "Revival Campaign at Bethel Temple." *LRE* 15 (8, May 1922): 14–15.

Forsberg, "Medicine." Forsberg, Vivian Mildred. "T'boli Medicine and the Supernatural." MA thesis, Fuller Theological Seminary, 1988.

Forsman, "Double Agency." Forsman, Rodger. "'Double Agency' and Identifying Reference to God." Pages 123–42 in *Divine Action: Studies Inspired by the Philosophical Theology of Austin Farrer*. Edited by Brian Hebblethwaite and Edward Henderson. Edinburgh: T&T Clark, 1990.

Fortune, "Healed." Fortune, Bonnie. "Healed Instantly of Tumor." *PentEv* 523 (Nov. 24, 1924): 19.

Fosl, "Hume." Fosl, Peter S. "Hume, Skepticism, and Early American Deism." *HumSt* 25 (1–2, 1999): 171–92.

Fosmark, "Sketch." Fosmark, Aagoth. "Brief Sketch of Life of Nien Ho-san." *CGl* 12 (1, Jan. 1935): 10–11.

Foster, "Etiologies." Foster, George M. "Disease Etiologies in Non-Western Medical Systems." *AmAnth* 78 (1976): 773–82.

Foster, "Miracles." Foster, Frank H. "The New Testament Miracles: An Investigation of Their Function." *AmJTh* 12 (1908): 369–91.

Fountain, *Medicine*. Fountain, Daniel E. *God, Medicine, and Miracles: The Spiritual Factor in Healing*. Wheaton: Harold Shaw, 1999.

Fox, "Structure." Fox, John W. "The Structure, Stability, and Social Antecedents of Reported Paranormal Experiences." *SocAn* 53 (1992): 417–31.

Fox, "Witchcraft." Fox, J. Robin. "Witchcraft and Clanship in Cochiti Therapy." Pages 174–200 in *Magic, Faith, and Healing: Studies in Primitive Psychiatry Today*. Edited by Ari Kiev. Foreword by Jerome D. Frank. New York: Free Press, 1964.

France, "Authenticity." France, R. T. "The Authenticity of the Sayings of Jesus." Pages 101–43 in *History, Criticism, and Faith*. Edited by Colin Brown. Downers Grove, Ill.: InterVarsity, 1976.

Francis, "Conflict." Francis, V. Ezekia. "Spiritual Conflict in the Indian Context." Pages 152–59 in *Deliver Us from Evil: An Uneasy Frontier in Christian Mission*. Edited by A. Scott Moreau, Tokunboh Adeyemo, David G. Burnett, Bryant L. Myers, and Hwa Yung. Monrovia, Calif.: Lausanne Committee for World Evangelization, 2002.

Francis and Kaldor, "Relationship." Francis, Leslie J., and Peter Kaldor. "The Relationship between Psychological Well-Being and Christian Faith and Practice in an Australian Population Sample." *JSSR* 41 (1, 2002): 179–84.

Francis et al., "Correlation." Francis, Leslie J., Mandy Robbins, et al. "Correlation between Religion and Happiness: A Replication." *PsycRep* 92 (1, 2003): 51–52.

Frank, *Aspects*. Frank, Tenney. *Aspects of Social Behavior in Ancient Rome*. Cambridge, Mass.: Harvard University Press, 1932.

Frank, "Devotion." Frank, Georgia. "Lay Devotion in Context." Pages 531–47 in *Constantine to c. 600*. Edited by Augustine Casiday and Frederick W. Norris. Vol. 2 of *The Cambridge History of Christianity*. 9 vols. Cambridge: Cambridge University Press, 2007.

Frank, *Persuasion*. Frank, Jerome D. *Persuasion and Healing: A Comparative Study of Psychotherapy*. Baltimore: Johns Hopkins University Press, 1961.

Frankenberry, *Faith*. Frankenberry, Nancy K. *The Faith of Scientists in Their Words*. Princeton, N.J.: Princeton University Press, 2008.

Frankforter, *History*. Frankforter, A. Daniel. *A History of the Christian Movement: The Development of Christian Institutions*. Chicago: Nelson-Hall, 1978.

Frankfurter, "Christianity and Paganism." Frankfurter, David. "Christianity and Paganism, I: Egypt." Pages 173–88 in *Constantine to c. 600*. Edited by

Augustine Casiday and Frederick W. Norris. Vol. 2 of *The Cambridge History of Christianity*. 9 vols. Cambridge: Cambridge University Press, 2007.

Frankfurter, "Curses." Frankfurter, David. "Curses, Blessings, and Ritual Authority: Egyptian Magic in Comparative Perspective." *JANER* 5 (2005): 157–85.

Frankfurter, "Magic." Frankfurter, David. "The Magic of Writing and the Writing of Magic: The Power of the Word in Egyptian and Greek Traditions." *Helios* 21 (1994): 189–221.

Frankfurter, "Perils." Frankfurter, David. "The Perils of Love: Magic and Countermagic in Coptic Egypt." *JHistSex* 10 (3–4, 2001): 480–500.

Frankfurter, *Religion in Egypt*. Frankfurter, David. *Religion in Roman Egypt: Assimilation and Resistance*. Princeton, N.J.: Princeton University Press, 1998.

Franzini, Ribble, and Wingfield, "Religion." Franzini, Luisa, John C. Ribble, and Katherine A. Wingfield. "Religion, Sociodemographic and Personal Characteristics, and Self-Reported Health in Whites, Blacks, and Hispanics Living in Low-Socioeconomic-Status Neighborhoods." *EthDis* 15 (3, 2005): 469–84.

Frateantonio, "Miracles." Frateantonio, Christa. "Miracles, Miracle Workers: Greco-Roman." Pages 52–53 in vol. 9 of *Brill's New Pauly: Encyclopaedia of the Ancient World*. Edited by Hubert Cancik and Helmuth Schneider. 20 vols. English ed. Christine F. Salazar. Leiden: Brill, 2010.

Frazer et al., "Effects." Frazer, G. E., et al. "Effects of Traditional Coronary Risk Factors on Rates of Incident Coronary Events in a Low-Risk Population: The Adventist Health Study." *Circ* 86 (1992): 406–13.

Frazier, *Healing*. Frazier, Claude A., comp. *Faith Healing: Finger of God? Or, Scientific Curiosity?* New York: Thomas Nelson, 1973.

Freddoso, "Aristotelianism." Freddoso, Alfred J. "Medieval Aristotelianism and the Case against Secondary Causation in Nature." Pages 74–118 in *Divine and Human Action: Essays in the Metaphysics of Theism*. Edited by Thomas V. Morris. Ithaca, N.Y.: Cornell University Press, 1988.

Freed and Freed, "Possession." Freed, Stanley S., and Ruth R. Freed. "Spirit Possession as an Illness in a North Indian Village." *Ethnology* 3 (1964): 152–97.

Freeman, "Famous Miracle." Freeman, Thomas S. "Through a Venice Glass Darkly: John Foxe's Most Famous Miracle." Pages 307–20 in *Signs, Wonders, Miracles: Representations of Divine Power in the Life of the Church. Papers Read at the 2003 Summer Meeting and the 2004 Winter Meeting of the Ecclesiastical History Society*. Edited by Kate Cooper and Jeremy Gregory. Rochester: Boydell & Brewer, for the Ecclesiastical History Society, 2005.

Frei, *Eclipse*. Frei, Hans W. *The Eclipse of Biblical Narrative: A Study in Eighteenth- and Nineteenth-Century Hermeneutics*. New Haven: Yale University Press, 1974.

Freidzon, *Spirit*. Freidzon, Claudio. *Holy Spirit, I Hunger for You*. Lake Mary, Fla.: Charisma House, Strang Communications, 1997.

Frend, "Place of Miracles." Frend, W. H. C. "The Place of Miracles in the Conversion of the Ancient World to Christianity." Pages 11–21 in *Signs, Wonders, Miracles: Representations of Divine Power in the Life of the Church. Papers Read at the 2003 Summer Meeting and the 2004 Winter Meeting of the Ecclesiastical History Society*. Edited by Kate Cooper and Jeremy Gregory. Rochester: Boydell & Brewer, for the Ecclesiastical History Society, 2005.

Frend, *Rise*. Frend, W. H. C. *The Rise of Christianity*. Philadelphia: Fortress, 1984.

Freston, "Contours." Freston, Paul. "Contours of Latin American Pentecostalism." Pages 221–70 in *Christianity Reborn: The Global Expansion of Evangelicalism in the Twentieth Century*. Edited by Donald M. Lewis. SHCM. Grand Rapids: Eerdmans, 2004.

Freston, "Transnationalisation." Freston, Paul. "The Transnationalisation of Brazilian Pentecostalism: The Universal Church of the Kingdom of God." Pages 196–215 in *Between Babel and Pentecost: Transnational Pentecostalism in Africa and Latin America*. Edited by André Corten and Ruth Marshall-Fratani. Bloomington: Indiana University Press, 2001.

Fretheim, "Plagues." Fretheim, Terence E. "The Plagues as Ecological Signs of Historical Disaster." *JBL* 110 (1991): 385–96.

Freud, *Interpretation*. Freud, Sigmund. *The Interpretation of Dreams*. Harmondsworth: Penguin, 1977.

Freud, "Neurosis." Freud, Sigmund. "A Seventeenth-Century Demonological Neurosis." Pages 21–61 in *Possession and Exorcism*. Vol. 9 of *Articles on Witchcraft, Magic, and Demonology: A Twelve-Volume Anthology of Scholarly Articles*. Edited by Brian P. Levack. New York: Garland, 1992. Reprinted from pages 67–105 in *The Standard Edition of the Complete Psychological Works of Sigmund Freud*. Edited by James Strachey. London: Hogarth Press, 1975.

Frey and Roysircar, "Acculturation and Worldview." Frey, Lisa L., and Gargi Roysircar. "Effects of Acculturation and Worldview for White American, South American, South Asian, and Southeast Asian Students." *IJAC* 26 (3, Sept. 2004): 229–48.

Frickenschmidt, *Evangelium als Biographie*. Frickenschmidt, Dirk. *Evangelium als Biographie. Die vier Evangelien im Rahmen antiker Erzählkunst*. TANZ 22. Tübingen: Francke, 1997.

Fried et al., "Pseudocyesis." Fried, P. H., et al. "Pseudocyesis: A Psychosomatic Study in Gynecology." *JAMA* 145 (1951): 1329–35.

Friedländer, *Life*. Friedländer, Ludwig. *Roman Life and Manners under the Early Empire*. 4 vols. Translated from the 7th rev. ed. by Leonard A. Magnus, J. H. Freese, and A. B. Gough. Vols. 1 and 4: New York: Barnes & Noble, 1907, 1965. Vols. 2 and 3: New York: E. P. Dutton, 1908, 1913.

Friedman, "Miracle." Friedman, Yvonne. "Miracle, Meaning, and Narrative in the Latin East." Pages 123–34 in *Signs, Wonders, Miracles: Representations of Divine Power in the Life of the Church. Papers Read at the 2003 Summer Meeting and the 2004 Winter Meeting of the Ecclesiastical History Society*. Edited by Kate Cooper and Jeremy Gregory. Rochester: Boydell & Brewer, for the Ecclesiastical History Society, 2005.

Friedman et al., "Predictors." Friedman, Lois C., et al. "Medical and Psychosocial Predictors of Delay in Seeking Medical Consultation for Breast Symptoms in Women in a Public Sector Setting." *JBehMed* 29 (4, 2006): 327–34.

Friedrich, "Fighter." Friedrich, Paul. "An Agrarian Fighter." Pages 117–43 in *Culture and Meaning in Cultural Anthropology: In Honor of A. Irving Hallowell*. Edited by Melford E. Spiro. New York: Free Press; London: Collier-Macmillan, 1965.

Friedson, *Prophets*. Friedson, Steven. *Dancing Prophets: Musical Experiences in Tumbuka Healing*. Chicago: University of Chicago Press, 1996.

Friesen, *Mystery*. Friesen, James G. *Uncovering the Mystery of MPD: Its Shocking Origins . . . Its Surprising Cure*. San Bernardino, Calif.: Here's Life, 1991.

Frodsham, *Apostle*. Frodsham, Stanley. *Smith Wigglesworth: Apostle of Faith*. Springfield, Mo.: Gospel Publishing House, 1948.

Frodsham, "Victories." Frodsham, Stanley H. "Glorious Victories of God in Dallas, Texas." *WWit* 9 (Jan. 20, 1913): 1.

Fröhlich, "Invoke." Fröhlich, I. "'Invoke at Any Time . . .' Apotropaic Texts and Belief in Demons in the Literature of the Qumran Community." *BN* 137 (2008): 41–74.

Frölich, "Saints." Fröhlich, Roland. "Saints, Veneration of Saints." Pages 870–73 in vol. 12 of *Brill's New Pauly: Encyclopaedia of the Ancient World*. Edited by Hubert Cancik and Helmuth Schneider. 20 vols. English ed. Christine F. Salazar. Leiden: Brill, 2010.

Frohock, *Healing Powers*. Frohock, Fred M. *Healing Powers: Alternative Medicine, Spiritual Communities, and the State*. Chicago: University of Chicago Press, 1992.

Frost, *Healing*. Frost, Evelyn. *Christian Healing: A Consideration of the Place of Spiritual Healing in the Church of Today in the Light of the Doctrine and Practice of the Ante-Nicene Church*. Foreword by T. W. Crafer. London: A. R. Mowbray, 1940.

Fry, *Spirits*. Fry, Peter. *Spirits of Protest: Spirit-Mediums and the Articulation of Consensus among Zezuru of Southern Rhodesia (Zimbabwe)*. Cambridge: Cambridge University Press, 1976.

Frye, "Analogies in Literatures." Frye, Roland Mushat. "The Synoptic Problems and Analogies in Other Literatures." Pages 261–302 in *The Relationships among the Gospels: An Interdisciplinary Dialogue*. Edited by William O. Walker Jr. San Antonio: Trinity University Press, 1978.

Frye, "Faith Healing." Frye, Glenn R. "Faith Healing." Pages 12–18 in *Healing and Religious Faith*. Edited by Claude A. Frazier. Philadelphia: Pilgrim Press, United Church Press, 1974.

Frykenberg, *Christianity in India*. Frykenberg, Robert Eric. *Christianity in India: From Beginnings to the Present*. OHCC. New York: Oxford University Press, 2010.

Frykenberg, "Globalization." Frykenberg, Robert Eric. "Gospel, Globalization, and Hindutva: The Politics of 'Conversion' in India." Pages 108–32 in *Christianity Reborn: The Global Expansion of Evangelicalism in the Twentieth Century*. Edited by Donald M. Lewis. SHCM. Grand Rapids: Eerdmans, 2004.

Frykenberg, "Introduction." Frykenberg, Robert Eric. "Introduction: Dealing with Contested Definitions and Controversial Perspectives." Pages 1–32 in *Christians and Missionaries in India: Cross-Cultural Communication Since 1500, with Special Reference to Caste, Conversion, and Colonialism*. Edited by Robert Eric Frykenberg with Alaine Low. SHCM. Grand Rapids: Eerdmans, 2003.

Fuchs, "Techniques." Fuchs, Stephen. "Magic Healing Techniques among the Balahis in Central India." Pages 121–38 in *Magic, Faith, and Healing: Studies in Primitive Psychiatry Today*. Edited by Ari Kiev. Foreword by Jerome D. Frank. New York: Free Press, 1964.

Fuh, "China." Fuh, P'eng. "The China of Today." *CGl* 13 (2, April 1936): 16–17.

Fuh, "Hope." Fuh, P'eng. "Is There No Hope for the Church of Christ in China?" *CGl* 9 (3, July 1932): 9.

Fuller, "Classics." Fuller, Reginald H. "Classics and the Gospels: The Seminar." Pages 173–92 in *The Relationships among the Gospels: An Interdisciplinary Dialogue*. Edited by William O. Walker Jr. San Antonio: Trinity University Press, 1978.

Fuller, "Harman." Fuller, Lois. "Harman, James Tswanya." *DACB*. http://www.dacb.org/stories/nigeria/harman_james.html.

Fuller, *Miracles*. Fuller, Reginald H. *Interpreting the Miracles*. Philadelphia: Westminster, 1963.

Fuller, "Taiwo." Fuller, Lois. "Taiwo, Paul." *DACB*. http://www.dacb.org/stories/nigeria/taiwo_paul .html.

Fuller, "Tsado." Fuller, Lois. "Tsado, Paul Jiya." *DACB*. http://www.dacb.org/stories/nigeria/tsado_paul .html.

Fung and Fung, "Prayer Studies." Fung, Gregory, and Christopher Fung. "What Do Prayer Studies Prove?" *CT* 53 (5, May 2009): 42–44.

Funk, "Form." Funk, Robert W. "The Form of the New Testament Healing Miracle Story." *Semeia* 12 (1978): 57–96.

Funk et al., *Acts of Jesus*. Funk, Robert W., and the Jesus Seminar. *The Acts of Jesus: The Search for the Authentic Deeds of Jesus*. New York: Polebridge, HarperSanFrancisco, 1998.

Furley, "Epicurus." Furley, David John. "Epicurus." Pages 532–34 in *OCD*.

Furnham and Wong, "Comparison." Furnham, Adrian, and Linda Wong. "A Cross-Cultural Comparison of British and Chinese Beliefs about the Causes, Behaviour Manifestations, and Treatment of Schizophrenia." *PsycRes* 151 (1–2, 2007): 123–38.

Fusco, "Sezioni-noi." Fusco, Vittorio. "Le sezioni-noi degli Atti nella discussione recente." *BeO* 25 (2, 1983): 73–86.

Gaffin, *Perspectives*. Gaffin, Richard B., Jr. *Perspectives on Pentecost: Studies in New Testament Teaching on the Gifts of the Holy Spirit*. Phillipsburg, N.J.: Presbyterian and Reformed, 1979.

Gaffin, "View." Gaffin, Richard B., Jr. "A Cessationist View." Pages 25–64 in *Are Miraculous Gifts for Today? Four Views*. Edited by Wayne A. Grudem. Grand Rapids: Zondervan, 1996.

Gager, *Moses*. Gager, John G. *Moses in Greco-Roman Paganism*. SBLMS 16. Nashville: Abingdon, for the Society of Biblical Literature, 1972.

Gaines, "Lilith." Gaines, Janet Howe. "Lilith: Seductress, Heroine, Murderer?" *BRev* 17 (5, 2001): 12–20, 43–44.

Gaiser, *Healing*. Gaiser, Frederick J. *Healing in the Bible: Theological Insight for Christian Ministry*. Grand Rapids: Baker Academic, 2010.

Gaiser, "Touch." Gaiser, Frederick J. "In Touch with Jesus: Healing in Mark 5:21-43." *WW* 30 (1, 2010): 5–15.

Gaiya, "Gindiri." Gaiya, Musa A. B. "Paul Gofo Gunen Gindiri." *DACB*. http://www.dacb.org/stories /nigeria/gindiri_paul.html.

Gale and Pruss, "Argument." Gale, Richard M., and Alexander Pruss. "A New Cosmological Argument." *RelS* 35 (1999): 461–76.

Gale and Pruss, *Existence*. Gale, Richard M., and Alexander Pruss. *The Existence of God*. Aldershot: Ashgate; Burlington, Vt.: Dartmouth, 2003.

Galea et al., "Abuse." Galea, Michael, Joseph W. Ciarrocchi, Ralph L. Piedmont, and Robert J. Wicks. "Child Abuse, Personality, and Spirituality as Predictors of Happiness in Maltese College Students." *RSSSR* 18 (2007): 141–54.

Gallagher, *Divine Man*. Gallagher, Eugene V. *Divine Man or Magician? Celsus and Origen on Jesus*. SBLDS 64. Chico, Calif.: Scholars Press, 1982.

Gallagher, "Hope." Gallagher, Robert L. "Hope in the Midst of Trial, Acts 12:1–11." Pages 157–66 in *Mission in Acts: Ancient Narratives in Contemporary Context*. Edited by Robert L. Gallagher and Paul Hertig. AmSocMissS 34. Maryknoll, N.Y.: Orbis, 2004.

Galley, "Heilige." Galley, Susanne. "Jüdische und christliche Heilige—Ein Vergleich." *ZRGG* 57 (1, 2005): 29–47.

Gallup and Castelli, *Religion*. Gallup, George, Jr., and Jim Castelli. *The People's Religion: American Faith in the 90s*. New York: Macmillan, 1989.

Garbett, "Mediums." Garbett, G. Kingsley. "Spirit Mediums as Mediators in Valley Korekore Society." Pages 104–27 in *Spirit Mediumship and Society in Africa*. Edited by John Beattie and John Middleton. Foreword by Raymond Firth. New York: Africana Publishing Corporation, 1969.

Garcia, "Minds." Garcia, Robert K. "Minds sans Miracles: Colin McGinn's Naturalized Mysterianism." *PhilChr* 2 (2, 2000): 227–42.

Gardner, "Ghosts." Gardner, Daniel K. "Ghosts and Spirits in the Sung Neo-Confucian World: Chu Hsi on *Kuei-Shen*." *JAOS* 115 (4, Oct. 1995): 598–611.

Gardner, *Healing Miracles*. Gardner, Rex. *Healing Miracles: A Doctor Investigates*. London: Darton, Longman and Todd, 1986.

Gardner, "Miracles." Gardner, Rex. "Miracles of Healing in Anglo-Celtic Northumbria as Recorded by the Venerable Bede and His Contemporaries: A Reappraisal in the Light of Twentieth-Century Experience." *BMedJ* 287 (Dec. 24–31, 1983): 1927–33.

Gardner-Smith, *Gospels*. Gardner-Smith, Percival. *Saint John and the Synoptic Gospels*. Cambridge: Cambridge University Press, 1938.

Garma Navarro, "Socialization." Garma Navarro, Carlos. "The Socialization of the Gifts of Tongues and Healing in Mexican Pentecostalism." *JCommRel* 13 (3, 1998): 353–61.

Garner, "Regressions." Garner, Jim. "Spontaneous Regressions: Scientific Documentation as a Basis for the Declaration of Miracles." *CMAJ* 111 (Dec. 7, 1974): 1254–63.

Garnett, *Duma*. Garnett, Mary. *Take Your Glory, Lord: William Duma, His Life Story*. Roodepoort, South Africa: Baptist Publishing House, 1979.

Garnett, *Mountains*. Garnett, Eve. *To Greenland's Icy Mountains: The Story of Hans Egede, Explorer, Coloniser, Missionary*. London: Heinemann, 1968.

Garnham, "Stage." Garnham, P. C. C. "At Some Stage in Evolution, God Created the Human Soul." Pages 172–73 in *Cosmos, Bios, and Theos: Scientists Reflect on Science, God, and the Origins of the Universe, Life, and Homo Sapiens*. Edited by Henry Margenau and Roy Abraham Varghese. La Salle, Ill.: Open Court, 1992.

Garrard-Burnett, "Demons." Garrard-Burnett, Virginia. "Casting Out Demons in Almolonga: Spiritual Warfare and Economic Development in a Maya Town." Pages 209–25 in *Global Pentecostalism: Encounters with Other Religious Traditions*. Edited by David Westerlund. New York: I. B. Taurus, 2009.

Garrett, *Demise*. Garrett, Susan R. *The Demise of the Devil: Magic and the Demonic in Luke's Writings*. Minneapolis: Fortress, 1989.

Garrison, "Syndrome." Garrison, Vivian. "The 'Puerto Rican Syndrome' in Psychiatry and *Espiritismo*." Pages 383–449 in *Case Studies in Spirit Possession*. Edited by Vincent Crapanzaro and Vivian Garrison. New York: John Wiley & Sons, 1977.

Garrow, "Acts." Garrow, Alan. "The Paranormal Acts of Jesus." *ExpT* 118 (2006): 133.

Gaskin, *Philosophy*. Gaskin, J. C. A. *Hume's Philosophy of Religion*. London: Macmillan, 1978.

Gaster, *Scriptures*. Gaster, Theodor H. *The Dead Sea Scriptures*. Garden City, N.Y.: Doubleday, 1976.

Gaster, *Studies*. Gaster, Moses. *Studies and Texts in Folklore, Magic, Mediaeval Romance, Hebrew Apocrypha, and Samaritan Archaeology*. 3 vols. New York: KTAV, 1971.

Gaztambide, "Psychoimmunology." Gaztambide, Daniel J. "Psychoimmunology and Jesus' Healing Miracles." Pages 94–113 in *Medical and Therapeutic Events*. Vol. 2 of *Miracles: God, Science, and Psychology in the Paranormal*. Edited by J. Harold Ellens. Westport, Conn.; London: Praeger, 2008.

Gaztambide, "Relocating." Gaztambide, Daniel J. "Relocating, Reanalyzing, and Redefining Miracles: A Psychodynamic Exploration of the Miraculous." Pages 27–48 in *Medical and Therapeutic Events*. Vol. 2 of *Miracles: God, Science, and Psychology in the Paranormal*. Edited by J. Harold Ellens. Westport, Conn.; London: Praeger, 2008.

Gaztambide, "Role." Gaztambide, Daniel J. "The Role of the Placebo Effect, Individual Psychology, and Immune Response in Regulating the Effects of Religion on Health." Pages 302–24 in *Psychodynamics*. Vol. 3 of *The Healing Power of Spirituality: How Faith Helps Humans Thrive*. Edited by J. Harold Ellens. Santa Barbara, Calif.: Praeger, 2010.

Gautheret, "Spirit." Gautheret, Roger J. "A Spirit Which Has Established the Universe and Its Laws." Pages 174–76 in *Cosmos, Bios, and Theos: Scientists Reflect on Science, God, and the Origins of the Universe, Life, and* Homo Sapiens. Edited by Henry Margenau and Roy Abraham Varghese. La Salle, Ill.: Open Court, 1992.

Gaxiola, "Serpent." Gaxiola, Manuel Jésus G. "The Serpent and the Dove." MA project, Fuller Theological Seminary, 1978.

Geary, Ciarrocchi, and Scheers, "Spirituality." Geary, Brendan, Joseph W. Ciarrocchi, and N. J. Scheers. "Spirituality and Religious Variables as Predictors of Well-Being in Sex Offenders." *RSSSR* 15 (2004): 167–87.

Gee, "Apostles." Gee, Donald. "Calling Themselves 'Apostles.'" *VOH* (June 1953): 8.

Gee, "Foreword." Gee, Donald. "Foreword." Pages 11–14 in *The Anointing of His Spirit*, by Smith Wigglesworth. Compiled and edited by Wayne Warner. Ann Arbor, Mich.: Servant, 1994.

Gee, *Trophimus*. Gee, Donald. *Trophimus I Left Sick: Our Problems of Divine Healing*. London: Elim, 1952.

Gehman, "Communion." Gehman, Richard J. "Communion with the Dead according to the Scriptures." *AJET* 25 (1, 2006): 9–31.

Geisler, *Miracles*. Geisler, Norman L. *Miracles and the Modern Mind: A Defense of Biblical Miracles*. Grand Rapids: Baker, 1992.

Geisler, "Miracles." Geisler, Norman L. "Miracles and the Modern Mind." Pages 73–85 in *In Defense of Miracles: A Comprehensive Case for God's Action in History*. Edited by R. Douglas Geivett and Gary R. Habermas. Downers Grove, Ill.: InterVarsity, 1997.

Geivett, "Value." Geivett, R. Douglas. "The Evidential Value of Miracles." Pages 178–95 in *In Defense of Miracles: A Comprehensive Case for God's Action in History*. Edited by R. Douglas Geivett and Gary R. Habermas. Downers Grove, Ill.: InterVarsity, 1997.

Geivett and Habermas, "Introduction." Geivett, R. Douglas, and Gary R. Habermas. "Introduction." Pages 9–26 in *In Defense of Miracles: A Comprehensive Case for God's Action in History*. Edited by R. Douglas Geivett and Gary R. Habermas. Downers Grove, Ill.: InterVarsity, 1997.

Geivett and Habermas, *Miracles*. Geivett, R. Douglas, and Gary R. Habermas, eds. *In Defense of Miracles: A Comprehensive Case for God's Action in History*. Downers Grove, Ill.: InterVarsity, 1997.

Geleta, "Demonization." Geleta, Amsalu Tadesse. "Demonization and Exorcism in Ethiopian Churches." Pages 91–103 in *Deliver Us from Evil:*

An Uneasy Frontier in Christian Mission. Edited by A. Scott Moreau, Tokunboh Adeyemo, David G. Burnett, Bryant L. Myers, and Hwa Yung. Monrovia, Calif.: Lausanne Committee for World Evangelization, 2002.

Gelfand, "Disorders." Gelfand, Michael. "Psychiatric Disorders as Recognized by the Shona." Pages 156–73 in *Magic, Faith, and Healing: Studies in Primitive Psychiatry Today.* Edited by Ari Kiev. Foreword by Jerome D. Frank. New York: Free Press, 1964.

Gelfand, *Religion.* Gelfand, Michael. *Shona Religion: With Special Reference to the Makorekore.* Foreword by M. Hannan. Cape Town: Juta & Company, 1962.

Gelfand, *Witch Doctor.* Gelfand, Michael. *Witch Doctor: The Traditional Medicine Man of Rhodesia.* London: Harvill, 1964.

"General News." "General News." *CGl* 2 (1, Oct. 1920): 1–2.

George, "Beginnings." George, A. C. "Pentecostal Beginnings in Travancore, South India." *AJPS* 4 (2, 2002): 215–37.

George, "Growth." George, Thackil Chacko. "The Growth of the Pentecostal Churches in South India." MA project, Fuller Theological Seminary, 1975.

George, "Miracle." George, Augustin. "Le miracle dans l'oeuvre de Luc." Pages 249–68 in *Les Miracles de Jésus selon le Nouveau Testament,* by J.-N. Aletti et al. Edited by Xavier Léon-Dufour. Paris: Éditions du Seuil, 1977.

George, "Miracles." George, Augustin. "Miracles dans le Monde Hellénistique." Pages 95–108 in *Les Miracles de Jésus selon le Nouveau Testament,* by J.-N. Aletti et al. Edited by Xavier Léon-Dufour. Paris: Éditions du Seuil, 1977.

Georgi, *Opponents.* Georgi, Dieter. *The Opponents of Paul in Second Corinthians.* Philadelphia: Fortress, 1986.

Gerber, "Psychotherapy." Gerber, Lane. "Psychotherapy with Southeast Asian Refugees: Implications for Treatment of Western Patients." *AmJPsychT* 48 (2, Spring 1994): 280–95.

Gerhart and Russell, "Mathematics." Gerhart, Mary, and Allan Melvin Russell. "Mathematics, Empirical Science, and Religion." Pages 121–29 in *Religion and Science: History, Method, Dialogue.* Edited by W. Mark Richardson and Wesley J. Wildman. Foreword by Ian G. Barbour. New York: Routledge, 1996.

German, "Mysterious Ways." German, Jeanie. "Mysterious Ways." *MounM* (May 1994): 29.

Ghéon, *The Secret.* Ghéon, Henri. *The Secret of the Curé d'Ars.* London: Sheed & Ward, 1952.

Gibbs, "Wimber." Gibbs, Eddie. "My Friend, John Wimber." Pages 147–55 in *Signs and Wonders Today: The Story of Fuller Theological Seminary's Remarkable Course on Spiritual Power.* Rev. ed. Edited by C. Peter Wagner. Altamonte Springs, Fla.: Creation House, Strang Communications, 1987.

Gibbs, "Miracles." Gibbs, Nancy. "The Message of Miracles." *Time* 145 (15, April 10, 1995): 64–73.

Giberson and Artigas, *Oracles.* Giberson, Karl, and Mariano Artigas. *Oracles of Science: Celebrity Scientists versus God and Religion.* New York: Oxford University Press, 2007.

Gibson, "New Eyes." Gibson, John. "New Eyes in Answer to Prayer: Remarkable Story of George Evison." *LRE* (Nov. 1915): 7–10.

Giere, "Naturalism." Giere, Ronald N. "Naturalism." Pages 213–23 in *The Routledge Companion to Philosophy of Science.* Edited by Stathis Psillos and Martin Curd. New York: Routledge, 2008.

Gifford, "Developments." Gifford, Paul. "Some Recent Developments in African Christianity." *African Affairs* 93 (1994): 513–34.

Gifford, "Healing." Gifford, Paul. "Healing in African Pentecostalism: The 'Victorious Living' of David Oyedepo." Pages 251–66 in *Global Pentecostal and Charismatic Healing.* Edited by Candy Gunther Brown. Foreword by Harvey Cox. Oxford: Oxford University Press, 2011.

Gifford, "Miracles." Gifford, Paul. "Expecting Miracles." *ChrCent* 124 (14, July 10, 2007): 20–24.

Gifford, *Pentecostalism.* Gifford, Paul. *Ghana's New Christianity: Pentecostalism in a Globalizing African Economy.* Bloomington: Indiana Univerity Press, 2004.

Gifford, "Provenance." Gifford, Paul. "The Complex Provenance of Some Elements of African Pentecostal Theology." Pages 62–79 in *Between Babel and Pentecost: Transnational Pentecostalism in Africa and Latin America.* Edited by André Corten and Ruth Marshall-Fratani. Bloomington: Indiana University Press, 2001.

"Gift of Tongues." "Gift of Tongues." *New Zealand Christian Record* (April 14, 1881): 11.

Gildea, "Possession." Gildea, Peter. "Demoniacal Possession." *ITQ* 41 (4, Oct. 1974): 289–311.

Giles, "Possession." Giles, Linda L. "Spirit Possession and the Symbolic Construction of Swahili Society." Pages 142–64 in *Spirit Possession, Modernity and Power in Africa.* Edited by Heike Behrend and Ute Luig. Madison: University of Wisconsin Press, 1999.

Giles, "Possession Cults." Giles, Linda L. "Possession Cults on the Swahili Coast: A Re-examination of Theories of Marginality." *Africa* 57 (2, 1987): 234–58.

Giles, "Spirits." Giles, Linda. "The Role of Spirits in Swahili Coastal Society." Pages 61–85 in *Studies in Witchcraft, Magic, War, and Peace in Africa.* Edited by Beatrice Nicolini. Lewiston, N.Y.: Edwin Mellen, 2006.

Gill, "Veil." Gill, Lesley. "'Like a Veil to Cover Them': Women and the Pentecostal Movement in La Paz." Pages 191–97 in *Latin American Religions: Histories and Documents in Context*. Edited by Anna L. Peterson and Manuel A. Vasquez. New York: New York University Press, 2008.

Gillies, "Proof." Gillies, Donald. "A Bayesian Proof of a Humean Principle." *BJPhilSc* 42 (1991): 255–56.

Gilliland, "Churches." Gilliland, Dean. "How 'Christian' Are African Independent Churches?" *Missiology* 14 (3, July 1986): 259–72.

Gillum, "Frequency." Gillum, Richard F. "Frequency of Attendance at Religious Services and Leisure-Time Physical Activity in American Women and Men: The Third National Health and Nutrition Examination Survey." *AnnBehMed* 31 (1, 2006): 30–35.

Gillum and Ingram, "Frequency." Gillum, Richard F., and Deborah D. Ingram. "Frequency of Attendance at Religious Services, Hypertension, and Blood Pressure: The Third National Health and Nutrition Examination Survey." *PsychMed* 68 (2006): 382–85.

Gillum, Sullivan, and Bybee, "Importance." Gillum, T. L., C. M. Sullivan, and D. I. Bybee. "The Importance of Spirituality in the Lives of Domestic Violence Survivors." *ViolWom* 12 (3, 2006): 240–50.

Gilman, "Miracles." Gilman, James E. "Reconceiving Miracles." *RelS* 25 (4, 1989): 477–87.

Gingerich, *Book*. Gingerich, Owen. *The Book Nobody Read: Chasing the Revolutions of Nicolaus Copernicus*. New York: Walker, 2004.

Gingerich, "Copernicus." Gingerich, Owen. "Did the Reformers Reject Copernicus?" *ChH* 76 (4, 2002): 22–23.

Gingerich, "Scientist." Gingerich, Owen. "Dare a Scientist Believe in Design?" Pages 21–32 in *Evidence of Purpose: Scientists Discover the Creator*. Edited by John Marks Templeton. New York: Continuum, 1994.

Gispert-Sauch, "Upanisad." Gispert-Sauch, George. "Brhadaranyaka Upanisad 1.3.28 in Greek Literature?" *Vid* 40 (4, 1976): 177–80.

Githieya, "Church." Githieya, Francis Kimani. "The Church of the Holy Spirit: Biblical Beliefs and Practices of the Arathi of Kenya, 1926–50." Pages 231–43 in *East African Expressions of Christianity*. Edited by Thomas Spear and Isaria N. Kimambo. EAfSt. Athens: Ohio University Press; Oxford: James Currey; Dar es Salaam: Mkuki na Nyota; Nairobi: East African Educational Publishers, 1999.

Glasson, *Moses*. Glasson, T. Francis. *Moses in the Fourth Gospel*. SBT. Naperville, Ill.: Alec R. Allenson, 1963.

Gleim, "Ministering." Gleim, Pauline. "Ministering to the Sick." *PentEv* 513 (Sept. 8, 1923): 12.

Glennon, "Religion." Glennon, Fred. "Religion and Healing for Physician's Assistants." Pages 293–306 in *Teaching Religion and Healing*. Edited by Linda L. Barnes and Inés Talamantez. AARTRSS. Oxford: Oxford University Press, 2006.

Glew, "Experience." Glew, Anne M. S. "Personal Experience in Faith Healing." Pages 81–86 in *Faith Healing: Finger of God? Or, Scientific Curiosity?* Compiled by Claude A. Frazier. New York: Thomas Nelson, 1973.

Glover, "Healings." Glover, Kelso R. "Some Recent Healings in the Stone Church." *LRE* 15 (2, Dec. 1921): 15–17.

Glover, "Miracles of Healing." Glover, Kelso R. "Miracles of Healing in the Stone Church." *LRE* 15 (11, Aug. 1922): 5–6.

Glover, "Modern Miracles." Glover, Kelso R. "Modern Miracles." *LRE* 15 (11, Aug. 1922): 2–5.

Glover, "Recent Healings." Glover, Kelso R. "Recent Healings by the Lord." *LRE* 15 (8, May 1922): 13–14.

Glueck, *Side*. Glueck, Nelson. *The Other Side of the Jordan*. Cambridge: American Schools of Oriental Research, 1970.

Gmur and Tschopp, "Factors." Gmur, M., and A. Tschopp. "Factors Determining the Success of Nicotine Withdrawal: Twelve-Year Followup of 532 Smokers after Suggestion Therapy (by a Faith Healer)." *IntJAd* 22 (12, 1987): 1189–1200.

Gnuse, "Temple Experience." Gnuse, Robert K. "The Temple Experience of Jaddus in the *Antiquities* of Josephus: A Report of Jewish Dream Incubation." *JQR* 83 (1993): 349–68.

Go, "Ministry." Go, Peter Kwang-Seog. "Healing Ministry in Kingdom Perspective." ThM thesis, Fuller School of World Mission, 1993.

Goddu, "Failure." Goddu, André. "The Failure of Exorcism in the Middle Ages." Pages 2–19 in *Possession and Exorcism*. Vol. 9 of *Articles on Witchcraft, Magic, and Demonology: A Twelve-Volume Anthology of Scholarly Articles*. Edited by Brian P. Levack. New York: Garland, 1992. Reprinted from *Soziale Ordnungen im Selbstverständnis des Mittelalters* 12 (1980): 540–57.

Godron, "Healings." Godron, Gérard. "Healings in Coptic Literature." Pages 1212–14 in vol. 4 of *The Coptic Encyclopedia*. Edited by Aziz S. Atiya. 8 vols. New York: Macmillan, 1991.

Godwin, *Strategy*. Godwin, Ben. *God's Strategy for Tragedy: A Documented Modern-day Miracle*. Cleveland, Tenn.: Deeper Revelation, 2008.

Goergen, *Mission*. Goergen, D. J. *The Mission and Ministry of Jesus*. Wilmington, Del.: Michael Glazier, 1986.

Goforth, *Goforth*. Goforth, Rosalind. *Goforth of China*. Grand Rapids: Zondervan, 1937.

Goguel, *Life*. Goguel, Maurice. *The Life of Jesus*. Translated by Olive Wyon. New York: Macmillan, 1948.

Golden et al., "Spirituality." Golden, Jonathan, Ralph L. Piedmont, Joseph W. Ciarrocchi, and Thomas Rodgerson. "Spirituality and Burnout: An Incremental Validity Study." *JPsyTh* 32 (2, 2004): 115–25.

Goldin, "Magic." Goldin, Judah. "The Magic of Magic and Superstition." Pages 115–47 in *Aspects of Religious Propaganda in Judaism and Early Christianity*. Edited by Elisabeth Schüssler Fiorenza. UNDCSJCA 2. Notre Dame, Ind.: University of Notre Dame Press, 1976.

Gómez, *Mission*. Gómez, Ricardo. *The Mission of God in Latin America*. ATSSWCRMIS 4. Lexington, Ky.: Emeth, 2010.

Gomm, "Spirit Possession." Gomm, Roger. "Bargaining from Weakness: Spirit Possession on the South Kenya Coast." *Man* 10 (1975): 530–43.

Gondola, "Kimbangu." Gondola, Charles Didier. "Kimbangu, Simon, and Kimbanguism." Pages 766–67 in vol. 2 of *Encyclopedia of African History*. Edited by Kevin Shillington. 3 vols. New York: Fitzroy Dearborn, 2005.

González, *Acts*. González, Justo L. *Acts: The Gospel of the Spirit*. Maryknoll, N.Y.: Orbis, 2001.

González, *Guide*. González, Justo L. *Church History: An Essential Guide*. Nashville: Abingdon, 1996.

González, *Months*. González, Justo L. *Three Months with the Spirit*. Nashville: Abingdon, 2003.

González, *Story*. González, Justo L. *The Story of Christianity: The Early Church to the Present Day*. 2 vols. Peabody, Mass.: Hendrickson, 1999.

González, *Tribe*. González, Justo L. *Out of Every Tribe and Nation: Christian Theology at the Ethnic Roundtable*. Nashville: Abingdon, 1992.

Goodacre and Perrin, *Questioning*. Goodacre, Mark, and Nicholas Perrin, eds. *Questioning Q: A Multidimensional Critique*. Foreword by N. T. Wright. Downers Grove, Ill.: InterVarsity, 2004.

Goodare, "Act." Goodare, Julian. "The Scottish Witchcraft Act." *CH* 74 (1, 2005): 39–67.

Goodare, "Knox." Goodare, Julian. "John Knox on Demonology and Witchcraft." *ARG* 96 (2005): 221–45.

Gooden, *Faith Cures*. Gooden, Rosemary D., ed. *Faith Cures and Answers to Prayer by Mrs. Sarah Edward Mix*. Syracuse, N.Y.: Syracuse University Press, 2002.

Gooden, "Help." Gooden, Rosemary D. "Seeking Help for the Body in the Well-Being of the Soul." Pages 147–59 in *Faith, Health, and Healing in African-American Life*. Edited by Stephanie Y. Mitchem

and Emilie M. Townes. RelHHeal. Westport, Conn.: Praeger, 2008.

Goodenough, *Symbols*. Goodenough, Erwin R. *Jewish Symbols in the Greco-Roman Period*. 13 vols. BollS 37. Vols. 1–12: New York: Pantheon Books, for Bollingen Foundation, 1953–65. Vol. 13: Princeton, N.J.: Princeton University Press, for Bollingen Foundation, 1968.

Goodich, "History." Goodich, Michael. "*Mirabilis Deus in Sanctis Suis*: Social History and Medieval Miracles." Pages 135–56 in *Signs, Wonders, Miracles: Representations of Divine Power in the Life of the Church. Papers Read at the 2003 Summer Meeting and the 2004 Winter Meeting of the Ecclesiastical History Society*. Edited by Kate Cooper and Jeremy Gregory. Rochester: Boydell & Brewer, for the Ecclesiastical History Society, 2005.

Goodich, *Miracles*. Goodich, Michael E. *Miracles and Wonders: The Development of the Concept of Miracle, 1150–1350. Church, Faith, and Culture in the Medieval West*. Burlington, Vt.: Ashgate, 2007.

Goodman, *Demons*. Goodman, Felicitas D. *How about Demons? Possession and Exorcism in the Modern World*. Bloomington: Indiana University Press, 1988.

Goodman, "Disturbances." Goodman, Felicitas D. "Disturbances in the Apostolic Church: A Trance-Based Upheaval in Yucatán." Pages 227–364 in *Trance, Healing, and Hallucination: Three Field Studies in Religious Experience* by Felicitas D. Goodman, Jeannette H. Henney, and Esther Pressel. New York: John Wiley & Sons, 1974.

Goodman, *Ecstasy*. Goodman, Felicitas D. *Ecstasy, Ritual, and Alternate Reality: Religion in a Pluralistic World*. Bloomington: Indiana University Press, 1988.

Goodman, "Glossolalia." Goodman, Felicitas D. "Phonetic Analysis of Glossolalia in Four Cultural Settings." *JSSR* 8 (2, 1969): 227–39.

Goodman, *Speaking in Tongues*. Goodman, Felicitas D. *Speaking in Tongues: A Cross-Cultural Study of Glossolalia*. Chicago: University of Chicago Press, 1972.

Goodman, *State*. Goodman, Martin. *State and Society in Roman Galilee, A.D. 132–212*. OCPHS. Totowa, N.J.: Rowman & Allanfeld, 1983.

Goodman, *Trance Journeys*. Goodman, Felicitas D. *Trance Journeys and Other Ecstatic Experiences*. Bloomington: Indiana University Press, 1990.

Goodman, "Workshop." Goodman, Felicitas D. "Experiential Workshop." Pages 112–15 in *Proceedings of the Fourth International Conference on the Study of Shamanism and Alternate Modes of Healing, Held at the St. Sabina Center, San Rafael, California, September 5–7, 1987*. Edited by Ruth-Inge Heinze. N.p.:

Independent Scholars of Asia; Madison, Wis.: A-R Editions, 1988.

Goodman, Henney, and Pressel, *Trance*. Goodman, Felicitas D., Jeannette H. Henney, and Esther Pressel. *Trance, Healing, and Hallucination: Three Field Studies in Religious Experience*. New York: John Wiley & Sons, 1974.

Goppelt, *Jesus, Paul and Judaism*. Goppelt, Leonhard. *Jesus, Paul and Judaism*. Translated by Edward Schroeder. New York: Thomas Nelson, 1964.

Goppelt, *Theology*. Goppelt, Leonhard. *Theology of the New Testament*. Edited by Jürgen Roloff. Translated by John E. Alsup. 2 vols. Grand Rapids: Eerdmans, 1981–82.

Gordon, *Civilizations*. Gordon, Cyrus H. *The Common Background of Greek and Hebrew Civilizations*. New York: W. W. Norton, 1965.

Gordon, "Cosmology." Gordon, Bruce L. "Inflationary Cosmology and the String Multiverse." Pages 75–103 in *New Proofs for the Existence of God: Contributions of Contemporary Physics and Philosophy*, by Robert J. Spitzer. Grand Rapids: Eerdmans, 2010.

Gordon, "Incantations." Gordon, Cyrus H. "Two Aramaic Incantations." Pages 231–44 in *Biblical and Near Eastern Studies: Essays in Honor of William Sanford LaSor*. Edited by Gary A. Tuttle. Grand Rapids: Eerdmans, 1978.

Gordon, "Ministry of Healing." Gordon, A. J. "The Ministry of Healing." Pages 119–282 in *Healing: The Three Great Classics on Divine Healing*. Edited by Jonathan L. Graf. Camp Hill, Pa.: Christian Publications, 1992.

Gordon, *Near East*. Gordon, Cyrus H. *The Ancient Near East*. New York: W. W. Norton, 1965.

Gorsuch, "Limits." Gorsuch, Richard L. "On the Limits of Scientific Investigation: Miracles and Intercessory Prayer." Pages 280–99 in *Religious and Spiritual Events*. Vol. 1 of *Miracles: God, Science, and Psychology in the Paranormal*. Edited by J. Harold Ellens. Westport, Conn.; London: Praeger, 2008.

Goudge, *Ascent*. Goudge, Thomas A. *The Ascent of Life: A Philosophical Study of the Theory of Evolution*. Toronto: University of Toronto Press, 1961.

Gould, *Dinosaur*. Gould, Stephen Jay. *Dinosaur in a Haystack: Reflections in Natural History*. New York: Harmony, 1995.

Gould, *Mismeasure*. Gould, Stephen Jay. *The Mismeasure of Man*. New York: W. W. Norton, 1981.

Gould, *Philosophy of Chrysippus*. Gould, Josiah B., Jr. *The Philosophy of Chrysippus*. Leiden: Brill, 1970.

Gould, *Rocks*. Gould, Stephen Jay. *Rocks of Ages: Science and Religion*. New York: Ballantine, Random House, 1989.

Goulet, "Dreams." Goulet, Jean-Guy. "Dreams and Visions in Other Lifeworlds." Pages 16–38 in *Being Changed: The Anthropology of Extraordinary Experience*. Edited by David E. Young and Jean-Guy Goulet. Peterborough, Ont.: Broadview, 1994.

Goulet, "Ways of Knowing." Goulet, Jean-Guy. "Ways of Knowing: Toward a Narrative Ethnography of Experiences among the Dene Tha." *JAnthRes* 50 (1994): 113–39.

Goulet and Young, "Issues." Goulet, Jean-Guy, and David Young. "Theoretical and Methodological Issues." Pages 298–335 in *Being Changed: The Anthropology of Extraordinary Experience*. Edited by David E. Young and Jean-Guy Goulet. Peterborough, Ont.: Broadview, 1994.

Gounelle, "Théologien." Gounelle, Remi. "Un théologien face aux miracles: Augustin." *FoiVie* 108 (2, 2009): 63–68.

Gousmett, "Miracle." Gousmett, Chris. "Creation Order and Miracle according to Augustine." *EvQ* 60 (3, 1988): 217–40.

Gower, "Probability." Gower, Barry. "David Hume and the Probability of Miracles." *HumSt* 16 (1, April 1990): 17–32.

Gräbe, "Discovery." Gräbe, Peter J. "The Pentecostal Discovery of the New Testament Theme of God's Power and Its Relevance to the African Context." *Pneuma* 24 (2, 2002): 225–42.

Grady, "Followers." Grady, J. Lee. "Nigerian Healer T. B. Joshua Still Attracts Followers from Abroad." *Charisma* 29 (5, Dec. 2003): 16–19.

Graf, "Death." Graf, Fritz. "Untimely Death, Witchcraft, and Divine Vengeance: A Reasoned Epigraphical Catalog." *Zeitschrift für Papyrologie und Epigraphik* 162 (2007): 139–50.

Graf, "Ecstasy." Graf, Fritz. "Ecstasy: Greek and Roman Antiquity." Pages 799–801 in vol. 4 of *Brill's New Pauly: Encyclopaedia of the Ancient World*. Edited by Hubert Cancik and Helmuth Schneider. 20 vols. English ed. Christine F. Salazar. Leiden: Brill, 2010.

Graf, "Healing Deities." Graf, Fritz. "Healing Deities, Healing Cults: Greece and Rome." Pages 22–26 in vol. 6 of *Brill's New Pauly: Encyclopaedia of the Ancient World*. Edited by Hubert Cancik and Helmuth Schneider. 20 vols. English ed. Christine F. Salazar. Leiden: Brill, 2010.

Graf, "Initiation." Graf, Fritz. "The Magician's Initiation." *Helios* 21 (2, 1994): 161–77.

Graham, *Just As I Am*. Graham, Billy. *Just As I Am: The Autobiography of Billy Graham*. New York: HarperCollins, 1997.

Graham, "Materialism." Graham, Lloyd. "From Materialism to Miracles: Connections and Contradictions." *ModCh* 34 (4, 1993): 44–48.

Graham, *Spirit*. Graham, Billy. *The Holy Spirit*. Dallas: Word, 1988.

Graham et al., "Frequency." Graham, T. W., et al. "Frequency of Church Attendance and Blood Pressure Elevation." *JBehMed* 1 (1978): 37–43.

Grange, "Globalization." Grange, John M. "Globalization, Health Sector Reform and Justice." *IntRevMiss* 90 (356/357, Jan./Apr. 2001): 160–65.

Granit, "Attitude." Granit, Ragnar. "I Have a Religious Attitude toward the Unknown." Pages 177–78 in *Cosmos, Bios, and Theos: Scientists Reflect on Science, God, and the Origins of the Universe, Life, and* Homo Sapiens. Edited by Henry Margenau and Roy Abraham Varghese. La Salle, Ill.: Open Court, 1992.

Granjo, "Rituals." Granjo, Paulo. "Back Home: Post-War Cleansing Rituals in Mozambique." Pages 277–94 in *Studies in Witchcraft, Magic, War, and Peace in Africa*. Edited by Beatrice Nicolini. Lewiston, N.Y.: Edwin Mellen, 2006.

Grant, "Folk Religion." Grant, Earl E. "Folk Religion in Islam." PhD diss., Fuller Theological Seminary, 1987.

Grant, *Gods*. Grant, Robert M. *Gods and the One God*. LEC 1. Philadelphia: Westminster, 1986.

Grant, *Miracle*. Grant, Robert M. *Miracle and Natural Law in Greco-Roman and Early Christian Thought*. Amsterdam: North-Holland Publishing Company, 1952.

Grant, *Paul*. Grant, Robert M. *Paul in the Roman World: The Conflict at Corinth*. Louisville: Westminster John Knox, 2001.

Grant, *Religions*. Grant, Frederick C., ed. *Hellenistic Religions: The Age of Syncretism*. The Library of Liberal Arts. Indianapolis: Bobbs-Merrill, The Liberal Arts Press, 1953.

Gray, "Christianity." Gray, Richard. "Christianity." Pages 140–90 in *From 1905–1940*. Edited by A. D. Roberts. Vol. 7 of *The Cambridge History of Africa*. Edited by J. D. Fage and Roland Oliver. 8 vols. Cambridge: Cambridge University Press 1986.

Gray, "Cult." Gray, Robert F. "The Shetani Cult among the Segeju of Tanzania." Pages 171–87 in *Spirit Mediumship and Society in Africa*. Edited by John Beattie and John Middleton. Foreword by Raymond Firth. New York: Africana Publishing Corporation, 1969.

Gray, "Exorcism." Gray, John N. "Bayu Utarnu: Ghost Exorcism and Sacrifice in Nepal." *Ethnology* 26 (1987): 179–99.

Gray, *Figures*. Gray, Rebecca. *Prophetic Figures in Late Second Temple Jewish Palestine: The Evidence from Josephus*. New York: Oxford University Press, 1993.

Grayson, "Elements." Grayson, James H. "Elements of Protestant Accommodation to Korean Religious Culture: A Personal Ethnographic Perspective." *Missiology* 23 (1, 1995): 43–59.

Grazier, *Power Beyond*. Grazier, Jack. *The Power Beyond: In Search of Miraculous Healing*. New York: Macmillan, 1989.

Greeley, *Sociology*. Greeley, Andrew M. *The Sociology of the Paranormal: A Reconnaissance*. Sage Research Papers in the Social Sciences, Studies in Religion and Ethnicity. Beverly Hills, Calif.: Sage, 1975.

Green, *Asian Tigers*. Green, Michael. *Asian Tigers for Christ: The Dynamic Growth of the Church in South East Asia*. Foreword by Datuk Yong Ping Chung. London: SPCK, 2001.

Green, "Daughter of Abraham." Green, Joel B. "Jesus and a Daughter of Abraham (Luke 13:10–17): Test Case for a Lucan Perspective on Jesus' Miracles." *CBQ* 51 (1989): 643–54.

Green, "Good News." Green, Joel B. "Good News to Whom? Jesus and the 'Poor' in the Gospel of Luke." Pages 59–74 in *Jesus of Nazareth: Lord and Christ; Essays on the Historical Jesus and New Testament Christology*. Edited by J. B. Green and M. Turner. Grand Rapids: Eerdmans, 1990.

Green, "Healing." Green, Joel B. "Healing." Pages 755–59 in vol. 2 of *The New Interpreter's Dictionary of the Bible*. Edited by Katharine Doob Sakenfeld et al. 5 vols. Nashville: Abingdon, 2007.

Green, *History*. Green, Vivian H. H. *A New History of Christianity*. New York: Continuum, 1996.

Green, *Holy Spirit*. Green, Michael. *I Believe in the Holy Spirit*. 2nd ed. Grand Rapids: Eerdmans, 1989.

Green, *Life*. Green, Joel B. *Body, Soul, and Human Life*. StThIn. Grand Rapids: Baker Academic, 2008.

Green, *Thirty Years*. Green, Michael. *Thirty Years That Changed the World: The Book of Acts for Today*. Grand Rapids: Eerdmans, 2002.

Green and Hazard, *No Compromise*. Green, Melody, and David Hazard. *No Compromise: The Life Story of Keith Green*. Foreword by Winkie Pratney. Chatworth, Calif.: Sparrow, 1989.

Green and Sim, *Relevance Theory*. Green, Gene L., and Ronald J. Sim. *Relevance Theory and Biblical Interpretation*. SBLSymS. Atlanta: Society of Biblical Literature, forthcoming.

Greenbaum, "Possession Trance." Greenbaum, Lenora. "Possession Trance in Sub-Saharan Africa: A Descriptive Analysis of Fourteen Societies." Pages 58–87 in *Religion, Altered States of Consciousness, and Social Change*. Edited by Erika Bourguignon. Columbus: Ohio State University Press, 1973.

Greenbaum, "Societal Correlates." Greenbaum, Lenora. "Societal Correlates of Possession Trance in Sub-Saharan Africa." Pages 39–57 in *Religion, Altered States of Consciousness, and Social Change*. Edited by Erika Bourguignon. Columbus: Ohio State University Press, 1973.

Greenfield, *Spirits*. Greenfield, Sidney M. *Spirits with Scalpels: The Culturalbiology of Religious Healing in Brazil*. Walnut Creek, Calif.: Left Coast Press, 2008.

Greenspahn, "Prophecy." Greenspahn, Frederick E. "Why Prophecy Ceased." *JBL* 108 (1, 1989): 37–49.

Greenstone, *Messiah*. Greenstone, Julius H. *The Messiah Idea in Jewish History*. Philadelphia: Jewish Publication Society of America, 1906.

Greer, "Care." Greer, Rowan A. "Pastoral Care and Discipline." Pages 567–84 in *Constantine to c. 600*. Edited by Augustine Casiday and Frederick W. Norris. Vol. 2 of *The Cambridge History of Christianity*. 9 vols. Cambridge: Cambridge University Press, 2007.

Gregersen, "Emergence." Gregersen, Niels Henrik. "Emergence: What Is at Stake for Religious Reflection?" Pages 279–302 in *The Re-Emergence of Emergence: The Emergentist Hypothesis from Science to Religion*. Edited by Philip Clayton and Paul Davies. Oxford: Oxford University Press, 2006.

Gregory, "Healed." Gregory, Cora B. "Healed of Blindness Through Prayer." *PentEv* 420–21 (Nov. 26, 1921): 9.

Gregory, "Introduction." Gregory, Anita Kohsen. "Introduction." Pages v–xvi in *Possession: Demoniacal and Other among Primitive Races, in Antiquity, the Middle Ages, and Modern Times*, by T. K. Oesterreich. Translated by D. Ibberson. New Hyde Park, N.Y.: University Books, 1966.

Gregory, "Secular Bias." Gregory, Brad S. "The Other Confessional History: On Secular Bias in the Study of Religion." *HistTh*, theme issue 45 (4, Dec. 2006): 132–49.

Grelot, "Démonologie." Grelot, Pierre. "Miracles de Jésus et Démonologie Juive." Pages 59–72 in *Les Miracles de Jésus selon le Nouveau Testament*, by J.-N. Aletti et al. Edited by Xavier Léon-Dufour. Paris: Éditions du Seuil, 1977.

Grenz and Olson, *Theology*. Grenz, Stanley J., and Roger E. Olson. *Twentieth-Century Theology: God and the World in a Transitional Age*. Downers Grove, Ill.: InterVarsity, 1992.

Greyson, "Experiences." Greyson, Bruce. "Near-Death Experiences." Pages 315–52 in *Varieties of Anomalous Experience: Examining the Scientific Evidence*. Edited by Etzel Cardeña, Steven Jay Lynn, and Stanley Krippner. Washington, D.C.: American Psychological Association, 2000.

Griffith, "Miracles." Griffith, Stephen. "Miracles and the Shroud of Turin." *FPhil* 13 (1, 1996): 34–49.

Griffith, "Signs." Griffith, Sidney H. "The Signs and Wonders of Orthodoxy: Miracles and Monks' Lives in Sixth-Century Palestine." Pages 139–68 in *Miracles in Jewish and Christian Antiquity: Imagining Truth*. Edited by John C. Cavadini. NDST 3. Notre Dame, Ind.: University of Notre Dame Press, 1999.

Griffiths, "Fruit." Griffiths, Tudor. "The Fruit of Revival in Uganda." Pages 233–42 in *Revival, Renewal, and the Holy Spirit*. Edited by Dyfed Wyn Roberts. SEHT. Eugene, Ore.: Wipf & Stock, 2009.

Griffiths and Cheetham, "Priests." Griffiths, J. A., and R. W. S. Cheetham. "Priests Before Healers—An Appraisal of the *isangoma* or *isanusi* in Nguni Society." Pages 295–303 in *Afro-Christian Religion and Healing in Southern Africa*. Edited by G. C. Oosthuizen, S. D. Edwards, W. H. Wessels, and I. Hexham. AfSt 8. Lewiston, N.Y.: Edwin Mellen, 1989.

"Grimsby Testimony." "Grimsby Testimony: Woman, Helpless for Eleven Years, Walks About Cured." *Conf* 129 (April 1922): 28–29.

Grindal, "Heart." Grindal, Bruce T. "Into the Heart of Sisala Experience: Witnessing Death Divination." *JAnthRes* 39 (1983): 60–80.

Grof, "Potential." Grof, Stanislav. "Healing Potential of Spiritual Experiences: Observations from Modern Consciousness Research." Pages 126–46 in *Psychodynamics*. Vol. 3 of *The Healing Power of Spirituality: How Faith Helps Humans Thrive*. Edited by J. Harold Ellens. Santa Barbara, Calif.: Praeger, 2010.

Gronewold, "Cushing." Gronewold, Sylvia. "Did Frank Hamilton Cushing Go Native?" Pages 33–50 in *Crossing Cultural Boundaries: The Anthropological Experience*. Edited by Solon T. Kimball and James B. Watson. San Francisco: Chandler, 1972.

Groothuis, *Religions*. Groothuis, Douglas. *Are All Religions One?* Downers Grove, Ill.: InterVarsity, 1996.

Groseth, "Killed." Groseth, Ida. "The First Christians Killed by Bandits in the Tengchow District." *CGl* 6 (3, April 1925): 18.

Gross, *Spiritual Healing*. Gross, Don H. *The Case for Spiritual Healing*. New York: Thomas Nelson, 1958.

Gruchy and Chirongoma, "Elements." Gruchy, Steve de, and Sophie Chirongoma. "Earth, Water, Fire, and Wind: Elements of African Ecclesiologies." Pages 291–305 in *The Routledge Companion to the Christian Church*. Edited by Gerard Mannion and Lewis S. Mudge. New York: Routledge, 2008.

Grudem, *Gifts*. Grudem, Wayne A., ed. *Are Miraculous Gifts for Today? Four Views*. Grand Rapids: Zondervan, 1996.

Grudem, *Theology*. Grudem, Wayne. *Systematic Theology: An Introduction to Biblical Doctrine*. Grand Rapids: Zondervan; Leicester: Inter-Varsity, 1994.

Grundmann, *Heal*. Grundmann, Christoffer H. *Sent to Heal! Emergence and Development of Medical Missions*. Lanham, Md.: University Press of America, 2005.

Grundmann, "Healing." Grundmann, Christoffer H. "Healing—A Challenge to Church and Theology." *IntRevMiss* 90 (356/357, Jan./Apr. 2001): 26–40.

Grundmann, "Inviting." Grundmann, Christoffer H. "Inviting the Spirit to Fight the Spirits? Pneumatological Challenges for Missions in Healing and Exorcism." *IntRevMiss* 94 (255, 2005): 51–73.

Gruson, "Josephe." Gruson, Marie-Odile. "Flavius Josèphe. Miracles de Jésus et de Moise." *MScRel* 65 (4, 2008): 51–62.

Guédon, "Ways." Guédon, Marie Francoise. "Dene Ways and the Ethnographer's Culture." Pages 39–70 in *Being Changed: The Anthropology of Extraordinary Experience*. Edited by David E. Young and Jean-Guy Goulet. Peterborough, Ont.: Broadview, 1994.

Guevara, "Campaign." Guevara, Emiliano. "Outstanding Campaign Held in Olongapo City." *PentV* (Manila) 4 (5–7, June–July 1967): 12–13.

Guijarro, "Politics." Guijarro, Santiago. "The Politics of Exorcism: Jesus' Reaction to Negative Labels in the Beelzebul Controversy." *BTB* 29 (3, 1999): 118–29.

Guijarro Oporto, "Articulación literaria." Guijarro Oporto, Santiago. "La articulación literaria del Libro de los Hechos." *EstBib* 62 (2, 2004): 185–204.

Guillemette, "Forme." Guillemette, Pierre. "La forme des récits d'exorcisme de Bultmann. Un dogme à reconsidérer." *ÉgT* 11 (2, 1980): 177–93.

Guldseth, "Cases." Guldseth, Gustav. "Some Hospital Cases." *CGl* 12 (3, July 1935): 16–17.

Guldseth, "Hospital." Guldseth, Gustav. "Luther Hospital, Hwangchuan." *CGl* 14 (4, Oct. 1937): 9–12.

Guldseth, "Power." Guldseth, Gustav J. "All Power Is Given Me . . . Go Ye Therefore . . ." *CGl* 14 (1, Jan. 1937): 2–4.

Gumede, "Healers." Gumede, M. V. "Healers: Modern and Traditional." Pages 319–28 in *Afro-Christian Religion and Healing in Southern Africa*. Edited by G. C. Oosthuizen, S. D. Edwards, W. H. Wessels, and I. Hexham. AfSt 8. Lewiston, N.Y.: Edwin Mellen, 1989.

Gundry, *Commentary*. Gundry, Robert H. *Matthew: A Commentary on His Literary and Theological Art*. Grand Rapids: Eerdmans, 1982.

Gundry, "Genre." Gundry, Robert H. "Recent Investigations into the Literary Genre 'Gospel.'" Pages 97–114 in *New Dimensions in New Testament Study*. Edited by Richard N. Longenecker and Merrill C. Tenney. Grand Rapids: Zondervan, 1974.

Gundry, *Use*. Gundry, Robert H. *The Use of the Old Testament in St. Matthew's Gospel: With Special Reference to the Messianic Hope*. NovTSup 18. Leiden: Brill, 1975.

Gurney, *Aspects*. Gurney, O. R. *Some Aspects of Hittite Religion*. Oxford: Oxford University Press, 1977.

Gusmer, *Healing*. Gusmer, Charles W. *The Ministry of Healing in the Church of England: An Ecumen-ical-Liturgical Study*. Alcuin Club Collections 56. Great Wakering, England: Alcuin Club, Mayhew-McCrimmon, 1974.

Gussler, "Change." Gussler, Judith D. "Social Change, Ecology, and Spirit Possession among the South African Nguni." Pages 88–126 in *Religion, Altered States of Consciousness, and Social Change*. Edited by Erika Bourguignon. Columbus: Ohio State University Press, 1973.

Guthrie, "Breakthrough." Guthrie, Stan. "Muslim Mission Breakthrough." *CT* (Dec. 13, 1993): 20–26.

Guthrie, *Disorder*. Guthrie, George M. *Culture and Mental Disorder*. ModAnth 39. Reading, Mass.: Addison-Wesley, 1973.

Guthrie, *Orpheus*. Guthrie, W. K. C. *Orpheus and Greek Religion: A Study of the Orphic Movement*. 2nd ed. New York: Norton, 1966.

Guthrie and Szanton, "Diagnosis." Guthrie, B., and D. Szanton. "Folk Diagnosis and Treatment of Schizophrenia: Bargaining with Spirits in the Philippines." Pages 147–63 in *Culture-Bound Syndromes, Ethno-Psychiatry, and Alternate Therapies*. Edited by W. Lebra. Honolulu: University of Hawaii Press, 1976.

Gutierrez, *Mujer de Milagros*. Gutierrez, Angel Luis. *Mujer de Milagros*. Guaynabo, Puerto Rico: Editorial Chari, 1991.

Gutting, *Paradigms*. Gutting, Gary, ed. *Paradigms and Revolutions: Appraisals and Applications of Thomas Kuhn's Philosophy of Science*. Notre Dame, Ind.: University of Notre Dame Press, 1980.

Guttmann, "Miracles." Guttmann, Alexander. "The Significance of Miracles for Talmudic Judaism." *HUCA* 20 (1947): 363–406.

Guy, "Miracles." Guy, Laurie. "Miracles, Messiahs, and the Media: The Ministry of A. H. Dallimore in Auckland in the 1930s." Pages 453–63 in *Signs, Wonders, Miracles: Representations of Divine Power in the Life of the Church. Papers Read at the 2003 Summer Meeting and the 2004 Winter Meeting of the Ecclesiastical History Society*. Edited by Kate Cooper and Jeremy Gregory. Rochester: Boydell & Brewer, for the Ecclesiastical History Society, 2005.

Guy, "Physician." Guy, John R. "Archbishop Secker as a Physician." Pages 127–35 in *The Church and Healing: Papers Read at the Twentieth Summer Meeting and the Twenty-first Winter Meeting of the Ecclesiastical History Society*. StChHist 19. Edited by W. J. Sheils. Oxford: Basil Blackwell, 1982.

Gwynne, *Action*. Gwynne, Paul. *Special Divine Action: Key Issues in the Contemporary Debate (1965–1995)*. Tesi Gregoriana, Serie Teologia 12. Rome: Gregorian University Press, 1996.

Haacker, *Theology*. Haacker, Klaus. *The Theology of Paul's Letter to the Romans*. Cambridge: Cambridge University Press, 2003.

Haar and Ellis, "Possession." Haar, Gerrie ter, and Stephen Ellis. "Spirit Possession and Healing in Modern Zambia: An Analysis of Letters to Archbishop Milingo." *African Affairs* 87 (347, 1988): 185–206.

Haar and Platvoet, "Bezetenheid." Haar, Gerrie ter, and Jan Platvoet. "Bezetenheid en christendom." *NedTT* 43 (3, 1989): 177–91.

Habermas, *Evidence.* Habermas, Gary R. *Ancient Evidence for the Life of Jesus: Historical Records of His Death and Resurrection.* Nashville: Thomas Nelson, 1984.

Habermas and Moreland, *Immortality.* Habermas, Gary R., and J. P. Moreland. *Immortality: The Other Side of Death.* Nashville: Thomas Nelson, 1992.

Habermas, "Miracles." Habermas, Gary R. "Did Jesus Perform Miracles?" Pages 117–40 in *Jesus Under Fire.* Edited by Michael J. Wilkins and J. P. Moreland. Grand Rapids: Zondervan, 1995.

Habermas, *Risen Jesus.* Habermas, Gary R. *The Risen Jesus and Future Hope.* Lanham, Md.: Rowman and Littlefield, 2003.

Hadaway, Elifson, and Peterson, "Involvement." Hadaway, C. K., K. W. Elifson, and D. M. M. Peterson. "Religious Involvement and Drug Use among Urban Adolescents." *JSSR* 23 (2, 1984): 109–28.

Hagerland, "Review." Hagerland, Tobias. Review of Eric Eve, *The Healer from Nazareth. RBL* 11 (2009).

Hagin, *Midas Touch.* Hagin, Kenneth E. *The Midas Touch: A Balanced Approach to Biblical Prosperity.* Tulsa: Faith Library Publications, 2000.

Hai-po, "Works." Hai-po, Fang. "Great Works Manifested at Popeiho." *CGl* 12 (4, Oct. 1935): 20.

Hair, "Witches." Hair, P. E. H. "Heretics, Slaves, and Witches—as Seen by Guinea Jesuits c. 1610." *JRelAf* 28 (2, 1998): 131–44.

Haldon, "Essay." Haldon, John. "Supplementary Essay: The Miracles of Artemios and Contemporary Attitudes: Context and Significance." Pages 33–56 in *The Miracles of St. Artemios: A Collection of Miracle Stories by an Anonymous Author of Seventh-Century Byzantium.* Edited by Virgil S. Crisafulli and John W. Nesbitt. Translated by Virgil S. Crisafulli. Introduction by John W. Nesbitt. Commentary by Virgil S. Crisafulli and John W. Nesbitt. Leiden: Brill, 1997.

Haliburton, *Harris.* Haliburton, Gordon Mackay. *The Prophet Harris.* London: Longmans, 1973.

Hall, "Attendance." Hall, Daniel E. "Religious Attendance: More Cost-Effective Than Lipitor?" *JABFM* 19 (2, March 2006): 103–9.

Hall, *Worlds.* Hall, David D. *Worlds of Wonder, Days of Judgment: Popular Religious Belief in Early New England.* New York: Alfred A. Knopf, 1989.

Halverson, "Dynamics." Halverson, John. "Dynamics of Exorcism: The Sinhalese Sanniyakuma." *HR* 10 (1971): 334–59.

Hambourger, "Belief." Hambourger, Robert. "Belief in Miracles and Hume's Essay." *Nous* 14 (1980): 587–604.

Hamilton, *Revolt.* Hamilton, Kenneth. *Revolt against Heaven: An Enquiry into Anti-Supernaturalism.* Grand Rapids: Eerdmans, 1965.

Hamilton, "Signs." Hamilton, Bernard. "'God Wills It': Signs of Divine Approval in the Crusade Movement." Pages 88–98 in *Signs, Wonders, Miracles: Representations of Divine Power in the Life of the Church. Papers Read at the 2003 Summer Meeting and the 2004 Winter Meeting of the Ecclesiastical History Society.* Edited by Kate Cooper and Jeremy Gregory. Rochester: Boydell & Brewer, for the Ecclesiastical History Society, 2005.

Hamilton and Levine, "Preferences." Hamilton, Jennifer L., and Jeffrey P. Levine. "Neo-Pagan Patients' Preferences Regarding Physician Discussion of Spirituality." *FamMed* 38 (2, 2006): 83–84.

Hammerschlag, "Offering." Hammerschlag, Carl Allen. "The Huichol Offering: A Shamanic Healing Journey." *JRH* 48 (2, 2009): 246–58.

Hammond-Tooke, "Aetiology." Hammond-Tooke, W. D. "The Aetiology of Spirit in Southern Africa." Pages 43–65 in *Afro-Christian Religion and Healing in Southern Africa.* Edited by G. C. Oosthuizen, S. D. Edwards, W. H. Wessels, and I. Hexham. AfSt 8. Lewiston, N.Y.: Edwin Mellen, 1989.

Hamrick and Diefenbach, "Religion." Hamrick, Natalie, and Michael A. Diefenbach. "Religion and Spirituality among Patients with Localized Prostate Cancer." *PallSCare* 4 (4, 2006): 345–55.

Hanciles, *Beyond Christendom.* Hanciles, Jehu J. *Beyond Christendom: Globalization, African Migration, and the Transformation of the West.* Maryknoll, N.Y.: Orbis, 2008.

Hanciles, "Conversion." Hanciles, Jehu J. "Conversion and Social Change: A Review of the 'Unfinished Task' in West Africa." Pages 157–80 in *Christianity Reborn: The Global Expansion of Evangelicalism in the Twentieth Century.* Edited by Donald M. Lewis. SHCM. Grand Rapids: Eerdmans, 2004.

Hand, *Magical Medicine.* Hand, Wayland D. *Magical Medicine: The Folkloric Component of Medicine in the Folk Belief, Custom, and Ritual of the Peoples of Europe and America.* Berkeley: University of California Press, 1980.

Handley, "Ghosts." Handley, Sasha. "Reclaiming Ghosts in 1690s England." Pages 345–55 in *Signs, Wonders, Miracles: Representations of Divine Power in the Life of the Church; Papers Read at the 2003 Summer Meeting and the 2004 Winter Meeting of the Ecclesiastical History Society.* Edited by Kate Cooper and Jeremy Gregory. Rochester, N.Y.: Boydell & Brewer, for the Ecclesiastical History Society, 2005.

Handley, *Visions*. Handley, Sasha. *Visions of an Unseen World: Ghost Beliefs and Ghost Stories in Eighteenth-Century England*. Religious Cultures in the Early Modern World 2. London; Brookfield, Vt.: Pickering & Chatto, 2007.

Hansen, "Cures." Hansen, E. "Cures by Prayer: A Doctor's Personal Experience in the Course of His Practice." *Conf* 9 (7, July 1916): 114–15.

Hanson, *Acts*. Hanson, R. P. C. *The Acts in the Revised Standard Version, with Introduction and Commentary*. Oxford: Clarendon, 1967.

Hanson, "Dreams and Visions." Hanson, John S. "Dreams and Visions in the Graeco-Roman World and Early Christianity." *ANRW* 2.(Principat) 23.2.1395–1427.

Hanson, "Theory." Hanson, Norwood Russell. "A Picture Theory of Theory Meaning." Pages 233–74 in *The Nature and Function of Scientific Theories: Essays in Contemporary Science and Philosophy*. Edited by Robert G. Colodny. Pittsburgh: University of Pittsburgh Press, 1970.

Haq, "Culture." Haq, Syed Nomanul. "That Medieval Islamic Culture Was Inhospitable to Science." Pages 35–42 in *Galileo Goes to Jail and Other Myths about Science and Religion*. Edited by Ronald L. Numbers. Cambridge, Mass.: Harvard University Press, 2009.

Harakas, "Sacrament." Harakas, Stanley S. "The Sacrament of Healing." *IntRevMiss* 90 (356/357, Jan./Apr. 2001): 81–86.

Hard, "Animism." Hard, Theodore. "Does Animism Die in the City?" *UrbMiss* 6 (3, 1989): 45–46.

Harder, "Defixio." Harder, Ruth Elisabeth. "Defixio." Pages 175–78 in vol. 4 of *Brill's New Pauly: Encyclopaedia of the Ancient World*. Edited by Hubert Cancik and Helmuth Schneider. 20 vols. English ed. Christine F. Salazar. Leiden: Brill, 2010.

Hardesty, *Faith Cure*. Hardesty, Nancy A. *Faith Cure: Divine Healing in the Holiness and Pentecostal Movements*. Peabody, Mass.: Hendrickson, 2003.

Hardon, "Concept." Hardon, John A. "The Concept of Miracle from St. Augustine to Modern Apologetics." *TS* 15 (1954): 229–57.

Hardon, "Miracle Narratives." Hardon, John A. "The Miracle Narratives in the Acts of the Apostles." *CBQ* 16 (3, 1954): 303–18.

Hargreaves, "Miracles." Hargreaves, A. C. M. "Eastern Christendom and the Miracles of Jesus." *IJT* 10 (1961): 25–33.

Harinath et al., "Effects." Harinath, Kasiganesan, Anand Sawarup Malhotra, Karan Pal, et al. "Effects of Hatha Yoga and Omkar Meditation on Cardiorespiratory Performance, Psychologic Profile, and Melatonin Secretion." *JAlComMed* 10 (2004): 261–68.

Harline, "Miracles." Harline, Craig. "Miracles and This World: The Battle for the Jesus Oak." *ARG* 93 (2002): 217–38.

Harnack, *Acts*. Harnack, Adolf von. *The Acts of the Apostles*. New Testament Studies 3. Translated by J. R. Wilkinson. New York: G. P. Putnam's Sons; London: Williams and Norgate, 1909.

Harner, *Way of Shaman*. Harner, Michael. *The Way of the Shaman: A Guide to Power and Healing*. San Francisco: Harper & Row, 1980.

Harper, *Healings*. Harper, Michael. *The Healings of Jesus*. Downers Grove, Ill.: InterVarsity, 1986.

Harper, "Pollution." Harper, Edward B. "Ritual Pollution as an Integrator of Caste and Religion." Pages 151–96 in *Religion in South Asia*. Edited by Edward B. Harper. Seattle: University of Washington Press, 1964.

Harpur, *Touch*. Harpur, Tom. *The Uncommon Touch: An Investigation of Spiritual Healing*. Toronto: McClelland and Stewart, 1994.

Harrauer, "Agnostos Theos." Harrauer, Christine. "Agnostos Theos." Pages 346–47 in vol. 1 of *Brill's New Pauly: Encyclopaedia of the Ancient World*. Edited by Hubert Cancik and Helmuth Schneider. 20 vols. English ed. Christine F. Salazar. Leiden: Brill, 2010.

Harré, *Introduction*. Harré, Romano. *An Introduction to the Logic of the Sciences*. London: Macmillan; New York: St. Martin's Press, 1967.

Harrell, "Divine Healing." Harrell, David Edwin, Jr. "Divine Healing in Modern American Protestantism." Pages 215–27 in *Other Healers: Unorthodox Medicine in America*. Edited by Norman Gevitz. Baltimore: Johns Hopkins University Press, 1988.

Harrell, "Healers." Harrell, David E., Jr. "Healers and Televangelists after World War II." Pages 325–47 in *The Century of the Holy Spirit: One Hundred Years of Pentecostal and Charismatic Renewal, 1901–2001*. Edited by Vinson Synan. Nashville: Thomas Nelson, 2001.

Harrell, *Portrait*. Harrell, David Edwin, Jr. *Pat Robertson: A Personal, Religious, and Political Portrait*. San Francisco: Harper & Row, 1987.

Harrell, *Possible*. Harrell, David Edwin, Jr. *All Things Are Possible: The Healing and Charismatic Revivals in Modern America*. Bloomington: Indiana University Press, 1975.

Harrell, *Robertson*. Harrell, David Edwin, Jr. *Pat Robertson: A Life and a Legacy*. Grand Rapids: Eerdmans, 2010.

Harrelson, *Cult*. Harrelson, Walter. *From Fertility Cult to Worship*. Garden City, N.Y.: Doubleday, 1969.

Harries, "Nature." Harries, Jim. "The Perceived Nature of God in Europe and in Africa: Dealing with 'Difference' in Theology, Focusing on 'Altered States of Consciousness.'" *Missiology* 38 (4, Oct. 2010): 395–409.

Harries, "Worldview." Harries, Jim. "The Magical Worldview in the African Church: What Is Going On?" *Missiology* 28 (4, 2000): 487–502.

Harris, *Acts Today*. Harris, Ralph W. *Acts Today: Signs and Wonders of the Holy Spirit*. Springfield, Mo.: Gospel Publishing House, 1995.

Harris, "Dead." Harris, Murray J. "'The Dead Are Restored to Life': Miracles of Revivification in the Gospels." Pages 295–326 in *The Miracles of Jesus*. Edited by David Wenham and Craig Blomberg. Vol. 6 of *GosPersp*. Sheffield: JSOT Press, 1986.

Harris, "Healing in Wicca." Harris, Grove. "Healing in Feminist Wicca." Pages 253–63 in *Religion and Healing in America*. Edited by Linda L. Barnes and Susan S. Sered. New York: Oxford University Press, 2005.

Harris, "Miracle in Poland." Harris, J. A. "A Gracious Miracle in Poland." *PentEv* 696 (May 7, 1927): 5.

Harris, "Possession Hysteria." Harris, Grace. "Possession 'Hysteria' in a Kenya Tribe." *AmAnth* 59 (6, 1957): 1046–66.

Harris, Edlund, and Larson, "Involvement." Harris, Kathleen M., Mark J. Edlund, and Sharon L. Larson. "Religious Involvement and the Use of Mental Health Care." *HealthSR* 41 (2, 2006): 395–410.

Harris et al., "Trial." Harris, W. S., et al. "A Randomized, Controlled Trial of the Effects of Remote, Intercessory Prayer on Outcomes in Patients Admitted to the Coronary Care Unit." *ArchIntMed* 159 (Oct. 25, 1999): 2273–78.

Harrison, "Descartes." Harrison, Peter. "That René Descartes Originated the Mind-Body Distinction." Pages 107–14 in *Galileo Goes to Jail and Other Myths about Science and Religion*. Edited by Ronald L. Numbers. Cambridge, Mass.: Harvard University Press, 2009.

Harrison, "Miracles." Harrison, Peter. "Miracles, Early Modern Science, and Rational Religion." *CH* 75 (3, Sept. 2006): 493–510.

Harrison, *Riches*. Harrison, Milmon. *Righteous Riches: The Word of Faith Movement in Contemporary African American Religion*. New York: Oxford University Press, 2005.

Harrison et al., "Pain." Harrison, Myleme O., et al. "Religiosity/Spirituality and Pain in Patients with Sickle Cell Disease." *JNMDis* 193 (4, 2005): 250–57.

Hart, *Delusions*. Hart, David Bentley. *Atheist Delusions: The Christian Revolution and Its Fashionable Enemies*. New Haven: Yale University Press, 2009.

Hartley, *Evangelicals*. Hartley, Benjamin L. *Evangelicals at a Crossroads: Revivalism and Social Reform in Boston, 1860–1910*. RNENR. Durham, N.H.:

University of New Hampshire Press; published by University Press of New England, 2011.

Harvey, "Agony." Harvey, John. "The Agony in the Garden: Visions of the 1904 Revival." Pages 129–38 in *Revival, Renewal, and the Holy Spirit*. Edited by Dyfed Wyn Roberts. SEHT. Eugene, Ore.: Wipf & Stock, 2009.

Harvey, *Historian*. Harvey, Van. *The Historian and the Believer*. New York: Macmillan, 1966.

Harvey, *History*. Harvey, A. E. *Jesus and the Constraints of History*. Philadelphia: Westminster, 1982.

Harvey, "Victory." Harvey, Esther B. "Victory . . . Healings . . . Miracles." *PentEv* 1247 (April 2, 1938): 9.

Harwood, *Spiritist*. Harwood, Alan. *Rx: Spiritist as Needed; A Study of a Puerto Rican Community Mental Health Resource*. New York: Wiley, 1977; repr., Ithaca, N.Y.: Cornell University Press, 1987.

Hasel, *Theology*. Hasel, Gerhard F. *New Testament Theology: Basic Issues in the Current Debate*. Grand Rapids: Eerdmans, 1978.

Haught, *Atheism*. Haught, John F. *God and the New Atheism: A Critical Response to Dawkins, Harris, and Hitchens*. Louisville: Westminster John Knox, 2008.

Hausfeld, "Understanding." Hausfeld, Mark. "Islam in America: Understanding and Engaging Diaspora Muslims through the Local Church." JPHWMSM 2. Springfield, Mo.: Assemblies of God Theological Seminary, 2007.

Hawking and Mlodinow, "Theory." Hawking, Stephen, and Leonard Mlodinow. "The Elusive Theory of Everything." *ScAm* 303 (Oct. 2010): 68–71.

Hawking and Penrose, *Space and Time*. Hawking, Stephen, and Roger Penrose. *The Nature of Space and Time*. Princeton, N.J.: Princeton University Press, 1996.

Hawthorne, *Questions*. Hawthorne, J. N. *Questions of Science and Faith*. London: Tyndale, 1960.

Hawthorne, *Windows*. Hawthorne, Tim. *Windows on Science and Faith*. Leicester: Inter-Varsity Press, 1986.

Hay, "Concept." Hay, Eldon. "The Concept of Miracle: A Process Perspective." *Enc* 47 (3, 1986): 183–203.

Hay, "Contranatural View." Hay, Eldon. "A Contranatural View of Miracle." *CJT* 13 (4, 1967): 266–80.

Hay, "View." Hay, Eldon. "Bultmann's View of Miracle." *LQ* 24 (3, 1972): 286–300.

Hayes, "Limits." Hayes, Kelly E. "Caught in the Crossfire: Considering the Limits of Spirit Possession. A Brazilian Case Study." *CulRel* 7 (2, 2006): 155–75.

Hayes, "Mthembu." Hayes, Stephen. "Mthembu, Toitoi Smart." *DACB*. http://www.dacb.org/stories /botswana/mthembu_toitoismart.html.

Hayes, "Responses." Hayes, Stephen. "Christian Responses to Witchcraft and Sorcery." *Missionalia* 23 (3, 1995): 339–54.

"Healed from Trauma." "Healed from the After Effects of a Cranio-cerebral Trauma." *Ten Years of Grace* (2004): 39–41.

"Healed the Scar." "God Healed the Scar on Alexander's Heart." *Ten Years of Grace* (2004): 44–46.

"Healeth: in India." "'I Am the Lord That Healeth Thee.' Healings in India." *PentEv* 523 (Nov. 24, 1923): 18.

"Healing from Side." "Healing from His Wounded Side." *LRE* 13 (1, Oct. 1920): 5.

"Healings among Baptists." "Healings among Baptists." *PentEv* 566 (Oct. 4, 1924): 9, 13.

"Healings at Victoria." "Healings at Victoria, B.C." *PentEv* 513 (Sept. 8, 1923): 9, 15.

"Healing Service." "Healing Service at Canton, Ohio." *PentEv* (Dec. 10, 1921): 26.

"Healings in Australia." "Healings in Australia." *Conf* 129 (April 1922): 27–28.

"Healings in India." "Healings in India." *PentEv* 513 (Sept. 8, 1923): 9.

Heard, *Introduction.* Heard, Richard. *An Introduction to the New Testament.* New York: Harper & Brothers, 1950.

Hearn, "Purpose." Hearn, Walter R. "Evidence of Purpose in the Universe." Pages 57–69 in *Evidence of Purpose: Scientists Discover the Creator.* Edited by John Marks Templeton. New York: Continuum, 1994.

Hebblethwaite and Henderson, *Divine Action.* Hebblethwaite, Brian, and Edward Henderson, eds. *Divine Action: Studies Inspired by the Philosophical Theology of Austin Farrer.* Edinburgh: T&T Clark, 1990.

Hebert, *Raised.* Hebert, Albert J. *Raised from the Dead: True Stories of 400 Resurrection Miracles.* Rockford, Ill.: Tan, 1986.

Hebert, Dang, and Schulz, "Beliefs." Hebert, Randy S., Qianyu Dang, and Richard Schulz. "Religious Beliefs and Practices Are Associated with Better Mental Health in Family Caregivers of Patients with Dementia: Findings from the REACH Study." *AmJGerPsy* 15 (4, April 2007): 292–300.

Hedges, "Prosperity Theology." Hedges, Daniel. "Prosperity Theology." Pages 348–49 in vol. 1 of *Encyclopedia of Religious Revivals in America.* Edited by Michael McClymond. 2 vols. Westport, Conn: Greenwood, 2007.

Hedgespeth, "Power." Hedgespeth, Joanne. "The Healing Power of the Will to Live." Pages 235–48 in *Medical and Therapeutic Events.* Vol. 2 of *Miracles: God, Science, and Psychology in the Paranormal.*

Edited by J. Harold Ellens. Westport, Conn.; London: Praeger, 2008.

Hedrick, "Miracles." Hedrick, Charles W. "Miracles in Mark: A Study in Markan Theology and Its Implications for Modern Religious Thought." *PRSt* 34 (3, 2007): 297–313.

Hedrick, "Stalemate." Hedrick, Charles W. "The Secret Gospel of Mark: Stalemate in the Academy." *JECS* 11 (2, Summer 2003): 133–45.

Hege, *Prayers.* Hege, Nathan B. *Beyond Our Prayers: Anabaptist Church Growth in Ethiopia, 1948–1998.* Scottsdale, Pa.: Herald Press, 1998.

Heidelberger, "Astronomy." Heidelberger, Michael. "Some Intertheoretic Relations between Ptolemean and Copernican Astronomy." Pages 271–83 in *Paradigms and Revolutions: Appraisals and Applications of Thomas Kuhn's Philosophy of Science.* Edited by Gary Gutting. Notre Dame, Ind.: University of Notre Dame Press, 1980.

Heil, "Aspects." Heil, John Paul. "Significant Aspects of the Healing Miracles in Matthew." *CBQ* 41 (1979): 274–87.

Heim, *Transcendent.* Heim, Karl. *God Transcendent: Foundation for a Christian Metaphysic.* 3rd ed. Translated by Edgar Primrose Dickie. Revised by Edwyn Bevan. London: Nisbet, 1935.

Heim, *Transformation.* Heim, Karl. *The Transformation of the Scientific World View.* New York: Harper & Brothers, 1953.

Heimann, "Enlightenment." Heimann, Mary. "Christianity in Western Europe from the Enlightenment." Pages 458–507 in *A World History of Christianity.* Edited by Adrian Hastings. Grand Rapids: Eerdmans, 1999.

Heinrich, "Medicines." Heinrich, Michael. "Herbal and Symbolic Medicines of the Lowland Mixe (Oaxaca, Mexico): Disease Concepts, Healer's Roles, and Plant Use." *Anthropos* 89 (1–3, 1994): 73–83.

Heinze, "Introduction." Heinze, Ruth-Inge. "Introduction." Pages 1–18 in *Proceedings of the Fourth International Conference on the Study of Shamanism and Alternate Modes of Healing, Held at the St. Sabina Center, San Rafael, California, September 5–7, 1987.* Edited by Ruth-Inge Heinze. N.p.: Independent Scholars of Asia; Madison, Wis.: A-R Editions, 1988.

Heinze, *Reform.* Heinze, Rudolph W. *Reform and Conflict: From the Medieval World to the Wars of Religion, A.D. 1350–1648.* Vol. 4 of *The Baker History of the Church.* Grand Rapids: Baker Books, 2005.

Hellestad, "More." Hellestad, Mrs. Oscar. "They That Are with Us Are More Than They That Are with Them." *CGl* 9 (2, April 1932): 16.

Hellestad, "Prayer." Hellestad, Mrs. Oscar. "Prayer Changes Things." *CGl* 12 (2, April 1935): 16–17.

Helm, "Miraculous." Helm, Paul. "The Miraculous." *ScChrB* 3 (1, 1991): 83–95.

Helm et al., "Activity." Helm, Hughes M., Judith C. Hays, Elizabeth P. Flint, Harold G. Koenig, and Dan G. Blazer. "Does Private Religious Activity Prolong Survival? A Six-Year Follow-up Study of 3,851 Older Adults." *JGBSMS* 55 (7, 2000): M400–405.

Helmbrecht, "Leper." Helmbrecht, Anna. "Only a Leper, but—!" *PentEv* 513 (Sept. 8, 1923): 12.

Hemer, *Acts in History*. Hemer, Colin J. *The Book of Acts in the Setting of Hellenistic History*. Edited by Conrad H. Gempf. WUNT 49. Tübingen: Mohr Siebeck, 1989.

Hemer, *Letters*. Hemer, Colin J. *The Letters to the Seven Churches of Asia in Their Local Setting*. JSNTSup 11. Sheffield: Department of Biblical Studies, University of Sheffield, 1986.

Hendricks, *Politics*. Hendricks, Obery M. *The Politics of Jesus: Rediscovering the True Revolutionary Nature of the Teachings of Jesus and How They Have Been Corrupted*. New York: Doubleday, 2006.

Hengel, *Judaism and Hellenism*. Hengel, Martin. *Judaism and Hellenism: Studies in Their Encounter in Palestine During the Early Hellenistic Period*. Translated by John Bowden. 2 vols. Philadelphia: Fortress, 1974.

Hengel, *Mark*. Hengel, Martin. *Studies in the Gospel of Mark*. Translated by John Bowden. Philadelphia: Fortress, 1985.

Hengel and Schwemer, *Between Damascus and Antioch*. Hengel, Martin, and Anna Maria Schwemer. *Paul between Damascus and Antioch: The Unknown Years*. Translated by John Bowden. London: SCM; Louisville: Westminster John Knox, 1997.

Henney, "Belief." Henney, Jeannette H. "Spirit-Possession Belief and Trance Behavior in Two Fundamentalist Groups in St. Vincent." Pages 1–111 in *Trance, Healing, and Hallucination: Three Field Studies in Religious Experience*, by Felicitas D. Goodman, Jeannette H. Henney, and Esther Pressel. New York: John Wiley & Sons, 1974.

Henson, *Notes*. Henson, Herbert Hensley. *Notes on Spiritual Healing*. London: Williams and Norgate, 1925.

Herford, *Christianity*. Herford, R. Travers. *Christianity in Talmud and Midrash*. Library of Philosophical and Religious Thought. Clifton, N.J.: Reference Book Publishers, 1966.

Hermansen, "Healing." Hermansen, Marcia. "Dimensions of Islamic Religious Healing in America." Pages 407–22 in *Religion and Healing in America*. Edited by Linda L. Barnes and Susan S. Sered. New York: Oxford University Press, 2005.

Hernández-Ávila, "Dance Tradition." Hernández-Ávila, Inés. "La Mesa del Santo Niño de Atocha and

the Conchero Dance Tradition of Mexico-Tenochtitlán: Religious Healing in Urban Mexico and the United States." Pages 359–74 in *Religion and Healing in America*. Edited by Linda L. Barnes and Susan S. Sered. New York: Oxford University Press, 2005.

Hernández-Ávila, "Ometeotl Moyocoyatzin." Hernández-Ávila, Inés. "Ometeotl Moyocoyatzin: Nahuatl Spiritual Foundations for Holistic Healing." Pages 127–38 in *Teaching Religion and Healing*. Edited by Linda L. Barnes and Inés Talamantez. AARTRSS. Oxford: Oxford University Press, 2006.

Hernando, "Function." Hernando, James D. "Pneumatological Function in the Narrative of Acts: Drawing Foundational Insight for a Pentecostal Missiology." Pages 241–76 in *Trajectories in the Book of Acts: Essays in Honor of John Wesley Wyckoff*. Edited by Paul Alexander, Jordan Daniel May, and Robert G. Reid. Eugene, Ore.: Wipf & Stock, 2010.

Heron, *Channels*. Heron, Benedict. *Channels of Healing Prayer*. Foreword by Francis MacNutt. Notre Dame, Ind.: Ave Maria, 1992; London: Darton, Longman and Todd, 1989.

Herrick, *Mythologies*. Herrick, James A. *Scientific Mythologies: How Science and Science Fiction Forge New Religious Beliefs*. Downers Grove, Ill.: IVP Academic, 2008.

Herrlich, *Wunderkuren*. Herrlich, Samuel. *Antike Wunderkuren: Beiträge zu ihrer Beurteilung*. Berlin: Weidmann, 1911.

Herskovits, *Life*. Herskovitz, Melville J. *Life in a Haitian Valley*. New York: Doubleday, 1971.

Herum, "Theology." Herum, Nathan M. "Augustine's Theology of the Miraculous." MDiv thesis, Beeson Divinity School, 2009.

Herzog, *Jesus*. Herzog, William R., II. *Jesus, Justice, and the Reign of God: A Ministry of Liberation*. Louisville: Westminster John Knox, 2000.

Hes, "Role." Hes, Jozef Ph. "The Changing Social Role of the Yemenite *Mori*." Pages 364–83 in *Magic, Faith, and Healing: Studies in Primitive Psychiatry Today*. Edited by Ari Kiev. Foreword by Jerome D. Frank. New York: Free Press, 1964.

Hesse, "Language." Hesse, Mary. "Is There an Independent Observation Language?" Pages 35–77 in *The Nature and Function of Scientific Theories: Essays in Contemporary Science and Philosophy*. Edited by Robert G. Colodny. Pittsburgh: University of Pittsburgh Press, 1970.

Hesse, "Miracles." Hesse, Mary. "Miracles and the Laws of Nature." Pages 33–42 in *Miracles: Cambridge Studies in Their Philosophy and History*. Edited by C. F. D. Moule. New York: Morehouse-Barlow, 1965.

Hesselgrave, *Movements*. Hesselgrave, David J. *Dynamic Religious Movements: Case Studies of Rapidly*

Growing Religious Movements Around the World. Grand Rapids: Baker, 1978.

Heth, "Demonization." Heth, William A. "Demonization Then and Now: How Contemporary Cases Fill in the Biblical Data." Paper presented to the Evangelical Theological Society, Washington, D.C., Nov. 16, 2006.

Heth, "Remarriage." Heth, William A. "Remarriage for Adultery or Desertion." Pages 59–83 in *Remarriage after Divorce in Today's Church: Three Views* by Gordon J. Wenham, William A. Heth, and Craig S. Keener. Edited by Mark L. Strauss and Paul E. Engle. Grand Rapids: Zondervan, 2006.

Heth and Wenham, *Divorce.* Heth, William A., and Gordon J. Wenham. *Jesus and Divorce: The Problem with the Evangelical Consensus.* Nashville: Thomas Nelson, 1984.

Heuch, Jacobsen, and Fraser, "Study." Heuch, Ivar, Bjarne K. Jacobsen, and Gary E. Fraser. "A Cohort Study Found That Earlier and Longer Seventh-Day Adventist Church Membership Was Associated with Reduced Male Mortality." *JClinEpid* 58 (1, 2005): 83–91.

Hexham, "Exorcism." Hexham, Irving. "Theology, Exorcism, and the Amplification of Deviancy." *EvQ* 49 (1977): 111–16.

Hexham, "Religion." Hexham, Irving. "Some Aspects of Religion and Spiritual Healing in Cultsville, a Contemporary North American City." Pages 415–29 in *The Church and Healing: Papers Read at the Twentieth Summer Meeting and the Twenty-first Winter Meeting of the Ecclesiastical History Society.* StChHist 19. Edited by W. J. Sheils. Oxford: Basil Blackwell, 1982.

Hexham, "Shembe." Hexham, Irving. "Shembe, Isaiah Mdliwamafa." *DACB.* http://www.dacb.org/stories /southafrica/shembe2_isaiah.html.

Hexham and Poewe, "Churches." Hexham, Irving, and Karla Poewe. "Charismatic Churches in South Africa: A Critique of Criticisms and Problems of Bias." Pages 50–69 in *Charismatic Christianity as a Global Culture.* Edited by Karla Poewe. SCR. Columbia: University of South Carolina Press, 1994.

Heyer, *Jesus Matters.* Heyer, C. J. den. *Jesus Matters: 150 Years of Research.* Valley Forge, Pa.: Trinity Press International, 1997.

Heyob, *Isis.* Heyob, Sharon Kelly. *The Cult of Isis among Women in the Graco-Roman World.* ÉPROER 51. Publiées par M. J. Vermaseren. Leiden: Brill, 1975.

Hiatt, "Vision." Hiatt, Oscar. "Vision and Healing." *WWit* 9 (Jan. 20, 1913): 1.

Hickling, "Portrait in Acts 26." Hickling, C. J. A. "The Portrait of Paul in Acts 26." Pages 499–503 in *Les Actes des Apôtres: Traditions, Rédaction, Théologie.*

Edited by Jacob Kremer. BETL 48. Leuven: Leuven University Press, 1979.

Hickson, *Bridegroom.* Hickson, James Moore. *Behold, the Bridegroom Cometh: Addresses Given at the Services of Healing in Christ Church Westminster 1931 to 1933.* Edited by Sister Constance. London: Methuen & Co., 1937.

Hickson, *Heal.* Hickson, James Moore. *Heal the Sick.* 2nd ed. London: Methuen, 1924.

Hiebert, "Excluded Middle." Hiebert, Paul G. "The Flaw of the Excluded Middle." *Missiology* 10 (1, Jan. 1982): 35–47.

Hiebert, "Power Encounter." Hiebert, Paul. "Power Encounter in Folk Islam." Pages 45–61 in *Muslims and Christians on the Emmaus Road.* Edited by J. Dudley Woodberry. Monrovia, Calif.: MARC, 1989.

Hiebert, *Reflections.* Hiebert, Paul G. *Anthropological Reflections on Missiological Issues.* Grand Rapids: Baker, 1994.

Hien, "Yin Illness." Hien, Nguyen Thi. "Yin Illness: Its Diagnosis and Healing Within Lên Đồng (Spirit Possession) Rituals of the Viêt." *AsEthn* 67 (2, 2008): 305–21.

Hiers, "Satan." Hiers, Richard H. "Satan, Demons, and the Kingdom of God." *SJT* 27 (1, Feb. 1974): 35–47.

Higgins, *Historicity.* Higgins, A. J. B. *The Historicity of the Fourth Gospel.* London: Lutterworth, 1960.

Hilborn, "Glossolalia." Hilborn, David. "Glossolalia as Communication: A Linguistic-Pragmatic Perspective." Pages 111–46 in *Speaking in Tongues: Multi-Disciplinary Perspectives.* Edited by Mark J. Cartledge. SPCI. Waynesboro, Ga.: Paternoster, 2006.

Hill, *Prophecy.* Hill, David. *New Testament Prophecy.* NFTL. Atlanta: John Knox, 1979.

Hill, "Temple of Asclepius." Hill, Andrew E. "The Temple of Asclepius: An Alternative Source for Paul's Body Theology?" *JBL* 99 (3, Sept. 1980): 437–39.

Hill, "Witchcraft." Hill, Harriet. "Witchcraft and the Gospel: Insights from Africa." *Missiology* 24 (3, 1996): 323–44.

Hill, Kopp, and Bollinger, "Measures." Hill, Peter C., Katie J. Kopp, and Richard A. Bollinger. "A Few Good Measures: Assessing Religion and Spirituality in Relation to Health." Pages 25–38 in *Spirit, Science, and Health: How the Spiritual Mind Fuels Physical Wellness.* Edited by Thomas G. Plante and Carl E. Thoresen. Foreword by Albert Bandura. Westport, Conn.: Praeger, 2007.

Hill et al., "Attendance." Hill, Terrence D., Amy M. Burdette, Jacqueline L. Angel, and Ronald J. Angel. "Religious Attendance and Cognitive Functioning among Older Mexican Americans." *JGPSSS* 61 (1, 2006): P3–9.

Hill et al., "Attendance and Mortality." Hill, Terrence D., Jacqueline L. Angel, Christopher G. Ellison, and Ronald J. Angel. "Religious Attendance and Mortality: An 8-Year Follow-up of Older Mexican Americans." *JGPSSS* 60 (2, 2005): S102–9.

Hill et al., "Behaviors." Hill, Terrence D., Amy M. Burdette, Christopher G. Ellison, and Marc A. Musick. "Religious Attendance and the Health Behaviors of Texas Adults." *PrevMed* 42 (4, 2006): 309–12.

Hillerbrand, "Historicity." Hillerbrand, Hans J. "The Historicity of Miracles: The Early Eighteenth-Century Debate among Woolston, Annet, Sherlock, and West." *SR/SR* 3 (2, 1973): 132–51.

Hillgarth, *Paganism*. Hillgarth, J. N. *Christianity and Paganism, 350–750: The Conversion of Western Europe*. Rev. ed. Philadelphia: University of Pennsylvania Press, 1986.

Himmelfarb, "Impurity and Sin." Himmelfarb, Martha. "Impurity and Sin in 4QD, 1QS, and 4Q512." *DSD* 8 (1, 2001): 9–37.

Hinchliff, "Africa." Hinchliff, Peter. "Africa." Pages 455–87 in *The Oxford Illustrated History of Christianity*. Edited by John McManners. Oxford: Oxford University Press, 1990.

Hindle, "Heart." Hindle, Louise. "Missionary's Heart Healed." *PentEv* 647 (May 15, 1926): 10.

Hinn, *Miracle*. Hinn, Benny. *This Is Your Day for a Miracle*. Lake Mary, Fla.: Creation House, 1996.

Hinson, "Healings." Hinson, Gladys. "Healings at the National Children's Home." *PentEv* 1771 (April 17, 1948): 12.

Hirschberg and Barasch, *Recovery*. Hirschberg, Caryle, and Marc Ian Barasch, *Remarkable Recovery: What Extraordinary Healings Tell Us about Getting Well and Staying Well*. New York: Riverhead, 1995.

Hirschfeld and Solar, "Baths." Hirschfeld, Yizhar, and Giora Solar. "Sumptuous Roman Baths Uncovered Near Sea of Galilee: Hot Springs Drew the Afflicted from Around the World." *BAR* 10 (1984): 22–40.

Hirschfeld and Solar, "Hmrhs'wt." Hirschfeld, Yizhar, and Giora Solar. "Hmrhs'wt hrwmyym sl hmtgdr—slws 'wnwt-hpyrh (The Roman Thermae at Hammath-Gader—Three Seasons of Excavations)." *Qad* 13 (1980): 66–70.

Hitchcock and Jones, *Spirit Possession*. Hitchcock, John T., and Rex L. Jones, eds. *Spirit Possession in the Nepal Himalayas*. New Delhi: Vikas, 1976.

Hminga, "Life." Hminga, C. L. "The Life and Witness of Churches in Mizoram." DMiss diss., Fuller Theological Seminary, 1976.

Hoare, "Approach." Hoare, Frank. "A Pastoral Approach to Spirit Possession and Witchcraft Manifestations among the Fijian People." *MissSt* 21 (1, 2004): 113–37.

Hobart, *Performance*. Hobart, Angela. *Healing Performance of Bali: Between Darkness and Light*. New York: Berghahn Books, 2003.

Hobbs, "Miracle Story." Hobbs, Edward C. "Gospel Miracle Story and Modern Miracle Stories." *AThR* Suppl. 3 (1974): 117–26.

Hobson, *Chemistry*. Hobson, J. Allan. *The Chemistry of Conscious States: How the Brain Changes Its Mind*. Boston: Little, Brown, 1994.

Hock, *Miracles*. Hock, Harry D. *Miracles from the Lord*. Harrisburg, Pa.: McFarland, 1966.

Hocken, "Renewal." Hocken, Peter. "The Catholic Charismatic Renewal." Pages 209–32 in *The Century of the Holy Spirit: One Hundred Years of Pentecostal and Charismatic Renewal, 1901–2001*. Edited by Vinson Synan. Nashville: Thomas Nelson, 2001.

Hodges, *Indigenous Church*. Hodges, Melvin L. *The Indigenous Church*. Springfield, Mo.: Gospel Publishing House, 1976.

Hodgson, "Sorcerer." Hodgson, Edmund. "Christ Conquers a Cannibalistic Sorcerer." *PentEv* 1771 (April 17, 1948): 5–14.

Hoff, "Planters." Hoff, Paul. "Church Planters under Construction." *MounM* (Nov. 1991): 6–7.

Hoffman, "Comments." Hoffman, Joshua. "Comments on 'Miracles and the Laws of Nature.'" *FPhil* 2 (4, 1985): 347–52.

Hoffman and Fehl, "Spiritualizing." Hoffman, Louis, and Steve Fehl. "Spiritualizing the Unknown." Pages 194–209 in *Parapsychological Perspectives*. Vol. 3 of *Miracles: God, Science, and Psychology in the Paranormal*. Edited by J. Harold Ellens. Westport, Conn.; London: Praeger, 2008.

Hoffman and Kurzenberger, "Miraculous." Hoffman, Louis, and Marika Kurzenberger. "The Miraculous and Mental Illness." Pages 65–93 in *Parapsychological Perspectives*. Vol. 3 of *Miracles: God, Science, and Psychology in the Paranormal*. Edited by J. Harold Ellens. Westport, Conn.; London: Praeger, 2008.

Hoffman and McGuire, "Miracles." Hoffman, Louis, and Katherine McGuire. "Are Miracles Essential or Peripheral to Faith Traditions?" Pages 221–40 in *Religious and Spiritual Events*. Vol. 1 of *Miracles: God, Science, and Psychology in the Paranormal*. Edited by J. Harold Ellens. Westport, Conn.; London: Praeger, 2008.

Hoffman, Moriarty, and Williamson, "Dynamics." Hoffman, Louis, Glendon L. Moriarty, and Natalie Williamson. "The Dynamics of Religious Experience and Psychological Health: An Existential-Psychodynamic Perspective." Pages 147–70 in *Psychodynamics*. Vol. 3 of *The Healing Power of Spirituality: How Faith Helps Humans Thrive*. Edited by J. Harold Ellens. Santa Barbara, Calif.: Praeger, 2010.

Hoffmeier, *Israel.* Hoffmeier, James K. *Israel in Egypt: The Evidence for the Authenticity of the Exodus Tradition.* Oxford: Oxford University Press, 1997.

Hofmann, "Novels: Christian." Hofmann, Heinz. "Novels: Christian." Pages 846–49 in vol. 9 of *Brill's New Pauly: Encyclopaedia of the Ancient World.* Edited by Hubert Cancik and Helmuth Schneider. 20 vols. English ed. Christine F. Salazar. Leiden: Brill, 2010.

Holder, "Hume." Holder, Rodney D. "Hume on Miracles: Bayesian Interpretation, Multiple Testimony, and the Existence of God." *BJPhilSc* 49 (1, March 1998): 49–65.

Holder, "Revival." Holder, Ralph R. "Revival in China." *PentEv* 1814 (Feb. 12, 1949): 7.

Holladay, *Theios Anēr.* Holladay, Carl R. *Theios Anēr in Hellenistic Judaism: A Critique of the Use of This Category in New Testament Christology.* SBLDS 40. Missoula, Mont.: Scholars Press, 1977.

Hollan, "Culture." Hollan, Douglas. "Culture and Dissociation in Toraja." *TranscPsyc* 37 (2000): 545–59.

Holland, "Miraculous." Holland, R. F. "The Miraculous." Pages 53–69 in *Miracles.* Edited by Richard Swinburne. New York: Macmillan, 1989. See also *AmPhilQ* 2 (1965): 43–51.

Hollenbach, "Demoniacs." Hollenbach, Paul W. "Jesus, Demoniacs, and Public Authorities: A Socio-Historical Study." *JAAR* 49 (1981): 567–88.

Hollenweger, "Azusa Street." Hollenweger, Walter J. "From Azusa Street to the Toronto Phenomenon: Historical Roots of the Pentecostal Movement." Pages 3–14 in *Pentecostal Movements as an Ecumenical Challenge.* Edited by Jürgen Moltmann and Karl-Josef Kuschel. Concilium 3. London: SCM; Maryknoll, N.Y.: Orbis, 1996.

Hollenweger, "Elites." Hollenweger, W. J. "The Pentecostal Elites and the Pentecostal Poor: A Missed Dialogue?" Pages 200–214 in *Charismatic Christianity as a Global Culture.* Edited by Karla Poewe. SCR. Columbia: University of South Carolina Press, 1994.

Hollenweger, *Pentecostals.* Hollenweger, Walter J. *The Pentecostals.* Peabody, Mass.: Hendrickson, 1988.

Holley, "Existence." Holley, Robert W. "I Consider the Existence of God as Unknowable." Pages 179–80 in *Cosmos, Bios, and Theos: Scientists Reflect on Science, God, and the Origins of the Universe, Life, and Homo Sapiens.* Edited by Henry Margenau and Roy Abraham Varghese. La Salle, Ill.: Open Court, 1992.

Höllinger and Smith, "Religion." Höllinger, Franz, and Timothy B. Smith. "Religion and Esotericism among Students: A Cross-Cultural Comparative Study." *JContRel* 17 (2, May 2002): 229–49.

Holm, "Awakening." Holm, Geo. O. "The Awakening in the Churches of Honan and Hupeh." *CGl* 10 (4, Oct. 1933): 7–10.

Holmén and Porter, *Handbook.* Holmén, Tom, and Stanley E. Porter, eds. *Handbook for the Study of the Historical Jesus.* 4 vols. Boston: Brill, 2010.

Holmes, Rabow, and Dibble, "Screening." Holmes, Seth M., Michael W. Rabow, and Suzanne L. Dibble. "Screening the Soul: Communication Regarding Spiritual Concerns among Primary Care Physicians and Seriously Ill Patients Approaching the End of Life." *AmJHPallCare* 23 (1, 2006): 25–33.

Hong, "Mission." Hong, Young-Gi. "Church and Mission: A Pentecostal Perspective." *IntRevMiss* 90 (358, July 2001): 289–308.

Hood, "Mysticism." Hood, Ralph W., Jr. "Mysticism and the Paranormal." Pages 16–37 in *Parapsychological Perspectives.* Vol. 3 of *Miracles: God, Science, and Psychology in the Paranormal.* Edited by J. Harold Ellens. Westport, Conn.; London: Praeger, 2008.

Hood and Byrom, "Mysticism." Hood, Ralph W., Jr., and Greg N. Byrom. "Mysticism, Madness, and Mental Health." Pages 171–91 in *Psychodynamics.* Vol. 3 of *The Healing Power of Spirituality: How Faith Helps Humans Thrive.* Edited by J. Harold Ellens. Santa Barbara, Calif.: Praeger, 2010.

Hopkins, "Status." Hopkins, Jamal-Dominique. "The Authoritative Status of *Jubilees* at Qumran." *Hen* 31 (1, 2009): 97–104.

Horden, "Saints." Horden, Peregrine. "Saints and Doctors in the Early Byzantine Empire: The Case of Theodore of Sykeon." Pages 1–13 in *The Church and Healing: Papers Read at the Twentieth Summer Meeting and the Twenty-first Winter Meeting of the Ecclesiastical History Society.* StChHist 19. Edited by W. J. Sheils. Oxford: Basil Blackwell, 1982.

Hornblower, "Introduction." Hornblower, Simon. "Introduction." Pages 1–72 in *Greek Historiography.* Edited by Simon Hornblower. New York: Oxford University Press, 1994.

Horsley, "Death." Horsley, Richard A. "The Death of Jesus." Pages 395–422 in *Studying the Historical Jesus: Evaluations of the State of Current Research.* NTTS 19. Edited by Bruce Chilton and Craig A. Evans. Leiden: Brill, 1994.

Horsley, *Documents* 1. Horsley, G. H. R., ed. *New Documents Illustrating Early Christianity: A Review of the Greek Inscriptions and Papyri Published in 1976.* Vol. 1. North Ryde, N.S.W.: The Ancient History Documentary Research Center, Macquarie University, 1981.

Horsley, *Documents* 2. Horsley, G. H. R., ed. *New Documents Illustrating Early Christianity: A Review of the Greek Inscriptions and Papyri Published in 1977.* Vol. 2. North Ryde, N.S.W.: The Ancient History Documentary Research Center, Macquarie University, 1982.

Horsley, "Law of Nature." Horsley, Richard A. "The Law of Nature in Philo and Cicero." *HTR* 71 (1–2, 1978): 35–59.

Horsley and Hanson, *Bandits.* Horsley, Richard A, and John S. Hanson. *Bandits, Prophets, and Messiahs: Popular Movements in the Time of Jesus.* Minneapolis: A Seabury Book, Winston Press, 1985.

Hort, "Plagues." Hort, Greta. "The Plagues of Egypt." *ZAW* 69 (1957): 84–103; 70 (1957): 48–59.

Horton, *Corinthians.* Horton, Stanley M. *I and II Corinthians: A Logion Press Commentary.* Springfield, Mo.: Logion, 1999.

Horton, "Possession." Horton, Robin. "Types of Spirit Possession in Kalabari Religion." Pages 14–49 in *Spirit Mediumship and Society in Africa.* Edited by John Beattie and John Middleton. Foreword by Raymond Firth. New York: Africana Publishing Corporation, 1969.

Horwitz et al., "Adherence." Horwitz, R. I., et al. "Treatment Adherence and Risk of Death after a Myocardial Infarction." *Lancet* 336 (1990): 542–45.

Hosack, "Arrival." Hosack, James. "The Arrival of Pentecostals and Charismatics in Thailand." *AJPS* 4 (1, 2001): 109–17.

Hosack, "Church." Hosack, James. "The 'Accidental' Church." *MounM* (March 1989): 6–7.

Houston, *Miracles.* Houston, J. *Reported Miracles: A Critique of Hume.* Cambridge: Cambridge University Press, 1994.

Howard-Snyder, "Case." Howard-Snyder, Daniel. "On Hume's Philosophical Case against Miracles." Pages 395–411 in *God Matters: Readings in the Philosophy of Religion.* Edited by Raymond Martin and Christopher Bernard. New York: Longman, Pearson Education, 2003.

Howson, "Bayesianism." Howson, Colin. "Bayesianism." Pages 103–14 in *The Routledge Companion to Philosophy of Science.* Edited by Stathis Psillos and Martin Curd. New York: Routledge, 2008.

Hruby, "Perspectives Rabbiniques." Hruby, Kurt. "Perspectives Rabbiniques sur le Miracle." Pages 73–94 in *Les Miracles de Jésus selon le Nouveau Testament,* by J.-N. Aletti et al. Edited by Xavier Léon-Dufour. Paris: Éditions du Seuil, 1977.

Huang, "Effects." Huang, Guozhi. "Physiological Effects During Relaxation Qigong Exercise." *Psych Med* 53 (1991): 228.

Hubbard, "Hazarding." Hubbard, David Allan. "Hazarding the Risks." Pages 13–17 in *Signs and Wonders Today: The Story of Fuller Theological Seminary's Remarkable Course on Spiritual Power.* Rev. ed. Edited by C. Peter Wagner. Altamonte Springs, Fla.: Creation House, 1987.

Hudson, "British Pentecostals." Hudson, Neil. "Early British Pentecostals and Their Relationship to Health, Healing, and Medicine." *AJPS* 6 (2, July 2003): 283–301.

Hudson, *Doubts.* Hudson, Charles. *Doubts Concerning the Battle of Bunker's Hill.* Boston/Cambridge: James Munroe and Co., 1857.

Hudson, "Strange Words." Hudson, Neil. "Strange Words and Their Impact on Early Pentecostals: A Historical Perspective." Pages 52–80 in *Speaking in Tongues: Multi-Disciplinary Perspectives.* Edited by Mark J. Cartledge. SPCI. Waynesboro, Ga.: Paternoster, 2006.

Hufford, "Epistemologies." Hufford, David J. "Epistemologies in Religious Healing." *JMedPhil* 18 (1993): 175–94.

Hufford, "Folk Healers." Hufford, David J. "Folk Healers." Pages 306–19 in *Handbook of American Folklore.* Edited by Richard M. Dorson. Bloomington: Indiana University Press, 1983.

Hufford, "Folk Medicine." Hufford, David J. "Contemporary Folk Medicine." Pages 228–64 in *Unorthodox Medicine in America.* Edited by Norman Gevitz. Baltimore: Johns Hopkins University Press, 1988.

Hufford, *Terror.* Hufford, David J. *The Terror That Comes in the Night: An Experience-Centered Study of Supernatural Assault Traditions.* Philadelphia: University of Pennsylvania Press, 1982.

Hughes et al., "Support." Hughes, Joel W., Alisha Tomlinson, J. A. Blumenthal, J. Davidson, M. H. Sketch, and L. L. Watkins. "Social Support and Religiosity as Coping Strategies for Anxiety in Hospitalized Cardiac Patients." *AnnBehMed* 28 (3, 2004): 179–85.

Huguelet et al., "Spirituality." Huguelet, Philippe, Sylvia Mohr, Laurence Borras, Christiane Gillieron, and Pierre-Yves Brandt. "Spirituality and Religious Practices among Outpatients with Schizophrenia and Their Clinicians." *PsychServ* 57 (3, 2006): 366–72.

Hull, *Magic.* Hull, John M. *Hellenistic Magic and the Synoptic Tradition.* SBT, 2nd ser., 28. Naperville, Ill.: Alec R. Allenson, 1974.

Hultgren, "Stories." Hultgren, Arland J. "The Miracle Stories in the Gospels: The Continuing Challenge for Interpreters." *WW* 29 (2, Spring 2009): 129–35.

Hultkrantz, *Healing.* Hultkrantz, Åke. *Shamanic Healing and Ritual Drama: Health and Medicine in Native North American Religious Traditions.* HMFT. New York: Crossroad Herder, 1997. Original copyright, Lutheran General Health System, 1992.

Hume, *Ancestral Power.* Hume, Lynne. *Ancestral Power: The Dreaming, Consciousness, and Aboriginal Australians.* 2nd ed. Edinburgh: T&T Clark, 1998.

Hume, *History of Religion.* Hume, David. *The Natural History of Religion.* Edited by H. E. Root. London: Adam & Charles Black, 1956.

Hume, "Life." Hume, David. "The Life of David Hume, Esq. Written by Himself" (1776). Pages 232–40 in *Hume's Dialogues Concerning Natural Reason.* Edited by Norman Kemp Smith. 2nd ed. New York: Thomas Nelson, 1947.

Hume, *Miracles.* Hume, David. *Of Miracles.* Introduction by Antony Flew. La Salle, Ill.: Open Court, 1985.

Hume, "Miracles." Hume, David. "Of Miracles." Pages 29–44 in *In Defense of Miracles: A Comprehensive Case for God's Action in History.* Edited by R. Douglas Geivett and Gary R. Habermas. Downers Grove, Ill.: InterVarsity, 1997. The same essay (Hume, "Of Miracles") appears (with different pagination) in pages 23–40 in Richard Swinburne, ed., *Miracles* (New York: Macmillan; London: Collier Macmillan, 1989); in pages 68–87 in Robert J. Fogelin, *A Defense of Hume on Miracles* (PrMPhil; Princeton, N.J.: Princeton University, 2003); and in pages 140–57 in John Earman, *Hume's Abject Failure: The Argument Against Miracles* (Oxford: Oxford University, 2000).

Hume, *Works.* Hume, David. *The Philosophical Works of David Hume.* Edited by Thomas Hill Green and Thomas Hodge Grose. 4 vols. London: Longmans, 1886.

Hummel, *Connection.* Hummel, Charles. *The Galileo Connection.* Downers Grove, Ill.: InterVarsity, 1986.

Hunt, "Sociology." Hunt, Stephen. "Sociology of Religion." Pages 179–201 in *Studying Global Pentecostalism: Theories and Methods.* Edited by Allan Anderson, Michael Bergunder, André Droogers, and Cornelis van der Laan. Berkeley: University of California Press, 2010.

Hunter, *Christianity Beyond Belief.* Hunter, Todd D. *Christianity Beyond Belief: Following Jesus for the Sake of Others.* Foreword by Eugene H. Peterson. Downers Grove, Ill.: InterVarsity, 2009.

Hunter, *John.* Hunter, Archibald M. *The Gospel According to John.* CBC. Cambridge: Cambridge University Press, 1965.

Hunter, "Spinoza." Hunter, Graeme. "Spinoza on Miracles." *IJPhilRel* 56 (1, 2004): 41–51.

Hunter, *Theology.* Hunter, A. M. *Introducing New Testament Theology.* London: SCM, 1957.

Hunter, *Work.* Hunter, Archibald M. *The Work and Words of Jesus.* Rev. ed. Philadelphia: Westminster; London: SCM, 1973.

Hunter and Chan, *Protestantism.* Hunter, Alan, and Kim-Kwong Chan. *Protestantism in Contemporary China.* Cambridge: Cambridge University Press, 1993.

Hunter and Linn, "Differences." Hunter, Kathleen I., and Margaret W. Linn. "Psychosocial Differences between Elderly Volunteers and Non-Volunteers." *IJAHD* 12 (1980–81): 205–13.

Huntingford, "Takla." Huntingford, G. W. B. "The Lives of Takla Häymänot." *JEthS* 4 (July 1966): 35–40.

Hurbon, "Pentecostalism." Hurbon, Laënnec. "Pentecostalism and Transnationalisation in the Caribbean." Pages 124–41 in *Between Babel and Pentecost: Transnational Pentecostalism in Africa and Latin America.* Edited by André Corten and Ruth Marshall-Fratani. Bloomington: Indiana University Press, 2001.

Hurreiz, "Zar." Hurreiz, Sayyid. "Zar as a Ritual Psychodrama: From Cult to Club." Pages 147–55 in *Women's Medicine: The Zar-Bori Cult in Africa and Beyond.* Edited by I. M. Lewis, Ahmed Al-Safi, and Sayyid Hurreiz. Edinburgh: International African Institute/Edinburgh University Press, 1991.

Hurst, "Healings." Hurst, Wesley R., Sr. "Jesus' Healings Do Last." *PentEv* (May 19, 1968): 5.

Hurtado, *Become God.* Hurtado, Larry W. *How on Earth Did Jesus Become a God? Historical Questions about Earliest Devotion to Jesus.* Grand Rapids: Eerdmans, 2005.

Hurtado, *Lord Jesus Christ.* Hurtado, Larry W. *Lord Jesus Christ: Devotion to Jesus in Earliest Christianity.* Grand Rapids: Eerdmans, 2003.

Hurtado, *Mark.* Hurtado, Larry W. *Mark.* GNC. San Francisco: Harper & Row, 1983.

Hurtado, *One God.* Hurtado, Larry W. *One God, One Lord: Early Christian Devotion and Ancient Jewish Monotheism.* Philadelphia: Fortress, 1988.

Hutton, "Status." Hutton, Ronald. "The Status of Witchcraft in the Modern World." *Pom* 9 (2, 2007): 121–31.

Huyssen, *Saw.* Huyssen, Chester, and Lucille Huyssen. *I Saw the Lord.* Tarrytown, N.Y.: Chosen, Fleming H. Revell, 1977, 1992.

Hyatt, *Years.* Hyatt, Eddie L. *Two Thousand Years of Charismatic Christianity: A Twentieth-Century Look at Church History from a Pentecostal/Charismatic Perspective.* Foreword by Vinson Synan. Chicota, Tex.: Hyatt International Ministries, 1996.

Hyatt, "Women." Hyatt, Susan C. "Spirit-Filled Women." Pages 233–63 in *The Century of the Holy Spirit: One Hundred Years of Pentecostal and Charismatic Renewal, 1901–2001.* Edited by Vinson Synan. Nashville: Thomas Nelson, 2001.

Ibba, "Spirits." Ibba, Giovanni. "The Evil Spirits in Jubilees and the Spirit of the Bastards in 4Q510 with Some Remarks on Other Qumran Manuscripts." *Hen* 31 (1, 2009): 111–16.

Idler and Kasl, "Religion." Idler, Ellen L., and Stanislav V. Kasl. "Religion among Disabled and Nondisabled Elderly Persons, II: Attendance at Religious Services as a Predictor of the Course of Disability." *JGer* 52B (1997): S306–16.

Ikeobi, "Healing." Ikeobi, Goddy. "Healing and Exorcism: The Nigerian Pastoral Experience." Pages 55–104 in *Healing and Exorcism: The Nigerian Experience. Proceedings, Lectures, Discussions, and Conclusions of the First Missiology Symposium on Healing and Exorcism, Organized by the Spiritan International School of Theology, Attakwu, Enugu, May 18–20, 1989.* Edited by Chris U. Manus, Luke N. Mbefo, and E. E. Uzukwu. Attakwu, Enugu: Spiritan International School of Theology, 1992.

Ikin, *Concepts.* Ikin, Alice Graham. *New Concepts of Healing: Medical, Psychological, and Religious.* Introduction by Wayne E. Oates. New York: Association Press, 1956.

Iler, Obenshain, and Camac, "Impact." Iler, A. L., D. Obenshain, and M. Camac. "The Impact of Daily Visits from Chaplains on Patients with Chronic Obstructive Pulmonary Disease (COPD): A Pilot Study." *ChapT* 17 (2001): 5–11.

Imasogie, *Guidelines.* Imasogie, Osadolor. *Guidelines for Christian Theology in Africa.* 2nd ed. Achimota: Africa Christian, 1993.

Instone-Brewer, "Psychiatrists." Instone-Brewer, David. "Jesus and the Psychiatrists." Pages 133–48 in *The Unseen World: Christian Reflections on Angels, Demons, and the Heavenly Realm.* Edited by Anthony N. S. Lane. Grand Rapids: Baker, 1996.

Inwagen, "Chance." Inwagen, Peter van. "The Place of Chance in a World Sustained by God." Pages 211–35 in *Divine and Human Action: Essays in the Metaphysics of Theism.* Edited by Thomas V. Morris. Ithaca, N.Y.: Cornell University Press, 1988.

Inwood, "Natural Law." Inwood, Brad. "Natural Law in Seneca." *SPhilA* 15 (2003): 81–99.

Ironson et al., "Increase." Ironson, G., R. Stuetzie, and M. A. Fletcher. "An Increase in Religiousness/Spirituality Occurs after HIV Diagnosis and Predicts Slower Disease Progression over Four Years in People with HIV." *JGenIntMed* 21 (2006): S62–68.

Ironson et al., "Spirituality." Ironson, G., G. F. Solomon, E. G. Balbin, et al. "Spirituality and Religiousness Are Associated with Long Survival, Health Behaviors, Less Distress, and Lower Cortisol in People Living with HIV/AIDS: The IWORSHIP Scale, Its Validity and Reliability." *AnnBehMed* 24 (2002): 34–48.

Irvin and Sunquist, *History.* Irvin, Dale T., and Scott W. Sunquist. *History of the World Christian Movement.* Vol. 1: *Earliest Christianity to 1453.* Maryknoll, N.Y.: Orbis, 2001.

Isaacs, "Disorder." Isaacs, T. Craig. "The Possessive States Disorder: The Diagnosis of Demonic Possession." *PastPsy* 35 (4, Summer 1987): 263–73.

Isaacs, *Spirit.* Isaacs, Marie E. *The Concept of Spirit: A Study of Pneuma in Hellenistic Judaism and Its Bearing on the New Testament.* HeyM 1. London: Heythrop College, 1976.

Isbell, *Bowls.* Isbell, Charles D. *Corpus of the Aramaic Incantation Bowls.* SBLDS 17. Missoula, Mont.: Scholars Press, 1975.

Isbell, "Story." Isbell, Charles D. "The Story of the Aramaic Magical Incantation Bowls." *BA* 41 (1, March 1978): 5–16.

Isichei, *History.* Isichei, Elizabeth. *A History of Christianity in Africa from Antiquity to the Present.* Lawrenceville, N.J.: Africa World Press; Grand Rapids: Eerdmans, 1995.

Isichei, "Soul of Fire." Isichei, Elizabeth. "A Soul of Fire." *ChH* 79 (2003): 22–25.

Ising, *Blumhardt.* Ising, Dieter. *Johann Christoph Blumhardt, Life and Work: A New Biography.* Translated by Monty Ledford. Eugene, Ore.: Cascade, 2009. Translated from *Johann Christoph Blumhardt: Leben und Werk.* Göttingen: Vandenhoeck & Ruprecht, 2002.

"Islam and Christianity." "Islam and Christianity in Sub-Saharan Africa." Pew Forum on Religion and Public Life, April 2010. Available at www.pewforum.org.

Itioka, "Umbanda." Itioka, Neuza. "Umbanda in Brazil." Pages 104–16 in *Deliver Us from Evil: An Uneasy Frontier in Christian Mission.* Edited by A. Scott Moreau, Tokunboh Adeyemo, David G. Burnett, Bryant L. Myers, and Hwa Yung. Monrovia, Calif.: Lausanne Committee for World Evangelization, 2002.

Ivey, "Discourses." Ivey, Gavin. "Diabolical Discourses: Demonic Possession and Evil in Modern Psychopathology." *SAJPsyc* 32 (4, Dec. 2002): 54–59.

Jackson, "Back." Jackson, Neels. "Back from the Dead." *News24* (May 27, 2002). http://www.news24.com /News24/Archive/0,,2-1659_1190553,00.html. Accessed June 13, 2009.

Jackson, *Quest.* Jackson, Bill. *The Quest for the Radical Middle: A History of the Vineyard.* Foreword by Todd Hunter. Cape Town: Vineyard International, 1999.

Jackson-McCabe, "Implanted Preconceptions." Jackson-McCabe, Matt. "The Stoic Theory of Implanted Preconceptions." *Phronesis* 49 (4, 2004): 323–47.

Jacob, "Introduction." Jacob, W. Lindsay. "Introduction." Pages xi–xiv in *Kathryn Kuhlman: The Woman Who Believes in Miracles,* by Allen Spraggett. Cleveland, N.Y.: World, 1970.

Jacobs, "Possession." Jacobs, Donald R. "Possession, Trance State, and Exorcism in Two East African Communities." Pages 175–87 in *Demon Possession: A Medical, Historical, Anthropological, and Theological Symposium*. Papers presented at the University of Notre Dame, January 8–11, 1975, under the auspices of the Christian Medical Association. Edited by John Warwick Montgomery. Minneapolis: Bethany House, 1976.

Jacobs, "Rituals." Jacobs, Claude F. "Rituals of Healing in African American Spiritual Churches." Pages 333–41 in *Religion and Healing in America*. Edited by Linda L. Barnes and Susan S. Sered. New York: Oxford University Press, 2005.

Jacobsen, *Thinking in Spirit*. Jacobsen, Douglas. *Thinking in the Spirit: Theologies of the Early Pentecostal Movement*. Bloomington: Indiana University Press, 2003.

Jacquette, "Divinity." Jacquette, Dale. "Zeno of Citium on the Divinity of the Cosmos." *SR/SR* 24 (4, 1995): 415–31.

Jaeger, "Suggestionstherapeut." Jaeger, J. "Ist Jesus Christus ein Suggestionstherapeut gewesen?" *NKZ* 8 (1897): 454–81.

Jaffarian, "Statistical State." Jaffarian, Michael. "The Statistical State of the Missionary Enterprise." *Missiology* 30 (1, Jan. 2000): 15–32.

Jaffe et al., "Neighborhood." Jaffe, D. H., Z. Eisenbach, Y. D. Neumark, and O. Manor. "Does Living in a Religiously Affiliated Neighborhood Lower Mortality?" *AnnEpid* 15 (10, 2005): 804–10.

Jaillard, "Plutarque et divination." Jaillard, Dominique. "Plutarque et la divination: la piété d'un prêtre philosophe." *RHR* 224 (2, 2007): 149–69.

Jaki, *Miracles and Physics*. Jaki, Stanley. *Miracles and Physics*. Front Royal, Va.: Christendom, 1989.

Jaki, "Miracles and Physics." Jaki, Stanley. "Miracles and Physics." *AsTJ* 42 (1, 1987): 5–42.

Jaki, *Patterns*. Jaki, Stanley L. *Patterns or Principles and Other Essays*. Wilmington, Del.: Intercollegiate Studies Institute, 1995.

James, *Varieties*. James, William. *The Varieties of Religious Experience: A Study in Human Nature. Being the Gifford Lectures on Natural Religion Delivered at Edinburgh in 1901–1902*. Enlarged ed. Introduction by Joseph Ratner. New Hyde Park, N.Y.: University Books, 1963.

Jamieson, "Healings." Jamieson, S. A. "Healings That Remain." *LRE* 25 (4, Jan. 1933): 11.

Janney, *Who Goes There?* Janney, Rebecca Price. *Who Goes There? A Cultural History of Heaven and Hell*. Chicago: Moody Press, 2009.

Jansen, "Crucifixes." Jansen, Katherine L. "Miraculous Crucifixes in Late Medieval Italy." Pages 203–27 in *Signs, Wonders, Miracles: Representations of Divine Power in the Life of the Church. Papers Read at the 2003 Summer Meeting and the 2004 Winter Meeting of the Ecclesiastical History Society*. Edited by Kate Cooper and Jeremy Gregory. Rochester: Boydell & Brewer, for the Ecclesiastical History Society, 2005.

Jansen-Winkeln, "Healing Deities." Jansen-Winkeln, Karl. "Healing Deities, Healing Cults: Egypt." Pages 21–22 in vol. 6 of *Brill's New Pauly: Encyclopaedia of the Ancient World*. Edited by Hubert Cancik and Helmuth Schneider. 20 vols. English ed. Christine F. Salazar. Leiden: Brill, 2010.

Jantzen, "Hume." Jantzen, Grace M. "Hume on Miracles, History, and Politics." *CSR* 8 (4, 1979): 318–25.

Jantzen, "Miracles." Jantzen, Grace. "Miracles Reconsidered." *CSR* 9 (4, 1980): 354–58.

Jastrow, *Dictionary*. Jastrow, Marcus. *Dictionary of the Targumim, Talmud Babli, Yerushalmi, and Midrashic Literature*. New York: Judaica Press, 1971.

Jastrow, "Forces." Jastrow, Robert. "What Forces Filled the Universe with Energy Fifteen Billion Years Ago?" Pages 45–49 in *Cosmos, Bios, and Theos: Scientists Reflect on Science, God, and the Origins of the Universe, Life, and* Homo Sapiens. Edited by Henry Margenau and Roy Abraham Varghese. La Salle, Ill.: Open Court, 1992.

Jeffers, *World*. Jeffers, James S. *The Greco-Roman World of the New Testament Era: Exploring the Background of Early Christianity*. Downers Grove, Ill.: InterVarsity, 1999.

Jeffery, *Secret Gospel*. Jeffery, Peter. *The Secret Gospel of Mark Unveiled: Imagined Rituals of Sex, Death, and Madness in a Biblical Forgery*. New Haven: Yale University Press, 2007.

Jeffries, "Healing." Jeffries, M. D. "Miraculous Healing, as Recorded in the Scriptures, and as Claimed Since That Day." *RevExp* 19 (1, Jan. 1922): 64–73.

Jenkins, *New Faces*. Jenkins, Philip. *The New Faces of Christianity: Believing the Bible in the Global South*. New York: Oxford University Press, 2006.

Jenkins, *Next Christendom*. Jenkins, Philip. *The Next Christendom: The Coming of Global Christianity*. New York: Oxford University Press, 2002.

Jenkins, "Reading." Jenkins, Philip. "Reading the Bible in the Global South." *IBMR* 30 (2, April 2006): 67–73.

Jenkins, "Reindorf." Jenkins, Paul. "Reindorf, Carl Christian." *DACB*. http://www.dacb.org/stories/ghana/reindorf2_carl.html.

Jenkins, "South Africa." Jenkins, Eleazar, and Lizzie Ann Jenkins. "South Africa." *Conf* 4 (Jan. 1911): 18.

Jensen, "Calvin." Jensen, Peter F. "Calvin, Charismatics, and Miracles." *EvQ* 51 (3, 1979): 131–44.

Jensen, "Logic." Jensen, Dennis. "The Logic of Miracles." *JASA* 33 (3, Sept. 1981): 145–53.

Jensen, "Risk." Jensen, O. M. "Cancer Risk among Danish Male Seventh-Day Adventists and Other Temperance Society Members." *JNatCInst* 70 (1983): 1011–14.

Jeremias, *Sermon*. Jeremias, Joachim. *The Sermon on the Mount*. Translated by Norman Perrin. Philadelphia: Fortress, 1963.

Jeremias, *Theology*. Jeremias, Joachim. *New Testament Theology*. New York: Charles Scribner's Sons, 1971.

Jervell, *Apostelgeschichte*. Jervell, Jacob. *Die Apostelgeschichte*. KEKNT 17. Göttingen: Vandenhoeck & Ruprecht, 1998.

Jervell, "Paul in Acts: Theology." Jervell, Jacob. "Paul in the Acts of the Apostles: Tradition, History, Theology." Pages 297–306 in *Les Actes des Apôtres: Traditions, Rédaction, Théologie*. Edited by Jacob Kremer. BETL 48. Leuven: Leuven University Press, 1979.

Jervell, *Unknown Paul*. Jervell, Jacob. *The Unknown Paul: Essays on Luke-Acts and Early Christian History*. Partly translated by Roy A. Harrisville. Minneapolis: Augsburg, 1984.

Jervis, "Law." Jervis, L. Ann. "Law/Nomos in Greco-Roman World." Pages 631–36 in *DNTB*.

Jessup, "Healings." Jessup, E. W. "Remarkable Healings in Hattiesburg, Miss." *PentEv* 368–369 (Nov. 27, 1920): 2.

Jewett, *Romans*. Jewett, Robert. *Romans: A Commentary*. Assisted by Roy D. Kotansky. Edited by Eldon Jay Epp. Hermeneia. Minneapolis: Fortress, 2007.

Jewsiewicki, "Belgian Africa." Jewsiewicki, B. "Belgian Africa." Pages 460–93 in *From 1905–1940*. Edited by A. D. Roberts. Vol. 7 of *The Cambridge History of Africa*. Edited by J. D. Fage and Roland Oliver. 8 vols. Cambridge: Cambridge University Press, 1986.

Jilek, "Brainwashing." Jilek, Wolfgang. "Brainwashing as a Therapeutic Technique in Contemporary Canadian Indian Spirit Dancing: A Case of Theory-Building." Pages 201–13 in *Anthropology and Mental Health*. Edited by Joseph Westermeyer. The Hague: Mouton, 1976.

Jilek, "Therapeutic Use." Jilek, Wolfgang G. "Therapeutic Use of Altered States of Consciousness in Contemporary North American Indian Dance Ceremonials." Pages 167–85 in *Altered States of Consciousness and Mental Health: A Cross-Cultural Perspective*. Edited by Colleen A. Ward. CCRMS 12. Newbury Park, Calif.: Sage, 1989.

Jochim, *Religions*. Jochim, Christian. *Chinese Religions: A Cultural Perspective*. Prentice-Hall Series in World Religions. Englewood Cliffs, N.J.: Prentice-Hall, 1986.

Johns, "Healing." Johns, Cheryl Bridges. "Healing and Deliverance: A Pentecostal Perspective." Pages 45–51 in *Pentecostal Movements as an Ecumenical Challenge*. Edited by Jürgen Moltmann and Karl-Josef Kuschel. Concilium 3. London: SCM; Maryknoll, N.Y.: Orbis, 1996.

Johns, "Name." Johns, Greg. "His Name Can Heal You!" *MounM* (June 1995): 8–9.

Johns, "Results." Johns, Mr. and Mrs. H. J. "Results of Faithful Witnessing in Hawaii: Healings of Leprosy and Incurable Diseases." *LRE* 9 (May 1917): 10–11.

Johns and Miller, "Signs." Johns, L. L., and D. B. Miller. "The Signs as Witnesses in the Fourth Gospel: Reexamining the Evidence." *CBQ* 56 (3, 1994): 519–35.

Johnson, *Acts*. Johnson, Luke Timothy. *The Acts of the Apostles*. SP 5. Collegeville, Minn.: Liturgical Press, 1992.

Johnson, "Alone." Johnson, Gerald. "Alone in the Mountains." *MounM* (Nov. 1995): 20–21.

Johnson, "Authority." Johnson, Harmon A. "Authority over the Spirits: Brazilian Spiritism and Evangelical Church Growth." MA thesis, Fuller Theological Seminary, May 1969.

Johnson, "Growing Church." Johnson, Harmon A. "The Growing Church in Haiti." Coral Gables, Fla.: West Indies Mission, 1970.

Johnson, *Heaven*. Johnson, Bill. *When Heaven Invades Earth: A Practical Guide to a Life of Miracles*. Forewords by Jack Taylor and Randy Clark. Shippensburg, Pa.: Destiny Image, 2003.

Johnson, *History*. Johnson, David M. *Led by the Spirit: The History of the American Assemblies of God Missionaries in the Philippines*. Foreword by L. John Bueno. Manila: ICI Ministries, 2009.

Johnson, *Hume*. Johnson, David. *Hume, Holism, and Miracles*. CSPhilRel. Ithaca, N.Y.: Cornell University Press, 1999.

Johnson, "Impact." Johnson, Byron R. "Assessing the Impact of Religious Programs and Prison Industry on Recidivism: An Exploratory Study." *TexJC* 28 (Feb. 2002): 7–11.

Johnson, "Luke-Acts." Johnson, Luke Timothy. "Luke-Acts, Book of." Pages 403–20 in vol. 4 of *ABD*.

Johnson, *Mind*. Johnson, Bill. *The Supernatural Power of a Transformed Mind: Access to a Life of Miracles*. Shippensburg, Pa.: Destiny Image, 2005.

Johnson, "Miracles and History." Johnson, William. "Miracles and History." *PTR* 8 (4, Oct. 1910): 529–59.

Johnson, "Model." Johnson, Willard. "A Multidimensional Model to Interpret Shamanistic and Other Attention Shifting Dissociative States." Pages 19–30 in *Proceedings of the Fourth International Conference on the Study of Shamanism and Alternate Modes of*

Healing, Held at the St. Sabina Center, San Rafael, California, September 5–7, 1987. Edited by Ruth-Inge Heinze. N.p.: Independent Scholars of Asia; Madison, Wis.: A-R Editions, 1988.

Johnson, "Neurotheology." Johnson, Ron. "Neurotheology: The Interface of Neuropsychology and Theology." Pages 207–29 in *Psychodynamics*. Vol. 3 of *The Healing Power of Spirituality: How Faith Helps Humans Thrive*. Edited by J. Harold Ellens. Santa Barbara, Calif.: Praeger, 2010.

Johnson, "Possession." Johnson, Walter C. "Demon Possession and Mental Illness." *JASA* 34 (3, 1982): 149–54.

Johnson, "Psychotherapy." Johnson, Ron. "The Miracle of Psychotherapy." Pages 187–93 in *Parapsychological Perspectives*. Vol. 3 of *Miracles: God, Science, and Psychology in the Paranormal*. Edited by J. Harold Ellens. Westport, Conn.; London: Praeger, 2008.

Johnson, "Work." Johnson, Bernhard. "A Pure and Lasting Work." *MounM* (May 1993): 11.

Johnson, Barrett, and Crossing, "Christianity 2010." Johnson, Todd M., David B. Barrett, and Peter F. Crossing. "Christianity 2010: A View from the *New Atlas of Global Christianity*." *IBMR* 34 (1, Jan. 2010): 29–36.

Johnson, Elbert-Avila, and Tulsky, "Influence." Johnson, K. S., K. I. Elbert-Avila, and J. A. Tulsky. "The Influence of Spiritual Beliefs and Practices on the Treatment Preferences of African-Americans: A Review of the Literature." *JAmGerAss* 53 (2005): 711–19.

Johnson, Larson, and Pitts, "Programs." Johnson, Byron R., D. B. Larson, and T. C. Pitts. "Religious Programs, Institutional Adjustment, and Recidivism Among Former Inmates in Prison Fellowship Programs." *Justice Quarterly* 14 (1, March 1997): 145–66.

Johnson and Butzen, "Prayer." Johnson, Judith L., and Nathan D. Butzen. "Intercessory Prayer, Group Psychology, and Medical Healing." Pages 249–61 in *Medical and Therapeutic Events*. Vol. 2 of *Miracles: God, Science, and Psychology in the Paranormal*. Edited by J. Harold Ellens. Westport, Conn.; London: Praeger, 2008.

Johnson and Keller, "Possession." Johnson, Paul Christopher, and Mary Keller. "The Word of Possession(s)." *CulRel* 7 (2, 2006): 111–22.

Johnson and Ross, *Atlas*. Johnson, Todd M., and Kenneth R. Ross, eds. *Atlas of Global Christianity, 1910–2010*. Managing editor, Sandra S. K. Lee. Edinburgh: Center for the Study of Global Christianity, 2009.

Johnston, *Baxter*. Johnston, E. A. *J. Sidlow Baxter: A Heart Awake: The Authorized Biography*. Grand Rapids: Baker Books, 2005.

Johnston, "Ordination." Johnston, Flo. "Ordination Will Cross Racial Lines." *The Chicago Tribune* (Aug. 9, 1991): section 2, 9.

Johnston, "Rain." Johnston, Bill. "Miracle Rain." *MounM* (Jan. 1996): 29.

Johnston, "Version." Johnston, Edwin D. "The Johannine Version of the Feeding of the Five Thousand—An Independent Tradition?" *NTS* 8 (2, January 1962): 151–54.

Johnstone, "Intercession." Johnstone, Patrick. "Biblical Intercession: Spiritual Power to Change Our World." Pages 137–63 in *Spiritual Power and Missions: Raising the Issues*. Edited by Edward Rommen. EvMissSS 3. Pasadena, Calif.: William Carey Library, 1995.

Johnstone and Mandryk, *Operation World*. Johnstone, Patrick, and Jason Mandryk, with Robyn Johnstone. *Operation World*. 6th ed. Waynesboro, Ga.; Carlisle: Paternoster, 2001.

Jonas and Crawford, "Presence." Jonas, Wayne B., and Cindy C. Crawford. "The Healing Presence: Can It Be Reliably Measured?" *JAlComMed* 10 (2004): 751–56.

Jonas and Fischer, "Management." Jonas, Eva, and Peter Fischer. "Terror Management and Religion: Evidence That Intrinsic Religiousness Mitigates Worldview Defense Following Mortality Salience." *JPerSocPsy* 91 (3, 2006): 553–67.

Jones, "Fire." Jones, Arun. "Playing with Fire." Pages 209–24 in *A New Day: Essays on World Christianity in Honor of Lamin Sanneh*. Edited by Akintunde E. Akinade. Foreword by Andrew F. Walls. New York: Peter Lang, 2010.

Jones, *Hobbes to Hume*. Jones, W. T. *Hobbes to Hume: A History of Western Philosophy*. 2nd ed. New York: Harcourt, Brace, 1969.

Jones, *Kings*. Jones, Gwilyn H. *1 and 2 Kings*. Vol. 2: *1 Kings 17:1–2 Kings 25:30*. NCBC. Grand Rapids: Eerdmans; London: Marshall, Morgan & Scott, 1984.

Jones, "Passage." Jones, C. P. "Apollonius of Tyana's Passage to India." *GRBS* 42 (2, 2001): 185–99.

Jones, "Rumors." Jones, Timothy. "Rumors of Angels?" *CT* (April 5, 1993): 18–22.

Jones, *Wonders*. Jones, Philip Hanson. *Wonders, Signs, Miracles … Why Not? Tales of a Missionary in China*. New York: Exposition Press, 1966.

Jones and Jones, *Women*. Jones, Violet Rhoda, and L. Bevan Jones. *Women in Islam*. Lucknow: Lucknow Publishing House, 1941.

Joos, "Emergence." Joos, Erich. "The Emergence of Classicality from Quantum Theory." Pages 53–78 in *The Re-Emergence of Emergence: The Emergentist Hypothesis from Science to Religion*. Edited by Philip

Clayton and Paul Davies. Oxford: Oxford University Press, 2006.

Jordan, "Classification." Jordan, G. J. "The Classification of the Miracles." *ExpT* 46 (1934–35): 310–16.

Jordan, *Egypt*. Jordan, Paul. *Egypt the Black Land*. Oxford: Phaidon; New York: E. P. Dutton, 1976.

Jordan, "Erotic Spell." Jordan, David R. "P.Duk.inv. 230, an Erotic Spell." *GRBS* 40 (2, 1999): 159–70.

Jordan, "New Curse Tablets." Jordan, David R. "New Greek Curse Tablets (1985–2000)." *GRBS* 41 (1, 2000): 5–46.

Jörgensen, *Francis*. Jörgensen, Johannes. *St. Francis of Assisi: A Biography*. Translated by T. O'Conor Sloane. Garden City, N.Y.: Image Books, Doubleday, 1955.

Josephson, "Conflict." Josephson, B. D. "There Need Be No Ultimate Conflict between Science and Religion." Page 50 in *Cosmos, Bios, and Theos: Scientists Reflect on Science, God, and the Origins of the Universe, Life, and Homo Sapiens*. Edited by Henry Margenau and Roy Abraham Varghese. La Salle, Ill.: Open Court, 1992.

Joshua, "Pentecostalism in Vietnam." Joshua (pseudonym). "Pentecostalism in Vietnam: A History of the Assemblies of God." *AJPS* 4 (2, 2001): 307–26.

Joubert, "Perspective." Joubert, Nicolene. "An African Perspective on Miracles." Pages 117–38 in *Parapsychological Perspectives*. Vol. 3 of *Miracles: God, Science, and Psychology in the Paranormal*. Edited by J. Harold Ellens. Westport, Conn.; London: Praeger, 2008.

Joubert, "Spirituality." Joubert, Nicolene. "How Christian Spirituality Spurs Mental Health." Pages 238–66 in *Religion*. Vol. 2 of *The Healing Power of Spirituality: How Faith Helps Humans Thrive*. Edited by J. Harold Ellens. Santa Barbara, Calif.: Praeger, 2010.

Judge, *Athens*. Judge, Edwin A. *Jerusalem and Athens: Cultural Transformation in Late Antiquity*. Edited by Alanna Nobbs. Tübingen: Mohr Siebeck, 2010.

Judge, *First Christians*. Judge, Edwin A. *The First Christians in the Roman World: Augustan and New Testament Essays*. Edited by James R. Harrison. WUNT 229. Tübingen: Mohr Siebeck, 2008.

Juel, *Messiah and Temple*. Juel, Donald. *Messiah and Temple: The Trial of Jesus in the Gospel of Mark*. SBLDS 31. Missoula, Mont.: Scholars Press, 1977.

Jules-Rosette, "Healers." Jules-Rosette, Bennetta. "Faith Healers and Folk Healers: The Symbolism and Practice of Indigenous Therapy in Urban Africa." *Religion* 11 (1981): 127–49.

Jules-Rosette, "Spirituality." Jules-Rosette, Bennetta. "Creative Spirituality from Africa to America: Cross-Cultural Influences in Contemporary Religious Forms." *WJBlSt* 4 (4, Winter 1980): 273–85.

Jumbo, "Healed." Jumbo, Henderson E. S. "God Healed My Broken Spine." *Living Testimonies* (Oct. 2000): 5–18.

Jung, "Symbolic Life." Jung, Carl G. *The Symbolic Life*. Vol. 18 of *The Collected Works of C. G. Jung*. 20 vols. Princeton, N.J.: Princeton University Press, 1977.

Kabat-Zinn et al., "Influence." Kabat-Zinn, J., et al. "Influence of a Mindfulness Meditation-Based Stress Reduction Intervention on Rates of Skin Clearing in Patients with Moderate to Severe Psoriasis Undergoing Phototherapy (UVB) and Photochemotherapy (PUVA)." *PsychMed* 60 (5, 1998): 625–32.

Kadetotad, "Practices." Kadetotad, N. K. "Religious Practices of a Mysore Village." Pages 379–87 in *The Realm of the Extra-Human: Ideas and Actions*. Edited by Agehananda Bharati. The Hague: Mouton, 1976.

Kahakwa, "Theology." Kahakwa, Sylvester B. "Theology of Ancestors from African Perspective." *AfThJ* 30 (1, 2007): 4–25.

Kahana, "Zar Spirits." Kahana, Yael. "The Zar Spirits, a Category of Magic in the System of Mental Health Care in Ethiopia." *IJSocPsyc* 31 (Summer 1985): 125–43.

Kahl, *Miracle Stories*. Kahl, Werner. *New Testament Miracle Stories in Their Religious-Historical Setting: A Religionsgeschichtliche Comparison from a Structural Perspective*. Göttingen: Vandenhoeck & Ruprecht, 1994.

Kahl, "Überlegungen." Kahl, Werner. "Überlegungen zu einer interkulturellen Verständigung über Neutestamentliche Wunder." *ZMR* 82 (2, 1998): 98–106.

Kaiser, "Complementarity." Kaiser, Christopher B. "Quantum Complementarity and Christological Dialectic." Pages 291–98 in *Religion and Science: History, Method, Dialogue*. Edited by W. Mark Richardson and Wesley J. Wildman. Foreword by Ian G. Barbour. New York: Routledge, 1996.

Kaiser, "Pantheon." Kaiser, Walter C., Jr. "The Ugaritic Pantheon." PhD diss., Brandeis University Department of Mediterranean Studies, 1973.

Kallas, *Significance*. Kallas, James. *The Significance of the Synoptic Miracles*. London: SPCK, 1961.

Kallas, *View*. Kallas, James. *The Satanward View: A Study in Pauline Theology*. Philadelphia: Westminster, 1966.

Kalu, "Afraid." Kalu, Ogbu U. "'Who Is Afraid of the Holy Ghost?' Presbyterians and the Charismatic Movement in Nigeria, 1966–1996." *Missionalia* 35 (3, Nov. 2007): 5–29.

Kalu, *African Pentecostalism*. Kalu, Ogbu. *African Pentecostalism: An Introduction*. Oxford: Oxford University Press, 2008.

Kalu, "Lijadu." Kalu, Ogbu U. "Lijadu, Emmanuel Moses." *DACB*. http://www.dacb.org/stories /nigeria/lijadu2_emmanuel.html.

Kalu, "Mission." Kalu, Ogbu U. "Pentecostalism and Mission in Africa, 1970–2000." *MissSt* 24 (2007): 9–45.

Kamen, *Inquisition*. Kamen, Henry. *The Spanish Inquisition: A Historical Revision*. New Haven: Yale University Press, 1998.

Kamsteeg, "Healing." Kamsteeg, Frans H. "Pentecostal Healing and Power: A Peruvian Case." Pages 196–218 in *Popular Power in Latin American Religions*. Edited by André Droogers, Gerrit Huizer, and Hans Siebers. Saarbrücken: Verlag Breitenbach, 1991.

Kamsteeg, "Message." Kamsteeg, Frans H. "The Message and the People—The Different Meanings of a Pentecostal Evangelistic Campaign: A Case from Southern Peru." Pages 127–44 in *The Popular Use of Popular Religion in Latin America*. Edited by Susanna Rostas and André Droogers. Amsterdam: CEDLA, 1993.

Kamsteeg, *Pentecostalism*. Kamsteeg, Frans H. *Prophetic Pentecostalism in Chile: A Case Study on Religion and Development Policy*. StEv 15. Lanham, Md.: Scarecrow, 1998.

Kanda, "Form." Kanda, Shigeo Harold. "The Form and Function of the Petrine and Pauline Miracle Stories in the Acts of the Apostles." PhD diss., Claremont Graduate School, 1973.

Kane, *Growth*. Kane, J. Herbert. *Twofold Growth*. Philadelphia: China Inland Mission, 1947.

Kang, "Resources." Kang, Chang-soo. "Resources for Studies of David Yonggi Cho." Pages 273–302 in *David Yonggi Cho: A Close Look at His Theology and Ministry*. Edited by Wonsuk Ma, William W. Menzies, and Hyeon-sung Bae. AJPSS 1. Baguio City, Philippines: APTS Press, Hansei University Press, 2004.

Kang, "World." Kang, Namsoon. "*Whose/Which* World in *World Christianity*? Toward *World Christianity* as Christianity of *Worldly-Responsibility*." Pages 31–48 in *A New Day: Essays on World Christianity in Honor of Lamin Sanneh*. Edited by Akintunde E. Akinade. Foreword by Andrew F. Walls. New York: Peter Lang, 2010.

Kant, Immanuel. *Observations on the Feeling of the Beautiful and the Sublime*. Berkeley: University of California Press, 1991.

Kantel, "Revival." Kantel, Donald R. "The 'Toronto Blessing' Revival and Its Continuing Impact on Mission in Mozambique." DMin diss., Regent University, 2007.

Kao, *Tales*. Kao, Karl S. Y., ed. *Classical Chinese Tales of the Supernatural and the Fantastic Selections from*

the Third to the Tenth Century. Bloomington: Indiana University Press, 1985.

Kapferer, *Exorcism*. Kapferer, Bruce. *A Celebration of Demons: Exorcism and the Aesthetics of Healing in Sri Lanka*. 2nd ed. Oxford: Berg Publishers, 1991.

Kaplan, Schwartz, and Jones, "View." Kaplan, Kalman J., Matthew B. Schwartz, and Elizabeth Recht Jones. "A Biblical View of Health, Sickness, and Healing: Overcoming the Traditional Greek View of Medicine." Pages 230–42 in *Psychodynamics*. Vol. 3 of *The Healing Power of Spirituality: How Faith Helps Humans Thrive*. Edited by J. Harold Ellens. Santa Barbara, Calif.: Praeger, 2010.

Kaplan and Johnson, "Navajo Psychopathology." Kaplan, Bert, and Dale Johnson. "The Social Meaning of Navajo Psychopathology and Psychotherapy." Pages 203–29 in *Magic, Faith, and Healing: Studies in Primitive Psychiatry Today*. Edited by Ari Kiev. Foreword by Jerome D. Frank. New York: Free Press, 1964.

Kaplan and Sadock, *Psychiatry*. Kaplan, Harold I., and Benjamin J. Sadock. *Comprehensive Textbook of Psychiatry*. 4th ed. Baltimore: Williams & Wilkins, 1985.

Kapolyo, *Condition*. Kapolyo, Joe M. *The Human Condition: Christian Perspectives through African Eyes*. Downers Grove, Ill.: InterVarsity, 2005.

Kareem, "Attitude." Kareem, M. A. "The Attitude of Nigerian Muslims to Traditional Medicine." Pages 76–82 in *Religion, Medicine, and Healing*. Edited by Gbola Aderibigbe and Deji Ayegboyin. Lagos: Nigerian Association for the Study of Religions and Education, 1995.

Karle, "No Way." Karle, Jerome. "I Have No Way of Knowing Whether God Exists." Pages 181–83 in *Cosmos, Bios, and Theos: Scientists Reflect on Science, God, and the Origins of the Universe, Life, and Homo Sapiens*. Edited by Henry Margenau and Roy Abraham Varghese. La Salle, Ill.: Open Court, 1992.

Karnofsky, "Vision." Karnofsky, E. S. "The Vision of Tainard, *miraculum de quodam canonico Guatenensi per Sanctum Donatianum curato*." Pages 15–24 in *The Church and Healing: Papers Read at the Twentieth Summer Meeting and the Twenty-first Winter Meeting of the Ecclesiastical History Society*. StChHist 19. Edited by W. J. Sheils. Oxford: Basil Blackwell, 1982.

Karris, *Saying*. Karris, Robert J. *What Are They Saying about Luke and Acts? A Theology of the Faithful God*. New York: Paulist Press, 1979.

Kasher, "Miracles." Kasher, Rimon. "Miracles in the Bible" (in Hebrew). *BMik* 104 (1985): 40–58. (RTA)

Kassimir, "Politics." Kassimir, Ronald. "The Politics of Popular Catholicism in Uganda." Pages 248–74 in *East African Expressions of Christianity*. Edited by Thomas Spear and Isaria N. Kimambo. EAfSt.

Athens: Ohio University Press; Oxford: James Currey; Dar es Salaam: Mkuki na Nyota; Nairobi: East African Educational Publishers, 1999.

Kasten, "Shamanism." Kasten, Erich. "Sami Shamanism: Variations of a Religious Concept under the Impact of Culture Contact." Pages 64–69 in *Proceedings of the Fourth International Conference on the Study of Shamanism and Alternate Modes of Healing, Held at the St. Sabina Center, San Rafael, California, September 5–7, 1987.* Edited by Ruth-Inge Heinze. N.p.: Independent Scholars of Asia; Madison, Wis.: A-R Editions, 1988.

Kasule, "Possession." Kasule, Sam. "Possession, Trance, Ritual, and Popular Performance: The Transformation of Theater in Post-Idi Amin Uganda." Pages 295–317 in *Studies in Witchcraft, Magic, War, and Peace in Africa.* Edited by Beatrice Nicolini. Lewiston, N.Y.: Edwin Mellen, 2006.

Katz, *Energy.* Katz, Richard. *Boiling Energy: Community Healing among the Kalahari Kung.* Cambridge, Mass.: Harvard University Press, 1982.

Katz, "Healing." Katz, Richard. "Healing and Transformation: Perspectives from !Kung Hunter-Gatherers." Pages 207–27 in *Altered States of Consciousness and Mental Health: A Cross-Cultural Perspective.* Edited by Colleen A. Ward. CCRMS 12. Newbury Park, Calif.: Sage, 1989.

Kauffman, "Introduction." Kauffman, Richard A. "Introduction." Pages 6–9 in *Essays on Spiritual Bondage and Deliverance.* Edited by Willard M. Swartley. Occasional Papers 11. Elkhart, Ind.: Institute of Mennonite Studies, 1988.

Kauffman, "Representations." Kauffman, Gerald. "Representations of God and the Devil: A Psychiatric Perspective from Object Relations Theory." Pages 150–62 in *Essays on Spiritual Bondage and Deliverance.* Edited by Willard M. Swartley. Occasional Papers 11. Elkhart, Ind.: Institute of Mennonite Studies, 1988.

Kaufman et al., "Decline." Kaufman, Yakir, David Anaki, Malcolm Binns, and Morris Freedman. "Cognitive Decline in Alzheimer's Disease: Impact of Spirituality, Religiosity, and QOL." *Neurology* 68 (2007): 1509–14.

Kay, *Networks.* Kay, William K. *Apostolic Networks in Britain: New Ways of Being Church.* Studies in Evangelical History and Thought. Carlisle: Paternoster, 2007.

Kay, *Pentecostalism.* Kay, William K. *Pentecostalism.* SCM Core Text. London: SCM, 2009.

Kay, *Pentecostals.* Kay, William K. *Pentecostals in Britain.* Carlisle: Paternoster, 2000.

Kay and Parry, *Exorcism.* Kay, William K., and Robin Parry, eds. *Exorcism and Deliverance: Multi-Disciplinary Perspectives.* Milton Keynes, UK: Paternoster, forthcoming.

Kee, "Aretalogy." Kee, Howard Clark. "Aretalogy and Gospel." *JBL* 92 (3, Sept. 1973): 402–22.

Kee, "Hippocratic Letters." Kee, Howard Clark. "Hippocratic Letters." Pages 498–99 in *DNTB.*

Kee, *Miracle.* Kee, Howard Clark. *Miracle in the Early Christian World: A Study in Sociohistorical Method.* New Haven: Yale University Press, 1983.

Kee, *Origins.* Kee, Howard Clark. *Christian Origins in Sociological Perspective: Methods and Resources.* Philadelphia: Westminster, 1980.

Kee, "Quests." Kee, Howard Clark. "A Century of Quests for the Culturally Compatible Jesus." *ThTo* 52 (1, 1995): 17–28.

Kee, "Self-Definition." Kee, Howard Clark. "Self-Definition in the Asclepius Cult." Pages 118–36 in *Self-Definition in the Greco-Roman World* (1982). Edited by Ben F. Meyer and E. P. Sanders. Vol. 3 of *Jewish and Christian Self-Definition.* Edited by E. P. Sanders. 3 vols. Philadelphia: Fortress, 1980–82.

Kee, "Terminology." Kee, Howard Clark. "The Terminology of Mark's Exorcism Stories." *NTS* 14 (2, Jan. 1968): 232–46.

Keene, "Possibility of Miracles." Keene, J. Calvin. "The Possibility of Miracles." *CrQ* 26 (3, July 1949): 208–14.

Keener, *Acts.* Keener, Craig S. *Acts: An Exegetical Commentary.* 4 vols. Grand Rapids: Baker Academic, forthcoming.

Keener, "Acts 2:1–21." Keener, Craig S. "Day of Pentecost, Years A, B, C. First Lesson: Acts 2:1–21." Pages 524–28 in *The First Readings: The Old Testament and Acts.* Vol. 1 of *The Lectionary Commentary: Theological Exegesis for Sunday's Texts.* Edited by Roger E. Van Harn. 3 vols. Grand Rapids: Eerdmans; London: Continuum, 2001.

Keener, "Asia." Keener, Craig S. "Between Asia and Europe: Postcolonial Mission in Acts 16:8–10." *AJPS* 11 (1–2, 2008): 3–14.

Keener, "Assumptions." Keener, Craig S. "Assumptions in Historical Jesus Research: Using Ancient Biographies and Disciples' Traditioning as a Control." *JSHJ* 9 (1, 2011): forthcoming.

Keener, "Biographies." Keener, Craig S. "Reading the Gospels as Biographies of a Sage." In *Buried History.* Forthcoming.

Keener, "Comparative Studies." Keener, Craig S. "The Value of Comparative Studies for Controlling Bias." Invited paper for the Historical Jesus section of the Society of Biblical Literature, Atlanta, Nov. 21, 2010.

Keener, "Comparisons." Keener, Craig S. "Cultural Comparisons for Healing and Exorcism Narratives in Matthew's Gospel." *HTS/TS* 66 (1, 2010). Art. #808, 7 pages. DOI: 10.4102/hts.v66i1.808. Available at http://www.hts.org.za.

Keener, "Corinthian Believers." Keener, Craig S. "Paul and the Corinthian Believers." Pages 46–62 in *The Blackwell Companion to Paul*. Edited by Stephen Westerholm. Malden, Mass.: Blackwell, 2011.

Keener, *Corinthians*. Keener, Craig S. *1 and 2 Corinthians*. NCamBC. Cambridge: Cambridge University Press, 2005.

Keener, "Diversity." Keener, Craig S. "Embracing God's Passion for Diversity: A Theology of Racial and Ethnic Plurality." *Enr* 12 (3, Summer 2007): 20–28.

Keener, "Fever." Keener, Craig S. "Fever and Dysentery in Acts 28:8 and Ancient Medicine." *BBR* 19 (2, 2009): 393–402.

Keener, *Gift*. Keener, Craig S. *Gift and Giver: The Holy Spirit for Today*. Grand Rapids: Baker Academic, 2001.

Keener, *Historical Jesus*. Keener, Craig S. *The Historical Jesus of the Gospels*. Grand Rapids: Eerdmans, 2009.

Keener, "Human Stones." Keener, Craig S. "Human Stones in a Greek Setting—Luke 3.8; Matthew 3.9; Luke 19.40." *JGRCJ* 6 (2009): 28–36.

Keener, *John*. Keener, Craig S. *The Gospel of John: A Commentary*. 2 vols. Peabody, Mass.: Hendrickson; now Grand Rapids: Baker Academic, 2003.

Keener, "Luke-Acts and Historical Jesus." Keener, Craig S. "Luke-Acts and Historical Jesus." Presented on April 19 at the Second Princeton-Prague Symposium on the Historical Jesus: Methodological Approaches to the Historical Jesus, April 18–21, 2007, Princeton, N.J. To be published in a collection of essays edited by James H. Charlesworth. Grand Rapids: Eerdmans, forthcoming.

Keener, *Marries Another*. Keener, Craig S. *... And Marries Another: Divorce and Remarriage in the Teaching of the New Testament*. Peabody, Mass.: Hendrickson; now Grand Rapids: Baker Academic, 1991.

Keener, *Matthew*. Keener, Craig S. *A Commentary on the Gospel of Matthew*. Grand Rapids: Eerdmans, 1999. Reprinted with additional introductory material as *The Gospel of Matthew: A Socio-Rhetorical Commentary*. Grand Rapids: Eerdmans, 2009.

Keener, "Miracles." Keener, Craig S. "Miracles: An Examination of Contemporary Miracle Testimony in the Majority World and the Implications of These Testimonies for Assessing the Plausibility of Miracle Claims in the Gospels and Acts." Public lecture, Wheaton College, Wheaton, Ill., March 16, 2009.

Keener, "Moussounga." Keener, Médine Moussounga. "Jacques Moussounga." *DACB*. http://www.dacb.org/stories/congo/moussounga_jacques.html.

Keener, "Ndoundou." Keener, Médine Moussounga. "Daniel Ndoundou." *DACB*. http://www.dacb.org/stories/congo/ndoundou_daniel.html.

Keener, "Notes." Keener, Craig S. "Three Notes on Figurative Language: Inverted Guilt in Acts 7:55–60, Paul's Figurative Vote in Acts 26:10, Figurative Eyes in Galatians 4:15." *JGRCJ* 5 (2008): 41–49.

Keener, "Official." Keener, Craig S. "Novels' 'Exotic' Places and Luke's African Official (Acts 8:27)." *AUSS* 46 (1, 2008): 5–20.

Keener, "Otho." Keener, Craig S. "Otho: A Targeted Comparison of Suetonius' Biography and Tacitus' History, with Implications for the Gospels' Historical Reliability." *BBR* 21 (3, 2011): forthcoming.

Keener, "Perspectives." Keener, Craig S. "'Fleshly' versus Spirit Perspectives in Romans 8:5–8." Pages 211–29 in *Paul: Jew, Greek, and Roman*. Edited by Stanley Porter. PAST 5. Leiden: Brill, 2008.

Keener, "Plausibility." Keener, Craig S. "The Plausibility of Luke's Growth Figures in Acts 2.41; 4.4; 21.20." *JGRCJ* 7 (2010): 140–63.

Keener, "Possession." Keener, Craig S. "Spirit Possession as a Cross-Cultural Experience." *BBR* 20 (2, 2010): 161–82.

Keener, "Readings." Keener, Craig S. "Sage Rhetoric and Majority World Readings of Miracle Narratives in Matthew." Paper presented to the Matthew section of the Society of Biblical Literature, New Orleans, Nov. 22, 2009.

Keener, "Reassessment." Keener, Craig S. "A Reassessment of Hume's Case Against Miracles in Light of Testimony from the Majority World Today." *PRSt* 38 (3, Fall 2011): forthcoming.

Keener, *Revelation*. Keener, Craig S. *Revelation*. NIVAC. Grand Rapids: Zondervan, 2000.

Keener, "Review of Bauckham." Keener, Craig S. "Review of Richard Bauckham, *Jesus and the Eyewitnesses*." *BBR* 19 (1, 2009): 130–32.

Keener, *Romans*. Keener, Craig S. *Romans*. NCCS 6. Eugene, Ore.: Cascade, 2009.

Keener, "2 Corinthians." Keener, Craig S. "2 Corinthians." Pages 809–24 in *The New Interpreter's Bible One Volume Commentary*. Edited by Beverly Roberts Gaventa and David Petersen. Nashville: Abingdon, 2010.

Keener, "Special Men." Keener, Médine Moussounga. "Special Men in a Life of a Congolese Professor." Pages 9–25 in *Some Men Are Our Heroes: Stories by Women about the Men Who Have Greatly Influenced Them*. Edited by KeumJu Jewel Hyun and Cynthia Davis Lathrop. Eugene, Ore.: Wipf & Stock, 2010.

Keener, *Spirit*. Keener, Craig S. *The Spirit in the Gospels and Acts: Divine Purity and Power*. Peabody, Mass.: Hendrickson; now Grand Rapids: Baker Academic, 1997.

Keener, "Spirit." Keener, Craig S. "The Holy Spirit." Pages 159–73 in *The Oxford Handbook of Evangelical*

Theology. Edited by Gerald R. McDermott. Oxford: Oxford University Press, 2010.

Keener, "Warfare." Keener, Craig S. "Paul and Spiritual Warfare." In *Missions according to Paul* (probable title). Edited by Robert Plummer and J. Mark Terry. Colorado Springs: Biblica, 2012, forthcoming.

Kelhoffer, "Miracle Workers." Kelhoffer, James A. "Ordinary Christians as Miracle Workers in the New Testament and the Second and Third Century Christian Apologists." *BR* 44 (1999): 23–34.

Kelhoffer, "Paul and Justin." Kelhoffer, James A. "The Apostle Paul and Justin Martyr on the Miraculous: A Comparison of Appeals to Authority." *GRBS* 42 (2, 2001): 163–84.

Kellenberger, "Miracles." Kellenberger, J. "Miracles." *IJPhilRel* 10 (3, 1979): 145–63.

Keller, "Argument." Keller, James A. "A Moral Argument against Miracles." *FPhil* 12 (1, Jan. 1995): 54–78.

Keller, "Glimpses." Keller, Edmund B. "Glimpses of Exorcism in Religion." Pages 259–311 in *Exorcism Through the Ages*. Edited by St. Elmo Nauman. New York: Philosophical Library, 1974.

Keller, *Hammer*. Keller, Mary. *The Hammer and the Flute: Women, Power, and Spirit Possession*. Baltimore: Johns Hopkins University Press, 2002.

Keller, "Healings." Keller, Marian Wittich. "Healings among the Heathen." *LRE* (May 1925): 14.

Keller, *Miracles*. Keller, Ernst, and Marie-Luise Keller. *Miracles in Dispute: A Continuing Debate*. Translated by Margaret Kohl. London: SCM, 1969.

Keller, "Power." Keller, James A. "The Power of God and Miracles in Process Theism." *JAAR* 63 (1, 1995): 105–26.

Kelly and Floyd, "Impact." Kelly, S., and F. J. Floyd. "Impact of Racial Perspectives and Contextual Variables on Marital Trust and Adjustment for African American Couples." *JFamPsych* 20 (1, 2006): 79–87.

Kelly, "Miracle." Kelly, Stewart E. "Miracle, Method, and Metaphysics: Philosophy and the Quest for the Historical Jesus." *TJ*, n.s., 29 (1, 2008): 45–63.

Kelsey, *Healing*. Kelsey, Morton T. *Healing and Christianity in Ancient Thought and Modern Times*. New York: Harper & Row, 1973.

Kemp, "Ravished." Kemp, Simon. "'Ravished of a Fiend': Demonology and Medieval Madness." Pages 67–78 in *Altered States of Consciousness and Mental Health: A Cross-Cultural Perspective*. Edited by Colleen A. Ward. CCRMS 12. Newbury Park, Calif.: Sage, 1989.

Kendler and Liu et al., "Dimensions." Kendler, Kenneth S., Xiao-Qing Liu, et al. "Dimensions of Religiosity and Their Relationship to Lifetime Psychiatric

and Substance Use Disorders." *AmJPsyc* 160 (3, 2003): 496–503.

Kennedy, "Customers." Kennedy, Paul. "Satisfied Customers: Miracles at the Vineyard Christian Fellowship." *MHRC* 1 (2, 1998): 135–52.

Kennedy, *Dream*. Kennedy, Nell L. *Dream Your Way to Success: The Story of Dr. Yonggi Cho and Korea*. Plainfield, N.J.: Logos International, 1980.

Kennedy, "Miracles." Kennedy, Rick. "Miracles in the Dock: A Critique of the Historical Profession's Special Treatment of Alleged Spiritual Events." *FidHist* 26 (2, 1994): 7–22.

Kennedy, "Source Criticism." Kennedy, George A. "Classical and Christian Source Criticism." Pages 125–55 in *The Relationships among the Gospels: An Interdisciplinary Dialogue*. Edited by William O. Walker Jr. San Antonio: Trinity University Press, 1978.

Kennedy, "Zar Ceremonies." Kennedy, John G. "Nubian *Zar* Ceremonies as Psychotherapy." *Human Organization* 26 (1967): 185–94.

Kent, *Inscriptions*. Kent, John Harvey. *The Inscriptions 1926–1950*. Vol. 8, part 3 of *Corinth: Results of Excavations Conducted by the American School of Classical Studies at Athens*. Princeton, N.J.: The American School of Classical Studies at Athens, 1966.

Kent and Fotherby, *Frontier*. Kent, Richard, and Val Fotherby. *The Final Frontier: Incredible Stories of Near-Death Experiences*. London: Marshall Pickering, HarperCollins, 1997.

Kent and Waite, *Beyond*. Kent, Richard, and David Waite. *Beyond the Final Frontier*. London: Marshall Pickering, HarperCollins, 2000.

Kenyon, "Case." Kenyon, Susan M. "The Case of the Butcher's Wife: Illness, Possession and Power in Central Sudan." Pages 89–108 in *Spirit Possession, Modernity and Power in Africa*. Edited by Heike Behrend and Ute Luig. Madison: University of Wisconsin Press, 1999.

Kenyon, "Zar." Kenyon, Susan M. "The Story of a Tin Box: *Zar* in the Sudanese Town of Sennar." Pages 100–117 in *Women's Medicine: The Zar-Bori Cult in Africa and Beyond*. Edited by I. M. Lewis, Ahmed Al-Safi, and Sayyid Hurreiz. Edinburgh: International African Institute, Edinburgh University Press, 1991.

Kepler, *Astronomy*. Kepler, Johannes. *Johannes Kepler's New Astronomy*. Translated by William H. Donahue and O. Gingerich. Cambridge: Cambridge University Press, 1992.

Kepler, *Harmony*. Kepler, Johannes. *The Harmony of the World*. Translated by E. J. Aiton, A. M. Duncan, and J. V. Field. Philadelphia: American Philosophical Society, 1997.

Kerin, *Fulfilling*. Kerin, Dorothy. *Fulfilling: A Sequel to* The Living Touch. 3rd ed. Foreword by Bishop

Cuthbert Bardsley. Tunbridge Wells: K&SC (Printers), 1960.

Kerin, *Touch*. Kerin, Dorothy. *The Living Touch*. Kent: Courier Printing and Publishing, 1914.

Kerns, *People's Temple*. Kerns, Phil, with Doug Wead. *People's Temple—People's Tomb*. Plainfield, N.J.: Logos, 1979.

Kern-Ulmer, "Evil Eye." Kern-Ulmer, Brigitte. "The Power of the Evil Eye and the Good Eye in Midrashic Literature." *Judaism* 40 (3, 1991): 344–53.

Kesselring et al., "Attitudes." Kesselring, A., M. J. Dodd, A. M. Lindsey, and A. L. Strauss. "Attitudes of Patients Living in Switzerland about Cancer and Its Treatment." *CanNur* 9 (1986): 77–85.

Kessler, "Conflict." Kessler, Clive S. "Conflict and Sovereignty in Kelantanese Malay Spirit Seances." Pages 295–332 in *Case Studies in Spirit Possession*. Edited by Vincent Crapanzaro and Vivian Garrison. New York: John Wiley & Sons, 1977.

Key, Leppien, and Smith, "Model." Key, B. F., F. Leppien, and J. B. Smith. "Journey Out of Night: Spiritual Renewal for Combat Veterans." *VA Practitioner* 11 (1, 1994): 60–62.

Keylock, "Distinctness." Keylock, Leslie R. "Bultmann's Law of Increasing Distinctness." Pages 193–210 in *Current Issues in Biblical and Patristic Interpretation: Studies in Honor of Merrill C. Tenney Presented by His Former Students*. Edited by Gerald F. Hawthorne. Grand Rapids: Eerdmans, 1975.

Keyser, "Rationale." Keyser, Leander S. "The Rationale of Christ's Miracles." *EvQ* 5 (1933): 357–64.

Kgatla, "Moloi." Kgatla, S. T. "'Moloi ga a na mmala' [A Witch Has No Color]: Witchcraft Accusations in South Africa." *Missionalia* 32 (1, 2004): 84–101.

Kgwatalala, Villiers, and Lubbe, "Behaviours." Kgwatalala, Gomotsang, Louise de Villiers, and Gerrie J. A. Lubbe. "Health-Seeking Behaviours of the Members of the Africa Gospel Church." *Missionalia* 34 (2–3, Aug. 2006): 267–84.

Khai, *Cross*. Khai, Chin Khua. *The Cross Among Pagodas: A History of the Assemblies of God in Myanmar*. Baguio City, Philippines: APTS, 2003.

Khai, "Legacy." Khai, Chin Khua. "Legacy of Hau Lian Kham (1944–1995): A Revivalist, Equipper, and Transformer for the Zomi-Chin People of Myanmar." *AJPS* 4 (1, Jan. 2001): 99–107.

Khai, "Overview." Khai, Chin Khua. "Pentecostalism in Myanmar: An Overview." *AJPS* 5 (1, 2002): 51–71.

Khai, "Pentecostalism." Khai, Chin Khua. "The Assemblies of God and Pentecostalism in Myanmar." Pages 261–80 in *Asian and Pentecostal: The Charismatic Face of Christianity in Asia*. Edited by Allan Anderson and Edmond Tang. Foreword by Cecil

M. Robeck. Regnum Studies in Mission, AJPSS 3. Oxford: Regnum; Baguio City, Philippines: APTS Press, 2005.

Kham, "Story." Kham, Cin Do. "The Untold Story: The Impact of Revival among the Chin People in Myanmar (Burma)." *JAM* 1 (2, Sept. 1999): 205–22.

Khouzam, Smith and Bissett, "Therapy." Khouzam, H. R., C. E. Smith, and B. Bissett. "Bible Therapy: A Treatment of Agitation in Elderly Patients with Alzheimer's Disease." *Clinical Gerontologist* 15 (2, 1994): 71–74.

Kibicho, "Continuity." Kibicho, Samuel G. "The Continuity of the African Conception of God into and through Christianity: A Kikuyu Case Study." Pages 370–88 in *Christianity in Independent Africa*. Edited by Edward Fasholé-Luke, Richard Gray, Adrian Hastings, and Godwin Tasie. Bloomington: Indiana University Press, 1978.

Kidd, *Awakening*. Kidd, Thomas S. *The Great Awakening: The Roots of Evangelical Christianity in Colonial America*. New Haven: Yale University Press, 2007.

Kidd, "Healing." Kidd, Thomas S. "The Healing of Mercy Wheeler: Illness and Miracles among Early American Evangelicals." *WMQ* 63 (1, Jan. 2006): 149–70.

Kiev, *Magic*. Kiev, Ari, ed. *Magic, Faith, and Healing: Studies in Primitive Psychiatry Today*. Foreword by Jerome D. Frank. New York: Free Press, 1964.

Kiev, "Value." Kiev, Ari. "The Psychotherapeutic Value of Spirit-Possession in Haiti." Pages 143–48 in *Trance and Possession States*. Proceedings of the Second Annual Conference, R. M. Bucke Memorial Society, March 4–6, 1966. Edited by Raymond Prince. Montreal: R. M. Bucke Memorial Society, 1968.

Kim, "Apocalypse." Kim, Chong Bum. "Preaching the Apocalypse in Colonial Korea: The Protestant Millennialism of Kil Son-ju." Pages 149–66 in *Christianity in Korea*. Edited by Robert E. Buswell Jr. and Timothy S. Lee. Honolulu: University of Hawai'i Press, 2006.

Kim, "Foreword." Kim, Sung-hae (Grace). "Foreword." Page iii in *David Yonggi Cho: A Close Look at His Theology and Ministry*. Edited by Wonsuk Ma, William W. Menzies, and Hyeon-sung Bae. AJPSS 1. Baguio City, Philippines: APTS Press, Hansei University Press, 2004.

Kim, "Healing." Kim, Sean C. "Reenchanted: Divine Healing in Korean Protestantism." Pages 267–85 in *Global Pentecostal and Charismatic Healing*. Edited by Candy Gunther Brown. Foreword by Harvey Cox. Oxford: Oxford University Press, 2011.

Kim, "Influence." Kim, Kwan Soo. "A Study of the Influence of Healing Ministry to Church Growth with Reference to Korea Evangelical Church." DMin diss., Fuller Theological Seminary and Asian Center for Theological Studies and Mission, Seoul, 1987.

Kim, "Pentecostalism." Kim, Sung-Gun. "Pentecostalism, Shamanism, and Capitalism Within Contemporary Korean Society." Pages 23–38 in *Spirits of Globalization: The Growth of Pentecostalism and Experiential Spiritualities in a Global Age*. Edited by Sturla J. Stålsett. London: SCM, 2006.

Kim, "Prominent Woman." Kim, Ig-Jin. "A Prominent Woman in Early Korean Pentecostal Movement: Gui-Im Park (1912–1994)." *AJPS* 9 (2, July 2006): 199–218.

Kim, "Realistic." Kim, Jaegwon. "Being Realistic about Emergence." Pages 189–202 in *The Re-Emergence of Emergence: The Emergentist Hypothesis from Science to Religion*. Edited by Philip Clayton and Paul Davies. Oxford: Oxford University Press, 2006.

Kim, "Significance." Kim, Stephen S. "The Significance of Jesus' Healing the Blind Man in John 9." *BSac* 167 (667, 2010): 307–18.

Kim, "Spirit." Kim, Kirsteen. "The Holy Spirit and Spirituality." Pages 88–94 in *A Commentary on 1 & 2 Corinthians*, by J. Ayodeji Adewuya. London: SPCK, 2009.

Kimball, "Learning." Kimball, Solon T. "Learning a New Culture." Pages 182–92 in *Crossing Cultural Boundaries: The Anthropological Experience*. Edited by Solon T. Kimball and James B. Watson. San Francisco: Chandler, 1972.

King, Mainous, and Pearson, "Protein." King, D. E., A. G. Mainous III, and W. S. Pearson. "C-reactive Protein, Diabetes, and Attendance at Religious Services." *DiabC* 25 (7, 2002): 1172–76.

King, Sobal, and DeForge, "Experience." King, D. E., J. Sobal, and B. R. DeForge. "Family Practice Patients' Experience and Beliefs in Faith Healing." *JFamPr* 27 (5, 1988): 505–8.

King and Bushwick, "Beliefs." King, D. E., and B. Bushwick. "Beliefs and Attitudes of Hospital Inpatients about Faith Healing and Prayer." *JFamPr* 39 (1994): 349–52.

King et al., "Relationship." King, D. E., A. G. Mainous, T. E. Steyer, and W. Pearson. "Relationship between Attendance at Religious Services and Cardiovascular Inflammatory Markers." *IntJPsyMed* 31 (2001): 415–26.

King-Farlow, "Insights." King-Farlow, John. "Historical Insights on Miracles: Babbage, Hume, Aquinas." *IJPhilRel* 13 (4, 1982): 209–18.

Kinghorn, *Story*. Kinghorn, Kenneth Cain. *The Story of Asbury Theological Seminary*. Lexington, Ky.: Emeth, 2010.

Kingsbury, *Christology*. Kingsbury, Jack Dean. *The Christology of Mark's Gospel*. Philadelphia: Fortress, 1983.

Kinnear, *Tide*. Kinnear, Angus. *Against the Tide: The Story of Watchman Nee*. Wheaton: Tyndale, 1978.

Kinney et al., "Involvement." Kinney, Anita Yeomans, et al. "Roles of Religious Involvement and Social Support in the Risk of Colon Cancer among Blacks and Whites." *AmJEpid* 158 (11, 2003): 1097–107.

Kippenberg, "Magic." Kippenberg, Hans G. "Magic in Roman Civil Discourse: Why Rituals Could Be Illegal." Pages 137–63 in *Envisioning Magic: A Princeton Seminar and Symposium*. Edited by Peter Schäfer and Hans G. Kippenberg. SHR 75. Leiden: Brill, 1997.

Kirby, "Recovery." Kirby, Jeff. "The Recovery of Healing Gifts." Pages 101–20 in *Those Controversial Gifts: Prophecy, Dreams, Visions, Tongues, Interpretation, Healing*. Edited by George Mallone. Foreword by Michael Green. Downers Grove, Ill.: InterVarsity, 1983.

Kirchschläger, "Exorzismus." Kirchschläger, W. "Exorzismus in Qumran?" *Kairos* 18 (1976): 135–53.

Kirkaldy, "Vhuloi." Kirkaldy, Alan. "Vhuloi and Witch Hunting in Late Nineteenth-Century Vendaland." Pages 87–113 in *Studies in Witchcraft, Magic, War, and Peace in Africa*. Edited by Beatrice Nicolini. Lewiston, N.Y.: Edwin Mellen, 2006.

Kistiakowsky, "Order." Kistiakowsky, Vera. "The Exquisite Order of the Physical World Calls for the Divine." Pages 51–53 in *Cosmos, Bios, and Theos: Scientists Reflect on Science, God, and the Origins of the Universe, Life, and Homo Sapiens*. Edited by Henry Margenau and Roy Abraham Varghese. La Salle, Ill.: Open Court, 1992.

Klassen, "Fire." Klassen, J. P. "Fire in the Pararno." MA thesis, Fuller Theological Seminary, 1975.

Klassen, "Healing." Klassen, Pamela E. "Religion, Ritual, and Healing in North America." Pages 329–40 in *Teaching Religion and Healing*. Edited by Linda L. Barnes and Inés Talamantez. AARTRSS. Oxford: Oxford University Press, 2006.

Klauck, "Ärzten." Klauck, Hans-Josef. "Von Ärzten und Wundertätern. Heil und Heilung in der Antike." *BK* 61 (2, 2006): 94–98.

Klauck, *Context*. Klauck, Hans-Josef. *The Religious Context of Early Christianity: A Guide to Graeco-Roman Religions*. Translated by Brian McNeil. Minneapolis: Fortress, 2003.

Klaus, "Foreword." Klaus, Byron D. "Foreword." Pages xi–xv in *Miracles, Missions, and American Pentecostalism*, by Gary B. McGee. AmSocMissS 45. Maryknoll, N.Y.: Orbis, 2010.

Klaus, "Global Culture." Klaus, Byron D. "Pentecostalism as a Global Culture: An Introductory Overview." Pages 127–30 in *The Globalization of Pentecostalism: A Religion Made to Travel*. Edited by Murray W. Dempster, Byron D. Klaus, and Douglas Petersen. Foreword by Russell P. Spittler. Carlisle: Paternoster; Oxford: Regnum, 1999.

Klaus, "Miracle." Klaus, Byron. "A Miracle Named Rudi." *MounM* (June 1993): 16–17.

Klausner, *Jesus.* Klausner, Joseph. *Jesus: His Life, Times, and Teaching.* Translated by Herbert Danby. Foreword by Sidney B. Hoenig. Reprint, New York: Menorah Publishing Company, 1979; n.p.: Macmillan Company, 1925.

Klawans, "Idolatry." Klawans, Jonathan. "Idolatry, Incest, and Impurity: Moral Defilement in Ancient Judaism." *JSJ* 29 (4, 1998): 391–415.

Klawans, "Impurity." Klawans, Jonathan. "The Impurity of Immorality in Ancient Judaism." *JJS* 48 (1, 1997): 1–16.

Klein, "Anglicanism." Klein, Herbert S. "Anglicanism, Catholicism, and the Negro Slave." Pages 137–90 in *The Debate Over Slavery.* Edited by Ann Lane. Urbana: University of Illinois Press, 1971.

Klein-Braslavy, "Use." Klein-Braslavy, Sara. "Gersonides' Use of Aristotle's Meteorology in His Accounts of Some Biblical Miracles." *Aleph* 10 (2, 2010): 241–313.

Kleine, "Wissenschaft." Kleine, Christoph. "Die Wissenschaft und das Wunder. Überlegungen zum Umgang der Religionswissenschaft mit dem 'Paranormalen.'" *ZR* 7 (2, 1999): 121–44.

Kleiner, "Tumor." Kleiner, Sarah. "Tumor Healed." *WWit* 9 (6, June 20, 1913): 7.

Kleinman, *Healers.* Kleinman, Arthur. *Patients and Healers in the Context of Culture: An Exploration of the Borderland between Anthropology, Medicine, and Psychiatry.* CSHSMC 3. Berkeley: University of California Press, 1980.

Kleinman and Sung, "Practitioners." Kleinman, Arthur, and L. H. Sung. "Why Do Indigenous Practitioners Successfully Heal? A Follow-up Study of Indigenous Practice in Taiwan." *SSMed* 13B (1979): 7–26.

Kleve, "Daimon." Kleve, K. "The Daimon of Socrates." *SIFC* 4 (1986): 5–18.

Kluger, "Biology." Kluger, Jeffrey. "The Biology of Belief." *Time* (Feb. 23, 2009): 62–72.

Klutz, *Exorcism Stories.* Klutz, Todd. *The Exorcism Stories in Luke-Acts: A Sociostylistic Reading.* SNTSMS 129. Cambridge: Cambridge University Press, 2004.

Knapp, *Thunder.* Knapp, Doug, and Evelyn Knapp, with Robert O'Brien. *Thunder in the Valley: The Amazing Spiritual Harvest in Tanzania.* Foreword by Owen Cooper. Nashville: Broadman, 1986.

Knapstad, "Power." Knapstad, Bård Løkken. "Show Us the Power! A Study of the Influence of Miracles on the Conversion Process from Islam to Christianity in an Indonesian Context." ThM thesis, Norwegian Lutheran School of Theology, 2005.

Knight, "Pregnancy." Knight, J. A. "False Pregnancy in a Male." *PsychMed* 22 (1960): 260–66.

Knox, *Acts.* Knox, Wilfred L. *The Acts of the Apostles.* Cambridge: Cambridge University Press, 1948.

Kobelski, "Melchizedek." Kobelski, P. J. "Melchizedek and Melchiresa: The Heavenly Prince of Light and the Prince of Darkness in the Qumran Literature." PhD diss., Fordham University, 1978.

Koch, *Bondage.* Koch, Kurt. *Occult Bondage and Deliverance: Advice for Counselling the Sick, the Troubled and the Occultly Oppressed.* Grand Rapids: Kregel, 1971.

Koch, *Gifts.* Koch, Kurt. *Charismatic Gifts.* Quebec: Association for Christian Evangelism, 1975.

Koch, *Revival.* Koch, Kurt. *The Revival in Indonesia.* Baden: Evangelization Publishers; Grand Rapids: Kregel, 1970.

Koch, *Strife.* Koch, Kurt E. *The Strife of Tongues.* Grand Rapids: Kregel, 1971.

Koch, *Zulus.* Koch, Kurt E. *God Among the Zulus.* Translated by Justin Michell and Waldemar Engelbrecht. Natal, R.S.A.: Mission Kwa Sizabanu, 1981.

Koenig, "Afterword." Koenig, Harold G. "Afterword: A Physician's Reflections." Pages 505–7 in *Religion and Healing in America.* Edited by Linda L. Barnes and Susan S. Sered. New York: Oxford University Press, 2005.

Koenig, *Hospitality.* Koenig, John. *New Testament Hospitality: Partnership with Strangers as Promise and Mission.* OBT 17. Philadelphia: Fortress, 1985.

Koenig, "Inpatients." Koenig, Harold G. "Religion and Depression in Older Medical Inpatients." *AmJGerPsy* 15 (4, 2007): 282–91.

Koenig, *Medicine.* Koenig, Harold G. *Medicine, Religion, and Health: Where Science and Spirituality Meet.* Templeton Science and Religion Series. West Conshohocken, Pa.: Templeton Foundation Press, 2008.

Koenig, "Prison." Koenig, Harold G. "Religion and Older Men in Prison." *IJGerPsyc* 10 (3, March 1995): 219–30.

Koenig, *Religion.* Koenig, Harold G. *Is Religion Good for Your Health? The Effects of Religion on Physical and Mental Health.* New York: Haworth Press, 1997.

Koenig, "Remission." Koenig, Harold G. "Religion and Remission of Depression in Medical Inpatients with Heart Failure/Pulmonary Disease." *JNMDis* 195 (2007): 389–95.

Koenig, George, Cohen, et al., "Relationship." Koenig, Harold G., L. K. George, H. J. Cohen, et al. "The Relationship between Religious Activities and Blood Pressure in Older Adults." *IntJPsyMed* 28 (1998): 189–213.

Koenig, George, and Titus, "Ill Patients." Koenig, Harold G., L. K. George, and P. Titus. "Religion, Spirituality, and Health in Medically Ill Hospitalized Older Patients." *JAmGerAss* 52 (2004): 554–62.

Koenig, McCullough, and Larson, *Handbook*. Koenig, Harold G., Michael E. McCullough, and David B. Larson. *Handbook of Religion and Health*. New York: Oxford University Press, 2001.

Koenig, Moberg, and Kvale, "Activities." Koenig, Harold G., D. O. Moberg, and J. N. Kvale. "Religious Activities and Attitudes of Older Adults in a Geriatric Assessment Clinic." *JAmGerSoc* 36 (1988): 362–74.

Koenig et al., "Care Use." Koenig, Harold G., L. K. George, P. Titus, and K. G. Meador. "Religion, Spirituality, Acute Hospital and Long-Term Care Use by Older Patients." *ArchIntMed* 164 (2004): 1579–85.

Koenig et al., "Religion and Use." Koenig, Harold G., L. K. George, P. Titus, and K. G. Meador. "Religion, Spirituality and Health Service Use by Older Hospitalized Patients." *JRelHealth* 42 (4, 2003): 301–14.

Koester, "Gospels." Koester, Helmut. "One Jesus and Four Primitive Gospels." *HTR* 61 (1968): 203–47.

Koester, *Introduction*. Koester, Helmut. *Introduction to the New Testament*. 2 vols. Hermeneia Foundations and Facets Series. Vol. 1: *History, Culture, and Religion of the Hellenistic Age*. Vol. 2: *History and Literature of Early Christianity*. Philadelphia: Fortress, 1982.

Koester, *Paul and World*. Koester, Helmut. *Paul and His World: Interpreting the New Testament in Its Context*. Minneapolis: Fortress, 2007.

Koestler, "Kepler." Koestler, Arthur. "Kepler and the Psychology of Discovery." Pages 49–57 in *The Logic of Personal Knowledge: Essays Presented to Michael Polanyi on His Seventieth Birthday 11 March 1961*. London: Routledge & Kegan Paul, 1961.

Konkel, *Kings*. Konkel, August H. *1 and 2 Kings*. NIVAC. Grand Rapids: Zondervan, 2006.

Koons, *Realism*. Koons, Robert C. *Realism Regained: An Exact Theory of Causation, Teleology, and the Mind*. Oxford: Oxford University Press, 2000.

Kortkamp, "Healings." Kortkamp, A. W. "Remarkable Healings at Alton, Ill." *PentEv* 338–339 (May 1, 1920): 9.

Koschorke, Ludwig, and Delgado, *History*. Koschorke, Klaus, Frieder Ludwig, and Mariano Delgado, eds., with Roland Spliesgart. *History of Christianity in Asia, Africa, and Latin America, 1450–1990: A Documentary Sourcebook*. Grand Rapids: Eerdmans, 2007.

Koskenniemi, "Apollonius." Koskenniemi, Erkki. "Apollonius of Tyana: A Typical θεῖος ἀνήρ?" *JBL* 117 (3, 1998): 455–67.

Koskenniemi, "Background." Koskenniemi, Erkki. "The Religious-Historical Background of the New Testament Miracles." Pages 103–16 in *Religious and Spiritual Events*. Vol. 1 of *Miracles: God, Science, and Psychology in the Paranormal*. Edited by J. Harold Ellens. Westport, Conn.; London: Praeger, 2008.

Koskenniemi, "Figures." Koskenniemi, Erkki. "Old Testament Figures as Miracle Workers." Pages 77–87 in *Religious and Spiritual Events*. Vol. 1 of *Miracles: God, Science, and Psychology in the Paranormal*. Edited by J. Harold Ellens. Westport, Conn.; London: Praeger, 2008.

Koskenniemi, *Miracle-Workers*. Koskenniemi, Erkki. *The Old Testament Miracle-Workers in Early Judaism*. WUNT 2.206. Tübingen: Mohr Siebeck, 2005.

Koss, "Spirits." Koss, Joan D. "Spirits as Socializing Agents: A Case Study of a Puerto Rican Girl Reared in a Matrocentric Family." Pages 365–82 in *Case Studies in Spirit Possession*. Edited by Vincent Crapanzaro and Vivian Garrison. New York: John Wiley & Sons, 1977.

Koss-Chioino, "Transformation." Koss-Chioino, Joan D. "Spiritual Transformation, Radical Empathy, and Embodied Emotion in Healing Ritual." Pages 51–67 in *Religion*. Vol. 2 of *The Healing Power of Spirituality: How Faith Helps Humans Thrive*. Edited by J. Harold Ellens. Santa Barbara, Calif.: Praeger, 2010.

Köstenberger, *Encountering John*. Köstenberger, Andreas J. *Encountering John: The Gospel in Historical, Literary, and Theological Perspective*. Grand Rapids: Baker, 1999.

Kotansky, "Demonology." Kotansky, Roy. "Demonology." Pages 269–73 in *DNTB*.

Kotansky, "Remnants." Kotansky, Roy. "Remnants of a Liturgical Exorcism on a Gem." *Muséon* 108 (1–2, 1995): 143–56.

Kraemer, "Doctor." Kraemer, David. "Why Your Son (or Daughter), the Doctor, Really Is God." *ConsJud* 59 (1, 2006): 72–79.

Kraemer, "Ecstasy." Kraemer, Ross Shepard. "Ecstasy and Possession: The Attraction of Women to the Cult of Dionysus." *HTR* 72 (1, Jan. 1979): 55–80.

Kraft, "Animism." Kraft, Charles H. "'Christian Animism' or God-Given Authority?" Pages 88–135 in *Spiritual Power and Missions: Raising the Issues*. Edited by Edward Rommen. EvMissSS 3. Pasadena, Calif.: William Carey Library, 1995.

Kraft, *Christianity in Culture*. Kraft, Charles H. *Christianity in Culture: A Study in Dynamic Biblical Theologizing in Cross-Cultural Perspective*. Foreword by Bernard Ramm. Maryknoll, N.Y.: Orbis, 1981.

Kraft, *Power*. Kraft, Charles H., with Christie Varney and Ellen Kearney. *Christianity with Power: Your Worldview and Your Experience of the Supernatural*. Foreword by Clark H. Pinnock. Ann Arbor, Mich.: Servant, 1989.

Kraft, *Worldview*. Kraft, Charles H. *Worldview for Christian Witness*. Pasadena, Calif.: William Carey Library, 2008.

Kraft, "Worldviews." Kraft, Charles. "Shifting World-views, Sifting Attitudes." Pages 57–68 in *Power Encounters Among Christians in the Western World.* Edited by Kevin Springer, with an introduction and afterword by John Wimber. San Francisco: Harper & Row, 1988.

Kraft, "Years." Kraft, Charles H. "Five Years Later." Pages 115–23 in *Signs and Wonders Today: The Story of Fuller Theological Seminary's Remarkable Course on Spiritual Power.* Rev. ed. Edited by C. Peter Wagner. Altamonte Springs, Fla.: Creation House, 1987.

Krasser, "Reading." Krasser, Helmut. "Light Reading." Pages 553–55 in vol. 7 of *Brill's New Pauly: Encyclopaedia of the Ancient World.* Edited by Hubert Cancik and Helmuth Schneider. 20 vols. English ed. Christine F. Salazar. Leiden: Brill, 2010.

Krause, "Exploring." Krause, Neal. "Exploring the Stress-Buffering Effects of Church-Based and Secular Social Support on Self-Rated Health in Late Life." *JGPSSS* 61 (1, 2006): S35–43.

Krause, "Facets." Krause, Neal. "Common Facets of Religion, Unique Facets of Religion, and Life Satisfaction among Older African Americans." *JGPSSS* 59 (2, 2004): S109–17.

Krause, "Meaning." Krause, Neal. "Religious Meaning and Subjective Well-Being in Late Life." *JGer* 58 (3, 2003): S160–70.

Krause, "Support." Krause, Neal. "Church-Based Social Support and Mortality." *JGPSSS* 61 (3, 2006): S140–46.

Krause et al., "Death." Krause, Neal, Jersey Liang, et al. "Religion, Death of a Loved One, and Hypertension among Older Adults in Japan." *JGPSSS* 57B (2, 2002): S96–107.

Krauss, "Religion." Krauss, Lawrence M. "Religion vs. Science?" Pages 125–53 in *The Religion and Science Debate: Why Does It Continue?* Edited by Harold W. Attridge. New Haven: Yale University Press, 2009.

Kraut et al., "Association." Kraut, Allen, Samuel Melamed, et al. "Association of Self-Reported Religiosity and Mortality in Industrial Employees: The CORDIS Study." *SSMed* 58 (3, 2004): 595–602.

Kravig, "Heal." Kravig, Clara. "Heal the Sick." *CGl* 9 (3, July 1932): 12–14.

Kreeft and Tacelli, *Handbook.* Kreeft, Peter, and Ronald K. Tacelli. *Handbook of Christian Apologetics: Hundreds of Answers to Crucial Questions.* Downers Grove, Ill.: InterVarsity, 1994.

Kreisel, "Miracles." Kreisel, Howard. "Miracles in Medieval Jewish Philosophy." *JQR* 75 (2, 1984): 99–133.

Kreiser, "Devils." Kreiser, B. Robert. "The Devils of Toulon: Demonic Possession and Religious Politics in Eighteenth-Century Provence." Pages 63–111 in *Possession and Exorcism.* Vol. 9 of *Articles on Witchcraft, Magic, and Demonology: A Twelve-Volume Anthology of Scholarly Articles.* Edited by Brian P. Levack. New York: Garland, 1992. Reprinted from pages 173–221 in *Church, State, and Society under the Bourbon Kings of France.* Edited by Richard M. Golden. Lawrence, Kans.: Coronado Press, 1982.

Kreiser, *Miracles.* Kreiser, B. Robert. *Miracles, Convulsions, and Ecclesiastical Politics in Early Eighteenth-Century Paris.* Princeton, N.J.: Princeton University Press, 1978.

Kremer, "Tales of Power." Kremer, Jürgen W. "Tales of Power." Pages 31–49 in *Proceedings of the Fourth International Conference on the Study of Shamanism and Alternate Modes of Healing, Held at the St. Sabina Center, San Rafael, California, September 5–7, 1987.* Edited by Ruth-Inge Heinze. N.p.: Independent Scholars of Asia; Madison, Wis.: A-R Editions, 1988.

Kremer and Ironson, "Spirituality." Kremer, Heidemarie, and Gail Ironson. "Spirituality and HIV/AIDS." Pages 176–90 in *Spirit, Science, and Health: How the Spiritual Mind Fuels Physical Wellness.* Edited by Thomas G. Plante and Carl E. Thoresen. Foreword by Albert Bandura. Westport, Conn.: Praeger, 2007.

Krings, "History." Krings, Matthias. "On History and Language of the 'European' *Bori* Spirits of Kano, Nigeria." Pages 53–67 in *Spirit Possession, Modernity and Power in Africa.* Edited by Heike Behrend and Ute Luig. Madison: University of Wisconsin Press, 1999.

Krippner, "Call." Krippner, Stanley. "A Call to Heal: Entry Patterns in Brazilian Mediumship." Pages 186–206 in *Altered States of Consciousness and Mental Health: A Cross-Cultural Perspective.* Edited by Colleen A. Ward. CCRMS 12. Newbury Park, Calif.: Sage, 1989.

Krippner, "Disorders." Krippner, Stanley. "Cross-Cultural Treatment Perspectives on Dissociative Disorders." Pages 338–61 in *Dissociation: Clinical and Theoretical Perspectives.* Edited by S. J. Lynn and J. W. Rhue. New York: Guilford, 1994.

Krippner, "Medicine." Krippner, Stanley. "'Energy Medicine' in Indigenous Healing Systems." Pages 191–202 in *Proceedings of the Fourth International Conference on the Study of Shamanism and Alternate Modes of Healing, Held at the St. Sabina Center, San Rafael, California, September 5–7, 1987.* Edited by Ruth-Inge Heinze. N.p.: Independent Scholars of Asia; Madison, Wis.: A-R Editions, 1988.

Krippner, "Perspectives." Krippner, Stanley C. "Conflicting Perspectives on Shamans and Shamanism: Points and Counterpoints." *AmPsyc* (Nov. 2002): 962–77.

Krippner, Friedman, and Johnson, "Spirituality." Krippner, Stanley, Harris L. Friedman, and Chad

V. Johnson. "Indigenous Spirituality and Psychological Healing." Pages 122–43 in *Personal Spirituality*. Vol. 1 of *The Healing Power of Spirituality: How Faith Helps Humans Thrive*. Edited by J. Harold Ellens. Santa Barbara, Calif.: Praeger, 2010.

Krippner and Achterberg, "Experiences." Krippner, Stanley, and Jeanne Achterberg. "Anomalous Healing Experiences." Pages 353–96 in *Varieties of Anomalous Experience: Examining the Scientific Evidence*. Edited by Etzel Cardeña, Steven Jay Lynn, and Stanley Krippner. Washington, D.C.: American Psychological Association, 2000.

Krippner and Kirkwood, "Bleeding." Krippner, Stanley, and Jeffrey Kirkwood. "Sacred Bleeding: The Language of Stigmata." Pages 154–75 in *Medical and Therapeutic Events*. Vol. 2 of *Miracles: God, Science, and Psychology in the Paranormal*. Edited by J. Harold Ellens. Westport, Conn.; London: Praeger, 2008.

Krisanaprakornkit et al., "Therapy." Krisanaprakornkit, T., W. Krisanaprakornkit, N. Piyavhatkul, and M. Laopaiboon. "Meditation Therapy for Anxiety Disorders." *CDSR* 1 (2006). Online: http://online library.wiley.com/o/cochrane/clsysrev/articles/CD004998/frame.html.

Kristeller et al., "Study." Kristeller, Jean L., Mark Rhodes, Larry D. Cripe, and Virgil Sheets. "Oncologist Assisted Spiritual Intervention Study (OASIS): Patient Acceptability and Initial Evidence of Effects." *IntJPsyMed* 35 (2005): 329–47.

Krucoff et al., "Music." Krucoff, M. W., et al. "Music, Imagery, Touch, and Prayer as Adjuncts to Interventional Cardiac Care: The Monitoring and Actualization of Noetic Trainings (MANTRA) II Randomized Study." *Lancet* 366 (9481, 2005): 211–17.

Krupski et al., "Spirituality." Krupski, T. L., L. Kwan, A. Fink, et al. "Spirituality Influences Health Related Quality of Life in Men with Prostate Cancer." *Psycho-Oncology* 15 (2006): 121–31.

Kselman, *Miracles*. Kselman, Thomas A. *Miracles and Prophecies in Nineteenth-Century France*. New Brunswick, N.J.: Rutgers University Press, 1983.

Kub, "Miracles." Kub, Joan. "Miracles and Medicine: An Annotated Bibliography." *SMedJ* 100 (12, Dec. 2007): 1273–76.

Kucera, "South India." Kucera, Martha M. "South India." *PentEv* 1047 (May 5, 1934): 10.

Kugel, *Bible*. Kugel, James L. *How to Read the Bible: A Guide to Scripture, Then and Now*. New York: Free Press, 2007.

Kugler, "History." Kugler, Michael. "Enlightenment History, Objectivity, and the Moral Imagination." Pages 128–52 in *Confessing History: Explorations in Christian Faith and the Historian's Vocation*. Edited by John Fea, Jay Green, and Eric Miller. Notre Dame, Ind.: University of Notre Dame Press, 2010.

Kuhlman, *Again*. Kuhlman, Kathryn. *God Can Do It Again: Amazing Testimonies Wrought by God's Extraordinary Servant*. Englewood Cliffs, N.J.: Prentice-Hall, 1969; rev. ed.: Gainesville, Fla.: Bridge-Logos, 1993.

Kuhlman, *Impossible*. Kuhlman, Kathryn. *Nothing Is Impossible with God: Modern-Day Miracles in the Ministry of a Daughter of Destiny*. Englewood Cliffs, N.J.: Prentice-Hall, 1974; rev. ed., Gainesville, Fla.: Bridge-Logos, 1999.

Kuhlman, *Late*. Kuhlman, Kathryn. *Never Too Late*. Plainfield, N.J.: Logos, 1975.

Kuhlman, *LeVrier*. Kuhlman, Kathryn. *Captain LeVrier*. Plainfield, N.J.: Logos, 1973.

Kuhlman, *Miracles*. Kuhlman, Kathryn. *I Believe in Miracles*. New York: Pyramid Books, Prentice-Hall, 1962.

Kuhn, *Structure*. Kuhn, Thomas S. *The Structure of Scientific Revolutions*. 2nd ed. Chicago: University of Chicago Press, 1970.

Kuligin, "Church." Kuligin, Victor. "The New Apostolic Church." *AJET* 24 (1, 2005): 63–79.

Kümmel, *Introduction*. Kümmel, Werner George. *Introduction to the New Testament*. London: SCM, 1965.

Kundsin, "Christianity." Kundsin, Karl. "Primitive Christianity in the Light of Gospel Research." Pages 77–161 in *Form Criticism: Two Essays on New Testament Research*, by Rudolf Bultmann and Karl Kundsin. Translated by Frederick C. Grant. New York: Harper & Brothers, 1962.

Kure, "Light." Kure, Emmanuel Nuhu. "Bringing Light to the Muslims." Pages 172–86 in *Out of Africa: How the Spiritual Explosion Among Nigerians Is Impacting the World*. Edited by C. Peter Wagner and Joseph Thompson. Ventura, Calif.: Regal, 2004.

Kvalbein, "Wonders." Kvalbein, Hans. "The Wonders of the End-Time: Metaphoric Language in 4Q521 and the Interpretation of Matthew 11.5 par." *JSP* 18 (1998): 87–110.

Kvalbein, "Wunder." Kvalbein, Hans. "Die Wunder der Endzeit. Beobachtungen zu 4Q521 und Matth 11,5p." *ZNW* 88 (1–2, 1997): 111–25.

Kvamme, "Raised." Kvamme, Martin. "Child Raised from Death's Door." *PentEv* 1020 (Oct. 21, 1933): 6.

Kvanvig and McCann, "Conservation." Kvanvig, Jonathan L., and Hugh J. McCann. "Divine Conservation and the Persistence of the World." Pages 13–49 in *Divine and Human Action: Essays in the Metaphysics of Theism*. Edited by Thomas V. Morris. Ithaca, N.Y.: Cornell University Press, 1988.

Kwan, "Argument." Kwan, Kai-Man. "The Argument from Religious Experience." Pages 498–552 in *The Blackwell Companion to Natural Theology*. Edited by William Lane Craig and J. P. Moreland. Malden, Mass.: Blackwell, 2009.

Kwon, "Foundations." Kwon, Tack Joe. "The Theoretical Foundations of Healing Ministry and the Applications to Church Growth." DMin diss., Fuller Theological Seminary, 1985.

Kydd, *Gifts*. Kydd, Ronald A. N. *Charismatic Gifts in the Early Church*. Peabody, Mass.: Hendrickson, 1984.

Kydd, *Healing*. Kydd, Ronald A. N. *Healing Through the Centuries: Models for Understanding*. Peabody, Mass.: Hendrickson, 1998.

Kyomo, "Healing." Kyomo, Andrew A. "Faith and Healing in the African Context." Pages 145–56 in *Charismatic Renewal in Africa: A Challenge for African Christianity*. Edited by Mika Vähäkangas and Andrew A. Kyomo. Nairobi: Acton Publishers, 2003.

Laato, "Miracles." Laato, Antti. "Miracles in the Old Testament." Pages 57–76 in *Religious and Spiritual Events*. Vol. 1 of *Miracles: God, Science, and Psychology in the Paranormal*. Edited by J. Harold Ellens. Westport, Conn.; London: Praeger, 2008.

LaBerge and Gackenbach, "Dreaming." LaBerge, Stephen, and Jayne Gackenbach. "Lucid Dreaming." Pages 151–82 in *Varieties of Anomalous Experience: Examining the Scientific Evidence*. Edited by Etzel Cardeña, Steven Jay Lynn, and Stanley Krippner. Washington, D.C.: American Psychological Association, 2000.

Lacey, *Nature*. Lacey, Thomas Alexander. *Nature, Miracle, and Sin: A Study of St. Augustine's Conception of the Natural Order*. The Pringle Stuart Lectures for 1914. New York: Longmans, Green, 1916.

Lachs, *Commentary*. Lachs, Samuel Tobias. *A Rabbinic Commentary on the New Testament: The Gospels of Matthew, Mark, and Luke*. Hoboken, N.J.: KTAV; New York: Anti-Defamation League of B'Nai B'Rith, 1987.

LaCocque, "Competition." LaCocque, Andre. "Moses' Competition with Pharaoh's Magicians." Pages 87–102 in *Religious and Spiritual Events*. Vol. 1 of *Miracles: God, Science, and Psychology in the Paranormal*. Edited by J. Harold Ellens. Westport, Conn.; London: Praeger, 2008.

Ladd, *Kingdom*. Ladd, G. E. *The Gospel of the Kingdom*. Grand Rapids: Eerdmans, 1978.

Ladd, *Theology*. Ladd, George Eldon. *A Theology of the New Testament*. Grand Rapids: Eerdmans, 1974.

Lagerwerf, *Witchcraft*. Lagerwerf, Leny. *Witchcraft, Sorcery and Spirit Possession: Pastoral Responses in Africa*. Gweru, Zimbabwe: Mambo Press, 1987.

Laing, "Face." Laing, Mark. "The Changing Face of Mission: Implications for the Southern Shift in Christianity." *Missiology* 34 (2, April 2006): 165–77.

Laistner, *Historians*. Laistner, M. L. W. *The Greater Roman Historians*. Berkeley: University of California Press; London: Cambridge University Press, 1947.

Lake, *Healer*. Lake, Robert G. (Medicine Grizzlybear Lake). *Native Healer: Initiation into an Ancient Art*. Wheaton: Quest Books, Theosophical Publishing House, 1991.

Lake, *Sermons*. Lake, John G. *The John G. Lake Sermons on Dominion over Demons, Disease, and Death*. 4th ed. Edited by Gordon Lindsay. Shreveport, La.: Gordon Lindsay, 1949; repr., Dallas: Christ for the Nations, 1995.

Lake and Cadbury, *Commentary*. Lake, Kirsopp, and Henry J. Cadbury. *English Translation and Commentary*. Vol. 4 of *The Beginnings of Christianity*. Edited by F. J. Foakes Jackson and Kirsopp Lake. Grand Rapids: Baker, 1979.

Lalleman, "Apocryphal Acts." Lalleman, Pieter J. "Apocryphal Acts and Epistles." Pages 66–69 in *DNTB*.

Lamarche, "Miracles." Lamarche, Paul. "Les miracles de Jésus selon Marc." Pages 213–26 in *Les Miracles de Jésus selon le Nouveau Testament*, by J.-N. Aletti et al. Edited by Xavier Léon-Dufour. Paris: Éditions du Seuil, 1977.

Lambek, "Disease." Lambek, Michael. "From Disease to Discourse: Remarks on the Conceptualization of Trance and Spirit Possession." Pages 36–61 in *Altered States of Consciousness and Mental Health: A Cross-Cultural Perspective*. Edited by Colleen A. Ward. CCRMS 12. Newbury Park, Calif.: Sage, 1989.

Lambek, *Knowledge*. Lambek, Michael. *Knowledge and Practice in Mayotte: Local Discourses of Islam, Sorcery, and Spirit Possession*. Toronto: University of Toronto Press, 1993.

Lambert, *Millions*. Lambert, Tony. *China's Christian Millions: The Costly Revival*. London: Monarch, 1999.

Lambert, *Resurrection*. Lambert, Tony. *The Resurrection of the Chinese Church*. Foreword by David Adeney. Wheaton: Harold Shaw, 1994. Revised from London: Hodder & Stoughton, 1991.

Lampe, "Miracles." Lampe, G. W. H. "Miracles in the Acts of the Apostles." Pages 163–78 in *Miracles: Cambridge Studies in Their Philosophy and History*. Edited by C. F. D. Moule. London: A. R. Mowbray; New York: Morehouse-Barlow, 1965.

Landesman, *Epistemology*. Landesman, Charles. *An Introduction to Epistemology*. Cambridge, Mass.; Oxford: Blackwell, 1997.

Landmann, "Agape." Landmann, Salcia. "Agape Satana: Katholische Exorzismen." *ZRGG* 28 (3, 1976): 265–67.

Landrum, "Miracle." Landrum, George. "What a Miracle Really Is." *RelS* 12 (1, 1976): 49–57.

"Landscape Survey." *U.S. Religious Landscape Survey: Religious Beliefs and Practices: Diverse and Politically Relevant*. Washington, D.C.: The Pew Forum on Religion and Public Life, June 2008. http://religions .pewforum.org/pdf/report2-religious-landscape-study-full.pdf. Accessed Dec, 2, 2008.

Lane, *Mark*. Lane, William L. *The Gospel According to Mark*. NICNT. Grand Rapids: Eerdmans, 1974.

Lane, "*Theios Anēr*." Lane, William L. "*Theios Anēr* Christology and the Gospel of Mark." Pages 144–61 in *New Dimensions in New Testament Study*. Edited by Richard N. Longenecker and Merrill C. Tenney. Grand Rapids: Zondervan, 1974.

Lang, *History*. Lang, G. H., ed. *The History and Diaries of an Indian Christian*. London: Thynne & Co., 1939.

Lang, *Lives*. Lang, D. M., ed. *Lives and Legends of the Georgian Saints*. 2nd ed. Crestwood, N.Y.: St. Vladimir's Seminary Press, 1976.

Lang, "Toland." Lang, Marijke H. de. "John Toland en Hermann Samuel Reimarus over de wonderen in het Oude Testament." *NedTT* 46 (1, 1992): 1–9.

Lang'at, "Experience." Lang'at, Robert K. "The Holiness-Pentecostal Experience in South African Zionism." *Missionalia* 35 (2, Aug. 2007): 89–107.

Lange, "Laws." Lange, Marc. "Laws of Nature." Pages 203–12 in *The Routledge Companion to Philosophy of Science*. Edited by Stathis Psillos and Martin Curd. New York: Routledge, 2008.

Langermann, "Maimonides." Langermann, Y. Tzvi. "Maimonides and Miracles: The Growth of a (Dis) Belief." *JewishHist* 18 (2, 2004): 147–72.

Langford, "Problem." Langford, Michael J. "The Problem of the Meaning of Miracle." *RelS* 7 (1, 1971): 43–52.

Langtry, "Miracles." Langtry, Bruce. "Miracles and Principles of Relative Likelihood." *IJPhilRel* 18 (3, 1985): 123–31.

Langtry, "Probability." Langtry, Bruce. "Hume, Probability, Lotteries, and Miracles." *HumSt* 16 (1, April 1990): 67–74.

Lanternari, "Dreams." Lanternari, Vittorio. "Dreams as Charismatic Significants: Their Bearing on the Rise of New Religious Movements." Pages 321–35 in *The Realm of the Extra-Human: Ideas and Actions*. Edited by Agehananda Bharati. The Hague: Mouton, 1976.

Lappin, "Miracles." Lappin, Anthony. "Miracles in the Making of Twentieth-Century Spanishness: Ramón Menéndez Pidal, Buñuel's *Viridiana* and *Isidro El Labrador*." Pages 464–75 in *Signs, Wonders, Miracles: Representations of Divine Power in the Life of the Church. Papers Read at the 2003 Summer Meeting and*

the 2004 Winter Meeting of the Ecclesiastical History Society. Edited by Kate Cooper and Jeremy Gregory. Rochester: Boydell & Brewer, for the Ecclesiastical History Society, 2005.

Lara, "Joachim." Lara, Jaime. "A Vulcanological Joachim of Fiore and an Aerodynamic Francis of Assisi in Colonial Latin America." Pages 249–72 in *Signs, Wonders, Miracles: Representations of Divine Power in the Life of the Church. Papers Read at the 2003 Summer Meeting and the 2004 Winter Meeting of the Ecclesiastical History Society*. Edited by Kate Cooper and Jeremy Gregory. Rochester: Boydell & Brewer, for the Ecclesiastical History Society, 2005.

Lara, "Report." Lara, Mariano B. "Dr. Lara's Report of the Amazing Case of Clarita Villanueva." *VOH* (Jan. 1955): 5, 18.

Larbi, "Anim." Larbi, E. Kingsley. "Peter Newman Anim." *DACB*. http://www.dacb.org/stories/ghana /anim_peter.html.

Larbi, "Healing." Larbi, Kingsley. "Healing." Page 47 in *Africa Bible Commentary*. Edited by Tokunboh Adeyemo. Grand Rapids: Zondervan; Nairobi: WordAlive, 2006.

Larmer, "Apology." Larmer, Robert. "Miracles and Overall: An Apology for Atheism?" *Dial* 43 (3, 2004): 555–68.

Larmer, "Criteria." Larmer, Robert. "Miracles and Criteria." *Soph* 23 (1, April 1984): 4–10.

Larmer, "Critique." Larmer, Robert A. "C. S. Lewis's Critique of Hume's 'Of Miracles.'" *FPhil* 25 (2, 2008): 154–71.

Larmer, "Evidence." Larmer, Robert. "Miracles, Evidence, and Theism: A Further Apologia." *Soph* 33 (1, March 1994): 53–57.

Larmer, "Explanations." Larmer, Robert A. "Miracles and Natural Explanations: A Rejoinder." *Soph* 28 (1989): 7–12.

Larmer, "Interpreting Hume." Larmer, Robert A. "Interpreting Hume on Miracles." *RelS* 45 (3, 2009): 325–38.

Larmer, "Laws." Larmer, Robert A. "Miracles and the Laws of Nature." *Dial* 24 (1985): 227–35.

Larmer, "Manuscript." Larmer, Robert A. Unpublished manuscript. Forwarded to Craig Keener with personal correspondence, Aug. 4, 2009.

Larmer, "Physicalism." Larmer, Robert A. "Miracles, Physicalism, and the Laws of Nature." *RelS* 44 (2, 2008): 149–59.

Larmer, *Water*. Larmer, Robert A. *Water into Wine? An Investigation of the Concept of Miracle*. Kingston and Montreal: McGill-Queen's University, 1988.

Larson, "Centuries." Larson, Mark J. "Three Centuries of Objections to Biblical Miracles." *BSac* 160 (255, 2003): 77–100.

Larson, "Migration." Larson, Peter A. "Migration and Church Growth in Argentina." DMiss diss., Fuller Theological Seminary, 1973.

Larson, "Trial." Larson, Edward J. "That the Scopes Trial Ended in Defeat for Antievolutionism." Pages 178–86 in Galileo Goes to Jail and Other Myths about Science and Religion. Edited by Ronald L. Numbers. Cambridge, Mass.: Harvard University Press, 2009.

Larson and Wilson, "Religious Life." Larson, David B., and W. P. Wilson. "Religious Life of Alcoholics." SMedJ 73 (1980): 723–27.

Larson and Witham, "Keeping." Larson, Edward J., and Larry Witham. "Scientists Are Still Keeping the Faith." Nature 386 (Apr. 3, 1997): 435–36.

Larson and Witham, "Reject." Larson, Edward J., and Larry Witham. "Leading Scientists Still Reject God." Nature 394 (6691, July 23, 1998): 313.

Larson et al., "Impact." Larson, David B., et al. "The Impact of Religion on Men's Blood Pressure." JRelHealth 28 (1989): 265–78.

Last, "Bori." Last, Murray. "Spirit Possession as Therapy: Bori among Non-Muslims in Nigeria." Pages 49–63 in Women's Medicine: The Zar-Bori Cult in Africa and Beyond. Edited by I. M. Lewis, Ahmed Al-Safi, and Sayyid Hurreiz. Edinburgh: International African Institute, Edinburgh University Press, 1991.

Latour and Woolgar, Laboratory Life. Latour, Bruno, and Steve Woolgar. Laboratory Life: The Construction of Scientific Facts. Rev. ed. Princeton, N.J.: Princeton University Press, 1986.

Latourette, History of Christianity. Latourette, Kenneth Scott. A History of Christianity. Vol. 1: Beginnings to A.D. 1500. San Francisco: HarperSanFrancisco, 1975.

Laughlin, "Energy." Laughlin, Charles D., Jr. "Psychic Energy and Transpersonal Experience: A Biogenetic Structural Account of the Tibetan Dumo Yoga Practice." Pages 99–134 in Being Changed: The Anthropology of Extraordinary Experience. Edited by David E. Young and Jean-Guy Goulet. Peterborough, Ont.: Broadview, 1994.

Laurent, "Transnationalisation." Laurent, Pierre Joseph. "Transnationalisation and Local Transformations: The Example of the Church of Assemblies of God in Burkina Faso." Pages 256–73 in Between Babel and Pentecost: Transnational Pentecostalism in Africa and Latin America. Edited by André Corten and Ruth Marshall-Fratani. Bloomington: Indiana University Press, 2001.

Laurentin, Catholic Pentecostalism. Laurentin, René. Catholic Pentecostalism. Translated by Matthew J. O'Connell. Garden City, N.Y.: Doubleday, 1977.

Laurentin, Medjugorje. Laurentin, René. Is the Virgin Mary Appearing at Medjugorje? An Urgent Message for the World Given in a Marxist Country. Washington, D.C.: World Among Us, 1984.

Laurentin, Miracles. Laurentin, René. Miracles in El Paso? Ann Arbor, Mich.: Servant, 1982.

Lawal, "Psychology." Lawal, Olufemi A. "Miracles and Crowd Psychology in African Culture." Pages 134–53 in Medical and Therapeutic Events. Vol. 2 of Miracles: God, Science, and Psychology in the Paranormal. Edited by J. Harold Ellens. Westport, Conn.; London: Praeger, 2008.

Law and Tang, "Analysis." Law, M., and J. L. Tang. "An Analysis of the Effectiveness of Interventions Intended to Help People Stop Smoking." ArchIntMed 155 (18, 1995): 1933.

Lawrence, Healing. Lawrence, Roy. Christian Healing Rediscovered: A Guide to Spiritual, Mental, Physical Wholeness. Downers Grove, Ill.: InterVarsity, 1980.

Lawrence, Practice. Lawrence, Roy. The Practice of Christian Healing: A Guide for Beginners. Downers Grove, Ill.: InterVarsity, 1996.

Lawton, Miracles. Lawton, John Stewart. Miracles and Revelation. New York: Association Press, 1960.

Lazar, "Aggression." Lazar, Ineke Maria. "Management of Aggression in a Male-Dominated Culture: Samoan Migrant Women in Distress." Paper presented at the National Women's Studies Association Conference, Arcata, Calif., June 1982.

Leavitt, "Trance." Leavitt, Johan. "Are Trance and Possession Disorders?" TranscPsycRR 30 (1993): 51–57.

Lebra, Patterns. Lebra, Takie Sugiyama. Japanese Patterns of Behavior. Honolulu: University Press of Hawaii, 1976.

Lechler, Ratsel. Lechler, Alfred. Das Ratsel von Konnersreuth im Lichte eines neuen Falles von Stigmatisation. Elberfeld, Germany: Licht und Leben, 1933.

Lechner et al., "Associations." Lechner, Suzanne C., Charles S. Carver, Michael H. Antoni, Kathryn E. Weaver, and K. M. Phillips. "Curvilinear Associations between Benefit Finding and Psychosocial Adjustment to Breast Cancer." JConClPsy 74 (5, 2006): 828–40.

Leclaire, "Cardiologist." Leclaire, Jennifer. "Florida Cardiologist Documents Miracles." Charisma (May 2008): 38.

Le Cornu, Acts. Le Cornu, Hilary, with Joseph Shulam. A Commentary on the Jewish Roots of Acts. Jerusalem: Netivyah Bible Instruction Ministry, 2003.

Lederer, "Healing." Lederer, Christina. "A Wonderful Healing." PentEv (July 22, 1922): 5.

Lee, "Church Growth." Lee, Chang-Shik. "Church Growth in Korea: 1834–1910." ThM thesis, Fuller School of World Mission, 1976.

Lee, "Development." Lee, Young-Hoon. "The Holy Spirit Movement in Korea: Its Historical and Doctrinal Development." PhD diss., Temple University, 1996.

Lee, "Distinctives." Lee, Jae Bum. "Pentecostal Type Distinctives and Korean Protestant Church Growth." PhD diss., Fuller Theological Seminary, 1986.

Lee, "Future." Lee, Moonjang. "Future of Global Christianity." Pages 104–5 in *Atlas of Global Christianity, 1910–2010*. Edited by Todd M. Johnson and Kenneth R. Ross; managing editor, Sandra S. K. Lee. Edinburgh: Center for the Study of Global Christianity, 2009.

Lee, "Galileo." Lee, H. J. "'Men of Galilee, Why Stand Gazing Up into Heaven': Revisiting Galileo, Astronomy, and the Authority of the Bible." *JETS* 53 (1, March 2010): 103–16.

Lee, "Juning." Lee, Thomas. "Juning." *CGl* 9 (2, April 1932): 8–11.

Lee, "Korean Pentecost." Lee, Young-Hoon. "Korean Pentecost: The Great Revival of 1907." *AJPS* 4 (1, 2001): 73–83.

Lee, *Movement*. Lee, Young-Hoon (Yi, Yong-hun). *The Holy Spirit Movement in Korea: Its Historical and Theological Development*. Forewords by David Yonggi Cho and Andrew F. Walls. RStMiss. Eugene, Ore.: Wipf & Stock, 2009.

Lee, "Movement." Lee, Young-Hoon. "The Korean Holy Spirit Movement in Relation to Pentecostalism." Pages 509–26 in *Asian and Pentecostal: The Charismatic Face of Christianity in Asia*. Edited by Allan Anderson and Edmond Tang. Foreword by Cecil M. Robeck. Regnum Studies in Mission, AJPSS 3. Oxford: Regnum; Baguio City, Philippines: APTS Press, 2005.

Lee, "Possession." Lee, S. G. "Spirit Possession among the Zulu." Pages 128–56 in *Spirit Mediumship and Society in Africa*. Edited by John Beattie and John Middleton. Foreword by Raymond Firth. New York: Africana Publishing Corporation, 1969.

Lee, "Powers." Lee, Jung Young. "Interpreting the Demonic Powers in Pauline Thought." *NovT* 12 (1, 1970): 54–69.

Lee, "Rulers." Lee, Thomas I. "Against the Rulers of Darkness." *CGl* 14 (3, July 1937): 4–7.

Lee, "Self-Presentation." Lee, Raymond L. M. "Self-Presentation in Malaysian Spirit Seances: A Dramaturgical Perspective on Altered States of Consciousness in Healing Ceremonies." Pages 251–66 in *Altered States of Consciousness and Mental Health: A Cross-Cultural Perspective*. Edited by Colleen A. Ward. CCRMS 12. Newbury Park, Calif.: Sage, 1989.

Lee, "Sociology." Lee, Richard B. "The Sociology of !Kung Bushman Trance Performances." Pages 35–54 in *Trance and Possession States*. Proceedings of the Second Annual Conference, R. M. Bucke Memorial Society, March 4–6, 1966. Edited by Raymond Prince. Montreal: R. M. Bucke Memorial Society, 1968.

Lee, "Ta-Tung-Chai." Lee, Thomas I. "Ta-Tung-Chai." *CGl* 11 (4, Oct. 1934): 15–16.

Lee and Poloma, *Commandment*. Lee, Matthew T., and Margaret M. Poloma. *A Sociological Study of the Great Commandment in Pentecostalism: The Practice of Godly Love as Benevolent Service*. Lewiston, N.Y.: Mellen, 2009.

Leek, *Story*. Leek, Sybil. *The Story of Faith Healing*. New York: Macmillan, 1973.

Leeper, "Connection." Leeper, Elizabeth A. "From Alexandria to Rome: The Valentinian Connection to the Incorporation of Exorcism as a Prebaptismal Rite." *VC* 44 (1, 1990): 6–24.

Leeper, "Exorcism." Leeper, Elizabeth A. "The Role of Exorcism in Early Christianity." *StPatr* 26 (1993): 59–62.

Lees and Fiddes, "Healed." Lees, Bill, and Paul Fiddes. "How Are People Healed Today? The Relationship between the 'Medical' and the 'Spiritual' in Healing." Pages 5–30 in *Christian Healing: What Can We Believe?* Edited by Ernest Lucas. London: Lynx Communications, SPCK, 1997.

Légasse, "L'Historien." Légasse, Simon. "L'historien en quête de l'événement." Pages 109–45 in *Les Miracles de Jésus selon le Nouveau Testament*, by J.-N. Aletti et al. Edited by Xavier Léon-Dufour. Paris: Éditions du Seuil, 1977.

Légasse, "Miracles." Légasse, Simon. "Les miracles de Jésus selon Matthieu." Pages 227–47 in *Les Miracles de Jésus selon le Nouveau Testament*, by J.-N. Aletti et al. Edited by Xavier Léon-Dufour. Paris: Éditions du Seuil, 1977.

Legrand, "Miracle." Legrand, Thierry. "Qu'est-ce qu'un miracle? Une perspective en histoire des religions." *FoiVie* 108 (2, 2009): 12–27.

Lehmann, "Miracles." Lehmann, Hartmut. "Miracles Within Catastrophes: Some Examples from Early Modern Germany." Pages 321–34 in *Signs, Wonders, Miracles: Representations of Divine Power in the Life of the Church. Papers Read at the 2003 Summer Meeting and the 2004 Winter Meeting of the Ecclesiastical History Society*. Edited by Kate Cooper and Jeremy Gregory. Rochester: Boydell & Brewer, for the Ecclesiastical History Society, 2005.

Lehmann, *Struggle*. Lehmann, David. *Struggle for the Spirit: Religious Transformation and Popular Culture in Brazil and Latin America*. Cambridge: Polity Press (with Blackwell), 1996.

Lehmann, *Study*. Lehmann, Martin E. *A Biographical Study of Ingwer Ludwig Nommensen (1834–1918)*,

Pioneer Missionary to the Bataks of Sumatra. Lewiston, N.Y.: Mellen, 1996.

Leicht, "Mashbia." Leicht, Reimund. "Mashbia' Ani 'Alekha: Types and Patterns of Ancient Jewish and Christian Exorcism Formulae." *JSQ* 13 (4, 2006): 319–43.

Leiris, *Possession.* Leiris, Michel. *La possession et ses aspects theatreaux chez les Ethiopiens de Gender.* Paris: Librarie Plon, 1958.

Lema, "Chaga Religion." Lema, Anza A. "Chaga Religion and Missionary Christianity on Kilimanjaro. The Initial Phase, 1893–1916." Pages 39–62 in *East African Expressions of Christianity.* Edited by Thomas Spear and Isaria N. Kimambo. EAfSt. Athens: Ohio University Press; Oxford: James Currey; Dar es Salaam: Mkuki na Nyota; Nairobi: East African Educational Publishers, 1999.

LeMarquand, "Readings." LeMarquand, Grant. "African Readings of Paul." Pages 488–503 in *The Blackwell Companion to Paul.* Edited by Stephen Westerholm. Malden, Mass.: Blackwell, 2011.

Lenzer, "Citizen." Lenzer, Jeanne. "Citizen, Heal Thyself." *Discover: Science, Technology, and the Future* 28 (9, Sept. 2007): 54–59, 73.

Leonard, "Spirit Mediums." Leonard, Anne P. "Spirit Mediums in Palau: Transformations in a Traditional System." Pages 129–77 in *Religion, Altered States of Consciousness, and Social Change.* Edited by Erika Bourguignon. Columbus: Ohio State University Press, 1973.

Léon-Dufour, "Approches." Léon-Dufour, Xavier. "Approches diverses du miracle." Pages 11–39 in *Les Miracles de Jésus selon le Nouveau Testament,* by J.-N. Aletti et al. Edited by Xavier Léon-Dufour. Paris: Éditions du Seuil, 1977.

Léon-Dufour, "Conclusion." Léon-Dufour, Xavier. "Conclusion." Pages 355–74 in *Les Miracles de Jésus selon le Nouveau Testament,* by J.-N. Aletti et al. Edited by Xavier Léon-Dufour. Paris: Éditions du Seuil, 1977.

Léon-Dufour, "Fonction." Léon-Dufour, Xavier. "Structure et fonction du récit de miracle." Pages 289–353 in *Les Miracles de Jésus selon le Nouveau Testament,* by J.-N. Aletti et al. Edited by Xavier Léon-Dufour. Paris: Éditions du Seuil, 1977.

Léon-Dufour, "Miracles." Léon-Dufour, Xavier. "Les miracles de Jésus selon Jean." Pages 269–87 in *Les Miracles de Jésus selon le Nouveau Testament,* by J.-N. Aletti et al. Edited by Xavier Léon-Dufour. Paris: Éditions du Seuil, 1977.

Lerman, "Arthritis." Lerman, C. E. "Rheumatoid arthritis: psychological factors in the etiology, course, and treatment." *ClinPsyRev* 7 (1987): 413–25.

Le Roux, "Le Roux." Le Roux, Harold. "White Afrikaner Zionist Pieter Louis Le Roux (1865–1943)." *StHistEc* 33 (2, Sept. 2007): 45–65.

Leshan, *Medium.* Leshan, Lawrence. *The Medium, the Mystic, and the Physicist: Toward a General Theory of the Paranormal.* New York: Ballantine, 1975.

Lesher, "Response." Lesher, Ruth Detweiler. "Psychiatry/Psychology: A Response." Pages 163–73 in *Essays on Spiritual Bondage and Deliverance.* Edited by Willard M. Swartley. Occasional Papers 11. Elkhart, Ind.: Institute of Mennonite Studies, 1988.

Leslie, *Universes.* Leslie, John. *Universes.* New York: Routledge & Kegan Paul, 1989.

Lesniak et al., "Distress." Lesniak, K. T., W. Rudman, M. B. Rector, and T. Elkin. "Psychological Distress, Stressful Life Events, and Religiosity in Younger African American Adults." *MHRC* 9 (1, 2006): 15–28.

Lesslie, *Angels.* Lesslie, Robert D. *Angels in the ER: Inspiring True Stories from an Emergency Room Doctor.* Eugene, Ore.: Harvest House, 2008.

Leung, "Conversion." Leung, Philip Yuen-Sang. "Conversion, Commitment, and Culture: Christian Experience in China, 1949–99." Pages 87–107 in *Christianity Reborn: The Global Expansion of Evangelicalism in the Twentieth Century.* Edited by Donald M. Lewis. SHCM. Grand Rapids: Eerdmans, 2004.

Levene, "Heal." Levene, Dan. "Heal O' Israel: A Pair of Duplicate Magic Bowls from the Pergamon Museum in Berlin." *JJS* 54 (1, 2003): 104–21.

Levin and Schiller, "Factor." Levin, J. S., and P. L. Schiller. "Is There a Religious Factor in Health?" *JRelHealth* 26 (1, 1987): 9–36.

Levine, "Belief." Levine, M. "Belief in Miracles: Tillotson's Argument against Transubstantiation as a Model for Hume." *IJPhilRel* 23 (3, May 1988): 125–60.

Levine, *Hellenism.* Levine, Lee I. *Judaism and Hellenism in Antiquity: Conflict or Confluence?* Peabody, Mass.: Hendrickson, 1998.

Levine, *Problem.* Levine, Michael P. *Hume and the Problem of Miracles: A Solution.* PhilSS. Dordrecht: Kluwer Academic, 1989.

Levine, "Twice." Levine, Nachman. "Twice as Much of Your Spirit: Pattern, Parallel, and Paronomasia in the Miracles of Elijah and Elisha." *JSOT* 85 (1999): 25–46.

Levitt, *Beef.* Levitt, Zola. *Corned Beef, Knishes, and Christ.* Wheaton: Tyndale, 1975.

Lewis, "Analysis." Lewis, David C. "A Social Anthropologist's Analysis of Contemporary Healing." *Pneuma Review* 11 (4, Fall 2008): 20–37; 12 (1, Winter 2009): 6–18.

Lewis, "Deprivation Cults." Lewis, I. M. "Spirit Possession and Deprivation Cults." Pages 311–33 in

Possession and Exorcism. Vol. 9 of *Articles on Witchcraft, Magic, and Demonology: A Twelve-Volume Anthology of Scholarly Articles.* Edited by Brian P. Levack. New York: Garland, 1992. Reprinted from *Man* 1 (1966): 307–29.

Lewis, *Ecstatic Religion.* Lewis, I. [Ioan] M. *Ecstatic Religion: An Anthropological Study of Spirit Possession and Shamanism.* Pelican Anthropology Library. Middlesex: Penguin, 1971.

Lewis, *Healing.* Lewis, David C. *Healing: Fiction, Fantasy, or Fact?* London: Hodder & Stoughton, 1989.

Lewis, "Introduction." Lewis, I. M. "Introduction: Zar in Context: The Past, the Present and Future of an African Healing Cult." Pages 1–16 in *Women's Medicine: The Zar-Bori Cult in Africa and Beyond.* Edited by I. M. Lewis, Ahmed Al-Safi, and Sayyid Hurreiz. Edinburgh: International African Institute, Edinburgh University Press, 1991.

Lewis, *Life.* Lewis, Naphtali. *Life in Egypt under Roman Rule.* Oxford: Clarendon, 1983.

Lewis, "Martyrdom." Lewis, Justin Jaron. "Miracles and Martyrdom: The Theology of a Yiddish-Language Memorial Book of Hasidic Tales in the Context of Earlier Hasidic Hagiography" (in Hebrew). *JStIJ* 6 (2007).

Lewis, *Miracles.* Lewis, C. S. *Miracles: A Preliminary Study.* New York: Macmillan, 1948.

Lewis, "Possession." Lewis, I. M. "Spirit Possession in Northern Somaliland." Pages 188–219 in *Spirit Mediumship and Society in Africa.* Edited by John Beattie and John Middleton. Foreword by Raymond Firth. New York: Africana Publishing Corporation, 1969.

Lewis, "Signs." Lewis, David C. "Appendix F: Signs and Wonders in Sheffield: A Social Anthropologist's Analysis of Words of Knowledge, Manifestations of the Spirit, and the Effectiveness of Divine Healing." Pages 248–69 in *Power Healing,* by John Wimber with Kevin Springer. San Francisco: Harper & Row, 1987.

Lewis, "Spirits and Sex War." Lewis, I. M. "Correspondence: Spirits and the Sex War." *Man,* n.s., 2 (4, Dec. 1967): 626–28.

Lewis, Al-Safi, and Hurreiz, *Medicine.* Lewis, I. M., Ahmed Al-Safi, and Sayyid Hurreiz, eds. *Women's Medicine: The Zar-Bori Cult in Africa and Beyond.* Edinburgh: International African Institute, Edinburgh University Press, 1991.

Lewis-Williams and Dawson, "Signs." Lewis-Williams, J. David, and Thomas A. Dawson. "The Signs of All Times: Entoptic Phenomena in Upper Paleolithic Art." *CurAnth* 29 (1988): 201–45.

Li, "Abirewa." Li, Anshan. "Abirewa: A Religious Movement in the Gold Coast, 1906–8." *JRH* 20 (1, 1996): 32–52.

Li, "Theology of Exorcism." Li, Lawrence. "Theology of Exorcism." *ThLife* 20 (1998): 97–109.

Liang, Krause, and Bennett, "Exchange." Liang, Jersey, Neal M. Krause, and Joan M. Bennett. "Social Exchange and Well-Being: Is Giving Better Than Receiving?" *PsyAg* 16 (3, 2001): 511–23.

Liardon, *Generals.* Liardon, Roberts. *God's Generals: Why They Succeeded and Why Some Failed.* New Kensington, Pa.: Whitaker House, 1996.

Liardon, *Wigglesworth.* Liardon, Roberts, ed. *Smith Wigglesworth: The Complete Collection of His Life and Teachings.* Foreword by Alice Berry neé Wigglesworth. Tulsa: Albury Publishing, 1996.

Libersat, "Epilogue." Libersat, Henry. "Epilogue." Pages 139–42 in *Miracles Do Happen,* by Briege McKenna with Henry Libersat. New York: St. Martin's Press, 1987.

Licauco, "Psychic Healing." Licauco, Jaime. "Psychic Healing in the Philippines." Pages 93–96 in *Proceedings of the Fourth International Conference on the Study of Shamanism and Alternate Modes of Healing, Held at the St. Sabina Center, San Rafael, California, September 5–7, 1987.* Edited by Ruth-Inge Heinze. N.p.: Independent Scholars of Asia; Madison, Wis.: A-R Editions, 1988.

Licauco, "Realities." Licauco, Jaime. "Close In: Strange Realities." Pages 262–69 in *Proceedings of the Fourth International Conference on the Study of Shamanism and Alternate Modes of Healing, Held at the St. Sabina Center, San Rafael, California, September 5–7, 1987.* Edited by Ruth-Inge Heinze. N.p.: Independent Scholars of Asia; Madison, Wis.: A-R Editions, 1988.

Licona, "Historicity of Resurrection." Licona, Michael R. "The Historicity of the Resurrection of Christ: Historiographical Considerations in the Light of Recent Debates." PhD diss., University of Pretoria, 2008.

Licona, *Resurrection.* Licona, Michael R. *The Resurrection of Jesus: A New Historiographical Approach.* Downers Grove, Ill.: InterVarsity; Nottingham: Apollos, 2010.

Licona and Van der Watt, "Adjudication of Miracles." Licona, Michael R., and Jan G. Van der Watt. "The Adjudication of Miracles: Rethinking the Criteria of Historicity." *HTS/TS* 65 (1, 2009): article 130, 7 pages. http://www.hts.org.za.

Licona and Van der Watt, "Historians and Miracles." Licona, Michael R., and Jan G. Van der Watt. "Historians and Miracles: The Principle of Analogy and Antecedent Probability Reconsidered." *HTS/TS* 65 (1, 2009): article 129, 6 pages. http://www.hts.org.za.

Liddell and Scott, *Lexicon.* Liddell, Henry George, and Robert Scott. *A Greek-English Lexicon.* Revised by Henry Stuart Jones and Roderick McKenzie. Oxford: Clarendon, 1968.

Lieberman, "Dybbuk." Lieberman, Leo. "The Concept of the 'Dybbuk' (Demon) in Hebrew Literature and Thought." Pages 99–104 in *Exorcism Through the Ages*. Edited by St. Elmo Nauman. New York: Philosophical Library, 1974.

Lieberman, "Golem." Lieberman, Leo. "The Legend of the Golem." Pages 105–10 in *Exorcism Through the Ages*. Edited by St. Elmo Nauman. New York: Philosophical Library, 1974.

Liefeld, "Divine Man." Liefeld, Walter L. "The Hellenistic 'Divine Man' and the Figure of Jesus in the Gospels." *JETS* 16 (1973): 195–205.

Lienhardt, "Death." Lienhardt, Godfrey. "The Situation of Death: An Aspect of Anuak Philosophy." *AnthrQ* 35 (2, April 1962): 74–85.

Lietaer and Corveleyn, "Interpretation." Lietaer, Hugo, and Jozef Corveleyn. "Psychoanalytical Interpretation of the Demoniacal Possession and the Mystical Development of Sister Jeanne des Anges from Loudun." *IntJPsRel* 5 (4, 1995): 259–76.

Lietzmann, *History.* Lietzmann, Hans. *A History of the Early Church.* Translated by Bertram Lee Woolf. 4 vols. Cleveland: Meridian Books, World, 1961.

"Life of Ramabai." "From a Child of the Forest to a Power that Sways India: Incidents in the Life of Pandita Ramabai." *LRE* 15 (8, May 1922): 15–17.

Lim, "Challenges." Lim, David S. "The Challenges of Empowering Philippine Churches for Effective Missions in China (and Beyond)." Pages 195–210 in *Asian Church and God's Mission: Studies Presented in the International Symposium on Asian Mission in Manila, January 2002.* Edited by Wonsuk Ma and Julie C. Ma. Manila: OMF Literature; West Caldwell, N.J.: MWM, 2003.

Lim, "Evaluation." Lim, David S. "A Missiological Evaluation of David Yonggi Cho's Church Growth." Pages 181–207 in *David Yonggi Cho: A Close Look at his Theology and Ministry.* Edited by Wonsuk Ma, William W. Menzies, and Hyeon-sung Bae. AJPSS 1. Baguio City, Philippines: APTS Press, Hansei University Press, 2004.

Lincoln, *John.* Lincoln, Andrew T. *The Gospel According to Saint John.* BNTC. Peabody, Mass.: Hendrickson; London: Continuum, 2005.

Lincoln, *Paradise.* Lincoln, Andrew T. *Paradise Now and Not Yet: Studies in the Role of the Heavenly Dimension in Paul's Thought with Special Reference to His Eschatology.* SNTSM 43. Cambridge: Cambridge University Press, 1981.

Lindberg, "Adversaries." Lindberg, David. "Natural Adversaries?" *ChH* 76 (4, 2002): 44–46.

Lindberg, *Beginnings.* Lindberg, David. *The Beginnings of Western Science: The European Scientific Tradition in Philosophical, Religious, and Institutional Context, Prehistory to A.D. 1450.* 2nd ed. Chicago: University of Chicago Press, 2008.

Lindberg, "Rise." Lindberg, David C. "That the Rise of Christianity Was Responsible for the Demise of Ancient Science." Pages 8–18 in *Galileo Goes to Jail and Other Myths about Science and Religion.* Edited by Ronald L. Numbers. Cambridge, Mass.: Harvard University Press, 2009.

Lindberg and Numbers, *Essays.* Lindberg, David, and Ronald Numbers, eds. *God and Nature: Historical Essays on the Encounter between Christianity and Science.* Berkeley: University of California Press, 1986.

Lindholm, "Healings." Lindholm, Grace, with Gail Winters. "Healings in Congo." *PentEv* 1422 (Aug. 9, 1941): 9.

Lindsay, *Lake.* Lindsay, Gordon. *John G. Lake: Apostle to Africa.* Dallas: Christ for the Nations, 1981.

Lindsay, *Not Healed.* Lindsay, Gordon. *Why Some Are Not Healed.* Dallas: Christ for the Nations, n.d.

Little, *Believe.* Little, Paul E. *Know Why You Believe.* Downers Grove, Ill.: InterVarsity, 1973.

Little, *Faith.* Little, Paul E. *How to Give Away Your Faith.* Revised by Marie Little. Foreword by Leighton Ford. Downers Grove, Ill.: InterVarsity, 1988.

Little, "Planned." Little, William A. "Was It Planned, Is It Part of a Grander Scheme of Things?" Pages 54–56 in *Cosmos, Bios, and Theos: Scientists Reflect on Science, God, and the Origins of the Universe, Life, and Homo Sapiens.* Edited by Henry Margenau and Roy Abraham Varghese. La Salle, Ill.: Open Court, 1992.

Litwin, "Association." Litwin, Howard. "What Really Matters in the Social Network Mortality Association? A Multivariate Examination among Older Jewish Israelis." *EurJAg* 4 (2, June 2007): 71–82.

Liu, "Evaluation." Liu, Herrick P. "A Theological Evaluation on Charles Kraft's Theory of Inner Healing" (in Chinese). *Jian Dao* 31 (2009): 53–81. (RTA)

Livingstone, *Defenders.* Livingstone, David N. *Darwin's Forgotten Defenders: The Encounter between Evangelical Theology and Evolutionary Thought.* Grand Rapids: Eerdmans; Edinburgh: Scottish Academic Press, 1987.

Livingstone, "Huxley." Livingstone, David N. "That Huxley Defeated Wilberforce in Their Debate over Evolution and Religion." Pages 152–60 in *Galileo Goes to Jail and Other Myths about Science and Religion.* Edited by Ronald L. Numbers. Cambridge, Mass.: Harvard University Press, 2009.

Livingstone, *Last Journals.* Livingstone, David. *The Last Journals of David Livingstone, in Central Africa, from 1865 to His Death, with a Narrative of His Last*

Moments and Sufferings. Hartford, Conn.: R. W. Bliss; Chicago: American Publishing Company, 1875.

Livingstone, Hart, and Noll, *Perspective*. Livingstone, David N., D. G. Hart, and Mark A. Noll, eds. *Evangelicals and Science in Historical Perspective*. Religion in America. New York: Oxford University Press, 1999.

Llewellyn, "Events." Llewellyn, Russ. "Religious and Spiritual Miracle Events in Real-Life Experience." Pages 241–63 in *Religious and Spiritual Events*. Vol. 1 of *Miracles: God, Science, and Psychology in the Paranormal*. Edited by J. Harold Ellens. Westport, Conn.; London: Praeger, 2008.

Lloyd-Jones, *Spirit*. Lloyd-Jones, Martyn. *The Sovereign Spirit: Discerning His Gifts*. Wheaton: Harold Shaw, 1985.

Loder and Neidhardt, "Dialectic." Loder, James E., and W. Jim Neidhardt. "Barth, Bohr, and Dialectic." Pages 271–89 in *Religion and Science: History, Method, Dialogue*. Edited by W. Mark Richardson and Wesley J. Wildman. Foreword by Ian G. Barbour. New York: Routledge, 1996.

Loewen, "Possession." Loewen, Jacob A. "Demon Possession and Exorcism in Africa, in the New Testament Context, and in North America; or: Toward a Western Scientific Model of Demon Possession and Exorcism." Pages 118–45 in *Essays on Spiritual Bondage and Deliverance*. Edited by Willard M. Swartley. Occasional Papers 11. Elkhart, Ind.: Institute of Mennonite Studies, 1988.

Loewer, "Determinism." Loewer, Barry. "Determinism." Pages 327–36 in *The Routledge Companion to Philosophy of Science*. Edited by Stathis Psillos and Martin Curd. New York: Routledge, 2008.

Lonczak et al., "Coping." Lonczak, Heather S., Seema Clifasefi, G. Alan Marlatt, Arthur Blume, and Dennis M. Donovan. "Religious Coping and Psychological Functioning in a Correctional Population." *MHRC* 9 (2, 2006): 171–92.

Lonergan, *Insight*. Lonergan, Bernard J. F. *Insight: A Study of Human Understanding*. Rev. ed. New York: Philosophical Library; London: Longmans, Green and Co., 1958.

Lonergan, *Method*. Lonergan, Bernard J. F. *Method in Theology*. 2nd ed. New York: Herder and Herder, 1973.

Lonergan, *Understanding*. Lonergan, Bernard. *Understanding and Being: An Introduction and Companion to Insight*. Edited by Elizabeth A. Morrelli and Mark D. Morelli. TorStTh 5. Lewiston, N.Y.: Edwin Mellen, 1980.

Long, *Ecology*. Long, Joseph K., ed. *Extrasensory Ecology: Parapsychology and Anthropology*. Metuchen, N.J.: Scarecrow, 1977.

Long, "Samuel." Long, V. Philips. "1 Samuel." Pages 266–411 in vol. 2 of *Zondervan Illustrated Bible*

Backgrounds Commentary: Old Testament. Edited by John H. Walton. 5 vols. Grand Rapids: Zondervan, 2009.

Long, *Philosophy*. Long, A. A. *Hellenistic Philosophy: Stoics, Epicureans, Sceptics*. New York: Charles Scribner's Sons, 1974.

Longenecker, *Paul*. Longenecker, Richard N. *Paul, Apostle of Liberty*. Grand Rapids: Baker, 1976.

Longkumer, "Study." Longkumer, H. "A Study of the Revival Movement in Nagaland." MTh thesis, Fuller Theological Seminary, 1981.

Loos, *Miracles*. Loos, Hendrik van der. *The Miracles of Jesus*. NovTSup 9. Leiden: Brill, 1965.

Lotufo and Lotufo-Neto, "Religiosity." Lotufo, Zenon, Jr., and Francisco Lotufo-Neto. "Healthy Religiosity that Generates Illness." Pages 287–302 in *Religion*. Vol. 2 of *The Healing Power of Spirituality: How Faith Helps Humans Thrive*. Edited by J. Harold Ellens. Santa Barbara, Calif.: Praeger, 2010.

Lotufo-Neto, "Influences." Lotufo-Neto, Francisco. "Religious Influences on Psychotherapy in Brazil." Pages 192–206 in *Psychodynamics*. Vol. 3 of *The Healing Power of Spirituality: How Faith Helps Humans Thrive*. Edited by J. Harold Ellens. Santa Barbara, Calif.: Praeger, 2010.

Loubser, "Possession." Loubser, J. A. "Possession and Sacrifice in the New Testament and African Traditional Religion: The Oral Forms and Conventions behind the Literary Genres." *Neot* 37 (2, 2003): 221–45.

Loud, "Miracles." Loud, G. A. "Monastic Miracles in Southern Italy, c. 1040–1140." Pages 109–22 in *Signs, Wonders, Miracles: Representations of Divine Power in the Life of the Church. Papers Read at the 2003 Summer Meeting and the 2004 Winter Meeting of the Ecclesiastical History Society*. Edited by Kate Cooper and Jeremy Gregory. Rochester: Boydell & Brewer, for the Ecclesiastical History Society, 2005.

Love, *Stewart*. Love, N. B. C. *John Stewart: Missionary to the Wyandots*. New York: Missionary Society of the Methodist Episcopal Church, n.d.

Lovelace, *Dynamics*. Lovelace, Richard F. *Dynamics of Spiritual Life: An Evangelical Theology of Renewal*. Exeter: Paternoster; Downers Grove, Ill.: InterVarsity, 1979.

Lovett, "Pentecostalism." Lovett, Leonard. "Black Holiness-Pentecostalism." Pages 76–84 in *Dictionary of Pentecostal and Charismatic Movements*. Edited by Stanley M. Burgess, Gary B. McGee, and Patrick H. Alexander. Grand Rapids: Zondervan, 1988.

Lowe, "Miracles." Lowe, E. J. "Miracles and Laws of Nature." *RelS* 23 (2, 1987): 263–78.

Lowe, *Spirits*. Lowe, Chuck. *Territorial Spirits and World Evangelisation?* Kent: OMF International, 1998.

Lowie, *Religion*. Lowie, Robert H. *Primitive Religion*. New York: Liveright, 1948.

Lown, "Miraculous." Lown, John S. "The Miraculous in the Greco-Roman Historians." *Forum* 2 (4, Dec. 1986): 36–42.

Lozano, *Unbound*. Lozano, Neal. *Unbound: A Practical Guide to Deliverance from Evil Spirits*. Foreword by Francis MacNutt. Grand Rapids: Chosen, 2003.

Lubkemann, "Ancestor." Lubkemann, Stephen C. "Where to Be an Ancestor? Reconstituting Socio-Spiritual Worlds among Displaced Mozambicans." Pages 319–50 in *Studies in Witchcraft, Magic, War, and Peace in Africa*. Edited by Beatrice Nicolini. Lewiston, N.Y.: Edwin Mellen, 2006. Reprinted from *Journal of Refugee Studies* 15 (2, 2002): 189–212.

Lucas, "Foundations." Lucas, John R. "Foundations for the Healing Ministry in the Uniting Church in Australia." DMin diss., Fuller Theological Seminary, 1992.

Lucas, *Healing*. Lucas, Ernest, ed. *Christian Healing: What Can We Believe?* London: Lynx Communications, SPCK, 1997.

Luck, "Defense." Luck, Morgan. "In Defense of Mumford's Definition of a Miracle." *RelS* 39 (4, 2003): 465–69.

Lüdemann, *Acts*. Lüdemann, Gerd. *The Acts of the Apostles: What Really Happened in the Earliest Days of the Church*. Assisted by Tom Hall. Amherst, N.Y.: Prometheus, 2005.

Lüdemann, *Two Thousand Years*. Lüdemann, Gerd. *Jesus after Two Thousand Years: What He Really Said and Did*. With contributions from Frank Schleritt and Martina Janssen. Amherst, N.Y.: Prometheus, 2001.

Ludwig, "Altered States." Ludwig, Arnold M. "Altered States of Consciousness." Pages 69–95 in *Trance and Possession States*. Proceedings of the Second Annual Conference, R. M. Bucke Memorial Society, March 4–6, 1966. Edited by Raymond Prince. Montreal: R. M. Bucke Memorial Society, 1968.

Ludwig, *Order Restored*. Ludwig, Garth D. *Order Restored: A Biblical Interpretation of Health, Medicine, and Healing*. St. Louis: Concordia Academic Press, 1999.

Luft, "Unfolding." Luft, Eric von der. "Review Article: The Unfolding of Hegel's Berlin Philosophy of Religion." *IJPhilRel* 25 (1989): 53–64.

Lugazia, "Movements." Lugazia, Faith J. "Charismatic Movements and the Evangelical Lutheran Church in Tanzania." Pages 45–65 in *Charismatic Renewal in Africa: A Challenge for African Christianity*. Edited by Mika Vähäkangas and Andrew A. Kyomo. Nairobi: Acton Publishers, 2003.

Lugt, "Incubus." Lugt, Maaike van der. "The *Incubus* in Scholastic Debate: Medicine, Theology and Popular Belief." Pages 175–200 in *Religion and Medicine in the Middle Ages*. Edited by Peter Biller and Joseph Ziegler. YSMT 3. Woodbridge, Suffolk: York Medieval Press, The University of York (with Boydell Press), 2001.

Luig, "Worlds." Luig, Ute. "Constructing Local Worlds: Spirit Possession in the Gwembe Valley, Zambia." Pages 124–41 in *Spirit Possession, Modernity and Power in Africa*. Edited by Heike Behrend and Ute Luig. Madison: University of Wisconsin Press, 1999.

Luks, *Power*. Luks, Allan. *The Healing Power of Doing Good*. New York: Ballantine, 1993.

Luling, "Possession Cults." Luling, Virginia. "Some Possession Cults in Southern Somalia." Pages 167–77 in *Women's Medicine: The Zar-Bori Cult in Africa and Beyond*. Edited by I. M. Lewis, Ahmed Al-Safi, and Sayyid Hurreiz. Edinburgh: International African Institute, Edinburgh University Press, 1991.

Lumahan, "Fact and Figures." Lumahan, Conrado P. "Facts and Figures: A History of the Origin and Development of the Assemblies of God Churches in Southern Ilocos Region." ThM thesis, Asia Pacific Theological Seminary, 2003.

Lumby, "Feeding." Lumby, J. R. "Christ Feeding the Multitudes." *Exp*, 1st ser., 8 (1878): 148–55.

Lutgendorf et al., "Participation." Lutgendorf, Susan K., Daniel Russell, Philip Ullrich, Tamara B. Harris, and Robert Wallace. "Religious Participation, Interleukin-6, and Mortality in Older Adults." *HealthPsy* 23 (5, 2004): 465–75.

Lutzer, *Miracles*. Lutzer, Erwin W. *Seven Convincing Miracles: Understanding the Claims of Christ in Today's Culture*. Chicago: Moody Press, 1999.

Luzbetak, *Church and Cultures*. Luzbetak, Louis J. *The Church and Cultures*. Techny, Ill.: Divine Word, 1970; Pasadena, Calif.: William Carey Library, 1976.

Lygunda li-M, "Pelendo." Lygunda li-M, Fohle. "Pelendo, Isaac." *DACB*. http://www.dacb.org/stories/demrepcongo/f-pelendo_isaac.html.

Lynch-Watson, *Robe*. Lynch-Watson, Janet. *The Saffron Robe: A Life of Sadhu Sundar Singh*. London: Hodder & Stoughton, 1975.

Lyon, "Prophecies." Lyon, William S. "The Prophecies of Black Elk." Pages 70–86 in *Proceedings of the Fourth International Conference on the Study of Shamanism and Alternate Modes of Healing, Held at the St. Sabina Center, San Rafael, California, September 5–7, 1987*. Edited by Ruth-Inge Heinze. N.p.: Independent Scholars of Asia; Madison, Wis.: A-R Editions, 1988.

Ma, "Challenges." Ma, Jungja. "Pentecostal Challenges in East and South-East Asia." Pages 183–202 in *The Globalization of Pentecostalism: A Religion Made to Travel*. Edited by Murray W. Dempster,

Byron D. Klaus, and Douglas Petersen. Foreword by Russell P. Spittler. Carlisle: Paternoster; Oxford: Regnum, 1999.

Ma, "Church Planting." Ma, Julie C. "Church Planting: Strategy for Mission among Pentecostals." *JAM* 6 (2, Sept. 2004): 213–33.

Ma, "Encounter." Ma, Julie C. "'A Close Encounter with the Transcendental': Proclamation and Manifestation in Pentecostal Worship in Asian Context." Pages 127–45 in *Asian Church and God's Mission: Studies Presented in the International Symposium on Asian Mission in Manila, January 2002.* Edited by Wonsuk Ma and Julie C. Ma. Manila: OMF Literature; West Caldwell, N.J.: MWM, 2003.

Ma, "Manifestations." Ma, Julie C. "Manifestations of Supernatural Power in Luke-Acts and the Kankana-eys Tribe of the Philippines." *SpCh* 4 (2, 2002): 109–28.

Ma, "Ministry." Ma, Julie. "Ministry of the Assemblies of God among the Kankana-ey Tribe in the Northern Philippines: A History of a Theological Encounter." PhD diss., Fuller Theological Seminary, 1996.

Ma, *Mission.* Ma, Julie C. *Mission Possible: The Biblical Strategy for Reaching the Lost.* RStMiss. Foreword by Walter C. Kaiser Jr. Eugene, Ore.: Wipf & Stock, 2005.

Ma, "Mission." Ma, Julie C. "Pentecostalism and Asian Mission." *Missiology* 35 (1, Jan. 2007): 23–37.

Ma, "Planting." Ma, Julie C. "Church Planting: Pentecostal Strategy for Mission." Pages 323–55 in *Reflections on Developing Asian Pentecostal Leaders: Essays in Honor of Harold Kohl.* Edited by A. Kay Fountain. Baguio City, Philippines: APTS Press, 2004.

Ma, "Presence." Ma, Wonsuk. "The Presence of Evil and Human Response in the Old Testament." *AJPS* 11 (1–2, 2008): 15–32.

Ma, "Santuala." Ma, Julie C. "Santuala: A Case of Pentecostal Syncretism." *AJPS* 3 (1, 2000): 61–82.

Ma, *Spirit.* Ma, Julie C. *When the Spirit Meets the Spirits: Pentecostal Ministry among the Kankana-ey Tribe in the Philippines.* SICHC 118. Frankfurt: Peter Lang, Wien, 2000.

Ma, "Theology." Ma, Wonsuk. "Asian (Classical) Pentecostal Theology in Context." Pages 59–91 in *Asian and Pentecostal: The Charismatic Face of Christianity in Asia.* Edited by Allan Anderson and Edmond Tang. Foreword by Cecil M. Robeck. Regnum Studies in Mission, AJPSS 3. Oxford: Regnum; Baguio City, Philippines: APTS Press, 2005.

Ma, "Types." Ma, Wonsuk. "Three Types of Ancestor Veneration in Asia: An Anthropological Analysis." *JAM* 4 (2, Sept. 2002): 201–15.

Ma, "Vanderbout." Ma, Julie C. "Elva Vanderbout: A Woman Pioneer of Pentecostal Mission among Igorots." *JAM* 3 (1, March 2001): 121–40.

Ma, "Veneration." Ma, Wonsuk. "Three Types of Ancestor Veneration in Asia: An Anthropological Analysis." Pages 163–77 in *Asian Church and God's Mission: Studies Presented in the International Symposium on Asian Mission in Manila, January 2002.* Edited by Wonsuk Ma and Julie C. Ma. Manila: OMF Literature; West Caldwell, N.J.: MWM, 2003.

Ma, "Worldviews." Ma, Julie C. "Asian Religious Worldviews and Their Missiological Implications." *Journal of Asian Mission* 7 (1, March 2005): 3–22.

Ma, Menzies, and Bae, Cho. Ma, Wonsuk, William W. Menzies, and Hyeon-sung Bae, eds. *David Yonggi Cho: A Close Look at His Theology and Ministry.* AJPSS 1. Baguio City, Philippines: APTS Press, Hansei University Press, 2004.

Ma and Anderson, "Renewalists." Ma, Julie, and Allan Anderson. "Pentecostals (Renewalists), 1910–2010." Pages 100–101 in *Atlas of Global Christianity, 1910–2010.* Edited by Todd M. Johnson, Kenneth R. Ross, and Sandra S. K. Lee. Edinburgh: Center for the Study of Global Christianity, 2009.

MacArthur, *Chaos.* MacArthur, John F., Jr. *Charismatic Chaos.* Grand Rapids: Zondervan, 1992.

Macchia, "Deliverance." Macchia, Frank. "Deliverance and Deliverance Ministry." Pages 140–41 in vol. 1 of *Encyclopedia of Religious Revivals in America.* Edited by Michael McClymond. 2 vols. Westport, Conn: Greenwood, 2007.

Macchia, *Spirituality.* Macchia, Frank D. *Spirituality and Social Liberation: The Message of the Blumhardts in the Light of Wuerttemburg Pietism.* PWS 4. Metuchen, N.J.: Scarecrow, 1993.

MacCulloch, *Christianity.* MacCulloch, Diarmaid. *Christianity: The First Three Thousand Years.* New York: Viking Penguin, 2009.

MacDonald, "Healing." MacDonald, Michael. "Religion, Social Change, and Psychological Healing in England, 1600–1800." Pages 101–25 in *The Church and Healing: Papers Read at the Twentieth Summer Meeting and the Twenty-first Winter Meeting of the Ecclesiastical History Society.* StChHist 19. Edited by W. J. Sheils. Oxford: Basil Blackwell, 1982.

MacGaffey, "Epistemological Ethnocentrism." MacGaffey, Wyatt. "Epistemological Ethnocentrism in African Studies." Pages 42–48 in *African Historiographies: What History for Which Africa?* Edited by Bogumil Jewsiewicki and David Newbury. SSAMD 12. Beverly Hills, Calif.: Sage, 1986.

MacGaffey, "Ideology." MacGaffey, Wyatt. "African Ideology and Belief: A Survey." *AfSR* 24 (2–3, 1981): 227–74.

MacIntosh and Anstey, "Boyle." MacIntosh, J. J., and Peter Anstey. "Robert Boyle." *Stanford Encyclopedia of Philosophy.* http://plato.stanford.edu/entries/boyle. Rev. July 6, 2010. Accessed Sept. 4, 2010.

MacIntyre, "Crises." MacIntyre, Alasdaire. "Episte-mological Crises, Dramatic Narrative, and the Phi-losophy of Science." Pages 54–74 in *Paradigms and Revolutions: Appraisals and Applications of Thomas Kuhn's Philosophy of Science*. Edited by Gary Gut-ting. Notre Dame, Ind.: University of Notre Dame Press, 1980.

Mack, *Abduction*. Mack, John E. *Abduction: Human Encounters with Aliens*. New York: Scribner's Sons, 1995.

Mack, *Lost Gospel*. Mack, Burton L. *The Lost Gospel: The Book of Q and Christian Origins*. San Francisco: HarperSanFrancisco, 1993.

Mack, *Myth*. Mack, Burton L. *A Myth of Innocence: Mark and Christian Origins*. Philadelphia: Fortress, 1988.

Mackay, "Plutarch." Mackay, Barry S. "Plutarch and the Miraculous." Pages 93–112 in *Miracles: Cam-bridge Studies in Their Philosophy and History*. Edited by C. F. D. Moule. London: A. R. Mowbray; New York: Morehouse-Barlow, 1965.

MacKay, *Science*. MacKay, Donald M. *Science and Christian Faith Today*. 2nd ed. London: Falcon, 1973.

Mackie, "Miracles and Testimony." Mackie, J. L. "Miracles and Testimony." Pages 85–96 in *Miracles*. Edited by Richard Swinburne. New York: Macmil-lan, 1989.

MacKinnon, "Complementarity." MacKinnon, Ed-ward. "Complementarity." Pages 255–70 in *Religion and Science: History, Method, Dialogue*. Edited by W. Mark Richardson and Wesley J. Wildman. Foreword by Ian G. Barbour. New York: Routledge, 1996.

Macklin, "Yankee." Macklin, June. "A Connecticut Yankee in Summer Land." Pages 41–86 in *Case Stud-ies in Spirit Possession*. Edited by Vincent Crapan-zaro and Vivian Garrison. New York: John Wiley & Sons, 1977.

Maclean, "Miracles." Maclean, A. J. "Miracles." Pages 39–42 in vol. 2 of *Dictionary of the Apostolic Church*. Edited by James Hastings. 2 vols. New York: Charles Scribner's Sons, 1915–18.

Maclean, "Misconceptions." Maclean, Meg. "Some Misconceptions about Death in Papua New Guinea." *MJT* 5 (2, 1989): 70–73.

Maclean and Aitken, *Heroikos*. Maclean, Jennifer K. Berenson, and Ellen Bradshaw Aitken. *Flavius Philostratus: Heroikos*. SBLWGRW 1. Edited by Jackson P. Hershbell. Atlanta: Society of Biblical Literature, 2001.

MacLeod, "Surprised." MacLeod, David J. "Sur-prised by the Power of the Spirit: A Review Article (Are Miracle Workers and the Gift of Miracles for Today?)" *EmmJ* 10 (1, 2001): 115–51.

MacMullen, *Christianizing*. MacMullen, Ramsay. *Christianizing the Roman Empire*. New Haven: Yale University Press, 1984.

MacMullen, *Enemies*. MacMullen, Ramsay. *Enemies of the Roman Order: Treason, Unrest, and Alienation in the Empire*. Cambridge, Mass.: Harvard University Press, 1966.

MacMullen, *Second Church*. MacMullen, Ramsay. *The Second Church: Popular Christianity A.D. 200–400*. WGRWSup 1. Atlanta: Society of Biblical Litera-ture, 2009.

MacNutt, *Crime*. MacNutt, Francis. *The Nearly Perfect Crime: How the Church Almost Killed the Ministry of Healing*. Grand Rapids: Chosen, 2005.

MacNutt, *Healing*. MacNutt, Francis. *Healing*. Notre Dame, Ind.: Ave Maria Press, 1974.

MacNutt, *Power*. MacNutt, Francis. *The Power to Heal*. Notre Dame, Ind.: Ave Maria Press, 1977.

MacPhail, "Path." MacPhail, Richard D. "Finding a Path in Others' Worlds—The Emic Challenges of Exorcism." *BangTF* 31 (1, 1999): 168–204.

MacRae, "Miracle." MacRae, George. "Miracle in *The Antiquities* of Josephus." Pages 127–48 in *Miracles: Cambridge Studies in Their Philosophy and History*. Edited by C. F. D. Moule. London: A. R. Mowbray; New York: Morehouse-Barlow, 1965.

Maddocks, *Call*. Maddocks, Morris. *God's Call to Heal: A Life in Music and Healing*. London: SPCK, 2008.

Maddocks, *Hildegard*. Maddocks, Fiona. *Hildegard of Bingen: The Woman of Her Age*. New York: Double-day, 2001.

Maddocks, *Ministry*. Maddocks, Morris. *The Chris-tian Healing Ministry*. 3rd ed. London: SPCK, 1995.

Maddox, "Cigogo." Maddox, Gregory H. "The Church and Cigogo: Father Stephen Mlundi and Christianity in Central Tanzania." Pages 150–66 in *East African Expressions of Christianity*. Edited by Thomas Spear and Isaria N. Kimambo. EAfSt. Athens: Ohio University Press; Oxford: James Cur-rey; Dar es Salaam: Mkuki na Nyota; Nairobi: East African Educational Publishers, 1999.

Magaji and Danmallam, "Magaji." Magaji, Sule, and Galadima Danmallam. "Magaji, Sule." *DACB*. http://www.dacb.org/stories/nigeria/magaji1 _sule.html.

Maggay, "Issues." Maggay, Melba Padilla. "Early Protestant Missionary Efforts in the Philippines: Some Intercultural Issues." Pages 29–41 in *Asian Church and God's Mission: Studies Presented in the International Symposium on Asian Mission in Manila, January 2002*. Edited by Wonsuk Ma and Julie C. Ma. Manila: OMF Literature; West Caldwell, N.J.: MWM, 2003.

Magliocco, "Spells." Magliocco, Sabina. "Spells, Saints, and Streghe: Witchcraft, Folk Magic, and Healing in Italy." *Pom* 13 (2000): 4–22.

Maharam, "Genius." Maharam, Wolfram-Aslan. "Genius." Pages 756–58 in vol. 5 of *Brill's New Pauly: Encyclopaedia of the Ancient World*. Edited by Hubert Cancik and Helmuth Schneider. 20 vols. English ed. Christine F. Salazar. Leiden: Brill, 2010.

Maher, "Writings." Maher, Michael. "Recent Writings on the Miracles." *NBf* 56 (1975): 165–74.

Major, *Faiths.* Major, Ralph H. *Faiths That Healed.* New York: D. Appleton-Century, 1940.

Makarfi, "Bedrock." Makarfi, Ya'u Ismaila. "Islam as the Bedrock of Medicine." Pages 63–71 in *Religion, Medicine, and Healing*. Edited by Gbola Aderibigbe and Deji Ayegboyin. Lagos: Nigerian Association for the Study of Religions and Education, 1995.

Makarius, "Violation." Makarius, Laura. "The Violation of Taboo and Magical Power." Pages 231–35 in *The Realm of the Extra-Human: Ideas and Actions*. Edited by Agehananda Bharati. The Hague: Mouton, 1976.

"Making Room." "Making Room for Alternatives." *HastCRep* 30 (3, May 2000): 26–28.

Makris and Al-Safi, "Spirit Possession Cult." Makris, Gerasimos P., and Ahmad Al-Safi. "The *Tumbura* Spirit Possession Cult of the Sudan." Pages 118–36 in *Women's Medicine: The* Zar-Bori *Cult in Africa and Beyond*. Edited by I. M. Lewis, Ahmed Al-Safi, and Sayyid Hurreiz. Edinburgh: International African Institute, Edinburgh University Press, 1991.

Makris and Natvig, "Bibliography." Makris, G. P., and Richard Natvig. "The *Zar, Tumbura* and *Bori* Cults: A Select Annotated Bibliography." Pages 233–82 in *Women's Medicine: The* Zar-Bori *Cult in Africa and Beyond*. Edited by I. M. Lewis, Ahmed Al-Safi, and Sayyid Hurreiz. Edinburgh: International African Institute, Edinburgh University Press, 1991.

Malarkey, *Boy.* Malarkey, Kevin and Alex. *The Boy Who Came Back from Heaven: A Remarkable Account of Miracles, Angels, and Life Beyond This World*. Carol Stream, Ill.: Tyndale, 2010.

Malek, "Stranger." Malek, Jeri Sue. "The Kind, Quiet Stranger." *MounM* (Oct. 1994): 16–17.

Malherbe, "Not in a Corner." Malherbe, Abraham J. "Not in a Corner: Early Christian Apologetic in Acts 26:26." *SecCent* 5 (4, 1986): 193–210.

Malia, "Look." Malia, Linda. "A Fresh Look at a Remarkable Document: Exorcism: The Report of a Commission Convened by the Bishop of Exeter." *AThR* 83 (1, 2001): 65–88.

Malick, "Sowing." Malick, Y. G. "Sowing and Reaping in Syria." *PentEv* 647 (May 15, 1926): 11.

Malina, "Assessing Historicity." Malina, Bruce J. "Assessing the Historicity of Jesus' Walking on the Sea: Insights from Cross-Cultural Social Psychology." Pages 351–71 in *Authenticating the Activities of Jesus*. Edited by Bruce Chilton and Craig A. Evans. Leiden: Brill, 1999.

Malina, "Thinking." Malina, Bruce J. "Religious Thinking: Key to Experiencing Miracles." *BibT* 90 (1977): 1199–205.

Malina, *Windows.* Malina, Bruce J. *Windows on the World of Jesus: Time Travel to Ancient Judea*. Louisville: Westminster John Knox, 1993.

Malina and Pilch, *Acts.* Malina, Bruce J., and John J. Pilch. *Social-Science Commentary on the Book of Acts*. Minneapolis: Fortress, 2008.

Malina and Pilch, *Letters.* Malina, Bruce J., and John J. Pilch. *Social-Science Commentary on the Letters of Paul*. Minneapolis: Fortress, 2006.

Maluleke and Nadar, "Pentecostalisation." Maluleke, Tinyiko Sam, and Sarojini Nadar. "Guest Editorial: The Pentecostalisation of African Christianity." *Missionalia* 35 (3, Nov. 2007): 1–4.

Manala, "Witchcraft." Manala, Matsobane J. "Witchcraft and Its Impact on Black African Christians: A Lacuna in the Ministry of the Hervormde Kerk in Suidelike Afrika." *HTS/TS* 60 (4, 2004): 1491–511.

Manala and Theron, "Need." Manala, Matsobane J., and Jacques P. J. Theron. "The Need for the Healing Ministry in the Maranatha Reformed Church of Christ." *Missionalia* 37 (2, Aug. 2009): 165–79.

Manana, "Kitonga." Manana, Francis. "Kitonga, Arthur." *DACB*. http://www.dacb.org/stories/kenya /kitonga_arthur.html.

Manana, "Magaji." Manana, Francis. "Magaji, Sule." *DACB*. http://www.dacb.org/stories/nigeria /magaji_sule.html.

Manana, "Ndaruhutse." Manana, Francis. "Ndaruhutse, David." *DACB*. http://www.dacb.org/stories /burundi/ndaruhutse_david.html.

Mandryk, *Operation World.* Mandryk, Jason. *Operation World*. 7th ed. Colorado Springs: Biblica, 2010.

Manns, "Jacob." Manns, Fréderic. "Jacob, le Min, selon la Tosephta Hulin 2,22–24. Contribution à l'étude du christianisme primitif." *CNS* 10 (3, 1989): 449–65.

Manschreck, *History.* Manschreck, Clyde L. *A History of Christianity: Readings in the History of the Church from the Reformation to the Present*. Englewood Cliffs, N.J.: Prentice-Hall, 1964.

Mansfield, *Pentecost.* Mansfield, Patti Gallagher. *As by a New Pentecost: The Dramatic Beginning of the Catholic Charismatic Renewal*. Foreword by Léon-Joseph Cardinal Suenens. Steubenville, Ohio: Franciscan University Press, 1992.

Mansfield, Mitchell, and King, "Doctor." Mansfield, Christopher J., Jim Mitchell, and Dana E. King. "The Doctor as God's Mechanic? Beliefs in the Southeastern United States." *SSMed* 54 (2004): 399–409.

Manson, *Design.* Manson, Neil, ed. *God and Design: The Teleological Argument and Modern Science.* London: Routledge, 2003.

Mansour, Mehio-Sibai, Walsh et al., "Jesus and Eye." Mansour, A. M., A. Mehio-Sibai, J. B. Walsh, et al. "Jesus and the Eye: New Testament Miracles of Vision." *AcOphSc* 83 (2005): 739–45.

Manuel, *Factor.* Manuel, David, with Don Wilkerson and Reginald Yake. *The Jesus Factor.* Plainfield, N.J.: Logos, 1977.

Manus, "Healing." Manus, Ukachukwu Chris. "Healing and Exorcism: The Scriptural Viewpoint." Pages 84–104 in *Healing and Exorcism: The Nigerian Experience.* Proceedings, Lectures, Discussions, and Conclusions of the First Missiology Symposium on Healing and Exorcism, organized by the Spiritan International School of Theology, Attakwu, Enugu, May 18–20, 1989. Edited by Chris U. Manus, Luke N. Mbefo, and E. E. Uzukwu. Attakwu, Enugu: Spiritan International School of Theology, 1992.

Manus, "Parallels." Manus, Ukachukwu Chris. "John 6:1–15 and Its Synoptic Parallels: An African Approach toward the Solution of a Johannine Critical Problem." *JITC* 19 (1–2, 1991–92): 47–71.

Map Manual. *Student Map Manual: Historical Geography of the Bible Lands.* Edited by J. Monson. Grand Rapids: Zondervan; Jerusalem: Pictorial Archive (Near Eastern History), 1979.

Maquet, "Shaman." Maquet, Jacques. "Introduction: Scholar and Shaman." Pages 1–6 in *Ecstasy and Healing in Nepal: An Ethnopsychiatric Study of Tamang Shamanism,* by Larry Peters. Malibu: Undena Publications, 1981.

Margenau, "Laws." Margenau, Henry. "The Laws of Nature Are Created by God." Pages 57–63 in *Cosmos, Bios, and Theos: Scientists Reflect on Science, God, and the Origins of the Universe, Life, and Homo Sapiens.* Edited by Henry Margenau and Roy Abraham Varghese. La Salle, Ill.: Open Court, 1992.

Margenau and Varghese, *Cosmos.* Margenau, Henry, and Roy Abraham Varghese, eds. *Cosmos, Bios, and Theos: Scientists Reflect on Science, God, and the Origins of the Universe, Life, and Homo Sapiens.* La Salle, Ill.: Open Court, 1992.

Marguerat, *Actes.* Marguerat, Daniel. *Les Actes des Apôtres (1–12).* Commentaire du Nouveau Testament, 2nd series, 5 A. Genève: Labor et Fides, 2007.

Marguerat, *Histoire.* Marguerat, Daniel. *La Première Histoire du Christianisme (Les Actes des apôtres).* LD 180. Paris: Cerf, 1999.

Marguerat, "Pionnier." Marguerat, Daniel. "Luc, pionnier de l'historiographie chrétienne." *RSR* 92 (4, 2004): 513–38.

Mariz, "Pentecostalism." Mariz, Cecilia Loreto. "Pentecostalism and Confrontation with Poverty in Brazil." Pages 129–46 in *In the Power of the Spirit: The Pentecostal Challenge to Historical Churches in Latin America.* Edited by Benjamin F. Gutiérrez and Dennis A. Smith. Mexico City: Asociación de Iglesias Presbiterianias y Reformadas en América Latina; Guatemala City: Centro Evangélico Latinoamericano de Estudios Pastorales; Louisville: Presbyterian Church (U.S.A.), 1996.

Mark, "Myth." Mark, James. "Myth and Miracle, or the Ambiguity of Bultmann." *Theology* 66 (514, April 1963): 134–40.

Markle, "Body." Markle, George B., IV. "Body, Mind, and Faith." Pages 15–20 in *Faith Healing: Finger of God? Or, Scientific Curiosity?* Compiled by Claude A. Frazier. New York: Thomas Nelson, 1973.

Markschies, "Schlafkulte." Markschies, Christoph. "Gesund werden im Schlaf? Die antiken Schlafkulte und das Christentum." *TLZ* 131 (12, 2006): 1233–44.

Marmorstein, *Names.* Marmorstein, A. *The Old Rabbinic Doctrine of God: The Names and Attributes of God.* New York: KTAV, 1968.

Marnham, *Lourdes.* Marnham, Patrick. *Lourdes: A Modern Pilgrimage.* New York: Coward, McCann & Geoghegan, 1981.

Marostica, "Learning." Marostica, Matthew. "Learning from the Master: Carlos Annacondia and the Standardization of Pentecostal Practices in and beyond Argentina." Pages 207–27 in *Global Pentecostal and Charismatic Healing.* Edited by Candy Gunther Brown. Foreword by Harvey Cox. Oxford: Oxford University Press, 2011.

Marsden, *Outrageous Idea.* Marsden, George M. *The Outrageous Idea of Christian Scholarship.* New York: Oxford University Press, 1997.

Marsden, *Soul of University.* Marsden, George M. *The Soul of the American University: From Protestant Establishment to Established Nonbelief.* New York: Oxford University Press, 1994.

Marsella et al., "Aspects." Marsella, Anthony J., Matthew J. Friedman, and E. Huland Spain. "Ethnocultural Aspects of PTSD: An Overview of Research and Research Directions." Pages 105–29 in *Ethnocultural Aspects of Posttraumatic Stress Disorder: Issues, Research, and Clinical Applications.* Edited by Anthony J. Marsella, Matthew J. Friedman, Ellen T. Gerrity, and Raymond M. Scurfield. Washington, D.C.: American Psychological Association, 1996.

Marsh, *John.* Marsh, John. *Saint John.* WPC. Philadelphia: Westminster, 1968.

Marshall, *Beyond Ourselves*. Marshall, Catherine. *Beyond Ourselves*. New York: McGraw-Hill, 1961.

Marshall, *Helper*. Marshall, Catherine. *The Helper*. Waco, Tex.: Chosen, 1978.

Marshall-Fratani, "Mediating." Marshall-Fratani, Ruth. "Mediating the Global and Local in Nigerian Pentecostalism." Pages 80–105 in *Between Babel and Pentecost: Transnational Pentecostalism in Africa and Latin America*. Edited by André Corten and Ruth Marshall-Fratani. Bloomington: Indiana University Press, 2001.

Marshman, "Exorcism." Marshman, Michelle. "Exorcism as Empowerment: A New Idiom." *JRelHealth* 23 (3, 1999): 265–81.

Marszalek, *Miracles*. Marszalek, Therese. *Extraordinary Miracles in the Lives of Ordinary People: Inspiring Stories of Divine Intervention*. Tulsa: Harrison House, 2007.

Martell-Otero, "Liberating News." Martell-Otero, Loida I. "Liberating News: An Emerging U.S. Hispanic/Latina Soteriology of the Crossroads." PhD diss., Fordham University Department of Theology, 2004.

Martell-Otero, "Satos." Martell-Otero, Loida I. "Of Satos and Saints: Salvation from the Periphery." Pages 7–33 in *Perspectivas*. HTIOPS 4, Summer 2001. Edited by Renata Furst-Lambert.

Martens, "Unwritten Law." Martens, John W. "Unwritten Law in Philo: A Response to Naomi G. Cohen." *JJS* 43 (1, 1992): 38–45.

Martin, *Acts*. Martin, Francis, ed., with Evan Smith. *Acts*. ACCS 5. Downers Grove, Ill.: InterVarsity, 2006.

Martin, "Artemidorus." Martin, Luther H. "Artemidorus: Dream Theory in Late Antiquity." *SecCent* 8 (1991): 97–108.

Martin, "Christianity." Martin, David. "Evangelical and Charismatic Christianity in Latin America." Pages 73–86 in *Charismatic Christianity as a Global Culture*. Edited by Karla Poewe. SCR. Columbia: University of South Carolina Press, 1994.

Martin, "Expansion." Martin, David. "Evangelical Expansion in Global Society." Pages 273–94 in *Christianity Reborn: The Global Expansion of Evangelicalism in the Twentieth Century*. Edited by Donald M. Lewis. SHCM. Grand Rapids: Eerdmans, 2004.

Martin, *Foundations*. Martin, Ralph P. *New Testament Foundations: A Guide for Christian Students*. Vol. 2: *The Acts, The Letters, The Apocalypse*. Grand Rapids: Eerdmans, 1978.

Martin, *Healing*. Martin, George. *Healing: Reflections on the Gospel*. Ann Arbor, Mich.: Servant, 1977.

Martin, "Healings at Kilsyth." Martin, John. "Healings at Kilsyth." *Conf* 2 (May 1908): 17.

Martin, "Historians on Miracles." Martin, Raymond. "Historians on Miracles." Pages 412–27 in *God Matters: Readings in the Philosophy of Religion*. Edited by Raymond Martin and Christopher Bernard. New York: Longman, Pearson Education, 2003.

Martin, *Kimbangu*. Martin, M.-L. *Kimbangu: An African Prophet and His Church*. Translated by D. M. Moore. Oxford: Basil Blackwell, 1975; Grand Rapids: Eerdmans, 1976.

Martin, *Pentecostalism*. Martin, David. *Pentecostalism: The World Their Parish*. Oxford: Basil Blackwell, 2001.

Martin, *Religions*. Martin, Luther H. *Hellenistic Religions: An Introduction*. New York: Oxford University Press, 1987.

Martin, "Resisting." Martin, Dennis. "Resisting the Devil in the Patristic, Medieval, and Reformation Church." Pages 46–71 in *Essays on Spiritual Bondage and Deliverance*. Edited by Willard M. Swartley. Occasional Papers 11. Elkhart, Ind.: Institute of Mennonite Studies, 1988.

Martin, *Tongues*. Martin, David. *Tongues of Fire: The Explosion of Protestantism in Latin America*. Oxford: Basil Blackwell, 1990.

Martínez-Taboas, "Seizures." Martínez-Taboas, Alfonso. "Psychogenic Seizures in an Espiritismo Context: The Role of Culturally Sensitive Psychotherapy." *PsycTRPT* 42 (1, Spring 2005): 6–13.

Martínez-Taboas, "World." Martínez-Taboas, Alfonso. "The Plural World of Culturally Sensitive Psychotherapy: A Response to Castro-Blanco's (2005) Comments." *PsycTRPT* 42 (1, Spring 2005): 17–19.

Martins Terra, "Milagres." Martins Terra, J. E. "Os Milagres Helenisticos." *RCB* 4 (15–16, 1980): 229–62.

Martitz, "Υἱός." Martitz, Wülfing von. "Υἱός in Greek." Pages 335–40 in vol. 8 of *TDNT*.

Marton, "Approach." Marton, Yves. "The Experiential Approach to Anthropology and Castaneda's Ambiguous Legacy." Pages 273–97 in *Being Changed: The Anthropology of Extraordinary Experience*. Edited by David E. Young and Jean-Guy Goulet. Peterborough, Ont.: Broadview, 1994.

Maselko et al., "Attendance." Maselko, Joanna, Laura Kubzansky, Ichiro Kawachi, Teresa Seeman, and Lisa Berkman. "Religious Service Attendance and Allostatic Load among High-Functioning Elderly." *PsychMed* 69 (5, 2007): 464–72.

Mashau, "Occultism." Mashau, T. D. "Occultism in an African Context: A Case for the Vhavenda-Speaking People of the Limpopo Province." *IDS* 41 (4, 2007): 637–53.

Mason, *History*. Mason, Stephen F. *A History of the Sciences*. Rev. ed. New York: Collier Books, 1973.

Mason, *Ko Thah Byu.* Mason, Francis. *The Karen Apostle; or, Memoir of Ko Thah Byu.* Bassein, Burma: SGAU Karen Press, 1884.

Mason, "Rocamadour." Mason, Emma. "'Rocamadour in Quercy above All Other Churches': The Healing of Henry II." Pages 39–54 in *The Church and Healing: Papers Read at the Twentieth Summer Meeting and the Twenty-first Winter Meeting of the Ecclesiastical History Society.* StChHist 19. Edited by W. J. Sheils. Oxford: Basil Blackwell, 1982.

Masquelier, "Invention." Masquelier, Adeline. "The Invention of Anti-Tradition: Dodo Spirits in Southern Nigeria." Pages 34–49 in *Spirit Possession, Modernity and Power in Africa.* Edited by Heike Behrend and Ute Luig. Madison: University of Wisconsin Press, 1999.

Mast, "Training." Mast, H. Michael. "Theological Training among the Tobas of Argentina." MA thesis, Fuller Theological Seminary, 1972.

Masters, "Disconnect." Masters, Kevin S. "Research on the Healing Power of Distant Intercessory Prayer: Disconnect between Science and Faith." *JPsyTh* 33 (4, 2005): 268–77.

Masters, "Prayer." Masters, Kevin S. "Prayer and Health." Pages 11–24 in *Spirit, Science, and Health: How the Spiritual Mind Fuels Physical Wellness.* Edited by Thomas G. Plante and Carl E. Thoresen. Foreword by Albert Bandura. Westport, Conn.: Praeger, 2007.

Masters et al., "Orientation." Masters, Kevin S., Robert D. Hill, John Kircher, Tera Lensegrav Benson, and Jennifer A. Fallon. "Religious Orientation, Aging, and Blood Pressure Reactivity to Interpersonal and Cognitive Stressors." *AnnBehMed* 28 (3, 2004): 171–78.

Mather, *Providences.* Mather, Cotton. *Memorable Providences Relating to Witchcrafts and Possessions . . . clearly manifesting, not only that there are witches, but that good men (as well as others) may possibly have their lives shortned by such evil instruments of Satan.* London: Thomas Parkhurst, 1691.

Matsuoka, "Fox Possession." Matsuoka, E. "The Interpretations of Fox Possession: Illness as Metaphor." *CMPsy* 15 (1991): 453–77.

Matthews, "Eunapius." Matthews, John F. "Eunapius." Pages 568–69 in *OCD.*

Matthews and Benjamin, "Leper." Matthews, Victor H., and Don C. Benjamin. "The Leper." *BibT* 29 (1991): 292–97.

Matthews and Clark, *Faith Factor.* Matthews, Dale A., with Connie Clark. *The Faith Factor: Proof of the Healing Power of Prayer.* New York: Viking Penguin, 1998.

Matthews, Larson, and Barry, *Bibliography.* Matthews, Dale A., David B. Larson, and Constance

P. Barry. *The Faith Factor: An Annotated Bibliography of Clinical Research on Spiritual Subjects.* National Institute for Healthcare Research, presented to the John Templeton Foundation, 1993.

Matthews, Marlowe, and MacNutt, "Effects." Matthews, Dale A., Sally M. Marlowe, and Francis S. MacNutt. "Effects of Intercessory Prayer on Patients with Rheumatoid Arthritis." *SMedJ* 93 (Dec. 2000): 1177–86.

Mattis et al., "Religiosity." Mattis, Jacqueline S., D. L. Fontenot, et al. "Religiosity, Racism, and Dispositional Optimism among African Americans." *PerIndDif* 34 (6, 2003): 1025–38.

Maurizio, "Pythia's Role." Maurizio, Lisa. "Anthropology and Spirit Possession: A Reconsideration of the Pythia's Role at Delphi." *JHS* 115 (1995): 69–86.

Mavrodes, "Hume." Mavrodes, George I. "David Hume and the Probability of Miracles." *IJPhilRel* 43 (3, 1998): 167–82.

Mavrodes, "Miracles." Mavrodes, George I. "Miracles and the Laws of Nature." *FPhil* 2 (4, 1985): 333–46.

Mavrodes, "Theorem." Mavrodes, George I. "Bayes' Theorem and Hume's Treatment of Miracles." *TJ* 1 (1, 1980): 47–61.

Mawson, "Miracles." Mawson, T. J. "Miracles and Laws of Nature." *RelS* 37 (1, March 2001): 33–58.

Maxwell, *African Gifts.* Maxwell, David. *African Gifts of the Spirit: Pentecostalism and the Rise of a Zimbabwean Transnational Religious Movement.* Oxford: James Currey; Harare: Weaver Press; Athens: Ohio University Press, 2006.

Maxwell, "Theories." Maxwell, Grover. "Theories, Perception, and Structural Realism." Pages 3–34 in *The Nature and Function of Scientific Theories: Essays in Contemporary Science and Philosophy.* Edited by Robert G. Colodny. Pittsburgh: University of Pittsburgh Press, 1970.

Maxwell, "Witches." Maxwell, David. "Witches, Prophets, and Avenging Spirits: The Second Christian Movement in North-East Zimbabwe." *JRelAf* 25 (3, 1995): 309–39.

May, "Miracles." May, Peter. "Claimed Contemporary Miracles." *Medico-Legal Journal* 71 (4, 2003): 144–58.

Mayhue, *Healing.* Mayhue, Richard. *Divine Healing Today.* Chicago: Moody Press, 1983.

Mayrargue, "Expansion." Mayrargue, Cédric. "The Expansion of Pentecostalism in Benin: Individual Rationales and Transnational Dynamics." Pages 274–92 in *Between Babel and Pentecost: Transnational Pentecostalism in Africa and Latin America.* Edited by André Corten and Ruth Marshall-Fratani. Bloomington: Indiana University Press, 2001.

Mbiti, *Religions*. Mbiti, John S. *African Religions and Philosophies*. Garden City, N.Y.: Doubleday, 1970.

McAll, "Deliverance." McAll, R. Kenneth. "The Ministry of Deliverance." *ExpT* 86 (10, July 1975): 296–98.

McAll, "Taste." McAll, R. Kenneth. "Taste and See." Pages 269–78 in *Demon Possession: A Medical, Historical, Anthropological, and Theological Symposium*. Papers presented at the University of Notre Dame, January 8–11, 1975, under the auspices of the Christian Medical Association. Edited by John Warwick Montgomery. Minneapolis: Bethany House, 1976.

McBane, "Bhils." McBane, George William. "The Bhils on the Indian Subcontinent (with Emphasis for Church Growth in Pakistan)." ThM thesis, Fuller School of World Mission, 1976.

McCain, "Faith." McCain, Dorothy Nabriet. "Using Faith as a Copy-Cat Version of Constraint-Induced Movement Therapy to Regain a Richer Quality of Life." Paper submitted for Social Research Seminar 1, LaSalle University, Philadelphia, Dec. 4, 2007.

McCall, "Peace." McCall, John. "Making Peace with the Agwu." *AnthHum* 18 (1993): 56–66.

McCallie, *Trophy*. McCallie, Bertha. *A Trophy of Redeeming Grace and the Story of My Healing of a Broken Neck*. Indianapolis: Bertha McCallie, n.d.

McCasland, *Finger*. McCasland, S. Vernon. *By the Finger of God: Demon Possession and Exorcism in Early Christianity in the Light of Modern Views of Mental Illness*. Introduction by David Cole Wilson. New York: Macmillan, 1951.

McCasland, "Signs." McCasland, S. Vernon. "Signs and Wonders." *JBL* 76 (1957): 149–52.

McCauley et al., "Beliefs." McCauley, Jeanne, M. W. Jenckes, M. J. Tarpley, H. G. Koenig, L. R. Yanek, and D. M. Becker. "Spiritual Beliefs and Barriers among Managed Care Practitioners." *JRelHealth* 44 (2, 2005): 137–46.

McClain, Rosenfeld, and Breithart, "Effect." McClain, C. S., B. Rosenfeld, and W. Breithart. "Effect of Spiritual Well-Being on End-of-Life Despair in Terminally Ill Cancer Patients." *Lancet* 361 (2003): 1603–7.

McCleery, "Curing." McCleery, Iona. "*Multos Ex Medicinae Arte Curaverat, Multos Verbo et Oratione*: Curing in Medieval Portuguese Saints' Lives." Pages 192–202 in *Signs, Wonders, Miracles: Representations of Divine Power in the Life of the Church. Papers Read at the 2003 Summer Meeting and the 2004 Winter Meeting of the Ecclesiastical History Society*. Edited by Kate Cooper and Jeremy Gregory. Rochester: Boydell & Brewer, for the Ecclesiastical History Society, 2005.

McClenon, "Analysis." McClenon, James. "Content Analysis of an Anomalous Memorate Collection: Testing Hypotheses Regarding Universal Features." *SocRel* 61 (2000): 155–69.

McClenon, *Events*. McClenon, James. *Wondrous Events: Foundations of Religious Belief*. Philadelphia: University of Pennsylvania Press, 1994.

McClenon, "Experiential Foundations." McClenon, James. "The Experiential Foundations of Shamanic Healing." *JMedPhil* 18 (1993): 107–27.

McClenon, *Healing*. McClenon, James. *Wondrous Healing: Shamanism, Human Evolution, and the Origin of Religion*. DeKalb, Ill.: Northern Illinois University Press, 2002.

McClenon, "Healing." McClenon, James. "Spiritual Healing and the Ritual Healing Theory: Qualitative Foundations." Pages 32–50 in *Religion*. Vol. 2 of *The Healing Power of Spirituality: How Faith Helps Humans Thrive*. Edited by J. Harold Ellens. Santa Barbara, Calif.: Praeger, 2010.

McClenon, "Miracles." McClenon, James. "Miracles in Kongo Religious History: Evaluating the Ritual Healing Theory." Pages 176–97 in *Medical and Therapeutic Events*. Vol. 2 of *Miracles: God, Science, and Psychology in the Paranormal*. Edited by J. Harold Ellens. Westport, Conn.; London: Praeger, 2008.

McClenon, "Shamanic Healing." McClenon, James. "Shamanic Healing, Human Evolution, and the Origin of Religion." *JSSR* 36 (1997): 323–37.

McClenon and Nooney, "Experiences." McClenon, James, and Jennifer Nooney. "Anomalous Experiences Reported by Field Anthropologists: Evaluating Theories Regarding Religion." *AnthConsc* 13 (2, 2002): 46–60.

McCluney, "Correspondence." McCluney, Frank. "Correspondence." *Nazarene Messenger* 12 (2, July 11, 1907): 3–4.

McClymond, "Mason." McClymond, Michael. "The Early Life of Black Holiness and Pentecostal Pioneer Charles Mason." Pages 250–53 in vol. 2 of *Encyclopedia of Religious Revivals in America*. Edited by Michael McClymond. 2 vols. Westport, Conn: Greenwood, 2007.

McClymond, *Stranger*. McClymond, Michael J. *Familiar Stranger: An Introduction to Jesus of Nazareth*. Grand Rapids: Eerdmans, 2004.

McConnell et al., "Links." McConnell, Kelly M., Kenneth I. Pargament, Christopher G. Ellison, and Kevin J. Flannelly. "Examining the Links between Spiritual Struggles and Symptoms of Psychopathology in a National Sample." *JClPsychol* 62 (12, 2006): 1469–84.

McConvery, "Ancient Physicians." McConvery, Brendan. "Ancient Physicians and Their Art." *BibT* 36 (5, 1998): 306–12.

McConvery, "Praise." McConvery, Brendan. "Ben Sira's 'Praise of the Physician' (Sir 38:1–15) in the Light of Some Hippocratic Writings." *PIBA* 21 (1998): 62–86.

McCormick and Gerlitz, "Nature." McCormick, Rod, and Julia Gerlitz. "Nature as Healer: Aboriginal Ways of Healing through Nature." *CounsSp* 28 (1, 2009): 55–72.

McCready, *Miracles*. McCready, William D. *Miracles and the Venerable Bede*. Pontifical Institute of Mediaeval Studies, Studies and Texts 118. Toronto: Pontifical Institute of Mediaeval Studies, 1994.

McCullough and Laurenceau, "Religiousness." McCullough, Michael E., and Jean-Philippe Laurenceau. "Religiousness and the Trajectory of Self-Rated Health across Adulthood." *PSocPsyBull* 31 (4, 2005): 560–73.

McCullough et al., "Disposition." McCullough, M. E., R. A. Emmons, et al. "The Grateful Disposition: A Conceptual and Empirical Topography." *JPerSocPsy* 82 (1, 2002): 112–27.

McDaniel, "States." McDaniel, June. "Possession States among the Saktas of West Bengal." *JRitSt* 2 (1, 1988): 87–99.

McDannell and Lang, *Heaven*. McDannell, Colleen, and Bernhard Lang. *Heaven: A History*. 2nd ed. New Haven: Yale University Press, 2001.

McDermid, "Miracles." McDermid, Kirk. "Miracles: Metaphysics, Physics, and Physicalism." *RelS* 44 (2, 2008): 125–47.

McDonald, "Herodotus." McDonald, A. H. "Herodotus on the Miraculous." Pages 81–92 in *Miracles: Cambridge Studies in Their Philosophy and History*. Edited by C. F. D. Moule. New York: Morehouse-Barlow, 1965.

McDonnell and Montague, *Initiation*. McDonnell, Kilian, and George T. Montague. *Christian Initiation and Baptism in the Holy Spirit: Evidence from the First Eight Centuries*. Collegeville, Minn.: Liturgical Press, 1991.

McFadden, "Elements." McFadden, Brian. "The Elements of Discourse: Orality, Literacy, and Nature in the Elemental Miracles of Bede's Ecclesiastical History." *AmBenRev* 55 (4, 2004): 442–63.

McGavran, "Faith Healing." McGavran, Donald. "Faith Healing and Church Growth—Ivory Coast." *CGB* 10 (2, 1973): 376–77.

McGavran, "Healing." McGavran, Donald A. "Divine Healing and Church Growth." Pages 71–78 in *Signs and Wonders Today: The Story of Fuller Theological Seminary's Remarkable Course on Spiritual Power*. Rev. ed. Edited by C. Peter Wagner. Altamonte Springs, Fla.: Creation House, 1987.

McGavran, "Healing and Evangelization." McGavran, Donald. "Healing and the Evangelization of the World." Pages 289–99 in *1979 Brasilia Church Growth Seminar*. Brazil: Sevic, 1979.

McGavran, "Healing and Growth." McGavran, Donald. "Divine Healing and Church Growth." *RenJ* 17 (1, 2001): 1.

McGavran, "Seeing." McGavran, Donald. "Seeing Is Believing." Pages 65–69 in *Signs and Wonders Today: The Story of Fuller Theological Seminary's Remarkable Course on Spiritual Power*. Rev. ed. Edited by C. Peter Wagner. Altamonte Springs, Fla.: Creation House, 1987.

McGee, "Hermeneutics." McGee, Gary B. "Early Pentecostal Hermeneutics: Tongues as Evidence in the Book of Acts." Pages 96–118 in *Initial Evidence: Historical and Biblical Perspectives on the Pentecostal Doctrine of Spirit Baptism*. Edited by Gary B. McGee. Peabody, Mass.: Hendrickson, 1991.

McGee, *Miracles*. McGee, Gary B. *Miracles, Missions, and American Pentecostalism*. AmSocMissS 45. Maryknoll, N.Y.: Orbis, 2010.

McGee, "Miracles." McGee, Gary B. "Miracles." Pages 252–54 in *Encyclopedia of Mission and Missionaries*. Edited by Jonathan J. Bonk. New York: Routledge, 2007.

McGee, "Miracles and Mission." McGee, Gary B. "Miracles and Mission Revisited." *IBMR* 25 (Oct. 2001): 146–56.

McGee, *People of Spirit*. McGee, Gary B. *People of the Spirit: The Assemblies of God*. Springfield, Mo.: Gospel Publishing House, 2004.

McGee, "Radical Strategy." McGee, Gary B. "The Radical Strategy in Modern Mission: The Linkage of Paranormal Phenomena with Evangelism." Pages 69–95 in *The Holy Spirit and Mission Dynamics*. Edited by C. Douglas McConnell. EvMissSS 5. Pasadena, Calif.: William Carey Library, 1997.

McGee, "Regions Beyond." McGee, Gary B. "To the Regions Beyond: The Global Expansion of Pentecostalism." Pages 69–95 in *The Century of the Holy Spirit: One Hundred Years of Pentecostal and Charismatic Renewal, 1901–2001*. Edited by Vinson Synan. Nashville: Thomas Nelson, 2001.

McGee, "Revivals in India." McGee, Gary B. "Pentecostal Phenomena and Revivals in India: Implications for Indigenous Church Leadership." *IBMR* 20 (July 1996): 112–17.

McGee, "Shortcut." McGee, Gary B. "Shortcut to Language Preparation? Radical Evangelicals, Missions, and the Gift of Tongues." *IBMR* 25 (July 2001): 118–23.

McGee, "Strategies." McGee, Gary B. "Strategies for Global Mission." Pages 203–24 in *Called and Empowered: Global Mission in Pentecostal Perspective*.

Edited by Murray A. Dempster, Byron D. Klaus, and Douglas Petersen. Peabody, Mass.: Hendrickson, 1991.

McGee, "Strategy." McGee, Gary B. "The Radical Strategy." Pages 47–59 in *Signs and Wonders in Ministry Today*. Edited by Benny C. Aker and Gary B. McGee. Foreword by Thomas E. Trask. Springfield, Mo.: Gospel Publishing House, 1996.

McGinley, *Form-Criticism*. McGinley, Laurence J. *Form-Criticism of the Synoptic Healing Narratives: A Study in the Theories of Martin Dibelius and Rudolf Bultmann*. Woodstock, Md.: Woodstock College Press, 1944.

McGowan, *Authenticity*. McGowan, A. T. B. *The Divine Authenticity of Scripture: Retrieving an Evangelical Heritage*. Downers Grove, Ill.: IVP Academic, 2007.

McGrath, *Dialogue*. McGrath, Alister E. *The Foundations of Dialogue in Science and Religion*. Malden, Mass.: Blackwell, 1998.

McGrath, *Heaven*. McGrath, Alister E. *A Brief History of Heaven*. Blackwell Brief Histories of Religion. Malden, Mass.: Blackwell, 2003.

McGrath, "Mill." McGrath, P. J. "John Stuart Mill and the Concept of a Miracle." *ITQ* 59 (3, 1993): 211–17.

McGrath, *Science and Religion*. McGrath, Alister E. *Science and Religion: An Introduction*. Malden, Mass.: Blackwell, 1999.

McGrath, *Universe*. McGrath, Alister E. *A Fine-Tuned Universe: The Quest for God in Science and Theology*. Louisville: Westminster John Knox, 2009.

McGreevy, "Histories." McGreevy, John. "Faith Histories." Pages 63–75 in *Religion, Scholarship, Higher Education: Perspectives, Models, and Future Prospects*. Edited by Andrea Sterk. Notre Dame, Ind.: University of Notre Dame Press, 2001.

McGrew, "Argument." McGrew, Timothy. "The Argument from Miracles: A Cumulative Case for the Resurrection of Jesus of Nazareth." Pages 593–662 in *The Blackwell Companion to Natural Theology*. Edited by J. P. Moreland and William Lane Craig. Malden, Mass.: Blackwell, 2009.

McGrew, "Miracles." McGrew, Timothy. "Miracles." *The Stanford Encyclopedia of Philosophy*. Winter 2010 edition. Edited by Edward N. Zalta. http://plato.stanford.edu/entries/miracles/. Accessed Oct. 11, 2010.

Mchami, "Gifts." Mchami, Ronilick E. K. "Apostle Paul on Charismatic Gifts." Pages 169–88 in *Charismatic Renewal in Africa: A Challenge for African Christianity*. Edited by Mika Vähäkangas and Andrew A. Kyomo. Nairobi: Acton Publishers, 2003.

Mchami, "Possession." Mchami, R. E. K. "Demon Possession and Exorcism in Mark 1:21–28." *AfThJ* 24 (1, 2001): 17–37.

McIllmurray et al., "Needs." McIllmurray, M. B., B. Francis, et al. "Psychosocial Needs in Cancer Patients Related to Religious Belief." *PallMed* 17 (1, 2003): 49–54.

McInerny, *Miracles*. McInerny, Ralph M. *Miracles: A Catholic View*. Huntington, Ind.: Our Sunday Visitor Publishing Division, 1986.

McKenna, *Miracles*. McKenna, Briege, with Henry Libersat. *Miracles Do Happen*. New York: St. Martin's Press, 1987.

McKenzie, "Miracles." McKenzie, David. "Miracles Are Not Immoral: A Response to James Keller's Moral Argument against Miracles." *RelS* 35 (1, 1999): 73–88.

McKenzie, "Signs." McKenzie, John L. "Signs and Power: The New Testament Presentation of Miracles." *ChicSt* 3 (1, Spring 1964): 5–18.

"McKenzie Story." "Miracles: The Randy McKenzie Story." DVD, 2006. See http://teamfamilyonline.com/miracles/; www.RandyandSusan.org.

McKim, "View." McKim, Donald K. "The Puritan View of History or Providence Without and Within." *EvQ* 52 (1980): 215–37.

McKinnon, "Miracle." McKinnon, Alastair. "Miracle." Pages 49–52 in *Miracles*. Edited by Richard Swinburne. New York: Macmillan, 1989.

McLaughlin, *Ethics*. McLaughlin, Raymond W. *The Ethics of Persuasive Preaching*. Grand Rapids: Baker, 1979.

McMullin, "Virtues." McMullin, Ernan. "The Virtues of a Good Theory." Pages 498–508 in *The Routledge Companion to Philosophy of Science*. Edited by Stathis Psillos and Martin Curd. New York: Routledge, 2008.

McNamara, *Judaism*. McNamara, Martin. *Palestinian Judaism and the New Testament*. Good News Studies 4. Wilmington, Del.: Michael Glazier, 1983.

McNamara, "Nature." McNamara, Kevin. "The Nature and Recognition of Miracles." *ITQ* 27 (1960): 294–322.

McNamara and Szent-Imrey, "Learn." McNamara, Patrick, and Reka Szent-Imrey. "What We Can Learn from Miraculous Healings and Cures." Pages 208–20 in *Religious and Spiritual Events*. Vol. 1 of *Miracles: God, Science, and Psychology in the Paranormal*. Edited by J. Harold Ellens. Westport, Conn.; London: Praeger, 2008.

McNaughton, *Blacksmiths*. McNaughton, Patrick R. *The Mande Blacksmiths: Knowledge, Power, and Art in West Africa*. Bloomington: Indiana University Press, 1988.

McNichols and Feldman, "Spirituality." McNichols, Kathryn Z., and David B. Feldman. "Spirituality at the End of Life: Issues and Guidelines for Care."

Pages 191–203 in *Spirit, Science, and Health: How the Spiritual Mind Fuels Physical Wellness*. Edited by Thomas G. Plante and Carl E. Thoresen. Foreword by Albert Bandura. Westport, Conn.: Praeger, 2007.

McNutt, "Healed." McNutt, Mrs. Arthur. "Healed of Bright's Disease and Other Complications." *PentEv* 523 (Nov. 24, 1923): 18–19.

McRay, *Archaeology and New Testament*. McRay, John. *Archaeology and the New Testament*. Grand Rapids: Baker, 1991.

McVeigh, "Possession." McVeigh, Brian. "Spirit Possession in Suky, Mahikari: A Variety of Sociopsychological Experience." *JapRel* 21 (2, 1996): 283–98.

"Medical News." "Medical News." *CGl* 4 (2, Jan. 1923): 13.

Medina, "Religion." Medina, Lara. "Chicanos/as, Religion, and Healing: Traditions and Transformations." Pages 139–55 in *Teaching Religion and Healing*. Edited by Linda L. Barnes and Inés Talamantez. AARTRSS. Oxford: Oxford University Press, 2006.

Meeks, *Prophet-King*. Meeks, Wayne A. *The Prophet-King: Moses Traditions and the Johannine Christology*. NovTSup 14. Leiden: Brill, 1967.

Meeks, "Why Study?" Meeks, Wayne A. "Why Study the New Testament?" *NTS* 51 (2, April 2005): 155–70.

Meier, *Marginal Jew*. Meier, John P. *A Marginal Jew: Rethinking the Historical Jesus*. ABRL. Vol. 1: *The Roots of the Problem and the Person*. New York: Doubleday, 1991. Vol. 2: *Mentor, Message, and Miracles*. New York: Doubleday, 1994.

Meier, "Quest." Meier, John P. "The Quest for the Historical Jesus as a Truly Historical Project." *Grail* 12 (3, 1996): 43–52.

Meier, "Reflections." Meier, John P. "Reflections on Jesus-of-History Research Today." Pages 84–107 in *Jesus' Jewishness: Exploring the Place of Jesus Within Early Judaism*. Edited by James H. Charlesworth. New York: The American Interfaith Institute, Crossroad, 1991.

Meier, "Signs." Meier, Samuel A. "Signs and Wonders." Pages 755–62 in *Dictionary of the Old Testament: Pentateuch*. Edited by T. Desmond Alexander and David W. Baker. Downers Grove, Ill.: InterVarsity, 2003.

Meier, "Third Quest." Meier, John P. "The Present State of the 'Third Quest' for the Historical Jesus: Loss and Gain." *Bib* 80 (4, 1999): 459–87.

Melinsky, *Miracles*. Melinsky, M. A. H. *Healing Miracles: An Examination from History and Experience of the Place of Miracle in Christian Thought and Medical Practice*. London: A. R. Mowbray, 1968.

Menberu, "Abraham." Menberu, Dirshaye. "Emmanuel Abraham." *DACB*. http://www.dacb.org /stories/ethiopia/emmanuel_abraham.html.

Menberu, "Estifanos." Menberu, Dirshaye. "Abba Estifanos." *DACB*. http://www.dacb.org/stories /ethiopia/estifanos_.html.

Menberu, "Mekonnen Negera." Menberu, Dirshaye. "Mekonnen Negera." *DACB*. http://www.dacb.org /stories/ethiopia/mekonnen_negera.html.

Menberu, "Regassa Feysa." Menberu, Dirshaye. "Regassa Feysa." *DACB*. http://www.dacb.org/stories /ethiopia/regassa_feysa.html.

Mendonca et al., "Spirituality." Mendonca, Dudley, K. Elizabeth Oakes, Joseph W. Ciarrocchi, W. J. Sneck, and K. Gillespie. "Spirituality and God Attachment as Predictors of Subjective Well-Being for Seminarians and Nuns in India." *RSSSR* 18 (2007): 121–40.

Mensah, "Basis." Mensah, Felix Augustine. "The Spiritual Basis of Health and Illness in Africa." Pages 171–80 in *Health Knowledge and Belief Systems in Africa*. Edited by Toyin Falola and Matthew M. Heaton. Durham, N.C.: Carolina Academic Press, 2008.

Menzies, *Anointed*. Menzies, William W. *Anointed to Serve: The Story of the Assemblies of God*. Springfield, Mo.: Gospel Publishing House, 1971.

Menzies, "Paradigm." Menzies, Robert P. "Acts 2.17–21: A Paradigm for Pentecostal Mission." *JPT* 17 (2, 2008): 200–218.

Menzies, "Sending." Menzies, Robert P. "The Sending of the Seventy and Luke's Purpose." Pages 87–113 in *Trajectories in the Book of Acts: Essays in Honor of John Wesley Wyckoff*. Edited by Paul Alexander, Jordan Daniel May, and Robert G. Reid. Eugene, Ore.: Wipf & Stock, 2010.

Menzies, *Young*. Menzies, Doris Dresselhaus. *Young at Heart: The Story of a Heart Transplant Recipient*. Springfield, Mo.: Celebration Publishing, 2007.

Mercado, "Power." Mercado, Leonardo. "Power and Spiritual Discipline among Philippine Folk Healers." *DialAll* 3 (4, 1989): 55–63.

Merenlahti, "Reality." Merenlahti, Petri. "Distorted Reality or Transitional Space? Biblical Miracle Stories in Psychoanalytic Perspective." Pages 15–35 in *Religious and Spiritual Events*. Vol. 1 of *Miracles: God, Science, and Psychology in the Paranormal*. Edited by J. Harold Ellens. Westport, Conn.; London: Praeger, 2008.

Merkur, "Revelation." Merkur, Dan. "Revelation and the Practice of Prophecy: With Special Reference to Rabbi Nachman of Breslov." Pages 253–300 in *Parapsychological Perspectives*. Vol. 3 of *Miracles: God, Science, and Psychology in the Paranormal*. Edited by J. Harold Ellens. Westport, Conn.; London: Praeger, 2008.

Merwe, "Relevance." Merwe, J. C. van der. "The Relevance of Worldview Interpretation to Health Care in South Africa." Pages 55–66 in *Health Knowledge and Belief Systems in Africa*. Edited by Toyin Falola and Matthew M. Heaton. Durham, N.C.: Carolina Academic Press, 2008.

Merz, "Witch." Merz, Johannes. "'I am a Witch in the Holy Spirit': Rupture and Continuity of Witchcraft Beliefs in African Christianity." *Missiology* 36 (2, April 2008): 201–17.

Messina et al., "Study." Messina, Giuseppina, Paolo Lissoni, et al. "A Psychoncological Study of Lymphocyte Subpopulations in Relation to Pleasure-Related Neurobiochemistry and Sexual and Spiritual Profile to Rorschach's Test in Early or Advanced Cancer Patients." *JBiolRegHomA* 17 (4, 2003): 322–26.

Messing, "Zar Cult." Messing, Simon D. "Group Therapy and Social Status in the *Zar* Cult of Ethiopia." *AmAnth* 60 (6, 1958): 1120–47.

Metzger, *Index*. Metzger, Bruce M. *Index to Periodical Literature on Christ and the Gospels*. NTTS 6. Grand Rapids: Eerdmans, 1962; Leiden: Brill, 1966.

Metzger, *Text*. Metzger, Bruce Manning. *The Text of the New Testament: Its Transmission, Corruption, and Restoration*. 2nd ed. New York: Oxford University Press, 1968.

Metzger, *Textual Commentary*. Metzger, Bruce M. *A Textual Commentary on the Greek New Testament*. Corrected edition. New York: United Bible Societies, 1975.

Metzner, "Hallucinogens." Metzner, Ralph. "Hallucinogens in Contemporary North American Shamanic Practice." Pages 170–75 in *Proceedings of the Fourth International Conference on the Study of Shamanism and Alternate Modes of Healing, Held at the St. Sabina Center, San Rafael, California, September 5–7, 1987*. Edited by Ruth-Inge Heinze. N.p.: Independent Scholars of Asia; Madison, Wis.: A-R Editions, 1988.

Mews, "Revival." Mews, Stuart. "The Revival of Spiritual Healing in the Church of England 1920–26." Pages 299–331 in *The Church and Healing: Papers Read at the Twentieth Summer Meeting and the Twenty-first Winter Meeting of the Ecclesiastical History Society*. StChHist 19. Edited by W. J. Sheils. Oxford: Basil Blackwell, 1982.

Meyer, "Evidence." Meyer, Stephen C. "Evidence for Design in Physics and Biology: From the Origin of the Universe to the Origin of Life." Pages 53–111 in *Science and Evidence for Design in the Universe*, by Michael J. Behe, William A. Dembski, and Stephen C. Meyer. The Proceedings of the Wethersfield Institute 9. San Francisco: Ignatius, 2000.

Meyer, *Realism*. Meyer, Ben F. *Critical Realism and the New Testament*. PrTMS 17. Allison Park, Pa.: Pickwick, 1989.

Meyer, "Scientific Status." Meyer, Stephen C. "The Scientific Status of Intelligent Design: The Methodological Equivalence of Naturalistic and Non-Naturalistic Origins Theories." Pages 151–211 in *Science and Evidence for Design in the Universe*, by Michael J. Behe, William A. Dembski, and Stephen C. Meyer. The Proceedings of the Wethersfield Institute 9. San Francisco: Ignatius, 2000.

Michael, "Gäbrä-Seyon." Michael, Belaynesh. "Gäbrä-Seyon." *DACB*. http://www.dacb.org/stories /ethiopia/gabra_seyon.html.

Michael-Dede, "Anastenari." Michael-Dede, Maria. "The Anastenari: From the Psychological and Sociological Viewpoint." *Thrakika* 46 (1973): 153–80.

Michaels, *Servant*. Michaels, J. Ramsey. *Servant and Son: Jesus in Parable and Gospel*. Atlanta: John Knox, 1981.

Michel, *Telling*. Michel, David. *Telling the Story: Black Pentecostals in the Church of God*. Cleveland, Tenn.: Pathway Press, 2000.

Michel, "Worlds." Michel, Claudine. "Of Worlds Seen and Unseen: The Educational Character of Haitian Vodou." Pages 32–45 in *Haitian Vodou: Spirit, Myth, and Reality*. Edited by Patrick Bellegarde-Smith and Claudine Michel. Bloomington: Indiana University Press, 2006.

Michel, Bellegarde-Smith, and Racine-Toussaint, "Mouths." Michel, Claudine, Patrick Bellegarde-Smith, and Marlène Racine-Toussaint. "From the Horses' Mouths: Women's Words/Women's Worlds." Pages 70–83 in *Haitian Vodou: Spirit, Myth, and Reality*. Edited by Patrick Bellegarde-Smith and Claudine Michel. Bloomington: Indiana University Press, 2006.

Middleton, "Growth." Middleton, V. J. "Church Growth in Tribal India." MA thesis, Fuller Theological Seminary, 1972.

Middleton, "Possession." Middleton, John. "Spirit Possession among the Lugbara." Pages 220–32 in *Spirit Mediumship and Society in Africa*. Edited by John Beattie and John Middleton. Foreword by Raymond Firth. New York: Africana Publishing Corporation, 1969.

Midelfort, "Possession." Midelfort, H. C. Erik. "The Devil and the German People: Reflections on the Popularity of Demon Possession in Sixteenth-Century Germany." Pages 113–33 in *Possession and Exorcism*. Vol. 9 of *Articles on Witchcraft, Magic, and Demonology: A Twelve-Volume Anthology of Scholarly Articles*. Edited by Brian P. Levack. New York: Garland, 1992. Reprinted from Steven Ozment, ed., *Religion and Culture in the Renaissance and Reformation, Sixteenth-Century Essays and Studies* 11 (1989): 99–119.

Midelfort, "Reactions." Midelfort, H. C. Erik. "Catholic and Lutheran Reactions to Demon Possession in the Late Seventeenth Century: Two Case Histories." Pages 135–60 in *Possession and Exorcism*. Vol. 9 of

Articles on Witchcraft, Magic, and Demonology: A Twelve-Volume Anthology of Scholarly Articles. Edited by Brian P. Levack. New York: Garland, 1992. Reprinted from *Daphnis* 15 (1986): 623–48.

Míguez-Bonino, "Acts 2." Míguez-Bonino, José. "Acts 2:1–42: A Latin American Perspective." Pages 161–65 in *Return to Babel: Global Perspectives on the Bible*. Edited by John R. Levison and Priscilla Pope-Levison. Louisville: Westminster John Knox, 1999.

Milbank, *Social Theory*. Milbank, John. *Theology and Social Theory*. Cambridge: Basil Blackwell, 1990.

Mill, *Logic*. Mill, John Stuart. *A System of Logic*. London: Longman's, 1967.

Millard, "Duma." Millard, J. A. "Duma, William." *DACB*. http://www.dacb.org/stories/southafrica/duma_william.html.

Millard, *Reading and Writing*. Millard, Alan. *Reading and Writing in the Time of Jesus*. The Biblical Seminar 69. Sheffield: Sheffield Academic Press, 2000.

Millay, "Time Travel." Millay, Jean. "Time Travel: A Guide for the Guide." Pages 100–106 in *Proceedings of the Fourth International Conference on the Study of Shamanism and Alternate Modes of Healing, Held at the St. Sabina Center, San Rafael, California, September 5–7, 1987*. Edited by Ruth-Inge Heinze. N.p.: Independent Scholars of Asia; Madison, Wis.: A-R Editions, 1988.

Miller, *Birth*. Miller, Timothy S. *The Birth of the Hospital in the Byzantine Empire*. The Henry E. Sigerist Supplements to the Bulletin of the History of Medicine, new series, 10. Baltimore: Johns Hopkins University Press, 1985.

Miller, *Convinced*. Miller, John B. F. *Convinced That God Had Called Us: Dreams, Visions, and the Perception of God's Will in Luke-Acts*. BIS 85. Leiden: Brill, 2007.

Miller, "Darwin." Miller, Kenneth R. "Darwin, God, and Dover: What the Collapse of 'Intelligent Design' Means for Science and Faith in America." Pages 55–92 in *The Religion and Science Debate: Why Does It Continue?* Edited by Harold W. Attridge. New Haven: Yale University Press, 2009.

Miller, "Miracle." Miller, John Franklin. "Is 'Miracle' an Intelligible Notion?" *SJT* 20 (1, 1967): 25–36.

Miller, *Miracle of Healing*. Miller, Basil. *The Miracle of Divine Healing*. Kansas City, Mo.: Beacon Hill, 1951.

Miller, "Miracle Worker." Miller, Louis G. "Jesus the Miracle Worker." *Lig* 77 (Aug. 1989): 20–26.

Miller, *Seminar*. Miller, Robert J. *The Jesus Seminar and Its Critics*. Santa Rosa, Calif.: Polebridge, 1999.

Miller, "Story." Miller, Jane. "Jane Miller's Story and Testimony (as told at the Conference)." Pages 174–78 in *Essays on Spiritual Bondage and Deliverance*.

Edited by Willard M. Swartley. Occasional Papers 11. Elkhart, Ind.: Institute of Mennonite Studies, 1988.

Miller and Gur, "Religiosity." Miller, Lisa, and Merav Gur. "Religiosity, Depression, and Physical Maturation in Adolescent Girls." *JAACAP* 41 (2, 2002): 206–14.

Miller and Samples, *Cult of Virgin*. Miller, Elliot, and Kenneth R. Samples. *The Cult of the Virgin: Catholic Mariology and the Apparitions of Mary*. Foreword by Norman L. Geisler. Grand Rapids: Baker, 1992.

Miller and Yamamori, *Pentecostalism*. Miller, Donald E., and Tetsunao Yamamori. *Global Pentecostalism: The New Face of Christian Social Engagement*. Berkeley: University of California Press, 2007.

Miller et al., "Needs." Miller, Brigitte E., Barbara Pittman, et al. "Gynecologic Cancer Patients' Psychosocial Needs and Their Views on the Physician's Role in Meeting Those Needs." *IJGynC* 13 (2, 2003): 111–19.

Millican, "Theorem." Millican, Peter. "Hume's Theorem Concerning Miracles." *PhilQ* 43 (1993): 489–95.

Mills, *Agents*. Mills, Mary E. *Human Agents of Cosmic Power in Hellenistic Judaism and the Synoptic Tradition*. JSNTSup 41. Sheffield: Sheffield Academic Press, 1990.

Mills, "Investigation." Mills, Antonia. "Making a Scientific Investigation of Ethnographic Cases Suggestive of Reincarnation." Pages 237–69 in *Being Changed: The Anthropology of Extraordinary Experience*. Edited by David E. Young and Jean-Guy Goulet. Peterborough, Ont.: Broadview, 1994.

Mills and Lynn, "Experiences." Mills, Antonia, and Steven Jay Lynn. "Past-Life Experiences." Pages 283–314 in *Varieties of Anomalous Experience: Examining the Scientific Evidence*. Edited by Etzel Cardeña, Steven Jay Lynn, and Stanley Krippner. Washington, D.C.: American Psychological Association, 2000.

Milner, "Exorcism." Milner, Neal. "Giving the Devil His Due Process: Exorcism in the Church of England." *JContRel* 15 (2, 2000): 247–72.

Min, *Solidarity*. Min, Anselm Kyongsuk. *The Solidarity of Others in a Divided World: A Postmodern Theology after Postmodernism*. New York: T&T Clark, 2004.

Minogue, "Religion." Minogue, Kenneth. "Religion, Reason and Conflict in the Twenty-first Century." *NatInt* (Summer 2003): 127–32.

"Miracle for Tamang." "A Miracle for Tamang." *Asian Report* 222 (March 1997): 8–9.

Miracle Investigation. *Miracle Investigation: 7 Miracles and a Martyr; 8 Stories of Supernatural Faith*. With Reinhard Bonnke. DVD. Orlando, Fla.: E-R Productions, 2005.

"Miracles, Miracle-Workers." "Miracles, Miracle-Workers: Biblical-Early Christian." Pages 53–56 in vol. 9 of Brill's New Pauly: Encyclopaedia of the Ancient World. Edited by Hubert Cancik and Helmuth Schneider. 20 vols. English ed. Christine F. Salazar. Leiden: Brill, 2010.

"Miracle Woman." "Miracle Woman." Time (Sept. 14, 1970): 62, 64.

Miraculous Healing. The Story of Jean Neil: A Miraculous Healing. Orlando, Fla.: E-R Productions, 2008.

"Miraculous Truth." "Miraculous Truth Can Stand a Test." CT (March 4, 1977): 30.

Mitchell, "Archaeology." Mitchell, Stephen. "Archaeology in Asia Minor 1990–1998." ArchRep 45 (1998–99): 125–92.

Mitchell, "Family Matters." Mitchell, Margaret M. "Why Family Matters for Early Christian Literature." Pages 345–58 in Early Christian Families in Context: An Interdisciplinary Dialogue. Edited by David L. Balch and Carolyn Osiek. Grand Rapids: Eerdmans, 2003.

Mitchem, Folk Healing. Mitchem, Stephanie Y. African-American Folk Healing. New York: New York University Press, 2007.

Mitchem, "Healing." Mitchem, Stephanie Y. "Religious Healing as Pedagogical Performance." Pages 219–29 in Teaching Religion and Healing. Edited by Linda L. Barnes and Inés Talamantez. AARTRSS. Oxford: Oxford University Press, 2006.

Mitsis, "Stoics and Aquinas." Mitsis, Phillip. "The Stoics and Aquinas on Virtue and Natural Law." SPhilA 15 (2003): 35–53.

Mittelstadt, Spirit. Mittelstadt, Martin William. The Spirit and Suffering in Luke-Acts: Implications for a Pentecostal Pneumatology. JPTSup 26. London, New York: T&T Clark International, 2004.

Miyamoto, "Possessed." Miyamoto, Yuki. "Possessed and Possessing: Fox-Possession and Discrimination against the Wealthy in the Modern Period in Japan." CulRel 7 (2, 2006): 139–54.

Mkhize, "Prayer-Healer." Mkhize, H. B. "The Umthandazi—Prayer-Healer." Pages 281–93 in Afro-Christian Religion and Healing in Southern Africa. Edited by G. C. Oosthuizen, S. D. Edwards, W. H. Wessels, and I. Hexham. AfSt 8. Lewiston, N.Y.: Edwin Mellen, 1989.

Mkhwanazi, "Psychotherapist." Mkhwanazi, I. "The iSangoma as Psychotherapist." Pages 261–79 in Afro-Christian Religion and Healing in Southern Africa. Edited by G. C. Oosthuizen, S. D. Edwards, W. H. Wessels, and I. Hexham. AfSt 8. Lewiston, N.Y.: Edwin Mellen, 1989.

Mlahagwa, "Contending." Mlahagwa, Josiah R. "Contending for the Faith: Spiritual Revival and the Fellowship Church in Tanzania." Pages 296–306 in East African Expressions of Christianity. Edited by Thomas Spear and Isaria N. Kimambo. EAfSt. Athens: Ohio University Press; Oxford: James Currey; Dar es Salaam: Mkuki na Nyota; Nairobi: East African Educational Publishers, 1999.

Modarressi, "Zar Cult." Modarressi, Taghi. "The Zar Cult in South Iran." Pages 149–55 in Trance and Possession States. Proceedings of the Second Annual Conference, R. M. Bucke Memorial Society, March 4–6, 1966. Edited by Raymond Prince. Montreal: R. M. Bucke Memorial Society, 1968.

Moerman, Meaning. Moerman, Daniel E. Meaning, Medicine, and the "Placebo Effect." Cambridge: Cambridge University Press, 2002.

Mofidi at al., "Spirituality." Mofidi, M., et al. "Spirituality and Depressive Symptoms in a Racially Diverse U.S. Sample of Community-Dwelling Adults." JNMDis 194 (2006): 975–77.

Mogashoa, "Survey." Mogashoa, H. "A Historical Survey of the Missionary Purposes of Baptist Medical Dispensaries to the 'Natives' (1904–1949)." StHistEc 28 (2, 2001): 74–97.

Mohammad, "Saw." Mohammad, "I Saw Jesus." MounM (Nov. 1990): 16–17.

Mohr, "Medicine." Mohr, Adam. "Missionary Medicine and Akan Therapeutics: Illness, Health and Healing in Southern Ghana's Basel Mission, 1828–1918." JRelAf 38 (4, 2009): 429–61.

Mohr, "Zion." Mohr, Adam. "Out of Zion Into Philadelphia and West Africa: Faith Tabernacle Congregation, 1897–1925." Pneuma 32 (2010): 56–79.

Mohr et al., "Integration." Mohr, S., P. Y. Brandt, L. Borras, C. Gillieron, and P. Huguelet. "Toward an Integration of Spirituality and Religiousness into the Psychosocial Dimension of Schizophrenia." AmJPsyc 163 (11, 2006): 1952–59.

Molalegn, Dawit. DVD. Vol. 2. Addis Ababa: Atsheber, Kingdom studio.

Molassiotis et al., "Medicine." Molassiotis, Alexander, et al. "Complementary and Alternative Medicine Use in Lung Cancer Patients in Eight European Countries." ComThClPrac 12 (1, 2006): 34–39.

Moll et al., "Networks." Moll, J., et al. "Human Fronto-mesolimbic Networks Guide Decisions about Charitable Donation." PNAS 103 (42, 2006): 15623–28.

Molobi, "Churches." Molobi, Victor S. "Do Zionist Churches Still Matter When Envisioning a Rainbow Nation?" MissFoc 17 (2009): 70–83.

Molobi, "Knowledge." Molobi, Victor S. "AIC Indigenous Knowledge and Theological Education Initiatives in Southern Africa." MissFoc 17 (2009): 83–99.

Molobi, "Veneration." Molobi, Victor. "Ancestral Veneration at the Core of African Spiritual Renewal among the AICs in South Africa." *StHistEc* 31 (1, 2005): 111–26.

Moltmann, "Blessing." Moltmann, Jürgen. "The Blessing of Hope: The Theology of Hope and the Full Gospel of Life." *JPT* 13 (2, 2005): 147–61.

Moltmann, *Broad Place*. Moltmann, Jürgen. *A Broad Place: An Autobiography*. Translated by Margaret Kohl. Minneapolis: Fortress, 2008.

Moltmann, "Resurrection." Moltmann, Jürgen. "The Resurrection of Christ and the New Earth." *CV* 49 (2, 2007): 141–49.

Monden, *Signs*. Monden, Louis. *Signs and Wonders: A Study of the Miraculous Element in Religion*. Foreword by Avery Dulles. New York: Desclee, 1966.

Monnin, *Curé d'Ars*. Monnin, Alfred. *The Curé d'Ars*. London: Sands, n.d. (ca. 1924).

Monroe et al., "Preferences." Monroe, Michael H., Deborah Bynum, et al. "Primary Care Physician Preferences Regarding Spiritual Behavior in Medical Practice." *ArchIntMed* 163 (22, 2003): 2751–56.

Montague, *Growth*. Montague, George T. *The Holy Spirit: Growth of a Biblical Tradition. A Commentary on the Principal Texts of the Old and New Testaments*. New York: Paulist, 1976.

Montague, *Spirit*. Montague, George T. *The Spirit and His Gifts: The Biblical Background of Spirit Baptism, Tongue Speaking, and Prophecy*. New York: Paulist, 1974.

Montefiore, *Gospels*. Montefiore, C. G. *The Synoptic Gospels*. 2 vols. Library of Biblical Studies. New York: KTAV, 1968.

Montefiore, *Miracles*. Montefiore, Hugh. *The Miracles of Jesus*. London: SPCK, 2005.

Montefiore and Loewe, *Anthology*. Montefiore, C. G., and Herbert Loewe, eds. and trans. *A Rabbinic Anthology*. New York: Schocken Books, 1974.

Montgomery, "Exorcism." Montgomery, John Warwick. "Exorcism: Is It for Real?" *CT* 18 (21, 1974): 1183–86.

Montgomery, *Faith*. Montgomery, Dan. *Faith Beyond Church Walls: Finding Freedom in Christ*. Montecito, Calif.: Compass Works, 2007.

Montgomery, "Fire." Montgomery, Jim. "New Testament Fire in the Philippines." C-Grip, Box 1416, Manila, Philippines, 1972.

Montgomery, *Kings*. Montgomery, James A. *A Critical and Exegetical Commentary on the Books of Kings*. Edited by Henry Snyder Gehman. ICC. Edinburgh: T&T Clark, 1951.

Montgomery, "Science." Montgomery, John Warwick. "Science, Theology, and the Miraculous." *JASA* 30 (4, 1978): 145–53.

Montgomery, *Trusting*. Montgomery, Dan and Kate. *Trusting in the Trinity: Compass Psychotheology Applied*. Montecito, Calif.: Compass Works, 2009.

Montilus, "Vodun." Montilus, Guérin C. "Vodun and Social Tranformation in the African Diasporic Experience: The Concept of Personhood in Haitian Vodun Religion." Pages 1–6 in *Haitian Vodou: Spirit, Myth, and Reality*. Edited by Patrick Bellegarde-Smith and Claudine Michel. Bloomington: Indiana University Press, 2006.

Moodley, *Shembe*. Moodley, Edley J. *Shembe, Ancestors, and Christ: A Christological Inquiry with Missiological Implications*. AmSocMissMonS 2. Foreword by Howard A. Snyder. Introduction by Eunice Irwin. Eugene, Ore.: Pickwick, 2008.

Moodley and Sutherland, "Healers." Moodley, Rod, and Patsy Sutherland. "Traditional and Cultural Healers and Healing: Dual Interventions in Counseling and Psychotherapy." *CounsSp* 28 (1, 2009): 11–31.

Moody, *Life*. Moody, Raymond A., Jr. *Life after Life*. Atlanta: Mockingbird, 1975.

Moog and Karenberg, "Francis." Moog, Ferdinand Peter, and Axel Karenberg. "St. Francis Came at Dawn—The Miraculous Recovery of a Hemiplegic Monk in the Middle Ages." *JNeurSc* 213 (1–2, 2003): 15–17.

Moolenburgh, *Meetings*. Moolenburgh, H. C. *Meetings with Angels: One Hundred and One Real-Life Encounters*. Translated by Tony Langham and Plym Peters. New York: Barnes & Noble, C. W. Daniel, 1995.

Mooney and Imbrosciano, "Case." Mooney, T. Brian, and Anthony Imbrosciano. "The Curious Case of Mr. Locke's Miracles." *IJPhilRel* 57 (3, 2005): 147–68.

Mooneyham, "Demonism." Mooneyham, W. Stanley. "Demonism on the Mission Field: Problems of Communicating a Difficult Phenomenon." Pages 209–19 in *Demon Possession: A Medical, Historical, Anthropological, and Theological Symposium*. Papers presented at the University of Notre Dame, January 8–11, 1975, under the auspices of the Christian Medical Association. Edited by John Warwick Montgomery. Minneapolis: Bethany House, 1976.

Moore, "Darwin's Faith." Moore, James. "That Evolution Destroyed Darwin's Faith in Christianity— Until He Reconverted on His Deathbed." Pages 142–51 in *Galileo Goes to Jail and Other Myths about Science and Religion*. Edited by Ronald L. Numbers. Cambridge, Mass.: Harvard University Press, 2009.

Moore, "Introduction." Moore, Charles E. "Introduction." Pages 9–29 in *Sadhu Sundar Singh: Essential Writings*. MSMS. Maryknoll, N.Y.: Orbis, 2005.

Moore, *Judaism*. Moore, George Foot. *Judaism in the First Centuries of the Christian Era*. 2 vols. Reprint,

New York: Schocken, 1971. Reprinted from Cambridge, Mass.: Harvard University Press, 1927.

Moore, "Quakerism." Moore, Rosemary. "Late Seventeenth-Century Quakerism and the Miraculous: A New Look at George Fox's 'Book of Miracles.'" Pages 335–44 in *Signs, Wonders, Miracles: Representations of Divine Power in the Life of the Church. Papers Read at the 2003 Summer Meeting and the 2004 Winter Meeting of the Ecclesiastical History Society*. Edited by Kate Cooper and Jeremy Gregory. Rochester: Boydell & Brewer, for the Ecclesiastical History Society, 2005.

Moore, "Raised." Moore, B. S. "Raised from the Dead thru Prayers of Natives." *LRE* 15 (2, Dec. 1921): 19–20.

Moreau, "Broadening." Moreau, A. Scott. "Broadening the Issues: Historiography, Advocacy, and Hermeneutics: Response to C. Peter Wagner." Pages 123–35 in *The Holy Spirit and Mission Dynamics*. Edited by C. Douglas McConnell. EvMissSS 5. Pasadena, Calif.: William Carey Library, 1997.

Moreau, "Perspective." Moreau, A. Scott. "Gaining Perspective on Territorial Spirits." Pages 259–75 in *Deliver Us from Evil: An Uneasy Frontier in Christian Mission*. Edited by A. Scott Moreau, Tokunboh Adeyemo, David G. Burnett, Bryant L. Myers, and Hwa Yung. Monrovia, Calif.: Lausanne Committee for World Evangelization, 2002.

Moreau, "Possession Phenomena." Moreau, A. Scott. "Possession Phenomena." Pages 771–72 in *Evangelical Dictionary of World Missions*. Edited by A. Scott Moreau. Grand Rapids: Baker, 2000.

Moreland, "Agency." Moreland, J. P. "Miracles, Agency, and Theistic Science: A Reply to Steven B. Cowan." *PhilChr* 4 (1, 2002): 139–60.

Moreland, "Miracles." Moreland, J. P. "Science, Miracles, Agency Theory, and the God-of-the-Gaps." Pages 132–48 in *In Defense of Miracles: A Comprehensive Case for God's Action in History*. Edited by R. Douglas Geivett and Gary R. Habermas. Downers Grove, Ill.: InterVarsity, 1997.

Moreland, *Triangle*. Moreland, J. P. *Kingdom Triangle: Recover the Christian Mind, Renovate the Soul, Restore the Spirit's Power*. Grand Rapids: Zondervan, 2007.

Moreland and Issler, *Faith*. Moreland, J. P., and Klaus Issler. *In Search of a Confident Faith: Overcoming Barriers to Trusting in God*. Downers Grove, Ill.: InterVarsity, 2008.

Morel-Vergniol, "Ève et Lilith." Morel-Vergniol, Danielle. "Adam, Ève . . . et Lilith?" *FoiVie* 99 (4, 2000): 39–51.

Morgan, "Heritability." Morgan, Arlene H. "The Heritability of Hypnotic Susceptibility in Twins." *JAbSocPsy* 82 (1973): 55–61.

Morgan, "Impasse." Morgan, Timothy C. "Egypt's Identity Impasse." *CT* 52 (4, April 2008): 60–61.

Morgan, *Sings*. Morgan, Robert J. *Then Sings My Soul: 150 of the World's Greatest Hymn Stories*. Nashville: Thomas Nelson, 2003.

Morphew, *Breakthrough*. Morphew, Derek J. *Breakthrough: Discovering the Kingdom*. Cape Town: Vineyard International, 1991.

Morris, "Introduction." Morris, Thomas V. "Introduction." Pages 1–9 in *Divine and Human Action: Essays in the Metaphysics of Theism*. Edited by Thomas V. Morris. Ithaca, N.Y.: Cornell University Press, 1988.

Morris, *Studies*. Morris, Leon. *Studies in the Fourth Gospel*. Grand Rapids: Eerdmans, 1969.

Morrison, "Miracles." Morrison, Molly. "Strange Miracles: A Study of the Peculiar Healings of St Maria Maddalena de' Pazzi." *Logos* 8 (1, 2005): 129–44.

Morrow-Howell et al., "Effects." Morrow-Howell, Nancy, et al. "Effects of Volunteering on the Well-Being of Older Adults." *JGPSSS* 58 (3, 2003): S137–45.

Morsy, "Possession." Morsy, Soheir A. "Spirit Possession in Egyptian Ethnomedicine: Origins, Comparison, and Historical Specificity." Pages 189–208 in *Women's Medicine: The Zar-Bori Cult in Africa and Beyond*. Edited by I. M. Lewis, Ahmed Al-Safi, and Sayyid Hurreiz. Edinburgh: International African Institute, Edinburgh University Press, 1991.

Morton, "*Dawit*." Morton, Alice. "*Dawit*: Competition and Integration in an Ethiopian Wuqabi Cult Group." Pages 193–234 in *Case Studies in Spirit Possession*. Edited by Vincent Crapanzaro and Vivian Garrison. New York: John Wiley & Sons, 1977.

Mosher and Jacobs, "Seminar." Mosher, Lucinda A., and Claude Jacobs. "The Worldviews Seminar: An Intensive Survey of American Urban Religious Diversity." Pages 261–75 in *Teaching Religion and Healing*. Edited by Linda L. Barnes and Inés Talamantez. AARTRSS. Oxford: Oxford University Press, 2006.

Motala, "Influence." Motala, Miriam B. "The Relative Influence of Participation in Zionist Church Services on the Emotional State of Participants." Pages 193–205 in *Afro-Christian Religion and Healing in Southern Africa*. Edited by G. C. Oosthuizen, S. D. Edwards, W. H. Wessels, and I. Hexham. AfSt 8. Lewiston, N.Y.: Edwin Mellen, 1989.

Mott, "Science." Mott, Nevill. "Science Will Never Give Us the Answers to All Our Questions." Pages 64–69 in *Cosmos, Bios, and Theos: Scientists Reflect on Science, God, and the Origins of the Universe, Life, and Homo Sapiens*. Edited by Henry Margenau and Roy Abraham Varghese. La Salle, Ill.: Open Court, 1992.

Moule, "Classification." Moule, C. F. D. "Excursus 2: The Classification of Miracle Stories." Pages 239–43 in *Miracles: Cambridge Studies in Their Philosophy and History*. Edited by C. F. D. Moule. London: Mowbray; New York: Morehouse-Barlow, 1965.

Mount, "Miracles?" Mount, Balfour M. "Healing Miracles Today?" Pages 19–26 in *Healing and Religious Faith*. Edited by Claude A. Frazier. Philadelphia: Pilgrim Press, United Church Press, 1974.

Mozley, *Lectures*. Mozley, J. B. *Eight Lectures on Miracles Preached Before the University of Oxford in the Year M.DCCC.LXV, on the Foundation of the Late Rev. John Bampton*. 3rd ed. New York: Scribner, Welford & Co., 1872.

Mthethwa, "Music." Mthethwa, B. N. "Music and Dance as Therapy in African Traditional Societies with Special Reference to the iBlandla lamaNazaretha (the Church of the Nazarites)." Pages 241–56 in *Afro-Christian Religion and Healing in Southern Africa*. Edited by G. C. Oosthuizen, S. D. Edwards, W. H. Wessels, and I. Hexham. AfSt 8. Lewiston, N.Y.: Edwin Mellen, 1989.

Mueller, "Blind, Deaf." Mueller, Rose. "The Blind See, the Deaf Hear, Cancers Healed." *LRE* 15 (7, April 1922): 20–22.

Mueller, "Healings." Mueller, Jennie Kirkland. "Healings among the Heathen." *LRE* (May 1925): 15.

Mueller, "Miraculously Healed." Mueller, Jacob J. "Many Miraculously Healed." *PentEv* 1020 (Oct. 21, 1933): 6.

Mull and Mull, "Leprosy." Mull, K. V., and C. S. Mull. "Biblical Leprosy—Is It Really?" *BAR* 8 (2, 1992): 32–39, 62.

Mullen, *Feel*. Mullen, Grant W. *Why Do I Feel So Down ... When My Faith Should Lift Me Up? How to Break the Three Links in the Chain of Emotional Bondage*. Foreword by Neil T. Anderson. Tonbridge: Sovereign World, 1999.

Müller, "Power." Müller, Barbara. "The Diabolical Power of Lettuce, or Garden Miracles in Gregory the Great's *Dialogues*." Pages 46–55 in *Signs, Wonders, Miracles: Representations of Divine Power in the Life of the Church. Papers Read at the 2003 Summer Meeting and the 2004 Winter Meeting of the Ecclesiastical History Society*. Edited by Kate Cooper and Jeremy Gregory. Rochester: Boydell & Brewer, for the Ecclesiastical History Society, 2005.

Mullet et al., "Involvement." Mullet, Etienne J., José Barros, et al. "Religious Involvement and the Forgiving Personality." *JPers* 71 (1, 2003): 1–19.

Mullin, "Bushnell." Mullin, Robert Bruce. "Horace Bushnell and the Question of Miracles." *CH* 58 (4, 1989): 460–73.

Mullin, *History*. Mullin, Robert Bruce. *A Short World History of Christianity*. Louisville: Westminster John Knox, 2008.

Mullin, *Miracles*. Mullin, Robert Bruce. *Miracles and the Modern Religious Imagination*. New Haven: Yale University Press, 1996.

Mullins, "Empire." Mullins, Mark R. "The Empire Strikes Back: Korean Pentecostal Mission to Japan." Pages 87–102 in *Charismatic Christianity as a Global Culture*. Edited by Karla Poewe. SCR. Columbia: University of South Carolina Press, 1994.

Mumford, "Laws." Mumford, Stephen. "Normative and Natural Laws." *Philosophy* 75 (292, April 2000): 265–82.

Mumford, "Miracles." Mumford, Stephen. "Miracles: Metaphysics, and Modality." *RelS* 37 (2, 2001): 191–202.

Munck, *Acts*. Munck, Johannes. *The Acts of the Apostles*. Revised by W. F. Albright and C. S. Mann. AB 31. Garden City, N.Y.: Doubleday, 1967.

Murdock, *Theories*. Murdock, George Peter. *Theories of Illness: A World Survey*. Pittsburgh: University of Pittsburgh Press, 1980.

Murphy, "Apologetics." Murphy, Nancey. "Postmodern Apologetics." Pages 105–20 in *Religion and Science: History, Method, Dialogue*. Edited by W. Mark Richardson and Wesley J. Wildman. Foreword by Ian G. Barbour. New York: Routledge, 1996.

Murphy, "Aspects of Shamanism." Murphy, Jane M. "Psychotherapeutic Aspects of Shamanism on St. Lawrence Island, Alaska." Pages 53–83 in *Magic, Faith, and Healing: Studies in Primitive Psychiatry Today*. Edited by Ari Kiev. Foreword by Jerome D. Frank. New York: Free Press, 1964.

Murphy, "Causation." Murphy, Nancey. "Emergence and Mental Causation." Pages 227–43 in *The Re-Emergence of Emergence: The Emergentist Hypothesis from Science to Religion*. Edited by Philip Clayton and Paul Davies. Oxford: Oxford University Press, 2006.

Murphy, "Evidence of Design." Murphy, Nancey. "Evidence of Design in the Fine-Tuning of the Universe." Pages 407–35 in *Quantum Cosmology and the Laws of Nature: Scientific Perspectives on Divine Action*. Edited by Robert John Russell, Nancey Murphy, and C. J. Isham. Berkeley: Center for Theology and the Natural Sciences, 1993.

Murphy, "Social Science." Murphy, Nancey. "Social Science, Ethics, and the Powers." Pages 29–38 in *Transforming the Powers: Peace, Justice, and the Domination System*. Edited by Ray Gingerich and Ted Grimsrud. Minneapolis: Fortress, 2006.

Murphy, Johnson, and Lohan, "Meaning." Murphy, S. A., L. C. Johnson, and J. Lohan. "Finding Meaning in a Child's Violent Death: A Five-Year Prospective Analysis of Parents' Personal Narratives and Empirical Data." *DeathS* 27 (5, 2003): 381–404.

Murphy and Ellis, *Nature*. Murphy, Nancey, and George F. R. Ellis. *On the Moral Nature of the Universe: Theology, Cosmology, and Ethics*. Minneapolis: Fortress, 1996.

Murphy et al., "Relation." Murphy, P. E., J. W. Ciarrocchi, R. L. Piedmont, S. Cheston, and M. Peyrot. "The Relation of Religious Belief and Practices, Depression, and Hopelessness in Persons with Clinical Depression." *JCounsClPs* 68 (6, 2000): 1102–6.

Murray, *Healing*. Murray, Andrew. *Divine Healing: A Series of Addresses and a Personal Testimony*. Reprint, Plainfield, N.J.: Logos, 1974.

Murray, "Healing." Murray, Andrew. "Divine Healing." Pages 3–117 in *Healing: The Three Great Classics on Divine Healing*. Edited by Jonathan L. Graf. Camp Hill, Pa.: Christian Publications, 1992.

Murray, *Stages*. Murray, Gilbert. *Five Stages of Greek Religion*. Westport, Conn.: Greenwood, 1976.

Murray, Gordon, and Simpson, *Healing*. Graf, Jonathan L., comp. and ed. *Healing: The Three Great Classics on Divine Healing*. Andrew Murray, *Divine Healing*; A. J. Gordon, *The Ministry of Healing*; A. B. Simpson, *The Gospel of Healing*. Camp Hill, Pa.: Christian Publications, 1992.

Murray-Swank et al., "Religiosity." Murray-Swank, A. B., et al. "Religiosity, Psychosocial Adjustment, and Subjective Burden of Persons Who Care for Those with Mental Illness." *PsychServ* 57 (2006): 361–65.

Musgrave, "Thoughts." Musgrave, Alan E. "Kuhn's Second Thoughts." Pages 39–53 in *Paradigms and Revolutions: Appraisals and Applications of Thomas Kuhn's Philosophy of Science*. Edited by Gary Gutting. Notre Dame, Ind.: University of Notre Dame Press, 1980.

Musi, "Shaman." Musi, Carla Corradi. "The Finno-Ugric Shaman and the West-European Magician." Pages 55–64 in *Proceedings of the Fourth International Conference on the Study of Shamanism and Alternate Modes of Healing, Held at the St. Sabina Center, San Rafael, California, September 5–7, 1987*. Edited by Ruth-Inge Heinze. N.p.: Independent Scholars of Asia; Madison, Wis.: A-R Editions, 1988.

Musick, House, and Williams, "Attendance and Mortality." Musick, Marc A., James S. House, and David R. Williams. "Attendance at Religious Services and Mortality in a National Sample." *JHSocBeh* 45 (2, 2004): 198–213.

Musk, "Popular Islam." Musk, Bill A. "Popular Islam: The Hunger of the Heart." Pages 208–15 in *The Gospel and Islam: A 1978 Compendium*. Edited by Don M. McCurry. Monrovia, Calif.: MARC, 1979.

Musk, "Strategy." Musk, Bill A. "Turkey, towards a Harvest Strategy." MTh thesis, Fuller Theological Seminary, 1980.

Mussner, *Miracles*. Mussner, Franz. *The Miracles of Jesus: An Introduction*. Translated by Albert Wimmer. Notre Dame, Ind.: University of Notre Dame Press, 1968.

Muzorewa, *Origins*. Muzorewa, Gwinyai H. *The Origins and Development of African Theology*. Maryknoll, N.Y.: Orbis, 1985.

Muzur and Skrobonja, "Healings." Muzur, Amir, and Ante Skrobonja. "Miraculous Healings as a Time-Space Conditioned Category—The Example of St. Thecla." *CollAntr* 26 (2, 1998): 325–32.

Mwaura, "Integrity." Mwaura, Philomena Njeri. "Integrity of Mission in the Light of the Gospel: Bearing Witness of the Spirit Among Africa's Gospel Bearers." *MissSt* 24 (2007): 189–212.

Mwaura, "Response." Mwaura, Philomena Njeri. "Response." *IntRevMiss* 90 (356/357, Jan./Apr. 2001): 65–69.

Mwaura, "Spirituality." Mwaura, Philomena Njeri. "A Spirituality of Resistance and Hope: African Instituted Churches' Response to Poverty." Pages 120–34 in *A New Day: Essays on World Christianity in Honor of Lamin Sanneh*. Edited by Akintunde E. Akinade. Foreword by Andrew F. Walls. New York: Peter Lang, 2010.

Myre, "Loi." Myre, André. "La loi dans l'ordre cosmique et politique selon Philon d'Alexandrie." *ScEs* 24 (2, 1972): 217–47.

Mzizi, "Images." Mzizi, Joshua Bheki. "Images of Isaiah Shembe: An Appraisal of the Views of Mthembeni Mpanza." *Missionalia* 32 (2, Aug. 2004): 190–209.

Naeem, "Culture." Naeem, A. G. "The Role of Culture and Religion in the Management of Diabetes: A Study of Kashmiri Men in Leeds." *JRSHealth* 123 (2, 2003): 110–16.

Naipaul, *Masque*. Naipaul, V. S. *The Masque of Africa: Glimpses of African Belief*. New York: Alfred A. Knopf, 2010.

Najman, "Authority." Najman, Hindy. "The Law of Nature and the Authority of Mosaic Law." *SPhilA* 11 (1999): 55–73.

Najman, "Written Copy." Najman, Hindy. "A Written Copy of the Law of Nature: An Unthinkable Paradox?" *SPhilA* 15 (2003): 54–63.

Nakasone, "Healing." Nakasone, Ronald Y. "Teaching Religion and Healing: Spirituality and Aging in the San Francisco Japanese Community." Pages 277–91 in *Teaching Religion and Healing*. Edited by Linda L. Barnes and Inés Talamantez. AARTRSS. Oxford: Oxford University Press, 2006.

Nanan, "Sorcerer." Nanan, Madame. "The Sorcerer and Pagan Practices." Pages 81–87 in *Our Time Has Come: African Christian Women Address the Issues of Today*. Edited by Judy Mbugua. Grand Rapids: Baker, 1994.

Narayanan, "Shanti." Narayanan, Vasudha. "Shanti: Peace for the Mind, Body, and Soul." Pages 61–82 in *Teaching Religion and Healing*. Edited by Linda L. Barnes and Inés Talamantez. AARTRSS. Oxford: Oxford University Press, 2006.

Nash, "Conceptual Systems." Nash, Ronald H. "Miracles and Conceptual Systems." Pages 115–31 in *In Defense of Miracles: A Comprehensive Case for God's Action in History*. Edited by R. Douglas Geivett and Gary R. Habermas. Downers Grove, Ill.: Inter-Varsity, 1997.

Naswem, "Healing." Naswem, R. A. "Healing in Twentieth-Century Christian Churches: Gimmicks, Reality, or Abuses?" Pages 26–32 in *Religion, Medicine, and Healing*. Edited by Gbola Aderibigbe and Deji Ayegboyin. Lagos: Nigerian Association for the Study of Religions and Education, 1995.

Nathan and Wilson, *Evangelicals*. Nathan, Rich, and Ken Wilson. *Empowered Evangelicals: Bringing Together the Best of the Evangelical and Charismatic Worlds*. Foreword by J. I. Packer. Ann Arbor, Mich.: Vine Books, 1995.

Natvig, "Rites." Natvig, Richard. "Liminal Rites and Female Symbolism in the Egyptian *Zar* Possession Cult." *Numen* 35 (1, 1988): 55–68.

Natvig, "*Zar* Cult." Natvig, Richard. "Some Notes on the History of the *Zar* Cult in Egypt." Pages 178–88 in *Women's Medicine: The Zar-Bori Cult in Africa and Beyond*. Edited by I. M. Lewis, Ahmed Al-Safi, and Sayyid Hurreiz. Edinburgh: International African Institute, Edinburgh University Press, 1991.

Natvig, "*Zar* Spirits." Natvig, Richard. "Oromos, Slaves, and the *Zar* Spirits: A Contribution to the History of the *Zar* Cult." *IJAHS* 20 (4, 1987): 669–89.

Nauman, "Exorcism." Nauman, St. Elmo. "Exorcism and Satanism in Medieval Germany." Pages 73–86 in *Exorcism Through the Ages*. Edited by St. Elmo Nauman. New York: Philosophical Library, 1974.

Naumann, "Religion." Naumann, Robert A. "Religion and Science Both Proceed from Acts of Faith." Pages 70–72 in *Cosmos, Bios, and Theos: Scientists Reflect on Science, God, and the Origins of the Universe, Life, and Homo Sapiens*. Edited by Henry Margenau and Roy Abraham Varghese. La Salle, Ill.: Open Court, 1992.

Naveh, "Fragments." Naveh, Joseph. "Fragments of an Aramaic Magic Book from Qumran." *IEJ* 48 (3–4, 1998): 252–61.

Ndofunsu, "Prayer." Ndofunsu, Diakanua. "The Role of Prayer in the Kimbanguist Church." Pages 577–96 in *Christianity in Independent Africa*. Edited by Edward Fasholé-Luke, Richard Gray, Adrian Hastings, and Godwin Tasie. Bloomington: Indiana University Press, 1978.

Ndubuisi, *Charisma*. Ndubuisi, Luke. *Paul's Concept of Charisma in 1 Corinthians 12: With Emphasis on the Nigerian Charismatic Movement*. Frankfurt am Main: Peter Lang, 2003.

Ndyabahika, "Attitude." Ndyabahika, James F. "The Attitude of the Historical Churches to Poverty and Wealth: A Challenge for African Christianity." *AJET* 23 (2, 2004): 199–214.

Neal, *Power*. Neal, Emily Gardiner. *The Healing Power of Christ*. New York: Hawthorn Books, 1972.

Neal, *Reporter*. Neal, Emily Gardiner. *A Reporter Finds God Through Spiritual Healing*. New York: Morehouse-Gorham, 1956.

Neal, *Smoke*. Neal, Emily Gardiner. *Where There's Smoke: The Mystery of Christian Healing*. New York: Morehouse-Barlow, 1967.

Neff, "Anglican." Neff, David. "The Accidental Anglican." *CT* 53 (9, Sept. 2009): 66–68.

Negash, "Demelash." Negash, Teshome. "Damtew Demelash." *DACB*. http://www.dacb.org/stories /ethiopia/demelash_damtew.html.

Neil, *Acts*. Neil, William. *The Acts of the Apostles*. NCBC. London: Marshall, Morgan & Scott; Grand Rapids: Eerdmans, 1973.

Neil, "Nature Miracles." Neil, William. "The Nature Miracles." *ExpT* 67 (Sept. 1956): 369–72.

Neill, "Demons." Neill, Stephen. "Demons, Demonology." Pages 161–62 in *Concise Dictionary of the Christian World Mission*. Edited by Stephen Neill, Gerald H. Anderson, and John Goodwin. Nashville: Abingdon, 1971.

Neill, *History of Missions*. Neill, Stephen. *A History of Christian Missions*. Harmondsworth: Penguin, 1964.

Nelsen, "Letter." Nelsen, Bergitha. "Letter." *CGl* 4 (2, Jan. 1923): 8–11.

Nelson, "Editorial." Nelson, D. "Editorial." *CGl* 9 (1, Jan. 1932): 1–2.

Nelson, "Editorial 2." Nelson, D. "Editorial." *CGl* 9 (4, Oct. 1932): 1.

Nelson, "Editorial 3." Nelson, D. "Editorial." *CGl* 10 (3, July 1933): 1.

Nelson, "Editorial 4." Nelson, D. "Editorial." *CGl* 11 (1, Jan. 1934): 1.

Nelson, "Study." Nelson, H. "A Study of the Protestant Churches in Madras." DMiss diss., Fuller Theological Seminary, 1974.

Nene, "Analysis." Nene, L. M. "A Preliminary Analysis of Student Attitudes towards Modern Doctors, Traditional Healers, and Faith Healers." Pages 35–41 in *Afro-Christian Religion and Healing in Southern Africa*. Edited by G. C. Oosthuizen, S. D. Edwards, W. H. Wessels, and I. Hexham. AfSt 8. Lewiston, N.Y.: Edwin Mellen, 1989.

Nesse, "Awakening." Nesse, Hans M. "The Awakening in China and the Young People." *CGl* 12 (2, April 1935): 15.

Nesse, "Psychology." Nesse, Hans M. "The Psychology of a Robber-Scare." *CGl* 4 (2, Jan. 1923): 11–12.

Netland, *Voices*. Netland, Harold H. *Dissonant Voices: Religious Pluralism and the Question of Truth*. Grand Rapids: Eerdmans, 1991.

Neusner, "Foreword." Neusner, Jacob. "Foreword." Pages xv–xlvi in *Memory and Manuscript: Oral Tradition and Written Transmission in Rabbinic Judaism and Early Christianity, with Tradition and Transmission in Early Christianity*, by Birger Gerhardsson. Grand Rapids: Eerdmans, 1998.

Neusner, *New Testament*. Neusner, Jacob. *Rabbinic Literature and the New Testament: What We Cannot Show, We Do Not Know*. Valley Forge, Pa.: Trinity Press International, 1994.

Neusner, *Sat.* Neusner, Jacob. *There We Sat Down: Talmudic Judaism in the Making*. Nashville: Abingdon, 1972.

Neusner, "Testimony." Neusner, Jacob. "'By the Testimony of Two Witnesses' in the Damascus Document IX, 17–22 and in Pharisaic-Rabbinic Law." *RevQ* 8 (30/2, March 1973): 197–217.

Nevius, *Possession*. Nevius, John L. *Demon Possession and Allied Themes*. Old Tappan, N.J.: Revell, 1894.

Newberg, d'Aquili, and Rause, *Brain Science*. Newberg, Andrew, Eugene d'Aquili, and Vince Rause. *Why God Won't Go Away: Brain Science and the Biology of Belief*. New York: Ballantine, 2001.

Newell, "Witchcraft." Newell, Sasha. "Pentecostal Witchcraft: Neoliberal Possession and Demonic Discourse in Ivorian Pentecostal Churches." *JRelAf* 37 (4, 2007): 461–90.

Newlin et al., "Relationship." Newlin, K., G. D. Melkus, D. Chyun, and V. Jefferson. "The Relationship of Spirituality and Health Outcomes in Black Women with Type II Diabetes." *EthDis* 13 (1, 2003): 61–68.

Newman, *Essays*. Newman, John Henry Cardinal. *Two Essays on Biblical and on Ecclesiastical Miracles*. 8th ed. Repr.; Eugene, Ore.: Wipf & Stock, 1998.

Newman, "Healings." Newman, Ethel. "Healings at Square Rock." *WWit* 9 (Jan. 20, 1913): 1.

Newman, "Prophecy." Newman, Robert C. "On Fulfilled Prophecy as Miracle." *PhilChr* 3 (1, 2001): 63–67.

Newmyer, "Climate." Newmyer, Stephen. "Climate and Health: Classical and Talmudic Perspective." *Judaism* 33 (4, Fall 1984): 426–38.

Newmyer, "Medicine." Newmyer, Stephen. "Talmudic Medicine: A Classicist's Perspective." *Judaism* 29 (3, Summer 1980): 360–67.

"New Spleen." "God Gave Tatiana a New Spleen." *Ten Years of Grace* (2004): 42–43.

Neyrey, "Miracles." Neyrey, Jerome H. "Miracles, In Other Words: Social Science Perspectives on Healings." Pages 19–56 in *Miracles in Jewish and Christian Antiquity: Imagining Truth*. Edited by John C. Cavadini. NDST 3. Notre Dame, Ind.: University of Notre Dame Press, 1999.

Niang, *Faith*. Niang, Aliou Cissé. *Faith and Freedom in Galatia and Senegal: The Apostle Paul, Colonists and Sending Gods*. BIS 97. Leiden: Brill, 2009.

Niccacci, "Faraone." Niccacci, Alviero. "Yahweh e il Faraone. Teologia biblica ed egiziana a confronto." *BN* 38/39 (1987): 85–102.

Nichols, *History*. Nichols, James Hastings. *History of Christianity 1650–1950: Secularization of the West*. New York: Ronald, 1956.

Nichols, "Miracles." Nichols, Terence L. "Miracles in Science and Theology." *Zyg* 37 (3, 2002): 703–15.

Nichols, "Supernatural." Nichols, Terence L. "Miracles, the Supernatural, and the Problem of Extrinsicism." *Greg* 71 (1, 1990): 23–41.

Nickles, "Discovery." Nickles, Thomas. "Scientific Discovery." Pages 442–51 in *The Routledge Companion to Philosophy of Science*. Edited by Stathis Psillos and Martin Curd. New York: Routledge, 2008.

Nicolini, "Notes." Nicolini, Beatrice. "Notes on Magical Practices in Zanzibar and Pemba: The Role of the *Waganga* During Colonial Times." Pages 115–26 in *Studies in Witchcraft, Magic, War, and Peace in Africa*. Edited by Beatrice Nicolini. Lewiston, N.Y.: Edwin Mellen, 2006.

Nicolls, "Laws." Nicolls, William K. "Physical Laws and Physical Miracles." *ITQ* 27 (1960): 49–56.

Nienkirchen, "Visions." Nienkirchen, Charles. "Conflicting Visions of the Past: The Prophetic Use of History in the Early American Pentecostal-Charismatic Movements." Pages 119–33 in *Charismatic Christianity as a Global Culture*. Edited by Karla Poewe. SCR. Columbia: University of South Carolina Press, 1994.

Nilsen, "Hospital." Nilsen, Bergitha. "From Siangyang Hospital." *CGl* 9 (2, April 1932): 25–26.

Nilsson, *Piety*. Nilsson, Martin Persson. *Greek Piety*. Translated by Herbert Jennings Rose. Oxford: Clarendon, 1948.

Nineham, *Mark*. Nineham, D. E. *Saint Mark*. Philadelphia: Westminster, 1977.

Nischan, "Baptism." Nischan, Bodo. "The Exorcism Controversy and Baptism in the Late Reformation." *SixtCenJ* 18 (1, 1987): 31–51.

Nischan, "Controversy." Nischan, Bodo. "The Exorcism Controversy and Baptism in the Late Reformation." Pages 161–80 in *Possession and Exorcism*. Vol. 9 of *Articles on Witchcraft, Magic, and Demonology: A*

Twelve-Volume Anthology of Scholarly Articles. Edited by Brian P. Levack. New York: Garland, 1992.

Noack, *Jesus Ananiassøn.* Noack, Bent. *Jesus Ananiassøn og Jesus fra Nasaret. En drøptelse af Josefus, Bellum Judaicum VI 5, 3.* Tkst of Tolkning 6. Copenhagen: Gyldendal, 1975.

Noack, "Qumran and Jubilees." Noack, Bent. "Qumran and the Book of Jubilees." *SEÅ* 22–23 (1957–58): 191–207.

Noam, "Cruse." Noam, Vered. "The Miracle of the Cruse of Oil: Questioning Its Use as a Source for Assessing the Sages' Attitude towards the Hasmoneans" (in Hebrew). *Zion* (2002): 67. (RTA)

Noam, "Miracle." Noam, Vered. "The Miracle of the Cruse of Oil: The Metamorphosis of a Legend." *HUCA* 73 (2002): 191–226.

Noble, "Possession." Noble, D. A. "Demoniacal Possession among the Giryama." *Man* 61 (1961): 50–52.

Nock, *Conversion.* Nock, Arthur Darby. *Conversion: The Old and the New in Religion from Alexander the Great to Augustine of Hippo.* Oxford: Clarendon, 1933.

Nock, *Essays.* Nock, Arthur Darby. *Essays on Religion and the Ancient World I and II.* Selected and edited by Zeph Stewart. Cambridge, Mass.: Harvard University Press, 1972.

Noel, *Hermeneutics.* Noel, Bradley Truman. *Pentecostal and Postmodern Hermeneutics: Comparisons and Contemporary Impact.* Eugene, Ore.: Wipf & Stock, 2010.

Nolen, *Healing.* Nolen, William A. *Healing: A Doctor in Search of a Miracle.* New York: Random House, 1974.

Nolen, "Woman." Nolen, William A. "The Woman Who Said No to Cancer." *ScDig* (Dec. 1982): 34–37.

Nolivos, "Paradigm." Nolivos, Virginia Trevino. "A Pentecostal Paradigm for the Latin American Family: An Instrument of Transformation." *AJPS* 5 (2, July 2002): 223–34.

Noll, "Evangelical." Noll, Mark A. "What is 'Evangelical'?" *The Oxford Handbook of Evangelical Theology.* Edited by Gerald R. McDermott. Oxford: Oxford University Press, 2010.

Noll, *History.* Noll, Mark A. *A History of Christianity in the United States and Canada.* Grand Rapids: Eerdmans, 1992.

Noll, *Rise.* Noll, Mark A. *The Rise of Evangelicalism: The Age of Edwards, Whitefield, and the Wesleys.* Vol. 1 of *A History of Evangelicalism: People Movements and Ideas in the English-Speaking World.* Downers Grove, Ill.: InterVarsity, 2003.

Noll, *Shape.* Noll, Mark A. *The New Shape of World Christianity: How American Experience Reflects*

Global Faith. Downers Grove, Ill.: IVP Academic, 2009.

Norman, "Healing." Norman, J. G. G. "Spiritual Healing." Page 927 in *The New International Dictionary of the Christian Church.* Grand Rapids: Zondervan, 1974.

Norwood, "Colloquium." Norwood, Douglass Paul. "A Reconciliation Colloquium for Church Leaders in Suriname." DMin project, Assemblies of God Theological Seminary, 2001.

Nowacki, *Argument.* Nowacki, Mark R. *The Kalam Cosmological Argument for God.* New York: Prometheus, 2007.

Nsenga, "Fuisa." Nsenga, Fidèle Bavuidinsi. "Joseph Fuisa Mbuku." *DACB.* http://www.dacb.org/stories/demrepcongo/f-fuisa_joseph.html.

Nudgett, "Healed." Nudgett, Myrtle A. "Healed of Tumor." *PentEv* 338–339 (May 1, 1920): 9.

Numbere, *Vision.* Numbere, Nonyem E. *A Man and a Vision: A Biography of Apostle Geoffrey D. Numbere.* Diobu, Nigeria: Greater Evangelism Publications, 2008.

Numbers, "Aggressors." Numbers, Ronald L. "Aggressors, Victims, and Peacemakers: Historical Actors in the Drama of Science and Religion." Pages 15–53 in *The Religion and Science Debate: Why Does It Continue?* Edited by Harold W. Attridge. New Haven: Yale University Press, 2009.

Numbers, *Galileo.* Numbers, Ronald L., ed. *Galileo Goes to Jail and Other Myths about Science and Religion.* Cambridge, Mass.: Harvard University Press, 2009.

Numbers, "Introduction." Numbers, Ronald L. "Introduction." Pages 1–7 in *The Religion and Science Debate: Why Does It Continue?* Edited by Harold W. Attridge. New Haven: Yale University Press, 2009.

Numbers, "Science." Numbers, Ronald L. "Science Without God: Natural Laws and Christian Beliefs." Pages 265–85 in *When Science and Christianity Meet.* Edited by David C. Lindberg and Ronald L. Numbers. Chicago: University of Chicago Press, 2003.

Numrich, "Medicine." Numrich, Paul David. "Complementary and Alternative Medicine in America's 'Two Buddhisms.'" Pages 343–57 in *Religion and Healing in America.* Edited by Linda L. Barnes and Susan S. Sered. New York: Oxford University Press, 2005.

Nunez, "Objectivity." Nunez, Theron A. "On Objectivity and Field Work." Pages 164–71 in *Crossing Cultural Boundaries: The Anthropological Experience.* Edited by Solon T. Kimball and James B. Watson. San Francisco: Chandler, 1972.

Nussbaum, "AICs." Nussbaum, Stan. "AICs as Astute Missiologists: Reflections on Fifty Years of

Mennonite-AIC Interaction." *MissFoc* 17 (2009): 100–112.

Nutton, "Galen." Nutton, Vivian. "God, Galen, and the Depaganization of Ancient Medicine." Pages 17–32 in *Religion and Medicine in the Middle Ages*. Edited by Peter Biller and Joseph Ziegler. YSMT 3. Woodbridge, Suffolk: York Medieval Press, The University of York (with Boydell Press), 2001.

Nutton, "Hospital." Nutton, Vivian. "Hospital." Pages 523–27 in vol. 6 of *Brill's New Pauly: Encyclopaedia of the Ancient World*. Edited by Hubert Cancik and Helmuth Schneider. 20 vols. English ed. Christine F. Salazar. Leiden: Brill, 2010.

Nutton, "Medical Ethics." Nutton, Vivian. "Medical Ethics." Pages 553–56 in vol. 8 of *Brill's New Pauly: Encyclopaedia of the Ancient World*. Edited by Hubert Cancik and Helmuth Schneider. 20 vols. English ed. Christine F. Salazar. Leiden: Brill, 2010.

Nutton, "Medicine." Nutton, Vivian. "Medicine." Pages 569–82 in vol. 8 of *Brill's New Pauly: Encyclopaedia of the Ancient World*. Edited by Hubert Cancik and Helmuth Schneider. 20 vols. English ed. Christine F. Salazar. Leiden: Brill, 2010.

Nuyen, "Kant on Miracles." Nuyen, A. T. "Kant on Miracles." *HistPhilQ* 19 (3, July 2002): 309–23.

Nyberg, "Field." Nyberg, L. "A New Field in Brazil for Scandinavians in Mission." MTh thesis, Fuller Theological Seminary, 1977.

O, "Volksglaube." O, Sek-Keun. "Der Volksglaube und das Christentum in Korea." PhD diss., Free University of Berlin, 1979. Munich: Arbeitsgemeinschaft für Religions- und Weltanschauungsfragen, 1979.

Oakes, "Experience." Oakes, Robert. "Religious Experience and Epistemological Miracles: A Moderate Defense of Theistic Mysticism." *IJPhilRel* 12 (2, 1981): 97–110.

Oates, "Roberts." Oates, Wayne E. "Oral Roberts: Oklahoma Evangelist and Faith Healer." Pages 235–38 in Alice Graham Ikin. *New Concepts of Healing: Medical, Psychological, and Religious*. Introduction by Wayne E. Oates. New York: Association Press, 1956.

Oberhelman, "Dreams." Oberhelman, Steven. "A Survey of Dreams in Ancient Greece." *CBull* 55 (1979): 36–40.

Obeyesekere, "Idiom." Obeyesekere, Gananath. "The Idiom of Demonic Possession: A Case Study." *SSMed* 4 (1970): 97–111.

Obeyesekere, "Possession." Obeyesekere, Gananath. "Psychocultural Exegesis of a Case of Spirit Possession in Sri Lanka." Pages 235–94 in *Case Studies in Spirit Possession*. Edited by Vincent Crapanzaro and Vivian Garrison. New York: John Wiley & Sons, 1977.

Obeyesekere, "Sorcery." Obeyesekere, Gananath. "Sorcery, Premeditated Murder, and the Canalization

of Aggression in Sri Lanka." *Ethnology* 14 (1975): 1–24.

Oblau, "Christianity in China." Oblau, Gotthard. "Pentecostal by Default? Contemporary Christianity in China." Pages 411–36 in *Asian and Pentecostal: The Charismatic Face of Christianity in Asia*. Edited by Allan Anderson and Edmond Tang. Foreword by Cecil M. Robeck. Regnum Studies in Mission, AJPSS 3. Oxford: Regnum; Baguio City, Philippines: APTS Press, 2005.

Oblau, "Healing." Oblau, Gotthard. "Divine Healing and the Growth of Practical Christianity in China." Pages 307–27 in *Global Pentecostal and Charismatic Healing*. Edited by Candy Gunther Brown. Foreword by Harvey Cox. Oxford: Oxford University Press, 2011.

O'Connell, "Hallucinations." O'Connell, Jake. "Jesus' Resurrection and Collective Hallucinations." *TynBul* 60 (1, 2009): 69–105.

O'Connell, "Miracles." O'Connell, Patrick. "Miracles: Sign and Fact." *Month* 36 (1966): 53–60.

O'Connell, "Possession." O'Connell, M. C. "Spirit Possession and Role Stress among the Xesibe of Eastern Transkei." *Ethnology* 21 (1, 1982): 21–37.

O'Connor, *Healing Traditions*. O'Connor, Bonnie Blair. *Healing Traditions: Alternative Medicine and the Health Professions*. Philadelphia: University of Pennsylvania Press, 1995.

O'Connor, *Movement*. O'Connor, Edward D. *The Pentecostal Movement in the Catholic Church*. Notre Dame, Ind.: Ave Maria Press, 1971.

O'Connor, "Science." O'Connor, Robert C. "Science on Trial: Exploring the Rationality of Methodological Naturalism." *PScChrF* 49 (1, March 1997): 15–30.

O'Connor, *Theism*. O'Connor, Timothy. *Theism and Ultimate Explanation*. Oxford: Basil Blackwell, 2008.

Odegard, "Miracles." Odegard, Douglas. "Miracles and Good Evidence." *RelS* 18 (1, 1982): 37–46.

Oderberg, "Argument." Oderberg, David S. "Traversal of the Infinite, the 'Big Bang' and the Kalam Cosmological Argument." *PhilChr* 4 (2002): 305–36.

Odili, "Agents." Odili, Jones Ugochukwu. "The Role of Indigenous Agents in the Advent and Growth of the Anglican Church in Emu Clan of Delta State 1911–2002." Master's thesis, Department of Religious and Cultural Studies, University of Port Harcourt, Choba, Rivers State, Nigeria.

Odili, "Okeriaka." Odili, Jones Ugochukwu. "Godwin Ikwuasum Okeriaka." *DACB*. http://www.dacb.org/stories/nigeria/okeriaka_godwin.html.

Odili, "Osaele." Odili, Jones Ugochukwu. "Abraham Osuam Osaele." *DACB*. http://www.dacb.org/stories/nigeria/osaele_abraham.html.

Oduyoye, "Value." Oduyoye, Mercy Amba. "The Value of African Religious Beliefs and Practices for Christian Theology." Pages 109–16 in *African Theology en Route: Papers from the Pan-African Conference of Third World Theologians, December 17–23, 1977, Accra, Ghana.* Edited by Kofi Appiah-Kubi and Sergio Torres. Maryknoll, N.Y.: Orbis, 1979.

Oepke, "Ὄναρ." Oepke, Albrecht. "Ὄναρ." Pages 220–38 in vol. 5 of *TDNT*.

Oesterreich, *Possession.* Oesterreich, T. K. *Possession: Demoniacal and Other among Primitive Races, in Antiquity, the Middle Ages, and Modern Times.* Translated by D. Ibberson. New Hyde Park, N.Y.: University Books, 1966.

Oesterreich, "Possession." Oesterreich, T. K. "The Genesis and Extinction of Possession." Pages 111–41 in *Exorcism Through the Ages.* Edited by St. Elmo Nauman. New York: Philosophical Library, 1974.

Ogilbee and Riess, *Pilgrimage.* Ogilbee, Mark, and Jana Riess. *American Pilgrimage: Sacred Journeys and Spiritual Destinations.* Brewster, Mass.: Paraclete, 2006.

Ogilvie, *Healing.* Ogilvie, Lloyd John. *Why Not? Accept Christ's Healing and Wholeness.* Minneapolis: Revell, 1985.

O'Grady, "Miracles." O'Grady, John F. "A Question of Miracles." *BibT* 25 (Nov. 1987): 367–73.

Ohnuki-Tierney, "Shamanism." Ohnuki-Tierney, Emiko. "Shamanism and World View: The Case of the Ainu of the Northwest Coast of Southern Sakhalin." Pages 175–200 in *The Realm of the Extra-Human: Ideas and Actions.* Edited by Agehananda Bharati. The Hague: Mouton, 1976.

Ojebode and Moronkola, "Healing Ministry." Ojebode, P. A., and O. A. Moronkola. "The Christian Faith and the Healing Ministry." Pages 38–43 in *Religion, Medicine, and Healing.* Edited by Gbola Aderibigbe and Deji Ayegboyin. Lagos: Nigerian Association for the Study of Religions and Education, 1995.

Ojo, "Miracles." Ojo, E. G. "The Healing Miracles of Jesus Christ and Its Relevance to the Contemporary Situation in Nigerian Churches." Pages 52–56 in *Religion, Medicine, and Healing.* Edited by Gbola Aderibigbe and Deji Ayegboyin. Lagos: Nigerian Association for the Study of Religions and Education, 1995.

Okello, *Case.* Okello, Joseph B. Onyango. *The Case for Miracles: A Defense of God's Action in the World.* Baltimore: PublishAmerica, 2007.

Okonkwo, "Sustaining." Okonkwo, Mike. "Sustaining the Move of God." Pages 56–77 in *Out of Africa: How the Spiritual Explosion Among Nigerians Is Impacting the World.* Edited by C. Peter Wagner and Joseph Thompson. Ventura, Calif.: Regal, 2004.

Okoye, "Healing." Okoye, P. I. "Healing in the Sabbath Churches: The View of Christ the King Holy Sabbath." Pages 19–25 in *Religion, Medicine, and Healing.* Edited by Gbola Aderibigbe and Deji Ayegboyin. Lagos: Nigerian Association for the Study of Religions and Education, 1995.

Oktavec, *Prayers.* Oktavec, Eileen. *Answered Prayers: Miracles and Milagros along the Border.* Tucson: University of Arizona Press, 1995.

Olaiya, "Praying." Olaiya, Joe. "Praying to See God's Promises." Pages 100–119 in *Out of Africa: How the Spiritual Explosion Among Nigerians Is Impacting the World.* Edited by C. Peter Wagner and Joseph Thompson. Ventura, Calif.: Regal, 2004.

Olena, *Horton.* Olena, Lois E., with Raymond L. Gannon. *Stanley M. Horton: Shaper of Pentecostal Theology.* Foreword by George O. Wood. Springfield, Mo.: Gospel Publishing House, 2009.

Oliver, "Riddle." Oliver, Roland. "The Riddle of Zimbabwe." Pages 53–59 in *The Dawn of African History.* Edited by Roland Oliver. London: Oxford University Press, 1961.

Oliver and Fage, *History.* Oliver, Roland, and J. D. Fage. *A Short History of Africa.* New York: Facts on File, 1989.

Ollson, "Healings." Ollson, Clarence W. "Healings in Venezuela." *PentEv* 1913 (Jan. 7, 1951): 9.

Olmstead, *Persian Empire.* Olmstead, A. T. *History of the Persian Empire.* Chicago: Phoenix Books, University of Chicago Press, 1959.

Olphen et al., "Involvement." Olphen, Juliana van, Amy Schulz, Barbara Israel, Linda Chatters, et al. "Religious Involvement, Social Support, and Health among African-American Women on the East Side of Detroit." *JGenIntMed* 18 (7, 2003): 549–57.

Olson, *Bruchko.* Olson, Bruce. *Bruchko.* Rev. ed. Lake Mary, Fla.: Creation House, 1995.

Olson, "Growth." Olson, G. W. "Church Growth in Tribal Sierra Leone." MA thesis, Fuller Theological Seminary, 1973.

Oman and Thoresen, "Spiritual." Oman, Doug, and Carl E. Thoresen. "How Does One Learn to Be Spiritual? The Neglected Role of Spiritual Modeling in Health." Pages 39–54 in *Spirit, Science, and Health: How the Spiritual Mind Fuels Physical Wellness.* Edited by Thomas G. Plante and Carl E. Thoresen. Foreword by Albert Bandura. Westport, Conn.: Praeger, 2007.

Oman et al., "Attendance." Oman, Doug, John H. Kurata, et al. "Religious Attendance and Cause of Death over Thirty-one Years." *IntJPsyMed* 32 (1, 2002): 69–89.

Omenyo, "Charismatization." Omenyo, Cephas. "Charismatization of the Mainline Churches in

Ghana." Pages 5–26 in *Charismatic Renewal in Africa: A Challenge for African Christianity*. Edited by Mika Vähäkangas and Andrew A. Kyomo. Nairobi: Acton Publishers, 2003.

Omenyo, "Healing." Omenyo, Cephas N. "New Wine in an Old Bottle? Charismatic Healing in the Mainline Churches in Ghana." Pages 231–49 in *Global Pentecostal and Charismatic Healing*. Edited by Candy Gunther Brown. Foreword by Harvey Cox. Oxford: Oxford University Press, 2011.

Omenyo, *Pentecost*. Omenyo, Cephas. *Pentecost Outside Pentecostalism: A Study of the Development of Charismatic Renewal in the Mainline Church in Ghana*. Zoetermeer: Uitgeverij Boekencentrum, 2002.

Omenyo, "Renewal." Omenyo, Cephas N. "Renewal, Christian Mission, and Encounter with the Other: Pentecostal-Type Movements Meeting Islam in Ghana and Nigeria." Pages 137–56 in *Global Renewal, Religious Pluralism, and the Great Commission: Towards a Renewal Theology of Mission and Interreligious Encounter*. Edited by Amos Yong and Clifton Clarke. ATSSWCRMPCS 4. Lexington, Ky.: Emeth, 2011.

Ong, *Spirits*. Ong, Aihwa. *Spirits of Resistance and Capitalist Discipline*. Albany: SUNY Press, 1987.

Onyinah, "Deliverance." Onyinah, Opoku. "Deliverance as a Way of Confronting Witchcraft in Modern Africa: Ghana as a Case History." *AJPS* 5 (1, Jan. 2002): 107–34.

Oosthuizen, "Baptism." Oosthuizen, G. C. "Baptism in the Context of the African Independent Churches." Pages 137–88 in *Afro-Christian Religion and Healing in Southern Africa*. Edited by G. C. Oosthuizen, S. D. Edwards, W. H. Wessels, and I. Hexham. AfSt 8. Lewiston, N.Y.: Edwin Mellen, 1989.

Oosthuizen, *Healer-Prophet*. Oosthuizen, Gerhardus C. *The Healer-Prophet in Afro-Christian Churches*. StChrMiss 3. Leiden: Brill, 1992.

Oosthuizen, "Healing." Oosthuizen, G. C. "Indigenous Healing Within the Context of African Independent Churches." Pages 71–90 in *Afro-Christian Religion and Healing in Southern Africa*. Edited by G. C. Oosthuizen, S. D. Edwards, W. H. Wessels, and I. Hexham. AfSt 8. Lewiston, N.Y.: Edwin Mellen, 1989.

Oosthuizen, *Penetration*. Oosthuizen, G. C. *Pentecostal Penetration into the Indian Community in South Africa*. Durban: Interprint, 1975.

Opp, *Lord for Body*. Opp, James. *The Lord for the Body: Religion, Medicine, and Protestant Faith Healing in Canada, 1880–1930*. Montreal: McGill-Queen's University Press, 2005.

Oquendo, Horwath, and Martinez, "Ataques." Oquendo, Maria, Ewald Horwath, and Abigail Martinez. "Ataques de nervios: Proposed diagnostic criteria for a culture specific syndrome." *CMPsy* 16 (1992): 367–76.

O'Regan and Hirschberg, *Remission*. O'Regan, Brendan, and Caryle Hirschberg. *Spontaneous Remission: An Annotated Bibliography*. Sausalito, Calif.: Institute of Noetic Sciences, 1993.

Oritsejafor, "Dealing." Oritsejafor, Ayo. "Dealing with the Demonic." Pages 78–99 in *Out of Africa: How the Spiritual Explosion Among Nigerians Is Impacting the World*. Edited by C. Peter Wagner and Joseph Thompson. Ventura, Calif.: Regal, 2004.

Oro and Semán, "Pentecostalism." Oro, Ari Pedro, and Pablo Semán. "Brazilian Pentecostalism Crosses National Borders." Pages 181–95 in *Between Babel and Pentecost: Transnational Pentecostalism in Africa and Latin America*. Edited by André Corten and Ruth Marshall-Fratani. Bloomington: Indiana University Press, 2001.

Orr, *Awakenings*. Orr, J. Edwin. *Evangelical Awakenings in Africa*. Minneapolis: Bethany House, 1975.

Orr, "Call." Orr, J. Edwin. "The Call to Spiritual Renewal." Pages 419–28 in *The Gospel and Islam: A 1978 Compendium*. Edited by Don M. McCurry. Monrovia, Calif.: MARC, 1979.

Osborn, *Christ*. Osborn, L. C. *Christ at the Bamboo Curtain*. Kansas City, Mo.: Beacon Hill, 1956.

Osborn, *Evangelism*. Osborn, T. L., and Daisy Osborn. *Faith Library in Twenty-three Volumes: Twentieth-Century Legacy of Apostolic Evangelism. Autobiographical Anthology*. Tulsa: Osfo International, 1923–97. Vol. 1: Dec. 1923–June 1953. Vol. 21: Dec. 1987–Dec. 1991. Vol. 22: Jan. 1992–Oct. 1994. Vol. 23: Nov. 1994–Sept. 1997.

Osborn, *Healing*. Osborn, T. L. *Healing the Sick: A Living Classic*. Rev. ed. Tulsa: Harrison House, 1992.

Osborne, "Miracles." Osborne, William. "Miracles, Mission, and Ministry." *AJT* 8 (2, 1994): 295–307.

Oshun, "Practices." Oshun, Chris O. "Healing Practices among Aladura Pentecostals: An Intercultural Study." *Missionalia* 28 (2, 2000): 242–52.

Osler, "Revolution." Osler, Margaret J. "That the Scientific Revolution Liberated Science from Religion." Pages 90–98 in *Galileo Goes to Jail and Other Myths about Science and Religion*. Edited by Ronald L. Numbers. Cambridge, Mass.: Harvard University Press, 2009.

Osmond, "Physiologist." Osmond, Daniel H. "A Physiologist Looks at Purpose and Meaning in Life." Pages 133–67 in *Evidence of Purpose: Scientists Discover the Creator*. Edited by John Marks Templeton. New York: Continuum, 1994.

Ostbye et al., "Investigators." Ostbye, Truls, K. M. Krause, M. C. Norton, J. Tschanz, L. Sanders,

K. Hayden, C. Pieper, and K. A. Welsh-Bohmer. "Cache County Investigators. Ten Dimensions of Health and Their Relationships with Overall Self-Reported Health and Survival in a Predominantly Religiously Active Elderly Population: The Cache County Memory Study." *JAmGerSoc* 54 (2, 2006): 199–209.

Otero, "Convention." Otero, Louis C. "Glorious Convention and Mighty Healings." *PentEv* 1047 (May 5, 1934): 10.

Otis, *Giants*. Otis, George, Jr. *The Last of the Giants*. Grand Rapids: Chosen, 1991.

O'Toole, "Parallels between Jesus and Disciples." O'Toole, Robert F. "Parallels between Jesus and His Disciples in Luke-Acts: A Further Study." *BZ*, n.s., 27 (2, 1983): 195–212.

Otte, "Schlesinger." Otte, Richard. "Schlesinger on Miracles." *FPhil* 10 (1, 1993): 93–98.

Otte, "Treatment." Otte, Richard. "Mackie's Treatment of Miracles." *IJPhilRel* 39 (3, 1996): 151–58.

"Our God Reigns." "Our God Reigns." Program book for The Holy Ghost Congress, Redeemed Christian Church of God, Lagos-Ibadan Expressway, Nigeria, Dec. 14–19, 2009.

Oursler, *Power*. Oursler, Will. *The Healing Power of Faith*. New York: Hawthorn, 1957.

Overall, "Larmer." Overall, Christine. "Miracles and Larmer." *Dial* 42 (1, 2003): 123–35.

Overall, "Miracles." Overall, Christine. "Miracles as Evidence Against the Existence of God." *SJPhil* 23 (3, 1985): 347–53.

Oxman, Freeman, and Manheimer, "Participation." Oxman, T. E., D. H. Freeman, and E. D. Manheimer. "Lack of Social Participation or Religious Strength and Comfort as Risk Factors for Death after Cardiac Surgery in the Elderly." *PsychMed* 57 (1995): 5–15.

Owen, "Probabilities." Owen, David. "Hume versus Price on Miracles and Prior Probabilities." Pages 115–32 in *Miracles*. Edited by Richard Swinburne. New York: Macmillan; London: Collier Macmillan, 1989.

Owens, *City*. Owens, E. J. *The City in the Greek and Roman World*. London: Routledge, 1991.

Owuor et al., "Reinventing." Owuor, O. Bethwell, et al. "Reinventing Therapo-Spiritual Fellowships: The Jolang'o in Luo African Independent Churches." *MHRC* 9 (5, 2006): 423–34.

Owusu, "Strings." Owusu, Maxwell. "Nanny's Apron Strings: Magic, 'Medicine,' Witchcraft, and Warfare in Colonial and Postcolonial West Africa." Pages 127–49 in *Studies in Witchcraft, Magic, War, and Peace in Africa*. Edited by Beatrice Nicolini. Lewiston, N.Y.: Edwin Mellen, 2006.

Packer, *Acts*. Packer, J. W. *Acts of the Apostles*. CBC. Cambridge: Cambridge University Press, 1966.

Padgett, "Advice." Padgett, Alan G. "Advice for Religious Historians: On the Myth of a Purely Historical Jesus." Pages 287–307 in *The Resurrection: An Interdisciplinary Symposium on the Resurrection of Jesus*. Edited by Stephen T. Davis, Daniel Kendall, and Gerald O'Collins. Oxford: Oxford University Press, 1997.

Pagaialii, "Assemblies." Pagaialii, Tavita. "The Assemblies of God in Samoa: History, Growth, and Challenges." DMin thesis, Asia Pacific Theological Seminary, 2005.

Pagán, "Miracles." Pagán, Joshua A. "Muhammad's Miracles: A Critical Examination." *Logia* 18 (4, 2009): 39–43.

Page, "Exorcism." Page, Sydney H. T. "Exorcism Revisited: A Response to Beck and Lewis and to Wilson." *JPsyTh* 17 (2, 1989): 140–43.

Page, "Role." Page, Sydney H. T. "The Role of Exorcism in Clinical Practice and Pastoral Care." *JPsyTh* 17 (2, 1989): 121–31.

Paget, "Quests." Paget, James Carleton. "Quests for the Historical Jesus." Pages 138–55 in *The Cambridge Companion to Jesus*. Edited by Markus Bockmuehl. Cambridge: Cambridge University Press, 2001.

Paige, "Demons." Paige, Terence. "Demons and Exorcism." Pages 209–11 in *DPL*.

Painter, "Tradition." Painter, John. "Tradition and Interpretation in John 6." *NTS* 35 (3, 1989): 421–50.

Paley, "Evidences." Paley, William. "Evidences of Christianity—Preparatory Considerations." Pages 41–47 in *Miracles*. Edited by Richard Swinburne. New York: Macmillan, 1989.

Palmer, "Growth." Palmer, Donald C. "The Growth of the Pentecostal Churches in Colombia." MA thesis, Trinity Evangelical Divinity School, May 1972.

Palmer, "Monograph" (1992). Palmer, Darryl W. "Acts and the Historical Monograph." *TynBul* 43 (2, 1992): 373–88.

Palmer, "Monograph" (1993). Palmer, Darryl W. "Acts and the Ancient Historical Monograph." Pages 1–29 in *The Book of Acts in Its Ancient Literary Setting*. Edited by Bruce W. Winter and Andrew D. Clarke. Vol. 1 of *The Book of Acts in Its First Century Setting*. Grand Rapids: Eerdmans, 1993.

Palmer, "Plague." Palmer, Richard. "The Church, Leprosy, and Plague in Medieval and Early Modern Europe." Pages 79–99 in *The Church and Healing: Papers Read at the Twentieth Summer Meeting and the Twenty-first Winter Meeting of the Ecclesiastical History Society*. StChHist 19. Edited by W. J. Sheils. Oxford: Basil Blackwell, 1982.

Paloutzian, Rogers, Swenson, and Lowe, "Attributions." Paloutzian, Raymond F., Steven A. Rogers,

Erica L. Swenson, and Deborah A. Lowe. "Miracle Attributions, Meaning, and Neuropsychology." Pages 49–66 in *Medical and Therapeutic Events.* Vol. 2 of *Miracles: God, Science, and Psychology in the Paranormal.* Edited by J. Harold Ellens. Westport, Conn.; London: Praeger, 2008.

Pankratz, "Magician." Pankratz, Loren. "Magician Accuses Faith Healers of Hoax." *JRelHealth* 26 (2, 1987): 115–24.

Pannenberg, "Concept." Pannenberg, Wolfhart. "The Concept of Miracle." *Zyg* 37 (3, 2002): 759–62.

Pannenberg, "History." Pannenberg, Wolfhart. "History and the Reality of the Resurrection." Pages 62–72 in *Resurrection Reconsidered.* Edited by Gavin D'Costa. Oxford: Oneworld, 1996.

Pannenberg, *Jesus.* Pannenberg, Wolfhart. *Jesus— God and Man.* Translated by L. L. Wilkins and D. A. Priebe. Philadelphia: Westminster, 1974.

Pao, *Isaianic Exodus.* Pao, David W. *Acts and the Isaianic New Exodus.* Grand Rapids: Baker Academic, 2002. Originally in WUNT series 2, number 130. Tübingen: Mohr Siebeck, 2000.

Papademetriou, "Exorcism." Papademetriou, George C. "Exorcism and the Greek Orthodox Church." Pages 43–56 in *Exorcism Through the Ages.* Edited by St. Elmo Nauman. New York: Philosophical Library, 1974.

Pargament et al., "Methods." Pargament, Kenneth I., Harold G. Koenig, Nalini Tarakeshwar, and June Hahn. "Religious Coping Methods as Predictors of Psychological, Physical and Spiritual Outcomes among Medically Ill Elderly Patients: A Two-Year Longitudinal Study." *JHPsych* 9 (6, 2004): 713–30.

Pargament et al., "Religious Struggle." Pargament, Kenneth I., Harold G. Koenig, Nalini Tarakeshwar, and June Hahn. "Religious Struggle as a Predictor of Mortality among Medically Ill Elderly Patients: A Two-Year Longitudinal Study." *ArchIntMed* 161 (2001): 1881–85.

Parish, "Histories." Parish, Helen. "'Lying Histories Fawning False Miracles': Magic, Miracles and Mediaeval History in Reformation Polemic." *RefRenRev* 4 (2, 2002): 230–40.

Park, "Dissection." Park, Katharine. "That the Medieval Church Prohibited Human Dissection." Pages 43–49 in *Galileo Goes to Jail and Other Myths about Science and Religion.* Edited by Ronald L. Numbers. Cambridge, Mass.: Harvard University Press, 2009.

Park, *Healing.* Park, Andrew Sung. *Racial Conflict and Healing: An Asian-American Theological Perspective.* Maryknoll, N.Y.: Orbis, 1996.

Park, "Relations." Park, Crystal L. "Exploring Relations among Religiousness, Meaning, and Adjustment to Lifetime and Current Stressful Encounters in Later Life." *AnxSC* 19 (1, 2006): 33–45.

Park, "Spirituality." Park, Myung Soo. "Korean Pentecostal Spirituality as Manifested in the Testimonies of Members of Yoido Full Gospel Church." Pages 43–67 in *David Yonggi Cho: A Close Look at His Theology and Ministry.* Edited by Wonsuk Ma, William W. Menzies, and Hyeon-sung Bae. AJPSS 1. Baguio City, Philippines: APTS Press, Hansei University Press, 2004.

Parker, "Suffering." Parker, Paul P. "Suffering, Prayer, and Miracles." *JRelHealth* 36 (3, 1997): 205–19.

Parrinder, "Learning." Parrinder, E. G. "Learning from Other Faiths: VI. African Religion." *ExpT* 83 (111, 1972): 324–28.

Parrinder, *Religion.* Parrinder, Geoffrey. *Religion in an African City.* New York: Oxford University Press, 1953.

Parshall, *Bridges.* Parshall, Phil. *Bridges to Islam: A Christian Perspective on Folk Islam.* Grand Rapids: Baker, 1983.

Parshall, "Lessons." Parshall, Phil. "Lessons Learned in Contextualization." Pages 251–72 in *Muslims and Christians on the Emmaus Road.* Edited by J. Dudley Woodberry. Monrovia, Calif.: MARC, 1989.

Parsitau, "Pentecostalisation." Parsitau, Damaris Seleina. "From the Periphery to the Center: The Pentecostalization of Mainline Christianity in Kenya." *Missionalia* 35 (3, Nov. 2007): 83–111.

Parsons, *Acts.* Parsons, Mikeal C. *Acts.* Paideia Commentaries on the New Testament. Grand Rapids: Baker Academic, 2008.

Parsons, *Luke.* Parsons, Mikeal C. *Luke: Storyteller, Interpreter, Evangelist.* Peabody, Mass.: Hendrickson, 2007.

Parsons, "Unity." Parsons, Mikeal C. "The Unity of Luke-Acts: Rethinking the *Opinio Communio.*" Pages 29–53 in *With Steadfast Purpose: Essays on Acts in Honor of Henry Jackson Flanders Jr.* Edited by N. H. Keathley. Waco: Baylor University Press, 1990.

Parsons et al., "Beliefs." Parsons, S. K., P. L. Cruise, W. M. Davenport, and V. Jones. "Religious Beliefs, Practices, and Treatment Adherence among Individuals with HIV in the Southern United States." *AIDSPCS* 20 (2, 2006): 97–111.

Pascal, *Life.* Pascal's *Short Life of Christ.* Translated and introduced by Emile Cailliet and John C. Blankenagel. PrPam 5. Princeton, N.J.: Princeton Theological Seminary, 1950.

Pascal, *Pensées.* Pascal, Blaise. *Pensées and Other Writings.* Translated by Honor Levi. Oxford: Oxford University Press, 1995.

Pate, "Missions." Pate, Larry D. "Pentecostal Missions from the Two-Thirds World." Pages 242–58 in *Called and Empowered: Global Mission in Pentecostal Perspective.* Edited by Murray A. Dempster, Byron

D. Klaus, and Douglas Petersen. Peabody, Mass.: Hendrickson, 1991.

Patel et al., "Variables." Patel, S. S., V. S. Shah, et al. "Psychosocial Variables, Quality of Life, and Religious Beliefs in ESRD Patients Treated with Hemodialysis." *AmJKDis* 40 (5, 2002): 13–22.

Pattison, "Interpretations." Pattison, E. Mansell. "Psychosocial Interpretations of Exorcism." Pages 203–17 in *Possession and Exorcism*. Vol. 9 of *Articles on Witchcraft, Magic, and Demonology: A Twelve-Volume Anthology of Scholarly Articles*. Edited by Brian P. Levack. New York: Garland, 1992. Reprinted from *JOpPsyc* 8 (1977): 5–19.

Pattison, "Meaning." Pattison, E. Mansell. "The Personal Meaning of Faith Healing." Pages 105–15 in *Faith Healing: Finger of God? Or, Scientific Curiosity?* Compiled by Claude A. Frazier. New York: Thomas Nelson, 1973.

Pattison, Lapins, and Doerr, "Faith Healing." Pattison, E. M., N. A. Lapins, and H. O. Doerr. "Faith Healing: A Study of Personality and Function." *JNMDis* 157 (6, 1973): 397–409.

Paul-Labrador et al., "Effects." Paul-Labrador, Maura, Donna Polk, James H. Dwyer, et al. "Effects of a Randomized Controlled Trial of Transcendental Meditation on Components of the Metabolic Syndrome in Subjects with Coronary Heart Disease." *ArchIntMed* 166 (11, 2006): 1218–24.

Payne-Jackson, "Illness." Payne-Jackson, Arvilla. "Spiritual Illness and Healing: 'If the Lord Wills.'" Pages 55–64 in *Faith, Health, and Healing in African-American Life*. Edited by Stephanie Y. Mitchem and Emilie M. Townes. RelHHeal. Westport, Conn.: Praeger, 2008.

Payne-Jackson, "Magic." Payne-Jackson, Arvilla. "Magic, Witchcraft, and Healing." Pages 229–43 in *Teaching Religion and Healing*. Edited by Linda L. Barnes and Inés Talamantez. AARTRSS. Oxford: Oxford University Press, 2006.

Peach, "Miracles." Peach, Bernard. "Miracles, Methodology, and Metaphysical Rationalism." *IJPhilRel* 9 (2, 1978): 66–84.

Peacocke, *Creation*. Peacocke, Arthur. *Creation and the World of Science: The Bampton Lectures, 1978*. Oxford: Clarendon, 1979.

Peacocke, "Emergence." Peacocke, Arthur. "Emergence, Mind, and Divine Action: The Hierarchy of the Sciences in Relation to the Human Mind—Brain—Body." Pages 257–78 in *The Re-Emergence of Emergence: The Emergentist Hypothesis from Science to Religion*. Edited by Philip Clayton and Paul Davies. Oxford: Oxford University Press, 2006.

Peacocke, "Incarnation." Peacocke, Arthur. "The Incarnation of the Informing Self-Expressive Word of God." Pages 321–39 in *Religion and Science: History,*

Method, Dialogue. Edited by W. Mark Richardson and Wesley J. Wildman. Foreword by Ian G. Barbour. New York: Routledge, 1996.

Peacocke, *Theology*. Peacocke, Arthur. *Theology for a Scientific Age: Being and Becoming—Natural, Divine, and Human*. Rev. ed. Minneapolis: Fortress, 1993.

Peake, "Colossians." Peake, A. S. "Colossians." Pages 477–547 in vol. 3 of *The Expositor's Greek Testament*. Edited by W. R. Nicoll. Grand Rapids: Eerdmans, 1979.

Pearce, Singer, and Prigerson, "Coping." Pearce, Michelle J., J. L. Singer, and H. G. Prigerson. "Religious Coping among Caregivers of Terminally Ill Cancer Patients: Main Effects and Psychosocial Mediators." *JHPsych* 11 (5, 2006): 743–59.

Pearce et al., "Symptoms." Pearce, Michelle J., Todd D. Little, et al. "Religiousness and Depressive Symptoms among Adolescents." *JCCAP* 32 (2, 2003): 267–76.

Pearl, "Miracles." Pearl, Leon. "Miracles and Theism." *RelS* 24 (4, 1988): 483–506.

Peat, "Science." Peat, F. David. "Science as Story." Pages 53–62 in *Sacred Stories: A Celebration of the Power of Story to Transform and Heal*. Edited by Charles Simpkinson and Anne Simpkinson. San Francisco: HarperSanFrancisco, 1993.

Peck, *Glimpses*. Peck, M. Scott. *Glimpses of the Devil: A Psychiatrist's Personal Accounts of Possession, Exorcism, and Redemption*. New York: Free Press, 2005.

Peckham, *Sounds*. Peckham, Colin, and Mary Peckham. *Sounds from Heaven: The Revival on the Isle of Lewis, 1949–1952*. Ross-shire, Scotland: Christian Focus, 2004.

Pedraja, "*Testimonios*." Pedraja, Luis G. "*Testimonios* and Popular Religion in Mainline North American Hispanic Protestantism." http://www.livedtheology.org/pdfs/Pedraja.pdf. Accessed Feb. 6, 2009.

Pekala and Cardeña, "Issues." Pekala, Ronald J., and Etzel Cardeña. "Methodological Issues in the Study of Altered States of Consciousness and Anomalous Experiences." Pages 47–82 in *Varieties of Anomalous Experience: Examining the Scientific Evidence*. Edited by Etzel Cardeña, Steven Jay Lynn, and Stanley Krippner. Washington, D.C.: American Psychological Association, 2000.

Pélaez del Rosal, "Reanimación." Pélaez del Rosal, Jésus. "'La reanimación de un cadáver.' Un problema de fuentes y géneros." *Alfinge* 1 (1983): 151–73.

Peltzer, "Faith Healing." Peltzer, Karl. "Faith Healing for Mental and Social Disorders in the Northern Province (South Africa)." *JRelAf* 29 (3, 1999): 387–402.

Penner, *Praise*. Penner, Todd. *In Praise of Christian Origins: Stephen and the Hellenists in Lukan Apologetic*

Historiography. Foreword by David L. Balch. New York: T&T Clark, 2004.

Penney, "Devils." Penney, Douglas L. "Finding the Devil in the Details: Onomastic Exegesis and the Naming of Evil in the World of the New Testament." Pages 37–52 in *New Testament Greek and Exegesis: Essays in Honor of Gerald F. Hawthorne*. Edited by Amy M. Donaldson and Timothy B. Sailors. Grand Rapids: Eerdmans, 2003.

Penney and Wise, "Beelzebub." Penney, Douglas L., and Michael O. Wise. "By the Power of Beelzebub: An Aramaic Incantation Formula from Qumran (4Q 560)." *JBL* 113 (1994): 627–50.

Pennington, "Relationship." Pennington, John E., Jr. "The Relationship of the Human Spirit to the Holy Spirit in the Process of Healing." Pages 156–63 in *Healing and Religious Faith*. Edited by Claude A. Frazier. Philadelphia: Pilgrim Press, United Church Press, 1974.

Penrose, *Mind*. Penrose, Roger. *The Emperor's New Mind*. Oxford: Oxford University Press, 1989.

Penzias, "Creation." Penzias, Arno. "Creation Is Supported by All the Data So Far." Pages 78–83 in *Cosmos, Bios, and Theos: Scientists Reflect on Science, God, and the Origins of the Universe, Life, and Homo Sapiens*. Edited by Henry Margenau and Roy Abraham Varghese. La Salle, Ill.: Open Court, 1992.

Percy, "Miracles." Percy, Martyn. "The Gospel Miracles and Modern Healing Movements." *Theology* 99 (Jan. 1997): 8–17.

Perkins, "World." Perkins, Judith B. "This World or Another? The Intertextuality of the Greek Romances, the Apocryphal Acts, and Apuleius' *Metamorphoses*." Pages 247–60 in *The Apocryphal Acts of the Apostles in Intertextual Perspectives*. Semeia 80. Edited by Robert F. Stoops. Atlanta: Scholars Press, 1997.

Perkinson, "Iron." Perkinson, Jim. "Ogou's Iron or Jesus' Irony: Who's Zooming Who in Diasporic Possession Cult Activity?" *JR* 81 (4, 2001): 566–94.

Perna, "Sicily." Perna, Alfred J. "Believes Sicily on Eve of Revival." *PentEv* 1913 (Jan. 7, 1951): 9.

Perrin, *Bultmann*. Perrin, Norman. *The Promise of Bultmann*. Philadelphia: Fortress, 1969.

Perrin, *Kingdom*. Perrin, Norman. *The Kingdom of God in the Teaching of Jesus*. Philadelphia: Westminster, 1963.

Perry, "Believing." Perry, Michael C. "Believing and Commending the Miracles." *ExpT* 73 (1962): 340–43.

Perry, "Course in Miracles." Perry, Robert. "Miracles in *A Course in Miracles*." Pages 162–86 in *Parapsychological Perspectives*. Vol. 3 of *Miracles: God, Science, and Psychology in the Paranormal*. Edited by J. Harold Ellens. Westport, Conn.; London: Praeger, 2008.

Perry, "Miracles." Perry, Michael C. "Believing the Miracles and Preaching the Resurrection." Pages 64–78 in *The Miracles and the Resurrection: Some Recent Studies by I. T. Ramsey, G. H. Boobyer, F. N. Davey, M. C. Perry, and Henry J. Cadbury*. Theological Collections 3. London: SPCK, 1964.

Perry, "Reporting." Perry, Alfred M. "On the Reporting of Miracles." *JBL* 45 (1926): 104–9.

Persinger and Makarec, "Signs." Persinger, Michael A., and Katherine Makarec. "Temporal Lobe Epileptic Signs and Correlative Behaviors Displayed by Normal Populations." *JGenPsy* 114 (1987): 179–95.

Persinger and Valliant, "Signs." Persinger, Michael A., and P. M. Valliant. "Temporal Lobe Signs and Reports of Subjective Paranormal Experiences in a Normal Population: A Replication." *PerMotSk* 60 (1985): 903–9.

"Personal and General." "Personal and General." *CGl* 8 (1, Nov. 1926): 8.

Pervo, *Dating Acts*. Pervo, Richard I. *Dating Acts: Between the Evangelists and the Apologists*. Santa Rosa, Calif.: Polebridge Press, 2006.

Peterman, *Healing*. Peterman, Mary E. *Healing: A Spiritual Adventure*. Philadelphia: Fortress, 1974.

Peters, *Healing in Nepal*. Peters, Larry. *Ecstasy and Healing in Nepal: An Ethnopsychiatric Study of Tamang Shamanism*. Malibu: Undena Publications, 1981.

Peters, *Revival*. Peters, George M. *Indonesia Revival: Focus on Timor*. Grand Rapids: Zondervan, 1973.

Petersen, "Genre." Petersen, Norman R. "Can One Speak of a Gospel Genre?" *Neot* 28 (3, 1994): 137–58.

Petersen, "Latin American Pentecostalism." Petersen, Douglas. "The Azusa Street Mission and Latin American Pentecostalism." *IBMR* 30 (2, April 2006): 66–67.

Petersen, *Might*. Petersen, Douglas. *Not by Might Nor by Power: A Pentecostal Theology of Social Concern in Latin America*. Preface by Jose Miguez Bonino. Oxford: Regnum; Carlisle: Paternoster, 1996.

Peterson, "Hospital." Peterson, Clara. "Luther Hospital, Kwang-Chow." *CGl* 10 (2, April 1933): 13–14.

Pettis, "Fourth Pentecost." Pettis, Stephen J. "The Fourth Pentecost: Paul and the Power of the Holy Spirit, Acts 19:1–22." Pages 248–56 in *Mission in Acts: Ancient Narratives in Contemporary Context*. Edited by Robert L. Gallagher and Paul Hertig. AmSocMissS 34. Maryknoll, N.Y.: Orbis, 2004.

Petts, "Healing and Atonement." Petts, David. "Healing and the Atonement." PhD diss., University of Nottingham, 1993.

Pfeiffer, *Psychiatrie*. Pfeiffer, W. M. *Transkulturelle Psychiatrie: Ergebnisse und Probleme*. Stuttgart: Georg Thieme Verlag, 1971.

Philip, "Growth." Philip, Puthvaíl Thomas. "The Growth of the Baptist Churches of Tribal Nagaland." MA thesis, Fuller School of World Mission, 1972.

Phillips, "Chiluba." Phillips, Barnaby. "Chiluba Worships in Controversial Church." BBC News, posted Nov. 12, 2000. http://news.bbc.co.uk/2/hi/africa/1020196.stm. Accessed June 12, 2009.

Phillips, "Miracles." Phillips, D. Z. "Miracles and Open-Door Epistemology." SJRS 14 (1, 1993): 33–40.

Phillips, "Restored." Phillips, Mrs. Paul. "Removed Vocal Cords Restored." VOH (May 1948): 9.

Phillips, "Science." Phillips, John G. "Science Asks What and How, While Religion Asks Why." Pages 84–85 in Cosmos, Bios, and Theos: Scientists Reflect on Science, God, and the Origins of the Universe, Life, and Homo Sapiens. Edited by Henry Margenau and Roy Abraham Varghese. La Salle, Ill.: Open Court, 1992.

Phillips, "Sings." Phillips, Mrs. Paul. "Girl with Severed Vocal Cords Sings over Radio." VOH (April 1951): 3.

Phillips, Van Vorhees, and Ruth, "Birthday." Phillips, D. P., C. A. Van Voorhees, and T. E. Ruth. "The Birthday: Lifeline or Deadline?" PsychMed 54 (1992): 532–42.

Phiri, "Witches." Phiri, Isaac. "Saving Witches in Kolwezi." CT 53 (9, Sept. 2009): 62–65.

Phiri and Maxwell, "Riches." Phiri, Isaac, and Joe Maxwell. "Gospel Riches." CT (July 2007): 22–29.

Pickstone, "Systems." Pickstone, John V. "Establishment and Dissent in Nineteenth-Century Medicine: An Exploration of Some Correspondence and Connections between Religious and Medical Belief-Systems in Early Industrial England." Pages 165–89 in The Church and Healing: Papers Read at the Twentieth Summer Meeting and the Twenty-first Winter Meeting of the Ecclesiastical History Society. StChHist 19. Edited by W. J. Sheils. Oxford: Basil Blackwell, 1982.

Pieris, "Humour." Pieris, Aloysius. "Prophetic Humour and the Exposure of Demons: Christian Hope in the Light of a Buddhist Exorcism." VidJTR 60 (5, 1996): 311–22.

Pierson, "Context." Pierson, Paul E. "The New Context of Christian Mission: Challenges and Opportunities for the Asian Church." Pages 11–28 in Asian Church and God's Mission: Studies Presented in the International Symposium on Asian Mission in Manila, January 2002. Edited by Wonsuk Ma and Julie C. Ma. Manila: OMF Literature; West Caldwell, N.J.: MWM, 2003.

Pikaza, "Jesús histórico." Pikaza, Xabier. "El Jesús histórico: Nota bibliográfico-temática." IgViv 210 (2002): 85–90.

Pilch, "Anthropology." Pilch, John J. "Insights and Models from Medical Anthropology for Understanding the Healing Activity of the Historical Jesus." HTS/TS 51 (2, 1995): 314–37.

Pilch, "Blindness." Pilch, John J. "Blindness." Pages 480–81 in vol. 1 of The New Interpreter's Dictionary of the Bible. Edited by Katharine Doob Sakenfeld et al. 5 vols. Nashville: Abingdon, 2006.

Pilch, Dictionary. Pilch, John J. The Cultural Dictionary of the Bible. Collegeville, Minn.: Liturgical Press, 1999.

Pilch, "Disease." Pilch, John J. "Disease." Pages 135–40 in vol. 2 of The New Interpreter's Dictionary of the Bible. Edited by Katharine Doob Sakenfeld et al. 5 vols. Nashville: Abingdon, 2007.

Pilch, "Eye." Pilch, John J. "The Evil Eye." BibT 42 (1, 2004): 49–53.

Pilch, Healing. Pilch, John J. Healing in the New Testament: Insights from Medical and Mediterranean Anthropology. Minneapolis: Fortress, 2000.

Pilch, "Sickness." Pilch, John J. "Sickness and Healing in Luke-Acts." Pages 181–209 in The Social World of Luke-Acts: Models for Interpretation. Edited by Jerome H. Neyrey. Peabody, Mass.: Hendrickson, 1991.

Pilch, "Sky Journeys." Pilch, John J. "The Holy Man, Enoch, and His Sky Journeys." Pages 103–11 in Shamans Unbound. Edited by Mihály Hoppál and Zsuzsanna Simonkay, with Kornélia Buday and Dávid Somfai Kara. BibSham 14. Budapest: Akadémiai Kiadó, 2008.

Pilch, "Trance Experience." Pilch, John J. "Paul's Ecstatic Trance Experience Near Damascus in Acts of the Apostles." HvTS 58 (2, 2002): 690–707.

Pilch, "Understanding Miracles." Pilch, John J. "Toward Understanding Miracles in the Bible." BibT 90 (1977): 1207–12.

Pilch, "Usefulness." Pilch, John J. "The Usefulness of the Meaning Response Concept for Interpreting Translations of Healing Accounts in Matthew's Gospel." Pages 97–108 in The Social Sciences of Biblical Translation. Edited by Dietmar Neufeld. SBLSymS 41. Atlanta: Society of Biblical Literature, 2008.

Pilch, Visions. Pilch, John J. Visions and Healing in the Acts of the Apostles: How the Early Believers Experienced God. Collegeville, Minn.: Liturgical Press, 2004.

Pilgaard, "Theios Anēr." Pilgaard, Aage. "The Hellenistic Theios Anēr—A Model for Early Christian Christology?" Pages 101–22 in The New Testament and Hellenistic Judaism. Edited by Peder Borgen and Søren Giversen. Peabody, Mass.: Hendrickson, 1997.

Pilsworth, "Miracles." Pilsworth, Clare. "Miracles, Missionaries, and Manuscripts in Eighth-Century

Southern Germany." Pages 67–76 in *Signs, Wonders, Miracles: Representations of Divine Power in the Life of the Church. Papers Read at the 2003 Summer Meeting and the 2004 Winter Meeting of the Ecclesiastical History Society*. Edited by Kate Cooper and Jeremy Gregory. Rochester: Boydell & Brewer, for the Ecclesiastical History Society, 2005.

Pink, *Healing*. Pink, Arthur W. *Divine Healing: Is It Scriptural?* Swengel, Pa.: Reiner Publications, 1952.

Pinkson, "Pilgrimage." Pinkson, Thomas L. "Huichol Pilgrimage Revisited." Pages 165–70 in *Proceedings of the Fourth International Conference on the Study of Shamanism and Alternate Modes of Healing, Held at the St. Sabina Center, San Rafael, California, September 5–7, 1987*. Edited by Ruth-Inge Heinze. N.p.: Independent Scholars of Asia; Madison, Wis.: A-R Editions, 1988.

Piper, *Minutes*. Piper, Don, with Cecil Murphey. *Ninety Minutes in Heaven: A True Story of Death and Life*. Grand Rapids: Revell, 2004.

Pirouet, *Christianity*. Pirouet, Louise. *Christianity Worldwide: A.D. 1800 Onwards*. Church History 4. TEFSG 22. London: SPCK, 1989.

Piroyansky, "Bloody Miracles." Piroyansky, Danna. "Bloody Miracles of a Political Martyr: The Case of Thomas Earl of Lancaster." Pages 228–38 in *Signs, Wonders, Miracles: Representations of Divine Power in the Life of the Church. Papers Read at the 2003 Summer Meeting and the 2004 Winter Meeting of the Ecclesiastical History Society*. Edited by Kate Cooper and Jeremy Gregory. Rochester: Boydell & Brewer, for the Ecclesiastical History Society, 2005.

Pittenger, "Miracles 1." Pittenger, Norman. "On Miracles: I." *ExpT* 80 (4, 1969): 104–7.

Pittenger, "Miracles 2." Pittenger, Norman. "On Miracles: II." *ExpT* 80 (5, 1969): 147–50.

Placher, *Mark*. Placher, William C. *Mark*. BTCB. Louisville: Westminster John Knox, 2010.

Plante, "Spirituality." Plante, Thomas G. "Spirituality, Religion, and Health: Ethical Issues to Consider." Pages 207–17 in *Spirit, Science, and Health: How the Spiritual Mind Fuels Physical Wellness*. Edited by Thomas G. Plante and Carl E. Thoresen. Foreword by Albert Bandura. Westport, Conn.: Praeger, 2007.

Plantinga, *Minds*. Plantinga, Alvin. *God and Other Minds: A Study of the Rational Justification of Belief in God*. Rev. ed. Ithaca, N.Y.: Cornell University Press, 1990.

Plantinga, "Science." Plantinga, Alvin. "Science and Religion: Why Does the Debate Continue?" Pages 93–123 in *The Religion and Science Debate: Why Does It Continue?* Edited by Harold W. Attridge. New Haven: Yale University Press, 2009.

Plantinga, *Warrant*. Plantinga, Alvin. *Warrant and Proper Function*. New York: Oxford University Press, 1993.

Platelle, "Miracle." Platelle, Henri. "Le miracle au moyen âge d'après un ouvrage récent." *MScRel* 42 (4, 1985): 177–84.

Platt, "Hope." Platt, D. L. "New Hope for Santo Domingo." MA thesis, Fuller Theological Seminary, 1975.

Platvoet, "Communication." Platvoet, Jan G. "Verbal Communication in an Akan Possession and Maintenance Rite." *NedTT* 37 (3, 1983): 202–15.

Platvoet, "Rule." Platvoet, Jan G. "The Rule and Its Exceptions: Spirit Possession in Two African Societies." *JStRel* 12 (1, 1999): 5–51.

Plümacher, "Cicero und Lukas." Plümacher, Eckhard. "Cicero und Lukas. Bemerkungen zu Stil und Zweck der historischen Monographie." Pages 759–75 in *The Unity of Luke-Acts*. Edited by Joseph Verheyden. BETL 142. Leuven: Leuven University Press, 1999.

Plümacher, *Geschichte*. Plümacher, Eckhard. *Geschichte und Geschichten: Aufsätze zur Apostelgeschichte und zu den Johannesakten*. Edited by Jens Schröter and Ralph Brucker. WUNT 170. Tübingen: Mohr Siebeck, 2004.

Plümacher, "Historiker." Plümacher, Eckhard. "Stichwort: Lukas, Historiker." *ZNW* 9 (18, 2006): 2–8.

Plümacher, *Lukas*. Plümacher, Eckhard. *Lukas als hellenisticher Schriftsteller: Studien zur Apostelgeschichte*. SUNT 9. Göttingen: Vandenhoeck & Ruprecht, 1972.

Plümacher, "Luke as Historian." Plümacher, Eckhard. "Luke as Historian." Translated by Dennis Martin. Pages 398–402 in vol. 4 of *ABD*.

Plümacher, "Monographie." Plümacher, Eckhard. "Die Apostelgeschichte also historiche Monographie." Pages 457–66 in *Les Actes des Apôtres: Tradition, rédaction, théologie*. Edited by Jacob Kremer. BETL 48. Gembloux: J. Duculot; Leuven: Leuven University Press, 1979.

Plümacher, "TERATEIA." Plümacher, Eckhard. "TERATEIA. Fiktion und Wunder in der hellenistisch-römischen Geschichtsschreibung und in der Apostelgeschichte." *ZNW* 89 (1–2, 1998): 66–90.

Pobee, "Health." Pobee, John S. "Health, Healing, and Religion: An African View." *IntRevMiss* 90 (356/357, Jan./Apr. 2001): 55–64.

Pocock, Van Rheenen, and McConnell, *Face*. Pocock, Michael, Gailyn Van Rheenen, and Douglas McConnell. *The Changing Face of World Missions: Engaging Contemporary Issues and Trends*. Grand Rapids: Baker Academic, 2005.

Poewe, "Nature." Poewe, Karla. "The Nature, Globality, and History of Charismatic Christianity." Pages

1–29 in *Charismatic Christianity as a Global Culture*. Edited by Karla Poewe. SCR. Columbia: University of South Carolina Press, 1994.

Poewe, "Rethinking." Poewe, Karla. "Rethinking the Relationship of Anthropology to Science and Religion." Pages 234–58 in *Charismatic Christianity as a Global Culture*. Edited by Karla Poewe. SCR. Columbia: University of South Carolina Press, 1994.

Poirier, "Consensus." Poirier, John C. "On the Use of Consensus in Historical Jesus Studies." *TZ* 56 (2, 2000): 97–107.

Poirier, "Linguistic Situation." Poirier, John C. "The Linguistic Situation in Jewish Palestine in Late Antiquity." *JGRCJ* 4 (2007): 55–134.

Poland, *Criticism*. Poland, Lynn M. *Literary Criticism and Biblical Hermeneutics*. AARAS 48. Atlanta: Scholars Press, 1985.

Polanyi, *Knowledge*. Polanyi, Michael. *Personal Knowledge: Towards a Post-Critical Philosophy*. Rev. ed. Chicago: University of Chicago Press, 1962.

Polanyi, *Science*. Polanyi, Michael. *Science, Faith and Society*. Chicago: University of Chicago Press, 1964.

Polen, "Church." Polen, O. W. "The East Flatbush Church of God." *ChGEv* (Jan. 1988): 27–28.

Polhill, "Perspectives." Polhill, John B. "Perspectives on the Miracle Stories." *RevExp* 74 (3, 1977): 389–99.

Polkinghorne, *Belief*. Polkinghorne, John. *Belief in God in an Age of Science*. The Terry Lectures. New Haven: Yale University Press, 1998.

Polkinghorne, "Chaos Theory." Polkinghorne, John. "Chaos Theory and Divine Action." Pages 243–52 in *Religion and Science: History, Method, Dialogue*. Edited by W. Mark Richardson and Wesley J. Wildman. Foreword by Ian G. Barbour. New York: Routledge, 1996.

Polkinghorne, *Faith*. Polkinghorne, John. *The Faith of a Physicist: Reflections of a Bottom-Up Thinker*. The Gifford Lectures, 1993–94. Minneapolis: Fortress, 1994.

Polkinghorne, "Origin." Polkinghorne, John. "Temporal Origin and Ontological Origin." Pages 86–88 in *Cosmos, Bios, and Theos: Scientists Reflect on Science, God, and the Origins of the Universe, Life, and Homo Sapiens*. Edited by Henry Margenau and Roy Abraham Varghese. La Salle, Ill.: Open Court, 1992.

Polkinghorne, *Physics*. Polkinghorne, John. *Quantum Physics and Theology: An Unexpected Kinship*. New Haven: Yale University Press, 2007.

Polkinghorne, *Quarks*. Polkinghorne, John. *Quarks, Chaos, and Christianity: Questions to Science and Religion*. 2nd ed. New York: Crossroad, 2006.

Polkinghorne, *Reality*. Polkinghorne, John. *Exploring Reality: The Intertwining of Science and Religion*. New Haven: Yale University Press, 2005.

Polkinghorne, *Science and Providence*. Polkinghorne, John. *Science and Providence: God's Interaction with the World*. Boston: New Science Library, Shambhala, 1989.

Polkinghorne, "Universe." Polkinghorne, John. "A Potent Universe." Pages 105–15 in *Evidence of Purpose: Scientists Discover the Creator*. Edited by John Marks Templeton. New York: Continuum, 1994.

Polkinghorne, *Way*. Polkinghorne, John. *The Way the World Is: The Christian Perspective of a Scientist*. Louisville: Westminster John Knox, 2007; London: SPCK, 1992.

Polkinghorne and Beale, *Questions*. Polkinghorne, John, and Nicholas Beale. *Questions of Truth: Fifty-one Responses to Questions about God, Science, and Belief*. Louisville: Westminster John Knox, 2009.

Poloma, *Assemblies*. Poloma, Margaret M. *The Assemblies of God at the Crossroads: Charisma and Institutional Dilemmas*. Knoxville: University of Tennessee Press, 1989.

Poloma and Gallup, *Prayer*. Poloma, Margaret M., and George H. Gallup Jr. *Varieties of Prayer: A Survey Report*. Philadelphia: Trinity Press International, 1991.

Pope-Levison, *Pulpit*. Pope-Levison, Priscilla. *Turn the Pulpit Loose: Two Centuries of American Women Evangelists*. New York: Palgrave Macmillan, 2004.

Pope-Levison and Levison, *Contexts*. Pope-Levison, Priscilla, and John R. Levison. *Jesus in Global Contexts*. Louisville: Westminster John Knox, 1992.

Popkin, "Bible Scholar." Popkin, Richard H. "Newton as a Bible Scholar." Pages 103–18 in *Essays on the Context, Nature, and Influence of Isaac Newton's Theology*, by James E. Force and Richard H. Popkin. IntArHistI 129. Dordrecht: Kluwer Academic, 1990.

Popkin, "Comments." Popkin, Richard H. "Some Further Comments on Newton and Maimonides." Pages 1–7 in *Essays on the Context, Nature, and Influence of Isaac Newton's Theology*, by James E. Force and Richard H. Popkin. IntArHistI 129. Dordrecht: Kluwer Academic, 1990.

Popkin, "Deism." Popkin, Richard H. "Polytheism, Deism, and Newton." Pages 27–42 in *Essays on the Context, Nature, and Influence of Isaac Newton's Theology*, by James E. Force and Richard H. Popkin. IntArHistI 129. Dordrecht: Kluwer Academic, 1990.

Popkin, "Fundamentalism." Popkin, Richard H. "Newton and Fundamentalism, II." Pages 165–80 in *Essays on the Context, Nature, and Influence of Isaac Newton's Theology*, by James E. Force and Richard H. Popkin. IntArHistI 129. Dordrecht: Kluwer Academic, 1990.

Popper, *Conjectures*. Popper, Karl R. *Conjectures and Refutations: The Growth of Scientific Knowledge*. 3rd rev. ed. London: Routledge & Kegan Paul, 1969.

Popper, *Historicism*. Popper, Karl R. *The Poverty of Historicism*. 3rd ed. New York: Harper & Row, 1961.

Popper, *Logic*. Popper, Karl R. *The Logic of Scientific Discovery*. London: Hutchinson, 1980.

Popper, *Myth of Framework*. Popper, Karl R. *The Myth of the Framework: In Defense of Science and Rationality*. Edited by M. A. Notturno. London: Routledge, 1994.

Porterfield, *Healing*. Porterfield, Amanda. *Healing in the History of Christianity*. New York: Oxford University Press, 2005.

Porterfield, "Shamanism." Porterfield, Amanda. "Shamanism as a Point of Departure: Two Courses on Christianity and Healing." Pages 159–69 in *Teaching Religion and Healing*. Edited by Linda L. Barnes and Inés Talamantez. AARTRSS. Oxford: Oxford University Press, 2006.

Portsmouth, *Prayer*. Portsmouth, William. *Healing Prayer: With Daily Prayers for a Month*. 5th ed. The Drift, Evesham, Worcs.: Arthur James, 1963.

Pospisil, "Deliverances." Pospisil, William. "Remarkable Deliverances." *VOH* (April 1954): 16.

Pothen, "Missions." Pothen, Abraham T. "Indigenous Cross-Cultural Missions in India and Their Contribution to Church Growth: With Special Emphasis on Pentecostal-Charismatic Missions." PhD diss., Fuller Theological Seminary, School of World Mission, 1990.

Potter, "Claros." Potter, David S. "Claros." Page 335 in *OCD*.

Power, "Response." Power, David N. "In Spirit, Mind, and Body: A Catholic Response." Pages 99–103 in *Pentecostal Movements as an Ecumenical Challenge*. Edited by Jürgen Moltmann and Karl-Josef Kuschel. Concilium 3. London: SCM; Maryknoll, N.Y.: Orbis, 1996.

Pradhan, Dalal, Khan, and Agrawal, "Fertility." Pradhan, M., A. Dalal, F. Khan, and S. Agrawal. "Fertility in Men with Down Sydrome: A Case Report." *FertSter* 86 (6, Dec. 2006): 1765.

Praise of Baal Shem Tov. *In Praise of the Baal Shem Tov (Shivhei ha-Besht): The Earliest Collection of Legends about the Founder of Hasidism*. Translated and edited by Dan Ben-Amos and Jerome R. Mintz. Bloomington: Indiana University Press, 1970; New York: Schocken, 1984.

Prakash, *Preaching*. Prakash, Perumalla Surya. *The Preaching of Sadhu Sundar Singh: A Homiletic Analysis of Independent Preaching and Personal Christianity*. Bangalore: Wordmakers, 1991.

Prather, *Miracles*. Prather, Paul. *Modern-Day Miracles: How Ordinary People Experience Supernatural Acts of God*. Kansas City, Mo.: Andrews McMeel, 1996.

"Prayer and Outcomes." "Intercessory Prayer and Patient Outcomes in Coronary Care Units."

AmFamPhys 61 (3, Feb. 1, 2000). http://www.aafp.org/afp/20000201/tips/13.html. Accessed June 22, 2009.

Pressel, "Possession." Pressel, Esther. "Negative Spirit Possession in Experienced Brazilian Umbanda Spirit Mediums." Pages 333–64 in *Case Studies in Spirit Possession*. Edited by Vincent Crapanzaro and Vivian Garrison. New York: John Wiley & Sons, 1977.

Pressel, "Trance." Pressel, Esther. "Umbanda Trance and Possession in São Paulo, Brazil." Pages 113–225 in *Trance, Healing, and Hallucination: Three Field Studies in Religious Experience*, by Felicitas D. Goodman, Jeannette H. Henney, and Esther Pressel. New York: John Wiley & Sons, 1974.

Pressel, "Umbanda." Pressel, Esther. "Umbanda in São Paulo: Religious Innovation in a Developing Society." Pages 264–318 in *Religion, Altered States of Consciousness, and Social Change*. Edited by Erika Bourguignon. Columbus: Ohio State University Press, 1973.

Price, "Dissertation." Price, Richard. "*Four Dissertations*: Dissertation IV, 'On the Importance of Christianity and the Nature of Historical Evidence, and Miracles.'" Pages 157–76 in *Hume's Abject Failure: The Argument against Miracles*, by John Earman. Oxford: Oxford University Press, 2000.

Price, "Easters." Price, Robert M. "Brand X Easters." *FourR* 20 (6, 2007): 13–15, 18–19, 23.

Price, "Healing." Price, Alfred W. "An Adventure in the Church's Ministry of Healing." Philadelphia: St. Stephen's Episcopal Church, n.d.

Price, *Faith*. Price, Charles S. *The "Real" Faith*. Pasadena, Calif.: C. S. Price, 1940.

Price, "Marian Miracles." Price, Richard M. "Marian Miracles and the Sacrament of Penance." *Maria* 2 (1, 2002): 46–56.

Price, "*Signo*." Price, Richard M. "*In Hoc Signo Vinces*: The Original Context of the Vision of Constantine." Pages 1–10 in *Signs, Wonders, Miracles: Representations of Divine Power in the Life of the Church. Papers Read at the 2003 Summer Meeting and the 2004 Winter Meeting of the Ecclesiastical History Society*. Edited by Kate Cooper and Jeremy Gregory. Rochester: Boydell & Brewer, for the Ecclesiastical History Society, 2005.

Price, *Signs Followed*. Price, Charles S. *And Signs Followed: The Story of Charles S. Price*. Rev. ed. Plainfield, N.J.: Logos, 1972.

Price, *Son of Man*. Price, Robert M. *The Incredible Shrinking Son of Man: How Reliable Is the Gospel Tradition?* Amherst, N.Y.: Prometheus, 2003.

Priest, Campbell, and Mullen, "Syncretism." Priest, Robert J., Thomas Campbell, and Bradford A. Mullen. "Missiological Syncretism: The New Animist Paradigm." Pages 9–87 in *Spiritual Power and*

Missions: Raising the Issues. Edited by Edward Rommen. EvMissSS 3. Pasadena, Calif.: William Carey Library, 1995.

"Priest in war." "Catholic priest in ancient war with 'demons.'" *The Manila Times*, April 16, 2011. http://www.manilatimes.net/news/topstories/catholic-priest-in-ancient-war-with-%e2%80%98demons%e2%80%99/. Accessed April 25, 2011.

Prince, "EEG." Prince, Raymond. "Can the EEG Be Used in the Study of Possession States?" Pages 121–37 in *Trance and Possession States*. Proceedings of the Second Annual Conference, R. M. Bucke Memorial Society, March 4–6, 1966. Edited by Raymond Prince. Montreal: R. M. Bucke Memorial Society, 1968.

Prince, "Foreword." Prince, Raymond. "Foreword." Pages xi–xvi in *Case Studies in Spirit Possession*. Edited by Vincent Crapanzaro and Vivian Garrison. New York: John Wiley & Sons, 1977.

Prince, "Possession Cults." Prince, Raymond. "Possession Cults and Social Cybernetics." Pages 157–65 in *Trance and Possession States*. Proceedings of the Second Annual Conference, R. M. Bucke Memorial Society, March 4–6, 1966. Edited by Raymond Prince. Montreal: R. M. Bucke Memorial Society, 1968.

Prince, "Variations." Prince, Raymond. "Variations in Psychotherapeutic Procedures." Pages 291–349 in vol. 6 of *Handbook of Cross-Cultural Psychology: Psychopathology*. Edited by H. C. Triandis and J. G. Draguns. Boston: Allyn & Bacon, 1980.

Prince, "Yoruba Psychiatry." Prince, Raymond. "Indigenous Yoruba Psychiatry." Pages 84–120 in *Magic, Faith, and Healing: Studies in Primitive Psychiatry Today*. Edited by Ari Kiev. Foreword by Jerome D. Frank. New York: Free Press, 1964.

Principe, "Catholics." Principe, Lawrence M. "That Catholics Did Not Contribute to the Scientific Revolution." Pages 99–106 in *Galileo Goes to Jail and Other Myths about Science and Religion*. Edited by Ronald L. Numbers. Cambridge, Mass.: Harvard University Press, 2009.

Pritz, *Nazarene Christianity*. Pritz, Ray A. *Nazarene Jewish Christianity: From the End of the New Testament Period Until Its Disappearance in the Fourth Century*. StPB. Jerusalem: Magnes Press, The Hebrew University; Leiden: Brill, 1988.

Propp, "Demons." Propp, William H. C. "Exorcising Demons." *BRev* 20 (5, 2004): 14–21, 47.

Protus, "Chukwu." Protus, Kemdirim O. "John (Nwagwu) Chukwu." *DACB*. http://www.dacb.org/stories/nigeria/chukwu_john.html.

Protus, "Latunde." Protus, Kemdirim O. "Elija Titus Latunde." *DACB*. http://www.dacb.org/stories/nigeria/latunde_.html.

Puddefoot, "Information Theory." Puddefoot, John C. "Information Theory, Biology, and Christology." Pages 301–19 in *Religion and Science: History, Method, Dialogue*. Edited by W. Mark Richardson and Wesley J. Wildman. Foreword by Ian G. Barbour. New York: Routledge, 1996.

Pugh, "Medicine." Pugh, Myrna M. "Where Medicine Ends and the Miraculous Begins in Mysterious Healings." Pages 198–212 in *Medical and Therapeutic Events*. Vol. 2 of *Miracles: God, Science, and Psychology in the Paranormal*. Edited by J. Harold Ellens. Westport, Conn.; London: Praeger, 2008.

Pugh, "Miracle." Pugh, Myrna M. "What Is a Medical or Therapeutic Miracle?" Pages 67–81 in *Medical and Therapeutic Events*. Vol. 2 of *Miracles: God, Science, and Psychology in the Paranormal*. Edited by J. Harold Ellens. Westport, Conn.; London: Praeger, 2008.

Puiggali, "Démonologie." Puiggali, J. "La démonologie de Philostrate." *RSPT* 67 (1983): 117–30.

Pui-lan, "Spirituality." Pui-lan, Kwok. "Spirituality of Healing." Pages 247–60 in *Teaching Religion and Healing*. Edited by Linda L. Barnes and Inés Talamantez. AARTRSS. Oxford: Oxford University Press, 2006.

Pulleyn, "Power of Names." Pulleyn, Simon. "The Power of Names in Classical Greek Religion." *CQ* 44 (1, 1994): 17–25.

Pullinger, *Dragon*. Pullinger, Jackie, with Andrew Quicke. *Chasing the Dragon*. London: Hodder & Stoughton, 1980.

Pullum, "Believe." Pullum, Stephen J. "'That They May Believe': Distinguishing the Miraculous from the Providential." Pages 135–58 in *Religious and Spiritual Events*. Vol. 1 of *Miracles: God, Science, and Psychology in the Paranormal*. Edited by J. Harold Ellens. Westport, Conn.; London: Praeger, 2008.

Pullum, "Selling." Pullum, Stephen J. "'Hallelujah! Thank You, Jesus!': Selling the Miraculous in the Preaching of Faith Healers." Pages 139–61 in *Parapsychological Perspectives*. Vol. 3 of *Miracles: God, Science, and Psychology in the Paranormal*. Edited by J. Harold Ellens. Westport, Conn.; London: Praeger, 2008.

Purkis, "Stigmata." Purkis, William J. "Stigmata on the First Crusade." Pages 99–108 in *Signs, Wonders, Miracles: Representations of Divine Power in the Life of the Church. Papers Read at the 2003 Summer Meeting and the 2004 Winter Meeting of the Ecclesiastical History Society*. Edited by Kate Cooper and Jeremy Gregory. Rochester: Boydell & Brewer, for the Ecclesiastical History Society, 2005.

Purtill, "Defining." Purtill, Richard L. "On Defining Miracles." *PhilChr* 3 (2, 2001): 37–39.

Purtill, "Defining Miracles." Purtill, Richard L. "Defining Miracles." Pages 61–72 in *In Defense of*

Miracles: A Comprehensive Case for God's Action in History. Edited by R. Douglas Geivett and Gary R. Habermas. Downers Grove, Ill.: InterVarsity, 1997.

Purtill, "Miracles." Purtill, Richard L. "Miracles: What If They Happen?" Pages 189–205 in *Miracles*. Edited by Richard Swinburne. New York: Macmillan, 1989.

Purtill, "Proofs." Purtill, Richard L. "Proofs of Miracles and Miracles as Proofs." *CSR* 6 (1, 1976): 39–51.

Putnam, "Tillich." Putnam, Leon J. "Tillich, Revelation, and Miracle." *ThLife* 9 (4, 1966): 355–70.

Puxley, "Experience." Puxley, H. L. "The Experience of Healing Prayer." Pages 164–74 in *Healing and Religious Faith*. Edited by Claude A. Frazier. Philadelphia: Pilgrim Press, United Church Press, 1974.

Pytches, "Anglican." Pytches, David. "Fully Anglican, Fully Renewed." Pages 186–97 in *Power Encounters Among Christians in the Western World*. Edited by Kevin Springer, with an introduction and afterword by John Wimber. San Francisco: Harper & Row, 1988.

Pytches, *Come*. Pytches, David. *Come Holy Spirit: Learning How to Minister in Power*. Foreword by John Wimber. London: Hodder & Stoughton, 1985.

Pytches, *Thundered*. Pytches, David. *Some Said It Thundered: A Personal Encounter with the Kansas City Prophets*. Foreword by John White. Afterword by Jamie Buckingham. Nashville: Thomas Nelson, 1991.

Pyysiäinen, "Fascination." Pyysiäinen, Ilkka. "The Enduring Fascination of Miracles." Pages 17–26 in *Medical and Therapeutic Events*. Vol. 2 of *Miracles: God, Science, and Psychology in the Paranormal*. Edited by J. Harold Ellens. Westport, Conn.; London: Praeger, 2008.

Pyysiäinen, "Mind." Pyysiäinen, Ilkka. "Mind and Miracles." *Zyg* 37 (3, 2002): 729–40.

Quast, *Reading*. Quast, Kevin. *Reading the Gospel of John: An Introduction*. New York: Paulist, 1991.

Quinn, "Conservation." Quinn, Philip P. "Divine Conservation, Secondary Causes, and Occasionalism." Pages 50–73 in *Divine and Human Action: Essays in the Metaphysics of Theism*. Edited by Thomas V. Morris. Ithaca, N.Y.: Cornell University Press, 1988.

Quinn, "Kivebulaya." Quinn, Frederick. "Apolo Kivebulaya." *DACB*. http://www.dacb.org/stories/demrepcongo/kivebulaya3_apollo.html.

Quintero Pérez, "Folleto." Quintero Pérez, Arianna. "Folleto sobre el surgimiento de la Iglesia Cristiana Pentecostal de Imías." Thesis for Instituto Bíblico ELIM, 2010.

Rabey, "Prophet." Rabey, Steve. "The People's Prophet." *ChH* 79 (2003): 32–34.

Rabinovitch, "Parallels." Rabinovitch, Nachum L. "Damascus Document IX, 17–22 and Rabbinic Parallels." *RevQ* 9 (1, 1977): 113–16.

Raboteau, *Slave Religion*. Raboteau, Albert J. *Slave Religion: The "Invisible Institution" in the Antebellum South*. Oxford: Oxford University Press, 1978.

Rack, "Healing." Rack, Henry D. "Doctors, Demons, and Early Methodist Healing." Pages 137–52 in *The Church and Healing: Papers Read at the Twentieth Summer Meeting and the Twenty-first Winter Meeting of the Ecclesiastical History Society*. StChHist 19. Edited by W. J. Sheils. Oxford: Basil Blackwell, 1982.

Rackham, *Acts*. Rackham, Richard Belward. *The Acts of the Apostles*. 4th ed. Grand Rapids: Baker, 1964.

Ragaz, *Kampf*. Ragaz, Leonhard. *Der Kampf um das Reich Gottes in Blumhardt, Vater und Sohn—und weiter!* Zürich: Rotaptfel Verlag, 1922.

Raguraman et al., "Presentation." Raguraman, Janakiraman, K. John Vijaysagar, and R. Chandrasekaran. "An Unusual Presentation of PTSD." *ANZJPsyc* 38 (9, Sept. 2004) [1 page, no pagination].

Rah, *Next Evangelicalism*. Rah, Soong-Chan. *The Next Evangelicalism: Freeing the Church from Western Cultural Captivity*. Downers Grove, Ill.: InterVarsity, 2009.

Rahim, "Zar." Rahim, S. I. "*Zar* among Middle-Aged Female Psychiatric Patients in the Sudan." Pages 137–46 in *Women's Medicine: The Zar-Bori Cult in Africa and Beyond*. Edited by I. M. Lewis, Ahmed Al-Safi, and Sayyid Hurreiz. Edinburgh: International African Institute, Edinburgh University Press, 1991.

Rahman, "Interpretation." Rahman, Muda Ismail Abd. "The Interpretation of the Birth of Jesus and His Miracles in the Writings of Sri Sayyid Ahmad Khan." *ICMR* 14 (1, 2003): 23–31.

Rahmani, "Amulet." Rahmani, L. Y. "A Magic Amulet from Nahariyya." *HTR* 74 (1981): 387–90.

Raised from the Dead. *Raised from the Dead*. DVD. Orlando, Fla.: E-R Productions, n.d.

"Raised from the Dead." "Raised from the Dead." *The Apostolic Faith* 1 (9, June 1907): 4.

Rajak, *Josephus*. Rajak, Tessa. *Josephus: The Historian and his Society*. Philadelphia: Fortress, 1984.

Rakoczy, "Renewal." Rakoczy, Susan. "Inculturation and Charismatic Renewal in Ghana." *Lit* 7 (3, 1988): 61–67.

Ramachandra, *Myths*. Ramachandra, Vinoth. *Subverting Global Myths: Theology and the Public Issues Shaping Our World*. Downers Grove, Ill.: IVP Academic, 2008.

Ramachandran and Blakeslee, *Phantoms*. Ramachandran, Vilayanur S., and Sandra Blakeslee. *Phantoms in* the Brain: Probing the Mysteries of the Human Mind. New York: William Morrow, 1998.

Ramirez, "Faiths." Ramirez, Daniel. "Migrating Faiths: A Social and Cultural History of Pentecostalism in the U.S.-Mexico Borderlands." PhD diss., Duke University, 2005.

Ramm, View. Ramm, Bernard. The Christian View of Science and Scripture. Grand Rapids: Eerdmans, 1954.

Ramsay, Letters. Ramsay, William M. The Letters to the Seven Churches of Asia. London: Hodder & Stoughton, 1904; repr., Grand Rapids: Baker, 1979.

Ramsay, Teaching. Ramsay, William M. The Teaching of St. Paul in Terms of the Present Day. 2nd ed. London: Hodder & Stoughton, 1913; repr., Grand Rapids: Baker, 1979.

Ramsey, "Miracles." Ramsey, Ian T. "Miracles: An Exercise in Logical Mapwork." An Inaugural Lecture Delivered before the University of Oxford, Dec. 7, 1951. Pages 1–30 in The Miracles and the Resurrection: Some Recent Studies by I. T. Ramsey, G. H. Boobyer, F. N. Davey, M. C. Perry, and Henry J. Cadbury. Theological Collections 3. London: SPCK, 1964.

Ran, "Church." Ran, Chu Hao. "Shanghai Lutheran Church." CGl 9 (4, Oct. 1932): 12.

Ran, "Experiences." Ran, Chu Hao. "My Experiences from 1926–1932." CGl 9 (4, Oct. 1932): 3–6.

Rana and Ross, Origins. Rana, Fazale, and Hugh Ross. Origins of Life: Biblical and Evolutionary Models Face Off. Colorado Springs: NavPress, 2004.

Rance, "Child." Rance, Alver. "For This Child They Prayed." MounM (Aug. 1992): 31.

Rance, "Fulfilling." Rance, DeLonn. "Fulfilling the Apostolic Mandate in Apostolic Power: Seeking a Spirit-Driven Missiology and Praxis." JPHWMSM 3. Springfield, Mo.: Assemblies of God Theological Seminary, 2008.

Randi, Faith Healers. Randi, James. The Faith Healers. Foreword by Carl Sagan. Buffalo: Prometheus, 1987.

Ranger, "Dilemma." Ranger, Terence. "Medical Science and Pentecost: The Dilemma of Anglicanism in Africa." Pages 333–65 in The Church and Healing: Papers Read at the Twentieth Summer Meeting and the Twenty-first Winter Meeting of the Ecclesiastical History Society. StChHist 19. Edited by W. J. Sheils. Oxford: Basil Blackwell, 1982.

Ranger, "Religion." Ranger, Terence. "African Religion, Witchcraft, and the Liberation War in Zimbabwe." Pages 351–78 in Studies in Witchcraft, Magic, War, and Peace in Africa. Edited by Beatrice Nicolini. Lewiston, N.Y.: Edwin Mellen, 2006.

Rapp, "Saints." Rapp, Claudia. "Saints and Holy Men." Pages 548–66 in Constantine to c. 600. Edited by

Augustine Casiday and Frederick W. Norris. Vol. 2 of The Cambridge History of Christianity. 9 vols. Cambridge: Cambridge University Press, 2007.

Rasolondraibe, "Ministry." Rasolondraibe, Péri. "Healing Ministry in Madagascar." WW 9 (4, 1989): 344–50.

Rawlings, "Introduction." Rawlings, Maurice. "Introduction: A Doctor Explains Near-Death Experiences." Pages ix–xiv in The Final Frontier: Incredible Stories of Near-Death Experiences, by Richard Kent and Val Fotherby. London: Marshall Pickering, HarperCollins, 1997.

Ray, "Aladura Christianity." Ray, Benjamin C. "Aladura Christianity: A Yoruba Religion." JRelAf 23 (3, 1993): 266–91.

Ray, "McPherson." Ray, Donna E. "Aimee Semple McPherson and Her Seriously Exciting Gospel." JPT 19 (1, 2010): 155–69.

Read, Monterroso, and Johnson, Growth. Read, William R., Victor M. Monterroso, and Harmon A. Johnson. Latin American Church Growth. Grand Rapids: Eerdmans, 1969.

Rebenich, "Historical Prose." Rebenich, Stefan. "Historical Prose." Pages 265–337 in Handbook of Classical Rhetoric in the Hellenistic Period 330 B.C.–A.D. 400. Edited by Stanley E. Porter. Leiden: Brill, 1997.

Redditt, "Nomos." Redditt, Paul L. "The Concept of Nomos in Fourth Maccabees." CBQ 45 (2, 1983): 249–70.

Redpath, "Change." Redpath, Bruce. "A Change of Blood." MounM (Feb. 1994): 11.

Reed, "Componential Analysis." Reed, J. F. "A Componential Analysis of the Ecuadorian Protestant Church." DMiss diss., Fuller Theological Seminary, 1974.

Reed, "Dead Raised." Reed, H. E. "Dead Raised." WWit 9 (6, June 20, 1913): 7.

Reed, Surgery. Reed, William Standish. Surgery of the Soul. Old Tappan, N.J.: Revell, 1969; Spire, 1973.

Regnerus, "Success." Regnerus, Mark D. "Shaping School Success: Religious Socialization and Educational Outcomes in Metropolitan Public Schools." JSSR 39 (3, 2000): 363–70.

Regnerus and Burdette, "Change." Regnerus, Mark D., and Amy Burdette. "Religious Change and Adolescent Family Dynamics." SocQ 47 (2006): 175–94.

Reiff, "Asleep." Reiff, Anna C. "Asleep in Jesus." LRE 4 (4, Jan. 1912): 2–4.

Reiff, "Healings." Reiff, Anna C. "Healings among the Natives." LRE 15 (11, Aug. 1922): 14.

Reiff, "Later Healings." Reiff, Anna C. "Later Healings." LRE 13 (1, Oct. 1920): 5–6.

Reiff, "Los Angeles Campmeeting." Reiff, Anna C. "Los Angeles Campmeeting." *LRE* (May 1913): 13–14.

Reimer, *Miracle*. Reimer, Andy. *Miracle and Magic: A Study in the Acts of the Apostles and the Life of Apollonius of Tyana*. JSNTSup 235. London: Sheffield Academic Press, 2002.

Reinhardt, "Movements." Reinhardt, Wolfgang. "Revival Movements in the Twentieth Century as an Urgent Task of the International Research Network." Pages 259–73 in *Revival, Renewal, and the Holy Spirit*. Edited by Dyfed Wyn Roberts. SEHT. Eugene, Ore.: Wipf & Stock, 2009.

Reinhardt, "Stripes." Reinhardt, Douglas. "With His Stripes We Are Healed: White Pentecostals and Faith Healing." Pages 126–42 in *Diversities of Gifts: Field Studies in Southern Religion*. Edited by Ruel W. Tyson Jr., James Peacock, and Daniel Patterson. Urbana: University of Illinois Press, 1988.

Reinhold, *Diaspora*. Reinhold, Meyer. *Diaspora: The Jews among the Greeks and Romans*. Sarasota, Fla.: Samuel Stevens & Company, 1983.

Reitzenstein, *Religions*. Reitzenstein, Richard. *Hellenistic Mystery Religions: Their Basic Ideas and Significance*. Translated by John E. Steeley. PTMS 15. Pittsburgh: Pickwick, 1978.

"Remarkable Healings in Australia." "Remarkable Healings in Australia." *PentEv* 696 (May 7, 1927): 6.

Remus, "Authority." Remus, Harold E. "Authority, Consent, Law: *Nomos, Physis*, and the Striving for a 'Given.'" *SR/SR* 13 (1, 1984): 5–18.

Remus, *Conflict*. Remus, Harold. *Pagan-Christian Conflict over Miracle in the Second Century*. Cambridge, Mass.: Philadelphia Patristic Foundation, 1983.

Remus, *Healer*. Remus, Harold. *Jesus as Healer*. UJT. Cambridge: Cambridge University Press, 1997.

Remus, "Magic or Miracle?" Remus, Harold. "'Magic or Miracle'? Some Second-Century Instances." *SecCent* 2 (3, 1982): 127–56.

Remus, "Terminology." Remus, Harold. "Does Terminology Distinguish Early Christian from Pagan Miracles?" *JBL* 101 (4, 1982): 531–51.

Renfrew and Bahn, *Archaeology*. Renfrew, Colin, and Paul Bahn. *Archaeology: Theories, Methods and Practice*. London: Thames and Hudson, 1991.

Repcheck, *Secret*. Repcheck, Jack. *Copernicus' Secret: How the Scientific Revolution Began*. New York: Simon & Schuster, 2007.

"Reports: Little Rock." "Reports from the Field: Little Rock, Ark." *PentEv* 513 (Sept. 8, 1925): 10.

Reppert, "Miracles." Reppert, Victor. "Miracles and the Case for Theism." *IJPhilRel* 25 (1, 1989): 35–51.

Rescher, *Studies*. Rescher, Nicholas. *Studies in Epistemology*. NRColPap 14. Frankfurt: Ontos Verlag, 2006.

Reville, "History." Reville, Albert. "History of the Devil." Pages 217–58 in *Exorcism Through the Ages*. Edited by St. Elmo Nauman. New York: Philosophical Library, 1974.

"Revival in England." "Revival in England." *PentEv* 696 (May 7, 1927): 5.

"Revival in London." "Pentecostal Revival in London." *LRE* 15 (2, Dec. 1921): 14–15.

Rew and Wong, "Review." Rew, Lynn, and Y. Joel Wong. "A Systematic Review of Associations among Religiosity/Spirituality and Adolescent Health Attitudes and Behaviors." *JAdHealth* 38 (2006): 433–42.

Rey, "Catholic Pentecostalism." Rey, Terry. "Catholic Pentecostalism in Haiti: Spirit, Politics, and Gender." *Pneuma* 32 (2010): 80–106.

Reyes, "Framework." Reyes, Erlinda T. "A Theological Framework on Non-Healing in the Pentecostal Perspective." ThM thesis, Asia Pacific Theological Seminary, 2007.

Reyes-Ortiz et al., "Attendance." Reyes-Ortiz, C. A., et al. "Higher Church Attendance Predicts Lower Fear of Falling in Older Mexican Americans." *AgMHealth* 10 (1, 2006): 13–18.

Reynolds, *Magic*. Reynolds, Barrie. *Magic, Divination and Witchcraft Among the Barotse of Northern Rhodesia*. Berkeley: University of California Press, 1963.

Rhoads and Michie, *Mark*. Rhoads, David, and Donald Michie. *Mark As Story: An Introduction to the Narrative of a Gospel*. Philadelphia: Fortress, 1982.

Ricci, "Ethiopian Literature." Ricci, Lanfranco. "Ethiopian Christian Literature." Pages 975–79 in vol. 3 of *The Coptic Encyclopedia*. Edited by Aziz S. Atiya. 8 vols. New York: Macmilan, 1991.

Richards, "Factors." Richards, Wes. "An Examination of Common Factors in the Growth of Global Pentecostalism: Observed in South Korea, Nigeria, and Argentina." *JAM* 7 (1, March 2005): 85–106.

Richards, "Healings." Richards, John. "Healings in South Africa." *LRE* 26 (5, Feb. 1934): 16.

Richardson, "Agency." Richardson, W. Mark. "The Theology of Human Agency and the Neurobiology of Learning." Pages 351–71 in *Religion and Science: History, Method, Dialogue*. Edited by W. Mark Richardson and Wesley J. Wildman. Foreword by Ian G. Barbour. New York: Routledge, 1996.

Richardson, *Age of Science*. Richardson, Alan. *The Bible in the Age of Science*. Philadelphia: Westminster, 1961.

Richardson, *Apologetics*. Richardson, Alan. *Christian Apologetics*. London: SCM, 1947.

Richardson, *Miracle-Stories*. Richardson, Alan. *The Miracle-Stories of the Gospels*. London: SCM, 1941.

Riddle, "Growth." Riddle, N. G. "Church Growth in Kinshasa." MA thesis, Fuller Theological Seminary, 1973.

Riesenfeld, Tradition. Riesenfeld, Harald. The Gospel Tradition. Philadelphia: Fortress, 1970.

Riesner, Early Period. Riesner, Rainer. Paul's Early Period: Chronology, Mission Strategy, Theology. Translated by Doug Stott. Grand Rapids: Eerdmans, 1998.

Riesner, "Zuverlässigkeit." Riesner, Rainer. "Die historische Zuverlässigkeit der Apostelgeschichte." ZNW 9 (18, 2006): 38–43.

Riggs, Witness. Riggs, Marcia Y., ed. Can I Get a Witness? Prophetic Religious Voices of African American Women: An Anthology. With Barbara Holmes. Maryknoll, N.Y.: Orbis, 1997.

Ring, Life. Ring, Kenneth. Life at Death: A Scientific Investigation of the Near-Death Experience. New York: Coward, McCann, and Geoghehan, 1980.

Ringgren, Religion. Ringgren, Helmer. Israelite Religion. Translated by David E. Green. Philadelphia: Fortress, 1966.

Ritchie, Spirit. Ritchie, Mark Andrew. Spirit of the Rainforest: A Yanomamö Shaman's Story. 2nd ed. Chicago: Island Lake Press, 2000.

Ritner, Mechanics. Ritner, Robert Kriech. The Mechanics of Ancient Egyptian Magical Practice. SAOC 54. Chicago: The Oriental Institute of the University of Chicago, 1993.

Rivera-Pagán, "Transformation." Rivera-Pagán, Luis N. "Pentecostal Transformation in Latin America." Pages 190–210 in Twentieth-Century Global Christianity. Edited by Mary Farrell Bednarowski. Vol. 7 of A People's History of Christianity. Minneapolis: Fortress, 2008.

Rivers, Medicine. Rivers, W. H. R. Medicine, Magic, and Religion. London: K. Paul, Trench, Trubner; New York: Harcourt, Brace, 1924.

Rives, "Magic in XII Tables." Rives, James B. "Magic in the XII Tables Revisited." CQ 52 (1, 2002): 270–90.

Rives, Religion. Rives, James B. Religion in the Roman Empire. Malden, Mass.; Oxford: Blackwell, 2007.

Robbins, "Exorcism." Robbins, Rossell Hope. "Exorcism." Pages 201–16 in Exorcism Through the Ages. Edited by St. Elmo Nauman. New York: Philosophical Library, 1974.

Robbins, Jesus the Teacher. Robbins, Vernon K. Jesus the Teacher: A Socio-Rhetorical Interpretation of Mark. Minneapolis: Augsburg Fortress, 1992.

Robbins, "Kastoreion." Robbins, Emmet. "Kastoreion." Page 26 in vol. 7 of Brill's New Pauly: Encyclopaedia of the Ancient World. Edited by Hubert Cancik and Helmuth Schneider. 20 vols. English ed. Christine F. Salazar. Leiden: Brill, 2010.

Robeck, "Charismatic Movements." Robeck, Cecil M., Jr. "Charismatic Movements." Pages 145–54 in Global Dictionary of Theology: A Resource for the Worldwide Church. Edited by William A. Dyrness and Veli-Matti Kärkkäinen, with Juan Francisco Martinez and Simon Chan. Downers Grove, Ill.: InterVarsity, 2008.

Robeck, Mission. Robeck, Cecil M., Jr. The Azusa Street Mission and Revival: The Birth of the Global Pentecostal Movement. Nashville: Thomas Nelson, 2006.

Robeck, "Seymour." Robeck, Cecil M., Jr. "William J. Seymour and 'The Bible Evidence.'" Pages 72–95 in Initial Evidence: Historical and Biblical Perspectives on the Pentecostal Doctrine of Spirit Baptism. Edited by Gary B. McGee. Peabody, Mass.: Hendrickson, 1991.

Robert, Claros. Robert, Jean and Louis. Claros 1. DécHell, fasc. 1. Paris: Éditions de Recherche sur les Civilisations, 1989.

Robert, Croyances. Robert, J. M. Croyances et Coutumes Magico-Religieuses des Wafipa Païens. Tabora, Tanzania: Tanganyika Mission Press, 1949.

Robert, "Introduction." Robert, Dana L. "Introduction: Historical Themes and Current Issues." Pages 1–28 in Gospel Bearers, Gender Barriers: Missionary Women in the Twentieth Century. Edited by Dana L. Robert. Maryknoll, N.Y.: Orbis, 2002.

Robert, "Pierson." Robert, Dana L. "Arthur Tappan Pierson and Forward Movements of Late-Nineteenth-Century Evangelicalism." PhD diss., Yale University, 1984.

Roberts, Coburn. Roberts, C. A. Vic Coburn: Man with the Healing Touch. Nashville: Thomas Nelson, 1975.

Roberts, "Contributions." Roberts, Thomas B. "Entheogenic Contributions to Self-Transcendence, Healing, Pastoral Counseling, and Evangelism." Pages 243–68 in Psychodynamics. Vol. 3 of The Healing Power of Spirituality: How Faith Helps Humans Thrive. Edited by J. Harold Ellens. Santa Barbara, Calif.: Praeger, 2010.

Roberts, "Darwin." Roberts, Jon H. "That Darwin Destroyed Natural Theology." Pages 161–69 in Galileo Goes to Jail and Other Myths about Science and Religion. Edited by Ronald L. Numbers. Cambridge, Mass.: Harvard University Press, 2009.

Roberts, "Study." Roberts, Thomas B. "Multistate and Entheogenic Contributions to the Study of Miracles and Experimental Religious Studies." Pages 38–64 in Parapsychological Perspectives. Vol. 3 of Miracles: God, Science, and Psychology in the Paranormal. Edited by J. Harold Ellens. Westport, Conn.; London: Praeger, 2008.

Robertson, "Epidauros to Lourdes." Robertson, David. "From Epidauros to Lourdes: A History of

Healing by Faith." Pages 179–89 in *Faith Healing: Finger of God? Or, Scientific Curiosity?* Compiled by Claude A. Frazier. New York: Thomas Nelson, 1973.

Robertson, *Futility*. Robertson, Morgan. *Futility*. New York: M. F. Mansfield, 1898.

Robertson, *Miracles*. Robertson, Pat. *Miracles Can Be Yours Today*. Brentwood, Tenn.: Integrity, 2006.

Robertson, *Word*. Robertson, O. Palmer. *The Final Word*. Carlisle, Pa.: Banner of Truth, 1993.

Robinson, "Causation." Robinson, J. A. "Causation, Probability, and Testimony." PhD diss., Princeton University, 1956.

Robinson, "Challenge." Robinson, Bernard. "The Challenge of the Gospel Miracle Stories." *NBf* 60 (1979): 321–34.

Robinson, "Growth." Robinson, Mark. "The Growth of Indonesian Pentecostalism." Pages 329–44 in *Asian and Pentecostal: The Charismatic Face of Christianity in Asia*. Edited by Allan Anderson and Edmond Tang. Foreword by Cecil M. Robeck. Regnum Studies in Mission, AJPSS 3. Oxford: Regnum; Baguio City, Philippines: APTS Press, 2005.

Robinson, "Power." Robinson, Mark. "Pentecostal Power among Pancasila People." Master's thesis, Griffith University, Australia, 2001.

Robinson, *Studies*. Robinson, John A. T. *Twelve New Testament Studies*. SBT 34. London: SCM, 1962.

Roebuck, *Asklepieion*. Roebuck, Carl. *The Asklepieion and Lerna*. Vol. 14 of *Corinth: Results of Excavations Conducted by the American School of Classical Studies at Athens*. Princeton, N.J.: The American School of Classical Studies at Athens, 1951.

Roelofs, "Thought." Roelofs, Gerard. "Charismatic Christian Thought: Experience, Metonymy, and Routinization." Pages 217–33 in *Charismatic Christianity as a Global Culture*. Edited by Karla Poewe. SCR. Columbia: University of South Carolina Press, 1994.

Roetzel, *Paul*. Roetzel, Calvin J. *Paul: A Jew on the Margins*. Louisville: Westminster John Knox, 2003.

Roff et al., "Limitations." Roff, Lucinda Lee, D. L. Klemmack, C. Simon, G. W. Cho, M. W. Parker, H. G. Koenig, P. Sawyer-Baker, and R. M. Allman. "Functional Limitations and Religious Service Attendance among African American and White Elders." *HSW* 31 (4, 2006): 246–55.

Roff et al., "Religiosity." Roff, Lucinda Lee, D. L. Klemmack, M. Parker, H. G. Koenig, P. Baker, and R. L. Allman. "Religiosity, Smoking, Exercise, and Obesity among Southern Community-Dwelling Older Adults." *JAppGer* 24 (2005): 337–54.

Rogers, *Miracles*. Rogers, Adrian. *Believe in Miracles but Trust in Jesus*. Wheaton: Crossway, 1997.

Rogers, "Miracles." Rogers, Steven A. "Miracles in the Frontal Lobes: A Neuropsychological Approach

to the Way We Make Miracle Attributions." Pages 94–116 in *Parapsychological Perspectives*. Vol. 3 of *Miracles: God, Science, and Psychology in the Paranormal*. Edited by J. Harold Ellens. Westport, Conn.; London: Praeger, 2008.

Rogers and Risher, "Religion." Rogers, Steven A., and Erin L. Risher. "Can We Recover Religion for Those with Schizophrenia?" Pages 283–301 in *Psychodynamics*. Vol. 3 of *The Healing Power of Spirituality: How Faith Helps Humans Thrive*. Edited by J. Harold Ellens. Santa Barbara, Calif.: Praeger, 2010.

Rogge, "Relationship." Rogge, Louis Philip. "The Relationship between the Sacrament of Anointing the Sick and the Charism of Healing Within the Catholic Charismatic Renewal." PhD diss., Union Theological Seminary, New York, 1984.

Rognon, "Relecture." Rognon, Frédéric. "Le miracle en philosophie: Une relecture critique." *FoiVie* 108 (2, 2009): 28–34.

Rollins, "Miracles." Rollins, Wayne G. "Jesus and Miracles in Historical, Biblical, and Psychological Perspective." Pages 36–56 in *Religious and Spiritual Events*. Vol. 1 of *Miracles: God, Science, and Psychology in the Paranormal*. Edited by J. Harold Ellens. Westport, Conn.; London: Praeger, 2008.

Rollins, "Wholeness." Rollins, Wayne G. "God, the Bible, and Human Wholeness in the Life and Thought of C. G. Jung." Pages 1–15 in *Psychodynamics*. Vol. 3 of *The Healing Power of Spirituality: How Faith Helps Humans Thrive*. Edited by J. Harold Ellens. Santa Barbara, Calif.: Praeger, 2010.

Rolston, "Science." Rolston, Holmes, III. "Science, Religion, and the Future." Pages 61–82 in *Religion and Science: History, Method, Dialogue*. Edited by W. Mark Richardson and Wesley J. Wildman. Foreword by Ian G. Barbour. New York: Routledge, 1996.

Romano, "Folk Healing." Romano, Octavio I. "Charismatic Medicine, Folk Healing and Folk-Sainthood." *AmAnth* 67 (1965): 1151–73.

"'Ronnie' Coyne." "'Ronnie' Coyne—The Boy Who Sees—with a Plastic Eye!" *VOH* (Feb. 1954): 6–7.

Ronning, "Mission." Ronning, Ella G. "Sinyeh Mission Thirtieth Anniversary." *CGl* 10 (2, April 1933): 7.

Root, "Introduction." Root, H. E. "Editor's Introduction." Pages 7–20 in *The Natural History of Religion*, by David Hume. Edited by H. E. Root. London: Adam & Charles Black, 1956.

Ropes, "Aspects." Ropes, James Hardy. "Some Aspects of the New Testament Miracles." *HTR* 3 (1910): 482–99.

Roque, "Mafumo." Roque, Ana Cristina. "Meeting Artur Murimo Mafumo and His Practices." Pages 171–90 in *Studies in Witchcraft, Magic, War, and*

Peace in Africa. Edited by Beatrice Nicolini. Lewiston, N.Y.: Edwin Mellen, 2006.

Roschke, "Healing." Roschke, Ronald W. "Healing in Luke, Madagascar, and Elsewhere." *CurTM* 33 (6, Dec. 2006): 459–71.

Rose, *Faith Healing.* Rose, Louis. *Faith Healing.* Edited by Bryan Morgan. Rev. ed. Baltimore: Penguin, 1971.

Rosen, "Psychopathology." Rosen, George. "Psychopathology in the Social Process: Dance Frenzies, Demonic Possession, Revival Movements, and Similar So-called Psychic Epidemics. An Interpretation." Pages 219–50 in *Possession and Exorcism.* Vol. 9 of *Articles on Witchcraft, Magic, and Demonology: A Twelve-Volume Anthology of Scholarly Articles.* Edited by Brian P. Levack. New York: Garland, 1992. Reprinted from *BullHistMed* 36 (1962): 13–44.

Rosenfeld, "Simeon b. Yohai." Rosenfeld, Ben-Zion. "R. Simeon b. Yohai—Wonder Worker and Magician—Scholar, *Saddiq* and Hasid." *REJ* 158 (3–4, 1999): 349–84.

Rosik, "Impact." Rosik, Christopher H. "The Impact of Religious Orientation in Conjugal Bereavement among Older Adults." *IntJAgHDev* 28 (4, 1989): 251–60.

Rosny, *Healers.* Rosny, Eric de. *Healers in the Night.* Translated by Robert R. Barr. Maryknoll, N.Y.: Orbis, 1985.

Ross, "Epileptic." Ross, John M. "Epileptic or Moonstruck?" *BTr* 29 (1978): 126–28.

Ross, "Murray." Ross, Andrew C. "Murray, Andrew, Jr." Pages 807–8 in *Dictionary of Evangelical Biography, 1730–1860.* Edited by Donald M. Lewis. 2 vols. Peabody, Mass.: Hendrickson, 2004; Oxford: Blackwell, 1995.

Ross, "Preaching." Ross, Kenneth R. "Preaching in Mainstream Christian Churches in Malawi: A Survey and Analysis." *JRelAf* 25 (1, Feb. 1995): 3–24.

Ross, "Review." Ross, Denise. Review of *Brother Yun and Paul Hattaway, The Heavenly Man. JAM* 6 (1, March 2004): 118–20.

Ross, "Search." Ross, C., Jr. "Search for Life." DMiss diss., Fuller Theological Seminary, 1969.

Rössler, "Mensch." Rössler, Andreas. "Jesus: ein blosser Mensch." *ZeitZeichen* 9 (1, 2008): 56–58.

Rosvold, "Conference." Rosvold, Nora. "L.U.M. Conference—1932." *CGl* 9 (4, Oct. 1932): 6–8.

Roth, "Piling." Roth, Jay. "The Piling of Coincidence on Coincidence." Pages 197–201 in *Cosmos, Bios, and Theos: Scientists Reflect on Science, God, and the Origins of the Universe, Life, and Homo Sapiens.* Edited by Henry Margenau and Roy Abraham Varghese. La Salle, Ill.: Open Court, 1992.

Rothaus, *Corinth.* Rothaus, Richard M. *Corinth: The First City of Greece: An Urban History of Late Antique Cult and Religion.* RGRW 139. Leiden: Brill, 2000.

Rothschild, "Emergence in Biology." Rothschild, Lynn J. "The Role of Emergence in Biology." Pages 151–65 in *The Re-Emergence of Emergence: The Emergentist Hypothesis from Science to Religion.* Edited by Philip Clayton and Paul Davies. Oxford: Oxford University Press, 2006.

Rothschild, *Rhetoric of History.* Rothschild, Clare K. *Luke-Acts and the Rhetoric of History: An Investigation of Early Christian Historiography.* WUNT 2.175. Tübingen: Mohr Siebeck, 2004.

Rousselle, "Cults." Rousselle, Robert. "Healing Cults in Antiquity: The Dream Cures of Asclepius of Epidaurus." *JPsycHist* 12 (3, Winter 1985): 339–52.

Rowland, *Origins.* Rowland, Christopher. *Christian Origins: From Messianic Movement to Christian Religion.* Minneapolis: Augsburg; London, SPCK, 1985.

Rozario, "Scientist." Rozario, Santi. "Allah Is the Scientist of the Scientists: Modern Medicine and Religious Healing among British Bangladeshis." *CulRel* 10 (2, 2009): 177–99.

Ruck, "Solving." Ruck, Carl A. P. "Solving the Eleusinian Mystery." Pages 35–50 in *The Road to Eleusis: Unveiling the Secret of the Mysteries,* by Robert Gordon Wasson, Albert Hofmann, and Carl A. P. Ruck. New York: A Helen and Kurt Wolff Book, Harcourt Brace Jovanovich, 1978.

Rudin and Rudin, *Prison.* Rudin, A. James, and Marcia R. Rudin. *Prison or Paradise: The New Religious Cults.* Philadelphia: Fortress, 1980.

Ruesga, "Healings." Ruesga, David G. "Healings among Mexicans." *PentEv* 647 (May 15, 1926): 10.

Rummans et al., "Quality." Rummans, Teresa A., et al. "Impacting Quality of Life for Patients with Advanced Cancer with a Structured Multidisciplinary Intervention: A Randomized Controlled Trial." *JClinOn* 24 (4, 2006): 635–42.

Rummel, "Parallels." Rummel, Stan. "Using Ancient Near Eastern Parallels in Old Testament Study." *BAR* 3 (3, Sept. 1977): 3–11.

Rumph, *Signs.* Rumph, Jane. *Signs and Wonders in America Today: Amazing Accounts of God's Power.* Ann Arbor, Mich.: Vine Books, 2003.

Rupke, "Theory." Rupke, Nicolaas A. "That the Theory of Organic Evolution Is Based on Circular Reasoning." Pages 131–41 in *Galileo Goes to Jail and Other Myths about Science and Religion.* Edited by Ronald L. Numbers. Cambridge, Mass.: Harvard University Press, 2009.

Rüsch, "Dämonenaus-Treibung." Rüsch, Ernst Gerhard. "Dämonenaus-Treibung in der Gallus-Vita und bei Blumhardt dem alteren." *TZ* 34 (2, 1978): 86–94.

Ruse, "Design." Ruse, Michael. "That 'Intelligent Design' Represents a Scientific Challenge to Evolution." Pages 206–14 in *Galileo Goes to Jail and Other Myths about Science and Religion*. Edited by Ronald L. Numbers. Cambridge, Mass.: Harvard University Press, 2009.

Rusecki, "Kryteria." Rusecki, M. "Kryteria historycznosci cudów Jezusa." *RocT* 54 (6, 2007): 317–34.

Rushton and Russell, "Language." Rushton, Cynda H., and Kathleen Russell. "The Language of Miracles: Ethical Challenges." *PedNurs* 22 (2, 1996): 64–67.

Russell, *Apocalyptic*. Russell, D. S. *The Method and Message of Jewish Apocalyptic*. Philadelphia: Westminster, 1964.

Russell, "Difficulty." Russell, John A. "I Have Difficulty Accepting That Matter Has Been in Existence Forever." Pages 89–92 in *Cosmos, Bios, and Theos: Scientists Reflect on Science, God, and the Origins of the Universe, Life, and* Homo Sapiens. Edited by Henry Margenau and Roy Abraham Varghese. La Salle, Ill.: Open Court, 1992.

Russell, *History of Western Philosophy*. Russell, Bertrand. *A History of Western Philosophy*. New York: Simon & Schuster, 1972.

Russell, "T = 0." Russell, Robert John. "T = 0: Is It Theologically Significant?" Pages 201–4 in *Religion and Science: History, Method, Dialogue*. Edited by W. Mark Richardson and Wesley J. Wildman. Foreword by Ian G. Barbour. New York: Routledge, 1996.

Rüther, "Representations." Rüther, Kirsten. "Representations of African Healers in the Popular Print Media: Inquiries into South African Understandings of Health and Popular Culture in the 1970s and 1980s." Pages 385–410 in *Health Knowledge and Belief Systems in Africa*. Edited by Toyin Falola and Matthew M. Heaton. Durham, N.C.: Carolina Academic Press, 2008.

Rutherford, "Tragedy." Rutherford, Richard. "Tragedy and History." Pages 504–14 in *A Companion to Greek and Roman Historiography*. Edited by John Marincola. 2 vols. Malden, Mass.: Blackwell, 2007.

Ruthven, *Cessation*. Ruthven, Jon. *On the Cessation of the Charismata: The Protestant Polemic on Postbiblical Miracles*. JPTSup 3. Sheffield: Sheffield Academic Press, 1993.

Ruthven, "Miracle." Ruthven, Jon. "Miracle." Pages 546–50 in *Global Dictionary of Theology: A Resource for the Worldwide Church*. Edited by William A. Dyrness and Veli-Matti Kärkkäinen, with Juan Francisco Martinez and Simon Chan. Downers Grove, Ill.: InterVarsity, 2008.

Rutz, *Megashift*. Rutz, James. *Megashift: Igniting Spiritual Power*. Colorado Springs: Empowerment Press, 2005.

Rycroft, *Innocence*. Rycroft, Charles. *The Innocence of Dreams*. New York: Pantheon, 1979.

Saayman, "Prophecy." Saayman, Willem. "Prophecy in the History of South Africa." *Missionalia* 33 (1, April 2005): 5–19.

Sabourin, "Healings." Sabourin, Leopold. "The Miracles of Jesus (III): Healings, Resuscitations, Nature Miracles." *BTB* 5 (2, 1975): 146–200.

Sabourin, *Miracles*. Sabourin, Leopold. *The Divine Miracles Discussed and Defended*. Rome: Officium Libri Catholici, 1977.

Sabourin, "Miracles." Sabourin, Leopold. "Hellenistic and Rabbinic 'Miracles.'" *BTB* 2 (3, 1972): 281–307.

Sabourin, "Powers." Sabourin, Leopold. "The Miracles of Jesus (II): Jesus and the Evil Powers." *BTB* 4 (2, 1974): 115–75.

Safrai, "Home." Safrai, S. "Home and Family." Pages 728–92 in *JPFC*.

Sahas, "Formation." Sahas, Daniel J. "The Formation of Later Islamic Doctrines as a Response to Byzantine Polemics: The Miracles of Muhammad." *GOTR* 27 (2, 1982): 307–26.

Saintyves, *Essais*. Saintyves, Pierre. *Essais de Folklore Biblique. Magie, Mythes et Miracles dans l'Ancien et le Nouveau Testament*. Paris: Émile Nourry, 1922.

Salam, "Science." Salam, Abdus. "Science and Religion: Reflections on Transcendence and Secularization." Pages 93–104 in *Cosmos, Bios, and Theos: Scientists Reflect on Science, God, and the Origins of the Universe, Life, and* Homo Sapiens. Edited by Henry Margenau and Roy Abraham Varghese. La Salle, Ill.: Open Court, 1992.

Salamone, "Bori." Salamone, Frank. "The Bori and I: Reflections of a Mature Anthropologist." *AnthHum* 20 (1995): 15–19.

Saler, "Supernatural." Saler, Benson. "Supernatural as a Western Category." *Ethos* 5 (1, Spring 1977): 31–53.

Salisbury, "Highlands." Salisbury, R. F. "Possession in the New Guinea Highlands." *IJSocPsyc* 14 (1968): 85–94.

Salisbury, "Possession." Salisbury, R. F. "Possession among the Siane (New Guinea)." *TranscPsycRR* 3 (1966): 108–16.

Sall, "Possession." Sall, Millard J. "Demon Possession or Psychopathology? A Clinical Differentiation." *JPsyTh* 4 (4, 1976): 286–90.

Sall, "Response." Sall, Millard J. "A Response to 'Demon Possession and Psychopathology: A Theological Relationship.'" *JPsyTh* 7 (1, Spring 1979): 27–30.

Salmon, "Explanation." Salmon, Wesley C. "Statistical Explanation." Pages 173–231 in *The Nature and Function of Scientific Theories: Essays in Contemporary*

Science and Philosophy. Edited by Robert G. Colodny. Pittsburgh: University of Pittsburgh Press, 1970.

Salmon, *Heals*. Salmon, Elsie H. *He Heals Today, or A Healer's Case Book*. 2nd ed. Foreword by W. E. Sangster. The Drift, Evesham, Worcs.: Arthur James, 1951.

Salomonsen, "Methods." Salomonsen, Jane. "Methods of Compassion or Pretension? Conducting Anthropological Fieldwork in Modern Magical Communities." *Pom* 8 (1999): 4–13.

Salsman, "Healing." Salsman, Leon. "Spiritual and Faith Healing." *JPastCare* 11 (1957): 146–55.

Salsman et al., "Link." Salsman, John M., Tamara L. Brown, Emily H. Brechting, and Charles R. Carlson. "The Link between Religion and Spirituality and Psychological Adjustment: The Mediating Role of Optimism and Social Support." *PSocPsyBull* 31 (4, 2005): 522–35.

Salvato, "Presence." Salvato, Rick. "'I Felt the Presence of God Descend into That Cubicle.'" *MounM* (Jan. 1990): 6–7.

Samuel, "Gatherings." Samuel, K. J. "India's Thousands Witness the Mighty Moving of God's Spirit as the M. A. Daouds Minister: Biggest Christian Gatherings India Ever Witnessed." *VOH* (April 1954): 16.

Sánchez, "Daimones." Sánchez, S. "Los 'daimones' del mundo helénico." *ByF* 2 (4, 1976): 47–59.

Sánchez Walsh, *Identity*. Sánchez Walsh, Arlene M. *Latino Pentecostal Identity: Evangelical Faith, Self, and Society*. New York: Columbia University Press, 2003.

Sánchez Walsh, "Santidad." Sánchez Walsh, Arlene. "Santidad, Salvación, Sanidad, Liberación: The Word of Faith Movement among Twenty-first Century Latina/o Pentecostals." Pages 151–67 in *Global Pentecostal and Charismatic Healing*. Edited by Candy Gunther Brown. Foreword by Harvey Cox. Oxford: Oxford University Press, 2011.

Sanday, "Miracles." Sanday, William. "Miracles and the Supernatural Character of the Gospels." *ExpT* 14 (1902–3): 62–66.

Sanders, *Figure*. Sanders, E. P. *The Historical Figure of Jesus*. New York: Allen Lane, Penguin, 1993.

Sanders, *Jesus and Judaism*. Sanders, E. P. *Jesus and Judaism*. Philadelphia: Fortress, 1985.

Sanders, *John*. Sanders, J. N. *A Commentary on the Gospel According to St. John*. Edited and completed by B. A. Mastin. Harper's New Testament Commentaries. New York: Harper & Row, 1968.

Sanders, *Tendencies*. Sanders, E. P. *The Tendencies of the Synoptic Tradition*. SNTSM 9. Cambridge: Cambridge University Press, 1969.

Sandgren, "Kamba Christianity." Sandgren, David. "Kamba Christianity: From Africa Inland Mission to African Brotherhood Church." Pages 169–95 in *East African Expressions of Christianity*. Edited by Thomas Spear and Isaria N. Kimambo. EAfSt. Athens: Ohio University Press; Oxford: James Currey; Dar es Salaam: Mkuki na Nyota; Nairobi: East African Educational Publishers, 1999.

Sandner, "Psychology." Sandner, Donald. "Analytical Psychology and Shamanism." Pages 277–83 in *Proceedings of the Fourth International Conference on the Study of Shamanism and Alternate Modes of Healing, Held at the St. Sabina Center, San Rafael, California, September 5–7, 1987*. Edited by Ruth-Inge Heinze. N.p.: Independent Scholars of Asia; Madison, Wis.: A-R Editions, 1988.

Sanford, *Gifts*. Sanford, Agnes. *The Healing Gifts of the Spirit*. San Francisco: Harper & Row, 1966.

Sangster, "Foreword." Sangster, W. E. "Foreword." Pages 5–8 in *He Heals Today, or A Healer's Case Book*, by Elsie H. Salmon. 2nd ed. The Drift, Evesham, Worcs.: Arthur James, 1951.

Sankey, "Method." Sankey, Howard. "Scientific Method." Pages 263–66 in *The Routledge Companion to Philosophy of Science*. Edited by Stathis Psillos and Martin Curd. New York: Routledge, 2008.

Sanneh, *Disciples*. Sanneh, Lamin. *Disciples of All Nations: Pillars of World Christianity*. New York: Oxford University Press, 2008.

Sanneh, *West African Christianity*. Sanneh, Lamin. *West African Christianity: The Religious Impact*. Maryknoll, N.Y.: Orbis, 1983.

Sanneh, *Whose Religion*. Sanneh, Lamin. *Whose Religion Is Christianity? The Gospel Beyond the West*. Grand Rapids: Eerdmans, 2003.

Sargunam, "Churches." Sargunam, Ezra. "Multiplying Churches in Urban India." MA thesis, Fuller Theological Seminary, 1973.

Sarna, *Exodus*. Sarna, Nahum M. *Exploring Exodus: The Heritage of Biblical Israel*. New York: Schocken, 1986.

Satellite Atlas. *The Holy Land Satellite Atlas*. Edited by R. L. W. Cleave. 2 vols. Nicosia, Cyprus: Rohr Productions, 1999. Vol. 1: *Terrain Recognition*; vol. 2: *The Regions*.

Satyavrata, "Globalization." Satyavrata, Ivan. "The Globalization of Pentecostal Missions in the Twenty-First Century." JPHWMSM 4. Springfield, Mo.: Assemblies of God Theological Seminary, 2009.

Satyavrata, "Perspectives." Satyavrata, Ivan M. "Contextual Perspectives on Pentecostalism as a Global Culture." Pages 203–21 in *The Globalization of Pentecostalism: A Religion Made to Travel*. Edited by Murray W. Dempster, Byron D. Klaus, and Douglas Petersen. Foreword by Russell P. Spittler. Carlisle: Paternoster; Oxford: Regnum, 1999.

Saucy, "Miracles." Saucy, Mark R. "Miracles and Jesus' Proclamation of the Kingdom of God." *BSac* 153 (255, 1996): 281–307.

Saucy, *Progressive Dispensationalism.* Saucy, Robert L. *The Case for Progressive Dispensationalism.* Grand Rapids: Zondervan, 1993.

Saucy, "View." Saucy, Robert L. "An Open but Cautious View." Pages 95–148 in *Are Miraculous Gifts for Today? Four Views.* Edited by Wayne A. Grudem. Grand Rapids: Zondervan, 1996.

Saulnier, "Josèphe." Saulnier, Christiane. "Flavius Josèphe et la propagande flavienne." *RB* 96 (4, 1989): 545–62.

Saunders, "Physics." Saunders, Simon. "Physics." Pages 567–80 in *The Routledge Companion to Philosophy of Science.* Edited by Stathis Psillos and Martin Curd. New York: Routledge, 2008.

Saunders, "Zar Experience." Saunders, Lucie Wood. "Variants in Zar Experience in an Egyptian Village." Pages 177–92 in *Case Studies in Spirit Possession.* Edited by Vincent Crapanzaro and Vivian Garrison. New York: John Wiley & Sons, 1977.

"Saw God." "Says She Saw God: Remarkable Experience of Eula Wilson." *The Wichita Eagle* (June 11, 1907): 5.

Sawyer and Wallace, *Afraid.* Sawyer, M. James, and Daniel B. Wallace, eds. *Who's Afraid of the Holy Spirit? An Investigation into the Ministry of the Spirit of God Today.* Dallas: Biblical Studies Press, 2005.

Sax, Weinhold, and Schweitzer, "Healing." Sax, William, Jan Weinhold, and Jochen Schweitzer. "Ritual Healing East and West: A Comparison of Ritual Healing in the Garhwal Himalayas and 'Family Constellation' in Germany." *JRitSt* 24 (1, 2010): 61–78.

Saxena, "Study." Saxena, S. "A Cross-Cultural Study of Spirituality, Religion, and Personal Beliefs as Components of Quality of Life." *SSMed* 62 (6, 2006): 1486–97.

Say, "History." Say, Saw Doh. "A Brief History and Development Factors of the Karen Baptist Church of Burma (Myanma)." ThM thesis, Fuller School of World Mission, 1990.

Scarre, "Tillotson." Scarre, Geoffrey. "Tillotson and Hume on Miracles." *DRev* 110 (255, 1992): 45–65.

Schaefer, "Miracles." Schaefer, Nancy A. "Some Will See Miracles: The Reception of Morris Cerullo World Evangelism in Britain." *JContRel* 14 (1, 1999): 111–26.

Schaeffer, *Tapestry.* Schaeffer, Edith. *The Tapestry: The Life and Times of Francis and Edith Schaeffer.* Waco: Word, 1981.

Schäfer, "Magic Literature." Schäfer, Peter. "Jewish Magic Literature in Late Antiquity and Early Middle Ages." *JJS* 41 (1, 1990): 75–91.

Schamoni, *Parallelen.* Schamoni, Wilhelm. *Parallelen zum Neuen Testament aus Heiligsprechungsakten.* Abensberg: Kral, 1971.

Schanowitz and Nicassio, "Predictors." Schanowitz, Jeff Y., and Perry M. Nicassio. "Predictors of Positive Psychosocial Functioning of Older Adults in Residential Care Facilities." *JBehMed* 29 (2, 2006): 191–201.

Schatzmann, *Charismata.* Schatzmann, Siegfried. *A Pauline Theology of Charismata.* Peabody, Mass.: Hendrickson, 1987.

Schawlow, "Why." Schawlow, Arthur L. "One Must Ask Why and Not Just How." Pages 105–7 in *Cosmos, Bios, and Theos: Scientists Reflect on Science, God, and the Origins of the Universe, Life, and* Homo Sapiens. Edited by Henry Margenau and Roy Abraham Varghese. La Salle, Ill.: Open Court, 1992.

Scherberger, "Shaman." Scherberger, Laura. "The Janus-Faced Shaman: The Role of Laughter in Sickness and Healing among the Makushi." *AnthHum* 30 (1, 2005): 55–69.

Scherer, "Miracles de Jésus." Scherer, E. "Des miracles de Jésus Christ." *RT* 4 (1852): 141–60.

Scherrer, "Signs." Scherrer, Steven J. "Signs and Wonders in the Imperial Cult: A New Look at a Roman Religious Institution in the Light of Rev 13:13–15." *JBL* 103 (4, 1984): 599–610.

Scherzer, *Healing.* Scherzer, Carl J. *The Church and Healing.* Philadelphia: Westminster, 1950.

Schiappacasse, *Heals.* Schiappacasse, Chuck. *God Heals Today.* N.p.: Chuck Schiappacasse, 1993.

Schiefelbein, "Oil." Schiefelbein, Kyle K. "'Receive this oil as a sign of forgiveness and healing': A Brief History of the Anointing of the Sick and Its Use in Lutheran Worship." *WW* 30 (1, 2010): 51–62.

Schiff, "Shadow." Schiff, Miriam. "Living in the Shadow of Terrorism: Psychological Distress and Alcohol Use among Religious and Non-Religious Adolescents in Jerusalem." *SSMed* 62 (9, 2006): 2301–12.

Schindler, *Nervensystem.* Schindler, R. *Nervensystem und spontane Blutungen: Mit besonderer Berücksichtigung der hysterischen Ecchymosen und der Systematik der hämorrhagischen Diathesen.* Berlin: Karger, 1927.

Schipkowensky, *Feuertanz.* Schipkowensky, Nikola. *Der Feuertanz als magischer Brauch, als mystische Psychokatharsis und als Freudenspiel.* Summarized in *TranscPsycR* 15 (1963): 67–68.

Schipperges, *Hildegard.* Schipperges, Heinrich. *Hildegard of Bingen: Healing and the Nature of the Cosmos.* Translated by John A. Broadwin. Princeton, N.J.: Markus Wiener, 1997.

Schlatter, *Wunder.* Schlatter, Adolf. *Das Wunder in der Synagoge.* Gütersloh: Bertelsmann, 1912.

Schlemon, *Prayer.*   Schlemon, Barbara Leahy. *Healing Prayer.* Foreword by Francis MacNutt. Notre Dame, Ind.: Ave Maria, 1976.

Schlesinger, "Credibility."   Schlesinger, George. "The Credibility of Extraordinary Events." *Analysis* 51 (1991): 120–26.

Schlesinger, "Miracles."   Schlesinger, George. "Miracles and Probabilities." *Nous* 21 (1987): 219–32.

Schlink, *World.*   Schlink, Basilea. *The Unseen World of Angels and Demons.* Old Tappan, N.J.: Revell, 1985.

Schloz-Durr, "Exorzismus."   Schloz-Durr, Adelbert. "Der traditionelle kirchliche Exorzismus im Rituale Romanum—biblisch-systematisch Betrachtet." *EvT* 52 (1, 1992): 56–65.

Schmidt, "Bones."   Schmidt, F. W. "The Lord Heals Broken Bones." *LRE* (May 1925): 21–22.

Schmidt, *Influence.*   Schmidt, Alvin J. *Under the Influence: How Christianity Transfomed Civilization.* Foreword by Paul L. Maier. Grand Rapids: Zondervan, 2001.

Schmidt, "Influences."   Schmidt, Daryl D. "Rhetorical Influences and Genre: Luke's Preface and the Rhetoric of Hellenistic Historiography." Pages 27–60 in *Jesus and the Heritage of Israel: Luke's Narrative Claim upon Israel's Legacy.* Vol. 1 of *Luke the Interpreter of Israel.* Edited by David P. Moessner. Harrisburg, Pa.: Trinity Press International, 1999.

Schmidt, "Possession."   Schmidt, Leigh Eric. "From Demon Possession to Magic Show: Ventriloquism, Religion, and the Enlightenment." *CH* 67 (2, 1998): 274–304.

Schmidt, "Psychiatry."   Schmidt, K. E. "Folk Psychiatry in Sarawak: A Tentative System of Psychiatry of the Iban." Pages 139–55 in *Magic, Faith, and Healing: Studies in Primitive Psychiatry Today.* Edited by Ari Kiev. Foreword by Jerome D. Frank. New York: Free Press, 1964.

Schnackenburg, *John.*   Schnackenburg, Rudolf. *The Gospel According to St. John.* 3 vols. Vol. 1: Translated by Kevin Smyth. Edited by J. Massingberd Ford and Kevin Smyth. New York: Herder & Herder, 1968. Vol. 2: New York: Seabury, 1980. Vol. 3: Crossroad, 1982.

Schneider et al, "Trial."   Schneider, R. H., F. Staggers, C. Alexander, et al. "A Randomized Controlled Trial of Stress Reduction for Hypertension in Older African Americans." *Hypertension* 26 (1995): 820–29.

Schneider et al., "Year."   Schneider, R. H., C. N. Alexander, F. Staggers, et al. "A Randomized Controlled Trial of Stress Reduction in African Americans Treated for Hypertension for over One Year." *AmJHyp* 18 (1, 2005): 88–98.

Schoeneberger et al., "Abuse."   Schoeneberger, M. L., C. G. Leukefeld, M. L. Hiller, and T. Godlaski.

"Substance Abuse among Rural and Very Rural Drug Users at Treatment Entry." *AJDAA* 32 (1, 2006): 87–110.

Schoepflin, "Anesthesia."   Schoepflin, Rennie B. "That the Church Denounced Anesthesia in Childbirth on Biblical Grounds." Pages 123–30 in *Galileo Goes to Jail and Other Myths about Science and Religion.* Edited by Ronald L. Numbers. Cambridge, Mass.: Harvard University Press, 2009.

Schofer, "Cosmology."   Schofer, Jonathan Wyn. "Theology and Cosmology in Rabbinic Ethics: The Pedagogical Significance of Rainmaking Narratives." *JSQ* 12 (3, 2005): 227–59.

Scholem, *Gnosticism.*   Scholem, Gershom G. *Jewish Gnosticism, Merkabah Mysticism, and Talmudic Tradition.* New York: The Jewish Theological Seminary of America, 1965.

Scholem, *Sabbatai Sevi.*   Scholem, Gershom. *Sabbatai Sevi: The Mystical Messiah.* Princeton, N.J.: Princeton University Press, 1973.

Schottenbauer et al., "Coping Research."   Schottenbauer, Michele A., Benjamin F. Rodriguez, Carol R. Glass, and Diane B. Arnkoff. "Religious Coping Research and Contemporary Personality Theory: An Exploration of Endler's (1977) Integrative Personality Theory." *BJPsy* 97 (4, 2006): 499–519.

Schuetze, "Role."   Schuetze, Christy. "Examining the Role of Language in Healing: Comparison of Two Therapeutic Interventions for Spirit Possession." Pages 33–54 in *Health Knowledge and Belief Systems in Africa.* Edited by Toyin Falola and Matthew M. Heaton. Durham, N.C.: Carolina Academic Press, 2008.

Schulz, "Ende."   Schulz, Heiko. "Das Ende des common sense: Kritische Überlegungen zur Wunderkritik David Humes." *ZNThG* 3 (1, 1996): 1–38.

Schumaker, "Suggestibility."   Schumaker, J. F. "The Adaptive Value of Suggestibility and Dissociation." Pages 108–31 in *Human Suggestibility: Advances in Theory, Research, and Application.* Edited by J. F. Schumaker. Florence, Ky.: Taylor and Francis/ Routledge, 1991.

Schwab, "Psychosomatic Medicine."   Schwab, John J. "Psychosomatic Medicine: Its Past and Present." *Psychosomatics* 26 (7, July 1985): 583–93.

Schwartz, "Global History."   Schwartz, Nancy. "Christianity and the Construction of Global History: The Example of Legio Maria." Pages 134–74 in *Charismatic Christianity as a Global Culture.* Edited by Karla Poewe. SCR. Columbia: University of South Carolina Press, 1994.

Schwartz, "Possession."   Schwartz, Howard. "Spirit Possession in Judaism." *Parab* 19 (4, 1994): 72–76.

Schwartz et al., "Behaviors."   Schwartz, Carolyn, Janice Bell Meisenhelder, Yunsheng Ma, and George Reed.

"Altruistic Social Interest Behaviors Are Associated with Better Mental Health." *PsychMed* 65 (5, 2003): 778–85.

Schwarz, *Healing*. Schwarz, Ted. *Healing in the Name of God: Faith or Fraud?* Grand Rapids: Zondervan, 1993.

Schweitzer, *Quest*. Schweitzer, Albert. *The Quest of the Historical Jesus*. Introduction by James M. Robinson. New York: Collier Books, Macmillan, 1968.

Schweizer, *Parable*. Schweizer, Eduard. *Jesus the Parable of God: What Do We Really Know About Jesus?* PrTMS 37. Allison Park, Pa.: Pickwick, 1994.

"Science or Miracle." "Science or Miracle? Holiday Season Survey Reveals Physicians' Views of Faith, Prayer, and Miracles." Business Wire, Dec. 20, 2004. http://www.businesswire.com/portal/site/google/index.jsp?ndmViewID=news_view&news&newsID=20041220005244&newsLang=en. Accessed May 12, 2009.

Scorgie, "Weapons." Scorgie, Fiona. "Weapons of Faith in a World of Illness: Zionist Prophet-Healers and HIV/AIDS in Rural KwaZulu-Natal." Pages 83–106 in *Health Knowledge and Belief Systems in Africa*. Edited by Toyin Falola and Matthew M. Heaton. Durham, N.C.: Carolina Academic Press, 2008.

"Scotland Stirred." "Scotland Being Stirred." *PentEv* 696 (May 7, 1927): 5–6.

Scott, "Attitudes." Scott, David A. "Buddhist Attitudes to Hellenism: A Review of the Issue." *SR/SR* 15 (4, 1986): 433–41.

Scott, *Literature*. Scott, Ernest Findlay. *The Literature of the New Testament*. New York: Columbia University Press, 1936.

Scott, "Publics." Scott, J. Barton. "Miracle Publics: Theosophy, Christianity, and the Coulomb Affair." *HR* 49 (2, 2010): 172–96.

Scott, "Sect Leader." Scott, Dave. "Sect Leader, Three Others Killed in Plane Crash." *Akron Beacon Journal* (April 28, 1979): A1, 5.

Seagrave, "Cicero." Seagrave, S. Adam. "Cicero, Aquinas, and Contemporary Issues in Natural Law Theory." *RevMet* 62 (3, 2009): 491–523.

Seale, "Collaboration." Seale, J. Paul. "Christian Missionary Medicine and Traditional Healers: A Case Study in Collaboration from the Philippines." *Missiology* 21 (3, 1993): 311–20.

Sears, "View." Sears, Robert T. "A Catholic View of Exorcism and Deliverance." Pages 100–114 in *Essays on Spiritual Bondage and Deliverance*. Edited by Willard M. Swartley. Occasional Papers 11. Elkhart, Ind.: Institute of Mennonite Studies, 1988.

Sears and Wallace, "Spirituality." Sears, S. F., and R. L. Wallace. "Spirituality, Coping, and Survival." Pages 173–83 in *Biopsychosocial Perspectives on*

Transplantation. Edited by J. R. Rodrigue. New York: Kluwer Academic/Plenum, 2001.

Sebald, "Witchcraft." Sebald, Hans. "Franconian Witchcraft: The Demise of a Folk Magic." *AnthrQ* 53 (3, July 1980): 173–87.

Segal, "Few Contained Many." Segal, Eliezer. "'The Few Contained the Many': Rabbinic Perspectives on the Miraculous and the Impossible." *JJS* 54 (2, 2003): 273–82.

Segal, "Revolutionary." Segal, Alan F. "Jesus, the Jewish Revolutionary." Pages 199–225 in *Jesus' Jewishness: Exploring the Place of Jesus within Early Judaism*. Edited by James H. Charlesworth. New York: The American Interfaith Institute, Crossroad Publishing Company, 1991.

Segre, "Origin." Segre, Emilio. "The Origin of the Universe Does Not Seem to Me to Be a Scientific Question." Pages 108–10 in *Cosmos, Bios, and Theos: Scientists Reflect on Science, God, and the Origins of the Universe, Life, and* Homo Sapiens. Edited by Henry Margenau and Roy Abraham Varghese. La Salle, Ill.: Open Court, 1992.

Seibert, *Church*. Seibert, Jimmy. *The Church Can Change the World: Living from the Inside Out*. Waco, Tex.: Antioch Community Church, 2008.

Select Papyri. *Select Papyri*. Vol. 3: *Literary Papyri, Poetry*. Translated by D. L. Page. LCL. Cambridge, Mass.: Harvard University Press, 1941.

Sellers, "Zar." Sellers, Barbara. "The *Zar*: Women's Theater in the Southern Sudan." Pages 156–64 in *Women's Medicine: The Zar-Bori Cult in Africa and Beyond*. Edited by I. M. Lewis, Ahmed Al-Safi, and Sayyid Hurreiz. Edinburgh: International African Institute, Edinburgh University Press, 1991.

Selvanayagam, "Demons." Selvanayagam, Israel. "A. S. Peake Memorial Lecture: When Demons Speak the Truth! An Asian Reading of a New Testament Story of Exorcism." *EpwRev* 27 (3, 2000): 33–40.

Senior, "Swords." Senior, Donald. "'With Swords and Clubs . . .'—The Setting of Mark's Community and His Critique of Abusive Power." *BTB* 17 (1, 1987): 10–20.

Sephton et al., "Expression." Sephton, S. E., C. Koopman, M. Schaal, C. Thoreson, and D. Spiegel. "Spiritual Expression and Immune Status in Women with Metastatic Breast Cancer: An Exploratory Study." *Breast Journal* 7 (2001): 345–53.

Seybold and Mueller, *Sickness*. Seybold, Klaus, and Ulrich B. Mueller. *Sickness and Healing*. Translated by Douglas W. Stott. Nashville: Abingdon, 1981.

Shackelford, "Bruno." Shackelford, Jole. "That Giordano Bruno Was the First Martyr of Modern Science." Pages 59–67 in *Galileo Goes to Jail and Other Myths about Science and Religion*. Edited by Ronald

L. Numbers. Cambridge, Mass.: Harvard University Press, 2009.

Shakarian, *People.* Shakarian, Demos, with John and Elizabeth Sherrill. *The Happiest People on Earth.* London: Hodder and Stoughton, 1975.

Shank, "Prophet." Shank, David A. "A Prophet of Modern Times: The Thought of William Wadé Harris." 3 vols. PhD diss., University of Aberdeen, 1980.

Shank, *Prophet Harris.* Shank, David A. *Prophet Harris: The "Black Elijah" of West Africa.* Leiden: Brill, 1994.

Shank, "Suppressed." Shank, Michael H. "That the Medieval Christian Church Suppressed the Growth of Science." Pages 19–27 in *Galileo Goes to Jail and Other Myths about Science and Religion.* Edited by Ronald L. Numbers. Cambridge, Mass.: Harvard University Press, 2009.

Shao, "Heritage." Shao, Joseph Too. "Heritage of the Chinese-Filipino Protestant Churches." *JAM* 1 (1, March 1999): 93–99.

Shapere, "Structure." Shapere, Dudley. "The Structure of Scientific Revolutions." Pages 27–38 in *Paradigms and Revolutions: Appraisals and Applications of Thomas Kuhn's Philosophy of Science.* Edited by Gary Gutting. Notre Dame, Ind.: University of Notre Dame Press, 1980.

Shapiro, "History." Shapiro, Arthur K. "A Contribution to a History of the Placebo Effect." *BehSN* 5 (1960): 109–35.

Shapiro and Walsh, "Meditation." Shapiro, Shauna, and Roger Walsh. "Meditation: Exploring the Farther Reaches." Pages 57–71 in *Spirit, Science, and Health: How the Spiritual Mind Fuels Physical Wellness.* Edited by Thomas G. Plante and Carl E. Thoresen. Foreword by Albert Bandura. Westport, Conn.: Praeger, 2007.

Sharma, "History." Sharma, Bal Krishna. "A History of the Pentecostal Movement in Nepal." *AJPS* 4 (2, 2001): 295–305.

Sharp, "Miracles." Sharp, John C. "Miracles and the 'Laws of Nature.'" *SBET* 6 (1988): 1–19.

Sharp, *Possessed.* Sharp, Lesley A. *The Possessed and the Dispossessed: Spirits, Identity, and Power in a Madagascar Migrant Town.* CSHSMC. Berkeley: University of California Press, 1993.

Sharp, "Possessed." Sharp, Lesley A. "Possessed and Dispossessed Youth: Spirit Possession of School Children in Northwest Madagascar." *CMPsy* 14 (1990): 339–64.

Sharp, "Power of Possession." Sharp, Lesley A. "The Power of Possession in Northwest Madagascar: Contesting Colonial and National Hegemonies." Pages 3–19 in *Spirit Possession, Modernity and Power*

in Africa. Edited by Heike Behrend and Ute Luig. Madison: University of Wisconsin Press, 1999.

Shaub, "Analysis." Shaub, Robert William. "An Analysis of the Healing Ministries Conducted in Three Contemporary Churches." DMin thesis, Eastern Baptist Theological Seminary, 1980.

Shaull, "Reconstruction." Shaull, Richard. "The Reconstruction of Life in the Power of the Spirit." Pages 115–231 in Richard Shaull and Waldo Cesar, *Pentecostalism and the Future of the Christian Churches: Promises, Limitations, Challenges.* Grand Rapids: Eerdmans, 2000.

Shaw, "Agency." Shaw, David Gary. "Happy in Our Chains? Agency and Language in the Postmodern Age." *HistTh,* theme issue 40 (4, Dec. 2001): 1–9.

Shaw, *Awakening.* Shaw, Mark. *Global Awakening: How 20th-Century Revivals Triggered a Christian Revolution.* Downers Grove, Ill.: IVP Academic, 2010.

Shaw, *Kingdom.* Shaw, Mark. *The Kingdom of God in Africa: A Short History of African Christianity.* Grand Rapids: Baker, 1996.

Shaw, "Modernity." Shaw, David Gary. "Modernity between Us and Them: The Place of Religion within History." *HistTh,* theme issue 45 (4, Dec. 2006): 1–9.

Shearer, "Believe." Shearer, R. M. "Why I Believe in Divine Healings." *LRE* 21 (4, Dec. 1928): 5–9.

Sheils, *Healing.* Sheils, W. J., ed. *The Church and Healing: Papers Read at the Twentieth Summer Meeting and the Twenty-first Winter Meeting of the Ecclesiastical History Society.* StChHist 19. Oxford: Basil Blackwell, 1982.

Shelton, "Response." Shelton, James B. "'Not Like It Used to Be?' Jesus, Miracles, and Today." Response to Keith Warrington, "Healing Narratives." *JPT* 14 (2, 2006): 219–27.

Shemesh, "Reviving." Shemesh, Abraham Ofir. "Reviving the Children by Eliyau and Elisha: Medical Treatments or Miracles? (1 Kgs 17:8–17; 2 Kgs 4:1–8)" (in Hebrew). *BMik* 166 (2001): 248–60. (RTA)

Shenk, "Conversations." Shenk, David W. "Conversations Along the Way." Pages 1–17 in *Muslims and Christians on the Emmaus Road.* Edited by J. Dudley Woodberry. Monrovia, Calif.: MARC, 1989.

Sherman and Simonton, "Spirituality and Cancer." Sherman, Allen C., and Stephanie Simonton. "Spirituality and Cancer." Pages 157–75 in *Spirit, Science, and Health: How the Spiritual Mind Fuels Physical Wellness.* Edited by Thomas G. Plante and Carl E. Thoresen. Foreword by Albert Bandura. Westport, Conn.: Praeger, 2007.

Shermer, "Miracle." Shermer, Michael. "Miracle on Probability Street." *ScAm* 291 (2004): 32.

Sherrill, *Tongues.* Sherrill, John L. *They Speak with Other Tongues.* Old Tappan, N.J.: Revell, 1965.

Sherrill and Larson, "Anti-Tenure Factor." Sherrill, Kimberly A., and David B. Larson. "The Anti-Tenure Factor in Religious Research in Clinical Epidemiology and Aging." Pages 149–77 in *Religion in Aging and Health: Theoretical Foundations and Methodological Frontier.* Edited by Jeffrey S. Levin. Thousand Oaks, Calif.: Sage, 1994.

Shimony, "Scientific Inference." Shimony, Abner. "Scientific Inference." Pages 79–172 in *The Nature and Function of Scientific Theories: Essays in Contemporary Science and Philosophy.* Edited by Robert G. Colodny. Pittsburgh: University of Pittsburgh Press, 1970.

Shinde, "Animism." Shinde, B. P. "Animism in Popular Hinduism." DMiss diss., Fuller Theological Seminary, 1975.

Shinde, "Assemblies." Shinde, B. P. "The Assemblies of God in India." MA thesis, Fuller Theological Seminary, 1974.

Shishima, "Wholistic Nature." Shishima, D. S. "The Wholistic Nature of African Traditional Medicine: The Tiv Experience." Pages 119–26 in *Religion, Medicine and Healing.* Edited by Gbola Aderibigbe and Deji Ayegboyin. Lagos: Nigerian Association for the Study of Religions and Education, 1995.

Shogren, "Prophecy." Shogren, Gary Steven. "Christian Prophecy and Canon in the Second Century: A Response to B. B. Warfield." *JETS* 40 (4, Dec. 1997): 609–26.

Shoham-Steiner, "Healing." Shoham-Steiner, Ephraim. "Jews and Healing at Medieval Saints' Shrines: Participation, Polemics, and Shared Cultures." *HTR* 103 (1, 2010): 111–29.

Shoko, "Healing." Shoko, Tabona. "Healing in Hear the Word Ministries Pentecostal Church Zimbabwe." Pages 43–55 in *Global Pentecostalism: Encounters with Other Religious Traditions.* Edited by David Westerlund. New York: I. B. Taurus, 2009.

Shoko, *Religion.* Shoko, Tabona. *Karanga Indigenous Religion in Zimbabwe: Health and Well-Being.* VitIndRel. Foreword by James L. Cox. Burlington, Vt.: Ashgate, 2007.

Shorter, "Possession and Healing." Shorter, Aylward. "Spirit Possession and Christian Healing in Tanzania." *African Affairs* 79 (314, Jan. 1980): 45–53.

Shorter, "Spirit Possession." Shorter, Aylward. "The Migawo: Peripheral Spirit Possession and Christian Prejudice." *Anthropos* 65 (1970): 110–26.

Shorter, *Witch Doctor.* Shorter, Aylward. *Jesus and the Witch Doctor: An Approach to Healing and Wholeness.* Maryknoll, N.Y.: Orbis, 1985.

Shuler, *Genre.* Shuler, Philip L. *A Genre for the Gospels: The Biographical Character of Matthew.* Philadelphia: Fortress, 1982.

Sica et al., "Religiousness." Sica, Claudio, Caterina Novara, et al. "Religiousness and Obsessive-Compulsive Cognitions and Symptoms in an Italian Population." *BehResTher* 40 (7, 2002): 813–23.

Sider, "Historian." Sider, Ronald J. "The Historian, the Miraculous, and the Post-Newtonian Man." *SJT* 25 (1972): 309–19.

Sider, "Methodology." Sider, Ronald J. "Historical Methodology and Alleged Miracles: A Reply to Van Harvey." *FidHist* 3 (1, 1970): 22–40.

Siegel, *Medicine.* Siegel, Bernie S. *Law, Medicine & Miracles: Lessons Learned About Self-Healing from a Surgeon's Experience with Exceptional Patients.* New York: Harper & Row, 1986.

Sigal, *L'homme.* Sigal, Pierre-André. *L'homme et le miracle dans la France médiévale (XIᵉ-XIIᵉ siècles).* Paris: Cerf, 1985.

Signer, "Balance." Signer, Michael A. "Restoring the Balance: Musings on Miracles in Rabbinic Judaism." Pages 111–26 in *Miracles in Jewish and Christian Antiquity: Imagining Truth.* Edited by John C. Cavadini. NDST 3. Notre Dame, Ind.: University of Notre Dame Press, 1999.

Silberstein, "Defense." Silberstein, Michael. "In Defense of Ontological Emergence and Mental Causation." Pages 203–26 in *The Re-Emergence of Emergence: The Emergentist Hypothesis from Science to Religion.* Edited by Philip Clayton and Paul Davies. Oxford: Oxford University Press, 2006.

Silverman, "Ambiguation." Silverman, Martin G. "Ambiguation and Disambiguation in Field Work." Pages 204–29 in *Crossing Cultural Boundaries: The Anthropological Experience.* Edited by Solon T. Kimball and James B. Watson. San Francisco: Chandler, 1972.

Silvestri et al., "Importance." Silvestri, Gerard, Sommer Knittig, James Zoller, and Paul J. Nietert. "Importance of Faith on Medical Decisions Regarding Cancer Care." *JClinOn* 21 (2003): 1379–82.

Silvoso, *Perish.* Silvoso, Ed. *That None Should Perish: How to Reach Entire Cities for Christ Through Prayer Evangelism.* Foreword by C. Peter Wagner. Ventura, Calif.: Regal, 1994.

Simeon, "Datiro." Simeon, James Lomole. "Datiro, Yeremaya K." *DACB.* http://www.dacb.org/stories/sudan/datiro_yeremaya.html.

Simonton, Matthews-Simonton, and Creighton, *Getting Well.* Simonton, O. Carl, Stephanie Matthews-Simonton, and James L. Creighton. *Getting Well Again: A Step-by-Step, Self-Help Guide to Overcoming Cancer for Patients and Their Families.* Los Angeles: Jeremy P. Tarcher/St. Martin's Press, 1978.

Simpson, "Dead Raised." Simpson, W. W. "Man Pronounced Dead Raised to Life." *PentEv* 647 (May 15, 1926): 11.

Simpson, "Gospel of Healing." Simpson, A. B. "The Gospel of Healing." Pages 283–376 in *Healing: The Three Great Classics on Divine Healing*. Edited by Jonathan L. Graf. Camp Hill, Pa.: Christian Publications, 1992.

Simpson, "Utterance." Simpson, W. W. "'As the Spirit Gave Utterance.'" *PentEv* 1247 (April 2, 1938): 9.

Sindawi, "Head." Sindawi, Khalid. "The Head of Husayn Ibn 'Ali from Decapitation to Burial, Its Various Places of Burial, and the Miracles That It Performed." *ANES* 40 (2003): 245–58.

Singh, "Prophet." Singh, K. S. "The Making of a Prophet." Pages 106–14 in *Historical Anthropology*. Edited by Saurabh Dube. OIRSSA. New Delhi: Oxford University Press, 2007.

Singleton, "Spirits." Singleton, Michael. "Spirits and 'Spiritual Direction': The Pastoral Counseling of the Possessed." Pages 471–78 in *Christianity in Independent Africa*. Edited by Edward Fasholé-Luke, Richard Gray, Adrian Hastings, and Godwin Tasie. Bloomington: Indiana University Press, 1978.

Sivalon and Comoro, "Mouvement." Sivalon, John, and Christopher Comoro. "Le Mouvement pronant la guerison par la foi en Marie: changements sociaux et catholicisme populaire en Tanzanie." *SocCom* 45 (4, Dec. 1998): 575–93.

Skarsaune and Engelsviken, "Possession." Skarsaune, Oskar, and Tormed Engelsviken. "Possession and Exorcism in the History of the Church." Pages 65–87 in *Deliver Us from Evil: An Uneasy Frontier in Christian Mission*. Edited by A. Scott Moreau, Tokunboh Adeyemo, David G. Burnett, Bryant L. Myers, and Hwa Yung. Monrovia, Calif.: Lausanne Committee for World Evangelization, 2002.

Skepstad, "Call." Skepstad, John. "Call upon Me." *CGl* 15 (4, Oct. 1938): 4–5.

Skinsnes, "Healed." Skinsnes, C. C. "One of the Many Who Go Forth Healed." *CGl* 12 (1, Jan 1935): 14.

Skinsnes, "Hospital." Skinsnes, C. C. "Soth Honan Union Hospital." *CGl* 6 (4, June 1925): 30–31.

Skinsnes, "Incidents." Skinsnes, C. C. "Kioshan Hospital Incidents." *CGl* 15 (2, April 1938): 6.

Skinsnes, "Nelson." Skinsnes, C. C. "Rev. Bert Nelson." *CGl* 9 (2, April 1932): 13.

Skinsnes, "Reopening." Skinsnes, C. C. "Reopening of American Lutheran Hospital, Kioshan." *CGl* 15 (1, Jan. 1938): 2–4.

Skivington, "Strategy." Skivington, S. R. "Missiological Strategy for Mindanao." DMiss diss., Fuller Theological Seminary, 1976.

Slenczka, "Schopfung." Slenczka, Reinhard. "Schopfung und Wunder." *KD* 24 (2, 1978): 118–30.

Sluhovsky, "Apparition." Sluhovsky, Moshe. "A Divine Apparition or Demonic Possession? Female Agency and Church Authority in Demonic Possession in Sixteenth-Century France." *SixtCenJ* 27 (4, 1996): 1039–55.

Slupic, "Interpretation." Slupic, Chris. "A New Interpretation of Hume's *Of Miracles*." *RelS* 31 (4, 1995): 517–36.

Smalley, *John*. Smalley, Stephen S. *John: Evangelist and Interpreter*. Exeter: Paternoster, 1978.

Smart, *Experience*. Smart, Ninian. *The Religious Experience of Mankind*. New York: Charles Scribner's Sons, 1969.

Smart, *Philosophers*. Smart, Ninian. *Philosophers and Religious Truth*. 2nd ed. London: SCM, 1969.

Smart, *Philosophy of Religion*. Smart, Ninian. *The Philosophy of Religion*. New York: Random House, 1970.

Smedes, *Ministry*. Smedes, Louis B., ed. *Ministry and the Miraculous: A Case Study at Fuller Theological Seminary*. Foreword by David Allan Hubbard. Pasadena, Calif.: Fuller Theological Seminary, 1987.

Smith, *Animals*. Smith, Christian. *Moral, Believing Animals: Human Personhood and Culture*. Oxford: Oxford University Press, 2003.

Smith, *Autobiography*. Smith, Amanda. *An Autobiography: The Story of the Lord's Dealings with Mrs. Amanda Smith, the Colored Evangelist*. Chicago: Meyer and Brother, 1893.

Smith, "Baby." Smith, Ruthie. "Baby Restored to Life." *PentEv* (June 8, 1986): 15.

Smith, "Breakdowns." Smith, Glen. "Miraculous Breakdowns." *MounM* (May 1994): 28.

Smith, *Comparative Miracles*. Smith, Robert D. *Comparative Miracles*. St. Louis: Herder, 1965.

Smith, "Introduction." Smith, Norman Kemp. "Introduction." Pages 1–123 in *Hume's Dialogues Concerning Natural Reason*. Edited by Norman Kemp Smith. 2nd ed. New York: Thomas Nelson, 1947.

Smith, *John* (1999). Smith, D. Moody. *John*. ANTC. Nashville: Abingdon, 1999.

Smith, *John among Gospels*. Smith, D. Moody. *John among the Gospels: The Relationship in Twentieth-Century Research*. Minneapolis: Fortress, 1992.

Smith, "John and Synoptics." Smith, D. Moody. "John and the Synoptics: Some Dimensions of the Problem." *NTS* 26 (4, July 1980): 425–44.

Smith, *Magician*. Smith, Morton. *Jesus the Magician*. San Francisco: Harper & Row, 1978.

Smith, "Metaphilosophy." Smith, Quentin. "The Metaphilosophy of Naturalism." *Philo* 4 (2, Fall/Winter 2001): 195–215. Also available at http://www.philoonline.org/library/smith_4_2.htm.

Smith, "Method." Smith, Morton. "Historical Method in the Study of Religion." Pages 8–16 in *On Method in the History of Religions. HistTh* 8. Middletown, Conn.: Wesleyan University, 1968.

Smith, *Parallels.* Smith, Morton. *Tannaitic Parallels to the Gospels.* Philadelphia: Society of Biblical Literature, 1951.

Smith, *Physician.* Smith, Oswald J. *The Great Physician.* New York: Christian Alliance Publishing Company, 1927.

Smith, "Possession." Smith, James H. "Of Spirit Possession and Structural Adjustment Programs: Government Downsizing, Education and Their Enchantments in Neo-Liberal Kenya." *JRelAf* 31 (4, 2001): 427–56.

Smith, *Postmodernism.* Smith, James K. A. *Who's Afraid of Postmodernism? Taking Derrida, Lyotard, and Foucault to Church.* Grand Rapids: Baker Academic, 2006.

Smith, "Rethinking Secularization." Smith, Christian. "Introduction: Rethinking the Secularization of American Public Life." Pages 1–96 in *The Secular Revolution: Power, Interests, and Conflict in the Secularization of American Public Life.* Edited by Christian Smith. Berkeley: University of California Press, 2003.

Smith, "Secularizing Education." Smith, Christian. "Secularizing American Higher Education: The Case of Early American Sociology." Pages 97–159 in *The Secular Revolution: Power, Interests, and Conflict in the Secularization of American Public Life.* Edited by Christian Smith. Berkeley: University of California Press, 2003.

Smith, *Thinking.* Smith, James K. A. *Thinking in Tongues: Outline of a Pentecostal Philosophy.* Grand Rapids: Eerdmans, 2010.

Smith, "Tradition." Smith, Morton. "A Comparison of Early Christian and Early Rabbinic Tradition." *JBL* 82 (1963): 169–76.

Smith, "Universe." Smith, Wolfgang. "The Universe Is Ultimately to Be Explained in Terms of a Metacosmic Reality." Pages 111–18 in *Cosmos, Bios, and Theos: Scientists Reflect on Science, God, and the Origins of the Universe, Life, and* Homo Sapiens. Edited by Henry Margenau and Roy Abraham Varghese. La Salle, Ill.: Open Court, 1992.

Smith et al., "Religiousness." Smith, T. B., M. E. McCullough, et al. "Religiousness and Depression: Evidence for a Main Effect and the Moderating Influence of Stressful Life Events." *PsycBull* 129 (4, 2003): 614–36.

Smucker and Hostetler, "Case." Smucker, Mervin R., and John A. Hostetler. "The Case of Jane: Psychotherapy and Deliverance." Pages 179–91 in *Essays on Spiritual Bondage and Deliverance.* Edited by Willard M. Swartley. Occasional Papers 11. Elkhart, Ind.: Institute of Mennonite Studies, 1988.

Smythe, "Creation." Smythe, Kathleen R. "The Creation of a Catholic Fipa Society: Conversion in Nkansi District, Ufipa." Pages 129–49 in *East African Expressions of Christianity.* Edited by Thomas Spear and Isaria N. Kimambo. EAfSt. Athens: Ohio University Press; Oxford: James Currey; Dar es Salaam: Mkuki na Nyota; Nairobi: East African Educational Publishers, 1999.

Snell, "Science." Snell, George D. "I Do Not See How Science Can Shed Light on the Origins of Design." Pages 209–11 in *Cosmos, Bios, and Theos: Scientists Reflect on Science, God, and the Origins of the Universe, Life, and* Homo Sapiens. Edited by Henry Margenau and Roy Abraham Varghese. La Salle, Ill.: Open Court, 1992.

Snyder, "Gifts." Snyder, Howard A. "Spiritual Gifts." Pages 325–38 in *The Oxford Handbook of Evangelical Theology.* Edited by Gerald R. McDermott. Oxford: Oxford University Press, 2010.

Snyder, *Problem.* Snyder, Howard A. *The Problem of Wineskins: Church Structure in a Technological Age.* Downers Grove, Ill.: InterVarsity, 1975.

Snyder, *Renewal.* Snyder, Howard A. *Radical Renewal: The Problem of Wineskins Today.* Houston: Touch Publications, 1996.

Snyder, *Signs.* Snyder, Howard A. *Signs of the Spirit: How God Reshapes the Church.* Grand Rapids: Academie Books, Zondervan, 1989.

Sobel, "Evidence." Sobel, Jordan Howard. "On the Evidence of Testimony for Miracles: A Bayesian Interpretation of David Hume's Analysis." *PhilQ* 37 (1987): 166–86.

Sobel, *Logic.* Sobel, Jordan Howard. *Logic and Theism: Arguments for and against Beliefs in God.* Cambridge: Cambridge University Press, 2004.

Sobel, "Theorem." Sobel, Jordan H. "Hume's Theorem on Testimony Sufficient to Establish a Miracle." *PhilQ* 41 (1991): 229–37.

Sober, "Proposal." Sober, Elliott. "A Modest Proposal." *PhilPhenRes* 68 (2, March 2004): 487–94.

Sobrepeña, "Miracles." Sobrepeña, Victor E. "God Performed Miracles." *PentV* 2 (3, March 1965): 8, 14.

Sodowsky and Lai, "Variables." Sodowsky, Gargi Roysircar, and Edward Wai Ming Lai. "Asian Immigrant Variables and Structural Models of Cross-Cultural Distress." Pages 211–34 in *International Migration and Family Change: The Experience of U.S. Immigrants.* Edited by Alan Booth, Ann C. Crouter, and Nancy Landale. Mahwah, N.J.: Lawrence Erlbaum, 1997.

Soergel, "Legends." Soergel, Philip M. "From Legends to Lies: Protestant Attacks on Catholic Miracles in Late Reformation Germany." *FidHist* 21 (2, 1989): 21–29.

Sofowora, *Traditional Medicine.* Sofowora, Abayomi. *Medicinal Plants and Traditional Medicine in Africa.* New York: John Wiley & Sons, 1982.

Solivan, *Spirit.* Solivan, Samuel. *The Spirit, Pathos, and Liberation: Toward an Hispanic Pentecostal Theology.* JPTSup 14. Sheffield: Sheffield Academic Press, 1998.

Solomon, "Healing." Solomon, Robert. "Healing and Deliverance." Pages 361–68 in *Global Dictionary of Theology: A Resource for the Worldwide Church.* Edited by William A. Dyrness and Veli-Matti Kärkkäinen, with Juan Francisco Martinez and Simon Chan. Downers Grove, Ill.: InterVarsity, 2008.

Songer, "Possession." Songer, Harold S. "Demonic Possession and Mental Illness." *RelL* 36 (1, 1967): 119–27.

Sousa, "Women." Sousa, Alexandra O. de. "Defunct Women: Possession among the Bijagós Islanders." Pages 81–88 in *Spirit Possession, Modernity and Power in Africa.* Edited by Heike Behrend and Ute Luig. Madison: University of Wisconsin Press, 1999.

Southall, "Possession." Southall, Aidan. "Spirit Possession and Mediumship among the Alur." Pages 232–72 in *Spirit Mediumship and Society in Africa.* Edited by John Beattie and John Middleton. Foreword by Raymond Firth. New York: Africana Publishing Corporation, 1969.

Southon, *Methodism.* Southon, Arthur E. *Gold Coast Methodism.* Cape Coast: Methodist Book Depot; London: Cargate Press, 1934.

Sovik, "Experiences." Sovik, Mrs. Erik. "Kikungshan Experiences." *CGI* 9 (4, Oct. 1932): 13–14, 16–18.

Sövik, "Growing." Sövik, Erik. "Growing in Grace." *CGI* 11 (2, April 1934): 5–6.

Spahlinger, "Sueton-Studien II." Spahlinger, Lothar. "Sueton-Studien II: Der wundertätige Kaiser Vespasian (Sueton, Vesp. 7,2–3)." *Phil* 148 (2, 2004): 325–46.

Spanos, "Enactments." Spanos, Nicholas P. "Multiple Identity Enactments and Multiple Personality Disorder: A Sociocognitive Perspective." *PsycBull* 116 (1994): 143–65.

Spanos, "Hypnosis." Spanos, Nicholas P. "Hypnosis, Demonic Possession, and Multiple Personality: Strategic Enactments and Disavowals of Responsibility for Actions." Pages 96–124 in *Altered States of Consciousness and Mental Health: A Cross-Cultural Perspective.* Edited by Colleen A. Ward. CCRMS 12. Newbury Park, Calif.: Sage, 1989.

Spanos, *Identities.* Spanos, Nicholas P. *Multiple Identities and False Memories.* Washington, D.C.: American Psychological Association, 1996.

Spanos and Gottlieb, "Ergotism." Spanos, Nicholas P., and Jack Gottlieb. "Ergotism and the Salem Village Witch Trials." Pages 258–62 in *Possession and Exorcism.* Vol. 9 of *Articles on Witchcraft, Magic, and Demonology: A Twelve-Volume Anthology of Scholarly Articles.* Edited by Brian P. Levack. New York: Garland, 1992. Reprinted from *Science* 194 (1976): 1390–94.

Spanos and Gottlieb, "Possession." Spanos, Nicholas P., and Jack Gottlieb. "Demonic Possession, Mesmerism, and Hysteria: A Social Psychological Perspective on Their Historical Interrelations." Pages 263–82 in *Possession and Exorcism.* Vol. 9 of *Articles on Witchcraft, Magic, and Demonology: A Twelve-Volume Anthology of Scholarly Articles.* Edited by Brian P. Levack. New York: Garland, 1992. Reprinted from *Journal of Abnormal Psychology* 88 (1979): 527–46.

Spear, "History." Spear, Thomas. "Toward the History of African Christianity." Pages 3–24 in *East African Expressions of Christianity.* Edited by Thomas Spear and Isaria N. Kimambo. EAfSt. Athens: Ohio University Press; Oxford: James Currey; Dar es Salaam: Mkuki na Nyota; Nairobi: East African Educational Publishers, 1999.

Spear and Kimambo, "Prophecy." Spear, Thomas, and Isaria N. Kimambo. "Charismatic Prophecy and Healing." Pages 229–30 in *East African Expressions of Christianity.* Edited by Thomas Spear and Isaria N. Kimambo. EAfSt. Athens: Ohio University Press; Oxford: James Currey; Dar es Salaam: Mkuki na Nyota; Nairobi: East African Educational Publishers, 1999.

Spear and Kimambo, "Revival." Spear, Thomas, and Isaria N. Kimambo. "Protestant Revival and Popular Catholicism." Pages 245–47 in *East African Expressions of Christianity.* Edited by Thomas Spear and Isaria N. Kimambo. EAfSt. Athens: Ohio University Press; Oxford: James Currey; Dar es Salaam: Mkuki na Nyota; Nairobi: East African Educational Publishers, 1999.

Speed, *Incurables.* Speed, Teri. *The Incurables: Unlock Healing for Spirit, Mind, and Body.* Lake Mary, Fla.: Creation House, 2007.

Spencer, *Acts.* Spencer, F. Scott. *Acts.* Sheffield: Sheffield Academic Press, 1997.

Spencer, *Philip.* Spencer, F. Scott. *The Portrait of Philip in Acts: A Study of Role and Relations.* JSNTSup 67. Sheffield: Sheffield Academic Press, 1992.

Spicer, *Miracles.* Spicer, William A. *Miracles of Modern Missions.* Washington, D.C.: Review and Herald, 1926.

Spickard and Cragg, *Global History.* Spickard, Paul R., and Kevin M. Cragg. *A Global History of Christians.* Grand Rapids: Baker Academic, 2003. First published as *God's Peoples: A Social History of Christians,* 1994.

Spinks, "Growth." Spinks, Bryan D. "The Growth of Liturgy and the Church Year." Pages 601–17 in

Constantine to c. 600. Edited by Augustine Casiday and Frederick W. Norris. Vol. 2 of *The Cambridge History of Christianity.* 9 vols. Cambridge: Cambridge University Press, 2007.

"Spirit and Power." "Spirit and Power: A Ten-Country Survey of Pentecostals." Pew Forum Survey (2006). http://pewforum.org/survey/pentecostal. Accessed Jan. 4, 2009.

Spiro, *Supernaturalism.* Spiro, Melford E. *Burmese Supernaturalism.* Englewood Cliffs, N.J.: Prentice-Hall, 1967.

Spiro, "Systems." Spiro, Melford E. "Religious Systems as Culturally Conditioned Defense Mechanisms." Pages 100–113 in *Culture and Meaning in Cultural Anthropology: In Honor of A. Irving Hallowell.* Edited by Melford E. Spiro. New York: Free Press; London: Collier-Macmillan, 1965.

Spittler, "Review." Spittler, Russell P. "Are Pentecostals and Charismatics Fundamentalists? A Review of American Uses of These Categories." Pages 103–16 in *Charismatic Christianity as a Global Culture.* Edited by Karla Poewe. SCR. Columbia: University of South Carolina Press, 1994.

Spitzer, *Proofs.* Spitzer, Robert J. *New Proofs for the Existence of God: Contributions of Contemporary Physics and Philosophy.* Grand Rapids: Eerdmans, 2010.

Spraggett, *Kuhlman.* Spraggett, Allen. *Kathryn Kuhlman: The Woman Who Believes in Miracles.* Cleveland: World, 1970.

Spruth, "Mission." Spruth, Erwin L. "The Mission of God in the Wabag Area of New Guinea." MA thesis, Fuller Theological Seminary, 1970.

Spurgeon, *Autobiography.* Spurgeon, Charles H. *The Autobiography of Charles H. Spurgeon.* 4 vols. London: Curts & Jennings, 1899.

Spurr, "Miracles." Spurr, Frederic C. "The Miracles of Christ, and Their Modern Denial." *RevExp* 27 (3, July 1930): 324–34.

Squires, *Plan.* Squires, John T. *The Plan of God in Luke-Acts.* SNTSMS 76. Cambridge: Cambridge University Press, 1993.

Stabell, "Modernity." Stabell, Timothy D. "'The Modernity of Witchcraft' and the Gospel in Africa." *Missiology* 38 (4, Oct. 2010): 460–74.

Stacey, "Practice." Stacey, Vivienne. "The Practice of Exorcism and Healing." Pages 291–303 in *Muslims and Christians on the Emmaus Road.* Edited by J. Dudley Woodberry. Monrovia, Calif.: MARC, 1989.

Stackhouse, "Foreword." Stackhouse, Ian. "Foreword." Pages xv–xvi in *Exorcism and Deliverance Ministry in the Twentieth Century: An Analysis of the Practice and Theology of Exorcism in Modern Western Christianity,* by James M. Collins. Studies in Evangelical History and Thought. Colorado Springs: Paternoster, 2009.

Stadtner, "Review." Stadtner, Donald M. Review of Jan Van Alphen and Anthony Aris, eds., *Oriental Medicine: An Illustrated Guide to the Asian Arts of Healing. Asian Affairs* 29 (1, Feb. 1998): 73–74.

Stagg, *Acts.* Stagg, Frank. *The Book of Acts: The Early Struggle for an Unhindered Gospel.* Nashville: Broadman, 1955.

Stambaugh and Balch, *Environment.* Stambaugh, John E., and David L. Balch. *The New Testament in Its Social Environment.* LEC 2. Philadelphia: Westminster, 1986.

Stange, "Configurations." Stange, Paul D. "Configurations of Javanese Possession Experience." *RelT* 2 (2, Oct. 1979): 39–54.

Stanley, "Christianity." Stanley, Brian. "Twentieth-Century World Christianity: A Perspective from the History of Missions." Pages 52–83 in *Christianity Reborn: The Global Expansion of Evangelicalism in the Twentieth Century.* Edited by Donald M. Lewis. SHCM. Grand Rapids: Eerdmans, 2004.

Stanley, "Einstein." Stanley, Matthew. "That Einstein Believed in a Personal God." Pages 187–95 in *Galileo Goes to Jail and Other Myths about Science and Religion.* Edited by Ronald L. Numbers. Cambridge, Mass.: Harvard University Press, 2009.

Stanley, "Types." Stanley, Ruth. "Types of Prayer, Heart Rate Variability, and Innate Healing." *Zyg* 44 (4, 2009): 825–46.

Stannard, "Purpose." Stannard, Russell. "God's Purpose in and Beyond Time." Pages 33–43 in *Evidence of Purpose: Scientists Discover the Creator.* Edited by John Marks Templeton. New York: Continuum, 1994.

Stanton, *Gospels.* Stanton, Graham N. *The Gospels and Jesus.* OxBS. Oxford: Oxford University Press, 1989.

Stanton, *Gospel Truth.* Stanton, Graham N. *Gospel Truth? New Light on Jesus and the Gospels.* Valley Forge, Pa.: Trinity Press International, 1995.

Stanton, *Jesus of Nazareth.* Stanton, Graham N. *Jesus of Nazareth in New Testament Preaching.* Cambridge: Cambridge University Press, 1974.

Stanton, "Magician." Stanton, Graham N. "Jesus of Nazareth: A Magician and a False Prophet Who Deceived God's People?" Pages 164–80 in *Jesus of Nazareth: Lord and Christ. Essays on the Historical Jesus and New Testament Christology.* Edited by Joel B. Green and Max Turner. Grand Rapids: Eerdmans, 1994.

Stanton, "Message and Miracles." Stanton, Graham N. "Message and Miracles." Pages 56–71 in *The Cambridge Companion to Jesus.* Edited by Markus Bockmuehl. Cambridge: Cambridge University Press, 2001.

Stanton, *New People*. Stanton, Graham N. *A Gospel for a New People: Studies in Matthew*. Louisville: Westminster John Knox, 1993.

Stark, *Believe*. Stark, Rodney. *What Americans Really Believe*. Waco: Baylor University Press, 2008.

Stauffer, *Jesus*. Stauffer, Ethelbert. *Jesus and His Story*. Translated by Richard Winston and Clara Winston. New York: Alfred A. Knopf, 1960.

Stearns, *Vision*. Stearns, Bill, and Amy Stearns. *2020 Vision*. Minneapolis: Bethany House, 2005.

Stedman, *Life*. Stedman, Ray C. *Body Life*. Rev. James D. Denney. Grand Rapids: Discovery House, 1995.

Steele, *Plundering*. Steele, Ron. *Plundering Hell: The Reinhard Bonnke Story*. London: Pickering, 1984.

Steffen and Hinderliter, "Coping." Steffen, P. R., and A. L. Hinderliter. "Religious Coping, Ethnicity, and Ambulatory Blood Pressure." *PsychMed* 63 (4, 2001): 523–30.

Stegeman, "Faith." Stegeman, John. "A Woman's Faith." Pages 35–37 in *Faith Healing: Finger of God? Or, Scientific Curiosity?* Compiled by Claude A. Frazier. New York: Thomas Nelson, 1973.

Stegmüller, "Theory Change." Stegmüller, Wolfgang. "Accidental ('Non-Substantial') Theory Change and Theory Dislodgment." Pages 75–93 in *Paradigms and Revolutions: Appraisals and Applications of Thomas Kuhn's Philosophy of Science*. Edited by Gary Gutting. Notre Dame, Ind.: University of Notre Dame Press, 1980.

Stehly, "Upanishads." Stehly, Ralph. "Une citation des Upanishads dans Joseph et Aséneth." *RHPR* 55 (2, 1975): 209–13.

Steil, "Ears." Steil, Harry. "Deaf Ears Unstopped, Blind Eyes Opened." *PentEv* 1254 (May 21, 1938): 8–9.

Stein, "Criteria." Stein, Robert H. "The 'Criteria' for Authenticity." Pages 225–63 in vol. 1 of *GosPersp*.

Stein, *Messiah*. Stein, Robert H. *Jesus the Messiah: A Survey of the Life of Christ*. Downers Grove, Ill.: InterVarsity, 1996.

Stein, *Method and Message*. Stein, Robert H. *The Method and Message of Jesus' Teachings*. Philadelphia: Westminster, 1978.

Steinhauser et al., "Factors." Steinhauser, Karen E., Nicholas A. Christakis, Elizabeth C. Clipp, et al. "Factors Considered Important at the End of Life by Patients, Family, Physicians, and Other Care Providers." *JAMA* 284 (2000): 2476–82.

Steinhauser et al., "Peace." Steinhauser, Karen E., et al. "'Are You at Peace?': One Item to Probe Spiritual Concerns at the End of Life." *ArchIntMed* 166 (1, 2006): 101–5.

Steinmetz, "Wunder." Steinmetz, F.-J. "'Sie sahen die Wunder, die er tat' (Apg 8,6). Ereignis und Bedeutung religiöser Krafttaten in unserer Zeit." *GeistLeb* 46 (2, 1973): 99–114.

Stephanou, "Exorcisms." Stephanou, Eusebius A., trans. "Exorcisms or Prayers of Deliverance for General Use." Pages 57–72 in *Exorcism Through the Ages*. Edited by St. Elmo Nauman. New York: Philosophical Library, 1974.

Stephen, "Church." Stephen, Anil. "The Church at the Top of the World." *CT* (April 3, 2000): 56–59.

Stephens, "Destroyers." Stephens, Mark B. "Destroying the Destroyers of the Earth: The Meaning and Function of New Creation in the Book of Revelation." PhD diss., Department of Ancient History, Macquarie University, Sydney, Australia, April 2009.

Stephens, *Family*. Stephens, William N. *The Family in Cross-Cultural Perspective*. New York: Holt, Rinehart & Winston, 1963.

Stephens, *Healeth*. Stephens, Michael S. *Who Healeth All Thy Diseases: Health, Healing, and Holiness in the Church of God Reformation Movement*. ATSSW CRMPCS 1. Lanham, Md.: Scarecrow, 2008.

Sterling, *Ancestral Philosophy*. Sterling, Gregory E., ed. *The Ancestral Philosophy: Hellenistic Philosophy in Second Temple Judaism; Essays of David Winston*. BJS 331. SPhilMon 4. Providence: Brown University Press, 2001.

Sterling, *Sisters*. Sterling, Dorothy, ed. *We Are Your Sisters: Black Women in the Nineteenth Century*. New York: W. W. Norton & Company, 1984.

Sterling, "Universalizing the Particular." Sterling, Gregory E. "Universalizing the Particular: Natural Law in Second Temple Jewish Ethics." *SPhilA* 15 (2003): 64–80.

Stern, *Authors*. Stern, Menahem. *Greek and Latin Authors on Jews and Judaism: Edited with Introductions, Translations and Commentary*. Vol. 1: *From Herodotus to Plutarch*. Jerusalem: The Israel Academy of Sciences and Humanities, 1974. Vol. 2: *From Tacitus to Simplicius*. Jerusalem: The Israel Academy of Sciences and Humanities, 1980. Vol. 3: *Appendixes and Indexes*. Jerusalem: The Israel Academy of Sciences and Humanities, 1984.

Sternbach and Tusky, "Differences." Sternbach, R. A., and B. Tursky. "Ethnic Differences among Housewives in Psychophysical and Skin Potential Responses to Electric Shock." *Psychophysiology* 1 (1965): 241–46.

Stetz, "Blanket." Stetz, John. "The Blanket That Breathed." *MounM* (June 1995): 12–13.

Stewart, "Emphasis." Stewart, James S. "On a Neglected Emphasis in New Testament Theology." *SJT* 4 (1951): 292–301.

Stewart, "Firewagon." Stewart, David. "'Pentecostal Firewagon': Rescued by Angels?" *MounM* (Nov. 1992): 26–27.

Stewart, "Guardian Angel." Stewart, Lois. "Rice Straw and a Guardian Angel." *MounM* (March 1995): 12–13.

Stewart, *Only Believe.* Stewart, Don. *Only Believe: An Eyewitness Account of the Great Healing Revivals of the Twentieth Century.* Shippensburg, Pa.: Revival Press, Destiny Image, 1999.

Steyne, *Gods of Power.* Steyne, Philip M. *Gods of Power: A Study of the Beliefs and Practices of Animists.* Houston: Touch Publications, 1990.

Stibbe, *Prophetic Evangelism.* Stibbe, Mark. *Prophetic Evangelism: When God Speaks to Those Who Don't Know Him.* Milton Keynes: Authentic Media, 2004.

Stieglitz, "Records." Stieglitz, Robert R. "Ancient Records and the Exodus Plagues." *BAR* 13 (6, 1987): 46–49.

Stinton, *Jesus of Africa.* Stinton, Diane B. *Jesus of Africa: Voices of Contemporary African Christology.* Maryknoll, N.Y.: Orbis, 2004.

Stipp, "Vier Gestalten." Stipp, Hermann-Josef. "Vier Gestalten einer Totenerweckungserzählung (1 Kön 17,17–24; 2 Kön 4,8–37; Apg 9,36–42; Apg 20,7–12)." *Bib* 80 (1, 1999): 43–77.

Stirrat, "Possession." Stirrat, Richard L. "Demonic Possession In Roman Catholic Sri Lanka." *JAnthRes* 33 (1977): 122–57.

Stirrat, "Shrines." Stirrat, R. L. "Shrines, Pilgrimage, and Miraculous Powers in Roman Catholic Sri Lanka." Pages 385–413 in *The Church and Healing: Papers Read at the Twentieth Summer Meeting and the Twenty-first Winter Meeting of the Ecclesiastical History Society.* StChHist 19. Edited by W. J. Sheils. Oxford: Basil Blackwell, 1982.

Stock, "People Movements." Stock, F. E. "People Movements in the Punjab." MA thesis, Fuller Theological Seminary, 1974.

Stoeger, "Origin." Stoeger, William. "The Origin of the Universe in Science and Religion." Pages 254–69 in *Cosmos, Bios, and Theos: Scientists Reflect on Science, God, and the Origins of the Universe, Life, and Homo Sapiens.* Edited by Henry Margenau and Roy Abraham Varghese. La Salle, Ill.: Open Court, 1992.

Stoller, "Change." Stoller, Paul. "Stressing Social Change and Songhay Possession." Pages 267–84 in *Altered States of Consciousness and Mental Health: A Cross-Cultural Perspective.* Edited by Colleen A. Ward. CCRMS 12. Newbury Park, Calif.: Sage, 1989.

Stoller, "Eye." Stoller, Paul. "Eye, Mind, and Word in Anthropology." *L'Homme* 24 (3–4, 1984): 91–114.

Stoller and Olkes, *Shadow.* Stoller, Paul, and Cheryl Olkes. *In Sorcery's Shadow: A Memoir of*

Apprenticeship among the Songhay of Niger. Chicago: University of Chicago Press, 1987.

"Storm." "The Storm That Scared the U.S." *U.S. News & World Report* (Oct. 7, 1985): 11–12.

Stormont, *Wigglesworth.* Stormont, George. *Wigglesworth: A Man Who Walked with God. A Friend's Eyewitness Account.* Duluth, Minn.: Duluth Gospel Tabernacle, 1989.

Storms, *Convergence.* Storms, Sam. *Convergence: Spiritual Journeys of a Charismatic Calvinist.* Kansas City, Mo.: Enjoying God Ministries, 2005.

Storms, *Guide.* Storms, Sam. *The Beginner's Guide to Spiritual Gifts.* Ventura, Calif.: Regal, 2002.

Storms, *Healing.* Storms, C. Samuel. *Healing and Holiness: A Biblical Response to the Faith-Healing Phenomenon.* Phillipsburg, N.J.: Presbyterian and Reformed, 1990.

Storms, "View." Storms, Sam. "A Third Wave View." Pages 175–223 in *Are Miraculous Gifts for Today? Four Views.* Edited by Wayne A. Grudem. Grand Rapids: Zondervan, 1996.

Stout, *Dramatist.* Stout, Harry S. *The Divine Dramatist: George Whitefield and the Rise of Modern Evangelicalism.* LRB. Grand Rapids: Eerdmans, 1991.

Stowers, *Rereading of Romans.* Stowers, Stanley K. *A Rereading of Romans: Justice, Jews, and Gentiles.* New Haven: Yale University Press, 1994.

Strack, *Introduction.* Strack, Hermann L. *Introduction to the Talmud and Midrash.* New York: Atheneum, 1969.

Straight, *Miracles.* Straight, Bilinda. *Miracles and Extraordinary Experience in Northern Kenya.* Contemporary Ethnography. Philadelphia: University of Pennsylvania Press, 2007.

Strang, "Hinn." Strang, Stephen. "Benny Hinn Speaks Out." *Charisma* (Aug. 1993): 26–28.

Straton, *Healing.* Straton, John Roach. *Divine Healing in Scripture and Life.* New York: Christian Alliance Publishing House, 1927.

Stratton, "Imagining Power." Stratton, Kimberly. "Imagining Power: Magic, Miracle, and the Social Context of Rabbinic Self-Representation." *JAAR* 73 (2, 2005): 361–93.

Strawbridge et al., "Attendance." Strawbridge, W. J., S. J. Shema, et al. "Religious Attendance Increases Survival by Improving and Maintaining Good Health Behaviors, Mental Health, and Social Relationships." *AnnBehMed* 23 (1, 2001): 68–74.

Strawbridge et al., "Strength." Strawbridge, W. J., R. D. Cohen, et al. "Comparative Strength of Association between Religious Attendance and Survival." *IntJPsyMed* 30 (4, 2000): 299–308.

Streeter and Appasamy, *Message.* Streeter, B. H., and A. J. Appasamy. *The Message of Sadhu Sundar Singh:*

A Study in Mysticism on Practical Religion. New York: Macmillan, 1921.

Strelan, *Strange Acts.* Strelan, Rick. *Strange Acts: Studies in the Cultural World of the Acts of the Apostles.* BZNW 126. Berlin: Walter de Gruyter, 2004.

Strijdom, "Hallucinating." Strijdom, Johan. "A Historical Jesus Hallucinating During His Initial Spirit-Possession Experience: A Response to Stevan Davies' Interpretation of Jesus' Baptism by John." *HvTS* 54 (3, 1998): 588–602.

Strothers, "Objects." Strothers, R. "Unidentified Flying Objects in Classical Antiquity." *CJ* 103 (1, 2007): 79–92.

Stroumsa, "Testimony." Stroumsa, Guy G. "Comments on Charles Hedrick's Article: A Testimony." *JECS* 11 (2, Summer 2003): 147–53.

Stuckenbruck, "Angels of Nations." Stuckenbruck, Loren T. "Angels of the Nations." Pages 29–31 in *DNTB.*

Stump, "Prayer." Stump, Eleonore. "Petitionary Prayer." Pages 153–88 in *Miracles.* Edited by Richard Swinburne. New York: Macmillan; London: Collier Macmillan, 1989.

Stump and Kretzmann, "Being." Stump, Eleonore, and Norman Kretzmann. "Being and Goodness." Pages 281–312 in *Divine and Human Action: Essays in the Metaphysics of Theism.* Edited by Thomas V. Morris. Ithaca, N.Y.: Cornell University Press, 1988.

Stunt, "Trying Spirits." Stunt, Timothy C. F. "Trying the Spirits: Irvingite Signs and the Test of Doctrine." Pages 400–409 in *Signs, Wonders, Miracles: Representations of Divine Power in the Life of the Church. Papers Read at the 2003 Summer Meeting and the 2004 Winter Meeting of the Ecclesiastical History Society.* Edited by Kate Cooper and Jeremy Gregory. Rochester: Boydell & Brewer, for the Ecclesiastical History Society, 2005.

Sturch, "Probability." Sturch, R. L. "God and Probability." *RelS* 8 (1972): 351–54.

Suedfeld and Geiger, "Presence." Suedfeld, Peter, and John Geiger. "The Sensed Presence as a Coping Resource in Extreme Environments." Pages 1–15 in *Parapsychological Perspectives.* Vol. 3 of *Miracles: God, Science, and Psychology in the Paranormal.* Edited by J. Harold Ellens. Westport, Conn.; London: Praeger, 2008.

Suico, "Pentecostalism." Suico, Joseph. "Pentecostalism in the Philippines." Pages 345–62 in *Asian and Pentecostal: The Charismatic Face of Christianity in Asia.* Edited by Allan Anderson and Edmond Tang. Foreword by Cecil M. Robeck. Regnum Studies in Mission, AJPSS 3. Oxford: Regnum; Baguio City, Philippines: APTS Press, 2005.

Sullivan, "Foreword." Sullivan, Francis A. "Foreword." Pages vii–ix in *Miracles Do Happen,* by Briege

McKenna, with Henry Libersat. New York: St. Martin's Press, 1987.

Sullivan, "Healed." Sullivan, Beulah. "Stomach and Liver Healed by the Lord." *WWit* 9 (6, June 20, 1913): 7.

Sulmasy, "Issues." Sulmasy, Daniel P. "Spiritual Issues in the Care of Dying Patients: '... It's Okay between Me and God.'" *JAMA* 296 (2006): 1385–92.

Sumrall, *Story.* Sumrall, Lester, in collaboration with Mariano B. Lara and Ruben Candelaria. *The True Story of Clarita Villanueva: A Seventeen-Year-Old Girl Bitten by Devils in Bilibid Prison, Manila, Philippines.* Manila: Lester Sumrall; South Bend, Ind.: Calvary Book Store, 1955.

Sundkler, *Bara Bukoba.* Sundkler, Bengt. *Bara Bukoba: Church and Community in Tanzania.* London: C. Hurst, 1980.

Sundkler, "Worship." Sundkler, Bengt. "Worship and Spirituality." Pages 545–53 in *Christianity in Independent Africa.* Edited by Edward Fasholé-Luke, Richard Gray, Adrian Hastings, and Godwin Tasie. Bloomington: Indiana University Press, 1978.

Sundkler, *Zulu Zion.* Sundkler, Bengt. *Zulu Zion and Some Swazi Prophets.* London: Oxford University Press, 1976.

Sung, *Diaries.* Sung, John (Song, Shang-chieh). *The Diaries of John Sung: An Autbiography.* Translated by Stephen L. Sheng. Brighton, Mich.: Luke H. Sheng, Stephen L. Sheng, 1995.

Surgy, *L'Église.* Surgy, Albert de. *L'Église du Christianisme Céleste: un exemple d'Église prophétique au Bénin.* Paris: Karthala, 2001.

Swanson, "Trance." Swanson, G. E. "Trance and Possession: Studies of Charismatic Influence." *RRelRes* 19 (3, 1978): 253–78.

Swarz, "Changed." Swarz, Lise. "Being Changed by Cross-Cultural Encounters." Pages 209–36 in *Being Changed: The Anthropology of Extraordinary Experience.* Edited by David E. Young and Jean-Guy Goulet. Peterborough, Ont.: Broadview, 1994.

Sweeney, *Story.* Sweeney, Douglas A. *The American Evangelical Story: A History of the Movement.* Grand Rapids: Baker Academic, 2005.

Sweet, *Health.* Sweet, Leonard I. *Health and Medicine in the Evangelical Tradition: "Not By Might Nor Power."* Valley Forge, Pa.: Trinity Press International, 1994.

Swieson, *Angels.* Swieson, Eddy. *Why the Angels Laughed.* Winchester, Va.: Golden Morning, 2010.

Swinburne, "Evidence." Swinburne, Richard. "Evidence for the Resurrection." Pages 191–212 in *The Resurrection: An Interdisciplinary Symposium on the Resurrection of Jesus.* Edited by Stephen T. Davis,

Daniel Kendall, and Gerald O'Collins. Oxford: Oxford University Press, 1997.

Swinburne, *Existence*. Swinburne, Richard. *The Existence of God*. 2nd ed. New York: Oxford University Press, 2004.

Swinburne, "Historical Evidence." Swinburne, Richard. "Historical Evidence." Pages 133–51 in *Miracles*. Edited by Richard Swinburne. New York: Macmillan, 1989.

Swinburne, "Introduction." Swinburne, Richard. "Introduction." Pages 1–17 in *Miracles*. Edited by Richard Swinburne. New York: Macmillan, 1989.

Swinburne, *Miracle*. Swinburne, Richard. *The Concept of Miracle*. NSPR. London: Macmillan, 1970.

Swinburne, "Violation." Swinburne, Richard. "Violation of a Law of Nature." Pages 75–84 in *Miracles*. Edited by Richard Swinburne. New York: Macmillan, 1989.

Synan, "Charismatics." Synan, Vinson. "The 'Charismatics': Renewal in Major Protestant Denominations." Pages 177–208 in *The Century of the Holy Spirit: One Hundred Years of Pentecostal and Charismatic Renewal, 1901–2001*. Edited by Vinson Synan. Nashville: Thomas Nelson, 2001.

Synan, "Churches." Synan, Vinson. "The Holiness Pentecostal Churches." Pages 97–122 in *The Century of the Holy Spirit: One Hundred Years of Pentecostal and Charismatic Renewal, 1901–2001*. Edited by Vinson Synan. Nashville: Thomas Nelson, 2001.

Synan, "Foreword." Synan, Vinson. "Foreword." Pages 11–12 in Matthew W. Tallman, *Demos Shakarian: The Life, Legacy, and Vision of a Full Gospel Business Man*. ATSSWCRMPCS 2. Lexington, Ky.: Emeth, 2010.

Synan, *Grow*. Synan, Vinson. *The Spirit Said "Grow": The Astounding Worldwide Expansion of Pentecostal and Charismatic Churches*. Foreword by C. Peter Wagner. Innovations in Missions. Monrovia, Calif.: MARC (World Vision), 1992.

Synan, "Healer." Synan, Vinson. "A Healer in the House? A Historical Perspective on Healing in the Pentecostal/Charismatic Tradition." *AJPS* 3 (2, July 2000): 189–201.

Synan, "Legacies." Synan, Vinson. "The Lasting Legacies of the Azusa Street Revival." *Enr* 11 (2, Spring 2006): 142–52.

Synan, *Movement*. Synan, Vinson. *The Holiness-Pentecostal Movement in the United States*. Grand Rapids: Eerdmans, 1971.

Synan, "Renewal." Synan, Vinson. "Charismatic Renewal Enters the Mainline Churches." Pages 149–76 in *The Century of the Holy Spirit: One Hundred Years of Pentecostal and Charismatic Renewal, 1901–2001*. Edited by Vinson Synan. Nashville: Thomas Nelson, 2001.

Synan, "Revivals." Synan, Vinson. "Pentecostal Revivals." Pages 325–31 in vol. 1 of *Encyclopedia of Religious Revivals in America*. Edited by Michael McClymond. 2 vols. Westport, Conn: Greenwood, 2007.

Synan, "Seymour." Synan, Vinson. "Seymour, William Joseph." Pages 778–81 in *Dictionary of Pentecostal and Charismatic Movements*. Edited by Stanley M. Burgess, Gary B. McGee, and Patrick H. Alexander. Grand Rapids: Zondervan, 1988.

Synan, "Streams." Synan, Vinson. "Streams of Renewal at the End of the Century." Pages 349–80 in *The Century of the Holy Spirit: One Hundred Years of Pentecostal and Charismatic Renewal, 1901–2001*. Edited by Vinson Synan. Nashville: Thomas Nelson, 2001.

Synan, *Tradition*. Synan, Vinson. *The Holiness-Pentecostal Tradition: Charismatic Movements in the Twentieth Century*. Grand Rapids: Eerdmans, 1997.

Synan, *Voices*. Synan, Vinson. *Voices of Pentecost: Testimonies of Lives Touched by the Holy Spirit*. Ann Arbor, Mich.: Servant, 2003.

Syrdal, "Brigade." Syrdal, Rolf A. "The Bicycle Brigade." *CGl* 9 (4, Oct. 1932): 11.

Syrdal, "Byways." Syrdal, Rolf A. "Along Highways and Byways." *CGl* 10 (1, Jan. 1933): 11–12.

Syrdal, "Courses." Syrdal, Rolf A. "Bible Courses for Workers." *CGl* 10 (1, Jan. 1933): 4–5.

Syrdal, *Disciples*. Syrdal, Rolf A. *Go, Make Disciples*. Minneapolis: Augsburg, 1977.

Syrdal, "Editorial." Syrdal, Rolf A. "Editorial: 'And He Was Not, For God Took Him.'" *CGl* 10 (2, April 1933): 1–2.

Syrdal, "Editorial 2." Syrdal, Rolf A. "Editorial." *CGl* 12 (2, April 1935): 1.

Syrdal, "Editorial 3." Syrdal, Rolf A. "Editorial." *CGl* 12 (3, July 1935): 1.

Syrdal, *End*. Syrdal, Rolf A. *To the End of the Earth: Mission Concept in Principle and Practice*. Minneapolis: Augsburg, 1967.

Syrdal, "Gods." Syrdal, Rolf A. "Chinese Gods of the Home." *CGl* 12 (2, April 1935): 10–13.

Syrdal, "Graduation." Syrdal, Rolf A. "Graduation at the Bible School." *CGl* 10 (3, July 1933): 8–10.

Syrdal, "Highways." Syrdal, Rolf A. "Along Highways and Byways." *CGl* 9 (4, Oct. 1932): 8–9.

Syrdal, "Mission Work." Syrdal, Rolf A. "American Lutheran Mission Work in China." 2 vols. PhD diss., Drew Theological Seminary of Drew University, 1942.

Syrdal, "Seldom." Syrdal, Rolf A. "But You Come So Seldom." *CGl* 11 (3, July 1934): 19–20.

Syrdal, "Taipingtien." Syrdal, Rolf A. "Taipingtien, Hupeh." *CGl* 9 (2, April 1932): 7–8.

Syrdal, "Transcript." Syrdal, Rolf A. "Midwest China Oral History and Archives Project." A typed transcript of tape-recorded interviews. Midwest China Oral History and Archives Collection. St. Paul, Minn., 1976.

Szabo, "Healings." Szabo, Mary. "Divine Healings in Hungary." *PentEv* 1814 (Feb. 12, 1949): 7.

Szaflarski et al., "Modeling." Szaflarski, Magdalena, et al. "Modeling the Effects of Spirituality/Religion on Patients' Perceptions of Living with HIV/AIDS." *JGenIntMed* 21 (suppl. 5, 2006): S28–38.

Szentágothai, "Existence." Szentágothai, János. "The Existence of Some Creative Impulse at the Very Beginning." Pages 214–17 in *Cosmos, Bios, and Theos: Scientists Reflect on Science, God, and the Origins of the Universe, Life, and Homo Sapiens.* Edited by Henry Margenau and Roy Abraham Varghese. La Salle, Ill.: Open Court, 1992.

Taft, "Crash." Taft, Adon. "Guatemala Air Crash Kills Miami Preacher Who Led 'Body' Cult." *Miami Herald* (April 28, 1979): 4–A.

Taft, "Followers." Taft, Adon. "Four Thousand Followers of Brother Fife Get Ready for the 'End Days.'" *Miami Herald* (March 24, 1975): A1, 16.

Tajkumar, "Reading." Tajkumar, Peniel J. Rufus. "A Dalithos Reading of a Markan Exorcism." *ExpT* 118 (9, 2007): 428–35.

Talamantez, "Teaching." Talamantez, Inés M. "Teaching Native American Religious Traditions and Healing." Pages 113–26 in *Teaching Religion and Healing.* Edited by Linda L. Barnes and Inés Talamantez. AARTRSS. Oxford: Oxford University Press, 2006.

Talbert, *Acts.* Talbert, C. H. *Reading Acts: A Literary and Theological Commentary on the Acts of the Apostles.* Rev. ed. Macon, Ga.: Smyth & Helwys, 2005.

Talbert, *Gospel.* Talbert, C. H. *What Is a Gospel? The Genre of the Canonical Gospels.* Philadelphia: Fortress, 1977.

Talbert, *John.* Talbert, C. H. *Reading John: A Literary and Theological Commentary on the Fourth Gospel and the Johannine Epistles.* New York: Crossroad, 1992.

Talbert, *Matthew.* Talbert, Charles H. *Matthew.* Paideia Commentaries on the New Testament. Grand Rapids: Baker Academic, 2010.

Talbert, *Mediterranean Milieu.* Talbert, C. H. *Reading Luke-Acts in Its Mediterranean Milieu.* NovTSup 107. Leiden: Brill, 2003.

Talbot, *Healing in Byzantium.* Talbot, Alice-Mary M. *Faith Healing in Late Byzantium: The Posthumous Miracles of the Patriarch Athanasios I of Constantinople by Theoktistos the Stoudite.* AILEHS 8. Brookline, Mass.: Hellenic College Press, 1983.

Talbot, "Vision." Talbot, Susan Gabriel. "Dream/Vision: A Language of the Soul." Pages 274–82 in *Revival, Renewal, and the Holy Spirit.* Edited by Dyfed Wyn Roberts. SEHT. Eugene, Ore.: Wipf & Stock, 2009.

Taliaferro, "Argument." Taliaferro, Charles. "Cumulative Argument, Sustaining Causes, and Miracles." *PhilChr* 8 (2, 2006): 219–26.

Taliaferro and Hendrickson, "Racism." Taliaferro, Charles, and Anders Hendrickson. "Hume's Racism and His Case against the Miraculous." *PhilChr* 4 (2, 2002): 427–41.

Tallman, *Shakarian.* Tallman, Matthew W. *Demos Shakarian: The Life, Legacy, and Vision of a Full Gospel Business Man.* ATSSWCRMPCS 2. Lexington, Ky.: Emeth, 2010.

Tan, "Work." Tan, David. "The Secret Work of the Holy Spirit in China Through Madame Guyon." *JAM* 4 (1, March 2002): 97–110.

Tan, *Zion Traditions.* Tan, Kim Huat. *The Zion Traditions and the Aims of Jesus.* SNTSMS 91. Cambridge: Cambridge University Press, 1997.

Tan-Chow, *Theology.* Tan-Chow, May Ling. *Pentecostal Theology for the Twenty-First Century: Engaging with Multi-Faith Singapore.* ANCTRTBS. Burlington, Vt.: Ashgate, 2007.

Tang, "Healers." Tang, Edmond. "'Yellers' and Healers—Pentecostalism and the Study of Grassroots Christianity in China." Pages 467–86 in *Asian and Pentecostal: The Charismatic Face of Christianity in Asia.* Edited by Allan Anderson and Edmond Tang. Foreword by Cecil M. Robeck. Regnum Studies in Mission, AJPSS 3. Oxford: Regnum; Baguio City, Philippines: APTS Press, 2005.

Tanner, "Theory." Tanner, R. E. S. "The Theory and Practice of Sukuma Spirit Mediumship." Pages 273–89 in *Spirit Mediumship and Society in Africa.* Edited by John Beattie and John Middleton. Foreword by Raymond Firth. New York: Africana Publishing Corporation, 1969.

"Tapes Prove." "Tapes Prove Elders' Influence in (Body)." *North Charleston Banner* (Oct. 29, 1975): 1–2.

Tarakeshwar, Pearce, and Sikkema, "Development." Tarakeshwar, Nalini, Michelle J. Pearce, and K. J. Sikkema. "Development and Implementation of a Spiritual Coping Group Intervention for Adults Living with HIV/AIDS: A Pilot Study." *MHRC* 8 (3, 2005): 179–90.

Tarakeshwar et al., "Coping." Tarakeshwar, Nalini, et al. "Religious Coping Is Associated with the Quality of Life of Patients with Advanced Cancer." *JPallMed* 9 (3, 2006): 646–57.

Tarango, "Physician." Tarango, Angela. "Jesus as the 'Great Physician': Pentecostal Native North

Americans Within the Assemblies of God and New Understandings of Pentecostal Healing." Pages 107–27 in *Global Pentecostal and Charismatic Healing*. Edited by Candy Gunther Brown. Foreword by Harvey Cox. Oxford: Oxford University Press, 2011.

Targ, Schlitz, and Irwin, "Experiences." Targ, Elisabeth, Marilyn Schlitz, and Harvey J. Irwin. "Psi-Related Experiences." Pages 219–52 in *Varieties of Anomalous Experience: Examining the Scientific Evidence*. Edited by Etzel Cardeña, Steven Jay Lynn, and Stanley Krippner. Washington, D.C.: American Psychological Association, 2000.

Tari, *Breeze*. Tari, Mel, and Nona Tari. *The Gentle Breeze of Jesus*. Harrison, Ark.: New Leaf Press, 1974.

Tari, "Preface." Tari, Nona. "Preface." Pages 8–12 in *The Gentle Breeze of Jesus*. Harrison, Ark.: New Leaf Press, 1974.

Tari, *Wind*. Tari, Mel, with Cliff Dudley. *Like a Mighty Wind*. Carol Stream, Ill.: Creation House, 1971.

Tarr, *Foolishness*. Tarr, Del. *The Foolishness of God: A Linguist Looks at the Mystery of Tongues*. Foreword by Jack Hayford. Springfield, Mo.: Access, 2010.

"Tarry." "Tarry Until." *Tongues of Fire* (June 15, 1898): 93.

Taylor, *Adventures*. Taylor, William. *Christian Adventures in South Africa*. New York: Phillips and Hunt, 1880.

Taylor, *Formation*. Taylor, Vincent. *The Formation of the Gospel Tradition*. 2nd ed. London: Macmillan, 1960.

Taylor, "Future." Taylor, John. "The Future of Christianity." Pages 628–65 in *The Oxford Illustrated History of Christianity*. Edited by John McManners. Oxford: Oxford University Press, 1990.

Taylor, "Healings." Taylor, Mary. "Wonderful Healings in Kobe, Japan." *PentEv* 938 (March 5, 1932): 9, 11.

Taylor, *Hume*. Taylor, A. E. *David Hume and the Miraculous*. The Leslie Stephen Lecture, Cambridge University, 1927. Cambridge: Cambridge University Press, 1927.

Taylor, "Letters from Lourdes." Taylor, Thérèse. "'So Many Extraordinary Things To Tell': Letters from Lourdes, 1858." *JEH* 46 (3, 1995): 457–81.

Taylor, *Mark*. Taylor, Vincent. *The Gospel According to St. Mark*. London: Macmillan, 1952.

Taylor, *Metaphysics*. Taylor, Richard. *Metaphysics*. 2nd ed. Englewood Cliffs, N.J.: Prentice-Hall, 1974.

Taylor, *Missiology*. Taylor, William D., ed. *Global Missiology for the Twenty-first Century: The Iguassu Dialogue*. Foreword by Ravi Zacharias. Globalization of Mission series. Grand Rapids: Baker Academic, 2000.

Taylor, *Secret*. Taylor, Howard, and Geraldine Taylor. *Hudson Taylor's Spiritual Secret*. Chicago: Moody, 1987.

Taylor, "Wagner." Taylor, Bayard. "Wagner, C. Peter (1930–)." Pages 455–56 in vol. 1 of *Encyclopedia of Religious Revivals in America*. Edited by Michael McClymond. 2 vols. Westport, Conn: Greenwood, 2007.

Tedlock, "Dreams." Tedlock, Barbara. "The Role of Dreams and Visionary Narratives in Mayan Cultural Survival." *Ethos* 20 (4, Dec. 1992): 453–76.

Tedlock, "Observation." Tedlock, Barbara. "From Participant Observation to the Observation of Participation: The Emergence of Narrative Ethnography." *JAnthRes* 47 (1991): 69–94.

Teghrarian, "Al-Ghazali." Teghrarian, Souren. "Al-Ghazali and Hume on Causation and Miracles." *HamIsl* 14 (1, 1991): 21–28.

Telford, *Wesley*. Telford, John. *The Life of John Wesley*. 4th rev. ed. London: Epworth, 1924.

Templeton, "Introduction." Templeton, John Marks. "Introduction." Pages 7–20 in *Evidence of Purpose: Scientists Discover the Creator*. Edited by John Marks Templeton. New York: Continuum, 1994.

Ten, "Racism." Ten, C. L. "Hume's Racism and Miracles." *JVallnq* 36 (2002): 101–7.

Ten Boom, *Hiding Place*. Ten Boom, Corrie, with John and Elizabeth Sherrill. *The Hiding Place*. New York: Bantam, 1974.

Ten Boom, *Tramp*. Ten Boom, Corrie, with Jamie Buckingham. *Tramp for the Lord*. Old Tappan, N.J.: Fleming H. Revell, 1974.

Tenibemas, "Folk Islam." Tenibemas, Purnawan. "Folk Islam among the Sundanese People of Indonesia." PhD diss., Fuller School of World Missions, 1996.

Tennant, *Miracle*. Tennant, F. R. *Miracle and Its Philosophical Presuppositions: Three Lectures Delivered in the University of London 1924*. Cambridge: Cambridge University Press, 1925.

Tennant, *Theology*. Tennant, F. R. *Philosophical Theology*. 2 vols. Cambridge: Cambridge University Press, 1928–30. Vol. 1: *The Soul and Its Faculties*, 1928. Vol. 2: *The World, the Soul, and God*, 1930.

Tennent, *Christianity*. Tennent, Timothy C. *Theology in the Context of World Christianity: How the Global Church Is Influencing the Way We Think about and Discuss Theology*. Grand Rapids: Zondervan, 2007.

Tenzler, "Tiefenpsychologie." Tenzler, J. "Tiefenpsychologie und Wunderfrage. Der kognitive Teilbeitrag der Tiefenpsychologie zur Exegese biblischer Wunder." *BK* 29 (1, 1974): 6–10.

Thapar, *India*. Thapar, Romila. *A History of India*. Baltimore: Penguin, 1966.

Theissen, *Erleben.* Theissen, Gerd. *Erleben und Ver-halten der ersten Christen: Eine Psychologue des Ur-christentums.* Munich: Gütersloh, 2007.

Theissen, *Gospels in Context.* Theissen, Gerd. *The Gospels in Context: Social and Political History in the Synoptic Tradition.* Translated by Linda M. Maloney. Minneapolis: Fortress, 1991.

Theissen, *Miracle Stories.* Theissen, Gerd. *The Miracle Stories of the Early Christian Tradition.* Translated by Francis McDonagh. Edited by John Riches. Phila-delphia: Fortress, 1983.

Theissen and Merz, *Guide.* Theissen, Gerd, and An-nette Merz. *The Historical Jesus: A Comprehensive Guide.* Minneapolis: Fortress, 1998. Translated by John Bowden from *Der historische Jesus: Ein Lehr-buch.* Göttingen: Vandenhoeck & Ruprecht, 1996.

Theron, "Beste." Theron, J. P. J. "'Beste,' 'besete' of 'beserk'? besinning oor enkele begrippe binne die kerklike diens van bevryding van bose magte." *AcT* 23 (1, 2003): 194–212. (RTA)

Thielman, *Theology.* Thielman, Frank. *Theology of the New Testament.* Grand Rapids: Zondervan, 2005.

Thirring, "Guidance." Thirring, Walter. "The Guid-ance of Evolution Lets God Appear to Us in Many Guises." Pages 119–21 in *Cosmos, Bios, and Theos: Scientists Reflect on Science, God, and the Origins of the Universe, Life, and Homo Sapiens.* Edited by Henry Margenau and Roy Abraham Varghese. La Salle, Ill.: Open Court, 1992.

Thiselton, *Horizons.* Thiselton, Anthony C. *The Two Horizons: New Testament Hermeneutics and Philo-sophical Description.* Grand Rapids: Eerdmans, 1980.

Thollander, *Mathews.* Thollander, Jon. *He Saw a Man Named Mathews: A Brief Testimony of Thomas and Mary Mathews, Pioneer Missionaries to Rajasthan.* Udaipur, Rajasthan: Native Missionary Movement, Cross & Crown Publications, 2000.

Thomas, *Deliverance.* Thomas, John Christopher. *The Devil, Disease, and Deliverance: Origins of Illness in New Testament Thought.* JPTSup 13. Sheffield: Shef-field Academic Press, 1998.

Thomas, "Growth." Thomas, C. D. "Church Growth among Indians in West Malaysia." DMiss diss., Fuller Theological Seminary, 1976.

Thomas, "Health." Thomas, John Christopher. "Health and Healing: A Pentecostal Contribution." *ExAud* 21 (2005): 88–107.

Thomas, "Issues." Thomas, Juliet. "Issues from the Indian Perspective." Pages 146–51 in *Deliver Us from Evil: An Uneasy Frontier in Christian Mission.* Edited by A. Scott Moreau, Tokunboh Adeyemo, David A. Burnett, Bryant L. Myers, and Hwa Yung. Monrovia, Calif.: Lausanne Committee for World Evangelization, 2002.

Thomas, "Miracles." Thomas, David. "The Miracles of Jesus in Early Islamic Polemic." *JSS* 39 (2, 1994): 221–43.

Thomas, "Report." Thomas, H. "Report on the Chorti-Maya Indians of Guatemala." MA thesis, Fuller Theological Seminary, 1973.

Thomas, "Thought." Thomas, Owen. "Recent Thought on Divine Agency." Pages 35–50 in *Divine Action: Studies Inspired by the Philosophical Theology of Austin Farrer.* Edited by Brian Hebblethwaite and Edward Henderson. Edinburgh: T&T Clark, 1990.

Thomas, *Walls.* Thomas, Sandy. *Beyond Jungle Walls: Bringing Hope to the Forgotten Congo.* Springfield, Mo.: Twenty-first Century Press, 2005.

Thompson, *Motif-Index.* Thompson, Stith. *Motif-Index of Folk-Literature.* Vol. 3. Helsinki: Academia Scientiarum Fennica, 1934.

Thomson, "Sorcery." Thomson, Mike. "Child Sor-cery in DR Congo." http://news.bbc.co.uk/go/pr/fr/-/today/newsid_8530000/8530686.stm. Pub-lished and accessed March 1, 2010.

Thoresen, "Health." Thoresen, Carl E. "Spirituality, Religion, and Health: What's the Deal?" Pages 3–10 in *Spirit, Science, and Health: How the Spiritual Mind Fuels Physical Wellness.* Edited by Thomas G. Plante and Carl E. Thoresen. Foreword by Albert Bandura. Westport, Conn.: Praeger, 2007.

Thornton, *Zeuge.* Thornton, Claus-Jürgen. *Der Zeuge des Zeugen: Lukas als Historiker der Paulusreisen.* WUNT 56. Tübingen: Mohr Siebeck, 1991.

Thorsan, "Robbers." Thorsan, P. E. "Robbers Again." *CGl* 7 (1, Oct. 1925): 3.

"Thoughts Gleaned." "A Few Thoughts Gleaned from Sermons of Rev. Marcus Chen." *CGl* 6 (3, April 1925): 1.

Thouless, "Miracles." Thouless, Robert H. "Miracles and Psychical Research." *Theology* 72 (255, 1969): 253–58.

Thurs, "Quantum Physics." Thurs, Daniel Patrick. "That Quantum Physics Demonstrated the Doctrine of Free Will." Pages 196–205 in *Galileo Goes to Jail and Other Myths about Science and Religion.* Edited by Ronald L. Numbers. Cambridge, Mass.: Harvard University Press, 2009.

Thurston, *Phenomena.* Thurston, Herbert. *The Phys-ical Phenomena of Mysticism.* Chicago: Henry Reg-nery, 1952.

Tiede, *Figure.* Tiede, David Lenz. *The Charismatic Figure as Miracle Worker.* SBLDS 1. Missoula, Mont.: Society of Biblical Literature, 1972.

Tigchelaar, "Names of Spirits." Tigchelaar, Eibert J. C. "'These Are the Names of the Spirits of . . .': A Pre-liminary Edition of *4Qcatalogue of Spirits (4Q230)* and New Manuscript Evidence for the *Two Spirits*

Treatise (4Q257 and *1Q29a)." RevQ* 21 (84, 2004): 529–47.

Tilley, "Phenomenology." Tilley, James A. "A Phenomenology of the Christian Healer's Expeience." PhD diss., Fuller Graduate School of Psychology, 1989.

Tillich, "Revelation." Tillich, Paul. "Revelation and Miracle." Pages 71–74 in *Miracles.* Edited by Richard Swinburne. New York: Macmillan, 1989.

Timberlake et al., "Effects." Timberlake, D. S., et al. "The Moderating Effects of Religiosity on the Genetic and Environmental Determinants of Smoking Initiation." *NicTobRes* 8 (1, 2006): 123–33.

Tippett, *People Movements.* Tippett, Alan R. *People Movements in Southern Polynesia: Studies in the Dynamics of Church Planting and Growth in Tahiti, New Zealand, Tonga, and Samoa.* Chicago: Moody Press, 1971.

Tippett, "Possession." Tippett, A. R. "Spirit Possession as It Relates to Culture and Religion: A Survey of Anthropological Literature." Pages 143–74 in *Demon Possession: A Medical, Historical, Anthropological, and Theological Symposium.* Papers presented at the University of Notre Dame, January 8–11, 1975, under the auspices of the Christian Medical Association. Edited by John Warwick Montgomery. Minneapolis: Bethany House, 1976.

Tippett, *Solomon Islands Christianity.* Tippett, A. R. *Solomon Islands Christianity: A Study in Growth and Obstruction.* WSCM. London: Lutterworth, 1967.

Tippett, *Verdict Theology.* Tippett, Alan R. *Verdict Theology in Missionary Theory.* Pasadena, Calif.: William Carey Library, 1973.

Tobin, *Rhetoric in Contexts.* Tobin, Thomas H. *Paul's Rhetoric in Its Contexts: The Argument of Romans.* Peabody, Mass.: Hendrickson, 2004.

Todd, "Monism." Todd, Robert B. "Monism and Immanence: The Foundations of Stoic Physics." Pages 137–60 in *The Stoics.* Edited by John M. Rist. Berkeley: University of California Press, 1978.

Togarasei, "HIV/AIDS." Togarasei, Lovemore. "HIV/AIDS and the Role of the Churches in Zimbabwe." *AfThJ* 28 (1, 2005): 3–20.

Toland, John. *Christianity Not Mysterious: or, a Treatise shewing, that there is nothing in the Gospel contrary to reason, nor above it: and that no Christian doctrine can be properly call'd a mystery.* 2nd enlarged ed. London: Sam. Buckley, 1696.

Tombs, "Church." Tombs, David. "The Church in a Latin American Perspective." Pages 306–25 in *The Routledge Companion to the Christian Church.* Edited by Gerard Mannion and Lewis S. Mudge. New York: Routledge, 2008.

Tomkins, *History.* Tomkins, Stephen. *A Short History of Christianity.* Grand Rapids: Eerdmans, 2005.

Tomkins, *Wesley.* Tomkins, Stephen. *John Wesley: A Biography.* Grand Rapids: Eerdmans, 2003.

Tomlinson, "Magic Methodists." Tomlinson, John W. B. "The Magic Methodists and Their Influence on the Early Primitive Methodist Movement." Pages 389–99 in *Signs, Wonders, Miracles: Representations of Divine Power in the Life of the Church. Papers Read at the 2003 Summer Meeting and the 2004 Winter Meeting of the Ecclesiastical History Society.* Edited by Kate Cooper and Jeremy Gregory. Rochester: Boydell & Brewer, for the Ecclesiastical History Society, 2005.

Toner, *Culture.* Toner, Jerry. *Popular Culture in Ancient Rome.* Cambridge: Polity, 2009.

Toner, "Exorcism." Toner, Patrick J. "Exorcism and the Catholic Faith." Pages 31–41 in *Exorcism Through the Ages.* Edited by St. Elmo Nauman. New York: Philosophical Library, 1974.

Tonquédec, *Miracles.* Tonquédec, Joseph de. *Miracles.* Translated by Frank M. Oppenheim. West Baden Springs, Ind.: West Baden College, 1955. Translated from "Miracle," Pages 517–78 in vol. 3 of *Dictionnaire Apologétique de la Foi Catholique.* Edited by A. d'Alès. Paris: Beauchesne, 1926.

Toon, "Waldenses." Toon, Peter. "Waldenses." Pages 1025–26 in *The New International Dictionary of the Christian Church.* Grand Rapids: Zondervan, 1974.

Torrance, "Probability." Torrance, Alan J. "The Lazarus Narrative, Theological History, and Historical Probability." Pages 245–62 in *The Gospel of John and Christian Theology.* Edited by Richard Bauckham and Carl Mosser. Grand Rapids: Eerdmans, 2008.

Torrance, *Space.* Torrance, Thomas F. *Space, Time & Incarnation.* Oxford: Oxford University Press, 1969.

Torrey, *Healing.* Torrey, R. A. *Divine Healing.* Reprint, Grand Rapids: Baker, 1974.

Toulmin, *Philosophy.* Toulmin, Stephen Edelston. *Philosophy of Science.* London: Hutchinson University Library, 1967.

Tournier, *Casebook.* Tournier, Paul. *A Doctor's Casebook in the Light of the Bible.* Translated by Edwin Hudson. New York: Harper & Brothers, 1954.

Townes, "Question." Townes, Charles H. "The Question of Origin Seems Unanswered if We Explore from a Scientific View Alone." Pages 122–24 in *Cosmos, Bios, and Theos: Scientists Reflect on Science, God, and the Origins of the Universe, Life, and Homo Sapiens.* Edited by Henry Margenau and Roy Abraham Varghese. La Salle, Ill.: Open Court, 1992.

Trapnell, "Health." Trapnell, D. H. "Health, Disease and Healing." Pages 457–65 in *New Bible Dictionary.* 2nd ed. Edited by J. D. Douglas and N. Hillyer. Downers Grove, Ill.: InterVarsity, 1982.

Trapp, *Maximus*. Trapp, M. B., trans. and commentator. *Maximus of Tyre: The Philosophical Orations*. Oxford: Clarendon, 1997.

Trémel, "Risque de paganisation." Trémel, Yves-Bernard. "Voie du salut et religion populaire. Paul et Luc face au risque de paganisation." *LumVie* 30 (153–54, 1981): 87–108.

Trench, *Miracles*. Trench, Richard Chenevix. *Notes on the Miracles of Our Lord*. Reprint, New York: Revell, 1953.

Trigger, "Nubian." Trigger, Bruce G. "Nubian, Negro, Black, Nilotic?" Pages 26–35 in *Africa in Antiquity 1: The Arts of Ancient Nubia and the Sudan—The Essays*. Brooklyn, N.Y.: The Brooklyn Museum, 1978.

Trombley, "Paganism." Trombley, Frank R. "Christianity and Paganism, II: Asia Minor." Pages 189–209 in *Constantine to c. 600*. Edited by Augustine Casiday and Frederick W. Norris. Vol. 2 of *The Cambridge History of Christianity*. 9 vols. Cambridge: Cambridge University Press, 2007.

Trotter, "Dead Raised." Trotter, Alfred N. "Dead Raised." *PentEv* 738 (March 10, 1928): 5.

Tubiana, "Zar." Tubiana, Joseph. "*Zar* and *Buda* in Northern Ethiopia." Pages 19–33 in *Women's Medicine: The Zar-Bori Cult in Africa and Beyond*. Edited by I. M. Lewis, Ahmed Al-Safi, and Sayyid Hurreiz. Edinburgh: International African Institute, Edinburgh University Press, 1991.

Tucker, *Jerusalem*. Tucker, Ruth. *From Jerusalem to Irian Jaya: A Biographical History of Christian Missions*. Grand Rapids: Academie, Zondervan, 1983.

Tucker, *Knowledge*. Tucker, Aviezer. *Our Knowledge of the Past: A Philosophy of Historiography*. Cambridge: Cambridge University Press, 2004.

Tucker, "Miracles." Tucker, Aviezer. "Miracles, Historical Testimonies, and Probabilities." *HistTh* 44 (Oct. 2005): 373–90.

Tuckett, *Luke*. Tuckett, Christopher M. *Luke*. NTG. Sheffield: Sheffield Academic Press, 1996.

Tuckett, "Review." Tuckett, Christopher. Review of Richard Bauckham, *Jesus and the Eyewitnesses*. *RBL* 12 (2007).

Tully et al., "Factors." Tully, J., R. M. Viner, P. G. Coen, J. M. Stuart, M. Zambon, C. Peckham, C. Booth, N. Klein, E. Kaczmarski, and R. Booy. "Risk and Protective Factors for Meningococcal Disease in Adolescents: Matched Cohort Study." *BMedJ* 332 (7539, 2006): 445–50.

Tupper, "Healing." Tupper, Kenneth W. "Entheogenic Healing: The Spiritual Effects and Therapeutic Potential of Ceremonial Ayahuasca Use." Pages 269–82 in *Psychodynamics*. Vol. 3 of *The Healing Power of Spirituality: How Faith Helps Humans Thrive*. Edited by J. Harold Ellens. Santa Barbara, Calif.: Praeger, 2010.

Turaki, "Legacy." Turaki, Yusufu. "The British Colonial Legacy in Northern Nigeria." PhD diss., Boston University, 1982.

Turaki, "Missiology." Turaki, Yusufu. "Evangelical Missiology from Africa: Strengths and Weaknesses." Pages 271–83 in *Global Missiology for the 21st Century: The Iguassu Dialogue*. Edited by William D. Taylor. Grand Rapids: Baker Academic, 2000.

Turnbull, *Forest People*. Turnbull, Colin M. *The Forest People: A Study of the Pygmies of the Congo*. Foreword by Harry L. Shapiro. New York: Simon & Schuster, 1962.

Turner, "Actuality." Turner, Edith. "Psychology, Metaphor, or Actuality? A Probe into Iñupiat Eskimo Healing." *AnthConsc* 3 (1–2, 1992): 1–8.

Turner, "Advances." Turner, Edith. "Advances in the Study of Spirit Experience: Drawing Together Many Threads." *AnthConsc* 17 (2, 2006): 33–61.

Turner, "Anthropology." Turner, Edith. "The Anthropology of Experience: The Way to Teach Religion and Healing." Pages 193–205 in *Teaching Religion and Healing*. Edited by Linda L. Barnes and Inés Talamantez. AARTRSS. Oxford: Oxford University Press, 2006.

Turner, *Drums*. Turner, V. W. *The Drums of Affliction: A Study of Religious Processes among the Ndembu of Zambia*. Oxford: Clarendon and the International African Institute, 1968.

Turner, *Experiencing Ritual*. Turner, Edith, with William Blodgett, Singleton Kahoma, and Fideli Benwa. *Experiencing Ritual: A New Interpretation of African Healing*. SCEthn. Philadelphia: University of Pennsylvania Press, 1992.

Turner, "Field." Turner, Edith. "The Reality of Spirits: A Tabooed or Permitted Field of Study?" *AnthConsc* 4 (March 1993): 9–12.

Turner, *Gifts*. Turner, Max. *The Holy Spirit and Spiritual Gifts in the New Testament Church and Today*. Rev. ed. Peabody, Mass.: Hendrickson, 1998.

Turner, *Hands*. Turner, Edith. *The Hands Feel It: Healing and Spirit Presence among a Northern Alaskan People*. DeKalb: Northern Illinois University Press, 1996.

Turner, "Healed." Turner, William H. "Miraculously Healed after Two Years of Total Darkness." *LRE* (Feb. 1916): 7–8.

Turner, *Healers*. Turner, Edith. *Among the Healers: Stories of Spiritual and Ritual Healing Around the World*. Religion, Health, and Healing. Westport, Conn.: Praeger, 2006.

Turner, "Multiverse." Turner, Michael. "No Miracle in the Multiverse." *Nature* 467 (Oct. 2010): 657–58.

Turner, "Religious Healing." Turner, Edith. "Taking Seriously the Nature of Religious Healing in

America." Pages 387–404 in *Religion and Healing in America*. Edited by Linda L. Barnes and Susan S. Sered. New York: Oxford University Press, 2005.

Turner, "Reality." Turner, Edith. "The Reality of Spirits." *Re-Vision* 15 (1, 1992): 28–32.

Turner, "Reality of Spirits." Turner, Edith. "The Reality of Spirits." *Shamanism* 10 (1, Spring/Summer 1997).

Turner, "Spirit Form." Turner, Edith. "A Visible Spirit Form in Zambia." Pages 71–95 in *Being Changed: The Anthropology of Extraordinary Experience*. Edited by David E. Young and Jean-Guy Goulet. Peterborough, Ont.: Broadview, 1994.

Twelftree, "ΕΚΒΑΛΛΩ." Twelftree, Graham H. "'ΕΙ ΔΕ . . . ΕΓΩ ΕΚΒΑΛΛΩ ΤΑ ΔΑΙΜΟΝΙΑ . . .'" Pages 361–400 in *The Miracles of Jesus*. Edited by David Wenham and Craig Blomberg. Vol. 6 of *GosPersp*. Sheffield: JSOT Press, 1986.

Twelftree, *Exorcist*. Twelftree, Graham H. *Jesus the Exorcist: A Contribution to the Study of the Historical Jesus*. Peabody, Mass.: Hendrickson; Tübingen: Mohr Siebeck, 1993.

Twelftree, "Healing." Twelftree, Graham H. "Healing, Illness." Pages 378–81 in *DPL*.

Twelftree, "Message." Twelftree, Graham H. "The Message of Jesus I: Miracles, Continuing Controversies." Pages 2517–48 in *Handbook for the Study of the Historical Jesus*. Edited by Tom Holmén and Stanley E. Porter. 4 vols. Boston: Brill, 2010.

Twelftree, "Miracles." Twelftree, Graham H. "The Miracles of Jesus: Marginal or Mainstream?" *JSHJ* 1 (1, 2003): 104–24.

Twelftree, *Miracle Worker*. Twelftree, Graham H. *Jesus the Miracle Worker: A Historical and Theological Study*. Downers Grove, Ill.: InterVarsity, 1999.

Twelftree, *Name*. Twelftree, Graham H. *In the Name of Jesus: Exorcism among Early Christians*. Grand Rapids: Baker Academic, 2007.

Twelftree, "Signs." Twelftree, Graham H. "Signs, Wonders, Miracles." Pages 875–77 in *DPL*.

Twelftree, *Triumphant*. Twelftree, Graham H. *Christ Triumphant: Exorcism Then and Now*. London: Hodder & Stoughton, 1985.

Tyson, "Dates." Tyson, Joseph B. "Why Dates Matter: The Case of the Acts of the Apostles." *FourR* 18 (2, 2005): 8–11, 14, 17–18.

Tyson, *Marcion*. Tyson, Joseph B. *Marcion and Luke-Acts: A Defining Struggle*. Columbia: University of South Carolina Press, 2006.

Udoette, "Charismata." Udoette, Donatus. "Towards a Theology of Charismata for the Nigerian Church." *Encounter: A Journal of African Life and Religion* 2 (1993): 16–28.

Uhlig, "Origin." Uhlig, Herbert. "The Origin of the Universe Can Be Described Scientifically as a

Miracle." Pages 125–26 in *Cosmos, Bios, and Theos: Scientists Reflect on Science, God, and the Origins of the Universe, Life, and* Homo Sapiens. Edited by Henry Margenau and Roy Abraham Varghese. La Salle, Ill.: Open Court, 1992.

Ukachukwu Manus, "Miracle Workers." Ukachukwu Manus, Chris. "Miracle Workers/Healers as Divine Men: Their Role in the Nigerian Church and Society." *AJT* 3 (2, 1989): 658–69.

Ukah and Echtler, "Witches." Ukah, Asonzeh F.-K., and Magnus Echtler. "Born-Again Witches and Videos in Nigeria." Pages 73–92 in *Global Pentecostalism: Encounters with Other Religious Traditions*. Edited by David Westerlund. New York: I. B. Taurus, 2009.

Umeh, *Dibia*. Umeh, John Anenechukwu. *After God Is Dibia*. Vol. 2 of *Igbo Cosmology, Healing, Divination, and Sacred Science in Nigeria*. London: Karnak House, 1999.

Urbach, *Sages*. Urbach, Ephraim E. *The Sages: Their Concepts and Beliefs*. 2nd ed. Translated by Israel Abrahams. 2 vols. Jerusalem: Magnes Press, The Hebrew University, 1979.

Usry and Keener, *Religion*. Usry, Glenn, and Craig S. Keener. *Black Man's Religion: Can Christianity Be Afrocentric?* Downers Grove, Ill.: InterVarsity, 1996.

Uval, "Streams." Uval, Beth. "Streams of Living Water: The Feast of Tabernacles and the Holy Spirit." *JerPersp* 49 (1995): 22–23, 37.

Uyanga, "Characteristics." Uyanga, Joseph. "The Characteristics of Patients of Spiritual Healing Homes and Traditional Doctors in Southeastern Nigeria." *SSMed* 13 (1979): 323–29.

Uzukwu, "Address." Uzukwu, E. E. "Opening Address." Pages 7–10 in *Healing and Exorcism: The Nigerian Experience*. Proceedings, Lectures, Discussions, and Conclusions of the First Missiology Symposium on Healing and Exorcism, organized by the Spiritan International School of Theology, Attakwu, Enugu, May 18–20, 1989. Edited by Chris U. Manus, Luke N. Mbefo, and E. E. Uzukwu. Attakwu, Enugu: Spiritan International School of Theology, 1992.

Vähäkangas, "Responses." Vähäkangas, Auli. "Responses to Prayer Healing in the ELCT Northern Diocese." Pages 157–68 in *Charismatic Renewal in Africa: A Challenge for African Christianity*. Edited by Mika Vähäkangas and Andrew A. Kyomo. Nairobi: Acton Publishers, 2003.

Valla and Prince, "Experiences." Valla, Jean-Pierre, and Raymond H. Prince. "Religious Experiences as Self-Healing Mechanisms." Pages 149–66 in *Altered States of Consciousness and Mental Health: A Cross-Cultural Perspective*. Edited by Colleen A. Ward. CCRMS 12. Newbury Park, Calif.: Sage, 1989.

Vallance, "Anatomy." Vallance, J. T. "Anatomy and Physiology." Pages 82–85 in *OCD*.

Vambe, "Possession." Vambe, Maurice T. "Spirit Possession in the Zimbabwean Black Novel in English." *JStRel* 12 (1, 1999): 53–63.

Van Alphen and Aris, *Medicine*. Van Alphen, Jan, and Anthony Aris. *Oriental Medicine: An Illustrated Guide to the Asian Arts of Healing*. London: Serindia Publications, 1995.

Van Brenk, "Wagner." Van Brenk, Arie. "C. Peter Wagner: A Critical Analysis of His Work." DMin diss., Fuller Theological Seminary, 1993.

Van Cangh, "Miracles." Van Cangh, Jean-Marie. "Miracles de rabbins et miracles de Jésus. La tradition sur Honi et Hanina." *RTL* 15 (1, 1984): 28–53.

Van Cangh, "Miracles grecs." Van Cangh, Jean-Marie. "Miracles grecs, rabbiniques et évangéliques." Pages 213–36 in *Miracles and Imagery in Luke and John: Festschrift Ulrich Busse*. Edited by J. Verheyden, G. van Belle, and J. G. van der Watt. BETL 218. Leuven: Uitgeverij Peeters, 2008.

Van Cangh, "Sources." Van Cangh, Jean-Marie. "Les sources de l'Evangile: les collections prémarciennes de miracles." *RTL* 3 (1972): 76–85.

Van Dam, *Saints*. Van Dam, Raymond. *Saints and Their Miracles in Late Antique Gaul*. Princeton, N.J.: Princeton University Press, 1993.

Van den Berghe, "Wonderverhalen." Van den Berghe, P. "De wonderverhalen uit de evangeliën. Een handreiking." *Coll* 19 (4, 1973): 433–58.

Vander Broek, "*Sitz*." Vander Broek, Lyle D. "The Markan Sitz im Leben: A Critical Investigation." PhD diss., Drew University, 1983. Ann Arbor, Mich.: University Microfilms International, 1983.

Van der Horst, "Macrobius." Van der Horst, Pieter W. "Macrobius and the New Testament: A Contribution to the Corpus Hellenisticum." *NovT* 15 (3, July 1973): 220–32.

VanderKam, "Traditions." VanderKam, James C. "Enoch Traditions in Jubilees and Other Second-Century Sources." Pages 229–51 in vol. 1 of *SBLSP* 13. Missoula, Mont.: Scholars Press for SBL, 1978.

Vander Waerdt, "Theory." Vander Waerdt, Paul A. "The Original Theory of Natural Law." *SPhilA* 15 (2003): 17–34.

Van der Watt, "Relevance." Van der Watt, Jan G. "A Hermeneutics of Relevance: Reading the Bible in Dialogue in African Contexts." Pages 237–55 in *Miracles and Imagery in Luke and John: Festschrift Ulrich Busse*. Edited by J. Verheyden, G. van Belle, and J. G. van der Watt. BETL 218. Leuven: Uitgeverij Peeters, 2008.

Van der Woude, "Discussie." Van der Woude, C. "Een Discussie over het Christelijk Geloof en Zijn Wonderen, in de Tijd der Aufklarung." *GTT* 74 (2, 1974): 87–107.

Van de Vyfer, "Theology." Van de Vyfer, H. M. "Andrew Murray's Theology of Divine Healing." *VEE* 30 (1, 2009): 302–19.

Van De Walle, "Cobelligerence." Van De Walle, Bernie A. "Cautious Cobelligerence? The Late Nineteenth-Century American Divine Healing Movement and the Promise of Medical Science." Paper presented at the Society for Pentecostal Studies, Durham, N.C., March 13–15, 2008; *Pneuma Review* 13 (3, 2010): 20–44.

Van Dijk, "Miracles." Van Dijk, Mathilde. "Miracles and Visions in *Devotio Moderna* Biographies." Pages 239–48 in *Signs, Wonders, Miracles: Representations of Divine Power in the Life of the Church. Papers Read at the 2003 Summer Meeting and the 2004 Winter Meeting of the Ecclesiastical History Society*. Edited by Kate Cooper and Jeremy Gregory. Rochester: Boydell & Brewer, for the Ecclesiastical History Society, 2005.

Van Fraasen, *Laws and Symmetry*. Van Fraasen, Bas. *Laws and Symmetry*. Oxford: Clarendon, 1990.

Van Gelder, "Possession." Van Gelder, David W. "A Case of Demon Possession." *JPastCare* 41 (2, 1987): 151–61.

Van Gulick, "Charge." Van Gulick, Robert. "Who's in Charge Here? And Who's Doing All the Work?" Pages 233–56 in *Mental Causation*. Edited by John Heil and Alfred Mele. Oxford: Clarendon, 1995.

Vanhoozer, *Postmodern Theology*. Vanhoozer, Kevin J., ed. *The Cambridge Companion to Postmodern Theology*. Cambridge: Cambridge University Press, 2003.

Van Ness, Kasl and Jones, "Religion." Van Ness, Peter H., Stanislav V. Kasl, and Beth A. Jones. "Religion, Race, and Breast Cancer Survival." *IntJPsyMed* 33 (2003): 357–76.

Van Oyen, "Criteria." Van Oyen, Geert. "How Do We Know (What There Is to Know)? Criteria for Historical Jesus Research." *LouvS* 26 (3, 2001): 245–67.

Vansina, "Knowledge." Vansina, Jan. "Knowledge and Perceptions of the African Past." Pages 28–41 in *African Historiographies: What History for Which Africa?* Edited by Bogumil Jewsiewicki and David Newbury. SSAMD 12. Beverly Hills, Calif.: Sage, 1986.

Van Vliet, *No Single Testimony*. Van Vliet, Hendrik. *No Single Testimony: A Study of the Adoption of the Law of Deut. 19:5 par. into the New Testament*. Utrecht: Kemink, 1958.

Van Wyk and Viljoen, "Benaderings." Van Wyk, G. J., and Francois P. Viljoen. "Benaderings tot die interpretasie van die wonderverhale in Markus 8-10." *IDS* 43 (4, 2009): 879–94.

Varela et al., "Risk." Varela, J. Esteban, Orlando Gomez-Marin, et al. "The Risk of Death for Jehovah's Witnesses after Major Trauma." *JTIICC* 54 (5, 2003): 967–72.

Vargas-O'Bryan, "Balance." Vargas-O'Bryan, Ivette. "Keeping It All in Balance: Teaching Asian Religions Through Illness and Healing." Pages 83–94 in *Teaching Religion and Healing*. Edited by Linda L. Barnes and Inés Talamantez. AARTRSS. Oxford: Oxford University Press, 2006.

Varghese, "Introduction." Varghese, Roy Abraham. "Introduction." Pages 1–26 in *Cosmos, Bios, and Theos: Scientists Reflect on Science, God, and the Origins of the Universe, Life, and* Homo Sapiens. Edited by Henry Margenau and Roy Abraham Varghese. La Salle, Ill.: Open Court, 1992.

Venter, *Healing.* Venter, Alexander F. *Doing Healing: How to Minister God's Kingdom in the Power of the Spirit.* Cape Town: Vineyard International, 2008.

Venter, *Reconciliation.* Venter, Alexander. *Doing Reconciliation: Racism, Reconciliation, and Transformation in the Church and World.* Cape Town: Vineyard International, 2004.

Verger, "Trance." Verger, Pierre. "Trance and Convention in Nago-Yoruba Spirit Mediumship." Pages 50–66 in *Spirit Mediumship and Society in Africa*. Edited by John Beattie and John Middleton. Foreword by Raymond Firth. New York: Africana Publishing Corporation, 1969.

Verheyden, "Unity." Verheyden, Joseph. "The Unity of Luke-Acts: What Are We Up To?" Pages 3–56 in *The Unity of Luke-Acts*. Edited by Joseph Verheyden. BETL 142. Leuven: Leuven University Press, 1999.

Verman and Adler, "Path Jumping." Verman, M., and S. H. Adler. "Path Jumping in the Jewish Magical Tradition." *JSQ* 1 (2, 1993–94): 131–48.

Vermes, "Hanina." Vermes, Geza. "Hanina ben Dosa: A Controversial Galilean Saint from the First Century of the Christian Era." *JJS* 23 (1, Spring 1972): 28–50; 24 (1, Spring 1973): 51–64.

Vermes, *Jesus and Judaism.* Vermes, Geza. *Jesus and the World of Judaism.* Philadelphia: Fortress, 1984; London: SCM, 1983.

Vermes, *Jesus the Jew.* Vermes, Geza. *Jesus the Jew: A Historian's Reading of the Gospels.* Philadelphia: Fortress, 1973.

Vermes, "Notice." Vermes, Geza. "The Jesus Notice of Josephus Re-Examined." *JJS* 38 (1, Spring 1987): 1–10.

Vermes, *Religion.* Vermes, Geza. *The Religion of Jesus the Jew.* Minneapolis: Augsburg Fortress, 1993.

Versnel, "Miracles." Versnel, H. S. "Miracles." Page 989 in *OCD*.

Versteeg and Droogers, "Typology." Versteeg, P. G. A., and A. F. Droogers. "A Typology of Domestication in Exorcism." *CulRel* 8 (1, 2007): 15–32.

Vidler, *Revolution.* Vidler, Alec R. *The Church in an Age of Revolution: 1789 to the Present Day.* PHC 5. London: Penguin, 1974.

Viguerie, "Miracle." Viguerie, Jean de. "Le Miracle dans la France du XVIIᵉ siècle." *XVIIᵉ siècle* 35 (July 1983): 313–31.

Village, "Dimensions." Village, Andrew. "Dimensions of Belief about Miraculous Healing." *MHRC* 8 (2, 2005): 97–107.

Village, "Influence." Village, Andrew. "The Influence of Psychological Type Preferences on Readers Trying to Imagine Themselves in a New Testament Healing Story." *HTS/TS* 65 (1, 2009).

Vivian and Athanassakis, "Introduction." Vivian, Tim, and Apostolos N. Athanassakis. "Introduction." Pages 1–31 in *Life of Saint George of Choziba and the Miracles of the Most Holy Mother of God at Choziba,* by Antony of Choziba. Translated by Tim Vivian and Apostolos N. Athanassakis. San Francisco: International Scholars Publications, 1994.

Vogel, *Medicine.* Vogel, Virgil J. *American Indian Medicine.* Norman: University of Oklahoma, 1970.

Von Bendemann, "Arzt." Von Bendemann, R. "Christus der Arzt: Krankheitskonzepte in den Therapieerzahlungen des Markusevangeliums (Teil 1)." *BZ* 54 (1, 2010): 36–53.

Von Franz, "Daimons." Von Franz, Marie-Louise. "Daimons and the Inner Companion." *Parab* 6 (4, 1981): 36–44.

Voorst, *Jesus.* Voorst, Robert E. van. *Jesus Outside the New Testament: An Introduction to the Ancient Evidence.* Grand Rapids: Eerdmans, 2000.

Vries, "Miracles." Vries, Hent de. "Of Miracles and Special Effects." *IJPhilRel* 50 (1, 2001): 41–56.

Vries, "Situation." Vries, Christina L. de. "The Global Health Situation: Priorities for the Churches' Health Ministry Beyond A.D. 2000." *IntRevMiss* 90 (356/357, Jan./Apr. 2001): 149–59.

Waardt, "Witchcraft." Waardt, Hans de. "Dutch Witchcraft in the Sixteenth and Seventeenth Centuries." *SocG* 36 (3–4, May 1989): 224–44.

Wachholtz and Pearce, "Compassion." Wachholtz, Amy B., and Michelle Pearce. "Compassion and Health." Pages 115–28 in *Spirit, Science, and Health: How the Spiritual Mind Fuels Physical Wellness.* Edited by Thomas G. Plante and Carl E. Thoresen. Foreword by Albert Bandura. Westport, Conn.: Praeger, 2007.

Wacker, *Heaven Below.* Wacker, Grant. *Heaven Below: Early Pentecostals and American Culture.* Cambridge, Mass.: Harvard University Press, 2001.

Wacker, "Living." Wacker, Grant. "Living with Signs and Wonders: Parents and Children in Early Pentecostal Culture." Pages 423–42 in *Signs, Wonders, Miracles: Representations of Divine Power in the Life of the Church. Papers Read at the 2003 Summer Meeting and the 2004 Winter Meeting of the Ecclesiastical History Society.* Edited by Kate Cooper and Jeremy Gregory. Rochester: Boydell & Brewer, for the Ecclesiastical History Society, 2005.

Wacker, "Marching." Wacker, Grant. "Marching to Zion: Religion in a Modern Utopian Community." *CH* 54 (1985): 496–511.

Wacker, "Marching to Zion 1." Wacker, Grant. "Marching to Zion, Part 1: The Story of John Alexander Dowie's Twentieth-Century Utopian City—Zion, Illinois." *AGHer* 6 (2, Summer 1986): 6–9.

Wacker, "Marching to Zion 2." Wacker, Grant. "Marching to Zion, Concluding Part: The Story of John Alexander Dowie's Twentieth-Century Utopian City—Zion, Illinois." *AGHer* 6 (3, Fall 1986): 7–10.

Wacker, "Searching." Wacker, Grant. "Searching for Eden with a Satellite Dish: Primitivism, Pragmatism, and the Pentecostal Character." Pages 139–66 in *The Primitive Church in the Modern World.* Edited by Richard T. Hughes. Urbana: University of Illinois Press, 1995.

Wagner, *Acts.* Wagner, C. Peter. *The Acts of the Holy Spirit: A Modern Commentary on the Book of Acts.* Ventura, Calif.: Regal, 2000.

Wagner, "Dynamics." Wagner, C. Peter. "Contemporary Dynamics of the Holy Spirit in Missions: A Personal Pilgrimage." Pages 107–22 in *The Holy Spirit and Mission Dynamics.* Edited by C. Douglas McConnell. EvMissSS 5. Pasadena, Calif.: William Carey Library, 1997.

Wagner, "Genesis." Wagner, C. Peter. "Genesis." Pages 39–49 in *Signs and Wonders Today: The Story of Fuller Theological Seminary's Remarkable Course on Spiritual Power.* Rev. ed. Edited by C. Peter Wagner. Altamonte Springs, Fla.: Creation House, 1987.

Wagner, *Heiress.* Wagner, Petti. *Murdered Heiress . . . Living Witness.* Shreveport, La.: Huntington House, 1984.

Wagner, "Introduction." Wagner, C. Peter. "Introduction." Pages 3–11 in *Signs and Wonders Today: The Story of Fuller Theological Seminary's Remarkable Course on Spiritual Power.* Rev. ed. Edited by C. Peter Wagner. Altamonte Springs, Fla.: Creation House, 1987.

Wagner, "Introduction: Africa." Wagner, C. Peter. "Introduction." Pages 7–18 in *Out of Africa: How the Spiritual Explosion Among Nigerians Is Impacting the World.* Edited by C. Peter Wagner and Joseph Thompson. Ventura, Calif.: Regal, 2004.

Wagner, "Perspective." Wagner, C. Peter. "A Church Growth Perspective on Pentecostal Missions." Pages 265–84 in *Called and Empowered: Global Mission in Pentecostal Perspective.* Edited by Murray A. Dempster, Byron D. Klaus, and Douglas Petersen. Peabody, Mass.: Hendrickson, 1991.

Wagner, *Wave.* Wagner, C. Peter. *The Third Wave of the Holy Spirit.* Ann Arbor, Mich.: Vine Books, 1988.

Wagner, "Wonders." Wagner, Mark. "Signs and Wonders." Pages 875–76 in *Evangelical Dictionary of World Missions.* Edited by A. Scott Moreau. Grand Rapids: Baker, 2000.

Wagner, "World." Wagner, C. Peter. "Around the World." Pages 79–106 in *Signs and Wonders Today: The Story of Fuller Theological Seminary's Remarkable Course on Spiritual Power.* Rev. ed. Edited by C. Peter Wagner. Altamonte Springs, Fla.: Creation House, 1987.

Wagner and Higdon, "Issues." Wagner, J. T., and T. L. Higdon. "Spiritual Issues and Bioethics in the Intensive Care Unit: The Role of the Chaplain." *CrCareCl* 12 (1996): 15–27.

Wahlde, "Archaeology." Wahlde, Urban C. von. "Archaeology and John's Gospel." Pages 523–86 in *Jesus and Archaeology.* Edited by James H. Charlesworth. Grand Rapids: Eerdmans, 2006.

Währisch-Oblau, "Healing in Migrant Churches." Währisch-Oblau, Claudia. "Material Salvation: Healing, Deliverance, and 'Breakthrough' in African Migrant Churches in Germany." Pages 61–80 in *Global Pentecostal and Charismatic Healing.* Edited by Candy Gunther Brown. Foreword by Harvey Cox. Oxford: Oxford University Press, 2011.

Währisch-Oblau, "Healthy." Währisch-Oblau, Claudia. "God Can Make Us Healthy Through and Through: On Prayers for the Sick and the Interpretation of Healing Experiences in Christian Churches in China and African Immigrant Congregations in Germany." *IntRevMiss* 90 (356/357, Jan./Apr. 2001): 87–102.

Wakefield, *Miracle.* Wakefield, Dan. *Expect a Miracle: The Miraculous Things That Happen to Ordinary People.* San Francisco: HarperSanFrancisco, 1995.

Walbank, *Papers.* Walbank, Frank W. *Selected Papers: Studies in Greek and Roman History and Historiography.* Cambridge: Cambridge University Press, 1985.

Walbank, "Tragedy." Walbank, Frank W. "History and Tragedy." *Historia* 9 (1960): 216–34.

Walker, "Harrist Church." Walker, Sheila Suzanne. "Christianity African Style: The Harrist Church of the Ivory Coast." PhD diss., University of Chicago, 1976.

Walker, "Miracles." Walker, Ian. "Miracles and Violations." *IJPhilRel* 13 (2, 1982): 103–8.

Walker, "Propaganda." Walker, D. P. "Demonic Possession Used as Propaganda in the Later 16th Century." Pages 283–94 in *Possession and Exorcism*. Vol. 9 of *Articles on Witchcraft, Magic, and Demonology: A Twelve-Volume Anthology of Scholarly Articles*. Edited by Brian P. Levack. New York: Garland, 1992. Reprinted from pages 237–48 in *Scienze, Credenze Occulte Livelli di Cultura*. Florence: Olschki, 1982.

Walker, *Revolution*. Walker, Sheila Suzanne. *The Religious Revolution in the Ivory Coast: The Prophet Harris and His Church*. Chapel Hill: University of North Carolina Press, 1983.

Walker, *Siembra*. Walker, Luisa Jeter. *Siembra y cosecha*. Vol. 1–2. Miami: Editoria Vida, 1996.

Walker and Dickerman, "Influence." Walker, Anita M., and Edmund H. Dickerman. "'A Woman under the Influence': A Case of Alleged Possession in Sixteenth-Century France." Pages 183–202 in *Possession and Exorcism*. Vol. 9 of *Articles on Witchcraft, Magic, and Demonology: A Twelve-Volume Anthology of Scholarly Articles*. Edited by Brian P. Levack. New York: Garland, 1992.

Walker and Dickerman, "Woman." Walker, Anita M., and Edmund H. Dickerman. "'A Woman under the Influence': A Case of Alleged Possession in Sixteenth-Century France." *SixtCenJ* 22 (3, 1991): 535–54.

Wall, "Acts." Wall, Robert W. "The Acts of the Apostles." Pages 1–368 in vol. 10 of *The New Interpreter's Bible: A Commentary in Twelve Volumes*. Edited by Leander E. Keck et al. Nashville: Abingdon, 2002.

Wallace, "Debating." Wallace, Dale. "Debating the Witch in the South African Context: Issues Arising from the South African Pagan Council Conference of 2007." *Pom* 10 (1, 2008): 104–21.

Wallace, "Hume." Wallace, R. C. "Hume, Flew, and the Miraculous." *PhilQ* 20 (1970): 230–43.

Wallace, "Observations." Wallace, Robert. "Observations on the Account of the Miracles of the Abbé Paris." Pages 216–18 in Miguel A. Badía Cabrera. "Nota introductoria a la transcripción en inglés y a la traducción al español. *Diál* 83 (2004): 209–23.

Wallace and Forman, "Role." Wallace, John M., and Tyrone A. Forman. "Religion's Role in Promoting Health and Reducing the Risk among American Youth." *HealthEdBeh* 25 (1998): 721–41.

Wallis, "Healing." Wallis, Claudia. "Faith and Healing: Can Prayer, Faith, and Spirituality Really Improve Your Physical Health? A Growing and Surprising Body of Scientific Evidence Says They Can." *Time* 147 (26, June 24, 1996): 58–62, 64.

Walls, "Medical Missionary." Walls, A. F. "'The Heavy Artillery of the Missionary Army': The Domestic Importance of the Nineteenth-Century Medical Missionary." Pages 287–97 in *The Church and Healing: Papers Read at the Twentieth Summer Meeting and the Twenty-first Winter Meeting of the Ecclesiastical History Society*. StChHist 19. Edited by W. J. Sheils. Oxford: Basil Blackwell, 1982.

Walls, *Movement*. Walls, Andrew F. *The Missionary Movement in Christian History: Studies in the Transmission of Faith*. Maryknoll, N.Y.: Orbis, 1996.

Walsh, "Effect." Walsh, Anthony. "The Prophylactic Effect of Religion on Blood Pressure Levels Among a Sample of Immigrants." *SSMed* 14B (1980): 59–63.

Walsh, *Shamanism*. Walsh, Roger. *The World of Shamanism: New Views of an Ancient Tradition*. Woodbury, Minn.: Llewellyn Publications, 2007.

Walsham, "Miracles." Walsham, Alexandra. "Miracles in Post-Reformation England." Pages 273–306 in *Signs, Wonders, Miracles: Representations of Divine Power in the Life of the Church. Papers Read at the 2003 Summer Meeting and the 2004 Winter Meeting of the Ecclesiastical History Society*. Edited by Kate Cooper and Jeremy Gregory. Rochester: Boydell & Brewer, for the Ecclesiastical History Society, 2005.

Walsh et al., "Beliefs." Walsh, Kiri, Michael King, et al. "Spiritual Beliefs May Affect Outcome of Bereavement: Prospective Study." *BMedJ* 324 (7353, 2002): 1551–56.

Walsh et al., "Transcendence." Walsh, James W., Joseph W. Ciarrocchi, Ralph L. Piedmont, and Deborah Haskins. "Spiritual Transcendence and Religious Practices in Recovery from Pathological Gambling: Reducing Pain or Enhancing Quality of Life?" *RSSSR* 18 (2007): 155–75.

Walther, "Kritik." Walther, Manfred. "Spinozas Kritik der Wunder—ein Wunder der Kritik?" *ZTK* 88 (1, 1991): 68–80.

Walton, "Genesis." Walton, John H. "Genesis." Pages 2–159 in vol. 1 of *Zondervan Illustrated Bible Backgrounds Commentary*. Edited by John Walton. 5 vols. Grand Rapids: Zondervan, 2009.

Wanyama et al., "Belief." Wanyama, Jane, B. Castelnuovo, B. Wandera, P. Mwebaze, A. Kambugu, D. R. Bangsberg, et al. "Belief in Divine Healing Can Be a Barrier to Antiretroviral Therapy Adherence in Uganda." *AIDS* 21 (11, 2007): 1486–87.

Ward, "Believing." Ward, Keith. "Believing in Miracles." *Zyg* 37 (3, 2002): 741–50.

Ward, "Cross-Cultural Study." Ward, Colleen A. "The Cross-Cultural Study of Altered States of Consciousness and Mental Health." Pages 15–35 in *Altered States of Consciousness and Mental Health: A Cross-Cultural Perspective*. Edited by Colleen A. Ward. CCRMS 12. Newbury Park, Calif.: Sage, 1989.

Ward, "Introduction." Ward, Colleen A. "Introduction." Pages 8–10 in *Altered States of Consciousness and Mental Health: A Cross-Cultural Perspective*.

Edited by Colleen A. Ward. CCRMS 12. Newbury Park, Calif.: Sage, 1989.

Ward, *Miracles*. Ward, Benedicta. *Miracles and the Medieval Mind: Theory, Record, and Event: 1000–1215*. Philadelphia: University of Pennsylvania Press, 1982.

Ward, "Miracles and Testimony." Ward, Keith. "Miracles and Testimony." *RelS* 21 (1985): 134–45.

Ward, "Monks." Ward, Benedicta. "Monks and Miracle." Pages 127–37 in *Miracles in Jewish and Christian Antiquity: Imagining Truth*. Edited by John C. Cavadini. NDST 3. Notre Dame, Ind.: University of Notre Dame Press, 1999.

Ward, "Possession." Ward, Colleen A. "Possession and Exorcism: Psychopathology and Psychotherapy in a Magico-Religious Context." Pages 125–44 in *Altered States of Consciousness and Mental Health: A Cross-Cultural Perspective*. Edited by Colleen A. Ward. CCRMS 12. Newbury Park, Calif.: Sage, 1989.

Ward and Beaubrun, "Psychodynamics." Ward, Colleen, and Michael H. Beaubrun. "The Psychodynamics of Demon Possession." *JSSR* 19 (1980): 201–7.

Ward and Beaubrun, "Possession." Ward, Colleen, and Michael H. Beaubrun. "Spirit Possession and Neuroticism in a West Indian Pentecostal Community." *BSClinPsyc* 20 (4, Nov. 1981): 295–96.

"Warfare Report." "Appendix: Statement on Spiritual Warfare: A Working Group Report." Pages 309–12 in *Deliver Us from Evil: An Uneasy Frontier in Christian Mission*. Edited by A. Scott Moreau, Tokunboh Adeyemo, David G. Burnett, Bryant L. Myers, and Hwa Yung. Monrovia, Calif.: Lausanne Committee for World Evangelization, 2002.

Warfield, "Kikuyu." Warfield, Benjamin B. "Kikuyu, Clerical Veracity, and Miracles." *PTR* 12 (1914): 529–85.

Warfield, *Miracles*. Warfield, B. B. *Counterfeit Miracles*. Reprint, Carlisle, Pa.; Edinburgh: Banner of Truth Trust, 1972.

Warneck, *Christ*. Warneck, Johannes. *The Living Christ and Dying Heathenism*. 3rd ed. New York: Revell, n.d.

Warner, *Evangelist*. Warner, Wayne E. *The Woman Evangelist: The Life and Times of Charismatic Evangelist Maria B. Woodworth-Etter*. Studies in Evangelicalism 8. Metuchen, N.J.: Scarecrow, 1986.

Warner, "Introduction." Warner, Wayne E. "Introduction." Pages 15–24 in Smith Wigglesworth. *The Anointing of His Spirit*. Compiled and edited by Wayne Warner. Ann Arbor, Mich.: Servant, 1994.

Warner, *Kuhlman*. Warner, Wayne E. *Kathryn Kuhlman: The Woman Behind the Miracles*. Ann Arbor, Mich.: Servant, 1993.

Warner, "Living by Faith." Warner, Wayne E. "'Living by Faith': A Story of Paul and Betty Wells." *AGHer* 16 (4, Winter 1996–97): 3–4, 24.

Warner, "Position." Warner, Timothy M. "An Evangelical Position on Bondage and Exorcism." Pages 77–88 in *Essays on Spiritual Bondage and Deliverance*. Edited by Willard M. Swartley. Occasional Papers 11. Elkhart, Ind.: Institute of Mennonite Studies, 1988.

Warner, "Still Healed." Warner, Wayne E. "Still Healed of TB—after Fifty-two Years." *PentEv* (July 8, 2001): 28.

Warner, "Wigglesworth." Warner, Wayne E. "Wigglesworth, Smith." Pages 883–84 in *Dictionary of Pentecostal and Charismatic Movements*. Edited by Stanley M. Burgess, Gary B. McGee, and Patrick H. Alexander. Grand Rapids: Zondervan, 1988.

Warner, "Witchcraft." Warner, Richard. "Witchcraft and Soul Loss: Implications for Community Psychiatry." *HCPsy* 28 (9, 1977): 686–90.

Warrington, *Healer*. Warrington, Keith. *Jesus the Healer: Paradigm or Unique Phenomenon*. Carlisle: Paternoster, 2000.

Warrington, "Healing." Warrington, Keith. "Healing and Suffering in the Bible." *IntRevMiss* 95 (376–377, 2006): 154–65.

Warrington, "Healing Narratives." Warrington, Keith. "Acts and the Healing Narratives: Why?" *JPT* 14 (2, 2006): 189–217.

Warrington, "Response." Warrington, Keith. "A Response to James Shelton Concerning Jesus and Healing: Yesterday and Today." *JPT* 15 (2, 2007): 185–93.

Watlington and Murphy, "Roles." Watlington, Christina G., and Christopher M. Murphy. "The Roles of Religion and Spirituality among African American Survivors of Domestic Violence." *JClPsychol* 62 (7, 2006): 837–57.

Watson, "Leader." Watson, Dan. "Religious Commune Leader Indicted in '75 Kidnaping." *Dallas Morning News* (Nov. 25, 1976): D1.

Watson, "Natural Law." Watson, Gerard. "The Natural Law and Stoicism." Pages 216–38 in *Problems in Stoicism*. Edited by A. A. Long. London: University of London, Athlone Press, 1971.

Watt, "Dangers." Watt, Charles Peter. "Some Dangers in the Globalization of Pentecostalism: A South African Perspective." *Missionalia* 34 (2/3, Aug. 2006): 380–94.

Watt, "Demons." Watt, Jeffrey R. "The Demons of Carpi: Exorcism, Witchcraft, and the Inquisition in a Seventeenth-Century Convent." *ARG* 98 (2007): 107–33.

Watt, "Evidence." Watt, Ward B. "I Don't See How We Can Gather Empirical Evidence about How the Natural Order Itself Came into Being." Pages 220–24 in *Cosmos, Bios, and Theos: Scientists Reflect* on Science, God, and the Origins of the Universe, Life, and Homo Sapiens. Edited by Henry Margenau and Roy Abraham Varghese. La Salle, Ill.: Open Court, 1992.

Wayman, "Meaning." Wayman, Alex. "The Religious Meaning of Possession States (with Indo-Tibetan Emphasis)." Pages 167–79 in Trance and Possession States. Proceedings of the Second Annual Conference, R. M. Bucke Memorial Society, March 4–6, 1966. Edited by Raymond Prince. Montreal: R. M. Bucke Memorial Society, 1968.

Wazara, "Ministry." Wazara, Zach. "The Ministry and the Marketplace." Pages 151–71 in Out of Africa: How the Spiritual Explosion Among Nigerians Is Impacting the World. Edited by C. Peter Wagner and Joseph Thompson. Ventura, Calif.: Regal, 2004.

Weatherhead, Psychology. Weatherhead, Leslie D. Psychology, Religion. and Healing. New York: Abingdon-Cokesbury, 1952.

Weber, "Figure." Weber, Jeremy. "Go Figure." CT 53 (9, Sept. 2009): 20.

Webster, "Salvation." Webster, Robert. "Seeing Salvation: The Place of Dreams and Visions in John Wesley's Arminian Magazine." Pages 376–88 in Signs, Wonders, Miracles: Representations of Divine Power in the Life of the Church. Papers Read at the 2003 Summer Meeting and the 2004 Winter Meeting of the Ecclesiastical History Society. Edited by Kate Cooper and Jeremy Gregory. Rochester: Boydell & Brewer, for the Ecclesiastical History Society, 2005.

Webster, "Terrors." Webster, Robert. "'Those Distracting Terrors of the Enemy': Demonic Possession and Exorcism in the Thought of John Wesley." BJRL 85 (2/3, 2003): 373–85.

Weeden, "Heresy." Weeden, Theodore J. "The Heresy That Necessitated Mark's Gospel." ZNW 59 (1968): 145–58.

Weeden, Mark. Weeden, Theodore J., Sr. Mark—Traditions in Conflict. Philadelphia: Fortress, 1971.

Weeks, "Medicine." Weeks, Kent. "Medicine, Surgery, and Public Health in Ancient Egypt." Pages 1787–98 in vol. 3 of Civilizations of the Ancient Near East. Edited by Jack M. Sasson. 4 vols. New York: Scribner, 1995.

Wei, "Meaning." Wei, Tan Tai. "Professor Langford's Meaning of 'Miracle.'" RelS 8 (3, 1972): 251–55.

Wei, "Young." Wei, Tan Tei. "Mr. Young on Miracles." RelS 10 (1974): 333–37.

Weintraub, "Credibility." Weintraub, Ruth. "The Credibility of Miracles." PhilSt 82 (1996): 359–75.

Weisman and Hackett, "Predilection." Weisman, A. D., and T. P. Hackett. "Predilection to Death: Death and Dying as a Psychiatric Problem." PsychMed 23 (1961): 232–56.

Weiss, Zeichen. Weiss, Wolfgang. 'Zeichen und Wunder': Eine Studie zu der Sprachtradition und ihrer Verwendung im Neuen Testament. WMANT 67. Neukirchen-Vluyn: Neukirchener Verlag, 1995.

Weissenrieder, Images. Weissenrieder, Annette. Images of Illness in the Gospel of Luke: Insights of Ancient Medical Texts. WUNT 2.164. Tübingen: Mohr Siebeck, 2003.

Welbourn, "Exorcism." Welbourn, F. B. "Exorcism." Theology 75 (1972): 593–96.

Welbourn, "Healing." Welbourn, F. B. "Healing as a Psychosomatic Event." Pages 351–68 in Afro-Christian Religion and Healing in Southern Africa. Edited by G. C. Oosthuizen, S. D. Edwards, W. H. Wessels, and I. Hexham. AfSt 8. Lewiston, N.Y.: Edwin Mellen, 1989.

Welbourn, "Spirit Initiation." Welbourn, F. B. "Spirit Initiation in Ankole and a Christian Spirit Movement in Western Kenya." Pages 290–306 in Spirit Mediumship and Society in Africa. Edited by John Beattie and John Middleton. Foreword by Raymond Firth. New York: Africana Publishing Corporation, 1969.

Welch, "Miracles." Welch, John W. "Miracles, Maleficium, and Maiestas in the Trial of Jesus." Pages 349–83 in Jesus and Archaeology. Edited by James H. Charlesworth. Grand Rapids: Eerdmans, 2006.

Welch, "Myths." Welch, Claude. "Dispelling Some Myths about the Split between Theology and Science in the Nineteenth Century." Pages 29–40 in Religion and Science: History, Method, Dialogue. Edited by W. Mark Richardson and Wesley J. Wildman. Foreword by Ian G. Barbour. New York: Routledge, 1996.

Weld, "Impasse." Weld, W. C. "An Ecuadorian Impasse." MA thesis, Fuller Theological Seminary, 1968.

Welton, "Themes." Welton, Michael R. "Themes in African Traditional Belief and Ritual." PracAnth 18 (1971): 1–18.

Wendl, "Slavery." Wendl, Tobias. "Slavery, Spirit Possession and Ritual Consciousness: The Tchamba Cult among the Mina of Togo." Pages 111–23 in Spirit Possession, Modernity and Power in Africa. Edited by Heike Behrend and Ute Luig. Madison: University of Wisconsin Press, 1999.

Wenger and Carmel, "Religiosity." Wenger, Neil S., and Sara Carmel. "Physicians' Religiosity and End-of-Life Care Attitudes and Behaviors." MSJMed 71 (5, 2004): 335–43.

Wengert and Krey, "Exorcism." Wengert, Timothy J., and Philip D. W. Krey. "A June 1546 Exorcism in Wittenberg as a Pastoral Act." ARG 98 (2007): 71–83.

Wenham, Bible. Wenham, John W. Christ and the Bible. Downers Grove, Ill.: InterVarsity, 1977.

Wenham, "Story." Wenham, David. "The Story of Jesus Known to Paul." Pages 297–311 in *Jesus of Nazareth: Lord and Christ. Essays on the Historical Jesus and New Testament Christology.* Edited by Joel B. Green and Max Turner. Grand Rapids: Eerdmans, 1994.

Wenneberg et al., "Study." Wenneberg, S. R., R. H. Schneider, K. G. Walton, et al. "A Controlled Study for the Effects of the Transcendental Meditation Program on Cardiovascular Reactivity and Ambulatory Blood Pressure." *IJNeurSc* 89 (1–2, 1997): 15–28.

Wensinck, "Mu'djiza." Wensinck, A. J. "Mu'djiza." Page 295 in vol. 7 of *The Encyclopaedia of Islam.* New ed. Edited by C. E. Bosworth et al. 12 vols. Leiden: Brill, 1978–2004.

Werbner, "Truth." Werbner, Richard. "Truth-on-Balance: Knowing the Opaque Other in Tswapong Wisdom Divination." Pages 190–211 in *Witchcraft Dialogues: Anthropological and Philosophical Exchanges.* Edited by George Clement Bond and Diane M. Ciekawy. Athens: Center for International Studies, Ohio University, 2001.

Wesley, *Church.* Wesley, Luke. *The Church in China: Persecuted, Pentecostal, and Powerful.* Baguio City, Philippines: AJPS Books, 2004.

Wesley, *Journal.* Wesley, John. *The Journal of the Rev. John Wesley.* Edited by Nehemiah Curnock. 8 vols. London: Epworth, 1938.

Wesley, *Journal* (1974). Wesley, John. *The Journal of John Wesley.* Edited by Percy Livingstone Parker. Chicago: Moody Press, 1974.

Wesley, *Stories.* Wesley, Luke. *Stories from China: Fried Rice for the Soul.* Milton Keynes: Authentic Media, 2005.

Wessels, "Practices." Wessels, W. H. "Healing Practices in the African Independent Churches." Pages 91–108 in *Afro-Christian Religion and Healing in Southern Africa.* Edited by G. C. Oosthuizen, S. D. Edwards, W. H. Wessels, and I. Hexham. AfSt 8. Lewiston, N.Y.: Edwin Mellen, 1989.

West, *Inscriptions.* West, Allen Brown. *Latin Inscriptions 1896–1926.* Vol. 8, part 2 in *Corinth: Results of Excavations Conducted by the American School of Classical Studies at Athens.* Cambridge, Mass.: Harvard University Press, 1931.

West, "Introduction." West, Martin L. "Introduction." Pages 2–37 in *Greek Epic Fragments from the Seventh to the Fifth Centuries B.C.* Edited and translated by Martin L. West. LCL 497. Cambridge, Mass.: Harvard University Press, 2003.

West, *Miracles.* West, D. J. *Eleven Lourdes Miracles.* London: Gerald Duckworth & Co., 1957.

West, *Sorcery.* West, Harry G. *Ethnographic Sorcery.* Chicago: University of Chicago Press, 2007.

Westmeier, *Pentecostalism.* Westmeier, Karl-Wilhelm. *Protestant Pentecostalism in Latin America: A Study in the Dynamics of Missions.* Madison, N.J.: Fairleigh Dickinson University Press, 1999.

Wetering, "Effectiveness." Wetering, W. van. "The Effectiveness of a Rite: Exorcism of Demons in an Afro-American Religion." *NedTT* 37 (3, 1983): 216–29.

Whately, *Doubts.* Whately, Richard. *Historic Doubts Relative to Napoleon Bonaparte.* Andover: Warren F. Draper, 1874.

Wheeler, *Beyond Frontiers.* Wheeler, Sir Mortimer. *Rome Beyond the Imperial Frontiers.* Westport, Conn.: Greenwood, 1971.

Whisson, "Disorders." Whisson, Michael G. "Some Aspects of Functional Disorders among the Kenyan Luo." Pages 283–304 in *Magic, Faith, and Healing: Studies in Primitive Psychiatry Today.* Edited by Ari Kiev. Foreword by Jerome D. Frank. New York: Free Press, 1964.

Whitcomb, "Miracles." Whitcomb, John C., Jr. "Does God Want Christians to Perform Miracles Today?" *GrJ* 12 (3, 1971): 3–12.

White, *Adventure.* White, Anne S. *Healing Adventure.* Foreword by Dennis J. Bennett. Plainfield, N.J.: Logos, 1969.

White, *Artemidorus.* White, Robert J. "Commentary on Artemidorus." *The Interpretation of Dreams (Oneirocritica).* NCS. Park Ridge, N.J.: Noyes Press, 1975.

White, "Calling." White, Gayle. "Colorblind Calling." *The Atlanta Journal & Constitution* (Nov. 3, 1991): M1, 4.

White, "Lady." White, John. "Young Lady, Old Hag." Pages 69–86 in *Power Encounters among Christians in the Western World.* Edited by Kevin Springer, with an introduction and afterword by John Wimber. San Francisco: Harper & Row, 1988.

White, "Regrets." White, Loretta. "Laying Aside Regrets." Pages 175–85 in *Power Encounters Among Christians in the Western World.* Edited by Kevin Springer, with an introduction and afterword by John Wimber. San Francisco: Harper & Row, 1988.

White, "Revival." White, Eryn. "Revival and Renewal Amongst the Eighteenth-Century Welsh Methodists." Pages 1–12 in *Revival, Renewal, and the Holy Spirit.* Edited by Dyfed Wyn Roberts. SEHT. Eugene, Ore.: Wipf & Stock, 2009.

White, *Spirit.* White, John. *When the Spirit Comes with Power: Signs and Wonders among God's People.* Downers Grove, Ill.: InterVarsity, 1988.

White Crawford, "Folly." White Crawford, S. "Lady Wisdom and Dame Folly at Qumran." *DSD* 5 (3, 1998): 355–66.

Whittaker, *Jews and Christians*. Whittaker, Molly. *Jews and Christians: Graco-Roman Views*. CCWJCW 6. Cambridge: Cambridge University Press, 1984.

Wickkiser, "Asklepios." Wickkiser, Bronwen. "Asklepios Appears in a Dream: Antiquity's Greatest Healer." *ArchOd* 8 (4, 2005): 14–25, 48–49.

Wiebe, "Compatibility." Wiebe, Don. "Science and Religion: Is Compatibility Possible?" *JASA* 30 (4, 1978): 169–76.

Wiebe, "Persistence of Spiritism." Wiebe, James P. "Persistence of Spiritism in Brazil." DMiss diss., Fuller Theological Seminary, 1979.

Wigger, *Saint*. Wigger, John. *American Saint: Francis Asbury and the Methodists*. Oxford: Oxford University Press, 2009.

Wigginton, *Foxfire Book*. Wigginton, Eliot, ed. *The Foxfire Book: hog dressing; log cabin building; mountain crafts and food; planting by the signs; snake lore, hunting tales, faith healing; moonshining; and other affairs of plain living*. Garden City, N.Y.: Anchor, 1972.

Wigglesworth, *Anointing*. Wigglesworth, Smith. *The Anointing of His Spirit*. Compiled and edited by Wayne Warner. Ann Arbor, Mich.: Servant, 1994.

Wigner, "Relativity." Wigner, Eugene. "Relativity, Quantum Theory, and the Mystery of Life." Pages 270–77 in *Cosmos, Bios, and Theos: Scientists Reflect on Science, God, and the Origins of the Universe, Life, and Homo Sapiens*. Edited by Henry Margenau and Roy Abraham Varghese. La Salle, Ill.: Open Court, 1992.

Wikenhauser, "Doppelträume." Wikenhauser, Alfred. "Doppelträume." *Bib* 29 (1948): 100–111.

Wikenhauser, *Introduction*. Wikenhauser, Alfred. *New Testament Introduction*. New York: Herder & Herder, 1963.

Wikstrom, "Possession." Wikstrom, Owe. "Possession as Role-Taking." *JRelHealth* 28 (1, 1989): 26–35.

Wilcox, "Blind." Wilcox, David. "How Blind the Watchmaker?" Pages 168–81 in *Evidence of Purpose: Scientists Discover the Creator*. Edited by John Marks Templeton. New York: Continuum, 1994.

Wild, "Witchcraft." Wild, Emma. "Is It Witchcraft? Is It Satan? It Is a Miracle. Mai-Mai Soldiers and Christian Concepts of Evil in North-East Congo." *JRelAf* 28 (4, 1998): 450–67.

Wildman, "Quest." Wildman, Wesley J. "The Quest for Harmony: An Interpretation of Contemporary Theology and Science." Pages 41–60 in *Religion and Science: History, Method, Dialogue*. Edited by W. Mark Richardson and Wesley J. Wildman. Foreword by Ian G. Barbour. New York: Routledge, 1996.

Wiles, "Miracles." Wiles, Maurice F. "Miracles in the Early Church." Pages 219–34 in *Miracles: Cambridge Studies in Their Philosophy and History*. Edited by C. F. D. Moule. New York: Morehouse-Barlow, 1965.

Wilkerson, *Beyond*. Wilkerson, Ralph. *Beyond and Back: Those Who Died and Lived to Tell It!* Anaheim: Melodyland Productions, 1977.

Wilkerson, *Cross*. Wilkerson, David, with John Sherrill and Elizabeth Sherrill. *The Cross and the Switchblade*. New York: Pyramid, 1962.

Wilkie, "Imagination." Wilkie, Rab. "Spirited Imagination: Ways of Approaching the Shaman's World." Pages 135–64 in *Being Changed: The Anthropology of Extraordinary Experience*. Edited by David Young and Jean-Guy Goulet. Peterborough, Ont.: Broadview, 1994.

Wilkins, "Attitudes." Wilkins, Kay S. "Attitudes to Witchcraft and Demonic Possession in France During the Eighteenth Century." Pages 296–310 in *Possession and Exorcism*. Vol. 9 of *Articles on Witchcraft, Magic, and Demonology: A Twelve-Volume Anthology of Scholarly Articles*. Edited by Brian P. Levack. New York: Garland, 1992. Reprinted from *JEurSt* 3 (1973): 348–62.

Wilkins, "Mary and Demons." Wilkins, Katharina. "Mary and the Demons: Marian Devotion and Ritual Healing in Tanzania." *JRelAf* 39 (3, 2009): 295–318.

Wilkinson, *Healing*. Wilkinson, John. *The Bible and Healing: A Medical and Theological Commentary*. Edinburgh: Handsel; Grand Rapids: Eerdmans, 1998.

Wilkinson, *Health*. Wilkinson, John. *Health and Healing: Studies in New Testament Principles and Practice*. Edinburgh: Handsel Press, 1980.

Willemsen et al., "Upbringing." Willemsen, G., and D. I. Boomsma. "Religious Upbringing and Neuroticism in Dutch Twin Families." *TwinResHumGen* 10 (2, 2007): 327–33.

Williams, "Acts." Williams, Demetrius K. "The Acts of the Apostles." Pages 213–48 in *True to Our Native Land: An African American New Testament Commentary*. Edited by Brian K. Blount, with Cain Hope Felder, Clarice J. Martin, and Emerson Powery. Minneapolis: Fortress, 2007.

Williams, "Answer." Williams, Timothy. "Pentecostalism's Answer to Indonesia's Unreached Muslims." *JAM* 5 (1, 2003): 93–118.

Williams, "Bwaya." Williams, Mark S. "*Bwaya* as Spirit-Being: Filipino Islam and the Supernatural." *JAM* 7 (1, 2005): 119–31.

Williams, *Doctor*. Williams, Harley. *A Doctor Looks at Miracles*. London: Anthony Blond, 1959.

Williams, "Healing." Williams, C. Peter. "Healing and Evangelism: The Place of Medicine in Later Victorian Protestant Missionary Thinking." Pages 271–85 in *The Church and Healing: Papers Read at the Twentieth Summer Meeting and the Twenty-first Winter Meeting of the Ecclesiastical History Society*.

StChHist 19. Edited by W. J. Sheils. Oxford: Basil Blackwell, 1982.

Williams, *Miracle Stories*. Williams, Benjamin E. *Miracle Stories in the Biblical Book: Acts of the Apostles*. MBPS 59. Lewiston, N.Y.: Edwin Mellen, 2001.

Williams, *Miraculous*. Williams, T. C. *The Idea of the Miraculous: The Challenge to Science and Religion*. New York: St. Martin's Press, 1990.

Williams, *Radical Reformation*. Williams, George Huntston. *The Radical Reformation*. Philadelphia: Westminster, 1962.

Williams, *Renewal Theology*. Williams, J. Rodman. *Renewal Theology*. 3 vols. Vol. 2: *Salvation, the Holy Spirit, and Christian Living*. Grand Rapids: Academie Books, Zondervan, 1990.

Williams, "Seismology." Williams, Gareth D. "Greco-Roman Seismology and Seneca on Earthquakes in *Natural Questions 6*." *JRS* 96 (2006): 124–46.

Williams, *Signs*. Williams, Don. *Signs, Wonders, and the Kingdom of God: A Biblical Guide for the Reluctant Skeptic*. Ann Arbor, Mich.: Vine Books, 1989.

Williams, *Tokens*. Williams, Rowan. *Tokens of Trust: An Introduction to Christian Belief*. Louisville: Westminster John Knox, 2007.

Willis, *Revival*. Willis, Avery T., Jr. *Indonesian Revival: Why Two Million Came to Christ*. Pasadena, Calif.: William Carey Library, 1977.

Willis et al., *Spirits*. Willis, Roy, with K. B. S. Chisanga, H. M. K. Sikazwe, Kapembwa B. Sikazwe, and Sylvia Nanyangwe. *Some Spirits Heal, Others Only Dance: A Journey into Human Selfhood in an African Village*. Oxford: Berg, 1999.

Wills, "Miracles." Wills, James. "Miracles and Scientific Law." *RevExp* 59 (2, Spring 1962): 137–45.

Wills, Yaeger, and Sandy, "Effect." Wills, Thomas Ashby, Alison M. Yaeger, and James M. Sandy. "Buffering Effect of Religiosity for Adolescent Substance Use." *PsyAdBeh* 17 (1, 2003): 24–31.

Wilmore, *Religion*. Wilmore, Gayraud S. *Black Religion and Black Radicalism: An Interpretation of the Religious History of Afro-American People*. 2nd rev. ed. Maryknoll, N.Y.: Orbis, 1989.

Wilson, "Ambiguity." Wilson, Peter J. "Status Ambiguity and Spirit Possession." *Man*, n.s., 2 (3, Sept. 1967): 366–78.

Wilson, *Bleeding Mind*. Wilson, Ian. *The Bleeding Mind*. London: Weidenfeld and Nicolson, 1988.

Wilson, "Exorcism." Wilson, Michael. "Exorcism: A Clinical-Pastoral Practice Which Raises Serious Questions." *ExpT* 86 (10, 1975): 292–95.

Wilson, *Healing*. Wilson, Michael. *The Church Is Healing*. Naperville, Ill.: SCM, 1966.

Wilson, "Hysteria." Wilson, William P. "Hysteria and Demons, Depression and Oppression, Good and Evil." Pages 223–31 in *Demon Possession: A Medical, Historical, Anthropological, and Theological Symposium*. Papers presented at the University of Notre Dame, January 8–11, 1975, under the auspices of the Christian Medical Association. Edited by John Warwick Montgomery. Minneapolis: Bethany House, 1976.

Wilson, "Miracle Events." Wilson, William P. "How Religious or Spiritual Miracle Events Happen Today." Pages 264–79 in *Religious and Spiritual Events*. Vol. 1 of *Miracles: God, Science, and Psychology in the Paranormal*. Edited by J. Harold Ellens. Westport, Conn.; London: Praeger, 2008.

Wilson, "Miracles." Wilson, John. "The Miracles of the Gospels." *AmJTh* 9 (1905): 10–33.

Wilson, "Possession." Wilson, William P. "Demon Possession and Exorcism: A Reaction to Page." *JPsyTh* 17 (2, 1989): 135–39.

Wilson, *Power*. Wilson, Henry B. *The Power to Heal: A Handbook for the Practice of Healing according to the Methods of Jesus*. Foreword by C. H. Brent. Asheville, N.C.: Nazarene Press, 1923.

Wilson, "Revival." Wilson, Everett A. "Revival and Revolution in Latin America." Pages 180–93 in *Modern Christian Revivals*. Edited by Edith Blumhofer and Randall H. Balmer. Urbana: University of Illinois Press, 1993.

Wilson, "Seeing." Wilson, C. Roderick. "Seeing They See Not." Pages 197–208 in *Being Changed: The Anthropology of Extraordinary Experience*. Edited by David Young and Jean-Guy Goulet. Peterborough, Ont.: Broadview, 1994.

Wilson, "Spirits." Wilson, Peter J. "Correspondence: Spirits and the Sex War." *Man*, n.s., 2 (4, Dec. 1967): 628–29.

Wilson, *Swahili*. Wilson, Peter. *Simplified Swahili*. 2nd ed. Nairobi: Longman Kenya, 1985.

Wimber, *Healing*. Wimber, John, with Kevin Springer. *Power Healing*. San Francisco: Harper & Row, 1987.

Wimber, *Power Evangelism*. Wimber, John, with Kevin Springer. *Power Evangelism*. San Francisco: Harper & Row, 1986.

Wimber, *Wimber*. Wimber, Carol. *John Wimber: The Way It Was*. London: Hodder & Stoughton, 1999.

Wimber, "Zip." Wimber, John. "Zip to 3,000 in Five Years." Pages 27–37 in *Signs and Wonders Today: The Story of Fuller Theological Seminary's Remarkable Course on Spiritual Power*. Rev. ed. Edited by C. Peter Wagner. Altamonte Springs, Fla.: Creation House, 1987.

Winckley, "Healing." Winckley, Edward. "The Church's Ministry of Healing." Pages 175–81 in

Healing and Religious Faith. Edited by Claude A. Frazier. Philadelphia: Pilgrim Press, United Church Press, 1974.

Wink, "Reply." Wink, Walter. "Jesus' Reply to John: Matt 11:2–6/Luke 7:18–23." *Forum* 5 (1989): 121–28.

Wink, "Stories." Wink, Walter. "Our Stories, Cosmic Stories, and the Biblical Story." Pages 209–22 in *Sacred Stories: A Celebration of the Power of Story to Transform and Heal.* Edited by Charles Simpkinson and Anne Simpkinson. San Francisco: HarperSanFrancisco, 1993.

Wink, *Transformation.* Wink, Walter. *The Bible in Human Transformation.* Afterword by Marcus J. Borg. Minneapolis: Fortress, 2010.

Wink, "Worldview." Wink, Walter. "The New Worldview: Spirit at the Core of Everything." Pages 17–28 in *Transforming the Powers: Peace, Justice, and the Domination System.* Edited by Ray Gingerich and Ted Grimsrud. Minneapolis: Fortress, 2006.

Wink, "Write." Wink, Walter. "Write What You See." *FourR* 7 (3, May 1994): 3–9.

Wink, Larsen, and Dillon, "Religion." Wink, Paul, Britta Larsen, and Michele Dillon. "Religion as Moderator of the Depression-Health Connection: Findings from a Longitudinal Study." *ResAg* 27 (2, 2005): 197–220.

Wink and Dillon, "Development." Wink, Paul, and Michele Dillon. "Spiritual Development Across the Adult Life Course: Findings from a Longitudinal Study." *JAdDev* 9 (1, 2002): 79–94.

Wink and Scott, "Religiousness." Wink, Paul, and Julia Scott. "Does Religiousness Buffer against the Fear of Death and Dying in Late Adulthood? Findings from a Longitudinal Study." *JGer* 60 (4, 2005): P207–14.

Winkelman, "Shamanism." Winkelman, Michael. "Shamanism and the Origins of Spirituality and Ritual Healing." *JSRNC* 3 (4, 2009): 458–89.

Winkelman, "Spirituality." Winkelman, Michael. "Spirituality and the Healing of Addictions: A Shamanic Drumming Approach." Pages 455–70 in *Religion and Healing in America.* Edited by Linda L. Barnes and Susan S. Sered. New York: Oxford University Press, 2005.

Winkelman and Carr, "Approach." Winkelman, Michael, and Christopher Carr. "Teaching about Shamanism and Religious Healing: A Cross-Cultural, Biosocial-Spiritual Approach." Pages 171–90 in *Teaching Religion and Healing.* Edited by Linda L. Barnes and Inés Talamantez. AARTRSS. Oxford: Oxford University Press, 2006.

Winslow, "Care." Winslow, Mark H. "Pastoral Care of the Demonized Person." Pages 192–206 in *Essays on Spiritual Bondage and Deliverance.* Edited by Willard

M. Swartley. Occasional Papers 11. Elkhart, Ind.: Institute of Mennonite Studies, 1988.

Winston, *Faith.* Winston, Kimberly. *Faith Beyond Faith Healing: Finding Hope after Shattered Dreams.* Brewster, Mass.: Paraclete, 2002.

Winter, "Burden of Proof." Winter, Dagmar. "The Burden of Proof in Jesus Research." Pages 843–51 in *Handbook for the Study of the Historical Jesus.* Edited by Tom Holmén and Stanley E. Porter. 4 vols. Boston: Brill, 2010.

Wire, "Story." Wire, Antoinette Clark. "The Miracle Story as the Whole Story." *SEAJT* 22 (2, 1981): 29–37.

Wire, "Structure." Wire, Antoinette Clark. "The Structure of the Gospel Miracle Stories and Their Tellers." *Semeia* 11 (1978): 83–111.

Wise, "Healings." Wise, Henrietta. "Healings in India." *PentEv* 578 (Jan. 3, 1925): 6.

Wise, "Introduction" to 4Q242. Wise, Michael O. "Introduction" to 4Q242. Pages 265–66 in *The Dead Sea Scrolls: A New Translation,* by Michael Wise, Martin Abegg Jr., and Edward Cook. San Francisco: HarperSanFrancisco, 1999.

Wise, Abegg, and Cook, *Scrolls.* Wise, Michael, Martin Abegg Jr., and Edward Cook. *The Dead Sea Scrolls: A New Translation.* San Francisco: HarperSanFrancisco, 1996.

Wiseman, *Paradise.* Wiseman, Beth. *Plain Paradise.* Nashville: Thomas Nelson, 2010.

Witherington, *Acts.* Witherington, Ben, III. *The Acts of the Apostles: A Socio-Rhetorical Commentary.* Grand Rapids: Eerdmans, 1998.

Witherington, *Christology.* Witherington, Ben, III. *The Christology of Jesus.* Minneapolis: Augsburg Fortress, 1990.

Witherington, *Corinthians.* Witherington, Ben, III. *Conflict and Community in Corinth: A Socio-Rhetorical Commentary on 1 and 2 Corinthians.* Grand Rapids: Eerdmans, 1995.

Witherington, *End.* Witherington, Ben, III. *Jesus, Paul and the End of the World: A Comparative Study in New Testament Eschatology.* Downers Grove, Ill.: InterVarsity, 1992.

Witherington, *Money.* Witherington, Ben, III. *Jesus and Money.* Grand Rapids: Brazos, 2009.

Witherington, *Wisdom.* Witherington, Ben, III. *John's Wisdom: A Commentary on the Fourth Gospel.* Louisville: Westminster John Knox, 1995.

Witherington, *Women.* Witherington, Ben, III. *Women in the Ministry of Jesus: A Study of Jesus' Attitudes to Women and Their Roles as Reflected in His Earthly Life.* SNTSMS 51. Cambridge: Cambridge University Press, 1984.

Witmer, "Doctrine." Witmer, John A. "The Doctrine of Miracles." *BSac* 130 (255, 1973): 126–34.

Witty, *Healing*. Witty, Robert G. *Divine Healing: A Balanced Biblical View*. Foreword by Paul Yonggi Cho. Nashville: Broadman, 1989.

Wiyono, "Pentecostalism in Indonesia." Wiyono, Gani. "Pentecostalism in Indonesia." Pages 307–28 in *Asian and Pentecostal: The Charismatic Face of Christianity in Asia*. Edited by Allan Anderson and Edmond Tang. Foreword by Cecil M. Robeck. Regnum Studies in Mission, AJPSS 3. Oxford: Regnum; Baguio City, Philippines: APTS Press, 2005.

Wiyono, "Timor Revival." Wiyono, Gani. "Timor Revival: A Historical Study of the Great Twentieth-Century Revival in Indonesia." *AJPS* 4 (2, 2001): 269–93.

Wodi, "Wodi." Wodi, Sam. "Wodi, Herbert Nyemahame Amadi." *DACB*. http://www.dacb.org/stories/nigeria/wodi_amadi.html.

Woldu, *Gifts*. Woldu, Gebru. *Gifts of the Holy Spirit and How to Use Them*. Lake Mary, Fla.: Creation House, 2004.

Wolfe, "Potential." Wolfe, Alan. "The Potential for Pluralism: Religious Responses to the Triumph of Theory and Method in American Academic Culture." Pages 22–39 in *Religion, Scholarship, Higher Education: Perspectives, Models, and Future Prospects*. Edited by Andrea Sterk. Notre Dame, Ind.: University of Notre Dame Press, 2001.

Wolffe, *Expansion*. Wolffe, John. *The Expansion of Evangelicalism: The Age of Wilberforce, More, Chalmers and Finney*. Downers Grove, Ill.: InterVarsity, 2007.

Wolfson, *Philo*. Wolfson, Harry Austryn. *Philo: Foundations of Religious Philosophy in Judaism, Christianity, and Islam*. 4th rev. ed. 2 vols. Cambridge, Mass.: Harvard University Press, 1968.

Wollin et al., "Predictors." Wollin, S. R., J. L. Plummer, H. Owen, R. M. Hawkins, and F. Materazzo. "Predictors of Preoperative Anxiety in Children." *AnIntCare* 31 (1, 2003): 69–74.

Wolterstorff, "Theology and Science." Wolterstorff, Nicholas. "Theology and Science: Listening to Each Other." Pages 95–104 in *Religion and Science: History, Method, Dialogue*. Edited by W. Mark Richardson and Wesley J. Wildman. Foreword by Ian G. Barbour. New York: Routledge, 1996.

Wong, *Singapore*. Wong, James. *Singapore: The Church in the Midst of Change*. Singapore: Church Growth Study Center, 1973.

Wong et al., "Factors." Wong, Y. K., W. C. Tsai, J. C. Lin, C. K. Poon, S. Y. Chao, Y. L. Hsiao, et al. "Socio-demographic Factors in the Prognosis of Oral Cancer Patients." *OrOnc* 42 (9, 2006): 893–906.

Wood, "Appetites." Wood, Martin. "Divine Appetites: Food Miracles, Authority, and Religious Identities in the Gujarati Hindu Diaspora." *JContRel* 23 (3, 2008): 337–53.

Wood, "Healings in Argentina." Wood, Alice C. "Healings in Argentina." *PentEv* 430–431 (Feb. 4, 1922): 13.

Wood, "Preparation." Wood, R. Paul, and Wardine Wood. "Preparation for Signs and Wonders." Pages 60–73 in *Signs and Wonders in Ministry Today*. Edited by Benny C. Aker and Gary B. McGee. Foreword by Thomas E. Trask. Springfield, Mo.: Gospel Publishing House, 1996.

Woodard, *Faith*. Woodard, Christopher. *A Doctor's Faith Holds Fast*. Foreword by Robert Mortimer. London: Max Parrish, 1955.

Woodsmall, "Analysis." Woodsmall, Wyatt Lee. "An Analysis of the Use of Models in Science and Religion: A Clarification of the Notion of 'Theoretical Model' in Response to Some Misunderstandings of This Notion on the Part of Two Writers in the Philosophy of Religion." PhD diss., Columbia University, 1976.

Woodward, "Angels." Woodward, Kenneth. "Angels." *NW* (Dec. 27, 1993): 52–57.

Woodward, *Miracles*. Woodward, Kenneth L. *The Book of Miracles: The Meaning of the Miracle Stories in Christianity, Judaism, Buddhism, Hinduism, Islam*. New York: Simon & Schuster, 2000.

Woodward, "Miracles." Woodward, Kenneth L. "What Miracles Mean." *NW* (May 1, 2000): 54–60.

Woodworth-Etter, *Diary*. Woodworth-Etter, Maria. *A Diary of Signs and Wonders: A Classic*. Tulsa: Harrison House, reprint of 1916 ed.

Woodworth-Etter, *Miracles*. Woodworth-Etter, Maria. *Miracles, Signs, and Wonders Wrought in the Life and Ministry of Mrs. Woodworth-Etter from 1844–1916*. Portland: Apostolic Book Publishers, 1984.

Woolley, *Exorcism*. Woolley, Reginald Maxwell. *Exorcism and the Healing of the Sick*. London: SPCK, for the Church Historical Society, 1932.

Worrall, "Change." Worrall, John. "Theory-Change in Science." Pages 281–91 in *The Routledge Companion to Philosophy of Science*. Edited by Stathis Psillos and Martin Curd. New York: Routledge, 2008.

Wostyn, "Catholic Charismatics." Wostyn, Lode. "Catholic Charismatics in the Philippines." Pages 363–83 in *Asian and Pentecostal: The Charismatic Face of Christianity in Asia*. Edited by Allan Anderson and Edmond Tang. Foreword by Cecil M. Robeck. Regnum Studies in Mission, AJPSS 3. Oxford: Regnum; Baguio City, Philippines: APTS Press, 2005.

Wrede, *Secret*. Wrede, William. *The Messianic Secret*. Translated by J. C. G. Greig. Reprint, Cambridge: James Clarke, 1971.

Wrensch et al., "Factors." Wrensch, Margaret, Terri Chew, et al. "Risk Factors for Breast Cancer in a Population with High Incidence Rates." *BrCanRes* 5 (4, 2003): R88–102.

Wright, *Acts*. Wright, N. T. *Acts for Everyone*. Part 1: Chapters 1–12. Louisville: Westminster John Knox, 2008.

Wright, *Archaeology*. Wright, G. Ernest. *Biblical Archaeology*. Philadelphia: Westminster, 1962.

Wright, *God Who Acts*. Wright, G. Ernest. *God Who Acts: Biblical Theology as Recital*. SBT 8. London: SCM, 1952.

Wright, "Interpretations." Wright, Nigel G. "Charismatic Interpretations of the Demonic." Pages 149–63 in *The Unseen World: Christian Reflections on Angels, Demons, and the Heavenly Realm*. Edited by Anthony N. S. Lane. Grand Rapids: Baker, 1996.

Wright, *Miracle*. Wright, C. J. *Miracle in History and in Modern Thought; or, Miracle and Christian Apologetic*. New York: Henry Holt, 1930.

Wright, "Miracles." Wright, T. H. "Miracles." Pages 186–91 in vol. 2 of *Dictionary of Christ and the Gospels*. Edited by James Hastings. 2 vols. New York: Charles Scribner's Sons, 1906–8.

Wright, *Process*. Wright, J. Stafford. *Man in the Process of Time: A Christian Assessment of the Powers and Functions of Human Personality*. Grand Rapids: Eerdmans, 1955.

Wright, "Profiles." Wright, James. "Profiles of Divine Healing: Third Wave Theology Compared with Classical Pentecostal Theology." *AJPS* 5 (2, July 2002): 271–87.

Wright, "Prologue." Wright, G. Ernest. "Prologue: Introducing the Bible." Pages 11–51 in *The Book of the Acts of God: Modern Christian Scholarship Interprets the Bible*, by G. Ernest Wright and Reginald Fuller. Harmondsworth: Penguin, 1957.

Wright, *Resurrection*. Wright, N. T. *The Resurrection of the Son of God*. Christian Origins and the Question of God 3. Minneapolis: Fortress, 2003.

Wright, "Resurrection." Wright, N. T. "Resurrection and New Creation." *ChicSt* 46 (3, 2007): 270–86.

Wright, "Seminar." Wright, N. T. "Five Gospels but No Gospel: Jesus and the Seminar." Pages 83–120 in *Authenticating the Activities of Jesus*. Edited by Bruce Chilton and Craig A. Evans. NTTS 28.2. Leiden: Brill, 1999.

Wu, "Yu." Wu, Silas H. L. "Dora Yu (1873–1931): Foremost Female Evangelist in Twentieth-Century Chinese Revivalism." Pages 85–98 in *Gospel Bearers, Gender Barriers: Missionary Women in the Twentieth Century*. Edited by Dana L. Robert. Maryknoll, N.Y.: Orbis, 2002.

Wulff, "Experience." Wulff, David M. "Mystical Experience." Pages 397–40 in *Varieties of Anomalous Experience: Examining the Scientific Evidence*. Edited by Etzel Cardeña, Steven Jay Lynn, and Stanley Krippner. Washington, D.C.: American Psychological Association, 2000.

Wuthnow, "Contradictions." Wuthnow, Robert. "No Contradictions Here: Science, Religion, and the Culture of All Reasonable Possibilities." Pages 155–77 in *The Religion and Science Debate: Why Does It Continue?* Edited by Harold W. Attridge. New Haven: Yale University Press, 2009.

Wuthnow, *Heaven*. Wuthnow, Robert. *After Heaven: Spirituality in America since the 1950s*. Berkeley: University of California Press, 1998.

Wuthnow, "Teaching." Wuthnow, Robert. "Teaching and Religion in Sociology." Pages 184–92 in *Religion, Scholarship, Higher Education: Perspectives, Models, and Future Prospects*. Edited by Andrea Sterk. Notre Dame, Ind.: University of Notre Dame Press, 2001.

Wyk, "Witchcraft." Wyk, I. W. C. van. "African Witchcraft in Theological Perspective." *HvTS* 60 (3, 2004): 1201–28.

Wykstra, "Problem." Wykstra, Stephen J. "The Problem of Miracle in the Apologetic from History." *JASA* 30 (4, 1978): 154–63.

Wyllie, "Effutu." Wyllie, Robert W. "Do the Effutu Really Believe that the Spirits Cause Illness? A Ghanaian Case Study." *JRelAf* 24 (33, 1994): 228–40.

Xin, "Dynamics." Xin, Yalin. "Inner Dynamics of the Chinese House Church Movement: The Case of the Word of Life Community." *MissSt* 25 (2008): 157–84.

Xiong, "Shamanism." Xiong, Phua, et al. "Hmong Shamanism: Animist Spiritual Healing in America's Urban Heartland." Pages 439–54 in *Religion and Healing in America*. Edited by Linda L. Barnes and Susan S. Sered. New York: Oxford University Press, 2005.

Yadin, *Scroll of War*. Yadin, Yigael. *The Scroll of the War of the Sons of Light against the Sons of Darkness*. Translated by Batya Rabin and Chaim Rabin. Oxford: Oxford University Press, 1962.

Yalman, "Healing Rituals." Yalman, Nur. "The Structure of Sinhalese Healing Rituals." Pages 115–50 in *Religion in South Asia*. Edited by Edward B. Harper. Seattle: University of Washington Press, 1964.

Yamamori and Chan, *Witnesses*. Yamamori, Tetsunao, and Kim-kwong Chan. *Witnesses to Power: Stories of God's Quiet Work in a Changing China*. Waynesboro, Ga.: Paternoster, 2000.

Yamauchi, "Magic." Yamauchi, Edwin. "Magic or Miracle? Diseases, Demons, and Exorcisms." Pages 89–183 in *The Miracles of Jesus*. Edited by David

Wenham and Craig Blomberg. Vol. 6 of *GosPersp*. Sheffield: JSOT Press, 1986.

Yamauchi, *Persia*. Yamauchi, Edwin M. *Persia and the Bible*. Foreword by Donald J. Wiseman. Grand Rapids: Baker, 1990.

Yancey, "Miracle Worker." Yancey, Philip. "Jesus, the Reluctant Miracle Worker." *CT* (May 19, 1977): 80.

Yancey, *Scholarship*. Yancey, George. *Compromising Scholarship: Religious and Political Bias in American Higher Education*. Waco: Baylor University Press, 2011.

Yao, "Dynamics." Yao, Kevin Xiyi. "Dynamics of the Protestant Church in China Today." *MissFoc* 17 (2009): 23–33.

Yap, "Syndrome." Yap, P. M. "The Possession Syndrome: A Comparison of Hong Kong and French Findings." *JMenSc* 106 (Jan. 1960): 114–37.

Yates, *Expansion*. Yates, Timothy. *The Expansion of Christianity*. Downers Grove, Ill.: InterVarsity, 2004.

Yeager et al., "Involvement." Yeager, Diane M., Dana A. Glei, Melanie Au, Hui-Sheng Lin, Richard P. Sloan, and Maxine Weinstein. "Religious Involvement and Health Outcomes among Older Persons in Taiwan." *SSMed* 63 (2006): 2228–41.

Yee, *Feasts*. Yee, Gale A. *Jewish Feasts and the Gospel of John*. ZSNT. Wilmington, Del.: Michael Glazier, 1989.

Yeomans, *Healing*. Yeomans, Lilian B. *Healing from Heaven*. Springfield, Mo.: Gospel Publishing House, 1935.

Yeoward, "Miracle." Yeoward, A. E. "A Miracle." *PentEv* 523 (Nov. 24, 1923): 18.

Yi et al., "Religion." Yi, M. S., S. E. Luckhaupt, J. M. Mrus, et al. "Religion, Spirituality, and Depressive Symptoms in Primary Care House Officers." *AmbPed* 6 (2006): 84–90.

Yoder, "Church." Yoder, L. M. "The Church of the Muria." MTh thesis, Fuller Theological Seminary, 1981.

Yohannan, *Revolution*. Yohannan, K. P. *Revolution in World Missions*. Carrollton, Tex.: Gospel for Asia, 2004.

Yong, "Disability." Yong, Amos. "Disability and the Gifts of the Spirit: Pentecost and the Renewal of the Church." *JPT* 19 (1, 2010): 76–93.

Yong, "Independent Pentecostalism." Yong, Jeong Jae. "Filipino Independent Pentecostalism and Biblical Transformation." Pages 385–407 in *Asian and Pentecostal: The Charismatic Face of Christianity in Asia*. Edited by Allan Anderson and Edmond Tang. Foreword by Cecil M. Robeck. Regnum Studies in Mission, AJPSS 3. Oxford: Regnum; Baguio City, Philippines: APTS Press, 2005.

Yong, *Spirit Poured*. Yong, Amos. *The Spirit Poured Out on All Flesh: Pentecostalism and the Possibility of Global Theology*. Grand Rapids: Baker Academic, 2005.

York, "Indigenous Missionaries." York, Ted E. "Indigenous Missionaries—A Fruit of Revival: Lessons from the Indonesian Revival of 1965 to 1971." *JAM* 5 (2, Sept. 2003): 243–58.

York, *Missions*. York, John V. *Missions in the Age of the Spirit*. Foreword by Byron D. Klaus. Springfield, Mo.: Logion, 2000.

Yoshikawa, "Variables." Yoshikawa, Shoichi. "The Hidden Variables of Quantum Mechanics Are Under God's Power." Pages 133–35 in *Cosmos, Bios, and Theos: Scientists Reflect on Science, God, and the Origins of the Universe, Life, and* Homo Sapiens. Edited by Henry Margenau and Roy Abraham Varghese. La Salle, Ill.: Open Court, 1992.

Yoshimoto et al., "Coping." Yoshimoto, S. M., et al. "Religious Coping and Problem Solving by Couples Faced with Prostate Cancer." *EurJCC* 15 (5, 2006): 481–88.

Young, "Chaos." Young, Karl. "Deterministic Chaos and Quantum Chaology." Pages 227–42 in *Religion and Science: History, Method, Dialogue*. Edited by W. Mark Richardson and Wesley J. Wildman. Foreword by Ian G. Barbour. New York: Routledge, 1996.

Young, "Epistemology." Young, Robert. "Miracles and Epistemology." *RelS* 8 (2, 1972): 115–26.

Young, "Impossibility." Young, Robert. "Miracles and Physical Impossibility." *Soph* 11 (3, Oct. 1972): 29–35.

Young, "Miracles." Young, Robert. "Miracles and Credibility." *RelS* 16 (4, 1980): 465–68.

Young, "Miracles in History." Young, William. "Miracles in Church History." *Churchman* 102 (2, 1988): 102–21.

Young, "Petitioning." Young, Robert. "Petitioning God." *AmPhilQ* 11 (3, July 1974): 193–201.

Young, "Value." Young, M. L. "Evidential Value of the Miracles." *LQ* 22 (1892): 429–40.

Young, "Visitors." Young, David. "Visitors in the Night: A Creative Energy Model of Spontaneous Visions." Pages 273–97 in *Being Changed: The Anthropology of Extraordinary Experience*. Edited by David Young and Jean-Guy Goulet. Peterborough, Ont.: Broadview, 1994.

Young and Goulet, "Introduction." Young, David E., and Jean-Guy Goulet. "Introduction." Pages 7–13 in *Being Changed: The Anthropology of Extraordinary Experience*. Edited by David E. Young and Jean-Guy Goulet. Peterborough, Ont.: Broadview, 1994.

Young and Stewart, "Intervention." Young, D. R., and K. J. Stewart. "A Church-Based Physical

Activity Intervention for African American Women." *FamComHealth* 29 (2, 2006): 103–17.

Ytterbrink, *Biography*. Ytterbrink, Maria. *The Third Gospel for the First Time: Luke Within the Context of Ancient Biography*. Lund: Lund University, Centrum för teologi och religionsvetenskap, 2004.

Yuen, "Impact." Yuen, Hon K. "Impact of an Altruistic Activity on Life Satisfaction in Institutionalized Elders: A Pilot Study." *PhysOcTherGer* 20 (3–4, 2002): 125–35.

Yun, *Heavenly Man*. Yun, Brother, with Paul Hattaway. *The Heavenly Man: The Remarkable True Story of Chinese Christian Brother Yun*. London: Monarch, 2002.

Yung, "Case Studies." Yung, Hwa. "Case Studies in Spiritual Warfare from East Asia." Pages 138–45 in *Deliver Us from Evil: An Uneasy Frontier in Christian Mission*. Edited by A. Scott Moreau, Tokunboh Adeyemo, David G. Burnett, Bryant L. Myers, and Hwa Yung. Monrovia, Calif.: Lausanne Committee for World Evangelization, 2002.

Yung, "Integrity." Yung, Hwa. "The Integrity of Mission in the Light of the Gospel: Bearing the Witness of the Spirit." *MissSt* 24 (2007): 169–88.

Yung, "Pentecostalism." Yung, Hwa. "Pentecostalism and the Asian Church." Pages 37–57 in *Asian and Pentecostal: The Charismatic Face of Christianity in Asia*. Edited by Allan Anderson and Edmond Tang. Foreword by Cecil M. Robeck. Regnum Studies in Mission, AJPSS 3. Oxford: Regnum; Baguio City, Philippines: APTS Press, 2005.

Yung, "Power." Yung, Hwa. "Endued with Power: The Pentecostal-Charismatic Renewal and the Asian Church in the Twenty-first Century." *AJPS* 6 (1, 2003): 63–82.

Yung, *Quest*. Yung, Hwa. *Mangoes or Bananas? The Quest for an Authentic Asian Christian Theology. Biblical Theology in an Asian Context*. RStMiss. Oxford: Regnum, 1997.

Yung, "Reformation." Yung, Hwa. "A 21st Century Reformation: Recovering the Supernatural." The Lausanne Global Conversation. http://conversation.lausanne.org/en/conversations/detail/11041. Accessed Oct. 2, 2010.

Zabell, "Probabilistic Analysis." Zabell, S. L. "The Probabilistic Analysis of Testimony." *JStatPlInf* 20 (1988): 327–54.

Zachman, "Meaning." Zachman, Randall C. "The Meaning of Biblical Miracles in Light of the Modern Quest for Truth." Pages 1–18 in *Miracles in Jewish and Christian Antiquity: Imagining Truth*. Edited by John C. Cavadini. NDST 3. Notre Dame, Ind.: University of Notre Dame Press, 1999.

Zagrans, *Miracles*. Zagrans, Maura Poston. *Miracles Every Day: The Story of One Physician's Inspiring Faith and the Healing Power of Prayer*. New York: Doubleday, 2010.

Zaphiropoulos, "Sullivan." Zaphiropoulos, Miltiades L. "Harry Stack Sullivan." Pages 426–32 in *Comprehensive Textbook of Psychiatry*. 4th ed. Edited by Harold I. Kaplan and Benjamin J. Sadock. Baltimore: Williams & Wilkins, 1985.

Zaretsky, *Bibliography*. Zaretsky, I. I. *Bibliography on Spirit Possession and Spirit Mediumship*. Evanston, Ill.: Northwestern University Press, 1967.

Zebiri, "Understanding." Zebiri, Kate. "Contemporary Muslim Understanding of the Miracles of Jesus." *MusW* 90 (1, 2000): 71–90.

Zechariah, "Factors." Zechariah, C. "Factors Affecting the Growth of the Protestant Churches in Tamil Nadu and Kerala." MTh thesis, Fuller Theological Seminary, 1980.

Zechariah, "Strategy." Zechariah, C. "Missiological Strategy for the Assemblies of God in Tamil Nadu." DMiss diss., Fuller Theological Seminary, 1981.

Zehnder et al., "Study." Zehnder, Daniel, Alice Prchal, Margarete Vollrath, and Markus A. Landolt. "Prospective Study of the Effectiveness of Coping in Pediatric Patients." *ChPsyHumDev* 36 (3, 2006): 351–68.

Zeigler, "Lake." Zeigler, James R. "Lake, John Graham." Page 531 in *Dictionary of Pentecostal and Charismatic Movements*. Edited by Stanley M. Burgess, Gary B. McGee, and Patrick H. Alexander. Grand Rapids: Zondervan, 1988.

Zeilinger, "Wunderverständnis." Zeilinger, F. "Zum Wunderverständnis der Bibel." *BL* 42 (1969): 27–43.

Zeitlin, "Dreams." Zeitlin, Solomon. "Dreams and Their Interpretation from the Biblical Period to the Tannaitic Time: A Historical Study." *JQR* 66 (1975): 1–18.

Zempleni, "Symptom." Zempleni, Andras. "From Symptom to Sacrifice: The Story of Khady Fall." Translated by Karen Merveille. Pages 87–140 in *Case Studies in Spirit Possession*. Edited by Vincent Crapanzaro and Vivian Garrison. New York: John Wiley & Sons, 1977.

Zervakos, "Miracles." Zervakos, Philotheos. "Miracles of the Saint." Pages 80–101 in *St. Arsenios of Paros: Remarkable Confessor, Spiritual Guide, Educator, Ascetic, Miracle Worker, and Healer; An Account of His Life, Character, Message, and Miracles*, by Constantine Cavarnos. MOrthS 6. Belmont, Mass.: Institute for Byzantine and Modern Greek Studies, 1978.

Zevit, "Ways." Zevit, Ziony. "Three Ways to Look at the Ten Plagues." *BRev* 6 (3, 1990): 16–23, 42, 44.

Zhaoming, "Chinese Denominations." Zhaoming, Deng. "Indigenous Chinese Pentecostal Denominations." Pages 437–66 in *Asian and Pentecostal: The Charismatic Face of Christianity in Asia.* Edited by Allan Anderson and Edmond Tang. Foreword by Cecil M. Robeck. Regnum Studies in Mission, AJPSS 3. Oxford: Regnum; Baguio City, Philippines: APTS Press, 2005.

Zias, "Lust." Zias, Joseph. "Lust and Leprosy: Confusion or Correlation?" *BASOR* 275 (1989): 27–31.

Zipor, "Talebearers." Zipor, Moshe A. "Talebearers, Peddlers, Spies, and Converts: The Adventures of the Biblical and Post-Biblical Roots *rg"l* and *rk"l*." *HS* 46 (2005): 129–44.

Zusne, "States." Zusne, Leonard. "Altered States of Consciousness, Magical Thinking, and Psychopathology: The Case of Ludwig Staudenmaier." Pages 233–50 in *Altered States of Consciousness and Mental Health: A Cross-Cultural Perspective.* Edited by Colleen A. Ward. CCRMS 12. Newbury Park, Calif.: Sage, 1989.

Zvanaka, "Churches." Zvanaka, Solomon. "African Independent Churches in Context." *Missiology* 25 (1, 1997): 69–75.

Interviews and Personal Correspondence Cited

Note: I agreed with the Chinese pastors I interviewed in May 2007 to omit information about them to protect their privacy; also another Chinese minister on Jan. 30, 2009. A medical source (phone interviews, Dec. 17, 2008; March 27, 2009, and medical documentation that I received on Feb. 13, 2009) also asked that I withhold his name for the sake of his privacy; some other persons also requested anonymity (including conversation and correspondence, May 22, 26, 2010; June 7, 9, 2010). The other interviews and several transcriptions of others' interviews and correspondence appear below. I have included only the fraction of correspondence most relevant to the book, not a much larger range of correspondence for the book that did not ultimately prove as relevant.

Abraham, Alex. Interview, Irving, Tex., Oct. 29, 2009.

Achi, Gideon. Interview, Wynnewood, Pa., May 25, 2009.

Acosta Estévez, Eusbarina. Interview, Santiago de Cuba, Aug. 7, 2010.

Adelekan, Tahira G. Personal correspondence, April 6, 2009; phone interview, April 24, 2009.

Adewuya, J. Ayodeji. Phone interview, Dec. 14, 2009; personal correspondence, Dec. 16–17, 2009.

Ahanonu, Benjamin. Interview, Wynnewood, Pa., Sept. 29; Dec. 1, 2009; Sept. 4, 2010.

Ahanonu, Charity. Phone interview, May 19, 2010.

Alexander, Sheryl. Personal correspondence, Nov. 30, 2008; March 29, 2009.

Andrew Wommack Ministries. Personal correspondence (my specific respondent unspecified), June 22, 2009.

Aragona, Angela Salazar. Interview by Rosanny Engcoy, April 14, 2002. Transcribed by Gary Jay Engcoy.

APRC Oral History Transcriptions, Final and Authorized. Asia Pacific Research Center at Asia Pacific Theological Seminary, Baguio City, Philippines.

Arango, Obed. Personal correspondence, Aug. 27, 2008.

Arangote, Marcelo. Interview by Rosanny Engcoy, April 23, 2003. Transcribed by Rosanny Engcoy. APRC Oral History Transcriptions, Final and Authorized. Asia Pacific Research Center at Asia Pacific Theological Seminary, Baguio City, Philippines.

Arcila Gonzalez, Wilbert M. Personal correspondence, as translated by Eduardo Lara Reyes, Nov. 30, 2009.

Arukua, Donna. Interview, Baguio, Philippines, Jan. 23, 29, 2009.

Ascabano, Mervin. Personal correspondence, Feb. 6, 2009.

Asiimwe, Onesimus. Interview, Wynnewood, Pa., Oct. 12, 2008. Personal correspondence, April 4; May 2, 27, 2009.

Bagwell, Yulia Kolodotchka. Personal correspondence, July 1, 2010; discussion, Wynnewood, Pa., July 13, 2010.

Baker, James. Personal correspondence, April 3, 2008.

Baker, Rolland. Personal correspondence, April 26, 2008.

Bane, Sara. Personal correspondence, March 8, 2010.

Bawa, Leo. Personal correspondence, Aug. 10, 2009; Oct. 13, 2010.

Beera, Jacob. Personal correspondence, Nov. 2, 2009.

Best, Gary. Personal correspondence, July 21, 2008. Phone interview and follow-up personal correspondence, Sept. 25, 2008.

Bishop, Brianita. Personal correspondence, May 15, 17, 2010.

Bissouessoue, Albert. Interview, Brazzaville, Congo, July 29, 2008. Personal correspondence, Dec. 17, 2009 (reproducing an extensive interview with Emmanuel Moussounga, Dec. 16).

Bissouessoue, Julienne. Interview, Dec. 16, 2009, by Emmanuel Moussounga, received in personal correspondence Dec. 17, 2009.

Bonilla, Carlos, and Mayra (Giovanetti) Bonilla. Interview, Wynnewood, Pa., Sept. 13, 2008.

Bostrom, Kari. Personal correspondence, Sept. 8, 2009.

Briggs, Tonye. Phone interview, Dec. 14, 16, 2009.

Brodland, Wayne. Account written at the request of Robert Larmer, Oct. 13, 2007.

Brown, Candy Gunther. Personal correspondence, May 22, 26, 28, 2009; Jan. 1, 2011.

Brown, Marie. Personal correspondence, May 31, 2006.

Brown, Michael. Personal correspondence, Nov. 15, 2008.

Bruce, Bob. Personal correspondence, July 26, 2010.

Bungishabaku, Katho. Interview, Wynnewood, Pa., March 12, 2009.

Bustria, Dom. Interview, Baguio, Philippines, Jan. 29, 2009.

Butler, Pat. Personal correspondence, June 8, 14, 15, 16, 17, 2009; May 17, 2010.

Cagas, Roque, Sr. Interview by Rosanny Engcoy, April 11, 2002. Transcribed by Kay Garciano. APRC Oral History Transcriptions, Final and Authorized. Asia Pacific Research Center at Asia Pacific Theological Seminary, Baguio City, Philippines.

Cagle, Wayne, and Judy Cagle. Correspondence and verbal confirmation, Baguio, Philippines, Jan. 24, 25, 2009.

Cagle, Wayne. Personal correspondence, Feb. 10, 2009.

Camejo Tazé, Leonel. Interview, Havana, Cuba, Aug. 11, 2010.

Cho, Kumsook. Interview, Baguio, Philippines, Jan. 24, 2009.

Clark, Randy. Personal correspondence, April 1, 2011.

Claro Pupo, Alternan. Interviews, Santiago de Cuba, Aug. 3, 6, 2010.

Coats, John. Personal correspondence, Oct. 23, 24, 25; Nov. 6, 2009.

Cocherell, Carl E. Phone interview, May 2, 2009; medical documentation received, June 17, 2009.

Coffee, Lee Don. Phone interview, July 7, 2009.

Collins, Bruce. Phone interview, April 11, 2009. Personal correspondence, April 11, 2009, with supporting documentation.

Coulson, John. Discussion, Brisbane, Australia, April 18, 2011. Personal correspondence, April 26, 2011.

Crandall, Chauncey. Phone interviews, May 28, 30, 2010. Personal correspondence, Oct. 8, 2010.

Crute, Bryan. Personal correspondence, Jan. 17, 2011.

David, Prabhakar. Personal correspondence, shared with me Oct. 13, 2010 through Ivan Satyavrata and Jacob Mathew.

Dawkins, John. Personal correspondence, Nov. 20, 2009.

Dawson, John. Correspondence, May 18, 2007.

Dawson, Matthew. Personal correspondence, March 29; April 3, 4, 2009.

Devi, Lakshmi. Personal correspondence, shared with me Oct. 29, 2010 through Ivan Satyavrata and Jacob Mathew.

De Wet, Christiaan. Personal correspondence, March 25, 2008.

Dickinson, Gary. Personal correspondence, Aug. 5, 2008; June 3, 2010.

Dominong, David. Interview, Baguio, Philippines, Jan. 31, 2009.

Eddy, Paul R. Personal correspondence, Oct. 25–26, 2009.

Edward, Vasanth. Correspondence, March 2006; March, April 2007.

Eldevik, Bruce. Correspondence with Melody Mazuk, Oct. 12, 2009; with Craig Keener, Nov. 16, 2009.

En, Simon P. K. Personal correspondence, Sept. 11, 2009.

Evans, Kathy. Personal correspondence, Nov. 10, 2008.

Fadele, Manita. Personal correspondence, Nov. 14, 2009.

Fernando, Ajith. Phone interview, Oct. 1, 2008; personal correspondence, March 8, 12, 13, 2009.

Finley, Mike. Personal correspondence, Sept. 23; Oct. 10, 22, 31, 2010; phone interview, Oct. 2, 2010.

Fisk, Candace Dee Steelberg. Personal correspondence, May 20; June 25, 28, 2009.

Flores, Robin. Phone interview, May 23, 2010.

Fonseca Valdés, Iris Lilia. Interview, Havana, Cuba, Aug. 11, 2010.

Fountain, Kay. Interview, Baguio, Philippines, Jan. 29, 2009.

Ghosh, Nivedita. Personal correspondence, shared with me Oct. 13, 2010 through Ivan Satyavrata and Jacob Mathew.

Gibbs, Marva. Phone interview, Dec. 2, 2009; personal correspondence, Dec. 7, 2009.

Giovanetti (Bonilla), Mayra. Personal correspondence, July 9, 2009.

Godwin, Ben. Personal correspondence, May 23; May 28, 2009.

Gomero Borges, David. Interviews, Havana, Cuba, Aug. 12, 2010; Artemisa, Cuba, Aug. 13, 2010.

Gonzàlez Zorrilla, Rhode. Interview, Havana, Cuba, Aug. 11, 2010.

Greaux, Eric. Personal correspondence, Aug. 27–28, 2009.

Gulick, Anna. Personal correspondence, May 4; Aug. 10, 13, 14, 23–25; Dec. 2, 10, 2009; Jan. 14; Feb. 4; April 19, 23, 24, 25; May 8, 17, 29; June 4, 10, 11, 12; July 26–28, 31; Aug. 26, 28, 31; Sept. 3, 4, 9; Oct. 11, 30, 2010; Jan. 11; April 15; May 25; June 6, 7, 8, 9, 11, 13, 21; July 1, 2011. Interviews, March 9–11, 2011. Medical documentation sent June 14; July 28; Sept. 11, 2010; April 15, 2011.

Gutiérrez Valdés, Yaíma. Interview, Artemisa, Cuba, Aug. 13, 2010.

Harvey, Joseph. Interview, Brazzaville, Congo, July 25, 2008.

Hauger, Simon. Phone interview, Dec. 4, 2009.

Heneise, Steve, and Sheila Heneise. Personal correspondence, Aug. 20, 21, 22, 2008.

Heneise, Sheila. Interview, Ardmore, Pa., April 5, 2009.

Herman, Yusuf. Interview and documentation, Wilmore, Kentucky, July 10, 2011.

Hernández Guzmán, Yamilka. Interview, Santiago de Cuba, Aug. 8, 2010.

Hertweck, Galen. Interview, Baguio, Philippines, Jan. 26, 2009.

Hertweck, Galen. Personal correspondence, May 17, 2009.

Heth, James. Personal correspondence and blog postings, April 2008.

Heth, William. Personal correspondence, Sept. 12, 18, 2009.

Hicks, Flint. Interview, Baguio, Philippines, Jan. 29, 2009.

Hollis, Shelley. Phone interview, Jan. 10, 2009; personal correspondence, Nov. 6, 8, 2009; April 23, 2010.

Hommer, Yazmin. Personal correspondence, Oct. 26–27; Nov. 20; Dec. 1, 2009, with medical documentation.

Hortizuela, Ryan. Interview, Baguio, Philippines, Jan. 24, 2009.

Horton, Stanley. Personal correspondence, May 29, 2009.

Hsu, Renae Yu-Ching. Interview, Baguio, Philippines, Jan. 24, 2009. Personal correspondence, May 10; June 13, 24, 29, 2009.

Hunter, Todd. Phone interview, Jan. 5, 2009.

Irons, Barachias. Personal correspondence, Aug. 27, Sept. 13, 2009; Jan. 19, 21, 2010.

Israel, Suppogu. Discussion, Wynnewood, Pa., Nov. 2, 1997; May 6, 1998.

Itapson, Emmanuel. Interviews, Wynnewood, Pa., April 29, 2008; April 1, 8, 2011. Phone interview, Dec. 17, 2009.

Jackson, Bill. Interview, Corona, Calif., Nov. 13, 2007; personal correspondence, March 24, 2008.

Johnson, David M. Personal correspondence, Feb. 20, 2009.

Johnson, Kayon Murray. Interview, Oct. 14, 2010.

Johnson, Tamika. Personal correspondence, Dec. 2, 3, 4, 2010.

Jones-Anderson, Stacey. Phone interview, Dec. 9, 2009.

KC, Mina, and Nirmal (Nick) KC. Interview by John Lathrop (asking the healing-related questions for me). Sent to me by Nirmal KC (with John Lathrop) March 2, 2010. Follow-up correspondence with Nirmal KC, March 3, 2010; April 16, 2010.

Keating, Gwladys. Personal correspondence, July 25; Aug. 16, 2010.

Keener, Christopher. Personal correspondence, June 23, 2007; Jan. 27, 30, 2009; Feb. 8, 2009.

Keener, Craig. Personal journal entries, May 17; June 2, 9, 17, 1987; July 8–9, 1991; Nov. 6, 1993; Jan. 24–30, 1999; Feb. 5, 2001.

Keener, Médine Moussounga. Personal journal entries, Dolisie, Congo, June 23, 27; Aug. 29–Sept. 1, 1997; Feb. 27, 1999. Interview, Aug. 12, 2009.

Kefenie, Lidetu Alemu. Interview, Wynnewood, Pa., Sept. 30, 2010; personal correspondence, Oct. 1, 2010.

Kent, Anthony. Personal correspondence, Jan. 4; Feb. 18, 2010.

Kent, Jasper. Funeral reflections, Oct. 24, 2006.

Kent, Raymond. Phone confirmation, Feb. 11, 2010.

Kent, Thomas. Undated manuscript, mailed Feb. 19, 2010, received Feb. 22, 2010.

Kim, Joo Young. Interview, Baguio, Philippines, Jan. 24, 2009.

Kim, Jun. Interview, Baguio, Philippines, Jan. 24, 2009.

Kim, Mun Kil. Interview, Wynnewood, Pa., July 24, 2010.

Kinabrew, Bruce. Personal correspondence, June 23, 24, 2008; Feb. 10, 2011.

Klahr, Paul. Interview by Rosanny Engcoy, April 2006. APRC Oral History Transcriptions, Final and Authorized. Asia Pacific Research Center at Asia Pacific Theological Seminary, Baguio City, Philippines.

Klaus, Byron. Personal correspondence, July 6, 7, 2009; Sept. 24, 2010; documentation sent July 10, 2009.

Koehler, John. Interview, Wynnewood, Pa., May 22, 2009.

Koffa, Louise. Interview, Wynnewood, Pa., Oct. 6, 2010. Personal correspondence, Oct. 12, 2010.

Kolenda, Daniel. Personal correspondence, Dec. 11, 2009.

Krabill, Kelly. Personal correspondence, Aug. 24, 2009.

Kraybill, Sharon. Discussion, May 26; Nov. 10, 2009.

Kumar, Senthil. Personal correspondence, shared with me Oct. 29, 2010, through Ivan Satyavrata and Jacob Mathew.

Kyamanywa, Nathan. Personal correspondence, Sept. 2, 2009; Nov. 15, 27, 2010.

Laborde Figueras, Ismael. Interviews, Santiago de Cuba, Aug. 7, 8, 2010.

Lacy, Matthew. Interview, Wynnewood, Pa., Aug. 29, 2008.

Lai, Jenny. Personal correspondence, Aug. 2009.

Lapisac, Sharon. Interview, Baguio, Philippines, Jan. 31, 2009.

Lara Reyes, Eduardo. Personal correspondence, Sept. 23; Oct. 23, 2009.

Lara Reyes, Eduardo, and Nimsi A. Arcila Leal. Interview, Wynnewood, Pa., Sept. 17, 2009; Feb. 10, 2010.

Larmer, Robert. Personal correspondence, Aug. 4, 5, 2009.

Larsen, Cindy. Personal correspondence, Dec. 17, 2009.

Lathrop, John. Personal correspondence, Dec. 11, 2008.

LeRoy, Douglas. Personal correspondence, Nov. 9, 2009.

Lester, Craig. Interview, Baguio, Philippines, Jan. 28, 2009.

Lewis, Eveline Susanto. Interview, Baguio, Philippines, Jan. 23, 2009.

Licona, Michael. Personal correspondence, April 25; May 17, 2010. Interviews, Atlanta, Nov. 20, 22, 2010.

Luvutse, Bernard. Personal correspondence, Aug. 17, 2006.

Mabiala, Henriette. Interview, Brazzaville, Congo, July 24, 2008.

Mabiala, Jeanne. Interview, Brazzaville, Congo, July 29, 2008.

Macinskas-Le, Leah. Interview, April 25, 2010; personal correspondence, Oct. 18, 2010.

Malombé, Antoinette. Interviews, Dolisie, Congo, July 12–13, 2008.

Marchese, Joseph. Phone interview, May 11, 2009.

Marsak, Matt. Phone interview, Aug. 21, 2010.

Marshall, Aaron D. Personal correspondence, Dec. 16, 2009.

Marshall, Melaina. Personal correspondence, Dec. 16, 2009.

Martell-Otero, Loida. Discussion, Wynnewood, Pa., Feb. 23, 2010; interview, Wynnewood, Pa., April 22, 2010; personal correspondence, April 23, 2010.

Martin, Edith. Personal correspondence, June 3, 2010.

Marz, Fredrick. Discussion and personal correspondence, July 22, 2010.

Mason, Lauren. Personal correspondence, May 3, 5, 6, 8, 2010; interview, Wynnewood, Pa., June 3, 2010.

Mataika, Josiah. Interview, Baguio, Philippines, Jan. 29, 2009.

Matanguihan, John. Personal correspondence, Feb. 5, 2009.

Mathew, Raju. Interview, Wynnewood, Pa., Aug. 29, 2008.

Matthews, Nicole. Personal correspondence, April 1, 14; May 28; July 7; Aug. 16–17, 2009; May 25, 2010. Personal discussion, Philadelphia, Oct. 10, 2009.

Maxey, Gary. Personal correspondence, May 25, 2009; May 26, 2009.

McCain, Danny. Personal correspondence, June 1; July 11, 2009; Sept. 21, 22, 27, 2010; interview, Wilmore, Ky., July 17, 2011.

McCain, Yolanda. Personal correspondence, Oct. 3, 2008.

McClymond, Michael. Personal correspondence, unpublished manuscript, phone conversation, Jan. 3, 2011. Medical documentation sent Jan. 5, 2011.

McCormack, Ian. Personal correspondence, July 25, 2009.

McDougald, Lee. Personal correspondence, Aug. 28, 2008; May 24, 2009.

McGlaughlin, Flint. Personal correspondence, Feb. 6–7, 2009.

McGrew, Timothy. Personal correspondence, Nov. 26, 2009.

McKenzie, Susan. Personal correspondence, July 14, 20, 2010.

Mekonnen, Daniel. Phone interview, Dec. 10, 2009.

Miles, Henry H. W. Personal correspondence, April 21, 1980.

Miller, Craig. Personal correspondence, July 12–13, 2010.

Miller, Sondria. Personal correspondence, Dec. 12, 2009.

Mina, Len, with Wilfred Mina. Interview, Baguio, Philippines, Jan. 24, 2009.

Mina, Wilfred. Interview, Baguio, Philippines, Jan. 24, 2009.

Modina, Elena. Interview by Rosanny Engcoy, Jan. 7, 2005. Transcribed by Kay Garciano. APRC Oral History Transcriptions, Final and Authorized. Asia Pacific Research Center at Asia Pacific Theological Seminary, Baguio City, Philippines.

Moffett, Danielle Martin. Personal correspondence, Dec. 4, 2009.

Moïse, Ngoma. Phone interview (assisted by Médine Moussounga Keener), May 14, 2009.

Mokake, Paul. Interview, Wynnewood, Pa., June 3, 2006; May 13, 2009.

Moore, Donald. Personal correspondence, Oct. 28, 31; Dec. 4, 16, 2009; Jan. 3, 5, 2010.

Morphew, Derek. Interview, Corona, Calif., Nov. 12, 2007.

Mostert, Johan. Personal correspondence, July 4, 2009; Aug. 16, 2009.

Mouko, Jean. Interview, Brazzaville, Congo, July 31, 2008.

Moussounga, Emmanuel. Interviews, Brazzaville, Congo, July 25, 29, 2008. Phone interview, April 16, 2010. Correspondence, July 2, 2011.

Moussounga, Gracia. Interview, July 12, 2008.

Moussounga, Jacques. Personal correspondence, Sept. 8, 2005.

Mugari, Jorum. Discussion, Charlotte, N.C., March 27, 2010. Personal correspondence, April 1, 2, 5, 2010.

Mugshe, Henry. Phone interview, Oct. 23, 2008.

Mulindahabi, Frederic. Personal correspondence, Sept. 1, 2010.

Mullen, Grant. Personal correspondence, June 19, 20, 2009.

Navarro Jordan, Eliseo. Interview, Santiago de Cuba, Aug. 7, 2010.

Norwood, Douglass. Interview, Philadelphia, June 6, 2006. Interview, Wynnewood, Pa., Jan. 14, 2009. Medical documentation sent April 30, 2009.

Nsouami, Patrice. Phone interview, April 29, 2010.

Numbere, Nonyem E. Phone interview, Dec. 14, 2009; personal correspondence, Jan. 6, 13, 2010.

Nung, Suan Sian Tung. Phone interview, Sept. 9, 2009.

Nylund, Jan. Interview, New Orleans, Nov. 23, 2009.

Obeng, Joshua. Interview, Baguio, Philippines, Jan. 28, 2009.

O'Kelley, Edward and Frieda. Phone interview, July 7, 2009.

Oparanyawu, Chibuzo. Personal correspondence, Dec. 18, 2009; Feb. 22; June 7; Sept. 1, 2010.

Orombi, Henry. Interview, Wynnewood, Pa., Oct. 12, 2008.

Ortiz, Bonnie. Interview, Wynnewood, Pa., Jan. 10, 2009.

Ouoba, Elisée. Interview, Wheaton, Ill., March 16, 2009.

Palma, Claudia. Interview, Brisbane, Australia, April 19, 2011.

Palmquist, Dwight D. Personal correspondence, Feb. 2, 2009; Feb. 8, 2009.

Panelo, Elaine. Interview, Baguio, Philippines, Jan. 30, 2009. Personal correspondence, Oct. 8, 11, 18, 2009.

Pasamonte, Bishop Domingo. Interview by Rosanny Engcoy, March 2, 2005. Transcribed by Mishael Requina. APRC Oral History Transcriptions, Final and Authorized. Asia Pacific Research Center at Asia Pacific Theological Seminary, Baguio City, Philippines.

Philip, Finny. Personal correspondence, Aug. 14, 2008; correspondence, June 19, 2009.

Picos-Lee, Mayra. Personal correspondence, Sept. 30, 2009.

Pilch, John. Personal correspondence, Nov. 13, 2009.

Piippo, John. Personal correspondence, March 17, 2009; June 15, 18, 2009.

Pollard, Jonathan. Personal correspondence, May 12, 13, 15, 16, 19, 20, 22; June 18; July 16, 22, 2010.

Power, Jeff. Personal correspondence, July 24, 2010.

Price-Williams, Melanie. Interview, Wynnewood, Pa., Nov. 7, 2009; personal correspondence, Nov. 16, 2009.

Prysock, Lisa. Personal correspondence, Jan. 23, 2011.

Ragwan, Eva. Personal correspondence, Oct. 14, 2010.

Ragwan, Rodney. Interview, Wynnewood, Pa., Dec. 15, 17, 2009.

Rance, DeLonn. Personal correspondence, Sept. 25, 27, 2010.

Randolph, Gail. Personal correspondence, Oct. 9, 2009.

Reed, David M. Personal correspondence, May 27, 1980.

Regueiro Sanchéz, Raúl. Interview, Santiago de Cuba, Aug. 7, 2010.

Reid, Maggie. Personal correspondence, Nov. 19; Dec. 2, 2009; Jan. 3, 2010.

Rexho, Genti. Personal correspondence, May 25, 2009.

Riestra Matos, Juan Carlos. Interview, Santiago de Cuba, Aug. 7, 2010.

Riffle, Richard, and Debbie Riffle. Personal correspondence, Dec. 13, 2007.

Robinson, Yesenia. Phone interview, Dec. 15, 2009.

Rojas Cruz, Dorka R. Personal correspondence, Sept. 1; Oct. 5, 12, 17, 29, 2010.

Russell, Horace. Interviews, Wynnewood, Pa., July 2; Oct. 26, 2009.

Sarkauskas, Aldona. Phone interview, June 4, 2009.

Sayco, Ricky. Interview, Baguio, Philippines, Jan. 27, 2009.

Sebiano, Eleanor. Interview, Baguio, Philippines, Jan. 29, 2009; further discussion, Jan. 31, 2009; personal correspondence, Feb. 8, 2009.

Sharma, Udaya. Personal correspondence, March 29, 31, 2009.

Shaw, Mark. Personal correspondence, July 23, 2010.

Shields, Robin. Personal correspondence, Feb. 7, 8, 2009.

Singh, Lydia. Personal correspondence, shared with me Oct. 13, 2010 through Ivan Satyavrata and Jacob Mathew.

Soans, Willie. Personal correspondence, acquired for me and shared with me Nov. 3, 2010 through Ivan Satyavrata and Jacob Mathew.

Speer, Sarah. Phone interview, Jan. 7, 2009; personal correspondence, Aug. 20, 2009.

Spinosi, Pam. Personal correspondence, April 21, 2008.

Spittler, Russ, and Bobbie Spittler. Personal correspondence, June 2, 2009.

Stenhammar, Mikael. Personal correspondence, Oct. 4, 2010.

Stewart, Brian. Personal correspondence, June 7, 2010. Interviews, Aug. 7, 14, 2010.

Stewart, Don. Personal correspondence, Aug. 10, 2005.

Stiles, Peter. Discussion, Sydney, Australia, April 16, 2011. Personal correspondence, April 27, 28, 2011.

Sum, Thang. Personal correspondence, Sept. 5, 11, 2009.

Tarr, Del. Personal correspondence, Sept. 30; Oct. 5, 6, 20, 2010.

Terrell, Paulette. Personal correspondence, Dec. 16, 2009.

Tesoro, Chester Allen. Interview, Baguio, Philippines, Jan. 30, 2009.

Thomas, Sandy. Phone interview, Aug. 26, 2008.

Tovera, Gervacio. Interview by Rosanny Engcoy, July 6, 2001. Transcribed by Kay Garciano. APRC Oral History Transcriptions, Final and Authorized. Asia Pacific Research Center at Asia Pacific Theological Seminary, Baguio City, Philippines.

Turner, Angie. Personal correspondence, March 13, 2010.

Turner, Jonathan. Interview, Wynnewood, Pa., March 4; April 1, 2010; personal correspondence, March 4, 22, 2010.

Twyman, Bill. Interview, Corona, Calif., Nov. 11, 2007.

Uytanlet, Samson. Personal correspondence, Dec. 15, 2009.

Venero Boza, Mirtha. Interview, Santiago de Cuba, Aug. 6, 2010.

Vernaud, Jacques. Personal correspondence, Aug. 29, 2005; discussion, Kinshasa, Congo, July 23, 2008.

Vineyard Community Church, Cincinnati, Ohio, healing log, 2008.

Wahnefried, Joy. Personal correspondence, Nov. 4, 5, 6, 8, 20, 26, 2009.

Watson, Deborah E. Personal correspondence, Nov. 30; Dec. 9, 2009.

Watson, James E., Sr. Personal correspondence, Nov. 27, 2009.

Watts, Rikk E. Interview, Atlanta, Nov. 17, 2010.

Wheeler, Martha. Personal correspondence, Dec. 18, 2007.

Wilkins, Gene. Phone interview, May 17, 2009.

Wilkinson, Bradley E. Personal correspondence, May 17, 2009.

Wilkinson, Ed. Phone interview, Feb. 22, 2009; personal correspondence. March 11; April 3, 2009.

Woldetsadik, Melesse. Phone interview, Feb. 23, 2009.

Woldetsadik, Tadesse. Personal correspondence, Sept. 28, 2009 (with information and medical documentation from Tariku Kebede Woldeyes and Adanech Negash Tesema); Oct. 1, 17, 30 (with further documentation); Nov. 1, 2009.

Woldu, Gebru. Personal correspondence, Jan. 28; Feb. 5; May 21; June 3, 2010. Interview, Wynnewood, Pa., May 20, 2010.

Wood, Alycia. Personal correspondence, Sept. 2; Nov. 1, 2010.

Workman, Dave. Interview, Wynnewood, Pa., April 30, 2008.

Yoshihara, Miyuki, with Hiro Yoshihara. Interview, Baguio, Philippines, Jan. 30, 2009.

Zaritzky, David. Phone interview, May 24, 2009; medical documentation sent May 2009; personal correspondence, June 13, 2009; phone interview, July 24, 2009.

Index of Subjects

abolitionism, 225
abstract thinking (including abstract mathematics), 174, 701n337
accommodation
  to contemporary opinion, Jesus, 176, 632n161
  divine, 695n305
acculturation, 821n219
Acts, 2, 4, 5, 8, 9, 14, 16, 30n55, 31n62, 32, 52, 67, 71, 79, 82, 85–86, 91n40, 93n59, 100, 220, 240, 261, 262, 264, 268, 306, 329, 332n145, 506, 510
  dating, most common, 31, 71
  historiography, as ancient, 32n70, 35–36, 95n78, 736n140, 858
  miracle stories in, 9, 29, 31, 32–33, 509n5, 858, 876 (see also Luke-Acts, and miracle reports)
  models for ministry, construed as, 99, 523, 543
acts of God, 178n52, 589n541
acupuncture, 627n133
addiction
  cured, 287, 401, 473, 493n409, 642, 840
  prevention, 622
  recovery, 622, 624
Adelaja, Sunday, 491n389
Adventists, 392, 393n298, 394n314, 399n353, 451–52, 623n106, 624
Afghanistan, 512n26
Africa
  accounts of supernatural activity (besides Christian practice), 791n23, 792, 794n41
  beliefs in supernatural activity, 205, 216–19, 242n172, 311–13, 313n17, 327, 807n118, 807–8, 809, 826n261, 836, 837nn337, 340
  Central Africa, 313n20, 329n126, 514, 525, 551n335, 589n541–42, 597, 878n70, 880
  charismatic churches, 252n241 (see also Pentecostalism: African)
  Christianity, twentieth-century spread of, 734n132

  courtesy of, cultural, and belief statements, 804n104, 829n284, 837n337
  East Africa, 313n20, 314, 433n33, 792, 796n59, 803n96, 825n251, 835, 847n412, 875n51
  emphasis on healing and health, 217–19, 312, 617n67, 639, 640n212, 804n103
  miracle reports, ancient, 359, 362–65, 523n126
  miracle reports, modern, 241, 256n256, 259, 310–38, 330n132, 333, 514–18, 526, 530–31, 550–63, 589n540, 747, 748, 813, 847 (see also exorcism/deliverance)
  Southern Africa, 218n40, 323–24, 333n149, 368n62, 524, 586n529, 595, 792, 807n117, 813, 845, 847n412, 851n443, 875n51
  traditional civilizations, 223n67
  visions and dreams, 875–76
  West Africa, 313n20, 321–23, 515, 792, 796nn58–59, 803n96, 847n412
  worldview different from Enlightenment, 315n36
  See also specific countries
Africa Inland Church, 218n42, 312n15, 316
African American churches, 204, 392, 393, 414, 445n94, 456, 534n226, 622, 692n283, 795n50, 833n312
African Initiated Churches (African Independent Churches, AICs), 217, 218, 227n98, 228n104, 236n148, 238n, 312, 313n24, 326n116, 551–52, 641n215, 641n217, 794n40, 795n47, 798n73, 805n109, 813, 817n190, 827–28n270, 847n412, 875n51, 877nn64, 66
  valued for health functions, 218n39, 220n54, 639
African Methodist Episcopal Church (A.M.E.), 444n90, 448
African Methodist Episcopal Zion Church (A.M.E. Zion), 444n90, 447n102
African readings of Scripture, 15n29, 216–17n34, 221n58, 225–26

1057

Index of Authors, Interviewees, and Correspondents

Index of Scripture

Index of Other Ancient Sources

N ote: most disputed or pseudonymous works are listed under their putative or traditional authors.